EXAMINATION GUIDE FOR
WORLD GEOGRAPHY: PEOPLE AND PLACES

In *World Geography: People and Places,* special attention has been given to blending solid geography and regional content, skills development, and visual presentation. The Student Edition helps students understand their relationships with Earth and its people. It teaches them many of the skills geographers use in their work and skills needed to understand maps and other graphic illustrations. Many elements of the textbook are especially helpful in aiding student understanding. These elements, along with sample page references, are described below.

p. 1	The **Prologue** explains why the study of geography is important in today's world.
pp. 2-3, 598-599	**Unit Openers** contain full-color theme photographs, indicator maps, brief overviews of unit content, and tables of contents of the chapters in the units.
pp. 66, 202, 512, 578	**Chapter Openers** include colorful theme photographs, listings of chapter themes designed to acquaint students informally with the chapter objectives, and introductions that set the tone and topics of the chapter narrative.
pp. 68-69, 484-485	The **Chapter Narrative Organization,** consisting of numbered section headings and two levels of subheadings, provides a formal outline of chapter content.
pp. 59, 222	**Key Terms and Concepts** appear in boldface type when first introduced and are defined in context.
pp. 8, 136, 326, 431	**Pronunciations** of difficult or foreign terms and place-names are provided directly within the narrative for ease of reading and better understanding. Pronunciations are given as respellings of the words without the use of diacritical marks.
pp. 285, 447, 527, 639	**Content Checks** review exercises appearing after each numbered section, list important terms, people, and places and reinforce understanding of major concepts and factual content.
pp. 392, 406, 588, 606	Four types of special **Features,** color-coded for easy reference, enhance the presentation of material. **Thinking Like a Geographer** presents skills or vocabulary used by geographers; **Strange But True** describes unusual geographic phenomena; **Focus** shares studies of or stories about physical, cultural, economic, and historical geography; **The Urban World** teaches concepts in urban geography within descriptions of world cities.
pp. 96-97, 296, 382, 385, 395	More than 140 **Maps** provide visual content, showing the relationships among physical, cultural, economic, political, social, and historical factors. Every regional chapter has a set of three maps—physical, political, and land use and resources—that spotlights the region's geographic features. Each map is referenced in the chapter narrative and has a caption that asks a question about the map's content or about the accompanying narrative.
pp. 36-37, 47, 68, 560	Full-color **Graphic Illustrations,** including graphs, diagrams, charts, and tables, each referenced in the narrative, visually reinforce or extend concepts. Each graphic has a caption that asks a question related to the illustration or the accompanying narrative.
pp. 236, 394, 466	Full-color **Cultural Collages** in each regional unit visually show many of the cultural and historical themes of regions.
pp. 58, 99, 391, 460, 566, 581	Full-color **Photographs** and **Cartoons** have captions that identify the subject illustrated. Each caption ends in a question designed to relate the photograph or cartoon to the chapter narrative.
pp. 100-101, 186-187, 262-263	Skills features, **Using Graphic Skills,** in every chapter that teach students how to read, compare, analyze, and draw conclusions, as well as make generalizations and hypotheses, from data in maps and other graphic illustrations.
pp. 38-39, 448-449, 616-617	**Chapter Reviews** provide point summaries, vocabulary exercises, several sets of review questions that check knowledge, comprehension, and higher-level thinking and problem-solving skills, and further questions to reinforce graphic skills from the chapters.
pp. 160-161, 424-425	**Unit Reviews** provide point summaries of unit generalizations, cross-chapter review questions, suggested unit activities for groups or individuals, and social studies skills lessons applicable to geographic studies.
pp. 645, 650, 656-657, 660-661, 667	The **Appendix** provides study aids that include 14 **Atlas** maps of regions studied within the chapter content; a data chart, **National Profiles,** that gives vital statistics on all the independent nations of the world; a glossary and an index.
p. 681	The **Glossary** includes complete definitions of key terms and concepts with references to the pages on which the terms were defined briefly in context.
p. 689	The **Index** includes page references to concepts, places, terms, people, and so on, that are important to the study of world geography. Pronunciations are given in the index for many place-names.

PASSPORT

To geography success

MERRILL
PUBLISHING COMPANY
A Bell & Howell Information Company

CONTENTS

INTRODUCTION TO THE PROGRAM

INSTRUCTIONAL APPROACHES

TEXT IMPLEMENTATION

ISBN 0-675-02289-4

Published by

Merrill Publishing Company
A Bell & Howell Information Company
Columbus, Ohio 43216

Copyright © 1989, 1984 by Merrill Publishing Company

For citizens of tomorrow's world

Merrill WORLD GEOGRAPHY: PEOPLE AND PLACES is your passport . . . to helping students become informed citizens of tomorrow's world.

It's packed with information. With comprehensive coverage of geography concepts and world regions, Merrill WORLD GEOGRAPHY offers extensive coverage of all of the themes currently recommended by the Geographic Education National Implementation Project.

It's beautifully illustrated. Nearly every page features outstanding, four-color visuals that invite your students to think . . . to wonder . . . to imagine.

It goes beyond facts. Because your students live in an ever-changing world, Merrill WORLD GEOGRAPHY helps your students develop lasting skills. So they'll be prepared to learn on their own.

It has extensive urban content. Since most of today's students live in or near cities, Merrill WORLD GEOGRAPHY has more material on urban geography than any other program.

It has the teaching support you need. The core program—Student Edition, Teacher Annotated Edition, and Teacher Resource Book—is all you really need to offer a fascinating course in geography.

Of course, additional components are available to help fill special needs, for further teaching support, and to simplify evaluation.

Activity Book and TAE

Transparency Package

Test Generator

The Core Program

THE URBAN WORLD

LONDON: CULTURAL CENTER

relation to other cities and towns are
An important theory in urban geo
called the *central place theory*, says th
are some large cities that are used b
than just the people who live in
These cities become centers for certai
and services. People in smaller towns
ies all around these central places are
to travel many more miles, for exam
buy new cars or to talk with heart spe

Large cities are able to offer mo
of activities than most smaller cities ca
don is such a city. Its influence as a
center goes well beyond the city boun

London, both the capital and largest city

"Urban World" features are case studies about urban life and urban problems that bring out themes common to many cities.

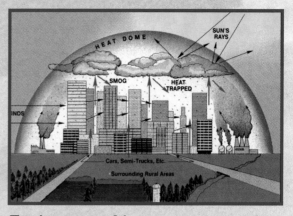

Environmental issues are examined in light of physical, as well as social, concerns.

A new chapter on urban patterns highlights worldwide urban growth and its importance to the people of the world.

CHAPTER 8

URBAN PATTERNS

In this chapter you will learn—
● What are the functions of urban areas.
● How cities developed from ancient to modern times.
● How urban environments are different from rural environments.
● What may be future changes and growth patterns of cities.

INTRODUCTION

To some people cities mean museums, beautiful parks, fancy restaurants, and crowds. Others think of tall buildings, noisy streets, crime, and dirt. To urban geographers cities mean all these things and much more.

Urban geographers want to learn how people live in today's cities. Some urban geographers study how cities are distributed inside a country or region. Others are more interested in a city's economic activities or politics. Still others are worried about the city environment in which people live.

For thousands of years, cities have been important as centers of trade, government, and culture. Today they are important to study because cities are where more and more of the world's population live.

1. CLASSIFYING URBAN AREAS

Urban generally means places in which most people make their living in ways other than farming. When urban geographers study an area, they start by classifying which parts are urban and which are rural. They may further classify urban areas more careful study. Urban areas can be grouped by population or by economic activities.

1.1 Kinds of Urban Are

Cities are a certain kind
Urban areas and cities are pl
law. Each country defines
an urban area and a city ins
For this reason, the defini
area and city can be differ
country. For example,
area is a town or indust
than 400 persons. But
50,000 or more perso
an urban area has
persons or more. C
are only those u
boundaries, or ar
There are se
think of urban
nities around
metropolitan
city and all
148 shows
Maryland
metropol
Area, on
W
study
tant
of
nu
a

T5

Broaden their horizons

Merrill WORLD GEOGRAPHY looks at the big picture . . . and that's an important difference for your students.

Merrill WORLD GEOGRAPHY looks at geography from a variety of perspectives:

- landscape and climate
- economic and cultural patterns
- influences of the past

With this balanced approach, your students get a better grasp of all the factors that combine to give a region its unique identity. This, combined with the most comprehensive content available, helps students make better sense of the diversity of the world.

Merrill WORLD GEOGRAPHY begins with the basics. Geography concepts are covered in detail in the first three units of WORLD GEOGRAPHY. Exceptional flexibility lets you teach these chapters first—or refer to them later as you focus on world regions.
Coverage of U.S. geography is thorough—so students have a chance to gain in-depth understanding of their own country.

FOCUS ON CULTURE

YOUTH SUBCULTURE

the United States, young people shave heads into punk hairstyles.

Teenagers also examine their own and the world. They may work to changes in these areas also. In China people are more and more frustrate their communist government's campa commit them to the goals of the Com Party. Some young Chinese feel that ment places too many restrictions on personal lives. They are willing to spo on issues much more than Chinese from years before. In South Africa youths recently protested against the

STRANGE BUT TRUE

DRIFTING CONTINENTS

strange as it may seem, scientists be hat about 135 million years ago the landmass that was made up of today's America and Africa started to split About 70 million years later, the new nts were separated by a new ocean, the Atlantic. The idea that continents have oving on the surface of Earth for bil f years is called the theory of *continental*

1912 a German scientist, Alfred We suggested the continental drift theory. pothesized that all the continents had art of one huge landmass about 200 years ago. Wegener believed that this

FUTURE EARTH

Adapted with permission from "The Breakup of Pangaea" Robert S. Dietz and John C. Holden Copyright © 1970 by Scientific American, Inc.

"Focus on . . ." features offer closer looks at culture, history, economy, or physical geography.

"Strange But True" features explore some of Earth's unusual geographic phenomena.

Plenty of cultural material helps your students understand the ways of life of people throughout the world.

NKRUMAH

A sense of place

Merrill WORLD GEOGRAPHY lets your students see the world . . . as well as read about it.

Stunning four-color photos and art clearly illustrate concepts . . . and give your students a sense of being there. And many of the photos are of places where most people never have the opportunity to go.

The superlative photos used in this edition have been hand-picked from sources all over the world.

Four-color art is used to make concepts clear—and all diagrams and charts are referred to in the text.

WORLD'S LARGEST METROPOLITAN AREAS

1.	Mexico City, Mexico	15,669,000	14. Bombay, India	8,243,000
2.	Shanghai, China	11,860,000	15. Tianjin, China	7,790,000
3.	Tokyo, Japan	11,671,000	16. Los Angeles, California (U.S.)	7,478,000
4.	São Paulo, Brazil	10,100,000	17. Chicago, Illinois (U.S.)	7,104,000
5.	Cairo, Egypt	10,000,000	18. London, England (U.K.)	6,755,000
6.	Buenos Aires, Argentina	9,968,000	19. Manila, Philippines	6,720,000
7.	Seoul, South Korea	9,501,000	20. Chongqing, China	6,511,000
8.	Beijing, China	9,231,000	21. Jakarta, Indonesia	6,503,000
9.	Calcutta, India	9,194,000	22. Wuhan, China	5,948,000
10.	New York, New York (U.S.)	9,120,000	23. Delhi, India	5,729,000
11.	Rio de Janeiro, Brazil	9,019,000	24. Changchun, China	5,705,000
12.	Moscow, U.S.S.R.	8,646.000	25. Shenyang, China	5,055,000
13.	Paris, France	8,510,000		

Maps, too, give students a sense of place . . . and help
them understand how their home compares to the rest
of the world. The in-text maps were rendered
specifically for Merrill by professional cartographers.
Special care was taken even in color selection—to help
color-deficient students better distinguish map features.

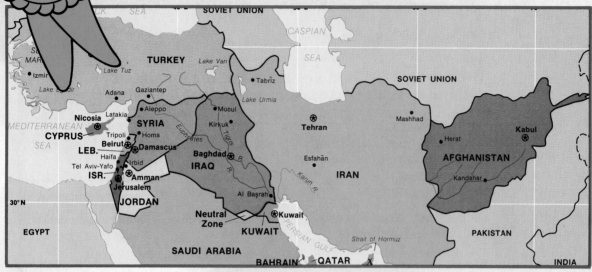

The Appendix includes an atlas with 14 professional-quality
reference maps, plus profiles of every nation in the world, in
easy-to-read chart form.

FLAG	COUNTRY Capital (Largest City)	AREA sq m (sq km) PERCENT ARABLE PERCENT URBAN	POPULATION DEN-SITY sq m (sq km) BIRTH/DEATH RATE ANNUAL GROWTH %	MAJOR LANGUAGES LITERACY RATE LIFE EXPECTANCY	PER CAPITA GNP MAJOR EXPORTS
		ASIA			
	BANGLADESH Dhaka	55,598 (143,998.7) 63 13	107,100,000 1,926 (743) 44/17 2.7	Bengali 23% 50 years	$150 raw & manufac-tured jute, leather, tea
	BHUTAN Thimphu	18,147 (47,000.7) 2 5	1,500,000 83 (32) 38/18 2.0	Dzongkha 5% 46 years	$160 agricultural and forestry products, coal
	BRUNEI Bandar Seri Begawan	2,228 (5,770.5) 1 64	200,000 90 (35) 30/4 2.6	Malay, English, Chinese 45% 62 years	$17,580 crude oil, liquefied natural gas, petro-leum products
	BURMA Rangoon	261,216 (676,548.9) 15	38,800,000 148 (57) 34/13 53 years	Burmese 78%	$190 teak, hardwoods, rice, beans, met-

Maps are accurate and easy to read . . . because
a professional scribing technique captures every
detail.

Mapping out success

The Student Edition is structured for maximum understanding . . . to aid independent learning.

The text is written in a clear, straightforward style that helps students comprehend basic ideas and relate concepts to what they are learning. And that means greater success in the classroom.

All of the regional chapters have consistent subheads that identify which aspect of geography is being studied. These sections are clearly numbered . . . and plenty of questions are provided to ensure that students are getting the main ideas.

Each major Slavic group has its own republic within Yugoslavia. The Yugoslav republics are Serbia, Croatia (kroh AY shuh), Slovenia, Bosnia and Herzegovina (HEHRT suh goh VEE nah), Macedonia, and Montenegro. The languages of the people are officially recognized by the Yugoslav government. However, Serbo-Croatian is the country's *lingua franca* (LING gwuh FRANG kuh), or common language of business and communication. It is written in two alphabets—Cyrillic, based on

Vocabulary terms are highlighted, and difficult place-names are followed in the text with easy-to-read pronunciations.

Content checks at the end of each section include plenty of vocabulary and recall questions.

CONTENT CHECK

1. **Define:** artisans, urbanization.
2. Where did the first cities develop?
3. What groups of workers developed in early cities?
4. During what time period did cities in Europe decline?
5. What helped European cities develop again in the mid-1000s?
6. **Challenge:** If new farm machinery had been invented 100 years before factory machinery, how do you think the development of cities would have been different?

Challenge questions are ideal for enlivening assignments or stimulating class discussions.

yerba mate (YEHR bah MAH tay)

Chapter reviews include different levels of questions, from vocabulary exercises . . . To recall questions . . .

REVIEWING VOCABULARY

Listed below are the vocabulary words in this chapter. Head a separate sheet of paper with th[e] Vocabulary of Physical and Human Geography. *Divide the paper into two columns with the* [headings] Physical Geography *and* Human Geography. *Then write each vocabulary word under the* [type of] geography *with which it can be classified. In a few cases, the word may be classified und[er both]* headings. *For this reason, be prepared to explain why you chose each classification.*

fjord	asbestos	fossil fuels	timberline	permafrost
cede	peat bogs	bilingual	reservations	subsidiaries
potash	truck farm	cordillera	separatists	hydroelectric

REMEMBERING THE FACTS

1. What oceans surround Canada?
2. What are the two major European groups that make up Canada's population?
3. What does bilingual mean?
4. What physical region covers nearly half of Canada's total land area?

6. What Canadian city is the busiest [West?] coast port in North America?
7. What groups of people live in the Cana- dian territories?
8. What province became home for [the United] sands of United Empire Loyalists [of?]

To comprehension . . .

7. What is the largest city in Brazil? The major language?
8. What are the four major physical regions of Argentina?
9. In what part of Argentina do most of the nation's people live? Why?

10. How would you describe the star[dard of] living in Argentina?
11. What is the highest mountain pea[k in the] Western Hemisphere? Where is it [located?]
12. Which one of the four Atlantic na[tions is] landlocked?

UNDERSTANDING THE FACTS

1. Why do some people say Brazil resembles the United States 100 years ago?
2. Why is rain-forest soil not fertile?
3. Why did Brazil decide to build its capital city, Brasília, far inland?
4. What differences are there in the ances- tries of people in Brazil and Argentina?

5. Why are the Pampas important [to the] people of Argentina?
6. What causes frequent fog in coast[al areas] of Patagonia?
7. In what ways is Brazil like two co[untries?]
8. Why has economic developmen[t been] slow in both Paraguay and Urugu[ay?]

To application, synthesis, and evaluation of content.

THINKING CRITICALLY AND CREATIVELY

1. What would you suggest a country do if it has little arable land and few natural resources but wants to build up its eco- nomic strength?
2. What makes a country a world power?

been between France and Spain[. How] might you explain this?
5. What is the relationship between [a country's] exports and the country's need f[or imports?] Where does France get its oil?

CHAPTER REVIEW

CHAPTER 22 — SOUTHWEST ASIA

SUMMARY

1. Southwest Asia lies at the meeting point of Europe, Africa, and Asia.
2. Southwest Asia can be divided into three parts—Arabian Peninsula, Middle East Core, and Northern Middle East.
3. Israel is the only Jewish nation in the world. It is isolated from its Arab neigh- bors by political and cultural differences. The conflict between Israel and Arab countries is a major source of tension in this part of the world.
4. Saudi Arabia is the largest country in Southwest Asia. It is important because of its huge deposits of oil.
5. Turkey is the most populous and the most industrialized country in Southwest Asia. In some ways it is more European than Asian in its outlook.

6. Iran is the largest country in the North- ern Middle East. Iran was once consid- ered a world leader in oil production, but a war and revolution have interfered with its economy.
7. The Fertile Crescent is a large area of fertile land running through the Middle East Core. Most of the people in this part of the Middle East live on this land.
8. Several small countries share the Arabian Peninsula with Saudi Arabia. The coun- tries in the south are mostly poor, while those in the east are among the richest in the world.
9. Since 1979 Afghanistan has been torn apart by fighting between Soviet military forces and Afghans opposing the coun- try's communist government.

REMEMBERING THE FACTS

1. What name is frequently given to the countries of the Southwest Asia region and Egypt?
2. What are some reasons why Southwest Asia is an important world region?
3. What are some waterways found in Isra- el's rift valley?
4. What is the most important source of wealth in Saudi Arabia?
5. What is the name of the peninsula where Saudi Arabia is located?

6. By what name was Iran known for many years?
7. What part of Iran receives the heavies[t] amount of rainfall?
8. In what part of Iran are most of the co[un]- try's oil deposits found?
9. What are *Shi'a* and *Sunni*?
10. What is the landscape like in the e[astern] most part of Turkey?
11. What accounts for the wealth of [some] States?

UNDERSTANDING THE FACTS

1. In what ways is Israel isolated from its neighbors?
2. Only three percent of Saudi Arabians are involved in the oil industry. Yet, oil ac- counts for a high percentage of the coun- try's income. How can this be explained?

3. Saudi Arabia has a relative[ly small popu]- lation. Why must it impo[rt labor from] many other countries?
4. Why is Turkey's location [important to] many other countries or [govern-?]
5. How did Iran's gover[nment change in] the revolution of 197[9?]

THINKING CRITICALLY AND CREATIVELY

1. If a new energy source developed that ended the need for oil, what do you think the impact would be on Saudi Arabia? Why do you think so?
2. **Challenge:** The Turkish leader Kemal Atatürk moved Turkey's capital from

Istanbul to A[nkara. Why] did this?
3. **Challenge[:** ...] fighting [...] pen to [...] tries st[...]

REINFORCING GRAPHIC SKIL[LS]

Study the map on page 457. Then answer the questions that [follow.]
1. What advantage does Israeli occupation of the Golan Heights give to Israel?
2. What are the physical [features? of the land] called the West Bank[?]

T11 Gaza Strip?

CHAPTER 22 SOUTHWEST ASIA

REVIEWING VOCABULARY

On a separate sheet of paper, write the word that is defined to the right of the blanks in each line. Then circle the letters in the words that show a star (*) below. Unscramble these letters to spell the mystery word, one of the countries of Southwest Asia.

meat that comes from sheep
ruler of the Ottoman Empire
collective farm settlement in Israel
cooperative where farms are individually owned
process of removing salt from seawater
pilgrimage to Mecca
[met]hod of irrigation that uses deep wells and
before 1979
[...]dings [...] leaders [...] UT 7

Confidence with skills

Give your students the tools to become better citizens of the world.

Building geography and social studies skills is as important for your students as building knowledge. A solid foundation in geography can be the key to success in other social studies disciplines.

Beyond the classroom, confidence with skills will give your students the ability to adapt to an ever-changing world.

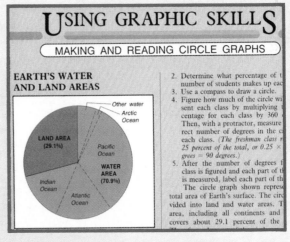

USING GRAPHIC SKILLS

MAKING AND READING CIRCLE GRAPHS

EARTH'S WATER AND LAND AREAS

- LAND AREA (29.1%)
- Other water
- Arctic Ocean
- Pacific Ocean
- WATER AREA (70.9%)
- Indian Ocean
- Atlantic Ocean

2. Determine what percentage of t number of students makes up eac
3. Use a compass to draw a circle.
4. Figure how much of the circle wi sent each class by multiplying t centage for each class by 360 Then, with a protractor, measure rect number of degrees in the c each class. *(The freshman class* r *25 percent of the total, or 0.25 × grees = 90 degrees.)*
5. After the number of degrees f class is figured and each part of t is measured, label each part of th
   The circle graph shown represe total area of Earth's surface. The circ vided into land and water areas. T area, including all continents and covers about 29.1 percent of the

Skills features in every chapter introduce and build on basic graphic skills.

Integrated skills program

The approach of Merrill WORLD GEOGRAPHY ensures that your students will always relate skills to content. And a proven teaching model helps you build important thinking skills from the ground up.

Our skills teaching model is based on a widely recognized approach for teaching thinking skills:

- Introduce
- Define
- Explain
- Demonstrate
- Apply

"Thinking Like a Geographer" features introduce skills or vocabulary that geographers use, so students see real examples of skills application.

Each chapter review includes questions that encourage students to use problem-solving and thinking skills . . . plus exercises for reinforcing graphic skills.

Unit review skill exercises help students synthesize the many skills they are learning into higher-level thinking skills.

Teaching companion

You won't have to look any farther than your Teacher Annotated Edition to find convenient planning and teaching materials for the whole program. The support you need for teaching geography is provided in a Teacher Guide in front and through extensive annotations on full-size student pages.

Whether you need a little help or a lot, consistent organization and plentiful labels throughout the Teacher Annotated Edition make it easy for you to find what you need.

Two activities are suggested for every chapter objective.

Teach, reinforce, and enrich content . . . with activities suggested in the Teacher Guide.

---

people in the nine regions that make up these sections use their land and natural resources is the chief theme of the chapter. Any major

feature of the chapter is a segment about the importance of the Gulf of Mexico to the United States economy.

CHAPTER 10 ACTIVITIES

● Teaching ■ Reinforcing ★ Enriching

Introducing Chapter 10

Have students choose a major American city to research while they are studying Chapter 10. Tell them to find out how and why the city grew. Students should research why the city was settled, who settled it, and when it was settled. If possible, students should find out how the city got its name, what major economic goods and services were first produced in the city, what effect the landscape and climate had on city growth, and population growth statistics. Tell students that they will prepare a research report from their findings that will be presented at the completion of the chapter's work.

If time does not allow such an extensive report, you might introduce the chapter with a short lecture about the growth of urbanization in the United States, using the history of one or two cities for exemplification.

Objective 1 Activities

● **Objective 1 Teaching Activity**
Refer to the guidelines for retrieval charts in the Instructional Approaches section of this Teacher Annotated Edition. Tell students tha there are many facts that contribute to region's economic and cultural developmen and these are described in their text. A r trieval chart will help them understand th facts.

Ask students to skim the chapter to how many regions are named. Place t regions down the left side of the chart. (subregions should be indented appropr under the four main regions.) Students s also skim the content of a couple of regi suggest headings for the top of this grid. Area and Features, Locations, States, C Agriculture, Industries, People, Cities students complete the retrieval chart Northeastern United States. Disc

10 Reading Assignments

Ed. pp. 183–189

Some modern technologies make pollution worse. Discarded steel cans soon rust in salt water, while plastic containers take many years to disintegrate.

Ecologists and other scientists have found that, in some cases, controlling pollution in one place may simply mean that it shifts to another place or takes another form. Therefore, researchers now are trying to find safer and cleaner raw materials and ways of manufacturing that make less waste.

See the *TAE* for an *Objective 4 Activity.*

3.2 Altering Waterways

People have changed the natural state of waterways to suit their needs and desires. For example, the Netherlands has added to its land by draining seawater from certain areas

Altering waterways can mean controversy; for example, upstream irrigation is often opposed by people in drier downstream areas.

the mainland that are made of sand and sediment, which protect the shoreline.

For thousands of years in Louisiana, the Mississippi River built up land with sediment. To prevent flooding, people built up ridges, called **levees** (LEHV eez) and channels to control the river. These levees caused sediment to move into the Gulf of Mexico. This led to the erosion of the built-up land, the rising of sea level, and the disappearance over time of the wetlands. These wetlands had at one time provided almost 30 percent of the fish harvest in the United States and a winter home for thousands of migratory birds.

See the *TRB* for *Chapter 4 Reading* on the use of waterways.

Teaching Options
TAE, Objective 3 Activities, pp. T298–T299
TRB, Chapter 30 Teacher Notes: Section 3, Extending the Lesson
Chapter 30 Skill Activity

Chapter 30 Review and Evaluation

Suggested Teaching Strategies	Review	Evaluation
TAE, Objective 4 Activities, p. T299 Concluding Chapter 30, p. T299	SE, Chapter 30 Review, pp. 630–631 TRB, Chapter 30 Review Worksheet	TRB, Chapter 30 Test TG, Chapter 30

Extensive annotations on full-size student pages include tips for extension, teaching strategies, cross-references, and background information.

Review and evaluation suggestions are offered to help you wrap up every chapter and unit.

Section lesson plans—correlated to chapter objectives—show you what components and teaching options are available.

Plan Suggestions—Chapter 10

SE—Student Edition   TAE—Teacher Annotated Edition   TG—Test Generator
TRB—Teacher Resource Book   TSP—Transparency Package

1 Northeastern United States (pp. 183–189)

Chapter Objectives	Suggested Teaching Strategies	Review
describe the major economic and cultural features of Northeastern United States.	**Teacher Preparation** SE, Reading Assignment, pp. 183–189 TAE, Unit 4 Suggested Resources Chapter 10 Overview, p. T130 Introducing Chapter 10, p. T130 TRB, Chapter 10 Teacher Notes: Section 1 **Teaching Options** TAE, Introducing Chapter 10, p. T130 Objective 1 Activities, pp. T130–T131 TRB, Chapter 10 Teacher Notes: Section 1, Extending the Lesson Chapter 10 Reading Chapter 10 Skill Activity TSP, Transparency 8 SE, *Using Graphic Skills,* "Reading Thematic Maps," pp. 186–187	SE, Content Check, p. 189
Skill Objective: read thematic maps.		

Section 2 North Central United States (pp. 189–192)

Chapter Objectives	Suggested Teaching Strategies	Review
major	**Teacher Preparation** SE, Reading Assignment, pp. 185–192 Suggested Resources T130	SE, Content Check, p. 192

Natural resource

The Teacher Resource Book lets you add worksheets, assignments, tests, and teaching aids to your plans without a lot of extra work on your part. That's why we're calling this Teacher Resource Book a "natural resource" for busy teachers.

Just choose the blackline masters you want, copy them—and you're ready to go. Once you've used the masters, it's easy to store them conveniently in the large three-ring binder.

Among the many masters provided are map, content, and review worksheets, chapter and unit tests, readings which feature primary and secondary sources, skill activities, career features, and a separate graphics section . . . with numerous outline maps you can use as teaching aids or for a variety of assignments.

Latin America

421

T16

Alternate routes

You can provide outstanding geography instruction using just the Student Edition, Teacher Annotated Edition, and Teacher Resource Book. Each contains plenty of options to help you plan a program that fits your students' needs . . . and your teaching style.

If you wish to emphasize certain aspects of the program . . . or if you are looking for special kinds of teaching support . . . look into the following optional components.

Student Activity Book . . . activities to reinforce concepts and skills. Ideal for homework or in-class assignments because many of the activities can be done before a chapter is completed. A **Teacher Annotated Edition** is available.

Transparency Package . . . seven colorful regional transparencies with overlays . . . plus outline maps of the United States and the world and a comparison of map projections. A booklet of teaching ideas is included.

Test Generator . . . easy-to-use software that puts a variety of test questions and formats at your fingertips. Includes a choice of questions, all conveniently correlated to learning objectives. Available for Apple II computers.

The Core Program

INTRODUCTION TO THE PROGRAM

PROGRAM RATIONALE

In the twentieth century, the world has been opened up for display. Advances in transportation, communication, and technology have made scenes from the most remote parts of the world only a satellite signal away from people on the other side of Earth. No longer can—or should—any one people remain ignorant of the ways of life of their fellow human beings in other parts of the world.

Since all people have very basic physical and social needs, some common characteristics will always be found in all cultures. At the same time, there will also be factors influencing cultures that make each one different from others. One such factor is physical environment. Each culture must adapt its surroundings to what fits the needs of its society and adapt its society to certain demands placed on it by the physical environment.

Learning about the ways of life of peoples around the world starts with understanding Earth's physical environments. The needs of people who live in an urban, industrial setting will be different from those of people who live in a small, rural community. Likewise, the wet, warm environment of people living in some coastal areas will make different demands on their lifestyles than a hot, dry desert environment will make on its peoples.

Another aspect of environment that influences cultural needs is supply of natural resources. What is plentiful in one part of Earth—water, oil, fertile soils—may be quite scarce in another part. Because of this, people in some parts of the world have become dependent upon people in other parts of the world for products and services they need and want. In some cases, having or not having needed resources has been a source of conflict. The reality of such conflict—and of growing global interdependence—is that both may grow and deepen during the twenty-first century.

The study of geography helps make sense of Earth and its peoples. It brings understanding of how Earth's physical features—land, water, and air—and the cultural features of its inhabitants—ethnicity, language, religion, customs—interact. It also helps people find patterns in the way nature fashions Earth and people fashion the world.

Today the world is grappling with many crises. In different places, people are without regular and nutritious food supplies; overcrowded urban centers offer few services or jobs to the thousands who move from rural areas in hopes of a better life; there is fighting over territorial rights; there are refugees seeking freedom from political repression; lack of natural resources or the means necessary to maximize them stymies economic development; and everywhere unsafe disposal of toxic materials threatens environments. These kinds of serious and complex problems are not quickly or easily solved. Without better understanding among Earth's peoples of the distinctive physical settings and particular ways of life of other peoples of the world, they probably cannot be solved at all.

Merrill *World Geography: People and Places* was specifically designed with the need of global understanding in mind. The total program is a resource rich in the facts, understandings, and skills today's students need to be effective and knowledgeable citizens in an interdependent world. It aids them in analyzing the physical, cultural, economic, political, social, and historical influences of the world and the many groups of people who live there.

PROGRAM OBJECTIVES

World Geography: People and Places is designed to achieve several general student objectives. These are linked to more specific unit goals and chapter objectives, which may be used to determine student mastery of the program. The program endeavors to help students of world geography to:

1. understand basic geographic concepts.
2. explain general physical characteristics of Earth.
3. explain human patterns that have developed because of physical environment.

4. describe relationships that develop between people and places as physical and cultural features interact.
5. summarize how people have changed their physical environment to suit the needs of their cultures and the effect these changes have had on Earth.
6. use maps to gather data, recognize physical and human patterns, and interpret the meaning of these patterns as they relate to people and places.
7. use the steps of geographic inquiry in their study of geography.
8. recognize regions and common characteristics that form regions.
9. gain insight in the ways of life of people from many different regions of the world.
10. increase awareness of the interdependence of cultures throughout the world.

PROGRAM COMPONENTS

World Geography: People and Places is a *complete* learning system. While encouraging the use of outside resources—statistical data, almanacs, newspapers, newsmagazines, audiovisual materials, community contacts, research documents, and so on—the authors recognize that locating all of these resources is often costly and always time-consuming for today's busy classroom teachers. For this reason, Merrill's program provides extensive content coverage, integrated skills development, and supplementary materials, supplying teachers and students with a comprehensive course in world geography.

STUDENT EDITION

World Geography: People and Places is a basal textbook designed to be used in secondary world geography courses. The text provides complete coverage of the concepts of geographic study and introduces students to the people and places around the world. The content is presented within an interdisciplinary approach, drawing on the physical sci-

ences, anthropology, sociology, economics, history, and political science. The material in the Student Edition is arranged so the students will be able to integrate the various physical aspects of Earth with the diverse activities of people within their physical environments.

Key features of the Student Edition are presented in a separate section described in detail on pages T24–T27 of this Teacher Annotated Edition.

TEACHER ANNOTATED EDITION

The Teacher Annotated Edition of *World Geography: People and Places* is designed to reduce teacher preparation time and to facilitate both teaching and learning. It has been organized to allow for easy adaptation to individual teaching styles and student needs. It includes both a teacher guide bound into the front of the Student Edition and teacher annotations printed throughout.

The annotations, printed in blue within the Student Edition pages, are of several basic types. Some provide additional or clarifying information about the content or accompanying photographs, maps, and other illustrations. Others offer topics of discussion and suggested activities. Still others point out relationships between the subject under discussion and material in other parts of the student text or program, including many helpful cross-references.

The teacher guide consists of the following four sections—Introduction to the Program, Instructional Approaches, Text Implementation, and Suggested Resources.

The **Introduction to the Program** contains the program rationale; program objectives; information on each of the program components; a description of the general content organization of the student text, skills program, and learning and visual aids; suggestions on text usage for year-long or semester courses; sample lesson plan suggestions that show the program's many teaching options; and a note about how teachers can evaluate Merrill *World Geography: People and Places* after the first year of implementation of the program.

The **Instructional Approaches** section contains general guidelines on teaching techniques commonly used to reinforce and enrich geography and other social studies classes. Among these are brainstorming, team learning, debates, and role plays and simulations. Ideas presented in this "how-to" section not only facilitate learning on several different levels but also add variety to daily lessons. A bibliography is also provided for other instructional assistance.

Many ideas described in the Instructional Approaches section appear as suggested unit activities in the student text and as suggested student activities in the Text Implementation section of this teacher guide. To aid in planning, a matrix has been included to identify the units and chapters where each approach is recommended within suggested activities. It is important to note, however, that these approaches may be applied to many other topics and used many times throughout the course. Furthermore, the guidelines provided can be easily adapted to various classroom situations. Before planning lessons, it may be helpful to refer back to this section for additional ideas and suggested procedures.

The **Text Implementation** section is the "heart" of the teacher guide and contains teaching ideas on a unit-chapter basis. As the longest section of the teacher guide, it is comprehensive and detailed. To begin the study of each unit, a list of general unit goals is given. It is followed by the unit skill objective, which indicates the geography skill that is taught in the Unit Review for that unit. The unit overview summarizes the content of the unit and explains how chapters within the unit relate to this content. A special activity to introduce the unit to students is described.

For each chapter in the unit, the teacher guide contains a list of specific chapter objectives. One or two of these chapter objectives are linked to the study of each section in the chapter. These objectives should be studied carefully because they correspond directly to the teaching, reinforcing, and enriching activities suggested later in the Text Implementation section. A skill objective is also listed for each chapter. It refers to the graphic skills lesson that is given in every chapter.

The chapter overview describes the major themes of the chapter, along with any special-interest features contained in the chapter. An activity to introduce the chapter is suggested, and reading assignments that link chapter objectives with individual sections are listed. The next part of the chapter implementation includes two suggested activities for each of the chapter objectives. Of these, one is designed to teach to the chapter objective. In addition, there is either a reinforcing activity or an enriching activity for the same objective. A special activity is summarized for concluding chapter study.

Many more activities have been given in each chapter's implementation section than is necessary for the effective teaching of the chapter. These activities give the teacher great flexibility in choosing the type of lesson necessary to suit the needs of the students.

Take special note that for Chapters 9–31—chapters with content on world regions—chapter objectives have been established that give the students a broad understanding of regions and countries profiled in the chapters. Physical, cultural, economic, and historical features are emphasized. In order to give the students a more in-depth look at regions, some of the activities suggested in the Text Implementation section for the regional chapters in this Teacher Annotated Edition have been directed toward a better understanding of one or two of these general geographic features. To inform the teacher of an activity's particular focus, letter markers appear at the beginning of the activity description. Unmarked activities deal with three or more features listed in the chapter objectives. Activities marked with the following letters deal with:
Ⓟ Physical features.
Ⓔ Economic features.
Ⓒ Cultural features.
Ⓗ Historical features.

Answers to Content Check questions, questions found in photograph, map, and other illustration captions, special features, Chapter Review, and Unit Review questions follow the activities section of each chapter. Answers are not provided for the Define and Identify parts of Content Checks. Definitions of terms found boldface in the narrative can be found in the section content or in the glossary. Place-names and people listed in the Identify section can be located and summarized from the section content.

Challenge questions found in Content Checks and the Chapter Review demand higher-level thinking processes. Answers for these questions cannot solely be found in section or chapter content. Students must apply facts, processes, and concepts learned in the chapter and in previous chapters to arrive at answers to Challenge questions. Within the Answers section of the teacher guide, several sample answers are given to help the teacher guide student discussion of these stimulating questions. In most cases, however, answers will vary, and teachers are encouraged to help students generalize and hypothesize rather than seek a particular answer for these thinking and problem-solving questions.

Possibly, the most useful tool for a teacher's day-to-day planning is the chart of lesson plan suggestions that concludes each chapter's implementation section. Each section has a separate plan that includes the chapter objectives related to that section, readings from the various program components to prepare for teaching that section, a listing of many teaching options from which teachers may select a number for their personal lesson plans, and the proper review and evaluation elements incorporated in the program. Again, many more options have been given in the lesson plan suggestions than are necessary or possible for the teaching of each section. Teachers may select those that fit their needs and schedule.

This order of chapter materials is repeated for each chapter in the unit. Following the last chapter in the unit, the teacher guide includes a special activity to conclude the study of the unit. Suggestions for evaluating student mastery of the unit content conclude the unit implementation section. The above procedure is then repeated for all 10 units of the Student Edition.

The **Suggested Resources** section contains books and articles for student use and books, articles, audiovisual and other supplementary materials for teacher use. It also gives a general bibliography of reference materials that will assist teachers, school librarians, and other media personnel in setting up necessary resources for a world geography curriculum. Many of the supplementary materials may be purchased at no or little cost by the school or located in area public or university libraries.

Following the Suggested Resources section is a survey form addressed to the classroom teacher. The form asks for an evaluation of the features of the Student Edition and other components in the *World Geography: People and Places* program. Merrill Publishing Company asks that the survey be completed and mailed after the teacher has used the program in the classroom for the first year after purchase.

TEACHER RESOURCE BOOK

The Teacher Resource Book is a timesaving teacher aid that provides a wealth of effective materials—for teaching content, reinforcing a variety of social studies skills, conducting hands-on activities, enriching lessons, practicing map and other graphic skills, and evaluating student performance.

It includes Teacher Notes that give the teacher a quick reference in presenting teacher material. A special section called Extending the Lesson is given for each section, which offers additional background information about a subject related to the section material but not presented in-depth in the student text. A Reading is provided for each chapter, which provides primary and secondary source materials. Skill Activities give teachers step-by-step instructions, as well as student handouts that are designed for student practice and application of the skill. The focus of each Reading and Skill Activity is labeled with a symbol representing either physical, cultural, economic, or historical geography. Review Worksheets are designed for each chapter as a quick review of the main points of each chapter.

Map and Content Worksheets have been devised for use with each of the regional units. In addition to providing exercises in locational geography, these worksheets may be used as pretests and posttests during the study of world regions. Students can be given both worksheets before a unit is studied. This will give both the student and teacher an idea of what facts and concepts about the region need to be stressed in chapter and unit study. At the end of the unit, the two worksheets can be used again to see how well the material in the unit was learned.

Career features are included in the Teacher Resource Book to introduce the many subfields of geography to students. The Teacher Resource Book also contains unit examinations and chapter tests for student evaluation. Unit examinations contain 40 objective questions, some of which test graphic skills learned within unit study, and 2–5 essay questions. Chapter tests are two pages and include 25 objective items and 2 optional essay questions. The Teacher Resource Book also contains more than 50 outline maps and graphs that may be duplicated for a variety of graphic exercises. Two correlations—skills and objectives—conclude the Teacher Resource Book.

STUDENT ACTIVITY BOOK

The Student Activity Book is organized on a unit-chapter basis with two activities per unit and three activities per chapter. The unit activities include a mapping worksheet, which gives students practice in map work and a skills worksheet that extends student practice of the geography skill taught in each Unit Review. The chapter activities include a reinforcement worksheet, which focuses on key concepts, important geography terms, and chapter content; a graphic skills worksheet, which gives students further practice in the graphic skills taught in each chapter; and an enrichment worksheet, which is designed to help students think critically and creatively through a variety of methods.

STUDENT ACTIVITY BOOK TEACHER EDITION

The Teacher Edition of the Student Activity Book contains the Student Edition plus answers for the student activities. The answers are printed in color in the answer spaces provided for the student.

TRANSPARENCY PACKAGE

The Transparency Package in the Merrill *World Geography: People and Places* program offers seven full-color regional transparencies that correlate with the seven regions presented in the Student Edition. Each transparency has two content overlays that help students understand the physical and cultural landscapes of the region. Transparencies of the world, the United States, and a comparison of map projections are also included. The package includes a booklet of teaching suggestions.

TEST GENERATOR SOFTWARE

The software package is a three-disk test generator that provides additional questions for each chapter objective. These questions can be combined to suit the needs of the students and the focus of the chapter study.

KEY FEATURES OF THE STUDENT EDITION

World Geography: People and Places is an *effective* learning system. Essential to the success of the total program is the content organization, skills development, learning and visual aids, and other key features.

CONTENT ORGANIZATION

The text provides a uniquely organized course in both topical and regional geography.

The text is organized on a unit-chapter basis with 10 units and 31 chapters. Units 1-3 use a topical approach to the discipline of geography. **Unit 1** lays the foundation for the study of geography by discussing the nature of the discipline and the manner in which geographers and students of geography study Earth and its people. It also teaches the necessary understanding of geographers' most important tool—maps. **Unit 2** presents the essential information and concepts of physical geography. **Unit 3** introduces to the students the important understandings of human, or cultural, geography.

Regional method of study is used in the remainder of the text—**Units 4-10.** The world has been divided for easier study into regions with common cultural characteristics, called culture areas. Culture areas have been further divided into smaller regions. In most cases a single culture area is studied in each unit. Regions then become the subject of each chapter in the unit. Within each regional chapter, the introduction presents an overview of the region as a whole. Individual profiles are then given of several countries within the region. These give students a closer look at physical and cultural characteristics and patterns of a particular region.

All chapters are organized on a formal outline basis, consisting of section and subsection arrangement. Regional chapters in Units 4-10 generally follow a similar pattern of presenting a section that studies landscape and climate, then a section on economic and cultural patterns, followed by a historical section—influences of the past.

SKILLS DEVELOPMENT

Special emphasis has been given throughout *World Geography: People and Places* to skills and skills development. Both social studies skills and graphic skills are stressed—in particular, those skills that geographers use in their research and studies. Social studies skills appear as a lesson in the Unit Reviews. Graphic skills appear as a lesson in every chapter. The skills are ordered so that those learned in the earlier units are built on in later units. The skills development scheme gives students much practice in higher-level thinking and problem-solving skills. The unit/chapter placement of these skills lessons and their titles are indicated in the following chart:

Chapter 1	Describing Exact and Relative Locations
Chapter 2	Understanding Scale
Unit 1 Review	Asking Effective Questions
Chapter 3	Understanding Diagrams
Chapter 4	Making and Reading Circle Graphs
Chapter 5	Reading Climographs
Unit 2 Review	Analyzing Photographs
Chapter 6	Comparing Tabular Data
Chapter 7	Comparing Data from Maps and Graphs
Chapter 8	Making Observations
Unit 3 Review	Developing a Global Point of View
Chapter 9	Understanding Maps with Insets
Chapter 10	Reading Thematic Maps
Chapter 11	Analyzing Historical Maps
Chapter 12	Interpreting Diagrams
Unit 4 Review	Observing in the Field
Chapter 13	Analyzing Demographic Maps
Chapter 14	Reading Topographic Maps
Chapter 15	Reading Transportation Maps
Chapter 16	Analyzing Data from Bar Graphs
Unit 5 Review	Classifying Information
Chapter 17	Making Generalizations
Chapter 18	Analyzing Line and Bar Graphs
Chapter 19	Reading Political Maps
Chapter 20	Comparing Land-Area Maps
Unit 6 Review	Making Comparisons
Chapter 21	Comparing Thematic Maps
Chapter 22	Reading Territorial Boundaries
Unit 7 Review	Making Inferences
Chapter 23	Reading Pictographs
Chapter 24	Interpreting Thematic Maps
Chapter 25	Analyzing Circle Graphs
Unit 8 Review	Supporting Generalizations
Chapter 26	Making Hypotheses
Chapter 27	Drawing Conclusions
Chapter 28	Reviewing Exact and Relative Locations
Unit 9 Review	Testing Hypotheses
Chapter 29	Reading Time-Zone Maps
Chapter 30	Reviewing Scale
Chapter 31	Evaluating Information
Unit 10 Review	Identifying Trends and Making Forecasts

Higher-level thinking and problem-solving is also strongly encouraged throughout the Student Edition. This is done within the many Challenge questions consistently provided in the Content Checks that appear at the end of chapter sections. Thinking Critically and Creatively questions in the Chapter Review also give students practice in thinking and problem-solving. The student is also given repeated practice throughout review materials in making hypotheses and making generalizations—important steps of geographic inquiry.

LEARNING AIDS

World Geography: People and Places includes a number of additional features designed to facilitate teaching and learning. A Preface familiarizes both teachers and students with the organization and format of the Student Edition. The Preface is followed by a table of contents and a list of special-interest features, skills lessons, and illustrations found throughout the Student Edition. A Prologue, designed to introduce students to the study and value of geography, immediately precedes Unit 1 material.

Valuable learning aids also have been incorporated in the unit and chapter presentation. Each unit opens with an identified colorful theme photograph, table of contents of the chapters in the unit, and a brief overview of unit content. Each chapter opens with an identified colorful photograph, a list of themes the students will read about within the chapter content, and an introduction that prepares the student for the major understandings presented in the chapter.

The chapter narrative itself is broken down into numbered sections. Key terms appear in boldface type and are immediately defined in context. Each numbered section is followed by Content Check questions that serve as a check on student comprehension. Each Unit Review contains a summary of major generalizations learned in unit content, several unit questions that attempt to help students synthesize all they have learned within the unit content, suggested unit activities for individual and group projects, and a thorough skills lesson on a skill important to the work of geographers. Each Chapter Review contains a useful summary of key understandings from the chapter, a vocabulary exercise that checks student comprehension of the important terms from the chapter content, and four sets of questions. Questions in Remembering the Facts are recall questions that test students' basic factual knowledge. Understanding the Facts check student comprehension of the meaning behind the facts. Thinking Critically and Creatively presents opportunities to students to apply, analyze, synthesize, and evaluate the information from the chapter. Challenge questions have been added to this section for use as classroom discussion topics, student research, and other enrichment application. Reinforcing Graphic Skills questions give students additional practice at the skill taught in the Using Graphic Skills exercise in the Student Edition.

To help students with the pronunciation of new terms and unfamiliar place-names, pronunciation respellings follow many words within the chapter narrative. The respellings show a primary accented syllable in capital letters and a secondary accented syllable in smaller capital letters. The pronunciations are easy to read because they are respellings of the words with no diacritical marks.

In view of the fact that, after English, Spanish is the most widely spoken language in the United States today, and the fact that Spanish is the language of most of the people in the Western Hemisphere, *World Geography: People and Places* has chosen to present pronunciation respellings of most Spanish and Latin American terms and place-names in a way that closely approximates their pronunciation in modern Spanish. This approach has been chosen for several reasons: to sensitize students gently to how Spanish and Latin American words sound in their own language; to introduce an aspect of the cultures of many of the people in the Western Hemisphere; and to stress to world geography students the importance of global perspectives. In doing so, *World Geography: People and Places* underlines one of its major themes—interdependence among nations of the world.

The Appendix to the text contains several helpful aids, including a set of 14 atlas maps—the world and its major regions; a 14-page data chart—National Profiles—that shows national flags and gives important statistical data on the independent nations of the world; a glossary, complete with references to the page on which important terms are introduced; and an index of the entire Student Edition.

VISUAL AIDS

Because the study of world geography depends on not only reading about the world but also seeing patterns of the world, *World Geography: People and Places* has given special attention to including additional visual features to help students visualize the world as it is. Full-color photographs have been specially selected from sources all over the world. Unit opening photographs were selected that show students natural landscapes; on the other hand, chapter opening photographs, in most chapters, emphasize cultural landscapes.

About 150 maps have been included in the Student Edition. In each regional chapter from Units 4–10, there is a set of maps that spotlight the region under study—a physical regions map, a political map, and a land use and resources map. Many chapters also show a historical map. Wherever possible, colors selected for use in the maps have been made with attention to the needs of visually color-deficient students. Colors hard to distinguish when side-by-side have been avoided, whenever possible.

Some graphic illustrations have been repeated throughout the text to help students compare similar information about different world regions. Compar-a-graphs show the population and land area of countries in comparison to the United States. At least one compar-a-graph has been included in each unit. A graphic on climate has also been included for each unit. It shows range of temperature and rainfall for a city within the region. Other charts that show comparative world information have been scattered throughout the Student Edition. For example, a map showing world population density is on page 117; a map on world literacy is on page 137; a chart of mountain peaks in the Americas is on page 299; a chart on world transportation systems is on page 419; and a map that shows several levels of economic development for the nations of the world is on page 510.

To encourage students to research further in the cultures of the many world regions studied in this text and to show students the richness and variety of cultural and historical influences in the world, seven cultural collages have been included as illustrations—one per unit.

TEXT USAGE

World Geography: People and Places includes ample material for a one-year course in world geography. However, the program may be adapted for use in shorter courses. Instructors of shorter courses may wish to select materials from the text that support such themes as Case Studies in World Geography; Culture Areas of the Eastern Hemisphere; The Developing World; Culture Areas of the Northern Hemisphere; and Culture Areas of the Western Hemisphere and the Pacific.

ONE-YEAR COURSES

Units and chapters in *World Geography: People and Places* are sequenced with a view to providing certain basic geographic understandings before introducing students to specific world regions. Though instructors may wish to alter the order in which specific world regions are introduced, it is recommended that the chapters in the first three units be taught as they appear in the textbook.

One of the difficulties of teaching a survey of world geography in two semesters is finding enough time to cover all of the material adequately. In most places the school year averages between 170 and 180 instructional days. Assuming an average school year of 175 days, an appropriate year-long course might devote between 4 and 7 days to each of the 31 chapters. Such a plan is suggested in the chart on page T28.

Each chapter is divided into sections. Teachers are encouraged to calculate how many sections should be covered each day. Keep in mind that the sections vary in length and difficulty. Assignments, too, need to be made after careful consideration of varying student needs and abilities.

World Geography Survey Course

Unit/Chapter	Title	Length of Study
Unit 1	Foundations of Geography	
Chapter 1	Nature of Geography	6 days
Chapter 2	Maps	6 days
Unit 1	Review and Evaluation	1 day
Unit 2	Physical Patterns	
Chapter 3	Landscapes	6 days
Chapter 4	Water and Waterways	5 days
Chapter 5	Climate	6 days
Unit 2	Review and Evaluation	1 day
Unit 3	Human Patterns	
Chapter 6	Population	5 days
Chapter 7	Culture	4 days
Chapter 8	Urban Patterns	4 days
Unit 3	Review and Evaluation	1 day
Unit 4	Anglo-America	
Chapter 9	United States: Landscape and Climate	5 days
Chapter 10	United States: Economic and Cultural Patterns	5 days
Chapter 11	United States: Influences of the Past	4 days
Chapter 12	Canada	6 days
Unit 4	Review and Evaluation	1 day
Unit 5	Latin America	
Chapter 13	Mexico and Central America	7 days
Chapter 14	The Caribbean	5 days
Chapter 15	South America: Atlantic Nations	6 days
Chapter 16	South America: Andean Nations	5 days
Unit 5	Review and Evaluation	1 day
Unit 6	Europe	
Chapter 17	Northwest Europe	6 days
Chapter 18	Mediterranean Europe	6 days
Chapter 19	Eastern Europe	5 days
Chapter 20	The Soviet Union	7 days
Unit 6	Review and Evaluation	1 day
Unit 7	North Africa and Southwest Asia	
Chapter 21	North Africa and the Sahel	5 days
Chapter 22	Southwest Asia	6 days
Unit 7	Review and Evaluation	1 day
Unit 8	Africa South of the Sahara	
Chapter 23	East Africa	5 days
Chapter 24	West and Central Africa	5 days
Chapter 25	Southern Africa	5 days
Unit 8	Review and Evaluation	1 day
Unit 9	Asia	
Chapter 26	South Asia	6 days
Chapter 27	East Asia	7 days
Chapter 28	Southeast Asia	6 days
Unit 9	Review and Evaluation	1 day
Unit 10	Oceania and Antarctica	
Chapter 29	Australia and New Zealand	4 days
Chapter 30	Pacific Islands	4 days
Chapter 31	Antarctica	3 days
Unit 10	Review and Evaluation	1 day
		175 days

ONE-SEMESTER COURSES

World Geography: People and Places may be adapted to a one-semester course of study. Choices may be made of which world regions will be studied in such shorter courses. Assuming that the average semester is about 90 days, various alternative courses are suggested on pages T29–T30 to show how this textbook can be taught based on curriculum demands of individual school districts.

Case Studies in World Geography

Chapter	Title	Length of Study
Chapter 1	Nature of Geography	5 days
Chapter 2	Maps	5 days
Chapter 3	Landscapes	6 days
Case Study: Chapter 21 East Africa		5 days
Chapter 4	Water and Waterways	5 days
Case Study: Chapter 27 East Asia		7 days
Chapter 5	Climate	4 days
Case Study: Chapter 29 Australia and New Zealand		4 days
Chapter 6	Population	5 days
Case Study: Chapter 26 South Asia		6 days
Chapter 7	Culture	4 days
Case Studies: Chapter 10 United States: Economic and Cultural Patterns		5 days
Chapter 17 Northwest Europe		6 days
Chapter 20 The Soviet Union		6 days
Chapter 22 Southwest Asia		6 days
Chapter 8	Urban Patterns	4 days
Case Study: Chapter 13 Mexico and Central America		7 days
		90 days

Culture Areas of the Eastern Hemisphere

Chapter	Title	Length of Study
Chapter 1	Nature of Geography	3 days
Chapter 2	Maps	4 days
Chapter 3	Landscapes	5 days
Chapter 4	Water and Waterways	4 days
Chapter 5	Climate	5 days
Chapter 6	Population	4 days
Chapter 8	Urban Patterns	4 days
Chapter 17	Northwest Europe	5 days
Chapter 18	Mediterranean Europe	5 days
Chapter 19	Eastern Europe	4 days
Chapter 20	The Soviet Union	6 days
Chapter 21	North Africa and the Sahel	4 days
Chapter 22	Southwest Asia	5 days
Chapter 23	East Africa	4 days
Chapter 24	West and Central Africa	4 days
Chapter 25	Southern Africa	4 days
Chapter 26	South Asia	5 days
Chapter 27	East Asia	6 days
Chapter 28	Southeast Asia	5 days
Chapter 29	Australia and New Zealand	4 days
		90 days

The Developing World

Chapter	Title	Length of Study
Chapter 1	Nature of Geography	4 days
Chapter 2	Maps	4 days
Chapter 3	Landscapes	4 days
Chapter 4	Water and Waterways	4 days
Chapter 5	Climate	4 days
Chapter 6	Population	5 days
Chapter 8	Urban Patterns	4 days
Chapter 13	Mexico and Central America	7 days
Chapter 14	The Caribbean	4 days
Chapter 15	South America: Atlantic Nations	5 days
Chapter 16	South America: Andean Nations	4 days
Chapter 21	North Africa and the Sahel	5 days
Chapter 22	Southwest Asia	6 days
Chapter 23	East Africa	5 days
Chapter 24	West and Central Africa	5 days
Chapter 26	South Asia	5 days
Chapter 27	East Asia	6 days
Chapter 28	Southeast Asia	5 days
Chapter 30	Pacific Islands	4 days
		90 days

Culture Areas of the Northern Hemisphere

Chapter 1	Nature of Geography	5 days
Chapter 2	Maps	5 days
Unit 1	Review and Evaluation	1 day
Chapter 9	United States: Landscape and Climate	3 days
Chapter 10	United States: Economic and Cultural Patterns	5 days
Chapter 11	United States: Influences of the Past	3 days
Chapter 12	Canada	5 days
Unit 4	Review and Evaluation	1 day
Chapter 17	Northwest Europe	5 days
Chapter 18	Mediterranean Europe	5 days
Chapter 19	Eastern Europe	4 days
Chapter 20	The Soviet Union	6 days
Unit 6	Review and Evaluation	1 day
Chapter 21	North Africa and the Sahel	4 days
Chapter 22	Southwest Asia	5 days
Unit 7	Review and Evaluation	1 day
Chapter 23	East Africa	4 days
Chapter 24	West and Central Africa	4 days
Chapter 25	Southern Africa	5 days
Unit 8	Review and Evaluation	1 day
Chapter 26	South Asia	5 days
Chapter 27	East Asia	6 days
Chapter 28	Southeast Asia	5 days
Unit 9	Review and Evaluation	1 day
		90 days

Culture Areas of the Western Hemisphere and the Pacific

Chapter 1	Nature of Geography	4 days
Chapter 2	Maps	5 days
Unit 1	Review and Evaluation	1 day
Chapter 3	Landscapes	5 days
Chapter 4	Water and Waterways	4 days
Chapter 5	Climate	5 days
Unit 2	Review and Evaluation	1 day
Chapter 6	Population	4 days
Chapter 7	Culture	4 days
Chapter 8	Urban Patterns	4 days
Unit 3	Review and Evaluation	1 day
Chapter 9	United States: Landscape and Climate	4 days
Chapter 10	United States: Economic and Cultural Patterns	5 days
Chapter 11	United States: Influences of the Past	4 days
Chapter 12	Canada	6 days
Unit 4	Review and Evaluation	1 day
Chapter 13	Mexico and Central America	7 days
Chapter 14	The Caribbean	5 days
Chapter 15	South America: Atlantic Nations	6 days
Chapter 16	South America: Andean Nations	5 days
Unit 5	Review and Evaluation	1 day
Chapter 29	Australia and New Zealand	4 days
Chapter 30	Pacific Islands	4 days
		90 days

TEACHING OPTIONS

After it is determined what text chapters will be included in a school's world geography course, day-to-day planning falls to classroom teachers. Their task is to plan lessons to achieve objectives for each of the selected chapters. To assist teachers in this task, the Text Implementation section of this Teacher Annotated Edition contains lesson plan suggestions in chart form for handy reference. Each chart indicates the objectives linked to a given section in a chapter, along with suggested teaching strategies to help in achieving those objectives. The strategies for a particular section include ideas for teacher preparation, as well as a list of teaching options for the section lesson. From the list of options, teachers may select those activities and exercises that best suit their teaching styles and the needs of their students. For example, when preparing plans for teaching "Making Maps," Section 3 of Chapter 2, the teacher would refer to the chart reproduced below that appears on page T70 in this Teacher Annotated Edition. From the information in the chart, individual lesson plans can be written. Three sample lesson plans follow the chart. These plans embody many of the teaching options suggested in the chart. They illustrate the flexibility fostered throughout this Teacher Annotated Edition.

Section 3   Making Maps (pp. 32–36)

Chapter Objectives	Suggested Teaching Strategies	Review

3. describe four properties maps may have.
 	
4. distinguish among cylindrical, conic, and flat-plane projections.
	Teacher Preparation
	    SE, Reading Assignment, pp. 32–37
	    TAE, Unit 1 Suggested Resources
	        Chapter 2 Overview, p. T64
	    TRB, Chapter 2 Teacher Notes: Section 3
	Teaching Options
	    SE, *Comparing Projections*, pp. 36–37
	    TAE, Objectives 3 and 4 Activities, pp. T66–T67
	    TRB, Chapter 2 Teacher Notes: Section 3, Extending the Lesson
	        Chapter 2 Skill Activity, B
		SE, Content Check, p. 36

Each of the following sample lesson plans, written from the suggestions in the chart above, will help students achieve the chapter objectives for Section 3 of Chapter 2. Each plan, however, teaches the section material from a different perspective and uses various teaching methods. Each plan assumes that both the teacher and students are prepared for the teaching of the section by Day 1. The students prepare for class by reading Section 3 on pages 32–36 of the Student Edition. The teacher prepares by following the Teacher Preparation guidelines of the Suggested Teaching Strategies column in the chart above. The guidelines suggest the reading of Section 3, along with portions of the Teacher Annotated Edition and the Teacher Resource Book.

PLAN A

Day 1 Review the reading of Section 3 by asking students to answer orally the questions in the Content Check on page 36 in the Student Edition. List the four properties of maps on the chalkboard. Conduct Objective 3 Teaching Activity. End the discussion on map properties by having students search through their textbooks for examples of maps with each of the four properties. Because the projection of each map in the Student Edition has been indicated, the names of the projections will assist the students in locating some maps with each of the four properties.

Day 2 Conduct both Objective 4 Teaching and Reinforcing Activities. Display the maps in the school hallway under letters that spell "Making Maps."

PLAN B

Day 1 Review the reading of Section 3 by asking students to define the terms listed in the Content Check on page 36 in the Student Edition. Have students examine the diagrams on mapmaking on pages 36-37 in the Comparing Projections feature. Have students make a list that matches properties of maps with types of projections. Then distribute the student handout for the Chapter 2 Skill Activity. Introduce the activity to students and assign the map as homework.

Day 2 Begin class by asking students the questions in the Content Check on page 36 in the Student Edition. Then give students time to work on their maps during class. Students may benefit by working in pairs to share ideas. Allow more time to complete the maps, or, if students finish, post the maps around the classroom or on a school bulletin board.

PLAN C

Day 1 Review the reading of Section 3 by asking students to answer orally the questions in the Content Check on page 36 in the Student Edition. Conduct Objective 4 Enriching Activity. After students have discussed the Chapter 2 Reading in the Teacher Resource Book, share with them the information in the Teacher Section 3

Extending the Lesson on new techniques in mapmaking. Have them look at the image on page 147 of the Student Edition to see how aerial photographs help define locations of highways, buildings, parks, and so on.

Day 2 Conduct the lecture described in Objective 4 Enriching Activity. Discuss the four map properties thoroughly, as you show the class various kinds of map projections. Debrief the class with the round-table discussion suggested in the activity.

EVALUATING THE PROGRAM

One of the best ways to ensure that effective learning-teaching materials are produced is to make your assessments of the materials you are using available to authors and publishers. This can be done by completing and mailing the survey form found on the last two pages of this teacher guide. Once you have completed the form and removed it from the book, fold and tape it so that the Merrill Publishing Company label shows. The authors and publishers appreciate hearing from you and will use your information in the planning of program revisions and new products.

INSTRUCTIONAL APPROACHES

In any course of study, teachers usually use a variety of approaches to provide students with opportunities for applying skills and factual knowledge, for gaining greater understanding of content, for enlivening the subject, or for expanding activities suggested in the Student Edition and Teacher Annotated Edition. Certain teaching approaches are particularly effective in a world geography course. This section is designed to provide guidelines on how to use several of these approaches in class. When planning lessons to meet unit goals and chapter objectives, you may wish to refer back to this section for additional ideas for structuring your class and for additional teaching approaches.

AUDIOVISUAL MATERIALS

Audiovisual materials offer an efficient and appealing means of conveying information. Their use in a world geography class can make people and places in other parts of the world more "real" to students. It is one thing to read about Sri Lanka, for example, and yet another thing to see the place and hear its people.

There are many kinds of audiovisual materials today. Some examples are 16-millimeter films, filmstrips, videocassettes, audiocassettes, records, 35-millimeter slides, still photographs, and computer software of all kinds. These materials can help focus attention on certain geographic topics or concepts and reinforce the geographic skills of observation and analysis. Students who have reading difficulties often benefit when audiovisual materials are used.

Selecting the Material. Audiovisual materials are available from a variety of sources, including media centers found in many school districts. Public libraries and school and university media centers are additional sources. In recent years, many school districts have acquired large libraries of computer software. A number of mail-order firms specialize in audiovisual material. Some travel agencies also have useful materials available. Additionally, several specific recommendations for audiovisual materials are listed in the Suggested Resources section of this Teacher Annotated Edition.

Preliminary Considerations. To attain the greatest educational benefit from a specific piece of audiovisual material, the teacher needs to be familiar with it. By previewing the material before introducing it to students, lesson plans can be devised that integrate the material smoothly into the unit of study. In doing this, it is well to think about which parts of the material are most relevant to what the class is doing. Often, only a portion of an item is needed for actual classroom instruction. Decisions need to be made about how much of an item to use and whether it should be presented to students continuously or by stopping it at selected places to allow for discussion.

Implementing the Method. Before the material is introduced, alert students to ideas and themes they are expected to grasp as a result of this learning experience. To prepare them for the activity, you may wish to distribute a set of focus questions to students. This can help them as they become involved in the activity. The questions can also provide a focus for debriefing.

Debriefing. A debriefing activity following work with audiovisual materials can take several forms. Often a discussion is effective. When leading a discussion, help students focus on the central points introduced in the audiovisual materials. It is important to establish the connection of the audiovisual material to the material in the unit being studied. At this time, individuals in the class can compare their perceptions with those of others. The debriefing session also allows you to correct bias, assure that all viewpoints are introduced, and encourage students to pursue additional research.

BRAINSTORMING

Geographers use brainstorming to gather information and ideas from one another through a free and open verbal exchange. Regardless of academic ability, students can successfully participate in classroom brainstorming because no evaluations or judgments concerning student responses are allowed.

In brainstorming, a topic is selected and students freely express ideas they think relate to the topic. The method provides students an opportunity to use ideas from their personal experiences in finding novel solutions to problems and puzzles, or creative ways for explaining situations and phenomena. Brainstorming can be used throughout the course of study to prompt student interest in a topic, expand the content of the text, assess student understanding of the material, or encourage class participation and student interaction.

Selecting the Topic. Almost any topic related to world geography would be suitable. The most effective ones, however, are those posing a problem or a puzzle. An example such as "Why is Mexico's largest city not a seaport?" would be an appropriate focus question for a brainstorming exercise linked to Chapter 13, Mexico and Central America.

Topics can also be expressed by a single word or phrase, such as "balkanization" or "pluralistic society." The most important thing to consider in choosing a topic is how the information and ideas generated by the students will be used. Keep this in mind when selecting brainstorming topics.

Preliminary Considerations. A simple way to explain the rules for a brainstorming exercise is to write them on the chalkboard and discuss each briefly. The following rules for brainstorming can serve as guidelines:
1. Say anything that comes to mind. Call out ideas as they occur to you.
2. Try to expand on the ideas of others.
3. If you cannot think of anything else to say, wait a minute and try again.
4. Never criticize what others say.

Implementing the Method. Write the topic on the chalkboard, and have students call out their ideas. If students have a difficult time generating ideas, get things started by calling out a few ideas. Your role is to write the student ideas on the board as rapidly as possible.

In listing the student responses, misconceptions that students might have about a situation or region may become evident. If that occurs, place a mark by the idea on the board in order to return to it after the brainstorming session. The session should be stopped when it becomes obvious that no new ideas are being presented. Ten to fifteen minutes is usually long enough.

Debriefing. Following the brainstorming session, reinforce information generated about the topic by reviewing the ideas mentioned by the students. This activity can take many forms. For example, the students can place the ideas in certain categories or list them according to certain priorities. Encourage students to draw conclusions and make generalizations from the information and ideas. It is important at this point to relate the ideas back to the subject of study.

CASE STUDIES

When geographers want to examine certain situations in-depth, they often follow a case study approach. It is a way to analyze and evaluate the facts of a situation and to reach and support a conclusion or generalization. Students of geography can also follow the same step-by-step evaluation procedure in an in-depth study of a variety of topics.

A case study requires students to ask questions; define elements important to a situation; analyze, synthesize, compare and contrast these elements; and make judgments in a case. In short, the case study provides the opportunity for students to practice all levels of thinking from recall to evaluation.

Selecting the Topic. Specific topics for case studies can be varied and numerous.

Limitations occur, however, with the time needed for case preparation and the availability of needed materials. For example, a case study focusing on the kinds of adaptations made by people in South America to living at a high altitude may be limited by the available data about life in this area. Topics such as an in-depth profile of the Argentine economy may prove to be more workable for both teachers and students.

Implementing the Method. First, select a case for study. Then, supply students with the necessary information about the situation in the case. In addition to statistical data, primary source material such as newspaper stories can be effective. Variety in the kind of information presented to students can add to the dimension of understanding that cannot be achieved by statistics alone. In some instances, films and other non-print materials may also be of value.

Allow sufficient time for students to review the case study information. Keep the material relatively short and to the point, trying not to overwhelm students with too much information at one time. Once the material has been reviewed, lead students through an evaluation of the material and the situation, using the information as it is presented in the case study.

Debriefing. Attempt to have students draw conclusions and make generalizations from the material. Depending on the objectives of the case study exercise, a variety of questions may be considered for the purpose of evaluating the situation and the data. Raise questions such as: Based on this information alone, how would you describe the situation? and Why are individual statistics often not enough to draw a proper conclusion?

Once students have drawn conclusions and made generalizations about the case, have them attempt to relate the in-depth study of the topic to the broader study of geography and the world situation. If the topic is an in-depth study of the economic situation in Argentina, have students relate the case to conditions in the subregion of the Atlantic Nations, the region of Latin America, the continent of South America, the Western Hemisphere, and the world.

COMMUNITY RESOURCE PERSONS

Every community has a wealth of resource persons willing to come into the classroom and share some of their knowledge about a particular aspect of world geography. Presentations made by people in the community can greatly enrich student learning. Such presentations, too, add an important dimension of "reality" to classroom instruction. People who have visited or lived for a time in other countries can bring these countries to life in ways that can never be duplicated by more typical classroom lessons.

Selecting the Participants. As a beginning, survey the local community to identify people who might be potential resources for each unit of the world geography course. For example, a list of people willing to speak to students about different aspects of Northwest Europe might be generated. Another list might include people willing to share information about "Earth and the Future."

Implementing the Method. Consult the master list to select a speaker. Then ask the individual to speak only on those topics with which he or she is most familiar. For example, someone who has lived in India probably could speak more knowledgeably about issues confronting Indians as they lead their day-to-day lives than someone who briefly toured the country. Yet, a tourist might have a considerable amount of information to share about the Taj Mahal or other favorite sites.

Provide the guest speaker with information about students in the class. This information might include what students have previously been taught, the general sophistication of students' vocabularies, and some of their areas of interest.

The prospective speaker also should be told about how long to speak. Generally, shorter presentations of 15 to 20 minutes, with time for questions, are more effective than longer ones. It is important that specific arrangements be made regarding such issues as the speaker's arrival time, where he or she should report, and who will meet and escort him or her to the classroom.

Students should be prepared for the speaker by having specific information about the subject of the speaker's talk. Often it is a good idea to provide students with a set of questions about the topic. These can then be used as a basis for note-taking. Also, debriefing is more productive with a common set of questions.

Debriefing. There may be a general debriefing discussion at the end of the speaker's presentation. Often a follow-up discussion will occur during the next class meeting. At this time, the speaker's remarks can be reinforced by reviewing main points with the class, keeping comments within the context of the world geography unit being studied. A concluding discussion might include such questions as: What new information did you learn? Was any of this information different from what you had learned from other sources? If so, how do you account for these differences? What did the speaker say that might lead you to seek additional information?

COOPERATIVE LEARNING

Cooperative learning approaches require students to work together as they pursue a common goal. Each member of a group is given a specific task to accomplish. Students are also given incentives to help one another accomplish tasks assigned to the group as a whole. Part of each student's evaluation is determined by the overall quality of the group's work.

Selecting the Topic. Cooperative learning is an especially useful approach when content being studied can be divided into parts. For example, there are many nations mentioned in Chapter 28, Southeast Asia. An assignment for students to "compare and contrast languages, religions, and racial characteristics in different countries of the Insular Southeast Asia region" would lend itself to cooperative learning.

Preliminary Considerations. A number of people have suggested cooperative learning guidelines. Aronson's "Jigsaw Method" (1978) is especially good for geography classes. In this method a number of learning tasks are identified, then the class is divided accordingly. If there are five tasks, five groups are needed. For example, five groups could be made for a lesson on the languages, religions, and racial characteristics of the Insular Southeast Asia region. Each group would focus on one of the following areas: (a) Indonesia, (b) the Philippines, (c) Malaysia, (d) Singapore, or (e) Brunei.

Five students could be assigned to each group, with each one having an approximately equal distribution of ability levels. In each group, one student should be assigned as the "expert" on each place (Indonesia, the Philippines, Malaysia, Singapore, and Brunei). Once groups are organized, the assigned task is again described. Students are directed to gather information about the languages, religions, and racial characteristics of the people.

Implementing the Method. Once basic group assignments have been made and students have been assigned to be "experts" on one of the five places, direct them to break out of their original groups to meet in "experts' groups." In other words, the students from each group assigned to "Indonesia" will meet together as will the students from each group assigned to each other place. Instruct students to work together in the experts' groups to gather information from Chapter 28 (and from supplementary sources) about the language, religions, and racial characteristics of their assigned place. Members of experts' groups should be encouraged to help one another.

After each experts' group has completed its task, members should reassemble into their original groups. In the original groups, the expert on each place shares with the others what he or she has learned.

Debriefing. Lead a class discussion. On the chalkboard, write names of the places studied in the groups, as well as information about languages, religions, and racial characteristics as such information surfaces. As a concluding activity, ask students to point out similarities and differences among places and suggest why these exist.

DEBATING

Geographers with opposing views of the world often debate topics in order to convince opponents that their own position is either correct or the most persuasive. For students, debating provides an opportunity for participants to conduct research, develop and articulate clear and logical arguments, and reach a reasonable conclusion. Debating requires students to exercise a wide range of research, thinking, and communication skills. Students who do not take part directly in the classroom debate are still involved in the learning process as they listen to new information, consider the arguments, make judgments about the quality of the presentation, and draw conclusions about the topic of the debate.

Selecting the Topic. There are numerous topics of debate appropriate for the world geography class. It may be worthwhile to involve students in selecting a subject in which they are particularly interested or about which they would like to learn more.

Sometimes the most effective topics for a classroom debate are those involving real or potential controversies. Depending on the lesson objective, the topic can be formulated into a resolution, such as "Resolved: All the people of Yugoslavia should be required to speak only Serbo-Croatian."

Selecting the Participants. Most classroom debates involve two competing teams. One team, the *pro* team, favors the resolution. The other team, the *con* team, opposes the resolution. Although each team generally consists of two or three members, larger teams can be used, depending on the topic and its objectives.

You can select the team members, or students can volunteer to be on one team or the other. A chairperson and timekeeper also should be named. As a general rule, the debate will be more successful if the opposing teams are fairly well balanced in terms of research and communication skills. To ensure order during the debate, you may have to assume the role of parliamentarian.

Preliminary Considerations. Both the debate topic and the participants should be selected several weeks in advance of the actual debate to allow students to research and prepare their arguments. In addition, participants should be given clear directions as to their assignment before they begin research. Debaters should be expected to develop their arguments based on from three to five major points. The arguments should be logically presented and substantiated by factual evidence. Explain these guidelines to both the debaters and observers so that everyone knows what to expect on the day of the debate.

During the time the debaters are completing their research, direct the other students in developing an observation sheet to monitor the progress of the debate. This will provide a focus for the observers and involve all the students in the activity.

Implementing the Method. The actual debate can be as formal or informal as desired to achieve the objectives of the lesson. The procedure outlined here is quite formal, but it can be easily adjusted as needed. It is important that before the debate begins, students are aware of the procedure that is to be followed.

The class should be arranged with the chairperson and the debating teams seated in the front of the room. The team in favor of the resolution should sit on one side of the chairperson; the team opposed, on the opposite side. The timekeeper should sit to one side at the front of the room.

The chairperson begins the debate by introducing the topic and reading the resolution. The chairperson then introduces a debater in support of the resolution to present the first argument. Then the chairperson assigns the speaker a predetermined amount of time for the presentation of the argument. Two minutes is usually sufficient. Following the presentation of the first debater, the chairperson introduces a debater from the opposing side. The chairperson continues to make the introductions as new speakers are presented.

As the debate proceeds, the role of the timekeeper becomes extremely important. The timekeeper should announce when each speaker's time has expired. No student should be allowed to exceed the prescribed time.

After all arguments have been presented by both sides, debaters are permitted time for rebuttal statements to refute what the opponents have said. The team in opposition to the resolution begins the rebuttal sequence. Note that these arguments may be anticipated, but cannot be prepared because their content depends upon material presented by the competing debaters.

Debriefing. This is an especially important step. Emphasize the major points presented by the debaters. Allow time for comments by the student observers to add additional points. When all the ideas about the resolution have been expressed, ask students for a show of hands to determine how many are in support of the resolution and how many are opposed. Tally the votes on the chalkboard. Conclude the session by asking students whether or not they changed their minds from a previous position due to the arguments presented.

DEMONSTRATION

Teacher-directed demonstrations have many applications in the world geography classroom. Perhaps one of the most important is showing students how to perform geographic skills.

Selecting the Topic. The topics best suited to this approach are those involving active student participation. In world geography, these range from locating places using latitude and longitude to demonstrating how the tilt of Earth on its axis results in changing seasons. A skill feature included in each chapter of the student text may be used as a source for demonstration topics.

Implementing the Method. Successful demonstrations follow a sound sequence of steps. It is also important to review each step of a demonstration to assure student understanding.

There are a number of possible steps that might be used in the demonstration approach. One that has been used with success is:

1. Teacher performs the entire activity in front of the class.
2. Teacher performs the activity a second time, dividing the activity into smaller tasks. Each task is written on the chalkboard.
3. Teacher discusses the tasks to assure student understanding. Each step is carefully reviewed.
4. Teacher has a student volunteer or the entire class perform the activity following the directions listed on the chalkboard.

Debriefing. This consists of the teacher monitoring student performance of a skill. When individual problems are spotted, have students orally review the steps to be followed. Then provide the needed assistance to assure student mastery of the skill.

DISCUSSION

The study of world geography can be difficult. Geographers often discuss complex topics to gather information and ideas and to bridge the gap between factual recall and understanding the implications of facts.

In a classroom discussion, students engage in teacher-directed verbal exchanges related to a selected topic. The method provides students an opportunity to demonstrate their understanding of geographic content. Classroom discussion also allows the teacher to evaluate students' levels of understanding and to act to remedy any misunderstanding.

Selecting the Topic. Virtually any topic studied in world geography can be used in a classroom discussion. Topics can be broad in scope, such as "the region of South Asia." Or, topics can be more focused, such as "the caste system of India." Generally, discussions are more productive when the range of content is not broad. In some instances, it may be convenient to conduct discussions after reading material the length of one subsection.

Preliminary Considerations. Successful discussions most often depend on properly sequencing questioning. To promote student participation early in the activity, ask questions requiring factual recall by the students. *Content Check* questions in the section reviews and *Remembering the Facts* questions in the chapter reviews of the text can be used as examples of this kind of questioning. Later in the discussion, ask questions requiring greater understanding of the facts. See the *Understanding the Facts* questions in the chapter reviews for examples.

In structuring the classroom discussion, it may be helpful to consider the three major categories of questions that were noted by researchers at the Northwest Educational Laboratory in 1972. These categories are (1) analysis of specifics questions, (2) analysis of relationships questions, and (3) generalizing or capstone questions.

Analysis of specifics questions calls upon students to recall specific pieces of information. Analysis of relationships questions requires students to compare, contrast, and analyze information. Generalizing or capstone questions require students to go beyond the given information to make judgments about the material.

Implementing the Method. One way to introduce the activity is to write the first question on the chalkboard. By writing *What is caste?* on the board, for example, student attention is focused on the topic. In some cases, it may be helpful to write each major question on the chalkboard to establish a line of questioning. In most cases, however, it is helpful to write only the most significant ones.

During the course of the activity, students are to answer verbally the teacher-directed questions. Also encourage students to ask their own questions about material that they do not fully understand. Conclude the session when it becomes obvious that no new questions and answers are being presented.

Debriefing. Following the discussion, reinforce information by reviewing the major points. This can be done by writing them on the chalkboard. Encourage students to draw conclusions and make generalizations from the points listed on the board. It is important to relate the information back to the general subject of study.

EXPERIMENTATION

Experimentation is a technique used to guide students toward discovery of important ideas. It involves hands-on activities that generate data students can use to make inferences and arrive at conclusions.

Selecting the Topic. Experimentation works best with data students can produce by manipulating things in the classroom. Consider, for example, the topic of contour maps. Many students have difficulty understanding the relationship between contour lines on a flat map and the three-dimensional surfaces these lines represent. An in-class experiment can help them grasp this concept.

Implementing the Method. Provide students with the necessary equipment and clear instructions for conducting the activity. You also may want to divide the class into groups.

For an experiment about contour maps, for example, provide the following equipment:

1. A clear plastic shoe box. Starting at the bottom of the box, place black marks every half inch with a grease pencil.
2. A clear plastic top to fit over the shoe box.
3. A clear overhead projector transparency and a marker to write on the transparency.
4. Some masking tape to attach the blank transparency to the clear plastic top of the shoe box.
5. Some modeling clay.
6. A one-gallon jug filled with water. (The experiment is easier to do if food coloring has been added to the water.)

Have students make a model of a mountain and some lowlands leading up to it with the modeling clay. Place this landform firmly inside the shoe box. Next, have them fill the shoe box with water up to the first half-inch line. Then place the lid on the box and tape a transparency to it.

At this point, one student in each group should draw a line with the transparency marker, marking the line of intersection between the water and the landform in the box. This line becomes the first contour line.

Once the first contour line has been drawn, remove the cover and the attached transparency with the contour line. Instruct students to add water to the second half-inch mark, replace the lid, then draw another line indicating the new intersection of water and landform. This results in a second contour line.

Continue the procedure until the landform has been completely covered or until the last half-inch line has been reached. The result is a contour map reflecting the elevation patterns of the landform.

Debriefing. Collect the transparencies from each group. Project one or more of them onto a screen or wall using an overhead projector. To prompt students to draw conclusions, ask questions such as the following:

1. What do contour lines that are far apart indicate about elevation?
2. What do contour lines that are close together indicate about elevation?
3. What kind of contour lines would indicate a mountain with an enormous cliff that ran vertically for 1,000 feet or more?

These questions relate to the experiment discussed as an example of the method. Questions will vary depending on the purpose of the individual experiment.

FIELD TRIPS

Field trips offer excellent opportunities for world geography students to experience their world more directly. They also allow students to encounter resources not available to them in the school. Field trips also can add realism to world geography instruction.

Selecting the Focus. A variety of places can be profitably visited. The basic limitation, however, is the range of options available locally or within a reasonable distance. Museums, international border stations, state border stations, universities, and international festivals are appropriate sites.

The local community also can serve as a productive resource for a field trip experience. A carefully structured field trip of the local community can help students understand basic street patterns, distributions of businesses and other services, local terrain features, and other information. This can provide a valuable store of information upon which the class can draw to compare and contrast local areas with other areas of the world.

Preliminary Considerations. The advanced planning for field trips is a must. Most school districts require that teachers follow specific procedures concerning transportation, chaperons, and parental permission. Arrangements often have to be made several weeks before the trip takes place.

Contacting people at the field trip destination is a major part of advance planning. A definite date and time of day must be decided. The staff at the site should be alerted to topics to be covered, interests of students, ages of students, and what previous exposure they might have received about the content of the field trip.

Students also must be prepared. They should be oriented to the place to be visited, the people they will meet, and their personal obligations. Often the latter will include specific kinds of information the students will be expected to bring back to the classroom. To help students do this, a field trip observation guide should be developed. This will help students take notes on the trip. These notes can be used during the debriefing discussion.

Implementing the Method. If planning has been well done, the actual point-to-point movement should go smoothly. Throughout the trip, the teacher should be alert to point out items of interest, answer questions, and provide additional clarification.

Debriefing. If possible, an initial debriefing should be conducted at the end of the field trip itself. Sometimes this can be done on the bus. Any students who have had difficulty completing observation guides can be helped at this time. During the next class period, a more formal debriefing discussion can be conducted. Among questions that might be asked are: What specific new information did you learn? How does this information compare with what you already knew from reading the text? What other places might you like to visit on your own to extend your understanding of this topic?

LECTURE

Lecture can be used to introduce a great deal of information about a given topic. In fact, the capability of the lecture to present great quantities of material in a short time is one of its potential pitfalls. Improperly used, lectures can overwhelm students with too much new content.

Lectures probably are best used to enrich coverage of a single topic or a limited range of topics. Keeping a lecture narrowly focused can

help overcome the potential for providing more content than students can absorb.

Selecting the Topic. Numerous topics lend themselves to lectures for the world geography class. The teacher might wish to involve students in selecting specific topics or issues that might become focal points for enrichment lectures. For example, a class might decide that it would like to know more about Liberia during the study of the chapter titled West and Central Africa.

Preliminary Considerations. Several key points should be kept in mind in preparing for a lecture. Among them are the following:

- **Identify present levels of understanding.** Find out what students already know about the topic so they will not have unrealistic expectations. Some questions to students will help the teacher gain insight into how much the students already understand.
- **Keep length short.** In planning a lecture, it is wise to keep length as short as possible consistent with the need to deal with the basic content.
- **Prepare an outline for students.** In preparation for a lecture, it is a good idea to provide a general outline for students to follow. This should list key points, and there should be space for students to take notes.
- **Highlight key points.** Plan to emphasize important points during the lecture. Alert students to critical material by cueing them with changes in voice, pitch, and intonation.

Implementing the Method. Provide students with a copy of an outline. For example, if the lecture were to focus on additional material on Liberia, the outline might be built around basic headings in the chapter on West and Central Africa. It could look something like this:

I. Landscape and Climate of Liberia
   A. Landscape
   B. Climate

II. Liberia: Economic and Cultural Patterns
   A. Regions
   B. Social and Economic Conditions
III. Liberia's Past

Be sure space is provided for students to take notes. This kind of an outline will help students organize information presented in the lecture.

Debriefing. Follow the lecture with a classroom discussion. The discussion should focus on some of the major points raised in the lecture. Ask some questions related to each of the major points listed on the lecture outline. Some suggestions to students for additional learning about the topic of the lecture also might be provided at this time.

READING GUIDES

A reading guide is a series of statements, each of which either accurately or inaccurately repeats an idea presented in the text. Reading Guides are designed to lead students through the various levels of reading comprehension.

Although *World Geography: People and Places* has a closely controlled reading level, some students may have difficulty with comprehension. Reading guides serve to help students comprehend on several levels what they read. Rather than being based on the assumption that students will read and understand text material, reading guides are based on the assumption that many students will have difficulty comprehending written material.

Reading guides may be used with sections, chapters, or units of study, depending on your objectives. They can be used as homework or seatwork and lend themselves readily to differentiation and individualization. When used in the form of a group activity in which students within a group compare responses and arrive at a consensus, they foster group interaction skills.

Selecting the Topic. Preview the material. Select a topic that you feel students might encounter difficulty in comprehending.

The topic should concern information important to subsequent student understanding of a broader concept.

Preliminary Considerations. Read the section or chapter related to the topic you have chosen with an eye to selecting the most important points and generalizations. Then determine whether you want to foster a literal or an interpretive level of reading comprehension. For the literal level, students are expected to read a statement from the guide and then read the text to determine if the statement in the guide accurately restates what has been said in the text. For the interpretive level, students are expected to determine whether or not a more general statement from the guide is a valid inference or generalization from the text.

For the literal level, develop statements that either accurately or inaccurately restate the points made in the text. For very slow readers, take the statements verbatim from the text. Then, to develop inaccuracies, incorporate gross errors. For better readers, adapt statements from the text by transposing words, using synonyms, or taking statements out of context. To develop an interpretive level guide, list accurate and/or inaccurate inferences or generalizations. A reading guide using questions instead of statements may be developed along the same guidelines, with questions leveled from knowledge and comprehension to higher levels of analysis and evaluation.

Implementing the Method. For the literal level, distribute in a handout the statements you developed that touch the points made in the text. Read each aloud to the class. Then have the students read the corresponding section in the text. As they read, have them refer back to the guide statements and indicate those they believe say what the authors *said*, not those that reflect what they believe the authors *meant* by what they said. To indicate that a statement is an accurate restatement of what was said in the text, have students place the page, column, and paragraph numbers to the left of the statement.

For the interpretive level, distribute in a handout the statements you developed that are inferences or generalizations based on the text content. Read each aloud to the class. Then have students read the corresponding section in the text and familiarize themselves with its content. Instruct them to place a checkmark next to each guide statement they believe represents what the authors *meant* by what they said.

Debriefing. For the literal level, starting with the first statement and continuing one by one until all statements have been covered, have students indicate by a show of hands whether or not they felt the statement was an accurate restatement of what the text authors said. Refer back to the indicated passage(s) of the text to confirm or dispute the students' decisions. If a guide statement is not an accurate restatement of the text material, determine why it is inaccurate.

For the interpretive level, go over each inference and generalization with the class, asking students to indicate whether or not it is valid. Have students refer back to the text to find bits of information that, when considered together, would form a relationship represented by the statement.

RETRIEVAL CHARTS

For students unfamiliar with content relating to places in the world, geography might appear to be a series of unrelated facts about individual countries. The retrieval chart method of organizing facts enables students of geography to organize information in such a way that patterns among countries and regions appear more clearly.

Retrieval charts are grids on which data are arranged under various headings. A completed retrieval chart can be used as a basis for class discussion. The charts are particularly useful when the class is reviewing content, enabling students to link information that might at first appear to be fragmented and disjointed.

Selecting the Topic. Topics for retrieval charts can be determined by using the regional division within the text. Countries not highlighted in each region may be appropriate subjects.

The kind of information also can be selected based on the categories in each of the regional chapters in the text. For example, in each of the regional chapters, information about climate in an area or country is presented. Thus, "climate types" might be one category choice.

COUNTRY: CHILE	
Physical Features	
Climate Types	
Forms of Government	

Depending on goals and objectives, the teacher can select categories that best relate to the material to be covered.

Implementing the Method. Supply students with a blank chart, such as the one shown on this page. In this example, the country of Chile is the place to be studied. Specific information on government, climate, and terrain of that country is to be gathered. Working with the class as a whole or divided into small groups, instruct students to complete each of the cells on the chart by reviewing the pertinent material in the text. In some cases, students may have to use other reference books.

Another approach might be to assign certain students or groups to complete sections of the chart. For example, one student or group might have to complete the cells pertaining to the government of Chile. Another student or group might have to complete the cells concerning climate. Also, consider drawing a blank retrieval chart on the chalkboard, with students writing in the information.

Debriefing. When adequate information has been logged on the retrieval chart, have students review the material. Help them compare and contrast the data. Then, have them compare and contrast the places studied. Raise questions such as: What are the similarities? What are the differences? and What patterns do you see? Have the students refer to the charts frequently for later discussions and review before test time.

ROLE-PLAYS AND SIMULATIONS

Role playing is an approach in which students assume the roles of other persons and act out what they believe those other persons would say or do in a given situation. The essence of role playing is people—what they feel and how they might typically respond. For example, a group of students might play the roles of people in different world cultures who would respond to situations in unique ways.

Simulations involve role playing, but the situation is designed to more closely model reality. For example, students might be involved in a simulated meeting of an international organization that is considering geographic features that might be used to determine where a new boundary line should be drawn.

Selecting the Topic. There are many situations that lend themselves to role plays and simulations. In world geography, these range from conducting an economic summit of representatives of countries within a region to reenacting events important to a region's history. In considering the topic, determine whether the situation is "action-oriented." Next, decide whether students will be able to enact clearly defined roles.

Preliminary Considerations. In role plays and simulations, it is important to ex- plain to students exactly what each person is to do. Any special rules involving such issues as how decisions are to be made, how characters are to act, time limits, and ranges of options need to be made clear. Explain the importance of all participants becoming actively involved.

Selecting Participants. Students may volunteer for roles, or the teacher may assign them. Depending on the lesson objectives, it may be worthwhile to ask students who have certain value positions to assume roles of persons whose values are different. If they have to articulate another person's point of view, they may better understand why others act as they do.

One way to assure that as many students as possible participate is to organize several concurrent role plays or simulations. Under these conditions, it is important to move from group to group. Further, this arrangement makes it easier for shy students to become active participants. Many who will hesitate to speak up in front of a group of 25 or 30 become willing participants in groups of 4, 5, or 6.

When it is not possible for all students in the class to become active participants in a role play or simulation, some can serve as observers. Before the role play or simulation begins, help these students develop an instruction sheet. The sheet may include a series of questions or a list of points to look for during the activity. The focus should be on patterns of interaction and on the general progress of the activity, rather than on judgments about individual performances.

Implementing the Method. After participants have been selected, the character- istics of each role should be described to the class. Sometimes this can be done by provid- ing participants with predesigned role cards that include such items as age, sex, racial or ethnic background, level of education, area of residence, and occupation. Depending on the objectives of the activity, you may wish to include any personality trait or value position that would make a difference in how the role should be played. If the activity is to simulate a real event, the situation should be described in detail before the action begins.

As the role play or the simulation begins, the room should be arranged to facilitate the interaction. It may be necessary to move desks and tables. Charts, maps, and other needed props should be arranged appropriately in the classroom.

Once the role play or simulation begins, it should be allowed to run its course. Intervene only to offer relevant information or to take other action designed to maintain the flow of the activity.

Debriefing. After the role play or simulation, review the action by considering outcomes and analyzing the nature of relationships among participants. Have observers refer to their observation sheets and actively involve these students in the discussion. Their contributions can be helpful to participants who often become so immersed in the activity that they fail to note much of what went on around them.

During the debriefing, raise questions such as: How did you feel about the activity? Was it realistic? What would you do differently if we did this again? Did your actions result in solving some problems you faced? and What did you learn from the experience?

TEAM LEARNING

A world geography course introduces a large volume of new content to students. Team learning is a procedure that involves organizing students into groups in order for them to study new material together. It provides students with opportunities to exchange information and ideas with other students as they are learning. Team learning emphasizes cooperation and communication skills.

Selecting the Topic. Many teachers find that this approach works particularly well in introducing entire sections of a chapter. For example, the basic information about Japan can be covered as a team learning exercise for the appropriate section of Chapter 27.

Preliminary Considerations. A simple way to explain the rules for team learning is to write them on the chalkboard and discuss each briefly. The following general rules for team learning can serve as guidelines:

1. Any team member can help any person on his or her team but not a member of another team.
2. Talking is encouraged, but do not disturb the work of other groups.
3. Each team member should try to answer all of the assigned tasks or questions. Do not rely on other team members to do all of the work.

Implementing the Method. Divide the class into teams of four to six members. Each team then selects one person to act as its recorder, or official notetaker. Provide each team with the same set of focus questions to be answered during the class period. These questions should be either written on the chalkboard or on a sheet of paper for each student. As the exercise progresses, move from group to group providing aid and direction. When all teams have completed the tasks, begin debriefing.

Debriefing. These steps can be followed during the debriefing:

1. Have the recorder of each team read aloud the findings of the team.
2. Discuss variations in the groups' findings. Attempt to arrive at a consensus.
3. Summarize the activity by writing the consensus answers on the chalkboard for the students to record.

CONCLUSION

The teaching approaches in this section of the Teacher Edition are only samples of those that might be appropriate for introducing students to geographic content. Even the approaches that have been described have been dealt with only briefly. For teachers interested in more detailed explanations of these techniques and of others, there are a number of good reference materials. Among these are:

Armstrong, David G. and Tom V. Savage. *Secondary Education: An Introduction.* New York: Macmillan Publishing Company, 1983.

Aronson, E. *The Jigsaw Classroom.* Beverly Hills, CA: Sage Publications, 1978.

Beebe, Steven A. and John Masterson. *Communicating in Small Groups.* Glenview, IL: Scott-Foresman Company, 1982.

Budin, Howard, Diane Kendall, and James Lengel. *Using Computers in the Social Studies.* New York: Teachers College Press, 1986.

Clark, Leonard S. and Irving S. Starr. *Secondary School Teaching Methods,* fourth edition. New York: Macmillan Publishing Company, 1981.

Dunn, Rita and Kenneth Dunn. *Practical Approaches to Individualizing Instruction.* West Nyack, NY: Parker Publishing Company, 1981.

Friant, Ray J. *Preparing Effective Presentations.* New York: Pilot Books, 1984.

Hunkins, Francis P. *Questioning Strategies and Techniques.* Boston: Allyn and Bacon, 1972.

Jacobsen, David, et al. *Methods for Teaching: A Skills Approach.* Columbus, OH: Merrill Publishing Company, 1981.

Jones, Ken. *Designing Your Own Simulations.* New York: Methuen, Inc., 1985.

Jones, Ken. *Simulations: A Handbook for Teachers.* New York: Nichols Publishing Company, 1980.

Nelson, Florence. *Yes, You Can Teach!* St. Paul, MN: Carma Press, 1982.

Northam, Saralie B., ed. *Instructor's Manual: Development of Higher Level Thinking Abilities.* Portland, OR: Northwest Regional Educational Laboratory, 1972.

References to Instructional Approaches

Instructional Approach	Introducing Unit 1	Chapter 1	Chapter 2	Concluding Unit 1	Introducing Unit 2	Chapter 3	Chapter 4	Chapter 5	Concluding Unit 2	Introducing Unit 3	Chapter 6	Chapter 7	Chapter 8	Concluding Unit 3	Introducing Unit 4	Chapter 9	Chapter 10	Chapter 11	Chapter 12	Concluding Unit 4	Introducing Unit 5	Chapter 13	Chapter 14	Chapter 15	Chapter 16
Audiovisual Materials		✓			✓	✓					✓		✓	✓			✓							✓	
Brainstorming		✓									✓		✓			✓		✓							
Case Studies							✓					✓													
Community Resource Persons						✓					✓		✓												
Cooperative Learning		✓						✓														✓		✓	
Debating						✓					✓														
Demonstration																	✓		✓						
Discussion	✓	✓	✓		✓		✓					✓			✓						✓	✓		✓	✓
Experimentation			✓		✓	✓																			
Field Trips			✓		✓													✓							
Lecture			✓		✓						✓		✓				✓	✓						✓	
Reading Guides		✓			✓													✓							
Retrieval Charts					✓		✓										✓		✓					✓	✓
Role Plays and Simulations		✓							✓		✓				✓							✓	✓		✓
Team Learning		✓		✓		✓										✓									✓

References to Instructional Approaches

	Concluding Unit 5	Introducing Unit 6	Chapter 17	Chapter 18	Chapter 19	Chapter 20	Concluding Unit 6	Introducing Unit 7	Chapter 21	Chapter 22	Concluding Unit 7	Introducing Unit 8	Chapter 23	Chapter 24	Chapter 25	Concluding Unit 8	Introducing Unit 9	Chapter 26	Chapter 27	Chapter 28	Concluding Unit 9	Introducing Unit 10	Chapter 29	Chapter 30	Chapter 31	Concluding Unit 10
Audiovisual Materials									✓	✓			✓	✓					✓	✓			✓			
Brainstorming									✓				✓					✓							✓	
Case Studies			✓						✓																	
Community Resource Persons				✓									✓					✓					✓			
Cooperative Learning										✓		✓	✓	✓	✓								✓			
Debating																		✓								
Demonstration																										
Discussion	✓	✓	✓	✓	✓	✓	✓	✓							✓			✓	✓	✓		✓		✓	✓	
Experimentation																										
Field Trips																							✓			
Lecture										✓				✓				✓	✓				✓			
Reading Guides																		✓								
Retrieval Charts			✓		✓											✓		✓		✓						
Role Plays and Simulations			✓		✓				✓	✓	✓		✓	✓	✓			✓						✓	✓	✓
Team Learning				✓														✓					✓	✓		

TEXT
IMPLEMENTATION

INTRODUCING
THE STUDENT EDITION

Besides the teacher, the students' most important classroom aid in the study of world geography is the textbook. Before the course of study begins, students should be familiar with the organization of the text so that they can make the best possible use of its contents.

As an introduction to the program, ask students to read the Prologue on page 1. This is a rationale for the study of geography.

A class reading and discussion of the Preface on page iii is one way to introduce students to the design of the text. The order of information in the Preface carries students through an explanation of the various parts of the text. As sections of the Preface are read in class, cite examples of each element mentioned, and have students turn to them in their texts. For each element, explain to students the purposes it serves. The Examination Guide presented on the inside cover of this Teacher Annotated Edition will help you locate sample pages for each of the special elements of the Student Edition.

Several other elements also may be used by students and teachers to reinforce chapter content. Specifically, point out that photographs, maps, and other illustrations have questions at the end of their captions. More questions, along with geography terms and important place-names, appear at the end of chapter sections called Content Checks. Chapter Review and Unit Review material can be used by students as self-checks on understanding. Teachers may use these same materials for review and evaluation purposes.

Following a discussion of the Preface, have students read through the Contents on pages v-xii. This listing of unit/chapter/section titles, in addition to titles of special-interest features, will illustrate the topics and the organization of the 10 units and 31 chapters of study. Have the students skim the list of skills they will be learning during the school year and the list of maps and other illustrations the

Student Edition has to offer them for visual clarification of geographic concepts and regions. Select one of the regional chapters in Chapters 12–29. Show students that in each of these chapters there are three maps of the region under study: a physical regions map, a land use and resources map, and a political map. Point out general reasons why each will be important to their study of the region.

Encourage the students to read some of the pronunciations of terms and place-names that are in the narrative. Point out that, in fact, the pronunciations are actually respellings of the words in syllables that have no diacritical marks and are easy to read.

Familiarize the students with the features in the Appendix, beginning on page 645. After they have looked over the list of Appendix features on page 645, ask them to study the legend for the atlas. Then encourage them to look at the atlas map of the United States on pages 648–649 to locate their state. Point out the other atlas maps of world regions. The data chart, National Profiles, on pages 667–680 will be of special interest to students. The chart shows the national flags of all the independent nations of the world, along with other vital statistics. One of the most helpful aids to show to students at the beginning of their study of geography is the glossary on pages 681–690. Each of the boldface terms and concepts used in the chapter narrative are listed in the glossary. Whereas the terms are usually defined in context in the narrative, the terms are often given a more complete definition in the glossary. The glossary also contains a pronunciation key to explain the sounds provided in the respellings. Inform students that the glossary will tell them on what page in the Student Edition a term is first introduced. The index on pages 691–707 will help students locate topics, people, and regions discussed in the text. The index also cross-references topics for further help to students.

UNIT 1 FOUNDATIONS OF GEOGRAPHY

Student Edition pp. 2–41

UNIT 1 GOALS

At the conclusion of this unit, students will be able to:

1. define *geography*, understand the importance of its study, and describe kinds and methods of study used by geographers.
2. understand maps and recognize how they serve as the principal tools of the geographer.
3. recognize various map projections, analyze their properties, and summarize the value of each.

UNIT 1 SKILL OBJECTIVE

After completing the *Developing Geography Skills* exercise in this unit, the student should be able to ask effective questions.

UNIT 1 OVERVIEW

The first unit of *World Geography: People and Places* focuses on the importance of geography and provides students with information about the tools and approaches used by geographers. *Chapter 1* discusses the value of the study of geography in today's world and the steps involved in geographic inquiry. Geography and its various branches of study are defined, and the topical and regional methods of geographic study are explained. Location and place as important concepts in understanding geography are introduced. Global interdependence and spatial interaction are additional concepts presented in Chapter 1 to help students realize that studying geography is more than memorizing facts about various countries. *Chapter 2* provides students with the fundamentals necessary to develop map skills, including recognition and use of the kinds of information maps present, the properties and parts of maps, and the kinds and uses of projections upon which maps are based.

Upon completion of this unit, students should have an enlarged concept and appreciation of the use and importance of geography, as well as a base from which to study any area of the world.

INTRODUCING UNIT 1

Have students turn to the Unit Opening Photograph on pages 2–3. Identify the photograph for the class as a harbor in the Aleutian Islands. Ask students if they know where these islands are located and what great landmasses they are near. Ask them to point out the location on a wall map and to indicate what the islands are near. Then, ask what direction one would have to travel from the Aleutians in order to reach the Soviet Union, Hawaii, and the California coast. Tell students to call out everything they see in the photograph, and write their responses on the chalkboard. Answers should include such things as vegetation, land formations, houses, other buildings, ships, docks, people, etc.

Raise the question: What do all of these things have to do with each other? Aid the class by asking such questions as: What does the location of the Aleutian Islands tell you about their climate? What do you see in the picture that confirms this? What season of the year do you suppose it was at the time the photograph was taken? What things in the illustration represent the workings of nature, and what things represent the workings of humans? How do you believe nature has affected what people have done, and how have people influenced nature here? How is this place different from the place where you live both in reference to location and place and to human-environment relationships? What does this photograph tell you about the mobility of

people, goods, and ideas in and from this place? Ask the class, considering the location, to hypothesize about why people live here, what life must be like here, what the seasons of the year are like, and how important this port might be and to which nations it would be most important. After this discussion, point out to students that they have been thinking like geographers—they have observed a specific place and formulated answers to questions about relationships between characteristics such as climate and physical features as well as how people are affected by and are affecting their environment.

As students learn new terms related to geology, have them include them in an "Illustrated Geology Dictionary" that they will make and keep in a notebook. The dictionary should include a verbal definition and an illustration that may be a drawing, diagram, or attached picture. Terms should be grouped together under headings or under introductory sentences.

CHAPTER 1 NATURE OF GEOGRAPHY

Student Edition pp. 5–21

CHAPTER 1 OBJECTIVES

At the conclusion of this chapter, students should be able to:

1. define *geography* and describe its different branches of study.
2. explain the way geographers identify and locate places.
3. distinguish between the topical and regional methods of geographic study.
4. list and apply the five steps of geographic inquiry.
5. describe the value of geography in today's world.

CHAPTER 1 SKILL OBJECTIVE

After completing the *Using Graphic Skills* exercise in this chapter, the student should be able to describe exact and relative locations.

CHAPTER 1 OVERVIEW

In this chapter the student is introduced to the concept of what geography is, and within that concept, what is included in the study of geography, how this study is approached, and its importance.

The student is led to see geography from the point of view of the geographer—understanding the importance of place, using geographic method in identifying and locating places, evaluating spatial interaction, and understanding the use of grids and hemispheric division. The physical and human aspects of geographic study are explained as well as methods used and the topics to which each method may be applied. The student is introduced to and given the opportunity to follow the steps of geographic inquiry.

A special chapter feature spotlights the achievements of Alexander Von Humboldt, emphasizing how he changed the process of geographic inquiry.

The chapter concludes with information regarding careers in geography, the usefulness of geography in many careers outside the field, and the importance of the study of geography in a shrinking world.

CHAPTER 1 ACTIVITIES

Introducing Chapter 1

Refer to the guidelines for audiovisuals in the Instructional Approaches section of this Teacher Annotated Edition, then show the film *The Solar System* listed under Unit 1 Suggested Resources. Alternate suggested audiovisuals are: *The Universe, Frontiers of Discovery Series, Part 1: The Solar System,* five sound filmstrips, 17–20 minutes each, 1984, available from National Geographic Educational Services, Washington, D.C. 20036, or *The Solar System,* color video or color film, 20 minutes, 1980, also available from National Geographic Educational Services.

During the debriefing, write the following statement on the chalkboard: ". . . absolutely essential is a coming together of the nations of the world to realize we have one small and fragile planet that we all share collectively, and that we will survive only if we work together." Explain to the class that this statement was made by Carl Sagan, an American astronomer. Ask the class to speculate on the role the study of geography could play to help preserve the life systems of Earth.

Then, explain to the students that some important and basic questions will be asked and answered during their study of this chapter. Prepare as part of a handout or write on the chalkboard the following questions: What is geography? What methods are used to study it? If you were a geographer, what questions would you ask to find out about a place? How would you locate the place you want to study? If you were a geographer, how could you help the people on Earth? Tell the students to answer these questions in short paragraphs before they begin their study of Chapter 1, and then to file the answers away in their notebooks. When they have concluded their study of Chapter 1, and as a part of Concluding Chapter 1, they will be asked to refer again to their answers to these questions.

Chapter 1 Reading Assignments

Objectives 1 and 2	Student Ed. pp. 5–13
Objectives 3 and 4	Student Ed. pp. 14–17
Objective 5	Student Ed. pp. 17–19

> ● Teaching   ■ Reinforcing   ★ Enriching

Objective 1 Activities

● Objective 1 Teaching Activity

Inform the class that they are going to begin to do the work of a geographer in relation to the place where they live. On the chalkboard, write the definition of geography given in the Student Edition, and below it, "describe, explain, and predict." Explain to the students that they will do all of these things in relation to the state where they live.

Have them begin by describing their state. Ask students: Are there many or few people in this state? How are these people distributed or arranged as to where they live and where they work? Have people changed this state? How? Where? Have the changes been for better or for worse? How can studying the geography of this area be of help to the people who live here?

When the class has reached a consensus on the correct answers to these questions, have them write the answers in notebooks. Tell them that these are the first notes that they will take in their geographic study of their state.

Now refer to the guidelines for team learning in the Instructional Approaches section of this Teacher Annotated Edition, and divide the class into groups, assigning each group a different branch of geographic study. Ask each group to answer the question, "How can this branch of geographic study be applied to or helpful to the area where we live?" Allow time for the various groups to research and write reports. Then, refer to the guidelines for discussions in the Instructional Approaches section of this Teacher Annotated Edition, and end this activity with a round-table discussion of how these various branches of geographic study relate and impinge upon each other, in particular with reference to the state where the students live.

Use the Teacher Resource Book, Chapter 1 Teacher Notes: Section 1, Extending the Lesson, "Economic Geography," as an aid to students in the preparation of this activity.

■ Objective 1 Reinforcing Activity

Refer to the guidelines for reading guides in the Instructional Approaches section of this Teacher Annotated Edition, and prepare a reading guide for Chapter 1 that will serve as the Reinforcing Activity for each objective related to this chapter. Statements or questions should be leveled from knowledge and comprehension to higher levels of analysis and evaluation. When each section of the chapter has been read, review the answers to the reading guide along with the answers to the Content Check questions.

Objective 2 Activities

● Objective 2 Teaching Activity

Provide the class with or have them bring in photographs of the state where they live, and ask them to describe the various areas. Provide photographs of any important geographic areas not shown in the photographs supplied by students. Ask students: Are all areas alike? Are some quite different? If so, in what way? Do any have special names?

Using latitude and longitude lines on a large globe, have students locate their state and identify it in terms of north or south latitude and hemisphere. On a large scale map of the state, point out the town or city in which the school is located. At this point, present the *Using Graphic Skills* feature on page 12 of the Student Edition, "Describing Exact and Relative Locations." When the students have gone through the skill, help them determine the degrees, minutes, and seconds for several locations within their state, including the city or town where their school is located. Next, have them locate areas within their state in terms of relative location.

Finally, provide the class with a world outline map with unnumbered longitude and latitude lines. Ask students to mark where the hemispheres are divided, and to label the latitude and longitude lines using degrees north, east, south, and west. Have students locate their state on this map and indicate it with a symbol. Ask the class to speculate about how the location of the state affects its physical environment.

■ Objective 2 Reinforcing Activity

Refer to Chapter 1, Objective 1 Reinforcing Activity, and have the class complete the reading guide and answer the Content Check questions for the reading assignment related to this objective.

★ Objective 2 Enriching Activity

Refer to the teacher annotation on page 10 of this Teacher Annotated Edition, and allow students to perform this exercise. Then have them give the grid location of their state using their new grid system. Emphasize that grid systems are arbitrary, and having a standard means for locating places is more important than the kind of system used.

Objective 3 Activities

● Objective 3 Teaching Activity

Explain to the class that they are continuing to apply the study of geography to the area where they live. After reviewing the topical and regional methods of inquiry with the students, refer to the guidelines for cooperative learning in the Instructional Approaches section of this Teacher Annotated Edition. Divide the class up into two-student teams, and assign half of the teams to do regional inquiry and the other half to do topical inquiry. Each team of the topical group should apply their method of inquiry to different topics such as a state industry, the state road system, forestry within the state, or any other single topic applicable to the state. The regional teams should investigate different features of the state such as ethnic groups in the region, religions of the region, cities of the region. Explain to the class that interviewing can be a part of their geographic inquiry. Before students begin working in teams, refer to the Teacher Resource Book, Chapter 1, Section 2: Extending the Lesson, "Interviewing." When investigations of the regional and topical features are completed, have each team report to the class.

■ Objective 3 Reinforcing Activity

Refer to Chapter 1, Objective 1 Reinforcing Activity, and have the class complete the reading guide and answer the Content Check questions for the reading assignment related to this objective.

★ Objective 3 Enriching Activity

Assign students the special feature in the Student Edition about Alexander Von Humboldt. Also have students read and answer questions related to the Chapter 1 Reading in the Teacher Resource Book. After students have studied about Humboldt, assign a book report about a famous person, geographer or not, who has made contributions to geographic knowledge. Examples of non-geographers who added to knowledge of Earth would be Marco Polo, the explorers of the New World, Ferdinand Magellan, Admiral Oliver Perry, the astronauts, and many others. Each book report should contain an explanation of the geographical activities of the person investigated, and a final paragraph explaining his or her contribution to geographic knowledge.

Objective 4 Activities

● Objective 4 Teaching Activity

As a continuation of the class's study of their state, choose one or more of its prominent geographical features and lead the class through the steps of geographic inquiry in relation to the feature(s). When the steps are understood by the class, have each student choose a state or world geographic feature not discussed in class and prepare a geographic study of it using the steps they have practiced. Photographs or drawings of the feature about which they are reporting should be included. Ask various volunteers to present their reports to the class. At the end of each report presented, involve the class in a discussion of the generalization arrived at in each case. Ask students if they believe the generalization is valid and to point out why the report substantiates or fails to substantiate the generalization. Refer to the guidelines for brainstorming in the Instructional Approaches section of this Teacher Annotated Edition, and ask the students to brainstorm predictions about the geographic future of the features studied.

■ Objective 4 Reinforcing Activity

Refer to Chapter 1, Objective 1 Reinforcing Activity, and have the class complete the reading guide and answer the Content Check questions for the reading assignment related to this objective. As an additional Reinforcing Activity, refer to the Chapter 1 Skill Activity

"Using the Steps of Geographic Inquiry," in the Teacher Resource Book, and have students complete it.

Objective 5 Activities

● Objective 5 Teaching Activity

Ask students to imagine that their state senate is considering a tax bill that would provide funds that would aid in expanding the geography curriculum in the schools. Refer to the guidelines for role plays and simulations in the Instructional Approaches section of this Teacher Annotated Edition, and prepare the students to role-play state senators involved in an informal debate of the issue dealing with whether or not geographic study is important enough to merit spending state funds on its development. This activity should be carried out using the parliamentary procedures practiced in the senate chambers, i.e., presided over by the Speaker of the House, with recognition of speakers, and a final vote taken on the proposed tax bill.

End this activity by having each student write a letter to his or her state senator explaining why the study of geography is important and deserves funds for special attention and expansion in the school curriculum.

■ Objective 5 Reinforcing Activity

Refer to Chapter 1, Objective 1 Reinforcing Activity, and have the class complete the reading guide and answer the Content Check questions for the reading assignment related to this objective.

★ Objective 5 Enriching Activity

Form a student panel and throw out the following topic question for their consideration: "We know the world has only so much land, clean water, oil, wood, and other natural resources. Therefore, should the larger and stronger nations secure enough for their own future needs and then decide on a plan for world distribution of what is left?" Have student panel members defend their positions and then open up the discussion to the whole class. Ask students to speculate about possible plans for the distribution of the world's natural resources. Through discussion, lead the class toward the understanding of the importance of interdependence among nations.

Concluding Chapter 1

Refer the students to the questions they answered in the Introducing Chapter 1 activity. Have students review their previous answers and re-answer any questions they feel were answered incorrectly or without sufficient information. Discuss with the class the way in which their answers have changed and what they have learned that caused them to change.

Finally, reemphasize to students that geography is much more than map locations and place-name recognition, reminding them that geographers study all the information about a place so that they can explain why it is important to all kinds of people. Have them look once more at the chapter opening photograph on page 4 of the Student Edition. Tell them that when one of the astronauts saw Earth from this perspective, he exclaimed, "I see just one planet Earth, having no frames, no boundaries." Ask the class to consider how this view and remark help to exemplify the last paragraph of Chapter 1.

ANSWERS TO CHAPTER 1 QUESTIONS

Content Check Questions
page 13

1. Refer to Glossary in Student Edition.

2. To describe, explain, and predict. (p. 6)

3. Place. (p. 7)

4. With a set of imaginary lines covering Earth. (p. 8)

5. Physical and human geography. (p. 11)

6. Answers will vary but students should include physical aspects such as what would happen if Earth experienced a warming

trend and human aspects such as the effect of possible future overpopulation.

page 17

1. Refer to Glossary in Student Edition.
2. To look at aspects of only one topic. To study region to discover how its many features fit together. (pp. 14–15)
3. Area that has one feature common to all its parts. An area that has many common features. (p. 15)
4. Observing, classifying, defining, comparing, and generalizing. (p. 15)
5. Topical. Sample steps: (1) Visit and observe shopping malls and centers. (2) Break malls and centers into groups by size and kind. (3) Decide on common definitions to be used in describing the malls and centers and use them consistently. (4) Compare features of the various malls and centers to determine how they are alike or different. Interview business people who own stores in the malls and centers to determine how successful their businesses are. (5) Correlate the success of the businesses with the type of and location of the mall or center in which they are found. From this, generalize about what type of business is successful in what type of mall or center.

page 19

1. Refer to Glossary in Student Edition.
2. Satisfy curiosity, develop career skills, help solve world problems to improve quality of life on Earth. (pp. 17–19)
3. World is growing "smaller," need to understand neighbor's and world's problems to protect Earth's future. (pp. 18–19)
4. Answers will vary but may include: by making clear how we depend on each other for necessities and how actions of groups of people can affect lives of other people.

Special Feature Questions
page 12, Using Graphic Skills: "Describing Exact and Relative Location"

1. Memphis: 35°N,90°W. Charleston: 34°N,90°W. Stillwater: 36°N,97°W. (p. 12)

2. Dallas: southeast of Oklahoma City, Oklahoma and east of Fort Worth, Texas. Baton Rouge: northwest of New Orleans, Louisiana and southwest of Jackson, Mississippi. Mobile: northeast of New Orleans, Louisiana and southwest of Montgomery, Alabama. (p. 12)
3. Answers will vary.
4. Answers will vary.

page 16, Focus on Geography: "Alexander Von Humboldt"

1. Nature and faraway lands.
2. Broadened the study of geography to include all life on Earth. Provided a system of geographic inquiry.

Photo/Illustration Caption Questions
page 6

Earth's rotation around its axis. (p. 5)

page 7

Human activities. (p. 7)

page 8

Atmosphere, hydrosphere, lithosphere. (p. 8)

page 9

0° latitude, 0° longitude. (pp. 8–9)

page 10

Northern and Western hemispheres. (p. 10)

page 11

Left: physical geographers, meteorologists. Right: cultural or social geographers. (p. 11)

page 14

Topical method. (p. 14)

page 18

Cartography, surveying, city planning, computer specialists, traffic supervision, aerial photography, real estate management, park rangers. (p. 18)

page 19

Food, clothing, metals, farm machinery. (pp. 18–19) Chemicals in a river flow through other countries; polluted air blows across borders. (p. 19)

Chapter 1 Review Questions
page 20, Reviewing Vocabulary

Answers will vary.

page 21, Remembering the Facts

1. One year. 24 hours. (p. 5)
2. Study of Earth and the people who live on it. (p. 6)
3. North America, South America, Europe, Asia, Africa, Australia, Antarctica. (p. 10)
4. Ural Mountains and the Caspian Sea. (p. 20)
5. Equator. (p. 10)
6. Climatology, meteorology, oceanography, biogeography, plant geography, or zoogeography. Culture/social geography, historical geography, demography, economic geography, political geography, or urban geography. (pp. 11–12)
7. Observing, classifying, defining, comparing, generalizing. (p. 15)

page 21, Understanding the Facts

1. Revolution. Rotation. (p. 5)
2. Numbered lines of latitude and longitude and direction. (p. 8)
3. Southern. Eastern.
4. Eastern. Because most of its land area is east of the Prime Meridian. (p. 10)
5. Relates to people and their activities whereas physical geography relates to things on Earth not made by people.

6. Regional.
7. Changed the way geographers study Earth by studying all living things through a system of geographic inquiry.

page 21, Thinking Critically and Creatively

1. Can be helpful in estimating distances; comparing maps to assess distortion. Also for distances; interpreting maps.
2. Answers will vary but may include: to understand relationships between regions; comparative study of a topic among many regions not possible. Point out features that make regions unique (regional) and highlight special features common to some or all regions (topical).
3. Answers will vary but should emphasize the importance of preserving its delicate balance.
4. Answers will vary but should mention the use of astronomy, land features, compass, and information passed on between navigators; many different grid systems were used before a standard was set.

page 21, Reinforcing Graphic Skills

1. 36° north parallel: Stillwater, Oklahoma; Tulsa, Oklahoma; Fayetteville, Arkansas; Nashville, Tennessee. 94° west meridian: Fayetteville, Arkansas; Shreveport, Louisiana; Beaumont, Texas. (p. 12)
2. Gadsden: 34°N,86°W. Pine Bluff: 34°N,92°W. (p. 12)
3. Austin: northeast of San Antonio, Texas and southwest of Waco, Texas. Jackson: northeast of Baton Rouge, Louisiana and southeast of Little Rock, Arkansas. (p. 12)

EVALUATING CHAPTER 1

World Geography: People and Places provides chapter tests to help evaluate student performance. To evaluate student mastery of Chapter 1, give students Chapter 1 Test from the Teacher Resource Book. This test may also be used for pretesting or retesting purposes. Other tests can be made from the questions available in the Test Generator Software.

Lesson Plan Suggestions—Chapter 1

Section 1   What is Geography? (pp. 5–13)

Chapter Objectives	Suggested Teaching Strategies	Review

1. define geography and describe its different branches of study.
 	
2. explain the way geographers identify and locate places.
 	
Skill feature describe the exact and relative location of places.
	Teacher Preparation
	   SE, Reading Assignment, pp. 5–13
	   TAE, Unit 1 Suggested Resources
	      Unit 1 Overview, p. T54
	      Introducing Unit 1, pp. T54–T55
	      Chapter 1 Overview, p. T56
	      Introducing Chapter 1, p. T56
	   TRB, Chapter 1 Teacher Notes: Section 1
	Teaching Options
	   TAE, Introducing Unit 1, pp. T54–T55
	      Introducing Chapter 1, p. T56
	      Objectives 1 and 2 Activities, pp. T56–T58
	   TRB, Chapter 1 Teacher Notes: Section 1, Extending the Lesson
	      Chapter 1 Reading
	   SE, *Using Graphic Skills*, "Describing Exact and Relative Locations," pp. 12–13
		SE, Content Check, p. 13

Section 2   The Study of Geography (pp. 14–17)

Chapter Objectives	Suggested Teaching Strategies	Review

3. distinguish between the topical and regional methods of geographic study.
 	
4. list the five steps of geographic inquiry.
	Teacher Preparation
	   SE, Reading Assignment, pp. 14–17
	   TAE, Unit 1 Suggested Resources
	   TRB, Chapter 1 Teacher Notes: Section 2
	Teaching Options
	   TAE, Objectives 3 and 4 Activities, pp. T58–T59
	   TRB, Chapter 1 Teacher Notes: Section 2, Extending the Lesson
	      Chapter 1 Reading
	      Chapter 1 Skill Activity
		SE, Content Check, p. 17

Chapter Objectives	Suggested Teaching Strategies	Review

5. describe the value of geography in today's world.	**Teacher Preparation**
	    SE, Reading Assignment, pp. 17–19
	    TAE, Unit 1 Suggested Resources
	    TRB, Chapter 1 Teacher Notes: Section 3
	Teaching Options
	    TAE, Objective 5 Activities, p. T59
	    TRB, Chapter 1 Teacher Notes: Section 3,
	        Extending the Lesson
		SE, Content Check, p. 19

Chapter 1 Review and Evaluation

Suggested Teaching Strategies	Review	Evaluation
TAE, Concluding Chapter 1, p. T59	SE, Chapter 1 Review, pp. 20–21 TRB, Chapter 1 Review Worksheet	TRB, Chapter 1 Test TG, Chapter 1

CHAPTER 2   MAPS

Student Edition pp. 22–41

CHAPTER 2 OBJECTIVES

At the conclusion of this chapter, students should be able to:
1. distinguish among different types of maps by the kinds of information they present.
2. read a map by using its basic parts.
3. describe the four properties maps may have.
4. distinguish among cylindrical, conic, and flat-plane projections.

CHAPTER 2 SKILL OBJECTIVE

After completing the *Using Graphic Skills* exercise in this chapter, the student should be able to calculate distance in miles and kilometers using a bar scale.

CHAPTER 2 OVERVIEW

With this chapter, students are introduced to skills necessary to the geographer—reading and using maps. In order to achieve this, students learn about some of the many kinds of maps created by cartographers and how to understand them using their basic parts and properties. Students are introduced to the concept of map projections, asked to distinguish among several types of maps, and asked to explain the usefulness of each.

Special features present the students with information necessary to develop various skills, such as understanding and using world time zones, and comparing map projections.

Also included in the chapter is information regarding how cartographers collect data and the problems presented by distortion in the representation of the world's surface areas. Great circle routes, how they are shown on globes and flat surface maps, and why distortion occurs are discussed.

Upon completion of this chapter, students should be able to appreciate the convenience and informational qualities of maps, recognize various kinds of maps and map projections, read and interpret maps, and understand why they are the basic tools of the geographer.

CHAPTER 2 ACTIVITIES

Introducing Chapter 2

Before beginning the study of this chapter, prepare a reference center for maps in the classroom. Collect and display maps of all types including folded general reference maps, topographical maps, atlases, and globes. Using an opaque projector, show students some old maps illustrating early ideas of Earth. Include the 1513 map from the Suleyman collection and Polynesian maps made from woven mats and shells. Let them point out the errors and speculate why errors were common on these maps. Then, show students several kinds of modern maps. Ask them to point out the differences they see among them. Inform students that in Chapter 2 they will learn many of the reasons behind these differences. Explain that the map is the most important tool for and product of geographic study, and that they will learn how different types of maps are used for different purposes. Next, project a photograph of Earth in space as seen from the moon. Explain that maps today are more accurate than ever. No part of our planet is unknown, although some areas contain mysteries waiting to be unraveled by future geographers.

Chapter 2 Reading Assignments

Objective 1   Student Ed. pp. 23–28
Objective 2   Student Ed. pp. 28–29
Objectives 3 and 4   Student Ed. pp. 32–37

● Teaching	■ Reinforcing	★ Enriching

Objective 1 Activities

● Objective 1 Teaching Activity

Have students create a general reference map and a thematic map using their school as the subject. The school office may be of assistance in this project by supplying maps of the school and data regarding number of students in home rooms and number of students in class and at lunch during one of the lunch periods.

Provide students with outline maps of the school. On the general reference map, ask students to indicate study areas, such as mathematics, music, social studies, home economics, gym, etc., using various colors. Other areas such as offices, cafeteria, and lounges could be indicated with special markings such as straight or slanted lines. Have students write out their daily schedule and show on the map how they move through the halls from class to class during the day.

Next, have students create a thematic map of their school showing distribution of the student body and school personnel during one or more periods of the school day. Provide them with the necessary figures and have them represent this information on their maps. They might, for example, show location of the student population during homeroom and then again, on another map, during one of the lunch periods. One round dot might represent 10 students. Dots of other colors could be used to represent teachers and other school employees with one dot representing one individual. Round off student population figures for easy representation. Help students create map keys.

When maps are completed, have students compare them and explain why one is a general reference map and the other two are thematic maps.

■ Objective 1 Reinforcing Activity

Allow students to select a map from the reference center. Have each student show the map selected to the class and tell what type of map it is and whether it provides general or specialized information. Ask the class whether they agree or disagree with the student's opinion, pointing out reasons. Remind students that some maps may be a combination of both general reference and thematic types.

★ Objective 1 Enriching Activity

Review the concept of relief and topographic maps with the class. Follow the instructions in the teacher annotation on page 24 of the Teacher Annotated Edition and create a model of a contour map. Explain to students that many maps show relief. Maps in the atlas section of the Student Edition are examples. However, maps with contour lines are less common and more specialized. Ask the class to whom they believe contour maps would be especially useful.

Students may also choose to make another type of model that demonstrates how contour maps are made. Refer to the guidelines for experimentation in the Instructional Approaches section of this Teacher Annotated Edition. Then, follow the suggested activity for making a contour map, or proceed in the following manner. In a large plastic or metal container with a flat bottom and high sides, have students use Play-Doh to construct an imaginary landscape with a mountain, a valley, low hills, and a plateau. Fill the container with water until water level reaches 1/2 inch up the sides of the container. Have a student use a waterproof marker pen to mark the water level line on the landscape. Then add another 1/2 inch of water, and repeat the procedure. When the top of the highest point has been covered, empty the water from the container and have the class note the contour lines running around the landscape features.

With a Polaroid camera, have a student take a photograph of the landscape from above, looking directly down over it. Then, using the opaque projector, project the image of the Polaroid print onto a large sheet of white poster board. Ask another student to copy the projected lines marking the contours of the landscape onto the poster board. Draw a border around the copied image on the poster board and label it "Contour Map of Imaginary Landscape."

Have students observe the drawing and the Play-Doh landscape carefully and note the following facts: (1) Contours are lines connecting points of equal height. (2) They are continuous lines. (3) They are drawn at fixed intervals. (4) Lines close together indicate a steep slope. (5) Lines far apart indicate a gentle slope.

Objective 2 Activities

● Objective 2 Teaching Activity

Have students bring in road maps or provide enough for your class. Ask them to identify each of the five basic parts and to indicate what the title and legend reveal about the maps. Compare the components of the road maps with those of the maps in the Student Edition atlas section. For example, most road maps will not have longitude and latitude lines. Some maps may have a grid system that does not represent longitude and latitude lines. Ask students to explain why the grid system is used and how to use it. To conclude this activity, have students plan a two-hour trip by car and decide in what direction and how far they will have to travel.

■ Objective 2 Reinforcing Activity

Divide the class into several groups, and pass out to each group a handout that includes several maps of various areas of the world and several historical maps. Have each group work together to identify and mark with a highlighter the five basic map parts on each map in the handout. On the last page of the handout, provide several grid locations and ask students to locate cities nearest them, or list several cities shown on the maps and have students indicate the coordinates for their grid location. You might ask questions related to the legend such as what shading or lines on the different maps mean. Also ask students how the information on the historical maps differs from that on the other maps. Then, aid the class in figuring out the RF for each of the maps in the handout. Be sure students understand the difference between large scale and small scale. Review the maps and the map parts identified by the students and discuss their significance on each map in the handout.

End this activity by conducting the Chapter 1 Skill Activity in the Teacher Resource Book, "Making Maps."

★ Objective 2 Enriching Activity

Refer to the guidelines for field trips in the Instructional Approaches section of this Teacher Annotated Edition and prepare the class for an orienteering trip into the countryside. Before the field trip, you may wish to demonstrate the use of compass and map for orienting and have students practice in class or on school grounds. A guest speaker might also be invited to tell the class about the sport of orienteering. Volunteers with a special interest in this area may prepare reports on the subject and present their reports to the class. Ask the students who have done the research into orienteering to be the "leaders" in the field during the field trip. Assign each leader a small group to direct. Take students to an area without known landmarks and have them practice orienteering with compass and map.

Objective 3 Activities

● Objective 3 Teaching Activity

Display around the room four large maps representing the different kinds of properties found on maps. One should be an equal-area map, such as a Gall-Peters projection, showing correct sizes of world areas. One should be a conformal map, such as a Lambert projection, showing the correct shapes of world areas. Another should be a consistent-scale map, such as an Albers projection, using the same scale for all parts, and another, a map showing true-compass direction, such as a Mercator projection. In leading students to understand the properties of these maps, ask questions like the following: What similarities do you notice among the maps? What differences are there? How can any differences be explained? In what cases would these different map properties be useful? Who would be likely to use the different types of maps? Explain.

Refer to the guidelines for discussion in the Instructional Approaches section of this Teacher Annotated Edition, and conclude this activity with a general discussion of the trade-offs that mapmakers make when deciding how to prepare a map.

■ Objective 3 Reinforcing Activity

Have each student imagine that he or she is a cartographer who has been assigned the task of making a map for a special purpose. Ask each to select a purpose for his or her map, and then choose a type of map that would be suitable for that purpose. Allow students to use the map reference center, their Student Edition texts, and the library if necessary. Have them use a copier to copy the maps that fit their purposes and below the map, have them write a paragraph explaining their choice and stating why that particular map is best. When paragraphs are completed, check the students' work and have students correct inaccuracies. Finally, display all completed work in the classroom.

Objective 4 Activities

● Objective 4 Teaching Activity

Write the terms *Conic, Cylindrical,* and *Flat-Plane* on the chalkboard. Ask students to describe each type of projection. Show the class various maps and have them call out the types of projections represented. Continue this procedure until they are able to distinguish among them. Then, write *Equatorial Africa, Major Rivers of Europe,* and *Arctic Ocean* on the chalkboard. Have students select the best projection(s) for showing each area with the least amount of distortion, give reasons for their selections, and reach a consensus on the best projections for the suggested areas.

■ Objective 4 Reinforcing Activity

Obtain an illuminated globe of the world. Prepare tracing paper backed with clear plastic for support to illustrate how cylindrical, conic, and flat-plane projections are made. See the feature *Map Projections* on pp. 36–37 of the Student Edition to determine the correct shapes in which to cut the paper and plastic. Place each shape in turn over the lighted globe and tape in place. Be certain that each student sees how the paper is applied to the globe. Ask a student with drawing ability to trace the outline of the landmasses as they are projected onto the paper-covered plastic shapes. Untape each map from the globe, label it, and display the maps in the classroom.

★ Objective 4 Enriching Activity

Refer to the guidelines for lectures in the Instructional Approaches section of this Teacher Annotated Edition, and prepare a short lecture about map projections. Before beginning the lecture, refer students to the Chapter 2 Reading, "Before Maps," in the Teacher Resource Book. Have students read the selection and answer the questions orally in class. Relate this reading to the importance of maps for navigation and to the work of Gerardus Mercator. You may also wish to prepare or have the class prepare a bulletin board display about the history of cartography and famous cartographers.

During the lecture, use an opaque projector to show the class various kinds of map projections including several not illustrated in Chapter 2 of the Student Edition, and explain their properties. Also explain in what way each of these projections is useful. As part of the debriefing after the lecture, lead the class in a round table discussion of "which map is best," helping them relate "best" to the purpose for which each map is used.

As an aid in preparing this activity, refer to the book *Mapping* by David Greenhood, the University of Chicago Press, Chicago, and the booklet, *Which Map is Best? Projections for World Maps,* by the Committee on Map Projections of the American Cartographic Association. This last booklet also contains illustrations of the various projections that would be useful as displays with an opaque projector. Both selections are referenced under *Unit 1 Suggested Resources* in this Teacher Annotated Edition.

Concluding Chapter 2

Write the following headings across the top of the chalkboard: *Kinds of Maps, Map Parts, Map Properties, Map Projections.* Ask students to supply specific information from the chapter to list under each heading.

Next, share with the class the information in the Teacher Resource Book, Chapter 2 Teacher Notes, "New Technology for Mapmaking." Ask questions like the following: What kinds of maps will space travelers need? Will they have the same parts and properties as the maps used for Earth? What will space travelers use to orient themselves? Where will up and down be? Where will north and south, east and west be? Lead students to consider computerized maps, possibilities for three-dimensional maps, and holographic maps. Finally, ask students how they would envision a map of the universe that would be equivalent to a globe of the world.

ANSWERS TO CHAPTER 2 QUESTIONS

Content Check Questions
page 28

1. Refer to Glossary in Student Edition.
2. General reference and thematic. (pp. 24–25)
3. Political maps and physical maps. (p. 24)
4. Shading and contour lines. (p. 25)
5. Answers will vary but may include maps from (a) atlas in Appendix and maps of physical regions, (b) historical, population distribution, ethnic and religious division maps, (c) land use and resource maps, (d) maps of countries, kingdoms, and changing boundaries.

page 30

1. Refer to Glossary in Student Edition.
2. Title, legend, grid system, direction indicator, scale. (p. 28)
3. North. (p. 28)
4. 1/50,000; 1:50,000. (pp. 28–29)
5. A compass rose is a direction indicator drawn on a map; a compass is a magnetic device for finding north. (pp. 28–29)
6. Cardinal directions—north, south, east, west. (p. 28)
7. Answers will vary but may include that a compass will not be accurate if used in the polar regions.
8. Answers will vary but should include: a large-scale map would show many details of an area but would not show where the area was situated compared with the rest of the world; a small-scale map would show an area's relationship with neighboring areas but few details.

page 36

1. Refer to Glossary in Student Edition.
2. Surveying, aerial photography, remote sensing. (p. 32)
3. Equal areas, conformality, consistent scale, and true-compass direction. (p. 33)
4. Cylindrical, conic, and flat-plane. (p. 34)
5. Conic. Flat-plane. Cylindrical. (pp. 34–35)

Special Feature Questions
page 27, Thinking Like a Geographer:
"World Time Zones"

1. Each 15 degrees of longitude represent one hour of time; 24 time zones of 15 degrees each equal a 24-hour day.
2. To prevent division of cities and small countries into two time zones.
3. 3 PM; 6 AM.
4. 11 AM.
5. 5 PM. Tuesday.
6. Answers will vary but may include Australia, Cocos Islands, India, Afghanistan, Iran.

page 31, Using Graphic Skills:
"Understanding Scale"

1. Approximately 125 miles (201 km). Approximately 150 miles (241 km). Approximately 175 miles (282 km).
2. Glendale.

Photo/Illustration Caption Answers
page 24

50 feet (15–15.5 m). Higher. (p. 24)

page 25

Rugged or steep topography. (p. 25)

page 29

With north to the top. (p. 29)

page 32

They pick up energy off Earth's features, change the energy into codes, and send signals to computers that assign a color to each level of energy. The computer puts the information together into a picture. (p. 32)

page 33

Size of the areas; shapes of the areas; consistent scale; true-compass direction. (p. 33)

page 34

Shortest distance between them. (p. 35)

Because a line between two points on a globe is actually a curved line. (p. 35)

page 37

Conic projection, such as the Lambert Conformal Conical. Flat-plane projection, such as the gnomonic. (pp. 34–36)

Chapter 2 Review Questions
page 39, Reviewing Vocabulary

1. DISTORTION. 2. PROJECTION.
3. CARTOGRAPHER.
4. PHOTOGRAMMETRY. 5. LEGEND.
6. COMPASS. 7. SCALE. 8. RELIEF.
9. PHOTOGRAPHY. 10. CAPITAL.
11. ELEVATION. 12. GNOMONIC.

Sentences will vary but should indicate that students understand the meaning of the words.

page 39, Remembering the Facts

1. Maps, photographs, books. (p. 23)
2. Physical features such as lakes, rivers, and mountains. Also may show elevation, relief, topographic features. (pp. 24–25)
3. Greenwich, England. (p. 26)
4. Thematic. (p. 25)
5. Title, legend, grid system, direction indicator, scale. (p. 28)
6. Large scale. (p. 29)
7. Distortion. (pp. 32–33)
8. Equal area. (p. 33)
9. True-compass direction map, such as the Mercator Projection. (pp. 33–34)
10. Cylindrical, conic, flat-plane. (pp. 34–35)
11. Great-circle route. (p. 35)

page 39, Understanding the Facts

1. To learn, record, and analyze information. (p. 23)
2. Relief shows difference in elevation between an area's highest and lowest points by shading and also by color and line patterns. Topography shows shape of land's surface by using contour lines; also may show relief and other features made by nature and by humans. (p. 25)
3. 1:63,360. (p. 29)

4. By using a compass and direction indicator on a map. (p. 29)
5. By using different map projections. (pp. 34–35)
6. Consistent scale and conformality. (p. 33)
7. Where cylinder touches the globe, probably at the Equator. Where cone touches the globe at the standard parallels. (p. 34)
8. True-compass direction for ease in setting their course, and consistent scale because distances may be measured accurately. (pp. 33–35)
9. Answers will vary but may include engineering, architecture, geology, mining, military.

page 39, Thinking Critically and Creatively

1. No. Terrain is too steep to effectively operate farm equipment.
2. Photogrammetry or remote sensing. Most accurate.
3. Answers will vary but may include: location and number of enemy troops and supplies revealed as well as the topography or "lay of the land." It is more difficult to hide from this type of scanning. Provided more accurate geographical information for future mapmaking.
4. Flat-plane is accurate for small areas such as the South Pole and is also good for plotting great-circle routes should navigation be the purpose of the map.
5. Curvature of latitude lines on other projections might fool the eye of an untrained map reader and make areas near sides of map seem to stretch up. This would be especially true were Maine on the edge of a conic projection map of the U.S. and therefore appeared to stretch upward.
6. North. East.

page 39, Reinforcing Graphic Skills

1. Routes and distances will vary.
2. Approximately 20 miles. Approximately 15 miles. A county map shows more detail than a state map. Since the county map's scale is larger, a short distance can be figured more accurately.

EVALUATING CHAPTER 2

World Geography: People and Places provides chapter tests to help evaluate student performance. To evaluate student mastery of Chapter 2, give student Chapter 2 test found in the Teacher Resource Book. This test may also be used for pretesting or retesting purposes. Other tests can be made from the questions available in the Test Generator Software.

Lesson Plan Suggestions—Chapter 2

SE—Student Edition   TAE—Teacher Annotated Edition   TG—Test Generator
TRB—Teacher Resource Book   TSP—Transparency Package

Section 1   *Kinds of Maps (pp. 24–28)*

Chapter Objectives	Suggested Teaching Strategies	Review
1. distinguish among different types of maps by the kinds of information they present.	**Teacher Preparation** SE, Reading Assignment, pp. 24–28 TAE, Unit 1 Suggested Resources 　　Chapter 2 Overview, p. T64 　　Introducing Chapter 2, p. T64 TRB, Chapter 2 Teacher Notes: Section 1 **Teaching Options** TAE, Introducing Chapter 2, p. T64 　　Objective 1 Activities, pp. T64–T65 TRB, Chapter 2 Teacher Notes: Section 1, 　　Extending the Lesson 　　Chapter 2 Skill Activity A 　　Chapter 2 Reading	SE, Content Check, p. 28

Section 2   *Reading Maps (pp. 28–31)*

Chapter Objectives	Suggested Teaching Strategies	Review
2. read a map by using its basic parts.	**Teacher Preparation** SE, Reading Assignment, pp. 28–31 TAE, Unit 1 Suggested Resources 　　Chapter 2 Overview, p. T64 TRB, Chapter 2 Teacher Notes: Section 2 **Teaching Options** TAE, Objective 2 Activities, pp. T65–T66 TRB, Chapter 2 Teacher Notes: Section 2, 　　Extending the Lesson	SE, Content Check, pp. 30–31

Skill feature: calculate distance in miles and kilometers using a bar scale.	SE, *Using Graphic Skills*, "Understanding Scale," pp. 30–31	

Section 3 *Making Maps (pp. 32–36)*

Chapter Objectives	Suggested Teaching Strategies	Review

3. describe four properties maps may have.
 	
4. distinguish among cylindrical, conic, and flat-plane projections
	Teacher Preparation
	SE, Reading Assignment, pp. 32–37
	TAE, Unit 1 Suggested Resources
	    Chapter 2 Overview, p. T64
	TRB, Chapter 2 Teacher Notes: Section 3
	Teaching Options
	SE, *Comparing Projections*, pp. 36–37
	TAE, Objectives 3 and 4 Activities, pp. T66–T67
	TRB, Chapter 2 Teacher Notes: Section 3, Extending the Lesson
	    Chapter 2 Skill Activity, B
		SE, Content Check, p. 36

Chapter 2 Review and Evaluation

Suggested Teaching Strategies	Review	Evaluation
TAE, Concluding Chapter 2, p. T67	SE, Chapter 2 Review, pp. 38–39 TRB, Chapter 2 Review Worksheet	TRB, Chapter 2 Test TG, Chapter 2

Unit 1 Review and Evaluation

Suggested Teaching Strategies	Review	Evaluation
TAE, Concluding Unit 1, p. T72 TRB, Unit 1 Career Worksheet	SE, Unit 1 Review, pp. 40–41	TRB, Unit 1 Exam

CONCLUDING UNIT 1

Introduce this activity to the students by telling them that they are to conduct a geographical survey. Refer to the guidelines for team learning in the Instructional Approaches section of this Teacher Annotated Edition. Divide the class into five groups to conduct the following activity. Provide the class with five large posters or pictures emphasizing five different kinds of geographical features from around the world, such as an island, a desert, a river basin, an urban area, and a mountainous region. Assign one of the pictures or posters to each group. Next, prepare a student worksheet or write the following tasks on the chalkboard: (1) Determine or guess the specific place shown in the picture; (2) Determine the exact location of the place; (3) Write three descriptions of the relative location of the place; (4) List five observations and generalizations about the place, including effects of humans on the environment and environment on humans; (5) Draw a small map of the place, including the five basic map parts.

Instruct each group to work together to complete the tasks relating to its assigned picture. When the tasks are completed, have each group present its geographical survey to the rest of the class. Conclude the lesson by congratulating the students for doing the work of a geographer. Then, ask students to read Unit 1 Careers "Cartography," in the Teacher Resource Book. Ask students how many believe they would enjoy being a cartographer and, for those who give a positive response, have them explain why they believe it might be an interesting career.

Unit 1 Exam in the Teacher Resource Book may be administered.

UNIT 1 REVIEW QUESTIONS

page 40, Thinking About the Unit

1. Answers will vary but should emphasize the relationships between geography, social science, and economics. Answers will vary but should bring out the fact that geography is a science and uses scientific methods. Answers will vary but should include the effects of society on its members, and the effects of society (people and their actions) on environment.

2. Scale, grid, title, legend, and directional arrow. Albers Equal Area Conical Projection shows greatest distortion in areas farthest away from standard parallels, i.e., top and bottom of map. Least distortion is along standard parallels ($29\frac{1}{2}°$ and $45\frac{1}{2}°$).

UNIT 2 PHYSICAL PATTERNS

Student Edition pp. 43–109

UNIT 2 GOALS

At the conclusion of this unit, students will be able to:
1. explain how landforms, waterways, soil, and plant and animal life make Earth's natural landscapes.
2. describe the elements of and controls on climate.
3. characterize how people have changed Earth's natural environments.

UNIT 2 SKILL OBJECTIVE

After completing the *Developing Geography Skills* exercise in this unit, the student should be able to analyze photographs.

UNIT 2 OVERVIEW

The second unit of *World Geography: People and Places* focuses on the principal physical patterns in Earth's biosphere—landforms, water and waterways, and climate. *Chapter 3* describes forces within Earth and how they relate to the formation of landforms. How forces on Earth's surface work to wear down landforms, causing weathering, erosion, mass movement, and deposition are examined, along with the formation of soil and the relationship of plants, animals, and humans to the physical patterns of Earth. *Chapter 4* emphasizes the importance of water to all Earth's life-forms and explains why it is Earth's most valuable resource. The effects of the many aquatic forces at work on our planet and how they create landscapes and influence life-forms are studied. Oceanography occupies an impor-

tant portion of the chapter's focus. Finally, the results of the actions of people upon Earth's water resources in terms of pollution and altered waterways are considered. Weather and climate are the central themes of *Chapter 5*. The elements that produce climate, the geographical facts that affect climate, and the major climate groups are presented. The concluding emphasis in this chapter is placed upon the effects of human activity on past, present, and future weather and climatic changes.

Upon completion of this unit, the student should have an understanding of forces at work above and below Earth's surface and the geographical patterns that result from these forces, including the impact of people on the world environment.

INTRODUCING UNIT 2

Review with the class the geological history of Earth, including how the solar system was formed, and forces that shaped land and water on Earth's surface. Ask students if they

know of other forces and weather patterns that shaped Earth and affected its life-forms. Students should be able to mention the Ice Ages and speculate about events that could have caused great changes on Earth, such as ash and dust clouds from volcanic eruptions and meteor strikes, or the shifting of the magnetic poles. Ask students to speculate about what changes these events might have caused, and how they could have affected life on Earth, including the disappearance of the dinosaurs.

Explain to students that in this unit they will discover how the activity of people can also affect Earth's physical features and climate and how either positive or negative changes in Earth's future could result.

As students learn new terms related to geology, have them include them in an "Illustrated Geology Dictionary" that they will make and keep in a notebook. The dictionary should contain a verbal definition and an illustration that may be a drawing, diagram, or attached picture. Terms should be grouped under headings or introductory sentences.

CHAPTER 3 LANDSCAPES

Student Edition pp. 44–65

CHAPTER 3 OBJECTIVES

At the conclusion of this chapter, students will be able to:

1. explain how forces within Earth's structure create landforms.
2. explain how forces on Earth's surface create landforms.
3. describe how soil is formed.
4. summarize what plants and animals live in similar environments.
5. analyze how people have changed the shape of Earth's land surface.

CHAPTER 3 SKILL OBJECTIVE

After completing the *Using Graphic Skills* exercise in this chapter, the student should be able to understand diagrams.

CHAPTER 3 OVERVIEW

In this chapter the student is introduced to the forces that have shaped the surface of Earth, landforms that result, how soil was formed, and the plants and animals of Earth's biomes. In addition to natural forces, people are presented as shapers of Earth's surface, and the past and possible future effects of human activity are studied.

The chapter's *Section 1* deals with primary and secondary landforms created by forces inside and on Earth's surface. *Section 2* explains the soil's formation and composition, including an explanation of the factors that combine to make soil. In *Section 3*, students learn about Earth's biomes with their plant and animal communities. Students are led in *Section 4* to explore the impact people have had on Earth's surface features. The advantages and disadvantages of the technological age in relation to landscapes and life on Earth are examined. Information is presented that challenges students to consider possible future effects of continued human activity.

A special feature presented in this chapter introduces the students to the theory of plate tectonics.

CHAPTER 3 ACTIVITIES

Introducing Chapter 3

Explain to students what landforms are, then have the class call out different kinds of landforms. Write their responses on the chalkboard. Ask students to speculate about how these landforms came into being. Explain what fossils are, and ask students if they have ever found any fossils. Some may have found rocks with shell fossils, and others may have found fossils such as sea urchins in rock formations along shorelines. Ask the class why fossils from the sea can be found in areas now far inland. Students may know that these areas were once covered by seas. Ask the students to bring any fossils they may have found to class. Some students may wish to look for fossils in their area. Contact with local universities might prove useful in relation to what fossils exist and where to find them in your area. Should no fossils be available, bring pictures of various kinds to class to show. Discuss the age of the fossils and why they were found where they were. Explain to the class that the face of Earth has changed many times, and that in this chapter they will study Earth's surface, the forces that shape it and change it, and the role people as well as nature have played in causing those changes.

Chapter 3 Reading Assignments

Objectives 1 and 2	Student Ed. pp. 45–54
Objective 3	Student Ed. pp. 55–57
Objective 4	Student Ed. pp. 57–61
Objective 5	Student Ed. pp. 62–63

● Teaching   ■ Reinforcing   ★ Enriching

Objective 1 Activities

● Objective 1 Teaching Activity

Provide students with a "You Are There" experience of the geologic forces described in Section 1 of Chapter 3 by showing a film or videocassette that illustrates the various kinds of landforms, tectonic movement, mountain formation, and continental drift. Refer to the guidelines for audiovisual materials in the Instructional Approaches section of this Teacher Annotated Edition. Then refer to the list of Supplementary Materials in the Unit 2 Suggested Resources and select a film or cassette to show before students read the assignment from their Student Edition. In this way, the visual images will help make the written explanations come alive. Emphasize the slow nature of most tectonic activity, and the fact that the film speeds up the reality that takes place over millions of years.

As students read the Student Edition, have them list the geologic terms used to name Earth's parts and movements. Use these lists as focus questions for a second viewing of the film or videocassette. During the debriefing, call on students to explain each new term illustrated in the artwork on the pages of their Student Edition.

■ Objective 1 Reinforcing Activity

Refer to the guidelines for reading guides in the Instructional Approaches section of this Teacher Annotated Edition. Prepare a handout for students to answer as they read or review Section 1 of Chapter 3. Provide questions on a literal and an interpretive level. Questions may be true and false, multiple choice, straight recall, or a combination of types. Charts might also be prepared for students to fill in, such as one showing Earth's structure with columns labeled Part, Made Of, Located, and Size/Extent. Parts may be prelisted and should include: Earth's crust, Earth's mantle, Earth's outer core, and Earth's inner core.

Before students begin using the reading guide, provide them with the following directions: "As you read your text, look for the answers to these questions. You will find some answers easily in the text, but you will have to think about others. To the left of each question, write the page, column, and paragraph numbers that helped you to answer it. Be ready to discuss your answers, explanations, and opinions in class."

Objective 2 Activities

● Objective 2 Teaching Activity

Ask students to add the terms explained in this chapter to their "Illustrated Geology Dictionary." At this time, read and discuss the skill feature "Understanding Diagrams" on page 52 of the Student Edition. Explain that under the main terms, "weathering," "erosion," "mass movement," "deposition," "plain," "plateau," and "hills," the various kinds of formations for each should be illustrated and labeled in their geology dictionaries. Remind students to use the glossary of the Student Edition as well as the text paragraphs for their definitions.

Have students complete the *Content Check* definitions on page 54 of the Student Edition by adding pages to their "Illustrated Geology Dictionary" under the major heading, "Forces within Earth's Structures Create Landforms."

Refer students to Chapter 3 Skill Activity in the Teacher Resource Book in relation to this objective.

■ Objective 2 Reinforcing Activity

Show the class a number of landform photographs from the library's picture file, calendars, travel posters, magazines, postcards, and the Student Edition. Include photographs of landforms in your local area, state, and region. Ask students to name the landforms they see, describe the landscapes, and explain as much as they can what geologic forces contributed to the building up or tearing down of Earth's surface in that place. Ask students: What is the overall effect for living things there? Lead the class to consider natural beauty, easy living, harsh environment, forced migration, or adaptation for survival, tourist attraction, and so on. For discussion of this section, focus students' attention on the natural landscape rather than on people-caused changes. Finally, challenge students to hold each of the landform photographs to a place on a map where it might have been taken; then point out the symbols on the map that give clues to the landforms such as mountains, hills, plains, plateaus, deltas, and so on. Some photographs might fit in different parts of the world. Students should discuss and challenge each other's hypotheses.

Refer students to Chapter 3 Reading in the Teacher Resource Book for further information in relation to this objective.

Objective 3 Activities

● Objective 3 Teaching Activity

Refer to the guidelines for community resource persons in the Instructional Approaches section of this Teacher Annotated Edition. Invite a speaker who works professionally with soil samples and the usefulness and problems of different kinds of soil to share practical information and samples with your class. This might be someone from an agricultural college, your farming community, a government agency, botanic gardens, a naturalist/environmental organization, or a museum or academy of natural sciences.

Give your speaker a copy of pages 55–56 of the Student Edition so that his or her presentation can be illustrative of the content, not overly technical, and show applications to your local soil structure as well as global patterns. Most of the sources mentioned have prepared demo kits with labeled soil samples and profiles that will provide illustrations of soil formation and should intrigue students. The speaker should explain the way in which the soils in question were formed. Allow time for questions and open discussion.

■ Objective 3 Reinforcing Activity

Have students add the terms from this section to their "Illustrated Geology Dictionary." Allow time to share, display, and discuss students' work on this project.

Call attention to the "Challenge" question under *Content Check* on page 57 of the Student Edition. Teach students the requirements for a generalization: conditions must be true for all like situations at all times in all places. Have students apply this rule as they discuss each of the five factors that affect soil formation to decide what kinds of parent material, climate, topography, plants and animals, and time conditions are optimal for making fertile soil.

Objective 4 Activities

● Objective 4 Teaching Activity

To help students understand the concept of biome, ask the class to call out words and phrases they associate with certain places, such as the Bahamas, Mt. Everest, Hawaii, Antarctica, Yellowstone National Park or a park area near your locale, Death Valley, and so on. Write student responses on the chalkboard, and circle those that describe the natural environment of each place. Lead students to name kinds of plants and animals if they have not done so. Explain that certain animals and plants live together naturally in certain landscapes and climates.

Discuss thoroughly students' previous understandings of the concepts *environment, ecology, community, biome, forest, grassland, dryland*. Using the glossary of the Student Edition and page 57, formulate working definitions of the first four terms and encourage students to add/illustrate these in their geology dictionary for this chapter. Discuss the plants and animals that live in each type of biome, emphasizing the key role of plants in each environment. Ask students: Why is each biome characterized more by its plant life than its animal life? Answers should indicate that plants *stay* there, whereas animals and people may adapt or migrate. Therefore, plants are indicators of the kinds of climate, soil, and landforms an environment contains naturally.

■ Objective 4 Reinforcing Activity

Refer to the guidelines for retrieval charts in the Instructional Approaches section of this Teacher Annotated Edition. Prepare a master chart on the chalkboard, on a blank transparency, or on a bulletin board poster. Indicate columns for types of biomes, location, examples, climate, soil, landforms, plants, and animals. Have students discuss and summarize what they have learned about biomes by orally contributing facts to complete the chart. Prepare a duplicate of the chart as a class handout or have each student copy the chart for future study and review.

Objective 5 Activities

● Objective 5 Teaching Activity

Refer to the guidelines for lecture in the Instructional Approaches section of this Teacher Annotated Edition. Provide handouts of your lecture outline with room for the students to take notes, such as:

People Change the Face of the Earth

I. All living things have special abilities to live on Earth.
   A. Plants
   B. Animals
   C. Human beings
II. People have always used the natural environment to fill human needs for food, shelter, warmth, clothing.
III. People began to change their environment when they learned to farm.
   A.
   B.
IV. People changed natural landscapes further when natural resources were needed from the land after industrialization began.
   A.
   B.
V. With greater industrialization and new technology, people are capable of either harming the environment or gaining more understanding and control over it.
   A.
   B.

For each part of the outline, explain and give examples of the early development, causes, and key inventions that enable the movement, how people dealt with it in different parts of the world, and the effects on the natural environment and Earth's storehouse of resources. Emphasize that every time a person uses any aspect of our natural environment, that environment is changed. Walking on a forest floor changes the composition of the plant and animal material stepped upon. Building a campfire or playing with rocks in a streambed leaves a changed environment. Ask students: What steps might people take to protect Earth's biomes? Lead students to see that people should make wise choices about how, to what extent, and for what purposes they change Earth's natural environment, and that every change is, to some degree, a permanent effect.

★ **Objective 5 Enriching Activity**

Refer to the guidelines for debating in the Instructional Approaches section of this Teacher Annotated Edition, and aid students to research and prepare debates on topics related to some of the current controversies between environmentalists and industrialists, such as, *Resolved: More of our natural environment should be protected by law in the form of National Parks or open spaces*, or *Resolved: The world's tropical rain forests should be systematically cleared and the areas developed for agriculture, factories, or cities.*

Concluding Chapter 3

Refer to the guidelines for field trips in the Instructional Approaches section of this Teacher Annotated Edition; then plan a trip to a natural history museum in your area. Show students displays that emphasize landforms and the forces that created them, relating the exhibits to what students have learned in the Student Edition.

If there are no natural history museums or universities that may have natural history displays in your area, you may wish to plan a group activity. Divide the class into nine groups. Tell the students that they are going to create a mural depicting Earth's biomes. Tape newsprint to the chalkboard around the classroom, and assign a section of the newsprint to each group. Assign a different biome to each group, and inform the groups that they are to depict the landforms, plants, and animals of their assigned biomes. The biome categories that should be assigned to the mural artists are: tropical rain forest, broadleaf forest, coniferous forest, shrub forest, prairie, steppe, tropical savanna, desert, and tundra. When the murals are completed, have each group explain its assigned biome in terms of landscape and inhabitants, both plant and animal, and then use colored pins as markers to indicate on a map of the world where biomes like theirs are located. End this activity with a discussion about how humans damage or improve each depicted biome.

ANSWERS TO CHAPTER 3 QUESTIONS

Content Check Questions
page 54

1. Refer to Glossary in Student Edition.

2. Forces inside and on surface of Earth. (p. 45)

3. Folded, fault-block, dome, and volcanic. (pp. 46–47)

4. Weathering, erosion, mass movement, and deposition. (pp. 49–51)

5. A plateau is a large raised area of level land that rises steeply from land around it on at least one side; a plain is a large area of mostly flat land. (pp. 51–52)

6. Constructional—formed from wind and from glacial deposits of rock and soil;

destructional—formed from piles of rock worn down by heavy erosion. (p. 53)

7. Answers will vary but should include that neither size nor kind alone gives accurate identification. Would indicate which force involved (kind) and the strength of that force (size); would facilitate comparison and categorizing.

page 57

1. Refer to Glossary in Student Edition.
2. Organic material such as leaves, stems, and other plant parts. Humus or topsoil. Rocks and plant roots. Original rock or bedrock. (pp. 55–56)
3. Parent material, climate, topography, plants and animals, time. (p. 56)
4. Answers will vary but may include: Fertile soil comes from weathered rocks within a relatively flat land area that has a warm, wet climate.

page 61

1. Refer to Glossary in Student Edition.
2. Forest, grassland, and dryland. (p. 57)
3. With enough rainfall. (p. 58)
4. Tropical rain forest. (p. 57)
5. About 30 years. (p. 59)
6. Prairies get more rain thus have longer grasses and richer soil than steppes. (p. 59)
7. Store water or get along with very little. (p. 60)
8. Unlike some farm crops, rain forest vegetation thrives on constant moisture, heat, and acidic soil, and has shallow root systems. Rain forest soil is low in nutrients needed by farm crops.

page 63

1. Refer to Section 4 content.
2. Refer to Glossary in Student Edition.
3. Farming. (p. 62)
4. Answers will vary but should include: changing landscapes due to mineral extraction; disappearing forest due to stripping for fuel and building; replacing natural surfaces with structures. (pp. 62–63)

5. Answers will vary but may include: city skylines that add variety, parks created by people, deserts made to bloom through irrigation.

Special Feature Questions
page 48, Strange But True: "Drifting Continents"

1. The idea that continents have been moving on the surface of Earth for billions of years.
2. Researchers could match fossils of similar extinct animals as well as similar rocks from different continents.
3. Answers will vary but should include: Australia has shifted northward; Europe and lower half of Africa have moved eastward; North and South America have moved westward; Prime Meridian no longer passes through Greenwich, England.

page 52, Using Graphic Skills, "Understanding Diagrams"

1. Eurasian, Indian-Australian, Pacific, North American, South American, African, Antarctic. The Pacific plate.
2. Northwest.
3. Himalayas.

Photo/Illustration Caption Questions
page 46

Mantle. (p. 46)

page 47

Appalachian Mountains. (p. 47)
Sierra Nevada. (p. 47)

page 49

From the sides and below. (p. 49)

page 50

Erosion, mass movement, deposition. (p. 50) Gravity pulls loose materials down slopes and as the materials move, they wear away the land surface. (p. 50)

page 51

The depositing, or laying down, in a new area of rock and soil carried by mass movement and other agents of erosion. (p. 50) Deposition. (pp. 50–51)

page 54

Answers will vary according to area.

page 55

Horizon A. (p. 55)

page 56

Parent material, climate, topography, plants and animals, time. (p. 56)

page 58

Leaves of deciduous trees often change color before falling off. (p. 58)
They have needlelike leaves, often bear cones, and keep their green leaves all year. (p. 58)

page 59

Fires. (pp. 58–59)
Argentina, Australia, South Africa, United States. (p. 59)

page 60

Bobcats, coyotes, owls, and lizards live in North American deserts; desert animals in Africa include gazelles and camels. (p. 60)
Tundra. (p. 60)
Lichens, mosses, and small shrubs. (p. 60)

page 61

Broadleaf, coniferous, taiga, shrub, tropical rain forest, middle-latitude grassland, desert, tundra, mountain. (p. 61)

page 62

Mining stripped the land of usefulness, forests were cut down, new fields were plowed, railroads and roads were cut through forests, towns and cities replaced forests. (pp. 62–63)

Chapter 3 Review Questions
page 64, Reviewing Vocabulary

LANDFORMS
lava, fault-block mountains, erosion, volcanoes, plateaus, canyon, glaciers, plate tectonics.

SOIL
permafrost, deposition, parent material, humus, bedrock, alluvial fan, (erosion), (lava), (glaciers).

BIOMES
tundra, tropical savanna, coniferous forests, desert, (plate tectonics), (erosion), (deposition).

page 64, Remembering the Facts

1. Crust, mantle, outer core, inner core. (p. 45)
2. From 1/2 inch (2.3 cm) to 4 inches (10.2 cm). (p. 46)
3. Pressure on Earth's crust. (pp. 46–47)
4. Magma is hot metal-rock inside Earth's core; lava is magma that has left Earth's core. (p. 47)
5. Mineral makeup of rock and climate. (p. 49)
6. Major landforms are large landforms such as mountains and plains; minor landforms are small such as alluvial fans and deltas. (p. 45) Primary landforms are those made originally by tectonic activity; secondary landforms are those made by wearing down primary landforms. (pp. 46, 51)
7. Tropical rain forest, broadleaf, coniferous, and shrub. Middle-latitude grassland and tropical savanna. Desert and tundra. (pp. 57–60)

page 65, Understanding the Facts

1. Earth's crust, made of rigid plates of rock, moves upon soft parts of mantle next to crust, making landforms on the ocean floor or on continents. (p. 46)
2. They weaken rock's base by making cracks in rocks wider and causing breakage. (p. 49)
3. When more snow falls in winter than melts in summer, it packs down, making heavy, thick ice. (p. 50)
4. Mountain streams have carried rock material from the mountains and left it in low areas (floodplains) along rivers and in

coastal areas where sediment has built up ocean floor. (pp. 50–51)

5. Constructional hills were formed from wind and glacial deposits and have never been worn down from large mountains; some hills are actually worn-down mountains. (p. 53)

6. Rock that has already been broken down and eroded away. Warm climate with much rainfall. (p. 56)

7. Grassland. (p. 59)

8. Through use of wise and careful practices such as contour plowing, terrace cropping, putting landfills in gullies and ravines. (p. 63)

page 65, Thinking Critically and Creatively

1. Answers will vary but should include the idea that landforms, continents, and the ocean floor will change in location and size with most continents moving farther away from each other.

2. Answers will vary but should include that the mountain ranges cover large areas of varied internal pressure within Earth's crust making for different tectonic movement; heavy movement near plate boundaries can cause folding in other nearby areas.

3. Answers will vary. Answers will vary. Answers will vary but should include the idea that life on a tundra would be very difficult, require appropriate warm clothing and protective shelter, food would be in short supply; few people would live in tundra conditions, no farming would be possible. In a tropical rain forest, minimal clothing would be required; shelter would be from the sun and rain, not the cold; forest would

supply food needs, but here also no farming would be possible.

4. Answers will vary but may include that forests provide many resources and advantages including beauty, fuel, building materials, recreation, shelter, nutrients, minerals, the slowing of erosion, and protection from enemies. A land without forests provides poor sustenance, shelter, etc., and without these, people would begin to die. Answers will vary. Answers will vary.

5. Answers will vary but should include that farming may suffer greatly because Horizon A is humus. Answers will vary but should include that less farmland could spur erosion, and loss of plants and animals in the area will create barren land; destruction of the soil may result in slow generation of new soil. Answers will vary but may include that nuclear power plants like the one in Chernobyl should no longer be constructed since it lacked proper safeguards; build safer nuclear power plants and maintain inspection and control of safety factors; continue research into safer forms of energy including less risky ways of using nuclear energy.

page 65, Reinforcing Graphic Skills

1. Answers will vary but may include: The Pacific is mostly made up of one plate, whereas the Atlantic is divided in the center by the Mid-Atlantic Ridge; the major plate in the Pacific is oceanic crust, whereas the major plates in the Atlantic have oceanic and continental crust, and so on.

2. Anchorage—North American and Pacific; Luzon—Philippine and Eurasian; Mexico City—North American and Cocos.

EVALUATING CHAPTER 3

World Geography: People and Places provides chapter tests to help evaluate student performance. To evaluate student mastery of Chapter 3, give students Chapter 3 Test from the Teacher Resource Book. This test may also be used for pretesting or retesting purposes. Other tests can be made from the questions available in the Test Generator Software.

Lesson Plan Suggestions—Chapter 3

SE—Student Edition   TAE—Teacher Annotated Edition   TG—Test Generator
TRB—Teacher Resource Book   TSP—Transparency Package

Section 1   Landforms (pp. 45–54)

Chapter Objectives	Suggested Teaching Strategies	Review

1. explain how forces within Earth's structure create landforms.
 	
2. explain how forces on Earth's surface create landforms.
 	
Skill Objective: describe subjects or explain processes illustrated in diagrams.
	Teacher Preparation
	SE, Reading Assignment, pp. 45–54
	TAE, Unit 2 Suggested Resources
	    Unit 2 Overview, p. T72
	    Introducing Unit 2, p. T72
	    Chapter 3 Overview, p. T73
	    Introducing Chapter 3, p. T74
	TRB, Chapter 3 Teacher Notes: Section 1
	Teaching Options
	TAE, Introducing Unit 2, p. T72
	    Introducing Chapter 3, p. T73
	    Objectives 1 and 2 Activities, pp. T74–T75
	TRB, Chapter 3 Teacher Notes: Section 1, Extending the Lesson
	    Chapter 3 Skill Activity
	    Chapter 3 Reading
	SE, *Using Graphic Skills*,
	    "Understanding Diagrams," pp. 52–53
		SE, Content Check, p. 54

Section 2   Soil (pp. 55–57)

Chapter Objectives	Suggested Teaching Strategies	Review
3. describe how soil is formed.	**Teacher Preparation** SE, Reading Assignment, pp. 55–56 TAE, Unit 2 Suggested Resources Chapter 3 Overview, p. T73 TRB, Chapter 3 Teacher Notes: Section 2 **Teaching Options** TAE, Objective 3 Activities, pp. T75–T76 TRB, Chapter 3 Teacher Notes: Section 2, Extending the Lesson	SE, Content Check, p. 57

Section 3   Plants and Animals (pp. 57–61)

Chapter Objectives	Suggested Teaching Strategies	Review
4. summarize what plants and animals live in similar environments.	**Teacher Preparation** SE, Reading Assignment, pp. 57–61 TAE, Unit 2 Suggested Resources 　　Chapter 3 Overview, p. T73 TRB, Chapter 3 Teacher Notes: Section 3 **Teaching Options** TAE, Objective 4 Activities, p. T76 TRB, Chapter 3 Teacher Notes: Section 3, 　　Extending the Lesson	SE, Content Check, p. 61

Section 4   Impact of People (pp. 62–63)

Chapter Objectives	Suggested Teaching Strategies	Review
5. analyze how people have changed the shape of Earth's land surface.	**Teacher Preparation** SE, Reading Assignment, pp. 62–63 TAE, Unit 2 Suggested Resources 　　Chapter 3 Overview, p. T72 TRB, Chapter 3 Teacher Notes: Section 4 **Teaching Options** TAE, Objective 5 Activities, pp. T76–T77 TRB, Chapter 3 Teacher Notes: Section 4, 　　Extending the Lesson	SE, Content Check, p. 63

Chapter 3   Review and Evaluation

Suggested Teaching Strategies	Review	Evaluation
TAE, Concluding Chapter 3, p. T77	SE, Chapter 3 Review, pp. 64–65 TRB, Chapter 3 Review Worksheet	TRB, Chapter 3 Test TG, Chapter 3

CHAPTER 4 WATER AND WATERWAYS

Student Edition pp. 66–83

CHAPTER 4 OBJECTIVES

At the conclusion of this chapter, students will be able to:

1. list the elements within the hydrosphere and explain how Earth's water cycle works.
2. describe changes on Earth's surface that are made by motions of ocean water and tectonic movement below the ocean floor.
3. summarize how lakes, streams, and glaciers each change natural landscapes.
4. specify ways people have changed water and waterways.

CHAPTER 4 SKILL OBJECTIVE

After completing the *Using Graphic Skills* exercise in this chapter, the student should be able to read circle graphs.

CHAPTER 4 OVERVIEW

In this chapter students learn about Earth's hydrosphere, including how the water cycle circulates the water supply, the changes brought about by movement of oceans and tectonic plates below them, the great variety of both plant and animal life in the oceans, how waterways change landscapes, and how people have caused changes in Earth's water supply and waterways with resultant ecological changes.

In *Section 1* water as a substance and the way the water cycle works are explained. The student is aided in understanding how and in what forms water is present on Earth, how the drying up and flooding of land areas may occur, and what the possible consequences are. *Section 2* deals with Earth's waterways. Topics of an oceanographic nature touch on the composition and motion of ocean water, tides, and the topography of the ocean floor.

Ocean biomes and their resources are explored as well as the dangers to the ocean's life-forms from overexploitation and pollution. Lakes and streams, where their water supply comes from, and how they change and evolve are described. Presentation of the important part played by glaciers in the hydrosphere and current studies being conducted on them closes this section.

Problems resulting from human activity touching Earth's water supply and waterways are considered in *Section 3*. Pollution, along with the changing of natural water courses, is studied, and students are challenged to find solutions.

Special chapter features inform students of irrigation technology and enhance students' knowledge of the proportion of land to water on Earth as they acquire skill in reading graphs.

CHAPTER 4 ACTIVITIES

Introducing Chapter 4

Prepare a pretest consisting of true and false statements covering the material presented in this chapter. You may find the Test Generator Software for this chapter useful in the preparation of this test. Have students go through the quiz and mark the statements by circling the T or the F preceding each, according to what they believe is correct. Create three or four statements for each chapter section. Sample statements for Section 1 might be:

1. T F   There is approximately as much water on Earth today as there was millions of years ago.
2. T F   Slow evaporation of water from Earth's surface has created a water crisis today.
3. T F   Plants use up water that is then lost to the hydrosphere.
4. T F   Sinkholes form where groundwater level in underground caves drops.

When students have completed the pretest, ask them to note the correct answers as they read assignments in the Student Edition, and to change their answers if necessary. Tell students to keep the pretest in their notebooks for use in the Concluding Chapter 4 activity.

Chapter 4 Reading Assignments

Objective 1	Student Ed. pp. 67–69
Objectives 2 and 3	Student Ed. pp. 69–78
Objective 4	Student Ed. pp. 79–81

● Teaching	■ Reinforcing	★ Enriching

Objective 1 Activities

● Objective 1 Teaching Activity

Use the terms and diagrams of the text content as focal points for teaching about Earth's hydrosphere and water cycle. Direct students to list terms that have to do with Earth's water supply. During class debriefing, make a composite list on the chalkboard as students volunteer to define and explain each term. Take time to thoroughly discuss and explain each of the diagrams that illustrate the main concepts of this section.

■ Objective 1 Reinforcing Activity

Ask students to note some interesting, and perhaps surprising, topic sentences about Earth's water from this section. Write on the chalkboard "EARTH'S WATER," and list students' contributions from the text. Sentences may state:

. . . covers 71% of its surface.
. . . is called the hydrosphere.
. . . includes oceans, lakes, streams, other bodies of water, underground water, water in the air, ice in glaciers and snow.
. . . is 97% ocean saltwater.
. . . is 3% fresh water, most of which is frozen in glaciers.
. . . is necessary for life on Earth.
. . . is about two-thirds of the human body.
. . . is not evenly distributed.
. . . has carved the details of landforms.
. . . is Earth's most valuable and most abundant resource.
. . . is unique because it is the only substance found in three natural states: liquid, solid, and gas.
. . . is about the same amount today as it was millions of years ago.
. . . is constantly changing its state and location in a process called the water cycle.
. . . is closer to the surface in some places than in others.

Allow time for class to thoroughly discuss each of these statements, citing examples and asking questions for further inquiry.

★ Objective 1 Enriching Activity

Challenge students to spontaneous creative storytelling about a single molecule of water that they imagine having been "born" when Earth was formed and colored or marked in some way to show its individuality. Where do students wish their molecule to be "born"—at the beginning of time? In a glacier? In the body of a prehistoric plant? In a raincloud? In the ocean? In groundwater? They should then show on a world map or globe a specific place they choose. Allow some time for students to review concepts in the chapter and use their imaginations to weave a fun—but scientifically possible—"biography" of one single molecule of water through space and time in geologic and human history, and then to either write, draw cartoon style, or tell its fascinating story. Encourage storytellers to use the chalkboard to illustrate their stories and to help the class visualize their fantasy.

Objective 2 Activities

● Objective 2 Teaching Activity

By means of an opaque projector, show class photographs or illustrations of landforms on Earth's surface that were created by motions of ocean water and tectonic movements below the ocean's floor. As students view the images, ask them what they believe caused the various formations. Be prepared to explain how each landform was shaped either by water or tectonic movement in case students are unable to guess correctly. Have students summarize what they have observed by adding the names of these landforms, a drawing or a description of each, and an explanation of how they were formed, to their geology dictionaries.

★ Objective 2 Enriching Activity

Refer to the guidelines for audiovisual materials in the Instructional Approaches section of this Teacher Annotated Edition. Show the filmstrip *The Ocean: Exploring Earth's Last Frontier*, listed in the Supplementary Materials for this unit in the Suggested Resources section of this Teacher Annotated Edition. During debriefing, challenge interested students to compose some Jeopardy-type answers (with brief questions) about the geology, water movements, biomes, resources, and importance to human history of Earth's oceans and seas. Allow sufficient time to play a short game

of Jeopardy using students' answers and questions that students have compiled.

Objective 3 Activities

● Objective 3 Teaching Activity

Show a map or series of maps from the library collection, a large atlas, or overhead projector transparencies, that show the continent of North America in various stages of glaciation. Have students identify the Great Lakes and other places at the edges of the glaciers and covered by them. Point out that Minnesota is nicknamed "the state of 1,000 lakes"—can students guess why?

Explain that since understanding the force of glaciation is a key to studying the waterways that are part of Earth's landscapes, you (or a pre-assigned student) have prepared a demonstration model of a glacier. Refer to the guidelines for experimentation in the Instructional Approaches section of this Teacher Annotated Edition. Select one or more experiment-demonstrations about glaciers from library references on science inquiry projects, science fairs, or earth-science activities manuals to prepare in advance for this class session. A simple one is to place some sand, gravel, and small rocks in a plastic container, filling it with water and letting it freeze for several hours. Next, make a clay model of a mountain and plain in a shallow pan. Push the frozen contents out of the plastic container in a solid piece and move it downward over the clay mountain; let it rest on the flat plain. Have students observe what the rough debris did to the smooth clay of the landscape and how it forms a small lake when it melts.

Demonstrate with experiments, models, pictures, and/or maps, the difference between continental glaciers and valley glaciers, the effects of gravity, and the kinds of changes glaciers have effected on Earth's landscape over millions of years.

■ Objective 3 Reinforcing Activity

Continue using the opaque projector as in the Objective 2 Teaching Activity to show photographs of landforms created or changed by lakes, streams, and glaciers. Have students guess the natural process that formed them, and instruct them about how the landforms were created should they guess incorrectly.

Assign students, individually or in pairs, to make clay and water models that illustrate the landscapes, terms, and movements related to waterways. They may choose to model oceans, seas, lakes, streams, or rivers. Display the models in the classroom.

Refer students to the Chapter 4 Skill Activity in the Teacher Resource Book as an adjunct to this activity.

Have students add new terms to their "Illustrated Geology Dictionary."

Objective 4 Activities

● Objective 4 Teaching Activity

Refer to the guidelines for case studies in the Instructional Approaches section of this Teacher Annotated Edition. Explain to students that by learning all we can about several case studies on one topic, we can make more reliable generalizations and decisions about issues. Tell them that they will apply the "case study approach" to the topic of this section to learn how human decisions and actions change Earth's water and waterways.

Read to the class and discuss one or two current news items as sample case studies of polluting water and/or altering waterways. For example, the following case could be studied: *On January 2, 1988, an Ashland Oil Company storage tank collapsed near Pittsburgh, pouring a million gallons of diesel fuel into the Monongahela River, which flows into the Ohio River and then into the Mississippi River.*

By January 12, the oil spill had spread 100 miles from where it began, polluting drinking water in three states—Pennsylvania, West Virginia, and Ohio—fouling rivers, and forcing some drinking water systems to shut down for several days. A month later, the slick arrived at Louisville, Kentucky, and February 24 at Joppa, Illinois, 30 miles upstream from the Mississippi.

Environmentalists were especially concerned about the effect of the oil spill on the Monongahela River that had already suffered from much pollution and mine spill-offs over a fifteen-year period. The river had been recovering from this history and had been reestablished as a source of fish and as a recreational resource. Since the Ashland oil spill on January 2, dead fish have been taken out of the river in large numbers.

In addition to articles similar to the above, the class might discuss the case studies of Israel's drip irrigation system that has been successful in the Negev Desert and the areas where it is used, and California's conversion of the Imperial Valley from desert into a productive agricultural region.

Direct students to read the case studies mentioned in Section 3 of this chapter in the Student Edition. Then, lead the class in a discussion of the various case studies cited, noting the complex effects of the different kinds of pollution and human activity described. Ask students: What are the good effects of such tampering? If there are so many harmful effects, why do people, industries, and governments continue to make decisions of which they can foresee the results? How local are the results, good and bad? How far-reaching? How global? With regard to the case studies in Israel and California, are there also disadvantages to these two success stories?

■ Objective 4 Reinforcing Activity

Refer to the guidelines for team learning in the Instructional Approaches section of this Teacher Annotated Edition. Divide the class into groups of five students, and ask each of the five to assume the roles of (1) industry spokesperson, (2) government agent, (3) environmental scientist, (4) citizen of the local area, and (5) futurist (one who projects and studies the future of a situation or place). Instruct the teams to decide on one case study they will research involving how people have changed water and waterways, each looking specifically for information from the viewpoint of his or her personal interests. Teams may choose among the case studies mentioned in the text, one which concerns your local area, or any other real situation about which they can readily find information. Check to see that no two teams are researching the same event.

When team members have had sufficient time to read about their problem, have students who researched the same case study sit in a semicircle before the class. Each group member should report what he or she learned about the problem from the point of view of the special interest he or she represents. After the group presentation, allow the class to challenge positions taken by group members. Encourage some informed arguing, informal debating, and speaking with conviction.

Refer students to Chapter 4 Reading in the Teacher Resource Book for additional information with regard to this objective.

Concluding Chapter 4

Ask students to retrieve the pretests completed before study of this chapter was begun and that they have been correcting as they studied the chapter. Now go through the true and false statements noting the correct answers and requiring students to give an explanation for each answer.

Assign students the reading of Unit 2 Careers, "Oceanography," in the Teacher Resource Book. Through informal class discussion, explore student interest in this career. Ask those students who would find a career in this field interesting to explain why they would like to be an oceanographer. Students with a special interest in this field may wish to research it further and make reports of their findings to the class.

ANSWERS TO CHAPTER 4 QUESTIONS

Content Check Questions
page 69

1. Refer to Glossary in Student Edition.
2. Can be found in three natural states of liquid, solid, and gas. (p. 67)
3. The sun evaporates water. (p. 67)
4. Transpiration—drawn into the roots of plants; groundwater—fills spaces between layers of rock. (p. 68)
5. Warm, moist ocean air flows over cooler land where it condenses and falls to Earth as precipitation.

page 78

1. Refer to Section 2 content.
2. Refer to Glossary in Student Edition.
3. Currents, waves, and tides. (pp. 70–71)
4. Through tectonic activity. (p. 73)
5. Streams, underground springs, and melting snow. (p. 76)
6. Large streams and rivers have served as boundaries, provided transportation, aided

irrigation, and produced power to generate electricity. (p. 78)

page 81

1. Refer to Glossary in Student Edition.
2. Through chemical, human, and industrial waste. (p. 79)
3. Farming and expanding cities. Transport people and goods and for irrigation. Control water for recreation, human use, flood control, and power generation. Cause marshes and wetlands to be worn away by the sea, threatening fish and natural wildlife. (p. 81)
4. Answers will vary but may include use of cleaner raw materials, more efficient waste disposal, more organic farming methods, air scrubbers and filters for industry.

Special Feature Questions
page 80, Focus on Geography: "Irrigation"

1. Irrigation increases food supply and growth of population.

2. Irrigation may be too costly and cause waste by evaporating water supply, lowering water table, changing or destroying courses of rivers, and making composition of soil unfavorable for farming.

page 72, Using Graphic Skills: "Making and Reading Circle Graphs"

1. Atlantic and Indian oceans.
2. Pacific Ocean.
3. 17%.

Photo/Illustration Caption Questions
page 68

Process by which precipitation moves into roots and up the stems then out through leaves of plants as water vapor. (p. 68)

page 69

The top of the aquifer zone. (p. 68)

page 69

Twice as large. (p. 69)

page 70

Earth's wind patterns. (p. 70)

page 71

The Bay of Fundy on the eastern coast of Canada. (p. 71)

page 73

Underwater land surface where a continent extends into the ocean. (p. 73)

page 74

Trenches. (p. 74)

page 75

The shaking of Earth's crust during tectonic movement. (p. 74)

page 76

North America. (p. 76)

page 77

Answers will vary. (p. 77)

page 78

Gravity. (p. 78)

page 79

Chemical spills; thermal pollution; burial of hazardous materials; pesticides and fertilizers washing into groundwater. (p. 79)

Chapter 4 Review Questions
page 82, Reviewing Vocabulary

1. g. 2. e. 3. a. 4. m. 5. b.
6. c. 7. f. 8. i. 9. j. 10. d.

page 83, Remembering the Facts

1. All Earth's water—oceans, lakes, streams, and other bodies of water, underground water, water in the air, ice in glaciers, and snow. (p. 67)
2. Currents, waves, and tides. (pp. 70–71)
3. Same landforms as on land surface as well as continental shelf and slopes, abyssal plain, rifts, and mountains called ridges. (pp. 71, 73)
4. The magnitude or energy release of earthquakes. (p. 74)
5. Fish, mammals, plants, and minerals such as gas, oil, gold, diamonds. (p. 76)
6. Polluting water, altering waterways. (p. 79)

page 83, Understanding the Facts

1. Answers will vary but should describe evaporation, absorption, water vapor, condensation, and precipitation. (pp. 67–68)
2. Currents influence temperature and moisture of land areas by carrying water from the poles to and from the Equator. (p. 71)
3. By causing erosion and deposition. (p. 71)
4. Pressure builds up from tectonic movement. (p. 74)
5. Life in the oceans needs sunlight and nutrients found in shallower waters. (p. 75)
6. Dry up from lack of rain; areas fill with sediment and vegetation takes root. (p. 76)
7. Provided irrigation, transportation, boundaries, food, water for industry, power to generate electricity. (p. 78)
8. Contain 75% of Earth's water, 90% of fresh water above ground. (p. 78)
9. Plant and wildlife deaths; contaminated drinking water. (p. 79)

page 83, Thinking Critically and Creatively

1. Changing state of water creates and continues the water cycle.
2. Answers will vary but may include: prevents flooding and can be purified and stored for future use.
3. Answers will vary but may include: need to gather food, control water supplies, obtain minerals to increase their wealth, and guard their boundaries from invasion.
4. Answers will vary but may include that irrigation can lower water levels in rivers, lakes, and in groundwater; this plus evaporation leaves salt and minerals behind making soil unsuitable for farming.
5. Answers will vary but may include that fish harvests go down, migratory birds and other wildlife leave the area or perish, and sediment from erosion causes sea level to rise.
6. Answers will vary but should include concepts such as allowing free access, control of spillage and pollution, restriction of excessive use for irrigation, and damming up.
7. Answers will vary but may include transporting it, getting fresh water from it to the land, controlling the melting process.

page 83, Reinforcing Graphic Skills

1. Indian and Arctic. Pacific and Atlantic.
2. Answers will vary but should include that Earth is a "water planet" with most of its surface covered with water; water areas on Earth's surface are larger than land areas.

EVALUATING CHAPTER 4

World Geography: People and Places provides chapter tests to help evaluate student performance. To evaluate student mastery of Chapter 4, give students Chapter 4 Test from the Teacher Resource Book. This test may also be used for pretesting or retesting purposes. Other tests can be made from the questions available in the Test Generator Software.

Lesson Plan Suggestions—Chapter 4

SE—Student Edition   TAE—Teacher Annotated Edition   TG—Test Generator
TRB—Teacher Resource Book   TSP—Transparency Package

Section 1   Water (pp. 67–69)

Chapter Objectives	Suggested Teaching Strategies	Review

1. list the elements within the hydrosphere and explain how Earth's water cycle works.	**Teacher Preparation**
	SE, Reading Assignment, pp. 67–69
	TAE, Unit 2 Suggested Resources
	    Chapter 4 Overview, p. T83
	    Introducing Chapter 4, p. T84
	TRB, Chapter 4 Teacher Notes: Section 1
	Teaching Options
	TAE, Introducing Chapter 4, p. T84
	    Objective 1 Activities, pp. T84–T85
	TRB, Chapter 4 Teacher Notes: Section 1,
	    Extending the Lesson
		SE, Content Check, p. 69

Section 2　Waterways (pp. 69–78)

Chapter Objectives	Suggested Teaching Strategies	Review
2. describe changes on Earth's surface that are made by motions of ocean water and tectonic movement below the ocean floor. 3. summarize how lakes, streams, and glaciers each change natural landscapes. Skill Objective: make and read circle graphs.	**Teacher Preparation** 　SE, Reading Assignment, pp. 69–78 　TAE, Unit 2 Suggested Resources 　　　Chapter 4 Overview, p. T83 　TRB, Chapter 4 Teacher Notes: Section 2 **Teaching Options** 　TAE, Objectives 2 and 3 Activities, pp. T84–T85 　TRB, Chapter 4 Teacher Notes: Section 2, Extending the Lesson 　　　Chapter 4 Skill Activity 　SE, *Using Graphic Skills,* "Making and Reading Circle Graphs," p. 72	SE, Content Check, p. 78

Section 3　Impact of People (pp. 79–81)

Chapter Objectives	Suggested Teaching Strategies	Review
4. specify ways people have changed water and waterways.	**Teacher Preparation** 　SE, Reading Assignment, pp. 79–81 　TAE, Unit 2 Suggested Resources 　　　Chapter 4 Overview, p. T84 　TRB, Chapter 4 Teacher Notes: Section 3 **Teaching Options** 　TAE, Objective 4 Activities, pp. T86–T87 　TRB, Chapter 4 Teacher Notes: Section 3, Extending the Lesson 　　　Chapter 4 Reading	SE, Content Check, p. 81

Chapter 4 Review and Evaluation

Suggested Teaching Strategies	Review	Evaluation
TAE, Concluding Chapter 4, p. T87	SE, Chapter 4 Review, pp. 82–83 TRB, Chapter 4 Review Worksheet	TRB, Chapter 4 Test TG, Chapter 4

CHAPTER 5   CLIMATE

Student Edition pp. 84–105

CHAPTER 5 OBJECTIVES

At the conclusion of this chapter, students will be able to:

1. explain how temperature, moisture, air pressure, and wind combine to produce climate.
2. describe how latitude, heating and cooling differences of land and water, prevailing wind patterns, and altitude affect climate.
3. list the five major types of climate and summarize typical characteristics of each.
4. discuss the ways people have changed weather and climate patterns.

CHAPTER 5 SKILL OBJECTIVE

After completing the *Using Graphic Skills* exercise in this chapter, the student should be able to read line and bar graphs (climographs).

CHAPTER 5 OVERVIEW

In this chapter students learn about climate, weather, and the differences between them. The study of climate in this chapter also incorporates how climate is produced, what elements affect climate, what the five major climate groups are, and how people influence weather and climate patterns.

In *Section 1*, different combinations of the elements that produce climate are studied to determine how varying climates occur. *Section 2* examines those things that act as controllers of climate such as altitude, latitude, land and water areas, and wind patterns. The five major climate groups are described in *Section 3*. Both the positive and negative results of human activity as it affects climate are presented in *Section 4*, and possible future consequences are considered. The importance of the study of Earth's climate is emphasized in the conclusion of this chapter.

A special chapter feature related to the study of the material presented in this chapter gives information on the weather phenomenon known as *El Niño*.

CHAPTER 5 ACTIVITIES

Introducing Chapter 5

Briefly compare the atmospheres of the various planets of the solar system to that of Earth. Ask students: How is Earth's atmosphere different from that of other planets in the solar system? Why is life as we know it possible only on Earth? Explain the difference between climate and weather, and ask students if they believe that climate and weather exist on all planets of the solar system. Why or why not? For example, what climates might exist on Mars? What might Mars' weather be like? Could people and animals live on Mars? Under what circumstances? Ask students if any of them have read *The Martian Chronicles* by Ray Bradbury. If so, they may recall the story of the Johnny Appleseed of Mars who planted trees over all the planet thus creating a breathable atmosphere. Ask the class if they understand why planting trees would help create an atmosphere that would support human life. Students should understand that trees put oxygen into the atmosphere. Explain that on Earth oxygen-producing plants such as those that exist in rain forests are important to human life. Ask the class to speculate about what would happen if Earth gradually lost its oxygen-producing plant life.

Using a world map or globe to point out climatic areas of the world, ask students what they think the climate of these various areas is like. Help them to determine possible climate through consideration of the areas' geographical features and global position. Ask them to imagine the kinds of vegetation and animals that could be common to these various climatic areas. Students should know about arctic, woodland, and tropical forest animals. Have students brainstorm ways plants, animals, and people adapt to these various climates. Explain that people of Earth have adapted to almost all climates on the planet.

During the study of this chapter, plan to have a brief simulated television weather broadcast each day at the beginning of the class on the weather in your area and immediate vicinity. Allow two different students acting as a team to present the program each day. Students should watch television and read newspapers to prepare each day's forecast and include simple visual aids such as wall maps, cut-out symbols, chalkboard drawings, or weather maps projected using an opaque or overhead projector.

Chapter 5 Reading Assignments

● Teaching   ■ Reinforcing   ★ Enriching

Objective 1 Activities

● Objective 1 Teaching Activity

Tell the class that you will use the first two sections of this chapter to help them learn how to take notes of essential points in a text for easy study purposes.

Write on the chalkboard: "EARTH'S ATMOSPHERE." Ask students to pick out key topic sentences from the text as they did for "Earth's Water" at the beginning of Chapter 4. List contributions under the topic on the chalkboard, and have students copy these phrases in their notebooks after thorough discussion of each. Statements should include:

. . . is a sea of gases.

. . . is the air part of Earth's biosphere.

. . . is most changeable of Earth's environments.

. . . protects people from harmful rays and materials from space.

. . . holds the air people need for life.

. . . is 78% nitrogen, 21% oxygen, argon, carbon dioxide, and other gases.

. . . is source of Earth's weather and climate patterns.

Suggest that sometimes notetaking can best be done graphically. For example, students might draw a circle graph to illustrate the important points in paragraph 2 of Section 1 in the Student Edition in Chapter 4. Review the circle graph for water, and allow time for students to draw one for air in their notebooks while a volunteer does so on the chalkboard.

Ask students to re-read paragraph 3 of the chapter introduction and tell what two essential points should be noted in their notebooks (definitions of *weather* and of *climate*). For paragraph 4, discuss the difference between *plant* and *animal adapting* and *people adjusting* to climates and environments. Have students define each in their notebooks, citing examples to illustrate.

Summarize for students the three ways of notetaking from text material you have just done together: (1) listing topic sentences about a major concept, (2) defining terms and citing examples when helpful, and (3) drawing simple graphics (diagram, chart, sketch, simple map).

Assign the reading of pp. 85–90, looking over the material first with class to organize notetaking procedure. Students should see that the main topic, or title, of this section's notes will be "ELEMENTS OF EARTH'S CLIMATES." Each of the four elements is a major concept, so students should look for and copy topic sentences about each. Under each concept, the related terms can be defined and some illustrated.

After the notes are completed, have students discuss from their notebooks and the text Figures 5–1 and 5–2. Be sure to clarify the difference between low and high latitudes and low and high pressure areas.

■ Objective 1 Reinforcing Activity

Refer to guidelines for experimentation in the Instructional Approaches section of this Teacher Annotated Edition. Many science books suggest experiments that demonstrate both the elements of climate, discussed in Section 1 of this chapter, and the controls on climate, discussed in Section 2. Prepare some for class demonstration, or preassign interested student volunteers to do so. Have demonstrators explain the experiments so that the rest of the class will be aided to understand and remember the key elements and forces involved in climate and weather.

Refer students to Chapter 5 Skill Activity in the Teacher Resource Book in relation to this activity.

Objective 2 Activities

● Objective 2 Teaching Activity

Before students read this section in the Student Edition, explain each climate control, relying on Figures 5-4, 5-5, 5-6, 5-7 as focal points of your discussion.

Assign text reading, asking students to continue their notetaking of topic sentences, terms, and graphics, as they did for the last section. Discuss each during the debriefing period. Allow time for demonstrations of any experiments prepared for this section as suggested in the Objective 1 Reinforcing Activity.

Have students read the special feature on *El Niño*, and discuss this and other anomalies of weather. Ask the class if they have heard about the "Siberian Express" often mentioned by TV meteorologists during the winter weather reports. Ask a volunteer to find out more about it and report to class.

Refer students to Chapter 5 Reading in the Teacher Resource Book for further information in relation to this activity.

■ Objective 2 Reinforcing Activity

Select a variety of maps, climate charts, and pictures from library collections, front parts of atlases, and such resources as National Geographic publications to illustrate some of the concepts of climate controls and how they operate in different parts of the world. For example, show pictures of Christmas time in Australia's and Argentina's mid-summer season. Compare maps that show length of growing seasons in different regions, such as Alaska, Canada, Southern United States, Argentina and other world areas. Have students locate snow-covered mountain peaks along the Equator in Asia and South America. Examine maps of Oregon and California to see how these states are cut lengthwise by high mountain ranges; show pictures of places along the coasts, in the valleys between the mountains, and on the eastern desert parts of each state.

Tell some anecdotes and stories from history, your own personal experiences, and current news items that include weather-related happenings in different climate areas with which you are familiar. Ask students who may have traveled elsewhere to share their stories or those of people they know. Have speakers point to locations on a wall map. After each story, ask the class to identify the specific elements or controls of climate in operation.

Objective 3 Activities

● Objective 3 Teaching Activity

Tell students that in addition to maps like the one for Earth's Climates on pages 96 and 97 of the Student Edition, another study tool useful for seeing patterns is a chart of notes under specified headings. Then, refer to the guidelines for retrieval charts in the Instructional Approaches section of this Teacher Annotated Edition. Draw a grid on the chalkboard or have one prepared on a transparency or handout. Across the top write the headings: "General Location, Global Examples, Temperature, Precipitation, Seasons, Vegetation, Animals, Human Living." You might suggest to students that two or more pieces of paper can be taped together to accommodate the size of the chart. Down the left side of the chart, write the five climate areas with indented subtypes as they are classified in the Student Edition.

Instruct students to take notes about each climate area in the appropriate squares as they read this section in the Student Edition, advising them that not all information is given here about every climate area. After the reading, divide class into thirteen groups. Group members should compare their charts to check each other for accuracy and to discuss their understanding of the text information.

★ Objective 3 Enriching Activity

Refer to the guidelines for cooperative learning in the Instructional Approaches section of this Teacher Annotated Edition. Ask each of the thirteen groups formed for the debriefing of the retrieval chart activity to choose a climate area to learn more about, or assign an area to each group. Allow time for groups to use library resources to complete the information grid on their charts for their one climate area. Direct students to use selected atlases that have good descriptions and maps to begin their research.

The designated "experts" from each group can then report collective findings about their respective climate areas to class, showing pictures, travel posters, or any audiovisual that might help to make the area real to students. Students should take notes from the talks of the experts to help them fill in all the squares on their grids.

Objective 4 Activities

● Objective 4 Teaching Activity

Remind students that another useful method for taking notes to remember the content of a reading is to outline it. Review with them that outlining may be done with very brief word headings, sentences, or topics with some explanatory notes after each. Suggest that students read the first paragraph of this section and skim the headings of the rest of it to see how they might organize their notetaking in outline form. Lead the class to contribute a skeletal outline that is similar to the one following. You may want to write the outline on the chalkboard.

People Change Weather and Climate

A. Through changing Earth's surface
   by deforestation
   by desertification
   by urbanization
B. Through polluting the air
   causing greenhouse effect
   causing acid rain
C. Through changing natural weather patterns
   by cloud seeding
   by frost prevention

Assign the reading of this section and tell students they may decide how much detail they need to complete the outline in their notebooks to enable them to recall the ideas in the debriefing discussion and for later study purposes.

Refer to the guidelines for discussion in the Instructional Approaches section of this Teacher Annotated Edition, then use notebook outlines and content check questions to lead class in discussion of this section, inviting students who are interested in specific topics to contribute information in addition to the text summaries.

Lesson Plan Suggestions—Chapter 5

| SE—Student Edition TAE—Teacher Annotated Edition TG—Test Generator |
| TRB—Teacher Resource Book TSP—Transparency Package |

Section 1 Elements of Climate (pp. 85–90)

Chapter Objectives	Suggested Teaching Strategies	Review

explain how temperature, moisture, air pressure, and wind combine to produce climate.	**Teacher Preparation**
	SE, Reading Assignment, pp. 85–90
	TAE, Unit 2 Suggested Resources
	  Chapter 5 Overview, p. T91
	  Introducing Chapter 5, pp. T91–T92
	TRB, Chapter 5 Teacher Notes: Section 1
	Teaching Options
	TAE, Introducing Chapter 5, pp. T91–T92
	  Objective 1 Activities, pp. T92–T93
	TRB, Chapter 5 Teacher Notes: Section 1,
	  Extending the Lesson
	  Chapter 5 Skill Activity
		SE, Content Check, p. 90

Section 2 Controls on Climate (pp. 90–94)

Chapter Objectives	Suggested Teaching Strategies	Review

describe how latitude, heating and cooling differences of land and water, prevailing wind patterns, and altitude, affect climate.	**Teacher Preparation**
	SE, Reading Assignment, pp. 90–94
	TAE, Unit 2 Suggested Resources
	  Chapter 5 Overview, p. T91
	TRB, Chapter 5 Teacher Notes: Section 2
	Teaching Options
	TAE, Objective 2 Activities, p. T93
	TRB, Chapter 5 Teacher Notes: Section 2,
	  Extending the Lesson
	  Chapter 5 Reading
	  Chapter 5 Skill Activity
		SE, Content Check, p. 94

★ Objective 4 Enriching Activity

Challenge students to research and present oral reports regarding the extent, methods, and possible global/future effects of human activity related to changing weather and climate patterns.

Assign several students to be classroom "reporters." The reporters should prepare summaries of the reports and create a magazine with a possible title "People and the Weather." This magazine should include articles based on their summaries as well as related illustrations, charts, diagrams, or photographs. Completed copies of the magazine should be distributed to the class.

Concluding Chapter 5

Assign each student team that presented a local weather report during the study of this chapter, and other student teams who may wish to volunteer, the presentation of weather reports based on other climate areas of the world, making certain no two teams select the same world area. Make the assignment sufficiently in advance to give each team time to prepare. When the teams are ready, have them present the weather programs during one class period. After each presentation, allow the class to comment on how they believe the climate of each of the subject areas affected the weather described in each report.

ANSWERS TO CHAPTER 5 QUESTIONS

Content Check Questions
page 90

1. Refer to Glossary of Student Edition.
2. Temperature, precipitation, air pressure, and wind. (p. 85)
3. Near Equator; 60°N; 60°S. 30°N; 30°S; at Poles. (p. 89)
4. Spreads heat more evenly over the surface of Earth. (p. 89)
5. Acts as buffer holding in infrared radiation; carbon dioxide and ozone take in some of the heat and send it back to warm Earth. (p. 86)

page 94

1. Refer to Glossary of Student Edition.
2. Latitude, heating and cooling of land and water, prevailing winds, altitude. (pp. 90–94)
3. They are opposites—winter, north; summer, south; and vice-versa. (p. 90)
4. Air forced to rise over mountains cools, clouds form, and precipitation falls. (p. 93)

pages 100–101

1. Refer to Glossary of Student Edition.
2. Tropical moist; dry; moist, mild winter; moist, cold winter; and polar. (p. 94)
3. Because when the monsoon blows from sea to land, it brings heavy rains. (p. 95)
4. Humid subtropical. (pp. 96–97)
5. Middle-latitude marine. (p. 98)
6. Humid continental, hot summer. (p. 98)
7. Humid subtropical; middle-latitude marine; Mediterranean. (p. 95)
8. Have no summers and are cold. (p. 99)
9. Answers will vary according to region.
10. Amazon River Basin in South America and the Zaire River Basin in Africa. (p. 95) Around Mediterranean Sea, California, parts of Chile, southern Australia, southern tip of Africa. (p. 98)
11. Amount of precipitation. (p. 95) Temperature and amount of precipitation. (p. 99)

page 103

1. Refer to Glossary of Student Edition.
2. Loss of moisture, plants, and animals; increase in carbon dioxide and erosion. (p. 102)
3. Tropical savanna and steppe. (p. 102)
4. Answers will vary but should include all effects of deforestation, desertification, urbanization, and pollution. (pp. 102–103)

Special Feature Questions
page 88, Strange But True: "Unusual Weather by El Niño"

1. A change in the normal wind and ocean current patterns in the Pacific near the Equator.
2. Warm ocean waters bring rain.
3. Created warmer than normal winter in northwestern U.S. and Canada, with winter storms on the west coast of the United States, while southeastern U.S. near Atlantic Ocean and South Africa near the Indian Ocean had lower than normal rainfall.

pages 100–101, Using Graphic Skills: "Reading Climographs"

1. Colombo. Point Barrow.
2. Colombo. Cairo.
3. Cairo. Answers will vary but should include: loss of growing season, drought, unpredictable precipitation, drain on stored water supplies, and so on. Answers will vary but may include: Egyptians have adapted to dry climate by living where water supply is adequate, farming in areas where irrigation is possible, and so on.

Photo/Illustration Caption Questions
page 86

World temperatures could rise enough to melt parts of the ice caps, causing oceans to rise and shorelines to flood. Farmland at or near sea level would be lost. It would become dangerous for plants and animals that are used to a certain climate. (pp. 86–87)

page 87

Actual amount of moisture in the air at a certain temperature compared with amount the air could hold at that temperature. (p. 87)

page 89

Northeast trade winds and southeast trade winds. (pp. 89–90)

page 91

Vertical rays cover a smaller surface area and give more energy for heat; somewhat vertical rays produce temperatures that are neither too hot nor too cold; non-vertical rays produce cold temperatures. (pp. 90–91)

page 92

The Northern Hemisphere is tilted away from the sun and the sun's direct radiation is over the Southern Hemisphere, producing longer days in the Southern Hemisphere and shorter days in the Northern Hemisphere. (p. 91)

page 93

Land. (p. 92)

page 94

Dry. (p. 94)

page 95

Tropical rain forest. (p. 95)

pages 96–97

Desert; steppe, tundra; humid subtropical; Mediterranean; middle-latitude marine; humid continental, hot summer; humid continental, warm summer; subarctic; savanna; tropical rain forest; mountain. (pp. 96–97)

page 98

Answers will vary according to region.

page 99

Mediterranean climate generally found in areas between 30° and 45° north and south latitude including areas around the Mediterranean Sea, California, parts of Chile, southern Australia, and the southern tip of Africa; Polar ice cap climate found at both poles, central and northern parts of Greenland, and Antarctica. (pp. 98–99)

page 102

Desertification. (p. 102)

Chapter 5 Review Questions
page 104, Reviewing Vocabulary

Answers will vary, but clues should indicate understanding of terms.

page 104, Remembering the Facts

1. Nitrogen and oxygen. (p. 85)

2. Clear skies and calm weather. Cloudy skies and stormy weather. (p. 89)
3. Trade winds. Prevailing westerlies. Polar easterlies. (pp. 89–90)
4. Near the Equator. (p. 90)
5. Summer. (pp. 90–91)
6. Leeward. Moisture from the clouds fell on the windward side. (p. 93)
7. Tropical moist, dry, moist and mild winter, moist and cold winter, polar. (p. 94)
8. Humid continental with warm summers, humid continental with hot summers, and subarctic. (p. 98)
9. By changing Earth's surface and by polluting the air. (p. 102)
10. Hard surfaces replace plants and trees and change temperature; factories pollute air with smog that blocks out sun's rays; tall buildings change wind patterns. (p. 103)

page 105, Understanding the Facts

1. Weather is the condition of the atmosphere at a certain place at a certain time; climate is the general or average atmospheric condition over a period of time. (p. 85)
2. Low. Little precipitation, few cloudy days, lots of sunshine. (p. 95)
3. Area's hot air weighs less than cold air and pushes less on Earth's surface. (p. 89)
4. Draw moisture overland as the wind flows from west to east; increase rainfall on western side, and eastern side is drier. (p. 90)
5. Makes it drier, causes greenhouse effect and temperature change. (p. 102)
6. Stripping of land surfaces leads to drier conditions and erosion. (p. 102)
7. Increases moisture and moderates temperature. (p. 92)

8. It is believed to increase effect. (p. 103)

page 105, Thinking Critically Creatively

1. Answers will vary but may or getting rid of plants an nate or enhance the greenh ting pollution into the atm
2. Answers will vary but sh greatly raises the surface t swers will vary but should of the atmosphere.
3. Answers will vary but sh take advantage of the curr
4. Answers will vary but sh buildings hold heat, chang
5. Answers will vary but ma tion of the farmers and grams directed toward p land.
6. Answers will vary but ma on a mountain top or at a
7. Answers will vary but sho low pressure areas and w

page 105, Reinforcing Grap

1. Cairo is located in a dry c has the least amount of aging 10 inches (25.4 ce for an entire year. Pert Mediterranean climate precipitation, especially months.
2. Perth is located in the sphere where winter oc July, and August.

EVALUATING CHAPTER 5

World Geography: People and Places provides chapter tests to help evaluate student performance. To evaluate student mastery of Chapter 5, give students Chapter 5 Test from

the Teacher Resource Book be used for pretesting or Other tests can be made available in the Test Gener

Section 3   Earth's Climates (pp. 94–101)

Chapter Objectives	Suggested Teaching Strategies	Review
3. list the five major types of climate and summarize typical characteristics of each. Skill Objective: read line and bar graphs (climographs).	**Teacher Preparation** 　SE, Reading Assignment, pp. 94–101 　TAE, Unit 2 Suggested Resources 　　Chapter 5 Overview, p. T91 　TRB, Chapter 5 Teacher Notes: Section 3 **Teaching Options** 　TAE, Objective 3 Activities, p. T94 　TRB, Chapter 5 Teacher Notes: Section 3, 　　Extending the Lesson 　SE, *Using Graphic Skills*, 　　"Reading Climographs," pp. 100–101	SE, Content Check, pp. 100–101

Section 4   Impact of People (pp. 102–103)

Chapter Objectives	Suggested Teaching Strategies	Review
4. discuss the ways people have changed weather and climate patterns.	**Teacher Preparation** 　SE, Reading Assignment, pp. 102–103 　TAE, Unit 2 Suggested Resources 　　Chapter 5 Overview, p. T91 　TRB, Chapter 5 Teacher Notes: Section 4 **Teaching Options** 　TAE, Objective 4 Activities, pp. T94–T95 　TRB, Chapter 5 Teacher Notes: Section 4, 　　Extending the Lesson	SE, Content Check, p. 103

Chapter 5   Review and Evaluation

Suggested Teaching Strategies	Review	Evaluation
TAE, Concluding Chapter 5, p. T95	SE, Chapter 5 Review, pp. 104–105 TRB, Chapter 5 Review Worksheet	TRB, Chapter 5 Test TG, Chapter 5

Unit 2 *Review and Evaluation*

Suggested Teaching Strategies	Review	Evaluation
TAE, Concluding Unit 2, p. T100 TRB, Unit 2 Career Worksheet	SE, Unit 2 Review, pp. 106–107	TRB, Unit 2 Exam

CONCLUDING THE UNIT

Ask the class to make predictions about Earth's future based on what they have learned in this unit. Suggest that they consider both events caused by nature and by people. Ask students: What things might be brought about by nature? By people? How could these occurrences affect life on Earth? Then ask: What might the role of the geographer be in preventing disasters and in bringing about positive changes? Students may consider purification of air and water, climate control, prevention of pollution, and the development of oceanographic potentials including farming the ocean and colonies of people living on the ocean floor.

Divide the class into groups of three or four and tell them that they are to prepare skits about life in an imaginary future environment. Ask half of the groups to focus on environments that are the result of natural occurrences and the other half of the groups to focus on environments created by humans. Scenarios might include: Life on Earth with a damaged ozone layer; life in a new ice age; life after a nuclear holocaust; life after an enormous volcanic eruption; life in an ocean-floor colony; life on Earth during a warming trend; and life on Earth as it would be with a perfectly controlled climate.

As an aid to your students in the preparation of their skits, refer to the General Geographic Resources in the Suggested Resources section in this Teacher Annotated Edition, and make use of suggestions contained in Chapter six of the book *The Study and Teaching of Geography*, under the section "Thinking Geographically About the Future."

Unit 2 Exam in the Teacher Resource Book may be administered.

UNIT 2 REVIEW QUESTIONS

page 106, Thinking About the Unit

1. Through plate tectonics and volcanic activity; weathering; erosion by action of wind, water, ice and gravity; human activity.
2. Answers will vary but should include better climate, transportation, recreation, water for irrigation and industry.
3. Temperature, precipitation, air pressure, and wind.
4. Answers will vary but may include irrigation projects to improve unwatered or desert areas, water purification to clean up waterways, and the planting of trees and other vegetation to improve the quality of air. Negative changes may include desertification, drying up and pollution of watered lands, creating a greenhouse effect through pollution.

★ Objective 4 Enriching Activity

Challenge students to research and present oral reports regarding the extent, methods, and possible global/future effects of human activity related to changing weather and climate patterns.

Assign several students to be classroom "reporters." The reporters should prepare summaries of the reports and create a magazine with a possible title "People and the Weather." This magazine should include articles based on their summaries as well as related illustrations, charts, diagrams, or photographs. Completed copies of the magazine should be distributed to the class.

Concluding Chapter 5

Assign each student team that presented a local weather report during the study of this chapter, and other student teams who may wish to volunteer, the presentation of weather reports based on other climate areas of the world, making certain no two teams select the same world area. Make the assignment sufficiently in advance to give each team time to prepare. When the teams are ready, have them present the weather programs during one class period. After each presentation, allow the class to comment on how they believe the climate of each of the subject areas affected the weather described in each report.

ANSWERS TO CHAPTER 5 QUESTIONS

Content Check Questions
page 90

1. Refer to Glossary of Student Edition.
2. Temperature, precipitation, air pressure, and wind. (p. 85)
3. Near Equator; 60°N; 60°S. 30°N; 30°S; at Poles. (p. 89)
4. Spreads heat more evenly over the surface of Earth. (p. 89)
5. Acts as buffer holding in infrared radiation; carbon dioxide and ozone take in some of the heat and send it back to warm Earth. (p. 86)

page 94

1. Refer to Glossary of Student Edition.
2. Latitude, heating and cooling of land and water, prevailing winds, altitude. (pp. 90–94)
3. They are opposites—winter, north; summer, south; and vice-versa. (p. 90)
4. Air forced to rise over mountains cools, clouds form, and precipitation falls. (p. 93)

pages 100–101

1. Refer to Glossary of Student Edition.
2. Tropical moist; dry; moist, mild winter; moist, cold winter; and polar. (p. 94)
3. Because when the monsoon blows from sea to land, it brings heavy rains. (p. 95)
4. Humid subtropical. (pp. 96–97)
5. Middle-latitude marine. (p. 98)
6. Humid continental, hot summer. (p. 98)
7. Humid subtropical; middle-latitude marine; Mediterranean. (p. 95)
8. Have no summers and are cold. (p. 99)
9. Answers will vary according to region.
10. Amazon River Basin in South America and the Zaire River Basin in Africa. (p. 95) Around Mediterranean Sea, California, parts of Chile, southern Australia, southern tip of Africa. (p. 98)
11. Amount of precipitation. (p. 95) Temperature and amount of precipitation. (p. 99)

page 103

1. Refer to Glossary of Student Edition.
2. Loss of moisture, plants, and animals; increase in carbon dioxide and erosion. (p. 102)
3. Tropical savanna and steppe. (p. 102)
4. Answers will vary but should include all effects of deforestation, desertification, urbanization, and pollution. (pp. 102–103)

Special Feature Questions
page 88, Strange But True: "Unusual Weather by El Niño"

1. A change in the normal wind and ocean current patterns in the Pacific near the Equator.
2. Warm ocean waters bring rain.
3. Created warmer than normal winter in northwestern U.S. and Canada, with winter storms on the west coast of the United States, while southeastern U.S. near Atlantic Ocean and South Africa near the Indian Ocean had lower than normal rainfall.

pages 100–101, Using Graphic Skills: "Reading Climographs"

1. Colombo. Point Barrow.
2. Colombo. Cairo.
3. Cairo. Answers will vary but should include: loss of growing season, drought, unpredictable precipitation, drain on stored water supplies, and so on. Answers will vary but may include: Egyptians have adapted to dry climate by living where water supply is adequate, farming in areas where irrigation is possible, and so on.

Photo/Illustration Caption Questions

page 86

World temperatures could rise enough to melt parts of the ice caps, causing oceans to rise and shorelines to flood. Farmland at or near sea level would be lost. It would become dangerous for plants and animals that are used to a certain climate. (pp. 86–87)

page 87

Actual amount of moisture in the air at a certain temperature compared with amount the air could hold at that temperature. (p. 87)

page 89

Northeast trade winds and southeast trade winds. (pp. 89–90)

page 91

Vertical rays cover a smaller surface area and give more energy for heat; somewhat vertical rays produce temperatures that are neither too hot nor too cold; non-vertical rays produce cold temperatures. (pp. 90–91)

page 92

The Northern Hemisphere is tilted away from the sun and the sun's direct radiation is over the Southern Hemisphere, producing longer days in the Southern Hemisphere and shorter days in the Northern Hemisphere. (p. 91)

page 93

Land. (p. 92)

page 94

Dry. (p. 94)

page 95

Tropical rain forest. (p. 95)

pages 96–97

Desert; steppe, tundra; humid subtropical; Mediterranean; middle-latitude marine; humid continental, hot summer; humid continental, warm summer; subarctic; savanna; tropical rain forest; mountain. (pp. 96–97)

page 98

Answers will vary according to region.

page 99

Mediterranean climate generally found in areas between 30° and 45° north and south latitude including areas around the Mediterranean Sea, California, parts of Chile, southern Australia, and the southern tip of Africa; Polar ice cap climate found at both poles, central and northern parts of Greenland, and Antarctica. (pp. 98–99)

page 102

Desertification. (p. 102)

Chapter 5 Review Questions
page 104, Reviewing Vocabulary

Answers will vary, but clues should indicate understanding of terms.

page 104, Remembering the Facts

1. Nitrogen and oxygen. (p. 85)

2. Clear skies and calm weather. Cloudy skies and stormy weather. (p. 89)
3. Trade winds. Prevailing westerlies. Polar easterlies. (pp. 89–90)
4. Near the Equator. (p. 90)
5. Summer. (pp. 90–91)
6. Leeward. Moisture from the clouds fell on the windward side. (p. 93)
7. Tropical moist, dry, moist and mild winter, moist and cold winter, polar. (p. 94)
8. Humid continental with warm summers, humid continental with hot summers, and subarctic. (p. 98)
9. By changing Earth's surface and by polluting the air. (p. 102)
10. Hard surfaces replace plants and trees and change temperature; factories pollute air with smog that blocks out sun's rays; tall buildings change wind patterns. (p. 103)

page 105, Understanding the Facts

1. Weather is the condition of the atmosphere at a certain place at a certain time; climate is the general or average atmospheric condition over a period of time. (p. 85)
2. Low. Little precipitation, few cloudy days, lots of sunshine. (p. 95)
3. Area's hot air weighs less than cold air and pushes less on Earth's surface. (p. 89)
4. Draw moisture overland as the wind flows from west to east; increase rainfall on western side, and eastern side is drier. (p. 90)
5. Makes it drier, causes greenhouse effect and temperature change. (p. 102)
6. Stripping of land surfaces leads to drier conditions and erosion. (p. 102)
7. Increases moisture and moderates temperature. (p. 92)

8. It is believed to increase the greenhouse effect. (p. 103)

page 105, Thinking Critically and Creatively

1. Answers will vary but may include adding or getting rid of plants and trees to eliminate or enhance the greenhouse effect; putting pollution into the atmosphere.
2. Answers will vary but should state that it greatly raises the surface temperature. Answers will vary but should include pollution of the atmosphere.
3. Answers will vary but should include to take advantage of the currents and winds.
4. Answers will vary but should include that buildings hold heat, change wind patterns.
5. Answers will vary but may include education of the farmers and government programs directed toward proper use of the land.
6. Answers will vary but may include location on a mountain top or at a high elevation.
7. Answers will vary but should note high and low pressure areas and wind pattern.

page 105, Reinforcing Graphic Skills

1. Cairo is located in a dry desert climate that has the least amount of precipitation averaging 10 inches (25.4 centimeters) or less for an entire year. Perth is located in a Mediterranean climate that does receive precipitation, especially during the winter months.
2. Perth is located in the Southern Hemisphere where winter occurs during June, July, and August.

EVALUATING CHAPTER 5

World Geography: People and Places provides chapter tests to help evaluate student performance. To evaluate student mastery of Chapter 5, give students Chapter 5 Test from the Teacher Resource Book. This test may also be used for pretesting or retesting purposes. Other tests can be made from the questions available in the Test Generator Software.

Lesson Plan Suggestions—Chapter 5

SE—Student Edition   TAE—Teacher Annotated Edition   TG—Test Generator
TRB—Teacher Resource Book   TSP—Transparency Package

Section 1   Elements of Climate (pp. 85–90)

Chapter Objectives	Suggested Teaching Strategies	Review
1. explain how temperature, moisture, air pressure, and wind combine to produce climate.	**Teacher Preparation** SE, Reading Assignment, pp. 85–90 TAE, Unit 2 Suggested Resources 　　Chapter 5 Overview, p. T91 　　Introducing Chapter 5, pp. T91–T92 TRB, Chapter 5 Teacher Notes: Section 1 **Teaching Options** TAE, Introducing Chapter 5, pp. T91–T92 　　Objective 1 Activities, pp. T92–T93 TRB, Chapter 5 Teacher Notes: Section 1, 　　Extending the Lesson 　　Chapter 5 Skill Activity	SE, Content Check, p. 90

Section 2   Controls on Climate (pp. 90–94)

Chapter Objectives	Suggested Teaching Strategies	Review
2. describe how latitude, heating and cooling differences of land and water, prevailing wind patterns, and altitude, affect climate.	**Teacher Preparation** SE, Reading Assignment, pp. 90–94 TAE, Unit 2 Suggested Resources 　　Chapter 5 Overview, p. T91 TRB, Chapter 5 Teacher Notes: Section 2 **Teaching Options** TAE, Objective 2 Activities, p. T93 TRB, Chapter 5 Teacher Notes: Section 2, 　　Extending the Lesson 　　Chapter 5 Reading 　　Chapter 5 Skill Activity	SE, Content Check, p. 94

Section 3 Earth's Climates (pp. 94–101)

Chapter Objectives	Suggested Teaching Strategies	Review
3. list the five major types of climate and summarize typical characteristics of each. Skill Objective: read line and bar graphs (climographs).	**Teacher Preparation** SE, Reading Assignment, pp. 94–101 TAE, Unit 2 Suggested Resources Chapter 5 Overview, p. T91 TRB, Chapter 5 Teacher Notes: Section 3 **Teaching Options** TAE, Objective 3 Activities, p. T94 TRB, Chapter 5 Teacher Notes: Section 3, Extending the Lesson SE, *Using Graphic Skills,* "Reading Climographs," pp. 100–101	SE, Content Check, pp. 100–101

Section 4 Impact of People (pp. 102–103)

Chapter Objectives	Suggested Teaching Strategies	Review
4. discuss the ways people have changed weather and climate patterns.	**Teacher Preparation** SE, Reading Assignment, pp. 102–103 TAE, Unit 2 Suggested Resources Chapter 5 Overview, p. T91 TRB, Chapter 5 Teacher Notes: Section 4 **Teaching Options** TAE, Objective 4 Activities, pp. T94–T95 TRB, Chapter 5 Teacher Notes: Section 4, Extending the Lesson	SE, Content Check, p. 103

Chapter 5 Review and Evaluation

Suggested Teaching Strategies	Review	Evaluation
TAE, Concluding Chapter 5, p. T95	SE, Chapter 5 Review, pp. 104–105 TRB, Chapter 5 Review Worksheet	TRB, Chapter 5 Test TG, Chapter 5

Unit 2 *Review and Evaluation*

Suggested Teaching Strategies	Review	Evaluation
TAE, Concluding Unit 2, p. T100 TRB, Unit 2 Career Worksheet	SE, Unit 2 Review, pp. 106–107	TRB, Unit 2 Exam

CONCLUDING THE UNIT

Ask the class to make predictions about Earth's future based on what they have learned in this unit. Suggest that they consider both events caused by nature and by people. Ask students: What things might be brought about by nature? By people? How could these occurrences affect life on Earth? Then ask: What might the role of the geographer be in preventing disasters and in bringing about positive changes? Students may consider purification of air and water, climate control, prevention of pollution, and the development of oceanographic potentials including farming the ocean and colonies of people living on the ocean floor.

Divide the class into groups of three or four and tell them that they are to prepare skits about life in an imaginary future environment. Ask half of the groups to focus on environments that are the result of natural occurrences and the other half of the groups to focus on environments created by humans. Scenarios might include: Life on Earth with a damaged ozone layer; life in a new ice age; life after a nuclear holocaust; life after an enormous volcanic eruption; life in an ocean-floor colony; life on Earth during a warming trend; and life on Earth as it would be with a perfectly controlled climate.

As an aid to your students in the preparation of their skits, refer to the General Geographic Resources in the Suggested Resources section in this Teacher Annotated Edition, and make use of suggestions contained in Chapter six of the book *The Study and Teaching of Geography*, under the section "Thinking Geographically About the Future."

Unit 2 Exam in the Teacher Resource Book may be administered.

UNIT 2 REVIEW QUESTIONS

page 106, Thinking About the Unit
1. Through plate tectonics and volcanic activity; weathering; erosion by action of wind, water, ice and gravity; human activity.
2. Answers will vary but should include better climate, transportation, recreation, water for irrigation and industry.
3. Temperature, precipitation, air pressure, and wind.

4. Answers will vary but may include irrigation projects to improve unwatered or desert areas, water purification to clean up waterways, and the planting of trees and other vegetation to improve the quality of air. Negative changes may include desertification, drying up and pollution of watered lands, creating a greenhouse effect through pollution.

UNIT 3 HUMAN PATTERNS

Student Edition pp. 108–161

UNIT GOALS

At the conclusion of this unit, students will be able to:

1. analyze how world population growth patterns are related to world economic growth patterns.
2. summarize the chief elements of culture areas throughout the world.
3. describe how urbanization has changed natural environments of the past and present.

UNIT 3 SKILL OBJECTIVE

After completing the *Developing Geography Skills* exercise in this unit, the student should be able to develop a global point of view.

UNIT 3 OVERVIEW

The third unit of *World Geography: People and Places* focuses on patterns made by people on Earth's surface. In this unit, these patterns are divided into three major categories—population, culture, and urban areas. *Chapter 6* explains the way Earth's population is grouped and scattered, the growth rate of the population, and the way the great increase in numbers of people living on Earth creates stress in providing for basic needs today and in the future. *Chapter 7* presents the fundamental concepts of culture and describes what a culture is, the stages of cultural development, and the characteristics of eleven culture areas of Earth. *Chapter 8* incorporates vital information about human patterns of urban development, including the functions of urban areas, how urban areas developed, and a contrast between urban and rural environments. Finally, the students are challenged to consider problems future growth patterns may present.

Upon completion of this unit, students should have a more developed idea of human patterns on Earth and a greater understanding of Earth's people. They should be able to recognize the importance of planning for the future well-being of Earth's growing population and the protection of Earth's environment.

INTRODUCING UNIT 3

Aid students to prepare an outline to be filled in as they study this unit. Use chapter titles as principal headings and chapter subheadings as subtitles. Explain to them that they are to fill in the outline with summaries of the related information. Remind students that outlining and summarizing are useful study techniques for any chapter or unit.

As students learn new terms related to geology, have them include them in an "Illustrated Geology Dictionary" that they will make and keep in a notebook. The dictionary should include a verbal definition and an illustration that may be a drawing, diagram, or attached picture. Terms should be grouped under headings or introductory sentences.

CHAPTER 6 POPULATION

Student Edition pp. 110–125

CHAPTER 6 OBJECTIVES

At the conclusion of this chapter, students will be able to:
1. identify the four stages of population growth countries may pass through as their economies develop.
2. differentiate between population distribution and population density.
3. state the four largest centers of population in the world.
4. suggest ways that problems with food supply, natural resources supply, population control, and migration may be solved.

CHAPTER 6 SKILL OBJECTIVE

After completing the *Using Graphic Skills* exercise in this chapter, the student should be able to compare tabular data.

CHAPTER 6 OVERVIEW

In this chapter, students are introduced to the study of population—how it is linked with economic factors, how Earth's population has grown in the past, and projections for future growth. In *Sections 1* and *2*, Earth's population distribution and the reasons for its uneven nature are combined with the study of the six continents and the way in which people have settled each. Also discussed in *Section 3* are the issues that affect the general population of Earth, such as the food supply, availability of natural resources, and the effects of population control and migration. A special feature in the chapter presents a synopsis of the work of Thomas Robert Malthus in the field of population study. The chapter concludes by emphasizing the importance of the study of issues related to population growth and distribution for the purpose of assuring the future success of humanity.

CHAPTER 6 ACTIVITIES

Introducing Chapter 6

Read with the class the introduction to this chapter on page 110 of the Student Edition. Then, using numerals, write the number five billion on the chalkboard. Beside it, write the population of your town or city. With the class, figure out how many times your town would have to be multiplied to represent the total world population. Or use the round figure of 10,000,000 to represent the population of the city of New York, and ask, "How many New Yorks would there have to be to represent the total world population?" Then on the map "World Population Density," on page 117 of the Student Edition, show students that the five billion people of Earth are not evenly distributed. Refer to the guidelines for brainstorming in the Instructional Approaches section of this Teacher Annotated Edition, and have students brainstorm answers to the question, "What do you believe may account for this uneven distribution?" Write student responses on the chalkboard, and have students copy them for later comparison with the text.

Chapter 6 Reading Assignments

> ● Teaching ■ Reinforcing ★ Enriching

Objective 1 Activities

● Objective 1 Teaching Activity

Ask students: What is a developing country? What is an industrialized country? Can you give examples of each? Then, have students define each stage of population growth and write their responses on the chalkboard.

Prepare a transparency for the overhead projector showing a chart that includes the following information: At the top of the chart, write in S1, S2, S3, and S4, to represent the four stages of population growth. Along the left side of the chart, write in D for developing and I for industrialized. Below the chart provide a list of countries, and then ask the students to place the countries into the proper categories provided on the chart. Explain to students that, in order to fill in the chart, they will have to identify whether the country is developing or industrialized, and determine the country's stage of population growth.

After students have completed the chart, ask them whether an industrialized country and a developing country can be at the same stage of population growth. Request explanations of answers.

Refer students to Chapter 6 Skill Activity in the Teacher Resource Book for another exercise related to world population growth.

■ Objective 1 Reinforcing Activity

Refer to the guidelines for audiovisual materials in the Instructional Approaches section of this Teacher Annotated Edition before directing this activity. Write the following points on the chalkboard: "famine, war, health care, domesticated animals," and "diet." Prepare the students for this activity by leading a discussion on how the items listed above contribute to population growth and decline. Then show a movie or filmstrip that includes the economy of an industrialized country and one picturing the economy of a developing country. Refer to Suggested Resources, Supplementary Materials, in this Teacher Annotated Edition, for audiovisuals related to this topic. Ask students to watch for the following points: type of agricultural techniques practiced; kinds of houses people live in; transportation; clothing; and food shown.

As part of the debriefing following the audiovisual presentation, have students relate what they have learned from the audiovisuals to the points made in the Student Edition about economic factors and population.

★ Objective 1 Enriching Activity

Refer to the guidelines for lecture in the Instructional Approaches section of this Teacher Annotated Edition, and then prepare a short lecture on the economic and social life of Colonial America. Have students determine Colonial America's stage of population growth. Then ask them to compare the Colonial stage to the United States' present stage of population growth. Finally, ask students to consider what factors have contributed to the changes since colonial times.

Objective 2 Activities

● Objective 2 Teaching Activity

Ask students to define population density and population distribution. Write their responses on the chalkboard, and then, place a population map of your state in front of the classroom. Give students the state's area and its estimated population, and then have them find the population density. Ask students to identify the densely populated areas and the sparsely populated areas on the map. Ask them how the population is distributed throughout the state and to suggest reasons for it. List their responses on the chalkboard and discuss them, relating their reasons to those explained in the Student Edition.

★ **Objective 2 Enriching Activity**

Locate an old and a current copy of a map of your town. Have students compare the changes in population and population distribution over time and conclude their study by writing a short paper on their observations. Provide them with a list of the following questions to think about while they are doing their research: Why did people move out of town? Why did people move into town? On what was the town's economy based? Did the type of businesses and industries change over time? If possible, provide students with copies of some old and some current town newspapers to help them with their research, or have them research the town's history in the public library. Refer to the guidelines for community resource persons in the Instructional Approaches section of this Teacher Annotated Edition and, if the town has a historian or librarian familiar with town history, invite him or her to speak to the class, emphasizing answers to the questions asked above.

Objective 3 Activities

● **Objective 3 Teaching Activity**

Lead a discussion in which the class may generalize about the things that attract people to certain world areas. Encourage students to tell the area of the world that appeals most to them as a place to live and why. On a handout list the four largest centers of population in the world. Ask students to list four countries located in each center. Ask them to explain why these areas are densely populated.

Refer students to the Chapter 6 Reading in the Teacher Resource Book for further information regarding this objective.

■ **Objective 3 Reinforcing Activity**

On the chalkboard list the six inhabited continents of the world. Then have students refer to pages 116–118 in the Student Edition to indicate either in a written form or orally the population centers on each continent and how population is distributed. Provide students with copies of the outline map of the world in the Teacher Resource Book and have them place a symbol for the centers on their maps.

Objective 4 Activities

● **Objective 4 Teaching Activity**

Refer to the guidelines for role plays and simulations in the Instructional Approaches section of this Teacher Annotated Edition. Tell the class that they will simulate a United Nations meeting with the purpose of deciding ways in which a population crisis can be avoided or made less severe. Have delegates from the various continents list the problems presented by overpopulation in their countries. They should consider problems of food supply, natural resources supply, population control, and migration. Then have delegates suggest solutions, forecast what might happen should no solution be forthcoming, and then forecast again the possible situation after a solution has been applied. Have delegates vote on solutions to be implemented.

Students may be interested in further investigation of the United Nations and the role this organization plays in solving Earth's population problems. The United Nations Information Center, 1889 F Street, N.W., Washington, D.C. 20006, can provide listings and audiovisual materials useful for teaching about Earth's peoples. Demographic studies published by the United Nations are available in many public and school libraries. For information on population issues, students may write to United Nations Fund for Population Activities, 220 East 42nd St., 19th Floor, New York, NY 10017.

Refer to Chapter 6 Teacher Notes, Section 3, Extending the Lesson, in the Teacher

Resource Book, for information about the United Nations and the World Food Council.

★ Objective 4 Enriching Activity

After students have read the *Focus on Geography* feature on Thomas Robert Malthus and his pioneering work in the field of geography on page 120 of the Student Edition, refer to the guidelines for debating in the Instructional Approaches section of this Teacher Annotated Edition. Prepare the class to debate the issue, *Resolved: The Malthusian theory of population growth and food production does not apply to the modern world.*

Concluding Chapter 6

Plan a food awareness day in your class, and begin by having the class choose a committee that will help plan the activities. Ideas for activities may include guest speakers, oral presentations by students, and audiovisuals relating to the topic. Some student volunteers could bring in sample foods from various world cultures to be shared among the class members and guests. Ask each student to pick a country and write a report to be presented orally to the class that should include the following: the types of food grown, the types of food imported and exported, daily caloric consumption per person, farming methods used, eating habits of the population, and whether or not the country grows a surplus of food. Encourage students to make posters, graphs, and charts to supplement their reports. Display their work in the classroom.

Refer to Unit 3 Careers in the Teacher Resource Book for information on the field of demography. Students especially interested in this career may wish to research this career in greater depth and make reports to the class.

ANSWERS TO CHAPTER 6 QUESTIONS

Content Check Questions
page 115

1. Refer to Glossary in Student Edition.
2. About five billion. (p. 111)
3. Stage One—high birth and death, little or no growth. Stage Two—high birth and falling death, rapid growth. Stage Three—falling birth and low death, slow growth. Stage Four—low birth and death, zero growth. (p. 113)
4. Answers will vary but may state that nations with good economies will reflect lower population growth. (p. 113)

page 119

1. Refer to Glossary in Student Edition.
2. Eastern Asia, Southern Asia, Western Europe, east central North America. (pp. 116–117)
3. 260 per sq. mi. or 78 per sq. km. (p. 118)

page 123

1. Refer to Glossary in Student Edition.

2. More land for farming, efficient eating habits, more productive farm methods, and new sources of food. (p. 119, p. 121)
3. Family planning and encouraged migration. (pp. 122–123)
4. Answers will vary but should include nutritional education.

Special Feature Questions
page 120, Focus on Geography: "Thomas Robert Malthus"

1. 1750 to 1800. Industrial Revolution.
2. The growth of the population would exceed the ability to feed humankind. The future would include famines and misery.

page 114, Using Graphic Skills: "Comparing Tabular Data"

1. Angola, Syria, India. Developing.
2. Percent farmland; death rate. In regard to all other data on chart.

Photo/Illustration Caption Questions
page 112

Industrialized. (p. 112)

page 113

6.1 billion. (p. 112)

page 115

Morocco. (p. 115)

page 117

Landscapes, waterways, ability of people to make a living. (p. 116)

page 118

By dividing number of people by number of square miles or square kilometers. (p. 118) Alexandria, El Giza, Cairo. (p. 118)

page 119

Affects over 500 million people. (p. 119)

page 121

Finding more productive farming techniques, using new food sources. (p. 121)

page 122

Many people want large families; people honor traditional values and religious beliefs opposed to birth control. (p. 123)

Chapter 6 Review Questions
page 124, Reviewing Vocabulary

1. Industrialized country.
2. Zero population growth.
3. Demographer.
4. Gross national product.
5. Density.
6. Population pyramid.
7. Economy.
8. Malnutrition.
9. Migration.

page 124, Remembering the Facts

1. Development of farming. (p. 111) Industrial Revolution. (p. 112)
2. Five billion. (p. 111) 6.1 billion. (p. 112)
3. 75%. (p. 113)

4. Stage two. (p. 113)
5. Eastern Asia, southern Asia, western Europe, east central North America. (p. 116)
6. China. (p. 116)
7. Find more productive farming techniques; use new food sources. (p. 121)
8. Successes included creation of new hybrid seeds that produced larger crops; failures involved weather, disease, insects, water supply, and economic problems. (p. 121)
9. Overpopulation. (p. 123)

page 125, Understanding the Facts

1. Disease, famine, wars. (p. 111)
2. Answers will vary but should include food, energy, health care, and education shortages. Answers will vary but may include impact on country's economy. (p. 113)
3. Inhospitable climates, poor soil, rugged terrain. (p. 116)
4. Waterways. Closeness to natural resources. (p. 116)
5. Climate limits the number of people who can live in an area, resulting in unique settlement patterns. (p. 116)
6. Encourage migration, provide family planning programs. (p. 123)

page 125, Thinking Critically and Creatively

1. Answers will vary but may suggest that while agriculture could have increased the birth rate by providing a larger food supply, increased death rate could be linked to problems resulting from overpopulation.
2. Answers will vary but may state that the population would move further north.
3. Answers will vary but may indicate that the land is probably flat (plain) and thus more accessible to natural resources and waterways, making it easier for farming and developing centers of population.
4. Answers will vary but may indicate that having children is easier than providing food for increased numbers of people. Answers will vary but may indicate agreement in that population pressure will use up all farm production land. Answers will vary

but may indicate disagreement in that farming techniques have increased food production and available crop land.

5. No. Answers will vary but should include improved food production, creation of more farmland, and population control.

6. Answers will vary but may indicate that there would be less oxygen available in the biosphere. Answers will vary but may indicate possible shortages of ocean plant and animal life, changed ocean biomes resulting in ecological imbalance.

7. Answers will vary but should indicate that is where most of the land area is.

8. Answers will vary but should indicate that people are not willing to lower their standard of living.

page 125, Reinforcing Graphic Skills

1. Birthrate and population growth of Syria is higher.

2. China has lower birthrate, lower death rate, larger population, larger farmland percent, slightly larger urban population, lower population growth.

3. Angola. Australia, U.S.S.R.

4. Population growth slows as economy improves (GNP increases).

EVALUATING CHAPTER 6

World Geography: People and Places provides chapter tests to help evaluate student performance. To evaluate student mastery of Chapter 6, give students Chapter 6 test found in the Teacher Resource Book. This test may also be used for pretesting or retesting purposes. Other tests can be made from the questions available in the Test Generator Software.

Lesson Plan Suggestions—Chapter 6

SE—Student Edition   TAE—Teacher Annotated Edition   TG—Test Generator
TRB—Teacher Resource Book   TSP—Transparency Package

Section 1   Earth's Growing Population (pp. 111–115)

Chapter Objectives	Suggested Teaching Strategies	Review

1. identify the four stages of population growth countries may pass through as their economies develop.	**Teacher Preparation**
	SE, Reading Assignment, pp. 111–115
	TAE, Unit 3 Suggested Resources
	    Unit 3 Overview, p. T101
	    Introducing Unit 3, p. T101
	    Chapter 6 Overview, p. T102
	    Introducing Chapter 6, pp. T102–T103
	TRB, Chapter 6 Teacher Notes: Section 1
	Teaching Options
	TAE, Introducing Unit 3, p. T101
	    Introducing Chapter 6, pp. T102–T103
	    Objective 1 Activities, p. T103
	TRB, Chapter 6 Teacher Notes: Section 1,
	    Extending the Lesson
	    Chapter 6 Skill Activity
		SE, Content Check, p. 115

Section 2 Population Patterns (pp. 116–119)

Chapter Objectives	Suggested Teaching Strategies	Review

2. differentiate between population distribution and population density.
 	
3. state the four largest centers of population in the world.
	Teacher Preparation
	SE, Reading Assignment, pp. 116–119
	TAE, Unit 3 Suggested Resources
	    Chapter 6 Overview, p. T102
	TRB, Chapter 6 Teacher Notes: Section 2
	Teaching Options
	TAE, Objectives 2 and 3 Activities, pp.
	    T103–T104
	TRB, Chapter 6 Teacher Notes: Section 2,
	    Extending the Lesson
	    Chapter 6 Reading
	    Chapter 6 Skill Activity
	TSP, Transparency 9
		SE, Content Check, p. 119

Section 3 Population Issues (pp. 119–123)

Chapter Objectives	Suggested Teaching Strategies	Review

4. suggest ways that problems with food supply, natural resources supply, population control, and migration may be solved.
 	
Skill Objective: compare tabular data.
	Teacher Preparation
	SE, Reading Assignment, pp. 119–123
	TAE, Unit 3 Suggested Resources
	    Chapter 6 Overview, p. T102
	TRB, Chapter 6 Teacher Notes: Section 3
	Teaching Options
	TAE, Objective 4 Activities, pp. T104–T105
	TRB, Chapter 6 Teacher Notes: Section 3,
	    Extending the Lesson
	    Chapter 6 Reading
	SE, *Using Graphic Skills*, "Comparing Tabular Data," pp. 114–115
		SE, Content Check, p. 123

Chapter 6 Review and Evaluation

Suggested Teaching Strategies	Review	Evaluation

TAE, Concluding Chapter 6, p. T105	SE, Chapter 6 Review,
	    pp. 124–125
	TRB, Chapter 6 Review
	    Worksheet
		TRB, Chapter 6 Test
		TG, Chapter 6

CHAPTER 7   CULTURE

Student Edition pp. 126–143

CHAPTER 7 OBJECTIVES

At the conclusion of this chapter, students will be able to:
1. describe what *culture* means and how cultures develop.
2. summarize the chief characteristics of each of 11 major culture areas.

CHAPTER 7 SKILL OBJECTIVE

After completing the *Using Graphic Skills* exercise in this chapter, the student should be able to compare data from maps and graphs.

CHAPTER 7 OVERVIEW

In this chapter the students are introduced both to the meaning of *culture* and to the important stages of early cultural development. They are familiarized with the principal characteristics of 11 cultural areas.

Section 1 explains what culture is, how cultures developed commonalities and differences, and what brings about these changes. *Section 2* explores 11 world culture areas and provides students with a brief description and history of each. Also included in this section is a special feature on youth subculture. The chapter reinforces the idea that cultural attitudes are learned, and cultural studies are important in order to improve relationships and promote understanding among Earth's peoples. Upon completion of this chapter, students will find that cultures grow to meet human needs and according to environment. Thus, since people are the basis of all cultures, it is possible to look for and find those common threads that bind all cultures together.

CHAPTER 7 ACTIVITIES

Introducing Chapter 7

Examine with the class the concept of "culture shock," and ask why some people have trouble adapting to cultures other than their own. Explain that sometimes culture shock occurs between generations of the same culture. Ask what changes students may notice in their own generation that their grandparents or great-grandparents would have difficulty accepting. Finally, explain that all cultures develop and change, but many of the most important elements do not change or change very slowly. Point out that all world cultures are ways of life created to accommodate people, and as a result, all cultures have common elements. For example, all must be concerned with things that affect human beings and their needs. Ask students to name elements that affect all people. They should note that all people have a basic need for shelter and food, and that all cultures have developed some type of communication systems and formed religious foundations.

Explain to students that in this chapter they will learn what culture is and identify the cultures of 11 world areas. Tell them that as they study each culture, they should attempt to answer the following questions: How might the natural environment have affected this culture? How have historical events affected this culture? What are the features of this culture that set it apart from others? What does this culture have in common with others?

Chapter 7 Reading Assignments

Objective 1   Student Ed. pp. 127–129
Objective 2   Student Ed. pp. 129–141

| ● Teaching | ■ Reinforcing | ★ Enriching |

Objective 1 Activities

● Objective 1 Teaching Activity

Tell the students that they are going to become anthropologists for a week. Explain that one way anthropologists study other cultures is by observing their everyday life. Prepare the students to observe and analyze their own culture by telling them to observe customs, traditions, technology, eating habits, clothing, work habits, family life, forms of transportation, and types of housing in their surroundings. Have them keep a notebook in which to record their observations. At the end of the week, have the students write a report summarizing their culture and explaining how some of the customs and traditions may have developed. Reports may include pictures, drawings, or models. When the projects are completed, have students share their reports with the class.

Refer students to the Chapter 7 Reading in the Teacher Resource Book for another source of information related to Objective 1.

★ Objective 1 Enriching Activity

Ask each student to create an imaginary culture that will include all the elements necessary to form a culture. Remind them of the elements that should be included such as type of food, housing, clothing, system for keeping order, ceremonies, and religions. Have them invent a history for their culture. Ask them to describe the environment that is the backdrop for their society and tell how their cultural landscape shows adaptation to that natural environment. Have students make posters describing and illustrating their imaginary cultures. Display the finished posters around the classroom.

Students may find the Chapter 7 Reading "The Beginnings of Culture," and the Chapter 7 Teacher Notes, Section 1, Extending the Lesson, "Egyptian Hieroglyphics," in the Teacher Resource Book helpful in preparing this assignment.

Objective 2 Activities

● Objective 2 Teaching Activity

Refer to the guidelines for case studies in the Instructional Approaches section of this Teacher Annotated Edition. Divide the class into 11 groups and assign a culture area to each one. Then have each group investigate in-depth one feature of the culture area assigned to them such as its history, economy, religion, form of government, language, or ethnic makeup of the population. Explain to the students that the investigation should be conducted and written by all members of the group because a group grade will be given for each case study.

When the research has been completed, discuss the results in class, and then aid the students to prepare a master chart that will summarize the chief characteristics of each of the 11 culture areas. Have students duplicate these charts in their notebooks.

For an exercise related to this activity, refer to the Chapter 7 Skill Activity in the Teacher Resource Book.

★ Objective 2 Enriching Activity

Appoint a student committee to write a letter requesting information on Legacy, an international youth program. The address is: International Youth Program of the Institute for Practical Idealism, Route 4, Box 265, Bedford, VA 24523. Legacy is a youth program for students age 11–18. The organization offers a variety of programs such as travel abroad, international summer camps, and international conferences. The goal of Legacy is to spread global understanding through the interaction of students from around the world. Encourage interested students in your school to participate in some aspects of Legacy.

Concluding Chapter 7

Review with students the concept of having a global viewpoint. Ask in what way they believe the study of this chapter has helped them develop a global perspective of the world's cultures.

Plan a world cultures day and invite visitors from as many of the cultural areas studied as possible. There may be exchange students in your school or at a nearby university. Many hospitals have interns from various cultures. Students may have friends or neighbors with differing ethnic backgrounds.

Have students set up tables with displays explaining and depicting the cultures of the invited guests. Request that representatives from countries with distinctive dress wear costumes that represent their cultures. Parents and students may volunteer to prepare foods from various ethnic groups. Some students may wish to make a special project of preparing and presenting music, dance, art, and literature from the countries that especially interest them.

After the world cultures day is over, have students write letters of thanks to their guests and express to them their appreciation of those features of their cultures that they found particularly appealing.

ANSWERS TO CHAPTER 7 QUESTIONS

Content Check Questions
page 129

1. Refer to Glossary in Student Edition.
2. Discovery of fire, invention of tools, growth of agriculture, use of writing. (p. 127)
3. People need food, homes, clothing, and a system of keeping order. (p. 128)
4. Answers will vary but may include religious beliefs, loyalties to family and nation, divisions of language, feelings of being "right" and "best," and political doctrines. (p. 128)

page 141

1. Refer to Chapter 7 content.
2. Refer to Glossary in Student Edition.
3. Anglo-America, Latin America, Western Europe, Eastern Europe and the Soviet Union, North Africa and Southwest Asia, Africa south of the Sahara, South Asia, East Asia, Southeast Asia, Australia and New Zealand, and the Pacific Islands. (pp. 129–130)

4. England. (p. 130) India and England. (p. 136)
5. Christian. (p. 132) Islam. (p. 133)
6. Communist. (pp. 132, 137)
7. Answers will vary but should include basic major differences in language, religion, and societies based on Indian culture. (pp. 131–132)

Special Features Questions
page 134, Focus on Culture: "Youth Subculture"

1. Groups with values and ways of life different from the majority.
2. They are in a time of life when they look at and judge themselves and their cultures; their ideas may change from those of the majority, and they may speak out and work to bring about change.
3. Chinese youth and South African youth who protest government policies; members of groups such as YES who work for environmental improvements and in-service projects.

1. North America, South America, Greenland, Europe, Asia, Africa, Australia. Africa, Asia. Asia. Asia.
2. Christianity.
3. Shintoism and Buddhism.
4. Asia, Africa, Australia, Middle East, South America, North America.
5. Local religions are divided into many groups without any one large following.
6. Eastern Europe and Soviet Union.
7. Answers will vary but should include that Hinduism has largest number of followers in relation to land area in which they live.
8. Christianity.
9. Answers will vary but may include influence of the number of European and Asian explorers and merchants who passed through this world area.
10. Live together in some area. Scattered around the world. Answers will vary but may include that the Jewish people lost their homeland and migrated to other countries.
11. Answers will vary but may follow the concept that religion is centered on people and its strength lies in its number of adherents and the strength of their faith.

Photo/Illustration Caption Questions
page 128

Ideas, objects, or behaviors of one culture are carried to another culture and made part of its own way of life. (p. 128)

page 129

Cities developed, people could study and share ideas, keep records, write down laws, and pass all these on to the next generation. (p. 128)

page 130

History, form of government, economy, language, religion. (p. 130)

page 131

Native Indian cultures, European settlement, democratic government, free enterprise and highly developed industrialized economies, high standard of living, English language, Christianity. (pp. 130–131)

page 133

Ural-Altaic, Hamito-Semitic. (pp. 132–133)

page 135

Bantu. (p. 135)

page 136

Japan's economy. is industrialized, China's is developing and relies on farming; Japan's government is democratic, China's is communist; Japanese and Chinese languages belong to two different language families; Japanese have a high literacy rate. (p. 137)

page 137

Anglo-America, Western Europe, Eastern Europe and the Soviet Union. (p. 137)

page 140

Prisoners jailed for not paying debts. (p. 141)

Chapter 7 Review Questions
page 142, Reviewing Vocabulary

Answers will vary but should indicate that student understands the concept of culture or cultural.

page 143, Remembering the Facts

1. A society with its own ways of life created to satisfy its needs. (p. 127)
2. The natural environment's impact upon the lives of the people. (p. 127)
3. The discovery of fire, invention of tools, development of agriculture, and use of writing. (p. 127)
4. The merging of two or more cultures. (p. 128)
5. Anglo-America, Latin America, Western Europe, Eastern Europe and the Soviet Union, North Africa and Southwest Asia, Africa south of the Sahara, South Asia, East Asia, Southeast Asia, Australia and New Zealand, and the Pacific Islands. (pp. 129–130)

6. Anglo-America, Latin America, Western Europe, Eastern Europe and the Soviet Union, Australia and New Zealand. (pp. 130–132, 141)
7. South Asia. (p. 136) North Africa and Southwest Asia. (p. 133) Southeast Asia. (p. 140)

page 143, Understanding the Facts

1. From their family and members of their ethnic group. (p. 127)
2. Culture is a society with its own ways of life created to satisfy its needs; civilization is a developed culture that includes a writing system. (p. 127)
3. Could live in colder climates and do things after (or in the) dark. (p. 127)
4. Both areas have been dominated by larger dominant cultures; Eastern Europe by the Soviet Union; Southeast Asia first by Europe and then China. (p. 132, p. 140)
5. It is where the first ideas about farming developed; the religions of Judaism, Christianity, and Islam developed in this area. (p. 133)

page 143, Thinking Critically and Creatively

1. Answers will vary according to area. Answers will vary by area. Answers will vary but may mention ten common cultural traits—language, religion, dress, the arts, education, economy, laws, form of government, technology, and history.
2. Answers will vary but may include that people share goods and ideas, transportation, and communication; they also have the ability to move and be conquered.

3. Answers will vary but should indicate that communication would be difficult, laws could not be written down and passed on to future generations, and no way to record history except through oral tradition.
4. Answers will vary but should contain the idea that *ethnocentric* means being loyal to the group within; *patriotism* refers to national loyalty.
5. Answers will vary but may suggest that as cultures develop in different surroundings, people have been able to adjust to environmental differences.
6. Answers will vary but may suggest the need for development of a common language and other unifying factors such as understanding between and appreciation of other cultures and a global point of view. Answers will vary but may include the need for total planning that would be utilized for quite a few areas, and it should eliminate the threat of wars. Answers will vary but may include lack of identity or difference from one area to another, loss of interesting linguistic and cultural heritages.

page 143, Reinforcing Graphic Skills

1. Europe, Asia, North America, South America, Africa.
2. Answers will vary but may include differences in religious beliefs and ideas; Muslim efforts to convert others and holy wars; possibility that trade and business took Muslims farther afield; some Muslims were war-like and conquered areas around them. Muslim invasions took them into other world areas such as Spain and India, resulting in spread of Islam.

EVALUATING CHAPTER 7

World Geography: People and Places provides chapter tests to help evaluate student performance. To evaluate student mastery of Chapter 7, give students Chapter 7 Test from the Teacher Resource Book. This test may also be used for pretesting or retesting purposes. Other tests can be made from the questions available in the Test Generator Software.

Lesson Plan Suggestions—Chapter 7

Section 1   Cultural Development and Change (pp. 127–129)

Chapter Objectives	Suggested Teaching Strategies	Review

1. describe what *culture* means and how cultures develop.	**Teacher Preparation**
	SE, Reading Assignment, pp. 127–129
	TAE, Unit 3 Suggested Resources
	    Chapter 7 Overview, p. T109
	    Introducing Chapter 7, p. T109
	TRB, Chapter 7 Teacher Notes: Section 1
	
	Teaching Options
	TAE, Introducing Chapter 7, p. T109
	    Objective 1 Activities, p. T110
	TRB, Chapter 7 Teacher Notes: Section 1,
	    Extending the Lesson
	    Chapter 7 Reading
	    Chapter 7 Skill Activity
		SE, Content Check, p. 129

Section 2   World Cultures (pp. 129–141)

Chapter Objectives	Suggested Teaching Strategies	Review

2. summarize the chief characteristics of each of 11 major culture areas.
 	
Skill Objective: compare data from maps and graphs.
	Teacher Preparation
	SE, Reading Assignment, pp. 129–141
	TAE, Unit 3 Suggested Resources
	    Chapter 7 Overview, p. T109
	TRB, Chapter 7 Teacher Notes: Section 2
	
	Teaching Options
	TAE, Objective 2 Activities, pp. T110–T111
	TRB, Chapter 7 Teacher Notes: Section 2,
	    Extending the Lesson
	    Chapter 7 Skill Activity
	TSP, Transparency 9
	SE, *Using Graphic Skills,*
	    "Comparing Data from Maps and
	    Graphs," pp. 138–139
		SE, Content Check, p. 141

Chapter 7 Review and Evaluation

Suggested Teaching Strategies	Review	Evaluation
TAE, Concluding Chapter 7, p. T111	SE, Chapter 7 Review, pp. 142–143 TRB, Chapter 7 Review Worksheet	TRB, Chapter 7 Test TG, Chapter 7

CHAPTER 8 URBAN PATTERNS

Student Edition pp. 144–159

CHAPTER 8 OBJECTIVES

At the conclusion of this chapter, students will be able to:
1. classify urban areas by kind or function.
2. discuss the development of cities from ancient to modern times.
3. characterize urban environments in terms of landscape, climate, and social interaction.
4. summarize the development today of citizens in industrialized nations and those in developing nations.

CHAPTER 8 SKILL OBJECTIVE

After completing the *Using Graphic Skills* exercise in this chapter, the student should be able to make observations.

CHAPTER 8 OVERVIEW

In this chapter students become familiar with urban geography, learning about the function, development, environments, and possible future patterns of urban growth.

Section 1 helps students classify urban areas and become aware of their functions. To better understand why cities came into being, *Section 2* explains the historical development of urban areas including the basic reasons behind their growth. How the natural environment influenced the sites of cities and the human activities that take place within them is proposed in *Section 3*. The environmental problems that resulted from city building are also examined. *Section 4* addresses the way in which urban patterns are developing worldwide today and looks at the trends that may affect the future growth of cities. A special feature in this chapter teaches students about aerial analysis of cities.

CHAPTER 8 ACTIVITIES

Introducing Chapter 8

Engage the class in a discussion centered around city, suburban, and country living. On one section of the chalkboard, write "CITY," on another "SUBURBAN," and on still another, "COUNTRY." Refer to the guidelines for brainstorming in the Instructional Approaches section of this Teacher Annotated Edition, and ask students to brainstorm advantages and disadvantages of each lifestyle. Write student responses on the chalkboard. Discuss the suggested differences, then ask students to indicate by a show of hands which lifestyle they prefer. Volunteers may explain their reasons.

Inform the class that in this chapter they will learn about the development and functions of urban life and how city patterns have developed throughout the world.

Chapter 8 Reading Assignments

Objective 1	Student Ed. pp. 145–149
Objective 2	Student Ed. pp. 149–151
Objective 3	Student Ed. pp. 151–156
Objective 4	Student Ed. pp. 156–157

● Teaching ■ Reinforcing ★ Enriching

Objective 1 Activities

● Objective 1 Teaching Activity

Prepare a large chart and hang it on the wall of the classroom. On the left axis of the chart, list the names of several urban areas. Across the top of the chart, list the following categories: Kind, Main Economic Activity, Government, Transportation, Trade, and Other Functions.

Have each student research one of the urban areas. They should find out the kind of area, its major economic activity, whether it is a national, state, or provincial capital, if it is a major transportation route, if it is a trade and office center, and what other functions it has.

After the students have completed their research, ask each to give his or her report to the class, point out the city in question on a map, and write in his or her findings on the chart.

■ Objective 1 Reinforcing Activity

Refer to the guidelines for community resource persons in the Instructional Approaches section of this Teacher Annotated Edition, then invite a city or town official to speak to your class. If your school is located in a country setting, invite an official from the nearest town or city. Have the class research your city's urban functions and prepare questions to ask the speaker related to manufacturing, government, transportation, trade and office, recreation, education, and religion. Finally, classify your city as to kind of urban area and as to urban function.

Objective 2 Activities

● Objective 2 Teaching Activity

Have students create a time line showing the development of cities over the 6,000-year period they are believed to have existed. Students may research names and dates of ancient cities (see Chapter 8 Suggested Resources in this Teacher Annotated Edition for reference books). Students should allow room on one side of the time line for a brief discussion of each city shown. On the other side of the time line, they should indicate trends that were affecting city development throughout this 6,000-year time span. Time lines should be created on large materials such as poster board, newsprint, or computer paper. Display completed time lines around the classroom.

■ Objective 2 Reinforcing Activity

Divide the class into three groups. Have the first group make a mural of an ancient city. Have the second group make a mural of a city at the time of the Industrial Revolution. Have the third group make a mural of a modern city. Ask each group to describe the characteristics of the city they have drawn. Display the murals in the class, then tell the students to write an essay for homework on the differences between the three cities drawn in the murals, explaining how cities developed over time and the characteristics of the cities of these three time periods. Several volunteers may share their essays with the class.

★ Objective 2 Enriching Activity

Refer to the guidelines for lecture in the Instructional Approaches section of this Teacher Annotated Edition, and prepare a short lecture on the everyday life of a person living in an eighteenth century city. A good reference to use for preparing this lecture is F. Braudel's *Capitalism and Material Life, 1400– 1800*, Harper and Row Publishers, New York, 1973. This book provides an excellent description of food and drink, houses, clothes, fashion, and technology of the period. Illustrate the lecture with drawings and photographs shown by means of an opaque projector. End the lecture by asking students if they would have enjoyed living in this time period, and why or why not.

Objective 3 Activities

● Objective 3 Teaching Activity

Prepare a handout with a list of 10 cities, then ask students to determine the site and situation of five of them. Allow them to choose one of the cities listed on which to write a short report. The report should include the following points: When and why was the city settled? What is the basis of its economy? What kind of climate does it have? What is its level of unemployment? What is its biggest source of environmental pollution? What, if any, problems does the city have with racial or religious conflicts? Conduct a general class discussion about the content of the reports.

Refer students to Chapter 8 Reading and Chapter 8 Skill Activity in the Teacher Resource Book as aids in preparing this activity.

★ Objective 3 Enriching Activity

Tell the class that each year certain cities are selected as "All American" cities. Using library resources, investigate with the class the criteria used in this selection and the names of cities so nominated in recent years. Relate this information to urban environment characterizations used in the Student Edition.

Have students collect newspaper clippings and articles about the All American cities. As students bring in clippings and articles, discuss them in terms of landscape, climate, and social interaction before placing material on the bulletin board.

Objective 4 Activities

● Objective 4 Teaching Activity

Refer to the guidelines for audiovisual materials in the Instructional Approaches section of this Teacher Annotated Edition. Select two films or cassettes, one about a city in an industrialized nation and one about a city in a developing nation. Ask students to take notes on the films and give them a list of questions to answer after they have viewed both films. The list should include questions on standard of living, employment, extended family, income, cost of food and housing, transportation, medical services, and government bureaucracy. As part of the debriefing, discuss the comparison of the two types of nations and cities.

Preparation of Chapter 8 Reading in the Teacher Resource Book will aid students in carrying out this activity.

■ Objective 4 Reinforcing Activity

Have students indicate on a world outline map the capital cities of each nation or certain specified nations. By means of symbols or colors, students should indicate which of these nations are developing and which are industrialized. Tell students to create a map key differentiating between industrialized nations and developing nations. This assignment may be done as a class project on a large outline map of the world or as individual projects on maps prepared by each student.

Concluding Chapter 8

Refer to the guidelines for discussion in the Instructional Approaches section of this Teacher Annotated Edition. Through class discussion, help students come to a consensus regarding the answers to the following questions: 1) How did cities develop? 2) Why do we have cities? 3) Who profits from having cities and in what ways? Opinions will probably differ, however, on answers to the next two questions. 4) In view of the disadvantages many people who live in cities suffer, do you think it would be better to organize society in a way that would not require cities? How might that society be organized (consider employment, health services, food supply, education, entertainment, and physical layout)?

5) You are the designer of a future city. Describe how you would design it. Have students draw up a plan for a future city with one artist working at the chalkboard and input by all students. Aid the class in comparing this super-modern city with plans of ancient cities. Help them discover elements that are similar and different with regard to transportation, food supply, living accommodations, type of commerce, and the fundamental reasons for the cities' existence. See Chapter 8 Suggested Resources in this Teacher Annotated Edition for reference sources on ancient cities.

ANSWERS TO CHAPTER 8 QUESTIONS

Content Check Questions
page 149

1. Refer to Glossary in Student Edition.
2. Metropolitan and suburban. (p. 145)
3. Manufacturing, government, transportation, trade, and office (also recreation, education, and religious). (pp. 148–149)
4. Answers will vary depending on location.

page 151

1. Refer to Glossary in Student Edition.
2. In the river valleys in Mesopotamia (Tigris and Euphrates); along Nile River and Indus River valleys in South Asia. (p. 150)
3. Artisans, merchants, and the ruling elite. (p. 150)
4. Early Middle Ages. (p. 150)
5. Farmers grew more crops, population grew, artisans and merchants reappeared, trade grew. (p. 150)
6. Answers will vary but may state that it is possible that increased farm production would have increased or speeded up city development. (pp. 150–151)

page 156

1. Refer to Glossary in Student Edition.
2. Site needs solidly based land, fertile farmland, good drainage, adequate water supply, natural resources nearby. A good situation requires central location, point along a transportation route, natural harbor, or land at confluence of rivers. (p. 152)
3. Hinterlands supply a city with raw materials and a city provides finished goods and services. (p. 152)
4. Cities tend to be warmer, cloudier, rainier, less windy, and less humid. (p. 153)
5. Answers will vary but may include calling a conference with both groups to help them plan the use of the park, stressing that it will benefit both by providing jobs and bringing them together.

page 157

1. Refer to Glossary in Student Edition.
2. Outward to the suburbs. (p. 156)
3. Latin America (Mexico City and São Paulo, Brazil); Tokyo-Yokohama, Japan; and Bombay-Calcutta, India. (p. 157)
4. Answers will vary but may include that suburban living is generally for the more affluent who can buy homes and have transportation, which requires a developed economy; in developing countries, the country poor move to the cities looking for jobs and a better life.

Special Features Questions
page 146, Thinking Like a Geographer: "Aerial Analysis of Cities"

1. Stadium north of the Astrodome and golf course in the north area of photo.

2. Businesses are located in the southeastern section of the map and along major highways; housing, within areas between major highways.
3. Clear, because water is a darker blue.
4. They analyze land use, locate polluted areas, assist in city planning and building, study water quality and plant life, show population growth and loss.

page 154, Using Graphic Skills: "Making Observations"

1. Shows Singapore is a coastal area, an island surrounded by water, and bordered by a large body of water on one side.
2. Singapore is located at a bottleneck through which shipping would have to pass on its way from the China Sea to the Indian Ocean.
3. It is located along the natural sailing route from the China Sea to the Indian Ocean. Its midway location makes it a convenient stopping-off point for ships in transit, loading and unloading goods, refueling, etc.

Photo/Illustration Caption Questions
page 148

Manufacturing, government, transportation, trade, and office. (p. 148)

page 149

Mecca, Saudi Arabia and Rome, Italy. (p. 149)

page 151

Trade and immigration. (p. 150)

page 153

Cities tend to be warmer, cloudier, rainier, less sunny, less windy, less humid. (p. 153)

page 157

Asia. (p. 157)

Chapter 8 Review Questions
page 158, Reviewing Vocabulary

Answers will vary but should indicate students' understanding of vocabulary.

page 159, Remembering the Facts

1. Metropolitan and suburban. (p. 145)
2. Manufacturing. (p. 148)
3. The Industrial and the Agricultural Revolutions. (p. 150)
4. Solidly based land, fertile farmland, good drainage, adequate water supply, available natural resources. (p. 152)
5. Unemployment, providing services, racial conflicts, pollution, rise of slums, migration to suburbs. (pp. 155–156)
6. About 45%. (p. 156)
7. Latin America, Asia. (p. 157)

page 159, Understanding the Facts

1. Because each country defines laws differently. (p. 145)
2. Site is the actual location of the city; the situation comprises the surroundings of the city. (p. 152)
3. Upsets natural land use patterns resulting in imbalance among air, soil, water, plants, and animals. (pp. 152–153)
4. Temperatures are higher, precipitation is greater, there is less wind. (p. 153)
5. People with the means move outward to get away from inner city problems like poverty, slums, pollution, and crime. (p. 156)
6. In 1800s there were many jobs and possibilities in cities for rural people; today there are fewer jobs. (pp. 150, 156–157)

page 159, Thinking Critically and Creatively

1. Answers will vary but may specify that there were fewer people; the Industrial Revolution created many job opportunities and attracted people to cities.
2. Answers will vary but should include the idea that pollution is not only a city problem; some pollution is generated by poor land use, poor drainage systems, building of outlying suburbs and shopping malls, and destruction of farm lands.
3. Answers will vary but should include that it should have room for expansion and development, allow for transportation, have adequate drainage for sewage, provide climate for farming and good farm lands, provide solid land for building construction, and be near natural resources.

4. Answers will vary but may include that they had nothing in the rural area, and cities provide hope and some help with various programs and benefits.

5. Answers will vary. Answers will vary but may indicate that it would take great cooperation, research, and expense.

6. Answers will vary but should state that cities are centers of art, culture, and education; they provide shopping choices, health facilities, public transportation, and jobs.

page 159, Reinforcing Graphic Skills

1. Answers will vary but may include that Singapore is a coastal area and a natural water route between the China Sea and the Indian Ocean.

2. Answers will vary but may include having an economy that is tied to transportation with easy access to world markets. Answers will vary but may state that climatic changes could greatly influence the trade and the economy of a country. Answers will vary.

EVALUATING CHAPTER 8

World Geography: People and Places provides chapter tests to help evaluate student performance. To evaluate student mastery of Chapter 8, give students Chapter 8 Test from the Teacher Resource Book. This test may also be used for pretesting or retesting purposes. Other tests can be made from the questions available in the Test Generator Software.

Lesson Plan Suggestions—Chapter 8

| SE—Student Edition   TAE—Teacher Annotated Edition   TG—Test Generator |
| TRB—Teacher Resource Book   TSP—Transparency Package |

Section 1   Classifying Urban Areas (pp. 145–149)

Chapter Objectives	Suggested Teaching Strategies	Review
1. classify urban areas by kind or function. Skill Objective: make observations.	**Teacher Preparation** SE, Reading Assignment, pp. 145–149 TAE, Unit 3 Suggested Resources Chapter 8 Overview, p. T115 Introducing Chapter 8, p. T116 **Teaching Options** TAE, Introducing Chapter 8, p. T116 Objective 1 Activities, p. T116 TRB, Chapter 8 Teacher Notes: Section 1, Extending the Lesson SE, *Using Graphic Skills,* "Making Observations," p. 154	SE, Content Check, p. 149

Section 2   History of Cities (pp. 149–151)

Chapter Objectives	Suggested Teaching Strategies	Review

2. discuss the development of cities from ancient to modern times.	**Teacher Preparation**
	SE, Reading Assignment, pp. 149–151
	TAE, Unit 3 Suggested Resources
	    Chapter 8 Overview, p. T115
	TRB, Chapter 8 Teacher Notes: Section 2
	Teaching Options
	TAE, Objective 2 Activities, pp. T116–T117
	TRB, Chapter 8 Teacher Notes: Section 2,
	    Extending the Lesson
	TSP, Transparencies 4 and 6
		SE, Content Check, p. 151

Section 3   Urban Environment (pp. 151–156)

Chapter Objectives	Suggested Teaching Strategies	Review

3. characterize urban environments in terms of landscape, climate, and social interaction.	**Teacher Preparation**
	SE, Reading Assignment, pp. 151–156
	TAE, Unit 3 Suggested Resources
	    Chapter 8 Overview, p. T115
	TRB, Chapter 8 Teacher Notes: Section 3
	Teaching Options
	TAE, Objective 3 Activities, p. T117
	TRB, Chapter 8 Teacher Notes: Section 3,
	    Extending the Lesson
	    Chapter 8 Reading
	    Chapter 8 Skill Activity
		SE, Content Check, p. 156

Section 4   World Patterns of Urban Development (pp. 156–157)

Chapter Objectives	Suggested Teaching Strategies	Review

4. summarize the development today of cities in industrialized nations and those in developing nations.	**Teacher Preparation**
	SE, Reading Assignment, pp. 156–157
	TAE, Unit 3 Suggested Resources
	    Chapter 8 Overview, p. T115
	TRB, Chapter 8 Teacher Notes: Section 4
	Teaching Options
	TAE, Objective 4 Activities, p. T117
	TRB, Chapter 8 Teacher Notes: Section 4,
	    Extending the Lesson
	    Chapter 8 Reading
	TSP, Transparencies 8 and 9
		SE, Content Check, p. 157

Chapter 8 Review and Evaluation

Suggested Teaching Strategies	Review	Evaluation
TAE, Concluding Chapter 8, pp. T117–T118	SE, Chapter 8 Review, pp. 158–159 TRB, Chapter 8 Review Worksheet	TRB, Chapter 8 Test TG, Chapter 8

Unit 3 Review and Evaluation

Suggested Teaching Strategies	Review	Evaluation
TAE, Concluding Unit 3, p. T122 TRB, Unit 3 Career Worksheet	SE, Unit 3 Review, pp. 160–161	TRB, Unit 3 Exam

CONCLUDING UNIT 3

Divide the class into six groups, each representing one of the following continents: North America, South America, Africa, Asia, Europe, and Australia. Each group should look back through this unit of the Student Edition and gather all available information on their assigned continents, including population centers and cultural characteristics. When information has been collected by the groups, have each present its continent to the class. Presentations may be supplemented by audio-visual materials. Aid groups to find materials adequate for their reports. Allow use of the library, reference books, maps, and atlases.

Unit 3 Exam in the Teacher Resource Book may be administered.

UNIT 3 REVIEW QUESTIONS

page 161, Thinking About the Unit

1. Answers will vary but should include increased food supply, better medical and health care, better standard of living through technology.
2. Answers will vary but should reflect necessary elements suggested in the Student Edition.
3. Answers will vary but should include overcrowding; crime; waste disposal; energy shortages, inadequate housing; inadequate public transport and transportation routes; pollution from cars, the burning of coal, and factory-produced smog; unemployment; poor planning in the development of suburbs; racial and religious conflicts.

UNIT 4 ANGLO-AMERICA

Student Edition pp. 162–241

UNIT 4 GOALS

At the conclusion of this unit, students will be able to:
1. describe the diverse physical, economic, and cultural features of the Anglo-American culture area.
2. list important similarities and differences between the United States and Canada.

UNIT 4 SKILL OBJECTIVE

After completing the *Developing Geography Skills* exercise in this unit, the student should be able to observe in the field.

UNIT 4 OVERVIEW

The fourth unit of *World Geography: People and Places*, Anglo-America, focuses on two of the leading industrial countries in the world, the United States and Canada. Although the two countries have diverse physical areas, they share many rich natural resources, common cultural backgrounds and language, and a high standard of living.

The major concentration of the unit centers on the geography of the United States. Three chapters provide extensive coverage of the land, culture, and historic influences on the American people. *Chapter 9* describes the 11 major physical regions found in the country. The chapter also describes major climate patterns in the United States.

Economic and cultural regions found in the United States are described in *Chapter 10*. Emphasis is placed on how the physical environment affects production of goods and services for the nation's economy and growth of its urban structure.

Chapter 11 takes students through the historical patterns of United States settlement as well as the major influences on its growth and development. Thus, the influence of immigration on the makeup of American society is incorporated into the chapter.

Concluding the unit is *Chapter 12*. This chapter concentrates on the geography of Canada with its huge land area, relatively small population density, and two cultural bases.

Upon completion of Unit 4, students should have a basic geographic knowledge of the Anglo-American culture area. They should also be able to describe the similarities and differences between the United States and Canada.

INTRODUCING UNIT 4

Ask students to describe the landscape of their community. Do they have rivers, lakes, an ocean, plains, or plateaus near their homes? If they live in the city, is the landscape relatively flat or are there hills in the area? Next, ask students to describe the climate of their area. Are the summers hot or cool? What type of winters do they usually have? How much rain falls in their area?

Continue with the discussion by asking students how the landscape and climate have affected the way their community has developed. Have these physical features affected where homes or apartments are built, businesses or farms are set up, streets or roads are developed? What effect has the climate had on community development?

Ask students to locate on a map the major cities of the United States and Canada. Have them explain why they think there are so many major cities in the northeast of the United States and why there are so many major cities in the southeast of Canada. Point out that cities often develop along trade and transportation routes and near sources of raw materials. How extensive this development is depends on how people adapt to the physical environment. Remind students to think of these reasons as they read about the development of the United States and Canada.

CHAPTER 9 U.S.: LANDSCAPE AND CLIMATE

Student Edition pp. 164–181

CHAPTER 9 OBJECTIVES

At the conclusion of this chapter, students will be able to:
1. locate the 11 major physical regions of the United States and summarize the characteristics of each.
2. describe the climates found in the United States.

CHAPTER 9 SKILL OBJECTIVE

After completing the *Using Graphic Skills* exercise in this chapter, the student should be able to read maps with insets.

CHAPTER 9 OVERVIEW

To understand the reasons behind the emergence of the United States as a highly developed country, students need to realize the country's special physical advantages. Thus, Chapter 9 describes the land area and climate found in the United States. In *Section 1*, the nation's landscape is broken into 11 physical regions, 8 of which lie in the 48 contiguous states. The other three are in Alaska and Hawaii. Because of their distinctive nature, some physical regions are further broken down into subregions.

Major elevations, landforms, waterways, and any physical characteristics unique to each region are described in this chapter. Vegetation commonly found is also detailed.

Section 2 of the chapter gives students a complete breakdown of climate types found in the United States. Based on the map of Earth's Climate Regions on pages 96–97 in the student text, the contiguous United States has eight climate types. Alaska has three, and

Hawaii has one. This section also gives average summer and winter high and low temperatures in selected areas within each climate region. Amounts of rainfall and any strong weather patterns are also described. The ironic difference in climate between Ketchikan, Alaska, and Minneapolis-St. Paul, Minnesota, is a feature of the chapter.

CHAPTER 9 ACTIVITIES

Introducing Chapter 9

Have students read and answer the questions at the end of Chapter 9 Reading in the Teacher Resource Book, the "Siege of Yorktown." Discuss the answers to the questions, and then hold a general class discussion about the effects of geography on settlement of the United States. Begin by asking students to name some of the geographic barriers settlers in the United States had to confront. For example, early settlers had to overcome rain, winds, temperature differences, and many changing weather patterns while crossing the oceans. Once on the continent, harsh winters and unfamiliar land features, especially in New England, caused many hardships. Complete the activity by having students search through American history texts to find additional examples of how settlement of the United States was affected by a geographic barrier.

Chapter 9 Reading Assignments

Objective 1	Student Ed. pp. 165–173
Objective 2	Student Ed. pp. 174–179

● Teaching   ■ Reinforcing   ★ Enriching

Objective 1 Activities

● Objective 1 Teaching Activity

Have students read and answer the questions from the *Using Graphic Skills* exercise, "Reading Maps with Insets," on page 170 of the Student Edition. Then distribute outline maps of the United States. Tell students that as they read about the physical features and characteristics of each region of the United States, they should draw and label them on their blank maps. Remind students to make a key that shows what each symbol and color on their map represents. Then have students prepare a brief outline of notes to help them identify the unique features of each of the 11 major regions and their subregions. Students might review the outline from Chapter 5, Objective 4 Teaching Activity. Explain that their notebook outlines will later help them to summarize the characteristics of each region. Let students know that they will be expected to locate the physical regions of the United States later on a test map, and name any region described.

Refer students to Chapter 9 Skill Activity in the Teacher Resource Book for another activity related to this objective.

■ Objective 1 Reinforcing Activity

Refer to the guidelines for team learning in the Instructional Approaches section of this Teacher Annotated Edition. Divide the class into eleven groups, and assign each one of the major landscape regions of the United States. Allow time for groups to prepare to "teach" the rest of the class about their respective regions. Team members should decide how they will present the information. Suggest some of the following procedures: a role play of an "old time resident"; a tour guide; a display of postcards, pictures, snapshots, or slides of the region's land features; a selected filmstrip or other audiovisual; or display of a large-scale relief map of the region.

★ Objective 1 Enriching Activity

In order to see maps as representations of real places on Earth, it is important to visualize map symbols as mental snapshots of real phenomena, whether physical, cultural, or statistical. Help students develop this ability by bringing to class (and asking them to bring) postcards, photos, calendar pictures, and travel brochures of land features of the United States. Make a bulletin board with these pinned around a United States map and connected by yarn to the places they show.

At the end of this section or chapter's study, take the pictures down, mix them up, and use them as flashcards for a quiz during which students must identify the region where each picture was taken. This part of the activity may take the form of a competition between two or more student teams.

Objective 2 Activities

● Objective 2 Teaching Activity

Refer to the guidelines for brainstorming in the Instructional Approaches section of this Teacher Annotated Edition. Then, ask students to brainstorm about the number and kinds of climate areas in the United States, putting together what they have studied about world climate areas in general, the elements and controls of climate, and the physical regions of the United States. Let students contribute information and hypothesize freely about the regions in any order. As regions are discussed, color a wall-size blank outline map using the same colors as the Earth's Climate map on pp. 96–97 of the Student Edition. Do not attempt to complete a perfect United States climate area map at this point, and do allow white areas to show so that students can hypothesize. After students have brainstormed, have them turn to the United States Climate Regions map to compare and discuss likenesses and discrepancies.

Refer students to the Chapter 9 Reading in the Teacher Resource Book for further information related to this objective.

★ Objective 2 Enriching Activity

Refer to the guidelines for role plays and simulations in the Instructional Approaches section of this Teacher Annotated Edition. Divide the class into groups of three. In each group, one student will be a tourist planning a trip, one a travel agent, and one the travel agent's experienced "boss" observing and critiquing the agent's job performance. The three students in each group will change roles so that each plays every role once. The tourist will choose a place to visit in the United States and ask the travel agent for advice in preparing for the trip: What kinds of clothes should be taken? What kinds of activities might be engaged in while there? What difficulties might be encountered? What might be especially enjoyable? The travel agent will advise the tourist, basing answers on the climate and landscape of the place. The boss, who will listen closely, may have a notebook open to write comments about the adequacy or omissions of the agent's advice.

When all three students have played each role, allow time for groups to debrief. Each member of the group should read his or her comments to the group for final discussion.

Concluding Chapter 9

Have students write a description of a hypothetical trip through one of the nine physical regions of the United States discussed in the chapter. Tell them to be as descriptive as possible about the landforms, waterways, vegetation, and weather that they encountered on the trip. If students have taken a trip through a region, they might enhance their descriptions with photographs or postcards. Share some of these reports with the remainder of the class.

ANSWERS TO CHAPTER 9 QUESTIONS

Content Check Questions
page 173

1. Refer to Section 1 content.

2. Refer to Glossary in Student Edition.

3. Interior Plains. (p. 169)

4. Answers will vary but could include that

land is gentler, flatter, and more accessible because of the many inlets and bays.

page 179

1. Hawaii. (p. 174)
2. Humid continental with hot summers, humid continental with warm summers, and humid subtropical. (pp. 176–177)
3. Enough rain for farming, and droughts are rare. (p. 177)
4. Answers should include influences of elevation and winds.

Special Feature Questions
page 170, Using Graphic Skills: "Reading Maps with Insets"

1. Contiguous United States.
2. Approx. 65°W to 125°W. Approx. 130°W to 173°E. Approx. 154°W to 161°W.
3. Alaska.

page 178, Focus on Geography: "Mild Winters in Southeast Alaska?"

1. West.
2. Wet. It is just off the coast of the ocean.
3. Middle latitude marine. Humid continental, warm or hot summer.

Photo/Illustration Caption Questions
page 166

Beaches, marshes, lagoons, barrier islands, hills, and swamps. (p. 166)

page 167

Rapids and waterfalls along the fall line provided water power to the area. (p. 167) Pennsylvania and Georgia. (p. 167)

page 168

Interior Low Plateau. (p. 169)

page 169

South. (p. 169)

page 172

Columbia Plateau, Colorado Plateau, Death Valley. (p. 172)

page 173

It is swampy lowland infested with mosquitoes in summer and frozen solid in winter. (p. 173)

page 174

Mount Waialeale. (p. 174)

page 175

Answers will vary.

page 176

Honolulu, Miami, Phoenix, Houston, and New Orleans. (p. 176)

page 177

The southeastern contiguous states, except for south Florida. Also, most of the Coastal Plains and Interior Highlands, and southern parts of the Appalachian Highlands and Interior Plains. (p. 176)

page 179

No, temperatures are above freezing for only a small part of the year and no month is free of frost. (p. 179)

Chapter 9 Review Questions
page 180, Reviewing Vocabulary

1. g.   2. e.   3. a.   4. d.   5. i.
6. f.   7. c.   8. b.

page 180, Remembering the Facts

1. Fourth. (p. 165)
2. Coastal Plains. (p. 165)
3. Appalachian. (p. 166)
4. Interior Plains. (p. 169)
5. Humid Subtropical. (p. 176)

page 181, Understanding the Facts

1. People could not travel any farther inland and rapids and waterfalls provided power. (p. 167)
2. Elevation. (pp. 166–168)
3. Water has dissolved limestone to form the caves. (p. 170)
4. It is the rain shadow of the Pacific mountains. (p. 172)
5. Oil is being piped from the region. (p. 173)

6. Warm summers and long, mild, moist winters. (p. 176–177)

page 181, Thinking Critically and Creatively

1. Answers will vary but may include that interior exploration and development would have been slower and later because of the mountains.
2. Answers will vary but may include that warmer water encourages growth of such life forms.
3. Answers will vary but may include that the Pacific mountains "drain" the air of precipitation as it passes over the tops of the coastal ranges on its way to the Rockies.
4. No. The area is too dry for such crops.
5. Answers will vary but may include that the area would become dry like areas of the west coast. Continental air masses from the north would also be more influential. Production of corn would drop because the hot, moist, growing season needed for corn production would be affected.

page 181, Reinforcing Graphic Skills

1. West.
2. Northeast to southwest. Northwest to southeast. North to south. Northeast to southwest. East to west.

EVALUATING CHAPTER 9

World Geography: People and Places provides chapter tests to help evaluate student performance. To evaluate student mastery of Chapter 9, give students Chapter 9 Test from the Teacher Resource Book. This test may also be used for pretesting or retesting purposes. Other tests can be made from the questions available in the Test Generator Software.

Lesson Plan Suggestions—Chapter 9

SE—Student Edition   TAE—Teacher Annotated Edition   TG—Test Generator
TRB—Teacher Resource Book   TSP—Transparency Package

Section 1   Landscape Patterns (pp. 165–173)

Chapter Objectives	Suggested Teaching Strategies	Review

1. locate the 11 major physical regions of the United States and summarize characteristics of each.	**Teacher Preparation**
	SE, Reading Assignment, pp. 165–173
	TAE, Unit 4 Suggested Resources
	    Unit 4 Overview p. T123
	    Introducing Unit 4, pp. T123–T124
	    Chapter 9 Overview, pp. T124–T125
	    Introducing Chapter 9, p. T125
	TRB, Chapter 9 Teacher Notes: Section 1
	Teaching Options
	TAE, Introducing Unit 4, pp. T123–T124
	    Introducing Chapter 9, p. T125
	    Objective 1 Activities, pp. T125–T126
	TRB, Chapter 9 Teacher Notes: Section 1,
	    Extending the Lesson
	    Chapter 9 Skill Activity
		SE, Content Check, p. 173

Section 2   Climate Patterns (pp. 174–179)

Chapter Objectives	Suggested Teaching Strategies	Review

2. describe the climates found in the United States.	**Teacher Preparation**
	SE, Reading Assignment, pp. 174–179
	TAE, Unit 4 Suggested Resources
	    Chapter 9 Overview, pp. T124–T125
	TRB, Chapter 9 Teacher Notes: Section 2
	Teaching Options
	TAE, Objective 2 Activities, p. T126
	TRB, Chapter 9 Teacher Notes: Section 2,
	    Extending the Lesson
	    Chapter 9 Reading
		SE, Content Check, p. 179

Skill Objective: read inset maps.	SE, *Using Graphic Skills*, "Reading Maps with Insets," pp. 170–171	

Chapter 9 Review and Evaluation

Suggested Teaching Strategies	Review	Evaluation

TAE, Concluding Chapter 9, p. T126	SE, Chapter 9 Review, pp. 180–181
	TRB, Chapter 9 Review Worksheet
		TRB, Chapter 9 Test
		    Unit 4 Pretest, Map and
		    Content Worksheets
		TG, Chapter 9

CHAPTER 10   U.S.: ECONOMIC AND CULTURAL PATTERNS

Student Edition pp. 182–201

CHAPTER 10 OBJECTIVES

At the conclusion of this chapter, students will be able to:

1. describe the major economic and cultural features of Northeastern United States.
2. describe the major economic and cultural features of North Central United States.
3. describe the major economic and cultural features of Southern United States.
4. describe the major economic and cultural features of Western United States.

CHAPTER 10 SKILL OBJECTIVE

After completing the *Using Graphic Skills* exercise in this chapter, the student should be able to read thematic maps.

CHAPTER 10 OVERVIEW

The focus of Chapter 10 is on the economic and cultural features of four geographic sections of the United States—the Northeast, North Central, South, and West. How the people in the nine regions that make up these sections use their land and natural resources is the chief theme of the chapter. Any major agricultural areas in each region are described and crops produced in them have been pointed out to students. Important urban centers and major industries are also given. A special feature of the chapter is a segment about the importance of the Gulf of Mexico to the United States economy.

CHAPTER 10 ACTIVITIES

Introducing Chapter 10

Have students choose a major American city to research while they are studying Chapter 10. Tell them to find out how and why the city grew. Students should research why the city was settled, who settled it, and when it was settled. If possible, students should find out how the city got its name, what major economic goods and services were first produced in the city, what effect the landscape and climate had on city growth, and population growth statistics. Tell students that they will prepare a research report from their findings that will be presented at the completion of the chapter's work.

If time does not allow such an extensive report, you might introduce the chapter with a short lecture about the growth of urbanization in the United States, using the history of one or two cities for exemplification.

Chapter 10 Reading Assignments

Objective 1	Student Ed. pp. 183–189
Objective 2	Student Ed. pp. 189–192
Objective 3	Student Ed. pp. 192–196
Objective 4	Student Ed. pp. 196–199

● Teaching	■ Reinforcing	★ Enriching

Objective 1 Activities

● Objective 1 Teaching Activity

Refer to the guidelines for retrieval charts in the Instructional Approaches section of this Teacher Annotated Edition. Tell students that there are many facts that contribute to a region's economic and cultural development, and these are described in their text. A retrieval chart will help them understand these facts.

Ask students to skim the chapter to see how many regions are named. Place these regions down the left side of the chart. (Nine subregions should be indented appropriately under the four main regions.) Students should also skim the content of a couple of regions to suggest headings for the top of this grid. (Land Area and Features, Locations, States, Climate, Agriculture, Industries, People, Cities.) Have students complete the retrieval chart for the Northeastern United States. Discuss and check factual understandings. Conclude the activity by having students complete *Using*

Graphic Skills exercise, "Reading Thematic Maps," on page 186 of the Student Edition.

Refer students to the Chapter 10 Reading in the Teacher Resource Book for further information related to this objective.

■ Objective 1 Reinforcing Activity

Refer to the guidelines for audiovisual materials in the Instructional Approaches section of this Teacher Annotated Edition. Also review the list of Supplementary Materials in the Suggested Resources for this unit. Select a set of filmstrips that divides the study of the United States into geographic regions. Plan to show each filmstrip in the set after the textbook reading about that region in this chapter. Debrief afterwards by asking how the filmstrips illustrated ideas explained in the textbook and what students may have learned in addition to their reading. They might also add information to their notebook charts.

Objective 2 Activities

● Objective 2 Teaching Activity

After reading the first paragraph of this section, have students study the map of the North Central United States on page 191 of the Student Edition. Ask students to recall what they learned about the Great Lakes in Chapter 4. (Great Lakes were formed by glaciers and are the largest lakes in North America.) Ask what they know about climate controls that affect the Great Lakes. (Nearness to a body of water moderates climate; the west side of the lakes is affected by the prevailing westerlies, so the east side of each lake is colder.) Help students see from the maps how and why people have changed the waterways of the Great Lakes-Mississippi waterway to create an even more useful transportation system to serve both agriculture and manufacturing for the whole country. After a discussion, show a filmstrip on the area, and then have students fill in their retrieval charts for this region.

★ Objective 2 Enriching Activity

Challenge students to become aware of current news items about the North Central United States. Ask them to cut them out of newspapers, magazines, or write a brief headline and explanation on a $3'' \times 5''$ card of a TV or radio announcement. Teach students to write the source of their information: date and title of newspaper, magazine, TV show and channel, or radio station. Then have students prepare a large scrapbook to display their news items. This exercise may be done for each region discussed in the chapter. Students can then study the scrapbooks prior to taking their chapter tests.

Objective 3 Activities

● Objective 3 Teaching Activity

Write on the chalkboard, "Southern United States is . . . " Ask students to complete the sentence. Write a few words from each student's contribution on the chalkboard, and then have students categorize these responses into landscape and climate, economy, culture, history, and major metropolitan areas. Leave this list on the chalkboard to discuss again after students read Section 3, and then correct any misconceptions or partial truths. Show a filmstrip on the region and have students fill in their retrieval charts.

■ Objective 3 Reinforcing Activity

Have students turn again to the *Using Graphic Skills* feature, "Reading Thematic Maps," on page 186 of the Student Edition. Have them closely examine the kinds of questions designed as study aids for careful interpretation of the map's language. Ask students to work in pairs composing a set of 10 similar questions for the map of the Southern United States. After questions are prepared, have pairs of students sit in groups of 4 to 6 to ask and answer questions of the other pair(s) in the group.

Objective 4 Activities

● Objective 4 Teaching Activity

Refer to the guidelines for demonstrations in the Instructional Approaches section of this

Teacher Annotated Edition. Put one end of a long string or yarn on the northeastern tip of the United States on a wall map, and draw the string taut along the east coast to the southeastern tip. Measure that length of string against a yardstick and write the measurement on the chalkboard. Again put one end of the string on the northeastern corner of the United States. Have a student hold it there as you carefully trace the entire eastern coastline with the rest of the string, making it go in and out of every bay and harbor to the southeastern tip. Then stretch the string out, measure this length, and write it under the first measurement as a fraction. (It will be about three times longer than the straight measurement.) Follow this same procedure for the west coast of the United States, again taking two measurements from the northwest corner to the southwest corner of the United States on the wall map. You will find the measurement "hugging the coastline" only about one-third longer than the measurement "as the crow flies." Lead students to conclude that this exercise demonstrates how many more harbors and potential places there are for ships to land on the east coast than on the west coast. Ask students: How might the changing of these two coastlines (uneven coast placed on the west and smooth coast on the east) have changed the historical, economic, and cultural development of the United States of America? Allow students to brainstorm, hypothesize, and discuss until the flow of ideas lessens. Then explain that you have chosen this demonstration question to show what ramifications a single geographic feature can have. Conclude the activity by showing a filmstrip on the region, and then have students fill in their retrieval charts.

★ **Objective 4 Enriching Activity**

Divide the class into four groups. Assign to each one of the major geographic regions studied in Chapter 10, and distribute large blank outline maps of that region or of the United States. Tell groups they are to decide on one geographic change they would make for their region, and draw that change on their outline map. For example, they might remove the Great Lakes, or change the directional flow of the Mississippi River, or lower the Rocky Mountains considerably, etc. Groups will then hypothesize about how such a change might have affected the economic and cultural development of their region.

As you walk around listening and observing, choose one or more groups to demonstrate its projected change and probable consequences for the whole class.

At this time, students may use the Chapter 10 Skill Activity in the Teacher Resource Book as an aid in reviewing the chapter.

Concluding Chapter 10

Read aloud some of the reports that students researched in the chapter opening activity. Then ask students if they found any unique characteristics about their individual cities that they would like to share with the rest of the class. Hold a class discussion about how 74 percent of Americans live on 2 percent of the country's land. Ask students to hypothesize why, when, how this came to be, what the known results are, and how the future may be affected or may change this statistic.

ANSWERS TO CHAPTER 10 QUESTIONS

Content Check Questions
page 189

1. Refer to Section 1 content.
2. Refer to Glossary in Student Edition.

3. Rocky soil and short growing season. (p. 184)
4. Fishing is important to the economy. (p. 185)
5. Southern region. (p. 185)

6. Small, but important source of food for nearby urban areas. (p. 185)
7. Services. (pp. 185–186)
8. Port, transportation center, national and international businesses and banking headquarters, printing, media, and cultural center. (pp. 186–187)
9. Answers will vary but may include that New York had better access to the Great Lakes, the Midwest, and the South.

page 192

1. Refer to Section 2 content.
2. Refer to Glossary in Student Edition.
3. Great Lakes, Ohio and Mississippi rivers. (p. 189)
4. Detroit. (p. 190)
5. Chicago. Great Lakes. (p. 190)
6. Iowa. (p. 190)
7. Answers will vary but may include that corporations have moved into food production and lowered production from the small family farm.

page 196

1. Refer to Section 3 content.
2. Refer to Glossary in Student Edition.
3. Farming. Light industry, textiles, lumber mills, farming, and tourism. (pp. 192–193)
4. Lower wages and costs, and mild climate. (p. 193)
5. Oil production. (p. 193)
6. Texas. (p. 195)
7. Answers will vary but may include to continue to stress livestock production.

pages 198–199

1. Refer to Section 4 content.
2. Refer to Glossary in Student Edition.
3. Rugged terrain and little rainfall.
4. Farming, fishing, lumbering, and mining. (p. 197)
5. Oil. (p. 197)
6. California. (p. 198)
7. It is a major part of its economy. Climate and natural beauty. (p. 198)

8. Answers will vary but could include that transportation and distant markets make it expensive to develop minerals.

Special Feature Questions
page 186, Using Graphic Skills: "Reading Thematic Maps"

1. Coal, fish, forests, granite, iron ore, natural gas, petroleum, and water power. Dairy, poultry, and mixed farming, little or no farming, specialized crops, and manufacturing areas.
2. New York, Maine, New Hampshire.
3. Camden, New Jersey; Hartford, Connecticut; and New York City.
4. Answers will vary but could include that most of the land in Northeastern United States is used for farming.

page 188, The Urban World: "N.E. United States: Megalopolis"

1. A continuous string of urban areas.
2. Between Boston and Washington D.C.
3. The northeast was settled early and had many later immigrants.
4. Between: Milwaukee, Chicago, Pittsburgh; San Francisco, Los Angeles, San Diego; Tokyo, Osaka; Leeds, Manchester, Birmingham, and London.

page 194, Focus on Geography: "Gulf of Mexico"

1. Chief source of precipitation makes farming possible.
2. Foundation for oil drilling platforms and important transportation link.

Photo/Illustration Caption Questions
page 184

The South. (p. 184)

page 185

Boston, Massachusetts. Gloucester, Massachusetts. Portland, Maine. (p. 185)

page 191

Milwaukee, Chicago, and Gary. (p. 191)

page 192

Tobacco, rice, soybeans, pecans, peanuts, citrus fruits, sugarcane, and vegetables. (p. 192)

page 195

Mississippi. (p. 195)

page 196

Farming is limited because of little water and people can make more money by raising livestock. (p. 196)

page 199

California. (p. 198)

Chapter 10 Review Questions
page 200, Reviewing Vocabulary

Molybdenum, barge, farm belt, sorghum, fodder, hollows, menhaden.

page 201, Remembering the Facts

1. New England, Middle Atlantic, Great Lakes, North Plains, South, South Plains, Rocky Mountain, Pacific Northwest, Pacific Southwest. (pp. 183–198)
2. Urban. (p. 185)
3. New York, Middle Atlantic. (p. 186)
4. Great Lakes. (p. 189)
5. Atlanta. (p. 193)
6. Phoenix and Denver. (p. 197)

page 201, Understanding the Facts

1. Climate is milder and area is more industrialized. (p. 185)
2. Services, light industry, high technology, and electronics. (pp. 185–186, 190)
3. Climate and landscape make grain production possible. (p. 190)
4. Farming. (p. 192)

5. In the Pacific Southwest crops are more tropical, such as fruits and vegetables. In the Great Lakes there is more grain farming. (pp. 190, 198)
6. Rocky Mountain and Pacific Northwest. (pp. 196–197)

page 201, Thinking Critically and Creatively

1. Answers will vary but may include that although the area is beautiful, it is rugged and dry, and thus it is hard to make a living. Transportation and markets are not accessible, and winters are hard.
2. Answers will vary but should include that it supplies water for drinking, industry, recreation, and transportation.
3. Answers will vary but may include that the location would create a need for jobs, but the problems of water and adequate transportation would hinder development.
4. Answers will vary but may include that the central location makes it a hub for movement in all directions.
5. Answers will vary but may include the information that the Ohio River flows through a major population and industrial heartland and connects the Midwest with the Gulf of Mexico. The Columbia does not have the well-developed industrial area and the sophisticated tributary system.

page 201, Reinforcing Graphic Skills

1. Refer to map key.
2. Answers will vary.
3. Answers will vary but may include that the state has much rough, rocky soil and a short growing season.

EVALUATING CHAPTER 10

World Geography: People and Places provides chapter tests to help evaluate student performance. To evaluate student mastery of Chapter 10, give students Chapter 10 Test from the Teacher Resource Book. This test may also be used for pretesting or retesting purposes. Other tests can be made from the questions available in the Test Generator Software.

Lesson Plan Suggestions—Chapter 10

SE—Student Edition TAE—Teacher Annotated Edition TG—Test Generator
TRB—Teacher Resource Book TSP—Transparency Package

Section 1 Northeastern United States (pp. 183–189)

Chapter Objectives	Suggested Teaching Strategies	Review

1. describe the major economic and cultural features of Northeastern United States.
 	
Skill Objective: read thematic maps.
	Teacher Preparation
	SE, Reading Assignment, pp. 183–189
	TAE, Unit 4 Suggested Resources
	    Chapter 10 Overview, p. T130
	    Introducing Chapter 10, p. T130
	TRB, Chapter 10 Teacher Notes: Section 1
	Teaching Options
	TAE, Introducing Chapter 10, p. T130
	    Objective 1 Activities, pp. T130–T131
	TRB, Chapter 10 Teacher Notes: Section 1,
	    Extending the Lesson
	    Chapter 10 Reading
	    Chapter 10 Skill Activity
	TSP, Transparency 8
	SE, *Using Graphic Skills*, "Reading Thematic
	    Maps," pp. 186–187
		SE, Content Check, p. 189

Section 2 North Central United States (pp. 189–192)

Chapter Objectives	Suggested Teaching Strategies	Review

2. describe the major economic and cultural features of North Central United States.	**Teacher Preparation**
	SE, Reading Assignment, pp. 185–192
	TAE, Unit 4 Suggested Resources
	    Chapter 10 Overview, p. T130
	TRB, Chapter 10 Teacher Notes: Section 2
	Teaching Options
	TAE, Objective 2 Activities, p. T131
	TRB, Chapter 10 Teacher Notes: Section 2,
	    Extending the Lesson
	    Chapter 10 Skill Activity
	TSP, Transparency 8
		SE, Content Check, p. 192

Section 3   Southern United States (pp. 192-196)

Chapter Objectives	Suggested Teaching Strategies	Review

3. describe the major economic and cultural features of Southern United States. .	**Teacher Preparation**
	SE, Reading Assignment, pp. 192-196
	TAE, Unit 4 Suggested Resources
	    Chapter 10 Overview, p. T130
	TRB, Chapter 10 Teacher Notes: Section 3
	Teaching Options
	TAE, Objective 3 Activities, p. T131
	TRB, Chapter 10 Teacher Notes: Section 3,
	    Extending the Lesson
	    Chapter 10 Skill Activity
	TSP, Transparency 8
		SE, Content Check, p. 196

Section 4   Western United States (pp. 196-199)

Chapter Objectives	Suggested Teaching Strategies	Review

4. describe the major economic and cultural features of Western United States.	**Teacher Preparation**
	SE, Reading Assignment, pp. 196-199
	TAE, Unit 4 Suggested Resources
	    Chapter 10 Overview, p. T130
	TRB, Chapter 10 Teacher Notes: Section 4
	Teaching Options
	TAE, Objective 4 Activities, pp. T131-T132
	TRB, Chapter 10 Teacher Notes: Section 4,
	    Extending the Lesson
	    Chapter 10 Skill Activity
	TSP, Transparency 8
		SE, Content Check, pp. 198-199

Chapter 10 Review and Evaluation

Suggested Teaching Strategies	Review	Evaluation
TAE, Concluding Chapter 10, p. T132	SE, Chapter 10 Review, pp. 200-201 TRB, Chapter 10 Review Worksheet	TRB, Chapter 10 Test TG, Chapter 10

CHAPTER 11 U.S.: INFLUENCES OF THE PAST

Student Edition pp. 202–217

CHAPTER 11 OBJECTIVES

At the conclusion of this chapter, students will be able to:
1. identify the important forces in the settlement of colonial America.
2. describe the settlement patterns of the United States and the influences upon them.
3. summarize the five major ethnic groups that make the United States a pluralistic society.

CHAPTER 11 SKILL OBJECTIVE

After completing the *Using Graphic Skills* exercise in this chapter, the student should be able to analyze historical maps.

CHAPTER 11 OVERVIEW

It took more than two hundred years for the colonies to become an independent country. During this colonial period, Europeans settled the country from east to west and from south to north. *Section 1* of Chapter 11 describes these two general European settlement patterns.

Expansion into the interior of the country as a result of historical acquisitions forms the foundation of *Section 2*. This section also describes other settlement patterns, such as urbanization. Concluding *Section 2* is a study of other factors that affected growth of the United States, such as transportation, industrialization, and immigration.

The historic origins of America's pluralistic society is covered in *Section 3* of the chapter. The influence of major ethnic groups and immigration on United States development is also given. A special feature found in the chapter is a segment about geographic and population centers.

CHAPTER 11 ACTIVITIES

Introducing Chapter 11

Secure a map of the Lewis and Clark expedition. Point out some of the major geographic features along the route. Ask students what effect these explorations had on United States settlement. Then ask what such an expedition would contribute economically to the country's growth. Conclude this activity by having students read "Explorations of Lewis and Clark," the reading for Chapter 11 in the Teacher Resource Book.

Chapter 11 Reading Assignments

Objective 1	Student Ed. pp. 203–206
Objective 2	Student Ed. pp. 206–213
Objective 3	Student Ed. pp. 213–215

Objective 1 Activities

● Objective 1 Teaching Activity

Refer to the guidelines for lecture in the Instructional Approaches section of this Teacher Annotated Edition. Because the first two sections of Chapter 11 cover so much history, help students see the relationships between events and trends by relating each section's content in a lively story fashion. Choose important points from the text, do some reading about these in other books, and weave these into an intriguing narrative delivered before the class reads the sections. After debriefing the lecture, have students study the map of Colonial Settlement Patterns on page 205 of the Student Edition. Encourage questions, hypotheses, and generalizations.

Refer students to the Chapter 11 Reading in the Teacher Resource Book for further information in relation to this objective.

★ Objective 1 Enriching Activity

Have students ask their parents and/or grandparents about their family roots in another part of the world and their migration to the United States. Ask them to write a one-page summary with an inset map illustration to display on the bulletin board. They may do this creatively in the form of an imagined letter from the first family member who came here, or excerpts from a diary or journal, or a newspaper article, etc. This completed activity will be appropriate to discuss during Section 3 as well, to show the pluralistic society of your own classroom.

Objective 2 Activities

● Objective 2 Teaching Activity

Continue part two of your lecture approach by relating a story about United States settlement patterns and the acquisition of each new segment of territory. You might illustrate your narrative with a series of historical maps on overhead transparencies, wall charts, or the textbook illustrations. Debrief by clarifying and summarizing.

■ Objective 2 Reinforcing Activity

Prior to beginning the activity, have a box or fishbowl with folded pieces of paper on which you have written the names of the 50 states, and such terms as: east-to-west, south-to-north, pocket settlements, land availability, transportation, industrialization, immigration, urbanization, manifest destiny, Northwest Ordinance, and Homestead Act. Also, the day before the class period, write Objective 2 on the chalkboard: "Describe the settlement patterns of the United States and the influences upon them." Tell students they will be called on to tell the story of each kind of settlement pattern, the various influences, and the acquisition of each new part of the United States of America. Allow some time for students to review the content of the section to prepare their explanations. Encourage them to use maps in the text and others from your lecture.

During the class period call on students at random to pull a piece of paper out of the box or bowl and describe the topic to the class.

Refer students to the Chapter 11 Skill Activity in the Teacher Resource Book in relation to this objective.

★ Objective 2 Enriching Activity

Suggest that some students read first-hand accounts of explorers, settlers, pioneers, frontiersmen, and immigrants. Bring to class a few selections from the library of the journals of Lewis and Clark, a diary of a covered wagon family, a collection of letters home from an immigrant, etc. Read portions to the class and suggest that some students may want to read more from these and other such primary sources. In a later class period, allow time for students to share interesting excerpts or retell stories they have read. Encourage them to imagine how they would have felt in the same circumstances, and to appreciate the character, qualities, and anxieties of the person(s) whose personal writings they have shared.

Objective 3 Activities

● **Objective 3 Teaching Activity**

Refer to the guidelines for reading guides in the Instructional Approaches section of this Teacher Annotated Edition. Develop some questions as a handout to guide your students through the reading of Section 3. Use these questions to help the class summarize the facts and understandings about the five major ethnic groups in the United States. Extend and enrich the discussion by encouraging students to share other information and personal experiences according to local history.

★ **Objective 3 Enriching Activity**

Refer to the guidelines for field trips in the Instructional Approaches section of this Teacher Annotated Edition. Plan a field trip to a nearby historical society to view displays about settlement and population makeup of your community. Or, visit a series of ethnic museums or exhibits that may be housed in neighborhood centers, church halls, libraries, schools, or community centers.

Concluding Chapter 11

Divide the class into three groups, assigning each group one of the sections from Chapter 11. Tell students to clip and bring to class photographs from newspapers or magazines that depict the section. Make a bulletin board display from the photographs, then hold a class discussion about future American settlement and ethnicity.

ANSWERS TO CHAPTER 11 QUESTIONS

Content Check Questions
page 206

1. Refer to Section 1 content.
2. Refer to Glossary in Student Edition.
3. Movement was east to west, then south to north. (p. 203)
4. France came for economic reasons and for exploitation. The English came for religious purposes and for settlement. (pp. 203–204)
5. Florida, Southwestern United States. (pp. 205–206)
6. Answers will vary but could include that Spanish settlements were military outposts and missions. The English colonies were set up to escape religious persecution and establish settlements.

page 213

1. Refer to Section 2 content.
2. Refer to Glossary in Student Edition.
3. Louisiana Territory, northern border, Florida, Texas, all land north of the Río Grande and Gila rivers, Oregon territory, and Gadsden Purchase. (pp. 206–209)
4. Westward movement, homesteading, pocket settlement, urbanization, transportation, industrialization. (pp. 210–212)
5. Answers will vary. Answers will vary but may include gold, jobs, chance to start over, and freedom.

page 215

1. Refer to Section 3 content.
2. Refer to Glossary in Student Edition.
3. Europeans, blacks, Hispanics, Asians, and American Indians. (pp. 213–215)
4. Europeans for their religion and taking jobs; blacks kept separate economically, politically, socially; Asians were sent to relocation camps; American Indians were driven from land, resettled, or killed. (pp. 213–215)
5. Answers will vary.

Special Feature Questions
pages 208–209, Using Graphic Skills: "Analyzing Historical Maps"

1. Britain, France, Spain.
2. Louisiana Purchase, 1803.
3. Revolutionary War.
4. France.

5. 1848.
6. 1853.
7. Revolutionary War, Louisiana Purchase, Convention with Britain.

page 210, Thinking Like a Geographer: "Geographic and Population Centers"

1. More land area to the north was added.
2. Based on census result and movement of population.
3. Possibly toward the southwest.
4. Growth of, and movement from, the north and east to the south and southwest.

Photo/Illustration Caption Questions
page 204

Religious freedom and to better their lives. (p. 204)

page 205

St. Augustine, Florida. (p. 205)

page 207

70 years after its independence. (p. 206)

page 211

Availability of cheap land. (p. 211)

page 213

Latin America. (p. 213, chart)

page 214

Blacks. (p. 215, graph)

page 215

Arizona, California, Colorado, Florida, New Mexico, New York, and Texas. (p. 214)

Chapter 11 Review Questions
page 216, Reviewing Vocabulary

Answers will vary.

page 217, Remembering the Facts

1. France and England. (p. 204)
2. The English and French moved from east to west and the Spanish moved from southwest to the north. (pp. 203–205)
3. As slaves. (p. 214)
4. Forty-ninth. (p. 207)
5. Río Grande river. (p. 209)

6. 43%. 12.2%. 7.3%. 2.1%. 0.6%. (pp. 213–215)

page 217, Understanding the Facts

1. Answers will vary but could include the following: Harsher climate in New England colonies made farming more difficult. Middle colonies were more diverse. Southern colonies established the plantation system of large specialized farms. Large cities developed most rapidly in the middle colonies. (pp. 203–206)
2. The flatter areas along the coast created areas of heavy population. (p. 204)
3. Spain ceded it to the United States. Republic of Texas asked to be annexed into the United States. Purchased from Russia. (pp. 206–209)
4. The Northwest Ordinance opened the present Great Lakes states to settlement with the offer of cheap land. (p. 206)
5. More people from eastern and southern Europe started coming. Asians began to settle along the West Coast. (pp. 213–215)

page 217, Thinking Critically and Creatively

1. Answers will vary but should include that people were drawn to an area to find wealth like gold, silver, etc.
2. Answers will vary but may include that people had a chance to start over and improve their lives.
3. Answers will vary but should state that cattle business spread throughout the West, the population spread to other market areas, and the railroads expanded.
4. Answers will vary but may state that the "melting pot" theory makes us both united and diverse. The world can see examples of success by people of all nationalities, races, and backgrounds. We stand as an example to the world.

page 217, Reinforcing Graphic Skills

1. 1800–1850.
2. Great Lakes, Mississippi River, Río Grande, and Missouri rivers.

EVALUATING CHAPTER 11

World Geography: People and Places pro-vides chapter tests to help evaluate student per-formance. To evaluate student mastery of Chapter 11, give students Chapter 11 Test from the Teacher Resource Book. This test may also be used for pretesting or retesting purposes. Other tests can be made from the questions available in the Test Generator Software.

Lesson Plan Suggestions—Chapter 11

SE—Student Edition   TAE—Teacher Annotated Edition   TG—Test Generator
TRB—Teacher Resource Book   TSP—Transparency Package

Section 1   Colonial Settlement (pp. 203–206)

Chapter Objectives	Suggested Teaching Strategies	Review
1. identify the important forces in the settlement of colonial America.	**Teacher Preparation** SE, Reading Assignment, pp. 203–206 TAE, Unit 4 Suggested Resources 　　Chapter 11 Overview, p. T137 　　Introducing Chapter 11, p. T137 TRB, Chapter 11 Teacher Notes: Section 1 **Teaching Options** TAE, Introducing Chapter 11, p. T137 　　Objective 1 Activities, p. T138 TRB, Chapter 11 Teacher Notes: Section 1, 　　Extending the Lesson 　　Chapter 11 Reading	SE, Content Check, p. 206

Section 2   Settling the United States (pp. 206–213)

Chapter Objectives	Suggested Teaching Strategies	Review
2. describe the settlement pat-terns of the United States and the influences upon them.	**Teacher Preparation** SE, Reading Assignment, pp. 206–213 TAE, Unit 4 Suggested Resources 　　Chapter 11 Overview, p. T137 TRB, Chapter 11 Teacher Notes: Section 2 **Teaching Options** TAE, Objective 2 Activities, p. T138 TRB, Chapter 11 Teacher Notes: Section 2, 　　Extending the Lesson 　　Chapter 11 Skill Activity	SE, Content Check, p. 213
Skill Objective: analyze histori-cal maps.	SE, *Using Graphic Skills*, 　　"Analyzing Historical Maps," pp. 208–209	

Chapter Objectives	Suggested Teaching Strategies	Review

3. summarize the five major ethnic groups that make the United States a pluralistic society.	**Teacher Preparation**
	SE, Reading Assignment, pp. 213–215
	TAE, Unit 4 Suggested Resources
	    Chapter 11 Overview, p. T137
	TRB, Chapter 11 Teacher Notes: Section 3
	Teaching Options
	TAE, Objective 3 Activities, p. T138
	TRB, Chapter 11 Teacher Notes: Section 3,
	    Extending the Lesson
	    Chapter 11 Skill Activity
		SE, Content Check, p. 215

Chapter 11 Review and Evaluation

Suggested Teaching Strategies	Review	Evaluation
TAE, Concluding Chapter 11, p. T139 TSP, Transparency 1	SE, Chapter 11 Review, pp. 216–217 TRB, Chapter 11 Review Worksheet	TRB, Chapter 11 Test TG, Chapter 11

CHAPTER 12   CANADA

Student Edition pp. 218–239

CHAPTER 12 OBJECTIVES

At the conclusion of this chapter, students will be able to:

1. describe the major landscape and climate patterns of Canada.
2. distinguish among the five economic-cultural regions and list which provinces or territories are in each.
3. outline the events important to the history of Canada.

CHAPTER 12 SKILL OBJECTIVE

After completing the *Using Graphic Skills* exercise in this chapter, the student should be able to interpret diagrams.

CHAPTER 12 OVERVIEW

Canada and the United States share many similar historical foundations and geographic features. Yet Canada, the second largest country in the world in land area, has unique geographic characteristics. Canada's location in the high latitudes of the Western Hemisphere has had a great impact upon its development. Climate and land use are two of several factors that have led to an uneven distribution of population. Canada, however, does enjoy certain advantages because of location. Its situation between two oceans makes possible easy access to both markets in Europe and Asia.

Thus, *Section 1* of Chapter 12 concentrates on the landscape and climate of Canada. Any significant mountain ranges, rivers, and elements of the terrain are described. Temperatures and amounts of rainfall for selected areas of the country also can be found in this section.

Section 2 of Chapter 12 breaks Canada into five regions for study of the country's economy and culture. Important natural resources as well as major economic activity found in the provinces of the regions are described. The section also gives population data for selected areas and calls out large metropolitan areas.

Like the United States, European settlement greatly influenced Canadian development. In *Section 3*, settlement by the English and the French is described. The section also includes the effect of that settlement on Canada today, for there is still conflict between those of English and French ancestry. How geographers mark borders and the purposes behind them is a special feature of the chapter.

CHAPTER 12 ACTIVITIES

Introducing Chapter 12

Refer to the guidelines for brainstorming in the Instructional Approaches section of this Teacher Annotated Edition. Write on chalkboard the focus questions, "What do we know about Canada? What do Canadians know about us?" Have students brainstorm answers to the first question, recalling where and what they have studied about Canada so far in their school studies at any grade level, and how much they hear about Canadian affairs in our news media. Assign some students to look through recent issues of United States news magazines to find articles about Canada. Challenge the class to be aware of any or all news items about Canada, in print or broadcast, during the length of time it takes to study the chapter. Discuss reasons why we should be more interested in our neighboring country.

Suggest that there are many interesting topics about Canada for students to read more about and share with classmates. Have students prepare brief oral reports that will be part of the study of Section 2 and the conclusion of this chapter's study. Examples include: Royal Canadian Mounted Police, totem poles of the Haidu Indians, world's largest shopping mall in Edmonton, Niagara Falls, Canadian Parliament, French Canada, Canadian art and artists, the problem of acid rain, why the metric system?, Canadian literature, Canada's flag and national anthem, refugee and immigration laws, consequences, prejudice, professional sports, and comparison of Indian reservations with those of the United States.

Discuss resources for information about Canada. In addition to library materials, there are Canadian Consulates, tourist bureaus, and Canadian studies projects in many parts of the United States from which students can request free print and film materials. If any of these are located in your community, students might interview persons associated with these bureaus, or invite a guest speaker to be interviewed by the class. The NCSS Bulletin #76 on Canada lists many of these addresses.

Chapter 12 Reading Assignments

● Teaching   ■ Reinforcing   ★ Enriching

Objective 1 Activities

● Objective 1 Teaching Activity

Hold a large globe so that Canada directly faces the class. Ask students to tell as many facts as they can about Canada by closely observing its position on the globe. (Students can describe Canada's shape, its location in the high latitudes of the Northern Hemisphere, its distance from England by reading the west longitude lines, and its relative location to other countries. They can read the names of the water and land areas that touch the borders, compare its size in relation to other countries and continents, hypothesize about its climate areas, count and name its political divisions, use the globe key to interpret its landscape features, and use a string and the globe scale to find its coast-to-coast measurements.) Have a student read aloud the first two paragraphs of page 219 of the Student Edition to confirm some of the class's observations.

Remind students that a great many facts can be visualized quickly on a map so mapmaking for the purpose of organizing and remembering facts is also an excellent way to take notes for a geographic content reading. Distribute blank outline maps of Canada, preferably with physical features and province borders drawn on them. Tell students that they will "take notes" on these maps as they read about the political, physical, economic,

cultural, and historical factors that describe Canada. They may devise their own legend symbols, identifying these on a map key. Have available an additional supply of blank maps for those who make errors or wish to repeat part of the exercise.

Require students to learn the locations and spellings of Canada's ten provinces, two territories, largest islands, and chief cities.

■ Objective 1 Reinforcing Activity

Ask students to imagine they are tourists crossing Canada for the first time. With a yellow see-through marker, they can draw their chosen route of travel on blank outline maps. They can choose a coast-to-coast route, or start from a point on the United States-Canada border and travel northward as far as they can go. Have students write a journal of their travels along the route based on their text reading about landscapes and climate, and on additional library reading as they wish. Remind them to describe means of travel they are using from point to point, to describe what they see, and to observe likenesses and differences between the places they visit and regions of the United States with their own travel and lifestyle experiences. Conclude the activity by reading to the class the summer journal of Lynn Ezell, a high school student from Michigan, that is contained in the NCSS Bulletin #76, *Canada in the Classroom*.

Objective 2 Activities

● Objective 2 Teaching Activity

Emphasize the facts stated in the two introductory paragraphs of Section 2 in the Student Edition as key ideas to be learned, remembered, and related to other facts from this chapter. Add to your discussion the facts from the Chapter 5 Summary, page 238 in the Student Edition, that "Ontario and Quebec . . . have 60% of the country's population and 80% of its industry." Then read and discuss the special feature, "Can You See Borders?," page 232 of the Student Edition.

Refer to the guidelines for demonstrations in the Instructional Approaches section of this Teacher Annotated Edition.

Prepare ahead of time and use an overhead projector to show the class: (1) A base map you have thermofaxed from the blank outline map of Canada you gave students at the beginning of this chapter; (2) The same map on another transparency to which you have added the landscape and climate information studied in Section 1; (3) Another transparency of the same base map to which you have added the borders and names of Canada's provinces, territories, and the cities identified throughout this chapter; (4) Another transparency of the same base map divided into the five economic-cultural regions specified in this section and showing symbols for the products, services, resources, and industries discussed in each part of Section 2.

Tell students that one map base can become very cluttered if all the information geographers study about a place is recorded on it. So, a helpful device for seeing the relationships between kinds of information is a series of overlay maps. In order to aid the students, show them an example of an overlay map. Also show students the way maps with overlays can be used by describing information learned from each overlay.

Tell students to make a similar series of overlay maps to record important facts about Canada. They might do this on clear plastic sheets the same size as their base maps from Section 1, or they might make separate maps on paper with lead pencil and then thermofax the series to obtain the clear plastic overlays. Color and detail can then be added, using projector pens.

★ **Objective 2 Enriching Activity**

Students who have prepared oral reports discussed in this chapter's opening activity related to economic and cultural topics might present these now.

Encourage reporters to use the overlay maps and any other illustrations they may have gathered to enrich their presentations.

Objective 3 Activities

● **Objective 3 Teaching Activity**

Refer to the guidelines for lecture in the Instructional Approaches section of this Teacher Annotated Edition. Storytell the history of Canada with a lively, easy-to-follow narrative. Illustrate your talk with pictures, maps, a time line, slides, or a filmstrip if these are available to you. The NCSS Bulletin #76, Chapter 2, may be helpful in your preparations. Reading excerpts from primary source journals will also add interest.

Assign the reading of Section 3 in the Student Edition, and debrief by asking students to retell the story and main points of each section in their own words. Especially discuss the significance of the Quebec Act of 1774, the migration from the United States of the United Empire Loyalists, the War of 1812, 1931 Independence, 1982 Constitution and Bill of Rights, and creation of the Canadian national flag.

■ **Objective 3 Reinforcing Activity**

With class participation, develop a time line of Canadian history, using the dates given in this section and filling in with some which you or students may judge significant from your readings. Write the time line on the chalkboard, a transparency, or on bulletin board paper. Have students copy it in their notebooks, reminding them to use a ruler to measure equal distances between the time segments you agree upon.

Concluding Chapter 12

Have students deliver the oral presentations about Canada assigned in the chapter's opening activity. Then, ask students which initial ideas about Canada were correct and which ones were misconceptions. Discuss with students why some of these misunderstandings came about.

Refer students to the Chapter 12 Reading and the Chapter 12 Skill Activity in the Teacher Resource Book.

ANSWERS TO CHAPTER 12 QUESTIONS

Content Check Questions
page 223

1. Refer to Section 1 content.
2. Refer to Glossary in Student Edition.
3. Saint Lawrence-Great Lakes Lowland. (p. 221)
4. Saint Lawrence. (p. 221)
5. Canadian Shield. (p. 221)
6. Cool or cold. (p. 223)
7. Answers will vary but include the fact that though rich in minerals, they are very costly to develop because of either hostile climate or rugged terrain.

page 231

1. Refer to Section 2 content.
2. Refer to Glossary in Student Edition.
3. Great Lakes-Saint Lawrence Provinces (Quebec and Ontario). (p. 225)
4. Toronto and Montreal. (p. 227)
5. Alberta and Saskatchewan. (p. 227)
6. Similarities include large size, wealth, industrialization, rich farmland, natural resources, education, transportation, language, economic levels, spectator sports. Differences are political organization into provinces and territories instead of states, popularity of winter sports, fear loss of national identity (to U.S.), regional language dominance (French in Quebec), fewer people. (pp. 230–231)
7. Answers should include inconsistent fishing yields, short growing season, rocky soil, and difficult transportation; to improve they could develop the mineral wealth, promote tourism. (pp. 224–225)

page 237

1. Refer to Section 3 content.
2. Refer to Glossary in Student Edition.
3. Inuit and American Indians (originally from Asia). (p. 231)
4. Ontario, Quebec, Nova Scotia, and New Brunswick. (p. 234)

5. Canada no longer needed British approval for changes. (p. 235)
6. The divisions between English- and French-speaking areas, and between the national government and provinces. (pp. 235–236)
7. Answers will vary but may indicate that Canada seemed to be a natural extension of the United States because of its physical and cultural similarities.

Special Feature Questions
page 226, Using Graphic Skills: "Interpreting Diagrams"

1. Northwest Territories.
2. Nova Scotia. Because its actual size is much smaller than Manitoba.

page 232, Strange But True: "Can You See Borders?"

1. Fences, walls.
2. Rivers, bodies of water, mountain ranges.
3. Separate nations, maintain cultural differences, many others.

Photo/Illustration Caption Questions
page 220

Canadian Shield. (p. 221)

page 221

Over one-half. (p. 221)
About 10 percent. (p. 221)

page 223

They cut into the coastline and are very deep. (p. 222)

page 224

Shipping, fishing, manufacturing, tourism, service industries. (pp. 224–225)

page 225

Five. (p. 224)

page 227

26 percent. (p. 227)

page 228

Near waterways. (p. 228)

page 229

That they would have light population density. (p. 228)

page 230

Eskimos, or Inuit, American Indians. (p. 230)

page 235

Ontario and Quebec. (p. 235)

page 236

Has made them tolerant of differences. (p. 237)

page 237

Changed the Canadian flag, made English and French official languages. (p. 236)

Chapter 12 Review Questions
page 238, Reviewing Vocabulary

Physical—fjord, peat bogs, cordillera, timberline, permafrost, asbestos, potash, fossil fuels. Human—cede, truck farm, bilingual, reservations, separatists, subsidiaries, hydroelectric power.
Both—potash, asbestos.

page 238, Remembering the Facts

1. Atlantic, Arctic, Pacific. (p. 220)
2. British and French. (p. 219)
3. Able to speak two languages fluently. (p. 219)
4. Canadian Shield. (p. 221)
5. Ottawa, Ontario. (p. 227)
6. Vancouver. (pp. 229–230)
7. Eskimos, or Inuit, and American Indians. (p. 230)
8. Ontario. (pp. 233–234)
9. English and French. (p. 219)

page 239, Understanding the Facts

1. Appalachian Highlands, Interior Plains, Rocky Mountains, Pacific Mountain and Valley System. (p. 220, map, pp. 221–222)
2. Keep it cool because of northern location in the high latitudes. (p. 223)
3. Border the Great Lakes and St. Lawrence river system for shipping goods, good natural resources, important manufacturing and agricultural areas. (p. 227)
4. Bad weather and agricultural usage, and poor transportation. (pp. 227–228)
5. After losing the Revolution and fearing U.S. takeover of Canada, Britain strengthened her hold, as more English loyalists moved in from the U.S.; Canadians feared American aims. (pp. 233–234)
6. Parliamentary self-government, completely independent of United Kingdom. (pp. 234–235)

page 239, Thinking Critically and Creatively

1. Answers will vary but should include that such changes will make economic activity less subject to the uncertainties of nature, will provide more diversity and create more jobs, thus contributing to the provinces' total wealth.
2. Answers will vary but should include that one reason for the friction is that both groups realize that language is an essential culture trait, defining their identity. The French speakers wish to maintain their identity, as do the English. Many French-speaking Canadians believe that the larger English-speaking group will overtake the French culture. Also, there is a feeling that discrimination exists toward the French in some quarters.
3. Answers will vary but should include the growth of surplus farm crops, especially wheat for which there is an international market, the development of mineral wealth, and improved transportation networks that allow these provinces to reach a larger national and world market.
4. Answers will vary but should include that Canadians want to keep their identity separate from the United States and that one such way is by making Canadian business less economically dependent on American control.
5. Answers will vary but may include that the relationship between Canada and the United States has been a positive example

to the world because of its long, friendly boundary, its ease of access back and forth, and the mutual respect shared. The early relationship between the two countries still holds true today, although Canada has taken a more forceful role in making its interests and concerns known to the U.S.

6. Answers will vary but may include that the people in these areas have become more in touch and in tune with the rest of Canada and the world. Before, these people were more attuned to local interests.

page 239, Reinforcing Graphic Skills

1. Larger.
2. Smaller.
3. Nova Scotia; a larger population lives within a smaller area.

EVALUATING CHAPTER 12

World Geography: People and Places provides chapter tests to help evaluate student performance. To evaluate student mastery of Chapter 12, give students Chapter 12 Test from the Teacher Resource Book. This test may also be used for pretesting or retesting purposes. Other tests can be made from the questions available in the Test Generator Software.

Lesson Plan Suggestions—Chapter 12

SE—Student Edition   TAE—Teacher Annotated Edition   TG—Test Generator
TRB—Teacher Resource Book   TSP—Transparency Package

Section 1   Landscape and Climate (pp. 219–223)

Chapter Objectives	Suggested Teaching Strategies	Review
1. describe the major landscape and climate patterns of Canada.	**Teacher Preparation** SE, Reading Assignment, pp. 219–223 TAE, Unit 4 Suggested Resources 　　　Chapter 12 Overview, p. T143 　　　Introducing Chapter 12, pp. T143–T144 TRB, Chapter 12 Teacher Notes: Section 1 **Teaching Options** TAE, Introducing Chapter 12, pp. T143–T144 　　　Objective 1 Activities, p. T144 TRB, Chapter 12 Teacher Notes: Section 1, 　　　Extending the Lesson 　　　Chapter 12 Reading 　　　Chapter 12 Skill Activity TSP, Transparency 1	SE, Content Check, p. 223

Section 2   *Economic and Cultural Patterns (pp. 224–231)*

Chapter Objectives	Suggested Teaching Strategies	Review

2. distinguish among the five economic-cultural regions and list which provinces or territories are in each.
 	
Skill Objective: interpret diagrams.
	Teacher Preparation
	SE, Reading Assignment, pp. 224–231
	TAE, Unit 4 Suggested Resources
	    Chapter 12 Overview, p. T143
	TRB, Chapter 12 Teacher Notes: Section 2
	Teaching Options
	TAE, Objective 2 Activities, pp. T144–T145
	TRB, Chapter 12 Teacher Notes: Section 2,
	    Extending the Lesson
	    Chapter 12 Reading
	    Chapter 12 Skill Activity
	SE, *Using Graphic Skills*, "Interpreting
	    Diagrams," p. 226
		SE, Content Check, p. 231

Section 3   *Influences of the Past (pp. 231–237)*

Chapter Objectives	Suggested Teaching Strategies	Review

3. outline the events important to the history of Canada.	**Teacher Preparation**
	SE, Reading Assignment, pp. 231–237
	TAE, Unit 4 Suggested Resources
	    Chapter 12 Overview, p. T143
	TRB, Chapter 12 Teacher Notes: Section 3
	Teaching Options
	TAE, Objective 3 Activities, p. T145
	TRB, Chapter 12 Teacher Notes: Section 3,
	    Extending the Lesson
		SE, Content Check, p. 237

Chapter 12 Review and Evaluation

Suggested Teaching Strategies	Review	Evaluation

TAE, Concluding Chapter 12,
    p. T145
	SE, Chapter 12 Review, pp.
	    238–239
	TRB, Chapter 12 Review
	    Worksheet
		TRB, Chapter 12 Test
		TG, Chapter 12

Unit 4 Review and Evaluation

Suggested Teaching Strategies	Review	Evaluation
TAE, Concluding Unit 4, p. T150 TRB, Unit 4 Career Worksheet	SE, Unit 4 Review, pp. 240–241	TRB, Unit 4 Exam Unit 4 Posttest, Map and Content Worksheets

CONCLUDING UNIT 4

Draw a large retrieval chart on the chalkboard. Across the top write these headings: "Major Physical Features, Climate Types, Land Area and Population, Major Language and Ethnic Groups, Major Economic Activities, 3 or 4 Major Events in History." On the side of the chart write "Canada," and below it, "United States." Then, create a grid with twelve squares by drawing lines between the categories. Divide the class into twelve groups, assigning one square to each. (For example, one group might have "Canada—Major Language and Ethnic Groups.") Have the students review Chapters 9–12 for the information to complete the grid. Invite them to write the information in the appropriate square on the chalkboard. This should result in a large matrix filled with information students can use to study for their unit test. Complete the review with a discussion about the similarities and differences between the United States and Canada.

Assign students the Unit 4 Career Worksheet in the Teacher Resource Book. Unit 4 Exam in the Teacher Resource Book may be administered at this time.

UNIT 4 REVIEW QUESTIONS

page 240, Thinking About the Unit

1. Answers will vary but should include that for an east-west route linking the coasts, rail lines might stop in New York, Chicago, and Los Angeles. A more southerly route would be through New York, Atlanta, New Orleans, Houston, San Antonio, and Los Angeles. A Canadian route linking east and west might stop in Montreal, Toronto, Winnipeg, Edmonton, Saskatoon, Vancouver. Highway systems might follow the same routes, but might have more stops at the population centers, such as Dallas, San Diego, and Albuquerque in the southern United States. Many of these same cities could be linked between the two countries.

2. Answers will vary but should include that the United States and Canada cover such a large land area and cross many latitudes. As a result, the landscape and climate are diverse and many economic activities are possible. Proximity to the oceans allows for extensive trade with other countries. Thus, people from all over the world have come to the region, making it one of the most diverse cultural areas.

UNIT 5 LATIN AMERICA

Student Edition pp. 242–331

UNIT 5 GOALS

At the conclusion of this unit, students will be able to:
1. list examples of the impact of various ethnic groups in shaping the cultural diversity of the Latin American culture area.
2. describe the major physical and economic characteristics of Latin American countries.
3. analyze how the historical development of Latin America has influenced its economic growth and cultural diversity.

UNIT 5 SKILL OBJECTIVE

After completing the *Developing Geography Skills* exercise in this unit, the student should be able to classify information.

UNIT 5 OVERVIEW

In this unit the great panoply of contrasts and similarities both in physical geography and cultures, stretching from Mexico's border with the United States southward to Tierra del Fuego, is presented for the student to discover and explore. There are descriptions of landscapes and climates, ranging from the rugged terrain of the Andes, to deserts, to productive farmlands, to tropical forests. The climatic factors influenced by elevation, important in the economies and lifestyles of many countries of this region, are clarified. The economic and historical backgrounds that have shaped each region are explained, along with the diverse ethnic mix that has caused Latin America to be called a "melting pot" of peoples and has created diverse regional characteristics in spite of the heritage common to all of Indian and Iberian cultures.

In each chapter, the major physical, economic, cultural, historical, and geographic features of one of four regions of Latin America are examined. *Chapter 13* focuses on Mexico and Central America, *Chapter 14* on the Caribbean, *Chapter 15* on the Atlantic nations of South America, and *Chapter 16* on the countries of the Andean region of South America.

Upon completion of this unit, the student should have a greater appreciation of the peoples and cultures of Latin America and an understanding of how history, economy, and physical geography have affected and continue to affect the growth and development of these diverse, yet sometimes similar, nations.

INTRODUCING UNIT 5

Create student interest in the study of Latin America by placing pictures and drawings that deal with this area of the world on a bulletin board. Discuss these illustrations in general terms, and then ask students what current events they are aware of that are occurring in Latin America. Assign the task of bringing in newspaper and magazine articles about news events and general interest items related to Latin America. As the students bring in the material, display it on the bulletin board, gradually replacing the original display.

Distribute to the class a blank outline map of Central and South America, including Mexico. Without using their texts, atlases, or other reference sources, students should fill in the maps with what they know about Latin America, including countries, capitals, mountain chains, principal rivers, etc. When students have completed the maps or after a short period of allotted time, place a wall map of Latin America before the class and have them compare it with their maps. Most students will discover from class discussion and their maps that they have much to learn about both the cultures and the physical geography of their neighbor countries in the Western Hemisphere. Ask them to save their maps until they have completed this unit when they will retrieve them for the Concluding Unit 5 activity.

CHAPTER 13 MEXICO AND CENTRAL AMERICA

Student Edition pp. 244–267

CHAPTER 13 OBJECTIVES

At the conclusion of this chapter, students will be able to:
1. describe the major physical, economic, cultural, and historical features of Mexico.
2. describe the major physical, economic, cultural, and historical features of Central America.
3. summarize the chief geographic features of Mexico and Central America.

CHAPTER 13 SKILL OBJECTIVE

After completing the *Using Graphic Skills* exercise in this chapter, the student should be able to analyze demographic maps.

CHAPTER 13 OVERVIEW

In this chapter the students are introduced to the varying landscapes and climates of Mexico and Central America. The relationship between geography and population density in terms of how landforms and climate affect living conditions and economic possibilities is explained, as well as the cultural and historic influences that weigh heavily on the economy and lifestyles of the people of the region. Mexico and each of the countries of Central America are profiled in respect to location, ethnic groups, population, history, and economy, yet the differences and uniqueness of each country are not neglected.

Section 1 of this chapter deals with Mexico, while *Section 2* examines the Central American nations with regard to physical, economic, cultural, and historical features. A special feature of the chapter provides background information on the ancient Maya.

CHAPTER 13 ACTIVITIES

Introducing Chapter 13

Create a large blank outline map of Mexico and Central America showing only the borders of the countries. Place this map before the class. In a container, mix strips of paper on which are written the names of countries, well-known cities, mountain ranges and peaks, the Panama Canal, and other physical and political features.

Have each student select a slip of paper and with a pin affix the name to the map in the area where it belongs. Ask the class to participate as a whole by correcting any errors they see. When all slips have been attached, place the wall map of Mexico and Central America before the class and compare results with the class' assessment of where things belong. Count and record the number of errors. Discuss the mistakes and place slips in the correct positions on the map. Inform the students that this activity will be repeated at the end of their study of this chapter.

Chapter 13 Reading Assignments

Objective 1   Student Ed. pp. 245–256
Objective 2   Student Ed. pp. 256–265

● Teaching   ■ Reinforcing   ★ Enriching

Unmarked activities deal with three or more features listed in the chapter objectives. Activities marked with the following letters deal with:
Ⓟ Physical features.
Ⓔ Economic features.
Ⓒ Cultural features.
Ⓗ Historical features.

Objective 1 Activities

● Objective 1 Teaching Activity

Obtain the *Area Handbooks* series on Mexico and other Central American countries from the United States Government Printing Office. Refer to the Suggested Resources in this Teacher Annotated Edition for the address. Hand out the booklets on Mexico, one to each student in the class. Reserve those on Central American countries for an Objective 2 activity.

Ask students to prepare an outline of the section on Mexico in their Student Edition. Under each heading, summarize material from the Student Edition. Use one page for each heading and subheading so that material may be added. Then have students read the handbook and add to each page of outlined material from the Student Edition any new information from the handbook. Review the summaries orally in class to be certain students have not omitted any important points. Discuss any new information from the handbooks that is not found in the Student Edition. Tell students to keep their outlines for study and review. You may wish to include material from the handbooks in your evaluation of this chapter or unit.

If for any reason you are unable to obtain the *Area Handbooks* as a resource, there are many other sources of information available. Most universities have Latin American study centers with materials available upon request. In addition, you may request materials from: Organization of American States, 19th Street and Constitution Avenue, Washington, D.C., 20036 (202) 789–3000; Stanford Program on International and Cross-Cultural Education (SPICE), 200 Lou Henry Hoover Building, Stanford University, Stanford, CA 94305–6012 (415) 723–1114; World Affairs Materials, Box 726, Kennett Square, PA 19348.

Refer students to the Chapter 13 Reading in the Teacher Resource Book for information related to this activity.

■ Objective 1 Reinforcing Activity   Ⓔ

Refer to the guidelines for discussion in the Instructional Approaches section of this Teacher Annotated Edition. Write the following heading on the chalkboard: "Mexico's Primary Economic Activities." Ask students to begin naming Mexico's economic activities, including any they may know about that are not mentioned in the text, or that they found in resource materials other than the Student Edition. Write their answers on the chalkboard under the heading. When the list is complete, discuss each item on the list with the class. Ask the following questions during the discussion: In what part of Mexico does this economic activity take place? Does the geography of the region play an important role in defining this economic activity? Explain.

★ **Objective 1 Enriching Activity** Ⓗ

Assign a book report on a topic related to the history of Mexico. Any period of history may be covered, ranging from pre-Columbian to the present. A committee might check the school library and the local public library for titles to prepare a list. Have students make their reports orally to the class.

Objective 2 Activities

● **Objective 2 Teaching Activity**

Use copies of the Area Handbooks from the United States Government Printing Office or other source material to perform the following activity. Also, refer to the guidelines for cooperative learning in the Instructional Approaches section of this Teacher Annotated Edition. Divide the class into groups, assigning each a country in Central America. Within the groups, assign individual members the investigation of the major physical, economic, cultural, or historical features of their country. When completed, have each group present a panel report on the country to the class.

Refer students to the Chapter 13 Reading in the Teacher Resource Book in relation to this activity.

★ **Objective 2 Enriching Activity**

Refer to the guidelines for role plays and simulations in the Instructional Approaches section of this Teacher Annotated Edition. Present the class with the following situation. The United States has just made a proposal to the government of Nicaragua for the building

of a new canal across its country. Appoint seven members of the class to role-play the decision-making committee. Other students in the class should be given roles, such as: (1) a Nicaraguan business executive who might report on the added income that the canal would bring to the country, (2) an engineer who might report on the advantage of either a sea level or locks canal, and (3) a politician who might feel that Nicaragua should own the new canal. Teachers may provide cards describing each role to help students decide upon their arguments. When all of the points of view have been expressed, the committee should vote whether or not to recommend construction of the new canal.

Refer students to Chapter 13 Skill Activity in the Teacher Resource Book for another related activity.

Objective 3 Activities

● **Objective 3 Teaching Activity** Ⓟ

After hanging a large map of Mexico and Central America in front of the class, divide the class into two teams. Ask each team one question at a time about the geography of Mexico and Central America. For example, you might ask for the name and location of Mexico's capital or for the location of the Sierra de Chiapas. Each team gets a question in turn. If one team answers the question incorrectly or is unable to answer it, the other team may try to answer the question. Each correct answer gives a team one point. Appoint a scorekeeper to keep track of the correct answers by team. The team with the greatest number of points wins.

■ **Objective 3 Reinforcing Activity**

On a large flat surface, such as wood or cardboard, have the class prepare a salt or papier mâché map of Mexico and Central America. The class may use paint and cutouts to show the countries' resources, products, population density, types of vegetation and landscapes, ethnic groups, and location of cities. In a class discussion, relate the information on the map to Mexico's population and economic problems, and any population or economic problems that may apply to the other countries of Central America. Compare the countries' geographic features.

Concluding Chapter 13

Repeat the Introducing Chapter 13 activity. Student knowledge should have benefited greatly from study of this chapter, and this should be reflected in a considerably reduced number of placement errors.

Next, give students a copy of a blank outline handout of this area from the Teacher Resource Book and have them fill in the same information as that contained on the slips of paper in the original activity, making certain that these maps are accurate. You may wish to make map tests a part of each regional chapter and unit evaluation. If so, inform students to reserve their maps for study and review.

ANSWERS TO CHAPTER 13 QUESTIONS

Content Check Questions
page 256

1. Refer to Section 1 content.
2. Refer to Glossary in Student Edition.
3. Dry or desert and rainy tropical moist. (p. 248)
4. Swampy, dotted with lagoons and sandbars. (p. 249) Southern part. (p. 248)
5. Decline in oil prices, expanding population, damage from earthquake, unemployment, foreign debt. (p. 252)
6. Answers will vary but should include the influences of the various groups who have had an effect on Mexican history including the Mexican Indians such as the Maya and Aztecs, the Spanish *mestizos*, Africans, and North Americans. (pp. 252–253, 255)

page 265

1. Refer to Section 2 content.
2. Refer to Glossary in Student Edition.
3. Nicaragua. Guatemala. (p. 256)
4. Tropical savanna and tropical rain forest. (p. 258)
5. Narrowest area. (pp. 260–261)
6. Many people think of Panamanian area as rightfully belonging to Colombia. (p. 265)
7. Answers should include the fact that changes in prices of coffee, bananas, and cotton can have a profound effect on their economies and markets are dependent upon open sea trade. (p. 259)

Special Feature Questions
page 254, Focus on History: "The Ancient Maya"

1. Yucatán peninsula in Mexico.
2. Numbering system was created that could accept anything from zero to millions.
3. Religion.

pages 262–263, Using Graphic Skills: "Analyzing Demographic Maps"

1. The central area of Mexico around Mexico City and the area in Central America where Guatemala, Honduras, and El Salvador join.
2. Above.
3. Because in an area closer to the Equator cooler and more comfortable climate conditions are found at a higher altitude and attract more people to live there.
4. It has a large population confined within a small area.
5. Because of its very small population.
6. Population distribution is heavier where the landscape is made up of highlands and at a relatively high altitude where the climate is cooler. Population distribution is lighter where the landscape is made up of desert, mountains, or low coastal areas and the climate is dry or tropical rain forest.

Photo/Illustration Caption Questions
page 246

Sierra de Chiapas. (p. 246)

81.9 million. (p. 246)

page 248

In the tropical moist climates south of the Tropic of Cancer. (p. 248)

Because of the city's location in the tierra fría climate zone at an elevation of 7,575 feet (2,308.9 m). (p. 248)

page 249

Along the coast. (p. 249)

page 250

The region contains good farming areas, large cities, the majority of the population, and the leading industrial cities are located in the region. (pp. 250–251)

page 251

Monterrey, Mexico City, Guadalajara. (p. 251)

page 252

Decline in world oil prices, expanding population, impact of 1985 Mexico City earthquake, emigration of wealth, unemployment, devaluation of currency, debt. (p. 252)

page 253

Nearly 300 years. (p. 253)

page 257

Belize, Guatemala, Honduras, El Salvador, Nicaragua, Costa Rica, Panama. (p. 256)

page 258

1976 in Guatemala; 1986 in El Salvador. (p. 258)

page 259

Coffee, sugar, seafood. (p. 259)

page 260

Guatemala and El Salvador. (p. 261)

page 261

The canal provides a direct crossing between the Atlantic Ocean and the Pacific Ocean. (pp. 260–261)

page 264

In the cool central highlands known as the Meseta Central. (p. 264)

Chapter 13 Review Questions
page 266, Reviewing Vocabulary

1. c h i c l e
2. m e s t i z o
3. p e n i n s u l a
4. l a d i n o s
5. b a u x i t e
6. t i e r r a f r í a
7. t i e r r a c a l i e n t e
8. c o l o n i e s   HONDURAS

pages 266–267, Remembering the Facts

1. Spain. (p. 245)
2. Lower. (p. 248)
3. The central plateau between the Sierra Madre Occidental and Sierra Madre Oriental mountain ranges. (p. 247)
4. Teotihuacán, Totonac, Zapotec, Maya. (p. 252)
5. Belize, Guatemala, Honduras, El Salvador, Nicaragua, Costa Rica, and Panama. (p. 256)
6. Farming. (p. 259)
7. Belize. (p. 261)
8. Costa Rica. (pp. 264–265)
9. Guatemala. (p. 261)

page 267, Understanding the Facts

1. Mexico's land increases in elevation from north to south. Elevations in the area of Mexico City are much higher than in northern Mexico. These higher elevations make for cooler temperatures. (pp. 247–248)
2. Most trading is done by train or truck with the U.S. (p. 250)
3. Many wealthy people are leaving the country, causing high unemployment, money with little value, and the need to borrow money from other countries. (p. 252)
4. Answers will vary but should include isolation because of the rugged land, similarity of products grown, political opposition to each other, few roads and railroads. (pp. 258–259)

5. Rugged and elevated. (p. 258)

6. Population density refers to the number of people per square mile or kilometer. Guatemala occupies a much larger land area than El Salvador. Though Guatemala's total population is larger than El Salvador's, its population is spread out across much more land area. For this reason, it is accurate to say that El Salvador is more densely populated. (pp. 256, 264)

page 267, Thinking Critically and Creatively

1. Answers will vary, but should include that a primary reason for building highways is to make shipment of goods easier. In the case of Central America, most trade has been ocean-going trade. These countries have had very little trade among themselves. Hence, there was little economic incentive to build expensive highways.

2. Answers will vary but should include Mexico's population has been growing very fast. A result has been a standard of living lower than that in the United States. People can make more money for the same work in the United States than in Mexico. The difference has been very important in drawing Mexicans' attention to the United States as a place to live and work.

3. Answers will vary but should state that climates were much more to their liking in the higher interior areas. Further, they found they could raise profitable crops in these areas where living conditions were more pleasant.

4. Answers will vary but should indicate that the United States was interested in building the Panama Canal. It was thought that permission could be obtained much easier from Panama than from Colombia.

5. Answers will vary but should include that Mexico has had a high birthrate for many years. Compare its birthrate of 31 per 1,000 to that of the United States at 16 per 1,000. Refer to the population pyramid diagram on page 115 that shows how a country with a rapid population growth shows a significant percentage of its population at younger ages. Morocco, shown on the population pyramid, and Mexico are also alike in that both countries have identical annual population growth percentages of 2.5%. (See National Profiles charts.)

6. Answers will vary but should include that El Salvador has so many people that its economy has a very difficult time providing work for all of them. There has been a tendency for people of El Salvador to "spill over" the border into neighboring countries. This produces resentment among workers in these countries. They feel jobs belonging to them are being taken away by people from El Salvador. This unwelcome migration has resulted in conflicts between El Salvador and its neighbors.

page 267, Reinforcing Graphic Skills

1. Plateau of Mexico. The land here is relatively flat, there is sufficient rainfall for growing crops, and there is a higher altitude and more comfortable climate.

2. The entire area is a coastal plain, some of which is tropical rain forest and other is near-desert.

3. Settlement along the coastlines of Mexico and Central America is lighter where the altitude is too high (mountains, uplands) or too low (coastal plains, lowlands). The terrain and climate associated with these coastal areas of Mexico and Central America discourage heavy settlement.

EVALUATING CHAPTER 13

World Geography: People and Places provides chapter tests to help evaluate student performance. To evaluate student mastery of Chapter 13, give students Chapter 13 Test from the Teacher Resource Book. This test may also be used for pretesting or retesting purposes. Other tests can be made from the questions available in the Test Generator Software.

Lesson Plan Suggestions—Chapter 13

Section 1   Mexico (pp. 245–256)

Chapter Objectives	Suggested Teaching Strategies	Review

1. describe the major physical, economic, cultural, and historical features of Mexico.	**Teacher Preparation**
	SE, Reading Assignment, pp. 245–256
	TAE, Unit 5 Suggested Resources
	    Unit 5 Overview, p. T151
	    Introducing Unit 5, pp. T151–T152
	    Chapter 13 Overview, p. T152
	    Introducing Chapter 13, p. T153
	TRB, Chapter 13 Teacher Notes: Section 1
	Teaching Options
	TAE, Introducing Unit 5, pp. T151–T152
	    Introducing Chapter 13, p. T153
	    Objective 1 Activities, pp. T153–T154
	TRB, Chapter 13 Teacher Notes: Section 1,
	    Extending the Lesson
	    Chapter 13 Reading
	TSP, Transparency 2
		SE, Content Check, p. 256

Section 2   Central America (pp. 256–265)

Chapter Objectives	Suggested Teaching Strategies	Review

2. describe the major physical, economic, cultural, and historical features of Central America.	**Teacher Preparation**
	SE, Reading Assignment, pp. 256–265
	TAE, Unit 5 Suggested Resources
	    Chapter 13 Overview, p. T152
	TRB, Chapter 13 Teacher Notes: Section 2
	Teaching Options
	TAE, Objective 2 Activities, p. T154
	TRB, Chapter 13 Teacher Notes: Section 2,
	    Extending the Lesson
	    Chapter 13 Reading
	    Chapter 13 Skill Activity
		SE, Content Check, p. 265

Skill Objective: analyze demographic maps.	SE, *Using Graphic Skills*, "Analyzing Demographic Maps," pp. 262–263	

Chapter 13 Review and Evaluation

Suggested Teaching Strategies	Review	Evaluation
TAE, Objective 3 Activities, pp. T154–T155 Concluding Chapter 13, p. T155	SE, Chapter 13 Review, pp. 266–267 TRB, Chapter 13 Review Worksheet	TRB, Chapter 13 Test Unit 5 Pretest, Map and Content Worksheets TG, Chapter 13

CHAPTER 14   THE CARIBBEAN

Student Edition pp. 268–287

CHAPTER 14 OBJECTIVES

At the conclusion of this chapter, students will be able to:

1. describe the major physical, economic, cultural, and historical features of the West Indies.
2. describe the major physical, economic, cultural, and historical features of the continental lands of the Caribbean.
3. summarize the chief geographic features of the Caribbean region.

CHAPTER 14 SKILL OBJECTIVE

After completing the *Using Graphic Skills* exercise in this chapter, the student should be able to read topographic maps.

CHAPTER 14 OVERVIEW

Some of the most beautiful areas of the world are located in the Caribbean region. Yet this region contains some of the poorest nations in the Latin American culture area. These developing countries have economies that range from one completely based on tourism and subsistence agriculture to one based on more advanced agricultural methods and some industrialization. Thus it is important to encourage a realistic portrayal of this varied land. It is home to people with origins from all over the world. It is also important for students to consider the role of these countries in the world today. The Caribbean region's stra-tegic location has implications for its future development.

The chapter breaks the region into two sections. *Section 1* describes the thousands of islands in the West Indies, concentrating primarily on three divisions—the Greater Antilles, the Lesser Antilles, and the Bahamas. *Section 2* discusses the continental lands at the northern part of South America, including Colombia, Venezuela, Guyana, Suriname, and French Guiana. A unique special feature of the chapter is a segment about the West Indian mongoose that was imported to control pests and became a pest himself.

CHAPTER 14 ACTIVITIES

Introducing Chapter 14

Ask a local travel agent for any advertising posters or brochures of the Caribbean area. Many cruise lines provide these for travel agencies. Some also can be found in magazines and newspapers. Bring some of these posters to class and display them around the room. Then pass out the brochures to students. Ask students to describe the landscapes and climate of the Caribbean region as shown on the posters and brochures. Ask what the advertisements say about life on the many islands. Do students think that a complete cultural picture of the region is shown? Why or why not? Tell students that they will find the answer to these questions as they study this chapter.

Chapter 14 Reading Assignments

Objective 1   Student Ed. pp. 269–281
Objective 2   Student Ed. pp. 281–285

● Teaching   ■ Reinforcing   ★ Enriching

Unmarked activities deal with three or more features listed in the chapter objectives. Activities marked with the following letters deal with:

(P) Physical features.
(E) Economic features.
(C) Cultural features.
(H) Historical features.

Objective 1 Activities

● Objective 1 Teaching Activity

Secure the supplementary map on the West Indies provided in the November 1987 edition of *National Geographic*, Volume 172, Number 51. Have students review the map, and then choose one of the countries identified and annotated on it. Tell students to make an illustration, write a brief story, or make a collage that uses the annotation as a foundation. When the projects are complete, display some of them throughout the classroom.

Refer students to Chapter 14 Reading in the Teacher Resource Book for additional information with regard to this activity.

■ Objective 1 Reinforcing Activity (H)

Have students create a time line of colonization of the West Indies by European countries. They should use their text as a foundation for the timeline, including Figure 14–3 on page 276. They may also want to research some of the information in other sources. Tell students to place the names of explorers and the European countries that colonized the Caribbean onto the time line. Then hold a discussion using the following questions as a guide: What was the first European country to influence the Caribbean? What other countries had colonies in the Caribbean? When did most of the Caribbean region gain independence? What countries have colonies in the Caribbean region today?

Objective 2 Activities

● Objective 2 Teaching Activity (P)

The climate of any equatorial region is affected by the elevation of the landscape. From sea level to around 3,000 feet (914.4 m) above sea level, the temperatures are generally warm, averaging 80°F (26.7°C) throughout the year. From 3,000 to 6,000 feet (914.4 to 1,828.8 m), daily average temperatures range from 65°F to 75°F (18.3°C to 23.9°C). From 6,000 to 10,000 feet (1,828.8 to 3,048 m), the range is from 55°F to 65°F (12.8°C to 18.3°C). Have students use an atlas to find cities on the continental lands that fit into this three-tiered breakdown. Then ask students: What kinds of vegetation and lifestyle are associated with these climate areas? In which city would you like to live, and why?

Refer students to Chapter 14 Skill Activity in the Teacher Resource Book for an activity related to this objective.

★ Objective 2 Enriching Activity (E)

Refer students to the map found on page 520 of the Student Edition, "Levels of Economic

Development." Point out some obstacles to economic growth, such as inability to support a large population, lack of education and technology, lack of natural resources, culture, religion, unstable or corrupt governments, and huge debts to other countries. Then ask students into which stage of economic development the continental lands of the Caribbean region fall. They should note that all fall into the developing nation categories. Explain that these categories are not fixed. They are simply groupings that describe the amount of economic growth that has taken place.

Objective 3 Activity

● **Objective 3 Teaching Activity**

Have students prepare a retrieval chart for the major geographic features of the countries of the Caribbean region. Students can review these charts when studying for their chapter test.

Concluding Chapter 14

Refer to the guidelines for role plays and simulations in the Instructional Approaches section of this Teacher Annotated Edition before directing this activity. Write the title "Important Roles in Caribbean History" on the chalkboard. Divide the class into six groups, assigning to each one of the following roles: (1) an Arawak Indian in Hispaniola, 1513; (2) a Spanish gold miner in Colombia, 1500; (3) a Caribbean pirate, 1600s; (4) the King of England, 1670; (5) owner of a sugar plantation in Cuba, 1827; and (6) a rebellious slave in Haiti, 1804. Write these questions on the board to help students identify information to use: What is the situation in your land and what caused it? What are likely to be the results? Finally, lead a class discussion in which students identify one or two characters that have had the most lasting effect upon the development of the Caribbean region.

ANSWERS TO CHAPTER 14 QUESTIONS

Content Check Questions
pages 280–281

1. Refer to Section 1 content.
2. Refer to Glossary in Student Edition.
3. Greater Antilles, Lesser Antilles, Bahamas. (p. 270)
4. Cuba. (pp. 271, 277)
5. Crops such as sugar, tobacco, cacao, and tourism. (p. 272)
6. Created slaves, first from Native Americans, later blacks from Africa. (p. 275)
7. Dutch trade threatened Spanish domination and distracted the Spanish. The French and English took advantage of Spain's distraction and weakening government to extend their colonization of the area. (p. 275)
8. A free and associated state, but people cannot vote for President, and the state does not have a voting representative in Congress. People are United States citizens and pay United States taxes. (p. 277)

9. Answers will vary but could include that Cuba's sugar business relied on slaves to be successful. Over-production caused sugar prices to decline, causing less to be produced; thus, the need for so many workers declined. (p. 276)

page 285

1. Refer to Section 2 content.
2. Refer to Glossary in Student Edition.
3. Colombia, Venezuela, Guyana, Suriname, French Guiana. (p. 281)
4. Colombia. (p. 281)
5. Highlands in the western half of the country. (p. 283)
6. Coffee. (p. 283)
7. Caracas. (p. 283)
8. Oil. (p. 284)
9. Hot, wet, tropical savanna. (p. 284)
10. Answers will vary but may state that oil helped develop an industrialized economy, both as resource and source of money.

Special Feature Questions
page 274, Focus on Geography: "Mongoose: Friend or Foe?"

1. A weasel-like small, meat-eating animal.
2. To get rid of rats that infested sugar fields.
3. Temporarily rid the land of rats; however, the mongoose became a threat because it started to destroy all chickens in the area.

page 278, Using Graphic Skills: "Reading Topographic Maps"

1. 750 meters. Northeast, east, and southwest of the town.
2. Northeast, southeast, and southwest.
3. Highways and roads, houses, buildings, church, cemetery, hospital, water plant, boundaries, contour lines, and elevation figures.
4. Buildings in the southern half of the area are located beside the highway and road.
5. Almost 2 miles.
6. Northwest, north, east, and south outside the city limits. These areas have low relief, indicating rather flat land surface that is the most suitable terrain for farming.

Photo/Illustration Caption Questions
page 270

Coastal plains. (p. 270)

page 271

Northeastern. (p. 271)

page 272

Goods bought by tourists and the money they spend on hotel rooms and food bring in much of the income for the people here. (p. 272)

page 273

Venezuela and Guyana; Suriname and French Guiana. (p. 273)

page 275

Indians, such as Arawaks and Caribs. (p. 275)

page 276

Cuba, Puerto Rico, Virgin Islands. (p. 276)

page 280

Coffee. (p. 280)

page 282

Cuba, Jamaica, Dominican Republic, Venezuela, Trinidad and Tobago, Guyana. (p. 282)

page 285

Jungle. (p. 284)

Chapter 14 Review Questions
page 286, Reviewing Vocabulary

1. Mulatto.
2. Archipelago.
3. Cays.
4. Cocaine.
5. Voodoo.
6. Abolition.

pages 286–287, Remembering the Facts

1. West Indies and continental lands of South America along the Caribbean. (p. 269)
2. Hispaniola. Haiti and Dominican Republic. (p. 269)
3. Cuba. (p. 271)
4. Plantation crops and tourism. (p. 272)
5. Haiti. (p. 280)
6. Sugarcane. (p. 279)
7. Subsistence farming. Roman Catholic. (p. 280)
8. Colombia. (p. 281)
9. Spanish. (pp. 283–284)
10. Magdalena and Orinoco. (pp. 281, 283)
11. Colombia. (p. 282)
12. Tropical. (p. 283)

page 287, Understanding the Facts

1. Greater are the larger islands that bind the Caribbean Sea to the north; lesser are the smaller ones that bind the Caribbean Sea on the east. (p. 269)
2. The positioning of the trade winds determines the amount of rainfall, which determines the side of the island people settled. (pp. 271–272)
3. The Caribbean Community and Common Market was set up to help the Caribbean nation countries cooperate economically instead of always trading with other countries. (p. 272)
4. Makes the Caribbean a haven for cruise ships, creates easy movement of trade to

the Panama Canal, closeness to the United States. (p. 272)

5. Cost of production is so high there is no demand to sell in other countries. (pp. 281–282)

6. Similar in land features, climates, and agriculture economies; differences are that each was settled by a different European country and people are from many different cultural backgrounds. (pp. 284–285)

page 287, Thinking Critically and Creatively

1. Many became sick and died; Spanish had to import labor from Africa.
2. Countries produce similar products so they have to go to the outside for goods they need.
3. Bases for trade in the West Indies and a base from which to attack Spanish ships.

4. As demand for sugar increased, plantations grew larger, and the number of slave workers increased.

5. Answers will vary but should stress that production amounts or crop failures determine the amount of profit or loss a nation faces that has no other major source of income.

6. Answers will vary but should point out the importance of elevation. The higher the elevation, the cooler the temperatures.

page 287, Reinforcing Graphic Skills

1. West Central.
2. 2.3 kilometers.
3. It is located in an area showing high relief, indicating a rugged land surface where the road has to curve around mountains.
4. 500 meters.

EVALUATING CHAPTER 14

World Geography: People and Places provides chapter tests to help evaluate student performance. To evaluate student mastery of Chapter 14, give students Chapter 14 Test from the Teacher Resource Book. This test may also be used for pretesting or restesting purposes. Other tests can be made from the questions available in the Test Generator Software.

Lesson Plan Suggestions—Chapter 14

SE—Student Edition TAE—Teacher Annotated Edition TG—Test Generator
TRB—Teacher Resource Book TSP—Transparency Package

Section 1 West Indies (pp. 269–281)

Chapter Objectives	Suggested Teaching Strategies	Review
1. describe the major physical, economic, cultural, and historical features of the West Indies.	**Teacher Preparation** SE, Reading Assignment, pp. 269–281 TAE, Unit 5 Suggested Resources 　　Chapter 14 Overview, p. T159 　　Introducing Chapter 14, p. T160 TRB, Chapter 14 Teacher Notes: Section 1	SE, Content Check, pp. 280–281

(Continued on next page.)

	Teaching Options	

Skill Objective: read topographic maps.	**Teaching Options**
	TAE, Introducing Chapter 14, p. T160
	    Objective 1 Activities, p. T160
	TRB, Chapter 14 Teacher Notes: Section 1,
	    Extending the Lesson
	    Chapter 14 Reading
	    Chapter 14 Skill Activity
	SE, *Using Graphic Skills*, "Reading
	    Topographic Maps," pp. 278–279	

Section 2   Continental Lands (pp. 281–285)

Chapter Objectives	Suggested Teaching Strategies	Review

2. describe the major physical, economic, cultural, and historical features of the continental lands of the Caribbean.	**Teacher Preparation**
	SE, Reading Assignment, pp. 281–285
	TAE, Unit 5 Suggested Resources
	    Chapter 14 Overview, p. T159
	    Introducing Chapter 14, p. T160
	TRB, Chapter 14 Teacher Notes: Section 2
	Teaching Options
	TAE, Introducing Chapter 14, p. T160
	    Objective 2 Activities, pp. T160–T161
	TRB, Chapter 14 Teacher Notes: Section 2,
	    Extending the Lesson
	    Chapter 14 Skill Activity
		SE, Content Check, p. 285

Chapter 14   Review and Evaluation

Suggested Teaching Strategies	Review	Evaluation
TAE, Objective 3 Activities, p. T161 Concluding Chapter 14, p. T161	SE, Chapter 14 Review, pp. 286–287 TRB, Chapter 14 Review Worksheet	TRB, Chapter 14 Test TG, Chapter 14

CHAPTER 15 SOUTH AMERICA: ATLANTIC NATIONS

Student Edition pp. 288–309

CHAPTER 15 OBJECTIVES

At the conclusion of this chapter, students will be able to:

1. describe the major physical, economic, cultural, and historical features of Brazil.
2. describe the major physical, economic, cultural, and historical features of Argentina.
3. describe the major physical, economic, cultural, and historical features of Paraguay and Uruguay.
4. summarize the chief geographic features of the Atlantic Nations region of South America.

CHAPTER 15 SKILL OBJECTIVE

After completing the *Using Graphic Skills* exercise in this chapter, the student should be able to read transportation maps.

CHAPTER 15 OVERVIEW

In this chapter, students are given the opportunity to discover the similarities and differences between those countries of South America that border the Atlantic Ocean, as well as Paraguay, a nation influenced by its link to the Atlantic by means of navigable rivers. The physical features and the climates of these nations vary greatly, due in part to the fact that they are located in many latitudes. In this chapter, Brazil, Argentina, Paraguay, and Uruguay are profiled in respect to physical, economic, cultural, and historical features, facilitating comparisons of these nations for the student. All of these features work together to influence the total portrait of each country with results as different as the ingredients that have combined to produce them. *Section 1* of this chapter discusses these features in relation to Brazil, *Section 2* in relation to Argentina, and *Section 3* covers both Paraguay and Uruguay.

Special chapter features provide background material in a *Strange But True* feature about the Manaus rubber boom and in *The Urban World* feature about the urban sprawl of Buenos Aires.

CHAPTER 15 ACTIVITIES

Introducing Chapter 15

Write the word "BRAZIL" on the chalkboard and ask the students to call out whatever comes to mind when they hear this name. Write their responses on the chalkboard. On another section, write the word "ARGENTINA" and follow the same procedure. Repeat with another section of chalkboard that is dedicated to Paraguay, and another to Uruguay. Any answer students may call out is valid. After students have exhausted their knowledge of these four countries, show them photographs that represent cities and regions of these nations. Ask students to guess what country each represents, and when the country has been identified, ask students if that photograph represents their ideas of the country and to explain why or why not. Go through the responses listed on the chalkboard and point out misconceptions. Inform the class that in reading this chapter, they should observe carefully which ideas they held in the past were incorrect. Have them copy the responses from the chalkboard and keep the lists for use in the Concluding Chapter 15 activity.

Chapter 15 Reading Assignments

● Teaching   ■ Reinforcing   ★ Enriching

Unmarked activities deal with three or more features listed in the chapter objectives. Activities marked with the following letters deal with:

Ⓟ Physical features.
Ⓔ Economic features.
Ⓒ Cultural features.
Ⓗ Historical features.

Objective 1 Activities

● Objective 1 Teaching Activity

Refer to the guidelines for audiovisuals in the Instructional Approaches section of this Teacher Annotated Edition, and show the film "Down the Amazon," one of the series *Flight of the Condor*, listed in the Suggested Resources in this Teacher Annotated Edition. Then, after students have read all material in this chapter related to Brazil, refer to the guidelines for cooperative learning in the Instructional Approaches section of this Teacher

Annotated Edition. Divide the class into four groups and assign each either the physical, economic, cultural, or historical features of Brazil. Have each group investigate the feature assigned to it by following procedures for cooperative learning. The *Area Handbooks* series from the Department of the Army, listed in the Suggested Resources for this unit in this Teacher Annotated Edition, might prove useful as supplements to material contained in the Student Edition.

Refer students to Chapter 15 Skill Activity in the Teacher Resource Book for another activity related to this objective.

■ Objective 1 Reinforcing Activity

Provide each student with an oversize sheet of paper, possibly from a sketch pad. Inform the students that they are to make a sketch of the map of Brazil large enough to fill the sheet of paper provided. Then, as they read the chapter, they are to sketch in on the map and label what the student text describes about the physical, economic, and cultural features of Brazil. At the end of the chapter, they will have a physical, political, and thematic map of the country. Each student should create a key for his or her map. Inform the class that making sketch maps and sketching in information on them is another form of note-taking that can be useful as a study technique, especially in the field of geography.

★ Objective 1 Enriching Activity

Refer to the guidelines for lecture in the Instructional Approaches section of this Teacher Annotated Edition, and prepare a lecture on the problems and controversies surrounding the destruction of the Amazon rain forests in Brazil. Provide the class with an outline of your lecture, and accompany the lecture with slides or photographs shown by means of an opaque projector. Explain the ecological function of a rain forest and its very important role in the production of oxygen for Earth and in the preserving of many life-forms.

After the lecture, ask students to look up and copy articles from books, newspapers, and magazines related to the subject. Based on what they have learned from the lecture and the articles, have students speculate about what can be done to prevent the loss of this vital resource. Students may wish to write letters to Brazilian representatives in the Organization of American States, to the Brazilian Embassy in Washington, D.C., and to world conservation organizations, to request information about what is being done and what they personally might do to contribute to a conservation program.

Create a bulletin board with articles from newspapers and magazines brought in by students, and include responses to any letters sent by the class. Encourage students to participate in conservation programs.

Objective 2 Activities

● Objective 2 Teaching Activity   Ⓔ

Refer to the guidelines for discussion in the Instructional Approaches section of this Teacher Annotated Edition, and lead the class in a discussion about the economy of Argentina. Begin by emphasizing the difference between a developed economy and the economy of a developing country. Explain that Argentina, unlike many other countries in Latin America, has a developed economy. Remind the class that Argentina's agriculture and livestock industries have made it a wealthy country, and that Argentina is a leading exporter of grain and meat. Ask students: How has Argentina's climate and geography contributed to its development? Are there other reasons beyond its physical geography that have contributed to its economic success? Lead students to understand that many developing nations have great resource potentials but have not used them. Ask students to speculate about the reasons for this. Tell them that, proportional to its population, Argentina has more physicians, dentists, and university students than any other Latin America country— even more than the United States. Food supply and life expectancy are higher in Argentina than in other Latin American countries. Have

them also consider Argentina's high literacy rate and its ethnic mix of peoples from many nations as possible factors contributing to economic development.

■ Objective 2 Reinforcing Activity

Have students create the same type of sketch map they prepared for Brazil showing Argentina's physical, economic, and cultural features. The key should be the same as the one used in their previous sketch map.

Refer students to the Chapter 15 Reading in the Teacher Resource Book for further information related to this activity.

Objective 3 Activities

● Objective 3 Teaching Activity

Explain to the class that as they read Section 3 about Paraguay and Uruguay, they will become aware of the extreme differences between these two countries. Refer to the guidelines for retrieval charts in the Instructional Approaches section of this Teacher Annotated Edition, and have students set up a chart that will aid them to contrast the physical, economic, cultural, and historical features of these two nations.

When the charts have been completed, discuss their contents in class. Ask students to explain why they believe there is such a disparity in the countries' features. Remind them to take into consideration all the geographical features of the two nations. Finally, ask students in which of the two countries, Paraguay or Uruguay, they would prefer to live, and why.

■ Objective 3 Reinforcing Activity

Have students create the same type of sketch map they prepared for the countries studied in the two previous sections, showing Uruguay's and Paraguay's physical, economic, and cultural features and again using the same key. Display the sketch maps around the classroom. Remind the students that these maps represent a type of note-taking that is valuable both to learn and review material. Return the maps in time for them to be used for review prior to evaluation.

Objective 4 Activities

● **Objective 4 Teaching Activity**

Divide the chalkboard into two sections. On one, place the heading "SIMILAR" and on the other, "DISSIMILAR." Consider all the nations studied in this chapter, and have the class call out ways in which they are similar and ways in which they are dissimilar. Write student responses in the appropriate sections. Consider all major physical, economic, cultural, and historical features. When all features have been covered, ask students to speculate about or explain reasons for these similarities and differences.

Refer students to Chapter 15 Skill Activity in the Teacher Resource Book for an activity related to this objective.

■ **Objective 4 Reinforcing Activity** Ⓗ

Ask students to prepare historical time lines designed to compare historical events of the countries studied in this chapter. Have them create four parallel time lines side by side. On the time lines, they should list events with a short summary of their importance. Explorers and leaders should be listed with one-sentence identifiers. Be certain that students read their Student Editions carefully in order to extract historical material that may be "hidden" in subsections not directly related to history. You may wish to make these time lines on the chalkboard as a class project, having the students copy them when they are complete. Or, each student may create his own, using his or her own format and possible illustrations.

★ **Objective 4 Enriching Activity**

Ask the class to find out about the music, art, and literature of Brazil, Argentina, Uruguay, and Paraguay. Have each student choose something to report on, making sure each investigates something different. After each student has made his or her report to the class with possible playing of music, showing of art, and reading of poems or passages, discuss with the class what they may see in the music, art, and literature of the countries that reflects influences of any aspect of their physical, economic, cultural, or historical background.

Concluding Chapter 15

Go through the responses copied from the chalkboard in the Introducing Chapter 15 activity. Discuss with the class how their ideas about the countries studied in this chapter have changed and review new things they have learned about them.

Make or have students working in groups divided according to country prepare a trivia game requiring answers about Brazil, Argentina, Paraguay, and Uruguay. Game cards could be prepared in advance as students read the chapter sections or as part of the chapter review. The questions should be in the categories of the features listed in each objective, that is, the physical, economic, cultural, and historical features of each nation. The game could be played with four groups competing. A large, cardboard trivia-type gameboard could be prepared and placed in the center of the classroom on a table or on the floor. A group captain from each group may be appointed to move the game pieces to their respective teams.

ANSWERS TO CHAPTER 15 QUESTIONS

Content Check Questions
page 298

1. Refer to Section 1 content.
2. Refer to Glossary in Student Edition.
3. There are lowland river basins, highlands with mountains and plateaus, as well as coastal plains. (p. 291)
4. Nearly all the country lies in the tropics and there are no extremes in elevation. (p. 292)
5. North, Northeast, Southeast, South, West Central. (pp. 292–293)
6. São Paulo, Rio de Janeiro. (p. 295)

7. As a commitment to settle the western highlands. (p. 295)
8. Portuguese. (p. 295)
9. Answers will vary but should stress that Brazil must import oil so they use surplus sugar cane to create alcohol fuel. (pp. 293, 297)

page 306

1. Refer to Section 2 content.
2. Refer to Glossary in Student Edition.
3. Patagonia, the rugged highlands. (p. 299)
4. The Pampas. (p. 301)
5. Grain (wheat and corn), cattle and sheep. (pp. 301–302)
6. Buenos Aires. (p. 301)
7. Provide electric power and water for irrigation; mining area; and a vacation area. (p. 303)
8. Answers will vary but should include some of these points. Britain, historically, was heavily involved in the development of Argentina. It was one of the first countries in the world to recognize Argentina's independence. British beef cattle provided the foundation for today's huge Pampas herds. British investors financed railroads to carry cattle and other agricultural goods to the port of Buenos Aires. In short, there had been a long, long history of cooperation between Argentina and Great Britain. (p. 303)

page 307

1. Refer to Section 3 content.
2. Refer to Glossary in Student Edition.
3. Paraguay. (p. 306)
4. Rolling plains and low hills. (p. 307)
5. Livestock products and goods manufactured from livestock. (p. 307)
6. Answers will vary but may include some of these points. Argentina and Brazil have large populations. It is likely that they might have conflicts resulting in difficulties along their border regions. Uruguay keeps a good distance between the densely populated parts of Argentina in and around Buenos Aires and people who are citizens of Brazil. The existence of Uruguay may have prevented conflicts between Argentina and Brazil as a result. The people of Brazil and Argentina are quite different. The languages of the two countries differ. There are numerous reasons why relations between the two countries from time to time might become strained.

Special Feature Questions
page 294, Strange But True: "Manaus Rubber Boom"

1. Rubber overshoes, Goodyear's process of vulcanization, rubber automobile tires.
2. People flocked to the city much like the "gold rush" of the American West.
3. Similar climates.

page 296, Using Graphic Skills: "Reading Transportation Maps"

1. Air; air and highway.
2. Railroad.
3. Southeast and South; these must be regions with large populations and cities, and relatively flat terrain for the construction of highways and railroads.
4. To link Brasília with Gôiania, which has an uninterrupted railroad link with São Paulo.
5. A city's population increases as a result of new people moving to the city. If a city is accessible by a variety of transportation routes, more people can reach the city. A city's economic growth depends on the ability to move products into and out of the city, for which transportation routes are necessary.

Photo/Illustration Caption Questions
page 290

Amazon. (p. 290)

page 291

4,000 miles (6,437.4 km). (p. 291)

page 292

Because of its location in the southern latitudes. (p. 292)

page 293

In the Northeast region. (p. 293)

page 295

1960. (p. 295)

page 298

The land is very rough, with many steep cliffs. Rivers and streams falling over these cliffs create waterfalls. (p. 299)

page 299

Chile. (p. 299)

page 301

One-third of Argentina's population. (p. 301)

page 302

Paraguay. (p. 302)

page 304

Argentina, Paraguay, Uruguay. (p. 304)

page 305

Brasília, Buenos Aires, Asunción, Montevideo. (p. 305)

Chapter 15 Review Questions
page 308, Reviewing Vocabulary

Sentences will vary.
v a q u e r o s;   l a n d l o c k e d;
e s c a r p m e n t;   c a a t i n g a;
a n a r c h y;   p a m p e r o s;
l o e s s;   t a n n i n.

pages 308–309, Remembering the Facts

1. Brazil, Argentina, Paraguay, Uruguay. (p. 289)
2. Brasília, Buenos Aires, Asunción, Montevideo. (p. 305, map)
3. Brazil. (p. 292)
4. Amazon. (p. 291)
5. Lowland river basins, highlands, coastal plains. (p. 291)
6. North, Northeast, Southeast, South, West Central. (pp. 292–293) Southeast. (p. 293)
7. São Paulo; Portuguese. (p. 295)
8. Pampas, Chaco and Mesopotamia, Patagonia, Andes. (pp. 298–299)
9. Pampas; Buenos Aires, where one-third of the population lives, is located here. (p. 301)
10. One of the highest in Latin America and one of the best in the world. (p. 303)
11. Mount Aconcagua; Argentina. (p. 299)
12. Paraguay. (p. 306)

page 309, Understanding the Facts

1. Areas are being developed on the frontier. (p. 292)
2. Nutrients in rain-forest soil are leached by heavy rains. (p. 293)
3. As a symbol for development and to encourage people to move inland. (p. 295)
4. Brazilians are a mixture of European, African, and Indian descent. (p. 295) Most Argentines are of European ancestry. (p. 303)
5. Its rich soil and mild climate make it suitable for human settlement, agriculture, and livestock. (pp. 301–302)
6. Cooler ocean-influenced air collides with warmer air overland. (p. 301)
7. Economic development is uneven. While some areas are industrial and urban, other areas are very little developed. (p. 297)
8. Paraguay is slowed by few resources, unemployment, and emigration. (p. 306) Uruguay is slowed by high prices, foreign debts, and emigration. (p. 307)

page 309, Thinking Critically and Creatively

1. Answers will vary but they may include some of these ideas: Major industrial powers tend to have very highly developed transportation, communication, and education systems in all parts of the country. While these are in place in parts of Brazil, by no means are they country-wide in their scope. Many areas of Brazil are very poor. These poor areas require funds from more well-to-do sections of the country. These funds are diverted from investment in industrial activity. Additionally, any new industrial competitor, such as Brazil, faces stiff competition in the world marketplace from already-industrialized nations of the world.

2. Answers will vary but should include that the mountain country of western Argentina has many hydroelectric plants. These plants send electricity to the heavily industrialized areas of the Pampas, especially to Buenos Aires and surrounding urban areas.

3. Answers will vary but should indicate that Brazil's mild climate and suitable terrain allow for sugarcane to be grown on a large scale. Further, there are relatively few sources of petroleum in Brazil. Though sugar beets can be grown in Argentina, the production of sugar is not as widespread here as in Brazil. Further, there have been some petroleum discoveries in Argentina in recent years. It simply has proved to be more cost-effective to experiment with alcohol in fuel in Brazil than in Argentina.

4. Answers will vary but some may logically argue that people in Uruguay are more similar to those in Argentina than to those in Brazil. For example, they speak Spanish, the language of Argentina. Also, people in Uruguay are heavily involved in cattle-raising, an extremely important economic activity in Argentina.

5. Answers will vary but should state that times were very bad for people in the cattle business. Because of the difficulty of getting beef out to England, there was a surplus. Prices fell. Many in the cattle business lost money.

page 309, Reinforcing Graphic Skills

1. São Paulo, Rio de Janeiro, Recife, Belem. São Paulo and Rio de Janeiro.

2. North and West. There are few people, few cities, and tropical rain forests in these parts of Brazil.

3. Ship. Answers will vary but may include that goods cannot be shipped directly to Brasília by sea, and that foreign products must be further transported to Brasília by means of air or highway routes adding to the cost. Added expenses for goods shipped by sea and then transshipped by air or overland could have an effect on Brasília's economic growth.

EVALUATING CHAPTER 15

World Geography: People and Places provides chapter tests to help evaluate student performance. To evaluate student mastery of Chapter 15, give students Chapter 15 Test from the Teacher Resource Book. This test may also be used for pretesting or retesting purposes. Other tests can be made from the questions available in the Test Generator Software.

Lesson Plan Suggestions—Chapter 15

SE—Student Edition   TAE—Teacher Annotated Edition   TG—Test Generator
TRB—Teacher Resource Book   TSP—Transparency Package

Section 1   Brazil (pp. 289–298)

Chapter Objectives	Suggested Teaching Strategies	Review
1. describe the major physical, economic, cultural, and historical features of Brazil.	**Teacher Preparation** SE, Reading Assignment, pp. 289–297 TAE, Unit 5 Suggested Resources	SE, Content Check, p. 298

(Continued on next page.)

	Chapter 15 Overview, p. T165 Introducing Chapter 15, pp. T165–T166 TRB, Chapter 15 Teacher Notes: Section 1 **Teaching Options** TAE, Introducing Chapter 15, pp. T165–T166 Objective 1 Activities, pp. T166–T167 TRB, Chapter 15 Teacher Notes: Section 1, Extending the Lesson Chapter 15 Skill Activity
Skill Objective: read transportation maps.	SE, *Using Graphic Skills,* "Reading Transportation Maps," p. 296

Section 2   *Argentina (pp. 298–306)*

Chapter Objectives	Suggested Teaching Strategies	Review
2. describe the major physical, economic, cultural, and historical features of Argentina.	**Teacher Preparation** SE, Reading Assignment, pp. 298–306 TAE, Unit 5 Suggested Resources Chapter 15 Overview, p. T165 TRB, Chapter 15 Teacher Notes: Section 1 **Teaching Options** TAE, Objective 2 Activities, p. T167 TRB, Chapter 15 Teacher Notes: Section 2, Extending the Lesson Chapter 15 Reading Chapter 15 Skill Activity	SE, Content Check, p. 306

Section 3   *Paraguay and Uruguay (pp. 306–307)*

Chapter Objectives	Suggested Teaching Strategies	Review
3. describe the major physical, economic, cultural, and historical features of Paraguay and Uruguay.	**Teacher Preparation** SE, Reading Assignment, pp. 306–307 TAE, Unit 5 Suggested Resources Chapter 15 Overview, p. T165 TRB, Chapter 15 Teacher Notes: Section 3 **Teaching Options** TAE, Objective 3 Activities, p. T167 TRB, Chapter 15 Teacher Notes: Section 3, Extending the Lesson Chapter 15 Skill Activity	SE, Content Check, p. 307

Chapter 15 *Review and Evaluation*

Suggested Teaching Strategies	Review	Evaluation
TAE, Objective 4 Activities, p. T168 Concluding Chapter 15, p. T168 TSP, Transparency 2	SE, Chapter 15 Review, pp. 308–309 TRB, Chapter 15 Review Worksheet	TRB, Chapter 15 Test TG, Chapter 15

CHAPTER 16 SOUTH AMERICA: ANDEAN NATIONS

Student Edition pp. 310–329

CHAPTER 16 OBJECTIVES

At the conclusion of this chapter, students will be able to:

1. describe the major physical, economic, cultural, and historical features of Chile.
2. describe the major physical, economic, cultural, and historical features of Peru.
3. describe the major physical, economic, cultural, and historical features of Bolivia and Ecuador.
4. summarize the chief geographic features of the Andean Nations of South America.

CHAPTER 16 SKILL OBJECTIVE

After completing the *Using Graphic Skills* exercise of this chapter, the student should be able to analyze bar graphs.

CHAPTER 16 OVERVIEW

The foundation of Chapter 16 is the Andes mountain range that stretches from the Caribbean Sea to the tip of South America. The Andes, with their massive height and length, play a major role in the geography of the countries that make up this region of South America, namely Chile, Peru, Bolivia, and Ecuador. From climate and land use patterns to transportation and communication linkages, the Andes influence daily life. Thus *Section 1* describes the physical, economic, cultural, and historical foundations of the largest country in the region, Chile. Peru's geography is described in *Section 2*. Bolivia and Ecuador are studied together in *Section 3*. A special feature of the chapter focuses on Cape Horn.

CHAPTER 16 ACTIVITIES

Introducing Chapter 16

Ask students to describe some of the effects of living on or near a mountain range. Discuss some of these, such as rugged terrain, colder temperatures as elevation increases, amount of rainfall on both sides of a mountain range, flow of water, types of resources usually found in mountainous regions, types of economic activity, transportation problems, population density, and any historical effects of having mountains as a natural barrier. Write student responses on the chalkboard, then have them copy these responses in their notebooks. Tell students that the countries in the region they are now studying have been grouped together because of the effects of the mountains on the life of the people who live there. As they study this region, tell them to periodically check to compare the actual result of living in mountainous areas with their previous ideas about the effects of mountains on the lifestyles of people.

Chapter 16 Reading Assignments

Objective 1   Student Ed. pp. 311–317
Objective 2   Student Ed. pp. 317–322
Objective 3   Student Ed. pp. 323–327

● Teaching	■ Reinforcing	★ Enriching

Unmarked activities deal with three or more features listed in the chapter objectives. Activities marked with the following letters deal with:
Ⓟ   Physical features.
Ⓔ   Economic features.
Ⓒ   Cultural features.
Ⓗ   Historical features.

Objective 1 Activities

● Objective 1 Teaching Activity   Ⓟ
Chile's diverse landscape provides a foundation for students to create a topographic map.

Prior to this activity, have the necessary materials on hand for making salt maps. Divide the class into small groups. Have each group make a salt map of Chile. Tell students to try to show some of the unique physical regions of the country on the map. After the maps are complete, have a spokesperson from each group describe a special feature of Chile's landscape as shown on the group's map.

■ Objective 1 Reinforcing Activity
Direct students to the maps found in the chapter. Using the maps, have students list everything indicated on the maps that refer to Chile. Once the lists are complete, have students group the items on the list according to the following characteristics: physical, economic, cultural, and political. Have students copy their lists in their notebooks. Then have students write a paragraph describing each aspect of Chile's geography.

Objective 2 Activities

● Objective 1 Teaching Activity
Ask students to note some topic sentences about Peru. Write on the chalkboard, "PERU HAS" and list students' contributions from the text. For example, sentences may include some of the following:

. . . the largest land area of the Andean Nations.
. . . many rich natural resources.
. . . a diverse climate.
. . . one of the world's leading fishing industries.
. . . a large Indian population.
. . . subsistence farmers.
. . . roads that need repair.

Allow time for the class to thoroughly discuss each of the statements, citing examples and asking questions for further inquiry. Have students organize the statements on the chalkboard into a descriptive paragraph about Peru.

■ Objective 2 Reinforcing Activity

Explain to the students that not only do the Andes mountains of Peru physically divide the country, they also act as an economic and cultural barrier. Ask the class to read Section 2 to get information about this observation, then hold a class discussion on the topic. As a final question, ask students the following: What is being done by the government of Peru to help bring the people closer together and help them have a higher standard of living? List student responses on the chalkboard and have them write the responses in their notebooks. Conclude this activity with Chapter 16 Reading in the Teacher Resource Book.

★ Objective 2 Enriching Activity Ⓗ Ⓒ

Have students read extensively about the Inca empire's rise and decline. Then, assign a one-page story about the feelings of an Inca who lived during the time of the Spanish conquest. Students can choose to tell the story from the point of view of a child, teenager, adult, grandparent, warrior, government official, farmer, or any particular person that comes to mind from their research. Once the stories are complete, share some of them with the rest of the class.

Objective 3 Activities

● Objective 3 Teaching Activity

Have students make a retrieval chart that analyzes the similarities and differences between the geography of Bolivia and that of Ecuador. Make sure that students include the five major divisions of landscape, climate, economy, culture, and historical influences on their charts. Once the charts are complete, hold a discussion clarifying any misconceptions held by students previously.

★ Objective 3 Enriching Activity Ⓒ

Have students research a cultural aspect of Bolivia or Ecuador by finding a cultural resource such as a poem, a song, an example of a piece of art, or sculpture. They should prepare a short (one- or two-minute) descriptive oral report on their cultural item. As they finish their reports, place some of the objects around the room. Items such as songs or poems could be copied and glued to cardboard or art paper to facilitate display.

Objective 4 Activities

● Objective 4 Teaching Activity

Have students design and construct a book jacket for a new travel book on one of the countries in this chapter. Students can cut out a magazine picture or draw a graphic illustration for the outside jacket. They will need to write a back cover blurb that will interest readers in opening the book. This blurb should mention some of the highlights in the travel guide. When finished, have students pass their jackets around so that others can see and read each one. Point out the types of photographs used on the jackets. Discuss the jackets of each country.

★ Objective 4 Enriching Activity Ⓔ

Divide students into four groups, assigning to each group one of the countries in this chapter. Have students assume the roles of economic analysts responsible for presenting the economic problems of their country at a meeting of the World Bank Organization. If the presentations are convincing, they will be awarded financial aid to solve economic problems. Begin by having each group review the chapter content and make a list of economic problems of its country. When the list is completed, the group should rank the problems with number one being the worst economic problem. As each presentation is given, write the lists on the board. After each country has been presented, lead a discussion based on these questions, "What problems are common to each country?" "What problems are unique to each country?" "What possible solutions do you see to these problems?" Discuss student responses.

Concluding Chapter 16

Have students choose a state located in the Rocky Mountain region of the United

States. Tell them to prepare a one-page comparison between that state and one of the countries in the Andean region of South America. Students should start their paper by completing the following statement: "The surprising difference (or similarity) between _____ (state) and _____ (country) is . . . ." Students can use information from Unit 4 in the Student Edition or from any other available resource.

ANSWERS TO CHAPTER 16 QUESTIONS

Content Check Questions
page 317

1. Refer to Section 1 content.
2. Refer to Glossary in Student Edition.
3. Mountains, desert, steppe, lowland. (pp. 312–313)
4. Wind patterns and the nearness of the Pacific Ocean. (p. 313)
5. Desert dry, steppe, Mediterranean, middle-latitude marine. (p. 313)
6. Desert North. Copper. (p. 315)
7. It is highly unlikely. Nitrates dissolve in water. The Los Canales region has much surface water. Nitrates would have been dissolved and washed away. (pp. 313, 315)

page 322

1. Refer to Section 2 content.
2. Refer to Glossary in Student Edition.
3. The Andes Highlands in the central part of the country, a desert coastal plain west of the Andes, and a lowland river basin east of the mountains. (p. 317)
4. A desert plain traversed by rivers; cool. (p. 318)
5. Attracts large numbers of fish to feed on it, making Peru a leading fishing nation and exporter of fish meal. (p. 319)
6. Agriculture and mining. (p. 319)
7. The two areas are separated by the steep Andes Mountains, and the country's major highway runs only north-south. (p. 320)
8. There are large numbers of Indians and mestizos, a much smaller group of people of pure European descent, and small numbers of people of African and Asian descent. (pp. 320–321)
9. The distinct physical characteristics of each region determine to a great extent what types of economic activity are possible there.

page 327

1. Refer to Section 3 content.
2. Refer to Glossary in Student Edition.
3. La Paz and Sucre. (p. 323)
4. Tin. (p. 325)
5. There is not good access between the lowlands and the highlands where most of the people presently live. (p. 325)
6. Highlands. (p. 325)
7. Coastal plain, Andes Highlands, tropical rain forests. (pp. 326–327)
8. Farming. (p. 327)
9. Oil. (p. 327)
10. Answers will vary but should include: All export goods must be shipped through territory of other nations, and so landlocked nations must be on good terms with their neighbors who have access to the sea. Also, landlocked countries have little control over freight rates in the parts of other nations through which their products must pass. Because imports must be off-loaded from ships and then delivered by truck or rail to the landlocked country, the costs for imported goods are often higher than they would be if there were direct sea access. Overall, landlocked countries, such as Bolivia, tend to pay higher transportation costs for exporting and importing goods.

Special Feature Questions
page 314, Focus on Geography: "Cape Horn"

1. The narrow passages are filled with icebergs, and the weather is often stormy.

2. The area is far south of the Equator, and not too far north of the Antarctic Circle.
3. Over 9,300 miles (14,967 km) are saved.

page 324, Using Graphic Skills: "Analyzing Data from Bar Graphs"

1. Chile.
2. Mestizo. About 7.6 million.
3. Chile. Bolivia.
4. Peru. Though Bolivia has a higher percentage of people who are Indians, the country has a much smaller total population than Peru. 55% of Bolivia's population (6.5 million) equals a total of about 3.6 million Indians. 45% of Peru's population (20.7 million) equals a total of about 9.3 million Indians.
5. Ecuador. Bolivia. Answers will vary but may include these points: Ethnic diversity provides a variety of cultural richness that other groups within a country can take advantage of (e.g. food, music, art). It also makes people tolerant of differences in their own and others' countries. On the other hand, people may become too closely identified with their own ethnic group and have little sense of national identity or unity.

Photo/Illustration Caption Questions
page 312

Andes Highlands. (p. 312)

page 315

Valparaiso is an important port city.
Concepción is an important industrial city. (p. 315)

page 316

Chile. (p. 316)

page 318

It is the world's highest navigable body of water. (p. 318)

page 319

Bolivia and Chile. (p. 319)

page 320

Oil. (p. 320)

page 321

About 1200 A.D. (p. 321)

page 322

Conquered the Incas, decimated the Indian population through diseases, introduced African slavery. (p. 322)

page 323

Bolivia. (p. 323)

page 325

When world prices of the export drop, the economy suffers. (p. 325)

page 326

Guayaquil. (p. 326)

Chapter 16 Review Questions
page 328, Reviewing Vocabulary

1. a.
2. k.
3. h.
4. e.
5. d.
6. c.
7. g.
8. l.
9. f.
10. i.

page 328, Remembering the Facts

1. Atacama Desert. (p. 312)
2. Lumber and dairy farming. (p. 315)
3. Peru. (p. 317)
4. The Incas. (p. 321)
5. Bolivia. (p. 323)
6. Tropical rain forests. (p. 327)

page 329, Understanding the Facts

1. Water always flows from higher elevations to lower elevations. It flows from high mountains in Eastern Chile west to the Pacific coast. (p. 313)
2. Transportation is difficult because of the many waterways that cut through the region, and it is not a rich agricultural section. (p. 315)
3. It has given Chile continued access to valuable nitrate deposits. (p. 317)
4. Peru has built a new oil pipeline and railroad to the Pacific coast, a new highway that is encouraging farming along the eastern slopes of the Andes, and a water project

that brings Amazon headwaters into streams flowing toward the Pacific. (p. 320)

5. This region supports the greatest amount of economic activity. There are fertile and productive areas in this generally very dry section. Fishing and industries based on iron and steel products are located here. The climate supports growth of many agricultural crops. (pp. 318–319)

6. During Spanish colonial rule, land ownership remained in European hands. Indians were subservient to Europeans whose descendants continued to govern and control the country's wealth. (p. 321)

7. Oil has been discovered here. Ecuador has enjoyed income from its export. (p. 327)

page 329, Thinking Critically and Creatively

1. Answers will vary but some of these ideas may be included: the nitrates industry could be wiped out; nitrates are water-soluble and could simply be washed away; if moisture persisted, agricultural activities might expand in this region; few flourish there now because of a lack of water.

2. Answers will vary but some of these ideas should be included: The *Los Canales* section is a land of inlets, rivers, and waterways; the land in this region is broken up by intrusions of water of various kinds; thousands of bridges would have to be built along any freeway route; the water problem is so severe that such a highway probably would be prohibitively expensive to build.

3. Answers will vary but should state that Chile has a much more diversified economy than Bolivia. Though copper is Chile's most important export, the nation's agricultural producers and domestic manufacturers provide income to the nation from other sources. A drop in copper prices does not hurt Chile, since the country has other income sources. Bolivia, on the other hand, has few developed industries. Farming income is not nearly so great as in Chile. The sale of tin is much more critical to Bolivia's overall economic well-being than the sale of copper is to Chile's.

4. Answers will vary but should indicate that the best answer to the question is probably Ecuador. Answers will vary but should include that though all these countries produce some oil, it is especially important to Ecuador's economy. It accounts for about half of its income. Hence, a drop in price can have very serious consequences.

5. Answers will vary but should state that Quito is located at a much higher elevation than Guayaquil. This elevation keeps temperatures quite cool. Bananas require warm weather. It is too cold for them to be grown in Quito.

page 329, Reinforcing Graphic Skills

1. Chile and Ecuador.

2. Africans and Asians. Answers will vary but may include these points: Ecuador has a larger percentage of other ethnic groups, perhaps because African descendants of the original slaves did not intermarry with other ethnic groups in Ecuador to the extent they did in other Andean countries. Also, some Africans would have settled in separate areas that remained isolated due to Ecuador's high terrain that discourages travel from one area to another. Any Asian who came to Ecuador, because it was close to the ocean and accessible for immigrants, probably did not intermarry with other groups and settled in isolated areas on the coast or further inland. As a result, both Africans and Asians maintained separate ethnic identities to a greater degree in Ecuador than elsewhere. Bolivia has no significant number of other ethnic groups because African slavery never took root there. Also, Bolivia's location further inland and its high physical terrain discouraged immigration by Asians or other groups. Therefore, Africans and Asians never became a significant part of Bolivia's population.

EVALUATING CHAPTER 16

World Geography: People and Places provides chapter tests to help evaluate student performance. To evaluate student mastery of Chapter 16, give students Chapter 16 Test from the Teacher Resource Book. This test may also be used for pretesting or retesting purposes. Other tests can be made from the questions available in the Test Generator Software.

Lesson Plan Suggestions—Chapter 16

SE—Student Edition   TAE—Teacher Annotated Edition   TG—Test Generator
TRB—Teacher Resource Book   TSP—Transparency Package

Section 1   Chile *(pp. 311–317)*

Chapter Objectives	Suggested Teaching Strategies	Review
1. describe the major physical, economic, cultural, and historical features of Chile.	**Teacher Preparation** SE, Reading Assignment, pp. 311–317 TAE, Unit 5 Suggested Resources 　　Chapter 16 Overview, p. T173 　　Introducing Chapter 16, p. T174 TRB, Chapter 16 Teacher Notes: Section 1 **Teaching Options** TAE, Introducing Chapter 16, p. T174 　　Objective 1 Activities, pp. T174 TRB, Chapter 16 Teacher Notes: Section 1, 　　Extending the Lesson 　　Chapter 16 Skill Activity	SE, Content Check, p. 317

Section 2   Peru *(pp. 317–322)*

Chapter Objectives	Suggested Teaching Strategies	Review
2. describe the major physical, economic, cultural, and historical features of Peru.	**Teacher Preparation** SE, Reading Assignment, pp. 317–322 TAE, Unit 5 Suggested Resources 　　Chapter 16 Overview, p. T173 TRB, Chapter 16 Teacher Notes: Section 2 **Teaching Options** TAE, Objective 2 Activities, pp. T174–T175 TRB, Chapter 16 Teacher Notes: Section 2, 　　Extending the Lesson 　　Chapter 16 Reading 　　Chapter 16 Skill Activity	SE, Content Check, p. 322

Chapter Objectives	Suggested Teaching Strategies	Review

3. describe the major physical, economic, cultural, and historical features of Bolivia and Ecuador.	**Teacher Preparation**
	SE, Reading Assignment, pp. 323–327
	TAE, Unit 5 Suggested Resources
	    Chapter 16 Overview, p. T173
	TRB, Chapter 16 Teacher Notes: Section 3
	Teaching Options
	TAE, Objective 3 Activities, p. T175
	TRB, Chapter 16 Teacher Notes: Section 3,
	    Extending the Lesson
	    Chapter 16 Skill Activity
		SE, Content Check, p. 327

Skill Objective: analyze data from bar graphs.	SE, *Using Graphic Skills*, "Analyzing Data from Bar Graphs," p. 324	

Chapter 16   Review and Evaluation

Suggested Teaching Strategies	Review	Evaluation

TAE, Objective 4 Activities,
    p. T175
    Concluding Chapter 16,
    pp. T175–T176
TSP, Transparency 2
	SE, Chapter 16 Review, pp. 328–329
	TRB, Chapter 16 Review
	    Worksheet
		TRB, Chapter 16 Test
		    Unit 5 Posttest, Map and
		    Content Worksheets
		TG, Chapter 16

Unit 5   Review and Evaluation

Suggested Teaching Strategies	Review	Evaluation
TAE, Concluding Unit 5, p. T180 TRB, Unit 5 Career Worksheet	SE, Unit 5 Review, pp. 330–331	TRB, Unit 5 Exam

CONCLUDING UNIT 5

Distribute outline maps of Latin America like those used in the Introducing Unit 5 activity. Ask students to fill in the same information as requested then without using the text or reference materials. When the maps are completed, ask students to compare them to the wall map of Latin America and to the ones they made before they began their study of this unit.

Discuss with students how their knowledge and perception of Latin America have changed and ask them in what areas their ideas have changed the most. Ask them what they have learned that has given them a better global viewpoint of this world area. Then, assign each student a country of Latin America about which to prepare a two-minute oral report. Inform students that each report should include physical, historical, economic, and cultural aspects of the assigned country.

As an outside project, students might enjoy making a jigsaw puzzle map of Latin America on posterboard or heavy cardboard with each country representing a piece of the puzzle. Making and putting these maps together would be a learning technique useful for memorizing countries' names and locations. Students should bring in their completed jigsaw puzzle maps for use in games and activities in class. If a student has a parent or friend who does woodwork and several students wish to undertake such a project under adult supervision, they could make a large jigsaw map in wood of Latin America that could be displayed on a table in the classroom. Painting the map could be a whole class project. One possible use of the map in the classroom would be to play a game in which competing teams would race against the clock in putting the map together. Another would be to mix the puzzle pieces up in a box, ask one student at a time to select a piece from the container, identify the country and give two facts about it. This may also be done as a game in teams, eliminating those people who are unable to respond. The team wins that has the most team members left.

Have students complete the Unit 5 Careers Worksheet in the Teacher Resource Book. Students with a special interest in this career may investigate further and make special reports.

Unit 5 Exam in the Teacher Resource Book may be administered.

UNIT 5 REVIEW QUESTIONS

Page 330, Thinking About the Unit

1. Answers will vary. Some students will suggest a single culture area because of the Spanish language, Catholic religion, Indian civilizations, European colonialism and especially Spanish colonization, ethnically mixed populations, the predominance of agriculture, and unstable governments found in both Middle America and South America. Other students will suggest two culture areas because Middle America is a collection of small countries whereas South America is composed of large nations; English, French, Dutch, and United States influence also entered into Middle America whereas only the Iberian countries were involved in South America; Indian populations make up a more significant percentage of the total population in South America than they do in Middle America; economies are more diversified in countries that are located in South America than in those in Middle America.

2. (a) Boston. (b) Buenos Aires. (c) Washington, D.C. at 77°0′W longitude is farther west than Lima at 76°55′W longitude. (d) Belmopan, Belize. (e) São Paulo, Brazil. (f) Guayaquil, Ecuador.

UNIT 6 EUROPE

Student Edition pp. 332–425

UNIT 6 GOALS

At the conclusion of this unit, students will be able to:
1. describe the unique cultural contributions the two culture areas of Europe have made to the rest of the world.
2. compare the physical, economic, and cultural patterns of Europe's four regions.

UNIT 6 SKILL OBJECTIVE

After completing the *Developing Graphic Skills* exercise in this unit, the student should be able to make comparisons.

UNIT 6 OVERVIEW

In the sixth unit of study in *World Geography: People and Places*, Europe is divided into four regions—Northwest Europe, Mediterranean Europe, Eastern Europe, and the Soviet Union. Despite the fact that more of the Soviet Union's land area lies on the eastern side of the Ural Mountains, the traditional dividing line between Europe and Asia, the Soviet population and its cultural heartland lie in Europe. This produces a national character more European than Asian.

In this unit, students will study the many geographic features that distinguish the two major world culture areas and 33 countries that are a part of them. Such features have fostered the development of many separate cultures. These countries have had a profound impact on the rest of the world.

From the warm, sunny beaches of the Iberian Peninsula to the cold, frozen flatlands of Siberia, students examine Europe's physical, economic, cultural, and geographic features. Thus, *Chapter 17* focuses on the countries in Northwest Europe, *Chapter 18* on those in Mediterranean Europe, *Chapter 19* on those in Eastern Europe, and *Chapter 20* on the Soviet Union. Upon completion of this unit, students should have obtained a greater understanding of the continent's features and its influences on the global culture.

INTRODUCING UNIT 6

Have students identify nations from which their ancestors came, locating the nations on a wall map. Ask students when most of the Europeans emigrated to the United States. Then have students turn to the patterns of immigration to the United States during selected periods of history found on page 213 of the Student Edition. Ask students to describe similarities and differences between the different periods. Point out that by the 1970s, Latin Americans and Asians had replaced Europeans as the largest groups of immigrants.

CHAPTER 17 NORTHWEST EUROPE

Student Edition pp. 334–357

CHAPTER 17 OBJECTIVES

At the conclusion of this chapter, students will be able to:

1. describe the major physical, economic, cultural, and historical features of the British Isles.
2. describe the major physical, economic, cultural, and historical features of France.
3. describe the major physical, economic, cultural, and historical features of West Germany.
4. describe the major physical, economic, cultural, and historical features of the Benelux countries, Norden, and the Alpine countries.
5. summarize the chief geographic features of Northwest Europe.

CHAPTER 17 SKILL OBJECTIVE

After completing the *Using Graphic Skills* exercise in this chapter, the student should be able to make generalizations.

CHAPTER 17 OVERVIEW

In this chapter, the student is introduced to Northwest Europe, a small, densely populated area of the world that is rich in natural resources and physical beauty. At its zenith, the region of 17 countries dominated large parts of the world and led the way to the industrial age. Although the countries of Northwest Europe are no longer the economic and political superpowers of days past, the region still has abundant resources, strong political leadership, and economies that are among the best developed in the world. Northwest Europe continues to exercise an important influence in global affairs.

Section 1 of the chapter concentrates on the geography of the British Isles, Europe's largest group of islands. *Section 2* includes a study of France, as well as the two small countries located along its southern borders—Monaco and Andorra. *Section 3* provides a study of the major geographic features of West Germany, and *Section 4* focuses upon the other countries of Northwest Europe. Special features of the chapter include a *Strange But True* segment about the discovery of bananas growing in Great Britain and an urban feature that describes the cultural aspects of London, England.

CHAPTER 17 ACTIVITIES

Introducing Chapter 17

Using a world map, point out to students cities along the 50°N latitude line in North America and cities along this line in Northwest Europe. Then have students use an atlas to find the average yearly temperatures of a few of the cities. Ask students to speculate about why temperatures are colder on the North American continent than they are in Northwest Europe along the same line of latitude.

Explain that Northwest Europe's closeness to the ocean helps warm temperatures over the region and keeps the region within a mild climate zone. Warm air blowing over the North Atlantic Current from the sea toward the land moderates the climate. Chapter 17 Skill Activity in the Teacher Resource Book may be used with this activity.

Chapter 17 Reading Assignments

Objective 1	Student Ed. pp. 335–343
Objective 2	Student Ed. pp. 343–347
Objective 3	Student Ed. pp. 347–352
Objective 4	Student Ed. pp. 352–355

● Teaching	■ Reinforcing	★ Enriching

Unmarked activities deal with three or more features listed in the chapter objectives. Activities marked with the following letters deal with:

- Ⓟ Physical features.
- Ⓔ Economic features.
- Ⓒ Cultural features.
- Ⓗ Historical features.

Objective 1 Activities

● Objective 1 Teaching Activity Ⓒ

Write some of the vocabulary from Section 1 on the chalkboard, such as moor, loch, glen, firth, and peat bog. Then read a story that describes an English, Scottish, or Irish countryside to create for students a sense of the surroundings in the lives of the people. The writings of James Herriot are often especially appealing to students. If these are not available, ask a librarian to assist you in finding an interesting story for students. After you have read the story, ask students to draw a scene that depicts some of the landscape described by the story so that the drawings are visible while students work through the chapter. Display some of these drawings around the room. Chapter 17 Reading in the Teacher Resource Book may be used after students have completed this activity.

★ Objective 1 Enriching Activity Ⓔ

The Industrial Revolution had a major impact on the geography of the British Isles. During this time, towns and cities sprang up where factories were built. Modern inventions brought more people out of rural areas into these towns and cities. Find a history textbook and read excerpts to the class about the Industrial Revolution. Then hold a class discussion about the effects of industrial growth. List on the chalkboard the changes that took place as a result of rapid growth, such as increased pollution, bad working and living conditions, child labor, and a new class of factory workers. Ask students what effect such changes would have on an area's landscape. Then ask if they know of any changes taking place in their communities or in nearby communities because of industrial growth. What is the effect of having a major corporation build a factory in a particular location? What does the business bring to a community? What effect does such a move have on supplying essential services, such as water and sewage, housing, education, police and fire protection? What effect does it have on the environment of an area? Conclude the discussion by asking what happens when a factory that is vital to a community's economy closes down. Conclude the activity by assigning the Career Feature on urban planning in the Teacher Resource Book.

Objective 2 Activities

● Objective 2 Teaching Activity
Because many students have heard of France and have prior ideas about the geography of the country, prepare a pretest that covers many of the major points discussed in Section 2 of the chapter. Ask students to answer the questions to the best of their ability. Tell them that they will not be graded on the test. Use the Test Generator for Chapter 17 to put together the ten questions, or use some or all of the following ones for the pretest. 1) What is the capital of France? 2) On which continent is France located? 3) Which countries border France on the south, west, east, and north? 4) What is the name of the river that runs through Paris? 5) Name the bodies of water that border France. 6) Name France's mountain ranges. 7) What are some of the major economic activities in France? 8) Who was Napoleon Bonaparte? 9) Who is the current President of France? 10) Name something for which the French are well-known. After students have read Section 2 of the chapter, go over the pretest questions again.

★ Objective 2 Enriching Activity Ⓒ
Plan a French cultural day. Some of the activities might include the following: inviting a guest of French nationality to speak to the class about France, bringing in examples of French food and music, placing pictures of France around the classroom, having students wear a traditional French costume, assigning French names to the students for the day, or having the students take a French lesson.

Objective 3 Activities

● Objective 3 Teaching Activity Ⓔ
Give students a blank outline map of West Germany. Tell them to make an economic map of the country, using their text and any additional sources necessary. Have them place the following in the correct geographical area on the maps: potatoes, apples, sugar beets, livestock, wheat, barley, oats, grapes, olives, iron and steel manufacturing, coal, iron ore, uranium, and timber. After the student maps are complete, display a blank outline map of West Germany on an overhead projector or on a large sheet of paper taped to the chalkboard. Ask the class to use their individual maps to suggest placement of the products onto the class map. Clear up any errors, and then ask students to correct their outline maps.

■ Objective 3 Reinforcing Activity Ⓗ
After World War II, the West German people had to rebuild their war-torn land. The rise and fall of Hitler's Germany left the nation with geographic devastation. Ask students to prepare a radio broadcast about the effects of the war. The broadcast should concentrate on one aspect of redevelopment. For example, they could describe the clean-up and rebuilding of a major city, the need for people to work toward building a new economy, or the effects of the split between West Germany and East Germany on families, especially in war-torn Berlin. To help students with the activity, bring to class photographs that show some of the aftermath of the war.

Objective 4 Activities

● Objective 4 Teaching Activity
Divide students into three groups. Assign one group the Benelux countries; one, Alpine countries; and one, Norden. Challenge each group to prepare a one-page informational brochure titled: "What You Will See When You Visit _____" (fill in the space with one of the regions). Encourage students to pack as much detail as possible regarding names of countries, landscape and climate patterns, and cultural features into the brochure. When groups have finished, share their work. Discuss the brochures and critique them as a class. Consider duplicating revised brochures and providing one for each class member.

■ Objective 4 Reinforcing Activity
Have students complete the *Using Graphic Skills* feature, "Making Generalizations," on

T185

page 354 of the Student Edition. Then, using the Student Edition and any additional resources available, have students form five generalizations about one of the countries, or some geographic aspect of one of the countries discussed in Section 4 of the chapter. Tell students to write several statements that support each generalization.

Objective 5 Activities

● **Objective 5 Teaching Activity**
Refer to the guidelines for case studies in the Instructional Approaches section of this Teacher Annotated Edition before directing the following activity. Assign each student a case study of some aspect of life in Western Europe. Some of these include sports, education, jobs, urban life, rural life, mountains, waterways, industries, farm products, languages, or government. Once the case studies are complete, have students share some of them with the remainder of the class.

■ **Objective 5 Reinforcing Activity** Ⓔ
Divide the class into five groups. Assign each one of the major rivers of Northwest Europe: Rhine, Seine, Elbe, Danube, Rhône. Draw a large retrieval chart on the chalkboard, listing the rivers down the left side and the following headings across the top: "Countries Crossed, Major Cities Along Route, Major Economic Activities Along Route, Where the River Empties." Students should be directed to find this information in their text, in other resource books, on maps, or in other materials in the library. Have students present their findings to the class and fill in the chart. Conclude by discussing how rivers influence the economic life of this region (transporting economic goods, sources of energy, and so forth). As an additional exercise, class members might trace courses of major United States rivers and note locations of major cities along their routes.

Concluding Chapter 17

Ask students to design a geography trivia game on Northwest Europe, using maps, atlases, and their textbooks. A question could ask for a simple response, might require a student to locate a place on the map, might ask a student to spell a place or geographic term, or it could require a student to define a term. Collect student questions and rewrite them on small cards. To play the game, break the class into two teams, with you as moderator.

ANSWERS TO CHAPTER 17 QUESTIONS

Content Check Questions
page 343

1. Refer to Section 1 content.
2. Refer to Glossary in Student Edition.
3. Britain and Ireland. (p. 335)
4. The Republic of Ireland and the United Kingdom of Great Britain and Northern Ireland. (p. 336)
5. Highlands and lowlands. (p. 337)
6. Middle latitude marine. (p. 339)
7. United Kingdom. (p. 339)
8. Respect for individual rights and tradition and the English language. Population density, urbanization, and religion. (p. 341)

9. Answers will vary but stress the importance of modernizing industry. Doubtful that England can regain its old position because it lost colonial possessions and its natural resources have been depleted, making it now heavily dependent on imports. (pp. 339, 342)

page 347

1. Refer to Section 2 content.
2. Refer to Glossary in Student Edition.
3. Mainland France and Corsica. (p. 343)
4. Paris. It is the seat of government that directs education, science, and industry. (p. 345)

5. Answers will vary; for example, it has experienced monarchy, dictatorships, empires, and republics. (pp. 345, 347)

page 352

1. Refer to Section 3 content.
2. Refer to Glossary in Student Edition.
3. East Germany and West Germany. (p. 347)
4. North German Plain; Central Uplands; Bavarian Alps. (pp. 347–348)
5. In the southern and eastern areas. (p. 349)
6. Fourth. (p. 349)
7. It is West Germany's main industrial area and one of the major industrial centers of the world. (p. 349)
8. The Rhine River connects West Germany with France and the Netherlands to the west all the way to the North Sea. The Danube River connects with countries to the east all the way to the Black Sea. The Elbe River connects with some countries to the east.

page 355

1. Refer to Section 4 content.
2. Refer to Glossary in Student Edition.
3. Low and flat. (p. 352)
4. Rotterdam; the Netherlands. (p. 353)
5. Sweden; cars and machine parts. (p. 353)
6. Since World War II, Eastern Europe has come under Soviet control and this has forced Austria to shift political and economic ties to Western Europe.

Special Feature Questions
page 338, Strange But True: "Bananas in Britain"

1. 28 miles (45 km) off the southwest coast of Britain.
2. They have a mild climate because of the North Atlantic Current and Gulf Stream.
3. Income from the sale of flowers and from tourism.
4. To see the flowers and the historic museum in Hugh Town.

page 340, The Urban World: "London: Cultural Center"

1. Size and location.

2. Publishing, broadcasting, music, dance, theater, museums.

page 354, Using Graphic Skills: "Making Generalizations"

1. France's west coast is affected by warm winds blowing across the North Atlantic Current, producing a mild climate. This climate affects the area of France where Paris is located. Vienna is far inland where the European landmass cools temperatures, producing colder winters. Vienna is also at a higher elevation than Paris.
2. San Juan's winter climate is very mild because of its location in the low latitudes toward the Equator and its low elevation.
3. Dublin's winter climate is relatively mild because air blowing over the North Atlantic Current from the west warms up and blows in over the land.

Photo/Illustration Caption Questions
page 336

Western Uplands. (p. 336)

page 337

Plains, valleys, rocky coastlines, lowlands, moors, glens, low hills. (pp. 337, 339)

page 339

Dublin. (p. 339)

page 342

48. (p. 343)

page 345

Over 200 miles (322 km) per hour. (p. 345)

page 346

England, Wales, Scotland, West Germany, Austria. (p. 346)

page 348

Answers will vary but should include Dublin, London, Paris, Brussels, Amsterdam, Luxembourg, Bern, Bonn, Vienna, Copenhagen, Oslo, Stockholm, Helsinki, Reykjavik.

page 350

Urban areas. (p. 350)

Britain, France, and the United States. (p. 351)

Because of the Netherlands' very high population density. (p. 352)

Chapter 17 Review Questions
page 356, Reviewing Vocabulary

l o̲ c h s,   p o l d̲ e r,   l i g n̲ i t e, m̲ o o r,   f i̲ r t h,   g r a p h i̲ t e, m o̲ n̲ a r c h y   DOMINION

page 357, Remembering the Facts

1. Slightly larger than the United States east of the Mississippi River. (p. 335)
2. England, Wales, Scotland, Northern Ireland. (p. 336)
3. Paris. (p. 344)
4. Benelux, Norden, Alpine. (p. 352)

page 357, Understanding the Facts

1. Warm, moist air from ocean currents passes over colder land, bringing rain that does not fully evaporate. (p. 339)
2. Ireland's economy is mainly agricultural; the United Kingdom's economy is mainly industrial. (pp. 339, 341)
3. Britain has more people, is more crowded, urban, and Protestant. Ireland has fewer people, is less crowded, rural, and Catholic. (p. 341)
4. Monarchy. (p. 347)
5. Northwesterly winds bring moisture off the sea over land. (p. 349)
6. Movement during the 1500s when Christians left the Catholic Church and formed Protestant churches. (p. 350)
7. Was divided into two governments, one democratic and the other communist. After the fall of Rome, was divided into many states; was religiously divided during and after the Reformation. (pp. 350–352)
8. Politically linked to Denmark, although geographically located in North America. (pp. 335, 353)

9. Austria has many mineral resources; Switzerland has none; Austria is overwhelmingly Catholic; Switzerland is both Protestant and Catholic. (p. 355)

page 357, Thinking Critically and Creatively

1. Answers will vary but may include some of these ideas: increasing farming and manufacturing productivity, modernizing industries, developing new ways of manufacturing, improving transportation systems for the delivery of goods, developing new markets with countries that have surplus agricultural products and resources to sell in exchange for needed goods they will buy, reducing tariff restrictions to allow needed goods not produced within the country to be imported and sold at lower costs, protecting domestic manufacturers by placing tariffs on similar manufactures imported from foreign countries.
2. Answers will vary but should stress the importance of economic power. A country should aim at being self-sufficient in providing food and necessary resources. It must have industrial manufacturing capabilities, good transportation facilities, a variety of foreign markets in which to sell its products, and a surplus of commodities to exchange with other countries.
3. Answers will vary but may include these ideas: Paris has an important continental location as well as an important location within France. Paris is the center of rail, highway, and river transport within France. In the context of the continent, Paris is central to transportation routes linking other areas of the continent.
4. Answers will vary but may include that the Pyrenees between France and Spain are a much more rugged mountain range than the Alps with very few passes through them. It has been extremely difficult to build highways across them. The Alps are broken by many more passes. There have long been well-traveled land routes through the Alps between France and Italy.

5. Income from French goods sold to foreign countries is used to pay for oil imports. The Middle East.
6. Rivers make it possible to ship goods within and outside of West Germany. Canals extend West Germany's internal waterway system and link the major cities and ports together.
7. Britain and Norway. Both have reserves of oil, making it an important export product for them. Falling oil prices would mean less income from the sale of oil.

page 357, Reinforcing Graphic Skills

1. Dublin and Oslo, Paris and Vienna, Paris and Portland.
2. Bogotá's winter climate is relatively cooler rather than milder, in spite of its proximity to the Equator, primarily because of its high elevation.

EVALUATING CHAPTER 17

World Geography: People and Places provides chapter tests to help evaluate student performance. To evaluate student mastery of Chapter 17, give students Chapter 17 Test from the Teacher Resource Book. This test may also be used for pretesting or retesting purposes. Other tests can be made from the questions available in the Test Generator Software.

Lesson Plan Suggestions—Chapter 17

SE—Student Edition   TAE—Teacher Annotated Edition   TG—Test Generator
TRB—Teacher Resource Book   TSP—Transparency Package

Section 1   British Isles (pp. 335–343)

Chapter Objectives	Suggested Teaching Strategies	Review
1. describe the major physical, economic, cultural, and historical features of the British Isles.	**Teacher Preparation** SE, Reading Assignment, pp. 335–343 TAE, Unit 6 Suggested Resources 　　Unit 6 Overview, p. T182 　　Introducing Unit 6, p. T182 　　Chapter 17 Overview, p. T183 　　Introducing Chapter 17, p. T184 TRB, Chapter 17 Teacher Notes: Section 1 **Teaching Options** TAE, Introducing Unit 6, p. T182 　　Introducing Chapter 17, p. T184 　　Objective 1 Activities, p. T184 TRB, Chapter 17 Teacher Notes: Section 1, 　　Extending the Lesson 　　Chapter 17 Reading 　　Chapter 17 Skill Activity TSP, Transparency 3	SE, Content Check, p. 343

Section 2   *France (pp. 343–347)*

Chapter Objectives	Suggested Teaching Strategies	Review

2. describe the major physical, economic, cultural, and historical features of France.	**Teacher Preparation**
	SE, Reading Assignment, pp. 343–347
	TAE, Unit 6 Suggested Resources
	    Chapter 17 Overview, p. T183
	TRB, Chapter 17 Teacher Notes: Section 2
	Teaching Options
	TAE, Objective 2 Activities, p. T185
	TRB, Chapter 17 Teacher Notes: Section 2,
	    Extending the Lesson
	    Chapter 17 Skill Activity
		SE, Content Check, p. 347

Section 3   *West Germany (pp. 347–352)*

Chapter Objectives	Suggested Teaching Strategies	Review

3. describe the major physical, economic, cultural, and historical features of West Germany.	**Teacher Preparation**
	SE, Reading Assignment, pp. 347–352
	TAE, Unit 6 Suggested Resources
	    Chapter 17 Overview, p. T183
	TRB, Chapter 17 Teacher Notes: Section 3
	Teaching Options
	TAE, Objective 3 Activities, p. T185
	TRB, Chapter 17 Teacher Notes: Section 3,
	    Extending the Lesson
	    Chapter 17 Skill Activity
		SE, Content Check, p. 352

Section 4   *Other Countries of Northwest Europe (pp. 352–355)*

Chapter Objectives	Suggested Teaching Strategies	Review

4. describe the major physical, economic, cultural, and historical features of the Benelux countries, Norden, and the Alpine countries.
 	
Skill Objective: make generalizations.
	Teacher Preparation
	SE, Reading Assignment, pp. 352–355
	TAE, Unit 6 Suggested Resources
	    Chapter 17 Overview, p. T183
	TRB, Chapter 17 Teacher Notes: Section 4
	Teaching Options
	TAE, Objective 4 Activities, pp. T185–T186
	TRB, Chapter 17 Teacher Notes: Section 4,
	    Extending the Lesson
	    Chapter 17 Skill Activity
	SE, *Using Graphic Skills*, "Making Generalizations," p. 354
		SE, Content Check, p. 355

Suggested Teaching Strategies	Review	Evaluation
TAE, Objective 5 Activities, p. T186 Concluding Chapter 17, p. T186	SE, Chapter 17 Review, pp. 356–357 TRB, Chapter 17 Review Worksheet	TRB, Chapter 17 Test Unit 6 Pretest, Map and Content Worksheets TG, Chapter 17

CHAPTER 18   MEDITERRANEAN EUROPE

Student Edition pp. 358–379

CHAPTER 18 OBJECTIVES

At the conclusion of this chapter, students will be able to:

1. describe the major physical, economic, cultural, and historical features of Spain and Portugal.

2. describe the major physical, economic, cultural, and historical features of Italy.

3. describe the major physical, economic, cultural, and historical features of Greece.

4. summarize the chief geographic features of Mediterranean Europe.

CHAPTER 18 SKILL OBJECTIVE

After completing the *Using Graphic Skills* exercise in this chapter, the student should be able to analyze line and bar graphs.

CHAPTER 18 OVERVIEW

In *Chapter 18,* students are introduced to the geography of the three peninsulas that make up Mediterranean Europe. The Iberian, Italian, and Balkan peninsulas that fork from the European continent into the Mediterranean Sea hold the countries of Spain, Portugal, Italy, and Greece. In contrast to the variety of landscapes and climates found in Northwest Europe, these four countries exhibit similar physical characteristics. Many ideas and ways of life basic to western culture began in this region, influencing much of the course of world history.

Today, Mediterranean Europe faces many problems and has relinquished its leadership position to other countries of Europe and the world. Students should come to recognize, however, that the region still occupies an important role because of its strategic position on the Mediterranean Sea. Thus, the chapter begins with a study of Spain and Portugal in *Section 1*. In *Section 2*, the concentration is on the geography of Italy, and in *Section 3* on Greece. A brief look at the postage-stamp countries of Europe is a special feature of the chapter.

CHAPTER 18 ACTIVITIES

Introducing Chapter 18

Tell students to review the photographs found in Chapter 18. Then hold a brainstorming session about what the photographs describe about Mediterranean Europe. Place student responses on the chalkboard. Categorize the responses by having students write a descriptive statement about the landscape and climate of the region, the economy and culture of the region, and the historical influence on the region's development. Share some of these statements with the rest of the class. Tell students to save the statements so that they can refer to their first impressions when they have completed their study of the chapter.

Use Chapter 18 Skill Activity in the Teacher Resource Book to conclude the introduction to this chapter.

Chapter 18 Reading Assignments

Objective 1   Student Ed. pp. 359–367
Objective 2   Student Ed. pp. 367–374
Objective 3   Student Ed. pp. 374–377

● Teaching	■ Reinforcing	★ Enriching

Unmarked activities deal with three or more features listed in the chapter objectives. Activities marked with the following letters deal with:
Ⓟ Physical features.
Ⓔ Economic features.
Ⓒ Cultural features.
Ⓗ Historical features.

Objective 1 Activities

● Objective 1 Teaching Activity
Have students write a total of eight or ten topic sentences that begin with each of the follow-

ing: "Unlike Spain, Portugal has. . ." and "Like Spain, Portugal has. . ." Then have students take four of the topic sentences and write a paragraph for each. Once the paragraphs are complete, set up a chart on the chalkboard with the following horizontal headings: "Similarities" and "Differences." On the side, write the two countries, "Spain" and "Portugal." Then ask for student input to fill in the chart.

Conclude the activity with the Chapter 18 Reading in the Teacher Resource Book.

■ Objective 1 Reinforcing Activity Ⓒ
Have students research recreation in Spain or Portugal. Try to get a variety of activities represented. Then ask students to create a vacation through one of the two countries. For example, students might describe a vacation in the Pyrenees Mountains, or a visit to a beach along the Mediterranean coast.

★ Objective 1 Enriching Activity Ⓗ
Have students write a short biographical sketch of one of the Spanish or Portuguese explorers. Ask students to research the life of the explorer, using at least three or four sources as background. Ask students to share their sketches with the class.

Objective 2 Activities

● Objective 2 Teaching Activity Ⓒ
Hold a discussion about the Italian influence on global culture. Inform students that during the height of the Roman empire, Rome's influence was felt throughout much of the world. Ask students to explain how the Italians have influenced American culture. They will probably answer in the food we eat. Encourage students to realize that the influence goes beyond food. The Italians have

influenced art, engineering, architecture, religion, music, and government. Then ask students why the American culture has had such a strong Italian influence. Students may answer that many Italians came to the United States as immigrants and brought their customs and culture with them.

Divide the class into groups to prepare a report on one aspect of the Italian influence on global culture. Groups should choose one of the following topics: language, food, art, architecture, or music.

■ Objective 2 Reinforcing Activity Ⓔ
Have students write an economic profile of Italy. Explain that an economic profile contains a summary of the types of industries, products manufactured, produce and livestock grown, natural resources, and products imported and exported. In their reports, students should keep in mind the difference in the level of economic activity between Northern Italy and Southern Italy.

★ Objective 2 Enriching Activity
Before directing this activity, refer to community resource persons in the Instructional Approaches section of this Teacher Annotated Edition. Italy attracts millions of visitors each year. Find a resource person who has visited Italy or someone who has migrated from Italy to the United States recently to speak to the class about the major geographic features of Italy. Other resource persons might include members of Italian-American culture groups, Italian university students, or travel agents. Prior to the visit, have students prepare specific questions on landscape and climate, economy, cultural life, and history. Inform the speaker ahead of time of the presentation's focus.

Objective 3 Activities

● Objective 3 Teaching Activity
Before directing the following activity, refer to team learning in the Instructional Approaches section of this Teacher Annotated Edition. Divide the class into teams. Have each team be responsible for teaching the class about one aspect of the geography of Greece. One team can describe the landscape and climate, one the economy, another the culture, and the last group, the history of Greece. Students should find unique ways of presenting the material, such as a role play, cartoon, sketch, or story.

★ Objective 3 Enriching Activity
Tourism in Greece is becoming an increasingly important economic activity. Tell students to create a newspaper or magazine advertisement for a vacation in Greece. Have them include in the advertisement one or two attractions that draw people to the country. Students may wish to interview a local travel agent to get more information about types of transportation available, and cost of lodging and meals. Once the advertisements are finished, ask a few students to explain to the remainder of the class what they found out about the geography of Greece.

Objective 4 Activities

● Objective 4 Teaching Activity
Organize a geography spelling bee. Begin by giving a student a word to spell from the chapter. The student must then spell the word correctly. If the word is a geographic term, the student must define it. If the word is a place-name, the student must locate the place on the map. Terms from each section's content will aid your preparation.

■ Objective 4 Reinforcing Activity
Clear a large space on one wall for a bulletin board headed "Economic and Cultural Characteristics of Mediterranean Europe." Cut out large letters to label the bulletin board. Encourage students to cut out photographs from such magazines as *National Geographic* that illustrate economic and cultural activities in either Spain, Portugal, Italy, or Greece. Photographs should be organized by country. Refer to the guidelines for discussion in the Instructional Approaches section of this Teacher Annotated Edition, and when students have completed the bulletin board, conduct a discussion. Ask students to recall their

reading, look at the photographs, and draw conclusions regarding economic and cultural characteristics of the region.

Concluding Chapter 18

Have students retrieve their statements formed from the brainstorming activity when Chapter 18 was introduced. Ask students if the photographs gave a complete overview of the geography of Mediterranean Europe. What else did students find out about the landscape

and climate, economy and culture, and history that could not be found in the photographs? Conclude the activity by having students describe six additional photographs they would like to have included in the chapter. The first two photographs should show additional features of the region's landscape and climate, the next two should summarize the region's economy and culture, and the last two photographs should show historical influences on the region's development.

ANSWERS TO CHAPTER 18 QUESTIONS

Content Check Questions
page 367

1. Refer to Section 1 content.
2. Refer to Glossary in Student Edition.
3. Pyrenees on northeast side, and water on all others (Bay of Biscay, Mediterranean Sea, Atlantic Ocean). (p. 359)
4. Both are high and rugged lands, but Portugal has more flat lowlands. (pp. 360–361)
5. Spain is larger in area and population and even though both are industrial, Portugal has remained more agricultural. (pp. 360–361, 364)
6. Poor soil and little rain; irrigation is needed. (p. 362)
7. Farm products are similar in Spain and Portugal. Grapes, olives, fruits, vegetables, livestock. (pp. 362–363)
8. In general wealth, it is one of the poorest nations in Europe. (p. 361)
9. Answers will vary. Catalonians may feel resentful of Castile's position of leadership. They may feel their prosperity helps support Castile. Language differences may cause misunderstandings. (p. 364)

page 374

1. Refer to Section 1 content.
2. Refer to Glossary in Student Edition.
3. Sicily and Sardinia. (p. 367)
4. High mountains (Alps) in the north, lower mountains (Apennines) extending into the central and southern areas, low hills on

either side of the Apennines, lowlands such as the Po River Valley in the north. (pp. 367–368)
5. Northern Italy is industrial and prosperous, while the South is poorer and less developed. (p. 368)
6. Roman Catholic. (p. 372)
7. Venice, Genoa, and Milan. (p. 373)
8. First, ranks only behind the Soviet Union and France. (p. 368)
9. Answers will vary but may include that the rough north-south terrain hampered transportation, movement, and communication. This would have contributed to more of a regional, rather than national, awareness.

page 377

1. Refer to Section 3 content.
2. Refer to Glossary in Student Edition.
3. Rugged terrain and mild wet winters and hot dry summers. (p. 374)
4. Smallest. (p. 376)
5. Much smaller, poorer, and less productive. (p. 375)
6. Greatly; contributes to fishing, trade, shipping, tourism. (p. 375)
7. Shipping. (p. 375)
8. Limestone is a porous mineral that absorbs water. This means that when rain falls, the moisture does not stay on the surface long. It quickly soaks through the soil and into the porous limestone below. This makes for very dry surface conditions.

Special Feature Questions
page 371, Focus on Geography: "Postage-Stamp Countries"

1. The name refers to their small size and to the fact that they earn money from the sale of postage stamps.
2. The Pyrenees between France and Spain.
3. Principality (ruled by a prince).
4. It is the headquarters of the Roman Catholic Church.

pages 362–363, Using Graphic Skills: "Analyzing Line and Bar Graphs"

1. Italy and Britain. Britain.
2. Portugal. West Germany.
3. The economy of Mediterranean Europe does not produce nearly as much in the way of goods and services as do the economies of Northwest European countries.

Photo/Illustration Caption Questions
page 360

Pyrenees, Alps, and Pindus. (p. 360)

page 361

Sierra Nevada. (p. 361)

page 364

Lisbon. (p. 364)

page 365

It is a leading seaport and industrial center. (p. 364)

page 366

Christianity, languages, laws, and architecture. (p. 366)

page 368

Northern Italy has more rainfall, is more prosperous, has modern, efficient industries and farms. Southern Italy is drier, poorer, less developed, and less industrialized. (p. 368)

page 369

Spain and Italy. (p. 369)

page 372

Britain. (p. 372)

page 373

Solar. (p. 373)

page 375

Crete. (p. 374)

page 376

Portugal. (p. 376)

Chapter 18 Review Questions
page 378, Reviewing Vocabulary

1. Hill-land economy.
2. Gross domestic product.
3. Expatriate workers.
4. City-state.
5. Acropolis.
6. Socialist.
7. Opera.

page 378, Remembering the Facts

1. Spain, Portugal, Italy, Greece. (p. 359)
2. Iberia. (p. 359)
3. Sunny climates with warm summers and moist, mild winters; large areas of mountains and highlands. (p. 359)
4. The Meseta. (p. 360)
5. Italy. (p. 368)
6. Northern, Po River Valley. (p. 372)
7. Rome. (p. 372)
8. The Hellenic Republic. (p. 374)
9. Athens. (pp. 374, 376)
10. The Peloponnesus. (p. 374)
11. Pindus. (p. 374)

page 379, Understanding the Facts

1. The Meseta is a dry plateau area with few forests, used for farming and livestock, while the Andalusian Lowland is more fertile and can hold a larger population. (pp. 360–361)
2. Warm winds blowing in off the Atlantic Ocean. (p. 361)
3. Northern Italy gets more rainfall than southern Italy. (p. 368)
4. Because of its large population, skilled workers, good climate for farming, sources of hydroelectric power, modern industries and farms, and urban centers. (pp. 368–369)

5. Available resources include coal, lead, water power, and fish. Scarce resources include petroleum and natural gas. (p. 369, map)
6. Because of dry rocky soil and not enough rain. (pp. 362, 368, 374)
7. Wealthy citizens began studying ancient Greek and Roman culture, which led to a renewed interest in art and literature. (p. 373)
8. The stress since World War II has been on the promotion of more democracy and greater freedom for the people. (pp. 367, 373, 377)

page 379, Thinking Critically and Creatively

1. Answers will vary but remember that the area has the problems of high prices, unemployment, and limited resources, so an ever-growing population must look elsewhere for jobs because of limited natural resources that limit industrialization.
2. Both ranges have rugged peaks. But there are many more passes through the Alps than through the Pyrenees. The existence of these passes has made it possible for people and goods to move relatively easily through the Alps for centuries. The Pyrenees, on the other hand, are a nearly impenetrable wall. They are extremely difficult to cross by land, and they have been a serious barrier to movement of peoples and goods between Spain and France.
3. Answers will vary but may include that Greece is located at a crossroads of trade between western Europe, southwestern Asia, and the Soviet Union; its location in the Mediterranean Sea gives it shipping access to Mediterranean ports, the Black Sea, and the Suez Canal.
4. Answers will vary but could include frequent changes in government, warfare, dictatorial rule, and struggles between opposing political forces.
5. Answers will vary but should include the following point. There could be a serious problem. Much of the electricity to run Italy's factories comes from hydroelectric plants in the Italian Alps. Were this supply cut off, many factories might have to shut down. Further, many Italian goods are shipped to markets in Europe through the Alps. If these routes were closed, Italian businesses might have difficulty in getting their products to their customers. Similarly, these routes provide a way to bring in raw materials. If new routes had to be found, cost of production could go up.
6. Answers will vary but could include these ideas: the statement means there is much in common between the countries of the Iberian Peninsula and Africa, especially North Africa. Landscape and climatic features are very similar. At one time, parts of Spain were under the control of Muslim Arabs, called Moors, who first invaded Spain by way of Africa. Some of their architecture remains even today. Thus, a case can be made for a certain African influence in parts of Spain. Answers will vary but should include that today Spain and Portugal's cultures are more related to Europe than to Africa.
7. Much of the interior terrain of both Greece and Italy is rugged. Land transportation was difficult. On the other hand, it was relatively easy to move from place to place on water. Hence, it was much easier to bring needed items in and to ship out products from coastal locations. This probably is one of the most compelling reasons for the coastal location.

page 379, Reinforcing Graphic Skills

1. Spain.
2. About 16 times greater. About 2 times greater.
3. Answers will vary but may include that the smaller populations of the Mediterranean countries, except Italy, mean that there will be a smaller work force to produce goods and services and that a smaller population will require less goods and services to be produced than in countries with larger populations such as Northwest Europe.

EVALUATING CHAPTER 18

World Geography: People and Places provides chapter tests to help evaluate student performance. To evaluate student mastery of Chapter 18, give students Chapter 18 Test from the Teacher Resource Book. This test may also be used for pretesting or retesting purposes. Other tests can be made from the questions available in the Test Generator Software.

Lesson Plan Suggestions—Chapter 18

SE—Student Edition TAE—Teacher Annotated Edition TG—Test Generator TRB—Teacher Resource Book TSP—Transparency Package

Section 1 *Iberian Peninsula (pp. 359–367)*

Chapter Objectives	Suggested Teaching Strategies	Review

1. describe the major physical, economic, cultural, and historical features of Spain and Portugal.
 	
Skill Objective: analyze line and bar graphs.
	Teacher Preparation
	SE, Reading Assignment, pp. 359–367
	TAE, Unit 6 Suggested Resources
	    Chapter 18 Overview, p. T191
	    Introducing Chapter 18, p. T192
	TRB, Chapter 18 Teacher Notes: Section 1
	Teaching Options
	TAE, Introducing Chapter 18, p. T192
	    Objective 1 Activities, p. T192
	TRB, Chapter 18 Teacher Notes: Section 1,
	    Extending the Lesson
	    Chapter 18 Reading
	    Chapter 18 Skill Activity
	SE, *Using Graphic Skills,*
	    "Analyzing Line and Bar Graphs," pp.
	    362–363
		SE, Content Check, p. 367

Section 2 *Italy (pp. 367–374)*

Chapter Objectives	Suggested Teachings Strategies	Review
2. describe the major physical, economic, cultural, and historical features of Italy.	**Teacher Preparation** SE, Reading Assignment, pp. 367–374 TAE, Unit 6 Suggested Resources Chapter 18 Overview, p. T191 TRB, Chapter 18 Teacher Notes: Section 2	SE, Content Check, p. 374

(Continued on next page.)

| | Teaching Options
TAE, Objective 2 Activities, pp. T192–T193
TRB, Chapter 18 Teacher Notes: Section 2,
    Extending the Lesson
    Chapter 18 Skill Activity | |

Section 3   Greece (pp. 374–377)

Chapter Objectives	Suggested Teaching Strategies	Review

3. describe the major physical, economic, cultural, and historical features of Greece.	**Teacher Preparation**
	SE, Reading Assignment, pp. 374–377
	TAE, Unit 6 Suggested Resources
	    Chapter 18 Overview, p. T191
	TRB, Chapter 18 Teacher Notes: Section 3
	Teaching Options
	TAE, Objective 3 Activities, p. T193
	TRB, Chapter 18 Teacher Notes: Section 3,
	    Extending the Lesson
	    Chapter 18 Skill Activity
		SE, Content Check, p. 377

Chapter 18   Review and Evaluation

Suggested Teaching Strategies	Review	Evaluation
TAE, Objective 4 Activities, pp. T193–T194 Concluding Chapter 18, p. T194	SE, Chapter 18 Review, pp. 378–379 TRB, Chapter 18 Review Worksheet	TRB, Chapter 18 Test TG, Chapter 18

CHAPTER 19   EASTERN EUROPE

Student Edition pp. 380–399

CHAPTER 19 OBJECTIVES

At the conclusion of this chapter, students will be able to:

1. describe the major physical, economic, cultural, and historical features of Northeastern Europe.
2. describe the major physical, economic, cultural, and historical features of Southeastern Europe.
3. summarize the chief geographic features of Eastern Europe.

CHAPTER 19 SKILL OBJECTIVE

After completing the *Using Graphic Skills* exercise in this chapter, the student should be able to read political maps.

CHAPTER 19 OVERVIEW

Eight countries make up the Eastern European region, the topic of Chapter 19. Poland, Czechoslovakia, and East Germany are studied in *Section 1*, Northeastern Europe. Hungary, Romania, Bulgaria, and Albania are covered in *Section 2*, Southeastern Europe. Students will find while studying this region that these lands have some of the most varied cultures in the world. Yet, they also have planned economies and close ties to the Soviet Union.

It is the advent of the influence of the Soviet Union in the area that has conditioned people to think of Eastern Europe as a separate region. Its obvious strategic position, both in terms of trade and defense, are such that almost every European country has, at one time or another, attempted to control all or part of it. In this chapter, students are also introduced to the term *balkanization* in a special feature.

CHAPTER 19 ACTIVITIES

Introducing Chapter 19

Distribute outline maps of Eastern Europe. Then, on a wall map, point out the location of the different mountain ranges, plains areas, and rivers in Eastern Europe. Have students fill in and label these on their outline maps. Explain to students that the mountains have acted as natural barriers for the countries of Eastern Europe, yet the plains have allowed these countries to be controlled by stronger European nations for centuries. Next, trace the course of the rivers in Eastern Europe. Show how the Danube cuts through eight nations on its journey to the Black Sea. Tell students that the Danube is the lifeline of Eastern Europe. It carries nearly 77 million tons of cargo each year and is used for irrigation, fishing, and hydroelectric power. Ask students to speculate what life would be like for Eastern Europeans without the Danube. What would the people have to do to get water for crops, living, and power? Would the region have developed differently? How? Tell students to keep the importance of the Danube in mind while they study this chapter. Conclude the activity with the Chapter 19 Reading, "The River Vanishes," in the Teacher Resource Book.

Chapter 19 Reading Assignments
Objective 1   Student Ed. pp. 382–389
Objective 2   Student Ed. pp. 389–397

● Teaching	■ Reinforcing	★ Enriching

Unmarked activities deal with three or more features listed in the chapter objectives. Activities marked with the following letters deal with:
Ⓟ Physical features.
Ⓔ Economic features.
Ⓒ Cultural features.
Ⓗ Historical features.

Objective 1 Activities

● Objective 1 Teaching Activity
Prepare a retrieval chart on the chalkboard. Along the top of the chart write "landscape and climate, major agricultural areas, major industrial areas, major cities, capital, ethnic

groups, language, and religion." On the side of the chart write three countries in Northeastern Europe, namely Poland, Czechoslovakia, and East Germany. Have students copy the blank chart into their notebooks. While they read the section about Northeastern Europe, they should fill in their charts. After completion, hold a class discussion about the contrast between Northeastern Europe and the countries that make up Northwest Europe.

★ **Objective 1 Enriching Activity** ©

Ask students to write a 2-week diary from the point of view of an American youth visiting one of the countries in Northeastern Europe. Ask them to focus on some of the rights that Eastern Europeans often do not have that are enjoyed by people in the West. For example, they often may not travel freely, many may not own or operate their own businesses, are often limited in the jobs they can have, what schools to attend and where to live. Ask students to focus on how they would feel if they were so limited.

Objective 2 Activities

● **Objective 2 Teaching Activity**

Divide the class into groups. Have each group make either a cultural map, a language map, or an economic map of either Hungary, Bulgaria, Albania, Yugoslavia, or Romania. Tell students to make the maps large enough to display around the room. After they have displayed the maps, tell students to form three generalizations about each country.

■ **Objective 2 Reinforcing Activity**

Place the names of the five countries that make up Southeastern Europe on separate slips of paper, fold the papers, then place them into a container. Divide the class into five groups and have each group draw one of the slips of paper. Assign each the task of preparing a ten-question quiz about their country. Five questions must be true or false; five questions must be completion. Students must use the information given in the Student Edition to formulate questions and answers. Collect the questions from each group, then choose five questions for each country and make up a 25-question quiz about Southeastern Europe.

Objective 3 Activity

● **Objective 3 Teaching Activity**

Have students write a poem or a short story using the geographic features of a country in Eastern Europe as background. Tell students to be as descriptive as possible. When their stories or poems are completed, have them share some of their writings with the class.

Concluding Chapter 19

Countries in Eastern Europe under the sphere of Soviet Union influence are often called satellites of the Soviet Union. Many people have fled the country because of tight control by the Soviets. Many East Germans especially have resented such dominance. The Berlin Wall stands as a symbol of these restrictions on the people's freedoms. Read a story or a description of life around the Berlin Wall, such as *Along the Edge of the Forest: An Iron Curtain Journey* by Anthony Baily, Random House, Inc., 1983. Then hold a class discussion about what life would be like in Eastern Europe without such barriers.

ANSWERS TO CHAPTER 19 QUESTIONS

Content Check Questions
page 389

1. Refer to Section 1 content.

2. Refer to Glossary in Student Edition.

3. East Germany, Poland, Czechoslovakia. (p. 383)

4. Flatlands, mountains, hills. (p. 383)

5. East Germany; Poland. (pp. 383, 384)

6. Government center, water and rail transportation center. (p. 385)

7. Austria. (p. 387)

8. Much of Northwest Europe benefits from the influence of the warm North Atlantic

Current. Prevailing westerly winds are warmed as they pass over the water. This heated air moderates winter temperatures. On the other hand, the countries of Northeastern Europe are far inland from the Atlantic. The prevailing westerlies pass over hundreds of miles of cool winter lands before they arrive here. Hence, they retain little of the warmth they have when they cross the Atlantic Coast.

page 397

1. Refer to Section 2 content.
2. Refer to Glossary in Student Edition.
3. Hungary, Yugoslavia, Romania, Bulgaria, Albania. (p. 389)
4. Balkan. (p. 389)
5. Landscape is mostly mountainous; interior climates are humid continental and humid subtropical; coastal areas have a Mediterranean climate. (p. 390)
6. Yugoslavia. (p. 391)
7. Oil. (pp. 391, 393)
8. The communist governments of Hungary, Romania, and Bulgaria are satellites of the Soviet Union. Yugoslavia and Albania have independent communist governments. Romania, Bulgaria, and Albania have government-controlled economies, while Yugoslavia has much less government control of its economy. Hungary allows some private enterprise. (pp. 390, 396)

Special Feature Questions
page 388, Using Graphic Skills: "Reading Political Maps"

1. Two areas. The one area was northwest and west along the Baltic coast and bordering East Germany and Czechoslovakia. The other area was northeast along the Baltic coast and bordering the U.S.S.R.
2. Warsaw and Posnań.
3. Brest.
4. Poland gained larger coastline along the Baltic Sea and increased territory in the north and west.

page 392, Thinking Like a Geographer: "Balkanization"

1. The breakup of an area into a number of small unstable parts or political units.
2. Mountainous terrain has fostered a sense of isolation and independence among the various ethnic groups.

Photo/Illustration Caption Questions
page 382

The Erzgebirge Mountains separate East Germany and Czechoslovakia; the Sudeten, Beskid, and Carpathian mountains separate Poland and Czechoslovakia. (pp. 382, 383)

page 384

1.2 million. (p. 384)

page 385

Coal, copper, forest, iron ore, lignite, petroleum, potash, salt, water power, zinc. (p. 385)

page 386

Collective or state farms. (p. 386)

page 387

1948. (p. 387)

page 390

Humid continental with warm to hot summers; humid subtropical with hot, humid summers; Mediterranean with long, warm summers. (p. 390)

page 391

The Adriatic coast experiences a Mediterranean climate. The Mediterranean countries of Greece and southern Italy, as well as Albania, have cities and towns that look like Dubrovnik. (p. 390)

page 393

Enough food is produced to feed the country, with enough left over to export. (p. 393)

page 394

Separate language, Roman Catholic and Protestant religions, fine food and drink, folk music, famous musical composers. (p. 394)

page 395

Bulgaria. (p. 395)

Greeks, Romans, Byzantines, Austrians, Russians, Germans, Soviets. (pp. 396–397)

Chapter 19 Review Questions
page 398, Reviewing Vocabulary

Cities—Bucharest, Budapest, Krakow, Łódź, Ploesti, Sofia, Warsaw
Physical features—Carpathian, Dinaric, Erzgebirge, Gerlachovka, Tatra
Waterways—Adriatic, Baltic, Danube, Labe, Vistula

page 398, Remembering the Facts

1. East Germany, Poland, Czechoslovakia; Hungary, Yugoslavia, Romania, Bulgaria, Albania. (pp. 383, 389)
2. Czechoslovakia, Hungary. (p. 395, map)
3. A nation that relies on another for authority and direction; all but Yugoslavia and Albania. (p. 381)
4. Economic goals and production are determined by the government. (pp. 381–382)
5. North European Plain. (p. 383)
6. Poland. (p. 383)
7. East Germany. (p. 383)
8. Yugoslavia. (p. 389)
9. Mediterranean. (p. 390)
10. Yugoslavia. (p. 391)

page 399, Understanding the Facts

1. State collectives; privately owned. (pp. 384, 390)
2. Poor soil; the best farmland is in central Poland. (p. 384)
3. Roman Catholic, Eastern Orthodox, Protestant Christian, Muslim. (pp. 384, 386, 391, 393–396)
4. Highlands form most of the landscape with only a few lowland areas. (p. 389)
5. It provides water transportation through this region to the Black Sea and provides borders, fertile plains, and inland ports. (pp. 389, 391)
6. Due to inland locations, mountains, and coastal areas, whereas most of Northeastern Europe is relatively flat. (pp. 383, 389–390)

7. Answers will vary but may include that in most satellite countries, there is stronger central control and central ownership of all aspects of economic life. In Yugoslavia, decision making is somewhat more decentralized. Much farm land is owned privately. This tends not to be true in most Soviet satellite countries. Individual farmers have a very strong voice in deciding what to produce and how to produce it. Yugoslavia tends to have much more extensive trade relationships with non-communist countries than do other Soviet satellite countries.

page 399, Thinking Critically and Creatively

1. Answers will vary but point out (a) most rivers flow to the sea or in a north to south direction so much bridging would have to be done and is costly, although the northern part of Northeastern Europe is quite flat; and (b) would have to cross rugged ranges of hills and mountains that go from north to south, and would be more costly.
2. Answers will vary but may include that lowland, flat areas tend to be better for farming than highland areas. Thus, the farm population tends to be attracted to more level areas. Highways, rail lines, high-power transmission lines, and other needed links are much easier to build in flat country than in mountain country. Land transport also moves faster in flat terrain than in rugged mountain country.
3. Answers will vary; privately owned farms are probably more efficient and productive because farmers have the incentive to produce and sell products for themselves rather than as state farmers working for the government.
4. The Soviet Union borders on the Black Sea. For security reasons, the Soviets often favor policies to assure friendly nations along the Black Sea. In addition, Bulgaria and Romania give the Soviet Union access in close proximity to the entrance into the Mediterranean Sea.

5. Answers will vary but may state that Poland's terrain might explain part of the difference. Major highways connect Warsaw to the coast. On the other hand, large cities in Yugoslavia such as Belgrade and Zagreb are separated from the Adriatic Sea by the Dinaric Alps. Major transportation lines tend to be located east of the Alps. Relatively few cut through to the coast. As a result, major population centers are not as oriented to the sea as are inland cities in the plains country of Poland.

6. Answers will vary but might include that limitation of contacts with other nations places constraints on markets for goods. Nations earn part of their income by selling their products to other countries that need them. When a country makes a decision to deny its products to world markets, then its national income is likely to fall. This can result in a decline in the rate of improvement of living standards. This attitude, too, can breed suspicion and increasing distrust of other people. Lack of contact with other people prevents the kind of give-and-take of information needed to contribute to understanding among people. In time, this can lead to very distorted views of other places and other peoples. Because of the increasing interdependence of the world's economies, any country that chooses to "stay out of the game" might find its economy falling farther and farther behind world standards.

page 399, Reinforcing Graphic Skills

1. U.S.S.R.
2. 1939–1945. All the area within the red line of Poland's border shows that this land was lost either to Germany or to the U.S.S.R. Also, the green line shows the division line between German-occupied territory and U.S.S.R.-occupied territory in 1939.

EVALUATING CHAPTER 19

World Geography: People and Places provides chapter tests to help evaluate student performance. To evaluate student mastery of Chapter 19, give students Chapter 19 Test from the Teacher Resource Book. This test may also be used for pretesting or retesting purposes. Other tests can be made from the questions available in the Test Generator Software.

Lesson Plan Suggestions—Chapter 19

SE—Student Edition   TAE—Teacher Annotated Edition   TG—Test Generator
TRB—Teacher Resource Book   TSP—Transparency Package

Section 1   Northeastern Europe (pp. 381–389)

Chapter Objectives	Suggested Teaching Strategies	Review

1. describe the major physical, economic, cultural, and historical features of Northeastern Europe.	**Teacher Preparation**
	SE, Reading Assignment, pp. 381–389
	TAE, Unit 6 Suggested Resources
	    Chapter 19 Overview, p. T199
	    Introducing Chapter 19, p. T199
	TRB, Chapter 19 Teacher Notes: Section 1
		SE, Content Check, p. 389

(Continued on next page.)

Section 1 Northeastern Europe (pp. 381–389) continued.

	Teaching Options	
	TAE, Introducing Chapter 19, p. T198	
	Objective 1 Activities, pp. T199–T200	
	TRB, Chapter 19 Teacher Notes: Section 1,	
	Extending the Lesson	
	Chapter 19 Reading	
	Chapter 19 Skill Activity	
Skill Objective: read political maps.	SE, *Using Graphic Skills*, "Reading Political Maps," p. 388	

Section 2 Southeastern Europe (pp. 389–397)

Chapter Objectives	Suggested Teaching Strategies	Review

2. describe the major physical, economic, cultural, and historical features of Southeastern Europe.	**Teacher Preparation**
	SE, Reading Assignment, pp. 389–397
	TAE, Unit 6 Suggested Resources
	    Chapter 19 Overview, p. T199
	TRB, Chapter 19 Teacher Notes: Section 2
	Teaching Options
	TAE, Objective 2 Activities, p. T200
	TRB, Chapter 19 Teacher Notes: Section 2,
	    Extending the Lesson
	    Chapter 19 Skill Activity
		SE, Content Check, p. 397

Chapter 19 Review and Evaluation

Suggested Teaching Strategies	Review	Evaluation
TAE, Objective 3 Activity p. T200 Concluding Chapter 19, p. T200	SE, Chapter 19 Review, pp. 398–399 TRB, Chapter 19 Review Worksheet	TRB, Chapter 19 Test TG, Chapter 19

CHAPTER 20 SOVIET UNION

Student Edition pp. 400–423

CHAPTER 20 OBJECTIVES

At the conclusion of this chapter, students will be able to:

1. describe the major landscape and climate patterns of the Soviet Union.
2. describe the major economic and cultural patterns of the Soviet Union.
3. describe the major historical patterns of the Soviet Union.

CHAPTER 20 SKILL OBJECTIVE

After completing the *Using Graphic Skills* exercise in this chapter, the student should be able to compare land area maps.

CHAPTER 20 OVERVIEW

Chapter 20 focuses on the geography of the Soviet Union. As students study the Soviet Union, they should develop an understanding of the country's tremendous physical area. Much of the country has a very northerly location. It is important to highlight this situation in discussions of Soviet agriculture and other aspects of life that are shaped, in part, by cold, winter climate considerations. Students should be helped to recognize that the Soviet Union's population includes people representing many diverse cultural groups. Finally, emphasize that the Soviet Union is seen as the world leader of the communist economic and political system. Life in the Soviet Union reflects that leadership.

CHAPTER 20 ACTIVITIES

Introducing Chapter 20

Draw students' attention to two large wall maps that you have placed in the classroom, one of the Soviet Union, the other of the United States. Ask a volunteer to use the map scale to make a rough estimate of the east-to-west extent of the Soviet Union. Then, have him or her do the same thing with the map of the United States. As a class, discuss the enormous difference. You may also want to do some north-to-south comparisons.

Next, point out differences in latitudes occupied by the bulk of the lands of the Soviet Union and the United States. Ask students to suggest possible consequences of the Soviet Union's generally more northern location. Finally, point out to students that, in general, population of the United States decreases in density from east to west. The pattern in the Soviet Union is reversed. Many more people live in the western part of the country than in the eastern part.

Conclude this activity with Chapter 20 Skill Activity in the Teacher Resource Book.

Chapter 20 Reading Assignments

Objective 1   Student Ed. pp. 401–407
Objective 2   Student Ed. pp. 407–417
Objective 3   Student Ed. pp. 417–421

● Teaching ■ Reinforcing ★ Enriching

Unmarked activities deal with three or more features listed in the chapter objectives. Activities marked with the following letters deal with:
Ⓟ Physical features.
Ⓔ Economic features.
Ⓒ Cultural features.
Ⓗ Historical features.

Objective 1 Activities

● **Objective 1 Teaching Activity** Ⓟ
Divide students into seven small groups. Assign each group one of the following physical regions of the Soviet Union: European Plain, Caucasus Region, Ural Mountains, Soviet Central Asia, West Siberian Plain, Central Siberian Plateau, East Siberian Mountains. Ask members of each group to prepare a small poster that includes specific information about its region. Names of the region should appear at the top of the poster. When students have concluded this activity, place posters on a wall beneath a large map of the Soviet Union. Use colored yarn or string to "tie" the descriptions of each region to the location of the region on

the large map of the Soviet Union. Conclude with a classroom discussion focusing on similarities and differences among regions.

★ **Objective 1 Enriching Activity** Ⓟ Ⓔ
Ask students to prepare a three- or four-page article for a newspaper travel section on "Rivers of the Soviet Union." In their articles, students should name the rivers, pinpoint their locations, cite their uses, and compare their importance to the Soviet Union with such rivers as the Mississippi in the United States and the Rhine in Northwest Europe. Critique student work.

Objective 2 Activities

● **Objective 2 Teaching Activity** Ⓒ
Prior to this activity, assign each student research on one of the major ethnic groups found in the Soviet Union. Have each student make a pictorial representation of the ethnic group. Then, place a large outline map of the Soviet Union on the wall of the classroom. Have the 15 republics of the Soviet Union outlined on the map. Tell students that they will plot the pictorial representations of the dominant ethnic groups in each republic, using Section 2.2 in the Student Edition as a guide. At the conclusion of the activity, ask students to compare the pluralistic society of the Soviet Union with that of the United States.

■ **Objective 2 Reinforcing Activity**
Hold a class discussion about the economy and culture of the Soviet Union by asking the questions that follow. What regions of the Soviet Union are the most important to the Soviet economy? Why? In what general parts of the country are these regions located? Are the kinds of economic activities in the Soviet Union varied, or are they much the same throughout the country? Are consumer goods available to all in the Soviet Union? What housing problems exist in the country? What is family life like in the Soviet Union? How are women treated? What is the status of religious freedom in the Soviet Union? What influence does the Communist Party have on the lives of

the people in the Soviet Union, such as where people live and where they work? Conclude the discussion by showing a short film or filmstrip about life in the Soviet Union using the Suggested Resources for Unit 6 in this Teacher Annotated Edition.

★ **Objective 2 Enriching Activity**
Enlist the aid of your school librarian to find photographs of old posters or handbills encouraging western territorial settlement of the United States. Circulate these among the class or display them on a bulletin board. Discuss with students the feelings these posters appeal to, such as freedom, adventure, the lure of riches, patriotism, and so forth. Next, divide students into groups. Each group should design and make a poster encouraging settlement of Siberia. Instruct students to look through the chapter for information they might wish to include. Display completed posters in your classroom. To conclude, lead students in a discussion of Siberian settlement. Raise questions such as these: Would high wages attract you to a place like Siberia? Would you sacrifice two or three years of hard work for a higher standard of living? You might point out the willingness of thousands of Americans to go to the North Slope of Alaska during the boom days of the Alaska pipeline.

Objective 3 Activities

● **Objective 3 Teaching Activity** Ⓗ
Have students prepare an oral report about an important historical figure in Russian history. Help students choose a person to avoid duplicate presentations. Tell students to relate the major contributions of each figure to life in the Soviet Union at the time the person lived. Once the reports are complete, assign Chapter 20 Reading in the Teacher Resource Book.

■ **Objective 3 Reinforcing Activity**
Ask students to research newspaper and magazine articles on American-Soviet relations during World War II, the cold war, detente, during the early 1980s, and current relations. Divide the class into groups and have each

group prepare a two-minute television newscast about a current topic concerning diplomatic relations between the United States and the Soviet Union.

Concluding Chapter 20

Divide the class into two teams. Then, write these labels on the chalkboard: "Landscape, Climate, How People Live, The Role of Government, Economic Patterns, Historical Events." Tell students that you will ask people, alternately, from each team to provide one piece of information that can be written under the first label, "Landscape." You will go back and forth between teams until no more ideas are forthcoming. Then, you will move on to "Climate" and follow a similar procedure. This pattern is carried through until information under all headings has been provided. The team with the largest number of contributions wins. Encourage students to copy the information from the board and keep it for review.

ANSWERS TO CHAPTER 20 QUESTIONS

Content Check Questions
page 407

1. Refer to Section 1 content.
2. Largest in area. (p. 401)
3. European Plain, Caucasus Mountains, Ural Mountains, Soviet Central Asia, West Siberian Plain, Central Siberian Plateau, East Siberian Mountains and Plateaus, Arctic Lowlands. (p. 403)
4. European Plain. (p. 403)
5. Ural Mountains. (p. 401)
6. Siberia. (pp. 403, 405)
7. Polar, subarctic, humid continental with warm summers, desert. (pp. 405, 407)
8. Despite the flat landscape on either side, these rivers flow south to north into the Arctic Ocean and are frozen most of the time because of the polar and subarctic climate. (p. 405)

page 417

1. Refer to Section 2 content.
2. Refer to Glossary in Student Edition.
3. The Communist Party. (p. 408)
4. Socialist. (p. 408)
5. Moscow—motor vehicles, chemicals, steel, textiles, electrical equipment; Leningrad—shipbuilding, light machinery, textiles, science and medical equipment; Ukraine—iron and steel, metal products and heavy machinery; Volga River and the Ural Mountains—oil and natural gas; Siberia—mineral resources; Caucasus region—oil and natural gas, appliances, textiles, chemicals; Soviet Central Asia—oil and natural gas, textiles, farm machinery, building equipment. (p. 410)
6. Major ethnic groups are Russians, Ukrainians, Byelorussians, Lithuanians, Latvians, Estonians, Georgians, Armenians, and Azerbaijanians. (pp. 411–413)
7. Family ties are strong although strained by housing shortages and crowded conditions, and families are becoming smaller. (p. 416)
8. Answers will vary but may state that city life is more progressive but has problems with crowding and shortages of consumer goods. Rural life is more primitive and backward. (pp. 415–416)

page 421

1. Refer to Section 3 content.
2. Refer to Glossary in Student Edition.
3. Around Kiev with the consolidation of the Slavs and Vikings. (p. 417)
4. Eastern Orthodox Christian religion. (p. 417)
5. Russia became isolated from Europe and the center of Russian culture shifted to Moscow. (p. 418)
6. To increase trade with Northwest and Mediterranean Europe. (p. 419)
7. Backward and locked in serfdom. (p. 419)
8. World War I. (p. 420)

9. Answers will vary but may include that tsars and nobles benefited from a continuation of serfdom that provided labor, taxes, and soldiers; tsars and nobles feared losing status and power if democratic reforms taking place elsewhere became established in Russia. (pp. 419–420)

Special Feature Questions
page 404, Using Graphic Skills: "Comparing Maps"

1. Soviet Union.
2. Volgograd and Novosibirsk.
3. If you use a different scale, then you cannot accurately compare the areas of the two countries.
4. Distance between Leningrad and Vladivostok is farther.

page 406, Focus on Geography: "World's Worst Climate"

1. In northeastern Siberia, 70 miles (112.6 km) north of the Arctic Circle.
2. 117.4 degrees Fahrenheit (65.2 degrees Celsius).
3. It never gets warm enough to evaporate all the moisture.
4. By working outside for only short periods of time, having heavily insulated buildings, and keeping engines constantly running.

Photo/Illustration Caption Questions
page 402

Ural Mountains. (p. 402)

page 403

To the north and east. (p. 403)

page 407

Moscow. (p. 407)

page 408

Communist Party. (p. 408)

page 409

The climate in these northern regions is too cold. (p. 409)

page 410

Kiev,   arkov, Rostov. (p. 410)

page 411

About two and one-third times larger. (p. 411)

page 412

Lithuanian, Latvian, and Estonian; they use the Latin alphabet, are Protestant and Catholic Christians, and have a higher standard of living. (pp. 412–413)

page 413

Flowers, tobacco, citrus fruit. (p. 413)

page 414

Moscow was the religious center of Eastern Orthodox Christianity and is the political center of world communism. (p. 414)

page 415

Shortages, long waiting lines, poor quality. (p. 415)
They are scarce and better quality goods are often imported. (p. 415)

page 416

Inferior housing facilities, lack of utilities, limited and inferior goods and services. (p. 416)

page 418

Alaska. (p. 418)

page 419

927 miles (1,491.9 km) longer than the Trans-Canada Highway; 2,437 miles (3,922 km) longer than the Inter-American Highway; 3,266 miles (5,256.2 km) longer than U.S. Interstate 80.

page 421

After World War II, the Soviet Union became mostly an industrial country and a major military power. (p. 420)

Chapter 20 Review Questions
page 422, Reviewing Vocabulary

1. bureaucracy; 2. sovkhozy; 3. kolkhozy; 4. five-year plans; 5. flax; 6. serfs; 7. clans; 8. confederation; 9. tsars; 10. atheistic; 11. abdicate; 12. Soviets

page 422, Remembering the Facts

1. Union of Soviet Socialist Republics. (p. 401)
2. One-sixth. (p. 401)
3. Communist countries. (p. 401)
4. Volga, European Plain. (p. 403)
5. Mount Elbrus, Caucasus Mountains. (p. 403)
6. One-half. (p. 405)
7. Plains, mountains, steppes, deserts, plateaus, lowlands. (pp. 402–403, 405)
8. Subarctic climate. (p. 405)
9. Northern location gives shorter growing season and in some areas it is too dry. (p. 411)
10. Russian Slavs. (p. 411)
11. Fifteen. (p. 411)
12. St. Petersburg; Leningrad. (p. 419)
13. Moscow. (pp. 414, 416)

page 423, Understanding the Facts

1. Caucasus are higher, more rugged, and more difficult to get through than the Urals. (p. 403)
2. Soil is salty and drier. (p. 405)
3. The Caucasus region is an area of highlands, high elevation, and cooler climate; the Ukraine is located on the European Plain and has a lower elevation and milder climate. (p. 402, map)
4. Like a pyramid with local, regional, and national levels headed by the Politburo and General Secretary. (p. 408)
5. Because there is so much to be developed and the government is pushing to expand its industry rapidly. (p. 410)
6. Considerably lower but improving. (pp. 415–416)
7. They historically were more aligned with Western Europe until World War II and culturally differ from Slavs in language and religion. (pp. 412–413)
8. Kiev, located on the steppe, was in the path of the Mongol invasions of Europe from Asia. (p. 418)
9. Factories, dams, bridges, roads were built; farms were collectivized and government control was tightened. (p. 420)

page 423, Thinking Critically and Creatively

1. Answers will vary but it should be stressed that the flat European Plain of Western Russia invited Slavic migration from the west and Mongol invasion from the east. With no natural protective barriers, Muscovy sought to protect itself through a policy of expansion and conquest. Population, agriculture, and industry became concentrated in the European Plain region with the Ural Mountains acting as an informal boundary with the more rugged area of highlands and forests to the east.
2. Answers will vary but may include that it is more difficult to conquer and occupy a large country. Further, with more land area, a large country has enough natural resources, several climate types, and a variety of food crops available. Answers will vary but may include that a large country tends to include different peoples speaking different languages causing problems of national unity. Also, it is difficult to provide transportation and move consumer goods in a large country.
3. Prevailing winds strike the Northwest European landmass after having first passed over the warm North Atlantic Current, causing warmer temperatures in Northwest Europe. Much of the Soviet Union lies too far north and inland to be affected by the North Atlantic Current. Thus, westerly winds passed over the cold landmass causing cold winter temperatures.
4. Answers will vary but may include that by cutting off the supply of young people with commitments to religious life, active interest in religion will diminish over time. Eventually, it is felt, the older church members will die off and there will be few young people ready to continue their work. In this way, the influence of the churches may decline even further in the future.
5. Answers will vary but may include that the western part of the Soviet Union is extremely flat. This has made the country relatively open to overland invasion from

the west. There are no mountain or water barriers to slow an invading army. By establishing satellite governments controlled by Moscow, the Soviet Union gained a buffer between potential western invaders and the Soviet frontier.

6. Answers will vary but some of the following may be included. One ethnic group, the Russians, exercises control over the central government and the entire Soviet Union. Though the Russians are the most numerous of the Soviet Union's peoples, still over one-half of the people are members of other ethnic groups. These ethnic minorities enjoy less influence in the Soviet Union than do the Russians. Hence, some have said that these ethnic groups stand in their relationship to the central government much as colonies stand in their relationship to their mother country within an empire.

page 423, Reinforcing Graphic Skills

1. Leningrad to Vladivostok is the greater distance.
2. Both areas are located far inland where their climates are affected by large landmass areas; also, both areas are located within the same general area of latitude.

EVALUATING CHAPTER 20

World Geography: People and Places provides chapter tests to help evaluate student performance. To evaluate student mastery of Chapter 20, give students Chapter 20 Test from the Teacher Resource Book. This test may also be used for pretesting or retesting purposes. Other tests can be made from the questions available in the Test Generator Software.

Lesson Plan Suggestions — Chapter 20

SE—Student Edition   TAE—Teacher Annotated Edition   TG—Test Generator
TRB—Teacher Resource Book   TSP—Transparency Package

Section 1   Landscape and Climate (pp. 401–407)

Chapter Objectives	Suggested Teaching Strategies	Review
1. describe the major landscape and climate patterns of the Soviet Union.	**Teacher Preparation** SE, Reading Assignment, pp. 401–407 TAE, Unit 6 Suggested Resources 　　Chapter 20 Overview, p. T205 　　Introducing Chapter 20, p. T205 TRB, Chapter 20 Teacher Notes: Section 1 **Teaching Options** TAE, Introducing Chapter 20, p. T205 　　Objective 1 Activities, pp. T205–T206 TRB, Chapter 20 Teacher Notes: Section 1, 　　Extending the Lesson TSP, Transparency 3 SE, *Using Graphic Skills,* 　　"Comparing Land Area Maps," p. 404	SE, Content Check, p. 407
Skill Objective: compare land area maps.		

Section 2   Economic and Cultural Patterns (pp. 408–417)

Chapter Objectives	Suggested Teaching Strategies	Review

2. describe the major economic and cultural patterns of the Soviet Union.	**Teacher Preparation**
	SE, Reading Assignment, pp. 408–417
	TAE, Unit 6 Suggested Resources
	     Chapter 20 Overview, p. T205
	TRB, Chapter 20 Teacher Notes: Section 2
	Teaching Options
	TAE, Objective 2 Activities, p. T206
	TRB, Chapter 20 Teacher Notes: Section 2,
	     Extending the Lesson
	     Chapter 20 Skill Activity
		SE, Content Check, p. 417

Section 3   Influences of the Past (pp. 417–421)

Chapter Objectives	Suggested Teaching Strategies	Review

3. describe the major historical patterns of the Soviet Union.	**Teacher Preparation**
	SE, Reading Assignment, pp. 417–421
	TAE, Unit 6 Suggested Resources
	     Chapter 20 Overview, p. T205
	TRB, Chapter 20 Teacher Notes: Section 3
	Teaching Options
	TAE, Objective 3 Activities, pp. T206–T207
	TRB, Chapter 20 Teacher Notes: Section 3,
	     Extending the Lesson
	     Chapter 20 Reading
	     Chapter 20 Skill Activity
		SE, Content Check, p. 421

Chapter 20   Review and Evaluation

Suggested Teaching Strategies	Review	Evaluation
TAE, Concluding Chapter 20, p. T207	SE, Chapter 20 Review, pp. 422–423 TRB, Chapter 20 Review Worksheet	TRB, Chapter 20 Test TG, Chapter 20

Unit 6   Review and Evaluation

Suggested Teaching Strategies	Review	Evaluation

TAE, Concluding Unit 6, p. T212
TRB, Unit 6 Career Worksheet
	SE, Unit 6 Review, pp. 424–425
	TSP, Transparency 3
		TRB, Unit 6 Exam
		     Unit 6 Posttest, Map and
		     Content Worksheets

CONCLUDING UNIT 6

Divide the class into four groups, assigning each group one of the regions of Europe. Have each group conduct a survey of its community in order to get an idea of the types of goods and services imported from each region to the United States. Members of each group should be sent to each of the following areas: (1) home, (2) local businesses, especially grocery, hardware, and clothing stores, (3) school, noting equipment used in sports, science, and home economics classrooms, and (4) parking lots, noting cars and motorcycles. Students should keep field notes of what type of products they find and their location. Allow several days for students to collect data. Finally, each group should present a summary of its findings to the rest of the class. Lead the class in a discussion comparing the types and quantities of products imported from each European region. Raise the questions, "From which region(s) did most imported products come?" "From which region(s) did most high-technology products come?" "Do you think your findings might vary if you lived in another part of the country?" Discuss student responses.

Unit 6 Exam in the Teacher Resource Book may be administered.

UNIT 6 REVIEW QUESTIONS

page 424, Thinking About the Unit

1. Oslo is located at approximately 60 degrees north latitude and 10 degrees east latitude. Moscow is located between 50 to 60 degrees north latitude and 30 to 40 degrees east longitude. Berlin is located between 50 to 60 degrees north latitude and 10 to 20 degrees east longitude. Moscow has the coldest winter temperatures. Moscow is located in a northerly latitude and far enough inland that its winter temperatures are not moderated by nearness to large water areas, as are Oslo and Berlin.

2. Answers will vary but may include that world economic development owes much to industrialization that began and developed in Europe and helped create a higher standard of living. Trade and technology associated with industrialism spread from Europe to other parts of the world. European colonialism, despite its negative impact on foreign peoples and appropriation of resources, helped to develop a viable economic base in many world areas. Trade relations continue to exist between Europe and former areas of European influence. Europe's highly skilled populations and prosperous industrial economies contribute to world economic development today.

3. Similarities are that Britain and Russia both established colonies between the 1500s and 1800s. Both brought peoples of different languages and cultures under their rule. Differences are that British colonial expansion was directed to various parts of the world, while Russian colonial expansion was directed toward adjoining land areas. British colonialism was based mainly on economic reasons, while Russian colonialism was based mainly on security reasons. British colonies became independent during the 1900s, while Russian colonial acquisitions still remain under Russian rule.

4. Answers will vary but may mention that the industrialized and mechanized warfare associated with World Wars I and II created severe physical devastation. World War I affected the physical environment of areas of Europe, whereas World War II affected a much larger area of the world and its physical environment. Culturally, both wars had destructive effects on national populations, cities, transportation systems, factories, farms, and trade.

UNIT 7 NORTH AFRICA AND SOUTHWEST ASIA

Student Edition pp. 426–475

UNIT 7 GOALS

At the conclusion of this unit, students will be able to:

1. explain the effects of the desert environment on the lives of the people who live in North Africa and Southwest Asia.
2. describe the importance of water and oil resources to the economies of the countries in North Africa and Southwest Asia.
3. identify three major religions that originated in the culture area of North Africa and Southwest Asia, and discuss their roles in shaping social, economic, and historical characteristics of the area.

UNIT 7 SKILL OBJECTIVE

After completing the *Developing Geography Skills* exercise in this unit, the student should be able to make inferences.

UNIT 7 OVERVIEW

North Africa and Southwest Asia share a large, physically similar area of dry, desertic characteristics. This region is unified by its geographic similarities and by an Arab-Islamic cultural heritage.

In this unit, the nations of this region are viewed not only from the perspective of their important economic positions in the modern world as oil producers, but also from the viewpoint of their historical roles in the development of Earth's first great civilizations in Mesopotamia, Egypt, and Africa, and as the birthplace of three major world religions. These religions and their common roots are examined in this unit, along with their cultural effects on this region.

Chapter 21 describes the major physical, economic, cultural, and historical features of North Africa and the Sahel, and the same features of Southwest Asia are the focus of *Chapter 22.*

Upon completion of this unit, the students should have a better understanding of the peoples of this world region and the effects of geography in its physical, economic, cultural, and historical aspects upon their lives, as well as be able to view their cultures and conflicts from a global perspective.

INTRODUCING UNIT 7

Introduce this unit to the class through a general discussion about deserts. First ask the class for a definition of a desert and allow students to express their ideas. Ask students: What is the climate of a desert? What is the weather usually like? Do many people live in deserts? Why or why not? What peoples do you know of that live in deserts? How do they live? Have you ever seen a desert? Describe what you saw.

On a wall map, help students locate the world's desert areas, ending with the Sahara. Then help them to locate the Sahel, which extends across the southern rim of the Sahara. Identify the countries located in this region. Then refer to the guidelines for brainstorming in the Instructional Approaches section of this Teacher Annotated Edition, and ask students to brainstorm what life would be like in an area similar to that of the desert zones of the southwestern United States. Students should take into consideration problems presented by such factors as the geography, the location, and the climate.

Explain to the class that the world region they are about to study is located in a large, desertic band spanning two continents, but that this region was, nevertheless, the cradle of two of Earth's earliest civilizations and three of its major religions. Tell them that through the study of this unit, they will learn how people adapted to this geography, developed their cultures and economies, and, because of their natural resources and history, have been placed in an increasingly significant position in world affairs.

CHAPTER 21   NORTH AFRICA AND THE SAHEL

Student Edition pp. 428–449

CHAPTER 21 OBJECTIVES

At the conclusion of this chapter, students will be able to:
1. describe the major physical, economic, cultural, and historical features of Egypt and Sudan.
2. describe the major physical, economic, cultural, and historical features of the Arab West.
3. describe the major physical, economic, cultural, and historical features of the Sahel.
4. summarize the chief geographic features of North Africa and the Sahel.

CHAPTER 21 SKILL OBJECTIVE

After completing the *Using Graphic Skills* exercise in this chapter, the student should be able to compare thematic maps.

CHAPTER 21 OVERVIEW

In this chapter, students are introduced to the world region that contains Earth's largest desert area. But this region is also the location of one of the river valleys that was the birthplace of one of the first great civilizations on Earth.

In *Section 1*, The Arab Republic of Egypt and the Democratic Republic of Sudan are presented with their major physical, economic, cultural, and historical features. Egypt's position as a world leader is discussed in light of the effects of history, economy, and cultural patterns. The Arab West, comprised of the four countries of Libya, Tunisia, Algeria, and Morocco, are similarly explored in *Section 2*, and the student is led to understand the present-day implications of this area's stormy past and cultural heritage. The nations of the Sahel and the geographical and climatic conditions that contribute to their economic and cultural state of transition are the subject of *Section 3*. This section also recalls the great African kingdoms of the Middle Ages and their cultural bequest, culminating in the empire of Mali, its ruler, Mansa Musa, and the fabled capital of Timbuktu.

Special features in this chapter give students background information on the overurbanization of Cairo and the Phoenician colony of Leptis Magna.

CHAPTER 21 ACTIVITIES

Introducing Chapter 21

Continue with the class the discussion begun in the Introducing Unit 7 activity about deserts. Show the class photographs of Bedouins and explain the lifestyle of this desert people. Have the students speculate about various questions to which you should be prepared with answers in case students' responses are incorrect. Ask the students: Why do Bedouins dress as they do? Why are they nomads? What would the inside of a Bedouin tent be like? What values do the Bedouins have and why? What would a Bedouin do if an enemy were lost in the desert but wandered into his camp? What does this demonstrate about the values of the Bedouins? In what ways is the camel a useful animal to the peoples of the desert? Students will probably mention that a camel is able to go for long periods without water. Also, bring out that it is a means of transportation, food storage unit for milk and sometimes meat, water purification plant converting pasturage into milk, and family pet. Explain to the students that the Bedouins have a great affection for their camels, kissing them, calling them by name, and even writing poetry about them. It appears that camels may become very attached to their owners, also. Tell students that the camel is being replaced by pickup trucks. Ask the class to comment on whether they believe that is good or bad, and why, mentioning the advantages and disadvantages of both. Tell students to pretend they are young Bedouins and to write a poem to one of their family's camels that is being sold to be replaced by a truck. Ask volunteers to share their creations.

The book *Arabian Peninsula*, Time-Life Books, Library of Nations series, 1986, would be a useful reference in preparing for this activity.

Chapter 21 Reading Assignments

Objective 1	Student Ed. pp. 429–436
Objective 2	Student Ed. pp. 437–443
Objective 3	Student Ed. pp. 443–447

● Teaching ■ Reinforcing ★ Enriching

Unmarked activities deal with three or more features listed in the chapter objectives. Activities marked with the following letters deal with:
Ⓟ Physical features.
Ⓔ Economic features.
Ⓒ Cultural features.
Ⓗ Historical features.

Objective 1 Activities

● Objective 1 Teaching Activity
Refer to the guidelines for audiovisuals in the Instructional Approaches section of this

Teacher Annotated Edition, and prepare the class to view two films. The first, *Preserving Egypt's Past*, will take students into the world of the ancient Egyptian civilization and show them how scientists today are endeavoring to preserve this monumental history. Follow this film with one entitled *Egypt*, that carries students to the modern Egypt of today and allows them to observe its major cities and its industry and agriculture along the Nile.

After students have viewed the films, ask them to contrast the old and the new in Egypt. Ask them also what they observed about the importance of the Nile River both in ancient times and in the present. Lead a discussion on the importance of the Nile River for the people of Egypt and the Sudan. Explain to the students that while the building of the Aswan High Dam benefited Egypt in some ways, it was also a source of problems for people living downstream from the dam. Ask students to recall the ways in which the dam benefited Egypt. Then ask them to imagine the ways in which it harmed the people living downstream. Ask students: What happens to a river downstream from a dam? What effect would this loss of water have on people living and farming near the river? Which Egyptians would most likely be affected by this partial drying up of the river? Ask students to hypothesize about how history would have been changed had the Nile dried up or changed its course in the year 1,000 AD; in the year 1,000 BC; in the year 5,000 BC. Have students point out the Nile River on a map and show where it flows. Ask students: What are the Nile's cataracts, where are they, and what effect do they have on navigation? Explain that nearly 99% of Egypt's population live within 20 miles of the Nile River. Students will probably be able to explain why this is so.

Refer students to the Chapter 21 Reading and the Chapter 21 Skill Activity in the Teacher Resource Book for further information and another activity for this objective.

■ Objective 1 Reinforcing Activity

Give students the assignment of writing a short story about a fellahin and his family who decide to move to the city. The story should explain why he reached this decision and the effect of this decision on family members. The story may be written from the point of view of a child or a young person in the family, and it should include a description of the life of a fellahin in the form of a first-person account. Aid students to see how Egypt's physical geography, economy, culture, and history could affect the story they will tell. Have students share their stories with the class.

Objective 2 Activities

● Objective 2 Teaching Activity

Provide the class with outline maps showing the Arab West, and tell them that they are going to create a historical map of the area. Help the students invent a key that will show invasions, occupations, and the appropriate dates. Research any dates not provided in the Student Edition. Below his or her map, have each student write a paragraph pointing out the most important and influential historical events and explaining their effects on the culture and economy, where applicable, of the area.

■ Objective 2 Reinforcing Activity ©

Explain to the students that the Arab culture had the most lasting influence on this world region. Refer to the guidelines for audiovisuals in the Instructional Approaches section of this Teacher Annotated Edition, and show the two-filmstrip series referenced in the Suggested Resources, *Islam, Its Power and Legacy*. As part of the debriefing, discuss with the class the things they learned from these filmstrips about the contributions of Islam to world civilization. Finally, ask them to speculate about what scientific changes might occur in the modern world should the Islamic culture never have developed. What things might we not have today? What things might we use instead? What events might never have occurred? Why?

Refer to the Chapter 21 Skill Activity in the Teacher Resource Book for this objective.

★ Objective 2 Enrichment Activity ©

Show the class examples of Egyptian hieroglyphics and explain that they represent an early system of writing. Tell students that Egyptians used hieroglyphics to record religious rituals, property ownership, and crop production. Hieroglyphics are made up of pictograms and ideograms. Pictograms are symbols that represent objects, and ideograms illustrate ideas or actions. Explain that later Egyptians developed hieroglyphics to represent sounds.

Have students invent their own hieroglyphics. Provide them with poster paper and tell them to use their imagination in creating their writing system. Ask volunteers to explain their hieroglyphics to the class, and display all posters in the classroom.

Objective 3 Activities

● Objective 3 Teaching Activity

Explain to the class that desertification leading to drought has occurred in part because well-intentioned American and European advisers taught the people of desertic African nations to dig deep wells to obtain water. But the natural ecology of the desert was very unlike that of the countries from which the advisers came, and the result was that the deep wells drained the groundwater and dried the land even further. The inhabitants of the Sahel were also advised to raise more livestock. Soon the lands became over-grazed, grasses were destroyed, and the natural ecosystem thrown even more out of balance. The threat of droughts and famine increased.

Divide the class into five groups and inform them that they will study the cause and effect of the drought that began in 1968 in the Sahel. Each group will research one of the following topics: The cause of the drought; the effect of the drought on the people of the Sahel; the coverage given to the drought by the press in the United States; the relief efforts instituted and whether or not they were successful and why; the changes in the region that resulted from the drought.

When the groups have researched their topics, have them present their findings to the class. Presentations may include audiovisual materials. After the presentations, ask the following question for class consideration: How has the harsh environment of the Sahel limited the economic potential of the countries within the region?

★ Objective 3 Enriching Activity

Students may find the ancient civilizations of Africa of special interest. Give them the assignment of gathering information on Mansa Musa, the empire of Mali, and the city of Timbuktu. Students may investigate one or all of these topics. Have each student take notes on what he or she is able to find out, and share the information in an informal class discussion. Students especially interested in this subject matter may continue researching the other kingdoms of Ghana and Songhai and share their special reports with the class.

Objective 4 Activities

● Objective 4 Teaching Activity

Write on the chalkboard "Is oil or water more important to the people of North Africa and the Sahel?" Instruct students to write down their responses using the pertinent material from the Student Edition to support their answers. Discuss the student responses, and list some of them on the chalkboard. Review in detail the pertinent material in the Student Edition. Take a class vote on the question. Then refer to the guidelines for discussion in the Instructional Approaches section of this Teacher Annotated Edition, and lead a class discussion about voting results. Ask questions like the following: What would happen if tomorrow all the water in North Africa and the Sahel turned to oil? What would happen if all the oil turned to water? Which situation would be worse and why?

■ Objective 4 Reinforcing Activity

Tell the class that the Mediterranean Sea has long been an important waterway for commerce. The Greeks, Romans, and Phoenicians used it for exploration, invasion, and commerce. Inform students that today the Suez Canal is strategically crucial to the shipment of oil to all parts of the world. Oil tankers fill up in the Middle East and then must travel through the Persian Gulf, the Arabian Sea, the Gulf of Aden, and the Red Sea before they reach the Suez Canal. Point out this passageway on a wall map, and show how passage through the Suez Canal allows ships to sail into the Mediterranean Sea.

Refer to the guidelines for role plays and simulations in the Instructional Approaches section of this Teacher Annotated Edition. Tell students they will act out the identity of one of the important people from the history of North Africa and the Sahel who used the Mediterranean to reach this area of the world. Possible personages could be: A Phoenician, a Roman, an Arab, a British subject, a Frenchman, a missionary (of any religion), a Kushite, a Muslim, and so on. Ask students to write out clues to their identity or a short speech that they will read to the class. The class will then try to guess their identities.

Concluding the Chapter

Develop a game for your classroom entitled, "What Do You Remember About North Africa?" Make a large chart with five horizontal and vertical columns. Write these headings across the top of the vertical columns: "Physical Features, Cultural Characteristics, Economic Patterns, Influences of the Past," and "Miscellaneous." Develop five questions for each column, and write them in the appropriate squares. Cover each separately with a removable piece of construction paper marked with a point value. As point values increase, so should the level of difficulty of the questions. The class can be divided into two or three teams. After selecting a column and point value, members should discuss their question before giving an answer. This is one way to review chapter material before a quiz.

Have students do the Chapter 7 Career Worksheet in the Teacher Resource Book for information about the career of hydrology. Students especially interested in this career could investigate it further and prepare reports to share with the class.

ANSWERS TO CHAPTER 21 QUESTIONS

Content Check Questions
page 436

1. Refer to Section 1 content.
2. Refer to Glossary in Student Edition.
3. Desert, Nile River Basin, plateaus. (p. 430, map)
4. Mostly desert; part desert with wetter tropical savanna. (p. 432)
5. Along the Nile River. (pp. 432–433)
6. Farming. (p. 432)
7. Answers will vary. It has brought irrigation, flood control, and electrical power. Problems are that the dam is holding back silt so that farmers must now use fertilizer, and the dam has reduced the river's flow, allowing Mediterranean salt water to erode the Nile Delta. Yes, because it has im-

proved living and economic conditions. (p. 433)

page 443

1. Refer to Section 2 content.
2. Refer to Glossary in Student Edition.
3. Along the coast. (p. 437)
4. The sale of oil and natural gas. (p. 439)
5. Expanding industry, building railroads and highways, improving ports. (pp. 439, 441)
6. Atlas Mountains enable winds coming off the Mediterranean Sea to drop their moisture, thus creating a fertile plain along the coast. The mountains prevent moisture from reaching further inland. The Atlas Mountains cause population and agriculture to be concentrated along the coast

while the interior is sparsely settled desert. (pp. 437–438)

page 447

1. Refer to Section 3 content.
2. Refer to Glossary in Student Edition.
3. Desert, tropical savanna, forest. (p. 443)
4. The unreliability of rain makes the region very dry. (p. 444)
5. Overgrazing, growing crops on arid land, overharvesting of timber. (p. 445)
6. Berbers, Arabs, black Africans of Ghana, Mali, and Songhai; the French. (p. 446)
7. The northern Sahel is desert, scarcely populated, devoid of farming; the southern Sahel is wooded tropical savanna, more heavily populated and agricultural. (p. 443)

Special Feature Questions
page 434, The Urban World: "Cairo: Urban Growth"

1. Too rapid a growth of population within a city area.
2. Lack of city services, inadequate housing, overcrowded living conditions, low standard of living.
3. Egypt is forced to spend its limited income and resources on solving the problems of one particular city rather than the nation's development as a whole.

page 440, Focus on History: "Ancient Leptis Magna"

1. East of modern Tripoli, Libya. Phoenicians. Romans.
2. The city was located in mountainous foothills that were used to grow olives and wheat. These products produced wealth and made Leptis Magna a cultural center.

page 438, Using Graphic Skills: "Comparing Thematic Maps"

1. Tropical monsoon and tropical rain forest climate regions have the greatest amount of rainfall. Dry desert climate region has the least amount of rainfall.
2. Population density is higher in those areas that have a greater amount of rainfall and lower in those areas that have a lesser amount of rainfall.

3. Answers may vary but should show that a relationship exists between annual rainfall, climate regions, and population density. A climate region determines how much rainfall occurs within the region, which in turn explains why many or few people live in the region.

Photo/Illustration Caption Questions
page 430

Mauritania. (p. 430)

page 431

Mediterranean Sea. (p. 430)

page 432

The White Nile and the Blue Nile. (p. 432)

page 435

Hieroglyphic writing, paper from papyrus, and a calendar for the growing season. (p. 435)

page 436

Nasser's nationalization of the Suez Canal led to British, French, and Israeli intervention to regain control of the canal and United States intervention to help stop the invasion. (p. 436)

page 437

The narrow coastal plain along the Mediterranean coast north of the Atlas Mountains. (p. 437)

page 441

The landscape and climate along the coast are suitable for this type of agriculture. (p. 441)

page 442

Islamic religion, Arabic language, also include styles of dress and architecture. (p. 442)

page 444

Morocco, Tunisia, Western Sahara. (p. 444)

page 445

Overgrazing, growing crops on arid land, overharvesting of timber. (p. 445)

page 446

The southern area. (p. 446)

page 447

Timbuktu. (p. 446)

Chapter 21 Review Questions
page 448, Reviewing Vocabulary

1. All deal with water.
2. All refer to or are in the Sahel.
3. All refer to areas in the Arab West.
4. Both refer to control by a foreign power.
5. All refer to desert features.
6. All refer to human features in the Nile Valley.

pages 448–449, Remembering the Facts

1. Flatlands, rock, gravel plateaus, and sand. (p. 429)
2. Egypt and Sudan; Arab West made up of Libya, Tunisia, Algeria, and Morocco. (p. 429)
3. Sinai Peninsula. (p. 431)
4. White Nile, Blue Nile. (p. 432)
5. 3.5 percent. (p. 433)
6. Cotton. (p. 433)
7. The shift toward large-scale farming has cost many fellahin their jobs, since fewer people are needed on farms. (p. 433)
8. Desert. (p. 437)
9. Mediterranean. (p. 437)
10. Dates, grapes, olives, citrus fruits, and cereal crops. (p. 438)
11. Oil and natural gas are energy resources; mineral resources include phosphates, iron ore, zinc, manganese, coal, lead, copper. (p. 439)
12. France. (pp. 442, 446)
13. Chad, Niger, Mali, Mauritania. (p. 443)
14. Southern part. (p. 445)

page 449, Understanding the Facts

1. Both are deserts in terms of their composition of rock, gravel, and sand; both are plateaus in terms of their elevation. (pp. 429, 431)
2. Due to numerous cataracts, or waterfalls, and long stretches of rapids. (p. 432)
3. Without the Nile River, Egypt might not even exist because it would be a barren desert with little population. (pp. 430–433)
4. Climate and topography form a fertile coastal plain between the Atlas Mountains and the Mediterranean coast. (pp. 437–438)
5. The economies of Egypt and Sudan are based on agriculture that thrives along the Nile River Basin. While many people of the Arab West are involved in agriculture, these countries are fortunate to have energy and mineral resources that have added wealth to their economies and enabled industrial growth to occur. (pp. 432–433, 438–441)
6. The money acquired from natural resources goes to expand industry and transportation, improve health care and education, and raise the living standards of the people. (pp. 439, 441)
7. They brought to North Africa the Islamic religion and the Arabic language. (p. 442)
8. Tunisia has very little energy or mineral wealth and must rely exclusively on farming; as a result it has remained less industrialized and developed than the other countries of the Arab West. (pp. 439, 441)
9. Both have large areas of desert and tropical savanna. (pp. 430, 443)
10. Little rain, little food, prolonged drought, starvation. (p. 444)

page 449, Thinking Critically and Creatively

1. Landscape and climate are prime determinants of where people live. Most of Egypt is desert except for the very small percentage of land along the Nile that can support people and agriculture.
2. Answers will vary but should indicate that Egypt's location at the junction of the Nile, the Suez Canal, and the Mediterranean Sea makes it a hub of transportation and cultural exchange. Egypt's long history also contributes to its cultural importance.

3. Answers may vary. Without the Atlas Mountains, there would be no orographic effect and little rain along the Tell, resulting in few people living near the coast, little agriculture, and more dependence on natural resources.

4. Answers will vary, but the region will continue to be affected by limited resources, harsh desert climate, desertification, and limited water. The region may be much the same in 2020 as it is today, with the problems much more intensified.

5. Answers will vary but could include: explore for and develop energy and mineral resources; promote modern agricultural practices; build reservoirs to control rainfall; tap underground water sources; plant more trees that can survive in a dry area; burn cow dung instead of wood.

page 449, Reinforcing Graphic Skills

1. Bamako, Mali. Largeau, Chad.
2. Under 10 inches (25 cm) for both countries.
3. The boundaries of climate regions and rainfall regions coincide very closely. Areas that have similar landscape and water features will often have similar types of climate and average rainfall amounts.

EVALUATING CHAPTER 21

World Geography: People and Places provides chapter tests to help evaluate student performance. To evaluate student mastery of Chapter 21, give students Chapter 21 Test from the Teacher Resource Book. This test may also be used for pretesting or retesting purposes. Other tests can be made from the questions available in the Test Generator Software.

Lesson Plan Suggestions—Chapter 21

SE—Student Edition   TAE—Teacher Annotated Edition   TG—Test Generator
TRB—Teacher Resource Book   TSP—Transparency Package

Section 1   Egypt and Sudan (pp. 429–436)

Chapter Objectives	Suggested Teaching Strategies	Review

1. describe the major physical, economic, cultural, and historical features of Egypt and Sudan.	**Teacher Preparation**
	SE, Reading Assignment, pp. 429–436
	TAE, Unit 7 Suggested Resources
	    Unit 7 Overview, p. T213
	    Introducing Unit 7, pp. T213–T214
	    Chapter 21 Overview, pp. T214–T215
	    Introducing Chapter 21, p. T215
	TRB, Chapter 21 Teacher Notes: Section 1
	Teaching Options
	TAE, Introducing Unit 7, pp. T213–T214
	    Introducing Chapter 21, p. T215
	    Objective 1 Activities, pp. T215–T216
	TRB, Chapter 21 Teacher Notes: Section 1,
	    Extending the Lesson
	    Chapter 21 Reading
	    Chapter 21 Skill Activity
		SE, Content Check, p. 436

Section 2   Arab West (pp. 437–443)

Chapter Objectives	Suggested Teaching Strategies	Review

2. describe the major physical, economic, cultural, and historical features of the Arab West.	**Teacher Preparation**
	SE, Reading Assignment, pp. 437–443
	TAE, Unit 7 Suggested Resources
	    Chapter 21 Overview, pp. T214–T215
	TRB, Chapter 21 Teacher Notes: Section 2
	Teaching Options
	TAE, Objective 2 Activities, pp. T216–T217
	TRB, Chapter 21 Teacher Notes: Section 2,
	    Extending the Lesson
	    Chapter 21 Skill Activity
		SE, Content Check, p. 443

Section 3   The Sahel (pp. 443–447)

Chapter Objectives	Suggested Teaching Strategies	Review

3. describe the major physical, economic, cultural, and historical features of the Sahel.
 	
Skill Objective: compare thematic maps.
	Teacher Preparation
	SE, Reading Assignment, pp. 443–447
	TAE, Unit 7 Suggested Resources
	    Chapter 21 Overview, pp. T214–T215
	TRB, Chapter 21 Teacher Notes: Section 3
	Teaching Options
	TAE, Objective 3 Activities, p. T217
	TRB, Chapter 21 Teacher Notes: Section 3,
	    Extending the Lesson
	    Chapter 21 Skill Activity
	SE, *Using Graphic Skills,*
	    "Comparing Thematic Maps,"
	    pp. 438–439
		SE, Content Check, p. 447

Chapter 21 Review and Evaluation

Suggested Teaching Strategies	Review	Evaluation

TAE, Objective 4 Activities,
    pp. T217–T218
    Concluding Chapter 21,
    p. T218
TSP, Transparency 4
	SE, Chapter 21 Review,
	    pp. 448–449
	TRB, Chapter 21 Review
	    Worksheet
		TRB, Chapter 21 Test
		    Unit 7 Pretest, Map and
		    Content Worksheets
		TG, Chapter 21

CHAPTER 22 SOUTHWEST ASIA

Student Edition pp. 450–473

CHAPTER 22 OBJECTIVES

At the conclusion of this chapter, students will be able to:

1. describe the major physical, economic, cultural, and historical features of Israel.
2. describe the major physical, economic, cultural, and historical features of Saudi Arabia.
3. describe the major physical, economic, cultural, and historical features of Turkey.
4. describe the major physical, economic, cultural, and historical features of Iran.
5. describe the major physical, economic, cultural, and historical features of the Middle East Core countries, Arabian Peninsula countries, and Northern Middle East countries.
6. summarize the chief geographic features of Southwest Asia.

CHAPTER 22 SKILL OBJECTIVE

After completing the *Using Graphic Skills* exercise in this chapter, the student should be able to read territorial boundaries.

CHAPTER 22 OVERVIEW

The countries of Southwest Asia are grouped for study in this chapter because of similarities in physical geography and because the majority are Muslim. However, this shared landscape and religion unite nations of great diversity in their cultural, historical, and ethnic backgrounds.

An illustration of this diversity is the nation to which *Section 1* of this chapter is dedicated—Israel. A small nation founded by immigrants from around the world, its healthy economy has been developed upon multiple bases and in spite of limited resources. Judaism and Christianity, religions now with followers worldwide, were born in this land and share common roots. Saudi Arabia, however, the subject of *Section 2,* is a giant Arab state

and a center of Islam—another religion that shares its source with Judaism and Christianity. With the discovery of oil in Saudi Arabia, this nation also became wealthy, but as a direct result of this natural resource. Turkey is a contrast to Saudi Arabia, and in *Section 3* the similarities and differences of its geographical features are explained. The student learns that it is a nation of highlands and plateaus with areas of rich farmland and where lifestyles are more European than Asian. Another country for which Islam is of great importance is Iran, and it is this nation that receives the focus of *Section 4.* Cultural and linguistic differences separate Iran from other Middle Eastern nations, and much of Iran's oil wealth has recently been spent to finance Iran's continuing war with neighboring Iraq. Other countries defined as Middle East Core countries, Arabian Peninsula countries, and Northern Middle East countries, are described in *Section 5*. These nations also share the Islamic religion but vary in wealth, ranging from developing nations to the world's richest.

This chapter's special feature explains the historical background and basic tenets of Judaism, Christianity, and Islam.

CHAPTER 22 ACTIVITIES

Introducing Chapter 22

Prepare a "mystery news" bulletin board with news items from the countries to be studied in this chapter. However, cut off the headings and date lines. Number the articles and identify them for your own reference. Mounting the articles on art paper or cardboard will facilitate handling and display. Tell the class that as they read about the countries of Southwest Asia, they will attempt to identify the country or region with which the news item is concerned. Read a few of the collected articles to the class and allow them to attempt to guess the country in question. Some students may be able to make fairly accurate identifications. Replace articles on the "mystery news" bulletin board when this activity is concluded. Explain to the class that when they have concluded their study of this chapter, they will once again use the articles in an activity.

Chapter 22 Reading Assignments

Objective 1	Student Ed. pp. 451–458
Objective 2	Student Ed. pp. 458–461
Objective 3	Student Ed. pp. 461–464
Objective 4	Student Ed. pp. 464–468
Objective 5	Student Ed. pp. 468–471

● Teaching ■ Reinforcing ★ Enriching

Unmarked activities deal with three or more features listed in the chapter objectives. Activities marked with the following letters deal with:
Ⓟ Physical features.
Ⓔ Economic features.
Ⓒ Cultural features.
Ⓗ Historical features.

Objective 1 Activities   Ⓟ Ⓒ

● Objective 1 Teaching Activity
Refer to the guidelines for audiovisuals in the Instructional Approaches section of this Teacher Annotated Edition, and show the film *An Israeli Family* listed in the Suggested Resources section. After the class has viewed the film, use a wall map to lead a discussion. Have students locate Israel, pointing out the exact location on the map. Ask students: Which countries border Israel? What are the important bodies of water in Israel? Where are the Golan Heights, the West Bank, and the Gaza Strip? What is the political significance of the Golan Heights and the West Bank? Name three cities in Israel. Next, review the film that was shown and ask pertinent questions developed from its content related to Israel today.

Refer students to Chapter 22 Reading in the Teacher Resource Book for further information related to this objective.

■ Objective 1 Reinforcing Activity
Show the filmstrip *Arabs and Jews* listed in the Suggested Resources in this Teacher Annotated Edition. After the class has viewed the filmstrip, have them suggest ways in which trust could be developed between Israelis and Palestinians. Refer to the guidelines for role plays and simulations in the Instructional Approaches section of this Teacher Annotated Edition, and prepare the class for a "Meet the Press" simulation. Ask for several student volunteers to represent Israelis, several to represent Palestinians, and several to represent

members of the press. Have press members prepare questions for the Israelis and the Palestinians on the issue of the Israeli presence in Palestine. Instruct the students representing the Israelis and the Palestinians to be prepared to answer the questions posed by the press and by each other, defending their positions on the issue. Group members should emphasize their ethnic loyalties and the histories that have brought them to this point. Provide a time limit for the press conference, after which students who did not have an active role may ask questions and challenge the press or members of either group.

Objective 2 Activities

● Objective 2 Teaching Activity
Give the students a pretest on Saudi Arabia consisting of ten questions. Explain to the class that they will not be graded on the test and that it is being given to test their present knowledge of Saudi Arabia. You may use the following questions or make your own. You could also refer to the Test Generator Software for Chapter 22 in order to make up an appropriate test.
1. Where is Saudi Arabia located?
2. What is the significance of Mecca?
3. What religious beliefs do the Saudi Arabians follow?
4. On what economic activity is the Saudi Arabian economy based?
5. Name one important body of water that surrounds Saudi Arabia.
6. Name one commodity imported by Saudi Arabia.
7. What is Saudi Arabia's major export?
8. What kind of government does Saudi Arabia have?
9. Describe its climate.
10. Is Saudi Arabia a wealthy country or a poor country? Explain.

Tell students to determine if their answers were right or wrong as they read Section 2 of Chapter 22. After the assignment has been read, review and correct the answers orally in class.

Refer students to the Chapter 22 Skill Activity in the Teacher Resource Book in relation to this objective.

★ Objective 2 Enriching Activity ©
Provide the class with handouts that contain the five basic teachings of Muhammad, the Ten Commandments from the Old Testament, and Christ's Sermon on the Mount from the New Testament. Ask students to study these tenets of Islam, Judaism, and Christianity, and prepare a chart that will show their similarities and differences. Hand out chart outlines to the class and fill in the chart with them, using an overhead projector or the chalkboard and discussing the various beliefs as you go. Ask the class what they see reflected in these beliefs that show their common roots.

An excellent resource for information on Islam is *The Middle East*, published by Congressional Quarterly, Inc., 1414 22nd St., N.W., Washington, D.C. 20037.

Objective 3 Activities

● Objective 3 Teaching Activity
Point out to students that the geography of Turkey is politically strategic. Inform them that Turkey is surrounded by waterways that are strategically important. Place a map of Turkey before the class, and ask: What important waterways surround Turkey? Students should indicate the Bosporus, Sea of Marmara, and the Dardanelles. Ask: Why are they strategically important? Why is Turkey particularly important to the Soviet Union? What is the collective name of the waterways? Have students point out on the map those features that make Turkey's geography different from that of other nations in this world region. Refer to the Student Edition to study the country's climate and point out the climate areas on the map. Ask students to speculate about what these differences mean in regard to lifestyle between Turkey and a country like Saudi Arabia. Next, review the bases for the economies of Saudi Arabia and Turkey, and have students speculate with regard to which type of economy is most desirable.

Refer students to the Chapter 22 Skill Activity in the Teacher Resource Book for another activity related to this objective.

■ Objective 3 Reinforcing Activity Ⓗ

Remind the students that Turkey has a long and colorful history with interesting events and historical figures, as do many of the countries of this world region. Refer to the guidelines for cooperative learning in the Instructional Approaches section of this Teacher Annotated Edition, and then provide topics for various groups such as the following: Early civilizations of the Tigris and Euphrates River Valleys; the Byzantine Empire; Constantinople/Istanbul; Justinian; the Christian Church in the Byzantine Empire; Byzantine culture, art, and law; the Ottoman Empire; Turkey's relations with the United States. Have the students present their research projects to the class and encourage them to supplement their oral reports with slides, photographs, illustrations that they make themselves, or posters that they have prepared.

Objective 4 Activities

● Objective 4 Teaching Activity

Refer to the guidelines for lecture in the Instructional Approaches section of this Teacher Annotated Edition, and prepare a very informal lecture about the geographical features of Iran. Use an opaque projector to show photographs and illustrations. At the end of the lecture, bring out the Soviet interest in this region, the war with Iraq, the importance of the Persian Gulf to the world's supply of oil, Iran's attitude toward the United States, and the current problems in the Persian Gulf. Follow the lecture with a discussion about the stereotypical ideas westerners have about Iranians and that Iranians have about westerners. Ask the class for ideas, and list their responses on the chalkboard. Ask students: Why do you believe these stereotypes exist? Do governments promote them? Does the press? End the discussion by having the class consider the pros and cons of living in a country that is governed by a theocracy.

Refer students to Chapter 22 Skill Activity in the Teacher Resource Book for another activity related to this objective.

■ Objective 4 Reinforcing Activity Ⓒ

Refer to the guidelines for case studies, and ask students to do in-depth studies of the two sects of Islam—*Shi'a* and *Sunni*. The class may be divided into two groups or broken down into smaller groups who will then pool their information. Explain to the class that Iranians are members of the *Shi'a* sect of Islam, while Muslims of Southwest Asia are of the *Sunni* sect. Have groups make their reports and, as reports are being given, draw up a chart on the chalkboard comparing the similarities and differences of the two sects. Ask the class to speculate about the relation between these religious beliefs and the political situation existing today in Iran and in other Muslim countries. How would these religious beliefs affect the attitude of Iranians toward foreigners and non-Muslims? Toward a more liberal neighbor? Does understanding the tenets of the *Shi'a* Muslims make it easier to understand Iranian attitudes and actions? Finally, have the class speculate about how relations with a Muslim country could be improved through the understanding of their religious beliefs.

Objective 5 Activities

● Objective 5 Teaching Activity

Write the names of the countries studied in Section 5 of this chapter on slips of paper and place them in a container. Ask each student, one at a time, to withdraw a slip of paper from the container. That student should then tell one fact, either of a historical, economic, cultural, or physical nature, about that country. Then he or she should replace the slip of paper in the container. If the next person who draws a slip gets the same country, he or she must still tell a fact about it, but it must be a different fact. The game may be played with teams competing against each other. If a person is unable to give a fact, he or she is "out." The team with the most people left at the end of the designated time allowed for the game is the winner.

Refer students to Chapter 22 Skill Activity in the Teacher Resource Book for another activity related to this objective.

■ Objective 5 Reinforcing Activity

Assign to each student the writing of a short statement consisting of one or two sentences describing either a person, place, thing, or event in one of the countries studied in this section, backed up by the section and page number where the information can be found in the Student Edition. Have each student in turn read his statement before the class, while the rest of the class tries to guess what or who is being described. If no one is able to guess correctly, have the student who made the statement give the page in the Student Edition where the information can be located, and, as a class, look up and read the passage indicated. If one student selects the same information to present in his or her statement that some other student has selected, he or she must find another person, place, thing, or event to describe. Continue with this activity until all students have had the opportunity to present a statement.

Objective 6 Activities

● Objective 6 Teaching Activity

Using statistics from reference books, have the students create a series of statistical charts for each country of Southwest Asia that will show the national wealth or GNP (Gross National Product); average income per person; average life span; percent of literacy; infant mortality rate; overall mortality rate; the population now and predicted for the year 2000; and other economic and cultural data. The charts may be prepared in advance as handouts showing the categories of information required. It would then be the students' job to do the research to fill in the correct amounts and percentages. Based on the information they gather in their statistical charts, have the class draw conclusions about the effects of national wealth on a country's people. End by asking the class under what circumstances might a country's wealth have no effect on the lifestyles of the majority of the people.

■ Objective 6 Reinforcing Activity

Have students each bring in a current editorial from newspapers about any of the countries studied in this chapter. Ask the students to re-write the editorial from the point of view of a citizen of the country the article discusses. Ask each student to share his or her original article and its revised version with the class and explain the effect writing from a citizen's point of view had on the slant of the editorial. Allow the remainder of the class to critique the way in which the editorial was changed and the reasons for changing it. Critics should be prepared to tell how they believe it should have been changed and why.

Concluding Chapter 22

Review the news articles on the "mystery news" bulletin board prepared in the Introducing Chapter 22 activity. Make several groups and give two or three articles to each group. Tell the groups that they will be asked to describe the contents of the articles in their own words and explain whether they relate to the economy, culture, history, or physical geography of the country. Explain that a current event would relate to current history, but might also contain elements of any of the countries' features. The groups should attempt to identify the countries the articles concern and then invent appropriate headlines for them. Have each group present its results to the class. Match the headlines you removed from the articles and reserved for use at this time. Put the headlines on the articles to which they belong, and replace them on the bulletin board as you discuss with the class the results of their efforts at identification. This activity would, perhaps, present a good opportunity to discuss the skill of recognizing and expressing the main idea in a paragraph or article, since it is this idea that would probably create the best headline.

ANSWERS TO CHAPTER 22 QUESTIONS

Content Check Questions
page 458

1. Refer to Section 1 content.
2. Refer to Glossary in Student Edition.
3. Mountains of Galilee, Golan Heights, Judean Hills, Negev Desert, Plain of Sharon, Great Rift Valley. (pp. 452–453)
4. Desert. (p. 453)
5. Potash, magnesium, bromide, salt, copper, phosphates, and a little oil. (p. 453)
6. Drained swamps, built irrigation systems, fertilized soils, and modernized farm machinery. (p. 453)
7. 1948. (p. 457)
8. Answers will vary but basically the Palestinians do not like having the Jewish people take over land they feel is theirs. (pp. 456–457)

page 461

1. Refer to Section 2 content.
2. Refer to Glossary in Student Edition.
3. Largest in area. (p. 458)
4. Plateaus, deserts, highlands, steppes, lowlands. (pp. 458–459)
5. Oil. (p. 459)
6. Religious pilgrimages to Mecca and Medina. (p. 460)
7. Answers will vary. Saudis view themselves as defenders of Islam. They only want people who believe in that faith to visit in fulfillment of their religious duty. They worry that the influences of non-Muslims could change the culture of Saudi Arabia.

page 464

1. Refer to Section 3 content.
2. Refer to Glossary in Student Edition.
3. Bosporus, Sea of Marmara, Dardanelles. (p. 461)
4. Highlands and plateaus. (p. 461)
5. Middle-latitude steppe and Mediterranean. (p. 462)
6. Coastal areas and the western Anatolian Plateau. (p. 462)

7. Muslim. (p. 463)
8. Answers will vary. One possibility is that geographically and historically Turkey has had more contact with the nations of Europe than with its Arab neighbors. Language differences, the status of women, and attempts at modernization have separated Turkey from its Arab neighbors.

page 468

1. Refer to Section 4 content.
2. Refer to Glossary in Student Edition.
3. Major oil-producing nations are located along the Persian Gulf. (pp. 459, 465)
4. Mountains and desert in central Iran, plateaus and desert in eastern Iran. (pp. 452, map; 465, map)
5. Oil. (p. 466)
6. Islam. (p. 464)
7. Theocracy, a government run by religious leaders. (p. 467)
8. Income from oil has gone to finance the war at the expense of industrial development; oil production has been reduced. (p. 466)

page 471

1. Refer to Section 5 content.
2. Jordan. (p. 469)
3. Damascus, Syria. (p. 469)
4. Very poorly; countries on the southern part of the Arabian Peninsula have little or no oil, whereas the Gulf States are oil-rich and among the world's wealthiest nations. (pp. 470–471)
5. To establish a satellite country that would give the Soviet Union closer access to the Persian Gulf and its oilfields. (p. 471)

Special Feature Questions
page 454, Focus on Culture: "Three Major Religions"

1. Judaism, Christianity, Islam; Judaism.
2. They all believe in only one god and consider Jerusalem a sacred city.

page 457, Using Graphic Skills: "Reading Territorial Boundaries"

1. Sinai Peninsula.
2. Lebanon.
3. Golan Heights, West Bank, Gaza Strip.
4. Provided a buffer zone between Israel and Egypt and gave Israel direct access to the Red Sea and to the Suez Canal.
5. The area bordering the Suez Canal.
6. The West Bank.

Photo/Illustration Caption Questions
page 452

Tigris and Euphrates Rivers. (p. 452)

page 453

Almost one-half of the country. (p. 452)

page 455

Israel's size, population, and military personnel are small in comparison to those of its Arab neighbors. (p. 455)

page 459

Oil makes up 99 percent of Saudi Arabia's exports. (p. 459)

page 460

The Muslim religion requires a pilgrimage to Mecca once during a lifetime. (p. 460)

page 462

Mediterranean. (p. 462)

page 463

Turkey. (p. 463)

page 465

The high Elburz Mountains along the Caspian Sea. (p. 465)

page 466

Farsi language, poetry, architecture, gardens, carpets, Islamic religion. (p. 467)

page 468

Tigris and Euphrates rivers. (p. 468)

page 469

Between Europe, Africa, and Asia. (p. 469)

page 470

Religious conflicts and civil war. (p. 470)

Chapter 22 Review Questions
page 472, Reviewing Vocabulary

1. m u t t o n
2. s u l t a n
3. k i b b u t z
4. m o s h a v
5. d e s a l i n i z a t i o n
6. h a j j
7. q a n a t s
8. s h a h
9. m i n a r e t
10. t h e o c r a c y   SAUDI ARABIA

page 473, Remembering the Facts

1. The Middle East. (p. 451)
2. Oil; crossroads between Europe, Africa, Asia; birthplace of western civilization. (p. 451)
3. Jordan River, Sea of Galilee, Dead Sea. (p. 453)
4. Oil. (p. 459)
5. Arabian Peninsula. (p. 458)
6. Persia. (p. 465)
7. The coast along the Caspian Sea. (p. 465)
8. South of the Khuzistan Plain along the Persian Gulf coast. (p. 466)
9. Sects of the Muslim religion. (p. 467)
10. Mountains. (p. 461)
11. Oil. (p. 471)

page 473, Understanding the Facts

1. Israel is isolated in terms of industrialization, urbanization, immigrant population, religion, language, and culture. (p. 454)
2. While only a small percent of people work in the oil industry, oil is just about Saudi Arabia's only export. (p. 459)
3. Limited rainfall, water, and arable land. (pp. 459–460)
4. Turkey overlaps between Europe and Asia and controls the Soviet Union's access to the Mediterranean Sea. (p. 461)

5. It went from the Shah's empire to a theocracy, a government run by religious leaders. (pp. 467–468)

page 473, Thinking Critically and Creatively

1. Severe. Answers will vary but should state Saudis would lose major source of income.
2. Answers will vary but should include that Ankara was more centralized and a more modern city than Istanbul.
3. Answers will vary but may include that these Muslim countries would be able to pool their resources in support of Arabs and Palestinians.

page 473, Reinforcing Graphic Skills

1. The Golan Heights is an elevated area that gives Israel surveillance over bordering areas of Lebanon and Syria.
2. The West Bank is a river valley lowland. The Gaza Strip is coastal plain. Israel contends that the West Bank up to the Jordan River forms a natural boundary, and the Gaza Strip is a natural extension of Israeli-held territory. Jordan and Israel contend their territory was illegally seized in war.
3. Answers will vary but could include that cultural differences, historical claims, and national pride are involved.

EVALUATING CHAPTER 22

World Geography: People and Places provides chapter tests to help evaluate student performance. To evaluate student mastery of Chapter 22, give students Chapter 22 Test from the Teacher Resource Book. This test may also be used for pretesting or retesting purposes. Other tests can be made from the questions available in the Test Generator Software.

Lesson Plan Suggestions — Chapter 22

| SE—Student Edition   TAE—Teacher Annotated Edition   TG—Test Generator |
| TRB—Teacher Resource Book   TSP—Transparency Package |

Section 1   Israel (pp. 451–458)

Chapter Objectives	Suggested Teaching Strategies	Review

1. describe the major physical, economic, cultural, and historical features of Israel.	**Teacher Preparation**
	SE, Reading Assignment, pp. 451–458
	TAE, Unit 7 Suggested Resources
	    Chapter 22 Overview, pp. T223–T224
	    Introducing Chapter 22, p. T224
	TRB, Chapter 22 Teacher Notes: Section 1
	Teaching Options
	TAE, Introducing Chapter 22, p. T224
	    Objective 1 Activities, pp. T224–T225
	TRB, Chapter 22 Teacher Notes: Section 1,
	    Extending the Lesson
	    Chapter 22 Reading
	    Chapter 22 Skill Activity
		SE, Content Check, p. 458

Section 2 Saudi Arabia (pp. 458–461)

Chapter Objectives	Suggested Teaching Strategies	Review
2. describe the major physical, economic, cultural, and historical features of Saudi Arabia.	**Teacher Preparation** SE, Reading Assignment, pp. 458–461 TAE, Unit 7 Suggested Resources Chapter 22 Overview, pp. T223–T224 TRB, Chapter 22 Teacher Notes: Section 2 **Teaching Options** TAE, Objective 2 Activities, p. T225 TRB, Chapter 22 Teacher Notes: Section 2, Extending the Lesson Chapter 22 Skill Activity	SE, Content Check, p. 461

Section 3 Turkey (pp. 461–464)

Chapter Objectives	Suggested Teaching Strategies	Review
3. describe the major physical, economic, cultural, and historical features of Turkey.	**Teacher Preparation** SE, Reading Assignment, pp. 461–464 TAE, Unit 7 Suggested Resources Chapter 22 Overview, pp. T223–T224 TRB, Chapter 22 Teacher Notes: Section 3 **Teaching Options** TAE, Objective 3 Activities, pp. T225–T226 TRB, Chapter 22 Teacher Notes: Section 3, Extending the Lesson Chapter 22 Skill Activity	SE, Content Check, p. 464

Section 4 Iran (pp. 464–468)

Chapter Objectives	Suggested Teaching Strategies	Review
4. describe the major physical, economic, cultural, and historical features of Iran.	**Teacher Preparation** SE, Reading Assignment, pp. 464–468 TAE, Unit 7 Suggested Resources Chapter 22 Overview, pp. T223–T224 TRB, Chapter 22 Teacher Notes: Section 4 **Teaching Options** TAE, Objective 4 Activities, p. T226 TRB, Chapter 22 Teacher Notes: Section 4, Extending the Lesson Chapter 22 Skill Activity	SE, Content Check, p. 468

Chapter Objectives	Suggested Teaching Strategies	Review

5. describe the major physical, economic, cultural, and historical features of the Middle East Core countries, Arabian Peninsula countries, and Northern Middle East countries.
 	
 Skill Objective: read territorial boundaries.
	Teacher Preparation
	 SE, Reading Assignment, pp. 468–471
	 TAE, Unit 7 Suggested Resources
	     Chapter 22 Overview, pp. T223–T224
	 TRB, Chapter 22 Teacher Notes: Section 5
	 Teaching Options
	 TAE, Objective 5 Activities, pp. T226–T227
	 TRB, Chapter 22 Teacher Notes: Section 5,
	     Extending the Lesson
	     Chapter 22 Skill Activity
	 SE, *Using Graphic Skills,*
	     "Reading Territorial Boundaries,"
	     pp. 456–457
		SE, Content Check, p. 471

Chapter 22 Review and Evaluation

Suggested Teaching Strategies	Review	Evaluation

TAE, Objective 6 Activities,
     p. T227
 Concluding Chapter 22,
     p. T227
	SE, Chapter 22 Review,
	     pp. 472–473
	 TRB, Chapter 22 Review
	     Worksheet
		TRB, Chapter 22 Test
		     Unit 7 Posttest, Map and
		     Content Worksheets
		 TG, Chapter 22

Unit 7 Review and Evaluation

Suggested Teaching Strategies	Review	Evaluation

TAE, Concluding Unit 7,
     pp. T232–T233
 TRB, Unit 7 Career
     Worksheet
 TSP, Transparency 4
	SE, Unit 7 Review, pp. 474–475	TRB, Unit 7

CONCLUDING UNIT 7

Circulate a list of all the countries studied in this unit. Each student should sign up for one. At the top of the list, it should read: "As representatives of your country, you are summoned to a meeting of the North Africa/ Southwest Asia Economic Symposium at which you will attempt to learn more about the economic problems and goals of your neighboring countries." Each student should use material from the text plus any other outside information available to help prepare a presentation. The presentation should answer questions such as these: How is your country different from the other nations present at this symposium economically, culturally, and historically? What are your country's immediate and long-range economic goals? What are the economic strengths and weaknesses of your country? How can cooperation with the other nations present here help your country? After the presentations, allow a few minutes for the representatives of the various nations to discuss possible cooperative plans. If any agreements are reached, write them on the chalkboard. When the symposium is over, draw up a document listing the agreements, have each representative sign it, and present copies to all participants. Create an agenda of outstanding disputes on which no agreement was reached during the symposium to take home to their countries for the consideration of their leaders. Discuss with students how they believe the leaders of various countries would vote on the disputes.

Unit 7 Exam in the Teacher Resource Book may be administered.

UNIT 7 REVIEW QUESTIONS

page 474, Thinking About the Unit

1. The general climate of North Africa and Southwest Asia is dry and hot, which influences people to live in areas where there is sufficient water and rainfall to support settlement and agriculture. Such areas are along the Mediterranean coast of North Africa and along the Mediterranean and Black Sea coasts of Southwest Asia, as well as along the Nile River Valley in Egypt and in the Tigris and Euphrates River Valley in Southwest Asia.

2. This area intersects Europe, Africa, and Asia and lies between two major water areas, the Mediterranean Sea and the Arabian Sea. North Africa borders the entire southern edge of Europe, while parts of Southwest Asia border the Soviet Union.

3. As Islam was carried from the Arabian Peninsula to Southwest Asia and North Africa, it became established as the major religion in all the countries of this region, with the exception of Israel. The Islamic religion has been part of the region's culture for centuries and has given a common cultural identification to the people of the region.

4. Egypt has a high population growth rate. Its agriculture is based on the dependable waters of the Nile River and is more productive, making it possible to support a larger population. The population of the Sahel, however, is affected by a combination of poor agricultural conditions that are the result of climate, desertification, drought, and famine.

UNIT 8 AFRICA SOUTH OF THE SAHARA

Student Edition pp. 476–535

UNIT 8 GOALS

At the conclusion of this unit, students will be able to:

1. recognize the diversity of physical features, climate, and cultures in Africa South of the Sahara.
2. identify natural resources of Africa South of the Sahara and their present and future role in the economic development of the nations in this area.
3. explain the problems created by European colonialism in the culture area of Africa South of the Sahara and ways its nations are trying to solve these problems.

UNIT 8 SKILL OBJECTIVE

After completing the *Developing Geography Skills* exercise in this unit, the student should be able to support generalizations.

UNIT 8 OVERVIEW

The focus of Unit 8 of *World Geography: People and Places* is on the physical, economic, cultural, and historical features of Africa South of the Sahara. This world area exemplifies the reason national unity has been difficult for many countries of Africa. It is made up of 2,000 different culture groups living in 40 independent nations, speaking 800 or more languages and dialects. National identity was made even more of a problem because the European colonial powers set national boundaries with no concern for keeping African ethnic groups together. Today these nations are struggling to give their citizens a nationalistic outlook centered on the government instead of ethnic loyalties, and they are also facing many other kinds of challenges.

This unit has been divided into three chapters, each focusing on a region of Africa South of the Sahara. *Chapter 23* deals with the nations of East Africa, almost all of which became independent in the 1960s. These developing nations have economies almost entirely dependent on agriculture. *Chapter 24* introduces West and Central Africa, a region of similar climates and landscapes and of diverse populations and resources where most of the people also are farmers. *Chapter 25* discusses Southern Africa where a once agrarian society was changed and challenged by the discovery of gold, diamonds, and copper. Yet, these nations have not yet solved many of their past problems.

Upon completion of this unit, the student should understand that the term *African* cannot be stereotyped in either human or physical terms, and, through the study of the features of each region, have a better grasp of what Africa South of the Sahara is today and may be in the future.

INTRODUCING UNIT 8

Explain to the class that since they are going to be studying the major physical, economic, cultural, and historical features of the nations that share the southern portion of the African continent that lies below the Sahara, the tasks for study and sharing of notes will be divided with one another. The class will be divided into four large committees, each to become "experts" and prepare summary handouts on the physical, economic, cultural, and historical features of each region. Since there are four regions to be studied—Eastern, Western, Central, and Southern—these committees will rotate topics for each chapter, so that every student has an opportunity to handle all of the kinds of geographic features that describe a place.

The Physical Features Committee will prepare an 8 1/2" × 11" paper map of each country, to be duplicated and given to all class members as a geographic features summary for their notebooks and individual study.

The Cultural Features Committee will be responsible for enriching the class's understanding about the peoples' way of life in each of the regions or countries of Africa as they are studied. This will include information about the people themselves and population statistics regarding distribution, density, composition, life expectancy, quality of life, and standard of living. Have students review what was learned in Chapter 6 of the Student Edition about these items and ways of analyzing and reporting them. The Cultural Features Committee should complete its work by attractively summarizing for the class on a bulletin board poster the cultural features of each country or region.

The Economic Features Committee will present to the class information about the kind of economic system a country has; its natural resources; the kinds of and products of agriculture, mining, manufacturing, and service; and the extent of tourism industries. Each country's economic facts and trends should be shown on an overhead projector transparency with appropriate graphics such as diagrams, charts, and pictures.

The Historical Features Committee will take notes from the Student Edition content regarding historical facts about the countries, read other sources to fill in information, and will present a time line for each country.

The presentations of the various committees will represent the Teaching or the Reinforcing Activity for each objective in this unit.

CHAPTER 23 EAST AFRICA

Student Edition pp. 478–495

CHAPTER 23 OBJECTIVES

At the conclusion of this chapter, students will be able to:
1. describe the major physical, economic, cultural, and historical features of Kenya.
2. describe the major physical, economic, cultural, and historical features of Tanzania.
3. describe the major physical, economic, cultural, and historical features of the countries of the Horn of Africa and the countries of the East African Highlands.
4. summarize the chief geographic features of East Africa.

CHAPTER 23 SKILL OBJECTIVE

After completing the *Using Graphic Skills* exercise in this chapter, the student should be able to read pictographs.

CHAPTER 23 OVERVIEW

The countries of East Africa as studied in this chapter share the unique physical feature called the Great Rift Valley. This dominant feature of East Africa was formed thousands of years ago through plate tectonics forces.

The countries that occupy this area also share similar economies and histories. All but one were once European colonies and have only recently gained independence. These developing nations are working hard today to create nationalistic feelings in their citizens. However, overcoming the effects of colonial decisions that divided the continent's ethnic groups has been difficult.

The countries of the region are different in the ways they have developed. Ethiopia, for example, has never been the colony of a foreign power. For many hundreds of years, it was ruled by an emperor and empress. In 1974 it became a republic with a socialist economy. Both Kenya and Tanzania, on the other hand, were British colonies. After they became independent, each turned to a different type of economic system. Today Kenya supports capitalism. Tanzania favors a form of socialism.

In this chapter, the region comprised by the African nations south of the Sahara has been divided into three parts for study. *Section 1* deals with the major physical, economic, cultural, and historical features of Kenya. *Section 2* describes these same features of Tanzania, and *Section 3* summarizes these features for the countries of the Horn of Africa and the East African Highlands. A special feature in this chapter provides background information on East African Parks and Reserves.

CHAPTER 23 ACTIVITIES

Introducing Chapter 23

Before students study this chapter, allow them time to organize into the various committees suggested in the Introducing Unit 8 activity and to confer about what they plan to do during the study of the countries of East Africa. They will probably wish to skim through the Student Edition and become familiar beforehand with the chapter content.

Transform a corner of the classroom into a learning center that might be called "The Story of East Africa." Obtain the aid of a school librarian in finding as many books and reference sources as possible about the East African culture, economy, history, and physical geography.

As the committees complete their presentations, display their work in this learning center. Committees may be given times to use the learning center as an aid in preparing their presentations.

Chapter 23 Reading Assignments

Objective 1	Student Ed. pp. 479–484
Objective 2	Student Ed. pp. 484–487
Objective 3	Student Ed. pp. 487–492

● Teaching	■ Reinforcing	★ Enriching

Unmarked activities deal with three or more features listed in the chapter objectives. Activities marked with the following letters deal with:

Ⓟ Physical features.
Ⓔ Economic features.
Ⓒ Cultural features.
Ⓗ Historical features.

Objective 1 Activities

● Objective 1 Teaching Activity

Have the students on the four committees present their reports on Kenya. Refer to Introducing Unit 8 in the Implementation section of this Teacher Annotated Edition for a description of this activity. In addition to their handout maps of Kenya, have the Physical Features Committee prepare 3-D relief maps out of salt and flour, clay, or plaster for classroom display and further study of the physical features of Africa. The map should show the Great Rift Valley that includes all of the East African countries, Kenya, Tanzania, the Horn of Africa countries, and the East African Highlands. Direct the committee to a few selected sources for needed information in addition to the textbook content, such as a very recent encyclopedia or atlas, a current year's almanac, or such resources as Grolier's *Lands and Peoples*, Reference: Vol. 1, *Africa*, and *National Geographic Picture Atlas of Our World*.

■ Objective 1 Reinforcing Activity

Refer to the guidelines for audiovisuals in the Instructional Approaches section of this Teacher Annotated Edition. Select a filmstrip or film about East Africa, preferably one that shows the geologic formation of the Great Rift Valley and that highlights the countries of Kenya and Tanzania as the Student Edition does.

Reinforce what students viewed in the film by using a large wall map to point out such land features as Mt. Kenya, Lake Victoria, the Rift Valley, and the highlands. Show students that Kenya sits squarely astride the Equator and that 75 percent of the nation is desert, semi-desert, or dry bush country with little rainfall. Point out that only 18 percent is highland steppe with temperate climate and fertile soil. Also point out the highlands, and inform students that over 70 percent of Kenya's population lives there. Discuss what this information reveals about the importance of land to Kenyans. Tell the class that in addition to freedom, land has been the most important factor in Kenyan history. Explain that because most Kenyans are pastoralists who raise and keep cattle, or agriculturists who farm, their lifestyles depend upon ownership of land. Without land for grazing or for growing crops, they cannot survive. If the Historical Features Committee did not bring out the problem of land disputes in their presentation, have them investigate the role land has played in Kenyan history before the British arrived, during British domination, and after independence, and make reports to the class concerning the role of land in Kenya.

Refer students to Chapter 23 Reading in the Teacher Resource Book for further information related to this objective.

★ Objective 1 Enriching Activity Ⓗ Ⓒ

Write on the chalkboard this statement from the Student Edition: "For Africans, Kenya is a symbol of freedom, pride, and self-reliance." Tell the class about Jomo Kenyatta, a Kikuyu folk hero who became Kenya's first president. Assign some students to find out about Jomo Kenyatta's life and significance. Then have them write a biographical sketch of Jomo Kenyatta and explain how his life is related to the fact that Kenya is a symbolic nation for other African countries. Have them share their findings about Kenya's first president with the remainder of the class.

Some other students might report on such topics as the Maasai, protected wildlife, Joy Adamson and her books and paintings, David Livingston, Olympic records for Kenya, and the flag and cities of Kenya. Ask all students to share their reports with the other members of the class.

Objective 2 Activities

● Objective 2 Teaching Activity

Have the various student committees make their presentations on Tanzania. Refer to Introducing Unit 8 in the Implementation section of this Teacher Annotated Edition for a description of how each committee is to prepare and present information.

■ Objective 2 Reinforcing Activity

Acquire travel folders, booklets, and posters about Tanzania from a local travel agency. Refer to the guidelines for role plays and simulations in the Instructional Approaches section of this Teacher Annotated Edition. Ask student volunteers to take turns acting in the role of travel guides conducting tours in different parts of Tanzania basing their actions on the information in the travel material and in the Student Edition. Have the rest of the class assume the role of tourists, asking questions of the tour guides. Tour guides should be prepared to answer questions on any of the geographical features of Tanzania.

Objective 3 Activities

● Objective 3 Teaching Activity

Ask the various student committees to present their reports on the countries of the Horn of Africa and of the East African Highlands. Refer to Introducing Unit 8 in the Implementation section of this Teacher Annotated Edition for a description of this activity.

■ Objective 3 Reinforcing Activity

Ask students to skim the Student Edition content for information about the historical features of the countries of the Horn of Africa and the East African Highlands. Discuss the role historical events and peoples' decisions play in the description of a country. Explain to the class that whether a country has been the homeland of one group of people or of several living in separate territories, or was conquered and reconquered by succeeding groups, this history will make an impact on the landscape, use of resources, economy, and present cultural features of a place. Revolutions, wars, and sudden changes in types of government will change the character of a place. Historical decisions, such as the building of a cross-country railroad or network of roads, and the growth of cities, are significant parts in the whole picture of a country. Refer to the guidelines for brainstorming in the Instructional Approaches section of this Teacher Annotated Edition, and then have the class look at the cultures, economies, and landscapes of the countries discussed in this section of the Student Edition and brainstorm the impact history had on each of their features. The Historical Features Committee may aid in carrying out this activity by showing their time lines once more and relating stories of some of the more interesting and significant events.

Refer students to Chapter 23 Skill Activity in the Teacher Resource Book for another activity related to this objective.

Objective 4 Activities

● Objective 4 Teaching Activity

Students are probably familiar with computer printouts of summarized facts or profiles generated after the computer sorts through a lot of input data.

Explain that after each of the four student committees has described the features of the many African nations, our minds might feel quite "scrambled" like a computer with input overload! So, to help sort and summarize the various data, a computer printout form might be helpful.

At the end of each chapter as the Teaching Activity for the summarizing objective, distribute to students duplicated handouts that simulate a computer printout and might take the following form:

AFRICAN NATION PROFILE:
Summary of Geographic Features

Legal Name:
Year of Independence:
Formerly a Colony of:
Kind of Government:
Location/Region:
Bordered by (N,S,E,W):
Landlocked:
Area Size (dimensions and comparisons):
Landscape Regions:
Outstanding Landforms & Water Bodies:
Climates:
Industries—Agriculture (crops):

Minerals:
Other:
Population—Statistics:
Distribution:
Composition:
Languages:
Religions:
Cities (*Capital):
Current Challenges:
Uniqueness:

Make it the responsibility of each student committee to specify what information is significant to record on this summary profile and to tell this to the class so that every student has a correctly filled-in printout at the end of each chapter's study. In this way students associate a few significant facts with the name of each African nation.

■ **Objective 4 Reinforcing Activity**

Ask each student to assume the role of an East African citizen with a particular career, such as an environmentalist, a business owner, an industry worker, a sociologist, a government official, a teacher, a parent, or a health worker. Then hold a discussion about the problems, challenges, and concerns that face his or her country as the 21st century approaches. What is being done about the issues now? What alternatives and consequences can be foreseen? Students should refer to the facts on their computer profiles to substantiate and support their opinions.

Concluding Chapter 23

Refer to the guidelines for community resource persons in the Instructional Approaches section of this Teacher Annotated Edition. Then, invite someone who is a native of an East African nation to speak to the class. Or, you may invite someone who has traveled to East Africa or lived there, such as a cultural attaché or a travel agent who can provide information on these countries. Ask students to prepare in advance appropriate questions related to all geographic features of the countries in the world region studied in this chapter. Display around the room all of the maps, time lines, posters, and graphs or diagrams prepared by the committees. Have the cultural committee prepare a short program of music, literature, and/or dance from East African nations as a form of entertainment for your guest as well as for others whom you may wish to invite to hear and meet your resource person.

ANSWERS TO CHAPTER 23 QUESTIONS

Content Check Questions
page 484

1. Refer to Section 1 content.
2. Refer to Glossary in Student Edition.
3. Lowlands, plains, highlands, plateaus. (p. 479)
4. The Equator passes through the middle of Kenya. (p. 480)
5. Farming and tourism. (p. 481)
6. The southern two-fifths of the country. (p. 481)
7. The Kikuyu. (p. 483)
8. The British took their land and controlled politics. (p. 484)

9. Answers will vary but may include: A national language would aid communication, travel, and technological development and help foster national unity. (p. 483)

page 487

1. Refer to Section 2 content.
2. Refer to Glossary in Student Edition.
3. Tanganyika and Zanzibar. (p. 484)
4. Coastal lowlands, plateaus, mountains, plains, and valleys. (p. 484)
5. Great Rift Valley. (p. 484)
6. Coastal areas, northern and southern highlands, and the western lake region. (p. 485)

7. As a socialist government, it owns many businesses and industries and controls co-operative farms. (p. 485)
8. The highlands, the coast, or along the shores of Lake Victoria. (p. 486)
9. The Arabs, Portuguese, Germans, and English. (p. 487)
10. Answers will vary but may include: Both are former British colonies; both depend primarily on agriculture, but most land is not suitable for farming; both have numerous ethnic groups; and both have high birthrates. Kenya has few mineral resources while Tanzania is rich in minerals. Tanzania's socialism does not give its people the economic freedom that Kenyans enjoy in a capitalistic society.

page 492

1. Refer to Section 3 content.
2. Agriculture. (pp. 488, 490)
3. All are hot and dry, and most of the people live in rural areas and are Muslims. (pp. 488–490)
4. Christianity, Judaism, Islam, and traditional African religions. (pp. 488, 490)
5. Ethiopia. (p. 488)
6. All have high elevations and mild climates, are small and landlocked, poor, densely populated, and were at one time ruled by European nations. (pp. 490–491)
7. They are mountainous, landlocked countries with few good roads or railroads. (p. 491)
8. Answers will vary but may include: Education, agricultural training, development of natural resources, and building industries.

Special Feature Questions
page 482, Focus on Geography: "National Parks and Reserves"

1. To protect natural landscapes and wildlife from being hunted or overrun.
2. Tsavo, in Kenya, and Tanzania's Serengeti.
3. Animals such as elephants, lions, apes, hippopotamuses, and giraffes.

page 492, Using Graphic Skills: "Reading Pictographs"

1. Ethiopia. 46 million.
2. Kenya. Ethiopia and Somalia.
3. 7.7 million. 15.9 million.
4. Two, Kenya and Tanzania. None.
5. Answers will vary but may state: Ethiopia's very large population means that not enough food can be grown to feed everyone, resulting in hunger, malnutrition, and starvation. Ethiopia's very large population causes overcrowding, resulting in disease, lack of sanitation, and poor health.

Photo/Illustration Caption Questions
page 480

Hot and humid. (p. 481)

page 481

Nairobi's high elevation. (p. 481)

page 483

About two million years ago. (p. 483)

page 485

In the Great Rift Valley of western Tanzania. (p. 484)

page 486

Kenya. (p. 486, map)

page 488

Ethiopia. (p. 488)

page 489

Ethiopia. (p. 489, map)

page 490

Because of its location as a port on the Gulf of Aden and its railroad link with Addis Ababa. (p. 490)

page 491

Burundi. (p. 491)

Chapter 23 Review Questions
page 494, Reviewing Vocabulary

1. cassava
2. sisal
3. clove
4. physical anthropologists
5. indigenous
6. pastoralists
7. subsistence crops
8. pyrethrum
9. tsetse flies
10. cash crops

page 495, Remembering the Facts

1. Coffee and tea. (p. 481)
2. About four percent per year. (p. 481)
3. Kiswahili. (p. 483)
4. To get their land back from the British. (p. 484)
5. Mount Kilimanjaro. Tanzania. (p. 484)
6. Arab traders. Portuguese. (p. 487)
7. Uganda, Rwanda, Burundi. (p. 490)

page 495, Understanding the Facts

1. The Great Rift Valley was formed when tectonic plates separated from each other, causing a severe chasm. (p. 479)
2. Differences in altitude. (pp. 480–481)
3. Both rely on farming although much of the land is not suitable. Tanzania is rich in minerals, but Kenya has few mineral resources. Tanzania's socialist government owns many businesses and industries and controls cooperative farms. (pp. 481, 485)
4. The disease-carrying tsetse fly. To change the capital to Dodom, a new city being built in the central plateau. (p. 486)

5. These countries control access to the Suez Canal through the Gulf of Aden and the Red Sea. (pp. 488–490)

page 495, Thinking Critically and Creatively

1. Answers will vary but should state that the northern part tends to be hot and dry. People prefer living in the south nearer the coast where rainfall is greater.
2. Answers will vary but may include: Programs in which people feel that they are involved in decision making or in which they have their time invested are probably more successful than those controlled by the government.
3. Answers will vary but may include: Try to eliminate the tsetse fly threat, improve transportation, and, as Tanzania is doing, move the capital inland to a new city and develop the area around it.
4. Answers will vary but may include: There may be pressure for the government to sell some of the park lands or to develop them for industry. As the economy grows, keeping parks open to attract tourists may not seem as important.

page 495, Reinforcing Graphic Skills

1. Kenya has the third largest population and the longest life expectancy among East African countries.
2. Answers will vary but could include that Africa's average life expectancy is so much lower than the world average because of substandard health and sanitation conditions, food production, medical care, and living conditions.

EVALUATING CHAPTER 23

World Geography: People and Places provides chapter tests to help evaluate student performance. To evaluate student mastery of Chapter 23, give students Chapter 23 Test from the Teacher Resource Book. This test may also be used for pretesting or retesting purposes. Other tests can be made from the questions available in the Test Generator Software.

Lesson Plan Suggestions—Chapter 23

Section 1 Kenya (pp. 479–484)

Chapter Objectives	Suggested Teaching Strategies	Review
1. describe the major physical, economic, cultural, and historical features of Kenya.	**Teacher Preparation** SE, Reading Assignment, pp. 479–484 TAE, Unit 8 Suggested Resources Unit 8 Overview, p. T234 Introducing Unit 8, p. T235 Chapter 23 Overview, p. T236 Introducing Chapter 23, p. T236 TRB, Chapter 23 Teacher Notes: Section 1 **Teaching Options** TAE, Introducing Unit 8, p. T235 Introducing Chapter 23, p. T236 Objective 1 Activities, p. T237 TRB, Chapter 23 Teacher Notes: Section 1, Extending the Lesson Chapter 23 Reading Chapter 23 Skill Activity TSP, Transparency 5 SE, *Using Graphic Skills*, "Reading Pictographs," pp. 492–493	SE, Content Check, p. 484
Skill Objective: read pictographs.		

Section 2 Tanzania (pp. 484–487)

Chapter Objectives	Suggested Teaching Strategies	Review
2. describe the major physical, economic, cultural, and historical features of Tanzania.	**Teacher Preparation** SE, Reading Assignment, pp. 484–487 TAE, Unit 8 Suggested Resources Chapter 23 Overview, p. T236 TRB, Chapter 23 Teacher Notes: Section 2 **Teaching Options** TAE, Objective 2 Activities, pp. T237–T238 TRB, Chapter 23 Teacher Notes: Section 2, Extending the Lesson Chapter 23 Reading Chapter 23 Skill Activity	SE, Content Check, p. 487

Chapter Objectives	Suggested Teaching Strategies	Review
3. describe the major physical, economic, cultural, and historical features of the countries of the Horn of Africa and the countries of the East African Highlands.	**Teacher Preparation** SE, Reading Assignment, pp. 487–492 TAE, Unit 8 Suggested Resources 　　Chapter 23 Overview, p. T236 TRB, Chapter 23 Teacher Notes: Section 3 **Teaching Options** TAE, Objective 3 Activities, p. T238 TRB, Chapter 23 Teacher Notes: Section 3, 　　Extending the Lesson 　　Chapter 23 Reading 　　Chapter 23 Skill Activity	SE, Content Check, p. 492

Chapter 23   Review and Evaluation

Suggested Teaching Strategies	Review	Evaluation
TAE, Objective 4 Activities, 　pp. T238–T239 　　Concluding Chapter 23, 　p. T239 TSP, Transparency 5	SE, Chapter 23 Review, pp. 　494–495 TRB, Chapter 23 Review 　　Worksheet	TRB, Chapter 23 Test 　　Unit 8 Pretest, Map and 　　Content Worksheets TG, Chapter 23

CHAPTER 24   WEST AND CENTRAL AFRICA

Student Edition pp. 496–513

CHAPTER 24 OBJECTIVES

At the conclusion of this chapter, students will be able to:

1. describe the major physical, economic, cultural, and historical features of Nigeria.

2. describe the major physical, economic, cultural, and historical features of other West African countries.

3. describe the major physical, economic, cultural, and historical features of Zaire.

4. describe the major physical, economic, cultural, and historical features of other Central African countries.

5. summarize the chief geographic features of West and Central Africa.

CHAPTER 24 SKILL OBJECTIVE

After completing the *Using Graphic Skills* exercise in this chapter, the student should be able to interpret thematic maps.

CHAPTER 24 OVERVIEW

West and Central Africa share much the same landscapes and climates. Composed of hundreds of ethnic groups with different ways of life, languages, and religions, the region is one of rich variety. Yet, it is one whose development is often hindered by this same diversity. Old loyalties to ethnic groups create problems for governments attempting to bind the identity of the people to their nation instead.

Section 1 of this chapter deals with West Africa, a region with a varied history and with many ethnic groups, each with its own traditions and languages. Among the nations of this area, Nigeria is the largest, and its major physical, economic, cultural, and historical features are an important focus of this section. The same geographic features of the other countries of West Africa are also described. Central Africa is the subject of *Section 2*, with special attention accorded the country of Zaire, the largest and most populous nation of Central Africa. This section also examines the geographic features of the other countries of Central Africa and their potential for rapid economic development. A special chapter feature refutes misconceptions about jungles and describes how they differ from rainforests.

CHAPTER 24 ACTIVITIES

Introducing Chapter 24

Follow the same cooperative learning technique for this chapter that you used for studying Chapter 23. Keep the same four student committee divisions of the class, but rotate the name of each committee to a different area of concentration.

Review the tasks of each student committee, sources of information readily available to them, and the means by which each group will share its findings with the whole class, as described in Introducing Unit 8 in the Implementation section of this Teacher Annotated Edition. Tell the student committees on which days each will make its presentation.

Allow students time to regroup, read the Introduction in their Student Editions, and skim the chapter in order to divide their areas of responsibility and begin to work on gathering information.

Arrange the learning center prepared for Chapter 23 to reflect the new regional study of West and Central Africa presented in this chapter.

Chapter 24 Reading Assignments
Objectives 1 and 2 Student Ed. pp. 497–503
Objectives 3 and 4 Student Ed. pp. 503–511

| ● Teaching | ■ Reinforcing | ★ Enriching |

Unmarked activities deal with three or more features listed in the chapter objectives. Activities marked with the following letters deal with:
- Ⓟ Physical features.
- Ⓔ Economic features.
- Ⓒ Cultural features.
- Ⓗ Historical features.

Objective 1 Activities

● Objective 1 Teaching Activity

Have student committees make their reports on Nigeria. Refer to Introducing Unit 8 in the Implementation section of this Teacher Annotated Edition for a description of this activity.

■ Objective 1 Reinforcing Activity

Call students' attention to the first sentence of this section in the Student Edition, "Some of the earliest and greatest kingdoms and empires of ancient times arose in West Africa." Refer to the guidelines for lecture in the Instructional Approaches section of this Teacher Annotated Edition, and prepare a lecture that might be entitled, "The Dark Continent." If possible, begin the lecture by reading to the class a primary source description of some of the advanced, wealthy ancient kingdoms of Africa where the people enjoyed a high standard of living. Ask students: Does it seem surprising that such advanced civilizations flourished in Africa before they did in Greece and Rome? Why or why not?

Write on the chalkboard, "The Dark Continent," and tell students that this is what Africa was called by Europeans and Americans until well into our own century. Explain that this was not because the peoples' skin was dark, but because Europeans' knowledge about Africa was very limited. Ask students to speculate about why this was so. Ask students to suggest reasons for prejudice, leading them to understand that prejudice is usually born out of ignorance about the realities of a place, people, or culture.

Next, use a physical map to demonstrate the great difficulties Europeans encountered if they did want to explore and learn more about this continent, the northern coast of which was so like their own Mediterranean lands. Overland they would have to successfully cross the huge Sahara Desert, and they did not know what awaited them on the other side of it. By water, their sailing ships could hardly sail around the western bulge because of the strong currents and wind patterns. Ships that did maintain course could not land anywhere—it was a smooth coast with steep escarpments to the sea. Once they reached the bays of West Central Africa, they could not sail up the waterfalls and torrential rivers that emptied off the cliffs. Then there was the jungle vegetation through which they could not pass, and the equatorial climate and insects for which they had no match in Europe.

Look with the students at the physical geography of Nigeria using maps in the student text and the salt map prepared by the student committee. Ask students: What geographical features of Nigeria would have made it a difficult country to explore?

End this activity by having the class read the chapter feature *Strange But True*, "That Is No Jungle," on page 504. Some students may also enjoy researching and reporting to the class on the adventures and discoveries of African explorers.

Objective 2 Activities

● Objective 2 Teaching Activity

Have student committees make their reports on the other countries of West Africa. Refer to Introducing Unit 8 in the Implementation section of this Teacher Annotated Edition for a description of this activity. Conclude these activities by having the students read Chapter 24 Reading in the Teacher Resource Book.

★ Objective 2 Enriching Activity Ⓗ Ⓒ

Tell the class that in Africa, a society's history and literature have traditionally been handed down from one generation to the next through the memories of the people. Explain that in West Africa, history is preserved and passed to others by *griots*, traditional historians who are also poets and musicians. Note that in the past, *griots* were the means by which rulers and the people communicated and that today they are often employed by wealthy patrons for the purpose of preserving and recounting family traditions and history.

Allow the students to use the library and the learning center to find stories from Africa.

Assign each student the reading of a different story. Tell the students that they must each remember the story and tell it to the class. Have the class sit in a semicircle, with each student taking his or her turn to be the *griot*. Students may accompany their stories with dramatic gestures, music, and embellishments such as "acting out" designed to capture the interest of their audience.

After the story-telling is over, challenge the class with questions: Africa's oral history was ignored for a long time. Why do you think this was so? Why do you think this oral history is now valued by western historians? What is the value of story-telling as opposed to watching movies or television? Does your family have any stories that have been passed down from other generations? What is the value of such oral traditions to you and your family? Students may volunteer to share one of their family stories with the class.

Objective 3 Activities

● Objective 3 Teaching Activity
Have the student committees present their reports on the country of Zaire. Refer to Introducing Unit 8 in the Implementation section of this Teacher Annotated Edition for a description of this activity.

■ Objective 3 Reinforcing Activity
Review with the class subsection 2.1 in this chapter of the Student Edition about Zaire and the information presented by the student committees. Refer to the guidelines for role plays and simulations in the Instructional Approaches section of this Teacher Annotated Edition. Tell students they will be role playing Zairean government officials and simulating a convocation called with the purpose of deciding what steps may be taken by the government to promote nationalism among the many ethnic groups of Zaire. The Cultural Features Committee may aid in this activity by giving information about the ethnic groups of Zaire, their beliefs, values, and histories, thus providing background information that may prove useful to the officials in understanding these groups and what is important to them. Have the convocation attendees write up their solutions and then discuss their feasibility and how they might be implemented.

Debrief the class after the convocation with a discussion of the advantages and disadvantages associated with ethnic loyalty, and have them speculate about the cultural losses among ethnic groups that might result from nationalization. Ask them for ideas about ways in which these losses might be minimized.

★ Objective 3 Enriching Activity Ⓗ Ⓒ
Refer to the guidelines for audiovisuals in the Instructional Approaches section of this Teacher Annotated Edition. Choose a film, filmstrip, or a "You Are There" type recorded news interview that tells about turmoil in the Congo of the 1960s and the efforts of the Zairean government of the 1970s to establish a new national peace. Ask students to note and point out the reasons underlying the turmoil.

Objective 4 Activities

● Objective 4 Teaching Activity
Have student committees present their reports on the other countries of Central Africa. Refer to Introducing Unit 8 in the Implementation section of this Teacher Annotated Edition for a description of this activity.

★ Objective 4 Enriching Activity Ⓟ
On a wall map, point to where the Equator crosses Central Africa and have students note that "all of Africa is not jungle," to counter a popular misconception. Have students compare places in Africa at 30°N and 30°S latitudes to places on other continents along those same parallels. Should we expect the climate to be the same? Recall the controls on climate that will cause differences, but make the point that only about one-third of Africa is tropical rain forest and another one-third is desert. Inform the students that, in fact, the continent has a sample of every climate type there is.

To counter another misconception, ask students: Which way do rivers always flow?

After they attempt to answer this question, explain to them that the only correct answer is *downward*, pulled by gravity from high places to lower places. The rivers of Africa demonstrate that we should not expect rivers to flow *southward*, simply down. Have students trace the rivers of West and Central Africa as well as other rivers of Africa from their sources to their mouths, naming the directions of flow as they demonstrate.

Objective 5 Activities

● Objective 5 Teaching Activity

Use handouts of the computer printout profile summaries described in the Chapter 23 Activities in the Implementation section of this Teacher Annotated Edition. Have students summarize the chief geographic features of West and Central African nations.

■ Objective 5 Reinforcing Activity

Have students suppose that they will be touring West and Central Africa for a month this summer. Each student should arrange an itinerary, or a proposed outline of a journey, to review the physical, economic, and social features of the countries. The itinerary should include a map or sketch of the route that the tour will take and a timetable explaining how much time to spend in each place. Remind students that the tour should include interesting physical features, economic highlights, and elements of cultural or social life in the countries. Ask student volunteers to share their proposed tours with their classmates.

Concluding Chapter 24

Have each student committee use old magazines, atlases, reference books, etc., to find pictures that exemplify their area of expertise during the study of this chapter. Ask them to draw or copy the people, landscapes, or items from the pictures, glue them to cardboard, and cut them out. Using string and coat hangers, each committee should construct a mobile to decorate the classroom. When the mobiles have been completed and displayed, lead the class in a discussion of what the drawings or copies tell about the geographic feature each committee investigated.

Conclude this chapter by having students do the Chapter 24 Skill exercise from the Teacher Resource Book.

ANSWERS TO CHAPTER 24 QUESTIONS

Content Check Questions
page 503

1. Refer to Section 1 content.
2. Refer to Glossary in Student Edition.
3. Nigeria, Benin, Togo, Ghana, Burkina Faso, Côte d'Ivoire, Liberia, Sierra Leone, Guinea, Guinea-Bissau, Senegal, The Gambia, Cape Verde. (p. 497)
4. Landscapes include coastal lowland, a gently sloping plain of tropical rain forests and palm bushes, a high plateau, and desert; the climate is tropical moist. (pp. 498–499)
5. Lagos; more than four million. (p. 500)
6. Farming. (p. 502)
7. Liberia. (p. 503)
8. Answers will vary. Probably a need to improve transportation, education, economic understanding, and government cooperation.

page 511

1. Refer to Section 2 content.
2. Refer to Glossary in Student Edition.
3. Zaire, Congo, Central African Republic, Gabon, Cameroon, Equatorial Guinea, São Tomé and Príncipe. (p. 497)
4. The area is susceptible to tsetse flies and locusts. (p. 507)

5. Regional conflicts and civil war kept the country divided. (p. 510)
6. Hot and humid tropical moist. (p. 510)
7. Oil and natural gas, diamonds, uranium, gold and manganese. (p. 511)
8. Answers will vary. The slave trade had an impact on the region in terms of the quantity and quality of Africans who were enslaved and created a sense of instability and distrust among the people of this region.

Special Feature Questions
page 504, Strange But True: "That Is No Jungle"

1. Brazil, West Africa, Central Africa, Southeast Asia.
2. A tropical rain forest has tree tops that block the sunlight, preventing the growth of dense jungle undergrowth.
3. Early explorers saw the jungle growth along rivers and assumed that the interior also had this dense undergrowth. Stories, books, and movies compounded the error.
4. In clearings, on slopes, along river banks, and where sunlight can penetrate the "umbrella" of the tropical rain forest.

page 506, Using Graphic Skills: "Interpreting Thematic Maps"

1. Ivory Coast, Nigeria, Gabon. Petroleum resources are located close to coastal areas.
2. Zaire. The map shows eight scattered areas in blue that indicate a second type of agriculture different from the agricultural area shown in green; symbols indicate a variety of resources are found in Zaire.
3. The information on this map argues against this view as the area is shown to possess a good many resources, including coal, iron ore, and petroleum, which have industrial importance.

Photo/Illustration Caption Questions
page 498

Burkina Faso, Cameroon, Nigeria. (p. 498, map)

page 499

Nigeria's population is almost one-half as large as that of the U.S. (p. 499)

page 500

A Muslim people called the Fulani established an Islamic empire that included the northern part of Nigeria. (p. 500)

page 501

Zimbabwe. (p. 501, map)

page 502

Peanuts and cotton. (p. 502)

page 503

57 percent. (p. 503)

page 505

On the coast. (p. 505, map)

page 508

Benefits are that they find and fill jobs in business, industry, and government. Problems are unemployment, overcrowding, and poor housing. (p. 508)

page 509

The slave trade. (p. 509)

page 510

Central America and areas of South America; areas of Southwest Asia, Southeast Asia, and East Asia; South Asia. (p. 510, map)

Chapter 24 Review Questions
page 512, Reviewing Vocabulary

1. cobalt
2. jungle
3. harmattan
4. cacao
5. periodic market
6. columbite

Sentences will vary.

page 513, Remembering the Facts

1. Tropical moist climate. (p. 499)
2. Hausa-Fulani, Yoruba, Ibo. (p. 499)
3. Peanuts, cotton, rubber, palm products, cacao. (pp. 499, 502)
4. Great Britain, Portugal, France, Germany. (pp. 500–503)
5. Tropical rain forests. (pp. 505, 511)
6. Farming. (pp. 506, 511)

page 513, Understanding the Facts

1. Its oil income and fairly developed economic base make it the economic leader of the region; its government has been successful in developing a national identity; it is also the largest country in size and population. (pp. 498–500)
2. Land becomes infertile and must be left to recover for extended periods of time. (p. 499)
3. These countries all grow mostly the same crops and therefore have no need to purchase from each other. (p. 502)
4. Zaire has important mineral and energy resources and the capability of supplying a significant amount of hydroelectric power. (p. 507)
5. Climate and rain forests, threats posed by tsetse flies and locusts, underdevelopment of resources, lack of efficient internal transportation systems. (pp. 505–507, 510–511)
6. Bantu-speaking peoples who came to the area almost 1,000 years ago. (p. 497)

page 513, Thinking Critically and Creatively

1. Answers will vary but should indicate that a nation should not be tied to a one-product economy, especially a non-renewable export such as oil, because it is susceptible to world prices and demand.
2. Answers will vary but may indicate that with more population distributed inland, the interior of the country will be developed further; such a plan has had success in Brasília; it will relieve the population strain in Nigeria's major cities.
3. Answers will vary but may include that the central government needs to educate the people to the strengths of national unity, stress a common language, form regional states whose activities are directed from the central government, and emphasize to all the people the advantages inherent in Nigeria's size and population.
4. Answers will vary but should stress that Portugal and Belgium were very much involved in Zaire's past, and both countries would have brought their Catholic influence with them.
5. Answers will vary but may state that with medical research, new ways of fighting diseases can be discovered. People can be educated to prevent disease by practicing proper hygiene. Utilize the services provided by the United Nations World Health Organization.
6. Answers will vary but should indicate that due to the vast potential in this area, it can only mean much good for the people of Zaire because cheap electricity can be a factor in everything from industry to technology to raising everyones' standard of living; it would provide a new source of income since Zaire could export power to neighboring countries; water power is renewable whereas oil is not.

page 513, Reinforcing Graphic Skills

1. Because of the prevalence of gold, silver, and diamonds found in this part of Africa.
2. Nigeria and Zaire. Rivers.

EVALUATING CHAPTER 24

World Geography: People and Places provides chapter tests to help evaluate student performance. To evaluate student mastery of Chapter 24, give students Chapter 24 Test from the Teacher Resource Book. This test may also be used for pretesting or retesting purposes. Other tests can be made from the questions available in the Test Generator Software.

Lesson Plan Suggestions—Chapter 24

Section 1   West Africa (pp. 497–503)

Chapter Objectives	Suggested Teaching Strategies	Review

1. describe the major physical, economic, cultural, and historical features of Nigeria.
 	
2. describe the major physical, economic, cultural, and historical features of other West African countries.
	Teacher Preparation
	SE, Reading Assignment, pp. 497–503
	TAE, Unit 8 Suggested Resources
	    Chapter 24 Overview, p. T244
	    Introducing Chapter 24, p. T244
	TRB, Chapter 24 Teacher Notes: Section 1
	    Chapter 24 Skill Activity
	Teaching Options
	TAE, Introducing Chapter 24, p. T244
	    Objectives 1 & 2 Activities,
	    pp. T245–T246
	TRB, Chapter 24 Teacher Notes: Section 1,
	    Extending the Lesson
	    Chapter 24 Reading
		SE, Content Check, p. 503

Section 2   Central Africa (pp. 503–511)

Chapter Objectives	Suggested Teaching Strategies	Review

3. describe the major physical, economic, cultural, and historical features of Zaire.
 	
4. describe the major physical, economic, cultural, and historical features of other Central African countries.
 	
Skill Objective: interpret thematic maps.
	Teacher Preparation
	SE, Reading Assignment, pp. 503–511
	TAE, Unit 8 Suggested Resources
	    Chapter 24 Overview, p. T244
	TRB, Chapter 24 Teacher Notes: Section 2
	    Chapter 24 Skill Activity
	Teaching Options
	TAE, Objectives 3 & 4 Activities,
	    pp. T246–T247
	TRB, Chapter 24 Teacher Notes: Section 2,
	    Extending the Lesson
	    Chapter 24 Skill Activity
	SE, *Using Graphic Skills,*
	    "Interpreting Thematic Maps,"
	    pp. 506–507
		SE, Content Check, p. 511

Suggested Teaching Strategies	Review	Evaluation
TAE, Objective 5 Activities, p. T247 Concluding Chapter 24, p. T247 TSP, Transparency 5	SE, Chapter 24 Review, pp. 512–513 TRB, Chapter 24 Review Worksheet	TRB, Chapter 24 Test TG, Chapter 24

CHAPTER 25 SOUTHERN AFRICA

Student Edition pp. 514–533

CHAPTER 25 OBJECTIVES

At the conclusion of this chapter, students will be able to:

1. describe the major physical, economic, cultural, and historical features of South Africa.
2. describe the major physical, economic, cultural, and historical features of Zimbabwe.
3. describe the major physical, economic, cultural, and historical features of Angola, Mozambique, Zambia, and Malawi.
4. describe the major physical, economic, cultural, and historical features of the island countries and South Africa dependencies of Southern Africa.
5. summarize the chief geographic features of Southern Africa.

CHAPTER 25 SKILL ACTIVITY

After completing the *Using Graphic Skills* exercise in this chapter, the student should be able to analyze circle graphs.

CHAPTER 25 OVERVIEW

Southern Africa is, in general, an area of rich resources that has not solved many of its problems from the past. It is an area of great conflict and tension between the majority black population and the minority white population. This social situation has drawn criticism from other countries of the world and has the potential to create conflict in sub-Saharan Africa. However, great developmental and social strides have been made by newly independent nations such as Zimbabwe, and potentials for advancement for the nations of this region are great.

Much of the racial tension in this subregion is focused on South Africa, the country with which *Section 1* of this chapter deals. It is the second largest country in area within Southern Africa and the largest in population. Economically, it is the most important and strongly influences neighboring Botswana, Swaziland, Lesotho, and the territory of Namibia.

Section 2 presents the geographic features of Zimbabwe, one of Africa's newest independent countries and also important economically in the region.

Section 3 analyzes the major geographic features of the other countries that are located in South Africa, with subsections dedicated to the countries of Angola, Mozambique, Zambia, Malawi, the island countries, and the South Africa dependencies.

The chapter contains two special features, one that highlights fabulous South African diamonds, and another describing the site and situation of Cape Town, South Africa.

CHAPTER 25 ACTIVITIES

Introducing Chapter 25

Have students again rotate the topics of study for their four student committees. Ask the entire class to brainstorm some ideas and resources for each committee's tasks and procedures. Review what is expected of each, what each committee will share with the class, and by what means of presentation. Refer to the suggestions given in the introduction to this unit and in the introductions to Chapters 23 and 24 of the Implementation section of this Teacher Annotated Edition.

Allow students time to regroup and make plans for their presentations. Arrange another learning center in the classroom centered around the region of Southern Africa.

Chapter 25 Reading Assignments

Objective 1   Student Ed. pp. 515–523
Objective 2   Student Ed. pp. 524–527
Objectives 3 and 4   Student Ed. pp. 527–531

● Teaching   ■ Reinforcing   ★ Enriching

Unmarked activities deal with three or more features listed in the chapter objectives. Activities marked with the following letters deal with:
- Ⓟ Physical features.
- Ⓔ Economic features.
- Ⓒ Cultural features.
- Ⓗ Historical features.

Objective 1 Activities

● Objective 1 Teaching Activity

Refer to the guidelines for discussion in the Instructional Approaches section of this Teacher Annotated Edition, and lead a class discussion about various topics regarding South Africa.

Ask students what they know about the country of South Africa from current news reports. For example, what industries is it known for? Some students may know that they are the mining of diamonds and gold. Write students' responses on the chalkboard. Also ask questions about the concept of apartheid. Ask students: What do you think about South Africa's position in world opinion today? Do you know how this has come about? How is the government of South Africa responding? What steps are some businesses, the United Nations, and other countries' governments taking to pressure South Africa into changing its policy?

Tell students about segregation in South Africa, the homelands, and such background as is necessary in order for them to comprehend the meaning of apartheid. Some of the books and materials listed under the Suggested Resources for this unit in this Teacher Annotated Edition will be helpful, both with background information and global perspective.

Indicate again South Africa's location on a map of Africa. Ask students: How does this location increase South Africa's significance in world opinion? Lead students to see that it is a crossroads for trading ships from all countries between Southeast Asia, Europe, and the Americas.

Write on the chalkboard, "site and situation," and "landlocked countries." Explain each term, pointing to examples on a world map. Have the class consider the advantages and disadvantages of various known cities' sites and situation features and the problems of being a landlocked country.

Point out that South Africa is in the middle latitudes and surrounded on three sides by water. What do they expect its climate to be like? Remind them of the moderating effects of latitude and water. Ask the students to name some other places in comparable geographic positions both north and south of the Equator.

Students may be referred to the Unit 8 Career Worksheet in the Teacher Resource Book on the career of mining, and those who have a special interest in this career might present more in-depth reports to the class about it.

■ Objective 1 Reinforcing Activity

Have the student committees present their reports on South Africa. Suggest to the Cultural Features Committee that they use a role-playing technique. Provide them with guidelines for this type of activity from the Instructional Approaches in this Teacher Annotated Edition, and have them lead the class in the activity. They should ask class members to form small groups and write skits in which they roleplay residents of South Africa in real situations. The Cultural Features Committee should provide background information and direct the class to books with first-hand accounts of the lives of South African residents. Have students check the learning center and the library, as well as listings under the Suggested Resources for this unit in this Teacher Annotated Edition for source material.

This activity may be concluded by having students complete the Chapter 25 Reading in the Teacher Resource Book.

Objective 2 Activities

● Objective 2 Teaching Activity

Have student committees present their reports on Zimbabwe. Refer to Introducing Unit 8 in the Implementation section of this Teacher Annotated Edition.

■ Objective 2 Reinforcing Activity

Tell the students that an on-the-street interview is one way in which views of private citizens are expressed in a public forum. Instruct students to review the text material concerning the road to independence for Zimbabwe and to prepare five questions that might have been part of an interview conducted in Zimbabwe in 1965. Questions might include: Do you think Rhodesia should be granted its independence? Who do you think should be in control of the Rhodesian government? While students are working on the questions, write the following on the chalkboard: "A black Rhodesian farmer, a white factory owner, a United Nations army officer stationed in Rhodesia, a descendant of the first settlers in the Great Dyke, the Prime Minister of Great Britain, a leader of the Mashona group." Have the students consider how each of the people listed would answer their questions. Review the outcome of the events in 1965 and 1980 in Zimbabwe, using the pertinent text material and any other available resources, such as newspaper and magazine articles from the periods in question.

★ Objective 2 Enriching Activity ©

Ask the class to investigate and take notes on the Shona culture of Zimbabwe. Where possible, find books with illustrations and photographs. Have an informal class presentation of the information the students found in their research with everyone contributing to the class discussion from their notes. Illustrations might be shown using an opaque projector.

Objective 3 Activities

● Objective 3 Teaching Activity

Have the student committees present their reports on Angola, Mozambique, Zambia, and

Malawi. Refer to Introducing Unit 8 in the Implementation section of this Teacher Annotated Edition for a description of this activity.

■ Objective 3 Reinforcing Activity

Ask students to choose either Angola, Mozambique, Zambia, or Malawi, and "run for political office" in that country. In order to do that, each student should write a speech explaining to the people of the nation chosen what he or she would do in order to improve the quality of life in that country and in order to bring that country's standard of living closer to that of the more economically advanced nations of Africa. When the speeches have been written, have volunteers read them to the class. On the chalkboard, note the ideas each candidate presents for his or her country's improvement. When the volunteers have given their speeches, discuss with the class the ideas written on the chalkboard. The class may then hold an election and vote for the candidate for political office (one of the volunteers who read his or her speech) who, in their opinion, had the best ideas for improving the selected country's quality of life.

Objective 4 Activities

● Objective 4 Teaching Activity

Have the student committees present their reports on the island countries and South Africa dependencies of Southern Africa. Refer to Introducing Unit 8 in the Implementation section of this Teacher Annotated Edition for a description of this activity.

■ Objective 4 Reinforcing Activity

Have students listen carefully to the committee presentations for details about the island countries of Southern Africa. Tell them to look for descriptions of these islands in other resource books and in magazines such as *National Geographic*. They might also find brochures from tourist agencies helpful, as well as the atlas entitled *National Geographic Picture Atlas of Our World*, published by the National Geographic Society. Explain to the class that they should each decide on which of the

islands they would prefer to live and then be prepared to explain orally to the class what the island is like and why he or she would prefer it before the others as a place to live.

Inform the students that they should include details about those features of the islands that affect quality of life—that is, physical geography, economics, impact of history on the way of life, and culture.

Objective 5 Activities

● Objective 5 Teaching Activity

Distribute and discuss the computer printout profile summaries described in the Chapter 23 Activities in the Implementation section of this Teacher Annotated Edition. Have students complete them for the countries of Southern Africa.

■ Objective 5 Reinforcing Activity

Using the same chart developed to play a game entitled "What Do You Remember About North Africa?" for the Concluding Chapter 21 activity in Unit 7, prepare a game using the same procedures entitled "What Do You Remember About Southern Africa?"

The class may be divided into two or three teams. Each team should in turn select a column and point value and then discuss their question before giving an answer.

Concluding Chapter 25

Write the statement "Southern Africa is a land of contrasts" on the chalkboard. Have the students find specific examples to support this statement in their Student Edition and make an outline of their findings under the heading on the chalkboard. The outline should be organized under the subheadings: Landscape and Climate; Economic and Cultural Patterns; and Influences of the Past. Tell the students that from this outline they will write an essay. Suggest that paragraphs can be organized around subheadings. There should also be a short introductory paragraph stating the main premise of the essay, and a closing paragraph restating the premise and summarizing the main points. Point out to students that their writing will be easier if they use specific examples. Ask volunteers to share their completed essays with the remainder of the class. Upon completing this chapter, students may do the Chapter 25 Skill Activity in the Teacher Resource Book.

ANSWERS TO CHAPTER 25 QUESTIONS

Content Check Questions
page 523

1. Refer to Section 1 content.
2. Refer to Glossary in Student Edition.
3. Lowlands, mountains, plateaus. (p. 516)
4. Diamonds and gold. (p. 517)
5. Whites, Coloreds, Asians, black Africans. (p. 519)
6. Mostly Dutch and British but some French and German, too. (p. 519)
7. Homelands, or bantustans, and townships. (p. 519)
8. Pretoria, Bloemfontein, and Cape Town. (p. 523)
9. Winds blowing over the cold Benguela Current in the Atlantic Ocean pick up little moisture, and as they move eastward and warm up over western South Africa, they retain moisture instead of releasing it. (p. 517)

page 527

1. Refer to Section 2 content.
2. Refer to Glossary in Student Edition.
3. Mozambique, Botswana, Zambia, and South Africa. (p. 524)
4. High rolling plateau. (p. 524)
5. Because of the high elevation of the plateau. (p. 524)
6. Sale of mineral resources of coal, chrome, gold, copper, asbestos, and iron ore. (p. 525)
7. Answers will vary but replies should indicate that the nation would probably be underdeveloped, have poor transportation, and English would not now be the official language.

page 531

1. Refer to Section 3 content.

2. Both are coastal countries with excellent harbors, have similar landscapes and climates, have adequate minerals and fertile land, Portuguese language. (pp. 527–528)
3. Zambia depends on its copper; Malawi depends on agriculture. (p. 528)
4. Differences include size, number of islands, mixtures of population, languages, religion, and foreign influences. (pp. 528–529)
5. Botswana, Lesotho, Swaziland, and Namibia. (p. 529)
6. Answers will vary, but stress that South Africa is a source of employment for many people in these countries. (pp. 530–531)

Special Feature Questions
page 518, The Urban World: "Cape Town: Site and Situation"

1. Near the southern tip of Africa where the Atlantic and Indian oceans meet.
2. Cape Town developed as a stopping-off point along an important east-west trade route and later grew as it was a point of arrival for settlers, miners, and suppliers.

page 520, Focus on Economy: "Fabulous Diamonds"

1. Around Kimberley, Bloemfontein, and Pretoria.
2. Kimberlite.
3. Most miners are black, and they are exploited and treated unfairly.

page 522, Using Graphic Skills: "Analyzing Circle Graphs"

1. 82 percent.
2. Almost four times larger.
3. Because the percentages on the "Black Population" graph are shown in proportion only to the black population, while the

percentages on the "Total Population" graph are shown in proportion to the entire population.

4. Racial attitudes and policies in South Africa have discouraged intermarriage between black Africans and Europeans, thus keeping Coloreds a separate, smaller minority.

Photo/Illustration Caption Questions
page 516

Botswana. (p. 516, map)

page 517

High, flat grasslands covering South Africa's central plateau. (p. 516)

page 519

Soweto. (p. 519)

page 521

Namibia, Botswana, Zimbabwe, Mozambique, Swaziland, Lesotho. (p. 521, map)

page 524

Zimbabwe and Zambia. (p. 524)

page 525

South Africa. (p. 525, map)

page 526

No, it also has resources and industrial areas. (p. 526)

page 529

Madagascar is the fourth largest island in the world. (p. 528)

page 530

Because so many of the men work in South Africa. (p. 530)

Chapter 25 Review Questions
page 532, Reviewing Vocabulary

Apartheid—an Afrikaans word meaning "apartness," it refers to South Africa's established government policy of separation of the races.

Economic sanctions—a policy decision designed to bring pressure on another country by limiting trade with it.

Bantustans—homelands set aside in South Africa for blacks only.

Highveld—high flat grasslands that cover South Africa's interior plateau.

Townships—large suburban areas set aside for blacks in South Africa.

The sentences will vary.

pages 532–533, Remembering the Facts

1. South Africa, Zimbabwe, Botswana, Swaziland, Lesotho, Zambia, Mozambique, Angola, and Malawi. (p. 515)
2. Namibia. (p. 531)
3. Angola. (p. 515)
4. Lowlands along the coast and high interior plateaus. (p. 515)
5. Kalahari Desert. (p. 517)
6. Gold and diamonds. (p. 517)
7. Corn. (p. 525)
8. Non-whites make up 82 percent of the total population, while whites make up only 18 percent. (p. 519)
9. Malawi. (p. 528)
10. Indonesia, East Africa, Arabian Peninsula, Portugal, Britain, France, China, India. (p. 528)
11. Botswana, Lesotho, and Swaziland. (pp. 530–531)

page 533, Understanding the Facts

1. Though the country has a long coastline, there are few good natural harbors. (p. 527)
2. The Drakensberg Escarpment which rises very sharply above the Natal Lowlands. (p. 516)
3. The west coast is extremely dry. (p. 517)
4. By and large there are two countries: the South Africa of the whites and the South Africa of blacks and non-whites, each having separate political, social, and economic distinctions. (pp. 519, 521)
5. A large percentage of land is suited for farming because of sufficient rainfall and a long growing season. (pp. 524–525)
6. Zambia is dependent on copper, its chief resource and export, and therefore its income from the sale of copper is dependent on world prices. (p. 528)

7. Answers will vary. South Africa's policy of apartheid exists nowhere else in the world. Other nations feel that this policy is a violation of human rights and that South Africa is unwilling to end it.

8. Answers will vary, but development of agriculture is dependent on and restricted by factors of landscape, climate, arable land, distribution of population, availability of transportation, to name a few.

page 533, Thinking Critically and Creatively

1. Answers will vary but should state that the western part is desert or dry, making it difficult to support agriculture or a large population.

2. Answers will vary but basically sanctions were seen as a means of economically crippling the white-controlled government and pressuring it to extend political power to the black majority in Rhodesia.

3. Answers will vary. The English language continues to be widely used; transportation networks, particularly railroads, the government, legal, and educational systems were established by the British.

4. Answers will vary but may state that to control the government means to control the military, police, courts, legislation, money, punishment and imprisonment, and other agencies of power.

5. Answers will vary but such differences have caused long-standing separateness, mistrust, and lack of cooperation. Racial, ethnic, and regional differences have made it difficult to establish political unity.

page 533, Reinforcing Graphic Skills

1. Xhosa.

2. The Zulu are more than twice as large as the Afrikaner population; the Zulu are more than three times as large as the British population.

EVALUATING CHAPTER 25

World Geography: People and Places provides chapter tests to help evaluate student performance. To evaluate student mastery of Chapter 25, give students Chapter 25 Test from the Teacher Resource Book. This test may also be used for pretesting or retesting purposes. Other tests can be made from the questions available in the Test Generator Software.

Lesson Plan Suggestions—Chapter 25

SE—Student Edition   TAE—Teacher Annotated Edition   TG—Test Generator
TRB—Teacher Resource Book   TSP—Transparency Package

Section 1   South Africa (pp. 515–523)

Chapter Objectives	Suggested Teaching Strategies	Review

1. describe the major physical, economic, cultural, and historical features of South Africa.	**Teacher Preparation**
	SE, Reading Assignment, pp. 515–523
	TAE, Unit 8 Suggested Resources
	    Chapter 25 Overview, pp. T251–T252
	    Introducing Chapter 25, p. T252
	TRB, Chapter 25 Teacher Notes: Section 1
		SE, Content Check, p. 523

(Continued on next page.)

Section 1 South Africa (pp. 515–523) continued.

	Teaching Options	

Skill Objective: analyze circle graphs.	TAE, Introducing Chapter 25, p. T252
	  Objective 1 Activities, pp. T252–T253
	TRB, Chapter 25 Teacher Notes: Section 1,
	  Extending the Lesson
	  Chapter 25 Reading
	  Chapter 25 Skill Activity
	SE, *Using Graphic Skills,*
	  "Analyzing Circle Graphs," p. 522	

Section 2 Zimbabwe (pp. 524–527)

Chapter Objectives	Suggested Teaching Strategies	Review

2. describe the major physical, economic, cultural, and historical features of Zimbabwe.	**Teacher Preparation**
	  SE, Reading Assignment, pp. 524–527
	  TAE, Unit 8 Suggested Resources
	    Chapter 25 Overview, pp. T251–T252
	  TRB, Chapter 25 Teacher Notes: Section 2
	Teaching Options
	  TAE, Objective 2 Activities, p. T253
	  TRB, Chapter 25 Teacher Notes: Section 2,
	    Extending the Lesson
	    Chapter 25 Skill Activity
		SE, Content Check, p. 527

Section 3 Other Countries of Southern Africa (pp. 527–531)

Chapter Objectives	Suggested Teaching Strategies	Review

3. describe the major physical, economic, cultural, and historical features of Angola, Mozambique, Zambia, and Malawi.
 	
4. describe the major physical, economic, cultural, and historical features of the island countries and South Africa dependencies of Southern Africa.
	Teacher Preparation
	  SE, Reading Assignment, pp. 527–531
	  TAE, Unit 8 Suggested Resources
	    Chapter 25 Overview, pp. T251–T252
	  TRB, Chapter 25 Teacher Notes: Section 3
	Teaching Options
	  TAE, Objectives 3 & 4 Activities,
	    pp. T253–T254
	  TRB, Chapter 25 Teacher Notes: Section 3,
	    Extending the Lesson
	    Chapter 25 Skill Activity
		SE, Content Check, p. 531

Chapter 25 *Review and Evaluation*

Suggested Teaching Strategies	Review	Evaluation
TAE, Objective 5 Activities, p. T254 Concluding Chapter 25, pp. T254–T255 TSP, Transparency 5	SE, Chapter 25 Review, pp. 532–533 TRB, Chapter 25 Review Worksheet	TRB, Chapter 25 Test TG, Chapter 25

Unit 8 *Review and Evaluation*

Suggested Teaching Strategies	Review	Evaluation
TAE, Concluding Unit 8, p. T259 TRB, Unit 8 Career Worksheet	SE, Unit 8 Review, pp. 534–535	TRB, Unit 8 Exam Unit 8 Posttest, Map and Content Worksheets

CONCLUDING UNIT 8

Refer to the guidelines for retrieval charts in the Instructional Approaches section of this Teacher Annotated Edition. Hold a class discussion in which you and the class compile a chart identifying the major problems, challenges, and prospects facing African nations into the 21st century.

Encourage students to use their computer profiles of each country, current events bulletin board, cultural features posters, textbook chapter summaries, and all the information they have learned during the course of this unit to summarize the problems, identify the challenges, and analyze the prospects for some of the countries of Africa. It is not useful to chart every nation, but have students suggest countries or groups of countries in the order that would facilitate their being able to chart them. For example, they may identify the Republic of South Africa first, with its problem of apartheid, the parallel challenge of human and civil rights for all its population groups, and the prospects for possible pressure on the government to change its official laws and policies, all-out civil war, economic ruin before recovery, and so on.

Some of the other problems that should be discussed are poor agricultural land where soil is leached or dry, overgrazing of grasslands, drought, shortage of food, disease, loss of tropical rain forests, challenge of self-government, lack of educated citizenry, few networks of intercontinental roads, railroads, and communication systems, lack of accurate knowledge and respect from European, American, and Soviet world opinion, and stereotyped status as third-, fourth-, or fifth-world countries.

Unit 8 Exam in the Teacher Resource Book may be administered.

UNIT 8 REVIEW QUESTIONS

page 534, Thinking About the Unit

1. The East African landscape is characterized by coastal lowlands that extend inward to plateau and highland areas. Temperatures are hot or warm with unpredictable rainfall. In West and Central Africa the coastal lowlands are long and swampy with rain forests. Farther inland is a dry plateau area with scattered highlands. There is a tropical moist climate. Southern Africa is surrounded by a small coastal lowland that rises sharply to plateau and highlands. Most of the region has a tropical moist and dry climate.

2. Some countries have discovered valuable mineral and energy resources. Sale of these results in income used to encourage other areas of industrial growth.

3. Answers will vary but may include the loyalty to ethnic groups rather than to nations. This is a result of borders established during European colonial rule without regard for ethnic regions. Another problem is poor race relations as a result of longtime rule by the white minority.

4. European colonization set borders without taking into account tribal loyalties and language differences. Therefore, there is a lack of national identity today. Colonial powers also failed to develop the countries, leaving them newly independent without industrial power.

UNIT 9 ASIA

UNIT 9 GOALS

At the conclusion of this unit, students will be able to:

1. describe the unique cultural contributions the three culture areas of Asia made to the rest of the world.
2. identify the chief physical features, economic activities, and historical influences of the countries of Asia.

UNIT 9 SKILL OBJECTIVE

After completing the *Developing Geography Skills* exercise in this unit, the student should be able to test hypotheses.

UNIT 9 OVERVIEW

In the ninth unit of *World Geography: People and Places*, students are introduced to the countries that make up much of the continent of Asia. Three regions are studied in this unit.

Some of the world's oldest civilizations have come from this vast, mountainous area that is rich in natural resources. Because the mountains in Asia limit agriculture, some of the highest yields per acre in the world feed some of the most densely populated areas of the world. Here, many ancient, traditional ways also mix with modern, industrial technology. *Chapter 26* covers the subcontinent of

South Asia, dominated by India. In *Chapter 27*, the culture area of East Asia, where one-fifth of the world's population live, is studied. The unit concludes with *Chapter 28*, Southeast Asia, that includes countries on the Asian mainland as well as thousands of islands in the Pacific. These two general areas make up Insular Southeast Asia.

At the conclusion of this unit, the student should be able to identify the basic cultures belonging to these three Asian regions and understand the role the geographic features of each area played in the development of its cultures.

INTRODUCING UNIT 9

Have students find Asia on a globe or a world map that shows physical features. Next, have students turn to the world climates map on pages 96–97 of the Student Edition to check Asia's climate patterns. Ask students to speculate where the population centers in Asia are located. Students should identify lowland areas, areas along coasts, and areas with warm climates. Then have students find world pop-

ulation figures in a current almanac. Read aloud the ten countries of the world with the largest populations. List on the chalkboard the names of the countries that are in Asia. Inform students that a major problem in Asia is the growing population. Two of the most populous countries in the world, China and India, are located here. Tell students to begin keeping a population almanac in their notebooks.

CHAPTER 26   SOUTH ASIA

Student Edition pp. 538–555

CHAPTER 26 OBJECTIVES

At the conclusion of this chapter, students will be able to:

1. describe the major physical, economic, cultural, and historical features of India.
2. describe the major physical, economic, cultural, and historical features of Pakistan.
3. describe the major physical, economic, cultural, and historical features of Sri Lanka, Bangladesh, Bhutan, and Nepal.
4. summarize the chief geographic features of South Asia.

CHAPTER 26 SKILL OBJECTIVE

After completing the *Using Graphic Skills* exercise in this chapter, the student should be able to make hypotheses.

CHAPTER 26 OVERVIEW

As pointed out in the Student Edition, South Asia is a huge subcontinent separated from the rest of Asia by rugged mountains— the Karakoram and Himalayas—that rim its northern border. Sometimes called the Indian subcontinent, this region is dominated by India's land area and population. Thus, *Section 1* of the chapter covers the diverse geography of India, where civilizations have lived for thousands of years. The physical geography of this massive land affects every aspect of the lives of this mostly Hindu population. *Section 2* concentrates on the primarily agricultural area of Pakistan, with its mainly Muslim people. In *Section 3*, the developing nations of Sri Lanka, Bangladesh, Bhutan, and Nepal, one of the most densely populated areas of the world, are described.

The poverty found in the city of Calcutta is an urban world feature of the chapter. The other special feature focuses on the economic importance of tea to the countries of Asia.

CHAPTER 26 ACTIVITIES

Introducing Chapter 26

Before directing this activity, refer to the guidelines for brainstorming in the Instructional Approaches section of this Teacher Annotated Edition. Have students brainstorm the word "water." Write all their responses on the chalkboard. The importance of water to survival should be brought out from the brainstorming session. Next, ask students what happens when a water emergency occurs in their community, such as when water has contaminated particles, when water in reservoirs are low, or when a major water main pipe breaks. How does such a situation affect the lives of people in their homes or businesses that depend on using water for producing goods or services? Point out to students that in many countries of the world, especially in those that they are going to study in Chapter 26, water not only acts as a vital source of physical and economic survival, but it also has religious and cultural importance to the people. Ask students if water has any religious or cultural importance to people in the United States. Students will probably describe religious ceremonies, such as baptism, that use water. Tell students to be aware of the importance of water to the people as they study this chapter.

Chapter 26 Reading Assignments

Objective 1   Student Ed. pp. 538–546
Objective 2   Student Ed. pp. 546–549
Objective 3   Student Ed. pp. 550–553

● Teaching   ■ Reinforcing   ★ Enriching

Unmarked activities deal with three or more features listed in the chapter objectives. Activities marked with the following letters deal with:

Ⓟ Physical features.
Ⓔ Economic features.
Ⓒ Cultural features.
Ⓗ Historical features.

Objective 1 Activities

● Objective 1 Teaching Activity   Ⓟ

Introduce India by pointing to it on a globe or a wall map of the world. Ask students how geographers would classify the shape of the landform (peninsula). Have students identify the bodies of water that surround India. Explain that because of the high mountain range that separates it from the rest of Asia, and because it is larger than peninsulas usually are, India is sometimes called a subcontinent. Ask the name of the mountains (Himalayas), and

what students might already know about them (tallest in the world; Mt. Everest is the world's highest peak on land; always snow-covered; sometimes people make the news by climbing various sides or faces of Mt. Everest and the Himalayas.) Next review the description of the tropical monsoon climate type in Chapter 5 on page 95 of the Student Edition. Then direct students to Figure 26-2 on page 542, "Monsoon Winds of India." After students have answered the question in the caption at the bottom of the illustration, read to them a description about life during a monsoon. Use the Unit 9 Resources to find an appropriate description.

Conclude the activity with Chapter 26 Skill Activity in the Teacher Resource Book.

■ Objective 1 Reinforcing Activity

Refer to the guidelines for reading guides in the Instructional Approaches section of this Teacher Annotated Edition. Prepare for your class a reading guide for India. Construct it so that questions are grouped under the following headings: Physical Features, Economic Features, Cultural Features, Historical Features. After completing the answers in the reading guide, have students write a brief summary of the geographic features of India.

★ Objective 1 Enriching Activity

Instruct students with last names beginning with the letters L to Z to move to the back seats of the classroom. Tell students that they will make no better than a "C" grade, no matter how hard they work. Students with last names beginning with the letters A to K are to sit in the front of the room. Tell students that they will be graded on performance. Instruct students in the front not to talk to students in the back. Use this class division to motivate a discussion of the caste system in India. After reviewing the origins and effects of the system, have students compare the concept of caste to social class in other countries. To conclude, point out to students that although the Indian government has tried to end the caste system, the practice is based on tradition, and it will be slow to change.

Objective 2 Activities

● Objective 2 Teaching Activity

Refer to the guidelines for lecture in the Instructional Approaches section of this Teacher Annotated Edition. Because differences in religious beliefs and practices form such a basic part of the cultural differences in South Asia, prepare a lecture comparing the major religions of this region, especially Islam and Hinduism. Use Unit 9 Suggested Resources in this Teacher Annotated Edition for reference material to aid in preparing the lecture. While giving the lecture, chart the major differences between the religions on the chalkboard. Also, when appropriate, include in the lecture reference to Figure 26-3 on page 543 of the Student Edition. After the lecture, ask students to explain why differences in religion would lead to conflict in the cultural and economic development of the places where belief is strong. Have students read Section 2.3 on page 549 of the Student Edition. Do students think that drawing political boundaries to divide land for separate nations was an adequate answer for the conflicting ways of life? What other ways might be tried to establish internal peace among the countries on the Indian subcontinent? Distribute handouts to the class summarizing your lecture and the chart from the chalkboard.

■ Objective 2 Reinforcing Activity

Before directing this activity, refer to the guidelines for team learning in the Instructional Approaches section of this Teacher Annotated Edition. Prepare the class for this team learning activity by dividing the class into two large teams. Divide each team into four smaller groups, and assign each smaller group either the physical, economic, cultural, or historic features of Pakistan. The small group should prepare five questions on its feature. Thus, each team will have a set of 20 questions to ask other class members. When the questions are complete, have teams ask each other the questions. Give members of the team with the most right answers three additional points on the chapter test.

Objective 3 Activities

● Objective 3 Teaching Activity ⓟ

Have additional resource material on the countries studied in Section 3 of the Student Edition available in the classroom before beginning the following activity. Divide the class into four groups, one for each country studied in Section 3. Give the groups a limited time period in which they are to prepare a presentation to the class about the most significant geographic feature of the assigned country. They can present the feature with a role play, discussion, drawing, piece of art, or anything that the group would like to use as a process.

Conclude the activity with the Chapter 26 Reading in the Teacher Resource Book.

■ Objective 3 Reinforcing Activity

Have students review page 128 of Chapter 7 in the Student Edition that discusses cultural diffusion. Then have them read the special feature, "A Story of Tea," on page 552 of the Student Edition. Hold a discussion about how the spread of tea is an example of cultural diffusion. Have students trace the spread of tea on an outline map of the world.

Objective 4 Activities

● Objective 4 Teaching Activity

Refer to the guidelines for retrieval charts in the Instructional Approaches section of this Teacher Annotated Edition. On the chalkboard or a transparency, construct a grid for the class to summarize the major geographic features of the six countries of South Asia. Down the left side, write the full name of each nation. Across the top, make five columns with the headings: Physical, Political, Economic, Cultural, Historical.

Tell students to use the charts as a study guide for chapter evaluation.

■ Objective 4 Reinforcing Activity

Refer to the guidelines for discussion in the Instructional Approaches section of this Teacher Annotated Edition. Give to each student a paper at the top of which is the question: Which kind of factors—physical, economic, cultural, historical—have had the greatest influence in shaping the boundaries and identities of the nations of South Asia? Allow students a few minutes to write a response on their papers. Then choose one of the following ways to discuss the topic with the class: (1) as a whole-class discussion, noting on the chalkboard key words of students' contributions; (2) small group discussions with debriefing afterward; or (3) team discussions, dividing the class into 4 teams (or 2 × 4), asking each to prepare debate-like defenses for one of the four categories.

Concluding Chapter 26

Refer to the guidelines for role plays and simulations in the Instructional Approaches section of this Teacher Annotated Edition. Have students role play several of the following situations, simulating a conversation between an American traveling through South Asia who meets one of the following people or groups of people and who chooses to meet them for dinner:

1. four families, each of a different Hindu caste in India.
2. a Muslim family who left India to live in Pakistan.
3. a British teacher who remains in India to teach school.
4. a grand-nephew of Mohandas Ghandi.
5. a college-educated woman who is working for change in the role of women in South Asia.
6. a member of the current government of India.
7. a relative of Indira Ghandi.
8. Mother Theresa of Calcutta.
9. a tea farmer of Sri Lanka.
10. a "typical" Bangladesh farmer.

ANSWERS TO CHAPTER 26 QUESTIONS

Content Check Questions
page 546

1. Refer to Section 1 content.
2. Refer to Glossary in Student Edition.
3. Mountain ranges, hills, plains, plateaus, lowlands, valleys, canyons, and a river delta. (pp. 539–541)
4. Monsoons blow two ways: dry winds come from the mountains during the cool and hot seasons; moist winds from the ocean bring rain during the rainy season. (p. 541)
5. Textile. (p. 543)
6. Hinduism. (p. 543)
7. To separate Hindus and Moslems. (p. 546)
8. Answers will vary but may include: India's factories, iron and steel mills, refineries, and other industries that give it a broad economic base. (p. 543)

page 549

1. Refer to Section 2 content.
2. Refer to Glossary in Student Edition.

3. Second in size and third in population. (p. 546)
4. Valleys of the Indus River and its tributaries. (p. 547)
5. Agriculture. (p. 547)
6. Government reforms have given more land to poor farmers, and they have begun to use fertilizers. (p. 547)
7. Arabs influenced art, architecture, and literature as well as bringing the Muslim faith. (p. 549)
8. Muslims wished to protect their own religion and culture and feared Hindu rule of India. (p. 549)
9. Answers will vary but may include: Pakistan has a shortage of natural resources, many workers have left to find jobs, they lack a common language, and the rugged landscape makes transportation difficult.

page 553

1. Refer to Section 3 content.
2. Refer to Glossary in Student Edition.

3. Sinhalese and Tamils. (p. 551)
4. Food shortages and overcrowding. (p. 553)
5. Forests, coal, minerals, wildlife, and rivers. (p. 553)
6. In rural areas on arable land which is only 10 percent of the country's total. (p. 553)
7. Answers will vary but may include: Rapid population growth, food shortages, floods, and typhoons are ongoing problems that would be difficult to quickly solve.

Special Feature Questions
page 544, The Urban World: "Calcutta: Poverty"

1. The influx of millions of jobless and homeless Hindus from East Pakistan in the 1940s and 1970s.
2. They live in shabby huts or on the streets and sift through garbage for food. They lack clean water and waste disposal.
3. It has improved with a slowdown in population growth; more sections have clean water and sewers; roads have been improved; more people are finding shelter.

page 552, Focus on Economy: "A Story of Tea"

1. Mountains of southeast Asia.
2. Tea became England's national drink, and the British East India Company made a great deal of money since it was the only company allowed to import it.
3. South Asia is the leading tea producer.

page 540, Using Graphic Skills: "Making Hypotheses"

1. Answers will vary, but the following are possible hypotheses: Pakistan has terrain and climate favorable for farming. Pakistan grows enough food to feed its own people and has a surplus left over that it can sell as exports. Pakistan's population has grown smaller so that it can now feed its people without buying or importing food. Pakistani farmers began using modern methods which increased their food supply.
2. Answers will vary, but the following are possible hypotheses: Bangladesh has a large population which drains the country's agricultural and natural resources. Bangladesh has few exports to sell abroad to raise money. There is little modern industry in Bangladesh to produce necessary goods. A dry climate and unfavorable terrain make for poor farming in Bangladesh, resulting in starvation and hunger.
3. Answers will vary, but the following are possible hypotheses: The Karakoram Mountains and the Himalayas are too high to cross. There are no mountain passes through these two ranges, similar to the Khyber Pass. Although India lies exposed to water, China has no water areas close to India that allowed for invasion by sea.

Photo/Illustration Caption Questions
page 541

Very heavy. (p. 541)

page 542

Because of the monsoon winds blowing inland off the Indian Ocean, and the orographic effect. (p. 542)

page 543

Pakistan. (p. 543)

page 545

The caste system and Hinduism. (p. 545)

page 547

The Khyber Pass. (p. 546)

page 548

Nomadic herding; growing corn, wheat, millet; growing rice; subsistence agriculture and livestock. (p. 548)

page 550

Sinhalese and Tamils. (p. 551)

page 551

It is largely made up of flat, low plains and has a tropical moist climate. (p. 551)

Chapter 26 Review Questions
page 554, Reviewing Vocabulary

1. teak.
2. caste system.

3. reincarnation.
4. chapatty.
5. cottage industry.
6. subcontinent.
Sentences will vary.

page 554, Remembering the Facts

1. India, Pakistan, Sri Lanka, Bangladesh, Nepal, Bhutan. (p. 539)
2. Calcutta, Bombay, and Karachi. (pp. 543, 549)
3. In rural villages. (p. 543)
4. Ganges Plain and Deccan Plateau. (p. 541)
5. Hinduism. (p. 543)
6. The rainy season is May through October. (p. 541)
7. Through more irrigation and better use of seeds and fertilizers. (p. 542)
8. Hindu Kush. (p. 546)
9. India and Bangladesh. (pp. 542, 551)
10. Mount Everest in Nepal. (p. 541)
11. Sri Lanka. (p. 551)
12. Bangladesh. (p. 551)

page 555, Understanding the Facts

1. From November through April, monsoon winds originating over land areas blow from the mountains across India toward the sea. These winds carry little moisture, and little rainfall occurs. The monsoon winds switch direction, and from May through October, they blow from the sea. They pick up moisture which is dropped in the form of rain over land areas. (p. 541)
2. Answers will vary but may include: Nearly 75 percent of the people live in rural villages. Industries depend on urban populations of trained workers. (p. 543)
3. Generally, Pakistan is drier. (p. 547)
4. Arabs and Turkish Muslims. (p. 549)
5. No, because the major crops are tea, rubber, and coconut. (p. 550)
6. Answers will vary but may include: The majority of the people of Bangladesh, like others of South Asia, are poor subsistence farmers living in rural areas. Most of the countries rely on some type of agricultural produce such as cotton, tea, jute, and rice for cash crops. Each of the countries, like Bangladesh, is taking steps to industrialize. (pp. 551, 553)

page 555, Thinking Critically and Creatively

1. Answers will vary but may include: The nations would probably have colder winters if the high mountain barriers were not there to block continental winds blowing from the interior of Asia.
2. Answers will vary but may include: British controlled government and the economy. All heads of industry and government were Britons. Indians worked the plantations, mines, and factories, but the British took the profits. The British did develop transportation and irrigation systems, but these tended to benefit them rather than Indians.
3. Answers will vary but may include: British India was divided to give separate countries to Hindus and Muslims. Many people gave up their homes as Hindus moved from Pakistan to India, and Muslims left India for Pakistan. Both countries have fought over control of Kashmir. An even greater problem was the division of Pakistan into East and West sections, more than 1,000 miles (1,609.3 km) of Indian territory. In addition to the distance, they were also divided by ethnic and language differences which led to civil war involving India. East Pakistan became the independent country of Bangladesh.
4. Answers will vary but may include: No, it would not be a wise investment because rice needs lots of water, and that area does not have adequate rainfall.
5. Answers will vary but may include: Civil war might result between the Tamils and majority Sinhalese who would probably oppose the creation of a separate country. Also, it would probably face economic problems.
6. Answers will vary but may include: One-crop or one-product economies are at the mercy of the world market. They must also depend on good weather for their crops.

page 555, Reinforcing Graphic Skills

1. Answers will vary, but the following are possible hypotheses: Bhutan has large areas of forests which allow it to produce wood and paper. Bhutan's population is not overcrowded and permits large areas for growing forests. Animals are raised for food and their hides. Many people in Bhutan are skilled artisans.

2. Answers will vary, but the following are possible hypotheses: Farmers have a special appreciation for land. The government giving land to poor farmers gave them an incentive to care for their farms and crops. Since Pakistani farmers have given more attention and care to their crops, they have produced crops with a greater yield and better quality.

EVALUATING CHAPTER 26

World Geography: People and Places provides chapter tests to help evaluate student performance. To evaluate student mastery of Chapter 26, give students Chapter 26 Test from the Teacher Resource Book. This test may also be used for pretesting or retesting purposes. Other tests can be made from the questions available in the Test Generator Software.

Lesson Plan Suggestions—Chapter 26

SE—Student Edition TAE—Teacher Annotated Edition TG—Test Generator
TRB—Teacher Resource Book TSP—Transparency Package

Section 1 India (pp. 538–546)

Chapter Objectives	Suggested Teaching Strategies	Review

1. describe the major physical, economic, cultural, and historical features of India.	**Teacher Preparation**
	SE, Reading Assignment, pp. 538–546
	TAE, Unit 9 Suggested Resources
	  Unit 9 Overview, p. T261
	  Introducing Unit 9, p. T261
	  Chapter 26 Overview, p. T262
	  Introducing Chapter 26, pp. T262–T263
	TRB, Chapter 26 Teacher Notes: Section 1
	Teaching Options
	TAE, Introducing Unit 9, p. T261
	  Introducing Chapter 26, p. T262
	  Objective 1 Activities, p. T263
	TRB, Chapter 26 Teacher Notes: Section 1,
	  Extending the Lesson
	  Chapter 26 Skill Activity
		SE, Content Check, p. 546

Skill Objective: make hypotheses.	TSP, Transparency 6 SE, *Using Graphic Skills*, "Making Hypotheses," p. 540	

Section 2   Pakistan (pp. 546–549)

Chapter Objectives	Suggested Teaching Strategies	Review

2. describe the major physical, economic, cultural, and historical features of Pakistan.	**Teacher Preparation**
	SE, Reading Assignment, pp. 546–549
	TAE, Unit 9 Suggested Resources
	    Chapter 26 Overview, p. T262
	TRB, Chapter 26 Teacher Notes: Section 2
	Teaching Options
	TAE, Objective 2 Activities, p. T264
	TRB, Chapter 26 Teacher Notes: Section 2,
	    Extending the Lesson
	    Chapter 26 Skill Activity
		SE, Content Check, p. 549

Section 3   Other Countries of South Asia (pp. 550–553)

Chapter Objectives	Suggested Teaching Strategies	Review

3. describe the major physical, economic, cultural, and historical features of Sri Lanka, Bangladesh, Bhutan, and Nepal.	**Teacher Preparation**
	SE, Reading Assignment, pp. 550–553
	TAE, Unit 9 Suggested Resources
	    Chapter 26 Overview, p. T262
	TRB, Chapter 26 Teacher Notes: Section 3
	Teaching Options
	TAE, Objective 3 Activities, p. T264
	TRB, Chapter 26 Teacher Notes: Section 3,
	    Extending the Lesson
	    Chapter 26 Reading
	    Chapter 26 Skill Activity
		SE, Content Check, p. 553

Chapter 26 Review and Evaluation

Suggested Teaching Strategies	Review	Evaluation

TAE, Objective 4 Activities,
    pp. T264–T265
    Concluding Chapter 26,
    p. T265
TSP, Transparency 6
	SE, Chapter 26 Review,
	    pp. 554–555
	TRB, Chapter 26 Review
	    Worksheet
		TRB, Chapter 26 Test
		    Unit 9 Pretest, Map and
		    Content Worksheets
		TG, Chapter 26

CHAPTER 27 EAST ASIA

Student Edition pp. 556–577

CHAPTER 27 OBJECTIVES

At the conclusion of this chapter, students will be able to:
1. describe the major physical, economic, cultural, and historical features of Japan.
2. describe the major physical, economic, cultural, and historical features of China.
3. describe the major physical, economic, cultural, and historical features of Taiwan, North and South Korea, Mongolia, Hong Kong, and Macao.
4. summarize the chief geographic features of East Asia.

CHAPTER 27 SKILL OBJECTIVE

After completing the *Using Graphic Skills* exercise in this chapter, the student should be able to synthesize information.

CHAPTER 27 OVERVIEW

East Asia, isolated from other regions in Asia by physical barriers including extensive deserts and the world's highest mountains, was once completely isolated from the rest of the world. Today, the region is not isolated. Yet it is one marked by political divisions, contrasting levels of economic development, and mixtures of traditional and contemporary societies. Thus, *Section 1* of Chapter 26 begins with a geographic study of the crowded island country of Japan with its advanced economy and adherence to tradition, simplicity, and beauty. In *Section 2*, the People's Republic of China, the third largest nation in the world that has more than four times as many people as the United States, is described. *Section 3* describes the other countries and territories of East Asia, including Taiwan, North Korea, South Korea, Mongolia, and the two territories of Hong Kong and Macao.

The special feature, *Thinking Like a Geographer*, expands upon Pinyin, China's new system of writing Chinese words with the Roman alphabet.

CHAPTER 27 ACTIVITIES

Introducing Chapter 27

Draw students' attention to a large wall map showing political boundaries and important physical features in Asia. Point out locations of the People's Republic of China, Japan, North Korea, South Korea, Mongolia, Hong Kong, and Macao. Have students note the great differences in physical size among these areas. Point out further that all but Mongolia have access to the sea. Ask students to recall the disadvantages of being landlocked. Students should remember to include less trade with other countries because of difficulty in getting goods to them and dependence upon other countries to ship goods through.

Next, have students turn to the map on Population Distribution of East Asia found on page 567 of the Student Edition. Ask students to form a generalization about the relationship between population distribution and access to the sea as exemplified by the map.

Chapter 27 Reading Assignments

● Teaching   ■ Reinforcing   ★ Enriching

Unmarked activities deal with three or more features listed in the chapter objectives. Activities marked with the following letters deal with:

Ⓟ Physical features.
Ⓔ Economic features.
Ⓒ Cultural features.
Ⓗ Historical features.

Objective 1 Activities

● Objective 1 Teaching Activity

Before students begin Section 1, slowly read to them the following story, pausing after each sentence so that students can think about the impact of each fact.

I live in a country whose total land area is smaller than the state of California, but whose population numbers about half of the entire United States. Our people all live on mountain tops separated by ocean water, for my country consists of about 4,000 islands which are really volcanic peaks of a huge underwater mountain range. Our homes often rock with earthquake movements and volcanic eruptions sometimes far beneath us. None of us lives more than 70 miles away from the sea.

I feel great pride in my country. I think of majestic Mount Fuji and the bright, rising sun as

the right symbols for my country's accomplishments and hopes for the future. But, we have very few natural resources that can be used in industry—only small amounts of farmland between our mountains and a little coal. But we have enough hydroelectric power to run factories if we import raw materials, and we have plenty of the most important natural resource of all: people who are intelligent, hardworking, loyal, and determined to work together. Our people have made our country the third highest-producing industrial nation in the world, ranking right after the United States and the Soviet Union.

So, in spite of our small land area, constant dangers of earthquakes, volcanic eruptions, and tidal waves, few industrial raw resources, overcrowded living conditions, history of wars and threats of being conquered and annexed to larger neighboring countries, we enjoy one of the highest standards of living in the world, and consider ourselves wonderfully rich in the things that we value most: pride, group loyalty, personal honor, family, friendship, natural beauty, joy in living, and long life.

Ask the class to guess where the writer lives: Japan. Then hold a discussion about which facts seemed surprising and why.

■ Objective 1 Reinforcing Activity Ⓔ

Before directing the following activity, review debates in the Instructional Approaches section of this Teacher Annotated Edition. Ask some students to look in a current almanac to find out how much Japan paid for raw materials purchased from the United States last year. How much did Japanese companies make on the manufactured goods sold here? What would happen if everyone in the United States obeyed the popular slogan to only "buy American," even for one year? (Japan would not have the money to buy our raw materials.) Consider the nations who owe us money, such as Mexico and Brazil. If Japan has the income from its manufactured goods to buy their raw materials, they will have more money to pay off their debt to us.

Have a mock United Nations debate on the topic of trade barriers. Have other countries included in the debate besides the United

States and Japan. Students may want to research current news magazines for information on the topic.

★ **Objective 1 Enriching Activity**

Role play a delegation from Japan visiting the United States for the purpose of observing and comparing differences in lifestyles between their countries and ours.

Objective 2 Activities

● **Objective 2 Teaching Activity**

Arouse students' interest in China by slowly reading to them the following story.

I live in the most populated country on Earth; in fact, one-fifth of all the world's people live here. We have four times the people of the United States, but only half the potential farmland of the United States to grow food to feed ourselves. So we know how to produce more food per acre than anyone else.

We are the third largest country in the world in land area, ranking after the Soviet Union and Canada, and we live on eight percent of the world's land area.

We are the world's oldest living civilization, with a written history from 3,500 years ago. Speaking of writing, we paint our words with brushes to make artworks out of them, and we must learn 2,000 to 3,000 characters equivalent to your 26-letter alphabet. This is hard to teach foreigners, so we invented a new alphabet and a new way of writing just 10 years ago.

We are good at inventions. Over the centuries we invented and taught the rest of the world how to use coal for fuel, how to make paper from wood pulp, how to make silk from the cocoons of worms, how to grow and brew tea, how to make and use glass, porcelain, lacquer, the magnetic compass, movable type printing press, seismograph, anesthesia, wheelbarrow, gunpowder, and paper money.

Our land is shaped like a huge bowl, with high sides surrounding flat plains and deserts, and we have tried many times in history to remain within this enclosure, to keep our affairs to ourselves, and not to be involved with the rest of the world. We have built a Great Wall, accepted a Bamboo Curtain, and during our Cultural Revolution of the 1960s decade, we blocked out all media information and communication ideas.

But we are a big part of the world, with the third largest land area and one-fifth of the people, so we are now determined to catch up with a modernization program which will make us industrial and educational leaders in the early 21st century.

Encourage students to discuss freely their previous perceptions of China, and what new facts they have learned from these descriptions. Refer to the list of recommended materials for this unit in the Suggested Resources section to obtain additional materials on China to present to the class. Conclude with Chapter 27 Reading in the Teacher Resource Book.

■ **Objective 2 Reinforcing Activity** Ⓒ Ⓗ

Refer to the guidelines for lecture in the Instructional Approaches section of this Teacher Annotated Edition and to the list of Suggested Resources for this unit as well as current periodicals. Prepare a lecture on "China's Many Cultural Revolutions" which will expand on the cultural themes hinted at in the reading from the preceding activity and mentioned in the Student Edition. Include explanations of Buddhism, Confucianism, Daoism, Christianity, writings of Chairman Mao, and contemporary Chinese communist philosophy. Also enlarge on the historical periods, the cultural blackout of the 1960s, and the opening of China to the West during the 1970s and 1980s, from "Ping Pong Diplomacy" to President Nixon's historic visit and enthusiastic exchange of visitors and ideas today. Conclude the lecture by developing with students a time line of events in Chinese history. Have them copy the time line into their notebooks.

★ **Objective 2 Enriching Activity** Ⓒ

Use a class period to display and discuss Chinese cultural items, which you and your class borrow from various sources, and current events news articles. Show samples of artwork, ancient and contemporary, play folk and modern music, read folklore, Marco Polo, and contemporary travelogues. Show a video or filmstrip about ancient Chinese ways of making paper, painting on silk, or other art and craft processes. Help the students to appreciate the beauty and labor of Chinese cultural contributions.

Ask students: For what historical reasons did these people so often prefer to withdraw their nation from interacting with others? Is it possible to do so in today's kind of world? What would be some consequences for China, for the United States, for the rest of the world, if their government's "Cultural Revolution of the 1960s" had succeeded and was still in effect?

Objective 3 Activities

● **Objective 3 Teaching Activity**
Read and discuss the following story.

I live on an island in the East China Sea, 100 miles from mainland China, which the Portuguese called "Beautiful," or "Formosa."

In 1949 the rulers and many people from China fled to my island to escape Communist conquerors of the mainland. These Chinese kept alive the hope of one day reestablishing the traditional political system for the whole nation. They said they were still the true rulers of all of China, and my island became known as The Republic of China. From 1949 to 1971, we voiced the vote of China in the United Nations, and successfully kept the take-over government of the mainland "People's Republic of China" out of the United Nations and world affairs altogether. Then, after 22 years, world opinion changed, and other nations acknowledged that the Communist governing party of the People's Republic had established itself firmly, and must be dealt with as representing the majority of the Chinese people. So in 1971, they were officially given recognition and the vote in the United Nations. My island country is now the home of the Nationalist Government in Taiwan, an ancient Chinese name.

We have made of ourselves an important manufacturing center, producing more than the

whole People's Republic of China. Look around your school and home to find products which were made in my country. We enjoy one of the highest standards of living in the world today, and we are determined to make our economic success mightier than our historical defeat, and our cultural impact stronger than anyone would expect from our geographic size and location.

Direct students to read Section 3.1 on page 570 of the Student Edition and compose a reading guide to help them remember significant facts. Next read the following story about North and South Korea.

We live on a very mountainous peninsula, about the size of your state of Utah. I live in the Republic of Korea, and my brother lives in the Democratic People's Republic of Korea. That just means that I live on the southern part of the peninsula and he lives on the northern part, but we might as well be on different continents, for we cannot travel across the 38th parallel of north latitude to visit each other.

If you look at where we live on a map, you will see that our peninsula has always been a convenient landbridge between Asia's mainland and Japan. Our history has been a true tug-of-war between the most powerful nations of Asia: China, Soviet Union, and Japan. Whoever was stronger at any time had us in their grip. For a long time before 1895, we were part of China; then Japan grabbed us as a colony they called "Chosen" until 1945, when they were defeated in World War II. Then the Soviet Union sent its armies from the north to set up a Communist government like China had, but the United States rushed in from the south to say that our people should be able to elect our own form of free government. About 10 years later in 1953, when our lands, and farms, cities and people had been devastated, it was agreed that we should be divided into two nations at the 38th parallel.

We really need each other, though, to become a good place to live. North Korea has only about half the number of people, while South Korea has much more land. The southern part of the peninsula has most of the good land to feed our people, but the northern part has the minerals and hydroelectric power for manufacturing. Our people are culturally one family. We speak the same language and share the same historical memories of suffering, war, devastation, conquest, and now forced separation, brother from brother.

Compose a reading guide on Sections 3.2 to 3.4 that begins on page 571 of the Student Edition.

★ Objective 3 Enriching Activity

Refer to the guidelines for community resource persons in the Instructional Approaches section of this Teacher Annotated Edition. Invite a guest speaker who is from East Asia or very knowledgeable about this region or one country in it. Prepare the speaker by sharing the text and your class' notebook contents, and prepare the class by having students list the questions they would like to ask.

Objective 4 Activities

● Objective 4 Teaching Activity

Refer to the guidelines for discussion in the Instructional Approaches section of this Teacher Annotated Edition.

Pose the following question for discussion: How important are the physical geographic features of a place—its location, site and situation, landscape, climate, and natural resources—in its development as an independent nation?

Suggest that students look at the map of East Asia and think about the descriptions of each country in the region to help them formulate their ideas and jot down notes for discussion. Approach this as a whole-class discussion, small-group discussions, informal debate teams or individually-prepared essay answers.

During debriefing, students should point out that in East Asia (as a case study for generalizations about world geography) there are the largest land areas and the smallest land areas as countries; there are mainland, island, peninsula, delta, and single-city countries. China has a rich and ample variety of resources; Japan and Taiwan have almost none to account for extraordinary industrial development; most places have a range of climate,

but Japan has definite natural adversities in its earthquakes, volcanoes, typhoons, and tidal waves.

Lead students to the following generalizations: (1) Like Earth's people, its countries come in all sizes and shapes and have pre-set conditions of native location, relationships, ethnic diversity, advantageous and disadvantageous features, and a set of circumstances created by past generations. (2) Different people—and nations of people—can decide to make their set features work for them or against them. They can use their circumstances as challenges and opportunities or as obstacles. They can even change some of the conditions. What is important are the decisions and movements of the people. Thus, like Japan, *people* are often the most important resource a country has.

★ Objective 4 Enriching Activity

Refer to the guidelines for audiovisual materials in the Instructional Approaches section of this Teacher Annotated Edition. Show a film, filmstrip, or videocassette, or have the class listen to a recorded program that describes how the people of East Asia deal with one or more of the features of their country or region. Debrief the class with a general discussion.

Concluding Chapter 27

Organize a symposium on "East Asia and the Future." Divide the class into five groups. Assign one group to each of these countries: Japan, China, North Korea, South Korea, and Taiwan. Groups for Japan and China may have more students than groups for the other countries. Ask members of each group to review information regarding patterns of government and economic development for each country. Have them prepare a one-page summary of "predictions" for the year 2000. Some questions might include the following: Will the government be the same? Will the country be more industrialized? What kinds of exports will be important? Give each student an opportunity to make a few comments from his or her paper. Then hold a general discussion about East Asia's future.

ANSWERS TO CHAPTER 27 QUESTIONS

Content Check Questions
page 563

1. Refer to Section 1 content.
2. Refer to Glossary in Student Edition.
3. Highlands surrounded by seas. (p. 557)
4. The cool Oyashio Current flows southward and cools northern Japan, while the warm Japan Current flows northward, warming southern Japan. Nearness to the sea brings a good deal of rain, but because of the orographic effect, more rain falls on the western side than on the eastern side of the islands. (p. 559)
5. Highly skilled work force. (p. 559)
6. Farmers use intensive cultivation which uses all available land, high quality fertilizers, and modern machinery. (p. 560)
7. In urban areas on coastal plains. (p. 560)
8. Defeated in World War II, Japan's cities lay in ruins, and its economy was near collapse. Under American direction the government and economy were rebuilt. (p. 562)
9. Answers will vary but may include: It would be severely limited unless an alternative power source could be found.

page 570

1. Refer to Section 2 content.
2. Refer to Glossary in Student Edition.
3. Largest by far. (p. 567)
4. Western China has rugged mountains, high plateaus, low basins, and barren desert. Eastern China has fertile river valleys, flat plains, and low hills. (p. 563)
5. Humid subtropical. (p. 564)
6. Agriculture. (p. 565)
7. The eastern third of the country. (p. 567)
8. Government controls over the economy have been reduced, and closer ties have been developed with western nations. (pp. 569–570)
9. Answers will vary but may include: China will have to overcome such problems as lack of transportation, outdated factories, and underdeveloped electrical power while still fulfilling the needs of its enormous population.

page 575

1. Refer to Section 3 content.
2. The Taiwanese Chinese and members of the Nationalist Party, or their descendants, from the mainland. (p. 570)
3. Taiwan grows most of its own food and trades extensively with foreign nations, including exporting a variety of goods. Both government and business aid manufacturing and trade. (pp. 570–571)
4. Mostly mountainous except along the eastern, southern, and western coasts where narrow lowlands and river valleys are found. (p. 572)
5. They share a common language and culture, similar landforms, and similar effects from monsoons. Until 1945 they shared a common history. Differences include South Korea's slightly warmer climate and types of government. North Korea has mineral and energy resources. South Korea has better farmland, more people, and a broad economic base, making it one of the world's most prosperous countries. (p. 572)
6. Tending livestock. (p. 573)
7. Location, smallness, Chinese people and language, trade and fishing centers, tourist spots. Both are foreign-ruled but will return to China in the 1990s. (pp. 574–575)
8. Answers will vary but may include: It has probably limited national unity and created serious divisiveness. On the other hand, the more democratic governments of Taiwan and South Korea have allowed these countries to become some of the world's most prosperous.

Special Feature Questions
page 566, Thinking Like a Geographer: "Pinyin"

1. It wanted a system providing standard spelling and pronunciation of Chinese

names in English or any other language using the Roman alphabet.

2. Wade-Giles.
3. Zhongguo. Beijing. Guangzhou.
4. Pinyin has not been totally accepted.

page 568, Using Graphic Skills: "Drawing Conclusions"

1. Answers will vary but could include: All began near and along rivers because they provided water, fertile land, and flat terrain, as well as a means of transportation.
2. Answers will vary but could include: River valleys provided access to a water supply and fertile land that encouraged permanent settlement; river valleys helped develop growth of towns and trades; river valleys may have acted as a barrier against invasions.

Photo/Illustration Caption Questions
page 558

The Gobi Desert. (p. 558)

page 559

Because of the orographic effect from the mountains. (p. 559)

page 560

Japan's population is one-half as large as that of the United States. Japanese agriculture is very efficient because of high quality fertilizers, modern farm machinery, and intensive cultivation. (p. 560)

page 561

Japanese transportation systems are advanced because of their high-speed trains and an interconnected network of roads and railroads. (p. 561) Shintoism; has given people a respect for nature, love of simple things, concern for cleanliness, and good manners. (p. 561)

page 562

Steel production. (p. 562)

page 563

Construction problems would have been caused in areas of rugged mountains and barren deserts. (p. 563)

page 565

Wheat. (p. 565)
Slightly larger. (p. 565)

page 567

Population distribution is heavily concentrated in eastern areas of China and fairly evenly distributed in North and South Korea, Japan, and Taiwan; population distribution is extremely sparse in western China and in Mongolia. (p. 567)

page 571

U.S.S.R. (p. 571)

page 572

Yes, its factories produce textiles, chemicals, steel, transportation equipment, electronics, cars. (p. 572)

page 573

North and South Korea are alike in their terrain and climate and in their common history, language, and culture; they are different in their governments, ownership of farms and factories, and populations. (p. 572)

page 574

Japan. (p. 574)

Chapter 27 Review Questions
page 576, Reviewing Vocabulary

1. South Korea.
2. North Korea.
3. West River.
4. Taiwan.
5. Xizang.
6. Guangzhou.
7. Yellow River.
8. Yangtze River.
9. Peking.

page 576, Remembering the Facts

1. Coastal plains. (p. 558)
2. Tokaido. (p. 560)
3. Shintoism and Buddhism. (p. 561)
4. Third largest in the world. (p. 563)
5. Mountains; the high, rugged Plateau of Tibet; and high valleys. (p. 564)

6. East central and southeastern. (p. 564)
7. Huang He because of its destructive floods. (p. 564)
8. Summer. (p. 564)
9. Confucius. (p. 567)
10. About 4,000 years. (p. 568)
11. The Nationalist Party of China. (p. 570)
12. Soviet Union. (p. 573)
13. People's Republic of China. (p. 575)

page 577, Understanding the Facts

1. Japan lies on the "ring of fire" where Earth's crust is unstable, and three tectonic plates meet near there. (p. 558)
2. Because of the orographic effect. (p. 559)
3. The cool Oyashio Current flows southward and cools northern Japan. The warm Japan Current flows northward and warms southern Japan. (p. 559)
4. Its highly skilled work force. (p. 559)
5. Mountainous landscape and growth of cities. (p. 559)
6. Flooding provides water and deposits rich silt which makes the farmland extremely fertile. (p. 564)
7. Southeastern China is humid subtropical with mild winters and hot and humid summers. Northwestern China is desert with cold winters and hot, dry summers. (p. 564)
8. Unevenly distributed with most people living in the eastern third of the country. (p. 567)
9. Both are mountainous and rugged with narrow coastal plains. Farms are small and privately owned, and farmers practice intensive cultivation using fertilizers and modern farm machinery. Hillsides are farmed by terracing, and patches of land between buildings and highways are planted. (pp. 557, 559–560, 572)
10. Nomadic herders and livestock farmers. (p. 573)

page 577, Thinking Critically and Creatively

1. Answers will vary, but students' replies may include the fact that it helps Japan show its technological progress and provides for rapid efficient movement of people and goods.
2. Answers will vary, but students' responses should recognize the fact that Japan was able to adopt the best features of western technology, establish trade for needed resources, and develop their markets for exports.
3. Answers will vary, but students' answers may take into account the following possibilities: Japanese industries emphasize strict quality control, involve workers in decision making, assign workers to teams with a variety of tasks, and do not segregate management from labor. These measures tend to foster a very loyal attitude among workers. Also, Japan has been able to devote almost all of its profits to developing the economy; very little of its budget is spent on national defense.
4. Answers will vary, but the following replies may be suggested: The Plateau is high, rugged, and mostly treeless with a dry and cool or cold climate. Nearly surrounded by high mountains, the Plateau is isolated from the rest of Asia. It may further be suggested that few people choose to live in such a harsh environment with limited economic opportunities and little communication or transportation.
5. Answers will vary, but students may consider the influences of China's large and industrious population, its relatively advanced culture, and its fertile eastern plains and excellent harbors would be enticing to invaders.
6. Answers will vary, but students may suggest the following situation as a response: China had been ravaged by war and years of misrule. On the surface, communism looked attractive to the poor Chinese peasants who were promised land taken from wealthy landowners and government reforms that would drastically change their society.
7. Answers will vary but may include: In Taiwan, unlike China, farms are privately

owned, and the government provides assistance to farmers. Taiwan has also welcomed trade with foreign countries, and manufacturing growth has been encouraged by government and business. Taiwan is much smaller than China with fewer people to govern; China has a great diversity of cultures and languages. The Taiwanese have an additional incentive for trying to remain economically strong in order to avoid takeover by the People's Republic of China.

page 577, Reinforcing Graphic Skills

1. Answers will vary but should stress that scientists rely on archaeological evidence such as ruins of buildings and artifacts, such as pottery, household items, tools, jewelry, and weapons.

2. Answers will vary, but one could conclude that the present environment of Asian river valleys would have large population areas, cities, many agricultural areas, and trading centers.

EVALUATING CHAPTER 27

World Geography: People and Places provides chapter tests to help evaluate student performance. To evaluate student mastery of Chapter 27, gives students Chapter 27 Test from the Teacher Resource Book. This test may also be used for pretesting or retesting purposes. Other tests can be made from the questions available in the Test Generator Software.

Lesson Plan Suggestions—Chapter 27

SE—Student Edition   TAE—Teacher Annotated Edition   TG—Test Generator
TRB—Teacher Resource Book   TSP—Transparency Package

Section 1   Japan   (pp. 556–563)

Chapter Objectives	Suggested Teaching Strategies	Review

1. describe the major physical, economic, cultural, and historical features of Japan.	**Teacher Preparation**
	SE, Reading Assignment, pp. 556–563
	TAE, Unit 9 Suggested Resources
	    Chapter 27 Overview, p. T270
	    Introducing Chapter 27, pp. T270–T271
	TRB, Chapter 27 Teacher Notes: Section 1
	Teaching Options
	TAE, Introducing Chapter 27, pp. T270–T271
	    Objective 1 Activities, pp. T271–T272
	TRB, Chapter 27 Teacher Notes: Section 1,
	    Extending the Lesson
	    Chapter 27 Skill Activity
		SE, Content Check, p. 563

Section 2   China   (pp. 563–570)

Chapter Objectives	Suggested Teaching Strategies	Review

2. describe the major physical, economic, cultural, and historical features of China.
 	
Skill Objective: draw a conclusion.
	Teacher Preparation
	  SE, Reading Assignment, pp. 563–570
	  TAE, Unit 9 Suggested Resources
	    Chapter 27 Overview, p. T270
	  TRB, Chapter 27 Teacher Notes: Section 2
	Teaching Options
	  TAE, Objective 2 Activities, pp. T272–T273
	  TRB, Chapter 27 Teacher Notes: Section 2,
	    Extending the Lesson
	    Chapter 27 Reading
	    Chapter 27 Skill Activity
	  SE, *Using Graphic Skills,*
	    "Drawing Conclusions," p. 568
		SE, Content Check, p. 570

Section 3   Other Countries and Territories of East Asia   (pp. 570–575)

Chapter Objectives	Suggested Teaching Strategies	Review

3. describe the major physical, economic, cultural, and historical features of Taiwan, North and South Korea, Mongolia, Hong Kong, and Macao.	**Teacher Preparation**
	  SE, Reading Assignment, pp. 570–575
	  TAE, Unit 9 Suggested Resources
	    Chapter 27 Overview, p. T270
	  TRB, Chapter 27 Teacher Notes: Section 3
	Teaching Options
	  TAE, Objective 3 Activities, pp. T273–T274
	  TRB, Chapter 27 Teacher Notes: Section 3,
	    Extending the Lesson
	    Chapter 27 Skill Activity
		SE, Content Check, p. 575

Chapter 27 Review and Evaluation

Suggested Teaching Strategies	Review	Evaluation

TAE, Objective 4 Activities,
  p. T274
    Concluding Chapter 27,
    p. T274
TSP, Transparency 6
	SE, Chapter 27 Review,
	  pp. 576–577
	TRB, Chapter 27 Review
	  Worksheet
		TRB, Chapter 27 Test
		TG, Chapter 27

CHAPTER 28   SOUTHEAST ASIA

Student Edition pp. 578–595

CHAPTER 28 OBJECTIVES

At the conclusion of this chapter, students will be able to:

1. describe the major physical, economic, cultural, and historical features of the continental lands of Southeast Asia.
2. describe the major physical, economic, cultural, and historical features of the islands of Southeast Asia.
3. summarize the chief geographic features of Southeast Asia.

CHAPTER 28 SKILL OBJECTIVE

After completing the *Using Graphic Skills* exercise in this chapter, the student should be able to confirm the skill of describing exact and relative locations of places.

CHAPTER 28 OVERVIEW

Southeast Asia consists of large island groups in the Pacific Ocean as well as countries on the Asian mainland. Thus, *Section 1* describes the major geographic features of countries such as Burma, Thailand, Laos, Kampuchea, and Vietnam that are located in continental Southeast Asia and are sometimes called Indochina. *Section 2* describes the major features of Insular Southeast Asia that includes large groups of islands in the Pacific as well as lands that touch the Asian mainland. The countries of Malaysia, Indonesia, Singapore, the Philippines, and Brunei are included in this study.

Unlike South Asia or East Asia, Southeast Asia is not dominated by any one culture. It has been influenced by outsiders from other parts of Asia as well as Europe and the United States. Like South Asia and East Asia, however, a rapidly growing population has hindered economic growth in many parts of the region. This area's growth has also been limited because of the debilitating effects of long wars fought over these lands.

CHAPTER 28 ACTIVITIES

Introducing Chapter 28

Using a large wall map depicting both physical features and political boundaries, point out the location of Southeast Asia to students. Then point out the countries comprising this region. If available, provide students with individual outline maps of Asia. Have them draw an enclosed line that includes all countries of the region. Regional boundaries are more difficult to draw in the case of Southeast Asia than with some other regions because so many of the lands within the region are scattered islands. Next, point out the locations of the Sulu Sea, the Celebes Sea, the Java Sea, the South China Sea, the Gulf of Thailand, the Strait of Malacca, and the Andaman Sea. Ask students to suppose that a hostile world power used its navy to seize control of these waters and that it closed them to all shipping. Challenge students to think about probable consequences for the economies of the countries of Southeast Asia. Share responses as a class.

Chapter 28 Reading Assignments

Objective 1   Student Ed. pp. 578–586
Objective 2   Student Ed. pp. 586–593

● Teaching   ■ Reinforcing   ★ Enriching

Unmarked activities deal with three or more features listed in the chapter objectives. Activities marked with the following letters deal with:

Ⓟ Physical features.
Ⓔ Economic features.
Ⓒ Cultural features.
Ⓗ Historical features.

Objective 1 Activities

● Objective 1 Teaching Activity
Display a large scale wall map of the continental lands of Southeast Asia. Also display a physical relief world map and a large globe. Have a set of overhead projector transparency maps of this area and maps of the individual countries located in it. Distribute to students blank outline maps of Southeast Asia.

As the class reads Section 1 that begins on page 579, allow them time to locate each of the places and natural features mentioned, using Figure 28-1 on page 580, wall maps, globe, and transparency maps. Students should label these places and features on their handout maps making their own key if necessary.

For further map practice, have the class read the graphic skills feature on exact and relative locations on page 590 of the Student Edition. Then challenge students to ask each

other in relay-team competition to describe the exact or relative locations of various places shown on the maps displayed and to name places for which others verbalize locations. Keep team scores on the chalkboard. It would be worthwhile to repeat this team location game on another day or two in the future to provide practice for skill development.

■ Objective 1 Reinforcing Activity
Show some photos, slides, or a filmstrip (without audio at first) of cities located on the continental lands of Southeast Asia. Ask students to identify observable influences of various cultures and ethnic groups in the pictures. Which of the places have the most mix of cultures? Then ask if this difference is because of location, history, or economics? Which of the Southeast Asian places will probably become more mixed in the 21st century? Why? Which will not? Why? What is the effect on the native people of the country?

With so much mixing of cultures in the population of almost every place in the world today, ask students if the word "foreigner" should be redefined or its connotation reevaluated. Hold a discussion about whether it is now more realistic to think of Earth's peoples as one human race rather than as ethnic and national classifications.

★ Objective 1 Enriching Activity
Ask the class to become aware of, collect, and display on a bulletin board, current events news articles about any of the countries in the continental lands of Southeast Asia. As you discuss these, question the media's bias, prejudice, or omission of news for some countries.

Objective 2 Activities

● Objective 2 Teaching Activity
Explain to the class that the countries of Insular Southeast Asia can provide a way to see the interrelationship between historical events and economic development. For example, in the center of downtown Singapore stands a very large statue of Sir Stamford Raffles, an Englishman whose fleet anchored at the mouth of the Singapore River on January 29, 1819.

There is some historical controversy about just how Raffles bargained with the then ruling Sultan of the land to have himself declared governor, but however that decision was made, just five years later Singapore was the busiest trading center in Southeast Asia with neighborhoods of European, Indian, Arab, Chinese, and Malay businesses. Today, the country of Singapore, whose total land area is almost exactly the same size as Chicago, Illinois, is a fully independent nation, Asia's busiest port, and the fifth largest port in the world. Its business language is English, although its national language taught in schools is Malay. Yet three-fourths of its people are Chinese, even though Singapore has never been a part of China. Ask students how such a small, overcrowded, multinational spot on an island can be a vital, independent nation where people maintain one of the highest standards of living in the world.

Malaysia's history was created to fill the economic needs of far-away Europe after the historic development there of the Industrial Revolution. British geologists found the world's lowest cost source of tin on the Malay Peninsula, and in 1895 a Chinese merchant brought seeds of rubber trees from Brazil to begin growth of that resource in Malaysia. Today, the country of Malaysia exists and prospers because it supplies about one-third of the world's supply of tin and one-half of the world's natural rubber. Ask students if they know of any other countries or regions of the world where this is true.

Indonesia—the largest nation of Insular Southeast Asia, composed of four and one-half large islands plus 13,600 small islands—was poorly prepared by history to develop in an economic way when it gained its independence from the Dutch in 1949. Only seven percent of its people were literate, and they spoke 200 separate languages. Ask students why this large nation has not yet caught up in living standards to tiny Singapore, or Brunei, a "postage stamp" on one of Indonesia's islands?

Brunei, a "tiny pocket of luxury," exports abundant oil and gas to the "big powers,"

Japan, the United States, and Singapore. How could history have dealt so differently with such a small spot on a big island divided between three countries, each of which is in a very different economic stage?

Point to the Philippines on a globe. Ask students: How has the geographic location of this country put it in the way of frequent invasions and conquests throughout its historic development? How do repeated wars and conquests by other nations with their own sets of objectives hinder economic development?

Challenge students to explore and report on these questions about the historic or economic development of each country. Then have them formulate two or three generalizations about the interplay between historic and economic features in a place. Share some of these generalizations with the class.

■ Objective 2 Reinforcing Activity

Have the class write a story about a country in Insular Southeast Asia beginning with "I live in a country where. . ." similar to the stories you read to them in Chapter 27. Tell students to take the point of view of a person who has lived in the area for a long time and can describe its geographic features accurately.

Objective 3 Activities

● Objective 3 Teaching Activity

Show the class an atlas map of the Pacific Ring of Fire region of volcanoes and frequent earthquakes. Ask for discussions about the consequences of this natural phenomenon for the Southeast Asia region. Effect on physical features: Which of the islands are the tops of volcanic mountain ranges? Which are not? Which land areas are formed by tectonic movement of continental plates? Which are not? Which countries have landscapes dominated by beautiful volcano peaks? By crevasses, canyons, and slides caused by earthquakes? Can islands suddenly disappear or appear above water because of tectonic movement? Have the class read the special feature on Krakatau, page 588 of the Student Edition.

Discuss the effect of the Ring of Fire proximity on the economic features of the region: What does a volcanic eruption or earthquake do to the soil? the water? Is it safe to farm there? to build homes? factories? cities?

What about the effects on cultural and historical features? How do students think families feel who live around the Ring of Fire? How does this compare with living in other potential natural disaster areas, such as Southeast United States where hurricanes occur, or the Great Plains, where tornadoes and dust storms are expected, or river valleys where flooding regularly happens. Why don't people move away from such areas?

■ **Objective 3 Reinforcing Activity**
Refer to the guidelines for retrieval charts in the Instructional Approaches section of this Teacher Annotated Edition. Have students as a class construct a summarizing chart. Discuss points of comparison, contrast, uniqueness,

and the interplay between the physical, economic, cultural, and historic features of the countries and the region.

Concluding Chapter 28

Ask students what the colors and symbols of the United States flag represent. Discuss these, and then inform students that the Japanese flag is a red sun on a white background. The Japanese call their country Nippon, or Nihon, meaning source of the sun. Divide the class into ten groups, assigning each one of the countries in Southeast Asia. Each group should first review the chapter material for what it feels is the most unique or outstanding aspect of the country; then design and construct a new national flag, using construction paper. Have each group present its flag to the class, explaining the reasons behind the chosen design. Some students may wish to research the actual flags of the countries and their symbolism.

ANSWERS TO CHAPTER 28 QUESTIONS

Content Check Questions
page 586

1. Refer to Section 1 content.
2. Refer to Glossary in Student Edition.
3. Mountains, plateaus, river basins, deltas, lowlands, rain forests. (pp. 580–581)
4. Farming. (p. 581)
5. Buddhist. (p. 582)
6. Vietnam. (p. 584)
7. Vietnam, Laos, Kampuchea. (p. 586)
8. Answers will vary but may state that most people live clustered in river valleys and deltas along the coast; mountainous regions and tropical rain forests are not capable of supporting large populations.

page 593

1. Refer to Section 2 content.
2. Refer to Glossary in Student Edition.
3. Several tectonic plates converge in this area. (p. 587)

4. Tropical rain forest. (p. 587)
5. Malays and Chinese. (p. 591)
6. It is a center of banking, insurance, manufacturing, and trade. (p. 592)
7. Answers will vary, but Insular Southeast Asia was a haven for settlement and trade by people from different areas of Asia and Europe, each with his or her own religion.

Special Feature Questions
page 588, Strange But True: "Mighty Blast at Krakatau"

1. It was completely blown away.
2. How to predict volcanoes and how to use their power.

page 590, Using Graphic Skills: "Reviewing Exact and Relative Locations"

1. Approximately 18°N, 121°E.
2. Between 10 and 11 degrees north latitude, and 124 degrees east longitude.

3. Sandakan.
4. Southwest of Mindoro and northeast of the Territory of Sabah in Malaysia.
5. Southeast of the island of Luzon and north of the island of Mindanao.
6. South China Sea: northwest. Philippine Sea: northeast. Sulu Sea: southwest.
7. Southeast.

Photo/Illustration Caption Questions
page 580

Insular Southeast Asia. (p. 580)

page 581

Shifting cultivation where trees are cleared and groundcover burned. (p. 581)

page 582

Chinese influence on business, European and American influence on religion and language. (pp. 582–583)

page 583

Rice farming in Java; subsistence farming and shifting cultivation in Borneo. (p. 583)

page 584

Bangkok, Thailand. (p. 584)

page 585

Portugal, Britain, France. (p. 585)

page 586

Vietnam, Laos, and Kampuchea became communist countries. (p. 586)

page 587

Sumatra, Java, Borneo, Celebes, Timor, western New Guinea. (p. 587)

page 589

Indonesia, Philippines, Singapore. (p. 589)

page 591

Its size is about one-fourth that of the U.S.; Its population is about three-fourths that of the U.S. (p. 591)

page 592

The Chinese have more wealth, but the Malays control the government. (p. 592)

Chapter 28 Review Questions
page 594, Reviewing Vocabulary

entrepôt—a center for storing and reshipping goods of other countries.

silvaculture—commercial tree-growing.

paddies—wet plots of land used for growing rice.

guerrilla warfare—type of warfare in which soldiers make attacks and then withdraw into forests or mountains.

page 594, Remembering the Facts

1. Continental Southeast Asia—Burma, Thailand, Laos, Kampuchea, Vietnam; Insular Southeast Asia—Malaysia, Indonesia, Singapore, the Philippines, Brunei. (p. 579)
2. The Mekong River. (p. 581)
3. Laos. (p. 584)
4. Indonesia. (p. 591)
5. Islam. (p. 591)
6. Tropical moist and humid subtropical. (p. 581)
7. Rice. (p. 582)

page 595, Understanding the Facts

1. Rice can be grown only where water is abundant. This suggests that Southeast Asia is an area with abundant rainfall and other water sources. (pp. 581, 589)
2. India, China, Europe, the United States. Religion, language, business, arts. (pp. 579, 582–583, 591–593)
3. Several tectonic plates meet in this area and are part of the Pacific "ring of fire." (p. 587)
4. Heavy rains leach the soil, washing away valuable minerals. Though there is abundant rain, the soils are not rich. Thus, crop production is not as good as in an area with more fertile soils. (p. 581)
5. Burma and Thailand are much more economically developed. A much higher percentage of their national income comes from industrial activity than is the case in Kampuchea and Laos. (pp. 583–584)
6. Singapore is heavily industrialized and a sophisticated trading country. Its prosperity is based on banking, insurance, manu-

facturing, and trade. Profits from these economic activities explain Singapore's high standard of living. (p. 592)

7. Singapore is more populous and has a highly developed and diverse economy. Brunei's economy is based primarily on oil. Singapore's prosperity is based on a wide variety of economic and industrial services, whereas Brunei's prosperity is tied to a single commodity, oil. (p. 592)

page 595, Thinking Critically and Creatively

1. Answers will vary, but student responses should indicate that people from India carried Hinduism to Insular Southeast Asia; people from India traveled on ships to this area.

2. Answers will vary, but student responses should take into account that most major cities are located at or near the mouths of rivers. Rivers have cut broad, fertile valleys where most of the people live. The locations of these cities give them access to world markets and to the most important food-producing sections of their countries.

3. Answers will vary but should note the location in Insular Southeast Asia. It may be further noted that water transport has made access to these lands easy for centuries. On the other hand, travel to the interior of Continental Southeast Asia was difficult. As a result, fewer outsiders visited and settled in this area.

4. Answers will vary, but students may note that the nation bears a legacy of Spanish rule in its Roman Catholic religion. The fact that English is widely spoken is a legacy of the Philippines' former status as a possession of the United States. Govern-

ment institutions are modeled after certain American and European practices.

5. Answers will vary, but students may note that advantages could include having a population that generally has the same expectations of life and the same assumptions about how people should behave. A common language makes it easier for people from various parts of the country to communicate with one another. It is easier for the government to promote the idea that citizens are part of large extended families. Disadvantages might be the development of attitudes that people of other ethnic groups are not to be trusted. It might breed intolerance. There might be less inclination to understand perspectives of people from other cultures.

6. Answers will vary but may include that this is a critically important sea link between the Bay of Bengal and (1) the China Sea and (2) the Java Sea. It is a critical link from East Asia and much of Southeast Asia to India and lands farther to the west. If this passage were closed, ships would be forced to divert miles to the south. This would add time and expense. Also, it probably would have a devastating impact on the economies of such cities as Singapore and Kuala Lumpur, which depend heavily on sea traffic through the Strait of Malacca.

page 595, Reinforcing Graphic Skills

1. Approximately 7°N, 122°E.
2. Zamboanga; northeast.
3. Between 4 and 5 degrees north latitude, and between 114 and 116 degrees east longitude.
4. Approximately 6°N, 118°E.

EVALUATING CHAPTER 28

World Geography: People and Places provides chapter tests to help evaluate student performance. To evaluate student mastery of Chapter 28, give students Chapter 28 Test from the Teacher Resource Book. This test may also be used for pretesting or retesting purposes. Other tests can be made from the questions available in the Test Generator Software.

Lesson Plan Suggestions—Chapter 28

SE—Student Edition TAE—Teacher Annotated Edition TG—Test Generator
TRB—Teacher Resource Book TSP—Transparency Package

Section 1 *Continental Southeast Asia* (*pp. 578–586*)

Chapter Objectives	Suggested Teaching Strategies	Review
1. describe the major physical, economic, cultural, and historical features of the continental lands of Southeast Asia.	**Teacher Preparation** SE, Reading Assignment, pp. 578–586 TAE, Unit 9 Suggested Resources Chapter 28 Overview, p. T280 Introducing Chapter 28, pp. T280–T281 TRB, Chapter 28 Teacher Notes: Section 1 **Teaching Options** TAE, Introducing Chapter 28, p. T280 Objective 1 Activities, p. T281 TRB, Chapter 28 Teacher Notes: Section 1, Extending the Lesson Chapter 28 Reading Chapter 28 Skill Activity	SE, Content Check, p. 586

Section 2 *Insular Southeast Asia* (*pp. 586–593*)

Chapter Objectives	Suggested Teaching Strategies	Review
2. describe the major physical, economic, cultural, and historical features of the islands of Southeast Asia. Skill Objective: review exact and relative locations.	**Teacher Preparation** SE, Reading Assignment, pp. 586–593 TAE, Unit 9 Suggested Resources Chapter 28 Overview, p. T280 TRB, Chapter 28 Teacher Notes: Section 2 **Teaching Options** TAE, Objective 2 Activities, pp. T281–T282 TRB, Chapter 28 Teacher Notes: Section 2, Extending the Lesson SE, *Using Graphic Skills,* "Reviewing Exact and Relative Locations," p. 590	SE, Content Check, p. 593

Chapter 28 Review and Evaluation

Suggested Teaching Strategies	Review	Evaluation
TAE, Objective 3 Activities, pp. T282–T283 Concluding Chapter 28, p. T283 TSP, Transparency 6	SE, Chapter 28 Review, pp. 594–595 TRB, Chapter 28 Review Worksheet	TRB, Chapter 28 Test TG, Chapter 28

Unit 9 Review and Evaluation

Suggested Teaching Strategies	Review	Evaluation
TAE, Concluding Unit 9, p. T287 TRB, Unit 9 Career Worksheet	SE, Unit 9 Review, pp. 596–597	TRB, Unit 9 Exam Unit 9 Posttest, Map and Content Worksheets

CONCLUDING UNIT 9

Divide the class into groups of four or five. Assign each group a pictorial collage of the Asian culture area. Tell the students to have landscape, climate, economy, culture, and history of the region represented on their collage. They should also be prepared to explain to other class members what each figure represents on the collage. Once collages are complete, have each group describe its work to the rest of the class.

Unit 9 Exam in the Teacher Resource Book may be administered.

UNIT 9 REVIEW QUESTIONS

page 596, Thinking About the Unit

1. South Asia and East Asia cover a greater land area and have a greater variety of landscapes with extensive plateau areas, some desert regions, and high mountains. Most of Southeast Asia stretches over a vast ocean area and has extensive areas of lowlands and river basins. Because of Southeast Asia's location relative to the Equator, it has a more tropical climate than South and East Asia.

2. Answers will vary but might include the British type of government in India, European and American technology in Japan, Soviet agricultural organization in China, and Chinese business practices throughout much of Southern Asia.

UNIT 10 OCEANIA AND ANTARCTICA

Student Edition pp. 598-643

UNIT 10 GOALS

At the conclusion of this unit, students will be able to:
1. recognize the diversity of physical features, climate, economic development, and cultural characteristics of Oceania and Antarctica.
2. describe the effects that isolation from most other world regions has on the two culture areas of Oceania.

UNIT 10 SKILL OBJECTIVE

After completing the *Developing Geography Skills* exercise in this unit, the student should be able to identify trends and make forecasts.

UNIT 10 OVERVIEW

In this unit, students will learn about Oceania, the world area that contains most of the insular territories of the Pacific Ocean, including Australia, New Zealand, and the Pacific Islands, and they will also study about Antarctica, the frozen continent surrounding the South Pole.

Australia and New Zealand, the subjects of *Chapter 29*, might be called neighbors in this Pacific world where the 1200-mile distance between them is a short hop between islands. Australia is an island continent with plants and animals as unusual as its landscapes. Here isolation has created a unique world where plants and animals have been allowed to reach their developmental potential undisturbed. The Australian Aborigines, believed by many anthropologists to be humanity's oldest surviving ethnic group, make the Australian outback a living laboratory for the study of a stone-age people.

In contrast to Australia, New Zealand has virtually no native animals, although today imported animals greatly outnumber the human inhabitants. In this island country with its moderate climate, people from many European and Asian nations have created an interesting pluralistic society. Also in contrast to Australia, where the Aborigines were separated from the European settlers, the Maori of New Zealand have been integrated into the nation's society.

Chapter 30 explores the geographical features of the Pacific Islands. These islands, so separated from each other and the rest of the world, developed many differing cultural traits and languages. However, all their inhabitants are believed to have come originally from Southeast Asia, settling first in Melanesia some 50,000 years ago, then in Micronesia around 4,000 years ago, and most recently, in Polynesia some 2,000 years ago.

Antarctica, described in *Chapter 31*, has only been inhabited by humans since scientists braved its inhospitable, icy wasteland to set up encampments for scientific inquiry. Their studies indicate that this continent may not, in fact, be a wasteland and may, in the future, yield important resources for humanity. Today, some 2,000 scientists from 18 nations accompany the only permanent residents—whales, seals, penguins, and other birds.

Upon completion of this unit, the student should understand that this vast Pacific world of Oceania and Antarctica is enormously varied in landscapes, climates, histories, economic patterns, flora, fauna, and peoples, creating a kaleidoscope of extreme contrasts between a land covered with thousands of feet of ice and unique island countries.

INTRODUCING UNIT 10

Look with the students at chapter and unit opening photographs for this unit in their Student Edition. Ask them to do once again the work of a geographer as they did with the unit opening photograph of Unit 1. Prepare the same kinds of questions, making them applicable to the photographs in this unit. Remind the students that these questions concerning location, place, human-environment relations, movement, and regions represent the work of a geographer. With the focus of the question in mind, ask students to make a rapid, comparative study of the regions covered in this unit based on the impressions gained from the unit and chapter opening photographs alone.

CHAPTER 29 AUSTRALIA AND NEW ZEALAND

Student Edition pp. 600–617

CHAPTER 29 OBJECTIVES

At the conclusion of this chapter, students should be able to:

1. describe the major physical, economic, cultural, and historical features of Australia.
2. describe the major physical, economic, cultural, and historical features of New Zealand.
3. summarize the chief geographic features of Australia and New Zealand.

CHAPTER 29 SKILL OBJECTIVE

After completing the *Using Graphic Skills* exercise in this chapter, the student should be able to read time-zone maps.

CHAPTER 29 OVERVIEW

Although Australia and New Zealand share common European cultural characteristics, their landscapes, economies, and histories are sufficiently different to provide themes for comparison and contrast. Students find that the differing Australian landscape with its even more unique plant and animal inhabitants, along with the pluralistic culture and mysterious background of the Maori of New Zealand, have high interest value.

In this chapter, *Section 1* describes the major physical, economic, cultural, and historical features of Australia, while *Section 2* focuses on the geographic features of New Zealand. Two special features in this chapter provide historical background on Captain Cook and on the planned city of Canberra, the capital of Australia.

CHAPTER 29 ACTIVITIES

Introducing Chapter 29

Have a student volunteer read aloud the introduction to Unit 10 on page 599 of the Student Edition as well as the introduction to Chapter 29 on page 600. You may also wish to allow the same or another volunteer to read Unit 10 Overview from this Teacher Annotated Edition. Then, instruct students to list 10 questions—5 for Australia and 5 for New Zealand—about landscape, climatic, cultural, economic, and historical features of these two countries. Select the best questions and write them on a piece of poster board and leave it in a visible spot in the classroom so that the questions may be answered as the study of this chapter proceeds.

Chapter 29   Reading Assignments

Objective 1   Student Ed. pp. 601–609
Objective 2   Student Ed. pp. 609–615

● Teaching	■ Reinforcing	★ Enriching

Unmarked activities deal with three or more features listed in the chapter objectives. Activities marked with the following letters deal with:

Ⓟ   Physical features.
Ⓔ   Economic features.
Ⓒ   Cultural features.
Ⓗ   Historical features.

Objective 1 Activities

● Objective 1 Teaching Activity
Refer to the guidelines for team learning in the Instructional Approaches section of this Teacher Annotated Edition. Divide the class into six groups and assign to each team one of the states of Australia. Each team should try to answer the following questions about its state: What are the major physical features? Where do most of the people live? What are the main economic activities? Students will find that the material in the text is not divided into state by state descriptions. Therefore, they will have to combine what is presented in the text with information from the maps in the chapter and from other resources. Once the questions are answered, information can be shared by filling in a chalkboard matrix.

Refer students to the Chapter 29 Reading in the Teacher Resource Book for background information related to this objective.

■ Objective 1 Reinforcing Activity
Refer to the guidelines for cooperative learning in the Instructional Approaches section of this Teacher Annotated Edition, and then divide the class into two large groups. Assign one group to study the Aborigines of Australia, and the other, American Indians. The two groups should conduct research in the following areas: Origins and characteristics of the ethnic group; encounters with people from other lands; present situation; and possibilities for the future. Within the two cooperative learning groups, responsibilities may be divided among committees or individuals. Have both groups present their findings to the class, and then conduct a class discussion about the similarities and differences between the Aborigines and the American Indians, their past, present, and future.

★ Objective 1 Enriching Activity
Form several groups to investigate several aspects of Australian life. One group may be

assigned to investigate the Australian vocabulary. Explain to the students that although Australia is an English-speaking country, many new words have been added to the vocabulary of the people, some of their own invention and some from the Aborigine language. Start the vocabulary group by providing the following words for them to investigate: squatters, drovers, home unit, veranda, station, paddock, homestead, outback, gum tree, mob, walk-about, boomerang, woomera, dingo, corroboree, billabong, and others. First, have them find the meanings, make sentences with them, and then see if the class can guess the meanings from their use in the sentences. After the class has attempted to guess the meanings, have the vocabulary group "translate" the sentences that they wrote and provide the class with a vocabulary list with translations in "American."

Another group may wish to investigate Australian animals. Provide this group with the following list to start them off: platypus, kookaburra, kangaroo, budgereegah, dugong, bandicoot, cassowary, cuscus, emu, koala, wallaby, phascogale, spiny anteater, Tasmanian devil, Tasmanian wolf, tiger cat, wallaby, joey, numbat, wallaroo, wombat. Tell the group reporting on animals to be able to explain the meaning of monotreme and marsupial and apply the terms to the animals they talk about. Have this group give the name of an animal to the class and ask the class to guess what kind of animal it is. Then they should show a photograph or illustration, possibly using an overhead projector, to show what the animal is really like. They should explain in what way it is unusual or how it is different to similar animals, if any, outside Australia.

A third group may report on Australian literature. Provide the names of some well-known poets to start them off. These might include: Adam Lindsay Gordon, Andrew Barton Paterson, Henry Lawson, David Campbell, Robert David Fitzgerald, Alec Durwent Hope, James Philip McAuley, Kenneth Slesson, Douglas Stewart, and Judith Wright. Ask this group to find poems by some of these authors and read them to the class, explaining their meanings.

A fourth group may investigate Australian plant life. Have the group prepare a felt board in the shape of the Australian continent and cutouts of plants native to Australia. Have them place the plants on the felt board map in the areas where they are found, give the names of the plants, explain the climate area in which they grow, and describe any features that make the plants unusual. When the class has had time to study the felt board, the plant group should take the plant cutouts off and then see how many of their classmates can remember where the different types of plants grow by replacing the cutouts where they belong on the map. This activity could take the form of a game with teams competing to replace plants correctly.

A fifth group might enjoy a more in-depth study of the life and culture of the Aborigines. Suggest Aborigine art as a possible theme as well as beliefs about the spirit world and Aborigine legends. Another group might like to research life in an Australian city, and still another, life in the Australian outback.

To end this activity, find copies of the music and lyrics for *Waltzing Matilda* and *Tie My Kangaroo Down*, and then explain any words the class might not yet know the meaning of, and teach the class to sing these songs.

Objective 2 Activities

● Objective 2 Teaching Activity

Explain to the class that this activity will take the form of writing a letter, and that they will write as if they were a New Zealand citizen. This New Zealander has been visiting in the United States and—has fallen in love! When he or she returns to his or her country, the New Zealander writes a letter to the American sweetheart to convince him or her to come to live in New Zealand. The problem is, how can the sad and lonely New Zealander convince the boy or girl of his or her dreams to come to live in New Zealand? Have each student write a letter to the American sweetheart explaining what a wonderful country New Zealand is and telling something about life there. Ask the students to share their "love letters" with the rest of the class.

■ Objective 2 Reinforcing Activity Ⓗ
Have the students prepare a series of "You Are There" broadcasts in the form of on-the-spot reports that may be prepared in advance as skits or performed extemporaneously. In each of the on-the-spot reports, a reporter should interview participants and get their opinions on what is happening, as well as obtain descriptions of what is going on. The reports should cover the following events: The Dutch try to land on New Zealand in 1642 but are prevented by fierce Maori warriors; Part of James Cook's expedition succeeds in landing on New Zealand; British immigrants begin arriving in New Zealand in the 1800s; The British and Maori negotiate a land rights treaty in exchange for British rule; New Zealand helps found the United Nations.

★ Objective 2 Enriching Activity Ⓒ
Refer to the guidelines for lecture in the Instructional Approaches section of this Teacher Annotated Edition. Give a short lecture on the Maori culture of New Zealand and illustrate it with photographs, slides, or a film strip. An alternate activity would be to refer to the guidelines for audiovisual materials in the Instructional Approaches section of this Teacher Annotated Edition, and show a movie or videocassette about the Maori. After the lecture or audiovisual, allow those students who are especially interested to make in-depth reports on special areas of the Maori culture, such as their art and music.

Objective 3 Activities

● Objective 3 Teaching Activity
In an informal class discussion, compare the features of Australia and New Zealand. Ask the class to help in deciding what things can be compared and/or contrasted. Make columns for each country on the chalkboard and compare and contrast as many things as the students can mention, writing student responses in the appropriate columns. Then have students decide four ways in which these countries are most alike and four ways in which they are most different. At this point, students should have some expertise in making retrieval charts, so have them make a chart in their notebooks of the aspects of Australia and New Zealand that are similar and different.

■ Objective 3 Reinforcing Activity
Remind the class that a sketch map is a form of note-taking especially applicable to the study of geography. Ask the class to make sketch outline maps of Australia and New Zealand on a large sheet of paper. Then have them review their Student Edition, filling in the map with the information from their texts. Have students draw in rivers and land formations, write in landscape and climate information, cultural and economic patterns, and create two small time lines beside the maps—one for Australia and one for New Zealand—showing events from the time of earliest Aborigine or Maori arrivals to the present. Students may invent their own map keys and the design of their time lines. Ask volunteers to explain their maps and time lines when the assignment is completed, and then display the sketch maps around the classroom.

Concluding Chapter 29

Appoint a committee to prepare a "Down Under Day." Show movies, tell stories, listen to the music of and sing songs from Australia and New Zealand. Some students may wish to find out who the popular music groups are from these countries and bring in recordings of their music to play. Invite guests from "down under" to meet the class and answer their questions. Display posters made by the students about the features they have studied. Instead of, or in addition to, the above activity, a trip to a zoo may be planned. Refer to the guidelines for field trips in the Instructional Approaches section of this Teacher Annotated Edition, and plan a trip to a local zoological park to see some of the animals studied in this chapter. A different trip might be planned to a botanical garden where some plants native to

Australia and New Zealand could be seen. Natural science museums might also have displays of Aborigine or Maori culture.

At this time, students may complete the Chapter 29 Skill Activity from the Teacher Resource Book.

ANSWERS TO CHAPTER 29 QUESTIONS

Content Check Questions
page 609

1. Refer to Section 1 content.
2. Refer to Glossary in Student Edition.
3. Coral reef, coastal plains, mountains, rugged hills, plateaus, deserts, river valleys, salt flats, basins, and deserts. (pp. 602–603)
4. Mostly dry. (p. 603)
5. Wheat, wool, and mutton. (p. 605)
6. Along the east and southeast coasts in some of the major cities; the west coast around Perth and southern coast around Adelaide are also heavily populated. (p. 607)
7. Answers will vary but may include: There is plenty of room for people to settle, and they could help develop the less-settled land. It is a bad idea in that much of the land will not accommodate a larger population. An increased population would demand more jobs, food supplies, and professional services, etc.

page 615

1. Refer to Section 2 content.
2. On North Island are, from west to east, coastal plains, volcanic highlands, and a high plateau. On South Island are rugged mountains running from north to south in the center and with coastal plains on the west, south, and east. (p. 611)
3. Middle-latitude marine. (pp. 610–611)
4. Raising and selling livestock. (p. 612)
5. Polynesians, including Maori, Samoans, Cook Islanders, and Tongans; Europeans; Indians, Chinese, and Southeast Asians. (p. 613)
6. North Island is smaller with lower mountains, has 72% of the population, has the largest cities, has less farmland than the more rural South Island, and is home to most of the Maori. (pp. 610–613)

Special Feature Questions
page 606, The Urban World: "Canberra: Urban Planning"

1. To establish a central location in the nation or to build in a particular area of the country so that people will move there and develop the area.
2. Near the Australian Alps 190 miles southwest of Sydney.

page 608, Focus on History: "Amazing Captain Cook"

1. To see what happens in the Southern Hemisphere when the planet Venus moves between Earth and the sun and to explore other parts of the Southern Hemisphere to search for another continent scientists believed existed.
2. In searching for Antarctica, he sailed farther south than anyone before him and mapped South Pacific and South Atlantic islands.
3. Answers will vary but may include: A northwest or northeast passage would save a great deal of time and money and would avoid overland travel which may involve crossing mountains, deserts, and other difficult terrain.

page 614, Using Graphic Skills: "Reading Time-Zone Maps"

1. 9:00 AM.
2. 1:00 AM Sunday.
3. 12:00 noon.

Photo/Illustration Caption Questions
page 602

Darling and Murray rivers. (p. 602)

page 603

Central Australia. (p. 603)
About 5 percent as large as the U.S. population. (p. 603)

page 604

Lower. (p. 604)

page 605

One-third. (p. 605)

page 607

Dairy farming, mixed farming, and livestock. (p. 607)

page 610

Queensland, New South Wales, Victoria, Darwin. (p. 610)

page 611

Mountains and fjords. (p. 611)

page 612

Its low elevation keeps Auckland relatively mild. (p. 612) The government is encouraging more manufacturing and industry. (p. 612)

page 613

The Maori, around 1300. (p. 613)

page 615

Many Maori have become actively involved in government and business. (p. 615)

Chapter 29 Review Questions
page 616, Reviewing Vocabulary

1. o U t b A c k
2. p e n A l c o L o n y
3. A r T e S I a n w e l l
4. f o d d e R   AUSTRALIA

pages 616–617, Remembering the Facts

1. World's smallest. (p. 601)
2. Eastern side in the Great Dividing Range. (p. 603)
3. The deserts in central Australia. (p. 603)
4. Two-thirds of Australia's people live along the east and southeast coasts with additional smaller population centers in the southern and western coastal areas. Few people live in the desert interior. (p. 607)
5. Southeast Asia. (p. 609)
6. Canterbury Plain in the east central coastal lowland of South Island. (p. 611)
7. Australia has gold, lead, zinc, bauxite, iron ore, rutile, zircon, diamonds, opals, coal, uranium, shale, and natural gas. New Zealand has asbestos, gold, copper, lead, and zinc. (pp. 605, 612)
8. Australia in 1901 and New Zealand in 1907. (pp. 609, 613)
9. Sydney, Melbourne, Brisbane, Canberra, Perth, and Adelaide in Australia; Auckland, Wellington, and Christchurch in New Zealand. (pp. 607, 613, 615)
10. Dutch sailors. (p. 613)

page 617, Understanding the Facts

1. The climate and landscape are best suited for sheep raising rather than growing crops. (pp. 605, 612)
2. Both countries have coastal lowlands. Australia's southeast highlands is the region most like New Zealand's mountains. Neither country has a large river network. Differences include Australia's relative flatness compared with New Zealand's high, rugged mountains. Australia has a greater variety of landforms. (pp. 601–603, 609–611)
3. Australia's farm economy was changed by the creation of a mining industry. This gave Australia a much broader economic base. (p. 605).
4. Both have common European, mostly British ancestry, religion, language, forms of government, and standards of living. Both also have significant indigenous populations and have also been enriched by Asian immigrants. (pp. 605, 609, 612–613)
5. New Zealand lies directly in the path of the westerly winds, and the eastern side is in the rain shadow of the Southern Alps. (p. 611)
6. The Treaty gave the Maori land rights in exchange for accepting British rule over the islands, making it officially a British colony. (p. 613)

page 617, Thinking Critically and Creatively

1. Answers will vary but may include: Australia's small population limits the size of the market for its products; there are not enough people to fully develop all the country's resources.
2. Answers will vary but may include that they are highly educated, industrious, were British colonies early, and now have had to develop as much of their own resources as possible to trade for what they need. They learned to be as self-sufficient as possible. Their remoteness tended to isolate them from invasions which allowed them a chance to prosper before becoming involved in world affairs.

3. Answers will vary but may include: Other groups are the native American Indians of North and South America, blacks of South Africa, and New Zealand's Maori. European explorers and colonists in search of wealth and land settled in areas with little regard for the Aborigines living there. In most cases Europeans felt that their culture was superior, and they had the weapons to back up their beliefs. Native peoples had to submit and adapt in order to survive.

page 617, Reinforcing Graphic Skills

1. Papua New Guinea.
2. Tokelau and Cook Islands.
3. Three.
4. Thursday, 12:00 noon.

EVALUATING CHAPTER 29

World Geography: People and Places provides chapter tests to help evaluate student performance. To evaluate student mastery of Chapter 29, give students Chapter 29 Test from the Teacher Resource Book. This test may also be used for pretesting or retesting purposes. Other tests can be made from the questions available in the Test Generator Software.

Lesson Plan Suggestions—Chapter 29

SE—Student Edition   TAE—Teacher Annotated Edition   TG—Test Generator
TRB—Teacher Resource Book   TSP—Transparency Package

Section 1   Australia (pp. 601–609)

Chapter Objectives	Suggested Teaching Strategies	Review

1. describe the major physical, economic, cultural, and historical features of Australia.	**Teacher Preparation**
	SE, Reading Assignment, pp. 601–609
	TAE, Unit 10 Suggested Resources
	    Unit 10 Overview, pp. T288–T289
	    Introducing Unit 10, p. T289
	    Chapter 29 Overview, pp. T289–T290
	    Introducing Chapter 29, p. T290
	TRB, Chapter 29 Teacher Notes: Section 1
		SE, Content Check, p. 609

(Continued on next page.)

Section 1 Australia (pp. 601–609) continued.

	Teaching Options	

	TAE, Introducing Unit 10, pp. T288–T289
	     Introducing Chapter 29, pp. T289–T290
	     Objective 1 Activities, pp. T290–T291
	TRB, Chapter 29 Teacher Notes: Section 1,
	     Extending the Lesson
	     Chapter 29 Reading
	     Chapter 29 Skill Activity
	TSP, Transparency 7	

Section 2 New Zealand (pp. 609–615)

Chapter Objectives	Suggested Teaching Strategies	Review

2. describe the major physical, economic, cultural, and historical features of New Zealand.	**Teacher Preparation**
	    SE, Reading Assignment, pp. 609–615
	    TAE, Unit 10 Suggested Resources
	         Chapter 29 Overview, pp. T289–T290
	    TRB, Chapter 29 Teacher Notes: Section 2
	Teaching Options
	    TAE, Objective 2 Activities, pp. T290–T291
	    TRB, Chapter 29 Teacher Notes: Section 2,
	         Extending the Lesson
	         Chapter 29 Skill Activity
		SE, Content Check, p. 615

Skill Objective: read time-zone maps.	SE, *Using Graphic Skills*, "Reading Time-Zone Maps," p. 614	

Chapter 29 Review and Evaluation

Suggested Teaching Strategies	Review	Evaluation

TAE, Objective 3 Activities,
     p. T292
    Concluding Chapter 29,
     pp. T292–T293
	SE, Chapter 29 Review,
	     pp. 616–617
	TRB, Chapter 29 Review
	     Worksheet
		TRB, Chapter 29 Test
		    Unit 10 Pretest, Map
		     and Content Worksheets
		TG, Chapter 29

CHAPTER 30 PACIFIC ISLANDS

Student Edition pp. 618–631

CHAPTER 30 OBJECTIVES

At the conclusion of this chapter, students will be able to:

1. describe the major physical, economic, cultural, and historical features of Melanesia.
2. describe the major physical, economic, cultural, and historical features of Micronesia.
3. describe the major physical, economic, cultural, and historical features of Polynesia.
4. summarize the chief geographic features of the Pacific Islands.

CHAPTER 30 SKILL OBJECTIVE

After completing the *Using Graphic Skills* exercise in this chapter, the student should be able to confirm the skill of calculating distance in miles and kilometers using a bar scale.

CHAPTER 30 OVERVIEW

The Pacific Islands comprise a fragmented region of the world covering a vast area of the Pacific Ocean. Students should come to appreciate the physical, economic, and cultural varieties that exist in this area. High islands mix with low islands, subsistence farmers mix with those who work in such industries as tourism or food processing, and countries that have achieved their independence mix with countries still controlled by colonial powers.

The chapter splits this vast area into three regions. *Section 1* describes the major geographic features of Melanesia, a region named for the people who live there. *Section 2* encompasses the islands of Micronesia, made up of many newly independent countries. These lands occupy a land and water area roughly the size of the United States. *Section 3* examines the varied islands that make up Polynesia. A special feature of the chapter focuses on the statues of Easter Island.

CHAPTER 30 ACTIVITIES

Introducing Chapter 30

For this activity display a large globe, a wall map of the world, and a transparency map of the Pacific Ocean area in the classroom. Have students work through the *Using* *Graphic Skills* feature on page 624 of the Student Edition. Once complete, call on different students to locate each island region and the individual islands discussed on page 619 of the text on the globe, wall map, and transparency map. As each place is located, have the class verbalize its exact location, relative location, size, and shape.

Chapter 30 Reading Assignments

Objective 1   Student Ed. pp. 619–622
Objective 2   Student Ed. pp. 622–626
Objective 3   Student Ed. pp. 626–629

● Teaching   ■ Reinforcing   ★ Enriching

Unmarked activities deal with three or more features listed in the chapter objectives. Activities marked with the following letters deal with:

Ⓟ Physical features.
Ⓔ Economic features.
Ⓒ Cultural features.
Ⓗ Historical features.

Objective 1 Activities

● Objective 1 Teaching Activity
Refer to the guidelines for team learning in the Instructional Approaches section of this Teacher Annotated Edition. Divide the class into groups, each of which will be responsible for researching one of the five island groups in Melanesia. Provide each team with a set of focus questions for its region. Once these questions are answered, teams should present their findings to the rest of the class.

■ Objective 1 Reinforcing Activity
Write the word "strategic" on the chalkboard, and ask students to define it. When a clear definition has been developed, identify this word as an important term for geographers, specifically in regard to the strategic location of a place. Point out that there are many areas of the world without valuable resources that give them a degree of influence in world affairs. Looking at a large world map, lead a class discussion on the strategic location of Melanesia. Raise the question: To which country or countries of the world would the location of

the islands of Melanesia be most important? Remind students that many of the islands in the Pacific have been used as military bases. Discuss student reactions.

Objective 2 Activities

● Objective 2 Teaching Activity
Pass out an outline map of the Micronesia area to each student. Then hold a discussion about the varied economic activities in the region. Some of these include subsistence farming and fishing, herding, cash farming of copra, light manufacturing of margarine, cooking oil, soap, phosphate mining, tourism, and strategic military activities. Because students have used economic development data in previous skills features, challenge them to find such information for the islands in Micronesia. They should then choose a way to graphically show that information on their outline maps.

Refer students to Chapter 30 Reading in the Teacher Resource Book for further information related to this objective.

■ Objective 2 Reinforcing Activity
Accompany students to the library or media center to explore picture files and audiovisual resources available of any of the countries or regions in Micronesia. Ask students to choose a unique feature about one of them to illustrate. They should choose either a physical, economic, cultural, or historical feature. The illustration could take the form of a postcard, calendar, magazine or travel brochure, or newspaper article. Display some of these illustrations around the classroom.

Objective 3 Activities

● Activity 3 Teaching Activity
Refer to the guidelines for discussion in the Instructional Approaches section of this Teacher Annotated Edition. Pose the following question for discussion: How do the decisions of history influence people to change their cultural decisions? Polynesia provides a case study for exploring that question. Have

students read Section 3 of the Student Edition to start them thinking about the question. Challenge them also to use library readings to cite examples. Encourage them to study pictures, artifacts, and economic charts of Polynesia to identify specific connections between history and cultural ways of doing things.

During debriefing have students contrast traditional cultures of the Pacific Islands with the cultural features a traveler finds there today. How might this be different if history had been different in any way? How might a future tourist describe the cultures?

★ **Objective 3 Enriching Activity**

Before directing the following activity, refer to role plays and simulations in the Instructional Approaches section of this Teacher Annotated Edition. Tourism is one of the biggest generators of income in Polynesia. Point out to students that many countries are hesitant about allowing tourism to become the base of their economies. Discuss with students why this might be true. Have a few students participate in a role play activity demonstrating this point. The scene should be a meeting of a governing council trying to decide whether or not to let a major hotel chain begin large-scale development of its island. Students should assume the roles of souvenir shopkeepers and travel agents, as well as those who might be against the proposal, such as scientists studying tropical wildlife and promoters of traditional culture.

Objective 4 Activities

● **Objective 4 Teaching Activity**

Tell students that they have an opportunity to travel by boat between the island regions of the South Pacific Ocean. They may each choose a starting point at a major continental port, chart a route of travel, decide which islands to visit (a minimum of 3 in each region), and where to end the journey—a place where he or she might like to live for some time.

Each student will keep a ship's log or a travel journal to record each day's movements, events, and observations, writing their descriptions in first person accounts. Explain that when you read this written diary, you want to be made to feel that you are traveling in the boat and experiencing the beauty and difficulties of the physical geography, observing the signs of historical geography in each place, and meeting the people to talk with them about their economic pursuits and enjoying their cultural gifts.

■ **Objective 4 Reinforcing Activity**

Hold a relay team competition in which a student says, "I am on an island . . .," describing one or more aspects of one of the islands in the Pacific culture area until the opposing team guesses the name of the island or island group.

Concluding Chapter 30

Have students prepare a display entitled "Lands of the Pacific." Suggest that they cover the entire chalkboard with blue construction paper. Use a black marker to draw longitude and latitude lines. Using green paper, students can cut out shapes for several of the major islands, and label them with the marker. Students should then cut out articles and pictures from newspapers, magazines, booklets, and travel folders. Glue them where they will not cover an island, and then run string from the pictures or articles to the island described.

Refer students to Chapter 30 Skill Activity in the Teacher Resource Book for another activity related to this objective.

ANSWERS TO CHAPTER 30 QUESTIONS

Content Check Questions
page 622

1. Refer to Section 1 content.
2. Refer to Glossary in Student Edition.
3. Papua New Guinea, Vanuatu, New Caledonia, Fiji, Solomon Islands. (p. 619)
4. Cacao, rubber, and coffee. (p. 621)
5. Malay Peninsula and Indonesia. (p. 622)

6. With over 700 local languages, pidgin is the only universal means of communication for business and government throughout Melanesia. (p. 621)

page 626

1. Refer to Section 2 content.
2. Refer to Glossary in Student Edition.
3. Guam. (p. 622)
4. Low islands. (p. 622)
5. Tropical rain forest. (p. 623)
6. Portugal, Spain, Germany, Japan, United States. (pp. 625–626)
7. Answers will vary, but Micronesia is a crossroads for shipping traffic between Asia, Australia, and North America; some of the islands are about equidistant between Hawaii, New Zealand, Australia, the Philippines, and Japan; the United States with its military bases is able to guard the free shipment of merchandise through important western Pacific sea lanes.

page 629

1. Refer to Section 3 content.
2. Refer to Glossary in Student Edition.
3. Tropical rain forest. (p. 627)
4. Sugarcane, cocoa, coffee, citrus fruits, pineapple, bananas, mother-of-pearl, and coconuts. (p. 627)
5. Tourism provides needed income, but the land development and increasing number of tourists can have a negative effect on the island's traditions. (p. 629)

Special Feature Questions
page 624, Using Graphic Skills: "Reviewing Scale"

1. Approximately 6,500 miles.
2. Measuring from near Midway Island to Easter Island, approximately 10,000 kilometers.
3. Hawaii.

page 628, Strange But True: "Statues of Easter Island"

1. At the easternmost edge. 2,300 miles.
2. Most are 10 to 20 feet (3 to 6 meters) high and weigh between 25 and 90 tons (23 and 82 metric tons).

3. Answers will vary but may indicate that they may have been carved for religious reasons, but no one is sure and no one knows why they all face inward.

Photo/Illustration Caption Questions
page 620

Mountains, forests, swamps, jungles, reefs. (p. 620)

page 621

100 degrees. (p. 621)

page 623

Melanesia. (p. 622)

page 625

Much of Nauru's soil has been ruined. (p. 625)

page 626

Landscape ranges from coral reefs to volcanic mountains; climate ranges from very wet to dry. (pp. 626–627)

page 627

4,000 miles north to south; 6,000 miles west to east. (p. 626)

Chapter 30 Review Questions
page 630, Reviewing Vocabulary

Answers will vary, but clues should indicate that students know the meanings of the words and recognize place-names.

pages 630–631, Remembering the Facts

1. Melanesia, Micronesia, and Polynesia. (p. 619)
2. Melanesia; Polynesia. (pp. 620, 624)
3. Papua New Guinea; Melanesia. (p. 620)
4. Malay Peninsula and Indonesia. (p. 622)
5. Tropical rain forest. (p. 623)
6. Farming and fishing. (p. 623)
7. Japan. (p. 626)
8. High islands produce cash crops; low islands are used for subsistence farming. (p. 627)
9. Polynesia. (p. 629)

page 631, Understanding the Facts

1. In or around Melanesia's major cities. (p. 621)

2. It is the common language of business and government. (p. 621)
3. All islands in Micronesia are quite small; some islands in Melanesia are very large. There is more cash crop farming in Melanesia, while Micronesia has subsistence farming. There are many more independent countries in Melanesia. (pp. 620–626)
4. Roman Catholic religion, family names, and customs. (p. 625)
5. Tourism is a growing industry in Polynesia, but has both advantages and disadvantages. Hawaii and Tahiti have been developed as tourist islands. Polynesians are looking at the effects of tourism in Hawaii and Tahiti to see if the economic advantages might outweigh any negative impacts on traditional culture and life in the Polynesian islands. (p. 629)
6. High islands have mountains and plateaus; low islands are made of coral and barely rise above sea level. (pp. 620, 622)

page 631, Thinking Critically and Creatively

1. Answers will vary, but some of these ideas should be included: They had military interests; they wanted to have control of areas to keep watch on important sea lanes; as maritime powers, they wanted dependable places to refuel and provision their ships; the tropical produce of some of these lands had markets in Europe.
2. Answers will vary but may observe that there is a chain of high mountains running down the center of the island. Temperatures at night can be quite cold at high elevations, even in latitudes fairly close to the Equator.
3. Answers will vary, but some might include: Hawaii is becoming increasingly crowded.

Some people prefer resorts that are less popular. Thus, some people who have been to Hawaii are looking for a similar Polynesian environment with fewer evidences of commercialism. Wide-bodied aircraft are available today that can traverse tremendous distances. It is no longer so difficult and time-consuming to get to Tahiti. Further, there are now more and more places for people to stay in Tahiti once they arrive. Interestingly, once tourists begin to arrive, they seem to demand the kinds of goods and services that the first tourists were "escaping" from as they searched for an alternative to Hawaii. Tahiti as a tourist destination is receiving more promotion from tourist agencies than it used to receive. Due to the fact that the total number of tourists looking for places to go has increased, and Tahiti offers what many tourists are searching for, it is getting its share of this increased total supply.

4. Answers will vary but may indicate that apparently they do not want the responsibility of local self-government but are content to be under the control of the United States. Answers will vary but should state that benefits would include self-determination in affairs directly affecting the islands, rights of United States citizenship, and United States military protection. Answers will vary but may include disadvantages such as a lack of complete independence and a view among neighboring island nations that the Palau Islands are too dependent on the United States.

page 631, Reinforcing Graphic Skills

1. New Caledonia.
2. Approximately 3,500 miles.

EVALUATING CHAPTER 30

World Geography: People and Places provides chapter tests to help evaluate student performance. To evaluate student mastery of Chapter 30, give students Chapter 30 Test from the Teacher Resource Book. This test may also be used for pretesting or retesting purposes. Other tests can be made from the questions available in the Test Generator Software.

Lesson Plan Suggestions—Chapter 30

SE—Student Edition   TAE—Teacher Annotated Edition   TG—Test Generator
TRB—Teacher Resource Book   TSP—Transparency Package

Section 1 Melanesia (pp. 619–622)

Chapter Objectives	Suggested Teaching Strategies	Review
1. describe the major physical, economic, cultural, and historical features of Melanesia.	**Teacher Preparation** SE, Reading Assignment, pp. 619–622 TAE, Unit 10 Suggested Resources 　　Chapter 30 Overview, p. T297 　　Introducing Chapter 30, pp. T297–T298 TRB, Chapter 30 Teacher Notes: Section 1 **Teaching Options** TAE, Introducing Chapter 30, pp. T297–T298 　　Objective 1 Activities, p. T298 TRB, Chapter 30 Teacher Notes: Section 1, 　　Extending the Lesson 　　Chapter 30 Skill Activity TSP, Transparency 7	SE, Content Check, p. 622

Section 2 Micronesia (pp. 622–626)

Chapter Objectives	Suggested Teaching Strategies	Review
2. describe the major physical, economic, cultural, and historical features of Micronesia.	**Teacher Preparation** SE, Reading Assignment, pp. 622–626 TAE, Unit 10 Suggested Resources 　　Chapter 30 Overview, p. T297 TRB, Chapter 30 Teacher Notes: Section 2 **Teaching Options** TAE, Objective 2 Activities, p. T298 TRB, Chapter 30 Teacher Notes: Section 2, 　　Extending the Lesson 　　Chapter 30 Reading 　　Chapter 30 Skill Activity	SE, Content Check, p. 626
Skill Objective: confirm skill in calculating distance in miles and kilometers using a bar scale.	SE, *Using Graphic Skills*, "Reviewing Scale," p. 624	

Chapter Objectives	Suggested Teaching Strategies	Review
3. describe the major physical, economic, cultural, and historical features of Polynesia.	**Teacher Preparation** SE, Reading Assignment, pp. 626–629 TAE, Unit 10 Suggested Resources 　　Chapter 30 Overview, p. T297 TRB, Chapter 30 Teacher Notes: Section 3 **Teaching Options** TAE, Objective 3 Activities, pp. T298–T299 TRB, Chapter 30 Teacher Notes: Section 3, 　　Extending the Lesson 　　Chapter 30 Skill Activity	SE, Content Check, p. 629

Chapter 30 Review and Evaluation

Suggested Teaching Strategies	Review	Evaluation
TAE, Objective 4 Activities, 　　p. T299 　　Concluding Chapter 30, 　　p. T299	SE, Chapter 30 Review, 　　pp. 630–631 TRB, Chapter 30 Review 　　Worksheet	TRB, Chapter 30 Test TG, Chapter 30

CHAPTER 31 ANTARCTICA

Student Edition pp. 632–641

CHAPTER 31 OBJECTIVES

At the conclusion of this chapter, students will be able to:
1. describe the physical features, climate, and natural resources of Antarctica.
2. characterize why Antarctica has been of interest to explorers and scientists and how their findings may help Earth's future.

CHAPTER 31 SKILL OBJECTIVE

After completing the *Using Graphic Skills* exercise in this chapter, the student should be able to evaluate information.

CHAPTER 31 OVERVIEW

Since the time humans first appeared on Earth, they have constantly faced challenges. Each century witnesses the appearance of new and different frontiers. In this century, everyone recognizes space as the newest geographic frontier to challenge people. However, there is still another frontier on Earth that has not yet been fully explored—the vast, stormy, frozen Antarctic. Today scientists from many nations work and live in several encampments on its icy surface, probing and testing to discover information about Antarctica's past and how its difficult-to-reach resources might be utilized in the future. Conservationists are also concerned about protecting the wildlife of the Antarctic, their natural habitats, and the natural environment.

In this chapter, *Section 1* describes the forbidding landscape and climate of Antarctica. *Section 2* concerns Antarctica's natural resources, including minerals and plant and animal life. *Section 3* recounts the Antarctic explorations and points out the work being done by scientists in the multi-national research stations. *Section 4* concerns what is happening today in Antarctica, and what the future possibilities and fears are for this continent.

A special feature in the chapter draws a relationship between Antarctica and outer space.

CHAPTER 31 ACTIVITIES

Introducing Chapter 31

Refer to the guidelines for brainstorming in the Instructional Approaches section of this Teacher Annotated Edition.

Obtain a copy of the *National Geographic* magazine, Vol. 171, No. 4, April 1987. Set the stage for a class brainstorming activity by reading aloud the first paragraph by Prut J. Vesilind, *National Geographic* senior writer, p. 557: "Antarctica, that bleak, white place, still defies full understanding. Man, earth's most meddlesome creature, has reached the moon but has yet to explore the frozen continent into submission."

Pause to invite students' initial response to this statement. Point out that the quote challenges us to study two main happenings in Antarctica—its natural features and its human features. Ask what students already know about each of these, and what questions their curiosity stimulates. Develop the following outline on an overhead transparency, jotting under each heading the descriptions students brainstorm. Later you can show this transparency again to compare with notes students take from reading the text.

Antarctica

I. Natural Features
   A. Physical
      1. Location (exact & relative)
      2. Size (exact & relative)
      3. Shape
      4. Land
      5. Water
   B. Climate
      1. Temperature
      2. Precipitation
      3. Wind
      4. Seasons
   C. Natural Resources
      1. Minerals
      2. Plants
      3. Animals
II. Human Features
   A. Exploration
      1. Who?
      2. When?
      3. Why?
   B. Scientific Research
      1. Geology
      2. Glaciology

3. Meteorology
4. Natural History
5. Human Physiology in Polar Environment
C. Future
   1. Tourism
   2. Potential
   3. Concerns
   4. Proposals

Chapter 31 Reading Assignments

| ● Teaching | ■ Reinforcing | ★ Enriching |

Unmarked activities deal with three or more features listed in the chapter objectives. Activities marked with the following letters deal with:

Ⓟ Physical features.
Ⓔ Economic features.
Ⓒ Cultural features.
Ⓗ Historical features.

Objective 1 Activities

● Objective 1 Teaching Activity

Use a large globe to help students brainstorm the likenesses and differences between the North and South Polar regions. They should observe that the Arctic is an ocean surrounded by land, whereas Antarctica is land surrounded by oceans. People inhabit the Arctic region, but there are no natives on Antarctica. There are many more species of plants and animals in the Arctic. Ask students: Do you recall the climate control of land and water modifications? Students should realize that Antarctica is much colder than the North Polar region because the interior is not modified by water bodies, and the exterior is not modified by closeness to landmasses. Demonstrate the two hemispheres with a globe. Explain that the Arctic is "warmed" by currents from the Atlantic. People in the Northern Hemisphere were able to migrate across the great land bridges from Asia to the Americas, and some moved east or north rather than south to populate the northern regions. Also, because of a less severe climate, more species of plants and animals could develop food chains that also support humans. Polar bears live only in the Arctic; penguins only in Antarctica. Whales and seals inhabit both areas.

Refer students to Chapter 31 Reading from the Teacher Resource Book for further information related to this objective.

■ Objective 1 Reinforcing Activity

Distribute handouts with the outline headings used in the chapter opening activity. Direct students to read pp. 633–637 to complete Part I of the outline. Use the outline as a focus for class discussion about the physical features, climate, and natural resources of Antarctica.

During debriefing, point out that Antarctica has one-tenth of the world's land area not covered by water, nine-tenths of Earth's permanent ice, and three-fourths of the world's fresh water solidly frozen. Ask students: Do these facts give us hints that Antarctica is a more important place to the well-being of Planet Earth and its people than most of us may realize?

Ask if students think most people realize that Antarctica is classified by geographers as a *desert*. Review the essential definition of a desert: less than 10 inches of precipitation per year. Explain that ice is not precipitation, and much snow is required to equal one inch of rain. Tell students that geographers know that Antarctica was not always a frozen desert. Millions of years ago it was a lush rain forest. Geologists have found fossil forms and tree trunks in the Queen Maud mountains as evidence of such vegetation and accompanying climate.

Have students look in an almanac or atlas to find other mountains of about 16,000 feet (4876.8m) to compare to the Transantarctic Range. How will these very real mountains offset the explorations of the continent? Can students imagine the added difficulties of climbing and crossing them in the climate conditions and remoteness of Antarctica?

Review the definition of "natural resource": something found in nature that people recognize as useful. Suggest that students speculate about possible natural resources in Antarctica that may be useful in the future that we do not even recognize yet, such as in medicine for diseases still unknown, or new kinds of industry not yet invented. This is why environmentalists fear future exploitation of Antarctica unless wise decisions and protective controls are implemented.

★ Objective 1 Enriching Activity

Ask the class to formulate interesting questions they have about the natural and human features of Antarctica. List these as topics on the chalkboard. Add some of your own, suggested by the chapter reading, such as comparison of Arctic and Antarctic exploration and exploitation; Earth's secrets uncovered by ice coring; krill as a human protein source; Cook, Shackleton, Amundsen, Scott, and Byrd expeditions; John Davis, a Connecticut seal hunter credited with first setting foot on the continent in 1821; International Geophysical Year Proceedings 1957–1958 related to Antarctica; Antarctic Treaty of 1959 and its review date of 1991; the "ozone hole" found in 1987; the proposal that Antarctica be made the first International World Park; and Antarctica's "fragile environment"; efforts of the organization, Greenpeace, to protect Antarctica.

Ask for volunteers to research these topics, either individually or in pairs, and prepare oral reports to share interesting information with the class at the end of the chapter's study. Suggest that when possible, presenters might use appropriate audiovisual accompaniments.

Objective 2 Activities

● Objective 2 Teaching Activity

Direct students to read Section 2 of the Student Edition and to complete the outline notes for Part II on the handout distributed earlier.

Read to the class the reflections of Sir Peter Scott, son of Captain Robert F. Scott, from the *National Geographic* magazine, April 1987, pp. 538–542. Explain that Peter was 2-1/2 years old when his famous father made the courageous journey that cost him and four other explorers their lives. Ask students: What lessons has Peter carried with him because of his father's work? What lessons does he hope the rest of us will learn from it? Would students characterize Robert Scott's expedition a failure or a success? Encourage a discussion about its ramifications for both.

Discuss how Amundsen and Scott knew when they reached the South Pole. Are magnetic compasses useful there? Point to the magnetic North Pole on a world map or globe. Ask a volunteer to look up information about magnetism in Antarctica and the kinds of scientific tools available to Amundsen and Scott in 1911. Inform the class that the world honors Robert F. Scott's expedition no less than Amundsen's by naming the science base at the South Pole the "Amundsen-Scott South Pole Station."

End this activity by emphasizing the nature and value of Antarctica's fragile environment by reading to the class the last five paragraphs on p. 541 and the first five on p. 542 of Sir Peter Scott's article in the *National Geographic* magazine, April 1987. Then invite open discussion of the last two sentences in the conclusion of this chapter in the Student Edition on page 640.

■ Objective 2 Reinforcing Activity

Guide students in developing a bulletin board time line for the human events that have taken place on Antarctica. Start with all the dates mentioned in this chapter, and leave room for students to add significant events from the research and reports they are preparing. Be sure the time line shows 1991 and a couple of decades into the 21st century to demonstrate the importance of keeping Antarctica's future in mind.

★ Objective 2 Enriching Activity

Obtain copies of the Antarctic Treaty and distribute them to the class, and then discuss its provisions. Refer to the guidelines for role plays and simulations in the Instructional

Approaches section of this Teacher Annotated Edition, and explain to students that they will play delegates attending the Antarctic Treaty Revision Conference. Determine what new issues will be considered at the revision conference. Some of the issues of importance for the new treaty are: development of oil, gas, and other mineral resources; restriction of tourism and population growth; nuclear activity; governance; weather-related activities and phenomena; fishing rights; and scientific research. Have students individually or in small groups represent the nations that have voting rights. The student(s) representing each nation should determine what interests their country has in Antarctica that would affect their vote(s) on the provisions of the new treaty and what positions they will take on the issues.

After students have performed any necessary research, convene the conference, have students discuss issues, write up new provisions, vote on them, and then finalize a New Antarctic Treaty.

Concluding Chapter 31

Refer to the guidelines for role plays and simulations in the Instructional Approaches section of this Teacher Annotated Edition. Have students role play explorers or settlers who are preparing their Antarctic expeditions. They can dialogue about the steps they need to take in preparing and the challenges and dangers they must be able to survive. (*National Geographic*, April 1987, pp. 544–555 recounts such a first-person narrative that a pair of students might read to prepare their role play presentation for class.)

At this time, students may do the Chapter 31 Skill Activity from the Teacher Resource Book.

ANSWERS TO CHAPTER 31 QUESTIONS

Content Check Questions
page 634

1. Refer to Section 1 content.
2. Refer to Glossary in Student Edition.
3. Because of harsh landscape and ice cap climate. (p. 633)
4. Ocean waters cool and become less salty. Plant and animal life changes. In winter the ocean freezes to form a solid pack of ice that floats on the surface. (p. 634)
5. Answers will vary but may include: Antarctica has a forbidding landscape of a barren ice-covered plateau with high rocky mountains and islands under thousands of feet of ice. Summer temperatures rarely rise above freezing. The interior is even colder. Winter months are shrouded in darkness. This would make exploration dangerously difficult and permanent settlement very unattractive in this region.

page 637

1. Refer to Glossary in Student Edition.

2. Probably coal, iron, copper, manganese and uranium; only mosses and lichens are found along the coast; penguins, other birds, whales, seals, fish, and krill. (pp. 635, 637)
3. Answers will vary but may include: Great care would have to be taken so as not to allow the by-products of mining or drilling to pollute the environment. Pollution could result in damaging the plants' and animals' natural habitats and breaking the food chain. Any increased human activity could frighten away animal life.

page 637

1. Refer to Section 3 content.
2. Nations would not push territorial claims or use Antarctica for military purposes, but scientists of all nations would be welcome. (p. 637)
3. Answers will vary but may include: Superpowers and others might have tried to lay claim to the land for their own self interest.

Results could have been disastrous for world peace.

page 639

1. Refer to Glossary in Student Edition.
2. As known resources decline, Antarctica's resources, especially minerals and krill, may become more attractive, icebergs may be a source of fresh water, and Antarctica may be used as a scientific laboratory. (p. 639)
3. Answers will vary but may include that provisions should be made for permanent settlement patterns, strict regulations for protecting the environment, and ways to share resources and scientific data.

Special Feature Questions
page 638, Focus on Geography: "Antarctica and Outer Space"

1. Did life exist on Mars some time in the past?
2. In fresh water areas below several feet of ice.
3. Microorganisms.
4. Chemical signatures of microorganisms.
5. Because they believe that at one time Mars was covered by huge bodies of water that may have been home to microorganisms like those found in Antarctica. If samples of dust particles can be brought back from Mars, the particles can be analyzed for chemical signatures and compared with those taken on Antarctica. This could give clues that life may have existed on Mars at some time.

page 636, Using Graphic Skills: "Evaluating Information"

1. Answers will vary.
2. Answers will vary.

Photo/Illustration Caption Questions
page 634

From permanent ice and a constant cold climate. (pp. 633–634)

page 635

The bar graph representing Antarctica's size would be extended out to 150 percent.

page 639

Eighteen nations. (p. 639)

Chapter 31 Review Questions
page 640, Reviewing Vocabulary

1. Krill.
2. Chemical signatures.
3. Ice shelves.
4. Calving.
5. Microorganisms.

page 641, Remembering the Facts

1. Animal and plant life include penguins, other birds, whales, fish, seals, krill, lichens, and mosses. Minerals found in Antarctica are coal, iron, copper, manganese, and uranium. (p. 635)
2. Commander Richard E. Byrd. (p. 637)
3. Scientific research stations were set up for scientists from around the world to study Antarctica's environment. (p. 637)
4. The Antarctic Treaty. (p. 639)

page 641, Understanding the Facts

1. Coastal temperatures are not as extreme as the interior. (p. 634)
2. The environment is too harsh—too cold and too dry and too little sunlight. (p. 634)
3. The food chain connects the continent's animal life. A break in one of the links would destroy the whole chain. (p. 637)
4. It gave the go ahead to twelve nations to build facilities for study and research and explore the continent. (p. 637)
5. Many are buried deep under ice; it is too expensive now to exploit the minerals. World shortages or depletion of known supplies could change the situation. (p. 635)
6. It might alter the ecological balance and lead to political conflict. (p. 639)

page 641, Thinking Critically and Creatively

1. Answers will vary but may include: It could indicate the shifting movement of the continents or climatic shifts over Earth.
2. Answers will vary but may include: Yes, because this action could be interpreted as a push to establish Argentina's territorial claims.
3. Answers will vary but may include: Those that agree may point for the need for the U.N. to govern Antarctica so that all member nations would be able to share the resources and scientific knowledge. Those that disagree may argue that nations that signed the original treaty have already invested a great deal of time and money and should not have to share with other countries that have done nothing to harvest resources or gather scientific data.
4. Answers will vary but may include: Continued harvesting of krill, especially if increased, could permanently damage the food chain and forever change Antarctica's wildlife.

page 641, Reinforcing Graphic Skills

1. Answers will vary.
2. Answers will vary.

EVALUATING CHAPTER 31

World Geography: People and Places provides chapter tests to help evaluate student performance. To evaluate student mastery of Chapter 31, give students Chapter 31 Test from the Teacher Resource Book. This test may also be used for pretesting or retesting purposes. Other tests can be made from the questions available in the Test Generator Software.

Lesson Plan Suggestions—Chapter 31

SE—Student Edition TAE—Teacher Annotated Edition TG—Test Generator
TRB—Teacher Resource Book TSP—Transparency Package

Section 1 Landscape and Climate and
Section 2 Natural Resources (pp. 633–637)

Chapter Objectives	Suggested Teaching Strategies	Review

1. describe the physical features, climate, and natural resources of Antarctica.	**Teacher Preparation**
	SE, Reading Assignment, pp. 633–637
	TAE, Unit 10 Suggested Resources
	   Chapter 31 Overview, p. T304
	   Introducing Chapter 31, pp. T304–T305
	TRB, Chapter 31 Teacher Notes: Sections 1 and 2
	Teaching Options
	TAE, Introducing Chapter 31, pp. T304–T305
	   Objective 1 Activities, pp. T305–T306
	TRB, Chapter 31 Teacher Notes: Sections 1 and 2, Extending the Lesson
	   Chapter 31 Reading
	   Chapter 31 Skill Activity
		SE, Content Check, pp. 634, 637

Chapter Objectives	Suggested Teaching Strategies	Review

2. characterize why Antarctica has been of interest to explorers and scientists and how their findings may help Earth's future.	**Teacher Preparation**
	SE, Reading Assignment, pp. 637–639
	TAE, Unit 10 Suggested Resources
	    Chapter 31 Overview, p. T304
	TRB, Chapter 31 Teacher Notes: Sections 3 and 4
	Teaching Options
	TAE, Objective 2 Activities,
	    pp. T306–T307
	TRB, Chapter 31 Teacher Notes: Sections 3 & 4, Extending the Lesson
	    Chapter 31 Skill Activity
		SE, Content Check, pp. 637, 639

Skill Objective: evaluate information.	SE, *Using Graphic Skills*, "Evaluating Information," p. 636	

Chapter 31 Review and Evaluation

Suggested Teaching Strategies	Review	Evaluation
TAE, Concluding Chapter 31, p. T307	SE, Chapter 31 Review, pp. 640–641 TRB, Chapter 31 Review Worksheet	TRB, Chapter 31 Test TG, Chapter 31

Unit 10 Review and Evaluation

Suggested Teaching Strategies	Review	Evaluation
TAE, Concluding Unit 10, pp. T310–T311 TRB, Unit 10 Career Worksheet	SE, Unit 10 Review, pp. 642–643 TSP, Transparency 7	TRB, Unit 10 Exam Unit 10 Posttest, Map and Content Worksheets

CONCLUDING UNIT 10

Have students simulate a broadcast of the Oceania Evening News. The television show should include elements of interest for Australia, New Zealand, and the Pacific Islands. Include an interview with scientists working at the McMurdo research base on Antarctica about their current research and what it is like to live and work there. Some students can team up to present different parts of the broadcast, including domestic news, world affairs, business, sports, special features, and weather. Other students may present an on-the-scene report near a volcanic eruption on one of the Pacific Islands or at the dedication of a new hotel in Polynesia. Students may need to do research on their topic, for example, to find out which sports are the most popular in New Zealand. The actual broadcast may mention fictitious accounts of a particular game.

Encourage students to base their program on fact, but to be as creative as possible. Newspapers from Australia might be found at newsstands or bookstores that carry newspapers from around the world. The class may decide to produce visuals to accompany the television broadcast and to invite a neighboring class in to view it.

The Unit 10 Career Worksheet from the Teacher Resource Book will aid students in the preparation of this activity. Allow those students with a special interest in meteorology to present the weather broadcast.

UNIT 10 REVIEW QUESTIONS

page 642, Thinking About the Unit

1. New Zealand's landscape is mountainous in the center with low plains along the coasts. The climate is warm and mild. Papua New Guinea's landscape is mountainous in the center with swamps and jungles bordering the mainland. The climate of the area is hot and humid.

2. Fragmentation of the islands over such a vast area of ocean.

3. Both countries trade extensively with countries throughout the world. They also maintain strong cultural ties with the rest of the English-speaking world.

4. Because it has no characteristic history, government, economy, language, or religion that identifies it as a specific world area. An area requires human habitation in order for culture traits to develop. Antarctica's landscape and climate are hostile to permanent human settlement.

SUGGESTED RESOURCES

GENERAL GEOGRAPHIC RESOURCES

Allen, John, ed. *Environment 87/88*. Annual Editions Series. Guilford, CT: Dushkin Publishing Group, 1987. Anthology of articles dealing with recent environmental issues. New edition annually.

Background Notes. Washington, DC: Department of State. Pamphlets containing information on the people, land, history, government, political conditions, economy, and foreign relations of world countries.

Broek, Jan O.M., et al. *The Study and Teaching of Geography*. Columbus, OH: Charles E. Merrill Publishing Co., 1980. Provides concrete inquiry strategies in the geographic field.

Brown, Lester R., et al. *State of the World, 1987*. New York: W.W. Norton & Co., 1987. Anthology of articles on world geographical issues.

Daniels, George, ed. *Planet Earth Series*. Chicago: Time-Life Books, 1982. Good series on physical geography.

de Blij, Harm J., and Peter O. Muller. *Geography: Regions and Concepts*. New York: John Wiley & Sons, 1988. College level regional geography textbook.

The Development Data Book. Washington, DC: World Bank Publications, 1984. Set of 11 booklets illustrating the differences between industrialized and developing countries and discussing population growth rates, GNP per capita, and more.

Espenshade, Edward B., ed. *Goode's World Atlas*. 17th ed. Chicago: Rand McNally & Co., 1987. The "standard" classroom atlas.

Friends of UNEP Newsletter. Wayland, MA: Friends of UNEP. Published quarterly. Spreads knowledge concerning the interdependence of environment and development.

Grant, Neil, and Nick Middleton. *Atlas of the World Today*. St. Paul, MN: Greenhaven, 1987. Features 37 full-color maps and 52 graphs, and provides immediate comparison in areas of climate, education, energy, trade, population, food production, and others.

Handbook of Economic Statistics. Washington, DC: Central Intelligence Agency. Published annually. A reference aid with economic statistics for selected countries.

Hursh, Heidi, and Michael Prevedel. *Activities Using the New State of the World Atlas*. Denver, CO: Center for Teaching International Relations, University of Denver, 1987. Provides activities to be used in conjunction with *The New State of the World Atlas*.

Information Please Almanac. Boston: Houghton Mifflin. Published annually. Reports on national and international events and vital statistics.

Jackson, Robert, ed. *Global Issues 87/88*. Guilford, CT: Dushkin Publishing Group, 1987. Annual publication on various world issues, most of which are geography related.

Kidron, Michael, and Ronald Segal. *The New State of the World Atlas*. New York: Simon and Schuster, 1984. Through colorful maps, depicts global pressures; ranks states by population.

Kurian, George Thomas. *Encyclopedia of the Third World*. New York: Facts on File, Inc., 1987. Features information on 126 countries, with 126 maps and more than 1,000 charts and tables.

Lounsbury, John F., and Frank T. Aldrich. *Introduction to Geographic Field Methods and Techniques*. Columbus, OH: Merrill Publishing Co., 1986. Presents approaches and methods concerned with the systematic acquisition of geographical data in the field.

Makower, Joel, ed. *The Map Catalog: Every Kind of Map and Chart on Earth and Even Some Above It*. New York: Random House, 1986. A comprehensive guide to all published maps. Includes map source addresses and costs. Invaluable.

McClintock, Jack, and David Helgren. *Everything is Somewhere: The Geography Quiz Book*. New York: William Morrow and Co.,

1986. A fascinating quiz book on world geography.

McKnight, Tom L. *Physical Geography: A Landscape Appreciation*. Englewood Cliffs, NJ: Prentice-Hall, 1987. Physical geography textbook.

Meyers, Norman, ed. *Gaia: An Atlas of Planet Management*. Garden City, NY: Anchor Press, Doubleday, 1984. An excellent guide to Earth's resources and human management of those resources.

Paxton, John, ed. *The Statesman's Year-Book*. New York: St. Martin's Press. Published annually. Provides information on international organizations and countries.

Pitzl, Gerald R., ed. *Geography 87/88*. Guilford, CT: Dushkin Publishing Group, 1987. Annual publication on world geographical issues.

Sheffield, Charles. *Earth Watch*. New York: Macmillan, 1981. A survey of the world from space.

Short, Nicholas M., et al. *Mission to Earth: Landsat Views the World*. Washington, DC: National Aeronautics and Space Administration, 1976. A collection of 400 Landsat photographs showing Earth's natural and cultural features.

Statistical Abstract of the United States. Washington, DC: U.S. Department of Commerce. Published annually. Convenient statistical reference and guide to other statistical publications and sources.

Thomas, William L., ed. *Man's Role in Changing the Face of the Earth*. Chicago: University of Chicago Press, 1956. A classic anthology produced by an international symposium of geographers in 1955. Highly useful and not outdated.

Vance, James E., Jr. *Capturing the Horizon: The Historical Geography of Transportation*. New York: Harper & Row, 1986. An excellent book on the theme of movement since the sixteenth century.

United Nations Radio and Visual Services Division, Department of Public Information, New York, NY 10017. Catalog describes UN films and videotapes available for sale or rental.

The World Almanac and Book of Facts. New York: Pharos Books. Published annually. Reports on national and international events and statistics.

The World Bank Atlas. Washington, DC: The World Bank. Published annually. Presents current economic and social indicators for countries of the world.

The World Factbook. Washington, DC: Central Intelligence Agency. Annual publication containing statistical information on the geography, people, government, economy, communications, and defense forces of world countries.

World Population Data Sheet. Washington, DC: Population Reference Bureau. Published annually. World and regional demographic information.

World Resources 1987. New York: Basic Books, 1987. A grand reference compiled by the International Institute for Environment and Development and the World Resources Institute. Articles and data tables for 146 countries.

Zimolzak, Chester E., and Charles A. Stansfield, Jr. *The Human Landscape: Geography and Culture*. Columbus, OH: Charles E. Merrill Publishing Co., 1983. Cultural geography college textbook.

UNIT 1 RESOURCES

Student Books and Articles

Babcock, William H. *Legendary Islands of the Atlantic*. Glen Arm, MD: The Sourcebook Project, 1984. Gives an account of geographic myths.

Beizer, Arthur. *Life Nature Library: The Earth*. New York: Time-Life Books, 1970. Provides an overview of planet Earth and its physical features.

Blandford, Percy W. *Maps & Compasses: A User's Handbook.* Blue Ridge Summit, PA: TAB Books, Inc., 1984. Guides people interested in doing fieldwork with maps and compasses; explains map orientation and orienteering.

Carey, Helen H. *How to Use Maps and Globes.* New York: Franklin Watts, 1983. Explains map symbols, projections, special-purpose maps, atlases, and drawing maps.

Fleming, June. *Staying Found: The Complete Map and Compass Handbook.* New York: Random House, 1982. Teaches practical use of orienteering skills.

Madden, James F. *The Wonderful World of Maps.* Maplewood, NJ: Hammond, 1982. Gives a well-illustrated treatment on how to read maps.

March, Susan. *All About Maps and Mapmaking.* New York: Random House, 1963. Represents a good resource for students.

Mathews, William H. *The Earth's Crust.* New York: Franklin Watts, 1971. Treats the major topics relating to the planet's crust.

McIntyre, Loren. "Humboldt's Way." *National Geographic,* September 1985. Describes a geography pioneer's travels and writings.

Millard, Reed. *Careers in the Earth Sciences.* New York: Julian Messner, 1975. Provides information on various careers in fields relating to the study of Earth.

Tannenbaum, Beulah, and Myra Stillman. *Understanding Maps.* New York: McGraw-Hill, 1969. Aids students to gain an in-depth understanding of maps.

Teacher Books and Articles

American Cartographic Association. *Which Map is Best?* Falls Church, VA: American Congress on Surveying and Mapping, 1986. Explains some of the better known map projections and their characteristics.

Bacon, Philip, ed. *Focus on Geography: Key Concepts and Teaching Strategies.* Washington, DC: National Council for the Social Studies, 1970. Provides a good overview of geography concepts and how to teach them.

Bagrow, Leo. *History of Cartography.* Cambridge, MA: Harvard University Press, 1964. Furnishes the reader with a detailed understanding of the field of cartography.

Broek, Jan O. M., et al. *The Study and Teaching of Geography.* Columbus, OH: Merrill Publishing Co., 1980. Provides basic concepts of geography and gives suggestions and activities for teaching these concepts.

Cuff, David J. and Mark T. Mattson. *Thematic Maps: Their Design and Production.* New York: Methuen, 1982. Presents a concise guide to the principles and practices of thematic mapping.

Gould, Peter. *The Geographer at Work.* Boston: Routledge and Kegan Paul Ltd., 1985. Provides information about what professional geographers do.

Greenhood, David. *Mapping.* Chicago: University of Chicago Press, 1964. Considered one of the best introductions to maps and map reading.

Haggett, Peter. *Geography: A Modern Synthesis.* New York: Harper & Row, 1983. Introduces thematic mapping.

Jay, L. J. *Geography Teaching With a Little Latitude.* Boston: George Allen & Unwin, 1981. Tells how to add a light-hearted approach in teaching geography.

Short, Nicholas M., et al. *Mission to Earth: Landsat Views the World.* Washington, DC: National Aeronautics and Space Administration, 1976. Shows images of natural and cultural features of Earth's surface through 400 Landsat photographs.

Supplementary Materials

Global Pursuit. The National Geographic Society, Educational Services, Dept. 87, Washington, DC 20036. Tests knowledge of world geography through the use of map puzzles and trivia questions.

The Language of Maps. Encyclopaedia Britannica Educational Corporation. 11 min. film/video. Color. Combines aerial photography and topographic models and shows how map symbols represent natural and human features.

Latitude and Longitude. Encyclopaedia Britannica Educational Corporation, 425 North Michigan Ave., Chicago, IL 60611. 14 min. film/video. Color. Explains the grid system, how it works, and why it is so accurate.

The Map Corner. Social Studies School Service, 10200 Jefferson Boulevard, P. O. Box 802, Culver City, CA 90232. Contains reproducible quizzes, activities, and maps.

Maps and What We Learn From Them. National Geographic Educational Services. Filmstrips/cassettes. Color. Concerns reading, using, and making maps.

Maps For a Changing World. Encyclopaedia Britannica Educational Corporation. 8 min. film/video. Color. Examines various map projections, distortion, symbols, and thematic features.

Mastering Geography. J. Weston Walch, P. O. Box 658, Portland, ME 04104. 26 spirit masters, 26 photocopy masters, teacher's guide. Consists of games, puzzles, teaching ideas, focusing on geographic skills and world geography.

More Than Maps: A Look at Geography. National Geographic Society, Educational Services. 3 filmstrips/cassettes. Color. Looks at fundamental themes in geography, using geography principles to understand the world as well as methods and tools used by geographers.

The Solar System. Encyclopaedia Britannica Educational Corporation. 18 min. film/video. Color. Examines the origins of the solar system and describes Earth in the context of the solar system.

UNIT 2 RESOURCES

Student Books and Articles

Asimov, Isaac. *How Did We Find Out About Volcanoes?* New York: Walker and Co., 1981. Traces volcanoes through history, analyzes volcanoes, describes what causes eruptions, and reveals where active volcanoes exist.

Eliot, John. "Glaciers on the Move," *National Geographic,* January 1987. Tells how scientists study Alaska's Hubbard Glaciers and why glaciers advance and retreat.

Frater, Alexander, ed. *Great Rivers of the World.* Boston: Little, Brown, 1984. Describes some of the most famous rivers in the world.

Gore, Rick. "No Way to Run a Desert," *National Geographic,* June 1985. Describes how record snowmelt and rain caused Utah's Great Salt Lake to flood its desert basin.

Gore, Rick. "Our Restless Planet Earth," *National Geographic,* August 1985. Discusses how Earth's face is changing and the tools scientists use to tell where Earth has been and where it is going.

Herman, John, and Richard Goldberg. *Weather and Climate.* New York: Dover Publications, 1985. Contains information on the various features associated with climate.

Lamb, H.H. *Climate, History, and the Modern World.* New York: Methuen, 1982. Describes some ways climate has influenced the development of the modern world.

Mulherin, Jenny. *Rivers and Lakes.* London: Franklin Watts, 1984. Gives illustrated presentation of how rivers and lakes are formed and their features on different continents.

National Geographic Society. *The Desert Realm.* Washington, DC: National Geographic Society, 1980. Surveys the great deserts of the world.

Polking, Kirk. *Oceans of the World.* New York: Philomel Books, 1983. Describes ocean topography and marine life, harnessing of marine energy, and the way sources of pollution are being handled.

Tuttle, Sherwood. *Landforms and Landscapes.* Dubuque, IA: William C. Brown, 1980. Provides a general overview of landforms.

Teacher Books and Articles

Allen, Oliver. *Atmosphere*. Alexandria, VA: Time-Life Books, 1983. Gives illustrated, factual treatment of the atmosphere, weather, and climate.

Bailey, Ronald. *Glacier*. Alexandria, VA: Time-Life Books, 1982. Examines the forces that shape and move glaciers.

Barry, Roger, and R.J. Chorley. *Atmosphere, Weather, and Climate*. New York: Methuen, 1982. Presents a overview of factors that influence climate.

Condie, Kent, ed. *Plate Tectonics and Crustal Evolution*. Elmsford, NY: Pergamon, 1982. Studies the effects of plate tectonics.

de Blij, Harm. *The Earth: A Topical Geography*. New York: John Wiley & Sons, 1980. Reveals how geographers study landscapes and the forces that forge them; also examines elements of climate.

Gibbons, Boyd. "Do We Treat Our Soil Like Dirt?" *National Geographic*, September 1984. Describes how soil is an essential bridge between the rock below and life above.

Gribbin, John, ed. *The Breathing Planet*. New York: Basil Blackwell & New Scientist, 1986. Discusses past and present climatic changes and the effects of human pollution on climate.

Gross, M. Grant. *Oceanography*. Columbus, OH: Charles E. Merrill Publishing Co., 1980. Introduces the fundamental features of the ocean.

Grove, Noel. "An Atmosphere of Uncertainty," *National Geographic*, April 1987. Discusses how human contaminants and global air pollution are a threat to life.

Miller, E. Willard. *Physical Geography*. Columbus, OH: Merrill Publishing Co., 1985. Examines landforms, their origins, and the forces that shape them; also discusses factors of climate, climatic systems, and climatic change.

Nebel, Bernard J. *Environmental Sciences: The Way the World Works*. Englewood Cliffs, NJ: Prentice-Hall, 1981. Contains chapters dealing with population, ecosystems, pollution, and resources.

Pringle, Laurence. *Rivers and Lakes*. Alexandria, VA: Time-Life Books, 1985. Presents an illustrated and factual treatment of inland waterways.

Thurman, Harold. *Essentials of Oceanography*. Columbus, OH: Merrill Publishing Co., 1987. Examines physical oceanography and problems resulting from human interaction with the ocean.

Weiner, Jonathan. *Planet Earth*. New York: Bantam, 1986. Gives illustrated treatment of forces that make and shape Earth.

Supplementary Materials

Continental Drift: The Theory of Plate Tectonics. Encyclopaedia Britannica Educational Corporation, 425 North Michigan Ave., Chicago, IL 60611. 22 min. film/video. Explores how continental drift occurs and its effect on the shapes and location of landmasses. It also examines the significance of plate tectonics in relation to earthquake prediction.

Dive to the Edge of Creation. National Geographic Society, P.O. Box 1640, Washington, DC 20013-9861. 59 min. film/video. Color. This film takes the viewer to the ocean floor to discover bacteria that convert chemicals into organic matter. The film also confirms various aspects of the theory of plate tectonics.

Earthquakes. Social Studies School Service, 10200 Jefferson Blvd., P.O. Box 802, Culver City, CA 90232. Wall poster with photographs of earthquake devastation and diagrams that give an explanation on how earthquakes happen.

Erosion and Weathering. Encyclopaedia Britannica Educational Corporation. 17 min. film/video. Shows the effects of weathering and erosional phenomena.

Ground Water. IBM, P. O. Box 2150, Atlanta, GA 30055. Software for IBM PC. Explores the relationship among groundwater, the environment, and people.

Hydrologic Cycle. IBM. Software for IBM PC. Examines the water cycle and the human impact on it.

The Oceans: Exploring Earth's Last Frontier. National Geographic Society, Educational Services, Dept. 87, Washington, DC 20036. Three 16 min. sound filmstrips. Shows the ocean floor, ocean plants and animals, as well as ocean resources and their uses.

Our Dynamic Earth. National Geographic Society, Educational Services. 23 min. film/ video. Contains footage of earthquakes, volcanoes, and animation explaining them in terms of plate tectonics.

Quake: Our Trembling Earth. Social Studies School Service, 10200 Jefferson Blvd., P.O. Box 802, Culver City, CA 90232. Filmstrips/cassettes. Illustrates the consequences of Earth's movement and the relationship between earthquakes and volcanoes.

Streams and Rivers. Aquarius, P.O. Box 128, Indian Rocks Beach, FL 33535. Software for Apple. Introduces rivers and streams.

The Earth's Climate. National Geographic Educational Services. Filmstrips/cassettes. Surveys the characteristics and causes of major types of climate.

The Oceans. Aquarius, P.O. Box 128, Indian Rocks Beach, FL 33535. Software for Apple. Instructs regarding the ocean.

The Temperate Deciduous Forest. Encyclopaedia Britannica Educational Corporation. 17 min. film/video. Illustrates the network of plant and animal relationships that makes up the community of the temperate deciduous forest.

Volcanoes. Social Studies School Service. Wallcharts with drawings and photographs show volcanic activity and how volcanoes contribute to the movement of Earth's crust.

What Makes Weather? Encyclopaedia Britannica Educational Corporation. 14 min. film/ video. Uses animation and photography to show the forces that produce weather.

UNIT 3 RESOURCES

Student Books and Articles

Caselli, Giovanni. *The First Civilizations: History of Everyday Things*. Culver City, CA: Social Studies School Service, 1985. Details the lives of many ancient peoples from earliest Stone Age to the great civilizations of Egypt, China, and Greece, including early agriculture and the first city.

Crosher, Judith. *The Greeks: Peoples of the Past*. Morristown, NJ: Silver Burdett. Describes building of city-states and way of life of ancient Greeks.

Duke, Dulcie. *The Growth of a Medieval Town*. Culver City, CA: Social Studies School Service, 1986. Records the growth of a typical European town between the eleventh and fifteenth centuries.

Gay, Kathlyn. *Cities Under Stress: Can Today's City Systems Be Made to Work?* Danbury, CT: Watts, 1985. Describes perspectives of the urban crisis and the process of cities' growth and development.

Higham, Charles. *The Earliest Farmers and the First Cities*. Culver City, CA: Social Studies School Service. Gives history of agriculture in the Middle East and its impact upon the life of the people.

Larned, Phyllis. *Industrial Giant: Richman, Poorman, Cattleman, Woman*. Culver City, CA: Social Studies School Service, 1982. Documents period from Reconstruction to World War I, including causes and growth of industrialization.

Macaulay, David. *City: A Story of Roman Planning and Construction*. Boston, MA: Houghton Mifflin. Depicts through text and illustrations the planning and step-by-step building of an imaginary Roman city.

Splendors of the Past: Lost Cities of the Ancient World. Washington, DC: National Geographic Educational Services, 1981. Recounts the glories of long-vanished peoples and civilizations.

The Story of America. National Geographic Educational Services, 1984. Gives information about presidents, population growth, and much more, with wall chart available in library edition.

Teacher Books and Articles

Caldwell, Lynton K. *Population and Environment: Unseparable Policy Issues.* Washington, DC: The Environmental Fund, 1985. Proposes that population considerations be included in environmental planning.

Drakakis-Smith, David. *Urbanization in the Developing World.* Wolfeboro, NH: Longwood Publishing Group, Inc., 1986. Focuses on patterns and causes of the rapid growth of cities in the developing world.

Ehrlich, Paul R., and Anne H. Ehrlich. *Population, Resources, Environment.* San Francisco: W. H. Freeman and Co., 1972. Deals with all phases of human ecology.

Food for All: Teaching Against Hunger. Intercom, No. 102. New York: Global Perspectives in Education, 1982. 40 pages of material suitable for photocopying that discusses, among other topics, the relationship between development and hunger.

Hanmer, Trudy. *The Growth of Cities.* Danbury, CT: Watts, 1985. Presents information on the development and growth of American cities.

Hartshorn, Truman A. *Interpreting the City: An Urban Geography.* New York: John Wiley & Sons, 1980. College-level text.

Haub, Carl, and Lindsey Grant. *Whatever Happened to the Population Bomb?* Washington, DC: The Environmental Fund. Answers the most frequently asked questions on world population growth and clarifies meaning of demographic projections.

The Hunger Project. *Ending Hunger: An Idea Whose Time Has Come.* New York: Praeger Publishers, 1985. Brings together major issues of food, population, and others, with 200 full-color photographs and many charts and graphs.

Marlin, John Tepper, and James S. Avery. *The Book of American City Rankings.* New York: Facts On File Publications, 1983. Charts standings of American cities on 267 issues.

McAuslan, Patrick. *Urban Land and Shelter for the Poor.* Washington, DC: International Institute for Environment and Development, 1985. Examines plight of urban poor and city building in developing nations.

Otero, George G., Jr. *Teaching About Population Growth.* Denver, CO: Center for Teaching International Relations, University of Denver, 1982. Creates awareness of current global population growth, the reasons for this growth, and long-term implications.

Sanborn, Michelle, et al. *Teaching About World Cultures: Focus on Developing Regions.* Denver, CO: Center for Teaching International Relations, University of Denver, 1986. Examines the relationship between culture and modernization, emphasizing the impact of development on people's lives.

Stuart, George E., ed. *Peoples and Places of the Past.* Washington, DC: National Geographic Society, 1983. Recreates the ancient world in form of an illustrated atlas.

Whitehouse, Ruth. *The First Cities.* Oxford, England: Phaidon Press Limited, 1977. Explores ancient cities of the Tigris and Indus River valleys and regions in between.

Supplementary Materials

Africa: Living in Two Worlds. Encyclopaedia Britannica Educational Corporation, 425 North Michigan Ave., Chicago, IL 60611. 17 min. film. Color. Contrasts old ethnic communities and new African nations with their growing city populations.

Backler, Alan L., ed. *The Geographic Route to a Global Perspective.* Global Perspectives in Education, Inc., 218 E. 18th St., New York, NY 10003. Provides 11 lesson plans with graphs, charts, maps, teaching suggestions, and activities.

The Canadians: Their Cities. Encyclopaedia Britannica Educational Corporation. 16 min. film. Color. Canadians tell about their people, economy, trade, architecture, industry, weather, foods, and history.

Connections: Our Developing World. Nancy Swing, Project Coordinator. Communications for Development, 634 F St. N.E., Washington, DC, 10002. Answers "What is a developing country?" with audiovisual presentation, printed handouts, and manual with teaching suggestions.

Hunger Hotline Revisited: Global Food Crisis. Church World Service, Office on Global Education, 2115 N. Charles St., Baltimore, MD 21218. 18 min. filmstrip. Color. Examines the global food crisis in-depth.

Immigrant. Educational Technical Center, Harvard Graduate School, Appian Way, Cambridge, MA. Software for Appleworks. Provides vehicle for student to trace voyage and new home of an immigrant family and make a 10-year economic projection for costs of home, food, transportation.

The Interior West: The Land Nobody Wanted. Encyclopaedia Britannica Educational Corporation. 20 min. film. Color. Shows how farming and building modern cities would be possible in this area through irrigation, water control, proper land and resource use.

International Youth Program of the Institute for Practical Idealism, (LEGACY), Route 4, Box 265, Bedford, VA 24523. Promotes global understanding and offers a variety of programs for youth ages 11–18.

International Film Foundation, Inc., 1987–88 Catalog of 16mm Films. International Film Foundation, Inc., P. O. Box 20115, Cathedral Finance Station, New York, NY 10025. Catalog offers 100 films for classroom.

King, David C., and Cathryn J. Long. *Environmental Issues and the Quality of Life*. Global Perspectives in Education, Inc. Material includes an urban planning simulation and selected readings for students on assessing "quality of life."

One World: Countries Database. Active Learning Systems. Available from Social Studies School Service, 10200 Jefferson Boulevard, Room B3, P.O. Box 802, Culver City, CA 90232–0802. 2 diskettes for Apple or Commodore. Requires 64K. Includes guide, reproducible activities, maps, and directions. Allows instant analysis and comparison of many aspects of 178 nations, including population and area, percent urbanization, and types of government.

Terry, Melinda Shaw. *R.A.P. on Culture Grades 6–9 (plus Teaching Guide)*. Center for Teaching International Relations, University of Denver, Denver, CO. Two kits contain activities designed to demonstrate and to encourage positive one-on-one encounters between students of different cultural backgrounds.

Venezuela: Oil Builds a Nation. Encyclopaedia Britannica Educational Corporation. 17 min. film. Color. Vividly contrasts skyscraper wealth of Caracas with the wooden shack existence of the outer-city slums and surrounding countryside.

UNIT 4 RESOURCES

Student Books and Articles

A Day in the Life of America, and *A Day in the Life of Canada*. New York: Collins Publishers, 1986. Selected views of the nations' people and landscapes.

Cameron, Robert. *Above San Francisco*. San Francisco: Cameron and Company, 1986. Excellent material for historical geography with photos of the same locations at different times. Other books in the series for the U.S. include *Above Hawaii*, *Above Los Angeles*, and *Above Washington D.C.*

Crump, Donald J., ed. *Exploring America's Valleys: From Shenandoah to the Rio Grande*. Washington, DC: National Geographic Society, 1984. Valleys and their role in the national life of the United States.

Fisher, Ron. *Our Threatened Inheritance: Natural Treasures of the United States*. Washington, DC: National Geographic Society, 1984. Examines physical features found in the United States.

Franklin, Paula. *Indians of North America.* New York: David McKay Co., Inc., 1979. Provides insights into the varied cultural perspectives of the many American Indian groups of the North American continent.

O'Neall, Thomas. *Back Roads America: A Portfolio of Her People.* Washington, DC: National Geographic Society, 1980. Photos and descriptions of people in non-urban America.

Smithsonian Institution. *The American Land: The Smithsonian Book of the American Environment.* New York: W.W. Norton Co., 1980. The landscapes of the United States with special emphasis on concerns of an ecological nature.

Tunner, Ogden, ed. *The Canadians.* Alexandria, VA: Time-Life Books, 1977. Emphasizes the westward expansion and growth of Canada.

Teacher Books and Articles

Allen, James Paul, and Eugene James Turner. *We the People: An Atlas of America's Ethnic Diversity.* New York: Macmillan, 1988. The best available atlas of ethnic distribution in the United States.

Birdshall, Stephen S., and John W. Florin. *Regional Landscapes of the United States and Canada.* New York: John Wiley & Sons, 1985. Survey of North American landscape features.

Garreau, Joel. *The Nine Nations of North America.* Boston: Houghton Mifflin, 1981. An examination of North America according to geographic regions rather than political boundaries.

Harris, R. Cole, ed. *Historical Atlas of Canada, Vol. I: From the Beginning to 1800.* Toronto: University of Toronto Press, 1987. The first of a proposed three-volume work. Excellent source of regional development of Canada.

Matthews, Rupert O. *America: An Aerial Closeup.* New York: Crescent Books, 1986. 412 pages of excellent color aerial photographs of all parts of the United States.

A great teaching tool for both physical and cultural geography of America.

Meinig, D.W. *The Shaping of America, Vol. 1: Atlantic America, 1492-1800.* New Haven: Yale University Press, 1986. First of a projected three-volume work on the development of America presented from a geographical perspective.

Metcalfe, William. *Understanding Canada: A Multidisciplinary Introduction to Canadian Studies.* New York: New York University Press, 1982. An overall view of Canada from seven disciplinary perspectives.

Mitchell, Robert D., and Paul A. Groves, eds. *North America: The Historical Geography of a Changing Continent.* Totowa, NJ: Rowman & Littlefield, Publishers, 1987. A collection of essays on the geographic-historical development of the United States and Canada.

Rooney, John F., Wilbur Zelinsky, and Dean R. Louder, eds. *This Remarkable Continent: An Atlas of United States and Canadian Society and Cultures.* College Station, TX: Texas A&M University Press, 1982. An anthology of 390 maps covering all significant aspects of North American society and culture.

Stegner, Wallace. *Beyond the Hundredth Meridian.* Lincoln, NE: University of Nebraska Press, 1982. A classic; essential to the understanding of the development of western America.

Thompson, Wayne C. *Canada 1987.* Washington, DC: Stryker-Post Publications, 1987. Current informational paperback on Canadian history, politics, resources, culture, and economy. This publication is updated on a yearly basis.

Supplementary Materials

Building a Nation: The Story of Immigration. National Geographic Educational Services, Dept. 88, Washington, DC 20036. 2 filmstrips/cassettes. Why immigrants came to the U.S., their obstacles and contributions.

Canada. National Geographic Educational Services. 5 filmstrips/cassettes. Examines the people and geography of Canada's different regions.

Canadian Geographic. A bi-monthly publication of the Royal Canadian Geographical Society, 488 Wilbrod St., Ottawa, Ont. KIN 6MB. Excellent publication on Canadian geographical topics.

The Canadians: Their Land. Encyclopaedia Britannica Educational Corporation, 425 North Michigan Ave., Chicago, IL 60611. 16 min. film/video. A view of Canada with emphasis on its people.

Geography of the United States. National Geographic Educational Services. 10 filmstrips/cassettes. A five-part series on the regions of the U.S.

Hands-on Geography: North America, and *Hands-On Geography: United States.* Nystrom, 3333 Elston Ave., Chicago, IL 60618. Activity set of high-quality laminated desk maps with copymasters for students.

Indians of North America. National Geographic Educational Services. 5 filmstrips/cassettes. North America's native peoples from ancient to modern times.

National Atlas of Canada. Royal Canadian Geographical Society, 488 Wilbrod St., Ottawa, Ont. K1N 6MB. Collection of Canadian maps from the Surveys and Mapping Branch: Energy, Mines & Resources of Canada. Individual maps available.

North America. National Geographic Educational Services. Filmstrip/cassette. Explores the physical regions and major geographical features of North America.

Our Canada Series. Social Studies School Service, 10200 Jefferson Blvd., P.O. Box 802, Culver City, CA 90232. 4 filmstrips/cassettes. A look at the people, history, geography, and government of Canada.

Regions of the United States. Social Studies School Service. 6 filmstrips/cassettes. Explores the climate, the topography, and other geographical features of the nation's regions.

United States Geography Series. National Geographic Educational Services. 23-27 min. films/videos. Ten films exploring the physical, cultural, and economic aspects of U.S. geography.

U.S. Regions: Contrasts of Land and People. Encyclopaedia Britannica Educational Corporation. 30 min. film/video. Examines the factors contributing to the cultural and economic development of the regions of the U.S.

UNIT 5 RESOURCES

Student Books and Articles

Bierhorst, John, ed. and trans. *Black Rainbow: Legends of the Incas and Myths of Ancient Peru.* New York: Farrar, Straus & Giroux, 1976. Provides a picture of the lifestyles of the people who once lived in Peru.

Cobb, Charles E. "Haiti—Against All Odds," *National Geographic,* November 1987. A poor nation's struggle to survive amid political turmoil.

Fincher, E.B. *Mexico and the United States: Their Linked Destinies.* New York: Thomas Y. Crowell Junior Books, 1983. An account of the interdependencies that cement the special relationship between Mexico and the United States.

Gardner, John L., ed. *Mysteries of the Ancient Americas.* Pleasantville, NY: The Reader's Digest Association, 1986. Reveals new facts and discoveries about the long-vanished civilizations on the American continent.

Griffiths, John. *Latin America in the Twentieth Century.* North Pomfret, VT: David and Charles, 1985. Presents an overview of this region of the Western Hemisphere in modern times.

Hinds, Harold E., Jr., and Charles M. Tatum, eds. *Handbook of Latin American Popular Culture.* Westport, CT: Greenwood Press, 1985. Contains articles on popular music, religion, comics, sports, films, and other topics.

Hodgson, Bryan. "Argentina's New Beginning," *National Geographic*, August 1986. Argentina looks to democracy after a decade of military rule.

Keen, Benjamin. *A Short History of Latin America*. 2nd ed. Boston: Houghton Mifflin, 1983. An abbreviated history of Latin America.

McIntyre, Loren. "The High Andes," *National Geographic*, April 1987. Traditional Indian communities and modern cities in South America's highest mountains.

Vesilind, Priit. "Brazil: The Promise and Pain," *National Geographic*, March 1987. Brazil's emergence as a world economic power despite a huge foreign debt.

Wilkes, John. *Hernan Cortés, Conquistador in Mexico*. Minneapolis, MN: Lerner, 1977. A biography of Cortés with emphasis upon his experiences in the New World.

Teacher Books and Articles

Blakemore, Harold, et al., eds. *The Cambridge Encyclopedia of Latin America and the Caribbean*. London: Cambridge University Press, 1985. Authoritative source of information on facts relating to Latin America.

Cleary, Edward L. *Crises and Change: The Church in Latin America Today*. New York: Orbis Books, 1985. Offers the account of a Maryknoll father in Latin America for 20 years and of the situation of the Catholic Church in today's Latin America.

Dostert, Pierre Etienne. *Latin America 1987*. Washington, DC: Stryker-Post Publications, 1987. Annual update on Latin America; part of "The World Today" series.

James, Preston E., and Clarence W. Minkel. *Latin America*. 5th ed. New York: John Wiley & Sons, 1986. Revised edition of a classic text on Central and South America. Also contains a comprehensive bibliography for each country.

Latin America 87/88. Annual Editions. Guilford, CT: Dushkin Publishing Group, 1987. Various selections on contemporary Latin American issues.

Martin, Michael R., and Gabriel H. Lovett, eds. *Encyclopedia of Latin American History*. Westport, CT: Greenwood Press, 1981. A reference work for facts, dates, people, and events in the history of Latin America.

Mintz, Sidney W., and Sally Price, eds. *Caribbean Contours*. Baltimore, MD: The John Hopkins University Press, 1985. Describes ethnic and cultural diversity of the region.

Morner, Magnus. *The Andean Past: Land, Societies, and Conflicts*. New York: Columbia University Press, 1985. Focuses on social and physical adaptation within political and economic frameworks in Bolivia, Peru, and Ecuador.

Preston, D. London. *Latin American Development: Geographical Perspectives*. New York: John Wiley & Sons, 1987. A look at recent growth and development in Latin America.

Rudolph, James B., ed. *Mexico: A Country Study*. 3rd ed. Washington, DC: American University, 1985. Discusses the social, economic, and political development in modern Mexico.

Sexton, James D., ed. *Campesino: The Diary of a Guatemalan Indian*. Tucson, AZ: University of Arizona Press, 1985. Focuses on life of a Guatemalan Indian in troubled times.

Switzer, Kenneth A., and Charlotte A. Redden. *Teaching About Diversity: Latin America*. Denver, CO: Center for Teaching International Relations, University of Denver, 1982. Stresses the complexity and diversity of the world community, using the Latin American region as an example.

Supplementary Materials

The Amazon. Encyclopaedia Britannica Educational Corporation, 425 North Michigan Ave., Chicago, IL 60611. 22 min. film/video. Examines the people and environment along the Amazon River.

Amazon Frontier. BBC-TV: Films Incorporated. 20 min. film. Color. Examines the high cost of economic development in the Amazon River Basin, focusing on effects on the rain forest and people who live there.

Area Handbook Series. Department of the Army, U.S. Government Printing Office, Washington, DC. Handbooks on many countries of the world including Brazil, Chile, Guatemala, Panama, and others.

The Caribbean Basin. Social Studies School Service, 10200 Jefferson Boulevard, P.O. Box 802, Culver City, CA 90232. 4 filmstrips/cassettes. Studies the geography, history, and politics of the Caribbean region.

Central America. National Geographic Educational Services, Dept. 88, Washington, DC 20036. 4 filmstrips/cassettes. Examines geography, cultural heritage, and conflicts in Central America.

Central America. National Geographic Educational Services. 25 min. film/video. Explains how Central American countries differ in economic development, cultural traditions, and political stability.

Digging Up America's Past. National Geographic Educational Services. 5 filmstrips/cassettes. An archaeological and historical study of Latin America's past before and after European colonization.

Flight of the Condor. WNET-BBC-TV, Films Incorporated. Series of films in color, 60 minutes each. Consists of "Down the Amazon," "Ice, Wind, Fire," and "Ocean, Desert, and Thin Air." All present geographic pictures of Latin America including plants, animals, and their natural habitats.

Hands-On Geography: South America. Nystrom, 3333 Elston Ave., Chicago, IL 60618. Activity set of high-quality laminated desk maps with copymasters for students.

Latin America. Social Studies School Service. 2 filmstrips/cassettes. Explores the diversity of the region's history, geography, and economic systems.

The Latin American Project. SPICE, 200 Lou Henry, Hoover Bldg., Stanford, CA 94305. A series of resources for teaching about Latin America including booklets, slides, bibliographies, cassette tapes, and activities.

Latin America Today. Social Studies School Service. 150 reproducible maps, tables, and graphs on frequently studied topics relating to Latin America.

Mexico. National Geographic Educational Services. 26 min. film/video. Looks at Mexico's geographical and cultural variety.

Mexico: The Land and the People. Encyclopaedia Britannica Educational Corporation. 22 min. film/video. How the growth of cities and other changes are shaping Mexico.

South America. National Geographic Educational Services. Filmstrip/cassette. Explores the physical regions and major geographical features of South America.

Women in Latin America. Social Studies School Service. Filmstrip/cassette. Shows the diversity of women's status and roles throughout Latin American history.

UNIT 6 RESOURCES

Student Books and Articles

A Day in the Life of the Soviet Union. New York: Collins Publishers, 1987. A pictorial sampling of Soviet life and culture.

Asimov, Isaac. *The Shaping of France*. Boston: Houghton Mifflin, 1972. Overview of France with an emphasis on history.

Binyon, Michael. *Life in Russia*. New York: Pantheon Books, 1983. Explains how ordinary Soviets live, their preoccupations, and their attitudes.

Chelminski, Rudolph. "Coldest Town in the World." *Reader's Digest*, November 1982. Gives an account of climatic conditions in Oymyakon, Soviet Union, where the lowest recorded temperatures exist for inhabitable places.

Edwards, Mike. "Ukraine." *National Geographic*, May 1987. Examines the Ukrainians' struggle to maintain their language, religion, and identity.

Kroll, Jarrett, and Stanley Kroll. *Cruising the Inland Waterways of Europe*. New York: Harper & Row, 1979. Traveler's account of journeying on Europe's rivers and canals.

McDowell, Bart. "The Dutch Touch." *National Geographic*, October 1986. How people of the Netherlands apply practical solutions to their problems.

Putman, John J. "Switzerland: The Clockwork Country." *National Geographic*, January 1986. Examines the Swiss propensity for order.

Townson, Duncan. *Muslim Spain*. New York: Cambridge University Press, 1973. Overview of the spread of Muslim influence.

Teacher Books and Articles

Barzini, Luigi. *The Europeans*. New York: Penguin, 1984. Introduction to the people of Europe.

Clark, James. *The Soviet Union*. Evanston, IL: McDougal, Littell & Co., 1983. Describes peoples of the Soviet Union, using photographs, questions, and study aids.

Johnson, Jacquelyn S. *Teaching About Conflict: Northern Ireland*. Denver, CO: Center for Teaching International Relations, University of Denver, 1983. Examines the historical roots of the conflict in Northern Ireland while focusing on such global topics as propaganda and terrorism.

Kerblay, Basile. *Modern Soviet Society*. New York: Pantheon Books, 1983. Provides insights into the social and economic life of the Soviet Union.

Kostich, Dragos. *The Land and Peoples of the Balkans*. New York: Harper & Row, 1973. Survey of the cultures of Albania, Bulgaria, and Yugoslavia.

Kuter, Lois. *Introducing Western Europe*. Bloomington, IN: West European Center, Indiana University, 1982. Contains material designed to provide general geographical, historical, and cultural background on Western Europe.

"Teaching About Russia and the Soviet Union," *Social Education*, April 1981.
National Council for the Social Studies. A monthly magazine, with this entire issue devoted to teaching about the Soviet Union and including an extensive resources list.

Ustinov, Peter. *My Russia*. Boston: Little, Brown, 1983. Focuses on eradicating some of the misconceptions that have led to an atmosphere of suspicion and concern about the Soviet Union.

Willis, David K. *Klass: How Russians Really Live*. New York: St. Martin's Press, 1985. An account of how the Soviet system affects daily lives.

Zeldin, Theodore. *The French*. New York: Pantheon Books, 1982. Looks at the diversity of contemporary French attitudes and culture.

Supplementary Materials

The British Isles. Encyclopaedia Britannica Educational Corporation, 425 North Michigan Ave., Chicago, IL 60611. 21 min. film/video. Traces how physical geography has influenced life in Great Britain.

Eastern European Studies. Social Studies School Service, 10200 Jefferson Blvd., P.O. Box 802, Culver City, CA 90232. 6 filmstrips/cassettes. Focuses on the dichotomy between nationalistic elements and Soviet-dictated policies.

Europe. National Geographic Educational Services, Dept. 88, Washington, DC 20036. Filmstrip/cassette. Studies Europe's physical regions and major geographical features.

Geography of Europe Series. National Geographic Educational Services. 10 filmstrips/cassettes. An overview of culture and life in four European regions.

Hands-On Geography: Europe. Nystrom, 3333 Elston Ave., Chicago, IL 60618. Classroom activity set of high-quality laminated desk maps with copymasters for students.

Journey Across Russia: The Soviet Union Today. National Geographic Educational Services. 2 filmstrips/cassettes. This series provides an overview of Soviet ethnic groups and the regions where they live.

Nations of the World Series. National Geographic Educational Services. 25-28 min. film/video. A study of the geography and cultures of several nations. Separate films available on East Germany, West Germany, the Soviet Union, Yugoslavia.

Russia. Social Studies School Service. Set of 12 transparencies and duplicating masters. Includes a physical map of Russia, Russian expansion, and historical themes.

Siberia: The Endless Frontier. Social Studies School Service. Filmstrip/cassette. Unmasks numerous misconceptions and myths surrounding this great landmass and frontier area of the Soviet Union.

The Soviet Union: Epic Land. Encyclopaedia Britannica Educational Corporation. 29 min. film/video. Provides the viewer with a sweeping panorama of the Soviet land and people.

UNIT 7 RESOURCES

Student Books and Articles

Carpenter, Allan, and James Hughes. *Libya*. Chicago: Children's Press, Inc., 1977. Highlights the physical geography, history, and daily life of this country.

Clifford, Mary. *Land and People of the Arabian Peninsula*. Philadelphia: J.B. Lippincott, 1977. Emphasizes the effects of the area's physical environment on its people.

Le Carre, John. *The Little Drummer Girl*. New York: Knopf, 1983. Tells the story, in spy thriller form, of the deeply held and irreconcilable claims of Israelis and Palestinians.

Lengyel, Emil. *Oil Countries of the Middle East*. New York: Franklin Watts, 1973. Tells how the discovery of oil affected the Middle East.

Newton, Clark. *Middle East and Why*. New York: Dodd, Mead & Co., 1977. Explains the reasons for the area's importance in the world today.

Said, Edward W. *After the Last Sky*. New York: Pantheon Books, 1986. Through photographs and text, expresses the pain of dislocation and alienation of the Palestinian people from their ancient homeland.

Shapiro, William E. *Lebanon*. Danbury, CT: Watts, 1984. Provides an overview of historical background and explanations of recent events in Lebanon.

Shipler, David. *Arab and Jew: Wounded Spirits in a Promised Land*. New York: Times Books, 1986. Explores the images Arabs and Jews have of each other.

White, Peter T. "The Fascinating World of Trash," *National Geographic*, April 1983. Describes the Zabbalines and their efficient recycling system.

Teacher Books and Articles

Bakhash, Shaul. *The Reign of the Ayatollahs: Iran and the Islamic Revolution*. New York: Basic Books, 1984. Details the course and consequences of the revolution that began in Iran in the late 1970s.

Carter, Jimmy. *The Blood of Abraham: Insights into the Middle East*. Boston, MA: Houghton Mifflin, 1985. Explores the biblical, historical, and contemporary elements of the Arab-Israeli conflict.

Cottrell, Alvin J., ed. *The Persian Gulf States: A General Study*. Baltimore, MD: The Johns Hopkins University Press, 1980. Encompasses the geography, history, economics, culture, religion, literature, and arts of the Persian Gulf region of the Middle East.

Egypt: A Country Study. Area Handbook Series, Washington, DC: Department of the Army, U.S. Government Printing Office, 1983. Analyzes historical, social, economic, political, and national security aspects of Egypt.

Khouri, Fred J. *The Arab-Israeli Dilemma*. Syracuse, NY: Syracuse University Press, 1985. Offers documentary coverage of the Arab-Israeli conflict.

Lacey, Robert. *The Kingdom: Arabia and the House of Saud*. New York: Harcourt Brace Jovanovich, 1981. Describes Saudi Arabian beliefs, contrasts, and power.

Renda, Gunsel, and Max C. Kortepeter, eds. *The Transformation of Turkish Culture*. Princeton, NJ: The Kingston Press, 1986. Examines the changes in Turkish culture over the past 60 years.

Saudi Arabia: A Country Study. Area Handbook Series. Washington, DC: Department of the Army, U.S. Government Printing Office, 1983. Analyzes historical, social, economic, political, and national security aspects of Saudi Arabia.

Wormser, Michael D., ed. *The Middle East*. Washington DC: Congressional Quarterly Inc., 1981. Profiles the countries of the Middle East, gives a comprehensive history of Islam, and looks at modern events and conflicts.

Supplementary Materials

Arabs and Jews: The Crisis. World Studies. 6 filmstrips/cassettes. Summarizes major events from biblical times to 1973, including origins of Judaism, Christianity, Islam.

Egypt. National Geographic Educational Services Dept. 88, Washington, DC 20036. 25 min. film/video. Visits modern Cairo and Alexandria, and observes industry and agriculture along the Nile.

The Establishment of Israel. Social Studies School Service, 10200 Jefferson Blvd., P.O. Box 802, Culver City, CA 90232. 2 filmstrips/cassettes. Discusses the rise of Zionism and the conflicts which have resulted since Israel became a nation.

Hands-On Geography: Africa. Nystrom, 3333 Elston Ave., Chicago, IL 60618. Classroom activity set of high-quality laminated desk maps with copymasters for students.

Homeland: Israel and Palestine. Encyclopaedia Britannica Educational Corporation, 425 North Michigan Ave., Chicago, IL 60611. 25 min. film/video. Explains why both Jews and Palestinian Arabs believe the same territory is their homeland.

Islam, Its Power and Legacy. Bear Films, Inc. 2 filmstrips/cassettes. Looks at Islam and the contributions of Islamic culture.

An Israeli Family. International Film Foundation, Inc. 20 min. film. Reveals the life of an Israeli family and provides insights into what life is like in modern Israel.

Life in the Sahara. Encyclopaedia Britannica Educational Corporation. 15 min. film/video. Contrasts nomadic lifestyles with Arab and Berber settlements.

The Middle East. National Geographic Educational Services. 5 filmstrips/cassettes. Explores the complex geography, cultures, religions, and conflicts of the Middle East.

The Middle East: Its Lands, People and History. Social Studies School Service. Reproducible exercises, puzzles, maps, and fact sheets for studying the Middle East.

Preserving Egypt's Past. National Geographic Educational Services. 23 min. film/video. Working against time, scientists attempt to preserve Egypt's ancient monuments.

Revolution: Iraq and Iran. Encyclopaedia Britannica Educational Corporation. 25 min. film/video. How revolutionary activity sought to change the past in Iraq and recreate the past in Iran.

The World of Islam. Social Studies School Service. 2 filmstrips/cassettes. Presents the history of the Muslim world from the birth of Mohammed up to modern times.

UNIT 8 RESOURCES

Student Books and Articles

Amin, Mohamed. *Cradle of Mankind*. Woodstock, NY: The Overlook Press, 1983. Captures the atmosphere of the land and peoples of northern Kenya in photos and text.

Barthorp, Michael. *The Zulu War: A Pictorial History*. New York: Sterling Publishing Co.,

1984. Portrays the 1879 conflict between the Zulus and the British in southern Africa in pictures and prose.

Becker, Peter. *The Pathfinders: A Saga of Exploration in Southern Africa*. New York: Viking-Penguin, Inc., 1985. Includes accounts of early explorations into the interior of the southern African continent.

Gerster, George. "Tsetse—the Deadly Fly." *National Geographic*, December 1986. Investigates the continuing war to control the insect and how it stirs debate over land use.

Gilford, Henry. *Gambia, Ghana, Liberia, and Sierra Leone*. New York: Franklin Watts, 1981. A look at the small countries of West Africa with an emphasis on their people.

Harma, Robert W. *River of Wealth, River of Sorrow: The Central Zaire Basin in the Era of the Slave and Ivory Trade*. New Haven, CT: Yale University Press, 1981. Provides a fascinating account of lands surrounding the Congo River in the days of the slave and ivory traders.

Hilbert, Christopher. *Africa Explored*. New York: W.W. Norton, 1982. Gives the history and reasons behind the century of explorations in Africa, describes what explorers found, and discusses the various peoples they encountered.

Lanier, Alison R. *Update—Nigeria*. Yarmouth, ME: Intercultural Press, 1982. Introduces the reader to the land and people of Nigeria.

Laure, Jason, and Ettagale Laure. *South Africa, Coming of Age Under Apartheid*. New York: Farrar Straus Giroux, 1980. Presents several true personal accounts of young people living in contemporary South Africa.

Mathabane, Mark. *Kaffir Boy*. New York: Macmillan, 1986. Tells the true story of a black youth's coming of age in South Africa under apartheid.

Teacher Books and Articles

Africa South of the Sahara. London: Europa Publications, Ltd., 1986. Gives background information on the continent and countries of Africa, including statistical data.

Area Handbooks (example: *Zambia, A Country Study*). Washington, DC: U.S. Government Printing Office. A series of handbooks on most countries of Africa providing political, economic, and cultural information.

Cable, Mary. *The African Kings*. New York: Tree Communications, Inc., 1983. Explores the artifacts and history of the African kings. Contains picture essays and photographic portfolios.

Crofts, Marylee. "Africa." *Social Education*, September 1986, Vol. 50, No. 5. Examines how Africa is portrayed in United States textbooks.

Cultural Atlas of Africa. New York: Facts on File Publications, 1982. In a nation-by-nation format, covers Africa's natural geography, history, culture, and urbanization.

Lamb, David. *The Africans*. New York: Random House, 1987. An introduction to modern black Africa based on the author's observations and interviews with Africans from different cultural backgrounds.

Meredith, Martin. *The First Dance of Freedom*. New York: Harper & Row, 1984. Surveys Africa since independence, country by country, covering decolonization and the rise of independent African states.

Ungar, Sanford J. *Africa: the People and Politics of an Emerging Continent*. New York: Simon and Schuster, 1985. Explains politics of African nations and United States policy in Africa, calling attention to important but misunderstood events taking place in Africa today.

Wiley, Marylee. "Teaching About Africa," *Social Education*, November-December 1982, Vol. 46, No. 7. Includes articles on African history, arts, and Tanzania.

Williams, Oliver F. *The Apartheid Crisis: How We Can Do Justice in a Land of Violence*. New York: Harper & Row Junior Books, 1984. Describes the nature of the apartheid crisis and points out some responses to it.

Supplementary Materials

Africa: Its People and Promise. Social Studies School Service, 10200 Jefferson Blvd., P.O.

Box 802, Culver City, CA 90232. 6 film-strips/cassettes. Focuses on Africa's physical features, problems, and potential.

Africa: Living in Two Worlds. Encyclopaedia Britannica Educational Corporation, 425 North Michigan Ave., Chicago, IL 60611. 17 min. film/video. Contrasts centuries-old tribal communities and customs and the new African nations.

Africa Today: An Atlas of Reproducible Pages. Social Studies School Service. Contains 150 reproducible maps, graphs, and tables highlighting African topics.

Africa: A Voyage of Discovery with Basil Davidson. Social Studies School Service. Series of eight videocassettes. A comprehensive overview of African history, geography, and culture from ancient times to the present.

Development Decisions: Ghana's Volta River Project. SPICE, 200 Lou Henry Hoover Bldg., Stanford, CA 94305. Excellent case-study for third-world development and decision making.

Elephants: Their Last Stand. National Geographic Educational Services, Dept. 88, Washington, DC 20036. 22 min. film/video. Shows competition in Kenya between farmers and elephants for limited resources.

Hands-On Geography: Africa. Nystrom, 3333 Elston Ave., Chicago, IL 60618. Classroom activity set of high-quality laminated desk maps with copymasters for students.

The Kalahari Desert People. National Geographic Educational Services. 24 min. film/video. Shows how cattle-raising is changing the life of Kalahari nomads and the ecology of the desert.

Lessons on Africa. Social Studies School Service. A reproducible collection of activities, educational games, and skill-building exercises focusing on African studies.

South Africa: Economics and Politics of Apartheid. Social Studies School Service. Filmstrip/cassette. Traces the history of apartheid and the widespread internal and international opposition to it.

UNIT 9 RESOURCES

Student Books and Articles

Bolitho, Harold. *Meiji Japan*. Minneapolis, MN: Lerner, 1980. Story of the formation of the modern nation of Japan.

Buchanan, Keith. *China*. Boston: Little Brown, 1981. Provides a picture of Chinese civilization with many photographs, maps, charts, and diagrams.

Jhabvala, Ruth P. *The Householder*. Middlesex, England: Penguin Books, 1983. Novel about an Indian schoolteacher trying to come to terms with marriage and maturity.

Lawson, Don. *The New Philippines*. New York: Franklin Watts, 1986. Chronicles the overthrow of dictatorship in favor of democratic leader Corazon Aquino.

Lengyel, Emil. *Pakistan and Bangladesh*. New York: Franklin Watts, 1975. General overview of the two countries that border India.

Lewis, Brenda. *Growing Up in Samurai Japan*. North Pomfret, VT: David and Charles, 1981. Tells the story of life in Japan during the era of the samurai.

Nance, John. *The Land and People of the Philippines*. Philadelphia: J.B. Lippincott, 1977. Highlights the landscape and culture of the Philippine Islands.

Poole, Frederick King. *Mao Zedong*. Danbury, CT: Franklin Watts, 1982. Tells the story of the Chinese leader who transformed China into a Communist state.

Sanders, Tao Tao Liu. *Dragons, Gods and Spirits from Chinese Mythology*. New York: Schocken Books, 1983. Presents many representative Chinese myths and legends.

Seybolt, Peter. *Through Chinese Eyes*. New York: Center for International Education, 1981. A useful collection of primary sources for high school students.

White, Peter T. "Laos Today," *National Geographic*, June 1987. Reports how Laotians have adjusted to a decade of living under communist rule.

Teacher Books and Articles

Blunden, Carline. *Cultural Atlas of China*. New York: Facts on File Publications, 1983. Covers China's natural geography, history, and culture.

Burks, Ardath. *Japan*. Boulder, CO: Westview, 1981. Offers an introduction to the land and people of Japan.

Courdy, Jean Claude. *The Japanese: Everyday Life in the Empire of the Rising Sun*. New York: Harper & Row, 1984. Translated by Raymond Rosenthal. Observes Japanese folklore, religion, literature, business, politics, and international relations.

Danforth, Kenneth C. *Journey Into China*. Washington, DC: National Geographic Society, 1982. Beautiful resource of photographs and information.

Hook, Brian, ed. *The Cambridge Encyclopedia of China*. Cambridge, MA: Cambridge University Press, 1982. Provides basic information about traditional and modern China.

Hsu, Immanuel C. *The Rise of Modern China*. New York: Oxford University Press, 1983. Focuses on the major historical events of China from 1600 to the present, noting especially the role of foreign influence.

Kaplan, Fredric M., and Julian M. Sobin. *Encyclopedia of China Today*. New York: Harper & Row, 1981. Provides information on China's geography, politics, economics, and many other topics of interest. Includes several chronologies, maps, charts, a glossary, and an annotated bibliography.

Pye, Lucian. *China*. Boston: Little, Brown, 1984. 3rd ed. A general history of China, with many tables and maps.

Raghavan, G.N.S. *Introducing India*. New Delhi, India: Indian Council for Cultural Relations, 1978. Synthesizes and explains Indian history from Indus Valley civilization to modern times.

Reishchauer, Edwin O. *Japan*. Rev. ed. New York: Knopf, 1981. Required reading for any teacher of Asian studies.

Sakamoto, Taro. *Japanese History*. Tokyo: International Society for Education Information, 1980. Offers a brief account of Japan's history in English from an organization devoted to accurate information about Japan.

Wu, K.S. *The Chinese Heritage*. New York: Crown, 1982. Offers a general survey of China and its people.

Supplementary Materials

Asia. National Geographic Educational Services, Dept. 88, Washington, DC 20036. Filmstrip/cassette. Explores Siberia, the Himalayas, the Hindu Kush, and Indochina.

Child of Urban Thailand: A Place to Live. Encyclopaedia Britannica Educational Corporation, 425 North Michigan Ave., Chicago, IL 60611. 14 min. film/video. Examines the problems of inadequate shelter in overcrowded Bangkok.

China: A Portrait of the Land. Encyclopaedia Britannica Educational Corporation. 18 min. film/video. Examines China's six major regions and how their economic progress is determined by the land.

China in the Classroom: Resources Catalog 1987. US-China Peoples Friendship Association, The Center for Teaching About China, 2025 I St., N.W., Suite 715, Washington, DC 20006. A wealth of materials.

China: Sichuan Province. National Geographic Educational Services. 25 min. film/video. Focuses on China's most populous area.

Contemporary Family Life in Rural China. Center for Research in International Studies, Stanford University, Stanford, CA 94305. Excellent teaching unit including 66 slides.

Ganges: Sacred River. Encyclopaedia Britannica Educational Corporation. 27 min. film/video. A panorama of modern India showing its dependence on the water cycle.

Hands-On Geography: Asia. Nystrom, 3333 Elston Ave., Chicago, IL 60618. Classroom activity set of high-quality laminated desk maps with copymasters for students.

India Unveiled Series. Encyclopaedia Britannica Educational Corporation. 4 films/videos. A series of four 30-minute films;

explores India's many contradictions and shows how India has achieved self-reliance, social change, and modernization.

An Introduction to International Trade: Focus on Japan & the United States. The Japan Project/SPICE, 200 Lou Henry Hoover Bldg., Stanford, CA 94305. Excellent student activity investigation.

Japan. National Geographic Educational Services. 25 min. film/video. Presents Japan's villages, cities, manufacturing, and trade.

Japan: Miracle in Asia. Encyclopaedia Britannica Educational Corporation. 30 min. film/video. Describes Japan's rapid rise to a great industrial nation.

Lessons on Asia. Social Studies School Service, 10200 Jefferson Blvd., P.O. Box 802, Culver City, CA 90232. A reproducible collection of activities, educational games, and skill-building exercises focusing on Asian studies.

The People's Republic of China. National Geographic Educational Services. 3 filmstrips/cassettes. Shows how China is shaped by an ancient heritage, geographical diversity, and government policies.

UNIT 10 RESOURCES

Student Books and Articles

Australia. New York: Time-Life Books, 1986. An easy-to-read book that provides a general introduction to Australia.

Heyerdahl, Thor. *Fatu-Hiru: Back to Nature on a Pacific Island.* New York: Doubleday, 1975. Study of life in the Pacific Islands.

Jordan, Robert P. "New Zealand: the Last Utopia?" *National Geographic,* May 1987. How New Zealanders are grappling with world problems in a modern way.

King, Michael. *New Zealand in Color.* New York: St. Martin's Press, 1982. An introduction to New Zealand featuring many striking color photos.

Patterson, Carolyn Bennett. "New Nations in the Pacific." *National Geographic,* October 1986. A trust territory transforms itself into three new countries and a commonwealth.

Price, Christine. *Made in the South Pacific: Arts of the Sea People.* New York: E.P. Dutton, 1979. Photographs and written descriptions illustrate canoe building, weaving, pottery-making, and wood carving.

Robb, Joan, ed. *New Zealand Amphibians and Reptiles in Colour.* Sanibel, FL: R. Curtis Books, 1986. Vivid portrayals of some of New Zealand's fascinating fauna.

Scott, Peter. "The Antarctic Challenge." *National Geographic,* April 1987. Robert Scott's courageous journey to the South Pole inspires three men to set out on his path 74 years later.

Teacher Books and Articles

"Australia: A Bicentennial Down Under." *National Geographic,* February 1988. A variety of articles relating to Australia's past and present.

Baglin, Douglas and David R. Moore. *People of the Dream Time: The Australian Aborigines.* New York: Walker and Co., 1970. Explores the traditions and folklore of a unique people.

Brower, Kenneth. *Micronesia: the Land, the People, and the Sea.* Baton Rouge, LA: Louisiana State University Press, 1982. Provides a general introduction to lands and people in this important part of the Pacific Islands culture area.

Bunge, Frederica M. *Oceania: A Regional Study.* Washington, DC: United States Government Printing Office, 1985. A succinct introduction to this world region.

Christian, Erwin, and Raymond Bagnis. *Islands of Tahiti.* Bora Bora, French Polynesia: Kea Editions, 1985. A grand book on one area in the South Pacific.

Higham, Charles. *Maoris.* New York: Cambridge University Press, 1981. Describes the culture and traditions of these native people of New Zealand.

Jaffa, Herbert, "Australia Through Australian Eyes." *Social Education*, Vol. 48, No. 6, September/October, 1984. Contains a wealth of information and bibliographic material on Australia.

Sherington, Geoffrey. *Australian Immigrants: 1788-1978*. Winchester, MA: Allen Unwin, 1981. Describes Australian settlers and patterns of settlement spanning 200 years.

Vesilind, Priit. "Antarctica." *National Geographic*, April 1987. Outlines political, economic, and ecological status of Antarctica.

Supplementary Materials

Antarctica. National Geographic Educational Services, Dept. 88, Washington, DC 20036. Studies Antarctic glaciers, ice shelves, dry valleys, and research stations.

Antarctica: Exploring the Frozen Continent. Encyclopaedia Britannica Educational Corporation, 425 North Michigan Ave., Chicago, IL 60611. 23 min. film/video. Provides a history of major expeditions to Antarctica.

Australia. Encyclopaedia Britannica Educational Corporation. 22 min. film/video. Explores the continent's fringes and limitless outback.

Australia. National Geographic Educational Services. Filmstrip/cassette. Studies Australia's Western Plateau, Central Lowlands, and the Great Dividing Range.

Australia. National Geographic Educational Services. 26 min. film/video. A look at Australia's Aborigines, history, and wealth.

Australia and New Zealand. Social Studies School Service, 10200 Jefferson Blvd., P.O. Box 802, Culver City, CA 90232. 6 filmstrips/cassettes. Examines the people and geography of these two nations and their relationship to Great Britain.

Australia's Twilight of the Dreamtime. National Geographic Educational Services. 59 min. film/video. A study of Aborigine culture in Australia.

Child of Papua New Guinea. Encyclopaedia Britannica Educational Corporation. 14 min. film/video. Focuses on a boy and his family in a country with limited food production and commerce.

The Pacific World. Social Studies School Service. 5 filmstrips/cassettes. Contrasts the diverse economic, cultural, and historical conditions of the far-flung Pacific Islands.

SOURCES OF OTHER SUPPLEMENTARY MATERIALS

American Geographical Society; 156 Fifth Avenue, Suite 600; New York, NY 10010

American Heritage Publishing Company; 551 Fifth Avenue; New York, NY 10017

The Association of American Geographers; 1710 16th Street, N.W.; Washington, DC 20009; (202) 234-1450

Association of Pacific Coast Geographers; Geography Department; University of Nevada; Reno, NV 89557

The Christian Science Monitor; Education Services, P-204; One Norway Street; Boston, MA 02115-3195; (800) 225-7090

Corporation for Public Broadcasting (PBS); 1320 Braddock Place; Alexandria, VA 22314-1698; (703) 739-5000

The Cousteau Society; 930 West 21st Street; Norfolk, VA 23517

Current Affairs Films; 24 Danbury Road; Wilton, CT 60897

Earthwatch; Dept. 900 Box 403; Watertown, MA 02272; (617) 926-8200

Encyclopaedia Britannica Educational Corporation; 425 N. Michigan Avenue; Chicago, IL 60611

Eye Gate House; 146-01 Archer Avenue; Jamaica, NY 11435

Fodor's Travel Guides; Fodor's Travel Publications; 201 East 50th Street; New York, NY 10022

Guidance Associates; 41 Washington Avenue; Pleasantville, NY 10570

Indiana University Audiovisual Center; Bloomington, IN 47401

Insight Guides; Prentice Hall Press; Gulf & Western Building; One Gulf & Western Plaza; New York, NY 10023

Learning Corporation of America; 1350 Avenue of the Americas; New York, NY 10019

Mobil Travel Guides; Prentice Hall Press; 200 Old Tappan Road; Old Tappan, NJ 07675

National Council for Geographic Education; Western Illinois University; Macomb, IL 61455; (309) 298-2470. Publication—*Journal of Geography*

National Council for the Social Studies; 3501 Newark Street, N.W.; Washington, DC 20016; (202) 966-7840. Publication—*Social Education*

National Film Board of Canada; 1251 Avenue of the Americas; New York, NY 10020

National Geographic Society; Educational Services; 17th & M Streets, N.W.; Washington, DC 20036; (202) 857-7000

National Geographic Society Geographic Alliance Network; Educational Media Division; National Geographic Society; 17th & M Streets, N.W.; Washington, DC 20036; (202) 775-6731

Nova; P.O. Box 322; Boston, MA 02134. Television series

Nystrom; 3333 Elston Avenue; Chicago, IL 60618; (800) 621-8086

Population Reference Bureau; 777 14th Street, N.W., Suite 800; Washington, DC 20005

Rand McNally & Company; P.O. Box 7600; Chicago, IL 60680

The Royal Canadian Geographical Society; 488 Wilbrod Street; Ottawa, Ontario KIN 6MB

Smithsonian Associates; 900 Jefferson Drive; Washington, DC 20560

Social Studies School Service; 10200 Jefferson Boulevard; P.O. Box 802; Culver City, CA 90232-0802; (800) 421-4246

Stanford Program on International and Cross-cultural Education (SPICE); 200 Lou Henry Hoover Building; Stanford, CA 94305; (415) 723-1114

Sunset Travel Books; Lane Publishing Company; Menlo Park, CA 94025

Time-Life Books; 541 North Fairbanks Court; Chicago, IL 60611; Series; *Planet Earth, Library of Nations, The Great Cities, The World's Wild Places*, etc.

Time-Life Films; Rockefeller Center; New York, NY 10020

United Nations Children's Emergency Fund; 331 East 38th Street; New York, NY 10016. Publication—*UNICEF News*

U.S. Geological Survey; Federal Center; Denver, CO 80225

U.S. Information Agency; 1776 Pennsylvania Avenue; Washington, DC 20005

WETA Educational Activities; P.O. Box 2626; Washington, DC 20013; (703) 990-2709; Television series: "Global Links"

World Bank Film Library; Room D-845; 1818 H Street, N.W.; Washington, DC 20433

The World Bank Publications; Department 0552; Washington, DC 20073-0552. Publication—*Publications Update*

World Eagle, Inc.; 64 Washburn Avenue; Wellesley, MA 02181-9990. Publication—*World Eagle*

Regional studies resource centers located at universities throughout the United States can provide a wealth of information and services for the teacher, including curriculum materials, institutes, and training.

Suggested resources were compiled with the assistance of Muncel Chang, member of the National Commission on the Social Studies, Instructor for the National Geographic Society Summer Institute for Teachers, and Member of the Northern California Geographic Alliance Steering Committee.

WORLD GEOGRAPHY: PEOPLE AND PLACES ©1989
Evaluation of Total Program

Circle the number that corresponds most nearly to your opinion of each of the following items of the *World Geography: People and Places* program. Please also star (*) three factors that most influence your evaluation or choice of a text.

Student Edition	Excel-lent	Very Good	Satis-factory	Fair	Poor	Not Used	Comments
1. Visual Impact	1	2	3	4	5	N	_____
2. Approach	1	2	3	4	5	N	_____
3. Organization	1	2	3	4	5	N	_____
4. Readability	1	2	3	4	5	N	_____
5. Concept Development	1	2	3	4	5	N	_____
6. Content Coverage	1	2	3	4	5	N	_____
7. Factual Accuracy	1	2	3	4	5	N	_____
8. Using Graphic Skills Lessons	1	2	3	4	5	N	_____
9. Developing Geography Skills Lessons	1	2	3	4	5	N	_____
10. Special Features: Focus	1	2	3	4	5	N	_____
11. Special Features: Thinking Like a Geographer	1	2	3	4	5	N	_____
12. Special Features: Strange but True	1	2	3	4	5	N	_____
13. Content Check Questions	1	2	3	4	5	N	_____
14. Challenge Questions	1	2	3	4	5	N	_____
15. Boldface Terms	1	2	3	4	5	N	_____
16. Chapter Reviews	1	2	3	4	5	N	_____
17. Unit Reviews	1	2	3	4	5	N	_____
18. Maps	1	2	3	4	5	N	_____
19. Photographs	1	2	3	4	5	N	_____
20. Caption Questions	1	2	3	4	5	N	_____
21. Graphic Illustrations	1	2	3	4	5	N	_____
22. Atlas	1	2	3	4	5	N	_____
23. National Profiles Chart	1	2	3	4	5	N	_____
24. Glossary	1	2	3	4	5	N	_____
25. Index	1	2	3	4	5	N	_____

Teacher Annotated Edition							
1. Teachability	1	2	3	4	5	N	_____
2. Annotations in blue	1	2	3	4	5	N	_____
3. Introduction to the Program Section	1	2	3	4	5	N	_____
4. Instructional Approaches Section	1	2	3	4	5	N	_____
5. Activities	1	2	3	4	5	N	_____
6. Charts: Lesson Plan Suggestions	1	2	3	4	5	N	_____
7. Suggested Resources	1	2	3	4	5	N	_____

Teacher Resource Book							
1. Teacher Notes/Extending the Lesson	1	2	3	4	5	N	_____
2. Skill Activities	1	2	3	4	5	N	_____
3. Readings	1	2	3	4	5	N	_____
4. Chapter Review Worksheets	1	2	3	4	5	N	_____
5. Tests and Exams	1	2	3	4	5	N	_____
6. Map Worksheets	1	2	3	4	5	N	_____
7. Content Worksheets	1	2	3	4	5	N	_____
8. Careers	1	2	3	4	5	N	_____
9. Outline Maps/Transparency Masters	1	2	3	4	5	N	_____
10. Correlations—Skill/Objectives	1	2	3	4	5	N	_____

Student Activity Book	1	2	3	4	5	N	_____
Transparency Package	1	2	3	4	5	N	_____
Test Generator Software	1	2	3	4	5	N	_____

Circle the appropriate information.

1. Grade level of students	7	8	9	10	11	12
2. Enrollment of that grade	1–50		51–100	101–200		200+
3. Total school enrollment	1–200		201–500	501–1000		1000+
4. Locale of school	rural		small town	suburban		large city
5. Ability level of class	below average			average		above average
6. Appropriateness of text for your class	easy			about right		difficult
7. Number of years text used	1	2		3	4	5
8. May we quote you?	Yes		No			

Name _____

School _____ City _____ State _____ ZIP _____

Position _____ Date _____

You are encouraged to send more extensive comments to the address below at your convenience.

Fold and tape. Please do not staple.

MERRILL
WORLD GEOGRAPHY
PEOPLE AND PLACES

ARMSTRONG   HUNKINS

MERRILL
PUBLISHING COMPANY
A Bell & Howell Company
Columbus, Ohio
Toronto • London • Sydney

AUTHORS

David G. Armstrong is Professor of Educational Curriculum and Instruction at Texas A&M University. A social studies education specialist with additional advanced training in geography, Dr. Armstrong was educated at Stanford University, University of Montana, and University of Washington. He taught at the secondary level in the state of Washington before beginning a career in higher education. Dr. Armstrong has written books for students at the secondary and university levels, as well as for teachers and university professors. He maintains an active interest in travel, teaching, and social studies education.

Francis P. Hunkins is Professor of Education at the University of Washington. He began his professional career as a teacher in Massachusetts. He received his doctorate from Kent State University in general curriculum with a concentration in geography. Dr. Hunkins has written books and articles for students and teachers at the secondary and university levels. He has also written many professional articles and has assumed leadership roles in national professional organizations. As a student of geography, Dr. Hunkins has visited every continent but Antarctica.

ILLUSTRATORS

Map Illustrators	Maryland CartoGraphics, Inc.
Atlas Illustrators	R. R. Donnelley & Sons Co., Cartographic Services
Graphic Illustrator	David Germon
Collage Illustrator	Jim Pearson

Cover Illustrations: background, L. Guderian/Image Bank; inset photo, Tim Courlas.
Title Page and Table of Contents Photos: *i,* L. Guderian/Image Bank; *v,* NASA; *vi-vii,* Ed Kumler; *viii-ix, x-xi,* Michael Collier; *xii,* Steve Lissau.

ISBN 0–675–02288–6

Published by
Merrill Publishing Company
A Bell & Howell Information Company
Columbus, Ohio 43216

PREFACE

Merrill's *World Geography: People and Places* blends physical and human geography, helping students understand themselves and their relationship to Earth and to other peoples of the world. The text, introduced by a one-page Prologue that stresses the reasons for studying geography, is made up of 10 units divided into 31 chapters. The first three units introduce basic concepts within the disciplines of physical and human geography. Each of the remaining units focuses on a major world region, reinforcing the concepts introduced in the first three units.

Each unit opens with a descriptive photograph, an indicator map, a brief introduction to unit content, and a unit table of contents. Each concludes with a two-page Unit Review that includes a brief summary of unit generalizations; review questions; suggestions for group and individual activities; and a one-page skill-developing activity.

Each chapter opens with a colorful full-page photograph that highlights a theme from the chapter. Themes presented in the chapter are listed as a preview. An introduction helps set the tone for the narrative, which presents facts and concepts in a readable and interesting style. Supporting, reinforcing, and supplementing the narrative is a great variety of maps, full-color photographs, illustrations, graphs, diagrams, and charts. To promote ease of reading and comprehension, each chapter is divided into numbered sections and subsections, the headings of which serve as a content outline. Each section is followed by a Content Check that includes a list of concept terms, a list of important people and places, recall questions, and a challenge question that requires higher-level thinking and problem-solving skills.

At the end of each chapter is a Conclusion that summarizes the chapter narrative in light of any future changes faced by Earth and its people. This is followed by a two-page Chapter Review that consists of a summary of key points; a vocabulary exercise; three sets of questions that test knowledge, comprehension, and higher-level thinking and problem-solving skills; a geographic skills exercise; and several challenge questions.

Supplementing the basic chapter and unit content are four types of one-page special features—Thinking Like a Geographer, which discusses the important skills or vocabulary of geographers; Strange But True, which describes unusual geographic phenomena; Focus, which highlights studies of or stories about physical, cultural, economic, or historical geography; and The Urban World, which treats urban geography concepts as they relate to certain cities of the world. In addition, throughout *World Geography: People and Places,* special attention is given to skills development. Not only are social studies skills defined, taught, applied, and practiced in Unit Reviews, but each chapter contains a graphic skills feature as well.

At the end of the text is an Appendix that includes an atlas with general reference maps, a data chart that provides statistics and shows the flags of each independent nation of the world, a glossary that defines all boldfaced terms that appear in the text, and a comprehensive, cross-referenced index.

iv

CONTENTS

FEATURES

SKILLS

ILLUSTRATIONS

CULTURAL COLLAGES

CHARTS, DIAGRAMS, AND GRAPHS

PROLOGUE

[People] can no longer be studied apart from the ground which [they] fill, or the lands over which [they] travel, or the seas over which [they] trade, than polar bears or desert cactus can be understood apart from its habitat. [People's] relations to [their] environment are infinitely more numerous and complex than those of the most highly organized plant or animal. So complex are they that they constitute a legitimate and necessary object of special study.

The "special study" American geographer Ellen Churchill Semple spoke of in her 1911 book, *Influences of Geographic Environment,* is what is now called human geography. At the time, Semple was among a group of noted scientists that wanted geography to include more than just the study of Earth and its physical features. They believed that the study of relationships between Earth and the people who lived there was as important as physical geography.

Today, nearly a century later, the need for special study of both Earth and its people is even stronger. Educators and government leaders join geographers in promoting more geographic education for everyone. They strongly believe that, in the world we live in today, people need not only to understand themselves and their relationship to Earth but also their relationships to peoples all over the world.

In today's world people depend on each other for the needs of their daily lives. It is not unusual for an American teenager to wake up to an alarm clock manufactured in Taiwan, style his or her hair with a product from France, dress in jeans sewn in Honduras, and ride in a car made in Japan. With increased transportation, communication, and trade linking even the most faraway parts of Earth, people need to learn about cultures other than their own and know the environments in which they live. This will help them interact effectively not only in trade but in political and social situations as well. *World Geography: People and Places* seeks to provide the insights needed to begin understanding Earth's awesome environments and the world's fascinating cultures.

FOUNDATIONS
OF GEOGRAPHY

UNIT 1

Geography involves a special way of looking at planet Earth and its people. It looks at relationships between groups of people, between places, and between people and places.

The study of geography involves describing, explaining, and making forecasts about people and places. To do these tasks, the geographer uses special methods of inquiry and several different tools.

The most important tools are maps. Maps show information in picture form. They can show any of Earth's features that can be measured or counted. They give the geographer and the student of geography the information they need to learn more about this planet and the people who live on it.

Each unit of the text opens with a large identified photo designed to provide a colorful visual overview of the general topics or regions to be studied in the unit. The chapters within the unit are listed with opening page references, and a unit overview introduces the student to the content presented in the unit.

At the beginning of each unit, see the Text Implementation section in the *Teacher Annotated Edition* (*TAE*) for the Introducing the Unit Activity and Suggested Unit Resources.

Ship docked at Dutch Harbor in the Aleutian Islands of Alaska

CHAPTER 1

Each chapter of the text opens with a large identified photo designed to arouse student interest in the chapter. The photo provides visual impact for the subject of the chapter.

Earth viewed by the American *Apollo 17* crew on its way to the moon

NATURE OF GEOGRAPHY

See the Text Implementation section in the *TAE* for each chapter's objectives; overview of chapter content; suggested teaching strategies with activities for teaching content; answers to content check questions, questions in photo and illustration captions, special feature materials, and chapter review exercises; suggested lesson plans to teach each section of the chapter; and strategies for review and evaluation.

In this chapter you will learn—

- What geography is and what geographers study.
- How geographers identify and locate places.
- Why geographers use different methods of study.
- What the five steps of geographic inquiry are.
- Why the study of geography is valuable in today's world.

Metric forms are written out the first time each particular form appears. When the form is used later, it will be abbreviated.

Chapters are organized in outline form to help students work better with the content. Chapters are divided into sections, and sections are divided into subsections, all of which are numbered for ease of reference.

INTRODUCTION

From outer space the planet Earth looks like a beautiful blue and white ball shining in a black sky. It seems small to astronauts looking at it from the moon. It also seems small in photographs taken by spacecraft on the way to other planets.

Earth is one of nine known planets in the solar system. Earth is the fifth largest. Jupiter, Saturn, Uranus, and Neptune are larger. Venus, Mars, Mercury, and Pluto are smaller than Earth.

When compared with the planets in the solar system, the sun is huge. Its diameter, or distance through the middle, is 865,000 miles (1,392,082.5 kilometers). This is more than 109 times the diameter of Earth. The sun is a star made up of hydrogen, helium, and other gases. The sun works like a giant heating and lighting power plant. It gives off heat and light for all of the solar system.

The nine planets revolve around the sun in paths called orbits. They stay in these orbits because of two opposing forces. One of these is gravitational attraction. It pulls the planets toward the sun. The other is centrifugal force. It pulls them away from the sun. The two forces, however, balance each other.

Earth revolves around the sun at a speed of about 66,600 miles (107,182.3 km) per hour. It takes Earth 365.25 days, or one year, to complete one revolution. It is the revolution of Earth around the sun, as well as the tilt of Earth, that accounts for the change in seasons of the year.

Figure 1-1 on page 6 shows that Earth not only moves around the sun but that it also rotates, or spins, on its axis. The axis is an imaginary rod that passes through the center of Earth. The North Pole is at the northernmost end of the axis. The South Pole is at the southernmost end. It takes Earth 24 hours, or one day, to complete one rotation. It is the rotation of Earth that brings about night and day. Only one-half of Earth receives sunlight at one time. The other half is in darkness.

While Earth may appear small when seen from space, it has nearly 197 million square miles (510.2 million sq km) of surface area. The distance around Earth is about 24,900 miles (40,072.7 km). The diameter of Earth is 7,927 miles (12,757.3 km).

Whether a person thinks Earth is large or small, it is a unique planet. As far as scientists know, Earth is the only planet in the solar system that has life. It is the home of humanity—all the people who live on Earth.

REVOLUTION AND ROTATION OF EARTH

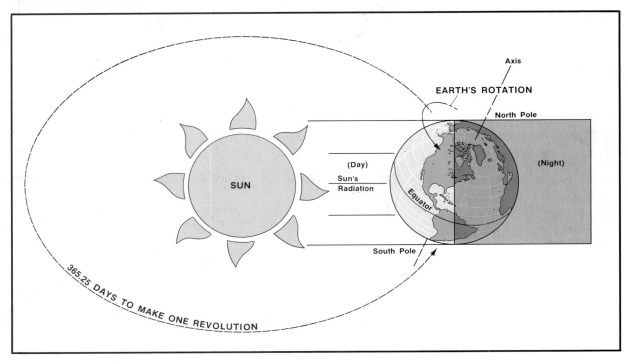

FIGURE 1-1
Earth revolves around the sun at the same time it rotates on its own axis. These two different kinds of motion bring about seasons and night and day. Which motion brings about night and day?

1. WHAT IS GEOGRAPHY?

Geography is the study of Earth and the people who live on it. The term geography comes from the Greek word *geographia*, meaning "description of Earth."

The people who practice the science of geography are known as geographers. Geographers study Earth and its people for three major reasons. First, they want to describe Earth. Second, they want to explain it. Third, they want to make predictions or forecasts about Earth's future.

To carry out their work, geographers try to understand relationships between people

and places on Earth. They also try to understand relationships between one place or group of places and another place or group of places. All of these relationships are called **spatial** (SPAY shuhl) **interaction.**

In their study of spatial interaction, geographers have found that people, places, and other features of Earth and its people are not equally spread across Earth's surface. For example, some places on Earth have many people. Other places on Earth, however, have few people. Geographers are interested in the distribution, or arrangement over an area, of people and places on Earth's surface. They can better describe and explain Earth and its features by studying the relationships and patterns made by people and places on Earth.

FOUNDATIONS OF GEOGRAPHY   UNIT 1

From studying Earth, geographers have learned that its features are always changing. Some changes take place over millions of years, while others happen in a day's time. Some changes are due to natural causes. For example, the effects of heavy rainfall can cause a hillside to change over time. Other changes, however, are due to human activities, such as the building of roads and cities or the clearing of forests for farming.

1.1 Importance of Places

It is the emphasis on *place* that makes geography different from other areas of study. For example, the study of history deals with people and places over time. In history, *time* is the main concern.

Time can be important in geography, too. In order to understand why New York City is so large or why Moscow is located where it is, geographers have to consider changes over time. But the main focus is on *place*, and not time.

Identifying Places. Each question that geographers seek to answer about Earth and its people deals with place. To identify a class or group of places that are alike in some way, geographers use general names such as *desert*. A desert is an area of very low rainfall and scarce vegetation. All areas of Earth meeting this description can be called deserts. To identify particular places within a general grouping, geographers use specific names. One such name is the Sahara. The Sahara is a particular desert with a definite space on Earth. No other place has the same location.

Locating Places. All kinds of places, both natural places and those made by humans, are found in a space on Earth known as the **biosphere** (BY uh SFIHR), or life-layer. All living things exist in this layer, which is at or near the surface of Earth. If the whole size of Earth is compared to an egg, the biosphere would be thinner than the egg's shell. It is this life-layer of Earth in which geographers are interested.

Geographers have divided Earth's biosphere into three parts—land, water, and air. They have a special name for each part. The

Erosion and volcanic activity are slowly changing the look of Mount Haleakala ("House of the Sun") in Hawaii. The world's largest inactive volcano, its crater measures 3,000 feet (914.4 meters) deep. What other activities change Earth's features?

At this California coast sky, sea, and shore all come together. What do geographers call the air, water, and land portions of Earth's life-layer?

land part is the **lithosphere** (LIHTH uh SFIHR). The water part is the **hydrosphere** (HY druh SFIHR). The air part is the **atmosphere** (AT muh SFIHR).

Because Earth is a sphere, or shaped like a ball, the best model of it is a globe. Using it, geographers have a way to locate places within the life-layer in order to study them.

To locate places, geographers, as well as others, use a set of imaginary lines that cover Earth. One set of lines crosses Earth's surface horizontally, circling east and west. Each of these lines is called a line of **latitude.** Each line of latitude is always an equal distance from the next. For this reason each is known also as a **parallel.** All latitude lines are parallel to each other.

A second set of lines runs vertically along Earth's surface from the North Pole to the South Pole. Each of these lines is called a line of **longitude,** or a **meridian** (muh RIHD ee uhn). On a globe, as shown in Figure 1-2 on page 9, these lines appear to form small wedges as they come together at the poles.

When lines of latitude cross lines of longitude, a grid is formed. It is used by geographers to locate certain places on Earth. This is done with the help of a numbering system.

Each line of latitude and longitude has an identifying number. These numbers are expressed in terms of *degrees*, or parts of a circle. The number given to each line is written using the symbol for a degree, such as 41°. Each degree can be further divided into *minutes*, or parts of a degree. There are 60 minutes in each degree. Minutes are written with one short line, such as 53'. They can be divided into even smaller parts called *seconds*. There are 60 seconds in each minute. Seconds are written with two short lines, such as 25".

It is important to know that when using the grid system, the numbered latitude and longitude lines are only part of the information needed to locate places on Earth. The other part is direction.

Lines of latitude are numbered based on how far north or south they are of an imaginary line called the **Equator.** The Equator circles Earth exactly halfway between the North Pole and the South Pole. The Equator is the starting point for lines of latitude. For this reason, its latitude is 0°. Between it and each of the poles, there are 90 degrees of latitude. The area between the Equator and the North Pole is known as *north* latitude. Any latitude line in this area must be followed by the word "north" or by an "N," such as 22°N. The area between the Equator and the South Pole is called *south* latitude. Any latitude line in this area must be followed by the word "south" or by an "S," such as 75°S.

Lines of longitude are numbered based on how far east or west they are of another imaginary line. This line is called the **Prime Meridian.** In 1884 geographers from around the world decided that the Prime Meridian would run through the Royal Astronomical Observatory that is in the city of Greenwich (GRIHN ihj), England. The Prime Meridian

FOUNDATIONS OF GEOGRAPHY UNIT 1

Explain that the fact that the Prime Meridian runs through Greenwich was an arbitrary one. It would have been possible to use any other location.

Remind students of the importance the grid system had for early navigators and how this improved their sailing and mapmaking accuracy.

is the starting point for lines of longitude. For this reason, its longitude is 0°. There are 180 degrees of longitude east of the Prime Meridian and 180 degrees west of it. The area east of the Prime Meridian is known as *east* longitude. Any line of longitude in this area must be followed by the word "east" or by an "E," such as 120°E. The area to the west of the Prime Meridian is known as *west* longitude. Any longitude line in this area must be followed by the word "west" or by a "W," such as 38°W.

Keep in mind that the Prime Meridian does not circle the globe as the Equator does. Instead it runs from the North Pole, through England, to the South Pole—covering only one-half of the globe. The line of longitude that runs from the North Pole to the South Pole on the other side of the globe is 180°. Most of this meridian serves as the **International Date Line,** an imaginary line that separates one calendar day from the next.

Using the grid system, a person can find each place on Earth by looking at the point where a line of latitude cuts across a line of longitude. The city of Nashville, Tennessee, for example, is found at 36° north latitude and 86° west longitude. Such a location, described by using latitude and longitude coordinates, is called the **exact location** of a place. The exact location of many places can

be even more precise. Using minutes as well as degrees, the exact location of Nashville is 36°10'N, 86°48'W. Using seconds, the exact location of the heart of the city is 36°10'10"N, 86°48'51"W.

Besides exact location, places also have **relative location.** This is the location of a place relative to, or compared with, another place. Direction is very important to relative location. North, south, east, and west are the chief directions. They are called **cardinal directions.** There are also four **intermediate directions**. They are northeast, southeast, northwest, and southwest. Northeast is midway between north and east. Southeast is midway between south and east, and so on.

All of these directions can be used to describe relative location. For example, you can say that New Orleans, Louisiana, is southwest of Washington, D.C., and north of the Gulf of Mexico. This is much like saying that one person is standing to the right or left of another person.

Geographers have another way of looking at relative location. They think of Earth as being divided into parts. By using latitude and longitude lines, for example, Earth can be divided into halves. Each of these halves is called a **hemisphere** (HEHM uh SFIHR).

Figure 1-3 on page 10 shows Earth divided into hemispheres at the Equator. The

LATITUDE AND LONGITUDE

FIGURE 1-2

Lines of latitude and longitude help people to locate places exactly on Earth's surface. Each of these lines is numbered for greater accuracy. What are the exact locations of the Equator and the Prime Meridian?

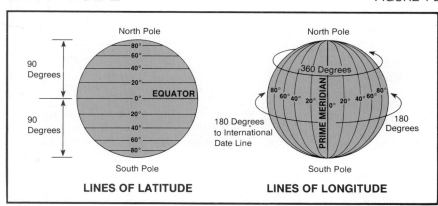

The boundaries between the Eastern and Western Hemispheres have not been definitely established. Some geographers use 20° west longitude and 160° east longitude. Explore with students why these meridians may be preferred rather than 0° and 180° longitude.

half that is north of the Equator is called the Northern Hemisphere. The half that is south of the Equator is referred to as the Southern Hemisphere.

Earth also can be divided into hemispheres at the circle formed by the Prime Meridian and the International Date Line. The half east of the Prime Meridian is called the Eastern Hemisphere. The half west of the Prime Meridian is the Western Hemisphere.

Earth may also be divided into land portions. There are seven major land areas called **continents.** The names of the continents are North America, South America, Europe, Africa, Asia, Australia, and Antarctica. Because Europe and Asia form one landmass, they are sometimes thought of as part of the same continent called Eurasia. To make it easier to study the continents, most geographers agree that two of the physical features that divide Europe and Asia are the Ural Mountains and the Caspian Sea. This places part of the Soviet Union in Europe and part in Asia. In this book the Soviet Union is studied with countries in Europe. This is because the Soviet culture, which includes its history and government, is tied closely to Europe.

Some of the continents are in more than two hemispheres. South America and Africa, for example, are both partly in the Northern Hemisphere and partly in the Southern Hemisphere. To make it easier to study, a continent is considered in the hemisphere where most of its land area lies.

HEMISPHERES

FIGURE 1-3

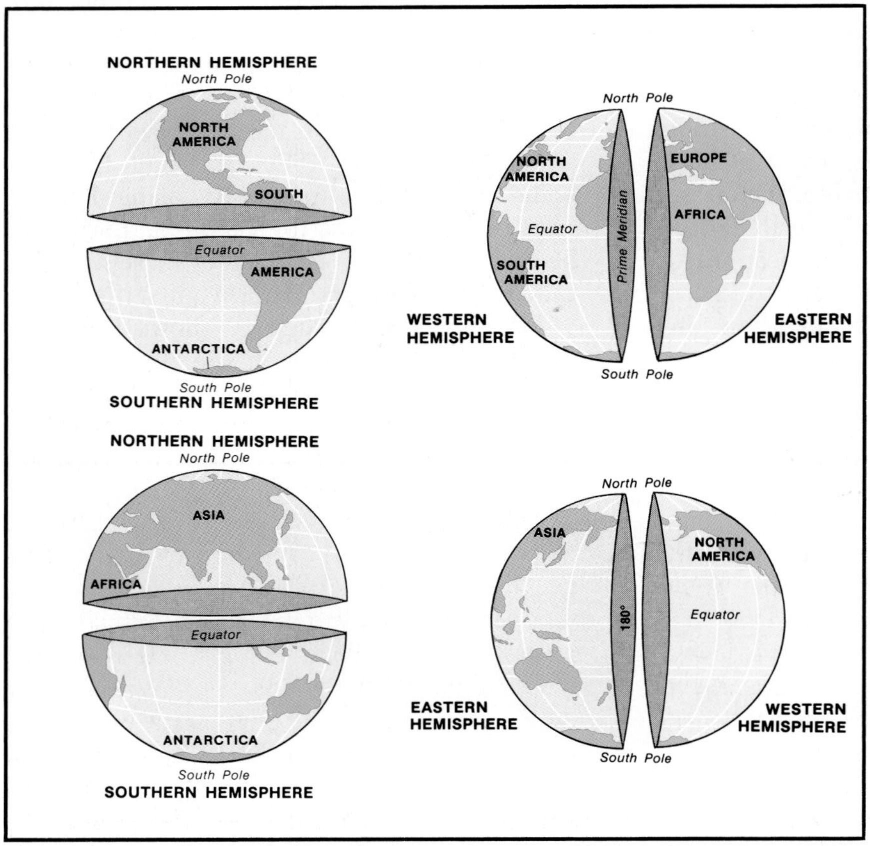

Geographers divide Earth into four different hemispheres to describe the general location of land and water areas. Hemispheres divide the globe into halves—*hemi* means half. In which two hemispheres do you live?

As a creative exercise, have students look at a globe and devise another grid system for locating points on the globe. For example, they might create a system in which an "east pole" and a "west pole" were identified with parallel lines running north to south.

Stress the fact that this book will be presenting the world through different branches of geography. Separate chapters are devoted to maps, climate, population, culture, and urban geography.

A weather satellite above the Pacific Ocean reports a hurricane near Hawaii (*left*). Followers of the Hindu religion bathe in the sacred water of the Ganges River in India (*right*). What kinds of geographers might be interested in each of these pictures?

Many physical geographers have specialized training in science as well as geography. For example, plant geographers with botany training may study the incidence of plant disease in an area with heavy air pollution.

1.2 Ways of Looking at Geography

People interested in finding out different facts about Earth and its people may study different branches of geography. The study of geography is generally divided into the study of physical Earth and the study of human activity on Earth.

Physical Geography. The study of Earth itself, as well as things on Earth not made by people, is called **physical geography.** There are many different branches of this kind of geography. Some physical geographers study landforms, such as mountains and plains. Others study *climate*—the pattern of weather in a place over a long time. This kind of geography is called *climatology.* Others study weather. They deal with temperature, clouds, wind, rain, and snow over a short time. This field of study is called *meteorology.* Still others study oceans. This branch of geography is called *oceanography.*

Another group of physical geographers studies how plant and animal life is distributed on Earth's surface. This field is called *natural geography* or *biogeography.* Some natural geographers study plants. This study is called *plant geography.* Others are interested in what kinds of animals and birds live in different areas. This is called *zoogeography* (ZOH uh jee AHG ruh fee).

Human Geography. The study of people and their activities within their **environment,** or surroundings, is called **human geography.** Human geographers study the places people live and the ways in which different groups live. These geographers are often called *cultural* or *social geographers.*

The field of human geography also has many different branches. For example, the study of people and places over time is called *historical geography.* The study of population in terms of births, deaths, marriages, and other data is called *demography* (dih MAHG ruh fee). *Economic geography* shows how the

Using Graphic Skills

DESCRIBING EXACT AND RELATIVE LOCATIONS

If you have ever found yourself lost and far away from your neighborhood, it would not have been easy to describe your location to someone else. If you were lost, you would not know your exact location, but you might know your relative location. You might describe this location by telling, for example, what direction you walked from the movie theater and how many blocks you are from the pizza shop on High Street.

Geographers use maps to describe both the exact and relative locations of places on Earth. For example, to describe the exact location of a city, they would first find on the map the line of latitude nearest to the city. Then they would follow this line until it cuts across the nearest line of longitude. The latitude and longitude coordinates together tell them the exact location of a certain place. For example, the exact location of the city of New Orleans, Louisiana, is 30°N, 90°W.

To describe the relative location of a city, geographers would first tell in what hemisphere, continent, and country the city could be found. They would then use cardinal and intermediate directions to tell in what specific part of the country the city is located. For example, the relative location of Oklahoma City, Oklahoma, is in the Western Hemisphere in the southern part of North America in the southwestern United States. The city is northwest of Little Rock, Arkansas, and southwest of Tulsa, Oklahoma.

Study the map on page 13 that shows south central United States. Then answer the questions that follow about the exact and relative locations of cities in that region.

1. What is the exact location of the city of Memphis, Tennessee? Of Charleston, Mississippi? Of Stillwater, Oklahoma?
2. What is the relative location of Dallas, Texas? Of Baton Rouge, Louisiana? Of Mobile, Alabama?
3. **Challenge:** What is the exact location of the city or town in which you live? Use the Atlas in the Appendix of this textbook for help.
4. **Challenge:** What is the relative location of your city or town?

places natural resources are found affect economic activities such as manufacturing and farming. *Political geography* deals with the relationship between an area's government and its physical features. *Urban geography* centers on the growth of cities and the areas around them. It studies how cities began and how they affect people.

These many branches of geography are just different ways of looking at Earth and its people. Many geographers would rather study how all of these ways interrelate in a certain part of the world. Others would rather study about a certain subject. They are interested in how these factors act together to make different patterns on Earth.

In this book attention is given to both physical and human geography. First, the book looks at the physical patterns of Earth such as landscape and climate. Second, it deals with general human patterns such as the growth of cities. Then, it tells about the different areas of the world and how the people in those areas live.

SOUTH CENTRAL UNITED STATES

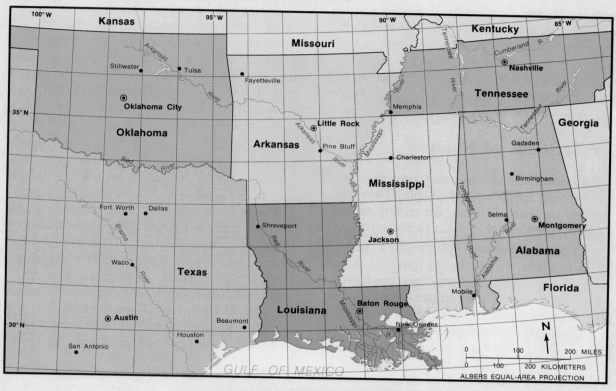

More review questions appear at the end of each chapter. Encourage students, however, to ask questions of their own about geography.

CONTENT CHECK

1. **Define:** geography, spatial interaction, biosphere, lithosphere, hydrosphere, atmosphere, latitude, parallel, longitude, meridian, Equator, Prime Meridian, International Date Line, exact location, relative location, cardinal directions, intermediate directions, hemisphere, continents, physical geography, environment, human geography.

2. For what three reasons do geographers study Earth and its people?

3. What emphasis sets geography apart from other areas of study?

4. How do geographers locate specific places on Earth's surface?

5. Into what two general categories can geography be divided?

6. **Challenge:** What might be two examples of predictions or forecasts about Earth that you think modern geographers may make?

CHAPTER 1   **NATURE OF GEOGRAPHY**

Suggest other subjects that can be investigated using the topical method, such as the distribution of steel mills or the location of sports stadiums.

Have students suggest regions that could be investigated. Have them consider regions they have visited or in which they have lived.

2. THE STUDY OF GEOGRAPHY

Geography is a social science. It is special because it acts as a bridge between science subjects, such as earth science and biology, and other social science subjects, such as psychology and economics. Like other social scientists, geographers have an organized way of studying their subject.

2.1 Methods of Study

Geographers use two methods, or plans, for studying Earth and its people. They may use one or both of these, depending on the kinds of questions they want to answer.

Topical Method. Suppose a person wants to know where lumber mills are found in the United States and why they are located there. To find out, geographers would use a plan of study called the **topical method.**

Using this method, geographers would look at one topic, such as lumber mills. In this case, they would try to discover patterns in the distribution of all lumber mills. They might find that most are found near large forests. Or they might find that more are found in one part of the country than in another.

Any number of topics can be studied by using the topical method. For example, it could be used to find out about the location of roads in a state, in several states, or in a country. It could be used to study in what countries a certain language, such as English, is spoken. No matter what areas of the world come into play, the focus is on one topic.

Regional Method. The **regional method** is used to study an area of the world that can be called a region. A **region** is an area that shows some sort of sameness. This sameness can be the physical look. It also can be the religious beliefs of the people who live there or some other feature common to the people who live in that area. The important point is that an area that forms a region has some things that are alike and some that make the area different from other areas.

Regions are categories. Categories help make better sense out of the world. By divid-

An area served by a major highway system like this one can be studied using the regional method. What plan of study can be used to find out the patterns of highways within large cities in a country?

In this textbook the topical method is followed in Units 1, 2 and 3. The regional method is used in Units 4-10.

ing Earth into regions, geographers can better describe it, explain it, and make predictions about it. By choosing the regional method, they can focus on a certain region to discover how its many features fit together.

Regions can be formed because of a single feature or because of several. An area with the same climate over all of its parts is an example of a single-feature region. An area in which the people share the same language but have different ways of making a living is an example of a multiple-feature region.

Regions can be as large as several countries or as small as part of a city. Their size depends upon the interests and needs of the individual geographer. It is important to remember that there are many ways to divide the world into regions. Not everyone agrees on the best way to do it.

Ask students to name "regions" in and around the school, such as the central office region, the parking lot region, etc.

2.2 Geographic Inquiry

No matter which method geographers use for a certain study, they follow some of the same steps in their work. These steps are (1) observing, (2) classifying, (3) defining, (4) comparing, and (5) generalizing. These are known as the steps of geographic inquiry.

Observing. The first step, observing, often means more than just looking at something. It might mean recording, or writing down, what is being observed. It also might mean counting or measuring what is being observed. For example, if a geographer is interested in the animals living in a certain place, he or she might record the number and kinds of animals observed from day to day or month to month. Such work, done directly with the subject under study, is called **fieldwork.**

Classifying. A second step is classifying. This means grouping things that are alike in some way. A geographer may classify kinds of animals into land animals and water ani-

mals or kinds of climates into moist climates and dry climates.

Defining. Once a subject has been classified, it is studied more closely. Certain characteristics of the subject are described, using special terms. This is when the third step, defining, becomes important. In this step, meanings are given to the many different terms used by geographers to describe Earth and its people.

So there is no confusion, different people must use definitions that are alike for things. This is as true for geographic inquiry as it is for everyday life. People who study geography must be able to understand the meaning of general terms such as *city* and *mountain,* as well as more specialized terms such as *megalopolis* and *volcano.*

Comparing. After things have been classified and defined, they can be compared with other things. For example, suppose that a geographer looks at two or three areas of the world and classifies them all as deserts. The next step would be to compare one desert with another to see how they are alike or different.

Generalizing. The last step is generalizing. This means making a statement that describes a relationship or condition between two or more things. Such a statement is called a **generalization.**

Geographers use many generalizations in their studies. One example might be "All mountain areas of the world have few people living in them." Another might be "The climate in mountain areas of the world is colder than that in the plains all around them."

Many generalizations are made only after a great deal of study. After their studies, geographers make generalizations if they see that certain relationships or conditions happen over and over again. Sometimes, however, a geographer will make a guess at a generalization before any studying has been done. In other words, he or she may decide to make

ALEXANDER VON HUMBOLDT

Another important early geographer was Carl Ritter. Ritter and von Humboldt were associates in Germany. Humboldt's interest was in physical geography, while Ritter focused on cultural geography.

Although you may never have heard of the scientist Alexander von Humboldt, he is viewed as a founder of modern geography.

Humboldt was born in 1769 in Berlin, Germany. As a child in school, Humboldt was not very interested in science. But he was interested in nature and lands far from Europe. Humboldt's dream was to travel and learn about Earth. When he was 27, he inherited enough money from his mother to plan his first trip. He prepared by learning how to use scientific instruments such as the sextant and the barometer.

Humboldt's first trip was to the German Alps. There he measured the atmospheric pressure, humidity, and oxygen content of the air in the region. Soon after, Humboldt and a fellow scientist were given permission by the king of Spain to visit colonies in Central and South America. Humboldt wrote to a friend, "I intend to walk from California to Patagonia—what a pleasure." From 1799 to 1804, they traveled more than 6,000 miles (9,656 km)—by foot, horseback, and canoe.

But the journey was not always easy for Humboldt and his companion. In the tropical forests, they lived on ground cacao beans and river water. While in the Andes, Humboldt suffered from mountain sickness. He was the first person to explain that a lack of oxygen causes mountain sickness.

During his travels Humboldt recorded all that he saw. He returned to Europe with data about land, sea, air, plants, animals, seeds, minerals, and mountains. For example, he recorded the daily temperatures and barometric pressure of Mexico and described 60,000 plant specimens. By the time he was 35, his maps, diagrams, and charts had made him famous.

His journeys over, Humboldt settled in Paris to sort through all the data. His goal was to organize and publish the information he had gathered during his travels within three years. Humboldt ended up spending 25 years writing 30 volumes on what he found in America.

Before Humboldt's observations were known, most geographers had studied only the shape of Earth and its regions. Humboldt gave them a new way of studying geography—measuring the land, air, and plants in an area, classifying them, and comparing them with what was in other places. He paid close attention to what happens on Earth and what *makes* it happen—cause-effect relationships. It was Humboldt who gave the world a system of geographic inquiry. Through his work Humboldt broadened geographic study to include all of Earth's life.

1. What were Alexander von Humboldt's interests in science?

2. In what ways did Humboldt change the field of geography?

a generalization first. Then, he or she will go through the other steps of geographic inquiry to see if it is true or needs to be changed. Such a generalization is called a **hypothesis** (hy PAHTH uh suhs). No matter the order in which they are taken, the five basic steps of geographic inquiry help geographers study and better understand Earth and its people.

CONTENT CHECK

1. **Define:** topical method, regional method, region, fieldwork, generalization, hypothesis.

2. For what reasons might a geographer choose the topical method of study? The regional method?

3. What is a single-feature region? A multiple-feature region?

4. What are the five basic steps to geographic inquiry?

5. **Challenge:** Suppose that you decided to study how the location of shopping centers and malls—large and small—in your community influenced the success or failure of individual businesses in those centers or malls. Which method of geographic study would you use? Make a list of the tasks that you would carry out as you follow the five steps of geographic inquiry.

Have students make a list of places they would like to visit or know more about. During the course of their study, allow them time to research these places.

3. THE VALUE OF GEOGRAPHY

Earlier parts of this chapter hinted at the value of studying geography. Because it is the study of Earth and its people, geography helps people to learn more about the place where they live. This means not only their own village, town, or city but also the world

community to which they belong. Such knowledge can be of great value both today and in the future.

3.1 Satisfying Curiosity

Have you ever wondered how the place where you live was first established? Perhaps there is a river that runs near your town. Do you know where the river begins? Do you know where it ends? Did the location of the river lead to the establishment of your town?

Most people are curious about their surroundings. Because geography is about rivers and towns, about how people live, and about any number of other things, studying geography can help to answer many of the questions people might have about their communities. It can help answer such questions as why a community is located where it is, how it has developed over the years, what its major businesses are, and why its houses are built with certain materials. It even can help you decide whether you should carry an umbrella today.

Keep in mind, however, that studying geography also can help to satisfy people's curiosity about faraway places. Nearly everyone likes to travel. One of the reasons is that travel provides people with the opportunity to see new places. When people travel, they want to know about the weather, the physical features, and the people of the area. They want to know about the area's geography.

Of course, people do not have to travel to a place to be curious about it. In today's world, people hear about distant places on television and radio or read about them in newspapers and books almost every day. After hearing the name of a new place, one of the first questions people ask is, "Where is this place located?" Geography can help answer this question. It also can help answer the question "Why should I know about this place?" Geography tells *where* places are located and *why* they are important.

Explain that many geographers work in occupations that contribute to the overall quality of daily life. Invite a city planner to class to explain how geography plays a part in his or her work.

Elicit from students examples of the "shrinking world." Compile a list of items that they have or know of that are from another area of the world.

This meteorologist gathers up-to-the-minute information on weather patterns across the United States. What she learns helps geographers to better understand how climate affects the way people live in different areas of the world. What other types of careers make use of geography skills?

See the *TAE* for an *Objective 5* Activity.

3.2 Developing Career Skills

Another reason the study of geography is so valuable is that it can help people learn the skills needed to find important information on their own. These skills include locating places, following directions, describing regions, and using sources to find geographic facts. By using such skills, people can learn more about Earth and its people.

Even further, however, geography skills can be useful in preparing for later in life. Students of geography can use their training to help them in a number of jobs. You may know of some of these jobs already—jobs such as cartographers and surveyors. There are more careers in geography than just these. They take in everything from city planners, computer specialists, traffic supervisors, and aerial photographers to meteorologists, real estate managers, and park rangers. Learning about geography will also help those who plan to work in other fields. Understanding more about Earth and its people will give a deeper understanding of the world to people in many

careers. All in all, knowing geography can be a valuable tool in preparing for a career.

3.3 Living in a Smaller World

Have you ever heard someone say that the world is getting smaller? This does not mean that the world is changing its size. What it really means is that today it takes less time to travel far distances. Better ways of communication and transportation have brought more people into closer contact with one another. Because of this contact, it has become easier to overcome the problems that distances and differences among people bring about.

One of the important results of today's smaller world is **global interdependence**. This means that people in one part of the world depend on people in other parts of the world for many of the things they need in order to live. The United States, for example, depends on countries throughout the world for certain foods, clothing, and metals, to name only a few. At the same time, other

18

FOUNDATIONS OF GEOGRAPHY UNIT 1

Ask students to bring in examples of environmental problems that demand the attention of people from more than one nation.

Explain the importance of taking careful notes. Point out that human memory is an imperfect guide, and geographic inquiry depends on an accurate record.

countries depend on the United States for such things as food, automobiles, and farm machinery. This idea of interdependence is discussed later in this book. It is important now, however, to think about what it means to the value of geography.

With people around the world in closer contact, it is more important than ever that they know more about one another. This is because living in a smaller world brings both benefits and problems. As people come into closer contact, the danger of conflict becomes greater. The world has only so much land, clean water, oil, wood, and other natural resources. There have been many wars in the past over control of these resources. Unlike in the past, countries in today's world have weapons for war that could be used to end life on Earth. By understanding other countries and their peoples' needs, government leaders can work so there is no conflict and war.

Countries must learn to work together—not only to stop wars before they start, but also to improve the quality of life on Earth. An important part of this is protecting Earth's resources. For example, the biosphere must be protected from permanent damage from pollutants, such as poisonous chemicals, factory wastes, and other such things.

Fish are not the only victims when chemicals are dumped into a river like this one. The drinking water of an entire city can be affected as well. How does pollution affect more than just a single country?

Protecting the environment is not the problem of just a single country. Chemicals dumped into a river might end up flowing through several different countries. Polluted air blows across borders. Protecting the world is every country's problem. The study of geography can help Americans better understand these problems. It can also help Americans understand people in other countries who can help them solve these problems.

Foreign automobiles, such as these sitting on a New Jersey pier, are major items of international trade. What other items are traded between nations?

CONTENT CHECK

1. **Define:** global interdependence.
2. List at least two reasons for studying geography.
3. Why is mastering basic geography skills important in today's world?
4. **Challenge:** How will your study of geography give you a better understanding of global interdependence?

CHAPTER 1   **NATURE OF GEOGRAPHY**

Each chapter ends with a brief conclusion. It provides a wrap-up for the chapter while providing students with ideas for further thought on the subjects discussed in the chapter.

CONCLUSION

Geography is important because it allows us to understand Earth and its people. Geography is more than learning many names and places. It deals with the relationships of people and their environments.

Earth is very large. For this reason, some geographers specialize in one of many fields in order to fully understand some of Earth's features. Others prefer to study all features about one part of the world. Most geographers use similar methods of investigation.

Key ideas such as spatial interaction and location are used by geographers. Their studies help not only to explain Earth but also to forecast what the years to come may bring to its people. By thinking like geographers, students too can better understand Earth.

CHAPTER REVIEW

CHAPTER 1   NATURE OF GEOGRAPHY

Each chapter ends with a CHAPTER REVIEW. The Summary is a wrap-up of the key points of the chapter.

SUMMARY

1. Geography studies Earth, its people, and their relationships and patterns.
2. Geography is different from other areas of study because it gives great importance to place.
3. To locate places on Earth, geographers use lines of latitude and longitude and the directions north, south, east, and west.
4. The study of geography is generally divided into physical geography and human geography.
5. Geographers use two basic plans of study. The topical method focuses on one topic in one or many areas of the world. The regional method allows close study of many topics within one region of the world.
6. Geographers follow the steps of geographic inquiry: observing, classifying, defining, comparing, and generalizing.
7. Geography can satisfy people's curiosity about faraway places. It also helps people learn how to find and understand information about people and places.
8. Global interdependence makes the study of geography necessary and valuable.

REVIEWING VOCABULARY gives students practice in understanding important terms necessary in geography. Answers to the following questions can be found on page T60.

REVIEWING VOCABULARY

Study the groups of terms listed below. Use each group of words in a complete sentence to show what the terms have in common.

1. biosphere, lithosphere, hydrosphere, atmosphere
2. exact location, latitude, longitude
3. relative location, directions, hemisphere
4. parallel, meridian, Equator
5. economic geography, human geography, urban geography, political geography
6. fieldwork, generalization, hypothesis

FOUNDATIONS OF GEOGRAPHY   UNIT 1

REMEMBERING THE FACTS

1. How long does it take for Earth to complete one revolution? One rotation?
2. What is geography?
3. What are the seven continents on Earth?
4. According to most geographers, what two features act as part of the boundary between the two continents in Eurasia?
5. What imaginary line divides the Northern Hemisphere from the Southern Hemisphere?
6. What are two branches of physical geography? Of human geography?
7. What are the five basic steps of geographic inquiry?

UNDERSTANDING THE FACTS

1. What movement of Earth brings about changes in the seasons? Night and day?
2. What information do geographers use to locate places with the grid system?
3. In what hemisphere is a city with the latitude of 35°S? The longitude of 110°E?
4. Would you place Africa in the Eastern or Western Hemisphere? Why?
5. How does human geography differ from physical geography?
6. What method of geographic study would you use to look at how people in a certain area earn a living, spend their free time, and elect their leaders?
7. Why is Alexander von Humboldt considered important to the field of geography?

THINKING CRITICALLY AND CREATIVELY

1. A degree of longitude equals about 69.2 miles (111.4 km) at the Equator. It gradually decreases to no distance at all at the poles. Of what value is this information to geographers? To navigators?
2. What do you think would happen if all geographic study were done by the regional method? What advantages are there in using both methods of geographic study?
3. **Challenge:** Knowing that the biosphere is so thin, what assumptions can you make about it?
4. **Challenge:** How do you suppose navigators located specific places before the grid system used today was established?

REINFORCING GRAPHIC SKILLS

Study the map on page 13. Then answer the questions that follow.

1. What four cities are near the 36° north parallel? The 94° west meridian?
2. What is the exact location of Gadsden?
3. What is the exact location of Pine Bluff?
4. What is the relative location of Austin, Texas? Of Jackson, Mississippi?

CHAPTER 2

Mount St. Helens, in southwestern Washington, erupted in 1980. The eruption blew away a crust about 1,800 feet (548.6 m) thick. Scientists expect more eruptions over the next several years.

Government surveyors on Mount St. Helens in Washington

MAPS

Although maps are the basic tool of geographers, periodically use a globe to orient students to places on Earth.

In this chapter you will learn—

- What kinds of information maps may present.
- How to read a map by using its basic parts.
- How information is gathered for making maps.
- What properties maps may have.
- What are the three basic kinds of map projection.

See the atlas in the Appendix for a map of Romania.

Explain to students that shapes and areas on globes closely match patterns actually found on Earth's surface.

INTRODUCTION

Geographers use many sources of information in their study of Earth. These sources can be thought of as their *tools*. Among these are books, photographs, and maps. Books can tell the stories of people from many countries. They can tell the population of a city or the number of cars owned by the people of a country. Other kinds of *statistics*, or mathematical facts, can also be found in books.

Photographs taken both from the ground and from the air are useful tools. They can show what the land of an area looks like, including such things as the arrangement of buildings and roads.

Of all the tools of the geographer, however, none is more important than maps. One reason maps are so useful is that they show in graphic form many different kinds of information—both simple and complex. Almost any feature on Earth that can be measured or counted can be shown on a map. Maps can be put to a wide variety of uses. They can help geographers learn, record, and analyze information about Earth and its people.

Keep in mind, however, that maps do not copy Earth's features perfectly. Actually, the best model of Earth is a globe. Yet in most cases, maps are more useful than globes. Globes have more disadvantages. For example, with a globe it is impossible to see more than one-half of Earth at any one time. Suppose that a geographer wanted to compare Brazil and Malaysia and needed to look at the two countries at the same time. This would be impossible using a single globe.

Another reason a globe is hard to work with is its size. Most standard globes are about 16 inches (40.6 centimeters) in diameter. On these globes, one inch (2.5 cm) represents about 500 miles (804.7 km).

Suppose that a person wanted to study the country of Romania. Romania is about 425 miles (684 km) wide from east to west. If you were looking on a 16-inch (40.6-cm) globe, Romania would be less than one inch (2.5 cm) wide from east to west. Very little information about Romania could be placed in that small space.

One possible way to fix this would be to make the globe larger in order to show more information. However, a globe large enough to show the details of cities, roads, railroads, or other features would be huge—even larger than most classrooms!

Maps do not have the disadvantages of globes. Using a map, a person can study several areas of Earth at one time. Maps can show a small area, such as Romania, in great detail. They are less costly to make than globes. They can be folded and stored easily. They lie flat and can be carried conveniently from place to place.

1. KINDS OF MAPS

There is almost no limit to the kinds of information that can be shown on maps. Maps can be divided into two broad categories, according to the type of information they show. Not all maps fit easily into one of these categories, and some maps can be placed in both. However, these categories do help provide a better understanding of the information maps may present.

Bring a standard highway map of your state to class. Point out examples of boundaries, county seats, and other general features discussed below.

1.1 General Reference Maps

A large category of maps is **general reference maps.** The purpose of this kind of map is to give the reader general information about an area or place. Such information may include the location of a place, its size, and its distance from other places.

Many general reference maps are political maps. They show the boundaries of political units, such as countries. Often they show the capital of each country. A **capital** is the city that serves as the seat, or the center, of the government.

Sometimes general reference maps also show other kinds of information, such as large cities, highways, and national parks.

Other general reference maps are physical maps. They show such physical features of an area as lakes, rivers, and mountains. Physical maps often show information about elevation. **Elevation** is the distance of land above or below **sea level,** or the position of the land that is level with the surface of a nearby ocean or sea. As shown in Figure 2-1 on this page, elevation may be shown on a map by using different colors. For example, all areas on the map that are between 50 feet (15.2 m) and 99 feet (30.2 m) above sea level are shown in one color. Areas between sea level and 50 feet (15.2 m) are a different color.

ELEVATION AND TOPOGRAPHY

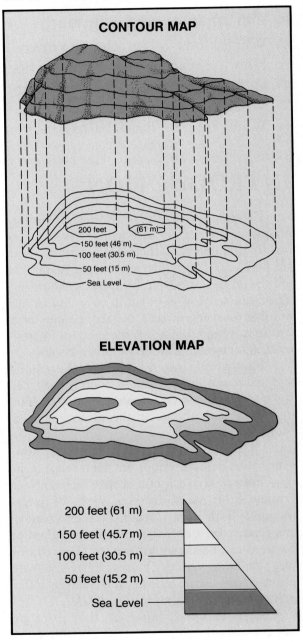

FIGURE 2-1
Contouring is an accurate way to show land shapes on a flat map. On the contour map above, what is the distance between contour lines? On the elevation map, is the brown area higher or lower than the yellow area?

24

FOUNDATIONS OF GEOGRAPHY UNIT 1

While general reference maps are useful for many applications, they often contain too much information that overwhelms some students. Many times it is better to select thematic maps that have fewer details, yet highlight significant features.

This 13-square-mile (33.7-sq-km) area of Dinosaur National Monument in Colorado shows great contrast in relief. What is the shape of land surface when contour lines are drawn close together?

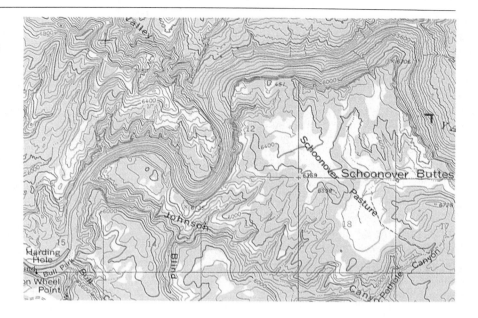

In addition to showing elevation, physical maps may show **relief,** or the difference in elevation between an area's lowest and highest points. Mountainous lands have *high relief* because the land's elevation rises and falls over and over again, making a rugged surface. Gently rolling lands have *low relief* because the land's elevation rises and falls only a little, making a rather flat surface. Relief may be shown on a map with shading. Dark shading may be used to show mountain areas with the highest relief. Lighter shading may be used to show mountains with less relief.

Physical maps may show the land's **topography** (tuh PAHG ruh fee)—the shape of the land's surface including relief and other features made by nature or by people. Topographic maps made in the United States use standard lines, colors, and symbols to show certain physical and cultural features of land. Figure 2-1 also shows contour lines—one of the most important parts of a topographic map. **Contour lines** connect points of equal elevation. To picture the topography of an area, study the space between contour lines.

If the contour lines on a certain part of a map are far apart, it means there is little change in elevation, or the area has low relief. If contour lines on a different part of the map are close together, it means there is great change in elevation, or the area has high relief.

Refer to any of the regional chapters for a sample political map.

1.2 Thematic Maps

A second category of maps is **thematic maps.** These maps show more specific information than general reference maps. Often the information is on a single topic. Thematic maps can show information about many geography topics. These include physical, cultural, historical, economic, and political information. A map showing religions is an example of a thematic map showing cultural information. This kind of map might contain information about the whole world. The areas of the world where people practice one certain religion may be colored on a map with one particular color.

WORLD TIME ZONES

At one time people set their own local time by the sun. When the sun was directly overhead, they set their clocks at 12 o'clock noon, marking "high noon." Because the sun is not directly overhead in all places at the same time, there were hundreds of different times in towns and cities all over Earth. Even places within several miles of each other observed slightly different times.

Having so many different times created problems, especially after transportation and communication improved. For example, travelers who took trains to faraway places had to guess at when they would arrive there.

In 1884 geographers and other scientists at an international conference agreed to set up standard world time zones. They based the new zones on Earth's rotation. Since Earth completes a rotation once every 24 hours, they established 24 time zones—one zone for each hour in a day's time. The scientists drew the boundaries of time zones 15 degrees of longitude apart. They figured this from knowing that Earth rotates 360 degrees in one day. That means that in one hour Earth moves a distance equal to 15 degrees of longitude. They decided that the point of reference for the zones would be the Prime Meridian in Greenwich, England. Each zone was centered around a meridian with 7½ degrees east and 7½ degrees west of it. Most countries in the world agreed to follow this plan.

Under this plan, when a person travels east from Greenwich to the next time zone, the time is one hour later. For example, if it is one o'clock in the afternoon in Greenwich, it is two o'clock in the afternoon in Paris. When a person travels west to the next time zone, it is one hour earlier.

One question remained even after the time zones were set—in what zone should

one calendar day end and the next day begin? The representatives at the conference agreed that the new calendar day should begin at the place where the zones east of Greenwich met the zones west of Greenwich. This place was on the other side of Earth along most of the 180° line of longitude. This line is called the International Date Line. When crossing this

STANDARD TIME ZONES

Data from Defense Mapping Agency, United States Department of Defense

line, a day is gained or lost, depending on the direction of travel. If you were traveling Sunday from Los Angeles, which is east of the line, you would arrive in Tokyo, Japan, Monday after crossing the line heading west. If it is Sunday in Canberra, Australia, it becomes Saturday after crossing the line going east to Lima, Peru.

The time zone lines and the International Date Line do not follow along lines of longitude perfectly. If they did, some cities or small countries might be divided into two time zones. Also some countries of the world have chosen to keep their own time. Despite these variations, travel and communications have benefited from standard time zones.

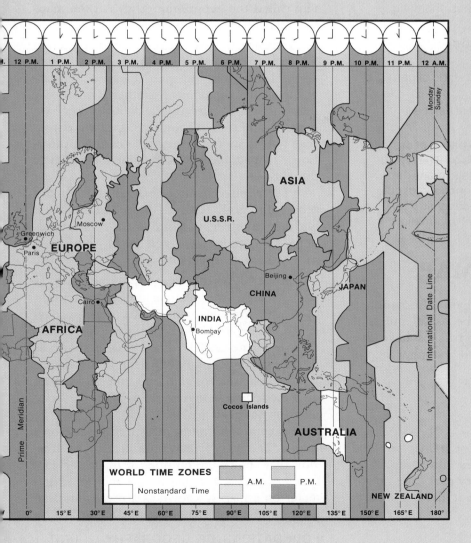

1. Why are the time zones spaced every 15 degrees of longitude apart?

2. For what reason are some time zone boundary lines not straight?

   Study the time zone map to the left. Then answer the questions that follow.

3. If it is noon in Greenwich, what time is it in Moscow? In Chicago?

4. If it is 4:00 PM in Washington, D.C., what time is it in Honolulu?

5. If it is noon Tuesday in São Paulo, Brazil, what day and time is it in Cairo, Egypt?

6. What are two countries that follow nonstandard times?

Another example of a thematic map is one showing *population density*—how closely people live together in a given area of land. Such a map might use dots to represent a number of people. Each dot, for example, may stand for 100,000 people. Areas with high population density would show many dots within a small area of land.

CONTENT CHECK

1. **Define:** general reference maps, capital, elevation, sea level, relief, topography, contour lines, thematic maps.
2. What are the two broad categories of maps?
3. What are two common kinds of general reference maps?
4. What are two ways relief can be shown on a map?
5. **Challenge:** Skim the pages of this book and list the pages on which you find examples of thematic maps that show (a) physical information, (b) cultural information, (c) economic information, and (d) political information.

2. READING MAPS

No matter what kind of information a map presents, it will not be useful unless it can be properly read. Most maps have five basic parts. The first step to reading a map is to study these parts.

2.1 Map Parts

The five basic parts of a map are the title, legend, grid system, direction, and scale. Not all maps use every part. Most maps do, however, use most, if not all, of the parts at one time.

Title. *All* maps should have a title, which tells the reader what the map is about.

Legend. Most maps have a legend, or key. A **legend** is the small boxed area that shows the colors, patterns, or symbols used on a map and explains what they represent. Sometimes, if several maps appear together, there might be one legend for all of the maps.

Grid System. Many maps have a grid system. It is a set of lines used to find the exact locations of places on a map. There are several different grid systems. Most maps, however, use the latitude and longitude system called the **geographic grid.** All the maps in this book use this system.

Direction. Most maps show direction with an arrow that points to the direction of *north*. From this the map reader can figure out the other directions. Another symbol on a map that shows direction is called a **compass rose.** In addition to showing north, a compass rose will show the other three cardinal directions. It may also show the four intermediate directions.

Direction can also be figured from the geographic grid. Latitude lines run east-west but their numbers indicate north-south direction. Longitude lines run north-south but show east-west direction.

Scale. Another important map part is scale. **Scale** is the relationship between a unit of measure on a map and a unit of measure on Earth. Many models of airplanes, cars, and ships are scale models. Their scale is shown as a fraction. A common scale for these models is 1/72. This means that one unit of measure on a model airplane is equal to 72 of the same units on the real airplane.

A common unit of measure for scale on a map is one inch or one centimeter. The fraction that shows the number of inches or centimeters on Earth equal to one inch or centimeter on a map is known as a **representative fraction,** or RF. An example of an RF is

FOUNDATIONS OF GEOGRAPHY   UNIT 1

Ask students to sketch the area surrounding their school. Their maps should have a title, legend, grid system, direction indicator, and scale.

Have students gather around you in a large circle. Place a large map on the floor and a compass beside it. Orient the map with the compass.

1/63,360. This means that one unit of measure, such as an inch or centimeter, on a map is equal to 63,360 units on Earth. It can also be written as a ratio—1:63,360. This RF is frequently used since one mile equals 63,360 inches, or one inch on a map represents 63,360 inches, or one mile, on the ground. Another example is 1/100,000 or 1:100,000.

It is important to know scale in order to measure distances. Most maps show scale with a line divided into several parts. Each part of the line is equal to a certain number of miles or kilometers. This line is called a *bar scale*. Its length can then be used to determine distances on the map. The information presented on the bar scale is sometimes written in sentence form, such as "One inch equals 560 miles" or "One centimeter equals 950 kilometers."

A map can be drawn to many different scales, depending on its purpose. If the purpose of a map is to show a large amount of detail about a small area, a **large-scale map** is drawn. An example of a large-scale map is a map that shows the streets and important buildings of a neighborhood area. The scale for such a map could be one inch to 1,000 feet (2.5 cm to 304.8 m). A **small-scale map** is a map that shows a small amount of detail about a large area. Such a map might show a continent or the world. Its scale might be one inch to 1,500 miles (2.5 cm to 2,414 km).

2.2 Map Orientation

Another step that can be taken to read a map has to do with direction.

Suppose you are walking along a trail in the woods. You have a map showing where a path from the trail leads to a country road. To find the path, you must first **orient**, or position, the map. This means that the map must be turned so that the part of the map indicating a particular direction actually is pointing toward that same direction. Then all the other directions can be found. You will then be able to walk in the right direction to find the path.

A **compass**, a magnetic device for finding north, is useful for orienting a map. In the Northern Hemisphere, the compass will point to the **magnetic north pole.** This is a point that marks Earth's northern magnetic field and is close to the geographic North Pole. Although the two points are not at exactly the same spot, they are close enough to orient maps for general purposes.

To orient a map toward north, you must place the compass directly on the map. The needle on the compass will stop moving when it is pointing north. You should then use the map's north arrow or compass rose to locate the northern areas on the map. When the map is turned toward the north, the map is oriented. You may then determine in what direction to go to reach your destination.

See the *TAE* for an *Objective 2* Activity.

A compass is being used to orient a topographic map. Directions on the map will then agree with directions marked on the compass. How is the map turned once compass direction of north is found?

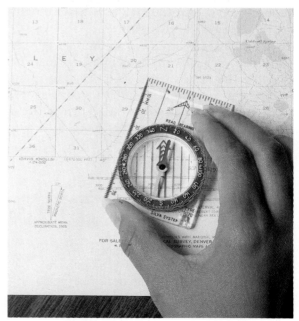

USING GRAPHIC SKILLS

UNDERSTANDING SCALE

The last time you read a road map, did you figure how far you were from your destination? Using the scale on a map will tell you that information. Geographers rely on scale to tell them distances between places nearby and faraway. They understand, however, that on all but the largest-scale maps, using the scale on maps gives only approximate distances.

The accuracy of the distances measured from a scale depends largely on how carefully the map is measured and the measurement is converted to actual miles or kilometers. Students, who usually do not have the special tools geographers use, can measure distances on maps by using the following methods.

To measure the direct distance between two places, place a piece of straight-edged paper on the map below the dots that mark the locations of two places. Carefully make marks on the paper below the dots. Then, below the zero mark on the map's bar scale, place the mark on the left. From the position of the other mark against the scale, calculate the distance between the two places.

To measure distances along road or sidewalk routes, place the paper on the map below the dot that marks your starting point. Follow the route until the road curves or a turn is made on a sidewalk. Then make a mark on the paper. Use this mark as a new

PHOENIX, ARIZONA

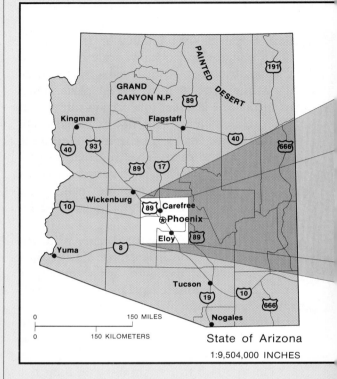

State of Arizona
1:9,504,000 INCHES

starting point. Continue to pivot and mark the paper along the curvy road or sidewalk route until you reach your destination. Make a final mark. Measure the distance between the first and last marks to calculate the actual distance between the two places.

CONTENT CHECK

1. **Define:** legend, geographic grid, compass rose, scale, representative fraction, large-scale map, small- scale map, orient, compass, magnetic north pole.

2. What are the five basic parts of a map?

3. What direction is shown most often on a map?

4. In what two ways can the scale "One inch equals 50,000 inches" be written as representative fractions?

FOUNDATIONS OF GEOGRAPHY UNIT 1

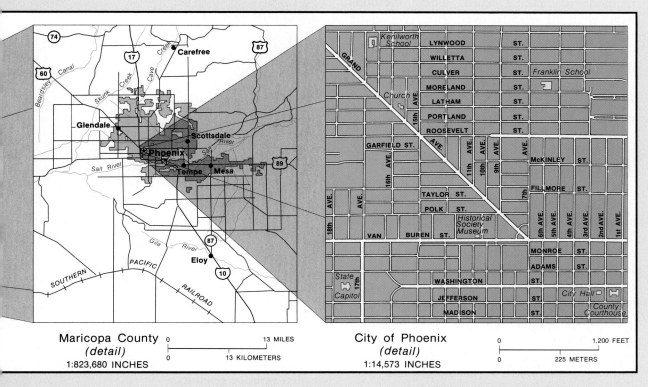

Maricopa County
(detail)
1:823,680 INCHES

0   13 MILES
0   13 KILOMETERS

City of Phoenix
(detail)
1:14,573 INCHES

0   1,200 FEET
0   225 METERS

Study the three maps above. Then use one of the methods described on page 30 to calculate the answers to the questions that follow.

1. According to the state map, what is the direct distance between Phoenix and Tucson? Phoenix and Flagstaff? Phoenix and Yuma?

2. Of three cities shown on the county map—Glendale, Tempe, and Scottsdale—which is by direct distance the closest to the heart of Phoenix?

5. What is the difference between a compass rose and a compass?

6. What directions usually are shown on a compass rose?

7. **Challenge:** Imagine that you were a navigator in an airplane flying across the north polar area. What might you have to consider when trying to chart an accurate flight direction?

8. **Challenge:** How may the general ideas geographers have about an area of the world be different if they study two maps of the area—each drawn at a different scale?

CHAPTER 2   **MAPS**

3. MAKING MAPS

Mapmakers, known as **cartographers** (kahr TAHG ruh fuhrs), use many different methods in making maps. These methods have changed greatly over time, especially with new technology. Today's cartographers, for example, use computers to sort and gather data into three-dimensional maps that appear on color computer screens. No matter what methods are used, however, making maps begins with gathering information.

See the *TRB* for the *Chapter 2 Skill Activity* on analyzing map projections.

3.1 Gathering Information

Cartographers need many people to gather information before a map is drawn. These people may be experts in different fields, such as photography or space science. Each uses special ways to gather information. Among these are surveying, aerial photography, and remote sensing.

Surveying. The oldest way to gather information about the land is surveying. **Surveying** is a method of measuring points and boundaries on Earth's surface. In the past surveyors gathered information by walking over the area they were studying and making drawings of what they saw. Then they drew maps. Today surveyors use mathematics and special tools to measure the land.

Aerial Photography. Another way to gather information for maps is through **aerial photography,** or taking pictures of Earth's surface from the air. Such pictures often are taken from low-flying airplanes or even hot-air balloons. With a picture taken from directly overhead, geographers can study larger areas in greater detail. The use of aerial photography for studying and measuring Earth is **photogrammetry** (FOHT uh GRAM uh tree).

Remote Sensing. Space technology gives cartographers by far the best informa-

This Landsat image shows San Francisco International Airport. Even from such a great distance, space-age technology makes it possible to see jets parked near the terminal. How do remote-sensing cameras work?

tion with which to make maps. As satellites circle Earth, highly sensitive cameras receive images of Earth from great distances. These cameras show images that cannot be seen in regular pictures. This kind of photography is called **remote sensing.**

Remote-sensing cameras work by picking up energy taken in and given off by features on Earth's surface. They change the energy into codes and send signals to computers in receiving stations on Earth. To make an image from the signals, a color is given to each level of energy. The computer then puts the information together into an image of Earth. The best known satellite images have come from five Landsat satellites.

See the *TAE* for an *Objective 3* Activity.

3.2 Problem of Distortion

Once the information to appear on a map is gathered, cartographers must deal with a major problem in making the map. That

The U.S. space-shuttle program has been experimenting with a combination of satellite photography and photogrammetry that might provide a new dimension to mapmaking.

problem centers on the facts that most maps are flat and Earth is a sphere. It is impossible to reproduce exactly on a flat surface an object shaped like a sphere.

To understand this better, think of a rubber ball. Suppose that a person wanted to lay the ball out completely flat. It cannot be done without tearing the ball and stretching it in some places.

There is the same problem in making a map of Earth's surface. In order to put Earth's features onto a map, they must be stretched in some way. This stretching is called **distortion.** Distortion simply means that maps do not represent Earth or its parts perfectly.

Cartographers understand the problem of distortion. They also understand ways to control distortion. By using different map projections, they design maps so there is as little distortion as possible in those areas that are of the most interest to the people using them. No matter how a cartographer makes a map, however, some distortion will remain.

Double-checking for accuracy requires much of a cartographer's time and attention. What four main properties must cartographers consider in making maps?

Point out that because of flat map distortion, Los Angeles looks west of Reno. However, according to its longitude, Reno is farther west than Los Angeles.

3.3 Map Properties

When they make maps, cartographers must consider four main properties, or characteristics of maps. These are (1) the size of the areas shown on a map, (2) the shapes of the areas, (3) consistent scale, and (4) true-compass direction. A map can be drawn so that it is correct in one or more of these properties. However, because of distortion, no map can be correct in all of them.

Equal Areas. One property that maps can have is that of equal areas. In an **equal-area map,** the places shown have the same proportions as they do on Earth. For example, the land area of Greenland is about one-eighth the land area of South America. Therefore, on an equal-area map, Greenland will be one-eighth the size of South America.

Conformality. A second map property is conformality, or having correct shapes. A flat map cannot show very large areas of Earth in their exact shapes. A **conformal map,** however, can show the true shapes of small areas accurately. It also can show larger areas as closely as possible to their true shapes.

Consistent Scale. A **consistent-scale map** uses the same scale for all parts of the map. It consistently shows the true distances between places on Earth. Because of distortion, other maps may show areas wider or longer than they really are. In most cases maps showing large areas cannot be consistent-scale maps.

True-Compass Direction. On a **true-compass direction map,** parallels and meridians appear as straight lines. By following these lines, a person will be following the cardinal directions of north, south, east, and west as correctly as possible. Navigators like to use true-compass direction maps. They know that if they draw a straight line between two points on the map, they can determine the exact direction and set their course.

3.4 Map Projections

What properties a map has depends on how Earth's features are transferred from a globe to a map's flat surface. The process is called **projection.** All maps are projections.

There are many different map projections. Each has a problem with distortion. For this reason, each has only certain map properties. A cartographer chooses a particular projection based on the purpose of the map, the size and location of the area to be shown, and the properties the projection has.

In today's technological world, most projections are made using complicated mathematics. However, the general ideas behind all map projections can be understood by looking at three general kinds of projection.

Cylindrical Projections. The **cylindrical** (suh LIHN drih kuhl) **projection** is most often used for maps of the world. Generally, it can be recognized by its straight lines of latitude and longitude that are perpendicular.

The idea behind the cylindrical projection comes from wrapping a cylinder of paper around a globe. A light from inside the globe projects the globe's features onto the paper. Distortion is least where the paper touches the globe. For example, suppose that the paper is wrapped so that it touches the globe at the Equator. The map from this projection would have little distortion near the Equator.

The best known cylindrical projection is the Mercator Projection. It was created in 1569 by Gerardus Mercator, a mapmaker from northwest Europe. It is a conformal and true-compass direction map. Geographers use this map when the shapes of areas or the directions between places are important. But the distortion on the Mercator map makes the size of land and water areas inaccurate. Mercator placed Europe near the center of his map, instead of the Equator, so Europe appears larger than South America. But South America is about twice as large as Europe.

Conic Projections. The **conic** (KAHN ihk) **projection** cannot map the entire world. It is often used to map areas in the middle latitudes. Many geographers consider the **middle latitudes** as those areas of Earth between 30° and 60° north latitude and between 30° and 60° south latitude. Maps of the United States are usually conic projections.

The name conic comes from the idea of wrapping a cone of paper around a globe. The cone touches the globe only along a certain parallel, called a **standard parallel,** where distortion is at its least.

With the help of mathematics, several conic map projections have been made that decrease the distortion along two or more standard parallels. One of the best known is the Lambert Conformal Conical Projection. This map is used when it is important to show the true shapes of areas. Another is the

See the *TAE* for an *Objective 4* Activity.

GREAT CIRCLE

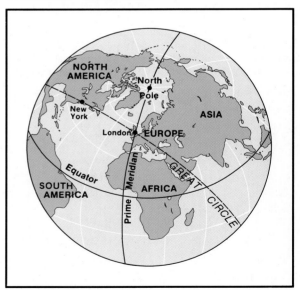

FIGURE 2-2
A great circle is any line that circles the globe and divides it into two equal halves. Any two places at a distance can be connected by a great circle. What does a great circle show between two points on a globe?

34   **FOUNDATIONS OF GEOGRAPHY**   UNIT 1

Use a globe to show students the middle latitudes. Ask students to find other areas, besides the United States, that lie in the middle latitudes.

Point out that airlines sometimes give passengers maps showing airline routes. They often are great circle routes that become stretched and distorted when printed on a two-dimensional map.

GREAT-CIRCLE ROUTE

A great circle route saves fuel costs and travel time for airplanes flying over a great distance. Why does the great circle route appear as a curved line on this map?

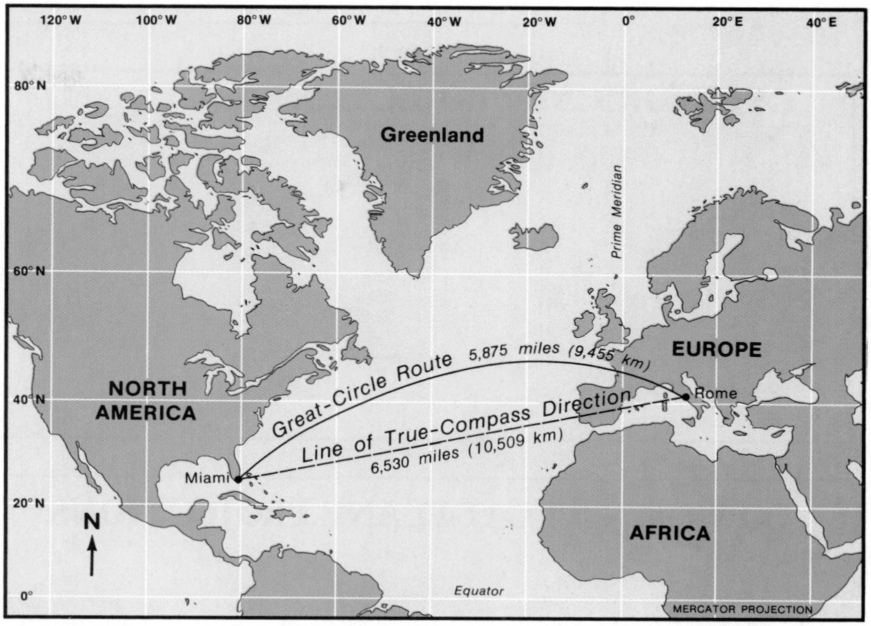

FIGURE 2-3

Have student volunteers research the magnetic north pole. Studies show that the pole has been moving northward about 6 miles (9.7 km) a year.

Albers Equal-Area Conical Projection. It has consistent scale and is used when the size of land and water areas must be accurate.

Flat-Plane Projections. A **flat-plane projection** is used to map the areas of the North and South Poles. The idea behind this projection comes from placing a flat piece of paper against a globe at only one point. Areas near that point show little distortion. The farther away one moves from the point, however, the greater the distortion of area, shape, and scale. This projection can show no more than one-half of Earth at one time. It is also called an **azimuthal projection.**

A flat-plane projection often used for the polar regions is a **gnomonic** (noh MAHN ihk) **projection.** On this projection, circles of latitude lines and straight longitude lines form a wheel-like pattern. A gnomonic projection is especially useful to navigators because the shortest distance between two places on the map is found by drawing a straight line between them. This line is actually a part of a **great circle,** any imaginary line that circles Earth and divides it into two equal parts. An example is shown in Figure 2-2 on page 34.

Great circles can best be understood by thinking of a globe. The shortest distance between two places on a globe can be found by stretching a string from one point to another. If the string were extended to wrap around the globe, it would make a great circle.

Because of distortion, most maps do not show great circles as straight lines. For example, a Mercator Projection is shown in Figure 2-3 above. From it navigators can find the true-compass direction to travel between Miami, Florida, and Rome, Italy. But drawing a straight line between the two places on the map will not tell them the shortest route. On the other hand, a gnomonic projection would show the most direct course between the two cities—the route of a great circle. For this reason navigators use gnomonic projections along with true-compass direction maps to make their travel plans.

MAP PROJECTIONS

COMPARING PROJECTIONS

CYLINDRICAL PROJECTION

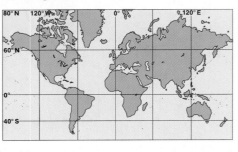

Paper Cylinder

Source of Light

MERCATOR
—true-compass direction
—conformal
—distortion near the poles
—valuable to navigators

CONIC AND FLAT-PLANE PROJECTIONS

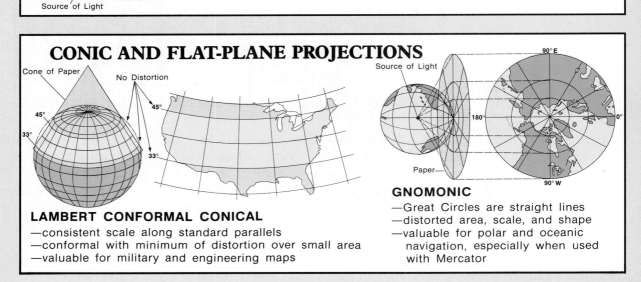

Cone of Paper

No Distortion

Source of Light

Paper

LAMBERT CONFORMAL CONICAL
—consistent scale along standard parallels
—conformal with minimum of distortion over small area
—valuable for military and engineering maps

GNOMONIC
—Great Circles are straight lines
—distorted area, scale, and shape
—valuable for polar and oceanic navigation, especially when used with Mercator

See the *TRB* for the *Section 3 Extending the Lesson* on new technology in mapmaking.

CONTENT CHECK

1. **Define:** cartographers, surveying, aerial photography, photogrammetry, remote sensing, distortion, equal-area map, conformal map, consistent-scale map, true-compass direction map, projection, cylindrical projection, conic projection, middle latitudes, standard parallel, flat-plane projec-tion, azimuthal projection, gnomonic projection, great circle.

2. What are three of the methods used to gather information for mapmaking?

3. What are four properties of maps?

4. Name three kinds of map projections.

5. **Challenge:** What kind of projection might cartographers choose to map the Soviet Union? Antarctica? India?

FOUNDATIONS OF GEOGRAPHY UNIT 1

MODIFIED PROJECTIONS

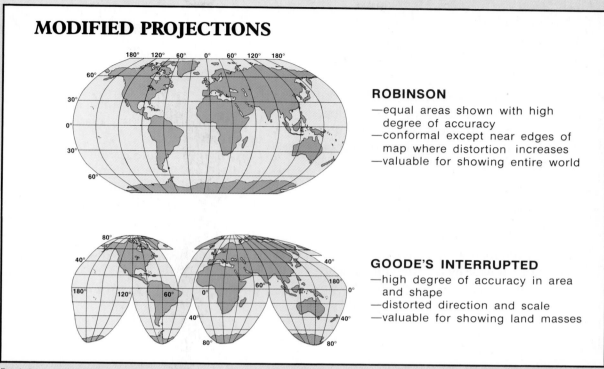

ROBINSON
—equal areas shown with high
  degree of accuracy
—conformal except near edges of
  map where distortion increases
—valuable for showing entire world

GOODE'S INTERRUPTED
—high degree of accuracy in area
  and shape
—distorted direction and scale
—valuable for showing land masses

Permission granted by University of Chicago Press to reproduce Goode's Interrupted Projection from *Mapping* by David Greenhood, copyright 1964.

Each map projection has advantages and disadvantages. The projection one chooses to use depends on the information one wants. For example, a conic projection is best used for showing countries like the United States that extend in an east-west direction. Which map projection would you use to compare the areas of Australia and the United States? Which projection would you use to plot a flight over the North Pole?

CONCLUSION

Geographic study would be impossible without maps. Maps show information in a graphic form that might otherwise take hundreds of words to explain. Geographers use maps to learn, record, and analyze all kinds of geographic information.

Maps contain a great variety of information about Earth and its people. To gather such information, experts rely upon modern technology to see Earth as it really is. To show Earth as correctly as possible, maps are made in many different ways. Because of the problem maps have in showing the round shape of Earth on a flat surface, students must understand maps in order to make the best use of them. Once understood, maps provide students with a solid foundation for their geographic study.

SUMMARY

1. Maps are geographers' main tools.
2. Globes are the best models of Earth, but they have more disadvantages than maps.
3. According to the kind of information they present, most maps are divided into two broad categories—general reference maps and thematic maps.
4. There are five basic parts of a map: (1) title, (2) legend, (3) grid system, (4) direction, and (5) scale.
5. Before reading a map, a person may have to orient the map with a compass.
6. Maps are drawn by cartographers who depend on experts in different fields to gather information through such ways as surveying, aerial photography, and remote sensing.
7. Because most maps are flat and Earth is round, maps have the disadvantage of distortion.
8. Cartographers make use of four different properties of maps to decrease distortion: (1) equal areas, (2) conformality, (3) consistent scale, and (4) true-compass direction. No map can have all of the properties at once.
9. There are three basic types of map projection: (1) cylindrical, (2) conic, and (3) flat-plane.

REVIEWING VOCABULARY

Unscramble the following vocabulary terms so that they are spelled correctly. Then use each word in a sentence that shows its meaning.

1. NDIOSITTOR
2. NIJTRCEOPO
3. TCGHEROPARRA
4. MOTTMOYGREHPAR
5. EDNGEL
6. MASCSPO
7. CASLE
8. ERFIEL
9. OGTRAYHPOP
10. PILATAC
11. LANIEOVTE
12. CONNOMIG

Answers to the following questions can be found on page T68.

REMEMBERING THE FACTS

1. What tools are used to study geography?
2. What information is on physical maps?
3. What place was chosen as the point of reference for the standard time zones?
4. What kind of map gives the reader specific information on a single topic?
5. What are the five basic parts of a map?
6. Which map—a large-scale map or a small-scale map—shows more detailed information about an area?
7. What problem results when globes are made into flat maps?
8. What property of maps shows places in the same proportion as they are on Earth?
9. On maps with what property can navigators draw a straight line between two places and set their direct course?
10. What are three basic types of projection?
11. What is the shortest route between two points on a globe called?

FOUNDATIONS OF GEOGRAPHY   UNIT 1

UNDERSTANDING THE FACTS

1. For what three purposes do geographers use maps?
2. What is the difference between relief and topography?
3. If the RFs of two maps are 1:75,000,000 and 1:63,360, which map is large-scale?
4. In what way can you orient a map?
5. How do cartographers control distortion?
6. What two properties are seen most often in maps of small areas?
7. Where is the least distortion in a cylindrical projection? In a conic projection?
8. What two map properties are most important to navigators? Why?
9. In what careers would topographic maps be used?

THINKING CRITICALLY AND CREATIVELY

1. If a place on a contour map has contour lines that are close to one another, would it be a good location for a wheat farm? Why or why not?
2. What method do you think is used to gather information that helps cartographers draw the exact shape of thousands of miles of coastline? Why would this method be the best to use?
3. Aerial photography was first used for military purposes. During the American Civil War, photographs were taken from balloons of enemy camps. During World War I, early airplanes scanned European forests for the enemy. What benefits do you think came from this information-gathering? What problems do you think it created? What good may the information have served after the wars?
4. Why do you suppose a cartographer would choose a flat-plane projection instead of a cylindrical projection to map the South Pole?
5. The northern tip of Maine is considerably south of the northern borders of Minnesota and North Dakota. This fact is seen easily on a cylindrical projection such as the Mercator, yet on other map projections this does not seem to be the case. How do you explain this?
6. **Challenge:** In what general direction is an airplane moving if it flies from 45° north latitude to 60° north latitude? From 40° west longitude to 10° west longitude?

REINFORCING GRAPHIC SKILLS

Study the maps on pages 30-31. Then answer the questions that follow.

1. The students in two downtown Phoenix schools plan to walk to the Historical Society Museum for a tour. Plan the sidewalk route each should follow. How much farther must the students from Kenilworth School walk than those from Franklin School?
2. Suppose you live in the town of Carefree and are going to drive to a concert in Phoenix. According to the state map, what distance would you travel? According to the county map, what distance would you travel? If the distances differ, how can you account for it?

UNIT REVIEW

SUMMARY

1. Geography is the study of Earth and the people who live on it. It focuses on studying the relationships between groups of people, between places, and between people and places.
2. Geographers are interested in the distribution of people and places on Earth's surface. They study the patterns nature and people make on Earth.
3. Geographers use special methods in their studies. They use a grid system to locate places. They study geography by topic or by region. They follow the same steps of geographic inquiry.
4. Geographers use special tools in their studies. They use books, photographs, globes, and especially maps. Globes best illustrate Earth's features, but they have many disadvantages. Maps are more convenient to use, but they do not illustrate Earth's features perfectly.
5. Maps may have the properties of equal area, conformality, consistent scale, or true-compass direction. No map can have all four properties at the same time.
6. Maps are projections of a round surface onto a flat surface. The problem of distortion can be lessened by using one of several types of map projections. The projection used depends on the purpose of the map and the area of the world shown on the map.

Answers to the following questions can be found on page T71.

THINKING ABOUT THE UNIT

1. Why do you think geography is often called a bridge between science subjects such as biology and social science subjects such as economics? In what ways is geographic study similar to scientific study? To the study of people and their relationships with one another?
2. Turn to the atlas in the Appendix of this book. Point out the five parts of the United States map. Note the projection used for this map and indicate where there is the most and least distortion in this kind of projection. Discuss what properties this map has.

SUGGESTED UNIT ACTIVITIES

1. List any five cities in North America. Using the North America map in the atlas, describe the exact and relative location of each place. Measure the distances, in both miles and kilometers, between your hometown and each of the cities.
2. Obtain old copies of newsmagazines and newspapers. Cut out ten general reference maps and ten thematic maps for display on a bulletin board. Label each, telling what its subject is and the kind of map it is.

DEVELOPING GEOGRAPHY SKILLS

ASKING EFFECTIVE QUESTIONS

An old proverb says that people do not become fools until they stop asking questions. You, as a student, must ask questions throughout your studies to learn even the most general information. A key to learning any kind of information is knowing how to ask questions that serve a specific purpose. Because these kinds of questions will better provide the information you need, they are called *effective questions*.

Asking effective questions cannot be done without preparation. Before you ask the questions, there are four things you must determine: (1) what you want to know; (2) what individuals or written materials you should consult; (3) what questions you should ask; and (4) how you should ask them.

Suppose, for example, that you have been assigned to find out what your classmates think of the food in the school cafeteria. The purpose of your investigation—what you want to know—is student opinion of cafeteria food. From what resource would you be most likely to find out what students think? Students are the *only* source that can give you firsthand information.

Now you can concentrate on what you need to ask. You would learn what you want by asking students what cafeteria foods they like; what foods they would like kept on the menu, added to it, or taken from it; or their general opinions of cafeteria food. For a question to be effective, it should be direct and free of your opinion. There is a large difference, for example, between asking Jennifer if she likes the cafeteria's pizza and asking if she likes "that yucky pizza."

Now you must decide how, or in what form, to ask the questions. Since you are questioning people you see every day at school, you might want to interview students in person. Or you could prepare written questionnaires for your classmates to fill out and return to you.

The same steps used for effective questioning about cafeteria food can also be used in studying geography. Suppose, for example, you were told to prepare an in-class report on how cartographers gather information to make maps. Using the guidelines discussed above, you probably would reason as follows:

1. I want to know what methods cartographers use to gather data, how each method works, and what kinds of information each method can provide.

2. Since I have to do this assignment in class, the best source is my textbook.

3. I should ask questions directly related to what I want to know, such as How many different ways do cartographers gather data? How does each way work? Which way will result in the best maps?

4. Since I am using my book, I can ask myself the questions and write down the answers, or I can write down both the questions and the answers.

As a result of this reasoning, your questions will be effective, and you will be able to use the answers as a basis for your report.

For practice in asking effective questions, use the suggested guidelines to prepare a list of eight effective questions on the following topic: "How the World Feels Smaller Because of Global Interdependence."

PHYSICAL PATTERNS

UNIT 2

Over the surface of Earth, many different patterns have formed. The patterns of land, water, and air in Earth's biosphere are called physical patterns. Land patterns are made from forces within Earth and forces on Earth's surface. These patterns involve Earth's land, soil, and plant and animal life. Water patterns in Earth's landscapes make life possible for all living things. Air patterns within Earth's atmosphere make many different climate conditions all over the world. Studying these physical patterns and the impact people have had on them helps people better understand Earth's life-layer.

Point out that the highlighted areas on the world map inset represent Earth's major mountain ranges.

Montana wheat fields

CHAPTER 3

Badlands landforms in Utah

LANDSCAPES

In this chapter you will learn—

● How forces within Earth and on Earth's surface create landforms.
● How soil is formed.
● What plants and animals live in similar environments.
● How people have changed Earth's land surface.

Landscapes can be thought of as nature's sculpture of Earth's surface.

INTRODUCTION

Most people have heard someone say "the face of the earth" and know that it means Earth's surface. While many people give little thought to what makes up this surface, geographers and students of geography give much thought to it. They need to know what the face of Earth looks like, why it looks that way, and how its appearance affects life.

Most of Earth's surface is made up of water. Only 29 percent of Earth's total surface is land. The lithosphere, or land surface, has a great many different shapes. Nature wrinkles, breaks, warps, and wears the land into many different forms. Through its actions, nature makes natural landscapes. **Landscapes** are the total ways areas look, including their land, soil, plants, and animals.

Soil covers most land surfaces. Without it, nothing could exist. For example, the soil provides plants with nutrients for them to grow. Animals depend on plants or on other animals that eat plants for their food. Thus, all living things need soil to live, and each of these is important to Earth's landscape.

The patterns of landscapes on Earth's surface affect where people live, how people make a living, and where transportation routes are built. So, to understand the relationships between people and places, it is important to study the patterns of landscapes.

Mountains and plateaus would be considered major landforms; deltas and alluvial fans, minor.

1. LANDFORMS

What most people notice first about landscapes is their landforms. **Landforms** are single physical features in landscapes that give the land its general shape and look. Large ones are called *major* landforms. Small ones are called *minor* landforms. Small landforms make up the significant details of landscapes. They give each area of Earth its individual look, just as little details, like the shapes of mouths or lines near eyes, give people individual appearances. It is these small details that make a hilly area of West Virginia look different from a hilly area in Hong Kong.

Landforms are caused by natural forces that shape the land on the surface of Earth. **Geologists** (jee AHL uh juhsts), or scientists who study Earth, have found that two different kinds of natural forces create landforms. One is forces inside Earth. The other is forces on the surface of Earth.

See the TAE for an Objective 1 Activity.

1.1 Forces Inside Earth

Forces inside Earth come from the movement of parts within Earth's structure.

Earth's Structure. Earth is made up of four parts: the crust, mantle, outer core, and inner core. Figure 3-1 on page 46 shows

45

Scientists estimate that oceanic crust can be about 3 miles (4.5 km) thick, while continental crust can be as thick as 22 miles (35.4 km).

Studies indicate that magma temperatures may range from 4,000°F (2,204.4°C) to 9,000°F (4,982°C).

these parts. The **crust** is the outer part of Earth. It is made of rock that is under the ocean floor and under continents.

Beneath the crust and running for nearly 1,800 miles (2,896.8 km) below the surface of Earth is the **mantle**, which is made of very hot solid rock. Below the mantle is the **outer core**, made mostly of molten, or melted, iron and nickel. This metal-rock, called **magma**, is very hot. At the center of Earth, with a diameter of 1,510 miles (2,430.1 km), is the **inner core**. It is thought to be made of very hot solid iron and nickel.

Tectonic Movement. The heat from the outer and inner cores causes rock in the mantle to rise toward the surface of Earth. This creates pressure on the thin crust, which may cause it to rise, fold, or break. Such movement is called **tectonic activity**. Scientists now agree that large pieces of Earth's crust are always moving or shifting. They call the study of tectonic activity **plate tectonics**.

In the diagram, the depth of Earth's crust is greatly exaggerated for illustrative purposes.

EARTH'S STRUCTURE

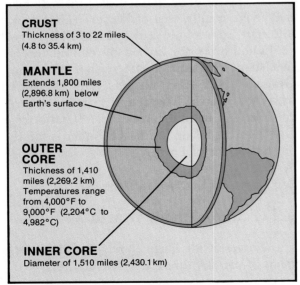

CRUST
Thickness of 3 to 22 miles
(4.8 to 35.4 km)

MANTLE
Extends 1,800 miles
(2,896.8 km) below
Earth's surface

OUTER CORE
Thickness of 1,410
miles (2,269.2 km)
Temperatures range
from 4,000°F to
9,000°F (2,204°C to
4,982°C)

INNER CORE
Diameter of 1,510 miles (2,430.1 km)

FIGURE 3-1
Recent discovery reveals mountains and valleys along Earth's core-mantle boundary. Which layer is deepest?

According to the theory of plate tectonics, Earth's crust is made of rigid plates of rock that move upon a soft part of the mantle next to the crust. In a year's time, the plates can move from one-half inch (1.3 cm) to four inches (10.2 cm).

Of the 14 plates that have been located by scientists, seven are major. The largest of these is made mostly of oceanic crust. The other six are made of both oceanic and continental crust. These plates are shown in the diagram on page 53.

Most tectonic activity happens along the edges of plates. The plates can slide over or under each other, or move away from each other. These movements make landforms on the ocean floor or on continents.

See the *TRB* for *Chapter 3 Reading* on plate tectonics.

1.2 Primary Landforms

Landforms made originally by tectonic activity are called **primary landforms**. These can be large pieces of rock in the crust that may warp or break from the tectonic pressure below and rise above the land surface. Many other primary landforms are **mountains**. Mountains are land features that have elevations of at least 2,000 feet (609.6 m) above sea level, with relief more than 1,000 feet (304.8 m), rather steep slopes, and small *summits*, or tops. There are four different kinds of mountains, each made by different tectonic activity. The four kinds are (1) folded, (2) fault-block, (3) dome, and (4) volcanic. Each is illustrated in Figure 3-2 on page 47.

Folded Mountains. Folded mountains are made when great tectonic forces press against Earth's crust, pushing pieces of it into folds or waves of mountains. Sometimes this folding happens along plate boundaries. At other times, it happens somewhere in the middle of the plate. This depends on how great the pressure is and against what parts of plates it presses. Folding is shown in

PHYSICAL PATTERNS UNIT 2

MAJOR KINDS OF MOUNTAINS

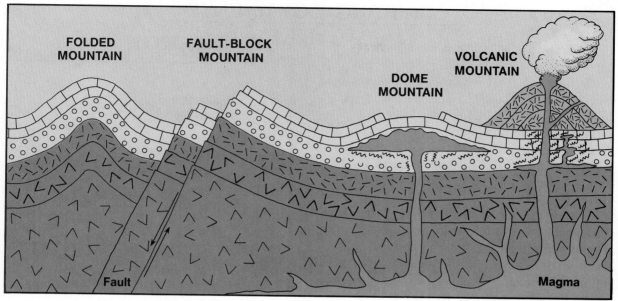

FIGURE 3-2
Tectonic activity creates pressures along Earth's surface, resulting in the formation of mountains. Forces from deep within Earth shape how mountains look. Which North American mountain chain is an example of folded mountains? Which is an example of fault-block mountains?

Humboldt's deep interest in volcanism convinced him that Earth's crust was formed more by volcanic force deep inside Earth than from oceanic deposition, as he had thought earlier.

Figure 3-3 on page 49. The Appalachian Mountains, which stretch from Canada to Birmingham, Alabama, are an example of folded mountains. Many of the world's largest mountain chains are made up mostly of folded mountains.

Fault-block Mountains. **Fault-block mountains** are made when two plates slide past each other and make breaks in Earth's crust. The breaks made by this movement are called *faults*. In many cases, faults become sites of earthquakes. Most earthquakes start along tectonic plate boundaries when plates move, causing vibrations on the surface of Earth on both sides of the fault line.

In some cases the crust at the fault line lifts and slowly tilts from pressures and movements of Earth. This motion forms fault-block mountains with steep slopes, such as the Sierra Nevada of California.

Dome Mountains. **Dome mountains** are made when Earth's crust is pushed up by one plate sliding under another. Sometimes, because of the kind of rock on the surface of Earth, the crust does not crease or fold. Instead, the movement puts pressure on magma in the outer core of Earth, and magma pushes up the rock and forms domes. The Black Hills of South Dakota are dome mountains.

Volcanoes. In other cases, when one plate slides under another, **volcanoes** may form. The movement puts pressure on magma, and it pushes up the rock. If there is a weak part of the mantle, the pressure cracks Earth's crust. As Figure 3-3 shows, magma either flows out slowly or is blown out with explosive force. Magma that has left Earth's core is called **lava**. Lava and ash pile up in layers on the surface of Earth, forming a volcanic mountain.

STRANGE BUT TRUE

DRIFTING CONTINENTS

As strange as it may seem, scientists believe that about 135 million years ago the large landmass that was made up of today's South America and Africa started to split apart. About 70 million years later, the new continents were separated by a new ocean, the South Atlantic. The idea that continents have been moving on the surface of Earth for billions of years is called the theory of *continental drift*.

In 1912 a German scientist, Alfred Wegener, suggested the continental drift theory. He hypothesized that all the continents had been part of one huge landmass about 200 million years ago. Wegener believed that this supercontinent, which he called Pangaea, broke into several pieces that drifted apart and formed the seven continents.

Like English scientist Francis Bacon in the 1600s and American scientist and leader Benjamin Franklin in the 1700s, Wegener wondered why continents on a world map looked like pieces of a large puzzle. He noted that the eastern half of South America looked as though it would fit in the western half of Africa. But other earth scientists pointed out to Wegener that his theory could not be proven by matching coastlines alone.

Through much further research Wegener learned that scientists had found fossils of NASA research shows that Europe and North America are drifting apart ½ inch (1.3 cm) a year.

PANGAEA

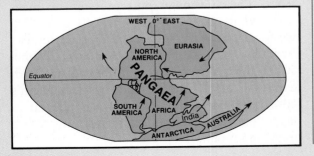

FUTURE EARTH

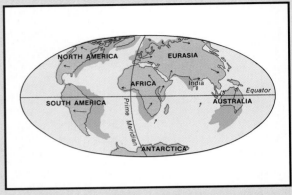

Adapted with permission from "The Breakup of Pangaea," Robert S. Dietz and John C. Holden. Copyright © 1970 by Scientific American, Inc.

similar extinct animals on different continents. Some rocks found in South America and Africa were alike, as were some in North America and Europe. Wegener used these findings to support his idea that these land areas were once connected. However, because he never could explain correctly what energy force moved the continents, there was little support for his theory until the 1960s.

During the 1950s and 1960s, the ocean floor was thoroughly studied. Scientists discovered a series of underwater mountains that made a ring around the edges of the continents. By 1968 their findings were combined with Wegener's continental drift theory into the theory of plate tectonics.

Today scientists interpret signals from satellites to forecast how far continents will have traveled in 50 million years.

1. What is the theory of continental drift?
2. What scientific evidence supported Alfred Wegener's theory?
3. Compare the map of the future Earth above to the world map on pages 646-647. What changes do you see?

TECTONIC MOUNTAIN-BUILDING

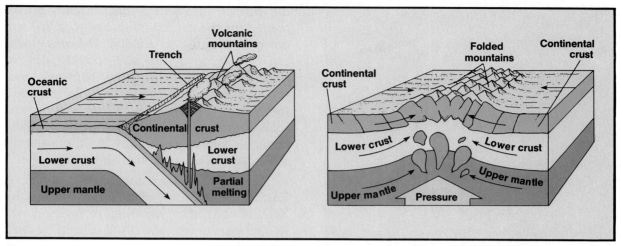

FIGURE 3-3
Pushing on either side of a flat piece of paper simulates the forces that form folded mountains. From which directions do the natural forces come?

See the *TAE* for an *Objective 2* Activity.

1.3 Forces on Earth's Surface

While forces from inside Earth build up the face of Earth, forces on the surface wear down Earth's landscapes. Major landforms, such as mountains and plains, can be worn down into many minor landforms. These forces include weathering, erosion, mass movement, and deposition.

Weathering. The breakdown of rock and soil is called **weathering**. Weathering can take a long time. How fast or slowly it takes place depends on the mineral makeup of the rock and the climate of the area. Air, water, and other substances react with minerals in rock and soil to wear them down.

Weathering comes about because of many actions. For example, water that leaks into or between rocks freezes and swells, causing the rocks to crack or break. Or rocks push or rub against each other, causing some to break into smaller pieces. This kind of weathering happens more often in areas where temperatures change greatly within a day or a season.

Plants and animals can cause weathering. Plants that have taken root between cracks in rocks grow, making the cracks wider and breaking the rocks apart. Burrowing animals can weaken a rock's base and cause it to fall and break into smaller pieces.

Some weathering happens when water mixes with other substances and causes a chemical action that weakens the rocks and makes them fall apart or dissolve. This happens more often in areas where temperatures and rainfall are always high.

Erosion. Another force that changes Earth's landscape is **erosion** (ih ROH zhuhn), the wearing away of Earth's surface through motion. The forces, or agents, of erosion are moving water, wind, moving ice, and gravity.

Moving water is the most persistent agent of erosion. Even one raindrop will change the surface of the soil upon which it falls. Rainwater carries rocks and soil to lower elevations, where they are then deposited in different places on Earth.

In dry areas, wind is the most active agent of erosion. Wind removes such loose

CHAPTER 3 **LANDSCAPES**

49

Relatively small glaciers that are confined to mountain valleys are termed *Alpine glaciers*. On a different scale, *continental glaciers*, or ice sheets, are massive accumulations of ice that are not confined to valleys, but cover a large portion of a landmass. Further coverage on glaciers is on page 78.

Solid rock is no obstacle for this wedged tree root that has split a granite boulder. Weathering forces change landforms over a long period of time. What other forces change Earth's landforms?

While there are thousands of Alpine glaciers on Earth today, there are only two continental glaciers—in Greenland and in Antarctica.

material as soil, leaves, and small rocks from the land surface. As these materials move in the air, they scour landforms and other surfaces, and in time, wear rugged surfaces down to flat ones.

Moving ice erodes land surfaces even more than water and wind. Huge rivers of moving ice, called **glaciers**, form when more snow falls in the winter than melts in the summer. The snow packs down and makes ice. When ice thickens, it becomes heavy. If the ice is on a slope, gravity causes it to move. As the ice moves, it erodes the land by picking up great amounts of rock, soil, and plants that scrape Earth's surface along its route. Glaciers can make lakes and change narrow, V-shaped valleys into wide, U-shaped valleys. A **valley** is a low, level section of land between two higher areas. Glaciers are most often found in areas near the North and South Poles or near the tops of high mountains.

Mass Movement. Another force on the surface of Earth is called **mass movement**. It is the natural motion of rock and soil down slopes due to gravity. The movement can be fast, as in the case of rockslides, or slow. Slow mass movement happens more times than fast. It happens on gentle slopes, for example, whenever rocks and soil become soaked with water. Gravity slowly pulls loose materials farther down hills. As the materials move, they wear away the land surface.

Deposition. Another major force on Earth's surface is **deposition** (dehp uh ZIHSH uhn), the depositing, or laying down, in a new area of rock and soil carried by mass movement and other agents of erosion. Low places in the land are often filled in by deposition. Rock, soil, and other loose materials pile up, layer upon layer, to make minor landforms. A **delta**, for example, is a triangular landform made by deposits of rock and soil carried to a river's mouth by moving wa-

Erosion wears away a Georgia hillside. Rockslides are beginning to fill in furrows that have been carved out by rainfall and loss of soil. How does mass movement act as a force to change land surface?

PHYSICAL PATTERNS UNIT 2

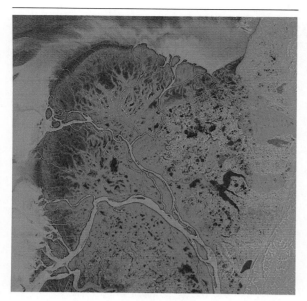

As seen from above, the delta at the mouth of Canada's Yukon River reveals the fan shape characteristic of river deltas. The Nile River in Egypt is another good example of delta deposition. What is deposition?

ter. An **alluvial** (uh LOO vee uhl) **fan** is a cone-shaped deposit of rock and soil carried to the foot of a mountain by moving water.

In most cases, weathering, erosion, mass movement, and deposition act together to tear down the high points and build up the low parts on Earth's surface. These actions cause new landforms to be made.

Ask students to describe the dominant landforms in your area. Are these primary or secondary?

1.4 Secondary Landforms

As soon as tectonic activity builds up primary landforms, forces on Earth's surface begin to wear them down. The landforms made from the wearing down of primary landforms are called **secondary landforms**. These landforms can be large or small. Some of them, as shown in Figure 3-4 on page 54, are plains, plateaus, and hills.

Plains. **Plains** are large areas of mostly level land. Most plains rise gradually to no more than 1,000 feet (304.8 m) above sea level with relief of less than 300 feet (91.4 m). Those with higher elevations are called *high plains*. Plains are often called *lowlands* because of their low elevation and level land.

Plains are found inland and along seacoasts. Those along seacoasts are called *coastal plains*. In some cases, coastal plains have been made by mountain streams depositing rock material into the sea. The seafloor is built up level with the shoreline and makes the land surface wider.

One of the largest plains in the world is the Great Plains of North America, which begins in Canada and runs inland 2,500 miles (4,023.4 km) southward into Texas. It is viewed as a high plains because its *altitude*, or elevation, is from about 2,500 feet (762 m) above sea level along its eastern boundary to about 6,500 feet (1,981.2 m) above sea level along its western boundary at the Rocky Mountains.

See the *TAE* for an *Objective 2* Activity.

An alluvial fan, such as the one in California's Death Valley, is the result of a mountain stream emptying onto a flat plain. Alluvial fans are formed in much the same way as deltas. How are both made?

USING GRAPHIC SKILLS

UNDERSTANDING DIAGRAMS

If you enjoy reading nonfiction books or working with computers, most likely you know what a diagram is. A diagram is a drawing that shows what something looks like or explains how something works. Diagrams are generally not drawn to represent their subjects exactly. Figure 1-3 on page 10, for example, does not show Earth's true size, nor do the map projection diagrams on pages 36-37 show exactly how each projection is done. The facts or ideas about each subject have been simplified to make it easier to understand.

The diagram on page 53 shows where the tectonic plates are located on Earth and where each meets its neighboring plates. The jagged lines of these boundaries represent the rough and uneven edges of Earth's tectonic plates. The arrows in the diagram show in what direction each plate moves. This illustration is considered more of a diagram than a map because the exact boundaries of plates in some areas are not known and not everyone agrees on how many tectonic plates there are.

To understand the theory of plate tectonics from this diagram, you must look carefully at the plate boundaries and the arrows. Since these have been placed on top of a map of the world, it is important to see the relationships of the plate boundaries to the boundaries of the continents.

Study the .diagram. Then answer the questions that follow.

1. What are the names of the seven major tectonic plates? Which is made up mostly of oceanic crust?

2. Locate the plate boundary in North America along which the San Andreas Fault in California is found. In what direction is the plate that includes the southwestern coastal areas of North America moving?

3. **Challenge:** Look at the map of South Asia in the Appendix. Which mountain range is at the same place as the boundary between the Eurasian and Indian-Australian plates?

Another important fertile plains region is the Pampas of Argentina in South America.

A kind of plain made by rock and soil deposits left on the land after a river overflows is a **floodplain**. During a flood, the floodplain becomes a part of the river floor. When high waters go down, some of the materials carried by the river stay in the floodplain, making rich soil for farming.

Plains are found on all continents except Antarctica. Because many plains have good soil, large numbers of people live on them.

Plateaus. Plateaus (pla TOHZ) are large raised areas of level land. They are a unique example of a landform with high relief and flat land. Plateaus may have elevations of less than 300 feet (91.4 m) to more than 3,000 feet (914.4 m) above sea level. They are different from plains in that they generally rise steeply from the land around them on at least one side. The steep cliff on the side of a plateau is called a *scarp*. Because the land is flat, plateaus are sometimes called *tablelands*.

Plateaus are generally close to or surrounded by mountains. Areas with mountains and plateaus are called *highlands* because of their high elevations. The highest plateau in the world is the Plateau of Tibet in Asia,

PHYSICAL PATTERNS   UNIT 2

PLATE TECTONICS

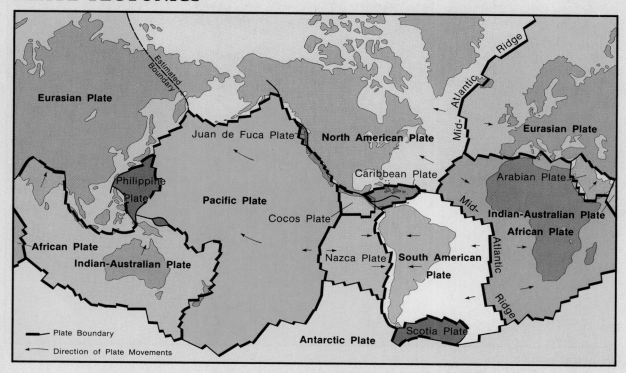

The area of earthquakes and volcanic activity that rings the Pacific Ocean has often been called the "Ring of Fire." Point out that this ring coincides with many of the tectonic plate boundaries. Lead a discussion on why many people choose to live near such boundaries even though earthquakes and volcanoes are likely to occur.

An excellent example of erosion in a plateau is the Grand Canyon in the Colorado Plateau in the western part of the United States.

which borders the Himalayas. Its elevation is about 14,000 feet (4,267.2 m) above sea level.

Some plateaus are formed when erosion wears down volcanic lava. Sometimes a plateau is eroded by streams that cut into the rock, making valleys or **canyons**, deep, narrow valleys with steep sides. There are plateaus on each of the continents. If their altitude is low, plateaus are commonly used for grazing livestock.

Hills. Another group of large secondary landforms is **hills**. Hills have much lower elevation and relief than mountains.

There are two types of hills, constructional and destructional. Hills made from wind and glacial deposits of rock and soil are known as *constructional hills*. Other hills begin as rock material piles up during tectonic activity. Heavy erosion wears down the rock into a hill. These are known as *destructional hills*. There are hills in every area of the world, including Antarctica, where they are mostly covered by ice. Some landforms are called hills but are really mountains. These include the Black Hills of South Dakota and the Naga Hills of India.

LANDFORMS

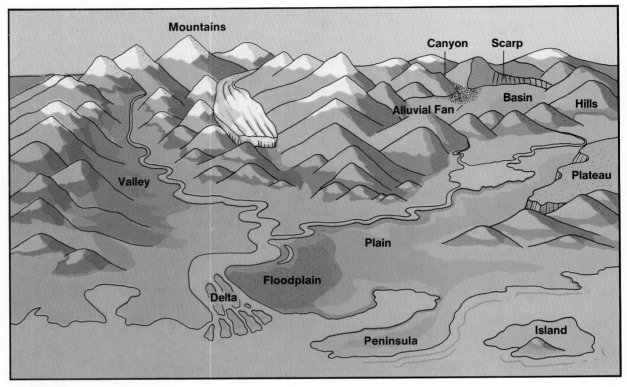

FIGURE 3-4
This diagram pictures an imaginary area that combines all the various landform types into one place. No such place exists on Earth. Which landform features are found where you live?

CONTENT CHECK

1. **Define:** landscapes, landforms, geologists, crust, mantle, outer core, magma, inner core, tectonic activity, plate tectonics, primary landforms, mountains, folded mountains, fault-block mountains, dome mountains, volcanoes, lava, weathering, erosion, glaciers, valley, mass movement, deposition, delta, alluvial fan, secondary landforms, plains, floodplain, plateaus, canyons, hills.

2. What are the two kinds of natural forces that create landforms?

3. What are the four kinds of mountains?

4. What are the four forces on Earth's surface that create secondary landforms?

5. How does a plateau differ from a plain?

6. What are two kinds of hills? How are they formed?

7. **Challenge:** Why do you think geographers and other scientists classify landforms according to their size and also according to how they were made? How would grouping landforms in these two different ways help them study Earth's landscapes more thoroughly?

PHYSICAL PATTERNS   UNIT 2

2. SOIL

Soil supports Earth's cover of plants, from patches of grass to tall forests. Anyone who has seen plowed fields knows that the soil of a plowed field in one area does not always look like the soil of a plowed field in another area. In some places the soil is a rich brown color and feels thick and heavy. In other areas it is shiny black and breaks easily into smaller chunks. In still other areas, it is a light ash color and very sandy.

Differences in soil color point to the fact that there are different kinds of soil. The differences in soil are due to the materials that nature makes to form soil. Yet, even though there are different soil groups, all soil is made of the same basic materials.

See the *TAE* for an *Objective 3* Activity.

2.1 Soil Composition

Soil takes hundreds of years to form. It can be many feet or meters deep or be only a thin layer on top of Earth's rocky crust. About one-half of good soil is rock material, minerals, and *organic matter*—living or dead plants and animals. The other half is made up of spaces that fill with water and air.

Most soil is made up of four layers called **soil horizons.** Each layer can be as thick as several feet or meters to less than an inch or centimeter. Geologists study soil by looking at a cross section that shows each horizon. This is called a **soil profile,** an example of which is shown in Figure 3-5 on this page.

The top layer of soil is called *Horizon O,* for organic. In this layer loose leaves, stems, and other plant parts can be seen. Directly below this layer is *Horizon A.* It is made up chiefly of organic matter called **humus** (HYOO muhs). Humus is made up of dead or decaying animals and plants. The soil in Horizon A is also called *topsoil.*

Below the humus is the third layer, *Horizon B.* This layer is a lighter color than the top layer. It has rock materials that have been carried down from the top layer and weathered pieces of rock material from the two lower layers. The roots of plants also work at this level, releasing chemicals into the soil. From Horizon A, minerals and other chemicals are *leached,* or washed out, by rain. In Horizons A and B, plant roots, worms, and insects help soil form by breaking down humus and rock and making more spaces for water and air to enter.

The fourth layer of soil is *Horizon C.* It is made up of the original rock material from which soil is "born." For this reason, this material is called the **parent material.** It can be

SOIL PROFILE

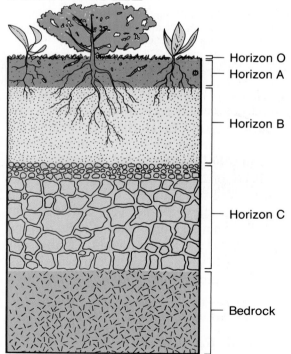

Horizon O
Horizon A

Horizon B

Horizon C

Bedrock

FIGURE 3-5
No two soils have exactly the same profile. Thus, by analyzing the differences in profiles, scientists can identify soil types. Topsoil is in which horizon?

CHAPTER 3   LANDSCAPES

A deep cut in the road gives this soil scientist an opportunity to study the weathering effects of a soil profile. Which five factors work together to form soil?

weathered rocks carried by erosion to the area or **bedrock**—solid rock from the upper part of Earth's crust. In Horizon C, weathering and soil formation are just beginning. Below Horizon C lies bedrock.

Each of the layers helps to determine what kind of soil is made. The chemicals and minerals in the soil also play an important part. The composition of soil tells its *fertility*, or usefulness for growing plants. Some soils are very rich and fertile, while others do not help plants grow at all.

Lead students in a discussion on how forest fires might affect the soil of an area.

2.2 Soil Formation

Five factors within an area's environment work together to make soil. They are (1) parent material, (2) climate, (3) topography, (4) plants and animals, and (5) time. Because each area has a different mix of these factors, there are many kinds of soil on Earth.

Parent Material. Soil begins to form when weathering breaks down parent material. If the original rock material is bedrock, it will take a long time to break down. If the parent material is rocks carried by erosion, breaking-down will already have begun, and soil will form more quickly. The chemical makeup of the original rocks will either help or stop plants from growing in the new soil.

Climate. The most important key to how soil forms in an area is climate. This is because the yearly range in temperatures and the amount of rainfall affect how quickly parent material is broken down or carried away. Water is important to making soil. It helps to wash out chemicals and to wash down rock pieces from one horizon to another. In general, soils form more quickly in warm climates with much rainfall than in colder and drier climates.

Topography. How well soil can form depends on an area's elevation and the slope of the land. If an area is mountainous or hilly, water may drain well, but soil will form poorly. On the other hand, valleys and plains have very deep soils because more water stays in the soil.

Plants and Animals. The growth of plants and the movement of animals through the top layers of soil make soil form faster. They mix the chemicals and move the rock pieces down to lower levels. The remains of plants and animals also make rich, fertile soil.

Time. The length of time needed to make thick layers of soil depends greatly on how the parent material, climate, topography, and plants and animals have worked together. Generally, the longer a soil has been forming, the thicker it becomes. If erosion has interrupted the process, the soil will be much less developed.

CONTENT CHECK

1. **Define:** soil horizons, soil profile, humus, parent material, bedrock.
2. What materials are found in the Horizon O layer of soil? In Horizon A? In Horizon B? In Horizon C?
3. What five factors within an area's environment interact to make soil?
4. **Challenge:** Make a generalization about what conditions make fertile soil.

3. PLANTS AND ANIMALS

Landscapes are made up of more than landforms and soil. They also include the many different kinds of plants and animals that grow and live within Earth's biosphere.

When people look at a landscape, often the first thing they see is plants. Plants are a major source of oxygen people breathe, and they support both animal and human life. If plants disappeared, so would all life.

The distribution of plants in the world is determined by each area's environment. For this reason, plants grow in uneven patterns on the surface of Earth. Geographers study the patterns made by plants and animals in each area all over Earth's surface.

See the *TAE* for an *Objective 4* Activity.

3.1 Plant Communities

Plants, like people, live in communities. A **plant community** is a grouping of plants that need a similar environment to grow. Climate, soil, and landforms play important parts in determining what plants grow in an area. In some plant communities, such as those in hot and wet areas, there are many different kinds of plants. In others, such as those in desert areas, there are fewer kinds. There is a plant community best suited for the environmental conditions of each area on Earth.

As each biome is studied, have students refer to the map of Earth's biomes in Figure 3-6 on page 61.

3.2 Plant and Animal Communities

The plant community growing in a certain area becomes a food source for a community of animals attracted to that area. **Ecologists** (ih KAHL uh juhsts), or scientists who study environment, have found that all over the world in areas with similar climates, certain plant and animal communities live together. Each combined community of plants and animals is called a **biome** (BY ohm).

Each biome is characterized more by its plant life than its animal life. For this reason, scientists have grouped biomes into three general categories—forest, grassland, and dryland. In each kind, a certain plant is most important and there are specific plant and animal communities. Figure 3-6 on page 61 shows many of Earth's biomes.

Forest Biomes. There are four forest biomes. They are tropical rain forests, broadleaf forests, coniferous forests, and shrub forests. Each kind of forest is determined by the major type of trees growing in it.

Tropical rain forests grow in areas near the Equator, where the temperature is hot all year round and it rains nearly every day. Many types of trees grow in rain forests. Many kinds of animals such as monkeys, parrots, butterflies, and snakes can also be found. There are more kinds of plants and animals in tropical rain forests than in all of the other biomes combined. Rain forests are found in Brazil, Puerto Rico, central and western Africa, and southeastern Asia.

Soil in a tropical rain forest is typically infertile. Great masses of plant materials fall to the forest floor where they decay in the hot, humid climate and become a quick and plentiful supply of nutrients to the trees. Destruction of the trees, therefore, means loss of the very source of the soil's fertility.

In recent years population in rain forest regions has grown rapidly. This has led to a need for more living space. Millions of acres or hectares of tropical rain forests have been cut or burned and cleared for housing or farming. The soil, however, in tropical rain forests is not fertile because it is poor in nutrients and very acidic. Clearing rain forests threatens life in this biome. With so much rain and no trees remaining to hold the soil, erosion begins soon after an area is deforested. Within a few years, fields no longer produce crops, and many animals die.

Broadleaf forests are made up of trees with broad leaves, such as oak or maple. In colder climates, broadleaf trees in these forests may be *deciduous* (dih SIHJ uh wuhs). This means their leaves fall off before winter and new ones grow back in warmer seasons. In warmer climates, broadleaf trees will keep their leaves throughout the year. Among other places, broadleaf forests can be found in the eastern United States and in eastern Australia. Some animals found in North American broadleaf forests are deer, squirrels, rabbits, and small birds. Some found in Australian forests are the koala bear and the echidna.

Point out to students that forests cover nearly one-third of Earth's surface.

Autumn color, a sign of winter's approach, paints a patch of broadleaf forest in New York State. Why are the trees pictured here deciduous?

Pine trees cover much of the forestland over the southeast portion of the United States. Why are pines classified as coniferous evergreens?

Coniferous (koh NIHF uh ruhs) **forests** have trees that have needlelike leaves and sometimes bear cones. Two examples are the spruce and pine. Because of the cones, the trees are called *conifers* (KAHN uh fuhrz). They are often known as evergreen trees, because they keep their deep green leaves all year. Coniferous forests in northern regions, such as Canada, Alaska, northern Europe, and the Soviet Union, are called *taiga* (TY guh). Animals in the taiga, such as moose, wolves, bears, and elk, are able to live in very cold climates.

Coniferous forests are also found in such middle-latitude areas as Australia, the western coast of North America, and the southeastern part of the United States. In these forests, animals are somewhat smaller than those in the taiga. They include porcupines, beavers, woodpeckers, and otters.

The forest biome with the smallest trees is the **shrub forest.** This forest is found in areas with warm climates that receive little rainfall, mostly during the coolest season. If there is enough rainfall, small trees, such as the olive, pine, and cork, grow. Otherwise, shrubs and other low-lying plants cover the area. Because the plants are very dry, fires

PHYSICAL PATTERNS UNIT 2

Small trees dot the hillsides along this coastline of Greece. Shrub forests are common in dry warm climates. What is a major danger in this biome?

Grasslands cover about one-fifth of Earth's surface.

often start and spread quickly. For several years after a fire, only grasses grow, and generally it takes 30 years for the plant life to return. Snakes, lizards, and other small animals live in this biome. Shrub forests are found in parts of southern California, Chile, South Africa, and the countries near the Mediterranean Sea.

Grassland Biomes. In addition to the forest biomes, there are two grassland biomes—middle-latitude grasslands and tropical savanna (suh VAN uh). These lie between forests and drylands, where wet and dry climates meet each other. Different combinations of soil and climate support each kind of grassland.

The **middle-latitude grasslands** are in areas where it is hot in summer and cold in winter. If there is enough rain, these grasslands may be *prairies* (PREHR eez), or continuous mats of tall grasses, sometimes as high as three feet (91.4 cm). Because prairies have rich soil, most are used for wheat farming. Some prairie animals are antelopes, coyotes, prairie dogs, foxes, and hawks. Prairies are found in parts of Argentina, Australia, South Africa, and the United States.

In middle-latitude areas that receive less rain, grasslands may be *steppes* (STEHPS). In steppes, the mat of grass is much shorter than prairie grass. In some areas where there is enough rain, wheat and corn are grown successfully. Livestock graze in this kind of grassland. Other steppe animals are wild sheep, hedgehogs, and roe deer. The largest steppe is in central Asia.

The **tropical savanna** is generally found between tropical rain forests and dryland biomes in areas where there is a rainy and a dry season. In the tropical savanna, grasses grow in clumps and sometimes there are palm trees and shrubs. Zebras, lions, rhinoceroses, hyenas, and reptiles are generally found in this biome. Some tropical savannas are found in Venezuela, Thailand, northern Australia, and the Sahel in Africa.

Dryland Biomes. There are two dryland biomes, the climates of which have very different temperatures. The one that is very hot is **desert,** an area of very little rain and scarce plant life. In some deserts, such as the southwestern part of North America, there are widely scattered clumps of grass, small shrubs, and plants such as cactus. In other deserts, such as the Sahara in Africa, there

Because rich grasslands attract agricultural development, much of the world's prairies have been plowed. Prairies are found in which countries?

There is no continuous vegetation cover in desert areas. Yet, deserts seldom lack some kind of plant life. What kinds of animal life are common in the deserts of North America and Africa?

Deserts cover about one-fifth of Earth's surface.

Steppe grassland usually consists of scattered clumps of grass and low-growing shrubs. Too dry for farming, these regions are used for grazing cattle and sheep. What is an example of a dryland biome?

are few or no plants at all. Bobcats, coyotes, owls, spiders, and lizards live in North American deserts. Some desert animals in Africa are gazelles and camels. These plants and animals must be able to store water or survive with very little water.

The other dryland biome is **tundra,** an area where cold temperatures all year round stop plants from growing. While there may be much water in some tundra areas, it is mostly in the form of ice. Tundra is found in both the Arctic region and mountains.

Arctic tundra is found in Greenland and in other areas near the Arctic Ocean in Alaska, Canada, Europe, and the Soviet Union. Few people choose to live in these areas. Because of the cold, there is a layer of soil called **permafrost** under the ground that is permanently frozen. Only when the soil above the permafrost thaws in warmer months can any plants grow. Tundra plants are lichens (LY kuhns), mosses, and small shrubs. Animals of the Arctic tundra are caribou, polar bears, walruses, and snow geese.

Mountainous tundras are found all over the world on mountains with very high alti-

tudes, where the average monthly temperature hardly ever is above 50°F (10°C). This kind of tundra does not have permafrost, and during the warmer months, small flowers may bloom. Among the animals in this kind of tundra are sheep, goats, woodchucks, mountain lions, and yaks.

Extremely cold temperatures, bitter winds, and permafrost create a harsh environment for plants, as seen in this Alaskan tundra. Trees will not grow in this climate. What types of plants grow in the tundra?

PHYSICAL PATTERNS   UNIT 2

EARTH'S BIOMES

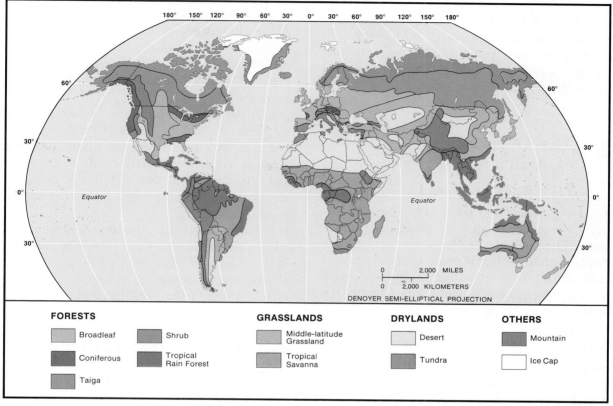

FIGURE 3-6
Earth's biosphere is divided into areas with similar types of plant and animal life. Known as biomes, these areas are controlled by particular climates, which set them apart. Human activity has changed many of Earth's natural biomes. Which biomes are found in the United States?

CONTENT CHECK

1. **Define:** plant community, ecologists, biome, tropical rain forests, broadleaf forests, coniferous forests, shrub forest, middle-latitude grasslands, tropical savanna, desert, tundra, permafrost.

2. What are the three general categories of biomes?

3. Under what condition do trees grow in the shrub forest biome?

4. In which biome do the most kinds of plant and animal life grow?

5. How long does it generally take for plant life to return after a fire?

6. What are differences between prairies and steppes?

7. What must plants and animals do to survive in the desert biome?

8. **Challenge:** Many trees and other plants grow in tropical rain forests, but the soil is viewed as too poor for farming. How can you explain this?

CHAPTER 3   **LANDSCAPES**

61

4. IMPACT OF PEOPLE

For thousands of years, people have changed the landscapes made by forces of nature to suit their needs and desires. For this reason, a full picture of landscapes must include the effects of people.

4.1 The Development of Agriculture

Many thousands of years ago people lived as hunters and gatherers. These people had little effect upon their natural surroundings. Then, about 11,000 years ago, people began to farm. They planted seeds and tamed animals. This is viewed as the first important period when people began to change the world around them.

The first to be affected by human changes to the environment were plants and animals. For people to farm, the land had to be cleared. When trees were cut down and grasses and weeds were killed, some animals did not have the plant life they needed to live. So they moved to other areas or died. Unlike plants and animals, the numbers of people grew as people became more able to raise more food.

After many people chose to make a living by farming the land, large groups of people began to live together in one place. The first farming villages appeared about 8,000 years ago. As the population continued to grow, these villages became small cities that served as trading centers.

Farms and cities became a permanent part of the world landscape. Cities became the first centers of education. Knowledge and abilities grew even more as people began the serious study of the world around them.

See the *TAE* for an *Objective 5* Activity.

4.2 The Industrial Revolution

Beginning in the 1700s, people in England invented machines that helped with many tasks. Steam-driven machines were used to power railroad locomotives and the machines in factories. Large numbers of people were brought together in the factories to make more goods than ever before. These changes spread to other countries in Europe and to the United States. People came to depend more on industry than agriculture. This industrial age that continued to develop into the 1800s is called the Industrial Revolution.

The Industrial Revolution is viewed as the second time period when the ability of people to change natural landscapes was suddenly advanced. For example, factories needed coal and other minerals, which were mined from beneath or on Earth's surface. Sometimes this left the land stripped of any further usefulness for many years. Forests were cut down to provide wood for fuel and

A painting, *The Miners*, shows a bleak picture of people trudging to work against a background of early factories. How did people change natural landscapes during the Industrial Revolution?

building materials. New fields were plowed and crops harvested with new farm machines. Railroads and roads cut through forests and hilly areas to link villages and cities. Forests that covered Europe and the eastern United States were replaced by hundreds of villages, towns, and cities. Many natural landscapes became human-made landscapes.

4.3 The Technological Age

The know-how from the Industrial Revolution exploded into the twentieth century. New scientific knowledge rapidly led to newer and more creative forms of technology. **Technology** is all the ways people use scientific knowledge to make what they need and want. It includes tools, machines, inventions, and special ways of doing things. New sources of power and energy, such as nuclear power, were discovered. Once again, people became even more able to change natural landscapes. Not everyone all over the world, however, has twentieth-century technology.

In industrialized areas technology has helped people gain more control over nature. Yet it presents grave threats to natural landscapes. For example, chemicals used on crops to rid them of destructive insects and animals often have harmful effects on other animals and humans. Nuclear power plants that make needed electrical power also make dangerous radioactive waste that is hard to get rid of safely. In using new technology, industrialized countries also find that they use more energy and make more waste. They need great supplies of wood, coal, and oil, as well as new places to dump wastes.

In some parts of the world, people are afraid that too many changes in natural landscapes will harm their environment. They encourage **conservation,** or the careful use and protection of Earth's resources. For example, farmers conserve land and slow down erosion

by contour plowing, or plowing across rather than up and down sloping fields.

Communities help in conserving land by building sanitary landfills to hold solid wastes and by filling ravines and other low-lying places. With proper treatment, landfills may help make soil. In many places, when forests are cleared, scientists study the effect on the land and plant and animal life.

Today there are few areas of Earth's natural landscapes that have not felt the impact of humans. Even the sides of hills have been cut to form terraces for growing crops. Over time, the human sculpturing of landscapes will change nature's land features.

CONTENT CHECK

1. **Identify:** Industrial Revolution.
2. **Define:** technology, conservation.
3. What development led to the first important period of people changing natural landscapes?
4. What changes took place in natural landscapes as a result of the Industrial Revolution?
5. **Challenge:** Of the many changes people have made to the surface of Earth, which do you think improved the natural landscape?

CONCLUSION

Although landscapes are made by the forces of nature, nature needs time to wrinkle, break, warp, and wear the land into many different forms. It may take a few years or as many as millions of years to change landscapes. Human changes to landscapes, however, have taken place well within the past 11,000 years. With the ever-growing need and use of technology, people will keep on having wide-ranging effects on landscapes.

CHAPTER REVIEW

SUMMARY

1. Landscapes are the total ways regions look, including their land, soil, plants, and animals.
2. The patterns of landscapes affect nearly every aspect of human life.
3. Single physical features in landscapes are called landforms. They can be classified by size.
4. Landforms can also be classified by how they are made. They are the result of forces within Earth and forces on Earth's surface.
5. The four kinds of mountains on Earth are (1) folded, (2) fault-block, (3) dome, and (4) volcanic.
6. Forces that wear down Earth's landscapes are weathering, erosion, mass movement, and deposition.
7. Soil is a combination of rock material, minerals, organic matter, air, and water.
8. The factors that interact to make soil are parent material, climate, topography, plants and animals, and time.
9. The three general categories of biomes are forests, grasslands, and drylands.
10. People have greatly changed the face of Earth. The development of agriculture, the Industrial Revolution, and the technological age have all increased humans' abilities to change natural landscapes.

Answers to the following questions can be found on page T79.

REVIEWING VOCABULARY

Listed below are some of the vocabulary words in this chapter. Head a separate sheet of paper with the words "Landscape Vocabulary." Divide the paper into three columns with the headings "Landforms," "Soil," and "Biomes." Then write each word below under the heading with which it is associated. In a few cases, the word may be associated with two headings.

lava	tundra	permafrost	deposition	fault-block mountains	parent material
humus	erosion	volcanoes	plateaus	tropical savanna	coniferous forests
desert	canyon	glaciers	bedrock	alluvial fan	plate tectonics

REMEMBERING THE FACTS

1. What are the four parts that make up Earth's structure?
2. In a year's time, how far may tectonic plates move?
3. What tectonic activity creates folded mountains?
4. What is the difference between magma and lava?
5. Upon what does the rate of weathering depend?
6. What is the difference between a major landform and a minor landform? What is the difference between a primary landform and a secondary landform?
7. What are four forest biomes? Two grasslands biomes? Two drylands biomes?

UNDERSTANDING THE FACTS

1. What is the theory of plate tectonics?
2. In what ways do plants and animals cause weathering?
3. Under what conditions do glaciers form?
4. How are floodplains and some coastal plains examples of deposition?
5. Why should all hills not be viewed as small mountains?
6. What kind of parent material will form soil more quickly? What kind of climate will form soil more quickly?
7. In which major type of biome is farming common?
8. How have conservation measures kept humans from making harmful changes to Earth's landscapes?

THINKING CRITICALLY AND CREATIVELY

1. If tectonic plates keep moving as far as scientists have learned in recent history, what major changes will happen to the continents 50 million years from now?
2. In some of the world's longest mountain chains, such as the Himalayas in Asia and the Rocky Mountains in North America, more than one kind of mountain can be found. How do you explain this?
3. In which biome type do you live? What plants and animals are commonly found in your area? How would your life be different if you lived in the tundra biome? The tropical rain forest biome?
4. An unknown poet once said, "A people without forests is a dying race." What do you think the poet meant? Do you agree or disagree? Why?
5. **Challenge:** In April 1986 there was a nuclear disaster at the Chernobyl power plant in the Soviet Union. Thirty-one persons were killed, and hundreds were injured. More than 100,000 people in many European countries were exposed to radiation. It was reported that topsoil was scraped up in most of the 1,000 square mile (1,609 sq km) evacuation zone. Horizon A soil was buried as nuclear waste. It was feared that contaminated forests would be burned. What effects may the loss of topsoil cause in the Chernobyl area? How may the landscape in the area change? What steps can be taken by people all over the world to make sure there is not another nuclear accident?

REINFORCING GRAPHIC SKILLS

Study the diagram on page 53. Then answer the questions below.

1. How do plates in the Pacific Ocean differ from plates in the Atlantic Ocean?
2. Earthquakes often happen along plate boundaries. Look at the world map in the atlas of the Appendix to locate the following places where there were earthquakes: Anchorage, Alaska (1964); Luzon, Philippines (1983); and Mexico City, Mexico (1985). Along what two plate boundaries is each located?

CHAPTER 4

Point out to students that, of all the planets in our solar system, only Earth has water.

A flowing woodland stream

WATER AND WATERWAYS

In this chapter you will learn—
- How Earth's water cycle works.
- What changes on Earth are made by the motions of ocean water and tectonic movement below the ocean floor.
- What forms of life and resources are found in the ocean.
- How other waterways change natural landscapes.
- How people have changed water and waterways.

INTRODUCTION

Some geographers call Earth the water planet because almost 71 percent of its surface is water. They call all of Earth's water—oceans, lakes, streams and other bodies of water, underground water, water in the air, ice in glaciers, and snow—the hydrosphere.

Ninety-seven percent of Earth's water is the salt water found in oceans. The other three percent is fresh water, most of which is frozen in glaciers.

Water is necessary for life on Earth. People, plants, and animals cannot survive without water. The human body, for example, is about two-thirds water. Manufacturing and other industries also depend on water.

Although there is plenty of water on Earth, it is not evenly distributed. Some areas never have enough to support life. Other places have enough some years and not enough other years. When some parts of Earth have no rain, other parts may have floods.

Water has helped carve the details of Earth's landforms. Ocean waves, for example, change the shape of shorelines, and streams make plateaus into canyons. Channels and bodies of water—waterways—are important parts of Earth's natural landscapes. The natural patterns made by water and waterways have been changed by human activity. Studying the natural and human-made patterns of water and waterways helps geographers and students of geography understand the many relationships between people and places.

See the *TAE* for an *Objective 1* Activity.

1. WATER

Water is Earth's most valuable and most abundant resource. There are about 326 million cubic miles (1.4 billion cu km) of water on Earth. Water is unique because it is the only substance on Earth that is found in three natural states: liquid, solid, and gas.

Emphasize that the water cycle can begin anywhere in the process (evaporation, condensation, runoff, etc.).

1.1 The Water Cycle

There is about as much water on Earth today as there was millions of years ago. However, most water near Earth's surface is constantly changing its state and location. This process is called the **water cycle.**

The sun begins the cycle when its heat evaporates water from the ocean and other wet surfaces. **Evaporation** is the process by which water changes from liquid to gas. Water as gas is called **water vapor.** When the water condenses, it returns to Earth's surface as rain, snow, hail, or sleet. These forms of water are called **precipitation.** Most precipitation falls on the ocean. The water that falls on land then either evaporates, goes through the

Set up in the classroom a terrarium with a glass cover. (An old aquarium filled with soil, a few plants, and some small rocks makes a good terrarium.) Call students' attention to any condensation of water vapor that may form on the inside of the glass cover. Explain that drops of this water will fall back onto the soil.

WATER CYCLE

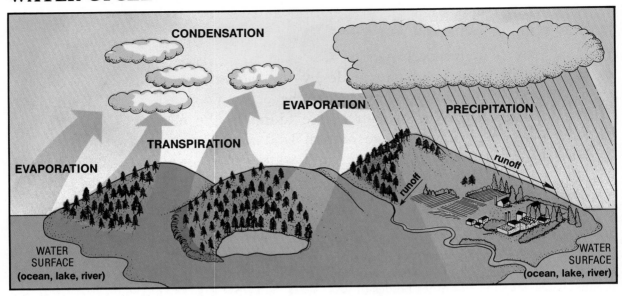

FIGURE 4-1
Between Earth's surface and the atmosphere, water is continually being recycled
from liquid to gas and back again by evaporation, condensation, and precipitation.
What is transpiration?

soil, or drains over land. One way water goes through soil is by being drawn into the roots of plants. This water then moves up the stems and out through the leaves as water vapor. This process is called **transpiration.** In the last stage of the water cycle, water moves back to the ocean or other waterways. Figure 4–1 on this page shows how water moves through the water cycle.

Some aquifers have been used so intensively for irrigation that future supplies have been threatened.

1.2 Groundwater

Another way water moves through soil is by filling spaces between layers of rock. This water is called **groundwater.** Through the force of gravity, it continues to flow down through the layers of rock until it fills all spaces. The body of rocks and soil that holds the water in this zone is called an **aquifer.** The top of the zone is called the **water table,** as shown in Figure 4–2 on page 69. The

water table may be closer to the surface in some places than in others. It even breaks the surface in places, forming swamps, ponds, and springs. Where the water table is close to the surface, wells can be drilled. Springs and wells are sources of water for drinking, industry, and **irrigation,** or bringing water to dry areas by canals or pipes.

If groundwater is taken out faster than nature's water cycle replaces it, the water table drops, and the dry soil and rock layers pack together more closely. This causes a slow sinking of the land, sometimes at a rate of 6 inches (15.2 cm) to 12 inches (30.5 cm) a year. Flooding happens if the sinking takes place along the shore. The foundations of buildings and roads can crack. Sinkholes form when groundwater no longer supports the roofs of underground caverns. In places all over the world, sinkholes suddenly swallow homes, automobiles, highways, forests, and farmland.

PHYSICAL PATTERNS UNIT 2

WATER TABLE

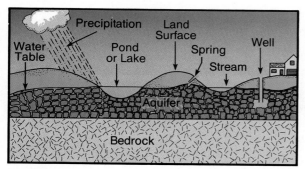

FIGURE 4-2
Aquifers may vary in depth from 200 feet (61 m) to 1,000 feet (304.8 m). What is a water table?

CONTENT CHECK

1. **Define:** water cycle, evaporation, water vapor, precipitation, transpiration, groundwater, aquifer, water table, irrigation.
2. What characteristic of water makes it unique among substances on Earth?
3. How does the water cycle begin?
4. What are two ways in which water travels through soil?
5. **Challenge:** Why do you think there is usually more precipitation along the shoreline than inland?

2. WATERWAYS

Channels and bodies of water are part of Earth's beauty. They are powerful in their shaping of all forms of life and Earth's natural landscapes. In oceans, seas, lakes, and streams all over Earth's surface, there are many kinds of plants and animals that support human life. Waterways have been important in human history. They have helped people build great civilizations and prosper.

On a globe or large world map, point out the locations of Earth's major oceans and seas.

2.1 Oceans and Seas

Earth may be thought of as one large ocean interrupted by areas of land. Continents and other land areas divide the world's ocean into smaller bodies of water. Most geographers study the four largest bodies of salt water as separate oceans. They are the Pacific, Atlantic, Indian, and Arctic (AHRK tihk) oceans. Figure 4–3 on this page compares these oceans.

The meaning of *sea* is not very precise. The term is used both for ocean water in general and also for such bodies of water as the Dead Sea in southwest Asia and the Caspian Sea in Eurasia. These two bodies of water are really saltwater lakes. However, in

EARTH'S LARGEST OCEANS

FIGURE 4–3

The planet Earth might better be called the planet Water. Most of Earth's surface is covered by water, of which 97 percent is found in the oceans. Approximately how much larger is the Pacific Ocean than the Atlantic Ocean?

OCEAN	AREA	AVERAGE DEPTH	DEEPEST POINT
Pacific	63,800,000 sq. mi. (165,242,000 sq. km.)	14,000 ft. (4,267.2 m.)	36,198 ft. (11,033.1 m.)
Atlantic	31,530,000 sq. mi. (81,663,000 sq. km.)	14,000 ft. (4,267.2 m.)	28,374 ft. (8,648.4 m.)
Indian	28,356,000 sq. mi. (73,442,000 sq. km.)	13,000 ft. (3,962.4 m.)	25,344 ft. (7,724.8 m.)
Arctic	3,662,000 sq. mi. (9,485,000 sq. km.)	4,362 ft. (1,329.5 m.)	17,880 ft. (5,449.8 m.)

EARTH'S OCEAN CURRENTS

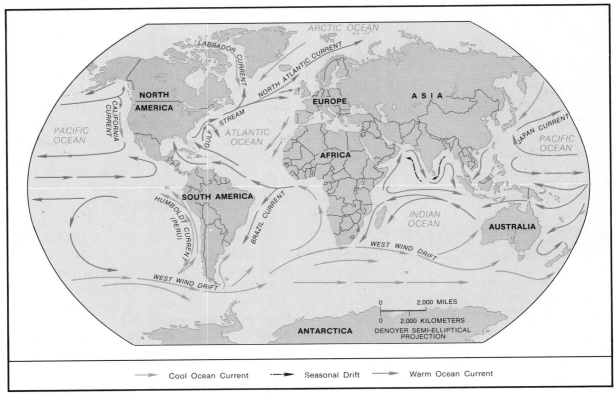

FIGURE 4-4
Ocean currents affect shipping and navigation as well as climates. What sets ocean currents in motion?

Of all the natural elements in ocean water, 85 percent is NaCl—common table salt.

See the *TAE* for an *Objective 2* Activity.

general, **sea** means a large body of salt water that is more or less surrounded by land except for a narrow opening to the ocean. The Mediterranean Sea, between Europe and Africa, is the world's largest sea. Other large seas are the Bering Sea, South China Sea, North Sea, and Caribbean Sea.

Composition of Ocean Water. Ocean water is made up of many substances. Only 96.5 percent is water. Dissolved in the water are nearly all of Earth's natural elements, some in only tiny amounts. Salts make up nearly 3.5 percent of ocean water. The amount of salts is about the same in all areas of the world's ocean because seawater is

mixed well during ocean motions. The salts make it easier to float in the ocean than in fresh water. All the ocean's substances are important because they combine to make the environment needed for ocean life.

Motions of Ocean Water. Ocean water is always moving across Earth's surface, as well as up and down below the surface. Scientists believe that water particles from the deepest parts of the ocean eventually return to the surface within 1,000 to 2,000 years.

Ocean water moves across Earth's surface in currents. They are like huge rivers of water inside the ocean, set in motion by Earth's wind patterns. In general, ocean cur-

PHYSICAL PATTERNS   UNIT 2

Many scientists consider Earth's ocean areas as one world ocean. To facilitate study, it is thought of as four separate oceans.

The sun influences tides. Maximum tides occur when the moon is either between Earth and the sun or on the opposite side of Earth from the sun.

rents move in a clockwise pattern in the Northern Hemisphere and a counterclockwise pattern in the Southern Hemisphere. As Figure 4-4 on page 70 shows, they carry cold water from the poles toward the Equator and warm water from the Equator toward the poles. These currents have a strong influence on the temperatures of land areas. They also are important to ocean transportation, since it is easier and faster for ships to move with the currents than against them.

Ocean water also moves up and down in waves. Only large waves, however, actually move water particles. When a large ocean wave reaches land, the bottom of the wave drags on the ocean floor. The top part pitches forward. These rolling waves, or *breakers*, slap the shore, causing erosion or deposition. Waves are constantly changing landforms close to the ocean. Cliffs are worn away and islands are built up.

Tides are still another example of how ocean water moves. **Tides** are the regular rise and fall of the surface of the ocean. They are caused by the gravitational pull of Earth toward the moon. This pull causes ocean water to bulge on the side nearer the moon and on the other side away from the moon. When this happens, land areas near the two bulges experience high tide, and those between the two bulges have low tide. At high tide the shore is covered with more seawater than it is at low tide. The long, narrow Bay of Fundy, on the eastern coast of Canada, has some of the highest and lowest tides in the world. The difference in water depth there has been as much as 50 feet (15.2 m). This process of high and low tides goes on as Earth spins on its axis. Most places along the shoreline have two high tides and two low tides about every 24 hours.

Topography of the Ocean Floor. At one time scientists thought that the ocean floor was smooth. It is now known that its surface has the same landforms found on land. It is also known that the force of ocean

In spite of its name, the Pacific (meaning peaceful) has violent storms, volcanic eruptions, and earthquakes.

Huge amounts of seawater flow in and out on the tides, as pictured here at the head of the bay in Eagle Harbor, Washington. Regular patterns of high tide (left) and low tide (right) are recorded and reported to people living near coastal areas. Where are some of the highest and lowest tides in the world located?

MAKING AND READING CIRCLE GRAPHS

EARTH'S WATER AND LAND AREAS

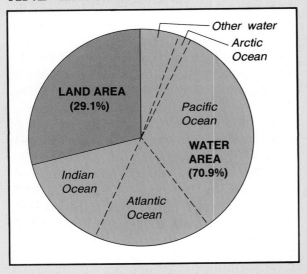

If you have ever tried to slice a pie into equal pieces for your family, you know that dividing a circle into equal parts takes practice and skill. Geographers often use a similar skill in their studies when it is necessary to compare statistics. They use circle graphs, also known as pie charts.

Circle graphs show relationships among parts of a whole. A circle is drawn to represent the total, or 100 percent. The total can then be broken down into parts called degrees. In a circle there are 360 degrees.

Suppose you are asked to show how many students in your school are in each grade. You would follow these steps to make a circle graph:

1. Find the statistics on your school's student population. (*For example, of 1,000 high school students, 200 are freshmen, 250 are sophomores, 300 are juniors, and 250 are seniors.*)

2. Determine what percentage of the total number of students makes up each class.
3. Use a compass to draw a circle.
4. Figure how much of the circle will represent each class by multiplying the percentage for each class by 360 degrees. Then, with a protractor, measure the correct number of degrees in the circle for each class. (*The freshman class represents 25 percent of the total, or 0.25 × 360 degrees = 90 degrees.*)
5. After the number of degrees for each class is figured and each part of the circle is measured, label each part of the circle.

The circle graph shown represents the total area of Earth's surface. The circle is divided into land and water areas. The land area, including all continents and islands, covers about 29.1 percent of the surface. Therefore, the part of the circle representing land area must be 29.1 percent of the circle, or about 105 degrees. Since water covers 70.9 percent of Earth's surface, the part of the circle representing water area is about 255 degrees. In the graph the water section is further divided into the area covered by the four major oceans and the other sources of water in the hydrosphere. Groundwater, streams, lakes, water vapor, precipitation, ice caps, and glaciers are included in the part of the circle labeled "Other Water."

Study the circle graph above. Then answer the questions that follow. It may be necessary to use a protractor.

1. Which two oceans cover about the same area?

2. Into which ocean would the entire land area of Earth's surface fit?

3. **Challenge:** What percent of Earth's total surface area does the Atlantic Ocean cover?

currents and waves carves major landforms on the ocean floor into many minor landforms.

From many shoreline areas, the ocean appears to be shallow. Actually, the continent's land extends into the ocean, sometimes for hundreds of miles or kilometers. This underwater land surface is called the **continental shelf.** If there are mountains near the shoreline, the continental shelf is usually narrow. From the end of the continental shelf, the land slopes underwater to the deep ocean floor. This land is called the **continental slope.** It slopes much more steeply into deep seawater than does the continental shelf.

At the end of the continental slope is a very flat surface called an **abyssal** (AH bihs uhl) **plain.** This is the actual floor of the ocean. With only a few feet or meters of relief, an abyssal plain is the most level plain on Earth's surface. Most abyssal plains are in the Atlantic Ocean and can be between 15,000 feet (4,572 m) and 20,000 feet (6,096 m) be-low the ocean surface. Abyssal plains are covered with *sediment*, or solid material, that has come down through seawater and settled at the bottom of the ocean floor. This sediment comes from soil erosion and the waste and remains of ocean life.

Some changes in the topography of the ocean floor come about because of tectonic activity on Earth's crust below the ocean floor. For example, the ocean floor spreads apart when oceanic plates move away from each other. This is called **seafloor spreading.** Into the opening moves magma from Earth's mantle, which piles up, making a ridge. The top of the ridge has a **rift,** or crack, through which new magma continually passes. As the lava cools, it becomes oceanic crust. Long underwater mountains form, called **midocean ridges.** These are found all over the ocean floor and almost make one long underwater mountain chain more than 40,000 miles (64,373.8 km) long.

The ocean floor contains a great variety of physical features. This is an artist's view of what scientists have learned about the floor of the Atlantic Ocean. Where is the continental shelf located?

TECTONIC MOVEMENT ON THE OCEAN FLOOR

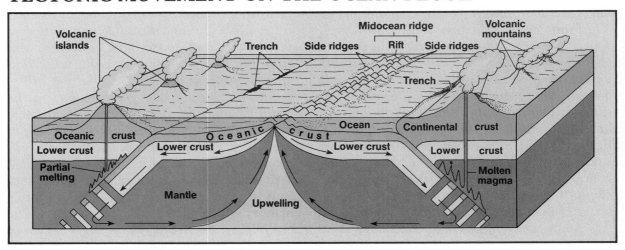

FIGURE 4-5
The same forces shape landforms on Earth's land surface and under the ocean floor. What are the deepest parts of oceans called?

Have volunteers report on such physical features of the ocean floor as mountains, trenches, and seamounts.

When the seafloor spreads, it causes an oceanic plate to hit a nearby plate. When they hit, the heavy oceanic plate goes under a lighter continental plate. As the oceanic plate moves down into the mantle, it makes a **trench,** or ditch, on the ocean floor. Trenches are the deepest parts of the ocean. The deepest trench is more than 6.8 miles (11 km) deep, and near the Marianas Islands in the Pacific Ocean. Figure 4–5 on this page shows how midocean ridges and trenches are made.

Because tectonic movements make great amounts of heat and energy in the mantle, they result in many earthquakes and volcanic eruptions in or near the ocean. This is especially true along midocean ridges and trenches. **Earthquakes** are caused by the shaking of Earth's crust during tectonic movement. The energy earthquakes release, called their *magnitude,* is measured by the Richter scale.

Earthquakes close to shoreline areas pose great danger to people who live there. The movement often forms **tsunami** (su NAHM ee), or seismic sea waves. They may carry huge amounts of water to the shoreline. These waves may reach heights of 50 feet (15.2 m) or more and travel at speeds of 400 miles (643.7 km) to 500 miles (804.7 km) per hour. Although these waves are often called tidal waves, they are not caused by tides.

Volcanoes are usually found near or in the ocean. Where trenches lie near land, volcanic mountains generally have formed close to the shoreline. Eruptions happen when pressure builds up from tectonic movement. On the ocean floor, volcanoes called **seamounts** form on the sides of midocean ridges and along abyssal plains. These seamounts may rise 3,285 feet (1,001.3 m) above the ocean floor. If their peaks rise above sea level, they become volcanic islands, like the Hawaiian Islands in the Pacific Ocean and the Azores in the Atlantic Ocean. Figure 4–6 on page 75 shows the places where volcanoes and earthquakes have been recorded.

Ocean Biomes. Because Earth's surface is covered more by water than by land, there are many more kinds and numbers of

The strength of earthquake vibrations, or seismic waves, is measured on the *Richter* scale. The damage earthquakes make is their intensity, which is measured by the *Mercalli* scale. This scale is based on the amount of earth movement felt by humans and the amount of physical damage caused by the earthquakes.

ZONES OF EARTHQUAKES AND VOLCANOES

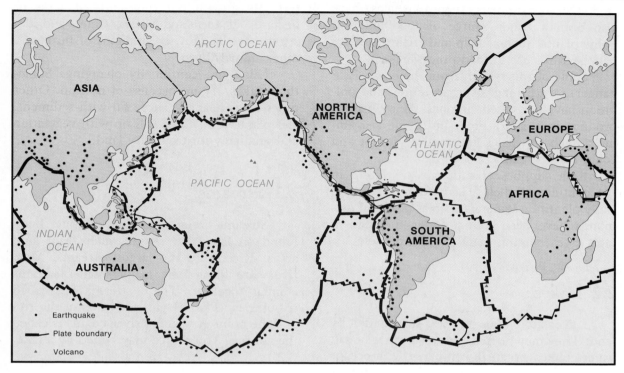

FIGURE 4-6
Most earthquakes occur in a belt, sometimes called the "Ring of Fire," which encircles the Pacific Ocean. What causes earthquakes?

plants and animals that live in the ocean than live in land areas. There are many different ocean biomes because conditions in some parts of the ocean are different from other parts. For example, plants and animals that live near the shore, such as algae, clams, and crabs, are able to live in both air and water. This is because their environment changes at high tide and low tide. On the other hand, in deep waters, plants cannot grow, and animals must be able to live in dark and cold waters.

Much like life on land, life in the ocean needs sunlight and nutrients. Depending on the latitude of the area, some parts of the ocean receive more energy from the sun than other parts. The amount of nutrients depends on the depth of the ocean water. Deep water,

which is thick with sediment, has many more nutrients than surface water. In some areas of the ocean, water from the ocean bottom rises to the top. This can happen when cold surface water sinks and warm bottom water rises. It can also happen when wind makes currents that move surface water. Then, bottom water rises to take its place. This movement of water from the ocean bottom to the top is called **upwelling.** Because their waters attract fish, areas of upwelling have some of Earth's best fisheries.

Resources of the Ocean. All forms of life in the ocean are important to the food chain on which all life depends. When you think of the ocean's resources, you probably think first of all the fish people use for food.

Manganese nodules are scattered throughout the ocean floor. Although the nodules average only about 25 percent manganese, they are attractive for mining because nearly 60 chemical elements have been found in them, including iron, nickel, cobalt, and copper.

Fish are also used as fertilizer and animal feed. Ocean mammals, such as whales, have also been a major source of food and oil. Some plants, such as kelp and Irish moss, are harvested for use in food processing.

Some of this wealth from the ocean is in danger. Overfishing, overharvesting, and pollution have decreased supplies. Many fish reproduce in a short time, but some sea animals, such as whales and turtles, do not and could become extinct.

Rich supplies of minerals are found in the continental shelf. Gas and oil are especially plentiful. Minerals such as gold and diamonds have been found under the sea. In most cases, mining them is too expensive.

See the *TAE* for an *Objective 3* Activity.

2.2 Lakes

Lakes are bodies of water surrounded by land. They may be made of fresh water or salt water. Lakes are small compared with oceans and seas. However, they are important as sources of water for plants, animals, and people.

Those parts of the world once covered by glaciers have the greatest number of lakes. Glaciers cut valleys and basins in Earth's surface. Water then filled the basins, forming lakes. North America has far more lakes than any other continent. The largest are the Great Lakes, which were partly made by glaciers. They are located in north central United States and south central Canada. About 350 miles (563.3 km) long and 160 miles (257.5 km) wide, Lake Superior is the largest of the Great Lakes and the largest body of fresh water in the world.

Water in lakes comes from many different sources. Some comes from streams and underground springs. Other water comes from melting snow on mountaintops. The size of lakes changes with different amounts of precipitation. For example, from 1963 to 1986 the Great Salt Lake in Utah tripled in size because of melting snow from heavy winters. Its growth put thousands of acres or hectares of farmland under water and destroyed wetlands where millions of birds and other animals lived.

Lakes are continually changing. Sometimes lakes dry up because of no rain. Other times areas near the shore fill with sediment, and plants root. Lakes fill up with vegetation and gradually turn into dry land.

2.3 Streams

Streams are another kind of water body found on land that drains water from land areas. Rivers are the largest streams. Most rivers are formed by many smaller streams coming together. These streams are called **tributaries** (TRIHB yuh TEHR eez) of the river. The point at which a river begins is called the **source**. The source may be fed by a lake,

Lakes provide peaceful scenery and excellent fishing. On which continent are most of the world's lakes found?

PHYSICAL PATTERNS   UNIT 2

On a large map of the United States, trace the Mississippi River from its mouth to its source in Minnesota, and identify its major tributaries.

The lakes that ultimately form from loops in an aging river are called *oxbow* lakes, because they resemble a U-shaped collar that fits around an ox's neck.

WATER FORMS

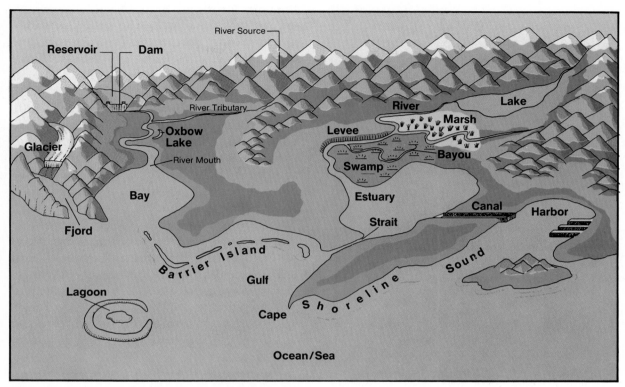

FIGURE 4-7
This diagram shows an imaginary area that combines the various types of waterways into one place. Which waterway features are found where you live?

a spring, melting snow and ice, and rainfall. The point at which a river empties into an ocean or other body of water is called the **mouth.** *Upstream* means moving away from the mouth and toward the source. *Downstream* means moving toward the mouth.

Every continent except Antarctica has important rivers. Most begin in and flow through areas of abundant rainfall. Two exceptions are the Colorado River of North America and the Nile River of Africa. Both begin in highlands where there is sufficient rainfall. However, both flow for much of their lengths through deserts. The Nile is the world's longest river. It flows 4,145 miles (6,670.7 km) from central Africa to its mouth in Egypt at the Mediterranean Sea.

The patterns streams make are constantly changing. Most major changes take a very long time. Young rivers cut deep, narrow valleys upstream. Downstream, their flow is greater, and they widen their valleys. As rivers age, their valleys become broad, flat floodplains. Because the natural patterns of streams are curved, they create loops in their floodplains. Eventually some of the loops may be cut off and become lakes. **Estuaries** (EHS chuh WEHR eez) have formed where some rivers meet the sea. They are deep, broad sections of rivers with water that is part salt water and part fresh water. Estuaries are noted for their many kinds of plants and animals that are suited to live in this special environment. Some of the other patterns and

Alaska's Hubbard Glacier has surged forward, damming up a nearby fjord and turning it into an enclosed lake. What force moves a glacier?

poles. About 98 percent of all glacial ice is in the polar ice sheets. A continental glacier covers most of Antarctica. The rest is in **valley glaciers,** long, narrow bodies of ice that flow downhill from mountains into valleys. There are 200,000 valley glaciers, with 5,000 in Alaska alone.

Most glaciers move slowly, some at 0.01 inch (0.025 cm) per hour. Others may move more than 2 miles (3.2 km) per hour. Gravity is the force that makes glaciers move. Snow and ice become heavy, and glaciers move down slopes. As they move, they scrape rock surfaces and move piles of material.

Scientists who study glaciers are trying to find out how water from glaciers can bring water to Earth's dry areas. They also study how the cold air above the polar ice caps affects climate patterns. And, they are drilling in Antarctica to study Earth's past ice ages and to forecast future changes.

CONTENT CHECK

1. **Identify:** Pacific Ocean, Atlantic Ocean, Indian Ocean, Arctic Ocean, Bay of Fundy, Richter scale, Lake Superior, Nile River.

2. **Define:** sea, tides, continental shelf, continental slope, abyssal plain, sea-floor spreading, rift, midocean ridges, trench, earthquakes, tsunami, sea-mounts, upwelling, lakes, streams, tributaries, source, mouth, estuaries, continental glaciers, valley glaciers.

3. In what three general ways does ocean water move?

4. How do underwater mountains form?

5. What are possible sources of lake water?

6. **Challenge:** In what ways have streams been important to the development of civilization?

forms waterways make are shown in Figure 4–7 on page 77.

Rivers have been important to people throughout human history. Many ancient centers of civilization developed near rivers. They have long been used for transportation. Although they hold only a small part of Earth's fresh water, they provide water for growing cities and for productive farmland. About one-fourth of the world's electrical power comes from hydroelectric plants.

Refer to discussion of glaciers on page 50.

2.4 Glaciers

Huge rivers of moving ice called glaciers cover more than 10 percent of Earth's land surface. Glaciers are an important part of the hydrosphere because they hold 75 percent of Earth's fresh water and 90 percent of all fresh water that is above ground. There are two kinds of glaciers. **Continental glaciers** are wide, thick sheets of ice that cover Earth's

PHYSICAL PATTERNS UNIT 2

Have students prepare a list of local bodies of water and their uses within the community. What impact, if any, have people had on these waterways?

Have students bring in articles on water pollution. Use these as a basis for class discussion, including student suggestions for solving the pollution problems.

3. IMPACT OF PEOPLE

Water and waterways have always been important parts of nature's landscapes. In addition to their beauty, they make great changes over time. Other changes to landscapes and waterways have been due to human activities. Two of the ways people have changed water and waterways is by polluting water and altering waterways.

See the *TAE* for an *Objective 4* Activity.

3.1 Polluting Water

Water becomes polluted when human or industrial wastes are dumped into waterways. It also can happen when chemicals used in farming run into groundwater supplies. For example, during the 1970s, oil spills in the ocean were a major cause of wastewater pollution. These were accidents involving tankers, or ships that carry petroleum. Many beaches were coated with oil and tar, and birds and fish died. Because of rules that have improved tanker safety, there was a decrease in oil spills in the 1980s.

Actually, the open ocean is far less polluted today than other waterways. In fact, most ocean pollution is along coastal areas. In the United States, 1,300 industrial plants and 500 cities send wastewater directly into estuaries and coastal waters. Sewage sludge is dumped into bays. Also, thousands of other pipelines carry wastes to rivers.

Pollution of rivers has long been a problem. For hundreds of years, cities have dumped wastes into streams. In recent years Europe's Rhine River, one of the world's busiest rivers, suffered from a number of chemical spills. The chemicals not only contaminated the river water, which is used by 20 million people in Europe for drinking, but also killed nearly all the river's fish and plant life. Also, chemicals released into the air by

Serious health hazards, caused by human carelessness, threaten waterways worldwide. Besides wastewater pollution, what are other means of polluting waterways?

industrial sources settle into river water. Ridding rivers of chemicals is not easy. Some chemicals stay in the sediment on the river bottom for many years. Dredging the river to get rid of the chemicals creates the problem of where to dump the sediment.

There is also a serious danger of pollution to rivers from another source. Industries cool equipment with water, and power plants heat water to produce steam. When they are finished with this hot wastewater, they empty it into waterways. This is called **thermal pollution.** The wastewater raises water temperature and is harmful to fish and plants.

Many wastes are not dumped into waterways but are put into dumps or buried. These hazardous materials come from industries and other sources. Some have polluted water supplies by seeping into groundwater. After heavy rains, pesticides and fertilizers used in farming move into groundwater. For example, a study of 500 wells in Iowa found that 39 percent of them had pesticides in the water.

FOCUS ON GEOGRAPHY

IRRIGATION

The technology of irrigation has made it possible to grow large quantities of food dependably in one place. Geographers and other scientists have found that if water is easily available in places around the world, it increases the amount of food supplies and the number of people who will live there.

Irrigation relies on great supplies of fresh water from lakes, streams, and groundwater sources. Ideally, water must be available consistently throughout the growing season. Rain should fall all through the year in such a way that water sources stay high enough to fill irrigation wells.

Irrigation also relies on a way to move the water from its source to the farmland. In many cases a system of canals, pipes, and ditches carries the water over many miles or kilometers of land to the fields.

Some of the most suitable areas for irrigation are in Asia. This is because Asia has many of the longest rivers in the world. Their great length allows millions of farmers to tap them for irrigation. These ready sources of water allow repeated use of farmland, and the result is high crop yields. The productivity of these lands helps support Asia's huge population. It is not a coincidence that Asia, with one-half the world's population, has more than two-thirds of the world's irrigated lands.

In many other parts of the world, people have been successful in increasing the amount of irrigated farmland. From 1950 to 1985, for example, the total amount of irrigated land in the world nearly tripled. However, today, there are concerns that irrigated lands are not increasing fast enough to feed the world's growing population. In some places water that could be used for irrigation must be used for homes, industry, or electricity. People in other places have found that large-scale irriga-

tion projects are too expensive. For example, the Soviet Union recently cancelled plans to irrigate lands around the Caspian Sea because it needs to modernize its industries instead.

Although irrigation has helped solve some problems, it has made some new problems as well. The greatest one is that 50 to 70 percent of water used in irrigation is lost through evaporation and transpiration. Also, when water evaporates, it leaves behind salt and other minerals. Some land can no longer be farmed because too much salt has ruined it. The natural course and state of rivers used for irrigation are changed, and their waters sometimes dry up before they reach areas downstream. Strange as it may seem, in some areas irrigation has actually increased the amount of land that is turning into desert. Water tables become too low, and land is overgrazed or overfarmed.

1. What is the relationship among irrigation, food supply, and population?

2. What geographic and economic factors must be considered before an area invests in irrigation projects?

Some modern technologies make pollution worse. Discarded steel cans soon rust in salt water, while plastic containers take many years to disintegrate.

Ecologists and other scientists have found that, in some cases, controlling pollution in one place may simply mean that it shifts to another place or takes another form. Therefore, researchers now are trying to find safer and cleaner raw materials and ways of manufacturing that make less waste.

See the TAE for an Objective 4 Activity.

3.2 Altering Waterways

People have changed the natural state of waterways to suit their needs and desires. For example, the Netherlands has added to its land by draining seawater from certain areas and building dikes to keep the water out. In many other parts of the world, land has been drained for farming and for expanding cities. Large business centers now stand in areas that were once wetlands.

People have changed the natural course of waterways by building canals, dams, and reservoirs. Some canals connect streams in order for boats to go longer distances, while other canals join bodies of water to make shorter routes. Many streams have been dammed so that people could control water for water supply and recreation. Dams and reservoirs also can generate hydroelectric power. However, damming a river in one place changes it miles or kilometers away. Less water flows down the river to its mouth, cutting down the amount of fresh water entering its estuary. Because places downstream have less water and more salt water enters the estuary, plant and animal life is threatened.

Because of human activity, the state of Louisiana has lost one million acres (404,685.6 hectares) of its wetlands since 1900. Today it is losing about 60 square miles (155.4 sq km) each year. These wetlands include marshes and barrier islands that are being worn away by the sea. **Marshes** are areas of soft, wet land, sometimes filled with grasses. **Barrier islands** are strips of land close to

Altering waterways can mean controversy; for example, upstream irrigation is often opposed by people in drier downstream areas.

the mainland that are made of sand and sediment, which protect the shoreline.

For thousands of years in Louisiana, the Mississippi River built up land with sediment. To prevent flooding, people built up ridges, called **levees** (LEHV eez), and channels to control the river. These levees caused sediment to move into the Gulf of Mexico. This led to the erosion of the built-up land, the rising of sea level, and the disappearance over time of the wetlands. These wetlands had at one time provided almost 30 percent of the fish harvest in the United States and a winter home for thousands of migratory birds.

See the TRB for Chapter 4 Reading on the use of waterways.

CONTENT CHECK

1. **Define:** thermal pollution, marshes, barrier islands, levees.

2. In what two general ways does water become polluted?

3. For what purposes do people drain seawater from wetlands? Build canals? Build dams and reservoirs? How do these human activities change the natural state of waterways?

4. **Challenge:** What steps can people take to keep water unpolluted?

CONCLUSION

Water is vital to all life. In addition, water is a great force for changing Earth's surface. Some parts of Earth do not have enough water. Other areas have too much. People have tried to control the supply of water in several ways. There have been some harmful effects on Earth's landscapes from the changes people have made. Efforts are being made to maintain the quantity and quality of water needed for modern life.

SUMMARY

1. There is more water on Earth's surface than land. The water part of Earth's biosphere, the hydrosphere, includes oceans, lakes, streams, groundwater, water vapor, glaciers, and precipitation.
2. Water is the only substance on Earth that is found in three natural states: liquid, solid, and gas.
3. Though it is an important and abundant resource, some places have too little water, and others have too much.
4. Condensed water vapor returns to Earth's surface as precipitation in the form of rain, snow, hail, or sleet.
5. By means of the water cycle, much of Earth's water is constantly changing its state and location.
6. Continents and other land areas divide Earth's large ocean area into smaller bodies of salt water that are studied as separate oceans.
7. Ocean water's motions include currents, waves, and tides.
8. The surface of the ocean floor has the same landforms that are found on land, such as mountains and plains.
9. Because of tectonic activity, the ocean floor is constantly changing. Earthquakes and volcanic eruptions are common in or near the ocean.
10. Oceans, lakes, and rivers all have their own biomes, and all are important to human life. There are many natural resources available in the ocean.
11. As lakes and rivers mature, they undergo natural changes.
12. Glaciers affect Earth's surface and climate, and their effect is under study by geographers and other scientists.
13. Human activities have caused water pollution and many changes in the natural state of waterways.

Answers to the following questions can be found on page T88.

REVIEWING VOCABULARY

Match each numbered definition with the correct lettered vocabulary term.

A. abyssal plain
B. continental shelf
C. earthquake
D. estuary

E. evaporation
F. irrigation
G. precipitation
H. seamounts
I. source

J. thermal pollution
K. tributaries
L. tsunami
M. water table

1. water that falls from the atmosphere
2. changing of water from liquid to vapor
3. flat area of ocean floor
4. top of aquifer
5. underwater extension of continent
6. shaking of Earth's crust
7. bringing water to dry land
8. beginning point of a river
9. changing a waterway by emptying warm water into it
10. deep, broad part of a river where it meets the sea

REMEMBERING THE FACTS

1. What makes up Earth's hydrosphere?
2. In what ways does ocean water move?
3. What are some of the topographic features of the ocean floor?
4. What does the Richter scale measure?
5. What resources are found in the ocean?
6. What are two general ways people have changed water and waterways?

UNDERSTANDING THE FACTS

1. What happens in the water cycle?
2. How do currents affect Earth's climate?
3. How do waves change shorelines?
4. Why do volcanic eruptions occur near ocean trenches?
5. Why is more ocean life found in the continental shelf than in deeper waters?
6. How can a lake die?
7. How have streams played a part in human history?
8. Why are glaciers an important part of the hydrosphere?
9. In what ways has water supply been affected by waste disposal?

THINKING CRITICALLY AND CREATIVELY

1. How can there be about as much water on Earth today as there was millions of years ago?
2. Why is it important that water continues to travel into areas below ground?
3. Aside from military matters, why are countries concerned with controlling ocean waters beyond their coastlines?
4. The world's growing population needs more food. To increase food production, more land is being set aside for farming. Much of this land is being irrigated. What long-range problems may result?
5. Why is losing wetlands a serious loss not only to nature but also to people?
6. **Challenge:** Some rivers flow through several countries, and many rivers are used by more than one city. What regulations would you propose in order to protect the rights of all the places that use a river?
7. **Challenge:** What would be some of the problems involved in using an iceberg broken off from the continental glacier of Antarctica to provide water for Mauritania in northern Africa?

REINFORCING GRAPHIC SKILLS

Study the graph on page 72. Then answer the questions that follow.

1. Which two oceans together cover about the same area as the Atlantic? Which cover about one-half of Earth's surface?
2. According to the graph, what generalization can you make about land and water areas on Earth's surface?

CHAPTER 5

Flashes of lightning during a thunderstorm

CLIMATE

In this chapter you will learn—

- How temperature, moisture, air pressure, and wind produce climate.
- How latitude, heating and cooling differences of land and water, wind patterns, and altitude affect climate.
- What the five major climate groups are.
- How people have changed weather and climate patterns.

INTRODUCTION

All around Earth is a sea of gases called the atmosphere. This is the air part of Earth's biosphere and the most changeable of Earth's environments. This sea of gases protects people from harmful rays and materials from space and holds the air people need for life.

Two gases—nitrogen and oxygen—make up most of the atmosphere. Nitrogen, which makes up about 78 percent, nourishes plant life. Oxygen, which makes up 21 percent, is needed by people to breathe. Other gases, such as argon and carbon dioxide, make up the rest.

The atmosphere is also the source of Earth's weather and climate patterns. Heavy rains, strong winds, cool days, and sunny skies are all common events that change from day to day all over the world. These events are called weather. **Weather** is the condition of the atmosphere at a certain place at any one time. **Climate** means the general kinds of weather a certain place has over a long time. All places in the world can be classified according to their climates.

Climate is important to plant, animal, and human life. Plants and animals can live only in certain climates. Some adapt in special ways. The needle-shaped leaves of conifers, for example, help the trees adjust to cold climates. The short fur of desert animals helps

See the *TAE* for an *Objective 1* Activity.

them to survive hot, dry climates. People also adjust what they wear, the kinds of homes they build, and the kinds of foods they grow.

The needle-shaped leaves of conifers and of many desert cactus plants minimize the amount of leaf surface exposed to extreme effects of harsh climate.

1. ELEMENTS OF CLIMATE

The main elements of climate are (1) temperature, (2) precipitation, (3) air pressure, and (4) wind. Different combinations of these elements make different climates.

1.1 Temperature and Precipitation

Generally when people talk about climate or weather, they are talking about temperature and precipitation. Temperature is the amount of heat found in the atmosphere. Precipitation is the moisture that falls from the atmosphere onto Earth's surface.

Temperature. The heat in the atmosphere comes from the sun. Each day a small amount of the sun's total energy reaches the top layers of Earth's atmosphere. Earth maintains an energy balance so that not all heat energy coming to it remains. In time, the energy held in the atmosphere and in Earth's surface escapes back into space.

In an effort to reduce the level of ozone-threatening chlorofluorocarbons (CFCs), many fast-food restaurants have stopped using plastic foam containers. These containers, along with refrigeration coolants and certain cleaning solvents, are thought to be the primary agents in the destruction of ozone.

GREENHOUSE EFFECT

FIGURE 5-1
Without the greenhouse effect, Earth's surface temperature would be nearly 60 degrees Fahrenheit (33.3 degrees Celsius) lower. Why do scientists fear too much heat in the atmosphere?

Earth's atmosphere acts like the glass roof of a greenhouse. In a greenhouse the sun's rays pass through the glass windows and warm the plants. These rays are short waves of light. On Earth they pass into the soil and ocean water. Those short waves that are reflected back into space change into longer heat waves called **infrared radiation**. They do not easily escape back through the atmosphere. This is because gases in the lower atmosphere, such as carbon dioxide and ozone, take in some of the heat energy and send it back to warm Earth. This natural process, called the **greenhouse effect**, greatly raises the surface temperature of Earth making better conditions for living things to grow in the biosphere. Figure 5-1 on this page shows how the greenhouse effect heats up Earth's surface.

Recently scientists have begun to worry that people are changing the natural greenhouse effect. Since the Industrial Revolution, with more burning of coal, oil, and natural gas, certain gases, especially carbon dioxide, go up into the atmosphere. When trees are cut down, the carbon dioxide they would have taken in is added to the atmosphere. Thus, more heat energy is taken in.

Scientists fear that if too much heat remains in the atmosphere, world temperatures could rise enough to melt parts of the ice caps at the North and South Poles. This would cause oceans to rise and shoreline areas to flood. Because of this, more areas at high alti-

PHYSICAL PATTERNS   UNIT 2

A constant source of water vapor is needed for the formation of hurricanes. A rise of four or five degrees in tropical air temperature may add thousands of tons of moisture to the air over a wide area.

tudes could be farmed, but much farmland at or near sea level would be lost. It would become dangerous for plants and animals that are used to a certain climate. The life-layer would be under great stress.

Precipitation. Moisture that reaches Earth's surface can be rain, snow, sleet, or hail. Moisture can also appear in the air as water vapor. The amount of moisture in the air depends on the temperature of the air. Warm air can hold more water than cold air. The temperature of the air also tells what kind of precipitation will fall. Rain, for example, generally falls during warm weather, while snow falls during cold weather.

Many people say it is "muggy" when the air is sticky with moisture. Muggy is not a scientific word. It really means that the **humidity**, or amount of water vapor in the air, is high. **Relative humidity** is the actual amount of moisture in the air at a certain temperature compared with the amount the air *could* hold at that temperature. If the air is holding only one-fourth of the moisture it could hold at a certain temperature, the relative humidity is 25 percent.

Hurricanes are names given to tropical cyclones near North America. In East Asia they are called typhoons; in India, cyclones; in Australia, willy-willies; and in China, baguios.

Storms are made when huge amounts of energy stored in the water vapor in the atmosphere let go. Fierce storms—called **hurricanes**—sometimes form in low-latitude areas of the Atlantic Ocean and Caribbean Sea. **Low latitudes** are from the Equator to 30° north and 30° south latitude. If these storms form in the Pacific Ocean and the China Sea, they are called **typhoons**. In other parts of the world, they are called **cyclones**. Such storms have very heavy rains and high winds.

Temperature and precipitation together help determine what plant and animal life grows in an area. In many areas with the same climate, similar biomes are found.

See the *TAE* for an *Objective 1* Activity.

1.2 Air Pressure and Wind

Air has weight. This weight pushing on Earth's surface makes air pressure. Differences in pressure areas cause wind.

Air Pressure. The uneven heating of Earth's surface by the sun leads indirectly to differences in air pressure. Through the movement of air in the atmosphere, warm air

Different combinations of temperature and moisture in the air produce these two contrasting scenes of climate. Air temperature affects what type of precipitation, if any, will fall. What is meant by relative humidity?

STRANGE BUT TRUE

UNUSUAL WEATHER BY EL NIÑO

Seven times from 1950 to 1983, geographers recorded a special change in wind patterns and ocean currents in parts of the Pacific Ocean near the Equator. This change, called **El Niño** (ehl NEEN yoh), brings unusual weather to much of the world. Peruvians who noticed that these special weather changes came to Peru around Christmas gave them the name El Niño, Spanish for "the child." The term refers to Christmas, when the birth of the Christ child is celebrated. Although geographers can explain how El Niño changes the world's weather, they do not know why.

In years when there is no El Niño, winds in the low latitudes blow from east to west. As these trade winds brush across the top of the ocean surface, warm top waters are moved, over time, to the west. In the Pacific Ocean, this makes deep warm water pile up in the western Pacific. Waters near the Philippines, Indonesia, and northeastern Australia tend to be quite warm. Air above these warm waters brings much rain to this part of the world.

When El Niño occurs, a different pattern develops. Trade winds either stop or actually reverse themselves. When this happens, water temperatures in different parts of the Pacific Ocean change. Instead of warm water piling up in the western Pacific, it piles up in the eastern Pacific and, helped by changing wind patterns, drifts eastward.

Many changes in Earth's weather came with El Niño in 1982-1983. In the western Pacific, the cooling seawater slowed the making of rain clouds. Because of this, Australia suffered its worst drought in over 200 years as shown in the photograph on this page.

On the eastern side of the Pacific, El Niño brought too much rain. Peru had more rain than it had received in more than 450 years. Some areas received 11 feet (3.4 m) of rain. Changes in water temperatures killed fish, and storms killed thousands of birds.

The 1982-1983 El Niño also affected climates in areas outside low latitudes. Northwestern United States and western Canada had warmer than average winter temperatures, while terrible winter storms reshaped some California beaches. Even southeastern United States near the Atlantic Ocean and South Africa near the Indian Ocean had lower than average rainfall.

Geographers know that El Niño occurs on the average about every 3 years and lasts about 12 to 18 months. Today they are beginning to use computers to forecast when conditions leading to it may occur. In time they hope to forecast El Niño well in advance of its arrival. This information will help farmers, government leaders, and others plan for protection against the unusual weather to come.

1. What is El Niño?
2. What is the relationship between warm ocean waters and rainfall?
3. What unusual weather did El Niño create in 1982-1983?

PRESSURE ZONES AND WIND PATTERNS

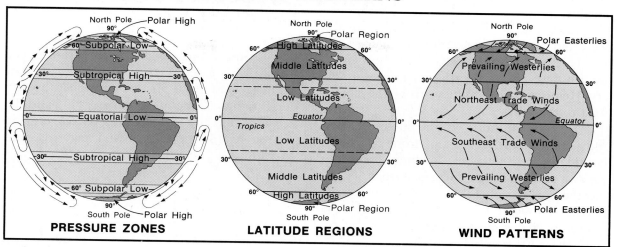

FIGURE 5-2
Wind motions in the atmosphere produce patterns that affect Earth's climates.
What are the prevailing wind patterns in the low latitudes?

from near the Equator is continually exchanged with colder air at the poles.

On Earth there are seven pressure zones, or areas with the same general air pressure. Two zones—those at each pole—are permanent. The other five, called belts, are semipermanent because the belts may move more north or south when seasons change. Near the Equator there is a belt of generally low pressure. Because the area's hot air weighs less than cold air, the air pushes less on Earth's surface. Near 30° north latitude and 30° south latitude, there are belts of high pressure. There, hot air from near the Equator rises, cools, and falls to Earth's surface, meeting colder air from the higher latitudes. The colder air falls below the warmer air and pushes down on Earth's surface. This action makes high pressure. High-pressure areas have clear skies and calm weather.

Near 60° north latitude and 60° south latitude, there are belts of low pressure. Here, warm air from high-pressure areas in lower latitudes rises above cold air from the poles. This action brings about low pressure. Low pressure areas have cloudy skies and stormy weather. At the North and South Poles, constant cold air makes high-pressure areas.

Wind. When air moves from a high-pressure area to a low-pressure area, it creates wind. The greater the difference between the two pressure areas, the faster the wind speed. If not for wind, areas near the Equator would become much too hot and areas near the poles much too cold. Wind spreads heat more evenly over the surface of Earth.

The pressure belts set up Earth's major wind patterns. These are highlighted in Figure 5-2 on this page. The wind patterns generally found in a place are called its *prevailing winds*. Near the Equator is a calm region called the **doldrums**. It has little or no wind. The prevailing winds in low latitudes are called **trade winds**. In the Northern Hemisphere, trade winds blow from the northeast to the southwest. In the Southern Hemisphere, they blow from the southeast to the northwest.

In middle latitudes winds blow from the west and are called **prevailing westerlies**. In the Northern Hemisphere, they blow from the southwest to the northeast. In the Southern Hemisphere, they blow from the northwest to the southeast.

In **high latitudes**—from 60° north latitude to the North Pole and from 60° south latitude to the South Pole—winds come from the east and are called **polar easterlies**. In the Northern Hemisphere, they blow out of the northeast toward the southwest and in the Southern Hemisphere from the southeast toward the northwest.

There are strong belts of wind high up in the air. These narrow belts of wind, called **jet streams**, flow from west to east. The jet streams form where warm air from the tropics meets cold air from the poles. These streams are much like a very fast-moving, winding river. Wind speeds in the jet streams range between 75 miles (120.7 km) and 280 miles (450.2 km) per hour. The jet streams change their positions in the atmosphere from day to day and season to season.

CONTENT CHECK

1. **Define:** infrared radiation, greenhouse effect, humidity, relative humidity, hurricanes, low latitudes, typhoons, cyclones, doldrums, trade winds, prevailing westerlies, high latitudes, polar easterlies, jet streams.
2. What are the four elements of climate?
3. Where are low-pressure zones located on Earth? High-pressure zones?
4. What is the purpose of wind?
5. **Challenge:** How does Earth's atmosphere act as a greenhouse for Earth's surface?

2. CONTROLS ON CLIMATE

Temperature, moisture, air pressure, and wind work together to produce climate. The climate they make may be controlled by several things. Among these are (1) latitude, (2) heating and cooling differences of land or water, (3) prevailing wind patterns, and (4) altitude.

2.1 Effects of Latitude

Latitude is the most important control on climate because it shows the angle at which the sun's rays hit Earth. Near the Equator these rays hit the surface of Earth more vertically—or straighter—than at other latitudes. As shown in Figure 5-3 on page 91, vertical rays cover a smaller surface area and give more energy for heat than indirect rays. For this reason, low-latitude areas near the Equator are nearly always warm for the whole year. Areas in the middle latitudes—called *temperate* areas—receive somewhat vertical rays part of the year and have temperatures that are neither too hot nor too cold. Areas in high latitudes never receive vertical rays and are cold all year.

Seasons are times of the year when different amounts of the sun's energy reach Earth. Seasons happen because of Earth's tilt on its axis. This exposes the Northern and Southern Hemispheres to the sun's more vertical rays at different times of the year. Figure 5-4 on page 92 shows how the sun's rays make seasons on Earth.

When the Northern Hemisphere is tilted toward the sun, it is summer there and winter in the Southern Hemisphere. Around June 22, the vertical radiation of the sun hits Earth the farthest north that it ever reaches—23½° north latitude. This line of latitude is called

Explain that all places on Earth's surface receive equal hours of sunlight. The extensive time of dark in Polar areas is offset by long periods of light.

About half of Earth's incoming solar radiation is either absorbed or scattered by clouds and air or is reflected by Earth's surface.

SUN'S RADIATION

FIGURE 5-3
Think of a flashlight shining on a basketball as an example of the sun's rays reaching Earth at different angles and intensity. How does the angle at which the sun's rays reach Earth's surface affect climate?

See the *TAE* for an *Objective 2* Activity.

the **Tropic of Cancer**. June 22 is called the **summer solstice** (SAHL stuhs). It marks the longest period of daylight in the Northern Hemisphere during a year.

During this time the sun never sets above the Arctic Circle and never rises below the Antarctic Circle. The **Arctic Circle** is an imaginary line circling Earth at 66½° north latitude. The **Antarctic Circle** is an imaginary line circling Earth at 66½° south latitude.

As Earth keeps revolving around the sun, the days in the Northern Hemisphere get shorter and cooler. Around September 23, the sun's rays hit vertically at the Equator. Since Earth's poles are not tilted toward or away from the sun, days and nights are of equal length in both hemispheres. This is called the **fall equinox** (EE kwuh NAHKS), and it marks the beginning of fall in the Northern Hemisphere. It also marks the beginning of spring in the Southern Hemisphere.

In December winter arrives in the Northern Hemisphere. Earth's North Pole is tilted away from the sun. Summer takes place in the Southern Hemisphere. About December 22, the sun's vertical rays hit Earth the farthest south that they ever reach—23½° south latitude. This line of latitude is known as the **Tropic of Capricorn**. December 22 is called the **winter solstice**. It marks the shortest period of daylight for the Northern Hemisphere and the longest day in the Southern Hemisphere.

In March the sun's radiation is again vertical at the Equator. On about March 21 comes the **spring equinox**, during which days and nights are again of equal length in both hemispheres. Spring starts in the Northern Hemisphere, and fall begins in the Southern Hemisphere. Daylight hours continue to increase in the Northern Hemisphere until late June when the cycle of the seasons repeats.

CHAPTER 5   **CLIMATE**

91

SEASONS

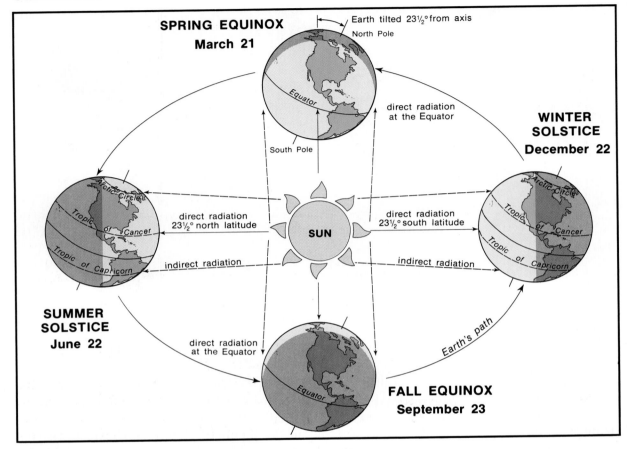

FIGURE 5-4
Seasons occur at opposite times of the year in the Northern and Southern Hemispheres. Why are winter days shorter in the Northern Hemisphere?

2.2 Effects of Land and Water

Another important control on climate is brought about by the heating and cooling of land and water. Land heats and cools more quickly than bodies of water.

Some land areas are warmed by ocean currents like the North Atlantic Current. As the current flows across the Atlantic Ocean from the Gulf of Mexico, it brings warmer temperatures to western Europe. Other land areas are cooled by ocean currents from the poles that bring cold temperatures.

The differences in the heating and cooling of land and water along coastlines also create light winds. During daylight hours, air over land is heated more quickly than air over bodies of water. This warmer air rises, resulting in a **sea breeze**. Figure 5-5 on page 93 shows how cooler air from the water blows in to take the place of rising warm air.

At night land loses its heat and cools more quickly than water. Warmer air over water rises, and cooler air blowing out from the land comes in and takes its place. This makes a **land breeze**.

PHYSICAL PATTERNS   UNIT 2

Have student volunteers research and report on some local winds, such as Santa Anas, mistrals, siroccos, boras, and chinooks.

Direct students to the photo of Mt. Kilimanjaro in Chapter 27. Ask why this peak, which is less than five degrees from the Equator, is snowcapped.

SEA AND LAND BREEZES

FIGURE 5-5
Cool air coming through an open window into a warm room has the same effect as the sea breeze (left) or the land breeze (right) pictured here. As warm air rises, one feels a cooler breeze blowing in. Which heats and cools faster, land or water?

See the *TRB* for the *Section 2 Extending the Lesson* on climate models.

2.3 Effects of Prevailing Wind Patterns

Winds tend to blow in some directions more than others. For example, in middle latitudes, the prevailing westerlies blow from west to east. Because of this, places on western sides of continents in the middle latitudes have much milder winters than places on eastern sides. Portland, Oregon, for example, benefits in winter from prevailing westerlies that pass over the warm waters of the Pacific Ocean before striking land. Portland, Maine, has colder winters because prevailing winds reach it after they have passed over much of the cold North American continent.

Westerlies also affect summer climates. Seattle, Washington, for example, has fewer hot summer days than Boston, Massachusetts. The reason for this is that the summer air is cooled by the waters of the Pacific Ocean before it blows across the west coast city of Seattle.

2.4 Effects of Altitude

The changes in climate one would feel climbing to the top of a high mountain are much like those experienced when moving from the Equator to one of the poles. For every 1,000 feet (304.8 m) of altitude, the temperature drops by almost three degrees Fahrenheit (1.7 degrees Celsius).

Because of the effects of altitude, it is possible to find a place with a cold climate in a larger area of warm climate. For example, California is mostly a warm-climate state. However, the top of Mount Whitney in California is covered with ice all year.

Altitude also controls climate through the **orographic** (OHR uh GRAF ihk) **effect**. This is the dropping of moisture as air moves up and over mountains. As air or wind reaches mountains, it is forced to rise over them. As it moves upward, it cools, causing clouds to form and precipitation to fall. The side of the mountains over which air is rising

Have a student volunteer research the effect that altitude has on the amount of oxygen in the air. How does the thinning of the atmosphere affect humans?

To introduce Section 3, list the five major climate areas on the chalkboard. Ask students to speculate how people live in these climates.

OROGRAPHIC EFFECT

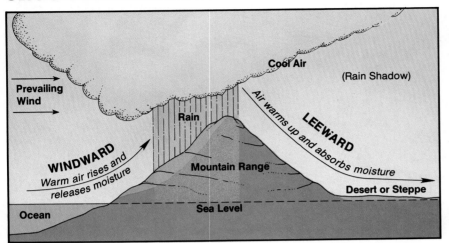

Large amounts of precipitation result when ocean winds blow over mountains, such as at Mt. Rainier in Washington, which averages 582 inches (1,478.3 cm) of rain or snow per year. What type of climate is found on a mountain's leeward side?

FIGURE 5-6

receives much rain or snow. This is called the **windward** side because it faces the wind.

As Figure 5-6 on this page shows, the other side of mountains receives little precipitation. This mountainside, called the **leeward** side, faces away from the wind. As air moves down the leeward side, it warms up and takes moisture from the land. Because it has no rain, the leeward mountainside is said to be in a *rain shadow*. Land on this side of mountains generally has a dry climate.

CONTENT CHECK

1. **Define:** seasons, Tropic of Cancer, summer solstice, Arctic Circle, Antarctic Circle, fall equinox, Tropic of Capricorn, winter solstice, spring equinox, sea breeze, land breeze, orographic effect, windward, leeward.

2. What are the four controls on climate?

3. How do seasons differ in the Northern and Southern Hemispheres?

4. **Challenge:** Explain how precipitation and air temperature change as air or wind moves over a mountain.

See the TRB for the Chapter 5 Skill Activity on making weather maps.

3. EARTH'S CLIMATES

Many different climates are found on Earth's surface. Geographers use different names and ways of classifying these into groups. Five major groups are (1) tropical moist, (2) dry, (3) moist, mild winter, (4) moist, cold winter, and (5) polar. Mountain or highland climates are found within larger climate regions. Where these climates are found on Earth is shown in Figure 5-7 on pages 96-97.

See the TAE for an Objective 3 Activity.

3.1 Tropical Moist Climates

The word tropical in tropical moist climates comes from **tropics**, the area of the world near the Equator between the Tropic of Cancer and the Tropic of Capricorn. This kind of climate is warm year round and has much precipitation.

There are three kinds of tropical moist climates: (1) tropical rain forest, (2) tropical savanna, and (3) tropical monsoon. All occur in low latitudes.

To help students associate each climate type with an actual location on Earth, refer to the map of global climates on pages 96-97 as each type is presented.

Have student volunteers research and report on ways people have tried to cause rain to fall in deserts or in drought areas.

Tropical Rain Forest Climate. In the tropical rain forest climate, temperatures are high—close to 80°F (26.7°C)—and it may rain as much as 100 inches (254 cm) a year. This climate is different from the other two tropical moist climates in that there is no dry season. For this reason, it supports the growth of thick vegetation. Two of the areas of the world that have tropical rain forest climates are the Amazon River Basin in South America and the Zaire River Basin in Africa.

Tropical Savanna Climate. In the tropical savanna climate, temperatures are high all through the year, and there is a dry season called a **drought**, when little, if any, rain falls. The dry season may last as long as six months. Only grasses, a few trees, and other small plants can live during the long drought. Tropical savanna climate is found in parts of South America, central Africa, southern Asia, southeastern Asia, and northern Australia.

Tropical Monsoon Climate. The word **monsoon** (mahn SOON) in tropical monsoon climates means a periodic change in the wind pattern that takes place in the Pacific and southeastern Asia. During the time the wind blows toward the land, there is a rainy season lasting up to four months. During the time it blows out toward the water, there is a drought that lasts about four months. Although forests are found in the tropical monsoon climate, trees are shorter than those in the tropical rain forest. There are also many small bushes and shrubs. Some of the areas of the world with this climate are the northeastern coast of South America, parts of western Africa and southeastern Asia, and the southwestern coast of India.

3.2 Dry Climates

Dry climates are found in areas where little precipitation falls. There are two kinds of dry climates—desert and steppe.

Desert Climate. The least amount of precipitation is found in the desert climate. There may be as little as 10 inches (25.4 cm) of rain a year or none at all. For much of the year, temperatures can be as high as 125°F (51.7°C) during the day and as low as 40°F (4.4°C) at night. The relative humidity is low, and there are few cloudy days and much sunshine. Desert climates are found in parts of Africa, Asia, Australia, and North America.

Steppe Climate. A dry climate with more precipitation is the steppe climate. In most areas yearly precipitation is from 10 inches (25.4 cm) to 20 inches (50.8 cm). This allows growth of short grass cover, but very few trees. In a middle-latitude steppe, it can be cold in the winter and quite hot in the summer. Steppe climates are found in North America, Africa, Asia, and Australia.

Steppe climate regions can be found near desert areas in Africa, Asia, Australia, and North America.

3.3 Moist, Mild Winter Climates

There are three kinds of moist, mild winter climates: (1) humid subtropical, (2) middle-latitude marine, and (3) Mediterranean. Most are found in middle latitudes. The major difference among the three kinds is temperature.

Lush vegetation is typical of this Amazon River Basin in Ecuador. What type of climate is shown here?

EARTH'S CLIMATE REGIONS

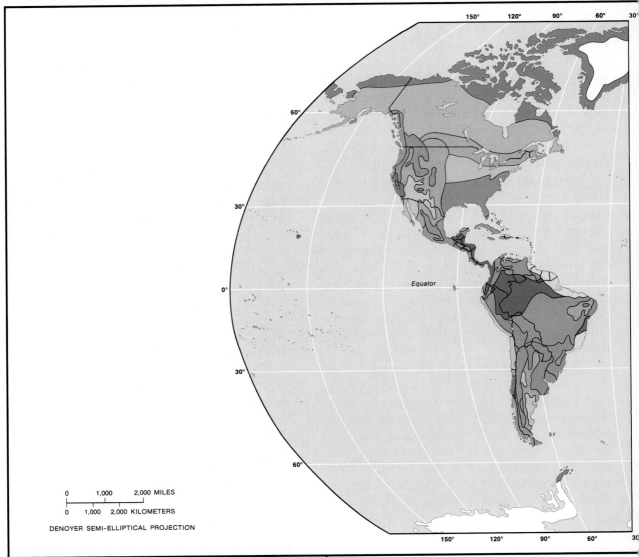

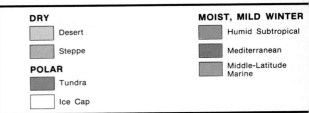

DRY		MOIST, MILD WINTER	
Desert		Humid Subtropical	
Steppe		Mediterranean	
POLAR		Middle-Latitude Marine	
Tundra			
Ice Cap			

FIGURE 5-7
A climate region is an area in which various elements of climate are about the same throughout the entire region. For example, all places within the same climate region have about (1) the same general range of tem-

Humid Subtropical Climate. The humid subtropical climate has hot summers and mild winters. **Subtropical** means areas near, but not in, the tropics. Generally, subtropical areas are just north of the Tropic of Cancer to 40° north latitude or just south of the Tropic of Capricorn to 40° south latitude. Average summer temperatures are 70°F (21.1°C) or above. Humidity is often high, and precipitation is heavy. Most of the time rain is spread

96

PHYSICAL PATTERNS UNIT 2

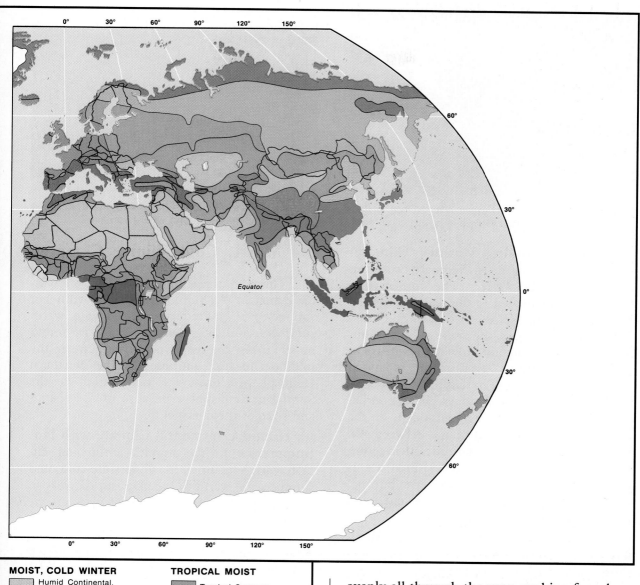

MOIST, COLD WINTER

Humid Continental,
Hot Summer

Humid Continental,
Warm Summer

Subarctic

TROPICAL MOIST

Tropical Savanna

Tropical Monsoon

Tropical Rain Forest

Mountain

perature with similar daily, monthly, and yearly variations of temperature; (2) the same amount of precipitation with a similar pattern of distribution; and (3) the same air pressure pattern and wind systems. Which climate regions are found in the United States?

evenly all through the year, making for a long growing season. Snow sometimes falls, but it does not stay on the ground long. The humid subtropical climate is generally found on the eastern sides of continents. It is found, for example, in southeastern United States, parts of southeastern South America, Japan, Korea, eastern Asia, and eastern Australia. Small areas with this climate are found also in Europe and South Africa.

CHAPTER 5   **CLIMATE**

Umbrellas do not seem to make a difference in the heavy rains of India's monsoons (left). Too little rain is the problem for people in Tunisia's sun-baked climate (right). What type of climate is found where you live?

Middle-Latitude Marine Climate. The middle-latitude marine climate has warm summers and mild winters. The word **marine** refers to things related to the sea, and marine climates are found close to oceans and seas. Precipitation is about the same as in the humid subtropical climate. However, because of cooler temperatures, evaporation is much slower, often making it damp or wet with many foggy and cloudy days. The middle-latitude marine climate is found mostly on the western side of continents and between 40° and 60° north and south latitude. It is found along the Pacific coast of the United States and Canada, in much of western Europe, southeastern Australia, New Zealand, and southern Chile in South America.

Mediterranean Climate. The Mediterranean climate has long summers and short, mild winters. Most precipitation falls during winter, while summer is mostly dry. This climate is generally found in areas between 30° and 45° north and south latitude. The Mediterranean climate is named after the Mediterranean Sea, and many areas of land around this sea have this kind of climate. Other areas of Mediterranean climate are found in California, parts of Chile in South America, southern Australia, and the southern tip of Africa.

3.4 Moist, Cold Winter Climates

There are three kinds of moist, cold winter climates: (1) humid continental with hot summers, (2) humid continental with warm summers, and (3) subarctic. They are found mostly in the central parts of continents in the middle and high latitudes of the Northern Hemisphere. They are not found in the Southern Hemisphere because of the shapes and sizes of the continents.

Humid Continental Climate with Hot Summers. In the humid continental climate with hot summers, winters are cold, and summers are warm to hot. During the year in most areas, differences are great between the highest and lowest temperatures, and the amount of precipitation is different from place to place. Some places receive much snow in winter and much rain in the summer, while others receive far less. Some areas with this type of climate are found in the northeastern United States and parts of northern China and Korea.

Humid Continental Climate with Warm Summers. In the humid continental climate with warm summers, monthly temperatures do not average above 70°F (21.1°C). In some places, precipitation falls evenly all through the year. In others, the

PHYSICAL PATTERNS UNIT 2

winter months are fairly dry. Areas with this climate are generally found between 50° and 60° north latitude. These include southern Canada, parts of the northern United States, eastern China, and much of eastern Europe.

Subarctic Climate. The word **subarctic** refers to areas between 50° and 70° north latitude just south of the North Pole. Subarctic climate areas have long, bitter cold winters with short, cool to warm summers. Frost forms even in summer. There are long days of sunlight during summer, with no fall or spring seasons. Temperatures above 50°F (10°C) last no longer than two or three months. During winter, temperatures can fall as low as −80°F (−62.2°C). Of all climates, this one has the greatest differences between highest and lowest temperatures during a year. Much of Alaska, Canada, Sweden, Finland, and the Soviet Union has this climate.

See the *TAE* for an *Objective 3* Activity.

3.5 Polar Climates

Polar climates are cold and have no summers. The name polar comes from the fact that polar climates are found near the North and South Poles. There are two kinds of polar climates—tundra and ice cap.

Tundra Climate. In the tundra climate no month is free of frost. Precipitation— snow—is very light, and temperatures seldom are above freezing. Winters are very long and cold. Summers are very short and cool. The temperatures, however, are not as extreme as in the subarctic climate because the nearby oceans warm the temperature. Because of the cold, areas with this climate are without trees. Some plants, such as mosses, lichens, and grasses, are able to grow in this climate. The tundra climate is found only in the continents of the Northern Hemisphere and the tip of the Antarctic Peninsula.

Ice Cap Climate. In areas with ice cap climate, temperatures are always below freezing, making it impossible for plants to grow. Snow and ice cover the surface all year and rarely melt. The sun appears during the summer months, but it is very low in the sky and gives little heat to the ground. Areas at both poles have this kind of climate. The central and northern parts of the island of Greenland and all of the continent of Antarctica have an ice cap climate.

Field workers harvesting a tomato orchard in sunny California (left) and the warm inviting glow of an Inuit igloo near bitter-cold Eskimo Point in Canada's Northwest Territory (right) contrast a Mediterranean and a polar ice cap climate. In what other areas are these two types of climate found?

USING GRAPHIC SKILLS

READING CLIMOGRAPHS

The daily weather report becomes important when planning a trip or picnic. People want to know if it will rain or snow and how hot or cold it will be. Geographers who study climate often show this information in line graphs and bar graphs. When the two graphs are combined, as on this page and page 101, the result is a *climograph*. A climograph shows information on climate for a certain place over a period of time.

The first step in reading a climograph is to read the title. It tells you the place where the statistics were recorded. The second step is to look at the bottom of the climograph. The letters there represent, in order, the months of the year from January to December. In each climograph shown here, temperature statistics are shown by a line graph. The numbers on the left side of the graph show temperature readings by intervals of 10 degrees Fahrenheit (5.6 degrees Celsius). The average temperature for each month can be read by locating the point at the top of the column for that particular month.

In each climograph, precipitation statistics are shown by a bar graph. The numbers on the right side of the graph show amounts of precipitation. The average monthly precipitation can be read by locating the top of the bar for that particular month.

Study the climographs found on pages 100-101. Then answer the questions that follow.

1. Which city shown has the highest average temperature for any month? Which has the lowest?

2. Which city has the greatest rainfall for any month? Which has the least?

3. **Challenge:** Which city has no rainfall at all during a span of several months? What problems do you think the people of that area have during this time? Make a hypothesis on how they may adapt to this climate.

COLOMBO, SRI LANKA

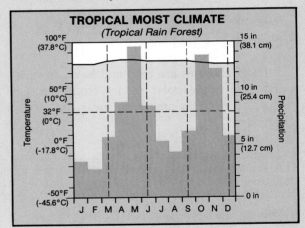

TROPICAL MOIST CLIMATE
(Tropical Rain Forest)

CONTENT CHECK

1. **Define:** tropics, drought, monsoon, subtropical, marine, subarctic.

2. What are the five ways of classifying climates?

3. Why do you think the word monsoon sometimes means "heavy rains"?

4. In which climate is rain spread evenly through the year, allowing a long growing season?

5. Which climate has many foggy and cloudy days?

PHYSICAL PATTERNS   UNIT 2

CAIRO, EGYPT

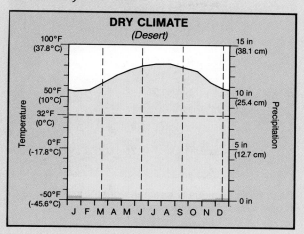

PERTH, AUSTRALIA

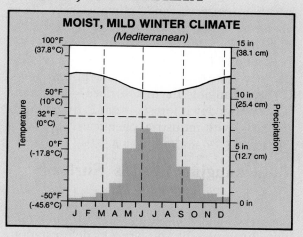

MOSCOW, U.S.S.R.

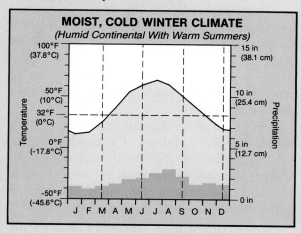

POINT BARROW, U.S.A.

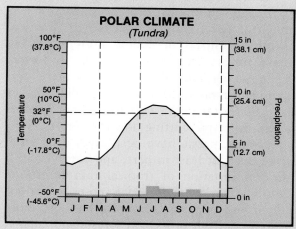

6. Which climate has the greatest differences between highest and lowest temperatures during a year?

7. What are the three kinds of moist, mild winter climates?

8. How are polar climates the opposite of tropical climates?

9. In which climate region do you live?

10. Which areas of the world have tropical rain forest climates? Mediterranean climates?

11. **Challenge:** What do you think the major difference is between tropical moist climates and dry climates? Between tropical moist climates and polar climates?

Geographers and other scientists estimate that desertification is happening in areas that affect about 15 percent of Earth's population. People's misuse of the land has caused desertification to an area about the size of China—approximately 3.7 million square miles (9.6 million sq km).

4. IMPACT OF PEOPLE

Throughout the history of Earth, weather patterns and climate have been changing. Many of these changes have been due to natural causes. Others, however, have been due to human activities. Generally, people affect weather and climate in two ways: (1) by changing Earth's surface—for example, cutting down forests—or (2) by polluting the air—with industrial chemicals.

See the *TAE* for an *Objective 4* Activity.

4.1 Changing Earth's Surface

People change weather and climate when they try to make natural areas into something else. Examples of this are (1) deforestation, (2) desertification, and (3) urbanization.

Deforestation. More than 10,000 years ago, enormous forests stretched across much of Asia, Europe, and North America. As the numbers of people grew, many of these forests were cleared to build towns. Then as agriculture developed, there was more and more need for more **arable** land, or land fit for farming. This led to more **deforestation**, or the cutting down of forests.

Some forests have been able, over time, to recover, at least in part, and survive. Still, the deforestation of tropical rain forests in South America and Africa poses a serious threat. Nigeria, for example, has lost more than 90 percent of its rain forests and Ghana, 80 percent. During the past 30 years, more than 40 percent of Earth's early rain forests have been cleared.

The loss of forests means the loss of a great many plants and animals. With fewer plants, there is less water in the air. There is also more carbon dioxide. This will set off the greenhouse effect and cause less rain to fall and temperatures to change. This, in turn, will cause deforested areas to become dry, barren, and eroded.

Pastureland gradually becomes desert in this area of Niger. What is this process of change called?

Some people fear that the effects of changing Earth's surface by deforestation will be felt in many parts of the world. For example, changes in the atmosphere upset the balance in Earth's biosphere, and climates all over the world will slowly change. Also, people who live in deforested areas move on to areas with arable land, causing unexpected population growth.

Steps to save tropical rain forests have begun in a few countries. The government of Brazil has made 46,000 square miles (119,140 sq km) into natural *reserves*, or land set aside for future needs, and the Congo has planted more than 10 million trees.

Desertification. People's actions are changing Earth's surface by increasing the number of dry climate areas. The process of arable land becoming desert is called **desertification**. This process is taking place because **semiarid** lands, or land that receives little rainfall, are not being used properly. Tropical savanna and steppe climate areas are semiarid. They have unpredictable amounts of rainfall that are different from season to season. In years of more rainfall, people add more animals to their herds and irrigate more

PHYSICAL PATTERNS   UNIT 2

fields for crops. When rainfall decreases, the land is not able to support the herds and crops. Animals overgraze the land, stripping it of its grasses. With little or no plant life, the land receives no rain and becomes drier. In this way each year millions of acres of Earth's surface become desert.

Urbanization. Climate changes caused by humans are especially seen in cities. Parking lots, streets, and sidewalks take the place of trees and other plants. Tall buildings are built that cause changes in wind patterns. Hot, waste heat from factories, buses, trucks, and cars rises into the air. Heavy industry and transportation cause thick polluted air called **smog**, or a combination of smoke and fog. Smog prevents some of the sun's rays from entering the city. Changes in warm temperatures and wind patterns often combine and trap chemicals in the air, making it harder for people to breathe. With cities around the world growing larger, serious and widespread changes to weather and climate may occur.

To exemplify heat absorption in asphalt and concrete cities, have students compare walking barefoot through grassy areas with walking across paved areas.

4.2 Polluting the Air

People also change weather and climate when they pollute the air. They have been doing this since fire was discovered. Today with more factories and machines than ever before, there may be great changes in climate. The increase of carbon dioxide in the atmosphere from the burning of coal, oil, and natural gas is thought to be increasing the greenhouse effect.

Climate is also changing because of acid rainfall. *Acid rain* is made when certain chemicals from cars, trucks, and factories, for example, are released into the atmosphere and mix together to form acids. These acids become a part of the water cycle and fall as rain or snow, often far away from where the chem-

icals first entered the air. Acid rain poisons lakes and other bodies of water, eats building surfaces, and takes nutrients away from soil.

See the *TRB* for the *Section 4 Extending the Lesson* on depletion of the ozone layer.

CONTENT CHECK

1. **Define:** arable, deforestation, semiarid, desertification, smog.
2. What are some effects caused by the destruction of tropical rain forests?
3. What general areas face especially great danger of becoming deserts?
4. **Challenge:** List all the ways you think humans affect climate in areas as small as your backyard to regions as large as a continent.

See the *TRB* for the *Chapter 5 Reading* on the next Ice Age.

CONCLUSION

When the atmosphere processes the energy of the sun, the result is weather and climate. The atmosphere receives the sun's energy, transfers heat and cold, and gives off an equal amount of energy. All this helps make sure that Earth will be able to support life.

All through history, people have tried to adjust to unfavorable climates. In the tropics, people have built houses that shade them from the hot sun and that allow breezes in. In high latitudes they have built houses that keep out as much cold air as possible. Today, specially designed buildings, clothing, and vehicles make living and exploration possible in places that are very hot or very cold.

Some people think that one day humans will be able to control climate or at least day-to-day weather. Others, however, worry that human activity is placing the atmosphere under great stress and will upset the delicate balance of Earth's climates. The study of climate will remain important for years to come.

SUMMARY

1. Surrounding Earth is a sea of gases called the atmosphere. It contains oxygen necessary for human life. It also produces weather and climate patterns.

2. The main elements of climate are temperature, precipitation, air pressure, and wind. Different combinations of these elements produce different climates.

3. Temperature and precipitation play an important part in determining what plant and animal life is found in an area.

4. Differences in air pressure from place to place cause winds. Winds help to spread heat and cold more evenly.

5. The four controls on climate are (1) latitude, (2) heating and cooling differences of land or water, (3) wind patterns, and (4) altitude.

6. Earth's climates can be classified into five major groups: (1) tropical moist, (2) dry, (3) moist, mild winter, (4) moist, cold winter, and (5) polar. In many parts of the world, mountain or highland climates occur within these other climate regions.

7. Although weather patterns and climate have been changing throughout Earth's history, recent activities of people are seriously altering weather and climate.

REVIEWING VOCABULARY

Imagine these terms from Chapter 5 are correct answers to 12 items in a crossword puzzle. Write the 12 clues for the answers. Then make the puzzle with some answers written down and some across.

climate	doldrums	precipitation	orographic effect
typhoon	trade winds	summer solstice	greenhouse effect
drought	front	fall equinox	deforestation

Answers to the following questions can be found on page T96.

REMEMBERING THE FACTS

1. What gases make up the major part of the atmosphere?

2. What weather do high-pressure areas generally have? Low-pressure areas?

3. What are the prevailing winds in low latitudes called? In middle latitudes? In high latitudes?

4. Why are low-latitude areas nearly always warm for the whole year?

5. During what time of the year are days longest in the Northern Hemisphere?

6. Because of the orographic effect, which side of a mountain receives little precipitation? Why?

7. What are the five major climate groups?

8. What climate group is found mostly in the central parts of continents in the Northern Hemisphere?

9. In what two general ways do people affect weather and climate?

10. How can a city's environment affect an area's climate?

UNDERSTANDING THE FACTS

1. What is the difference between weather and climate?
2. Would you expect to find high or low humidity in a desert area? Why?
3. Why would you expect to find an area of generally low pressure near the Equator?
4. How do prevailing winds in middle-latitude areas make climates on western sides of continents different from climates on eastern sides of continents?
5. How does deforestation cause changes in climate?
6. What kinds of human activities cause desertification to occur?
7. How does a body of water affect the air temperature of a nearby land area?
8. Why are increases in the amount of carbon dioxide in the atmosphere cause for worry among many geographers and other scientists?

THINKING CRITICALLY AND CREATIVELY

1. If you wanted to change the climate for your region, how would you go about it?
2. How has the greenhouse effect made better conditions for growth in the biosphere? How have humans interfered with this natural effect?
3. Why would sailing ships take one route from Europe to the Americas and a different route on the return voyage?
4. Urban areas tend to be cloudier and warmer than areas in the countryside. They also receive more precipitation than rural areas. Why do you suppose cities have this kind of weather?
5. **Challenge:** What do you think government leaders of semiarid lands could do with help and funds from international aid agencies to prevent desertification?
6. **Challenge:** If you are in the middle of a tropical moist climate region but the land around you has little vegetation and the air is cold, where are you?
7. **Challenge:** Use weather maps and local weather information to forecast probable local weather conditions for the next few days. Indicate the scientific basis for your predictions. After several days, evaluate the accuracy of your predictions.

REINFORCING GRAPHIC SKILLS

Study the climographs on pages 100 and 101. Then answer the questions that follow.

1. Cairo, Egypt, is located about the same distance north of the Equator as Perth, Australia, is south of the Equator. However, their rainfall patterns are very different. Based on their climates, how would you explain this?
2. Most precipitation in Mediterranean climates occurs during the winter months. The climograph shows that Perth, Australia, with a Mediterranean climate receives its greatest rainfall in June, July, and August. How do you explain this?

UNIT REVIEW

SUMMARY

1. Earth's biosphere is made up of the lithosphere—land, the hydrosphere—water, and the atmosphere—air.
2. Land and water occur on Earth in uneven patterns. This gives great variety to the natural landscape.
3. Forces within Earth and forces on its surface shape landforms. Earth's landforms can be classified by size as major and minor landforms or by how they were made as primary and secondary landforms.
4. Earth's land area is covered with many types of soils, plants, and animals.
5. Water covers almost 71 percent of Earth's total surface area. Without water, no life could exist on Earth.
6. The atmosphere surrounding Earth is the source of weather and climate patterns.
7. The four major elements of climate are temperature, moisture, air pressure, and wind. Latitude and altitude are two of the controls on climate.
8. Human activity has affected Earth's biosphere by changing landforms, waterways, and climate patterns, and polluting land, water, and air.

THINKING ABOUT THE UNIT

1. How do forces within Earth and on its surface shape its physical landscape?
2. Some regions on Earth have many lakes, rivers, and other interior waterways. Others lack them completely. What are some advantages enjoyed by a region with many interior waterways?
3. What factors must be considered when you analyze the climate of an area?
4. What positive influences have people had on the lithosphere, hydrosphere, and atmosphere? What negative influences? What do you predict about the biosphere's future?

Answers to the following questions can be found on page T100.

SUGGESTED UNIT ACTIVITIES

1. Suppose your class received a letter from a class in another part of the world asking for a description of landscape features of your city or town and state. Write a description of several paragraphs in which you describe these features.
2. Plan a bulletin board around the theme "Earth's Land and Water." Throughout the study of Unit 2, gather and display pictures of various landforms and bodies of water from around the world. Use old newsmagazines and newspapers.
3. Keep a weather notebook. Record daily high and low temperatures. Determine average monthly temperatures and prepare line graphs for temperature changes during each month of the school year.
4. Identify a problem with your hometown's physical environment. Conduct a survey to find out possible solutions.

DEVELOPING GEOGRAPHY SKILLS

ANALYZING PHOTOGRAPHS

Photographs are useful sources of information that can give you a sense of people, places, and events. Photographs can also give you misleading ideas of what is real by leaving important parts out of the picture or placing people or objects in unlikely situations. This happens when photographers choose to focus on just part of a larger scene. What is left out might be very important to our complete understanding of people or places. For this reason it is important to know how to *analyze* photographs, or look at them critically.

The photograph below is a reproduction of one that appears on page 98. The guidelines that follow the photo will help you analyze not only this photo but also others.

1. Look closely at the photograph.
2. Read any material accompanying the photograph. (*Read the caption on page 98.*)
3. Describe the content of the photograph, indicating such details as objects (*bicycles, umbrellas*), people (*adult men*), and actions (*people riding through a flooded street*). Point out clues in the photo as to

where it was taken (*Asian clothing on men, bicycle suggests developing country*). Determine what action is taking place and describe the relationship that seems to exist among people or objects in the photo (*people riding through streets; people dressed in similar kinds of clothes, suggesting they are from the same culture*).

4. Identify the main idea or purpose of the photograph. Ask yourself what impression the photograph creates about environments, lifestyles, customs, or beliefs. (*People must adapt to periodic heavy rains. Probably travel time is much longer during the rainy season.*) Determine what clues or details you saw in the photograph.

5. Determine the accuracy of the photograph by asking yourself what the photograph seems to emphasize. (*The rainy season results in much transportation difficulty for people in this part of the world because of the extensive street flooding it brings.*) What does the photo seem to leave out? (*Are bicycles the only mode of transportation? Or have the rains forced people to ride them who, otherwise, would ride other means of transportation? What about women? Aren't they out when there is flooding?*) To help determine what may be left out, compare the photograph with others of the same general subject or with other information sources on the topic.

6. Determine what generalization(s) you can make based on the photograph. (*The rainy season makes movement from place to place difficult and time-consuming.*)

For practice in this skill, use the suggested guidelines to analyze the landscape photographs on pages 44 and 78.

HUMAN PATTERNS

Where people live and how they act in their environment make patterns on Earth's surface. This unit explores these patterns—as they are made by population, culture, and urbanization. Population patterns show that people are spread unevenly over Earth's surface. Because each group of people has made a special way of life for itself, cultural patterns are different all over the world. The group's way of life is greatly influenced by the physical patterns of the place in which it lives. In today's world, for a variety of reasons, many people live in cities. Studying all these human patterns helps geographers and students of geography better understand Earth's people.

Point out to students that the highlighted areas on the world map inset represent the 16 largest metropolitan areas of the world.

Human landscape in Amsterdam, Netherlands

CHAPTER 6

Earth's population is estimated at 5 billion. In a class discussion, explore with students the magnitude of such a large number.

Participants at a sports festival in Czechoslovakia

POPULATION

In this chapter you will learn—

- How a country's economic growth is linked with its population growth.
- Where the most heavily populated areas of the world are.
- Why food supply, the supply of natural resources, population control, and migration are major world issues.

See the *TAE* for an *Objective 1* Activity.

INTRODUCTION

Geographers have long been interested in the study of human population. They study how landforms, waterways, climate, and vegetation influence where people live on Earth's surface. They also study how people affect their natural environment. Today, with more than five billion people living on Earth—more than ever before—the study of population becomes important for everyone.

Demography comes from two Greek words—*demos* (people) and *graphie* (study of).

1. EARTH'S GROWING POPULATION

An important first step in a study of population is to look at how the number of Earth's people has grown through time. Scientists who study this are called **demographers.** Through their studies they estimate the number of people who have lived on Earth at different times in history. They also look at what causes populations to grow. These causes help them explain why Earth's population has grown as it has and how population will grow in the years ahead.

The difference between the birth and death rates is the rate of the *natural* increase or decrease in a population. Many areas now having rapid population increases have continuing high birthrates and declining death rates.

1.1 Population Growth

For thousands of years, Earth's population grew at a very slow rate. This was because both the **birthrate**—the number of people born each year per thousand people—and the **death rate**—the number of people dying each year per thousand—were high. People knew little about staying healthy and preventing disease. With not enough food or the most nutritious food available in some areas, few ate good meals. Most did not live in clean or safe homes. These factors, as well as famines and wars, made life spans short.

The first important change in the population growth rate began with the development of agriculture. Taming animals to help with the farm work and to raise as sources of food helped make a more steady food supply. The harvests from fertile soils could support more people than had been possible when people were nomads and hunted and gathered food. Even with the beginning of agriculture, however, population growth was slow.

Scientists believe that in the year 1 AD the population of the world was about 250 million. By 1650 there were about 500 million people. It took more than 1,000 years for the number of people on Earth to double.

111

As contact among continents increased, crops from the Americas were taken back to Europe and Asia, while crops from Africa, Asia, and Europe were shared with the Americas. For instance, coffee now common in the Americas is indigenous to areas in Africa. Interested students might research and report on some of these crops.

This West German scene typifies Europe's urban population. Is Europe an industrialized or developing area?

The changes caused by the Industrial Revolution speeded up population growth in Europe. New machinery increased the number of factory goods. Better farming methods were tried, which increased food supplies. All of these changes brought about a better standard of living for many people. **Standard of living** means the quality of life people have because they own things that make life easier. Also, new medical discoveries, such as the smallpox vaccination, were put into use to fight diseases. As a result of these improvements in living conditions, **life expectancy,** or the average number of years people live, went up, and death rates went down.

More trade and contact among people from different continents spread ideas about growing crops and allowed the exchange of many foods. This helped improve the diets of millions of people. They became less dependent for their living on the natural resources of their own area. People who might have starved during hard times survived because they had learned to trade their labor for food.

Between 1650 and 1850, world population doubled, rising from 500 million to 1 billion. By 1960 it had reached 3 billion. This meant that world population had tripled in a

little more than 100 years. Such fast growth is called a **population explosion.** This is shown in Figure 6-1 on page 113.

Refer to the World Population Growth graph on page 113 during the study of this section.

1.2 Rates of Population Growth

Demographers agree that the world has not reached its highest population. Estimates are that the number of people will reach about 6.1 billion by the year 2000 and 8 billion by the year 2020. The rate of growth is about 1.7 percent each year. If this does not change, world population will double in 40 years. There are many things that can affect the rate of future growth.

During the 1800s birthrates in countries going through the Industrial Revolution went up quickly. By 1900 they began to go down. One reason for this is that in the past, when most of the people farmed for a living, they wanted large families to help with farm work. But after machines and new ways of farming eased their work load, they did not need as many children. Another reason was that methods of birth control became more generally known and used.

Differences in birth and death rates vary greatly from one part of the world to another. Because of this, population growth all through the world is far from uniform. In general, it is slowest today in countries that were first to experience the Industrial Revolution. Among these are many countries in Europe, as well as the United States and Canada in North America, and Japan in Asia. These countries are called **industrialized countries.** Each industrialized country's economy is based on manufacturing and is highly developed. An **economy** is an organized way that a country uses its resources to provide for the needs and wants of its people. Each industrialized country's **gross national product (GNP)**—the value of all goods and services produced during a year—is fairly high. They

HUMAN PATTERNS UNIT 3

have good transportation, information, and communication systems and offer public services such as education, health care, and housing to most people. Recently the population in industrialized countries has gone up at the rate of only 0.5 percent each year.

On the other hand, population growth is the greatest in **developing countries,** where three-fourths of Earth's people live. In developing countries the economy is based largely on farming, although in some, leaders are trying to industrialize. In general, the countries are poor, many with low food supplies and energy shortages. Many people also do not receive proper health care and education. The GNPs in these countries are very low. The number of people in some developing countries, such as Nicaragua and Kenya, has recently gone up three percent each year.

Advances in farming and manufacturing often cause variations in rates of population growth.

1.3 Stages of Growth

Demographers have identified four stages of population growth that they believe countries pass through as their economies go from developing to industrialized. They do not know if all countries will pass through each of these stages. They use them, however, as models to compare population patterns around the world.

Stage One shows high birth and death rates, causing little or no population growth. At present, there are no countries in the world in Stage One. Stage Two shows high birthrates and falling death rates, causing rapid growth in population. Unlike Stage One, there are many countries in Stage Two. Many of these developing countries are in Latin America and Africa south of the Sahara. Most must deal with the problems of short food supplies and high unemployment.

Stage Three shows falling birthrates and low death rates, causing slow population growth. Some countries in Stage Three are

WORLD POPULATION GROWTH

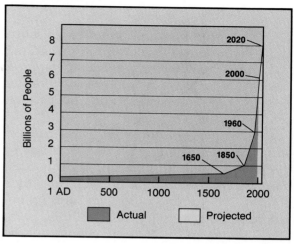

FIGURE 6-1   Data from Population Reference Bureau, Inc., 1987.
The slow growth of human population was followed by a recent explosion of rapid growth. What will the world's population be in the year 2000?

the United States and the People's Republic of China. Although China is not yet an industrialized country, its government leaders want people to have smaller families.

Stage Four shows low birth and low death rates, giving little or no growth. Countries in Stage Four have the least increase in population. Their birth and death rates remain about the same from year to year. When the birthrate equals the death rate, it is called **zero population growth,** or ZPG. Some Stage Four countries expect decreases in population in the near future. These are industrialized countries found mostly in Europe, such as Sweden and West Germany.

Important place-to-place differences in growth rates sometimes occur within an individual country.

1.4 Forecasting Growth

Two important keys to future population growth are the ages of the people and the number of males and females in a country. To study these, demographers make graphs

USING GRAPHIC SKILLS

COMPARING TABULAR DATA

How many RBIs did your favorite short-stop drive in? How many touchdowns did your favorite wide receiver score? If you are a baseball or football fan, you probably love to keep records of statistics. Such information can be presented in a table.

When geographers study world regions, they need to know facts. These facts can be placed in a table. When comparing countries, geographers look at tabular data from each country. They may compare land area, population, and other geographical features.

The table below shows population and economic data on some industrialized and de-

veloping countries. The headings identify the types of information being presented. The numerical information in the table is shown in percentages or in whole numbers.

Study the table below. Then answer the questions that follow.

1. What three countries shown have the highest birthrates? Are they industrialized or developing countries?

2. The population of Australia and Malaysia are nearly the same. In what other ways are the countries similar? In what ways are they different?

STATISTICS ON SELECTED COUNTRIES

	COUNTRY	AREA (sq. m.) (in sq. km.)	POPULATION (millions)	FARMLAND PERCENT	URBAN POP. PERCENT	POP. ANNUAL GROWTH RATE PERCENT	BIRTH/DEATH RATE (per 1,000)	PER CAPITA GNP (U.S. $)
INDUSTRIALIZED	UNITED STATES	3,615,104 (9,363,112.1)	243.8	20	74	0.7	16/9	16,400
	FRANCE	211,208 (547,028.3)	55.6	34	73	0.4	14/10	9,550
	JAPAN	143,749 (372,309.6)	122.2	13	76	0.6	12/6	11,330
	AUSTRALIA	2,967,896 (7,686,844.7)	16.2	6	86	0.8	16/8	10,840
	U.S.S.R.	8,649,498 (22,402,182.5)	284.0	10	65	0.9	19/11	7,400
DEVELOPING	ANGOLA	481,351 (1,246,698.1)	8.0	3	25	2.5	47/22	300
	SYRIA	71,498 (185,179.7)	11.3	31	49	3.8	47/9	1,630
	INDIA	1,269,340 (3,287,588.0)	800.3	51	25	2.1	33/12	250
	CHINA	3,705,390 (9,596,952.6)	1,062.0	11	32	1.3	21/8	310
	MALAYSIA	127,317 (329,750.8)	16.1	13	32	2.4	31/7	2,050

Data from *1987 World Population Data Sheet*, Population Reference Bureau, Inc.

A country with large numbers of young people must develop more education facilities and expand employment opportunities. A country with higher percentages of older people must plan for services geared toward an aging population—increased medical needs, for example.

POPULATION PYRAMIDS

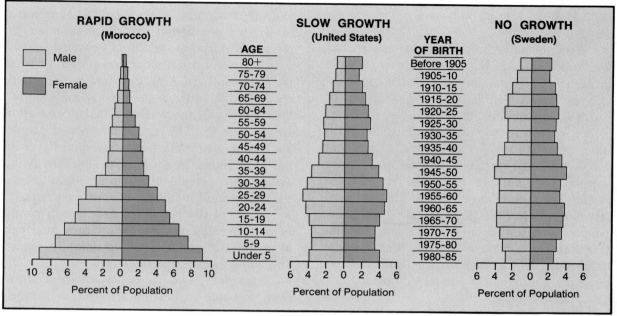

FIGURE 6-2

Data from Population Reference Bureau, Inc.

While population pyramids of developing countries, such as Morocco, often resemble a triangle, those of industrialized countries, such as the United States and Sweden, resemble a rectangle. Which of the three countries shown above has the highest percentage of young children?

See the *TRB* for the *Chapter 6 Skill Activity* on interpreting circle graphs.

called **population pyramids,** such as those shown in Figure 6–2 on this page. They use their findings to forecast population growth.

To make a population pyramid, demographers divide the population of a country into age groups. In some of these pyramids, each group covers five years. They then show the percentage of males and females in each age group. From this information demographers can draw conclusions about a country's growth. The number of males and females can show the effects of a country's past or the possible growth in the future. Countries may show a small percentage of males in young-adult age groups because of many deaths caused by war. A population with a large percentage of young females will likely have a high growth rate in the near future because the females will soon be of childbearing age.

CONTENT CHECK

1. **Define:** demographers, birthrate, death rate, standard of living, life expectancy, population explosion, industrialized countries, economy, gross national product, developing countries, zero population growth, population pyramids.

2. Approximately how many people are living on Earth today?

3. What kind of population growth happens in Stage One? Stage Two? Stage Three? Stage Four?

4. **Challenge:** What generalization can be made about the influence of a country's economy on its future population growth?

CHAPTER 6 **POPULATION**

2. POPULATION PATTERNS

For several reasons, people are spread very unevenly over Earth's surface, with some areas heavily populated and others uninhabited or nearly uninhabited. Some parts of Earth's surface are too cold for farming. Other parts are too dry for farming. Still other areas are too wet or too hot. Areas that are very rugged or that have poor soil cannot support large numbers of people. All of these factors affect population distribution and density. **Population distribution** tells how many people have settled in what places. **Population density** is the average number of people concentrated in a given area of land, such as per square mile or per square kilometer.

See the *TAE* for an *Objective 3* Activity.

2.1 Population Distribution

The patterns made by where people live in any part of Earth are determined by the landscapes and waterways of the area as well as by the ability of people to make a living in that area. An area's physical environment, especially climate, limits the number of people who can live there. Every area has a unique settlement pattern because people have adjusted to their natural environment in different ways.

In their studies, demographers have found four centers of heavy population in the world—eastern Asia, southern Asia, western Europe, and east central North America. As shown in Figure 6–3 on page 117, together they make up about 10 percent of the land surface of Earth, yet they hold more than 70 percent of Earth's people. These centers are described in the population distributions of the six inhabited continents that follow.

Asia. The greatest concentration of people on Earth is in eastern Asia, centered in the country of China. With its more than 1 billion people, China has more people than any other country in the world—21 percent of Earth's population. Most Chinese live in river valleys and along China's eastern coast.

The second largest concentration of people is in southern Asia, centered in the country of India. India is the second most populous country in the world, with 16 percent of Earth's people. The largest number of people are found in the valley of the Ganges River in northern India. In addition to southern Asia, about eight percent of Earth's people live in the islands and mainland of southeast Asia.

Most of the people of Asia live in rural, or countryside, settings. The largest number of people are farmers and live along the plains and valleys near large rivers.

Europe. The third largest concentration of people on Earth is in western Europe. Large numbers of people live in central and southern England, but mainland Europe has a major belt of heavy population. It begins along the southern coast of the North Sea, in the Netherlands and Belgium, and moves southward along the Rhine River between France and West Germany to northern Italy. This same band runs east through central Europe to the Ural Mountains in the Soviet Union. Unlike Asia, Europe's distribution of people is not tied to nearness to waterways, but more to where there are natural resources needed for industry.

North America. The fourth largest population center is in east central North America—in northeastern United States and southeastern Canada. Like Europe, North America's population is largely urban. In the United States, from the city of Boston, Massachusetts, south to Washington, D.C., there is an almost continuous series of cities and towns. In Canada the population also centers chiefly around cities. Heavy population areas circle Montreal in Quebec and Ottawa and Toronto in Ontario. Another area of heavy

Because humans are so adaptable, there are relatively few places where people have been unable to establish permanent settlements. In the 1980s several countries have even set up semi-permanent camps of scientists in various parts of Antarctica.

WORLD POPULATION DENSITY

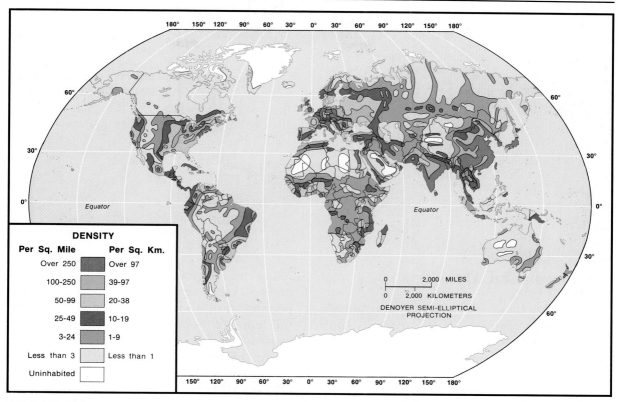

FIGURE 6-3

This map clearly shows the uneven patterns of world population over Earth's surface. Vast unsettled areas are located next to areas of heavy density. Population distribution is certainly not uniform. What three factors determine where people live in any part of Earth?

Have students compare the map above with the map of world economic development on page 510.

population in North America is found in southern Mexico.

Africa. Although Africa has 12 percent of Earth's population, it has only one heavily populated area that is like those in Asia, Europe, and North America. The largest cluster of people in Africa is found in the Nile River Valley. Smaller clusters of people in Africa are found around the large lakes of eastern Africa, along the Mediterranean coast of northwestern Africa and the southern coast of Africa's western bulge, and around the largest cities in southern Africa.

South America. South America, as a whole, is lightly populated compared with most of the other continents. Its population, however, has a distinct pattern—many people live along the edges of the continent, especially the southeastern Atlantic coast. There many people live in cities along the coast, such as Buenos Aires in Argentina, Montevideo in Uruguay, and Rio de Janeiro and Recife in Brazil.

Australia. Of all the inhabited continents, Australia has the fewest number of people. Population is concentrated along the eastern and southern coasts. In these areas there is fertile land and enough water. Much of the western half of Australia is desert, and few people live there.

Unfavorable physical geography alone does not control or limit population density. Ingenuity and inventiveness in Japan, for instance, have made possible a highly dense population in an extremely mountainous country with little good farmland.

POPULATION DENSITY

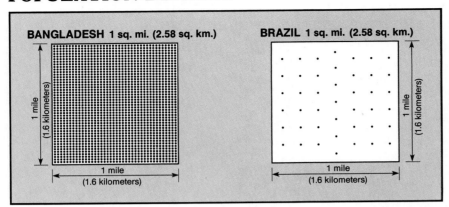

Population density in Bangladesh measures 1,926 people per square mile (743 per sq km), whereas Brazil measures 43 people per square mile (17 per sq km). How do you calculate population density?

FIGURE 6-4

See the *TRB* for the *Section 2 Extending the Lesson* on the family policy in China.

See the *TAE* for an *Objective 2* Activity.

2.2 Population Density

Closely related to population distribution is population density. It is generally not enough just to know where and how many people live in a certain land area. Density tells you how concentrated the numbers of people are in the area. For example, the state of

Massachusetts has an area of 8,300 square miles (21,497 sq km). It has an estimated population of about 5.8 million. By dividing the number of people by the number of square miles or square kilometers, you can figure that the population density of Massachusetts is about 700 people per square mile (270 per sq km).

Population density makes it possible to compare areas of different size and population all over the world. As Figure 6–4 above shows, for each person in Bangladesh, there is far less land area than there is for each person in Brazil.

In figuring population density, it is assumed that people are living all over the land area evenly. This is almost never true. Egypt, for example, has a population density of about 134 people per square mile (52 per sq km). This would mean that in every square mile throughout the country, 134 people live. Figure 6–5 on this page shows why population distribution and density should be studied together.

POPULATION OF EGYPT ___

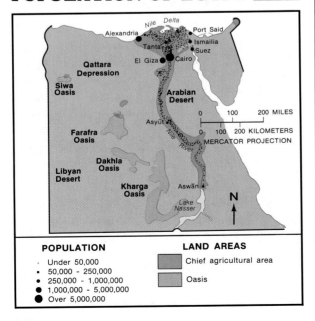

POPULATION

- · Under 50,000
- 50,000 – 250,000
- 250,000 – 1,000,000
- 1,000,000 – 5,000,000
- Over 5,000,000

LAND AREAS

Chief agricultural area

Oasis

FIGURE 6-5

Ninety-nine percent of Egyptians live in the Nile River valley and delta. According to this map, which three cities are the most populated?

118   **HUMAN PATTERNS**   UNIT 3

CONTENT CHECK

1. **Define:** population distribution, population density.
2. Where are the four largest centers of population in the world?
3. **Challenge:** What is the density of Europe, with 779 million people in a land area of about 3,835,000 square miles (9,932,642 sq km)?

See the *TAE* for an *Objective 4* Activity.

3. POPULATION ISSUES

The great increase in population that has taken place in the world raises a number of important issues. These deal with how Earth's people will handle the stress of growing numbers of people and still meet their basic needs today and in the years ahead.

3.1 Food Supply

One of the most basic needs threatened by overpopulation is food. Demographers and many other people worry that the world's food supply will not be able to keep up with the growing population. Estimates are that more than 10 million people die each year because they do not have a good diet. More than 500 million people suffer from **malnutrition,** or not enough nourishment.

During the 1970s the industrialized countries of the world increased food production by about 21 percent. During the same time, population in these countries went up about 8 percent. Food supply was no problem because they had food reserves, or stored food for the future. However, during the same time, food production in the developing countries, as a whole, went up 30 percent. Their population growth was 26 percent. In other words, the rate of population growth was more than the amount of food produced. In

Surplus grain from the United States is unloaded at a dock in Dakar, Senegal. Sharing food reserves remains a necessary, although short-range, remedy to the problem of uneven world food supplies. Why is malnutrition a serious problem?

The Food and Agricultural Organization and the World Bank of the United Nations are the two main international agencies that transport food from countries with surpluses to countries in need.

CHAPTER 6 **POPULATION**

FOCUS ON GEOGRAPHY

THOMAS ROBERT MALTHUS

In 1798 Thomas Malthus, an English economist and minister, wrote "An Essay on the Principle of Population as It Affects the Future Improvement of Society." Malthus wrote his ideas during the Industrial Revolution when England's population grew from about six million to nine million between 1750 and 1800.

In his paper Malthus stated his theory that the number of people tends to go up at a more rapid rate than food supplies. Food production is slower because it depends on Earth's limited amount of arable land. As the population grows, more people need food. Because food supplies cannot match this growth, many people get barely enough food. Malthus observed that natural ways to slow population growth—disease, war, starvation, and poor living and working conditions—would kill only some people. Malthus decided that if something was not done to control population, the world was headed for famine and misery.

Malthus' theory caused great debate about whether a country's government should help the poor. Those people who agreed with this theory believed that governments should not help because then population would grow and there would again be too many people. Others did not agree. They felt that people could increase food production if governments helped farmers financially. They also believed that if more people could get an education, they would learn how to slow down population growth.

By the mid-1800s, however, as more people began to live better, Malthus' ideas were forgotten. Even in overpopulated cities, heavy population was eased when many people *emigrated*, or moved away, from Europe to the Americas.

Yet Malthus' theory did not die. By the middle of the 1900s, the debate began again as rapid growth made world population much larger than even Malthus had thought possible. That growth continues today. Some population experts say that medical advances have helped people live longer. They also argue that food supplies in developing countries are increasing because governments are readying new lands for farming and are using new farming methods.

Nevertheless, some people argue that these changes have not proved Malthus wrong. Millions of people all over the world are starving. Supporters of Malthus' ideas say that improvements in medical care and farming only put off the time when there will be far too many people for Earth to support.

1. During what time did Malthus live? What was happening in Europe then?

2. What was Malthus' theory on population growth? What did he predict for Earth's future?

Studies show that nearly two-thirds of Earth's people either do not have enough food to eat or do not receive enough nutrition in the food they do have.

Other food sources being explored are wild vegetation such as prairie grasses and the use of animals native to the tropics as livestock in other areas.

fact, in some developing countries, there was less food to eat than before.

Although there are programs to ship food from countries with extra amounts to those who need it, many scientists and farm leaders feel that shipping food is not the way to help with food shortages. They feel that countries that do not have enough food must speed up their own food production.

More Land for Agriculture. Making land ready for farming is not easy. Since most of the best farmland in the world is already being used, it often means using land with poorer soil in areas with harsher climate. This is costly because much fertilizer and water for irrigation are needed.

Efficient Eating Habits. Another way to help with food shortages is for people to change some of their eating habits. For example, much of the grain grown around the world goes to feed animals, especially beef cattle. If less grain went to feeding cattle, more protein would be available for people. This solution, though, causes problems. For one thing, farmers in countries where most beef cattle are raised—the United States, Canada, Argentina, and Brazil—depend upon the sale of cattle for a living. They would not or could not easily switch to doing something else. For another, people do not easily change their eating habits.

Productive Farming Methods. The two most promising ways to help with food supply are finding more productive farming techniques and using new food sources. Current agricultural research is helping with both of these.

In the 1950s and 1960s, new ideas from agricultural research were tried in developing countries. New hybrid seeds for rice and wheat were planted that grew faster. This was because the plants could take large amounts of fertilizer. Harvests increased, and food supplies improved.

In the 1970s weather and economic problems caused the new crops to fail in many countries. To grow the new plants, which were easily attacked by disease and insects, continuous supplies of water, fertilizers, and pesticides were needed. There was so little water in many of the developing countries that irrigation was needed. Because most of these developing countries had little cash, they often could not pay to save the crops.

New Sources of Food. Today 90 percent of the world's food comes from 15 crops and 7 livestock animals. Yet, there are more

This "fish farm" in the Philippines is a new approach to increasing a country's food supply. Such methods are often used to solve food shortages. What are some other ways to increase a country's food supply?

To reduce food shortages more sources of protein need to be found. Oilseed crops such as cottonseed and peanuts, fish and plants from the ocean, and soybean products such as tofu are good sources of protein and are being developed into new or improved protein-rich food.

than 10 million kinds of plants and animals on Earth. Therefore, researchers are trying to find which of these can become new sources of food.

As supplies of natural resources become smaller, prices increase, prompting conservation and alternate sources.

3.2 Natural Resources Supply

A growing population puts pressure not only on the food supply but also on the supply of natural resources. If people today use up the resources, it will make problems for the future. Certain natural resources like petroleum are in limited supply.

The economies of industrialized countries depend on continuing supplies of petroleum. Oil and gas are used to heat homes, to make electricity, and to provide fuel. As industries grow to meet the needs of more people, greater demands are made on petroleum resources. Many experts fear that by early in the next century, there may be no petroleum. Conservation has led to less world energy use since 1980. Continued conservation could make energy resources last longer.

An even more basic resource being threatened is fresh water. Industrialized countries need larger and larger supplies for industry, and many developing countries are using huge amounts to irrigate dry lands. Also, water has been polluted in many places around the world. For these reasons, many water specialists think that having enough water will be a major problem by the year 2000.

Conversely, some countries in Eastern Europe are strongly encouraging larger families.

3.3 Population Control

Many people have come to believe that the solution to food shortages and dwindling natural resources is to reduce population growth. They believe that the birthrate of each country must be lowered until it is balanced with its death rate.

In developing countries, however, efforts to slow down the birthrate have met with lit-

"A small family is a happy family" is suggested in this Indian mural. Governments in many developing countries use such advertising to promote lower birthrates among their citizens. Why are such efforts not always successful?

Chinese law sets minimum ages for marriage at 22 for men and 20 for women. There is strong encouragement to marry late and to have only one child.

HUMAN PATTERNS   UNIT 3

tle success. Many people in these countries are **subsistence farmers**—farmers who grow most or all of the food their families need. Most of these people want large families. Children are needed to help with farm chores.

Since 1970 it has become the policy of many governments around the world to lower their population growth rates by offering programs for family planning. In this group are Asia's developing countries with the largest populations—China, India, Indonesia, Pakistan, and Bangladesh. Egypt, Kenya, Chile, and Honduras also have such programs. However, in some of these countries, people honor traditional values and strong religious beliefs that do not allow them to practice birth control.

Desertification in Africa is causing large-scale migration into cities and across borders.

3.4 Migration

In some overpopulated areas of the world, the number of people has gone down because of **migration,** or the movement of people from one place to another. In the past 400 years, when most large migrations have taken place, tens of millions of people have moved to other areas.

Demographers study migration because *immigrants,* people who move into another country, become part of the country's **census,** or count of people. They have found that, in general, immigrants move for either economic or political reasons. These reasons can be thought of as "push-pull" forces. The "push" comes from bad living conditions at home that make people want to leave. For example, people may leave because there is not enough food or jobs or they may not be able to practice their religion freely. The "pull" comes from better living conditions in other places. For example, people may want to go where land is promised if people settle or farm it or where full voting rights are given to all groups of people equally.

Migration has become an important issue in many parts of the world because rapid population growth and the living conditions it brings have made many more people move. Recently, there have been more moves from the countryside to urban areas and from developing to industrialized countries. When large numbers of immigrants go into a country, their need for food, jobs, and services such as health care places huge demands on the country's economy. In this way population explosions in developing countries are being felt in industrialized countries as well.

See the *TRB* for *Chapter 6 Reading* on United States population trends.

CONTENT CHECK

1. **Define:** malnutrition, subsistence farmers, migration, census.
2. What are four possible ways to increase the world's food supply?
3. What have many heavily populated developing countries done to control their rates of population growth?
4. **Challenge:** How would you go about encouraging people all over the world to eat more efficiently?

Initiate a class discussion on remedies students suggest for issues presented in this section.

CONCLUSION

People have settled various parts of Earth, forming many different patterns. The success of people in adapting to many physical environments is only one reason the number of Earth's people continues to grow.

Geographers are interested in more than the number of people and where they live. They are also interested in how people interact with their physical environments. Geographers want to know what people are doing to assure their success now and in the future. For that reason, population will remain an important focus of geographic study.

CHAPTER REVIEW

SUMMARY

1. For many years, the growth of Earth's population was slow. This changed with the development of agriculture.
2. The population of Earth in 1 AD is estimated at about 250 million. Today it is thought to be more than 5 billion.
3. Population growth rates are related to levels of economic development.
4. Demographers have identified four stages of population growth that countries may pass through as their economies go from developing to industrialized.
5. The population explosion has raised such issues as providing enough food, conserving supplies of natural resources, and controlling overpopulation.

Answers to the following questions can be found on page T106.

REVIEWING VOCABULARY

The definitions of several vocabulary words found in this chapter are listed below. Number your paper from 1 to 9. Next to each number, write the word that correctly fits each definition.

1. country whose economy is based on manufacturing and is highly developed
2. level of growth when the birthrate equals the death rate
3. type of scientist who studies human population growth
4. value of all goods and services produced in a country during a year
5. population of an area per unit of land
6. graph used by demographers to show the ages of the people in a country and the number of males and females
7. organized way that a country uses all of its resources to provide for the wants and needs of its people
8. lack of nourishment
9. movement of people from one place to another

REMEMBERING THE FACTS

1. What development brought about the first change in world population growth? The first great increase?
2. What is today's estimated world population? What is estimated as the world's population for the year 2000?
3. What percent of Earth's population lives in developing countries?
4. In what stage are nations that have the highest population growth rates?
5. Where are the four centers of heavy population in the world?
6. What country has more people than any other country in the world?
7. What are the two most promising solutions to world food supply shortages?
8. What were successes and failures in increasing food production in developing countries in the 1950s to 1970s?
9. What "pushes" people to migrate?

UNDERSTANDING THE FACTS

1. What were some of the reasons for shorter life spans in years past?
2. What problems does rapid population growth create for a country? No population growth?
3. Why are some world areas unpopulated?
4. What has influenced where people in Asia live? In Europe?
5. How has climate influenced the settlement of North America and Africa?
6. How may some governments take action to slow population growth?

THINKING CRITICALLY AND CREATIVELY

1. Do you think the development of agriculture increased the birthrate, the death rate, or both? Explain.
2. If the climate were to change so that Canada would be warmer than it is, what might be the influence on Canada's population pattern?
3. A geographer once observed that more than half of the people in the world live in areas less than 650 feet (198.1 m) above sea level. Why do you suppose an area's elevation would influence population distribution?
4. Thomas Malthus once said, "The power of population is infinitely greater than the power in the earth to produce subsistence for man." In your own words, what do you think Malthus means by this statement? In what ways do you agree with this statement? In what ways do you disagree with the statement?
5. Has the world population crisis that Malthus predicted happened yet? Why or why not?
6. One suggestion for dealing with the food crisis in the world is to use more plants and fish from the ocean as sources of protein. What effect may this have on the biosphere? What possible problems may there be with this plan?
7. **Challenge:** A startling population pattern is that more than 90 percent of Earth's population lives in the Northern Hemisphere. With the aid of a globe, analyze why this is true.
8. **Challenge:** If people are aware of problems with supplies of natural resources, why have the problems not been solved?

REINFORCING GRAPHIC SKILLS

Study the table on page 114. Then answer the questions that follow.

1. The United States and Syria have death rates of nine per thousand. How do their birthrates and annual population growth rates compare?
2. China and Angola have similar GNPs. How do they differ?
3. What developing countries in the table have 10 percent or less of their land area suitable for farming? What industrialized countries?
4. What generalization can you make about population growth and economic GNP?

CHAPTER 7

126

Busy marketplace in Patan, Nepal

CULTURE

In this chapter you will learn—

● What is meant by a culture.
● What stages were important in the development of early cultures.
● What the chief characteristics are of each of 11 culture areas.

INTRODUCTION

Many groups of people live on Earth. Each has its own traditions and customs, history, language, and religious beliefs and practices. Each also has its own ways of dressing and eating. Each has its own arts, technology, economy, laws, and form of government. Each is a **culture**—a society with its own way of life created to satisfy its needs. From the natural environment around it, each has shaped its own **cultural landscape**. This landscape greatly mirrors the people that made it.

Children learn about their culture from their families and other members of their group. They are shaped by their group's beliefs and ways. Learning their culture makes it possible for them to get along in their group.

A culture may be made up of people from more than one country. A country may be made up of people from more than one culture. No two cultures have adapted to their environments in the same way. All, however, have changed their environments in one way or another. They have built structures, tilled the earth, channeled water, and made lines of communication. Thus, all cultures, no matter how different they may be from one another, have something in common—a total way of life for themselves.

1. CULTURAL DEVELOPMENT AND CHANGE

Cultures do not just happen. They develop slowly over a very long time. In the view of human geographers, four stages were important to the development of early cultures. These were (1) the discovery of fire, (2) the invention of tools, (3) the growth of agriculture, and (4) the use of writing.

The discovery and use of fire made it possible for people to live in colder climates, and firelight allowed them to exchange information after dark. The invention of tools helped them hunt, prepare meat and animal skins, and do work. The growth of agriculture made it possible for them to stay in one place rather than move around in search of food. It also led them to tame animals to help them with their work and to be used for food. The use of writing allowed them to record information and pass it along. A group of people that has developed its culture and technology to include a writing system for itself is called a **civilization.**

Once people learned to grow crops, they began to settle in villages and raise enough food to feed growing numbers of people.

127

When there were too many people, some moved on and settled new villages. In time, cities developed. Since the people no longer had to spend all their time looking for or producing food, they were able to study and to take part in other activities. Since greater numbers of people were living closer to one another, it was easier for them to meet and share ideas. Once they knew how to write, they could keep records of their harvests and taxes and write down their laws. All of these could be passed on to the next generation.

As each culture developed, it changed. Changes still take place in cultures today. Sometimes the change is great. Other times it is not. Each culture develops at its own pace. A change that takes place in one culture may take place many years later in another, or it may not take place at all. Sometimes change comes about when the ideas, objects, or behaviors of one culture flow or are carried to another culture, which makes them a part of its own way of life. This is known as **cultural diffusion** (dihf YOO zhuhn). As shown in

See the *TAE* for an *Objective 1* Activity.

These Filipinos playing basketball reflect the worldwide popularity of certain sports that began in one particular area. What is meant by cultural diffusion?

Figure 7-1 on page 129, the methods of farming were carried to many parts of the world.

Other times, having close contact over a long time brings about change. One or both cultures may be greatly influenced in many ways by the other. They may even merge. This is known as **acculturation** (uh KUHL chuh RAY shuhn). This happened in the United States when different groups of people from many parts of the world came to settle a new land. Their cultures blended together over many, many years to form the culture of the American people.

People of all cultures need food, homes, and clothing. All need a system for keeping order. All have ceremonies for such events as birth, marriage, and death. In these ways, all cultures are the same. But the ways they go about meeting their needs and setting up their societies may be quite different.

One reason for the differences between cultures is environment. This is because people learn to adapt to their physical surroundings over time. People living in a warm climate, for example, will wear different kinds of clothes, build different kinds of houses, and grow different kinds of crops from those living in a cold climate. Those who live near rivers or oceans will make their livings in ways different from those who live on plains or in mountain areas.

Because of differences, people from one culture often have trouble understanding people of another culture. People feel most comfortable in their own group. Many are **ethnocentric**. This means that they believe that the ways and beliefs of their own culture are the best ones or the only right ones. These people think only in terms of what is most familiar. Often they are suspicious, unaware, or uncaring of people of other cultures.

In recent years cultures—and countries—trade more with one another than they did in the past. People from many parts of the world share goods and ideas. Because of more

HUMAN PATTERNS   UNIT 3

Point out that the process of acculturation is closely associated with that of westernization. Ask students if they know of instances of non-western cultures influencing western culture.

Material culture includes such physical things as buildings and art objects. Nonmaterial culture includes a group's customs and values, such as artistic expressions of beauty or customary greetings.

DIFFUSION OF AGRICULTURE

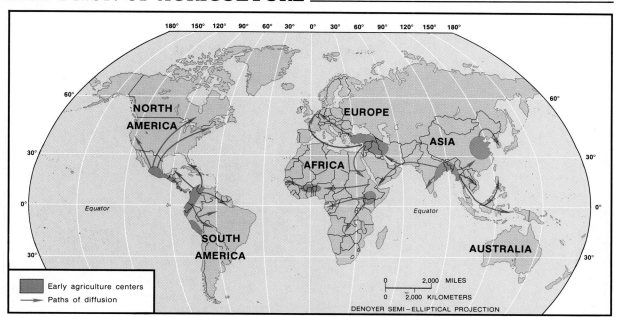

FIGURE 7-1
Agriculture began in the Middle East about 8000 BC and soon after in Asia and Mexico. How did agriculture help a culture develop?

and better transportation and communication systems, they have more contact with and know more about each other. In other words, they have become more interdependent. This has led many people to talk in terms of a global culture—one made up of many different cultures from all over the world, all of which have some things in common and depend in some way on one another.

CONTENT CHECK

1. **Define:** civilization, cultural diffusion, acculturation, ethnocentric.
2. What are the four stages important to the development of cultures?
3. In what ways are all cultures alike?
4. **Challenge:** How may ethnocentric feelings and actions prevent the development of a global culture?

2. WORLD CULTURES

Some social scientists use culture to divide the world into parts to make it easier to study. For example, **anthropologists**— those who study humans and human culture— speak of culture areas. **Culture areas** are large parts of the world in which one or more common culture traits are strong. **Culture traits** are the objects, ideas, behaviors, and other characteristics of a culture. A culture's objects, such as clothing and paintings, are part of its *material* culture. Its ideas, such as language and religion, are part of its *nonmaterial* culture.

Anthropologists have divided the world into the 11 major culture areas shown in Figure 7-2 on page 130. They are (1) Anglo-America, (2) Latin America, (3) Western Europe, (4) Eastern Europe and the Soviet

WORLD CULTURE AREAS

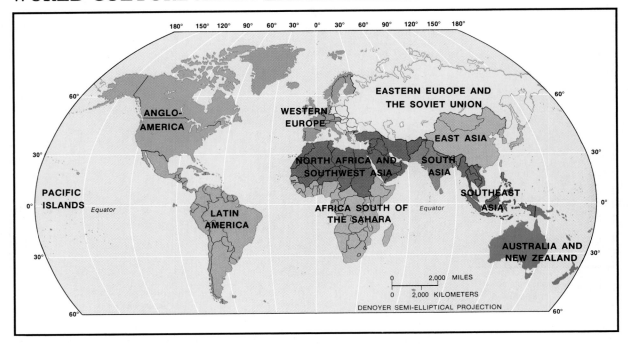

FIGURE 7-2
A map of the world can be divided according to particular topics, as in this map showing world areas whose cultures are alike. Such a map makes it possible to classify many countries under one area. What are some common characteristics that set apart one culture from another?

Have students prepare a display of marriage ceremonies in several world cultures. Information for the display can be found in such sources as the *Cultural Atlas* of various countries and *National Geographic*.

Union, (5) North Africa and Southwest Asia, (6) Africa south of the Sahara, (7) South Asia, (8) East Asia, (9) Southeast Asia, (10) Australia and New Zealand, and (11) the Pacific Islands. Each culture area can be further divided into regions in which many more culture traits are alike. There are other ways the world may be divided into culture areas and regions, but the way used in this book is accepted by many geographers.

Each culture area has certain common characteristics that set it apart from others. These are often its history, form of government, economy, language, and religion. The following descriptions of each culture area center around these common culture traits.

2.1 Anglo-America

The culture area named Anglo-America is made up of two regions that cover most of the North American continent—Canada and the United States. Each of these regions is also a **nation**, a group of people that has a territory of its own and is organized under one government.

For many centuries, native Indian cultures lived undisturbed in both regions of Anglo-America. Then settlers from Europe came to North America. Most of those who came to Canada were from France. Those who came to the United States were mainly from England. In the 1700s the British controlled the eastern parts of both regions. They

HUMAN PATTERNS   UNIT 3

The most densely populated French-speaking part of Canada is the province of Quebec.

Because the Andes are higher and more rugged than the Rockies, people on opposite sides of the mountains often have little contact with one another.

lost control of their American colonies when the United States won its independence in the late 1700s. Today each of the nations is a **democracy.** This is a form of government in which the people rule themselves by voting for their leaders and laws.

Canada and the United States have economies based on **free enterprise.** Under free enterprise, individuals and businesses have the freedom to make a living with little control by government. These regions both have highly developed industrialized economies. Large numbers of their people enjoy a high standard of living.

Even though French is spoken in parts of Canada and Spanish is spoken in parts of the United States, the majority of people in Anglo-America speak English. This is why this culture area is called Anglo-America. The word *Anglo* comes from the Angles, a people who settled in England during the late 400s BC. The majority of people in Anglo-America believe in Christianity, a religion that follows the teachings of Jesus Christ.

See the *TAE* for an *Objective 2* Activity.

2.2 Latin America

Latin America is made up of the regions of Mexico and Central America, the Caribbean islands, and all the countries in South America, including Argentina, Brazil, and Chile. Native Indian cultures built great civilizations in these regions between 1200 BC and 1500 AD. After Spain and Portugal conquered most of this part of the world in the 1500s and 1600s, traits from these cultures mixed with those from the European cultures. Further acculturation took place when European settlers brought Africans to these regions to work on their plantations.

Many countries in Latin America have **authoritarian** governments, in which one leader or a group of leaders rules the country and makes laws for the people. For the most part, these are developing countries faced with many economic problems.

The word *Latin* comes from the ancient Roman language. Spanish and Portuguese, the languages spoken in this culture area,

Downtown workers and visitors relax in a plaza near Toronto City Hall. Anglo-America is highly urban—76 percent of people in Canada and 74 percent of people in the United States live in cities. What other common traits do these two Anglo-American countries share?

were formed from Latin. Most Latin Americans are Roman Catholics, those who follow the beliefs of a Christian church that is led by the Pope, bishop of Rome.

2.3 Western Europe

Western Europe is made up of two regions—Northwest Europe and Mediterranean Europe. Within these regions are more than 25 nations, including the United Kingdom, France, West Germany, Spain, Italy, and Greece. Some of the countries are among the smallest in the world. The cultures in Western Europe are largely based on the great ancient civilizations of Greece and Rome. Many of the countries in Western Europe were once part of the Roman Empire. In later times in history, many were united under the same governments. Democracy is common in Western Europe.

Because the Industrial Revolution began in the Northwest Europe region, most of the countries in Western Europe are industrialized. Their people enjoy a high standard of living.

Most of the languages spoken in this culture area come from the same **language family**, or group of languages that come from the same common language. The many languages in the Indo-European family are shown in Figure 7-3 on page 133. Most Western Europeans are Christians—either Roman Catholics or Protestants, followers of different Christian beliefs and churches.

Parts of Eastern Europe, such as Albania, have large Muslim populations.

2.4 Eastern Europe and the Soviet Union

In this culture area, there are many **ethnic groups**, or people who share a common cultural heritage. Over many years in history,

groups in Eastern Europe were often stronger than any government or ruler that tried to unite them under its power. Within these groups, during the late 1800s, grew feelings of **nationalism**, or the demand by people for independent nations of their own. In the early 1900s, after World War I, many nations were formed in Eastern Europe. The Eastern European countries are East Germany, Poland, Czechoslovakia, Hungary, Yugoslavia, Romania, Bulgaria, and Albania.

At the same time, the Russian people revolted against their tsar, or king. The leaders of the revolution set up a communist government. **Communism** is an authoritarian government in which a small political group, members of the Communist Party, have total power over the people, laws, and economy of the country. Communist leaders renamed the country the Union of Soviet Socialist Republics. It is called the U.S.S.R., or the Soviet Union. In the mid-1900s, after World War II, most of the countries in Eastern Europe came under Soviet control and became communist. They were called *Soviet satellites*. Today some are less under the control of the Soviet Union than others. The Soviet Union and several countries in Eastern Europe have industrialized economies.

Most of the languages spoken in this culture area come from the Indo-European language family. Other languages in Eastern Europe come from the Ural-Altaic family. Each ethnic group speaks its own **dialect**, or special form of its language. The people in Eastern Europe and the Soviet Union are discouraged by their communist governments from practicing religion. However, many Christians follow the beliefs of the Roman Catholic Church or the Eastern Orthodox Church. The Eastern Orthodox Church is a group of Catholic churches that considers the patriarch in Istanbul (Constantinople) as their leader, rather than the Pope of the Roman Catholic Church in Rome, Italy.

Almost all of the three or four thousand languages spoken in the world are members of twenty known language families.

For the approximate number of followers of the world's major religions, refer to the table of World Religions on page 139.

INDO-EUROPEAN LANGUAGE FAMILY

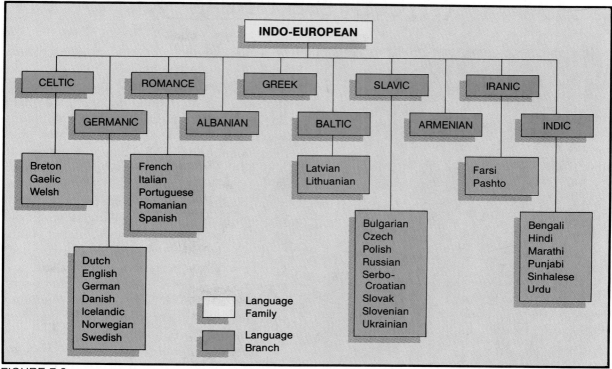

FIGURE 7-3
Nearly one-half—48 percent—of the world's population speak languages stemming from the Indo-European family group. This language family can be heard on continents around the world. What are names of some other language families?

Some conflicts in North Africa and Southwest Asia are between peoples belonging to different branches of Islam. For example, the *Sunni* Muslims of Iraq and the *Shiite* Muslims of Iran have fought during much of the 1980s.

2.5 North Africa and Southwest Asia

This culture area has two regions from different continents—North Africa and Southwest Asia. From this culture area in the valley of the Tigris and Euphrates rivers came one of the earliest civilizations. For this reason, the area has been called a **cultural hearth.** This means that it is an area where a culture begins and from which new ideas spread to other cultures in the world. It is from this cultural hearth that scientists think the first ideas of farming came. Also, in this area, the three great religions—Judaism, Christianity, and Islam—began. Judaism

(JYOOD uh IHZ uhm) is the religion of the early Hebrews, or Jews. It was the first major religion to believe in only one god. The belief in Islam, however, is the most common culture trait in North Africa and Southwest Asia. About 80 percent of the people are Muslims, followers of the teachings of Muhammad, the founder of Islam. Many of his teachings are based on Judaism and Christianity.

In addition to Islam, another common trait of this culture area is the Arabic language in the Hamito-Semitic family. Those who speak Arabic call themselves Arabs, even though each Arab country speaks a different dialect of the language. Only written Arabic is the same to all Arabs.

FOCUS ON CULTURE

YOUTH SUBCULTURE

Cultural geographers have observed that within a culture there may be several groups with values and ways of life different from those of the majority. These groups are called *subcultures*. They can be thought of as "cultures within a culture." Teenagers and young adults make up one such subculture that is found in cultures worldwide.

Many teenagers spend most of their time with other teenagers. They are in a time of life when they size up what they like or do not like about themselves as well as the people and world around them. Teenagers find this process easier to do with members of their own group. They experiment with different hairstyles, voice patterns, styles of dress—even personalities and behavior. Some changes set youth even farther apart from the rest of society. For example, during the 1980s in many European countries and in the United States, young people shaved their heads into punk hairstyles.

Teenagers also examine their own society and the world. They may work to make changes in these areas also. In China young people are more and more frustrated with their communist government's campaign to commit them to the goals of the Communist Party. Some young Chinese feel that government places too many restrictions on their personal lives. They are willing to speak out on issues much more than Chinese youths from years before. In South Africa black youths recently protested against their government's policies by wearing T-shirts with antigovernment slogans—dress commonly worn without worry by teens in countries with less restrictive governments.

Recently, some young people who are taking action to change their world organized Youths for Environment and Service (YES). Young people from many different countries—Spain, France, Greece, Turkey, Israel, Yugoslavia, Morocco, Egypt, Lebanon, Malta, and Jordan—work together on environmental studies like the group shown in the photograph on this page. The YES project for 1987 was cleaning up polluted areas along the Mediterranean coast. On some YES projects, young people work side-by-side with teens from other cultures. Many are from countries that are at war with one another. These young people more easily step across cultural barriers because of their age, their similar goals, and their being a part of youth subcultures.

1. What is a subculture?
2. Why do young people classify as a subculture in many world cultures?
3. What are some examples of youth working for change in their societies?

Because the area connects Europe, Asia, and Africa, it has always been a crossroads for trade routes. Today trade and transportation among these parts of the world greatly depend on the Suez Canal in North Africa. Even though some countries are wealthy from their oil resources, their economies are still viewed as developing. Only Israel is an industrialized country. Other countries are developing their economies at different rates.

2.6 Africa South of the Sahara

The part of Africa south of the Sahara includes the regions of East Africa, West and Central Africa, and Southern Africa. The Sahara has always physically kept the African people north of the desert from the African people south of the desert. As a result, different cultures developed in each part of the African continent.

Few written records were kept in the great cities and kingdoms that grew in this culture area from ancient times to the 1300s.

People from other parts of the world knew little about the African people. During the 1400s and 1500s, explorers and traders brought word to Europe about the riches of the land and the people in this culture area. From then until the 1800s, European countries took over most of the area. The countries there were ruled as European colonies. Only during the middle of the twentieth century did most of the countries gain independence. Many of these countries today are **republics**, governments in which people elect representatives to run their government. Even though the kinds of economies found in this area vary, the countries of Africa south of the Sahara are all viewed as developing countries, except for South Africa.

Many people in this area speak one of the 100 languages in the Bantu family. Each language also has many dialects. Many Africans from this area practice their own local religions. In many parts of the area, Christianity is followed. In others, the people follow the beliefs of Christianity along with their local religion.

Cool stone pillars provide a prayerful and restful setting inside this ancient Ethiopian church. Islam and Christianity blend with other traditional African religions in Ethiopia. Which language family is spoken in Africa south of the Sahara?

CHAPTER 7   **CULTURE**

2.7 South Asia

The culture area of South Asia is made up of the countries of India, Pakistan, Sri Lanka, the Maldives, Bangladesh, Nepal, and Bhutan. The history of this culture area dates back to 3000 BC when one of the oldest civilizations was founded in the Indus River Valley. Through the centuries the culture became diverse, largely because of influences from their Asian neighbors. It was also influenced by Great Britain, which controlled the area from the 1700s until the 1900s. Diversity continued as the nations gained independence and set up different forms of government and economies. Countries in this area are developing their economies at different rates.

The culture trait that binds this culture area together is religion. Hinduism is the religion followed by most of the people in this area. Hinduism developed in India from a number of different beliefs and practices from India's earliest times. It was also religion that divided the people in the mid-1900s when Britain created the nations of Pakistan for

Muslims and of India for Hindus. In order to practice their religion, many people had to leave their homes and resettle in another part of the area.

2.8 East Asia

The culture area of East Asia includes the countries of China, Taiwan, Japan, North Korea, South Korea, Mongolia, and the colonies of Hong Kong and Macao. The common culture characteristics of the East Asian area date back to the ancient Chinese, who created one of the oldest living civilizations. Most of the people in China and Taiwan are descendants of this society. From this culture hearth, Chinese culture spread to other parts of the area where their alphabet, styles of dress, religion, and art mixed with other East Asian cultures.

The people of East Asia follow many different religions. Three of the main religions are Buddhism (BOO DIHZ uhm), Shintoism, and Daoism (DOW IHZ uhm). Buddhism is a

See the *TAE* for an *Objective 2* Activity.

These young Tokyo students are learning calligraphy, an ancient artistic style of writing dating back to China in the fifth century BC and brought to Japan more than a thousand years ago. Although they share this common art form, in what cultural ways do Japan and China differ?

WORLD LITERACY

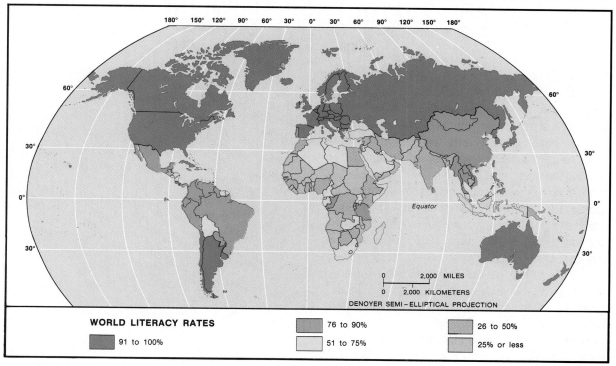

WORLD LITERACY RATES
91 to 100%   76 to 90%   51 to 75%   26 to 50%   25% or less

FIGURE 7-4
In today's world an ability to read and write are necessary for living and working, as well as for understanding one's own and other people's cultures. The importance that a country gives to education and schools helps to determine its literacy rate. The map shown here groups together countries whose literacy rates fall within certain ranges. Literacy rates are highest in which world culture areas?

religion founded in India during the 500s BC by Siddhartha Gautama, or Buddha. Shintoism grew in Japan and was, for a time, both the main religion and a form of patriotism. Daoism began in China at about the same time that Buddhism was growing in India. Many people throughout East Asia follow the practices and beliefs of more than one of these religions.

Some geographers have argued that Japan should not be viewed as part of the East Asian culture area, even though many of its culture traits have been borrowed from the Chinese culture. They point out that Japan is very different from the rest of the area. For

example, Japan is a highly developed industrialized country, whereas China's developing economy generally relies on farming. The government of Japan is democratic, while the government of China is communist. The Japanese language belongs to a different language family from the Sino-Tibetan family to which the Chinese language belongs. The Japanese have succeeded in teaching nearly 100 percent of their people to read and write, but only three-fourths of the Chinese people can. A country's **literacy rate** is the percent of the total number of people that can read and write their own language. Figure 7-4 on this page shows literacy rates of countries all over

USING GRAPHIC SKILLS

COMPARING DATA FROM MAPS AND GRAPHS

Your work on a social studies report is very frustrating. Even though you read a number of books that you stacked high on the study table at the library, you just do not understand that one key idea that *must* be in your report. Luckily, in the last book, you find a map that gives you the additional information you need. It finally makes sense!

Maps, graphs, and other illustrations are very important tools for studying geography. This is because they contain so much information. One small map, for example, can show the same data that would take several hundred words to describe. Illustrations are also helpful because they show you information in picture form that is often more easily understood than paragraphs of words.

Maps and graphs each show information in a different way. Maps use location, and graphs use numbers. Together they can give you much information about the same subject. Comparing data from maps and graphs on the same subject can help you understand certain generalizations about the subject.

In comparing data from maps and graphs, it is important to follow several steps. First, read the titles of the maps and graphs. The titles tell what kind of information is being illustrated. Second, determine the subject that they have in common. For example, the map and graph shown on page 139 both show information on the subject of religion. Next, study the colors and the symbols used in the map and in the graph. Then, begin to compare the information in the map with the information in the graph. Some information from each will tell you similar facts about the subject. Other information will tell you different facts. Finally, based on information from your comparisons, begin to draw conclusions about the subject.

Using the steps described, study the map and graph on page 139. Then answer the questions that follow.

1. On which continents are Christians found? Muslims? Hindus? Buddhists?

2. Which major religion has the largest number of followers who live within the largest total land area?

3. The followers of which religion live in the smallest land area?

4. In which culture areas of the world is more than one major religion practiced within the same area?

5. Within a large land area throughout the world, people practice local religions. Why are they not considered major religions?

6. In what culture area do the majority of Eastern Orthodox Christians live?

7. What conclusion or generalization can be made about Hinduism by comparing information on the map with information on the graph?

8. Compare the area and population of Islam with the area and population of Christianity. Which is larger?

9. **Challenge:** How do you explain the existence of so many religions in the islands of Southeast Asia?

10. **Challenge:** The numbers of Daoists and Jews in the world are about the same. What does the map tell you about where Daoists live? About where Jews live? Make a hypothesis about how Judaism spread to many parts of the world.

11. **Challenge:** In your opinion, what makes a religion a major religion: the number of its followers or the size of the total land area in which its followers live?

WORLD RELIGIONS

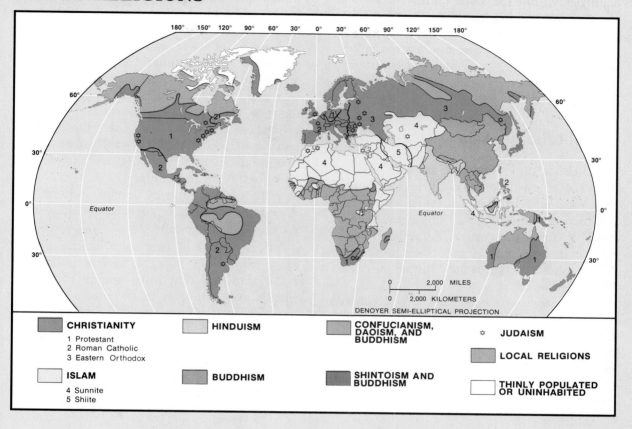

CHRISTIANITY
1 Protestant
2 Roman Catholic
3 Eastern Orthodox

ISLAM
4 Sunnite
5 Shiite

HINDUISM

BUDDHISM

CONFUCIANISM, DAOISM, AND BUDDHISM

SHINTOISM AND BUDDHISM

✡ **JUDAISM**

LOCAL RELIGIONS

THINLY POPULATED OR UNINHABITED

DENOYER SEMI-ELLIPTICAL PROJECTION

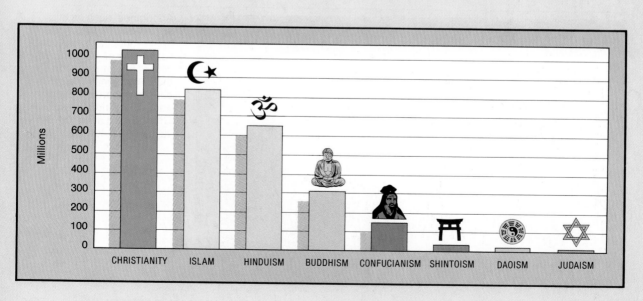

the world. These differences between two countries within the same culture area point out the problem in classifying the world into parts. Some regions in the same culture area may have much in common, while others within an area may have common beginnings but through the years develop very different individual culture traits.

2.9 Southeast Asia

The culture area of Southeast Asia is made up of two regions, Continental Southeast Asia and Insular Southeast Asia. The continental region is the countries in Asia south of China and east of India. The *insular*, or island, region is a group of more than 20,000 islands between the continental region and Australia.

Because Southeast Asia is at a crossroads location in the Pacific Ocean, this culture area has been visited and greatly influenced through the centuries by many other cultures in the world. It was Southeast Asia that had many of the spices sought by European explorers and traders during the 1400s and 1500s. The people of Southeast Asia also traded spices with merchants in North Africa, India, and China. These early contacts with people from other parts of the world led to changes in the ways of life for many people in the area. In later times European countries made much of Southeast Asia into colonies. In many cases the boundaries of the colonies did not keep members of the same ethnic groups together. This meant that the common culture of certain groups was broken apart, making different ways of life in many parts of Southeast Asia. In the mid-1900s, after World War II, many countries became independent nations. The forms of government their leaders chose are very different.

Some parts of this culture area are far away from other parts. It has been hard to make transportation links among the many islands and countries in the area. All countries, except for industrialized Singapore, are developing their economies.

In the continental region of Southeast Asia, nearly all people practice Buddhism. In the insular region, there are followers of many different religions.

Aborigines, such as this stockman, are the original native inhabitants of Australia. Making up about 1 percent of the total population, most Aborigines live in the country's more remote areas. What kind of people did Great Britain send to Australia in the eighteenth century?

HUMAN PATTERNS　　UNIT 3

Point out to students the great size of Australia. Explain that its small population is spread over an area as large as that of the contiguous United States.

In a discussion on development of global culture, point out that communication and transportation have expanding roles in creating such a culture. Ask students for examples of current global trends.

2.10 Australia and New Zealand

The two regions found in this culture area are the nations of Australia and New Zealand. Even though the area was originally settled 20,000 years ago by people from Southeast Asia, the culture that is found there today is based on the culture of Great Britain. This is because in the eighteenth century the British decided to send prisoners to faraway Australia as punishment. Many of these prisoners were not criminals but were in jail for not paying their bills. In time, many more people from England, Ireland, and Scotland that were not prisoners came to settle. The numbers grew larger after gold was found.

The people of Australia and New Zealand are ruled by democracies and have industrialized economies based on free enterprise. Most of the people speak English and practice Christianity.

Explain that some locations in the Pacific Islands are important tourist sites. Tahiti is an example.

2.11 Pacific Islands

The tens of thousands of islands in the Pacific Ocean that make up this culture area can be divided into three groups. These regions are Melanesia, Micronesia, and Polynesia. The regions are based generally on either the ethnic makeup of the people who live on the islands or the kinds of islands in the regions. They are viewed as a culture area more from their general location in the Pacific than from any common culture traits.

The countries in this area are among the poorest in the world. Their economies are very underdeveloped. As transportation costs become greater and greater, the crops these countries export are becoming more and more expensive to send to other parts of the world. Most of the people live in small villages and make a living by farming and fishing.

CONTENT CHECK

1. **Identify:** Christianity, Roman Catholics, Protestants, Eastern Orthodox Church, Judaism, Jews, Islam, Muslims, Hinduism, Buddhism.
2. **Define:** anthropologists, culture areas, culture traits, nation, democracy, free enterprise, authoritarian, language family, ethnic groups, nationalism, communism, dialect, cultural hearth, republics, literacy rate.
3. What are the 11 major culture areas?
4. From what country does the culture of Anglo-America stem? Of South Asia?
5. What religion is common among people in Western Europe? In North Africa and Southwest Asia?
6. What form of government is common to parts of Eastern Europe and the Soviet Union and East Asia?
7. **Challenge:** How might the culture area of Latin America be different if Europeans had never conquered it?

See the *TRB* for the *Chapter 7 Skill Activity* on recognizing cultural differences.

CONCLUSION

The study of culture in geography explores all the ways people live on Earth. Geographers have observed that groups of people in every place on Earth have unique ways of life. In one or more ways, each culture differs from every other culture in the world. Each has developed a different culture based on its group's needs. Geographers want to learn how and why certain culture traits are the same in groups in different parts of the world. They also want to know how and why other traits are different from those in other parts of the world. Studying culture helps geographers better understand relationships among people and places on Earth's surface.

SUMMARY

1. A culture is a society with its own way of life created to satisfy its needs.
2. Elements of culture include a group's traditions and customs, history, language, religious beliefs and practices, styles of dress, eating habits, arts, technology, economy, laws, and form of government.
3. People learn their culture by being members of their group.
4. Present-day cultures are the results of thousands of years of change. The stages important to the development of early cultures were (1) discovery of fire, (2) invention of tools, (3) growth of agriculture, and (4) use of writing.
5. In some ways cultures are the same. People in all cultures need food, homes, and clothing. Cultures are different in the ways they go about meeting their needs and setting up their societies.
6. One reason for the differences among cultures is the differences in physical environments. Each group has changed or adapted to its own environment.
7. The world can be divided into 11 major culture areas based on common culture traits. They are (1) Anglo-America, (2) Latin America, (3) Western Europe, (4) Eastern Europe and the Soviet Union, (5) North Africa and Southwest Asia, (6) Africa south of the Sahara, (7) South Asia, (8) East Asia, (9) Southeast Asia, (10) Australia and New Zealand, and (11) the Pacific Islands.

Answers to the following questions can be found on page T112.

REVIEWING VOCABULARY

Many words with general meanings may be made more specific by using a modifier. The modifier limits the word's meaning. Such is the case with several of the vocabulary words in this chapter. The words *culture* and *cultural* in the following list of words to the right limit the meanings of the general words in the list on the left.

<table>
<tr><td colspan="2">GENERAL WORDS</td><td colspan="2">SPECIFIC WORDS</td></tr>
<tr><td>area</td><td>landscape</td><td>culture area</td><td>cultural landscape</td></tr>
<tr><td>diffusion</td><td>trait</td><td>cultural diffusion</td><td>culture trait</td></tr>
<tr><td colspan="2" align="center">hearth</td><td colspan="2" align="center">cultural hearth</td></tr>
</table>

Use a dictionary to look up the definition of each of the general *words. Pick the definition for each word that relates most closely to the study of geography. Write the definitions on a sheet of paper, skipping several lines between each definition. On these extra lines, in your own words, modify, or change, the definition of each* general *word to define its related* specific *word. Try not to use the word* culture *or* cultural *in your definition.*

REMEMBERING THE FACTS

1. What is a culture?
2. What is a cultural landscape?
3. What were the four stages important to the development of early cultures?
4. What does acculturation mean?
5. What are the 11 major culture areas?
6. In what five culture areas are Indo-European languages common?
7. In what culture area is Hinduism common? Islam? Buddhism?

UNDERSTANDING THE FACTS

1. How do people learn their culture?
2. What is the difference between a culture and a civilization?
3. How did the discovery of fire help people adapt better to harsh environments?
4. What similar problems have ethnic groups in Eastern Europe and Southeast Asia experienced in the past?
5. Why is North Africa and Southwest Asia considered a cultural hearth?

THINKING CRITICALLY AND CREATIVELY

1. How would you describe the cultural landscape that surrounds you? How does it mirror the people of this country? What are ten common cultural traits of the people in this country?
2. How is it possible that a culture may be made up of people from more than one country?
3. How might the culture areas of the world be different if writing had never been developed?
4. What is the difference between being ethnocentric and being patriotic?
5. **Challenge:** In the past, some geographers believed that physical environment and climate determined the type of culture that a group had. Today many do not accept this view. What do you think are the reasons why this theory on culture was rejected?
6. **Challenge:** In your opinion, what actions and accomplishments by people in all the world's culture areas are needed before a global culture would develop? What might be the advantages of a global culture? The disadvantages? Explain.

REINFORCING GRAPHIC SKILLS

Study the map and graph on page 139. Then answer the questions that follow.

1. On which continents are followers of Judaism found?
2. **Challenge:** There are nearly as many Hindus in the world as there are Muslims. However, Muslims are spread over more land area than Hindus are. Make a hypothesis about why Hinduism remained in only one area of the world.

CHAPTER 8

Use the photograph below to point out that, in spite of many differences, all cities must be able to supply their inhabitants with resources such as food.

Floating city market on a canal in Bangkok, Thailand

URBAN PATTERNS

In this chapter you will learn—
- What are the functions of urban areas.
- How cities developed from ancient to modern times.
- How urban environments are different from rural environments.
- What may be future changes and growth patterns of cities.

Demographers frequently struggle to acquire accurate and consistent population statistics, especially for developing countries where census records are often incomplete and sometimes nonexistent.

INTRODUCTION

To some people cities mean museums, beautiful parks, fancy restaurants, and crowds. Others think of tall buildings, noisy streets, crime, and dirt. To urban geographers cities mean all these things and much more.

Urban geographers want to learn how people live in today's cities. Some urban geographers study how cities are distributed inside a country or region. Others are more interested in a city's economic activities or politics. Still others are worried about the city environment in which people live.

For thousands of years, cities have been important as centers of trade, government, and culture. Today they are important to study because cities are where more and more of the world's population live.

Ask students why an area with a population as small as 200 is considered an urban area in Iceland.

1. CLASSIFYING URBAN AREAS

Urban generally means places in which most people make their living in ways other than farming. When urban geographers study an area, they start by classifying which parts are urban and which are rural. They may further classify urban areas for more careful study. Urban areas can be grouped by population or by economic activities.

1.1 Kinds of Urban Areas

Cities are a certain kind of urban area. Urban areas and cities are places defined by law. Each country defines what it considers an urban area and a city inside its boundaries. For this reason, the definition for both urban area and city can be different from country to country. For example, in Albania an urban area is a town or industrial center with more than 400 persons. But in Japan it is an area of 50,000 or more persons. In the United States, an urban area has a concentration of 2,500 persons or more. Cities in the United States are only those urban areas that have legal boundaries, or are **incorporated.**

There are several other ways geographers think of urban areas. They call small communities around a large central city **suburbs.** A **metropolitan area** means the land of a central city and all of its suburbs. Figure 8-1 on page 148 shows the metropolitan area of Baltimore, Maryland. The Bureau of the Census calls a metropolitan area a **Metropolitan Statistical Area,** or MSA.

When population figures are used in studying an urban area or a city, it is important to know whether the figure is the number of people inside a city's boundaries or the number of people in the whole metropolitan area. For example, the population of the city of Baltimore from the 1980 census was 787,000. The 1980 metropolitan area, however, had a population of 2,174,000.

THINKING LIKE A GEOGRAPHER

AERIAL ANALYSIS OF CITIES

Since 1978 the United States Geological Survey, an office in the Department of the Interior, has coordinated the National High Altitude Photography program. In this program black-and-white photographs and color infrared images have been taken of all areas in the United States, except for Alaska and Hawaii. With the help of these aerial photographs, geographers and other scientists are now able to analyze land use, locate polluted areas, and determine how to manage the land's resources.

Color infrared images, such as the one that is shown on page 147, cover about 68 square miles (176.1 sq km). The photographs are taken at an altitude of 4,000 feet (1,219.2 m) above land.

The image on page 147 shows the southwest section of the city of Houston, Texas. Houston is the largest city in Texas with a metropolitan population of about 3.7 million. Studying the image shows you much information about the city. Notice the grid pattern of streets in most neighborhoods. This is generally found in cities in the United States. Major highways, such as the South Loop Freeway of Interstate 610 in the lower half of the image, can be easily seen. Notice that many office buildings have been built along highways. In some other large American cities, most large office buildings are in the center of downtown, in what is called the **central business district.**

Color infrared images do not show true colors. Additional color is added to make images easier to interpret. Bright pink or red colors indicate healthy vegetation. Notice that in the right center of the image there is much vegetation. Hermann Park is the area west of the north-south freeway in the far right part of the image. This park is north of the Brays Bayou, the winding stream that is shown in the lower half of the image. Water that is fairly clear shows up on infrared images as very deep blue. Water that is clouded with *silt*—small dirt particles—shows up light blue. Tall buildings cast shadows, which show up as black patches. Notice the black shadows of buildings southwest of Hermann Park.

One of the most useful functions of aerial photographs is that they help geographers to analyze land use. They can also help advise city planners and city officials when decisions must be made about where airports, highways, and parks should be built. From aerial photographs geographers can study an area's water quality and the condition of its plant life. Photographs also show which areas are becoming more populated and which areas are losing population. In short, photogrammetry helps people make better decisions about the places where they live, work, and play.

Study the infrared image on page 147. It may be helpful to use a magnifying glass. Then answer the questions that follow.

1. Locate the Houston Astrodome. What other sports-related structures have people built in the area of Houston shown in the image?

2. City leaders often designate—or zone—particular areas of a city for certain purposes. What Houston areas shown on the map appear to be commonly zoned for business? For housing?

3. Locate the Buffalo Bayou in the top part of the image. Does the bayou appear to have clear or polluted water?

4. What functions do aerial photographs serve?

1.2 Urban Functions

Another way of classifying urban areas is by what their people do for a living. In each urban area, there are some economic activities, such as retail trade, that are chiefly for the people who live in the area. Other activities are carried on for people who live outside the area. These goods and services bring in the money to make cities grow and prosper. The economic activities that go on are called an urban area's *functions*. Large metropolitan areas serve many functions. Small cities only serve a few.

Manufacturing. The function of many cities is manufacturing. Because cities generally have good transportation and communication systems, energy supplies, and many workers, they are ideal places to set up industry. This is certainly true when natural resources are nearby. For example, Birmingham, Alabama, became a steel center because iron ore, coal, and limestone are nearby.

Government. Some cities are national, state, or provincial capitals. These cities serve as government centers. Some centers, such as Washington, D.C., and Islāmābād, Pakistan, were planned and built as capital cities. They have government and politics at the center of most of their economic activities. Other cities developed around other functions and later were picked as capital cities. These cities serve other functions along with government.

Transportation. Most cities have good transportation systems; however some serve chiefly as transportation centers. They may be at river crossings, like Wuhan, China, or at the end of a mountain pass, like Turin, Italy. They may be port cities, such as Bombay, India, or Asunción, Paraguay, at the point where one physical region meets another.

Trade and Office. Trade and office centers generally develop in cities located in a central part of a region. From these centers goods or information are easily sent out to places in every part of the region. Atlanta,

BALTIMORE METROPOLITAN STATISTICAL AREA _____

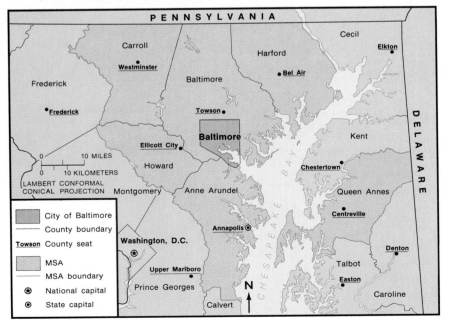

The Baltimore Metropolitan Statistical Area (MSA) includes the city of Baltimore and six surrounding counties. About three out of every four people in the United States live in one of the nation's 330 MSAs. What are some major functions of large metropolitan areas?

Until a few years ago, a Metropolitan Statistical Area (MSA) was called a Standard Metropolitan Statistical Area (SMSA). Students may encounter this term when doing research on cities.

FIGURE 8-1

Setting boundaries for urban areas is more difficult in some parts of the world than in others. Where automobile travel is common, workers can commute long distances. Changes from urban to rural areas may be gradual. In Seoul, South Korea, most people travel by bus, and the city boundary ends where the bus routes stop.

Chicago, Illinois (left), located near water, highway, and rail systems, is an example of a city's transportation function. Christian worshipers march in religious procession outside the old city of Jerusalem, Israel (right), which functions as a world religious center. What other cities are religious centers?

Georgia, serves as the trade and office center of the southeastern part of the United States.

Other Functions. Some cities like Las Vegas, Nevada; Acapulco, Mexico; and Monte Carlo, Monaco, serve as recreation centers for tourists. Other cities like Heidelberg, Germany, and Waterloo, Ontario, are education centers, around which, in many cases, research and development industries are growing. Cities like Mecca, Saudi Arabia, and Vatican City serve as religious centers.

See the TRB for Teacher Notes: Section 1 Extending the Lesson on the classification of urban patterns.

CONTENT CHECK

1. **Define:** urban, incorporated, suburbs, metropolitan area, Metropolitan Statistical Area, central business district.

2. By what two characteristics can urban areas be classified?

3. What are five kinds of urban functions?

4. **Challenge:** What are the economic functions served by a city near you?

See the TAE for an Objective 2 Activity.

2. HISTORY OF CITIES

It is important for urban geographers and students of geography to know how urban areas and cities developed through the course of human history. This helps them understand the problems and concerns of today's cities and forecast what cities of the future will face.

There have been cities on Earth for about 6,000 years. But until recent times, the number of people who lived in cities was small. Historians think the first cities developed about 4000 BC in Mesopotamia, an area in southwest Asia in the valley of the Tigris and Euphrates rivers.

These early cities had climates and water supplies that had made it possible for the people to farm. When farmers learned how to irrigate their fields, they were able to raise more food. This made them able to store what they did not need as *surplus*, or extra, food supply.

No longer did everyone have to be a farmer. Some of the workers not needed on the farms made things farmers wanted, which they then traded for some of the farmers' extra food. These workers were **artisans,** workers skilled in such trades as carpentry or pottery. There were other workers in the cities called merchants. In time they bought artisans' goods and farmers' surpluses and sold them to others for a profit. Also found in cities were religious or military leaders who kept written records of the city's growth, levied taxes on people, and supervised public building. They made up a small group called the ruling elite. Together the artisans, merchants, and ruling elite formed the beginnings of the urban functions of manufacturing, trade, and government.

One of the most famous of all ancient cities, Rome, became the center of a large empire. Rome's population reached nearly one million in the 100s AD. The Romans built cities in many places in Europe. The Roman cities were elaborately designed with public baths, theaters, arenas, gymnasiums, and water and sewage canals.

During the early Middle Ages, which lasted from about 500 AD to 1000 AD, cities in Africa, Asia, and the Americas grew and prospered. But most cities in Europe fell into ruin. This was because the Roman Empire began to fall apart when it was invaded by Germanic groups from northern Europe.

During the late Middle Ages, which lasted from about 1000 AD to 1500 AD, people began to put their lives back in order. Farmers grew more crops, which helped increase the population. Many villages once again became filled with artisans and merchants. Trade began to grow, and as it increased in larger villages, cities developed. For example, in 1370 Paris outgrew its walls, and new walls were built. By 1700 Paris was the center of culture and trade in France and had more than 300,000 people. By 1600 one-half million people were living inside London's walls and 125,000 outside.

Cities did not begin to grow quickly until the late 1700s when the Industrial Revolution took over northern Europe. Many new factories were built, and many people moved to cities in Europe to work. Many of these became manufacturing centers in Europe.

At the same time, an agricultural revolution took place. New farming machines greatly increased farm productivity so that fewer people were needed to farm the land. As Figure 8-2 on page 151 shows, for many people, these changes meant leaving the farm and going to the cities.

Cities also grew because of immigration. In the United States, for example, some cities had great population increases beginning in the mid-1800s. During that time many Europeans left their homes to settle in America. Because they needed work, they took factory jobs for low wages. Living conditions for workers in these industrial cities were generally poor.

The trend toward a greater percentage of people living in cities is called **urbanization.** Urbanization reached a turning point with the start of the twentieth century. In 1900 the world had 20 cities with more than 1 million people. Since that time cities have rapidly grown larger and larger. By 1950 there were almost 100 such cities. Today there are about 170 cities with more than 1 million people.

Before large-scale irrigation, it was dangerous for people to live in a densely populated area. The effects of serious drought could wipe out much of the population. Modern irrigation techniques and long-distance piping of fresh water have allowed cities to develop in areas previously unable to support large populations.

MIGRATION TO THE CITIES

Agricultural improvements, which made farming more productive and costly, pushed more people to leave the farms. At the same time, industrial improvements in manufacturing pulled more people to work and live in the cities. What other factors contributed to the growth of cities?

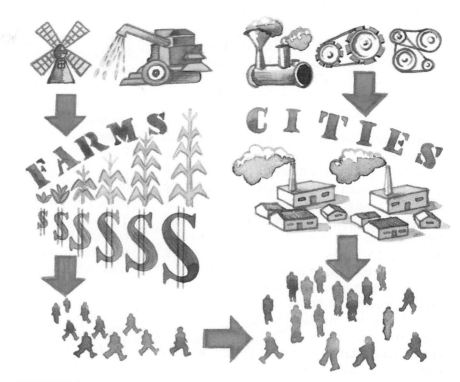

Cities have grown, not only because of migration from other countries, but also because of migration to cities by people unable to find work in rural areas. In addition, improved health standards have contributed to the population growth of many cities.

FIGURE 8-2

See the TRB for Teacher Notes: Section 2 Extending the Lesson on the history of cities.

CONTENT CHECK

1. **Define:** artisans, urbanization.
2. Where did the first cities develop?
3. What groups of workers developed in early cities?
4. During what time period did cities in Europe decline?
5. What helped European cities develop again in the mid-1000s?
6. **Challenge:** If new farm machinery had been invented 100 years before factory machinery, how do you think the development of cities would have been different?

See the TAE for an Objective 3 Activity

3. URBAN ENVIRONMENT

From the time cities began, their environments have been shaped by human activity. Changes that come about to the natural environment when cities are built up not only change the natural landscape and climate patterns but also present new challenges for people who live in cities and the officials who must govern them. These challenges often create problems for cities and their people. As a result cities are forced to deal with these problems as well as the increasing needs of their growing populations.

Not all cities have been built on well-drained sites. Leningrad, a large Soviet city, and Washington, D.C., are built on land that originally was marshy.

Politics can change a city's situation. Vienna, for example, was once the center of the Austria-Hungary empire. Today it has a very small hinterland.

3.1 Urban Landscape

The place where a city is settled has a great deal to do with whether or not it will quickly grow and prosper. Success may also be determined by the ways human activity has cut and molded the natural landscape into an urban landscape.

Site and Situation. The landscape of an area influences whether people will settle there. Whether a settlement then grows into a city is influenced by two factors. One is the settlement's **site,** the actual place where it is located with all its physical features—landforms, waterways, and climate. The other factor is the settlement's **situation,** the position of the place in relation to all the places around it. It is important to remember that a city's site is closely related to its exact location, whereas a city's situation is closely related to its relative location.

A good site for a city would be an area with some solidly based land for buildings and some fertile farmland. Both should be well drained. The land would have an adequate water supply with natural resources nearby. In earlier times a good site also would make it easy to defend a city from outsiders. For example, located in its strategic site on an island in the Seine River, Paris was able to control the river and protect itself. Today a good site is judged by whether it gives a city enough space to grow larger.

A good situation for a city would be an area in a central location inside a region, a significant point along a transportation route, a natural harbor, or land at a **confluence,** or a place where two or more rivers meet. For example, Pittsburgh's situation made it an important military post during the French and Indian War in the 1700s. It was situated at the confluence of the Allegheny and Monongahela rivers where they become the Ohio River. Since river transportation was common then, controlling the land meant controlling the river traffic. It also meant maintaining control over one of the major routes from the eastern coast of the United States to the interior of the country. A city's good situation can guarantee its influence over the area all around it.

A city's situation is very important to its survival. New York City prospered because a large nearby farming area supplied food. Boats used the nearby Hudson River to move goods from the rest of the country to the port of New York. New York's situation thus helped it grow and compete with other cities. The areas around a city that supply it with raw materials and farm products are called its **hinterland.** A city is supported by its hinterland, while the hinterland depends on the city for manufactured goods and services.

A city's site and situation can change over time. This can affect a city's growth and success. For example, a city along the coast can lose its site if it has lost its harbor because of erosion or heavy sediment. If a city is not made a part of a new modern transportation route, a city's good situation may be lost to new urban areas that spring up along the route. With today's technology people can also change a swampy site into dry land by filling in wetlands with soil moved from other regions. In this way human activity can make a poor site into a better one.

Impact of Urban Development. When natural landscapes are changed into urban landscapes, new environments are created. These environments usually go against natural land use patterns. When these patterns are broken down, the balance among air, soil, water, plants, and animals breaks down. This may cause problems.

Some problems develop when cities are built up. During this process land may be leveled, soil covered up or moved, and waterways filled in or rerouted. In many cases plant life is destroyed, which results in animal life moving to other places or dying. Paving over land surfaces means rain runs off more quickly and fills up streams higher than before. Natural drainage patterns may be broken during construction, which causes flooding.

Other problems come from changes in land use. In many parts of the world, arable land is being used for urban development. In many cases flat or gently rolling land that is well drained and fertile is desired for urban development and farming. After such land is used for urban development, it is rarely used again for food production. In a world with limited food supplies, the loss of farmland to urban development is a serious concern.

3.2 Urban Climate

Because the building up of urban areas changes Earth's natural landscapes, climate in cities is different from climate in nearby rural areas. Temperature, precipitation, and wind are especially affected by urbanization. Cities, then, tend to be warmer, cloudier, rainier, less sunny, less windy, and less humid.

Cities have warmer temperatures than nearby rural areas. Thousands of houses, apartments, factories, and office buildings give off waste heat that rises into the atmosphere above cities. This waste heat mixes with heat and dirt from automobiles, trucks,

Because of the warmer temperatures of the heat-island effect, the growing season in some cities may be three to eight weeks longer than in the surrounding countryside.

URBAN HEAT-ISLAND EFFECT

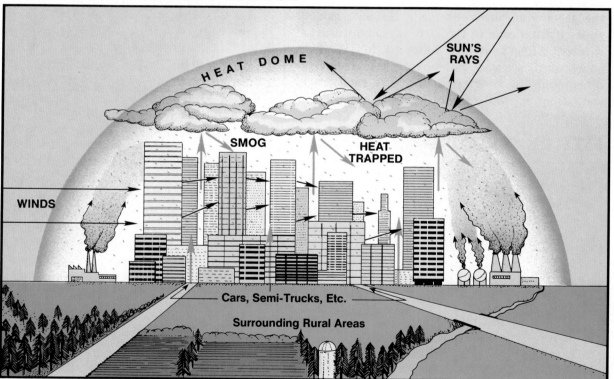

FIGURE 8-3
A heat dome forms above cities when smog fills the atmosphere. The smog, along with heat from buildings, factories, cars, and other vehicles, makes for more cloudy weather. In what other ways is the climate of cities different from surrounding rural areas?

CHAPTER 8   **URBAN PATTERNS**

USING GRAPHIC SKILLS

MAKING OBSERVATIONS

While walking past a large piece of land that you remember as woods, you notice that most of the trees have been cut down. You see workers in heavy machinery at work. In some places the ground has been bulldozed and smoothed over. What you have done is make an observation about the land.

An observation is noticing and recording something about a subject. For geographers, it is the first task of their work. After they have determined the subject of their study and the objectives, or goals, geographers begin observing the subject under study.

In making an observation, you must first look carefully at the subject. Make notes on the facts you have observed. Second, ask yourself what each of the facts says about the subject. After you have collected facts and analyzed them, you will be ready to tackle other steps in geographic inquiry, such as comparing, generalizing, or hypothesizing.

SITE OF SINGAPORE

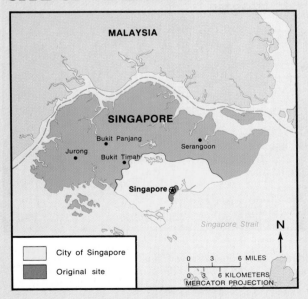

SITUATION OF SINGAPORE

Look at the two maps on this page. The map on the left shows the site of the country and city of Singapore in southeastern Asia. Observe the land and water features of the area. The map above shows the situation of Singapore. The objective of your study of Singapore is to make observations on the physical features and location of the country of Singapore and to analyze why the city of Singapore is a busy seaport city.

Study the maps. Then answer the questions that follow.

1. What do you observe about the site of the country of Singapore?

2. What do you observe about the situation of the country of Singapore?

3. Which of these observations accounts for its strong position as a commercial trading nation?

and buses and with smoke and other pollutants from factories. This combination makes smog, which can often be seen in daylight.

Heat stays in the air above cities for two reasons. First, clouds prevent most of the heat from escaping to upper levels of the atmosphere. Second, tall buildings built close together trap heat, while stone and brick buildings absorb and store heat.

Cities are set off from the rural areas around them by their warmer temperatures and their different climate conditions. For this reason geographers call cities **urban heat islands.** The urban-heat island effect warms up cities as much as 3 more degrees Fahrenheit (1.7 degrees Celsius).

With more cloudy weather, it is common for cities to receive more rain and less sunlight and radiation than the areas around them. As Figure 8-3 on page 153 shows, the sun's rays are often blocked by cloud and smog cover. Most rain runs off into sewers rather than into soil or plant roots. As a result, the water cycle slows down, and there is less evaporation. This makes cities lose cooling air, and they are less humid.

Natural wind patterns change when they meet city environments. Tall buildings, found in cities everywhere, block or change the flow of air. In most cases wind currents slow down as they pass through cities.

See the TRB for Teacher Notes: Section 3 Extending the Lesson on urban environments.

3.3 Urban Life

Because the number of people in urban areas is increasing, cities face many challenges. Cities everywhere have similar troubles, such as unemployment. In some ways cities in industrialized countries are experiencing somewhat different problems today than those problems developing countries are experiencing. These challenges will not be solved quickly or easily. Improving urban life will require much planning and cooperation.

Unemployment. Cities all over the world attract people who are looking for work. Rapid population growth in cities means there are many more people seeking jobs than there are jobs available.

Providing Services. Cities everywhere provide many services—transportation, health care, police and fire protection, education, recreation, and employment opportunities. If there are more people than the city government can provide these services for, the quality of life goes down for all.

Racial and Religious Conflict. In a city large numbers of people live and work in a relatively small area. Members of a racial, ethnic, or religious group may not be treated equally to other cultural groups in a city. They may live in **ghettos,** or parts of cities where minority groups live because they cannot afford or are not allowed to live in other parts of cities. Because certain groups are set apart from other groups, they do not understand each other's ways of life. Political leaders everywhere face the challenge of promoting good relations among various groups living in modern cities.

Environmental Pollution. Even during the 1600s, people in London complained that pollution was killing fish in the Thames River. Now nearly all cities in the world are affected by water, air, and noise pollution. Waste from sewage systems and industries has polluted the water supplies of many cities. Rivers and water supplies have become polluted by dumps and landfills. Pollution is increasing faster than many city governments can deal with it.

Decline of Central Cities. In many industrialized cities, especially in the United States, the central business district, also called downtown, is said to be dying. Some businesses and industries have moved out to industrial parks in the suburbs to get more room for lower rent and to be closer to where

Many businesses that have been established in suburban areas require highly skilled or vocationally trained workers. Unfortunately, many people in the inner cities lack the skills or training needed to qualify for employment in these businesses. Government and private agencies have been set up to provide job skills training.

customers live. The **inner city,** or the sections around downtown, has also changed. As wealthy families move farther out of the city, many of their former houses have become run-down or divided into apartments to house more families. Some inner-city areas have become **slums,** or parts of urban areas where many poor people live in run-down housing. Urban renewal projects have helped cities improve these sections. However, when old buildings are torn down, many low-income families are left without housing.

CONTENT CHECK

1. **Define:** site, situation, confluence, hinterland, urban heat islands, ghettos, inner city, slums.
2. What features make a good site for a city? A good situation?
3. How do a city and its hinterland support each other?
4. How is the climate of cities generally different from rural areas around it?
5. **Challenge:** Suppose you are mayor of a city that is trying to get two feuding neighborhood groups to share facilities in a park. What would you suggest to the citizens to gain their cooperation?

See the *TRB* for the *Chapter 8 Reading* on current trends in urban life.

4. WORLD PATTERNS OF URBAN DEVELOPMENT

Today nearly 45 percent of the world's people live in urban areas—about 75 percent of the people in industrialized countries and about 35 percent in developing countries. It is expected that by the year 2025, the world's urban population will be close to 5 billion. This means that, for the first time in history, more than one-half—60 percent—will be urban dwellers.

Population trends in industrialized countries are different from those in developing countries. For example, the rate of population growth of cities is slower in industrialized countries than in the developing world. Also, in industrialized countries, people who are very poor make up a much smaller part of the total population than in developing countries.

There are several reasons for the differences in these urban patterns. An important one is that today's largest urban centers in industrialized countries became urbanized slowly and then grew sharply during industrialization. Today's largest urban centers in developing countries became urbanized quickly. They are not major industrial centers. They started out with larger rates of population growth and now have larger numbers of people moving in from rural areas. If trends continue, these urban centers will not have the necessary resources they need to industrialize and grow.

Patterns of urban growth in industrialized countries have been changing. For example, in the United States over the last 100 years, there has been much movement from rural to urban areas. Within urban areas movement has been outward to the suburbs since the 1950s. Because of this, between 1950 and 1970, suburbs grew faster than central cities. Today the most rapid population growth seems to be in smaller cities and smaller metropolitan areas. In Japan thousands of people commute as much as two hours each way to work in Tokyo. Good train systems there have helped suburbs grow.

Today cities in developing areas are growing much faster than those in industrialized countries. Increases in population have caused grave problems. Because there are not enough jobs on farms, great numbers of peo-

HUMAN PATTERNS UNIT 3

Some countries have tried to restrict the large-scale migration from rural areas to cities. The Chinese government in the 1960s relocated trainloads of people from cities to the countryside. Also the Soviet Union limits migration into Moscow in order to control the city's growth.

WORLD'S LARGEST METROPOLITAN AREAS

1.	Mexico City, Mexico	15,669,000	14.	Bombay, India	8,243,000
2.	Shanghai, China	11,860,000	15.	Tianjin, China	7,790,000
3.	Tokyo, Japan	11,671,000	16.	Los Angeles, California (U.S.)	7,478,000
4.	São Paulo, Brazil	10,100,000	17.	Chicago, Illinois (U.S.)	7,104,000
5.	Cairo, Egypt	10,000,000	18.	London, England (U.K.)	6,755,000
6.	Buenos Aires, Argentina	9,968,000	19.	Manila, Philippines	6,720,000
7.	Seoul, South Korea	9,501,000	20.	Chongqing, China	6,511,000
8.	Beijing, China	9,231,000	21.	Jakarta, Indonesia	6,503,000
9.	Calcutta, India	9,194,000	22.	Wuhan, China	5,948,000
10.	New York, New York (U.S.)	9,120,000	23.	Delhi, India	5,729,000
11.	Rio de Janeiro, Brazil	9,019,000	24.	Changchun, China	5,705,000
12.	Moscow, U.S.S.R.	8,646.000	25.	Shenyang, China	5,055,000
13.	Paris, France	8,510,000			

FIGURE 8-4

Data from research conducted by Cartographic Services, a division of R. R. Donnelley & Sons. Inc . 1987

The combined populations of these 25 largest metropolitan areas equal almost 90 percent of the United States' total population. On which continent are most of these metropolitan areas located?

See the *TRB* for *Teacher Notes: Section 4 Extending the Lesson* on world patterns of urban development.

ple move into cities. But, more often than not, there are not enough jobs in cities either. Because people cannot earn money to pay for apartments or houses, **squatter settlements** have grown up near large cities, in which simple shelters have been made out of old boards, tar paper, and scraps. For example, in the cities of some of Africa's developing countries, as many as one-third of all people live in squatter settlements. Since squatters do not own their land or pay taxes, they generally do not receive such city services as water and electricity. In most of these settlements, health conditions are poor.

If present trends continue, the world's largest cities will be in developing countries. By the year 2025, cities in developing countries will have about 3.8 billion people. By then there are expected to be five metropolitan areas with a population of more than 16 million. All but one are in developing countries. The largest metropolitan area will probably be Mexico City, Mexico. The others will be São Paulo, Brazil; Tokyo-Yokohama, Japan; Calcutta, India; and Greater Bombay, India. Figure 8-4 on this page shows the world's largest metropolitan areas today.

CONTENT CHECK

1. **Define:** squatter settlements.
2. What type of urban movement has the United States been experiencing since the 1950s?
3. Where will the most populated cities be in the year 2025?
4. **Challenge:** Why are urban areas in developing countries not following the same growth pattern of urban areas in industrialized countries?

See the *TAE* for an *Objective 4* Activity.

CONCLUSION

Cities began to form about 4000 BC. Some of the first ones developed in Asian river valleys.

There were few large cities until the Industrial Revolution. These cities developed in Europe and the United States. Today the most rapidly growing cities are in developing nations. Since the population is growing so rapidly, not all people can find work in farms. Thousands have moved to the cities but are

Urban geographers are concerned about how people live in urban environments and how these environments change Earth's natural landscapes. They analyze the problems of urban living in relation to the problems of urban environment. Hopefully these analyses will provide insight into how to improve the quality of urban living.

unable to find work because industries cannot offer many jobs.

Even though living in cities has its problems, more and more people are moving to urban areas all over the world. In many places people have little choice in where they move. They move to urban areas to find food and work—to survive. In other places people choose to move to cities where they see many opportunities.

CHAPTER REVIEW

CHAPTER 8   URBAN PATTERNS

SUMMARY

1. Urban areas and cities are defined by law in each country. They are classified by population or by economic activity.
2. Urban areas and cities have functions based on their economic activity.
3. Improvements in agriculture led to the growth of early cities in Asian river valleys beginning in 4000 BC. Only after a surplus of food was produced could some people spend time doing things other than farming.
4. The Industrial Revolution led to the rapid growth of cities in Europe and North America during the late 1700s. Urbanization all over the world became rapid with the start of the 1900s.
5. Both the site of a city and its situation are important to its success.
6. Urban environments are not natural landscapes. Changes in the physical environment cause problems.
7. Cities generally have climates that are warmer, cloudier, rainier, less sunny, less windy, and less humid.
8. Cities all over the world face problems of unemployment, how to provide services to a growing population, racial and religious conflict, and pollution.
9. Industrialized nations have a larger percentage of their populations living in cities. Cities of the developing countries are growing at a faster rate.
10. By the year 2025, it is expected that, for the first time in history, more than one-half of the people in the world will be living in urban areas.

Answers to the following questions can be found on page T119.

REVIEWING VOCABULARY

Use the words that follow to make up 15 questions for a vocabulary quiz. Your quiz should include five fill-in-the-blank questions, five true or false questions, and five matching questions.

1. urbanization
2. incorporated
3. suburbs
4. site
5. situation
6. hinterland
7. artisans
8. confluence
9. urban heat island
10. metropolitan area
11. surplus
12. inner city
13. slums
14. ghetto
15. urban

REMEMBERING THE FACTS

1. In what two ways may urban areas be classified?
2. What is an example of an urban function that most cities serve?
3. What two revolutions spurred the growth of cities in the late 1700s and 1800s?
4. What features make for a good site?
5. What problems do all cities face?
6. About what percent of the world's people live in urban areas today?
7. In what parts of the world are cities growing fastest today?

UNDERSTANDING THE FACTS

1. Why is there not one standard definition for *city?*
2. How do site and situation differ?
3. What impact has urban development had on natural landscapes?
4. In general, how are urban climates different from rural climates?
5. What are some reasons for the growth of suburbs in the United States?
6. In the 1800s many people in Europe and the United States left farms for the cities. The same thing is taking place today in developing countries. How are the experiences of the two periods different?

THINKING CRITICALLY AND CREATIVELY

1. Why were ancient cities never so large as some of today's cities?
2. How might planning on a regional level instead of a city level help in solving the problem of environmental pollution?
3. How does the physical environment influence the location of cities?
4. Thousands of people in the cities of the developing world are unemployed. Yet thousands more move into these cities each year. Why do you think these people move to the cities when their chances for finding work are so poor?
5. **Challenge:** Some people who study future environments picture the world as one large domed city. In your opinion, could this be possible? Under what conditions could this be possible?
6. **Challenge:** Often people point out the problems of cities. Some people believe cities provide benefits to their residents. What are some of these benefits?

REINFORCING GRAPHIC SKILLS

Study the maps on page 154. Then answer the questions that follow.

1. From your observations on the site of the city of Singapore, why do you think Singapore is considered one of the busiest seaports in the world?
2. What advantages does the country of Singapore have in its location? Disadvantages? What problems might the city of Singapore have with its present location?

SUMMARY

1. Population is distributed on Earth in uneven patterns. The number of people found in different places is influenced by such factors as climatic conditions, landforms, amount of arable land, and the ability of people to make a living.
2. The number of people inhabiting Earth continues to increase dramatically. However, some areas are gaining population much more rapidly than others.
3. As a result of rapid global population growth, important issues have been raised, such as food supplies, supplies of natural resources, and pollution.
4. People of all cultures need certain things such as food, homes, clothing, and a system of order. The ways cultures go about meeting their people's needs and setting up their societies point out vast differences among many world cultures.
5. For purposes of study, the world can be divided into 11 culture areas. Each has characteristics that set it off from others.
6. Urban areas perform many important functions, such as manufacturing, trade and office, recreation, and government.
7. Cities began to grow for a number of reasons. In early river-valley civilizations, cities developed when a surplus of food was available. The Industrial Revolution created a need for many workers to be located in a single area.
8. Cities are growing more rapidly today in the developing countries of the world. These countries are experiencing difficulty in maintaining city services.

Answers to the following questions can be found on page T122.

THINKING ABOUT THE UNIT

1. Why has the rate of population growth increased over the past several centuries?
2. Develop your own definition for *culture*.
3. What factors contribute to heavy population density?
4. What are some of the important problems faced by leaders in urban areas?
5. How are human patterns in developing countries different from those of industrialized countries?

SUGGESTED UNIT ACTIVITIES

1. Invite a speaker from your local Chamber of Commerce to discuss population projections for your area.
2. Write to a student in a foreign country or interview an exchange student about what schools are like in the student's country. Prepare a chart on which you display similarities and differences between your school and the school in this foreign country.
3. Research newspaper and magazine articles that describe how different world cities are responding to such problems as environmental pollution, providing services, slums, and unemployment. Report to the class on your findings.

DEVELOPING GEOGRAPHY SKILLS

DEVELOPING A GLOBAL POINT OF VIEW

Suppose a magic carpet were to suddenly whirl you away to a city in England. Surprising and pleasant as this might be, you would find yourself faced with some puzzling situations. For one thing, you would notice cars driving smoothly along the left-hand, not the right-hand, side of the streets. Even though you would hear people speaking English on the street, it would sound unusual to your American ears. Some words, such as *spanner* and *lorry*, are easily understood by young Britons but may mean nothing to you.

High-speed air travel, satellite telecommunications, and other marvels of technology are "magic carpets" that make our world smaller. There is a need as never before to understand patterns of living developed by people in other cultures.

Global means "of, relating to, or involving the entire earth; worldwide." As people learn about a culture, if they consider it with a global point of view, it means that they are not judgmental about the culture and are not ethnocentric. People with a global point of view recognize that certain challenges of living face people everywhere. How these challenges are met varies greatly from place to place. There is not a perfect or ideal set of responses. People in different cultures have worked out solutions that make sense to them.

In learning to think globally, sometimes it is useful to consider four questions:

1. What are some basic problems of living that all cultures must solve?
2. What is the solution to these problems in the culture I am studying?

3. How well does this solution seem to work for these people?
4. What differences are there in their solutions and those worked out for the American people?

Apply this to the example of England. You might ask yourself, what problems are being responded to by the traffic patterns and the language differences? You could conclude that there is a need for an orderly pattern of traffic and for a system of language featuring words that most people in a country know. Certainly the left-side-of-the-street traffic pattern seems to work well. Most Britons seem to understand such words as *spanner* and *lorry*, even though you may not. The people of the United States simply adopted a different solution to traffic control—driving on the right. In the United States, *spanner* is called a *wrench* and a *lorry*, a *truck*. You may then conclude that people in the United Kingdom and people in the United States can communicate equally well about these things. You can see that British solutions to problems, though different from many American ones, work perfectly well in the United Kingdom.

Questions used to focus on studying life in the United Kingdom can be applied to other cultures. For practice in developing a global point of view, prepare a set of answers to the four questions on this page about one of the culture areas described in Chapter 7 or a city described in Chapter 8. You will need to research further in reference materials such as encyclopedias and news magazines to obtain complete answers to the four questions.

ANGLO-AMERICA

UNIT 4

Anglo-America includes the land of the North American continent north of Mexico and also the Hawaiian Islands in the Pacific Ocean. This land makes up the nations of the United States and Canada. As the name *Anglo-America* suggests, most people in this culture area speak English. This is because both the United States and Canada were at one time colonies of Great Britain. The United States and Canada also share other cultural traits. Both countries were settled mostly by people who came from Europe. Most of the people are Christians. Each country has a democratic form of government and an economy based on free enterprise. The land of the United States and Canada is rich with fertile soil, forests, minerals, and many other resources. These resources made it possible for the United States and Canada to industrialize. Today they are among the world's most economically developed countries. This is why the people of Anglo-America enjoy standards of living that are among the highest in the world.

Point out to students that the highlighted area on the world map inset represents the culture area of Anglo-America.

Horseshoe Falls in Niagara Falls, Canada

CHAPTER 9

The United States is a land of great physical variety ranging from rugged mountains and dense forests to the broad valley shown in this photograph.

Wheat field near Aspen, Colorado

UNITED STATES:

LANDSCAPE AND CLIMATE

In this chapter you will learn—

- What the 11 major physical regions of the United States are.
- What climates are found in the United States.

See the *TAE* for an *Objective 1* Activity.

INTRODUCTION

Most of the United States—48 of the country's 50 states—lies in North America between Canada to the north and Mexico to the south. Because these states are connected inside a common boundary, they are called the 48 **contiguous** (kuhn TIHG yuh wuhs) states. The largest state, Alaska, is outside this common boundary in the northwestern corner of the continent. The fiftieth state, Hawaii, is in the Pacific Ocean some 2,400 miles (3,862.4 km) southwest of the contiguous states.

The world's fourth largest country in land area, the United States takes up 3,615,104 square miles (9,363,112.1 sq km). Its westernmost point in Alaska to its easternmost point in the state of Maine spans more than 100 degrees in longitude. More than 50 degrees of latitude lie between its northernmost point in Alaska and its southernmost point in Hawaii.

The average altitude in the United States is 2,500 feet (762 m). Death Valley, California, has the lowest elevation, 282 feet (86 m) below sea level. The highest spot is Mount McKinley, Alaska, at 20,320 feet (6,193.5 m). The United States has many landforms. With so many different physical characteristics, it is not surprising that the United States has many kinds of climate.

1. LANDSCAPE PATTERNS

The United States is made up of three land areas—the 48 contiguous states, Alaska, and Hawaii. As the map on page 171 shows, these land areas may be divided into 11 physical regions. There are 8 regions in the contiguous 48 states: (1) Coastal Plains, (2) Appalachian (AP uh LAY chuhn) Highlands, (3) Interior Plains, (4) Interior Highlands, (5) Superior Upland, (6) Rocky Mountains, (7) Intermontane Plateaus and Basins, and (8) Pacific Mountain and Valley System. There are two more physical regions in Alaska: (1) Central Uplands and Lowlands and (2) North Slope. Hawaii is viewed as a single physical region—Volcanic Islands.

As each physical region is discussed, refer students to the map on page 171.

1.1 Coastal Plains

A broad lowland, which is more than 2,000 miles (3,218.7 km) long, extends from Massachusetts to Texas along the coasts of the Atlantic Ocean and the Gulf of Mexico. This plain can be divided into two parts, the Atlantic Coastal Plain and the Gulf Coastal Plain.

Atlantic Coastal Plain. This coastal plain runs along the Atlantic coast from Massachusetts to Florida. It is narrow in the

On a large wall map, point out some of the major harbors along the east coast, such as Long Island Sound, New York Bay, and Delaware Bay.

Explain that there are many ways of regionalizing an area. This textbook has divided regions generally into areas that share similar major landforms.

north, about 100 miles (160.9 km), but broadens to more than 200 miles (321.9 km) in the south. From its western boundary, it slopes gently eastward toward the Atlantic Ocean. Along its eastern boundary in the northern part of this plain, there are many good harbors.

In the southern part of the Atlantic Coastal Plain, there are fewer bays and harbors and more beaches. Marshes and **lagoons**—shallow bodies of water connected to larger ones—separate the beaches from hundreds of barrier islands along the southeastern coast of the United States. The southernmost part of this plain has low, rolling hills, marshes, and swamps such as those in the Everglades of Florida.

Gulf Coastal Plain. This plain runs along the coast of the Gulf of Mexico from the tip of southern Florida to the Rio Grande in Texas. It is much wider than the Atlantic Coastal Plain, about 150 miles (241.4 km) in the eastern part to about 600 miles (965.6 km) in the northern part, where it stretches far inland to the point where the Ohio River flows into the Mississippi River.

The Mississippi River is the largest river in the Gulf Coastal Plain that empties into the Gulf of Mexico. It flows through a broad plain bordered by rocky bluffs that rise as high as 200 feet (61 m) above the river. The Mississippi flows slowly through this plain and empties into the Gulf through the Mississippi Delta. This part of the plain is a wilderness of salt marshes and **bayous** (BY ooz), sluggish bodies of water that empty into larger bodies of water.

Sandy barrier islands, such as Padre Island, are common along much of the Atlantic and Gulf coastlines.

1.2 Appalachian Highlands

Just west of the Atlantic Coastal Plain are the Appalachian Highlands, which stretch about 1,200 miles (1,931.2 km) from northern Maine to western Alabama. This physical region takes its name from the Appalachian Mountains, the oldest mountains in North America. Included in the highlands are mountain ranges and plateaus. All the major mountain peaks of the eastern United States are in this region. The highest, Mount Mitchell in North Carolina, has an elevation of 6,684 feet (2,037.3 m). The six subregions of the Appalachian Highlands are (1) Piedmont, (2) Blue Ridge, (3) Ridge and Valley Section,

Natural harbors, such as the one pictured here along the Chesapeake Bay, indent the northern Atlantic Coastal Plain. What features are found along the southern part of the Atlantic Coastal Plain?

ANGLO-AMERICA   UNIT 4

FALL-LINE CITIES

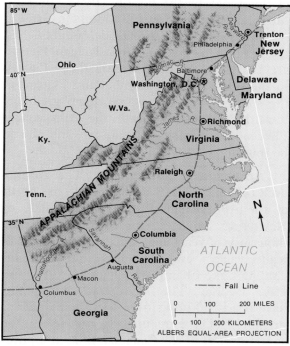

FIGURE 9-1
Cities were established on rivers upstream along the natural border between the Atlantic Coastal Plain and the Appalachian Highlands. Although the fall line restricted water travel, what benefit did it provide?

Stone Mountain, in Georgia, is a granite dome that rises more than 600 feet (182.9 m) in the Piedmont.

(4) Appalachian Plateau, (5) Adirondack Subregion, and (6) New England Section.

Piedmont. On the eastern edge of the Appalachian Highlands is the Piedmont (PEED MAHNT). It is a plateau, whose land rises sharply from the low-lying Atlantic Coastal Plain. Where fast-moving rivers drop from the low plateau to the plain, there are many rapids and waterfalls. The line formed where this drop takes place is called the **fall line.** During the early history of the United States, people could not travel by boats any farther inland than the fall line. Rapids and waterfalls provided water power to the area. Thus, many cities grew along this line as shown in Figure 9-1 on this page.

Blue Ridge. West of the Piedmont is the eastern range of the Appalachian Mountains called the Blue Ridge, which extends from Pennsylvania to Georgia. Where the Blue Ridge meets the Piedmont, there is a *ridge*, or a steep, rocky wall. It is called *blue* because the trees of the mountains appear blue when viewed from a distance. Many of the rounded summits are without trees, but the mountain slopes generally have forests.

The Blue Ridge is about 10 miles (16.1 km) to 15 miles (24.1 km) wide in the north. It widens as much as 80 miles (128.7 km) in its southern part, where the Appalachian Highlands' highest peaks reach elevations of 6,500 feet (1,981.2 m) above sea level. The Black Mountains of North Carolina and the Great Smoky Mountains of Tennessee and North Carolina are in the Blue Ridge.

Ridge and Valley Section. Beyond the Blue Ridge is the only lowland of the Appalachian Highlands, which runs the entire

The Blue Ridge, which includes some of North America's oldest mountains, is noted for its natural scenery. Between which two states does this subregion extend?

CHAPTER 9   **U.S.: LANDSCAPE AND CLIMATE**

On a large wall map of the United States, point out the locations of the Allegheny, Pocono, Catskill, and Cumberland mountains.

Most early settlers moving west of the Appalachians went through the mountains by way of the Cumberland Gap, a break in the Appalachian Plateau in Kentucky.

length of the physical region. The eastern part of the Ridge and Valley Section is made up of a chain of valleys, sometimes called the *Great Valley*. This includes the Hudson Valley in New York, the Lebanon Valley in Pennsylvania, and the Shenandoah Valley in Virginia. The rock in the western part has been folded into parallel ridges and valleys that are many miles long. In many areas of the Ridge and Valley Section, forests have been cleared to make use of very fertile soil.

Appalachian Plateau.
Farther west is the Appalachian Plateau, the largest part of the Appalachian Highlands. It extends about 1,000 miles (1,609.3 km) with a width from about 100 miles (160.9 km) to 200 miles (321.9 km).

In the eastern part of the Appalachian Plateau, there are more ranges of the Appalachian Mountains. The highest is the chain of Allegheny (AL uh GAY nee) Mountains, which stretches about 500 miles (804.7 km),

from central Pennsylvania to Virginia. North of this range lie the Pocono (POH kuh NOH) Mountains and the Catskill Mountains, and to the south lie the Cumberland Mountains. In the western part of the Appalachian Plateau are two large plateaus, the Allegheny Plateau in the north and the Cumberland Plateau in the south. They both slope down gradually toward the west. Beneath the Appalachian Plateau rich deposits of coal, gas, and oil can be found.

Adirondack Subregion.
The Adirondack (AD uh RAHN DAK) Subregion lies north of the Appalachian Plateau in the state of New York. Glaciers carved this landscape thousands of years ago. It has mountains, plateaus, valleys, and more than 200 lakes, including Lake Champlain (sham PLAYN) and Lake George. The Adirondack Mountains have nearly 50 peaks over 4,000 feet (1,219.2 m) high. These mountains are really the southern part of the Canadian Shield, a physical region of eastern Canada. North and east of the Adirondack Mountains in the St. Lawrence River Valley the landscape is flat or gently rolling.

New England Section.
Farther northeast of the Adirondack Subregion lies a heavily forested part of the Appalachian Highlands called the New England Section. It has plateaus, mountains, and hills. Glaciers in ancient times rounded the tops of most hills and mountains. The moving ice sheets carved out U-shaped valleys and basins, into which water drained, forming ponds and small lakes.

Two mountain ranges in this area are a part of the Appalachian Mountain system. The White Mountains stretch across parts of Maine and New Hampshire into northeast Vermont. Mount Washington is the highest peak, at 6,288 feet (1,916.6 m). The Green Mountains are somewhat lower in elevation and cover much of Vermont.

Kentucky's Bluegrass Country has long been associated with horse breeding. This horse farm is located near Lexington. In which subregion is this area located?

ANGLO-AMERICA   UNIT 4

1.3 Interior Plains

The enormous Interior Plains run from the Appalachian Highlands in the east, to the Gulf Coastal Plain in the south, and to the Rocky Mountains in the west. This is the heartland of the United States in which farmland is among the best in the world. Its four subregions are Interior Low Plateau, Central Lowland, Great Lakes Area, and Great Plains.

Interior Low Plateau. This plateau has low elevations between 500 feet (152.4 m) and 1,000 feet (304.8 m) above sea level. The famous Bluegrass Country of north central Kentucky is in this area. The gently rolling countryside is known for its very rich soil.

Central Lowland. The Central Lowland is a huge part of the United States that is drained by the Missouri and Mississippi river systems. Elevations vary from several hundred feet (more than 90 m) above sea level in the east to about 2,000 feet (609.6 m) above sea level in the west. The terrain includes rolling plains, flat lowlands, broad river valleys, and grassy hills.

Great Lakes Area. Much of the land located close to the five Great Lakes—Lake Superior, Lake Michigan, Lake Huron, Lake Erie, and Lake Ontario—is gently rolling. There are many other smaller lakes scattered all through the area.

Great Plains. The Great Plains lie west of the Central Lowland. They really begin in Canada and run 2,500 miles (4,023.4 km) southward into Texas. They are high plains because the land rises from about 2,500 feet (762 m) in the east to about 6,500 feet (981.2 m) in the west, where it meets the Rocky Mountains. The major rivers in the Great Plains generally flow eastward toward the Mississippi.

Most of the Great Plains is made up of dry, grassy, and very flat land with very few trees. The flattest is in the southernmost parts of the Interior Plains in Texas known as the *Llano Estacado* (LAN oh ЕHS tuh KAHD oh), or Staked Plain. A legend tells that this featureless land got its name when early travelers put stakes into the ground to help them find their way across the land.

Part of the Great Plains area, the Missouri Plateau, includes some scattered hills and highlands. In this area, the Black Hills of South Dakota have the highest peak in the United States east of the Rocky Mountains. It is Harney Peak, rising 7,242 feet (2,207.4 m) above sea level.

See the *TAE* for an *Objective 1* Activity.

1.4 Interior Highlands

The Interior Highlands region lies north of the Gulf Coastal Plain and south of the Interior Plains. Its major parts are the Ozark Plateau and the Ouachita (WAHSH ih TAW)

Blanchard Cavern in Arkansas is a popular tourist attraction in the Ozark Plateau. Where is this area located in relation to the Interior Plains?

USING GRAPHIC SKILLS

Have you ever tried to photograph a large group of people? Trying to fit everyone into the picture can be quite a challenge. When you finally think you have the people on one side of the picture, persons on the other side stray too far out of the frame.

Trying to show large parts of Earth's surface on a map often poses similar problems. When cartographers are making a map of a particular area, certain parts may not fit into the space they have for the map. They have solved this problem by using inset maps. They also use inset maps when they must show a large area in a map with a small part of the area shown in more detail.

The map on page 171 shows the physical regions of the United States. It has two inset maps inside it. The largest part of the map shows the 48 contiguous states. Because Alaska and Hawaii are far away from these states, a map showing the land areas of the United States would have to be much larger than this map. By using an inset map, these two states can be shown with the others.

The first step in reading maps with insets is to skim the whole map to see if the largest part of it and the insets contain the five basic parts of maps: title, legend, grid system, direction indicator, and scale. In looking at the United States map, you find that the main map and the insets share the same title and legend. This tells you that the general subject of the information in all parts of the map is similar—physical regions. You then notice that the main map and the insets have their own grid systems, direction indicators, and scales. This tells you that each of these basic parts is different.

The next step is to look closely at the map to observe why the parts are different. You see that each of the land areas of the United States lies inside a completely different part of the geographic grid. You also notice that it was necessary to adjust the direction and scale of each map to make the two inset maps fit within the whole map.

When you follow these steps to understand what is alike and what is different within a map with insets, it is easier to read the information within it.

Study the map with insets on page 171. Then answer the questions that follow.

1. Which is the largest-scale map—the one of the contiguous states, the inset of Alaska, or the inset of Hawaii?

2. Within what degrees of longitude do the 48 contiguous states lie? Alaska? Hawaii?

3. Within which of the areas is the westernmost part of the United States found?

Explain that the largest part of the Ozark Plateau lies in the states of Arkansas and Missouri.

Area. Deciduous broadleaf trees cover the highlands, and lead, zinc, coal, and iron are mined there.

Ozark Plateau. This flat or gently-rolling plateau is located between the Missouri and Arkansas rivers. Within it there are more than 400 underground caverns, streams, and springs. They have been formed by water dissolving the limestone that lies under much of the Ozark Plateau.

Ouachita Area. The Arkansas River Valley separates the Ozark Plateau from the Ouachita Area to the south. The Boston Mountains and the Ouachita Mountains reach elevations of 2,900 feet (883.9 m) above sea level, with relief of 1,500 feet (457.2 m).

See page 184 for a political map of the United States.

PHYSICAL REGIONS OF THE UNITED STATES

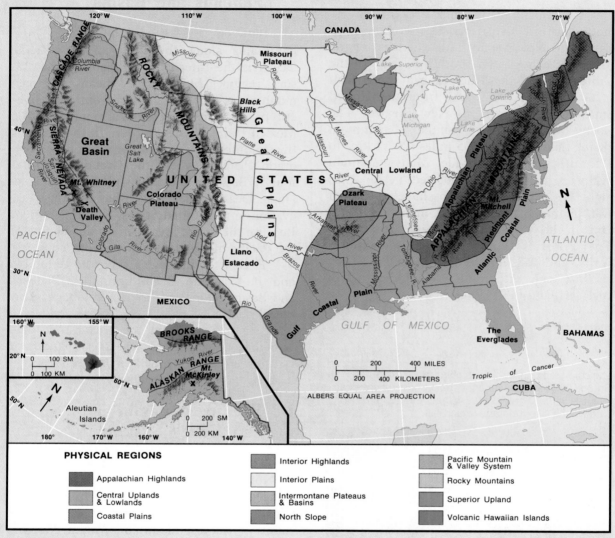

The Canadian Shield is discussed in greater detail in Chapter 12, "Canada."

1.5 Superior Upland

One of the smallest physical regions in the United States is an area that is found around part of the shore of Lake Superior called the Superior Upland. It is actually a part of the Canadian Shield. Thousands of years ago, this area was covered by glaciers.

Today the land is unsuitable for farming but rich in minerals. The Superior Upland has a rolling, lake-dotted surface rising from about 1,000 feet (304.8 m) to 1,700 feet (518.2 m) above sea level. There are several long, narrow ranges of hills, such as the Mesabi Range in Minnesota, where much of the country's iron ore is mined.

The continental divide runs along the main ridge of the Rocky Mountains. The divide separates rivers and streams that flow to opposite sides of North America.

To explain the dryness in intermontane areas, refer to information on the orographic effect on pp. 93-94.

1.6 Rocky Mountains

The Rocky Mountains are the largest mountains in North America, stretching from Canada to New Mexico. An extension of the Rockies reaches as far south as Texas. In the United States, the Rockies run more than 1,100 miles (1,770.3 km) from the United States-Canada border to New Mexico. The Rocky Mountains are a number of mountain chains that are about 125 miles (201.2 km) to 375 miles (603.5 km) wide. Many mountain peaks are more than 14,000 feet (4,267.2 m) high. The Rocky Mountains have high relief and are much more rugged than the mountains in the eastern half of the United States. They provide beautiful scenery, national parks, and vacation resorts for skiers. They also are rich with minerals and deposits of coal, gas, and oil.

Refer students to the chart on page 299 that provides data on some of the highest peaks in the Americas.

The colorful plunging gorges of northern Arizona's Grand Canyon are among the most beautiful physical features in the United States. What other features are found in the Intermontane region?

1.7 Intermontane Plateaus and Basins

Between the Rocky Mountains and mountains along the coast of the Pacific Ocean is the Intermontane Plateaus and Basins region. *Intermontane* means between mountains. This region runs from the northern part of the state of Washington to the Mexico-United States border. In the north is the Columbia Plateau. In the south is the Colorado Plateau, where the Grand Canyon is found. Between these two plateaus are lowlands. Death Valley, which has the lowest elevation in the United States, is in this region. Because the entire area is in a rain shadow of the Pacific mountains, it is very dry country.

Except for its large rivers, the Columbia and the Colorado, the Intermontane Plateaus and Basins region has **interior drainage.** This means that most streams and rivers drain into lakes or basins within the area rather than into the ocean. Most of the area's lakes and streams are dry for much of the year.

Have students research information on the May 18, 1980, eruption of Mount St. Helens.

1.8 Pacific Mountain and Valley System

This region runs along the western coast of North America from Alaska to Mexico along the Pacific Ocean. It has hills, mountains, lowlands, and river valleys. The country's highest mountain, Mount McKinley, at an elevation of 20,320 feet (6,193.5 m) above sea level, is in this region. Other mountain chains in this region are the Sierra Nevada with its highest, Mount Whitney, at 14,494 feet (4,417.8 m) and the Cascade Range with its highest, Mount Rainier, at 14,410 feet (4,392.2 m) above sea level. Another famous peak is Mount St. Helens, an active volcano, in the state of Washington.

Lowlands and valleys along the Pacific Ocean include the Susitna River Valley in

Point out that many towns in the Alaskan Panhandle can only be reached by boat or airplane. No roads connect the isolated communities.

Point out that even though there are no important rivers in Hawaii, rainfall and groundwater generally meet people's needs for fresh water.

Muskeg covers much of the surface area on the southern slopes of Alaska's Brooks Range. This is a sparsely populated part of the state. Why is it difficult for people to live here?

Alaska, the Puget (PYOO jiht) Sound Trough (TRAWF) in Washington, and the Central Valley in California. Rich soil is often found in these valleys. The east coast of the United States has more natural harbors than the west coast, but Puget Sound and San Francisco Bay serve as two good harbors on the Pacific Ocean.

See the TRB for Section 1 Extending the Lesson.

1.9 Central Uplands and Lowlands

This region is in the central part of Alaska. In the northern part are the mountains of the Brooks Range, which runs east-west about 600 miles (965.6 km) from western Alaska to Canada. South of the Brooks Range, the land is made up of plateaus and lowlands. This is **muskeg** country, swampy lowland that has mosquitoes in the summer and is frozen solid in the winter. In the southern part, the mountains of the Alaskan Range cut this region off from the Pacific Ocean.

1.10 North Slope

Land in the North Slope of Alaska is a plain that rises from the northern coast along the Arctic Ocean to the foothills of the Brooks Range. This area is mostly tundra. Even though there is poor soil in much of this area, the North Slope has seen much economic activity lately because of its huge deposits of natural gas and oil.

Explain to students that volcanic activity continues in Hawaii, sometimes disrupting human activities.

1.11 Volcanic Islands

All of the Hawaiian Islands are volcanic. This means they were made when lava erupted from underwater volcanoes and cooled. Some of the islands are **coral reefs,** or low-lying islands built up over time from the skeletons of certain kinds of tropical sea animals. These tiny animals attach themselves to the ocean floor or to each other. Over thousands of years, their remains pile up and make coral. In time, islands are made, or existing islands are made larger.

CONTENT CHECK

1. **Identify:** Coastal Plains, Appalachian Highlands, Interior Plains, Interior Highlands, Superior Upland, Rocky Mountains, Intermontane Plateaus and Basins, Pacific Mountain and Valley System, Central Uplands and Lowlands, North Slope, Volcanic Islands.

2. **Define:** contiguous, lagoons, bayous, fall line, interior drainage, muskeg, coral reefs.

3. What physical region is considered the heartland of the United States?

4. **Challenge:** Why are there are more good harbors on the east coast of the United States than on the west coast?

Refer students to pp. 96-97 to review the map on Earth's Climate Regions.

Stress to students that there are local variations in climate as well as the broader patterns of climatic differences.

2. CLIMATE PATTERNS

The physical location of the United States influences its patterns of climate. The country's territory lies across many latitudes. The northernmost, which are areas in Alaska, are north of the Arctic Circle. The southernmost areas, which are in Hawaii, lie entirely south of the Tropic of Cancer.

Along with differences in latitude, there are great differences in elevation all through the land of the United States from the Pacific to the Atlantic oceans. Furthermore, ocean currents and prevailing wind patterns exert their influences. All of these factors together make for many climates in the United States. Figure 9-2 on p. 175 shows that there are 8 climates in the contiguous 48 states and 3 in Alaska. All of Hawaii has the same general climate.

As each major climate region is studied, refer to the map of United States Climate Regions on page 175.

2.1 Tropical Moist Climates

Two tropical moist climates are found in the United States. These are tropical rain forest and tropical savanna.

Tropical Rain Forest. Hawaii has a tropical rain forest climate in which average temperatures, even during the coolest month of the year, are more than 64.4°F (18°C). Rain falls all through the year. Different amounts of rain cause contrasts that sometimes surprise visitors to the islands. Often receiving more than 460 inches (1,168.4 cm) of precipitation a year, Hawaii's Mount Waialeale (WAH ee AH leh AH leh) is one of the wettest spots on Earth. The orographic effect in these mountainous islands, however, causes some areas to receive as little as 20 inches (50.8 cm) or less each year.

Tropical Savanna. Only the southern part of Florida has a tropical savanna climate.

Hawaii's coastal areas are usually dry. The islands' highland interiors are often wet. This beach on Oahu receives about 22 inches (55.9 cm) of rain a year. Where is Hawaii's wettest spot located?

See the *TRB* for the *Chapter 9 Skill Activity* on comparing climate regions.

In winter, which has less rain than summer, freezing temperatures are rare. When they do occur, they sometimes damage citrus fruit crops. The average annual temperatures of Miami, Florida, in this climate area and of other cities all over the country are shown in Figure 9-3 on page 176.

See the *TAE* for an *Objective 2 Activity.*

2.2 Dry Climates

Two dry climates are found in the United States—desert and steppe.

Desert. Large areas in the southern part of the Intermontane Plateaus and Basins region of the United States have a desert climate. Desert areas to the north that have high elevations have cool temperatures during both summer and winter months. Desert areas to the south that have low elevations enjoy mild winter temperatures.

UNITED STATES CLIMATE REGIONS

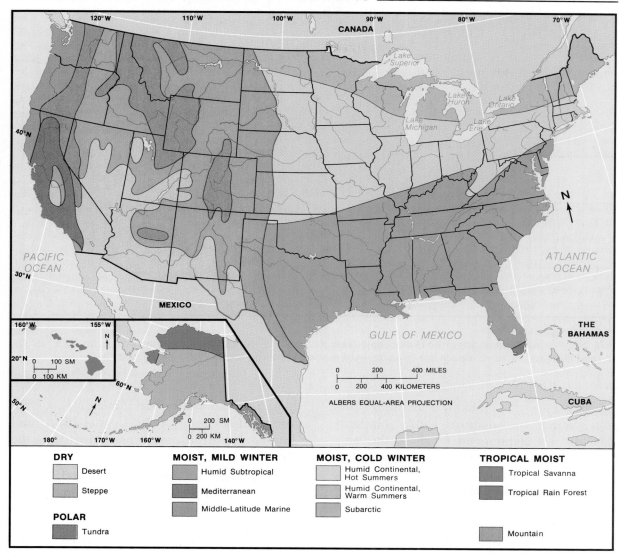

FIGURE 9-2
Oceans, the Gulf of Mexico, the Great Lakes, mountain ranges, prevailing wind patterns, elevation, and latitude all affect the many climates in the United States. In which climate region do you live?

Precipitation averages less than 8 inches (20.3 cm) a year. Because water is scarce, few crops are grown in most of this area. However, where water is available for irrigation and winter temperatures are mild, cotton, sugar beets, and citrus fruits are grown.

Steppe. Much of the Intermontane Plateaus and Basins and parts of the Great Plains regions have a steppe climate. Summers tend to be hot and dry and winters generally cold. This area is more likely to have violent weather than many other parts of the country.

People in some very dry areas, as around the Great Salt Lake in Utah, make careful use of the water from melting snow in the nearby mountains.

AVERAGE ANNUAL TEMPERATURES

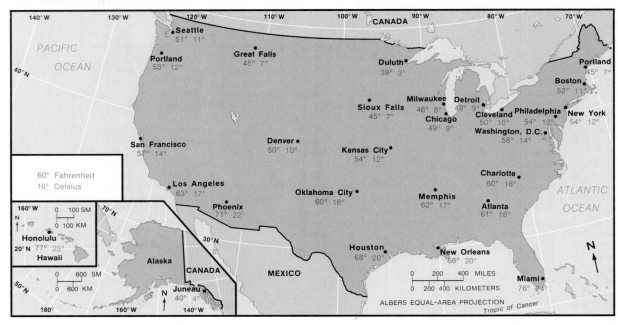

FIGURE 9-3
Average annual temperatures in the United States range from 9° F (−13° C) in Point Barrow, Alaska, to 78° F (26° C) in Death Valley, California. Which five cities have the warmest average annual temperature?

Strong winds are common, sometimes bringing summer tornadoes or winter blizzards. The dry air common in much of this area, however, makes both summer heat and winter cold more bearable than these temperatures might seem in more humid areas. Precipitation in this climate area averages between 8 inches (20.3 cm) and 20 inches (50.8 cm). As in areas with a desert climate, much of the farming here must be done with irrigation.

Explain that specialized vegetation grows in all deserts. None is completely vegetation-free.

2.3 Moist, Mild Winter Climates

The three moist, mild winter climates in the United States are humid subtropical, middle-latitude marine, and Mediterranean.

Humid Subtropical. The southeastern contiguous states, except for south Florida, have a humid subtropical climate. This large area includes most of the Coastal Plains and Interior Highlands, and southern parts of the Appalachian Highlands and Interior Plains.

Summers are hot and humid and winters generally mild and cool. In the summer severe thunderstorms are common. Rain falls mainly during the summer, but there can be precipitation during any month. Growing seasons can be as short as 7 months and as long as 11 months in areas to the south with low elevation. The long growing season and the variety of landscapes in this climate area net many different farm products such as peanuts, pecans, cotton, and tobacco.

Middle-Latitude Marine. The middle-latitude marine climate runs from the northern part of California along the Pacific coast to southeastern Alaska, covering a large part of the Pacific Mountain and Valley System. Because of prevailing westerlies, the summers in this area are warm but not hot. The winters are long and mild, but often damp and foggy. Growing seasons in the middle-latitude marine climate are surprisingly long, considering how far north this area is. In some places the growing season is as long as seven months.

Mediterranean. This climate is found in the United States only in parts of central and southern California. In the Mediterranean climate, winters are cool and somewhat rainy, but summers are warm to hot and very dry. In fact, sometimes the summers are so dry that forest fires become a serious problem.

The growing season in the Mediterranean climate is long. In some places, frosts that kill plants are rare. As a result, this is a rich farming area, especially for growing fruits and vegetables.

Explain that rain rarely falls in the summer in areas with Mediterranean climate because prevailing wind patterns are from the dry interior toward the coast.

2.4 Moist, Cold Winter Climates

The three moist, cold winter climates in the United States are humid continental with hot summers, humid continental with warm summers, and subarctic.

Humid Continental with Hot Summers. A broad band of land from the center of the contiguous 48 states to the east coast has this climate. It stretches through much of the central Interior Plains eastward through part of the Appalachian Highlands to the northeastern Atlantic Coastal Plain.

Areas with the humid continental with hot summers climate have great differences in temperature and many changes with each season. Summers are long and hot, and winters are cold. At least one month has average temperatures below freezing, 32°F (0°C). There is enough rain for farming, and droughts are

rare. Some of the country's most productive farmland is in this climate area.

Humid Continental with Warm Summers. This climate is found in parts of the northern Great Plains, the Superior Upland, and the northeastern stretches of the Appalachian Highlands. Summers are shorter and cooler here than in places with the humid continental with hot summers climate. Winter snowfall is typical, especially in areas near the Great Lakes. In fact, some areas have as much as 16 feet (4.9 m) of snow a year.

Although there is enough rain for farming in the region, the growing season is too short for many crops. Cornfields over time give way to pastureland and dairy farming or forestry in more northern parts of the area.

Subarctic. The subarctic climate covers more of Alaska's land than any other climate. Seldom in winter does the temperature rise above freezing. Although areas near the

Wind-blown trees and ocean surf signal an approaching thunderstorm, typical weather in a humid subtropical climate. Which areas have this type of climate?

STRANGE BUT TRUE

MILD WINTERS IN SOUTHEAST ALASKA?

When people think of winters in Alaska, they often imagine wind-driven snow and bone-chilling temperatures. There *are* parts of Alaska where winter temperatures are very low. However, winter temperatures in the southeastern part are surprisingly mild.

Consider Ketchikan, a small city located in the southeasternmost part of Alaska. Winter temperatures in this city might seem warm to someone used to winters in the Minneapolis-St. Paul area of eastern Minnesota. Compare the average winter low temperatures for both areas.

Even though it is farther north, Ketchikan has much warmer winters than the two Minnesota cities—called the Twin Cities. In the Twin City area, an average of 16 days each winter have temperatures below 0°F (−17.8°C). In a normal year in Ketchikan, the temperature does not drop that low for even a single day.

KETCHIKAN, ALASKA		
December	January	February
30.9°F (−0.6°C)	27.1°F (−2.7°C)	31.2°F (−0.4°C)

MINNEAPOLIS-ST. PAUL, MINNESOTA		
December	January	February
11.8°F (−11.2°C)	4.3°F (−15.4°C)	8.1°F (−13.3°C)

What accounts for the difference? Ketchikan is on the Pacific coast. Its climate is moderated by winds blowing off the ocean. Prevailing winds must pass over hundreds of miles or kilometers of land before reaching the Twin Cities. These winds do not have the moderating influences of water.

KETCHIKAN AND MINNEAPOLIS-ST. PAUL

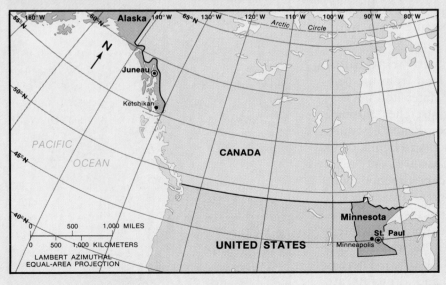

Locate Ketchikan and Minneapolis-St. Paul on the map. Then answer the questions that follow.

1. Is Ketchikan east or west of Minneapolis-St. Paul?

2. Would you expect Ketchikan to be a wet or a dry place? Explain.

3. Locate these two areas on the climate map on page 175. What climate does Ketchikan have? Minneapolis-St. Paul?

An Amish father and son bundle oats by hand. Humid hot summers allow for productive growing seasons on this Ohio farm. Does a tundra climate permit farming?

warmest part of summer rarely goes above 50°F (10°C), and no month is free of frost.

CONTENT CHECK

1. In what part of the United States are the precipitation levels and temperatures the highest?

2. What three climates cover the eastern half of the United States?

3. Much of the land with a humid continental with hot summers climate is flat to gently rolling. Some of the land with a desert climate is also flat. Why is agriculture so much more productive in the region with humid continental with hot summers climate than in the desert?

4. **Challenge:** The climate areas in the eastern half of the United States are contiguous. This is not the case in the western half. What factors concerning the western half of the United States have made its many climate types fall in uneven patterns?

See the TRB for the Section 2 Extending the Lesson on tornados and the NSSL.

CONCLUSION

The land of the United States—the 48 contiguous states, Alaska, and Hawaii—takes up a very large area. The country's landscapes include low plains, extensive plateaus, rolling hills, and rugged mountains. The area of the 48 contiguous states has coastlines on the east, southeast, and west, with ports on all three coasts.

The United States stretches across many degrees of latitude. Part of the country lies in the tropics. Part lies north of the Arctic Circle. This range of latitude makes for dramatic climatic differences. Landscape and climatic conditions in many parts of the United States make farming successful.

ocean are somewhat warmer, inland areas often record average winter temperatures of −40°F (−40°C). Besides cold temperatures, winters have long nights. From November to January, there are fewer than six hours of sunlight a day. Temperatures during the long summer days average as high as 60°F (15.6°C). Many inland areas have at least a few days with temperatures rising above 80°F (26.7°C). Annual precipitation over most of this climate area averages only about 15 inches (38.1 cm) to 20 inches (50.8 cm). However, areas near the ocean may receive 40 inches (101.6 cm) or more.

See the TAE for an Objective 2 Activity.

2.5 Polar Climates

The only polar climate found in the United States is tundra. This climate is found in the North Slope region of Alaska. Temperatures are above freezing for only a small part of the year. The average temperature for the

SUMMARY

1. The United States of America consists of 48 contiguous states, situated between Mexico and Canada, and two noncontiguous states, Alaska and Hawaii.
2. The United States ranks fourth in the world in land area. Its lands extend from north of the Arctic Circle to south of the Tropic of Cancer.
3. Many different types of terrain can be found throughout the United States.
4. There are 8 landscape regions in the contiguous 48 states and 3 in Alaska. Hawaii is a region of the Volcanic Islands.
5. The United States has many different climates. The variety is due to the large area of the country, its location, and place-to-place differences in the country.
6. There are 8 distinct climate regions in the contiguous 48 states and 2 in Alaska. Hawaii has a tropical rain forest climate.

Answers to the following questions can be found on page T127.

REVIEWING VOCABULARY

Number your paper from 1 to 8. Beside each number write the letter of the vocabulary word that best describes the numbered phrase. You will not use all the vocabulary words.

a. intermontane
b. muskeg
c. fall line
d. ridge
e. coral reef
f. bayou
g. lagoon
h. interior drainage
i. contiguous

1. shallow body of water that is connected to a much larger body of water
2. result of a buildup of skeletons of tiny marine animals
3. lying between mountains
4. steep, rocky wall
5. touching or connected within a common boundary
6. sluggish body of water that empties into a larger body of water
7. where fast-moving rivers drop from higher land areas to the lower coastal plain
8. land that is swampy and mosquito-infested in summer and frozen in winter

REMEMBERING THE FACTS

1. How does the land area of the United States compare with those of the other countries in the world?
2. What landscape region extends from Massachusetts to Texas along the Atlantic Ocean and the Gulf of Mexico?
3. What mountain range in the United States is the oldest in North America?
4. What landscape region occupies much of the interior of the contiguous 48 states?
5. What climate is found in much of the southeastern contiguous 48 states?

UNDERSTANDING THE FACTS

1. Why did cities develop along fall lines?
2. Several important rivers flow from the Great Plains region and eventually enter the Coastal Plains region. Why are there no rivers flowing from the Coastal Plains region to the Great Plains region?
3. How do you explain the presence of so many underground caves in the Interior Highlands region?
4. Why does the Intermontane Plateaus and Basins region get relatively little rain?
5. The North Slope region of Alaska has very poor land and a cold climate. However, there is much economic development there. Why?
6. What influence does their location near the ocean have on the Pacific coastal areas with a middle-latitude marine climate?

THINKING CRITICALLY AND CREATIVELY

1. How might settlement of North America by Europeans have been different if the features of the east coast were more like features of the west coast?
2. Coral reefs are found in Hawaii but not off the coasts of Alaska, Washington, Oregon, or Maine. Why not?
3. You have learned that western slopes of mountains in the western United States receive more precipitation than the eastern slopes. The western slopes of the Rocky Mountains receive less precipitation than the western slopes of Pacific Mountains such as the Sierra Nevada of California and the Cascade Range of Washington and Oregon farther west. How might this be explained?
4. **Challenge:** Use your Atlas in the Appendix of this book to locate Flagstaff, Arizona. Suppose you read an advertisement asking people to invest money in a project to plant orange groves just north of Flagstaff. Would you recommend this as a good investment? Why or why not?
5. **Challenge:** Much of the moisture that falls as rain in the humid continental with hot summers climate area is carried to the area by winds that blow inland from the Gulf of Mexico. Suppose an enormous chain of mountains developed, extending from central Texas to the Atlantic Ocean. What impact might this have on corn farmers in the humid continental with hot summers climate area?

REINFORCING GRAPHIC SKILLS

Study the map on page 171. Then answer the questions that follow.

1. Based on the longitude shown in the inset of Hawaii, would you travel east or west from Hawaii to cross the International Date Line?
2. What direction do the Appalachian Mountains follow? The Rocky Mountains? Cascade Range and the Sierra Nevada? The Brooks and Alaskan Ranges?

CHAPTER 10

In addition to the maps in this chapter, refer students to the physical and climate maps in Chapter 9 and the political map in Chapter 11.

New York Stock Exchange

UNITED STATES:

ECONOMIC AND CULTURAL PATTERNS

In this chapter you will learn—

● What economic and cultural regions make up the United States.

● What goods and services are produced in each region.

● How its physical features and climate help or hinder each region's economic growth.

The strong economy of the United States often faces stiff competition from foreign countries.

Because of declining industries, many northern cities have lost population to southern and western areas.

INTRODUCTION

The United States is one of the world's most developed countries. It has a large land area, many natural resources, and a skilled population. All of these factors help to give the United States a strong, productive economy.

The American economy is based on the free enterprise system. Under this system, people own and run businesses with only some government controls. Even in times of slow business or a rocky stock market, and with social differences between rich and poor, the American free enterprise system has, for the most part, worked well. Today the United States leads the world in industry and agriculture. It has made important advances in science, technology, education, and medicine. Because of the variety and growth of their economy, the American people have one of the highest standards of living in the world.

The United States has 243.8 million people. It is the fourth largest country in world population. Over the past 100 years, Americans have moved in large numbers from rural to urban areas. Today 74 percent of Americans live in urban areas. These urban areas cover less than two percent of the country's land area.

Americans come from many different national, ethnic, and religious backgrounds. They form a **pluralistic** culture. That means that large numbers of Americans keep many of the customs of their ancestors' cultures. However, Americans also have many things in common. They wear the same styles of clothes, eat the same kinds of foods, and almost all of them speak the English language.

Today the United States is a global economic power. It exports food and industrial goods to many areas of the world. However, it depends on other countries for many raw materials that major industries need. The United States often faces stiff competition from foreign countries. Yet other countries still look to the United States as a leader in space, computers, medicine, and entertainment.

Because of its variety, the United States is often divided by geographers into large areas: (1) Northeastern United States, (2) North Central United States, (3) Southern United States, and (4) Western United States. One way geographers divide these areas into smaller regions is described in the information that follows.

ECONOMIC AND CULTURAL REGIONS OF THE UNITED STATES

FIGURE 10-1
The United States can be divided into nine regions, each of which has economic and cultural characteristics in common. Which region includes the largest number of states?

A detailed map for each individual region appears with the description of the region.

See the *TAE* for an *Objective 1* Activity.

1. NORTHEASTERN UNITED STATES

The Northeastern United States covers only 5 percent of the country's land area. Yet it has 22 percent of its people. The Northeastern United States has two regions—New England and Middle Atlantic. The map on this page shows the northeastern regions of the United States.

Refer students to the map of Land Use and Resources on page 187.

1.1 New England Region

New England lies at the far northern tip of the Northeastern United States. It is made up of the states of Maine, New Hampshire, Vermont, Massachusetts, Rhode Island, and Connecticut.

In New England, farming is limited by its rocky soil and short growing season. Today only about 12 percent of New England's land area is farmed.

Some New England farmers grow many different kinds of fruits, vegetables, and plants to sell in their local communities. Others, however, have decided to grow one or two specialized crops to sell all over the nation. Aroostook (uh ROOS tuhk) County in Maine is one of the most famous potato-growing areas in the United States. Blueberries and apples are also important Maine crops. Dairy products and maple syrup come from New Hampshire and Vermont. Another important crop, tobacco, is grown in the fer-

184   **ANGLO-AMERICA   UNIT 4**

tile Connecticut River Valley. In swampy areas of Massachusetts, cranberries are grown.

Because of New England's long coastline, fishing plays an important role in its economy. Boston, New Bedford, Gloucester, and Portland are the leading fishing ports along the eastern coast of the United States. Ocean waters yield cod, haddock, and many other kinds of fish. Fewer New Englanders today, however, earn their living by fishing. In recent years offshore drilling by American oil companies has threatened New England fishing areas. At the same time, New England fisheries have felt strong competition from the fishing fleets of other countries.

The northern part of New England is rural with few people. The southern part, however, is urban and densely populated. This area was the first part of the country to industrialize in the 1800s. Most people in southern New England today work in industry, making goods ranging from steel and electronic parts to clothing and books. The most prosperous industries in the area are **high-technology industries.** These use the newest electronic discoveries to make products for their businesses and consumers. New England is ahead in this field because of the area's many fine colleges and universities. These include Yale, Harvard, and the Massachusetts Institute of Technology. Highly skilled people at these universities have helped the growth of the electronic and computer industries in the United States.

New England has several important cities. The largest is Boston, a seaport with about 574,000 people. Boston is the capital of Massachusetts. It is also one of the oldest and most historic cities in the United States. Other leading New England cities are Hartford and Providence. Hartford is Connecticut's state capital and the headquarters of many national insurance companies. Providence, the capital of Rhode Island, is a seaport and educational center.

1.2 Middle Atlantic Region

The Middle Atlantic region runs inland from the middle of the Atlantic coast to Lake Ontario and Lake Erie. It includes New York, Pennsylvania, New Jersey, Delaware, Maryland, and West Virginia.

Agriculture plays a small but important role in the economy of this region. Because of little good farmland, most farms are less than 200 acres (80.9 ha). The land of the Middle Atlantic is also used for poultry and dairy farming.

The Middle Atlantic region is an important industrial area. It was a leader in the early industrial growth of the United States. Railroads, steel mills, and coal mines were built in the western and southern sections of the region. Lately manufacturing is less important to the Middle Atlantic region. More and more economic activity there centers on

This fisherman makes his living by fishing in the waters off New Bedford. What other cities along the New England coast are leading fishing ports?

USING GRAPHIC SKILLS

Imagine that you have traveled to West Germany and you go to a large department store to shop. Unfortunately you cannot speak or read German. You are there because you must buy a new backpack for your stay. How could you find where the luggage or sporting goods departments are? What if there were no special organization of the department store's merchandise. Finding what you want to buy might involve a long and unsuccessful search.

However, if this store is organized like most large stores, there will be categories, or departments, where groups of products are sorted according to use. You would probably see displays of such items as clothing, household goods, and sports equipment. Because of such categories, your search for the backpack will probably be faster and easier.

In a similar way, some maps may contain so much information that they are hard to understand. Like finding particular products in a department store, finding certain facts may be difficult because even the simplest map contains a good deal of information.

Thematic maps combine general location information with information that might be seen on a chart or table. Like departments in stores that organize products in categories, thematic maps present information in categories. This helps you more easily find and identify certain facts.

One very useful way to present information about the economy of a country or region is with a map showing for what economic activities the land is used and what resources and farm products the land of the area produces. The map on page 187 shows land use, resources, and centers of industry for northeastern regions of the United States.

To read a thematic map, first read the title to find out the topic of the map. Next, locate and study the map legend that tells the categories of the information presented in the map. Often the legend uses symbols and colors to represent the categories. Finally, locate the symbols and colors on the map and determine in which places each resource is found and which places are manufacturing and agricultural areas.

Study the map on page 187. Then answer the questions that follow.

1. What resources are identified by symbols? What do the colors represent?
2. In which states are there large areas where little or no farming is done?
3. Name three of the largest manufacturing areas in Northeastern United States.
4. **Challenge:** According to the map, what generalization can you make about the general land use in Northeastern United States?

---

service functions. **Service industries** are businesses that give service to customers rather than agricultural or industrial products. Service industries include such activities as finance and banking, medical care, entertainment, education, and government.

The Middle Atlantic region has some of the country's largest cities. New York City, the most populous urban area in the country, has more than 7 million people. Its metropolitan area has almost 18 million. New York City is a major port and transportation center.

LAND USE AND RESOURCES OF NORTHEASTERN UNITED STATES

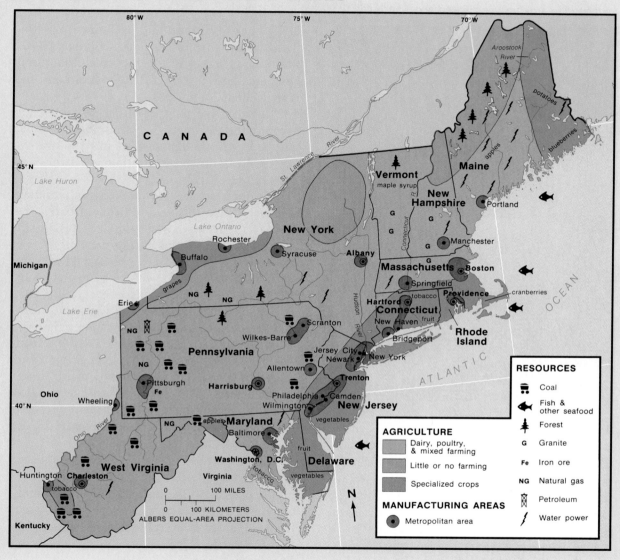

Philadelphia has a metropolitan population of more than 5.8 million.

It also is the headquarters for many national and international businesses and banks.

New York City is a leading cultural center. The city leads the country in publishing and is also the center of leading television and radio networks.

South of New York City are three other large urban areas along the Atlantic coast. Philadelphia, Pennsylvania, and Baltimore, Maryland, are both important ports and industrial centers. They are also famous for their historical and cultural attractions. The

THE URBAN WORLD

N.E. UNITED STATES: MEGALOPOLIS

In Japan the area between Tokyo and Osaka can be called a megalopolis.

The lights you see in the image above are not stars in a constellation but vibrant electricity of city lights. These lights are from the many urban areas of the northeastern coast of the United States. The urban areas form an almost continuous string of towns and cities. More than 25 years ago, a geographer created a new word and named this string of cities **megalopolis** (MEHG uh LAHP uh luhs). The new word combines two Greek words— *mega* meaning large and *polis* meaning city.

This relatively small area of the United States is one of the most densely settled areas of the world. More than 20 percent of the American people live there. The megalopolis runs from suburbs of Boston in southern New Hampshire to suburbs of Washington, D.C., in northern Virginia and is known as "Bowash." This strip is less than 500 miles (804.7 km) long. It takes in the 100-mile (160.9-km) wide area between the Atlantic Ocean and the Appalachian Mountains.

Because the megalopolis is so highly urbanized and productive, it continues to grow. On the north, the line of settlement is stretching to Portland, Maine. On the south, it is approaching Richmond, Virginia.

In their studies, urban geographers have discovered that this area of heavy urban activity grew in this way in the United States for two key reasons. First, this part of the country was one of the earliest areas to be settled. Towns sprang up in coastal areas close to the many natural harbors along the Atlantic coast. Other settlements came about along navigable rivers that flowed into the ocean. For a long time the Appalachian Mountains stopped settlers from moving farther inland. Consequently, towns grew larger and larger. Second, many immigrants in later years came through eastern ports when the rest of the country was being settled. Many of them stayed in the northeastern part of the United States.

This pattern of urban growth is being repeated for other reasons on a smaller scale in other parts of the United States. New megalopolises are growing between Milwaukee, Chicago, and Pittsburgh ("Chippits") and between San Francisco, Los Angeles, and San Diego ("San-San").

1. What is a megalopolis?
2. Where is the megalopolis in north-eastern United States located?
3. Why did this kind of urban growth happen in the United States?
4. Where in the United States are other megalopolises forming? In the world?

third city is Washington, D.C., the capital and center of the United States government. Metropolitan Washington has a population of 3.5 million.

Farther inland in the Middle Atlantic region are a number of other important urban areas. Buffalo, New York, is a grain-milling center and a port on Lake Erie. Pittsburgh, Pennsylvania, is an inland port where the Allegheny and Monongahela rivers join to form the Ohio River. It is a leading producer of iron and steel. Buffalo, Pittsburgh, and other inland urban centers of the Middle Atlantic region link the interior of the United States with ports on the Atlantic coast.

See the TRB for the Section 1 Extending the Lesson on the Statue of Liberty.

CONTENT CHECK

1. **Identify:** New England, Aroostook County, Boston, Middle Atlantic region, New York City, Philadelphia, Baltimore, Washington, D.C., Buffalo, Pittsburgh.

2. **Define:** high-technology industries, service industries, megalopolis.

3. What limits agriculture in the New England region?

4. What benefit does New England's coastline provide?

5. In what part of New England do most people live?

6. What role does agriculture play in the Middle Atlantic region's economy?

7. What industries are prospering in the Middle Atlantic region?

8. What urban functions does New York City serve?

9. **Challenge:** Boston was settled earlier than New York City, yet New York City became much larger in size and population than Boston. Why do you think this happened?

2. NORTH CENTRAL UNITED STATES

North Central United States is located west of the New England and Middle Atlantic states. This part of the country has two regions: the Great Lakes and the North Plains. Figure 10-2 on page 191 highlights the north central regions.

See the TAE for an Objective 2 Activity.

2.1 Great Lakes Region

The Great Lakes region includes Ohio, Indiana, Illinois, Wisconsin, and Michigan. The region borders Canada on the north. The Ohio River is to the south, and the Mississippi River is to the west.

A number of waterways are in the Great Lakes region. Among the most important are the Great Lakes themselves—Lake Superior, Lake Michigan, Lake Huron, Lake Erie, and Lake Ontario. Lake Michigan lies entirely within the United States. The others lie along the United States-Canada border.

The Great Lakes are linked to the Atlantic Ocean by the St. Lawrence Seaway. Built by Canada and the United States, the seaway runs from Lake Erie to the Canadian city of Montreal—a distance of about 450 miles (724.2 km). It is made up of lakes, canals, and the St. Lawrence River. The St. Lawrence Seaway provides an inexpensive way of carrying heavy farm and industrial goods. It has helped in the growth of farming and industry in the Great Lakes region.

Two rivers—the Ohio and Mississippi—are also important for carrying goods. Goods of all kinds ride on freight **barges**—large rafts that are towed by power vessels. Water transport in the Great Lakes region brings in raw materials from faraway places. Cities near the lake and river ports make finished products from the raw materials.

Many farmers borrowed money when land prices were high and crop prices were good. When crop prices fell, many farmers could not repay their debts.

On a large wall map of the United States, point out the location of Chicago. Have students suggest factors that encouraged the growth of a large city.

Fertile soils, plenty of rain, and scientific farming methods have made the Great Lakes an important farming area. Corn is the leading crop. The main areas of corn production are in Ohio, Indiana, and Illinois. Many farmers there use **crop rotation,** planting corn in a field one year and soybeans the next. This practice keeps nutrients in the soil. Grasses are also grown as hay to feed dairy cattle. Dairy products are important to the area's economy. Wisconsin is the leading dairy state in the United States. In recent years farmers in the Great Lakes region have had hard financial times. Many have left farming for other kinds of work.

The Great Lakes region is the industrial heart of the United States. Its factories make iron, steel, heavy machinery, and automotive products. Once centered in Detroit, Michigan, the automobile industry has spread to other cities in Great Lakes states. Parts are made and cars are assembled in Akron, Cleveland, Cincinnati, Milwaukee, and Indianapolis. Chicago and Gary are part of a large steel-making area.

Lately industrial growth has slowed in the Great Lakes region. The area has long relied on heavy industry. Recently, the greatest economic growth all over the country has taken place in light, high-technology industries, such as electronics. Older industries in the area have also faced greater competition in cars and steel from other countries. Automakers use large amounts of steel, glass, and rubber. Therefore, the slowdown in the auto industry has made itself felt in other industries.

Valuable coal and iron-ore deposits are easily transported to the cities of the Great Lakes region. This has helped them become important industrial and business areas. The Great Lakes region's largest city is Chicago. It is the third largest urban area in the country, after New York City and Los Angeles. Chicago has more than eight million people in its metropolitan area. The same waterways that helped develop the Great Lakes region have made Chicago important. Today Chicago is the country's busiest inland port. It is also the leading railroad and air transportation center. As a cultural center, Chicago has many museums, libraries, universities, and theaters.

High-grade iron ore from Minnesota is carried by waterways to steel centers in the Midwest.

2.2 North Plains Region

The North Plains region is made up of Minnesota, Iowa, Missouri, Kansas, Nebraska, South Dakota, and North Dakota. These states lie between the Mississippi River and the Rocky Mountains. They are north of Arkansas and Oklahoma.

The North Plains is the heart of the American **farm belt.** This is the area where many of the country's most productive farms are found. Farming gives jobs to many more people in this area than in any other part of the country. The crops grown in the North Plains vary from place to place. Wheat is an important crop in Kansas, Minnesota, Nebraska, North Dakota, and South Dakota. In these states the cooler, drier climate favors the growing of wheat. Wheat needs less water than other grains like corn. In fact, in the western part of the Great Plains, a certain kind of wheat is grown by **dry farming**—a method of farming dry areas without irrigation. Farmers make the most of what rain there is. They limit their use of water and plant crops that do not need much water.

Corn is the main crop in Iowa, Missouri, and other eastern parts of the Great Plains. More rain falls there than in the western part. Iowa is viewed as the richest farming state in the North Plains. It leads the United States in raising hogs and in corn production. In Iowa a large amount of corn is raised for **fodder,** or food for livestock.

In the North Plains, as in the country as a whole, the number of farms and farmers has

Another technique of dry farming is plowing the ground immediately after a rain, or as soon as the field is dry enough to support the equipment. Plowing during this time seals in moisture and slows evaporation.

LAND USE AND RESOURCES OF
NORTH CENTRAL UNITED STATES

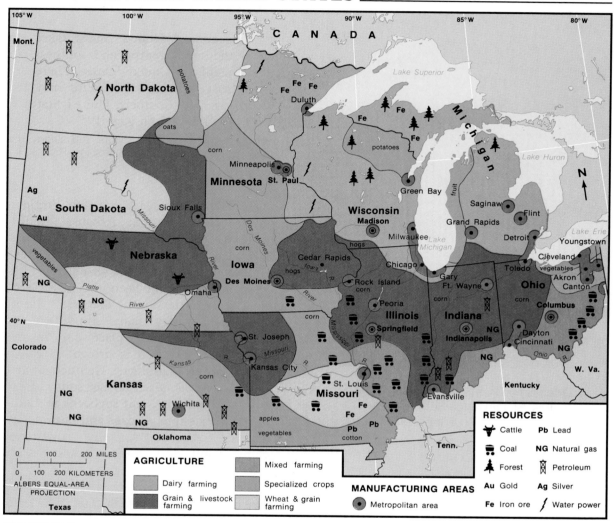

FIGURE 10-2
Agriculture and manufacturing share equal importance in the "American heartland" regions. Which three cities link to form a continuous manufacturing belt around the southern part of Lake Michigan?

Minneapolis and St. Paul are also important cultural centers. They have a number of nationally famous theaters and music groups as well as several sites of local historical interest.

been declining. At the same time, however, the amount of agricultural foods and products has increased. The most productive American farms are no longer the small family farms. Instead, many farms have become large businesses that produce huge amounts of food products for large numbers of people.

Cities play an important role in the North Plains region. Minneapolis and St. Paul are leading centers for flour production and the making of farm equipment. They also have many high-technology industries. Another important city is St. Louis, a leading transportation and industrial center.

CHAPTER 10   U.S.: ECONOMIC AND CULTURAL PATTERNS

191

Large farm machines, called combines, are needed to harvest Iowa's extensive cornfields. What are some important farm crops grown in the South?

CONTENT CHECK

1. **Identify:** Great Lakes region, Great Lakes, St. Lawrence Seaway, Chicago, North Plains, Minneapolis, St. Paul, St. Louis.

2. **Define:** barges, crop rotation, farm belt, dry farming, fodder.

3. What are the important waterways in North Central United States?

4. Around what city of the Great Lakes did the car industry develop?

5. What city is the country's busiest railroad center? In which region is it located?

6. What state leads the nation in corn production?

7. **Challenge:** Today many people find that they can no longer make a living in agriculture. This has forced many in the North Plains to leave farming. Why has this happened?

3. SOUTHERN UNITED STATES

The Southern United States takes up much of the south central and southeastern parts of mainland United States. There are two southern regions—the South and the South Plains. The Southern United States is shown in Figure 10-3 on page 195.

Except for Arkansas and Louisiana, the states that form the South are east of the Mississippi River.

3.1 The South

The South includes Kentucky, Virginia, Tennessee, North Carolina, Arkansas, Louisiana, Mississippi, Alabama, Georgia, South Carolina, and Florida. It is the southeastern one-fourth of the contiguous 48 states.

Farming has long been the major economic activity of the South. The area's warm, moist climate favors many crops that are hardly ever grown any place else in the United States. Tobacco is grown in North Carolina, South Carolina, Kentucky, and Tennessee. Rice is raised farther south in Arkansas and Louisiana, and soybeans in Louisiana and Mississippi. Pecans and peanuts are grown in Georgia. Citrus fruits, sugarcane, vegetables, and cattle are the leading farm products in Florida.

The South is where more than half of the fish are caught in the United States. The leading fishing areas are along the coast of the Gulf of Mexico. There, shrimp, oysters, and menhaden are found in large numbers. **Menhaden** are fish used in the production of fertilizer and fish oil. The waters around Florida are a source of turtles, sponges, and warm ocean fish. Rivers and ponds in the South provide catches of other fish, such as catfish, which are also raised on farms.

In recent years agriculture and fishing have been less important in the South's economy. Today industry is becoming the region's

ANGLO-AMERICA UNIT 4

major source of income. Light industries, textile factories, lumber mills, and farm production plants are now seen all through the
South. New automobile and truck factories
have opened in Tennessee and Kentucky.

Oil and natural gas are found in the
South. These minerals bring important income to the region. Most drilling for oil and
natural gas takes place along the coast of the
Gulf of Mexico. Louisiana is the South's leading producer of petroleum products.

Other areas of the South are rich in minerals. Some of the nation's largest coal deposits are found in Kentucky and Tennessee.
Coal and iron ore are mined in northern Alabama. They have made Birmingham, Alabama, an important steel center.

Recently, the South has drawn new businesses as well as people from all parts of the
country. Behind the South's growth is the
fact that wages and costs for businesses are
lower there than in other parts of the United
States. Also, people living in colder parts of
the country like the South's generally mild
winters.

Unfortunately, the growing prosperity is
not evenly distributed throughout the South.
Many poor people live in the **hollows,** or narrow mountain valleys, of Kentucky. Mississippi's per capita income is the lowest in the
United States. However, over time new industries will increase jobs in this region.

Cities in the South have grown along
with the region as a whole. Atlanta, the capital of Georgia, is the South's leading city and
most populous urban area. More than 2.5
million people live in metropolitan Atlanta.
Atlanta is a center of rail and air transportation. It is also a business, medical, and educational center.

Another important southern city is Miami, Florida. It is Florida's largest city. The
Miami metropolitan area has nearly three million people. It is closer to Central America
and South America than any other urban area

on the United States mainland. Miami's airport has many daily flights to cities in the
Caribbean and South America.

Other leading cities of the South include
New Orleans, Louisiana; Memphis, Tennessee; Nashville, Tennessee; and Louisville,
Kentucky. New Orleans is a busy seaport
near the mouth of the Mississippi River. It is
known for its historic buildings, French culture, and jazz music. Memphis is an important river port and makes chemicals, hard-
wood flooring, and cottonseed products. Nashville is a center for publishing and is the capital of the country music industry. Louisville
is a major industrial and transportation center. The Kentucky Derby, one of the world's
most famous horse races, is held each May in
Louisville.

3.2 South Plains Region

The South Plains region lies directly
south of the North Plains region. It includes
only two states: Texas and Oklahoma. These
states, however, cover a huge land area. Together, they are 60 percent as large as the
land area of all 7 states of the North Plains.

Oil production is the leading industry of
the South Plains region. When world oil
prices are high, Texas and Oklahoma are very
prosperous. When oil prices drop, the economies of these states suffer. Major centers of
the South Plains oil industry are Oklahoma
City and Tulsa in Oklahoma and Houston,
Dallas, and Corpus Christi in Texas.

Agriculture is also important in the
South Plains. Farmers in Oklahoma grow
wheat, cotton, corn, peanuts, and **sorghum,** a
grain used chiefly to feed livestock. However,
soil erosion has ruined farming in parts of
Oklahoma. In these areas, acres of fertile
farmland have become grassland. As a result,
cattle raising is now Oklahoma's chief agricultural activity.

FOCUS ON GEOGRAPHY

GULF OF MEXICO

The Gulf of Mexico is more than just a body of water bordering on the southern part of the United States. It is an important factor in the economic growth of the eastern half of the country and the United States in general.

The Gulf of Mexico is the chief source of precipitation for the eastern half of the United States. Without the Gulf, Missouri, Illinois, Wisconsin, Michigan, Ohio, Pennsylvania, and New York would be very dry.

Winds move in a northerly direction over the Gulf of Mexico. As they cross the Gulf, they pick up moisture. Because Earth rotates on its axis from east to west, the winds bend in a northeasterly direction. When the winds reach the land and move across it, the moisture falls as rain, sleet, or snow. This precipitation makes farming possible in much of the eastern half of the United States. Without the Gulf, American agriculture would not be nearly so productive.

In other ways the Gulf also benefits the whole country. For example, it is a shallow body of water. In some places the depth of the Gulf is only 31 feet (9.4 m) at points 62 miles (99.8 km) from the shore. This means that hundreds of oil drilling platforms were more easily built on the continental shelf. Oil from the Gulf of Mexico has added to United States energy supplies and jobs for workers in coastal states.

The Gulf serves as an important transportation link. From Gulf ports, ships can enter the Caribbean and the Atlantic. Another important water route is the Gulf Intercoastal Waterway. This series of canals and protected passages along the coast stretches from Brownsville, Texas, to Carrabelle, Florida. Barges can transport goods on this waterway at a reasonable cost.

1. What economic benefits does the Gulf of Mexico give the eastern half of the United States?
2. How does the Gulf help the nation as a whole?

ANGLO-AMERICA UNIT 4

LAND USE AND RESOURCES OF SOUTHERN UNITED STATES

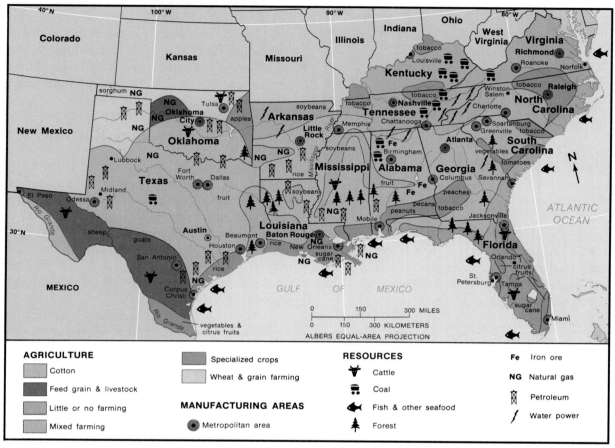

FIGURE 10-3
Favorable business conditions and a mild climate work together to attract increasing numbers of industries and workers to these regions. Which southern state in these regions has no manufacturing areas?

If the state continues to grow as it has, Texas will soon have more people than the state of New York.

Texas is a leading agricultural state. It has more farms than any other state in the country. The average size of a Texas farm is 733 acres (296.6 ha). Many farms in Texas are owned by large businesses. These farms average more than 1,000 acres (404.6 ha).

Texas leads the nation in raising cattle, sheep, and goats. Wheat is a major crop in northern Texas. Cotton is an important crop in central Texas. Vegetables and citrus fruits are grown in southern Texas.

Texas is one of the fastest growing states in the nation. With a population of more than 16 million, Texas has a larger population than any other state except California and New York.

Most Texans live in cities of more than 50,000 people. Houston and Dallas are among the ten largest cities in the country. Houston, with 1.8 million people, is the fourth largest city in the United States. It produces technology for space exploration use, energy, and

San Antonio, Texas, also one of the nation's largest cities, has a large Hispanic population. Spanish is almost as common as English.

Soil erosion has forced Oklahoma to raise cattle in place of crops. Why do people in the Rocky Mountain region raise livestock instead of crops?

medicine. Dallas is the eighth largest city in the country. Its economy is based on the manufacture of electrical equipment, airplane parts, and clothing.

Dallas is also a financial and insurance center.

CONTENT CHECK

1. **Identify:** South, Birmingham, Atlanta, Miami, South Plains, Oklahoma City, Houston, Dallas.

2. **Define:** menhaden, hollows, sorghum.

3. What has been the major economic activity in the South? What kinds of industry are becoming important in the South's economy today?

4. Why have so many people moved to the South in recent years?

5. What is the leading industry of the South Plains region?

6. Which southern state has more farms than any other state in the country?

7. **Challenge:** What would you recommend to Oklahoma farmers whose fertile land for crops has been eroded into grassland areas?

Refer students to the map of climate regions on page 175 and review the great variations in climate occurring in the Rocky Mountains.

4. WESTERN UNITED STATES

There are three regions in Western United States. They are Rocky Mountain, Pacific Northwest, and Pacific Southwest. These regions are shown in Figure 10-4 on page 199.

Refer students to the map of Land Use and Resources of Western United States on page 199.

4.1 Rocky Mountain Region

The Rocky Mountain region is made up of Arizona, Colorado, Montana, Nevada, New Mexico, Utah, and Wyoming. One of the most striking features of this area is its small population. Large stretches of land have few or no people. Very little rain is the chief reason for the low population. This will become more of a problem to the region's development in years to come.

With little water, farming is limited in the Rocky Mountain region. Farms are found only along waterways or where irrigation is available. Potatoes, hay, wheat, barley, and sugar beets are the region's major crops. In the far south, where climate is mild year round, cotton and citrus fruits are grown.

Many people in the Rocky Mountain region find that they can make more money by raising livestock instead of crops. In fact, cattle and sheep ranches there are bigger than most farms. Many of the ranches are as large as 2,000 acres (809.4 ha).

Although it does not have what it needs for agriculture, the Rocky Mountain region has rich mineral and energy resources. These include oil, natural gas, copper, mercury, and **molybdenum** (muh LIHB duh nuhm), a mineral used to strengthen steel. Coal and iron ore mined in Arizona, Colorado, and Utah support a regional steel industry.

Largely made up of mountains and open spaces, the Rocky Mountain region has few large cities. The two largest are Phoenix and

ANGLO-AMERICA UNIT 4

Point out that Denver is not located in the mountains but at the western edge of the Great Plains. It has one of the nation's busiest airports.

Review information on the orographic effect to explain the existence of two different farming zones in Oregon and Washington.

Denver. With people moving to this region, Phoenix has grown rapidly. Nearly two million people are now living in its metropolitan area. Phoenix is Arizona's state capital and an important industrial center. It makes electronic equipment, airplanes, steel, aluminum, and chemicals.

Denver has more than 1.8 million people in its metropolitan area. In addition to being Colorado's state capital, the city has many federal government offices. One of these is a branch of the United States Mint, a bureau that makes the nation's coins. Denver has many businesses that are related to oil and mining.

Other important cities in this area are Albuquerque (Al buh KUHR kee) and Salt Lake City. Albuquerque is New Mexico's largest city and a center for farm companies and scientific research. It produces electrical machinery and transportation equipment. Salt Lake City is Utah's state capital and the world center of the Mormon Church.

See the TAE for an Objective 4 Activity.

4.2 Pacific Northwest Region

The Pacific Northwest region is made up of Washington, Oregon, Idaho, and Alaska.

Agriculture in the Pacific Northwest is affected by differences in climate and landscape. In Alaska the growing season is short. However, the state's farmers are able to raise livestock, barley, hay, oats, and potatoes. About 75 percent of Alaskan farm products come from the central part of the state. This area receives the most sunlight during the short summer season.

In Oregon and Washington, the Cascade Range forms two separate agricultural areas. To the east, the climate is dry and cool. Farmers there raise wheat and cattle. Fruits and vegetables are grown on irrigated land along the Columbia River. However, some lands in this eastern area are nearly desert.

Because of the orographic effect, the western side of the Cascades is warmer, wetter, and more productive. In Oregon's Willamette Valley, regular rainfall and a mild climate bring good harvests of crops, such as beans, pears, onions, corn, and berries. Forests on the western slopes of the Cascades support a large timber industry in both Oregon and Washington.

Idaho also has separate agricultural areas. In the mountainous north, little agriculture is found. Lumbering and silver mining are the major economic activities. The southern part of the state is made up of dry plains. The Snake River, which winds through this dry landscape, provides water for irrigation.

Fishing is an important economic activity in Oregon, Washington, and Alaska. These states all have long Pacific coastlines. Salmon, halibut, and herring are among the most valuable fish caught in their waters.

Along with fishing, mining is a leading industry in Alaska. For many years, gold was Alaska's most important mining product. Today it is oil. Oil production began there in 1959. Nine years later the richest oil deposits were discovered near Prudhoe Bay. A pipeline running about 800 miles (1,287.5 km) was finished in 1977. It carries oil south to the port of Valdez near the Pacific Ocean.

Another source of income in the Pacific Northwest is **tourism**— the industry of traveling for recreation. Towering mountains, clear lakes, and sparkling rivers are found all over the region, many within a number of national and state parks.

Although largely made up of forests, wilderness, and farmland, the Pacific Northwest has a few important cities. The largest city in the region is Seattle, with about 2.3 million people in its metropolitan area. A leading seaport, Seattle is also the nation's largest manufacturer of commercial aircraft.

Portland, Oregon, is the second most populous city in the Pacific Northwest. It has a metropolitan population of 1.4 million. Portland is found on the Columbia River. Its industries center on lumbering, transportation, and shipping.

California's income from fish is higher than that of any other state.

4.3 Pacific Southwest Region

The Pacific Southwest includes two states: California and Hawaii. With 24 million people, California is the most populous state in the country. Known for its beautiful scenery, Hawaii is the only truly tropical state.

California leads the country in farming. Rice, cotton, citrus fruits, tomatoes, peppers, and wine grapes are among the state's many crops. Most of California's best farmland is found in the fertile Central Valley. California is also a leader in fishing. Anchovy, tuna, and mackerel are among the fish caught off California's coast.

Other important economic activities in California are found in the moutainous interior of the state. The Sierra Nevada range is a center of lumbering, mining, and tourism. There are many ski resorts and recreational camps in this area. Yosemite (yoh SEHM uht ee), one of the nation's leading national parks, is located in this part of California.

Two metropolitan areas on California's Pacific coast have most of the state's people. One of these is the San Francisco Bay area. The other is farther south, in the area stretching from Los Angeles to San Diego.

The metropolitan area of San Francisco has a population of nearly six million. It is a cultural center for artists, writers, and opera singers. San Francisco is a leading financial center and busy port.

The area south between San Francisco and San Jose has become the home of many high-technology firms. This area is called the famous "Silicon Valley." It is named for the **silicon chip,** an important part that is used in electronics.

Los Angeles, about 450 miles (724.2 km) south of San Francisco, has a population of more than 13 million people in its metropolitan area. It is the largest city in this region and the second largest city in the country.

Los Angeles has a varied economy. Oil refining, manufacturing, and many other business activities take place in the city. Hollywood, a city in the Los Angeles metropolitan area, is where most of the country's film industry is centered.

About 2,000 miles (3,218.7 km) southwest of California in the Pacific Ocean is Hawaii. Seven of its 132 islands hold most of the state's population of one million. About 80 percent of Hawaiians live on the island of Oahu (uh WAH hoo).

Hawaii's mild climate and fertile soils provide excellent conditions for growing tropical crops. Sugarcane and pineapples are the most important. Coffee, rice, bananas, and various kinds of nuts are also grown.

Tourism is Hawaii's major source of income. Tourists come not only from other parts of the United States but also from Japan and other Asian nations. People are attracted by the natural beauty of the islands.

Honolulu, the largest city in Hawaii, is also the state capital. It is found on the island of Oahu. The city's economy depends on tourism and United States military activities.

The Army, Navy, Air Force, and Marine Corps have bases near Honolulu.

CONTENT CHECK

1. **Identify:** Rocky Mountain region, Phoenix, Denver, Pacific Northwest region, Seattle, Portland, Pacific Southwest region, San Francisco, Silicon Valley, Los Angeles.

2. **Define:** molybdenum, tourism, silicon chip.

3. Why is farming a problem in the Rocky Mountain region?

ANGLO-AMERICA UNIT 4

LAND USE AND RESOURCES OF WESTERN UNITED STATES

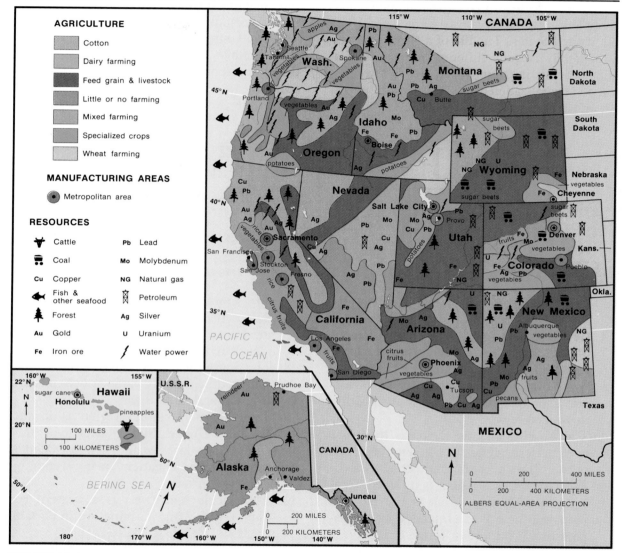

FIGURE 10-4

Agriculture and resources in these regions are as diversified as the landscapes and climates found here. The country's leading agricultural state is located in this area. Which state leads the country in farming?

Hawaii's flowers are sent by air to many cities on the United States mainland.

4. What economic activities are common in the Pacific Northwest?

5. What is Alaska's most important mining product?

6. What is the nation's leading agricultural state?

7. Why is tourism so important to Hawaii? What attracts tourists here?

8. **Challenge:** What do you see as the biggest problem in the economic development of the Rocky Mountain region in years to come?

CHAPTER 10   **U.S.: ECONOMIC AND CULTURAL PATTERNS**   199

CONCLUSION

It is difficult to make general statements about life in a country so large and varied as the United States. The life of a South Dakota farm family is quite different from that of a family living in New York City. However, some generalizations can be made about American society.

Today the United States is an urban nation. Its cities began as small centers for trade and manufacturing. Later they grew into large metropolitan areas.

The United States is a *mobile* nation—its people move from one region to another. Good transportation encourages trade and economic growth and communications networks link people from faraway places.

CHAPTER REVIEW

CHAPTER 10   U.S.: ECONOMIC AND CULTURAL PATTERNS

SUMMARY

1. The United States is one of the most developed countries in the world.
2. Geographers often divide the United States into economic and cultural regions, each with its own features.
3. New England is one region of Northeastern United States. Today it is a highly urbanized region.
4. The Middle Atlantic region is the other northeastern region. It has long been one of the nation's leading industrial areas.
5. The Great Lakes region is in North Central United States. This is the nation's industrial heartland. Inland water transportation is important to the economy.
6. In the North Plains region, the other north central region, a large percentage of the population is involved in farming.
7. The South is a region of Southern United States. It has long been a leading agricultural area. Today the South is becoming increasingly industrialized.
8. The Southern Plains region is the second southern region. It earns much income from oil and natural gas.
9. The Rocky Mountain region is in the Western United States. Much of this large region lacks water. Where water is available for irrigation, many types of crops are grown.
10. The Pacific Northwest is a western region. Fishing and farming are important there.
11. The Pacific Southwest is the third western region. Tourism is important throughout this region.

Answers to the following questions can be found on page T134.

REVIEWING VOCABULARY

Unscramble the following terms. Then write a sentence for each that shows you understand its meaning.

bylomundem   reagb   trebmafl   homsurg   dredof   swolloh   admeennh

ANGLO-AMERICA   UNIT 4

REMEMBERING THE FACTS

1. What are the nine economic and cultural regions of the United States?
2. Do more people in New England live in rural or urban areas?
3. What is the nation's largest city, and in which region is it located?
4. What region depends heavily on inland water transportation?
5. Which city is the most important transportation center in the South?
6. What are the two largest metropolitan areas in the Rocky Mountain region?

UNDERSTANDING THE FACTS

1. Why do more people live in southern New England than in the northern part?
2. What specialized industries are replacing heavy industries in regions such as the Middle Atlantic and the Great Lakes?
3. A higher percentage of people in the North Plains region lives on farms than in any other region. Why is this so?
4. What is the major economic activity of people who live in the South?
5. How do the kinds of crops grown in the Pacific Southwest region compare with the kinds of crops grown in the Great Lakes region?
6. In what regions is irrigation important to successful farming?

THINKING CRITICALLY AND CREATIVELY

1. Many people who visit northern Idaho are impressed by the region's magnificent mountains, pine forests, clear lakes, and rivers. Why does this beautiful area have such a small population?
2. Why is Lake Michigan so important to the city of Chicago?
3. Suppose the federal government decided to create a new city with about three million people in eastern Montana. What are some problems that might arise?
4. Why did Atlanta rather than Miami develop as a major transportation center?
5. **Challenge:** The Ohio River carries a great volume of barge traffic. The Columbia River of the Pacific Northwest has relatively little barge traffic. Why are there such differences?

REINFORCING GRAPHIC SKILLS

Study the map on page 187. Then answer the questions that follow.

1. In what states is tobacco grown? Fruit? Vegetables?
2. Which state do you think has the most diversified economy?
3. **Challenge:** Based on what you have learned about the physical geography of Maine, why do you think a large area of the state has little or no farming?

CHAPTER 11

The earliest European exploration and settlement was by Spain. Evidence of early Spanish influence remains throughout much of the United States.

Carmel Mission in California

UNITED STATES: INFLUENCES OF THE PAST

In this chapter you will learn—

Refer students to the world map on pages 646-647 to note how close the Alaskan peninsula is to northeastern Asia.

- How colonial America was settled.
- How the United States expanded its territories.
- What influenced settlement patterns in the United States.
- What general groups of people make up the population of the United States.

Explain that many people today prefer the term "Native American" to "Indian." They feel the use of "Indian" perpetuates the original mistake made when European voyagers thought they had reached the East Indies.

INTRODUCTION

For at least 10,000 years people have been living in the area now known as the United States. Scientists believe the earliest settlers came from Asia. During the last Ice Age, sea level was lower than it is now. It was low enough to create a land bridge across the Bering Strait. Animals and people walked across the bridge. The people were ancestors of today's Native Americans.

Many thousands of years later, settlers from Europe arrived. They set up **colonies**—settlements of people who moved from another country and in many cases kept ties with their parent country. There were two patterns of early European settlement. Some settlements spread from east to west, while others were built from south to north.

From its beginning the United States has been a country to which ethnic groups from many parts of the world—Asia, Europe, Africa—have come. They were looking for freedom, adventure, jobs, or a higher standard of living. Americans make up a pluralistic culture that blends many cultures.

1. COLONIAL SETTLEMENT

The American colonial period is a time when European countries ruled much of the land that today makes up the United States. This period was long—from the founding of St. Augustine in 1565 to the signing of the Declaration of Independence in 1776.

The colonial period lasted 211 years—nearly as long as the United States has existed as a country.

1.1 East-to-West Pattern

Though other countries played minor roles, the two countries most active in settling the eastern United States during the colonial period were England and France. England sent many more colonists than France did.

The French came to North America primarily for economic reasons. They were interested in the fur trade. French trappers, traveling such major rivers as the St. Lawrence and the Mississippi, settled at places along waterways where beaver pelts and other furs could be collected and shipped to Europe.

Point out to students that Sweden and Holland were among other European countries that established colonies along the eastern part of North America.

Although religious and political tolerance is widespread in modern America, some New England colonies refused to admit people whose beliefs differed.

This engraving shows an artist's idea of how the first English settlers of Jamestown arrived. Why did English settlers come to America?

Most did not plan to settle. They wanted to make money and then return to France.

English settlers had different reasons for coming to America. Many came for religious freedom. Others came to better their lives. Most who settled in America expected to stay.

Though the first permanent English settlement was at Jamestown, Virginia, in 1607, thirteen colonies stretched along the Atlantic coast from Maine to Georgia by 1732. At first, people settled in coastal areas, chiefly along the many rivers that flowed to the ocean. Little by little they moved inland as far west as the Appalachian Mountains.

The colonies could be divided into three groups. The New England Colonies were Rhode Island, Connecticut, New Hampshire, including Vermont, and Massachusetts, including Maine. The Middle Colonies were New York, New Jersey, Pennsylvania, and Delaware. The Southern Colonies were Maryland, Virginia, North Carolina, South Carolina, and Georgia. Each group had common features and settlement patterns.

New England Colonies. The settlers of the New England Colonies mainly came to America for religious freedom. The land was not very good for farming. Many turned to shipbuilding, the fur trade, or fishing to make a living. Trade became New England's major economic activity. Boston, the largest city, became the chief commercial center.

In New England there were many small villages. Because, for a time, the Appalachian Mountains stopped settlements from spreading inland, villages were built close together. This is one reason why the New England Colonies were more densely populated than either the Middle or Southern colonies.

Middle Colonies. The Middle Colonies had perhaps the most diverse features of the three groups. New York, settled by the Dutch, had many large farms, especially along the Hudson River. Swedes built a colony in Delaware. Quakers settled in both New Jersey and Pennsylvania, where they and others were granted pieces of land as long as they planted crops and built homes on the land. For this reason there were many small farms in these two colonies. Since Pennsylvania welcomed people from all over Europe—Germans and Scotch-Irish, for example—it had a more diverse population than other colonies.

Southern Colonies. In the Southern Colonies grants of land were also common. Many small farms produced corn and sugarcane. It was not until tobacco became an important crop, especially in Maryland and Virginia, that the **plantation system** came about. A small number of planters bought huge landholdings that were called plantations. Small farmers could not compete with these plantation owners who bought slaves to work the land. Africans were brought by force to the Southern Colonies during the early 1700s as plantation slaves. This was nearly 100 years after the first Africans came to America as **indentured servants**—workers who agree to work for a certain period of time for an employer who pays their way to America.

ANGLO-AMERICA UNIT 4

Coastal towns grew as centers of trade and transportation as goods from plantations were shipped downstream and reloaded for foreign shipment.

Rice, cotton, and indigo used to make blue dye soon became successful plantation crops. The population of the Southern Colonies was divided between many small farmers and few plantation owners. Because of the plantation system, few towns developed in the Southern Colonies.

Spanish influence in North America began soon after Columbus' arrival in 1492.

1.2 South-to-North Pattern

Whereas the English and French settled much of the eastern United States, other areas were settled during the colonial period by Spaniards. Spanish settlement generally followed a south-to-north pattern.

Spanish influence in the Americas became widespread during the sixteenth century. Spaniards came to gain wealth and increase their power. By the mid-1500s, Spain

Spanish legacy included the introduction of horses, sheep, pigs, and beef cattle. In fact, the first North American cowboys were Spanish *vaqueros*.

ruled much of South America, all of Central America, Mexico, and large areas of the United States west of the Mississippi River.

Spanish interest in Florida dates to as early as 1513, when Juan Ponce de León (POHN seh day lay OHN) explored much of the coast. In 1565 Spain set up the first European settlement in present-day United States at St. Augustine.

Most Spanish settlements made during the colonial period, however, were in the southwest—Texas, New Mexico, Arizona, and California. During the 1500s Spaniards explored the southwest seeking the legendary Indian "Seven Cities of Cibola" and a water passage to the Pacific. By the 1600s, however, they recognized the need to establish settlements to act as **buffers,** or barriers, to block potential expansion by such colonial powers as France and England.

COLONIAL EUROPEAN SETTLEMENT PATTERNS

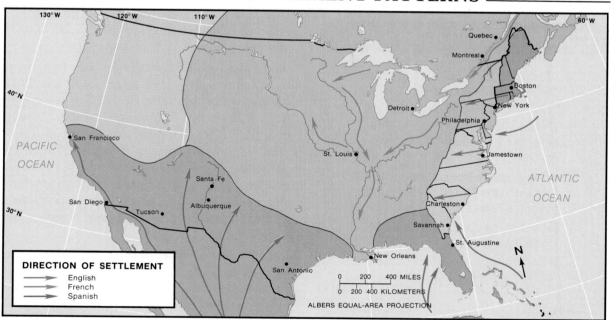

FIGURE 11-1
The names of early American cities give evidence to English, French, and Spanish influence in areas where each group explored and settled. Where was the first permanent European settlement established?

CHAPTER 11   **U.S.: INFLUENCES OF THE PAST**

Epidemics of diseases such as measles and smallpox reduced the population of Native Americans because they had no natural immunities to these diseases.

Unlike English settlements, Spanish settlements did not involve many people. Less than 25,000 Spaniards lived in areas west of the Mississippi River before the 1770s. Settlements were not only small in size but also scattered over a much greater area and separated by vast distances. This is highlighted in Figure 11-1 on page 205. The settlements served two purposes—as military outposts and as **missions,** or religious settlements.

The first settlements in the southwest were in New Mexico—Santa Fe in 1610 and Albuquerque in 1706. While some Spanish groups were settling New Mexico, others moved north from Mexico into Texas. A **presidio,** or fort, and mission were built at San Antonio in 1718. It was nearly 50 years later that Spaniards settled California. Spurred by the Roman Catholic Church's desire to convert the Indians, Spanish priests founded a string of missions along the Pacific coast from San Diego to San Francisco.

CONTENT CHECK

1. **Identify:** Jamestown, New England Colonies, Middle Colonies, Southern Colonies, St. Augustine.
2. **Define:** plantation system, indentured servants, buffers, missions, presidio.
3. What were the basic patterns of settlement of the United States during the colonial period?
4. How did French settlement differ from English settlement?
5. What areas of the United States did the Spanish settle during the colonial period?
6. **Challenge:** Spanish settlement during the colonial period involved fewer people than English settlement. How might this fact be explained?

Newly acquired territories did not automatically become states. Territories were admitted as states only when certain government requirements were met.

2. SETTLING THE UNITED STATES

With the signing of the Treaty of Paris in 1783, the United States won its independence. By terms of the treaty, it gained all land east of the Mississippi River, south of the Great Lakes, and north of Florida. During the next 70 years, the United States expanded to the present borders of the 48 contiguous states. In 1867 Alaska became an American territory after it was purchased from Russia. Hawaii, an independent country, became part of the United States in 1898. The 50 states that today make up the United States of America are shown in Figure 11-2 on page 207.

Zebulon Pike and Stephen Long also led expeditions to explore areas west of the Mississippi River.

2.1 Territorial Expansion

In 1783 the United States occupied 864,746 square miles (2,239,690.4 sq km). By 1853 it had expanded to three times its original size. The lands gained during this time are shown on the map on page 209.

Louisiana Territory. The first new lands came in 1803 with the Louisiana Purchase. In that year the United States bought from France the Louisiana Territory, nearly doubling the nation's size. Soon after, at President Thomas Jefferson's urging, Congress authorized a military expedition led by Meriwether Lewis and William Clark to explore and map the vast territory. The expedition's findings helped open up a new frontier for settlement.

Northern Border. Even before the Louisiana Purchase, Americans began moving west beyond the Appalachians. During the late 1700s and early 1800s, **pioneers,** or those who venture into unknown areas to settle, moved into the Ohio and lower Mississippi valleys. This led to problems with various In-

UNITED STATES OF AMERICA

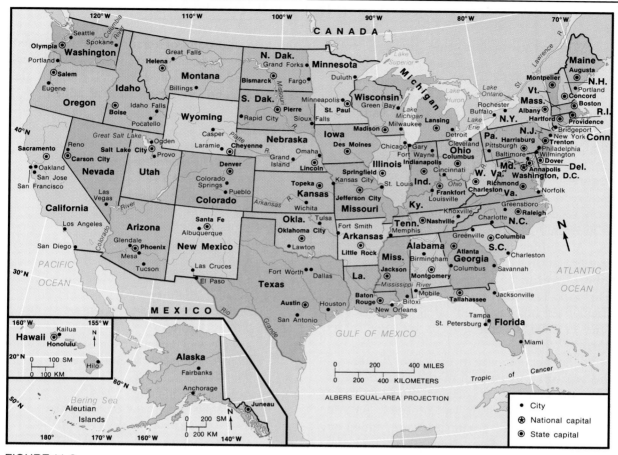

FIGURE 11-2
The United States is still a young nation when its history is compared with that of the European nations that first settled here. How long did it take the U.S. to expand to the present borders of the 48 contiguous states?

dian groups and with Britain and Spain. In time, the problems led to a second war between the United States and Great Britain.

The War of 1812, however, did not resolve the issues that caused the war. Nevertheless, in 1818 the two nations agreed to set the forty-ninth parallel as the northern boundary of the Louisiana Territory. In 1842 the Webster-Ashburton Treaty set the boundary between Maine and New Brunswick.

Florida Cession. Meanwhile, Spain and the United States came to a peaceful agreement over Florida. For some time Americans had wanted to add Florida to their territory. In 1819 Florida was **ceded,** or given up, by Spain in exchange for the United States giving up its claims to Texas, agreeing to take over $5 million in debts owed to Americans, and accepting southern and western boundaries of the Louisiana Territory.

Texas Annexation. Three years later Mexico became independent, and its government invited American settlers into its Texas territory. Mexican soldiers under Santa Anna

USING GRAPHIC SKILLS

When you take a ride through your town, you may see some changes in progress. A new, tall office building is being built downtown. A new fast-food restaurant has opened up near your school. Or you may know of a new road or a golf course or a shopping mall that was not in your town five years ago. Every town grows by adding new features—housing developments, businesses, and recreation areas, for example. As you grow older, you will see your town continue to grow and expand.

A country may grow in much the same way by adding new lands over a period of time. This can be shown on a *historical map*. This kind of a map shows a country's boundaries or territory as it looked at one particular time or over several periods of time in its history.

The historical map on page 209 shows the territorial expansion of the United States from the time of the original thirteen states up to the time Hawaii was annexed. As you can see, different territories were added at different times. The country's boundaries grew and expanded with each new addition. Different colors are used on the map to show the new additions of territory as the United States grew in size. As you look at the different colored blocks of territory, you can see both *when* and *how* new land was added.

Study the map on page 209. Then answer the questions that follow.

1. What European countries were involved in the territorial expansion of the United States?

2. How and when did most of the Great Plains come to be part of the United States?

3. What event led to most of the area east of the Mississippi River becoming part of the United States?

4. From which European country did the United States acquire the largest piece of territory?

5. In what year did the United States establish its present southernmost boundary?

6. According to the map in what year did the contiguous United States obtain its last piece of territory?

7. **Challenge:** How were the territories obtained that today make up the state of Minnesota?

Initiate a class discussion by asking students how life in this country might be different today had Mexico won the war with the United States. What effects might there have been on culture in the United States?

moved into Texas in 1836. They defeated 187 Americans defending Texas at the Alamo, a mission in San Antonio. Under Sam Houston, however, other Texan Americans fought and won Texan independence. Even though Texas petitioned the United States in 1837 for **annexation,** or to be joined to the Union, Congress did not annex Texas until 1845.

Mexican Cession. Annexation of Texas did not end problems between the United States and Mexico. Neither country could agree on the dividing boundary. The United States said it was the Rio Grande, whereas Mexico said it was the Nueces River. Unable to compromise, the United States government ordered military forces under Zachary Taylor to move from the Nueces to the Rio Grande in the spring of 1846. War then broke out. After much fighting, a peace treaty was signed in 1848. By its terms, Mexico gave up all claims to Texas north of the Rio Grande. It also ceded all Mexican land, including Cal-

TERRITORIAL EXPANSION OF THE UNITED STATES

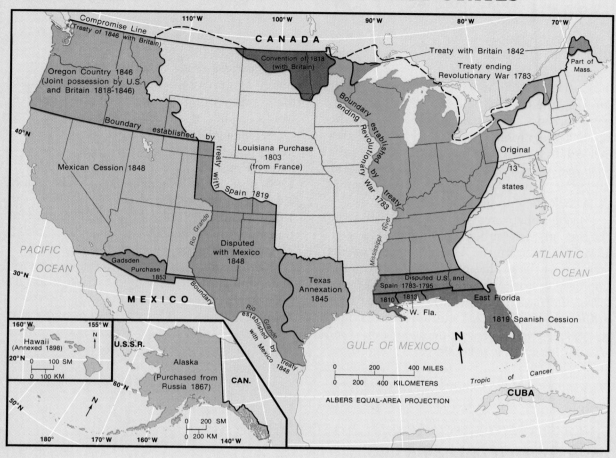

Russia and Spain had also claimed the Oregon Territory but had given up their claims by the early 1800s.

ifornia, north of the Gila River for payment of $15 million.

Oregon Territory. At the same time the United States was fighting Mexico, it reached a peaceful settlement with Great Britain on the Oregon Territory. Both nations for years had claimed Oregon. In 1818 they had agreed to allow settlers into Oregon from both countries. During the 1840s American settlers moved into the Willamette Valley. In 1846 the United States accepted a British proposal to extend the United States-Canadian border along the forty-ninth parallel from the Rocky Mountains to the Pacific Ocean.

Gadsden Purchase. In 1853 James Gadsden negotiated with Mexico for the United States to settle a boundary issue arising from the peace treaty ending the Mexican War. For payment of $10 million, the United States bought a strip of land south of the Gila River. It needed the territory as a route for a railroad to the Pacific coast.

CHAPTER 11   **U.S.: INFLUENCES OF THE PAST**

THINKING LIKE A GEOGRAPHER

GEOGRAPHIC AND POPULATION CENTERS

An important focus in the work of geographers is the distribution of people and places across Earth's surface and the patterns these distributions make. For example, after studying the distribution of land within a nation's territory, a geographer can calculate the nation's geographic center. If all the land area that makes up a nation were a flat surface, the *geographic center* would be the point—the center of gravity—where the surface would balance at the end of a stick.

Geographers are interested in studying changes in distribution over time. The geographic center of the United States, as the map below shows, has changed with the addition of new territories or new states. The center of the nation has moved west since 1783 until it made a dramatic shift north from 1848 to 1959. This tells geographers that more land area to the north was added to the country.

After geographers study the distribution of population in a country, they can also calculate the country's population center. If every person in the country weighed the same, the *population center* would be the point—the center of gravity—where a flat surface with the country's population distribution upon it would balance at the end of a stick.

A new population center of the United States can be figured after each census is taken. From the United States' first census in 1790 until 1970, the population center was always east of the Mississippi River. With the 1980 census and the estimated 1985 population, the population center is now west of the Mississippi River.

From studying changes in the geographic and population centers of the United States, geographers are able to make generalizations about the land and people. This study also makes it possible for geographers to identify trends in territorial gains and settlement patterns for the nation and forecast possible changes or developments to come.

GEOGRAPHIC AND POPULATION CENTERS OF THE UNITED STATES

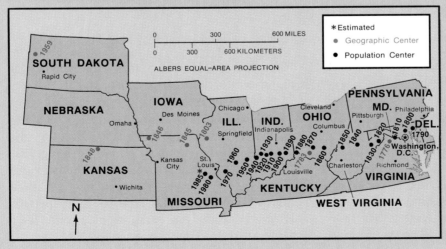

1. What accounted for the shift in the geographic center from 1848 to 1959?

2. Under what conditions would the geographic center move again?

3. In what direction would you forecast the population center to move in 1990?

4. How might you explain a gradual movement of the population center south and west?

Initiate a class discussion that compares the movement of Americans into Oregon, Texas, and California with the movement of Europeans to the New World.

Some supporters of manifest destiny wanted the northern border changed to 54°40′ north latitude. Show where this would have set the northern boundary.

2.2 Settlement Patterns

During territorial expansion, the basic pattern in settling the United States continued to be east-to-west. In the second half of the 1800s, however, other patterns of settlement developed.

Westward Movement. "Moving west" has always been an important part of American historical patterns. Until the 1900s, the availability of cheap land served as a magnet drawing pioneers west.

Right after the Revolutionary War, two important laws were passed that helped draw Americans into new western areas. The first was the Land Ordinance of 1785. It called for the Northwest Territory—the land south of the Great Lakes—to be surveyed and divided into townships. Each township was subdivided into sections that were sold to land companies or settlers. The second law was the Northwest Ordinance of 1787. It explained how territories would be governed and could become states. Thousands of families moved into the Northwest Territory.

By the 1830s Americans were crossing the Mississippi to settle in Missouri, Arkansas, Texas, and Iowa. It was at this time that a spirit of optimism spread across the nation and gave rise to **manifest destiny,** or belief that it was the nation's fate to have all North American lands from the Atlantic to the Pacific oceans. During the 1840s and 1850s, "western fever" encouraged many settlers to make the long, hazardous journey to Oregon and California. Discovery of gold near Sacramento in 1849 triggered a boom that saw over 80,000 people come to California that year. They came from the east as well as from Europe, Mexico, and China.

Last Frontier. After 1865 settlers moved into the last frontier—the area of the Great Plains, Rocky Mountains, and Great Basin. Though people kept moving west, settlement took a new pattern. Much was **pocket settlement**—settlements at single locations rather than settlements within a large area.

Settlement along the last frontier attracted three groups of people—miners, ranchers, and farmers. Lured by discoveries of gold and silver, miners set up mining camps near deposits. Once the deposits were mined out, they moved on, leaving behind **ghost towns,** or totally deserted settlements.

Settling the last frontier on a more permanent basis were ranchers and farmers. The grasslands of the region were well suited to raising cattle and sheep. At first, ranches were set up near military forts and mining towns. Later, they spread out over a wider area. In time, conflict, severe winter weather, and overgrazing brought an end to open-range ranching. By the late 1880s ranchers had fenced in their land.

Meanwhile, farm families, known as **homesteaders,** moved into the last frontier. Congress had passed the Homestead Act in 1862. Under it, settlers willing to settle and improve land for a five-year period were given 160 acres (64.7 ha). In the 1870s and 1880s

Because there were few trees, many homes in the Great Plains area were made with blocks of sod.

Log cabins became a symbol of pioneer life on the frontier. What attracted settlers to move west?

thousands moved into the Dakotas, Montana, Idaho, Wyoming, Colorado, and Utah. In 1890, with settlements spread all over the United States, the country's frontier had come to an end.

Urbanization. Another pattern of settlement as basic to the United States as the westward movement is urbanization. In 1790 only 5 percent of the population lived in cities and towns of 2,500 or more. By 1900 nearly 40 percent of the population was urban. Today more than 74 percent live in urban areas.

Along with an ever-increasing urban population has been the growth in the number of cities. In 1860 only 16 cities had populations of more than 50,000. By 1900 there were 80. Today there are more than 400.

Urbanization has also given rise to other settlement patterns. Americans have always been mobile. After World War I, many black Americans moved from southern rural areas to urban centers in the north and west. After World War II, many people began moving to suburbs. More recently, Americans have moved from harsh climates in the northeast and north central United States to milder climates in the southeast and the southwest.

A chart on page 419 compares U.S. Interstate 80 with other world transportation routes.

2.3 Factors Affecting Settlement

Throughout much of its history, the availability of cheap land played a major role in the settlement of the United States. Other factors also had an impact.

Transportation. The settling of the United States has always been linked closely to transportation. In the early years, people settled along the Atlantic coast and its navigable waterways. In time, they moved inland as trails became roadways, and canals were built to link waterways together.

During the 1830s a new mode of transportation—the railroad—opened settlement all over the eastern United States. During the late 1800s the building of transcontinental rail lines opened the western United States to heavy settlement.

Perhaps no single invention, however, had greater impact on settlement of the United States than the automobile. As roads crisscrossed the country in all directions, Americans were able to get to almost any place by car. After World War II, the automobile became the nation's chief means of transportation. It spurred the growth of suburbs, and it made a mobile people even more mobile.

Industrialization. Aided by improvements in transportation, industrialization is another factor that had significant impact on settlement patterns. As the country became more industrialized, cities expanded, drawing millions of Americans in search of employment and the lifestyles cities offered. The location of resources important to manufacturing gave rise to the development of industrial centers. Settlement no longer was linked to land but to where one could best earn a living.

Immigration. Another factor affecting settlement has been immigration. Before 1860 most people coming to live in the United States either emigrated from countries in northwest Europe or were brought from Africa. As Figure 11-3 shows on page 213, in the late 1800s, immigration patterns shifted. Many immigrants arrived from such European countries as Italy, Austria-Hungary, Poland, and Russia. Whereas early immigrants tended to settle in rural farm areas, these immigrants settled in large northeast and north central cities where they took jobs in factories.

Certainly not all immigrants in the late 1800s came from Europe. Many Asians came, especially from China, and settled chiefly in the west, where they helped build the transcontinental railroad. Later came Japanese and Filipinos who worked on farms along the west coast. Today much immigration comes from Asia and Latin America.

Immigration patterns throughout much of United States history have been greatly influenced by laws that have set immigration quotas for various nationalities. Sometimes immigration from certain areas was completely denied. A 1924 law, for instance, barred all Asian immigrants.

UNITED STATES IMMIGRATION PATTERNS—1820-1980

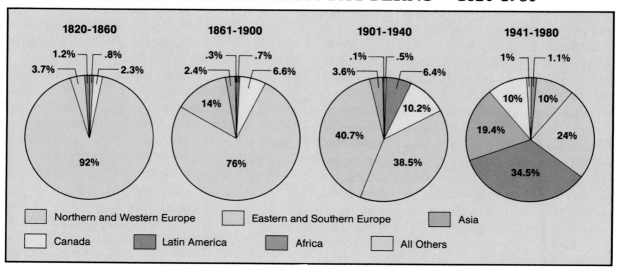

FIGURE 11-3

Data from *Historical Statistics of the United States* and *Statistical Abstract of the United States*.

Between 1820 and 1980, almost 50 million people immigrated to the United States. 73 percent of all immigrants came from Europe, 11 percent from Latin America, 9 percent from Canada, and 6 percent from Asia. From which area do most of today's immigrants come?

Sometimes economics, as much as politics or climate, influences people's decision to migrate. Many people may choose to move from areas of high unemployment to areas where they think work is more available.

CONTENT CHECK

1. **Identify:** Louisiana Purchase, Lewis and Clark, Florida Cession, Mexican Cession, Gadsden Purchase, Land Ordinance of 1785, Northwest Ordinance of 1787, Homestead Act.

2. **Define:** pioneers, ceded, annexation, manifest destiny, pocket settlement, ghost towns, homesteaders.

3. What were the territorial acquisitions of the United States between 1803 and 1853?

4. What physical and economic factors affected the settlement patterns of the United States?

5. **Challenge:** Frederick Jackson Turner, a noted American historian, believed land was the driving force behind westward expansion. Do you agree? What other factors do you think affected expansion?

3. THE AMERICAN PEOPLE

The United States has one of the most diverse populations in the world. The origins of its people can be traced to every area of the world. Though the cultural heritage of each ethnic group has not been forgotten, their cultures have blended to form a unique American culture.

See the *TRB* for the *Section 3 Extending the Lesson* on the plight of Native Americans.

3.1 Europeans

The largest cultural group in the United States is descendants of European immigrants. Today the descendants of immigrants from northwest Europe make up about 43 percent of the country's population. Descendants of immigrants from southern and eastern Europe make up about 35 percent.

Detroit and Chicago both attracted large numbers of immigrants from Poland. Employers in some eastern cities sometimes denied jobs to people from Ireland.

At times throughout American history, **prejudice,** or strong dislike formed from unsupported opinion, was directed at certain European immigrant groups. In the years before the Civil War, the Irish were discriminated against because of their Catholic beliefs. At the beginning of the 1900s, southern and eastern European immigrants found themselves targets of discrimination because of their religion. They also were discriminated against because of their different languages and customs not known to most Americans. Many Americans feared these newcomers would take their jobs. Nevertheless, in time, prejudice toward such groups decreased.

Some European immigrant groups tended to migrate to certain areas of the United States. For example, German descendants today can be found living in many places in Pennsylvania and Ohio, Scandinavians in Minnesota and the Dakotas, Irish and Italians in large eastern cities like New York City and Boston, and Poles and Slavs in north central cities like Chicago.

See the *TAE* for an *Objective 3* Activity.

These police officers of Santa Ana, California, reflect the diversity of the United States' population. Which is the country's second largest ethnic group?

In the South large numbers of black Americans are found in both rural and urban areas. In the North they are heavily concentrated in urban areas.

3.2 Black Americans

Today, black Americans make up 12.2 percent of the population. Most live in large metropolitan areas and in the south.

Granted freedom at the end of the Civil War, black Americans for years were kept politically, economically, and socially apart from the rest of the American population. For nearly 60 years, the United States government favored "separate but equal" for blacks. This attitude allowed segregation to keep blacks from receiving equal opportunities.

It was not until after World War II that steps were taken to end racial discrimination. The first step was desegregation of public schools. Congress also passed more civil rights laws.

With the civil rights movement in the 1950s and 1960s, blacks advanced themselves. They have many more high-paying jobs than before, and their median income and education levels have increased significantly. Nevertheless, young black men today have the highest unemployment rate in the United States.

Some authorities believe that Hispanic Americans may be the largest minority group in America by 2000.

3.3 Hispanics

Hispanics—people of Spanish descent—make up about 7.3 percent of the nation's population. Most live in Arizona, California, Colorado, Florida, New Mexico, New York, and Texas. Those who live in the southwest and west are mostly Mexican, whereas those who live in New York are mostly Puerto Rican, and those who live in Florida are mostly Cuban. Like many immigrants from southern and eastern Europe at the turn of the century, Hispanics have maintained their heritage. Where many Hispanics are concentrated in urban areas—for example, sections of Miami, San Antonio, and Los Angeles—business and other daily activities are often conducted in Spanish and English.

3.4 Asians

As Figure 11-4 on this page indicates, in the United States today, Asians and Polynesians, or people from South Pacific islands, make up about 2.1 percent of the population. Like other ethnic and racial groups, Asians have at times faced discrimination. In 1882 the Chinese were the first group to be restricted in immigrating to the United States. During World War II, over 100,000 Japanese, many of whom were American citizens, were forced to leave their homes in Hawaii and the Pacific coast states and move to relocation camps for security purposes. Many Asians who came to the United States in the 1970s and 1980s were **refugees,** or people fleeing from oppression, from Vietnam, Laos, and Kampuchea.

The New York Iroquois and the Florida Seminoles are among groups of Native Americans in other states.

3.5 Native Americans

Descendants of the first peoples to settle North America, Indians, or Native Americans, make up about 0.6 percent of the population. Today most reside in Oklahoma and the western states.

As European settlers moved west across the United States, Native Americans were pushed off their lands. Though various Indian nations fought back, many were killed in battles with settlers, thus decreasing their numbers significantly. From the 1830s to the 1890s, much of the Indian population was forced onto **reservations,** or lands specifically set aside by the federal government.

Even today many Native Americans remain largely apart from the mainstream of American society, both physically and socially. Government policies either try to help Indians blend into American culture or preserve Native American ways of life. Since the 1960s, however, some Indian groups have worked hard to further their political rights.

AMERICAN ETHNIC GROUPS

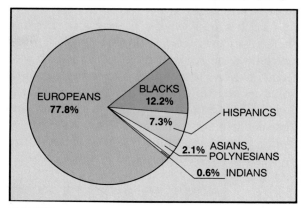

FIGURE 11-4
Although smaller than the black population, Hispanics are the fastest-growing ethnic group in the United States today. Where do most Hispanics live?

CONTENT CHECK

1. **Identify:** Hispanics, Native Americans.
2. **Define:** prejudice, refugees, reservations.
3. What general groups make up the American people?
4. What are some examples of prejudice that immigrant groups have faced in American history?
5. **Challenge:** The United States is a pluralistic society. What examples can you give to support this idea?

See the *TRB* for the *Chapter 11 Reading* on the explorations of Lewis and Clark.

CONCLUSION

When early European settlers came to North America, they brought with them their own ways of life, along with the hopes of success and freedom. Few, if any, realized they would not be continuing their ways of life but would be building a *new* American way of life. What helped them create this

American way of life were the physical features of the land.

Each group tackled its physical environment in its own way. At first, English settlers reacted to the Appalachians as barriers to settlement. Most settled down to farming, while some looked to the sea and forests to make a living. The French sought ways to avoid the Appalachians by using major waterways. Some farmed the land, but most let the fur trade take them inland. The Spanish pursued gold and glory. They explored the Florida swamps, the drylands of the Great Plains, and the Pacific coast ranges.

These early settlers established the hardy, independent image Americans still carry today. Since those early years, many more groups have come to settle. Still, each group of settlers—pioneers, indentured servants, homesteaders, immigrants, factory workers, and refugees—together has helped build today's American culture.

CHAPTER REVIEW

CHAPTER 11   U.S.: INFLUENCES OF THE PAST

SUMMARY

1. The earliest settlers of the area now occupied by the United States were ancestors of today's American Indians, who probably crossed over a land bridge from Asia.
2. Northwest Europeans arrived on the east coast. Gradually, their settlements pushed west. People from Spain entered from Mexico and the Caribbean and moved north into the southwest.
3. Most French settlers did not plan to settle permanently in America. Settlers from England, however, viewed themselves as permanent residents. In time their settlements became the New England, Middle, and Southern Colonies.

4. By 1898 the United States had all the territories that today make up its 50 states.
5. During the period of territorial expansion, the basic settlement pattern continued to be east-to-west. However, pocket settlements developed in the last frontier, and by the early 1900s there were many more settlements in urban areas than in rural areas.
6. There were several factors that helped settlement in the United States. These include transportation, industrialization, and immigration.
7. The American people make up a pluralistic society.

Answers to the following questions can be found on page T140.

REVIEWING VOCABULARY

Study the groups of terms listed below. Use each group of words in a complete sentence to show what the terms have in common.

1. buffers, missions, presidio
2. manifest destiny, cession, annexation
3. plantation system, indentured servants
4. homesteaders, colonies, reservations
5. pioneers, pocket settlement, ghost towns

ANGLO-AMERICA   UNIT 4

REMEMBERING THE FACTS

1. What two countries were most active in settling the eastern United States during the American colonial period?
2. What two patterns characterize early European settlement of the United States?
3. Under what conditions did the first Africans come to America?
4. What parallel serves as part of the border between Canada and the United States?
5. What serves as the border between Mexico and the United States?
6. What percent of the American population is of European descent? Black? Hispanic? Asian? Native American?

UNDERSTANDING THE FACTS

1. What were some differences in settlement patterns among the New England, Middle, and Southern Colonies?
2. How did the physical surroundings of the New England Colonies contribute to heavy population density?
3. How did Florida become a part of the United States? Texas? Alaska?
4. What encouraged thousands of pioneer families to cross the Appalachians?
5. How did immigration patterns shift in the late 1800s?

THINKING CRITICALLY AND CREATIVELY

1. Why do you think pocket settlement was common in the last frontier?
2. Why was the availability of land at little or no cost a leading reason in the rapid settlement of the United States?
3. In the mid-1800s there were a number of famous cattle trails running from Texas to railroad lines farther north. What do you suppose led to a decline in the use of these trails by 1890?
4. **Challenge:** The American writer John Gunther once wrote: "The United States is a country unique in the world because it was populated not merely by people who live in it by the accident of birth, but by those who willed to come here." Why does this fact make the United States special? In your opinion, what special privileges, if any, does this status bring to Americans in the world's eye?

REINFORCING GRAPHIC SKILLS

Study the map on page 209. Then answer the questions that follow.

1. During which 50-year period was the largest amount of land area added to the United States' territory: 1750-1800; 1800-1850; 1850-1900?
2. **Challenge:** What are four examples of waterways that served as natural boundaries for territories? Use the physical regions map on page 171 for help.

CHAPTER 12

Introduce the chapter by having students identify elements in the photograph that indicate similarities or differences between the United States and Canada.

St. John's harbor in Newfoundland, Canada

CANADA

In this chapter you will learn—

- What are the major physical regions and climates of Canada.
- How its physical environment has shaped Canada's economy and culture.
- What events have been important to Canada's growth as a nation.
- What major issues are facing Canada today.

The size of Canada's land area is second only to that of the Soviet Union.

See page 225 for a political map of Canada.

INTRODUCTION

Another country in the Anglo-American culture area is Canada. It is north of the 48 contiguous United States. Like the United States, it is bounded on the east by the Atlantic Ocean and on the west by the Pacific. To the north of Canada is the Arctic Ocean.

Canada is the second largest country in the world in land area. It takes up 3,851,792 square miles (9,976,133.5 sq km) of North America. Canada's land area is almost as large as all of Europe. It is 3,223 miles (5,186.9 km) from its easternmost point to its westernmost point. The distance from its northernmost point to its southernmost point is 2,875 miles (4,626.9 km) long.

For such a large country, Canada has a small population of 25.9 million people. Figure 12–2 on page 221 shows how its land area and population compare with those of the United States. About 87 percent of Canadians live within 200 miles (321.9 km) of the southern border.

The large majority of Canadians are of European ancestry. More than 40 percent are of British descent. It is from the United Kingdom that Canada has received much of its culture and its system of government.

While Canada can be viewed as part of Anglo-America, it has a large number of peo-ple of other backgrounds. Nearly 30 percent of all Canadians are of French ancestry. In many ways Canada is a nation of two cultures. Many Canadians, for example, are **bilingual,** which means they speak two languages. In Canada both English and French are spoken by the people.

In addition to British and French Canadi-ans, the country has people who settled there from many other European countries. Cana-da's population also is made up of Inuit (IHN yuh wuht) and other Native Americans, who were the original settlers of Canada. Further-more, there are Asians and blacks. This vari-ety of ethnic groups within the country has given Canada a rich cultural heritage.

Politically, Canada is divided into ten provinces and two territories. The provinces are Alberta, British Columbia, Manitoba, New Brunswick, Newfoundland (NOO fuhnd luhnd), Nova Scotia (NOH vuh SKOH shuh), Ontario, Prince Edward Island, Quebec (kwih BEHK), and Saskatchewan (suh SKACH uh wuhn). The territories are the Northwest Ter-ritories and the Yukon Territory.

Canada is a country rich in natural and human resources. The energy and skills of Canadians have helped to give this country one of the highest standards of living in the world. Canadians have made their country a major nation in world affairs.

PHYSICAL REGIONS OF CANADA

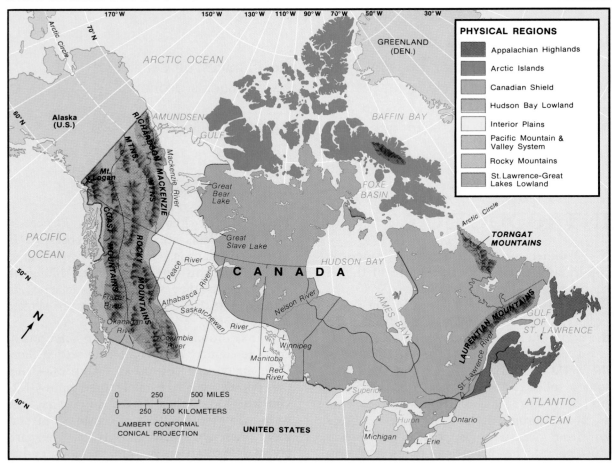

PHYSICAL REGIONS
- Appalachian Highlands
- Arctic Islands
- Canadian Shield
- Hudson Bay Lowland
- Interior Plains
- Pacific Mountain & Valley System
- Rocky Mountains
- St. Lawrence-Great Lakes Lowland

FIGURE 12-1

Canada's Appalachian Highlands, Interior Plains, Rocky Mountains, and Pacific Mountain and Valley System extend far south into the United States as well. Which physical region covers the largest area of Canada?

Refer to the map of Physical Regions of the United States on page 171. Ask students to describe how the physical regions of the United States and Canada are alike and how they are different.

Have students compare the map above with the map of Earth's Climate Regions on pages 96–97.

1. LANDSCAPE AND CLIMATE

Canada covers the northern part of North America except for Alaska. As in any area of such large size, many types of landscapes can be found. Its landscapes vary from rich, fertile farmlands to cold, arctic conditions. However, Canada does not have the many climates found in the United States.

1.1 Landscape

Canada's terrain generally can be compared with a large saucer. The center of the saucer is the lowlands all around Hudson Bay. The sides of the saucer are higher lands, moving out toward the east and west.

As Figure 12-1 on this page shows, the landscape of Canada can be divided into eight physical regions. These regions include (1) Appalachian Highlands, (2) St. Lawrence-

Great Lakes Lowland, (3) Canadian Shield, (4) Hudson Bay Lowland, (5) Interior Plains, (6) Rocky Mountains, (7) Pacific Mountain and Valley System, and (8) Arctic Islands.

Appalachian Highlands. Along the southeastern Atlantic coast of Canada are the Appalachian Highlands. They are part of the Appalachian Mountains, which run through the eastern United States. This area includes the island of Newfoundland, Nova Scotia, Prince Edward Island, New Brunswick, and southeastern Quebec.

The Appalachian Highlands are made up largely of hills and low mountains. Among the mountains and hills are valleys and plains. Much of this area is covered by forests. Fertile lowlands are found on Prince Edward Island and in parts of New Brunswick and Nova Scotia. The coast of this area is very jagged, providing many good harbors.

St. Lawrence-Great Lakes Lowland. Around the Great Lakes and the St. Lawrence River Valley is the St. Lawrence-Great Lakes Lowland. Although this is the smallest

See the *TAE* for an *Objective 1* Activity.

The surface of the Canadian Shield is dotted with lakes, bare rock hills, and vast forests. How large an area of Canada does the Canadian Shield cover?

COMPAR-A-GRAPH: CANADA-UNITED STATES

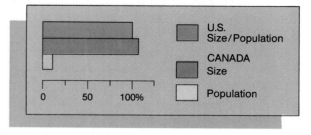

FIGURE 12-2
A compar-a-graph measures the size and population of a country in comparison with the United States. How large is Canada's population compared to the U.S.?

of Canada's physical regions, more than 60 percent of Canada's people live there. This is chiefly because the eastern half of the lowland is made up of rolling farmland. It follows the St. Lawrence River Valley toward the Atlantic Ocean. The St. Lawrence River is the outlet for water flowing from the Great Lakes to the Atlantic Ocean.

The western half of the lowland is a peninsula. This peninsula is in the southern part of the province of Ontario. It is surrounded on three sides by lakes Huron, Erie, and Ontario. Here the land is good for farming.

Canadian Shield. The largest natural landscape of Canada is called the Canadian Shield. It covers almost two million square miles (5,179,996 sq km). That is over half of the entire land area of Canada.

The Canadian Shield is shaped like a huge horseshoe that wraps around the Hudson Bay. It is made up of the oldest rock formation in North America. Geologists estimate that the rock in the Shield may be as old as five billion years. Hills, worn down by erosion, are common all through much of the region.

Although much of the Canadian Shield's central and northwestern parts are low and flat, hills may rise as high as 8,300 feet (2,590.8 m) in the highlands area. This area

A small part of the Canadian Shield extends into the United States. This is the Superior Upland in northern Minnesota, Wisconsin, and Michigan.

Once the Okanagan River in Canada crosses the United States border into Washington, the river's name is spelled Okanogan.

includes the Torngat Mountains in the northern part of Labrador, a large peninsula in the northeastern part of Canada. It also includes the Laurentian Highlands north of the St. Lawrence River.

The Canadian Shield also has hundreds of lakes that were carved by glaciers thousands of years ago. Many of these lakes are sources for rivers that often have rapids and waterfalls.

The northern part of the Canadian Shield has mostly tundra vegetation. However, much of the southern part is covered by great forests. The soil of the Shield is poor and not good for farming. Yet the region is rich in mineral resources, such as iron ore, cobalt, copper, and uranium.

Hudson Bay Lowland. Wedged between the Canadian Shield and Hudson Bay is the Hudson Bay Lowland. Most of this lowland runs along the southern and southwestern coasts of Hudson Bay.

The Hudson Bay Lowland is flat, and the land is poorly drained. In many places **peat bogs** have formed. These are areas of wet ground made up of many decaying plants. Peat is often used as fuel to heat homes. The soil in the Hudson Bay Lowland is generally poor.

Interior Plains. In the west central part of Canada is the Interior Plains. This is part of the Great Plains, which cover much of the central United States. The plains cover large parts of Alberta, Saskatchewan, Manitoba, and the northeastern corner of British Columbia.

The northern part of the plains is made up of forests. The southern part of the plains is a huge rolling prairie with very fertile soil. Most of the land is used for growing wheat and other grains.

Rocky Mountains. West of the Interior Plains are the Rocky Mountains. This region is made up of three chains of rugged mountains—the Rocky Mountains in the south and the Richardson and Mackenzie mountains in the north.

The mountains of the Rocky Mountain region are part of an even larger mountainous area that covers most of British Columbia, the Yukon Territory, and parts of western Alberta and the Northwest Territories. This huge area is called the Cordillera (KAWRD uhl EHR uh). A **cordillera** is a system of parallel mountain chains.

Canada's Rocky Mountains are an extension of the Rockies in the United States. This is an area of great natural beauty, visited regularly by thousands of tourists. Mount Robson, the highest mountain in the Canadian Rockies, rises 12,972 feet (3,953.9 m) above sea level. The Rocky Mountain area is heavily forested and rich in minerals. Rivers, such as the Fraser, the Columbia, and the Okanagan (OH kuh NAHG uhn), form narrow valleys of good soil.

Pacific Mountain and Valley System. The westernmost physical region of Canada is the Pacific Mountain and Valley System. It also includes a major group of the Cordillera—the Coast Mountains. Like the Rockies the Coast Mountains run northward from the United States. In Canada the two chains are separated by a narrow trench, or valley. Near Canada's border with Alaska are several mountains well over 15,000 feet (4,572 m). Among these is 19,850-foot (6,050.3-m) Mount Logan, Canada's highest peak.

The land west of the Coast Mountains to the Pacific Ocean is very rugged. Many offshore islands in the area are really the tops of mountains that rise from the floor of the Pacific Ocean. Many fjords cut into the coastline. A **fjord** (fee AWRD) is a narrow, winding inlet of the sea. Because they are very deep, the fjords make excellent harbors. However, the land along the sides of fjords is so steep that it is not easy for land transportation to reach the harbors.

Arctic Islands. The Arctic Islands are viewed as a region chiefly because of their cold climate. There are about ten large islands and hundreds of small ones. They are almost entirely north of the Arctic Circle.

Actually, there are many different landforms among the islands. For example, Baffin Island, the largest of the group, has high ice-capped mountains. On the eastern end of Victoria Island, the land is flat.

The Arctic Islands have permafrost, so there are no forests. The land is covered chiefly with such tundra plants as mosses and lichens. The northernmost islands are covered with glacial ice.

On the map on page 225, note that most of Canada's cities are concentrated south of 49° north latitude.

1.2 Climate

Canada has a generally cool or cold climate. This is because it is in the high latitudes of the Western Hemisphere. During winter months westerly winds sweeping across Hudson Bay bring cold Arctic air to central Canada. At the same time, the icy Labrador Current chills the eastern coast.

Conditions, however, vary from region to region all through the year. The far north has a tundra climate with year-round cold temperatures. Farther south, between 50° and 70° north latitude, an east-west band of territory across Canada has a subarctic climate with short, cool summers and long, cold winters. Southeastern Canada, where most Canadians live, has a humid continental climate with warm summers and cold winters.

The coast of British Columbia is Canada's only area of moist, mild winter climate— middle-latitude marine. There the Coast Mountains cause warm winds from the Pacific Ocean to release moisture. Thus, this area gets more rain than any other area in Canada. More than 100 inches (254 cm) of rain a year fall in some spots. The warm winds also keep temperatures from getting too cold.

This inlet along Big Bay in British Columbia is an example of the many fjords along Canada's Pacific coast. Why do you think fjords make excellent harbors?

See the *TAE* for an *Objective 1* Activity.

CONTENT CHECK

1. **Identify:** Appalachian Highlands, St. Lawrence-Great Lakes Lowland, Canadian Shield, Labrador, Hudson Bay Lowland, Interior Plains, Richardson Mountains, Mackenzie Mountains, Pacific Mountain and Valley System, Coast Mountains, Mount Logan, Arctic Islands.

2. **Define:** peat bogs, cordillera, fjord.

3. In what physical region do most of the people in Canada live?

4. What river flows from the Great Lakes to the Atlantic Ocean?

5. What is the largest of Canada's eight physical regions?

6. What general kind of climate does most of Canada have?

7. **Challenge:** Canada is a rich storehouse of minerals. Why do you think most of these minerals have not been fully tapped?

2. ECONOMIC AND CULTURAL PATTERNS

In spite of its large size and small population, Canada is a major industrial power. It is one of the world's richest and most economically developed countries. It has rich farmland and many natural resources.

About 76 percent of Canadians live in urban areas. They live in an area that covers only about one-tenth of Canada. Two provinces—Ontario and Quebec—form the heart of the country. Each is the center of one of Canada's two major cultures.

See the TAE for an Objective 2 Activity.

2.1 Provinces and Territories

Instead of states, Canada has provinces and territories. Figure 12-3 on page 225 shows that Canada has ten provinces and two

Apples in Nova Scotia are produced for local use and for sale to Canadian and foreign markets. What are other economic activities in the Atlantic Provinces?

St. John's and Halifax certainly qualify as urban centers, but they are very small compared with such major cities as Montréal, Toronto, and Vancouver.

territories. Geographers often group these into five economic and cultural regions. Each is different in natural resources, economic activities, and cultural life. The five regions of Canada are (1) Atlantic Provinces, (2) Great Lakes-St. Lawrence Provinces, (3) Prairie Provinces, (4) British Columbia, and (5) Canadian Territories.

Atlantic Provinces. Along the Atlantic coast are the four Atlantic provinces—New Brunswick, Newfoundland, Nova Scotia, and Prince Edward Island. Shipping and fishing have long been important activities in the Atlantic Provinces. St. John in New Brunswick, Halifax in Nova Scotia, and St. John's in Newfoundland are the region's chief shipping centers. The Grand Banks, an area of shallow water off the coast of Newfoundland, is one of the world's best fishing areas. Today about 75 percent of Canada's fish harvest comes from the Atlantic Provinces.

Fishing conditions have often brought hardships to the people of the Atlantic Provinces. The cold Atlantic waters bring thick fog, icebergs, and severe storms that make fishing difficult and dangerous. In some seasons fewer fish are caught. For this reason wages and living standards have been lower in the Provinces than in other parts of Canada.

Short growing seasons and thin, rocky soil limit farming in the Atlantic Provinces. However, small farms there grow many different crops. Potatoes are an important crop in New Brunswick and Prince Edward Island. Apples are grown in Nova Scotia and New Brunswick. Blueberries and cranberries are raised in Newfoundland. There also is some dairy farming through the region.

In recent years the Atlantic Provinces have helped their economies in different ways. They have developed their rich mineral deposits of iron ore, zinc, lead, copper, and coal. This has led to an increase in manufacturing in urban areas. Newfoundland has set up pulp and paper industries run by **hydro-**

PROVINCES AND TERRITORIES OF CANADA

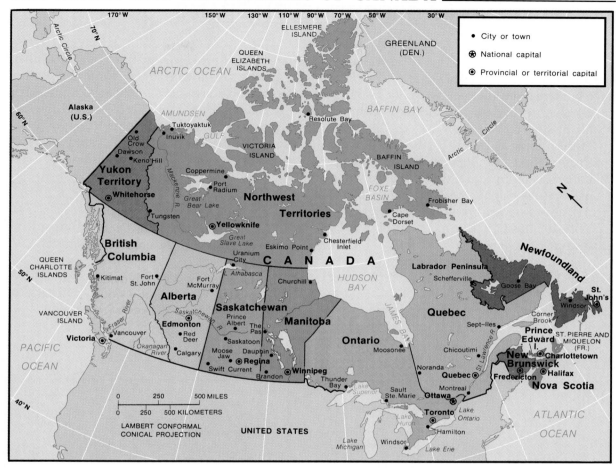

FIGURE 12-3

A relatively small population as well as rugged physical features may account for Canada's provinces and territories being few in number and large in size. Into how many economic and cultural regions is Canada divided?

electric power— electricity that is made by water turning turbines. Prince Edward Island and Nova Scotia have attracted many tourists to their beautiful coasts and beaches. Service industries, such as banking, government, and wholesale and retail trade, now account for nearly 75 percent of the yearly value of goods and services from the Atlantic Provinces.

The Atlantic Provinces were one of the first areas of Canada settled by Europeans. However, poor soil and the harsh climate have kept the population small. Today the Atlantic Provinces have only 10 percent of Canada's people. Most of the people of the region live in cities, towns, and villages along the coasts. About 70 percent are of British or Irish ancestry. Another 15 percent are of French origin.

Great Lakes-St. Lawrence Provinces. Together Quebec and Ontario form an economic-cultural region of Canada. These two provinces are the political and economic center of the country. They account for almost 80 percent of Canada's production and about 60 percent of the population.

USING GRAPHIC SKILLS

INTERPRETING DIAGRAMS

Have you ever needed to ask a friend to explain what a classmate's joke meant? It may have bothered you that you were not as quick to *interpret*, or explain, its meaning as other people had been.

Interpreting is an important skill for geographers and students of geography. Whether it is interpreting written information or interpreting graphics such as maps, charts, or diagrams, you learn a great deal when you are able to interpret the meaning of words, illustrations, or statistics.

The diagram below shows the population of Canada by provinces. Instead of showing the actual land area of each province, the diagram is drawn so that the provinces are shown according to the size of their popula-

tion. Those provinces with a greater number of people are drawn larger, while those with fewer people are drawn smaller. To interpret this diagram, you must keep in mind that its purpose is to show the population of each province or territory when compared with the population of the other areas of Canada.

Study the diagram below. Then answer the questions that follow.

1. Which province is the largest in terms of actual size and smallest in terms of population?
2. **Challenge:** Which province—Manitoba or Nova Scotia—would have the greatest population density? How do you explain this?

RELATIVE POPULATION OF CANADA

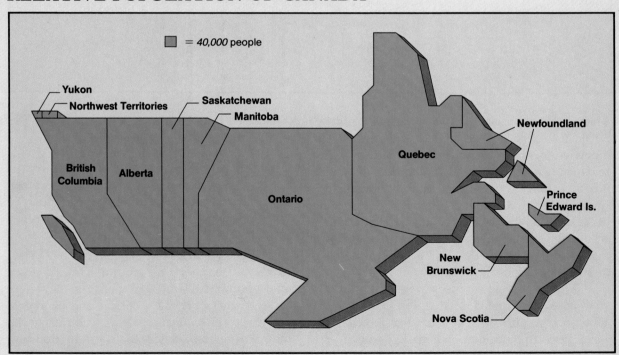

Data from Population Reference Bureau, Inc., 1987.

Quebec and Ontario border on the Great Lakes and the St. Lawrence River, which serve as a waterway for shipment of goods. Products, such as wheat and iron ore, are shipped through them to eastern Canada and to foreign markets. The Great Lakes-St. Lawrence system is not just a water highway. It also makes electric power for eastern Canada.

Quebec and Ontario are rich not only in water but also in other natural resources. Both have huge forests that supply wood products. They also have deposits of iron ore, copper, gold, and zinc. From Quebec comes nearly 90 percent of Canada's asbestos. **Asbestos** is a substance used in making products fireproof and resistant to chemicals.

Because of good transportation and resources, Quebec and Ontario are the leading manufacturing areas of Canada. Urban centers in both produce ships, cars, food products, clothing, and building materials.

Quebec and Ontario are also important agricultural areas. Most of Canada's fruits and vegetables come from southern Quebec and Ontario. Farmers in both provinces also raise beef and dairy cattle.

Canada's largest metropolitan areas are found in Quebec and Ontario. Toronto, the capital of Ontario, has 3.2 million people in its metropolitan area. It is Canada's largest city as well as its chief manufacturing, financial, and communications center. Montréal, Quebec, with a population of nearly 2.9 million people, is one of the world's largest inland ports and a major center of Canadian industry, culture, and education.

Another important city is Canada's national capital, Ottawa. It is located in eastern Ontario. With a population of nearly 300,000, Ottawa is known for its attractive parks and stately government buildings.

Quebec and Ontario are centers of two cultures. Quebec's culture is French. As Figure 12-4 on this page shows, about 80 percent of the people of Quebec are of French de-

FRENCH DOMINANCE IN QUEBEC

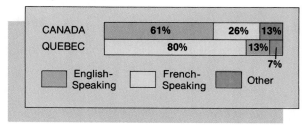

FIGURE 12-4
Quebec's French-speaking majority is a minority in Canada. How many Canadians speak French?

Use of asbestos has declined in recent years because of hazards such as respiratory ailments.

scent. French is Quebec's official language, and most of the people are Roman Catholics.

Ontario is the center of English-speaking Canada. Almost 60 percent of the people are of British or Irish descent. However, the province has other ethnic groups. This is because of a steady flow of immigrants to the province since World War II. Most of these new Canadians come from Germany, the Netherlands, Italy, Greece, and Portugal.

Prairie Provinces. West of Ontario lie the Prairie Provinces of Manitoba, Saskatchewan, and Alberta. These three provinces are largely flat. However, their landscape is different from place to place.

For years, the Prairie Provinces were largely agricultural. People in the region grew wheat and raised cattle. However, depending so much on farming brought problems. Farmers and ranchers often lost income as a result of bad weather, poor transportation, and low prices for their products.

The Prairie Provinces still raise most of Canada's grain and cattle. However, the region's economy is now mostly based on service industries. Also the discovery of oil and natural gas in Alberta and Saskatchewan has brought wealth to the region. These deposits of **fossil fuels**—fuels formed from organic matter—are among the largest reserves

LAND USE AND RESOURCES OF CANADA

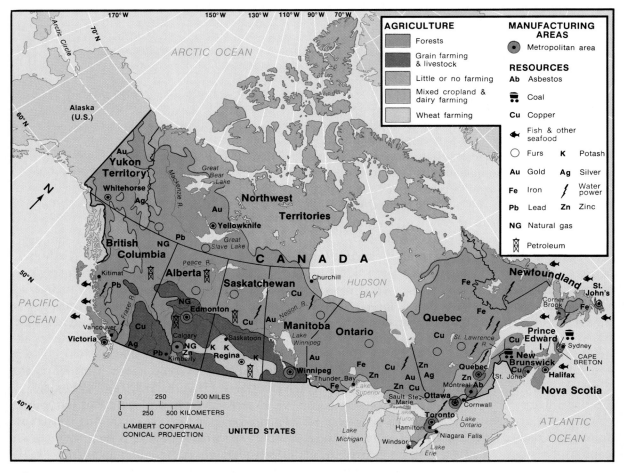

FIGURE 12-5

Vast stretches of forest blanket the Canadian landmass, while northern areas of the country allow little or no farming. Farming is restricted to Canada's southern areas. Where are most of the water power resources located?

A famous attraction in Calgary is the annual Calgary Stampede, which features outstanding rodeo talent.

known in the world. The Prairie Provinces are also rich in copper, lead, zinc, and **potash,** a mineral used in making fertilizer.

Despite the development of resources, the Prairie Provinces are lightly populated. The northern parts are mostly unsettled due to the harsh climate. The Prairie Provinces average fewer than three people per square mile (one per sq km). This amounts to about 17 percent of Canada's population. This region, however, has some of the fastest grow-

A chart on page 419 compares the Trans-Canada Highway with other transportation systems.

ing cities in Canada. Calgary, Alberta, is the largest city in the Prairie Provinces. Edmonton, also in Alberta, is the province's capital. Both Calgary and Edmonton are important service centers for the oil industry. Winnipeg—Manitoba's capital—is an important grain marketing center.

The Prairie Provinces were settled by Europeans in the late 1800s. Before this time the region was too far from the rest of Canada to appeal to settlers. However, the completion

ANGLO-AMERICA UNIT 4

of Canada's first railroad across the entire continent brought many Canadians and foreigners into the area. Today the people of the Prairie Provinces are of British, Irish, German, Polish, Ukrainian, and Scandinavian descent. Because of the oil industry, many Americans have settled here. Also many Native Americans live in the Prairie Provinces.

British Columbia. British Columbia is the westernmost province of Canada. It is made up of rugged mountains, large plateaus, and fertile river valleys. In the east the province is cut off from the rest of Canada by the Rocky Mountains. In the west it borders the Pacific Ocean.

British Columbia has many natural resources. The mild, wet climate of its Pacific coast is ideal for growing flowers, plants, and trees. Much of British Columbia is covered with forests. Timber, pulp, and paper provide most of the province's manufacturing income. British Columbia has plenty of water power for hydroelectricity. It also has deposits of coal, copper, asbestos, zinc, and lead. The mining of these minerals adds to the province's wealth.

Because much of British Columbia is mountainous, agriculture is limited to the narrow valleys of the Cordillera. In the southwest the Fraser River valley provides dairy products, meat, and vegetables. In the interior, fruit is grown in the Okanagan River Valley. These areas also have many poultry farms and **truck farms,** or market gardens, that raise vegetables for nearby urban areas.

Fishing is another major economic activity in British Columbia. Salmon is the major catch. Other important seafoods are halibut, clams, herring, and shrimp. The major fishing centers are small towns along the Pacific coast. Most canneries are found near the mouth of the Fraser River.

About one-half of British Columbia's 2,750,000 people live near two major cities— Vancouver and Victoria. Both of these cities are found in the southwestern corner of the province. Vancouver is the major city of British Columbia. It has about 1.3 million people in its metropolitan area. This makes Vancouver one of the largest cities in Canada. Lying near the mouth of the Fraser River, Vancouver is the busiest port on the Pacific coast of

Refer students to the chart on page 299 that provides data on the highest peaks in the Americas.

Because the mountains rise so sharply from sea level in the Vancouver area, there often is snow on the Grouse Mountain ski runs and rain in the city below.

The Saskatchewan wheat-growing community of Lajord is located on the Great Regina Plain. What does this photograph seem to suggest about the population density of the region of the Prairie Provinces?

Point out that British Columbia has outstanding timber resources. More than one-half of Canada's softwood reserves are here. Softwoods generally include conifers such as pines, firs, and balsams.

North America. The city is also an important business and financial center. Victoria is the capital and second largest city of British Columbia. Its metropolitan area has about 234,000 people. Victoria lies at the southern tip of Vancouver Island.

The people who live in British Columbia come from many different backgrounds. About 60 percent are of British ancestry. Asian as well as European groups are found in the province. They include people of Chinese, Japanese, Indian, and Pakistani descent. Many Native Americans also live in British Columbia.

Canadian Territories. In addition to the ten provinces, Canada includes two territories. These are the Yukon Territory and the

Northwest Territories. Both land areas are huge, together covering 40 percent of Canada. However, they have very few people. The Northwest Territories have about 50,000 people, and the Yukon Territory only 23,000. Together they have less than one-half of one percent of Canada's population.

There are no large cities in either of the territories. Even their capital cities are relatively small. Whitehorse, in the Yukon Territory, has about 15,000 people. Yellowknife, in the Northwest Territories, has about 10,000 people.

The people of the territories are mostly Eskimos, or Inuit, and other Native Americans. These groups make up two-thirds of the population of the region. The Inuit generally live north of the **timberline,** which marks the boundary between where trees can grow in cold winter climates and where trees cannot grow in polar climates. The Native Americans generally live in areas south of the line.

Some population growth is taking place in the territories due to the discovery of valuable natural resources. The major mineral resources are zinc, lead, and gold. Uranium and many rare metals have also been found. But they are not being mined at the present time. Roads and rail lines are being pushed farther north to reach these resources.

Lumber is the most important resource in the southern part of the territories. In the Yukon the tourist industry has taken the place of mining as the main source of income. However, despite many advances, the territories still remain largely undeveloped.

Much of the Yukon's tourist industry centers around the Alaskan Highway, which crosses western Canada as it connects Alaska with the contiguous United States.

2.2 Canadian Life

Canadian ways of life are similar to American ones. Like Americans, Canadians are wealthy by world standards. This is seen in a number of ways.

The artwork of this Native American of Canada reflects the wildlife and natural environment of his home near Hudson Bay. What people live in the territories?

Education is widespread among the people of Canada. Most Canadians are able to attend school from first grade through high school. The nation also has a large number of colleges and universities.

Canada also has good systems of transportation and communication. Private ownership of cars is common. Through the use of Canadian radio, television, newspapers, and magazines, people are able to keep in touch with national and world events. Since most Canadians live near the American border, they often read American newspapers and magazines. They also enjoy listening to American radio and watching American television programs.

Canadians enjoy many free-time activities that are similar to those in the United States. Not surprisingly, winter sports are very popular in Canada. These include ice skating, ice hockey, and skiing. Baseball and football are also popular spectator sports.

Canada's location next to the United States is very important economically. The two countries have long carried on a great amount of trade. Recently there has been a move toward economic cooperation between the United States and Canada. For example, large amounts of iron ore, lumber, and other raw materials are exported to the United States. In addition, many Canadian businesses are subsidiaries of American companies. **Subsidiaries** are companies owned or controlled by other firms. Many business decisions made in the United States have an important effect on Canadian life.

Canadians are concerned about keeping their sense of nationhood while living next to such a large and populous country as the United States. Recently the Canadian government has taken steps to reduce American control of businesses in Canada. It has also tried to limit the publication of books, magazines, and advertisements by American businesses in Canada.

CONTENT CHECK

1. **Identify:** Atlantic Provinces, New Brunswick, Newfoundland, Nova Scotia, Prince Edward Island, Halifax, Grand Banks, Great Lakes-St. Lawrence Provinces, Quebec, Ontario, Toronto, Montréal, Ottawa, Prairie Provinces, Manitoba, Saskatchewan, Alberta, Calgary, British Columbia, Vancouver, Victoria, Yukon Territory, Northwest Territories, Inuit.

2. **Define:** hydroelectric power, asbestos, fossil fuels, potash, truck farms, timberline, subsidiaries.

3. Which region is the political and economic center of Canada?

4. What are Canada's two most populated cities?

5. Which provinces have gained new wealth from oil?

6. How are Canadian life and American life similar? How are they different?

7. **Challenge:** What economic problems do the Atlantic Provinces have? What steps might they take to improve their economies?

See the *TAE* for an *Objective 3* Activity.

3. INFLUENCES OF THE PAST

Canada was originally settled by ancestors of the Inuit and other Native Americans. These people crossed the Bering Strait between Asia and North America more than 25,000 years ago. Today the majority of the country's Inuit live in northern Canada. Most of them fish and hunt for a living. Some work for mining and lumber companies. Other Native Americans generally live in western Canada on reservations, or separate land areas set aside for them by the government. Among the major Native American groups are the

STRANGE BUT TRUE

CAN YOU SEE BORDERS?

Borders are important in the study of political geography. All political divisions—cities, provinces, states, and countries—have borders. The borders give these political units their size and shape.

People deal with borders every day without even thinking about them. For example, when people go to a baseball game, they can see the boundaries of the field drawn on the grass or turf. These boundary lines show the base paths and the limits between foul territory and the playing field. Similar lines are drawn on basketball courts and football fields. All of these kinds of borders can be seen.

Other kinds of borders are invisible. For example, very young children are aware of the boundaries of the yards around their homes. Most school children could draw a map showing the boundaries of their school's property. When entering or leaving a city, people often notice a sign marking the city's border.

Because most borders between political divisions cannot be seen, it is often possible to leave a city without knowing it. If a person were traveling on a country road, there might not be a sign to tell where the city's borders are located. The same is true of a border between two countries.

Many natural features have been chosen as borders between political divisions. Rivers, lakes, and mountain ranges on many continents in the world serve as political borders. The Great Lakes, for example, mark part of the border between the United States and Canada. The Pyrenees serve as the border between France and Spain. Even though these natural features can be seen, the borders themselves are usually invisible. For example, the border may be the middle of a river.

Below is an aerial photograph taken of the border between the state of Montana in the United States and the province of Alberta in Canada. The border runs along the forty-ninth parallel and is visible because the difference in how each country uses the land causes contrasting patterns on each side of the border. In Montana much of the land is used for growing wheat. In Alberta, on the other hand, the land is used chiefly as grazing land for cattle and sheep.

The differences in land use shown in the photograph point to one of the reasons why borders are made in the first place. They are made to separate people with different ways of life into separate areas.

1. What are some boundaries that can be seen?
2. What natural features are commonly chosen to mark borders?
3. What are some of the purposes for having borders?

Algonquin, Athabaskan, Haida, Tlingit, and Iroquois. Many other groups have moved to Canada since the earliest peoples settled there. Most of them have been European. However, all have contributed to the making of the modern nation.

The first permanent settlement by France in Canada occurred just one year after Jamestown was started.

3.1 European Settlement

The first Europeans to settle Canada were the French. In 1534 Jacques Cartier sailed into the Gulf of St. Lawrence. He claimed the area for France. The first lasting French settlement was made at present-day Québec by Samuel de Champlain in 1608. For about 150 years, France ruled the area around the St. Lawrence and the Great Lakes as New France. During the time many settlers immigrated to Canada from France.

The English also explored Canada. In 1497 John Cabot landed on the Atlantic coast—at either Newfoundland or Nova Scotia—and claimed the area for England. For many years few English settlers came to Canada. Those who did come were mostly fur trappers.

In 1670 the Hudson's Bay Company was formed. The English government gave this group the right to control all of the fur trade in the Hudson Bay area. This helped to strengthen English claims to the lands that are now Canada.

Have students identify Native American place-names in their area and share any local folklore.

3.2 French-British Conflict

In the early 1700s, the English united with the Scots to form the United Kingdom. Together, they became known as the British. Soon the British and the French became rivals for large areas of land in North America. They had also been rivals in Europe for a long time. A series of wars was fought between the two peoples in the 1600s and 1700s.

The wars resulted in the gradual loss of French control over Canada. In 1713 France ceded, or gave over control of, what is now most of the Atlantic Provinces to the British. The most important war, known in America as the French and Indian War, was fought between 1754 and 1763. It ended in a British victory. With victory, the British gained control over most of New France.

Have interested students prepare a time line comparing events in both countries during this time.

3.3 Birth of a Nation

After their victory the British had to rule a new colony that had a large French population. By that time French settlers in Canada numbered some 65,000. There were important differences in culture between the British and the French. Some of these still affect Canada today. Besides having different languages, the French were mostly Roman Catholic, while the English were mostly Protestant. The French also had their own system of laws and courts.

The British government finally decided that the best way to rule over Canada was to allow the French to keep their own ways of living. This decision was affected in part by events in what is now the United States.

The population of the British colonies in what became the United States was growing rapidly. There were signs that these colonies might eventually seek independence. The British government hoped to keep Canada apart from these growing colonies to the south.

In the Quebec Act of 1774, the British promised to protect the French culture in Canada. The Act allowed French Canadians to keep their language, religion, and laws.

The Act, however, did not solve the problems of getting the two cultures to live side by side. Tensions continued between British Canadians and French Canadians. After the United States won its independence in

1783, several thousand people loyal to the British king moved to Canada. These people, known as United Empire Loyalists, settled mostly in what is now Ontario. In 1791 the British government divided Canada into two parts. Upper Canada—now Ontario—was where most English-speaking Canadians lived. Lower Canada—now Quebec—was where more French-speaking Canadians lived. Each part was given its own legislature and court system.

During the War of 1812, the United States tried to conquer Canada. Many people in the United States were convinced that Canada must one day be a part of their country. The American effort to rule Canada failed. However, many Canadians continued to fear American aims. To strengthen Canada, the British, in 1840, united the two parts of the country.

See the TRB for Teacher Notes: Section 1 Extending the Lesson on language equality.

3.4 Steps Toward Unity

All through the 1850s and 1860s, many Canadians wanted greater freedom under British rule. In 1867 the British set up a new country called the Dominion of Canada. As a result of this change, the Canadians gained control over their local affairs. However, foreign and military decisions were still made for them by the British. At this time Canada had only four provinces: Ontario, Quebec, Nova Scotia, and New Brunswick.

During the late 1800s, Canada grew rapidly in size and population. A railway was built across the country. As Figure 12-6 on page 235 shows, settlers moved west into an area called Hudson's Bay Territories that the Canadian government had received from the British. By the early 1900s, five new provinces had been added to Canada. They were Prince Edward Island in the east and Manitoba, British Columbia, Saskatchewan, and Alberta in the west.

Canada fought World War I on the side of the British and the other Allies. Because of its wartime efforts, Canada won more freedom in working out its military and foreign affairs. In 1931 the British recognized Canada as an independent nation. However, they kept the right to approve any changes made in Canada's form of government.

Following World War II, Canada enjoyed rapid economic growth. It also began to play an important role in world affairs. The nation finally reached its present size when Newfoundland became a province in 1949.

Refer to the map of Canada's growth on page 235 and the map of U.S. expansion on pages 208-209. Have students compare how the nations developed.

3.5 Canada Today and Tomorrow

As a nation Canada has developed slowly. In fact, it is still developing. There are many key issues that the country faces and will face in years to come.

One of the most important issues is the link between the national government and the provinces. Canada is a federation of provinces and territories. A **federation** is a system of government in which powers are shared between a central government and a number of regional governments. Problems for all of Canada are handled by the national government in Ottawa. However, each province has its own government for local problems.

When Canada took its first step toward nationhood in 1867, it set up a strong national government based on that of the United Kingdom. The British king or queen was recognized as king or queen of Canada. The actual head of government, however, was a Canadian prime minister. The prime minister and the Cabinet, or advisers, were leaders among the lawmakers who sat in Parliament, or the national legislature. The lawmakers, or members of Parliament, were representatives chosen by Canadian voters.

Nearly one-half million people migrated from the United States into the Canadian plains in the late 1800s and early 1900s. They took advantage of Canadian homesteads after lands for homesteading in the U.S. were gone. A railroad from the U.S. reached Winnipeg in 1878—seven years before one connected Winnipeg with Ontario.

GROWTH OF CANADA

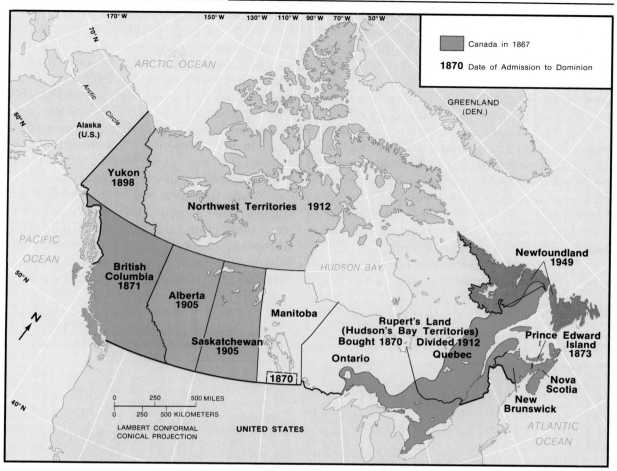

FIGURE 12-6
Rupert's Land was named for Prince Rupert, who was the first governor of the Hudson's Bay Company. This British company held control of the territory for 200 years. Which two provinces were formed out of Rupert's Land?

In the Canadian federation, provinces have more power. In the United States federal system, national government has more power. Both, however, are democracies.

Canada still has this form of national government today. However, during the past 100 years, little by little, the national government has given some of its powers to the governments of the provinces. Today, for example, the provinces control their own education, transportation, and social welfare. The territories are generally governed by the national government.

Some groups of Canadians want the national government to be stronger. However, most of the provinces have been against efforts to strengthen the national government. In fact, they want more power, especially over the use of natural resources inside their own borders.

In 1982 Canada put into effect a new constitution with a bill of rights. Before this time changes in Canada's government could take place only with British approval. Now the United Kingdom no longer has any say in Canadian affairs.

Another important issue facing Canada is the on-going division between English-speaking Canadians and French-speaking Canadians. While French speakers are the largest group in Quebec, English speakers are the dominant group in the country as a whole. As a result, English-speaking Canadians control the national government and economy.

In the 1960s French-speaking Canadians began to demand a greater part in Canadian affairs. They claimed that they could not get better jobs in government and industry. Most businesses in Quebec were owned by English-speaking Canadians or by Americans. French-speaking Canadians also wanted Canada to become officially a bilingual country.

The Canadian government began to meet some of these demands. The flag of Canada was changed to show a red maple leaf and two red stripes on a white background. Four years later it made both English and French the official languages of Canada.

In spite of these changes, some French-speaking Canadians in Quebec wanted the province to break away from Canada and become a separate country. These people were called **separatists.** Their demands were voted down in 1980. However, the difficulty of joining two cultures in one country will continue to face Canadians in the years to come.

While Canada's two major cultures are English and French, the country also has many other ethnic groups. They include other Europeans, Asians, Latin Americans, and Native Americans. Since World War II, more than 500,000 refugees have fled to Canada.

French and English historical flags in the collage are overlaid by the symbol of modern Canada—the maple leaf.

Modern Canada blends the heritage of France—Jacques Cartier, a fur trapper, the French language—and Britain—John Cabot, a redcoat soldier, the English language. How has this cultural diversity benefited Canada?

CARTIER · CABOT ·

ARRÊT STOP

While many people in Canada's ethnic groups are proud of their traditions, they also are proud of being Canadians. However, not all of them share equally in the benefits of Canadian life. The Canadian government is trying to develop policies to enable all Canadians to share in the country's prosperity and future growth.

Signs at a Montréal flea market give information in both French and English. This scene attests to the bilingual culture found in Canada's Quebec province. What steps did the Canadian government take to meet the demands of its French-speaking citizens?

See the TRB for the Chapter 12 Skill Activity on making inferences. Students will examine a map of Canada to infer possible demands of human settlement and future development.

See the TAE for an Objective 3 Activity.

See the TRB for the Chapter 12 Reading.

CONTENT CHECK

1. **Identify:** Bering Strait, Samuel de Champlain, New France, John Cabot, Hudson's Bay Company, French and Indian War, Quebec Act, War of 1812, Dominion of Canada.

2. **Define:** federation, separatists.

3. What groups of people originally settled in Canada?

4. What provinces made up the Dominion of Canada in 1867?

5. What changes did the 1982 constitution make in Canada's government?

6. What general issues are facing Canada today?

7. **Challenge:** Why do you think some Americans during the late 1700s and early 1800s thought that Canada should one day be part of the United States?

CONCLUSION

Canada, like many other countries, has had problems. Recently it has suffered from inflation and a relatively high level of unemployment. It needs to work out a better relationship between the federal government and the provinces. Tension between English and French Canadians is a major challenge.

Canada's weaknesses, however, are in some ways its strengths. Canadians are proud of the diversity of their nation. They feel that they are tolerant of differences. This tolerance allows the country to have two languages and two cultures, as well as great freedom for the provinces.

While Canada has evolved slowly as a country, it has nevertheless become one of the major nations of the world. Part of this is due to its great supply of natural resources. Much of it is due to the efforts of its people. Both seem to offer the country a prosperous future.

CHAPTER REVIEW

SUMMARY

1. Canada is the second largest country in the world in land area. However, it has a small population, numbering about 25.9 million.
2. There are eight major physical regions in Canada.
3. In general, Canada's climate is cool or cold over the whole country.
4. Canada's provinces can be grouped into five economic-cultural regions.
5. Ontario and Quebec form the economic and political heart of Canada. Combined they have 60 percent of the country's population and 80 percent of its industry.
6. Many natural resources have helped make Canada a leading industrialized country.
7. Canada exports many raw materials to the United States. Many companies in Canada are owned by American companies.
8. Canada is a country of two cultures—one is French and the other English.
9. Canada is a federation of ten provinces and two territories.

Answers to the following questions can be found on page T147.

REVIEWING VOCABULARY

Listed below are the vocabulary words in this chapter. Head a separate sheet of paper with the words Vocabulary of Physical and Human Geography. *Divide the paper into two columns with the headings* Physical Geography *and* Human Geography. *Then write each vocabulary word under the kind of geography with which it can be classified. In a few cases, the word may be classified under both headings. For this reason, be prepared to explain why you chose each classification.*

fjord	asbestos	fossil fuels	timberline	permafrost
cede	peat bogs	bilingual	reservations	subsidiaries
potash	truck farm	cordillera	separatists	hydroelectric power

REMEMBERING THE FACTS

1. What oceans surround Canada?
2. What are the two major European groups that make up Canada's population?
3. What does bilingual mean?
4. What physical region covers nearly half of Canada's total land area?
5. What city is the capital of Canada? In which province is it located?
6. What Canadian city is the busiest Pacific coast port in North America?
7. What groups of people live in the Canadian territories?
8. What province became home for thousands of United Empire Loyalists during and after the American Revolution?
9. What languages are spoken in Canada?

UNDERSTANDING THE FACTS

1. What physical regions of Canada are shared with the United States?
2. What control on climate does latitude have on Canada?
3. What factors explain the economic importance of Ontario and Quebec?
4. Why are the Prairie Provinces so lightly populated?
5. What was the effect of the American Revolution and the War of 1812 on Canada's history?
6. How is Canada governed?

THINKING CRITICALLY AND CREATIVELY

1. From their origin the Atlantic Provinces were involved in economic activities such as fishing, timbering, and farming. Today they are adding more variety to their economies by increasing manufacturing and service industries. How will these changes impact the provinces? Canada?
2. While Canada officially is a bilingual nation, there is some friction between French-speaking and English-speaking Canadians. What are some of the causes of this friction?
3. The Prairie Provinces were once poor economically. What factors have now allowed these provinces to prosper?
4. The government of Canada has taken several steps to reduce American control of business. Why do Canadians support such actions?
5. **Challenge:** A British historian and political leader, James Bryce, served as an ambassador from the United Kingdom to the United States from 1907–1913. He once said, "If Canada did not exist it would be to the interest of the United States to invent her." What do you think Bryce meant by this? What might he have been saying about the relationship between Canada and the United States during the early 1900s? Do you think this relationship still holds true today?
6. **Challenge:** A multimillion-dollar government program of the late 1970s offered airport services to all areas in the Northwest Territories with more than 100 persons. Also, through satellite technology, the people in these areas now have use of telephones, radios, and televisions. How do you think their lives have changed since the 1970s? What do you think their lives were like before these services were provided?

REINFORCING GRAPHIC SKILLS

Study the diagram on page 226 and the political map of Canada on page 225. Then answer the questions that follow.

1. How does the Yukon on the map compare with it in the diagram?
2. How does Nova Scotia on the map compare with the diagram?
3. Which area—the Yukon Territory or the province of Nova Scotia—has the greater population density? How do you explain this?

UNIT REVIEW

SUMMARY

1. Anglo-America is a culture area of two regions—the United States and Canada.
2. The United States and Canada have many physical regions, some of which are shared.
3. Because the area of the United States crosses through a broader range of latitudes than does Canada, the United States has a more diverse climate.
4. The populations of the United States and Canada are highly urbanized. Part of this pattern is the result of advanced agricultural practices. Together, the United States and Canada comprise one of the largest and most productive technical and industrial areas in the world.
5. Since most Canadian territory lies farther north than that of the United States, agriculture in the United States tends to be richer and more diversified than agriculture in Canada.
6. The United States and Canada are interdependent countries. There is a free flow of people, ideas, and goods across their common border.
7. The United States and Canada share common historical ties to the United Kingdom.
8. Both the United States and Canada have wrestled with difficult internal problems concerning population majorities and population minorities.

Answers to the following questions can be found on page T150.

THINKING ABOUT THE UNIT

1. Both the United States and Canada have transcontinental railroads and major interstate and interprovince highways. If you were to build a new transcontinental railroad, which cities would you link in each country? What major United States' and Canadian cities would you link with the new highway system? Why?
2. Anglo-America is a culture area known for its cultural diversity. What physical and economic characteristics of the area have encouraged this diversity?

SUGGESTED UNIT ACTIVITIES

1. Prepare a bulletin board comparing migration into the United States and Canada. For each country, indicate places from which most immigrants have come. Make comparisons at different periods of history.
2. Prepare weather reports for three areas of Anglo-America. Emphasize the type of information people in each area would want to hear, such as tides, storms, rain or snowfall.
3. Use advertisements in old copies of magazines and newspapers to prepare a bulletin board display on the economies in Anglo-America. Emphasize regional development of agriculture and industry.
4. Write an essay that describes what values are important in American culture.

240

DEVELOPING GEOGRAPHY SKILLS

OBSERVING IN THE FIELD

You can learn many wonderful things from books. But reading engages just one of your senses . . . sight. You learn better and remember better when more of your senses are involved. Going beyond books to smell, touch, hear, and, in some cases, even taste things gives you greater opportunity for learning. When you go out and directly observe Earth and its features, you are conducting field studies, just as many geographers do.

Good field observations require preparation. There is so much to be seen that you might miss important information if you fail to organize yourselves before you begin. You need to decide what to focus on, how to record your information, and how to think about what you have seen. Record your observations in a notebook that includes these categories:

1. *Date, time, and place of the observation.* This information helps the observer recall information that is being reported.
2. *Specific focus of the observation.* In any field observation, there are hundreds of things that distract attention. The careful observer wishes to focus only on one or two items of interest.
3. *Notes on what was observed.* Notes are complete descriptions of what was seen. The observer tries to describe it well enough for a reader to appreciate what has been seen even if he or she has never seen it personally.
4. *Comments and reactions to what has been seen.* The observer writes down thoughts about what has been seen. These might involve comparisons to other things. They might be personal feelings about what has been seen.

Suppose you lived in the corn-belt country of southern Minnesota and visited the Bitterroot Valley in western Montana. You might make field observations during your visit. You would begin by noting the date, time, and place. (*July 10, 1989; 10 AM: rural area just south of Victor, Montana.*)

Then you would indicate a focus (*landscape and crops*). This would be followed by your observations (*narrow valley with very high mountain range on the west side; mostly grazing land in the valley with a few sugar beets*). You could conclude with your comments (*very different appearance from the gently rolling landscape of southern Minnesota; no corn fields here in Montana; very different from farming country at home; must be some important climate and growing-conditions differences.*).

Field observations of your hometown can gather information useful in making comparisons with other places you have not visited. For example, you might focus on natural resources in your hometown. Then look at other regions of the United States, described in Chapter 10. How are natural resources found in your area similar and different from those in other parts of the country?

For practice in conducting field observations in your area, focus on land use. Use your notes to compare your hometown's land use to that in another region of the United States.

LATIN AMERICA

UNIT 5

Lake Atitlan in Guatemala

Latin America is a huge part of the world made up of 33 nations from two continents. Nearly two and one-half times larger than the United States' 48 contiguous states, it stretches from the Mexico-United States border in North America to the southernmost tip of South America. Latin America has four major regions—Mexico and Central America, the Caribbean, and two regions of South America separated by the massive Andes mountain chain.

Latin America is one of the world's major culture areas—one of many contrasts. Some of the world's smallest countries and one of the world's largest countries are part of it. Some have great mountain ranges, while others have miles of tropical rain forests. Some areas of Latin America have fertile fields, but others are desert. Even though most of the people of Latin America are descended from the Spanish and Portuguese, many Indians, Europeans, Africans, and Asians live there. What binds this large part of the world together are its common religion—Roman Catholicism—and languages—Spanish and Portuguese.

Point out to students that the highlighted area on the world map inset represents the culture area of Latin America.

CHAPTER 13

Often beginning and ending with fireworks and ringing bells, a Mexican *fiesta*, or party, is filled with music, dancing, and bright, colorful costumes.

Festival at the Basilica in Mexico City

MEXICO AND CENTRAL AMERICA

Although Latin America often is thought of as a land of continuous fiestas, the parties do not occur often, and when they do, they serve for many as a relief from the work and cares of everyday life.

In this chapter you will learn—

- What landscapes and climates are found in Mexico and Central America.
- How economic and cultural patterns of Mexico and Central America are the same and how they are different.
- How history has influenced Mexico and the countries of Central America.

Because of the growing Spanish-speaking minority in the United States, attempts have been made in this book to show the pronunciation of Spanish terms and place-names based on the modern Spanish language.

INTRODUCTION

Mexico and the Central American countries of Belize (bay LEEZ), Guatemala, Honduras, El Salvador, Nicaragua, Costa Rica, and Panama make up one of the regions of Latin America. Physically, the region is the southern part of the North American continent. Because it is between the United States and the continent of South America, it is sometimes called Middle America. The region sweeps in a southeasterly direction from its border with the United States on the north to its border with Colombia on the south. The Pacific Ocean is to the west of the region, and the Gulf of Mexico and the Caribbean Sea are to the east.

Because of its shape, the land looks like a tilted funnel on a map. The large end of the funnel is to the north and west. The small end is to the south and east. The distance from the large end of the funnel to the small end is about 2,500 miles (4,023.4 km). The northern border of Mexico across the large end is about 1,300 miles (2,092.1 km) long. The small end of the funnel, which is where central Panama crosses from the Pacific Ocean to the Caribbean Sea, is only about 50 miles (80.5 km) long.

The landscapes of the region include desert, plains, plateaus, and mountains. These are shown in Figure 13-1 on page 246. The highlands in the central part of the region divide the part in the north with dry climates from the part in the south with tropical moist climates.

The population density of Mexico and Central America is different from place to place. In Belize, for example, there are only about 23 persons per square mile (9 per sq km). On the other hand, in El Salvador there are 652 persons per square mile (252 per sq km). Parts of northern Mexico are among the least populated areas in the world. Yet Mexico City has the largest metropolitan area in the world.

Central America has many different cultures. In Guatemala, for example, more than one-half the people are of Indian descent. In Costa Rica more than one-half are descended from European settlers. Each country of the region, except Belize, was once a Spanish colony. Belize was at one time a British colony known as British Honduras.

The major language of the region is Spanish. In Belize, however, the official language is English. In areas where many Indians live, native Indian languages are common.

PHYSICAL REGIONS OF MEXICO AND CENTRAL AMERICA ___

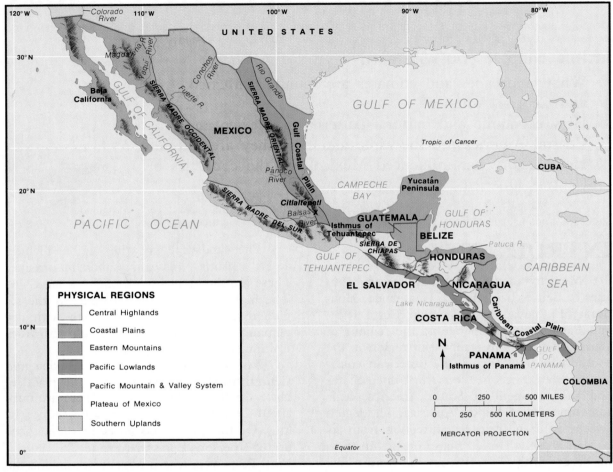

FIGURE 13-1
A great diversity of physical features is found in Mexico and Central America. At its extremes the region contains both deserts and rain forests. Four mountain ranges are located in Mexico. None extend throughout all the countries of Central America. Which of the four Mexican mountain ranges extends into Central America?

Mexico and Central America have gone from once-great ancient Indian civilizations to developing and struggling countries of the twentieth century. During these times, they have overcome many obstacles. However, there is still a large gap between rich and poor. Today there also are many social and political differences among the people. As a result, the eyes of the world often watch the struggles of this part of Latin America.

1. MEXICO

See the *TAE* for an *Objective 1* Activity.

Mexico, the largest country in the region, has most of its population. Figure 13-2 on page 247 shows how its land area and population compares with those of the United States. With 81.9 million people, Mexico has the greatest influence on the other countries in the area.

LATIN AMERICA UNIT 5

1.1 Landscape and Climate

Mexico is a rugged land of sharp physical differences. In the north there are deserts. In the south there are tropical rain forests. Mountains and a central plateau cover most of the landscape that is left. Because there are such differences in land and elevation, there are also great differences in climate.

Landscape. To the north, the widest part of the Mexican mainland borders the United States. To the south, the country narrows. It is narrowest at the Isthmus of Tehuantepec (teh wahn teh PEHK). An **isthmus** (IHS muhs) is a narrow piece of land connecting two larger land areas. At this point only about 140 miles (225.3 km) separate the Pacific Ocean from the Gulf of Mexico. South of the isthmus, the land broadens slightly as Mexico stretches toward the border with Belize and Guatemala.

West of the Mexican mainland is a narrow strip of land known as Baja (BAH hah) California. It is a long, thin **peninsula**—or piece of land surrounded on three sides by water—that is part of the Pacific Mountain and Valley System. It extends south from its northern border with California in the United States. The Gulf of California separates Baja California from the mainland of Mexico except near the border with the United States.

Two major mountain ranges dominate the Mexican mainland. The Sierra Madre Occidental runs north and south along the west coast of Mexico, not far inland from the Pacific Ocean. This area is also part of the Pacific Mountain and Valley System. On the east coast, the Sierra Madre Oriental, making up the Eastern Mountains region, runs north and south, not far inland from the Gulf of Mexico. Most of the people of Mexico live on the large central plateau between these two ranges. This relatively flat land is wedged between the two mountain chains, forming a V-shape.

COMPAR-A-GRAPH: MEXICO-UNITED STATES

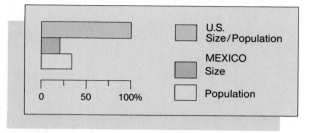

FIGURE 13-2
With the largest area and population in this region, Mexico's size is one-fifth as large as the United States, while it has one-third as many people as the United States. What is Mexico's actual population?

Many deep-sea-fishing enthusiasts favor the Cape San Lucas area at the southern tip of Baja California.

At the top of the "V," along the border with the United States, the land is mostly at sea level. Toward the south, the Plateau of Mexico rises slowly. From a low desert in the north, it rises to 8,000 feet (2,438.4 m) above sea level near Mexico City.

At the bottom of the "V," the two mountain ranges meet where the land narrows near the Isthmus of Tehuantepec. On the isthmus itself there are few mountains. South of it, however, mountains again dominate the landscape. This range is the Sierra de Chiapas (cheĉAH pahs). It reaches south into Central America.

East of the isthmus, the land broadens into a flat area of rain forest. North and east of this area is the Yucatán (yoo kah TAHN) Peninsula. This area is part of the coastal plains along the Gulf of Mexico. Some of the land of the peninsula is covered with tropical rain forest and part is near-desert. A thin layer of soil covers limestone all through this area, and rain drains easily from the surface.

Along the Pacific coast of Mexico, but west of the isthmus are the Southern Uplands. The Sierra Madre del Sur dominates this area. These mountains, distinguished by their sharp peaks, have streams that have

Refer students to pages 96-97 to review the map of Earth's Climate Regions.

Have students use an almanac or atlas to determine the major cities in each of Mexico's climate zones.

Northern Mexico's dry desert climate cannot support the growing of crops. The land here has some mineral wealth but has been used mostly for grazing livestock. Where do most people in Mexico live?

made gorges far into Earth's surface. These uplands also have beautiful beaches that line the coast and attract many tourists.

Climate. Because the land in the north of Mexico has a dry climate, most people live in the tropical moist climates south of the Tropic of Cancer. Despite this tropical location, however, not all of Mexico is hot and humid. At Mexico City, for example, the average high temperature drops from 74°F (23.3°C) in July to 66°F (18.9°C) in January. This is because the city's altitude is 7,575 feet (2,308.9 m) above sea level. Figure 13-3 on this page makes this clear.

People in Mexico use three terms to describe the kinds of climate in which they live, depending on the elevation. The first of these climate zones is the **tierra caliente** (tee AY rrah kah lee AYN teh), or hot country. In general, tierra caliente takes in lands that are at sea level to 1,500 feet (457.2 m) above sea level. Average yearly temperatures are between 77°F (25°C) and 82°F (27.8°C).

A little higher in elevation is the **tierra templada** (tehm PLAH dah), or temperate country. The tierra templada takes in lands between 1,501 feet (457.5 m) and 6,000 feet (1,828.8 m) above sea level. Average yearly temperatures in the tierra templada are between 70°F (21.1°C) and 75°F (23.9°C).

Higher still is the **tierra fría** (FREE ah), or cold country. The tierra fría takes in lands rising over 6,001 feet (1,829.1 m) above sea level. Temperatures during the year average below 68°F (20°C). The term "cold country," however, is misleading. Although lands in the tierra fria do not get very hot, they also do not get very cold. This is because they lie in the tropics.

Because of altitude, Mexico is greatly affected by a second element of climate—precipitation. In general, winds blowing from the Gulf of Mexico and the Pacific Ocean drop most of their rain on the low coastal areas. The Sierra Madre Oriental and Occidental chains stop the rain from reaching much of the central plateau.

Visitors often notice physical effects caused by the thinner atmosphere of Mexico City's high elevation.

CLIMATE: MEXICO CITY

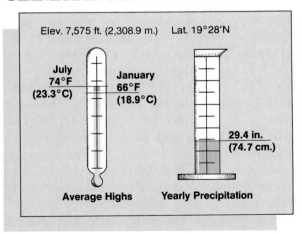

Elev. 7,575 ft. (2,308.9 m.)   Lat. 19°28′N

July 74°F (23.3°C)   January 66°F (18.9°C)

29.4 in. (74.7 cm.)

Average Highs   **Yearly Precipitation**

FIGURE 13-3
Surprisingly, July average high temperatures are the same for both Mexico City and Vancouver in Canada. Why are summer temperatures cool in Mexico City?

LATIN AMERICA   UNIT 5

A fisherman casts his butterfly net on Lake Pátzcuaro. Mexico's largest lakes are located in the central region of the country. Where in Mexico is fishing the major economic activity?

Review with students the principle of the orographic effect, which was presented in Chapter 5.

Ask students what effect the swampy coastline areas may have had on early settlement patterns in Mexico.

Because so little rain reaches the area, northern Mexico has a desert or steppe climate. Farther south, some sea winds break through the mountains to drop rain on the plateau. In Mexico, however, there is a rainy season and a dry season. The rainy season in Mexico City, for example, is from April to October. The dry season is from November through March.

See the *TAE* for an *Objective 1* Activity.

1.2 Economic and Cultural Patterns

The people of Mexico have adapted in many ways to the rugged land of their country. As can be seen in Figure 13-4 on page

250, it is a country with many rich mineral deposits and fertile farmlands.

Relative Location. Although it lies between the Pacific Ocean and the Gulf of Mexico, Mexico has taken little advantage of being so near these two large bodies of water. This is because of the inland settlement patterns on the central plateau. Only about 25 percent of the people live along the coast. Much of the coast tends to be swampy and dotted with lagoons and sandbars.

Mexico has about 6,190 miles (9,961.8 km) of coast. Fishing is the major economic activity there. It brings in more than 992,000 tons (899,927.5 metric tons) of shrimp, oysters, sardines, and other fish for foreign and home markets.

LAND USE AND RESOURCES OF MEXICO AND CENTRAL AMERICA

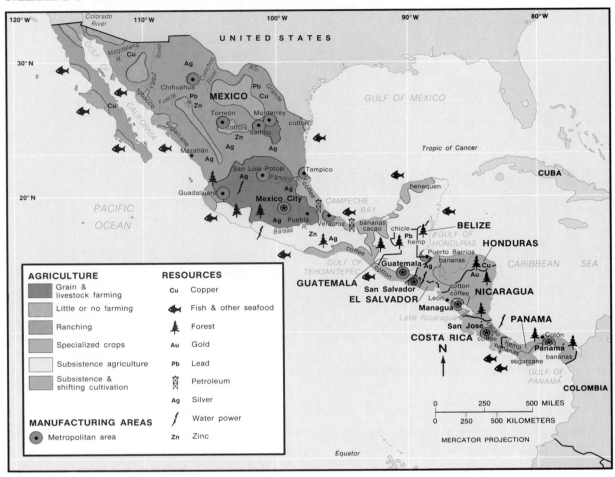

FIGURE 13-4
Landscape and climate features account for the predominance of ranching in Mexico's northern regions and various types of farming in its central and southern regions. Why is the central region the most important of Mexico's three economic regions?

Port cities such as Veracruz, Tampico, and Mazatlán handle relatively few factory and farm imports and exports. One reason is that trade with the United States has been so important. This trade has moved across the border by truck and train.

Economic Regions. Mexico can be divided into three economic regions. Its cultural and political heart is in the central region. A large part of this area is made up of the southern part of the central plateau. Enough rain and mild temperatures make the area good for farming. Corn is the major crop.

Large cities, such as Mexico City—the national capital—are found in the central region. Among the other large cities are Guadalajara (gwah dah lah HAH rah), León, and Puebla. The central region has more than half

250   **LATIN AMERICA**   UNIT 5

of Mexico's people. These cities are also among the leading industrial cities in the country. Their products include iron, steel, cement, fertilizer, artificial fibers, chemicals, and petroleum products.

A much different set of conditions is found in the northern region. This area has more than half of all the land in Mexico. However, it supports only one-fifth of the people. Much of the land is too dry to farm. Where irrigation is available, cotton, fruits, cereals, and vegetables are grown.

Some people in the region raise livestock such as cattle, sheep, goats, and pigs. Others work in mines and factories. Mines in this area produce much of the world's silver.

The largest city in the north is Monterrey (mohn teh *RRAY*). It leads the region and the country in steel production. In fact, Monterey, along with Mexico City and Guadalajara, continues to be one of the main manufacturing centers in Mexico.

The southern region is made up of highlands south of the central region and lowlands on the Yucatán Peninsula and along Mexico's southern border. In the mountains of the Southern Uplands, some farm towns have little contact with life in the rest of the country. For larger farms and plantations, coffee is the most important crop. On the dry part of the Yucatán, there are some farms. Deep wells bring water to the surface. The major crop is the henequen (HEHN ih kihn) cactus. Fibers from this plant are used in making packing string. In the rain forests of the south, rice, sugarcane, tomatoes, oranges, and bananas are grown.

Population and Economic Growth. Mexico has one of the fastest growing populations in the world. In 1970 it had 51 million people. In 1986 there were nearly 82 million. If present trends continue, it is estimated that there will be 110 million people in Mexico by the year 2000. This is almost one-half the present population of the United States.

The birthrate in Mexico is 31 per 1,000. This means that for every 1,000 people, 31 children are born every year. By comparison, the birthrate in the United States is 16 per 1,000. The birthrate of Mexico has been high

An expanding oil industry in Mexico has produced numerous new wells and refineries. What are some of the leading industrial cities in Mexico?

While Mexico's birthrate has remained high, the death rate has declined. Better food and health care are helping older people live longer.

The Inter-American Highway in Mexico and Central America is part of the Pan American Highway that connects the capitals of 17 countries in Latin America.

LATIN AMERICA'S LEADING OIL PRODUCERS

Production - *barrels* (1985)	
MEXICO	987 *million*
VENEZUELA	618 *million*
BRAZIL	206 *million*
ARGENTINA	168 *million*
ECUADOR	108 *million*

Data from *1987 Yearbook of World Energy Statistics*, United Nations

FIGURE 13-5
The discovery of major oil deposits during the 1970s made Mexico a world energy power. What events have hurt the Mexican economy in recent years?

for many years. In fact, 42 percent of Mexico's people are less than 15 years old, while only about 22 percent of the population in the United States is under this age.

The increase in the number of young people in Mexico means more people are entering school and the job market each year. The Mexican economy is hard-pressed to expand fast enough to keep up with the demands for education and jobs by its people. Many have moved to cities in search of work. More than 70 percent of the population now live in cities.

Many Mexicans have left the country to find work. Many have gone to the United States in search of jobs. Some of these people have entered the United States illegally. This situation has added to strained relations between Mexico and the United States.

Present-Day Conditions. Mexico tied many hopes for economic growth to the development of its mineral resources, especially oil. Some experts think Mexico has oil reserves nearly as large as those of Saudi Arabia, a country thought to have more oil than any other in the world. Figure 13-5 on this page shows how Mexico leads other Latin American countries in oil production.

In recent years, world oil prices have dropped. This fall came at a bad time for Mexico. In 1985 Mexico City and other areas in central Mexico suffered enormous damage from an earthquake. More than 5,000 people were killed. Tens of thousands of people became homeless. Millions and millions of dollars were needed to rebuild.

The decline in oil prices, expanding population, and damage from the earthquake have hurt the Mexican economy. Many of the wealthy people are leaving the country, taking much of their money with them. As a result, Mexico has many people out of work, its money has lost its value in world markets, and it has had to borrow a lot of money from other countries.

Although there are problems, Mexico has made progress in the twentieth century. The country has enjoyed a stable government for most of the 1900s. Many miles of roads have been built. The railroad system and seaports are being improved. People have more opportunities for education.

A chart on page 419 in Chapter 20 compares the Inter-American Highway with other world highways.

1.3 Influences of the Past

The history of Mexico falls into four time periods: (1) era of the Indian empires, (2) Spanish colonization, (3) national formation, and (4) era of revolution.

Indian Empires. Between 300 and 1000 AD, four Indian civilizations flourished in Mexico. The Teotihuacán (TAY oh tee wah KAHN) lived in central Mexico. The Totonac (toh toh NAHK) occupied eastern Mexico. The Zapotec (sah poh TEHK) lived in the southern highlands. The Maya (MAH yah) settled in the Yucatán Peninsula.

All of these groups were highly developed civilizations. They served as the cultural hearth of the Americas. Each had its own religion, written language, and form of government. Together their population was between 4 and 11 million.

These four centers of culture began to lose strength about 800 AD. Historians and archaeologists are not sure why this happened. There may have been an epidemic or some natural disaster. Farming may have worn out the soil so that the people could not grow as many crops. Or there may have been wars among the groups or with others.

By about 1000 AD, the four Indian civilizations left many of their population centers and drifted away. Only the Maya have descendants living in present-day southeastern Mexico and Guatemala.

During the next few hundred years, another group rose to power in central Mexico. This was the Toltec civilization. The center of its culture was the large city of Tula located in the present state of Hidalgo (ee DAHL goh). It had a large population and a well-ordered government.

In the early 1300s, wandering invaders destroyed Tula and the Toltec civilization. Among the invaders were the Aztecs, who set up a capital at Tenochtitlán (tay noch tee TLAHN), the site of present-day Mexico City. Moctezuma (mohk tay SOO mah) II was the Aztec leader at the time Spanish explorers arrived in Central America in 1519.

Spanish Colonization. Between 1519 and 1521, Spanish explorers conquered the Aztecs as well as people in much of Central America. They began forming colonies. One, called New Spain, was formed in 1535. Its capital was Mexico City, built over the ruins of the Aztec city of Tenochtitlán.

Mexico remained a Spanish colony for nearly 300 years. During that time, about 300,000 people moved to Mexico from Spain. Many married Indians. The name **mestizo** (mehs TEE soh) is given to people of mixed Indian and European ancestry. Today mestizos account for about 60 percent of the population of Mexico.

Some Indians, especially those of the southeastern highlands, had little contact with European settlers. Even today, Indians in isolated rural areas do not have many ties with non-Indians outside their home areas. At

A church rising above the houses and buildings of this Mexican town is a reminder of the Catholic religion first brought to Mexico by early Spanish explorers and colonists. For how long did Mexico remain a colony of Spain?

FOCUS ON CULTURE

THE ANCIENT MAYA

The Maya were people who lived in the area of the Yucatán Peninsula in Mexico. They developed a very advanced civilization hundreds of years before Europeans came to America.

Mayan history dates back at least as early as 1200 BC. This civilization reached its height in the years from 300 to 900 AD.

Evidence of Mayan civilization remains in southern Mexico and bordering areas of Central America. Much of this evidence is in the form of ruins of Mayan cities. Most of these cities had pyramids as well as other buildings built up on platforms as shown in the photo below.

Many of these cities featured upright stone shafts called stellae. They had carved messages on them. The messages were in hieroglyphics, a system of writing using picture symbols. Great care was taken on the stellae to date events correctly.

The dates of stellae give proof of the Mayan genius for mathematics. The Maya created a number system that allowed them to count into the millions and beyond. They also developed the concept of zero, hundreds of years before Europeans.

Time was important to the Maya. People today divide large units of time into smaller parts. These include days, months, years, and centuries. The Maya thought of time having more units. The basic unit was the *kin*, or day. Kins were grouped into *uinals* of 20 days each. Eighteen uinals formed one *tun*, or year. The Mayan year had 360 days and five "unlucky" days to equal 365 days.

That the Maya were interested in time and mathematics can be seen in their architecture. One of the greatest Mayan cities was Chichén Itzá (chee CHEHN eet SAH). The castle at Chichén Itzá has four sides. Each side has a stairway running to the top of a platform. There are 91 steps on each side, for a total of 364. The platform at the top makes 365, the number of days in a year.

Religion was the strongest force in Mayan society. The Maya worshipped things in nature, such as the sun, rain, and animals. In order to keep accurate times for their religious activities, the Maya also became very skillful in astronomy.

The cities of the Maya were gradually abandoned sometime after 800. It is not known why this civilization declined. Descendants of the Maya continue to live in southern Mexico and nearby areas of Guatemala.

1. Where did the Maya live?
2. What were some of their achievements in mathematics?
3. What was the strongest force in Mayan society?

Besides religion, the Spaniards introduced new grains and fruits, horses, and other domesticated animals. Over the years they added much to local economies.

Military leaders throughout Latin America in the 1800s were known as *caudillos*. Have interested students research and report on some of these leaders.

The collage portrays the diversity of Mexico's history and culture from early civilizations to modern times.

present, about 30 percent of the Mexican population is of pure Indian ancestry.

The smallest part of today's Mexican population is made up of people descended only from European colonists. Only nine percent of the population is classified as white or predominantly white.

Africans were brought to Mexico as slaves during the colonial period. They were forced to work in mines or on plantations. Once freed, they mixed with the rest of the people.

A further result of the heritage brought to Mexico from Spain is that most Mexicans today—about 97 percent—are Roman Catholics. Also there are small numbers who follow the Protestant and Jewish faiths.

National Formation. The move toward Mexican independence began between 1810 and 1815. The country finally won its independence from Spain in 1821.

Two problems were left from the years of Spanish rule. First, most Mexicans had not been allowed to take part in government. Second, much land and wealth was under the control of a few families.

In 1834 General Antonio López de Santa Anna became president of Mexico. During his rule of 20 years, little was done to improve life for the Mexican people. During this time, Mexico had serious trouble with the United States. Many settlers from the United States had gone to live in the Mexican province of Texas. In 1836 the Texans declared their independence from Mexico.

In 1845 the United States voted to annex Texas. Beginning in 1846, Mexico and the United States fought a war over Texas. By the terms of the 1848 Treaty of Guadalupe Hidalgo (gwah dah LOO peh ee DAHL goh), Mexico had to give up all claims to Texas. It

CHAPTER 13   **MEXICO AND CENTRAL AMERICA**

During World War I Germany tried to involve Mexico as an ally by promising to return to Mexico the areas it had lost to the United States in 1848.

Mexico has adopted September 16 as its national holiday for celebrating independence. The country's current constitution was adopted in 1917.

also lost present-day California and parts of New Mexico and several other states. As a result of the war, relations between Mexico and the United States have often been strained.

Era of Revolution. During much of the late 1800s and early 1900s, the Mexican people experienced many reform movements and had many presidents.

In 1861, Benito Juárez (HWAH rehs) became the leader of Mexico. Juárez was one of the most popular Mexican leaders in history. He ended the army and special privileges for the Catholic Church. Juárez wanted to hold democratic elections and educate the people. However, Juárez had trouble getting enough money to make many changes.

In 1877, Porfirio Díaz (pohr FEE reé oh DEE ahs) became president of Mexico. His goal was to reform the country's finances. Díaz, however, cared little about democratic elections. He favored the rich landowners. Díaz ordered land divided among large landowners, hoping to increase the amount produced on farms. Many people who lost their farms moved to the cities in search of jobs.

Díaz also allowed many foreign business people to set up companies in Mexico. This brought about some economic progress. People outside of Mexico built railroads, supplied electric power to Mexico City, and opened oil resources.

A revolution in 1910 changed much of this. Díaz was thrown out of office in 1911. The new Mexican government ended the privileges of foreign-owned companies. Many of these businesses were eventually taken over and controlled by the Mexican government. The oil industry is an example.

As Mexico became more industrialized, more and more people moved into the cities, creating urban slums. This migration continues, even though today it is believed that three million people have regained rights to their farmlands.

CONTENT CHECK

1. **Identify:** Mexico, Baja California, Sierra Madre Occidental, Sierra Madre Oriental, Plateau of Mexico, Sierra de Chiapas, Yucatán Peninsula, Mexico City, Monterrey, Teotihuacán, Totonac, Zapotec, Maya, Toltec, Aztecs, Tenochtitlán, Benito Juárez, Porfirio Díaz.

2. **Define:** isthmus, peninsula, tierra caliente, tierra templada, tierra fría, mestizo.

3. What are the two general kinds of climates in Mexico?

4. Why do most of the people in Mexico not live along the coasts? Where do most Mexicans live?

5. What problems in recent years have seriously hurt the Mexican economy?

6. **Challenge:** How is Mexico an excellent example of acculturation?

Refer students to the political map on page 257 and the map of Physical Regions on page 246 to note the many place-names that reflect a Spanish heritage.

2. CENTRAL AMERICA

South of Mexico and north of Colombia are the seven nations of Central America— Belize, Guatemala, Honduras, El Salvador, Nicaragua, Costa Rica, and Panama. These nations are shown in Figure 13-6 on page 257. The Mayan civilization lived on this land that covers 201,838 square miles (324,826.8 km). At its widest point, Central America is 300 miles (482.8 km). But it stretches more than 1,100 miles (1,770.3 km) in length.

The largest country in Central America is Nicaragua. Guatemala has the most people. However, El Salvador has more than three times the density that Guatemala has and nearly 10 times that of Nicaragua.

Central America was once a land of quiet villages and beautiful landscapes. It has be-

NATIONS OF MEXICO AND CENTRAL AMERICA

FIGURE 13-6

World attention continues to focus on this political region. Although Mexico is politically stable, turbulence and unrest have called attention to the neighboring countries of Central America. What are the seven nations that make up Central America?

On a physical map of North and South America that includes Central America, note that the mountains of Central America are, in general, part of a system of mountains extending down the western sides of both continents.

come an area of bitter struggles. Political and social unrest have become a normal way of life for many of its people.

See the *TAE* for an *Objective 2* Activity.

2.1 Landscape and Climate

All of Central America can be considered an isthmus that connects North America with South America. An important influence on

climate is the location of this isthmus. It lies south of the Tropic of Cancer.

Landscape. The landscape of Central America has three chief features. The first is a chain of volcanic mountains called the Central Highlands, running south from Mexico through much of Central America. Many of these are active volcanoes. In 1963 Mount Irazú erupted in Costa Rica, covering huge areas with volcanic ash.

Point out that land transportation between Central America's Pacific and Caribbean coasts has always been difficult. Even today, because the interior mountains have presented serious barriers to road-building, relatively few major highways connect the two coasts.

Earthquakes are all too common in Central America. This scene of destruction occurred after a 1985 earthquake in Mexico City. When and where did two other serious earthquakes take place in this region?

In addition to the destruction caused by periodic earthquakes, Central American countries also must deal with the damage to coastal areas caused by frequent tropical storms and hurricanes.

Earthquakes are also common. In 1976 some 23,000 people were killed in an earthquake in Guatemala. In 1986 an earthquake in El Salvador killed more than 1,000 people and injured about 10,000.

On both sides of the mountains are the two other features. One is the Pacific Lowlands. The other is the Caribbean Lowlands, a part of the coastal plain that runs from northern Mexico to the Colombian border. The band of lowlands on the Pacific side is much narrower than that on the Caribbean side. Many rivers flow from the mountains toward the Caribbean side. Farm products are shipped by way of these rivers to ports on the Caribbean, then on to world markets.

Climate. The climate in Central America depends on which side of the mountains the land area is. On the Pacific side of the mountains, the area has a tropical savanna climate with high temperatures all through the year and rainy and dry seasons. The rainy season is generally from May through November and the dry season from December through April.

On the Caribbean side of the mountains, the area has a tropical rain forest climate. Rain falls all year. There is as much as 100 inches (254 cm) to 250 inches (635 cm) of rain in a single year. Because of so much rain, soil in some areas is heavily leached. In other places water does not drain well. These conditions make it hard to grow crops.

Refer students to the map on page 250 to review the land use and resources of Central America.

2.2 Economic and Cultural Patterns

Travel has always been hard in Central America. Rough mountains and thick forests make travel slow along transportation routes. The rugged land also has the effect of isolating the people of Central America from one another. At times, individual countries had more contact with other areas of the world than they did with one another. Trying to improve cooperation among the nations often has been unsuccessful due to isolation.

More than 20 million people are unevenly distributed over Central America. On the other hand, each country of the subregion generally has one very large, densely populated city. This city generally dominates each country's economy, culture, and government. The populations of these cities are growing at a very rapid rate. Guatemala City, for example, zoomed from a population of 176,000 in 1940 to today's population of about 2 million.

Since people began settling in Central America, more have settled on the Pacific than on the Caribbean side. Only in recent years have people begun to settle in large numbers on the Caribbean side of the mountains due to overcrowding on the Pacific side.

Farming has always been the chief economic activity in Central America. Manufacturing plays a bigger part today, but the wealth from the soil remains most important. In the past indigo and cacao were leading crops. Today bananas, coffee, sugar, and seafood are the major export crops.

Along the coast, shrimp and lobster are harvested, mostly from the Pacific. Most of the seafood is exported to markets in the southern United States.

Central American countries trade mostly with the United States and Europe. In the past, they traded little among themselves. As shown in Figure 13-7 on page 260, many of the countries produce the same products for sale. In the 1960s, all of the countries except Panama agreed to form a **common market,** an agreement among several countries to lower or remove tariffs, or import taxes, on goods traded. The Central American Common Market worked to increase the trade of manufactured goods. However, a quarrel between Honduras and El Salvador in 1969 strained relations. This interfered with cooperation among the common market members.

Depending on the world to buy their products has had several consequences for the countries of Central America. For one thing, their economies may do well or poorly with changes in prices of coffee, bananas, and cot-

ton. Secondly, their economies depend upon open sea trade. Any condition such as a war or natural disaster that closes the sea-lanes hurts the Central American economy.

Dependence upon the sea for trade has had important effects on land transportation. Roads were slow to develop because they were not needed for export trade. Having few roads and railroads in the area has hampered efforts at cooperation and unity. As late as 1940, only Guatemala and El Salvador were connected by a paved road.

In the early 1950s, the building of the Inter-American Highway was started to connect all of the countries of Central America. This route was planned to stretch from the southern border of the United States to the border of Panama and Colombia. By 1973 the road was paved as far as southern Panama. It

Have students prepare to debate issues on the Panama Canal in the *TRB's* Chapter 13 Skill Activity

Bananas are an important cash crop for the economies of Central America because they are produced for sale to other countries. What are other major export crops?

LEADING EXPORTS OF CENTRAL AMERICA

	Sugar	Coffee	Bananas	Seafood	Cotton	Meat	Lumber
BELIZE	✓			✓			✓
COSTA RICA	✓	✓	✓			✓	
EL SALVADOR	✓	✓		✓	✓		
GUATEMALA	✓	✓	✓		✓	✓	
HONDURAS	✓	✓	✓	✓		✓	✓
NICARAGUA	✓	✓	✓	✓	✓		
PANAMA	✓		✓	✓			

FIGURE 13-7
Although the countries of Central America are separate and independent, they are economically similar in the products that they export to foreign markets. Changes in world market prices tend to affect the economies of Central America as a whole. Which two countries are the leading coffee producers in Central America?

Coffee and banana plantations became large-scale productions in Central America by the end of the 1800s.

has not been finished through the rain forest between Panama and the Colombian border. The project has encouraged other roads to be built in Central America to connect with this chief highway.

See the *TAE* for an *Objective 3* Activity.

2.3 Influences of the Past

As in Mexico, the history of the area under Spanish rule has had important effects on modern Central America. The economy, culture, population, and politics have all felt the influences of the past.

In most cases cities developed in areas where large settlements of Indian civilizations had been before the Europeans arrived. The Spanish took control of the densely populated areas first. Once these areas were under control, it was easier to take over the other areas. Under Spanish rule, the Central American colonies grew products for Spain.

Except for Belize and Panama, the Central American countries became independent from Spain in 1821. For several years, they joined together as the United Provinces of Central America. They broke up into separate

countries after 1838. However, their economies remained much the same.

Through most of Central America's history, there were small numbers of wealthy people owning huge tracts of land. It was very difficult for poor and middle-income people to own property. Large landholders also made or controlled most political decisions. It was not a common idea for all people to be a part of the government. This makes land reform a high priority even today in much of Central America. Some people feel this lack of a democratic history has helped make the governments of many Central American countries unstable.

Interest in building a canal across Central America increased around 1848. In that year, gold was discovered in California. People in the eastern United States as well as Europe wanted a faster route from the east coast to the west coast. Travel overland across the United States or by sea around South America took many months.

The isthmus of Central America had always been a barrier to travel between the Atlantic and Pacific oceans. As a barrier, the narrow isthmus offered the best place for a

LATIN AMERICA UNIT 5

direct ocean-to-ocean crossing. This fact can be seen in Figure 13-8 on page this page.

Between 1850 and 1900, several different places for a canal were studied. In 1881 a French company started to build a canal across the Isthmus of Panamá. This company ran out of money because many workers became ill and other difficulties surfaced. In 1903 the United States took over building the canal and it opened in 1914.

Have interested students research and report on how the United States helped Panama gain independence.

2.4 National Profiles

To understand Central America better, it helps to look closely at each individual country. Belize, Guatemala, Honduras, El Salvador, Nicaragua, Costa Rica, and Panama each reflects Central America's diversity.

Belize. Belize is smaller in size than all Central American countries except El Salvador. It is the least populous of the nations of Central America with a population of about 200,000. Belmopan is Belize's capital. Belize was the last British colony in the Americas to become independent. It became a self-governing nation in 1981. Guatemala claims the territory of Belize as its own and will not recognize the nation's independence.

Belize has a mixed population. Indians and people of mixed Indian and European and of African descent live in the country. English is the official language. Some Spanish and Indian dialects are also spoken.

Belize is primarily a farming country. Export crops are sugar, bananas, and citrus fruits. Fishing also helps bring in income. Some of the industrial products are clothing, wood, and wood products.

Guatemala. Guatemala has more people than any other country in Central America—about 8.4 million. Most live in the high basin area in the southern part of the country. The nation's capital, Guatemala City, is here.

With two million people, it is the largest city in Central America.

Most of the people are either Indians or of mixed Indian and European ancestry. More than 40 percent of the population maintain a way of life very similar to that of their Indian ancestors. Guatemalans use the term **ladinos** (lah DEE nohs) for people who speak Spanish and whose culture is like Europe's. Many ladinos are of mixed Indian and European descent, but they have ways of living that are more European than Indian.

The economy of Guatemala depends heavily on farming. Guatemala, along with El Salvador, is the leading coffee producer in Central America. It is also second after Mexico as a producer of **chicle** (CHEE klay), the main ingredient in chewing gum.

Honduras. Honduras lies generally northeast of Guatemala. Honduras is more

To encourage tourism, English-speaking Belize is trying to expand its tourist facilities.

PANAMA CANAL _____

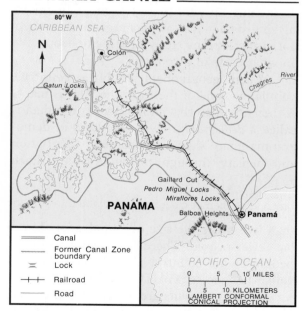

FIGURE 13-8
Construction of the Panama Canal is looked on as one of the major engineering accomplishments of the twentieth century. Why is this canal so important?

USING GRAPHIC SKILLS

ANALYZING DEMOGRAPHIC MAPS

If someone were taking you to a baseball game, you would probably want seats close to the infield—either behind first base, third base, or home plate. You would prefer to sit in one of these areas because you know this position gives you a better view of the players and the action of the game. You also have a much greater advantage in catching a foul ball there!

You may have noticed that infield seats are crowded with the most people. Seats near the outfield have fewer people, while seats in the upper decks have few people or none at all.

Consider some of the reasons that may influence where people sit in a stadium—ticket prices, view, nearness to favorite players, size of the crowd in each area, walking distance from the parking lot, and so on. In coming up with these reasons, you are analyzing data—just as geographers do, when, for example, they study how many people live in what parts of a country.

When geographers study a country's population, one of the tools they use is maps. A thematic map that shows population data is called a *demographic map*. One kind of demographic map shows population distribution and density through bands of color. Each color represents a range of numbers of people or density. An example of this kind of demographic map is on page 117. Another kind of demographic map also shows population distribution and density. This kind of map uses dots to locate where a certain number of people live. The map on page 263 is such a *dot-density map*. Each dot in this map represents 100,000 people. This kind of map shows you the areas where settlement is dense and the areas where it is scattered.

Geographers and demographers use both kinds of demographic maps to analyze where people settle and why they settle there. They take into consideration the type of climate, physical features of the area, the availability of a fresh water supply, and so on. For Mexico and Central America, one of the factors of settlement has been the altitude of the land area. On the map on page 263, altitudes above 2,000 feet (609.6 m) have been shaded.

Study the map on page 263. Then answer the questions that follow.

1. Which two areas of Mexico and Central America have the heaviest population density?

2. Do more people live above or below 2,000 feet (609.6 m)?

Use a large map or globe to show that the relative location of Honduras is almost directly south of Alabama.

than five times the size of El Salvador, but it has fewer people. There are about 4.7 million people in the country. Its capital is Tegucigalpa (tay goo see GAHL pah).

Most Hondurans are of mixed Indian and European descent. Others include blacks, people of European descent, and Indians.

Honduras is primarily a farming country. Many of the people are subsistence farmers.

Here and in areas of Nicaragua and Panama, farmers practice a farming method called **shifting cultivation**. Farmers use this as a way to rotate crops and put more nutrients back in the soil. They use machetes to cut all plants down and strip any trees of bark. After the plants and trees have dried out, the farmers set them on fire. After the fires have cleared the land, the farmers plant their

POPULATION DISTRIBUTION AND DENSITY

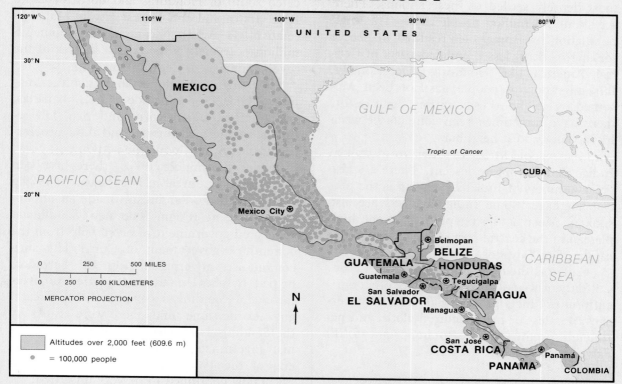

Data from Population Reference Bureau, Inc., 1987. Adapted from *Essentials of Geography and Development*, edited by Don R. Hoy. Charles E. Merrill Publishing Company, 1984.

3. Why would altitude be considered an important factor in determining the population distribution in this part of the world?

4. How can you explain why El Salvador has such heavy population density?

5. How can you explain why Belize has such scarce population density?

6. **Challenge:** What generalization can you make about how Mexico's landscape and climate affect its population distribution?

There is increasing environmental concern over the growing destruction of Central America's rain forests.

crops. This kind of farming is often called "slash and burn." In Honduras coffee, corn, and beans are grown in this way. Bananas are the most important export crop. Cement, clothing, textiles, and wood products make up most of the country's industrial wealth.

Honduras lies between Nicaragua and El Salvador. In recent years, there have been attempts by some in Nicaragua to overthrow the government of El Salvador. At the same time, some people in El Salvador and some outside the government in Nicaragua have tried to overthrow Nicaragua's government. Honduras has had to deal with people wanting to use its land to stage military operations directed either against El Salvador or against Nicaragua. Thus, the country has had to ask other nations for help.

El Salvador. El Salvador, the smallest country in size in Central America, is the most densely settled of these nations. There are about 5.3 million people there. This high population has sometimes resulted in people seeking work in less populated parts of Central America like Honduras. Occasionally, this migration of people has not been welcomed by neighboring countries. As a result, there have sometimes been conflicts between El Salvador and it neighbors.

Most people in El Salvador are of mixed Indian and European descent. There are also great numbers of Indians. Spanish is the official language. Some Indian dialects are also spoken. Most of the people live in the high plateau in the central part of the country. The capital, San Salvador, is in this area.

Coffee is the most important export crop. Cotton, corn, and sugar are among other agricultural products produced. Food and beverages, textiles, or manufactured cloth, and petroleum products are also important to El Salvador's economy.

El Salvador's northern section is mountainous with some volcanoes.

Even though Costa Rica is a densely populated country, its coastal areas have few inhabitants. Where do most of the people live in Costa Rica?

Nicaragua. Nicaragua occupies the middle section of Central America. It is located south of Honduras and north of Costa Rica. Its capital and largest city is Managua (mah NAH gwah). Nicaragua has about 3.5 million people. It is the largest in area of the seven countries of Central America.

Nicaragua is an important agricultural nation. Major crops include cotton, bananas, fruit, coffee, sugar, corn, and rice. Oil refining, textiles, chemicals, and food processing are important industrial activities.

Since the middle 1970s, there has been much political unrest in Nicaragua. In 1979 a group called the Sandinistas made an unpopular president resign. The new Sandinista-sponsored government received help from the communist government of Cuba. The anticommunist government of El Salvador, helped by the United States, tried to overthrow the Sandinista government of Nicaragua. At the same time, there were efforts by the Sandinistas to overthrow the anticommunist government of El Salvador. Toward the end of the 1980s, the political situation in Nicaragua continued to be very unsettled.

Costa Rica. A majority of Costa Rica's 2.8 million people live in a part of the cool central highlands known as the Meseta (meh SAY tah) Central. The national capital, San José (sahn hoh SAY), is in this area, as are most of the country's other cities.

The Indian cultures that once lived in Mexico and Guatemala did not reach as far south as present-day Costa Rica. Only a small number of the country's people claim any Indian heritage. Nine out of ten Costa Ricans are of European ancestry.

The absence of large numbers of Indians had an important effect on the development of Costa Rica. Early European settlers could not buy large plantations because of the shortage of workers. From the time of Spanish colonization, Costa Rica has been a land of small, privately owned farms. This tradition

LATIN AMERICA UNIT 5

of many people owning land goes on today. This makes Costa Rica very different from the rest of Central America. It is one of the reasons that Costa Rica has had a long tradition of stable and effective government.

Agriculture is most important to Costa Rica's economy. Coffee is the leading export. Bananas, beef, sugar, and cacao are other important farm products. About two-fifths of the people work in industry and commerce. There are some important minerals in the country, including **bauxite,** an ore used to make aluminum.

Panama.   Some other countries in Central America view Panama and its 2.3 million people as outsiders. This is due in part to Panama's once being part of Colombia. In 1903 it broke away from Colombia to become an independent country. The United States, wanting the right to build the Panama Canal, helped Panama against Colombia.

Under the terms of the treaty between Panama and the United States, a strip of land 10 miles (16.1 km) wide along the route of the canal was leased to the United States. Panamá, the capital of Panama, is located at the Pacific end of the canal.

For years many Panamanians wanted their country to have control of the canal. In 1977 the United States and Panama began negotiating about this again. A treaty was signed in 1978 providing for a takeover of the canal by Panama over time. The treaty gave the United States the right to defend the canal with full control until 1999.

Panama has a mixed population. About 70 percent of the people are of mixed Indian and European descent. Others include blacks from the West Indies, Indians, and people of European descent.

Along with activities connected with the canal, Panama's people earn their living from industrial, service, and agricultural activities. Bananas, sugarcane, rice, coffee, and livestock are important products.

CONTENT CHECK

1. **Identify:** Central America, Inter-American Highway, Panama Canal, Belize, Belmopan, Guatemala, Guatemala City, Honduras, Tegucigalpa, El Salvador, San Salvador, Nicaragua, Managua, Sandinistas, Costa Rica, San José, Panama, Panamá.

2. **Define:** common market, ladinos, chicle, shifting cultivation, bauxite.

3. What is the largest of the countries of Central America in land area? In total population?

4. What two kinds of tropical moist climates does Central America have?

5. Why was Central America considered a good place to build a canal connecting the Atlantic and the Pacific?

6. Why has Panama been considered an outsider by many of the other Central American countries?

7. **Challenge:** What are some of the possible problems for the countries of Central America because of their economic dependence on world markets?

Many Indians living in the low-lying plain between the Panama Canal and Panama's border with Colombia live much as their ancestors did centuries ago.

CONCLUSION

The region of Mexico and Central America is an important link between North and South America. This area is made up of a single large country and seven smaller ones. Yet each country is different and unique in its own way.

The smaller countries have neither the resources nor the population to be as important in the world scene as Mexico. The prosperity of these smaller countries is tied to a few export products. They depend heavily on trade with the United States. Today these countries are also trying to work out many political and social problems.

SUMMARY

1. Mexico and Central America lie between the United States and the continent of South America.
2. Mexico's population is growing very fast. Mexico City has the largest metropolitan area in the world.
3. The economy of Mexico is having difficulty providing jobs for all the people. More than 70 percent of the country's population lives in cities.
4. Mexico and most of the countries of Central America were once colonies of Spain.

From Spain, they acquired their language and the Roman Catholic religion. Various Indian languages are also important in several of the countries.
5. Each country in Central America tends to be dominated by one large city.
6. Central American countries produce much the same products for sale in world markets. For that reason, their economies are very dependent on world prices.
7. Many countries in Central America are having social and political problems.

Answers to the following questions can be found on page T156.

REVIEWING VOCABULARY

On a separate sheet of paper, write the word that is defined to the right of the blanks in each line. Then circle the letters in the words that show a star (★) below. These letters will spell the mystery word, one of the countries in Central America.

1. __ ★ __ __ __ __   a substance used in making chewing gum
2. __ __ __ __ __ __ ★   a term given to people who are of mixed European and Indian descent
3. __ __ ★ __ __ __ __ __ __   a piece of land surrounded on three sides by water
4. __ __ ★ __ __ __ __   term applied by Guatemalans to people who speak Spanish and whose culture is European
5. __ __ ★ __ __ __ __   an ore used to make aluminum
6. __ __ __ __ __ __
   __ ★ __ __   "cold country"; used to describe cold temperature lands found at higher elevations
7. __ __ __ __ __ __
   __ ★ __ __ __ __ __   "hot country;" used to describe hot temperature lands found at lower elevations
8. __ __ __ __ __ __ __ ★   lands controlled by an outside country

REMEMBERING THE FACTS

1. What European nation once owned Mexico and most of the countries of Central America as colonies?

2. Is the climate zone called "tierra caliente" found at lower or higher elevations than the climate zone called "tierra fría"?

3. In what region of Mexico are most of the country's people found?
4. What four Indian empires influenced Mexico's history?
5. What nations make up Central America?
6. What is the most important economic activity in Central America?

7. Which Central American country has English as its official language?
8. What country of Central America has had a long tradition of private ownership of small farms?
9. What nation of Central America has the largest population?

UNDERSTANDING THE FACTS

1. Why are temperatures in Mexico City, located far south of the Mexico-United States border, typically not so hot in the summer as temperatures are in the northern parts of Mexico?
2. Why does Mexico not have a very large and important ocean-shipping industry?
3. What effect has the drop in oil prices had on the economy of Mexico?

4. Why have the countries of Central America never traded very much with one another in the past?
5. In what kind of terrain do most people in Central America live?
6. El Salvador has fewer people than Guatemala, yet it is the most densely populated country in Central America. What are some reasons for this?

THINKING CRITICALLY AND CREATIVELY

1. Why were good highways that connected the countries of Central America slow to be built?
2. How do you explain why so many Mexicans have moved to the United States in recent years?
3. Why have few European immigrants to Central America settled close to the coast?

4. Why did the United States support the independence of Panama from Colombia?
5. **Challenge:** What factors have made Mexico's population so large and at the same time so young?
6. **Challenge:** How has the high population density in El Salvador affected its neighbors?

REINFORCING GRAPHIC SKILLS

Study the map on page 263. Then answer the questions that follow.

1. Compare the density map with the physical regions map on page 246. In what physical region of Mexico do most people live? Why?
2. What physical features of the Yucatan Peninsula discourage dense settlement there?
3. **Challenge:** What generalization can you make about the settlement of the coastlines of Mexico and Central America?

CHAPTER 14

San Juan was settled by followers of Ponce de León in 1521. El Morro Fortress, started by the Spaniards in 1539, was not complete until 1797.

El Morro castle, San Juan Bay, Puerto Rico

THE CARIBBEAN

- What landscapes and climates are found in the Caribbean.
- How successful economic development has been in the Caribbean.
- What cultural patterns are found in the Caribbean.
- How the past has influenced the countries of the Caribbean.

The Caribbean is a land of great economic contrasts. Venezuela has a prosperous economy based on oil, agriculture, and industry, while Haiti is one of the least prosperous countries in the world.

INTRODUCTION

Thousands of islands called the West Indies sweep in a clockwise direction from the Florida peninsula to the northeastern coast of South America. To the south and west of these islands are five countries that border the Caribbean Sea along the northern coast of South America. These two areas make up the Caribbean region of Latin America.

This region is named for the Caribbean Sea. Caribbean comes from *Carib*—Indian people living in the area in the late 1400s. The sea is bounded on the west by Central America, on the north by a chain of large islands known as the Greater Antilles, on the east by a chain of small islands called the Lesser Antilles, and on the south by South America.

The Greater Antilles include the four islands of Cuba, Jamaica, Hispaniola (ees pah nee OH lah), and Puerto Rico. Hispaniola is divided between the countries of Haiti on the western half and the Dominican Republic on the eastern half. The Lesser Antilles include many smaller islands. They stretch from the Virgin Islands in the north to Trinidad and Tobago in the south and the Netherlands Antilles in the west near the coast of South America. The Bahamas, a group of islands east of Florida, are also part of the region though they lie outside the Caribbean Sea.

The continental lands of the region include Colombia, Venezuela (veh neh soo AY lah), Guyana (goo JAH nah), Suriname (soo ree NAH meh), and French Guiana (gee AH nah). With the exception of French Guiana, each one of the continental lands is larger than any of the islands in the West Indies.

The Caribbean region lies chiefly in the tropics and has many different landscapes and climates. Some areas have plains and river basins, while others have many mountain ranges. The region is a zone of much tectonic activity where several tectonic plates meet. Some areas have dry climates, while others have tropical moist climates.

Although farming has been the major source of the Caribbean's income, some parts of the region are industrializing. However, the levels of economic growth among the countries of the region are very different.

Some places in the Caribbean have very large populations. Such West Indian islands as Barbados and Puerto Rico and the northern areas of Colombia and Venezuela are among the most densely populated in Latin America and the world.

The people of the Caribbean are descended chiefly from European and African settlers. Today most people are of mixed descent. Languages spoken in the Caribbean include Spanish, French, Dutch, and English.

Spanish explorers, who were led first by Christopher Columbus, laid the foundation for European influence in the Caribbean. Today, because it is so close to the area, the United States is a major influence in the Caribbean region.

PHYSICAL REGIONS OF THE CARIBBEAN

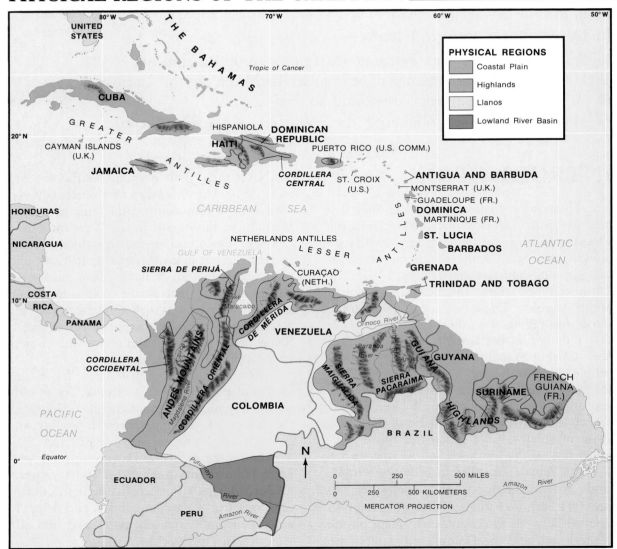

FIGURE 14-1
The Llanos physical region is an area of open grassy plain found in parts of Colombia and Venezuela. Which kind of physical region is found in all the Caribbean islands and continental lands shown on this map?

1. WEST INDIES

The West Indies are made up of the Greater Antilles, the Lesser Antilles, and the Bahamas. There are thousands of islands in the West Indies. Most have not been settled.

Many are **cays** (KEEZ), or tiny, low-lying islands of sand or coral.

Most countries or colonies in the West Indies are made up of many islands under a single name. The Bahamas, for example, are an **archipelago** (AHR kuh PEHL uh goh)—a

270   **LATIN AMERICA**   UNIT 5

Although there are only four islands in the Greater Antilles, their total land area far exceeds that of the islands in the Lesser Antilles.

Some areas get over 200 inches (508 cm) of rain a year, while the southwestern sides of many islands receive as little as 30 inches (76.2 cm) a year.

group of islands scattered within a large area of the ocean. The Lesser Antilles are made up of three chains of islands. The northern chain—from the Virgin Islands to Dominica—are sometimes called the Leeward Islands. They are called this because they face away from the northeast trade winds. This position gives them some protection from those winds. The southern islands—from Martinique to Trinidad and Tobago—are called the Windward Islands. They face into the northeast trade winds. The western islands—the Netherlands Antilles—are located along the coast of Venezuela.

Refer to the map of Earth's Climate Regions on pages 96–97 to determine the climate in the Caribbean.

1.1 Landscape and Climate

The lands of the West Indies are not all alike, despite all being islands. Likewise, there are some climatic differences among the islands. However, their location in the tropics ensures a warm climate for all areas.

Landscape. In the West Indies, there are islands, such as Barbados and Antigua in the Lesser Antilles, that are relatively flat. Some islands, as well as parts of others, are rugged and steep. Among these are Dominica, Grenada, Guadeloupe (GWAHD uhl OOP), Montserrat (MAHN suh RAT), northern and central Hispaniola, eastern Jamaica, and southeastern Cuba. Central and western Cuba have gently rolling hills and plains. The West Indies, however, generally have highlands in the middle of the islands that slope downward to a coastal plain by the sea. Many smaller islands of the West Indies are peaks of a vast underwater mountain range.

The islands are very different in size. Cuba, with 42,803 square miles (110,859.7 sq km) in land area, is the largest. This is about the same size as the state of Ohio. Anguilla (an GEE yah) is one of the smallest, with about 34 square miles (88 sq km) of land area.

The larger islands, such as Cuba, have pockets of fertile topsoil covering coral or limestone. In areas with much rain, tropical rain forests are common. Some mountain areas are covered by needleleaf forests.

Climate. The West Indies take in an area from about 10° to 27° north latitude and from about 59° to 85° west longitude. Other than the Bahamas, the islands all lie south of the Tropic of Cancer. Even the Bahamas lie close enough to the tropics to have a warm climate all year. Most of the West Indies has a tropical savanna climate with tropical monsoon climate on the northeastern part of Hispaniola and Puerto Rico.

More rain falls on the northeastern side of the West Indian islands because they lie in the path of the northeast trade winds. For example, Jamaica has a chain of mountains in the northeastern part of the island running

Lush vegetation covers areas of Jamaica. On which side of the West Indian islands does more rain fall?

from east to west. On the northeastern coast, it rains about 200 inches (508 cm) a year, while southwest of the mountains it rains only about 30 inches (76.2 cm) a year.

As can be seen in Figure 14–1 on page 270, the physical location of the West Indies gives them a generally mild climate. It also places the islands in the path of hurricanes in the summer months. These huge storms begin hundreds of miles to the east of the Caribbean over warm ocean waters within 10 degrees north or south of the Equator.

See the *TRB* for the *Chapter 14 Reading* on preservation of marine resources.

1.2 Economic and Cultural Patterns

The economies of the West Indies are based in large part on plantation crops and tourism. The islands produce many of the same kinds of farm products. Among these are sugar, tobacco, and cacao.

Sea, surf, sand, and sun attract vacationers to the Bahamas. How does tourism benefit the economies of the West Indies?

The warm climate and relative location of the West Indies are important for the economy. Cruise ships, especially from the United States and Europe, regularly visit the Caribbean. Goods bought by tourists and the money they spend on hotel rooms and food bring in much of the income for the people of the West Indies.

Their location along the waterway to the Panamá Canal places the West Indies on one of the major trade routes of the world. The closeness of the United States makes it the major trading partner of the Caribbean islands. These countries do trade with other countries—mostly those with coal or oil. They also trade with those countries who once ruled them as colonies.

The West Indies were ruled for years by different European countries. People from many different cultures live there today. Their languages include Spanish, English, or French. Many people are farmers, although much of the population lives in cities.

Despite the closeness of the islands to each other, the West Indies remain a group of separate countries and colonies. Figure 14–2 on page 273 shows the political divisions of the Caribbean region. Some people have tried to encourage greater unity among the islands. For example, the Caribbean Community and Common Market (CARICOM) was set up to help the countries cooperate economically. However, trade with outside countries still seems to be more important than trade with one another.

See the *TAE* for an *Objective 1* Activity.

1.3 Influences of the Past

The past tells why the population of the West Indies is so diverse. It is an area where immigrants from all over the world live.

Indian Peoples. About the same time that the Aztecs were controlling much of Mexico, three different Indian groups lived in

There continues to be debate over exactly which island was the site of Columbus' first landing in 1492. Although the island of San Salvador (also called Watling Island) has long been accepted by many as the exact site, recent studies indicate that the first landing was more likely on the island now called Samana Cay.

COUNTRIES OF THE CARIBBEAN

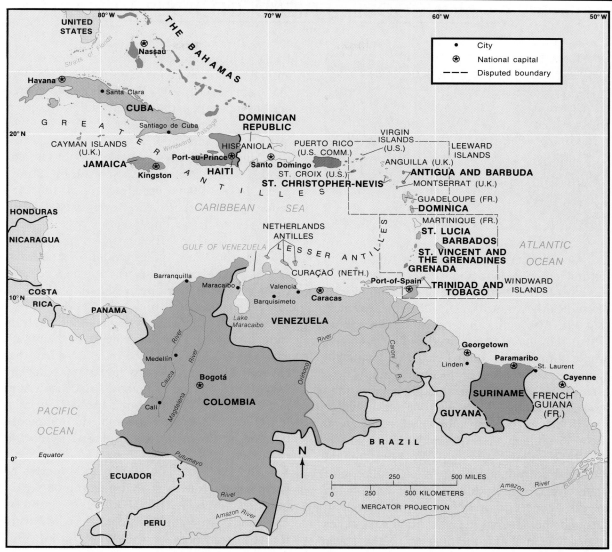

FIGURE 14-2
The Caribbean region is a mixture of independent nations and foreign dependencies. Which countries in this region have disputed boundaries?

the West Indies. These were the Ciboney (see boh NAY), the Arawak, and the Caribs. The oldest group in the West Indies was probably the Ciboney. The Arawak were the most numerous of the Indian peoples in the islands by the 1400s.

Sometime after 1400, the Caribs moved into the West Indies from the coast of Venezuela. They were very mobile people who either captured or destroyed most of the Arawak settlements in the eastern Caribbean. During the time they controlled the Lesser

FOCUS ON GEOGRAPHY

MONGOOSE: FRIEND OR FOE?

Geographers are concerned with how the natural environment and all forms of life in the biosphere interact. One of the many kinds of studies they have done has been on animals that are brought into new environments where they have never lived before. For example, during the 1800s, cages of European sparrows were brought to Argentina. These birds were released in the hope that they would kill moths. The sparrows multiplied so fast that they became more of a problem to the environment than the moths had been.

New animals to help the environment were also introduced in the West Indies. For many years planters there did not know what to do about the many rats that lived all through the sugarcane fields. Rats sometimes ruined as much as one-quarter of the sugar crop. In the mid-1700s planters tried to protect their crops from rats by placing weasels in the fields. However, the weasels were attacked by a certain species of burrowing fly and did not survive. Still later the planters chose a very aggressive species of ant to make the rats uncomfortable. But this did not help, either. Desperate planters even imported toads large enough to catch and eat young rats.

Nothing seemed to work until 1872 when the mongoose was brought to Jamaica from India. The mongoose is a small meat-eating animal that varies in length from 1.5 feet (45.7 cm) to 3.5 feet (106.7 cm). Mongooses tend to look like large weasels. They are fierce hunters of insects, snails, toads, snakes, birds, mice, and rats.

Nine mongooses were let go in the Jamaican sugarcane fields. Soon they multiplied. In less than a year, owners of the plantations noticed there were fewer rats. Within three years rats no longer were a serious problem in Jamaica. Plantations owners all through the West Indies praised the animal, and soon the mongoose was introduced into Cuba and other Caribbean islands.

The good news, however, was not to last. After about 10 years, people saw that rats were becoming a problem again in many areas. The reason is that the mongoose had discovered chickens. Many flocks of chickens were killed by the mongoose. Because many farmers in the West Indies depended on raising chickens for their income, the mongoose became a threat to the area's agricultural economy.

By 1900 the mongoose was viewed as such a dangerous pest that governments paid bounties for each animal killed by hunters. Even today, the animal is considered destructive by neighbors of the West Indies. For example, in the United States, it is illegal to bring mongooses into the country or even to display them in American zoos without a permit from the government.

1. What is a mongoose?
2. Why was the mongoose originally brought to the West Indies?
3. What effect did the mongoose have on the natural environment of the West Indies?

Antilles comes from the Spanish name "Antilla." Before Columbus' time, Antilla was the name of a mythical land thought to lie somewhere in the Atlantic.

Because of colonization and commercial exploitation by so many different countries, the West Indies today is very culturally and linguistically mixed.

trolled the Lesser Antilles, the Caribs took over much of the Arawak way of life. It is this mix of cultures that some people in the Caribbean today claim as their heritage.

Spanish Colonization.

In 1492, Christopher Columbus began his exploration of the Bahamas. From there, he went on to explore more of the islands that he called the Indies.

In 1502 Queen Isabella sent Nicolás de Ovando (nee koh LAHS day oh VAHN doh) and about 2,500 colonists to Hispaniola to make sure of Spain's claim to the area. Ovando became the founder of Spain's empire in America. By 1513 there were at least 13 Spanish towns and over 12,000 colonists in the West Indies.

Spanish colonists set up large farms and dug many mines. Because of their need for workers, they forced the Arawak into slavery. The Indian people were not used to harsh working conditions and were unable to fight diseases brought to the area by the Europeans. To replace the dying Arawak, Caribs from other islands were brought to Hispaniola. Later, Africans were brought to the Caribbean as slaves. Many colonists moved to other islands in the West Indies, such as Puerto Rico and Jamaica.

European Expansion.

For most of the sixteenth century, Spain controlled the Caribbean. By the early 1600s, however, Dutch traders set up several outposts on the northeastern coast of South America. From these bases they raided Spanish ships. These ships traded in the West Indies and carried cargoes of gold and other riches back to Spain.

Between 1630 and 1640, the Dutch seized several tiny islands among the Leeward Islands and Curaçao off the northern coast of Venezuela. By 1640 the Dutch became the most successful traders in the Caribbean.

This success threatened Spanish control of the Caribbean. While the Spanish tried to slow down the Dutch, other European countries, especially England and France, were able to build up settlements in the Caribbean.

The English moved into such islands as Barbados, Nevis, Antigua, and St. Lucia. Among the islands taken over by the French were Martinique and Guadeloupe. All of these islands were in the Lesser Antilles, which had long been neglected by Spain. It thought the islands were too small, too dry, and too far from the center of their Caribbean empire in the Greater Antilles.

The governments of England and France took advantage of a weakening government in Spain. In the late 1600s, England and France increased their holdings in the Caribbean. In 1670 Spain gave up Jamaica to England. In 1697 the western third of the island of Hispaniola was given to France. The French called the new colony Saint-Domingue. Today this country is Haiti. Figure 14–3 on page 276 shows the extent of European colonialism in the Caribbean.

The English and French developed their colonial economies in much the same manner as the Spanish. Farming, livestock, and mining all were important at first. By the end of the 1600s, however, sugar became the single most important product in the Caribbean. As

This engraving depicts African slaves working on an island sugar plantation. For over 300 years, slavery dominated the West Indies. Which people were forced into slavery in the West Indies before the Africans?

Refer students to the political map of the Caribbean on page 273 and have them compare the areas of foreign influence with the nations that occupy these areas today. Ask students to identify place-names that reflect foreign influences from colonial times. Ask students: Which of these areas are still under the control of foreign nations?

FOREIGN INFLUENCE IN THE CARIBBEAN

CARIBBEAN COUNTRY	FORMER COLONY/ DEPENDENCY OF:		DATE OF INDEPENDENCE
ANGUILLA	England		*
ANTIGUA & BARBUDA	England		1981
BAHAMAS	England		1973
BARBADOS	England		1966
COLOMBIA	Spain		1810
CUBA	Spain	United States	1898
DOMINICA	France	England	1978
DOMINICAN REPUBLIC	Spain		1844
FRENCH GUIANA	France		*
GRENADA	France	England	1974
GUADELOUPE	France		*
GUYANA	Netherlands	England	1966
HAITI	Spain	France	1804
JAMAICA	Spain	England	1962
MARTINIQUE	France		*
MONTSERRAT	England		*
NETHERLANDS ANTILLES	Spain	Netherlands	*
PUERTO RICO	Spain	United States	**
ST. CHRISTOPHER & NEVIS	England		1983
ST. LUCIA	France	England	1979
ST. VINCENT & GRENADINES	England		1979
SURINAME	England	Netherlands	1975
TRINIDAD & TOBAGO	Spain	England	1962
VENEZUELA	Spain		1811
VIRGIN ISLANDS	Denmark	United States	*

* Dependency ** Free Associated State

FIGURE 14–3

This chart shows the widespread colonial influence that some European nations exercised in the Caribbean region. While some Caribbean countries gained independence earlier, others remained under European rule until the 1960s and later. Some countries remain dependencies even today. United States involvement in the Caribbean grew significantly following the Spanish-American War. Over which three islands did the United States gain influence?

For a time, Spain considered Cuba its most valuable possession in the Western Hemisphere. Havana was an important collection point for colonial goods to be shipped to Spain or to other Spanish colonies.

the sugar business grew, so did the need for African slaves. Because so many Africans were brought to the West Indies, a large part of the Caribbean population today traces its ancestry to Africa.

In the 1800s sugar production grew so much that there was too much sugar. Within 100 years world sugar prices began to fall. Less successful plantations closed, and fewer workers were needed. Because of this, many people seriously considered the **abolition** of slavery—making slavery against the law.

At different times during the 1800s, slavery was abolished in different islands. Where sugar production was most efficient and the need for workers remained high, slavery lasted longer. One such place was Cuba, where slavery was not outlawed until 1886.

Remind students that slavery was abolished in the United States in 1865 with the ratification of the Thirteenth Amendment to the U.S. Constitution.

The island of Puerto Rico was originally San Juan Bautista, and the major port was Puerto Rico, which means "rich harbor." In time, the names changed.

When slavery was abolished, there was still a need for plantation workers. Some owners hesitated to hire former slaves because they did not want to pay wages to people who once worked without pay. Many landowners recruited indentured servants from Asia and other parts of the world, especially China, Japan, and India as well as western Europe. Indentured servants were persons who signed an agreement to work for a certain number of years for employers, who, in return, would pay for the servants' trip.

Have students collect advertisements for cruises to the West Indies. Ask: Are the tourist descriptions consistent with actual geographic information?

1.4 National Profiles

There are many similarities among the Caribbean islands. But differences among the islands are still important. Some of these differences are apparent in the cases of Puerto Rico, Cuba, and Haiti.

Puerto Rico. The island of Puerto Rico is the easternmost island in the Greater Antilles. It is 100 miles (160.9 km) east of Hispaniola. Puerto Rico is about 110 miles (177 km) long from east to west and about 35 miles (56.3 km) long from north to south.

The landscape of Puerto Rico includes a chain of inactive volcanic mountains running from east to west through the island. On both sides of the mountains there are fertile coastal plains. In general, rain falls more on the north side of the mountains than on the south. Temperatures average about 86°F (30°C) in the summer and about 83°F (28.3°C) in the winter.

From 1508 to 1898, Puerto Rico was a Spanish colony. As a result, Spanish is the dominant language, and Roman Catholicism is the major religion of the people today.

As part of the treaty that ended the Spanish-American War in 1898, Puerto Rico became a possession of the United States. American control opened markets in the United States to Puerto Rico. This was especially important for the sugar industry.

In 1950 the United States approved the right of the people of Puerto Rico to write a constitution and direct their home affairs. The constitution of 1952 set up the Commonwealth of Puerto Rico as "a free and associated state of the United States of America."

The people of Puerto Rico are American citizens, but Puerto Rico is not a state. The people cannot vote in elections for President, and they do not have a voting representative in the Congress. The people also do not have to pay federal income taxes.

Agriculture and tourism form the base of the Puerto Rican economy. Sugarcane and coffee are the major crops. Natural resources include only stone, gravel, and sand, which are used in their cement industry.

Puerto Rico has tried recently to increase its amount of industry. Many American companies have built factories in Puerto Rico. They are encouraged by laws that allow lower taxes on industry there than in the United States. Today Puerto Rico has more industry than any other area in the West Indies.

Despite much progress, Puerto Rico faces some important challenges in the years ahead. A growing population faces unemployment and scarce housing. With a population of 3.3 million, Puerto Rico is one of the most densely populated islands in the Caribbean.

The people of Puerto Rico face a decision about their relationship to the United States. Some favor Puerto Rico's independence. Others want Puerto Rico to become the fifty-first state of the United States. However, most favor the present commonwealth status.

Cuba. With 10.3 million people living there, Cuba is the most populous island in the West Indies. Most Cubans are descendants of the original Spanish settlers, African slaves, and European and Asian indentured servants. Almost 25 percent are **mulatto**—persons of

USING GRAPHIC SKILLS

READING TOPOGRAPHIC MAPS

Have you ever stood at the top of a very high building and looked out over a city far below you? Such a height may make you dizzy, but you can certainly see the layout of the city more clearly. The tops of buildings and houses tell you where the business areas and neighborhoods are located. Open areas—vacant lots, parking lots, city parks—are easy to spot. A river may be seen winding through the city. You can notice lines of traffic moving along the highways as well as the criss-cross pattern of the streets.

In much the same way, a topographic map gives a bird's-eye view of an area. This type of map is based on photogrammetry—photographs taken from the air. In Chapter 2 you learned that some physical maps show topography—the shape of the land's surface, including its relief and other natural or human-made features. Relief is shown on these maps by contour lines that connect points of the same elevation. If contour lines in an area are far apart, there is little change in elevation. The area has low relief. If contour lines are close together, there is great change in elevation. The area has high relief.

Look at the topographic map on page 279. It shows an area in the west central part of Puerto Rico surrounding the town of Ad-

juntas. Adjuntas is located within Cordillera Central—mountain ranges that cross Puerto Rico from west to east. The legend gives the scale and explains the symbols used on the map to represent certain physical and cultural features of the land. For example, each black square indicates a house or building. The numbers on the contour lines tell the elevation above sea level. On this map elevation is measured in meters.

Study the map on page 279. Then answer the questions that follow.

1. What is the highest elevation shown on the map? In what parts of the Adjuntas area is it located?

2. Use intermediate directions to indicate which parts of the area show very high relief.

3. What cultural, or human-made, features are shown on the map?

4. What generalization can you make about the location of buildings in the southern half of the area?

5. What is the approximate distance in miles from west to east on the map?

6. **Challenge:** Which parts of the area would be most suitable for farming? Why?

Cuba's government controls the economy, deciding what should be made and how much may be traded. Rationing is common; and, even though standards of health and education have improved, economic growth is slow.

mixed African and European ancestry. The language most Cubans speak is Spanish. Their major religion is Catholicism. However, the present communist government discourages all religious practices.

Christopher Columbus claimed Cuba for Spain in 1492, and Cuba remained a Spanish colony until 1898. As a result of the Spanish-American War, it became independent.

In 1959 Fidel Castro and his supporters won a revolution. This led to the establishment of a communist government in Cuba. American-owned property was taken over by the Cuban government. Today Cuba has established close ties with the Soviet Union and other communist countries in the world. Since 1959 the Soviet Union has been Cuba's favorite trading partner.

LATIN AMERICA   UNIT 5

ADJUNTAS, PUERTO RICO

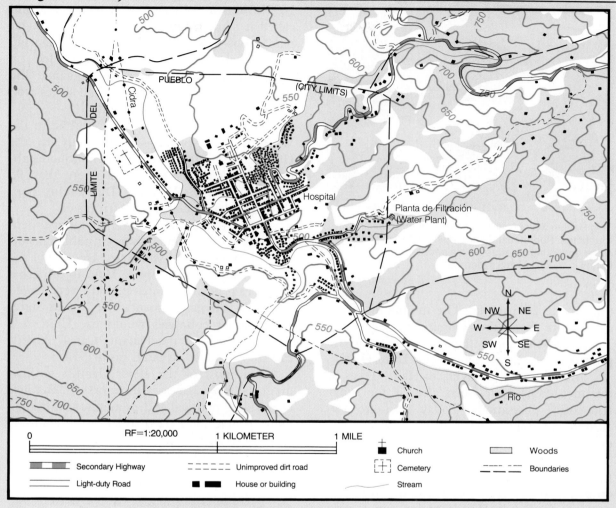

RF=1:20,000

0   1 KILOMETER   1 MILE

▬▬ Secondary Highway	┄┄┄┄ Unimproved dirt road	✚ Church
─── Light-duty Road	■■ House or building	⊞ Cemetery
		～ Stream
		▒ Woods
		─ ─ ─ Boundaries

Remind students that countries with an excessive reliance on a single commodity for their income are severely affected by changes in the world price of that commodity. Cuban economy suffers when sugar prices are low.

Sugar is not only Cuba's most important export but also accounts for most of the island's economic activity. In addition to sugarcane, Cuban farmers produce coffee, tobacco, rice, citrus and tropical fruits, and meat. Besides refining sugar, Cuban industry is a mix of processing food, producing cigars and cigarettes, and manufacturing light industrial goods.

Haiti. The country of Haiti (HAYT ee) takes up the western third of the island of Hispaniola. It is considered the poorest country in the Western Hemisphere. Haiti does not use its land for farming because two-thirds of the country is mountainous and has a very dry climate.

Haiti's dry climate is the result of its location on the western side of the mountains

This Haitian woman stands amid poverty-stricken surroundings. Poor housing, unemployment, and little income continue to plague Haiti's people. What crop brings in much of Haiti's income?

Many countries in the world have been trying to help Haiti overcome its environmental problems.

that divide Hispaniola. The mountains separate Haiti from the Dominican Republic. They keep much of the moisture from the prevailing northeast trade winds from Haiti.

Many forests are dying in Haiti. Trees in the mountains have been cleared for sugar and coffee plantations. Today trees are also cleared for fuel. The soil that is left has eroded and lost valuable nutrients.

About 80 percent of Haiti's 6.2 million people are subsistence farmers. Of the few crops grown for trade, coffee is the most important. Coffee is Haiti's major export and accounts for much of Haiti's income.

French is the official language of Haiti, but it is spoken by only about 10 percent of the population. Creole (KREE ohl) is spoken by most Haitians. It is a mixture of French, African, Spanish, English, and Arawakan words. Most Haitians are Roman Catholics, but voodoo is widely practiced in Haiti's rural areas. **Voodoo** is a religion taken from ancient African practices of ancestor worship. It is characterized by spells and the use of charms.

The western third of Hispaniola was given to France by Spain in a treaty signed in 1697. French colonists settled the area and called it Saint-Domingue. They started sugar plantations worked by African slaves. During the French Revolution, the slaves led by Toussaint L'Ouverture revolted against the French in the colony. By 1804 the slaves won and declared Haiti independent.

Haiti became the second republic in the Western Hemisphere—second only to the United States. It was the first republic established by Africans anywhere. More than 95 percent of today's Haitian (HAY shuhn) population is descended from Africans.

Even though Haiti was an independent country, its government was unstable and often plagued with violence. By 1915 the United States sent troops to Haiti to protect it from European countries that were owed money by the government. The United States feared other countries would use Haiti as a base to take over the Panama Canal. American troops stayed in Haiti until 1934.

For most of the 1900s, Haiti's government has been run as a dictatorship. Because of unstable political and economic conditions, many people have tried to leave the country. In 1980, for example, as many as 20,000 Haitians came to the United States.

See the *TRB* for the *Section 1 Extending the Lesson* on election-day violence in Haiti.

CONTENT CHECK

1. **Identify:** Greater Antilles, Lesser Antilles, the Bahamas, Leeward Islands, Windward Islands, Cuba, Hispaniola, Ciboney, Arawak, Caribs, Christopher Columbus, Saint-Domingue, Fidel Castro, Toussaint L'Ouverture.

2. **Define:** cays, archipelago, abolition, mulatto, voodoo.

3. What are the three island groups that make up the West Indies?

4. What is the largest and most populous island in the West Indies?

5. On what is the economy of most of the countries of the West Indies based?

6. How did the first Spanish settlers in the West Indies deal with too few laborers on plantations?

7. How were the Dutch important to French and English settlement of the Caribbean?

8. What is the political relationship of Puerto Rico to the United States?

9. **Challenge:** Slavery in Cuba lasted until the late nineteenth century. Why did slavery last so much longer there than elsewhere? Why was it finally abolished?

Refer students to the maps on pages 273 and 282 during their study of this section.

2. CONTINENTAL LANDS

The continental lands of the Caribbean wrap around the northern end of South America like a cap. The countries there are Colombia, Venezuela, Guyana, Suriname, and French Guiana. Colombia and Venezuela are large areas with large populations. In contrast, Guyana, Suriname, and French Guiana are small in area and in population.

Have students note from the map on page 273 that Colombia is the only country of South America that borders on both the Pacific and Atlantic oceans.

2.1 Colombia

With a land area of 439,734 square miles (1,138,910.2 sq km), Colombia (koh LOHM bee ah) is about three-fourths as large as the state of Alaska. The total population is 29.9 million. This makes Colombia the most populous country in the Caribbean.

Landscape and Climate. Several important physical features of South America are part of the landscape of Colombia. The Andes (AHN dehs) Mountains divide the country into a flat coastal area in the west, a central highland, and an eastern plain. In the west Colombia borders the Pacific Ocean. The eastern plain is called the Llanos (YAH nohs) and reaches into Venezuela. In southernmost Colombia, there is a lowland river basin that is part of the Amazon rain forest.

The Andes form a cordillera in Colombia, dividing into three chains. The Magdalena River, Colombia's most important river, flows in the valley between the central and eastern mountains. The Cauca (COW kah) River, a tributary of the Magdalena, flows between the central and western mountains.

Colombia is entirely within the tropics. The Equator runs through the southern part of the country. However, the country does not entirely have a tropical climate. Although most of Colombia has a tropical rain forest climate, areas in the north have a tropical savanna climate. The northernmost part of Colombia that juts into the Gulf of Venezuela has a dry steppe climate.

Altitude plays an important part in Colombia's climate. Elevation ranges from points in the Andes Mountains that are more than 18,000 feet (5,486.4 m) above sea level to lowlands along the coasts at sea level. As in Mexico, temperatures can be very cool in higher altitudes. High temperatures in the city of Bogotá (boh goh TAH), for example, at 8,355 feet (2,546.6 m) above sea level, average only 67°F (19.4°C). Low temperatures average about 50°F (10°C). In lowlands, weather can be typically tropical. The eastern part of the Llanos is also very hot.

Economic and Cultural Patterns. As shown in Figure 14–4 on page 282, the economy of Colombia is based on many different activities. The manufacture of textiles and clothing, cement, and processed foods and beverages plays an important part in Colombia's economy. Automobiles, metals, and machinery are among the country's industrial

Refer students to the political map on page 273 and the map of physical regions on page 270. Have them compare and contrast the information presented on the maps and to make some generalizations about the distribution of population and effects of physical features on accessibility and utilization of resources in the Caribbean.

LAND USE AND RESOURCES OF THE CARIBBEAN

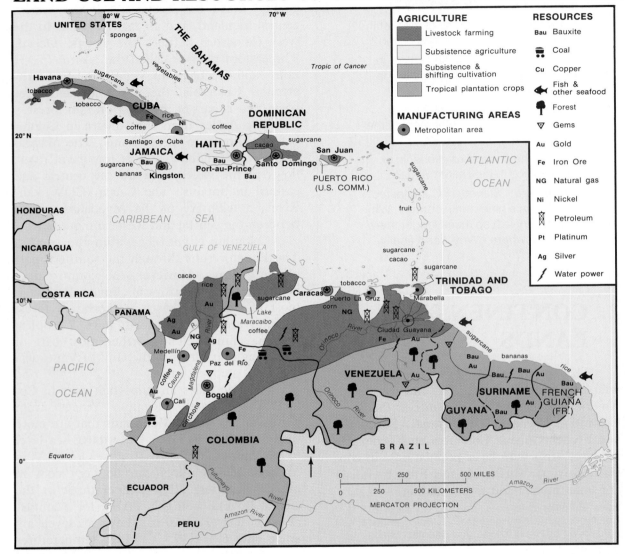

FIGURE 14-4
Sugar is an important agricultural product in many countries of the Caribbean region. Which countries in this region produce sugarcane?

products. The cost of making things tends to be high, however. This means Colombia's goods are expensive compared to goods made by other countries. As a result Colombia does not earn much money from exports.

Mining is another important part of the economy. Colombia produces more gold and coal than any other country in South America. Also 90 percent of the world's emeralds comes from Colombia.

Agriculture is most important to Colombia's economy. The great range of elevation in Colombia makes it possible to grow many different kinds of crops. In the low areas, bananas and other tropical crops are grown. At middle altitudes coffee is the major crop.

Coffee continues to be Colombia's main export. In fact, Colombia ranks second to Brazil as an exporter of coffee among countries of the world. Colombia also is believed to be a leading producer of **cocaine,** an illegal narcotic derived from the dried leaves of the coca plant. The governments of Colombia and the United States have been working together to curb the growing flow of such illegal drugs from Colombia into the United States.

Most Colombians live in the highlands found in the western half of the country. About 70 percent of the population lives in urban areas. Bogotá, the capital and largest city, has more than four million people.

The eastern part of Colombia is barely settled. It has been estimated that this part of the country has about 54 percent of the land, but less than 3 percent of the people.

During much of the 1800s and 1900s, the country experienced violence and political conflict. However, the people of Colombia have maintained a democratic government.

Influences of the Past. Not long after Spanish explorers landed in the West Indies, they went to the coasts of the continental lands. All through the 1500s, the Spanish used places in the area as bases from which to explore and to search for gold and other valuable resources.

Colombia became a Spanish colony with the capital at Bogotá. The city grew to become an important trading center of the Spanish empire. In 1717 the city became the capital of the Viceroyalty of New Granada. This also included the countries of Venezuela, Ecuador, and Panama.

In 1810 the people of the area declared their independence from Spain. The Republic of Greater Colombia was set up. In 1830 Ecuador and Venezuela broke away to become independent. Panama became an independent country in 1903.

During colonial days most mining in Colombia was done by Spanish settlers and Indians who were forced into working. In Colombia today about 58 percent of the population is of mixed Spanish and Indian ancestry.

On a map of North and South America, point out that most of Venezuela lies east of eastern United States.

2.2 Venezuela

Venezuela is a little smaller in size than Colombia, having 352,143 square miles (912,049.7 sq km) of land area. Its population of 18.3 million ranks it second to Colombia.

Landscape and Climate. The Andes Mountains do not dominate in Venezuela as in Colombia. The Sierra de Perijá (peh ree HAH) forms the western border of Venezuela with Colombia. Farther east is the Cordillera de Mérida. Between these ranges is Lake Maracaibo (mah rah KY boh), South America's largest lake.

The most important river of Venezuela is the Orinoco (oh ree NOH koh). The basin of the Orinoco lies between the coastal range and the Guiana Highlands of the southeast. The Llanos also form part of this basin.

Venezuela has tropical climates over most of the country. From one part of the country to another, differences in the amount of rain are more important than differences in temperatures. The southern part of Venezuela has a tropical rain forest climate, while north central areas have a tropical savanna climate. Dry climates cover the northernmost parts of Venezuela along the Gulf of Venezuela.

Economic and Cultural Patterns. In Venezuela most of the people live in urban areas, especially in the highlands along the Caribbean coast. Along with several other large cities and towns, Caracas, the capital and largest city, lies in the valleys of the coastal mountain range. Another large city, Maracaibo, lies on the shore of Lake Maracaibo in the western part of Venezuela.

Point out that Caracas, Venezuela, is the northern-most of South America's major cities. Frequent airline flights connect it with cities in North America.

Student volunteers might enjoy researching and reporting on Guyana's national hero, Cuffy, who led a major slave rebellion in 1763.

Venezuela is more an industrial country than an agricultural one. It has major deposits of iron ore and natural gas. The mining of gold continues to be a source of income for the country. The Orinoco River system also has great potential as a source of hydroelectric power for Venezuela's growing industries.

The most important economic resource for Venezuela is oil. The country is the fourth largest producer of oil in the world. It was one of the countries to establish the Organization of Petroleum Exporting Countries, or OPEC. This is a group of nations that work together to determine the amount of oil to pump and the price to charge for the oil. Two-thirds of Venezuela's income is from oil and oil products. Recently people from all over the world have come to Venezuela to work in the oil industry. They have come from Europe, India, southwest Asia, and north Africa.

Even though oil is so important, Venezuela does have other economic activities. A large number of different crops—rice, coffee, corn, sugarcane, and bananas—are grown in the country. Other farm products are poultry, meat, and dairy products. The Llanos is a major area where cattle are raised.

Influences of the Past. Venezuela's past has much in common with that of Colombia. It was first settled by Europeans looking for gold. Later it became a colony of Spain. Venezuela was part of Greater Colombia after breaking away from Spanish control. It became independent in 1811.

Both the people and the culture of Venezuela reflect its past. About 67 percent of the people are mestizos, 21 percent are of European ancestry, and about 10 percent are of African ancestry.

The major language of Venezuela is Spanish. Some Indian languages are spoken, especially by people living in the highlands of the southeast. Most of the people are Roman Catholics.

2.3 The Guianas

Guyana, Suriname, and French Guiana are known together as the Guianas. They have similar land features, climates, and agricultural economies.

Along the coast of Guyana is a swampy area in which most of the people live. Inland, it is heavily wooded. In the south and west, the land has mountains with tropical savanna vegetation. Sugarcane and bauxite are its largest industries. Georgetown is its capital and largest city, and English is spoken.

Suriname also has low coastal areas. In fact, most of the coast of the country would be underwater except for the dikes built by early settlers. The capital, Paramaribo (pah rah mah REE boh), is in this area. The central part of the country has woods and patches of tropical savanna. From the coast the highlands rise toward the south to more than 4,000 feet (1,219.2 m) above sea level. They cover 75 percent of the country. Much of this area is covered by thick jungle, much of which has never been explored. Many ethnic groups live in Suriname. About one-third are descendants of people from India called Hindustanis. Another one-third are people with mixed European and African ancestry. The Creole language is spoken by most people.

The coastal area of French Guiana reaches inland from 10 miles (16.1 km) to 30 miles (48.3 km). There the coastal plain meets the plateau. Farther south, there is a tropical rain forest covering low hills. The capital, Cayenne (ky EHN), is located in the coastal area. Although French Guiana's official language is French, Creole is also widely spoken.

Agriculture and mining remain the base of the economy in the Guianas. Rice and sugar are important farming products, while bauxite is a valuable mineral export.

Each of the Guianas was settled and made a colony by different European coun-

Guyana, Suriname, and French Guiana all have a tropical rain forest climate and large areas of dense jungles, much of which have never been explored.

Dugout canoes are Suriname's chief means of travel. What covers much of the country's terrain?

See the *TRB* for the *Chapter 14 Reading* on the Cayman Islands.

tries. Guyana was once a colony of Britain. Suriname was once held by the Netherlands. Only French Guiana remains a possession— of France.

The people of the Guianas come from many different backgrounds. Africans were brought into the area to work in the sugarcane fields. When slavery ended, people from India and the islands of the East Indies came to the Guianas looking for work. Today there are many people of Carib, East Indian, African, and European descent.

See the *TAE* for an *Objective 2 Activity.*

CONTENT CHECK

1. **Identify:** Colombia, Andes Mountains, Llanos, Magdalena River, Bogotá, New Granada, Venezuela, Lake Maracaibo, Orinoco River, Caracas, OPEC, the Guianas, Hindustanis, Creole.

Devil's Island, long famous as a French prison off the Guiana coast, is today a tourist site.

2. **Define:** cocaine.
3. What are the continental lands of the Caribbean?
4. What is the largest and most populous of the continental lands?
5. In what part of the country do most people in Colombia live?
6. From what product does Colombia make most of its money from exports?
7. What is the capital and most populous city of Venezuela?
8. What is the most important economic resource of Venezuela?
9. What general kind of climate do the Guianas have?
10. **Challenge:** Why do you think Venezuela is more industrialized than other countries of the Caribbean?

See the *TAE* for an *Objective 3 Activity.*

CONCLUSION

The lands of the Caribbean are all developing countries. Nearly all are small in both size and population. Even the largest— Colombia—lacks the size and population to be a major world power.

Variety is the key to the Caribbean area. Culturally, the region has as much variety as any place on Earth. The economies of the lands range from such slowly developing countries as Haiti to the fast-growing economy of Venezuela.

While lacking a major world power, the area is still important. The waters of the Caribbean and Atlantic have made it easy to reach the lands of the area for hundreds of years. Today the location of the region between North and South America makes it a crossroads of the Western Hemisphere. What happens in the years ahead will be important to the Caribbean's neighbors.

SUMMARY

1. There are two parts to the Caribbean region—the West Indies and the continental lands of South America that border the Caribbean Sea.
2. The West Indies consist of the Greater Antilles, Lesser Antilles, and Bahamas.
3. Landforms are different from island to island in the West Indies. The West Indies lie entirely within the tropics, where temperatures are warm throughout the year.
4. The West Indies have a great mix of people and cultures. Agriculture and tourism are the major economic activities of the islands.
5. The United States and European powers have had possessions in the Caribbean and have played an important role in influencing the history of the area.
6. Colombia, Venezuela, and the Guianas make up the continental lands of the Caribbean region.
7. Colombia is the largest and most populous country in the Caribbean region. Venezuela is more an industrial country than an agricultural one. Coffee is important to Colombia's economy, and oil to Venezuela's economy.
8. The Guianas have similar land features, climates, and agricultural economies.

Answers to the following questions can be found on page T162.

REVIEWING VOCABULARY

Number your paper from 1 to 6. Beside each number write the vocabulary word from the list below that best describes each phrase. Then use each word in a complete sentence that shows you understand the meaning of the word.

mulatto   voodoo   cocaine   cays   abolition   archipelago

1. person of mixed African and European ancestry
2. group of islands scattered through the ocean
3. tiny, low-lying islands
4. illegal narcotic derived from the dried leaves of the coca plant
5. religion derived from African practices of ancestor worship
6. act of doing away with

REMEMBERING THE FACTS

1. What are the two major parts of the Caribbean region?
2. What Greater Antilles island includes two countries? What are the countries?
3. What is the largest island in the West Indies?
4. What are major sources of income for people in the West Indies?
5. What nation of the West Indies became independent when slaves revolted against their French colonial masters?
6. What is Cuba's most important crop?

7. How do most Haitian people make a living? What religion do most follow?
8. Which is the largest and most populous of the continental lands of the Caribbean region?
9. What is the major language of both Colombia and Venezuela?
10. What are the most important rivers of Colombia and Venezuela?
11. Which continental country of the Caribbean produces more gold and coal than any other country in South America?
12. What kind of climate characterizes most of Venezuela?

UNDERSTANDING THE FACTS

1. What are the differences between the two terms "Greater Antilles" and "Lesser Antilles"?
2. What was the effect of the trade winds on the settlement of the eastern islands of the Caribbean?
3. For what purpose was the organization CARICOM established?
4. How does the location of the West Indies place them on one of the world's most heavily traveled sea trade routes?
5. Colombia manufactures automobiles, but few are exported. Why is this true?
6. What are some of the similarities and the differences among the countries of the Guianas?

THINKING CRITICALLY AND CREATIVELY

1. What problems did the Spanish encounter when they tried to make slaves of the Indians when Spain first took control of territories in the West Indies?
2. Why is trade of countries in the West Indies with countries outside the region more important than their trade with one another?
3. For what purpose did the Dutch establish outposts on the coast of South America in the early 1600s?
4. What was the relationship between the growth of sugar plantations and slavery in the West Indies?
5. **Challenge:** What potential economic problems might be faced by a nation such as Cuba that is heavily dependent on one product, such as sugarcane?
6. **Challenge:** Average summer temperatures in areas where most Colombians live are cooler than those where Venezuelans live. Why do these differences exist?

REINFORCING GRAPHIC SKILLS

Study the map on page 279. Then answer the questions that follow.

1. In what part of Adjuntas is the cemetery located?
2. What is the approximate distance in kilometers from north to south on the map?
3. Why does the highway in the northeastern part of this area have more curves in it than the other highways?
4. At what elevation is Adjuntas' center?

CHAPTER 15

Brazilians know Sugarloaf Mountain as Pao de Açúcar, which rises 1,325 feet (403.9 m) above sea level. Botafogo Bay is an inlet of the larger Guanabara Bay.

Botafogo Bay and Sugarloaf Mountain in Rio de Janeiro, Brazil

SOUTH AMERICA: ATLANTIC NATIONS

In this chapter you will learn—

● What landscapes and climates are found in the Atlantic nations.

● How physical features affect economic conditions in the Atlantic nations.

● What past civilizations influenced the development of the Atlantic nations.

INTRODUCTION

The Atlantic region of Latin America is made up of the countries of Brazil, Argentina, Paraguay, and Uruguay. Located on the Atlantic side of South America, these countries together make up about two-thirds of the continent's land area. All of the countries except Paraguay border the Atlantic Ocean. Paraguay, however, is linked to the Atlantic by way of deep, navigable rivers.

There are many important rivers in the Atlantic region. The largest and most famous is the Amazon. It flows from its source in the Andes Mountains of Peru eastward across Brazil to the Atlantic Ocean. Other rivers of the region besides the Amazon also empty into the Atlantic. Draining the northeastern side of Brazil's highlands is the São Francisco River. Draining Brazil's southeastern highlands is the Paraná (pah rah NAH) River. It links with the Uruguay River to form a long channel of water that ends at the Río de la Plata (REE oh deh lah PLAH tah).

Although the countries of the region are tied together by their closeness to the Atlantic Ocean, there are many differences, especially in landforms and climates. The lowlands of the Amazon River basin in Brazil hold many rich natural resources. With the highest point in the Western Hemisphere, the Andes Mountains stand tall over western Argentina. The grassy Pampas (PAHM pahs) in Argentina are the source of much of that country's wealth. The region's climates are diverse— from tropical moist to dry.

Like many countries in the Latin American culture area, the Atlantic nations have people who farm or hunt as they did hundreds of years ago. They live nearby those in highly industrialized cities.

Once colonies of Spain or Portugal, the Atlantic countries became independent nations in the 1800s. Independence, however, has not always brought stable government. Many rulers with different ideas have sometimes kept these lands in political turmoil. Today they all are working for stability and for better economies and standards of living.

1. BRAZIL

The Federative Republic of Brazil covers an area of 3,286,475 square miles (8,511,963.6 sq km). This makes it fifth in size among the

Refer students to the map of Land Use and Resources of the Atlantic Nations on page 302 and the political map of the Atlantic Nations on page 305.

PHYSICAL REGIONS OF THE ATLANTIC NATIONS _____

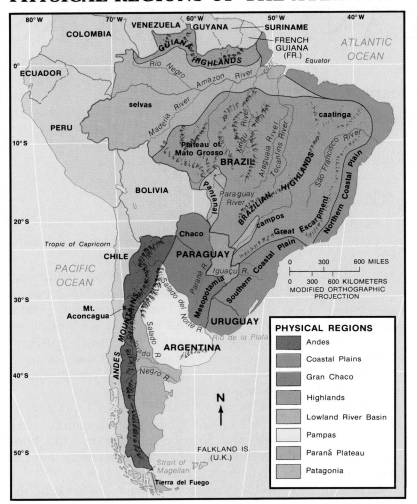

Two major highlands areas are prominent features of Brazil's landscape. These are the Brazilian Highlands and the Guiana Highlands. What river basin separates these areas?

Refer students to pages 96-97 to review the map of Earth's Climate Regions.

Cold weather is rare in Brazil. The cold air masses blowing north from Antarctica are warmed by warm ocean currents off the coast of southern Brazil.

FIGURE 15–1

largest countries of the world. As Figure 15-3 on page 293 shows, Brazil's land area is only slightly smaller than the area of the United States. With a population of 141.5 million people, Brazil ranks as the most populous Portuguese-speaking country in the world.

Brazil is a country of contrasts. In this nation traditional and modern exist side by side. Modern industry in the cities mixes with subsistence farming in rural areas. Its huge land area, large population, and many minerals supply it with enough resources to make it an economic world leader.

1.1 Landscape and Climate

For such a large area, Brazil has only a few landscapes and climates. The landscapes of the country do not show dramatic change from one place to another. The overall climate is warm or hot.

Brazil's rain forests are being destroyed at a rate of about 5,000 square miles (8,046.7 sq km) per year to make room for ranches, farms, and other projects.

Brazil's highest point, Pico da Neblina, which is 9,889 feet (3,014.2 m) above sea level, is found in the Guiana Highlands.

Landscape. In general, Brazil is made up of three physical regions. As shown in Figure 15–1 on page 290, these are lowland river basins, highlands with mountains and plateaus, and coastal plains.

The largest of the lowland river basins is that of the Amazon River in northern Brazil. The Amazon is the longest river in the Western Hemisphere and the second longest in the world. About 4,000 miles (6,437.4 km) long, it is navigable for about 2,300 miles (3,701.5 km) from the east coast of Brazil to the city of Iquitos (ee KEE tohs) in Peru. Counting its more than 200 tributaries, the Amazon drains more land than any other river in the world— some 2,700,000 square miles (6,992,994.6 sq km). Even though the river is filled with **silt**—tiny dirt particles—and is slow-moving, it drains 170 billion gallons (643.5 billion l) of water per hour into the Atlantic Ocean.

The Amazon River Basin is widest in the west near the Andes Mountains. It narrows close to the mouth of the river at the Atlantic Ocean. Most of the basin is covered by dense tropical rain forests called **selvas**.

A much smaller lowland area with swamps and marshes, called the Pantanal (pahn tah NAHL), is found in southwestern Brazil. It lies in the floodplain of the upper Paraguay River and its many tributaries.

Two other lowland river basins are found in Brazil. The area of the Paraná River in the southern part of Brazil and the area of the São Francisco River west of where it crosses the coastal plains are tropical savannas called **campos**. The rivers both begin in the central highlands of the country. The Paraná flows to the southwest, while the São Francisco flows to the northeast, emptying into the Atlantic.

Highland areas make up more than one-half of the land of Brazil. The largest is the Brazilian Highlands, which lie over the land of east central Brazil. They begin south of the Amazon River Basin. Within these highlands are low mountain ranges. The eastern edges

of the mountains drop sharply to the Atlantic Ocean. This is called the Great Escarpment. An **escarpment** (ihs KAHRP muhnt) is a steep slope between a higher surface and a lower one. Because travel over the Great Escarpment with its many waterfalls is difficult, most of the people of Brazil live between the escarpment and the Atlantic coast.

The Guiana Highlands are north of the Amazon River Basin along the border with Venezuela and the Guianas. In the north and west, there are other highlands such as the Mato Grosso Plateau.

Besides lowland river basins and highlands, Brazil has long coastal plains. These plains stretch along Brazil's 6,000-mile (9,656.1-km) Atlantic coast. From Brazil's border with French Guiana to the edge of the "bulge," the low, wide plains change from tropical rain forests in the west to tall tropical savanna grasses in the central coast. Most of the inland part of the bulge is a semiarid

The area drained by the Amazon is about three-fourths the size of the entire United States.

The Amazon River winds through dense rain forests near Iquitos, Peru, as it begins its long journey through Brazil. How long is the Amazon River?

shrub forest called the **caatinga** (kah TEEN gah). Farther south from the bulge to the city of Salvador, the coastal plains are forested areas mostly cleared for farmland. They are broken into the northern and southern coastal plains by the Great Escarpment.

Climate. Brazil's climate has no temperature extremes. This is because nearly all the country lies in the tropics, and there are no extremes in elevation.

The Amazon River Basin generally has two kinds of climate. The basin inland from the river's source to its center has a tropical rain forest climate. Temperatures are about 85°F (29.4°C) with little seasonal change. Rain is very heavy—as much as 120 inches (304.8 cm) per year—keeping humidity very high. The floodplain areas at the northwestern mouth of the Amazon River and the Atlantic coast have tropical monsoon climates.

The highlands are generally cool with a tropical savanna climate. For example, in January, which is summer in Brazil, tempera-

The city of Rio de Janeiro is close to the area where the Great Escarpment moves down to the ocean.

CLIMATE: RIO DE JANEIRO

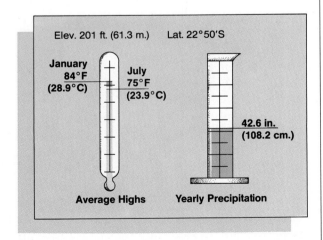

Elev. 201 ft. (61.3 m.)   Lat. 22°50′S

January 84°F (28.9°C)   July 75°F (23.9°C)

42.6 in. (108.2 cm.)

Average Highs   **Yearly Precipitation**

FIGURE 15-2
Rio de Janeiro's mid-summer temperature is the same as that of another summer resort—Atlantic City, New Jersey. Why is January a summer month in Brazil?

uary, which is summer in Brazil, temperatures in the city of Brasília (brah SEE lee ah) vary from 65°F (18.3°C) to 80°F (26.7°C). July's winter temperature varies from 51°F (10.6°C) to 78°F (25.6°C). In the highlands there are times of heavy rainfall and times of drought. The only dry climate in Brazil is steppe, which covers part of the caatinga in the northeastern highlands. This area is the hottest part of the country.

The east central coast of Brazil has a tropical rain forest climate. Farther south is a part of the northern coastal plain with a tropical monsoon climate. The rainy season lasts generally from October through April. Figure 15–2 on this page shows that in this climate area the city of Rio de Janeiro (REE oh day zhuh NAYR oh) has temperatures about 84°F (28.9°C) in summer and 75°F (23.9°C) in winter. Slightly inland from the southeastern coast is an area of the country with a middle-latitude marine climate. Temperatures there are warm year-round.

Farther inland in the southern coastal plain is an area of humid subtropical climate. This area has hot summers and mild winters. For the most part, rain falls evenly all through the year. This climate covers the southernmost part of Brazil, where freezing temperatures have been recorded.

Brazil's leading export is coffee. Recently, however, shoe exports have risen greatly.

1.2 Economic and Cultural Patterns

Brazil, the largest and most populous country in South America, takes up almost one-half of the continent. Some say that Brazil is a reminder of the way the United States was about 100 years ago. This is because lands are opening up for settlement and economic development as roads are built through highlands and the Amazon River Basin.

Economic Regions. Brazil can be divided into five major regions: (1) North, (2)

The destruction of Brazilian tropical rain forests worries many people. Widespread burning sends large amounts of carbon dioxide into the air. At the same time, the loss of forest reduces the amount of oxygen that goes into the atmosphere.

Northeast, (3) Southeast, (4) South, and (5) West Central.

The North is made up of the great Amazon River Basin and the Guiana Highlands. The area produces chiefly forest products, like rubber and cacao. The land is filled with dense forest and heavy plant growth. For many years this stopped people from clearing the land for farming.

In recent years, however, roads like the Trans-American Highway have been built. Since more people are now moving into the area, large parts of the Amazon River Basin have been cleared. However, only the soil in the narrow floodplains of the Amazon is fertile, because the nutrients in rain forest soil are constantly leached by heavy rains. Many scientists worry about destroying so much rain forest. They fear that if this continues, there may be serious environmental problems.

The Amazon River Basin continues to hold great potential for the country. The government is working to produce other products besides those that come from the rain forest. Making use of many mineral deposits in the area—bauxite, tin, iron, and manganese—is one way this is being done.

The North has about one-half of Brazil's land but only about five percent of its people. Most people live along the floodplains, where they depend almost totally on water transportation. Many farmers sell their goods and buy other products from floating markets. Trading companies in the cities of Belem (bay LEHM) and Manaus (mah NOWS) send riverboats up and down the rivers of the region. The boats stop at wharves to do business with the local people who offer to trade such products as rubber, nuts, hardwoods, animal hides, and flour made from cassava roots.

The second region of Brazil, the Northeast, has a wet coast and a dry interior. Along the coast the rain forest has largely been cleared for growing crops and raising cattle. Most cattle are raised on large ranches and

COMPAR-A-GRAPH: BRAZIL-UNITED STATES

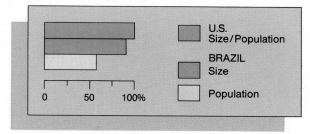

FIGURE 15-3
Despite its large size, many areas of Brazil are thinly populated. Where do most Brazilians live?

Ethyl alcohol is used in fuel for automobiles.

watched over by **vaqueiros** (vah KAYR ohs)—cowhands of Brazil. The people grow sugarcane, cotton, and cacao, as well as **sisal** (SY suhl), a plant whose fiber is used to make rope. Much of Brazil's sugarcane is used to produce a fuel called ethyl alcohol. Inland, the dry land is used for grazing goats, although tobacco is raised in some parts.

The Northeast, one of the most populated parts of Brazil, is one of the poorest. Some of the land has been ruined by overgrazing cattle and by frequent droughts. Large numbers of people have left rural areas to go to the many cities in the region. Among these are Salvador and Recife (reh SEE fay) with populations of more than two million. Each of these cities has slums, called **favelas** (fah VAY las), where people live in bad housing, in poor health, and with no jobs.

In contrast to the Northeast, the Southeast is as important to Brazil's economy as the central plateau area is to Mexico's. Settlement here was sparked by the discovery of gold in 1698. The discovery of diamonds shortly after also brought many people to the area. The region continues to be an important center for gold and industrial diamonds. Today manganese, quartz, and iron ore are also mined there. One of the world's largest iron ore deposits can be found in the Southeast.

STRANGE BUT TRUE

MANAUS RUBBER BOOM

Located about 1,000 miles (1,609.3 km) up the Amazon River is the city of Manaus, Brazil. Today a trading city of more than 600,000 people, Manaus was once one of the richest and most famous cities in the world. Its rise can be explained in one word—*rubber*.

Manaus is near the center of the huge Amazon rain forest. Rubber trees grow wild all through the selvas. But, before the late 1800s, there was little demand for rubber.

People started demanding rubber when rubber overshoes became popular. However, natural rubber hardened and cracked after a time. Charles Goodyear, an American, found a way to keep rubber soft and flexible. After his vulcanization process became known, rubber was used to make such things as fire hoses, seals, and other products.

Demand for rubber shot up with the invention of the automobile. Millions of rubber tires were needed for cars. A "rubber boom" hit Manaus much like the gold rushes in California and Alaska. Thousands of people from all over the world came to Manaus hoping to make a fortune.

As demand went up for rubber, so did the prices paid for it. Many "rubber barons" earned and spent huge fortunes. Elegant homes of every style were built only a few miles away from the rain forest. An electric streetcar system was built even before one appeared in cities like Boston. Some said that more people owned diamonds in Manaus than anywhere else. In the 1890s the opera house pictured on this page was built. It cost several million dollars, which, in those days, was worth many times more than what a million dollars is worth today. Opera companies from all over Europe were paid to make the long trip to Manaus.

The rubber boom did not last, however. In 1876 Henry Wickham of England had taken 70,000 rubber-tree seeds from the Amazon. He planted the seeds in hothouses in England. Later, plants were taken to an area that is now a part of Malaysia in southeast Asia. By the late 1890s, several rubber plantations there were producing natural rubber.

Plantation trees were far more productive than wild trees. Each provided as much as 11 pounds (5 kg) to 18 pounds (8.2 kg) of rubber a year instead of the 3.5 pounds (1.6 kg) of rubber each wild Amazon tree provided. The cost to produce rubber in southeast Asia was also much lower. As more rubber was made, world prices for it fell. Many people in Manaus were put out of business. When thousands of people left the city, the great Manaus rubber boom was over.

1. What led to the demand for rubber?
2. How did rubber change Manaus?
3. Why do you think rubber trees also grew well in southeast Asia?

294

Brazil's population is growing by leaps and bounds. Some think the country will have more people than the United States by the year 2000.

Point out that several capitals are planned cities; in addition to Brasília, there are Washington, D.C.; Ottawa, Canada; and Canberra, Australia.

Besides mineral wealth, the Southeast has rich farmlands. In fact, land and climate in this area allow Brazil to produce more coffee than any other country in the world.

Brazil's major cities are located in the Southeast. These cities are São Paulo (sow POW loh), with a population of more than seven million, and Rio de Janeiro, with a population of more than five million. São Paulo is one of the largest and fastest-growing cities in the world. Its metropolitan area ranks fourth in population in the world. Industries in the city make about every kind of product Brazil needs except tobacco, cacao, and some minerals. Coffee, sugar, cotton, and oranges are grown, and beef is raised. São Paulo is Brazil's industrial and financial center.

Rio de Janeiro, once the capital of Brazil, is one of the world's most beautiful cities. Its beaches attract many tourists from all parts of the world. Nearby at Volta Redonda is Brazil's largest steel mill.

Close to Brazil's border with Uruguay is the region of the South. Its major city is the port of Pôrto Alegre (PAWR too ah LEH grih), with a population of more than one million. This flat area has little mineral wealth but is rich with cattle. The region also makes **yerba mate** (YEHR bah MAH tay), a tea-like beverage.

The fifth major region of Brazil is West Central. It is made up of part of the western highlands, the Mato Grosso Plateau, and the Pantanal. This land is only lightly settled and somewhat isolated. The Brazilian government has urged more people to live there, but the land is not fertile and is damaged by too much grazing. The government hopes that if the land is used carefully, it could be made into a major agricultural area.

The government's commitment to western settlement was shown in 1960 when it planned and built a new capital for Brazil in the West Central region. The government moved the capital from Rio de Janeiro to the new city, Brasília. Brasília was designed and planned for 500,000 people. By 1980 it had grown to a city of more than 1.1 million people. Even though Brasília is now a symbol of the country's expansion and economic development, it has failed to bring Brazil much economic strength.

Population and Culture. Portuguese immigrants brought with them two important parts of Brazilian culture—the Portuguese language, which became the official language, and Roman Catholicism, which became the major religion.

Besides the Portuguese, immigrants from around the world have come to Brazil. They have given the country one of the world's most diverse populations. Today 55 percent of the people are of European descent. About 38 percent are of mixed European and African or mixed European and Indian descent.

Brazil Today. In recent years Brazil has experienced problems with growth. Government spending to improve the economy

See the TRB for Teacher Notes: Section 1 Extending the Lesson on Brasília.

Modern architecture gives Brasília the look and feel of a fast-growing, progressive city. When did Brasília become the new capital city of Brazil?

USING GRAPHIC SKILLS

READING TRANSPORTATION MAPS

If your family is taking a trip by car, a road map is sure to be first on your packing list. A road map tells you how many and what kinds of roads can take you from one place to another. Depending on where you are going, you may have a choice of roads or you may have only one road available.

A road map is the most common type of transportation map. It gives information about *accessibility*—how hard or easy it is to get to a certain place. When traveling, people need to know not only how far and in what direction a place is but also how accessible it

is. A place that has no transportation routes leading to it is not very accessible.

Below is a map that shows Brazil's chief transportation routes. It shows the accessibility of Brazil's capital, Brasília, to other cities in the country. It also shows how accessible these cities are to one another. The map indicates three kinds of transportation routes— air routes, main highways, and main railroads—that connect cities in Brazil. To read this transportation map, notice in the legend that each transportation route is shown in a different color.

TRANSPORTATION ROUTES TO BRASÍLIA

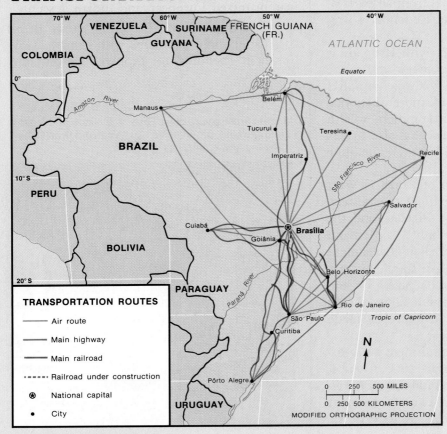

Study the map below. Then answer the questions that follow.

1. What method of transportation would take you from Brasília to Manaus? From Brasília to São Paulo?

2. What method of transportation provides the fewest routes to and from Brasília?

3. In what regions of Brazil are the most transportation routes? Make a hypothesis about why this is true.

4. Why do you think a railroad is being constructed between Brasília and Goiânia?

5. **Challenge:** In what ways do you think accessibility is important to a city's population growth? To its economic growth?

The wealthiest one percent of Brazil's people earn as much as the poorest fifty percent.

Scientists have recently concluded that human beings inhabited parts of Brazil at least 32,000 years ago.

and the lives of the people has brought about high prices for many goods and services. Poor land use and overcrowding in areas like the Northeast have added to Brazil's problems. Also, wealth is not evenly spread among the people of Brazil. There have always been a few very wealthy people and many poor.

Brazil has had other economic problems. It owes great debts to other countries of the world. Because it does not have enough petroleum to meet the demands of its people, Brazil must import large amounts.

Unlike some developing countries, Brazil has the potential to become a major world power. It is the most industrial country in South America. Cities such as São Paulo and Rio de Janeiro are as modern as many other world cities. On the other hand, parts of Brazil have had very little development. In some areas life is much as it was 100 or more years ago. Economically, Brazil is almost two countries. One is very advanced. The other looks like one of the least developed countries in the world.

See the TAE for an Objective 1 Activity.

1.3 Influences of the Past

In the year 1500, a Portuguese sea captain, Pedro Álvares Cabral, was blown off course sailing south from Portugal to Africa. His ship landed near the bulge of South America. He claimed the area for Portugal. Today this area is Brazil.

Colonization. Portuguese explorers did not meet an Indian civilization in Brazil like the Aztecs in Mexico. Instead they met groups of widely scattered people who lived by hunting, gathering, and fishing. Many of these people belonged to the Guaraní, Tupí, and Arawak Indian groups.

The Portuguese settled in northeast Brazil. There they set up plantations and forced the Indians to work as slaves in the fields.

Many Indians died from overwork and disease. Others fled into the interior. Today most of the estimated 200,000 Indians of Brazil live in the Amazon River Basin.

Between 1500 and 1800, almost four million Africans were brought to the Northeast. When gold was discovered in the 1700s in the Southeast, many slaves were moved to these mining areas. Slavery was finally abolished in Brazil in 1888. Many Africans left the areas where they had once worked as slaves to look for work elsewhere. Today those of African descent—six percent of the population—still live in the northeastern part of Brazil.

National Development. The Portuguese population in Brazil grew rapidly during the gold-rush days. Up to 1822, when Brazil became an independent country, most people who lived there were Portuguese or African. By the end of the 1800s, however, people from many countries had moved to Brazil—Italians, Germans, Poles, Syrians, Lebanese, Japanese, and East Indian.

During the mid-1800s, a ruler named Pedro II did much for the development of Brazil. He set up schools and banks and brought industry to the area. In addition, many new roads and railroad lines were started during the years of his reign.

Brazil became a republic in 1889. However, the country continued to go through many political changes in the late 1800s. Different rulers, another constitution, and revolts often kept the country in a state of confusion. During the 1900s Brazil has gone through years of dictatorship, democracy, and **anarchy**—or no orderly government—followed again by dictatorship.

Recently, however, there has been a more sound government and growth in industry and in the economy. The people of Brazil are determined to help their country develop and to enjoy its enormous potential in the coming years.

CONTENT CHECK

1. **Identify:** Federative Republic of Brazil, Amazon River, Amazon River Basin, Pantanal, Brazilian Highlands, Great Escarpment, Guiana Highlands, Mato Grosso Plateau, São Paulo, Rio de Janeiro, Pôrto Alegre, Brasília, Pedro Álvares Cabral, Pedro II.

2. **Define:** silt, selvas, campos, escarpment, caatinga, vaqueiros, sisal, favelas, yerba mate, anarchy.

3. What three general kinds of landscapes are in Brazil?

4. Why are there no temperature extremes in Brazil's climate?

5. What are the major economic regions of Brazil?

6. What are Brazil's major cities?

7. Why was Brasília built?

8. What is the most common language spoken in Brazil?

9. **Challenge:** What special conditions have helped to make Brazil a world leader in the use of alcohol as fuel?

2. ARGENTINA

Argentina, the second largest country in South America, is one of the region's richest in natural resources. It covers an area of about 1,068,297 square miles (2,766,887 sq km)—about the same amount of land as the United States east of the Mississippi River. Argentina is about one-third the size of Brazil. However, unlike Brazil, its landscape and climate are not the same from one part of the country to another. Also different from Brazil is the language spoken. Most people speak Spanish.

2.1 Landscape and Climate

Argentina is a long country—about 2,300 miles (3,701.5 km) long from north to south. Its widest part is in the north, above the Tropic of Capricorn. As it narrows to the south, its southernmost point lies less than 10 degrees from the Antarctic Circle.

Landscape. The landscape of this long, narrow country changes from thick woodlands and grassy plains to rugged mountains and desert shrub. It can be grouped into four physical regions: Pampas, Chaco and Mesopotamia, Patagonia, and Andes.

In the center of Argentina is the Pampas. From the Río de la Plata, this plain of rich soil fans out almost 500 miles (804.7 km) north to the Salado del Norte River and south

The southernmost town in the world, Ushuaia, is in Argentina on the island of Tierra del Fuego.

Iguazú Falls, seen here from the Brazilian side, are higher and wider than North America's Niagara Falls. Why are waterfalls common along the Paraná Plateau?

298

Use the map of Physical Regions of the Atlantic Nations on page 290 to point out that Chaco is part of the Gran Chaco, a 200,000-square-mile (517,999.6-sq-km) savanna that takes in parts of Paraguay and Bolivia, as well as Argentina.

SELECTED PEAKS OF THE AMERICAS

The Andes Mountains, with 37 mountain peaks higher than Alaska's Mount McKinley, are the highest mountain range in the Western Hemisphere. The mountains shown on this chart are the highest peaks in different areas of North and South America. The Andes Mountains form a natural boundary between Argentina and which other country?

MOUNTAIN	RANGE	LOCATION	ELEVATION
Aconcagua	Andes	Argentina	22,834 ft. (6,959.8 m.)
McKinley	Alaska	Alaska (U.S.)	20,320 ft. (6,193.5 m.)
Logan	Coast	Canada	19,850 ft. (6,050.3 m.)
Citlaltépetl	Sierra Madre Oriental	Mexico	18,700 ft. (5,699.8 m.)
Whitney	Sierra Nevada	California (U.S.)	14,494 ft. (4,417.8 m.)

FIGURE 15-4

See the *TAE* for an *Objective 2* Activity.

to the Colorado River. The flat surface is broken only by a few low mountains in the southeast and the northwest. Much of the country's wealth comes from this area.

In the north Argentina has two lowland areas—Chaco and Mesopotamia. Chaco is between the Andes Mountains in the west and the Paraná River in the east. Much of it is covered by tropical savanna somewhat like the caatinga of Brazil.

To the east of Chaco and between the Uruguay and Paraná rivers lies another lowland known as Mesopotamia. Its southern and central parts have some low rolling hills and swampy valleys with thick forests.

As the land rises to the north, the Paraná Plateau sticks out from the rest of Argentina like an arm between Paraguay and Brazil. On the Paraná Plateau, the land is very rough, with many steep cliffs. Rivers and other streams falling over these cliffs create many waterfalls. Among the most noted of these is Iguazú Falls (ee gwah SOO), found on the border between Argentina and Brazil. The Iguazú River tumbles 237 feet (72.2 m) over a number of islands.

A region that seems far away and separate from the rest of Argentina is the Patagonia (pat tah GOH neȇah). This area of rugged highlands is south of the Pampas. It runs from the Colorado River in the north to the Strait of Magellan in the south. Many canyons in the region were formed by glaciers and rivers that cut into Earth's surface thousands of years ago. Steppe grasslands and desert also take up part of the landscape.

Argentina in the west is dominated by the Andes Mountains and its foothills. This range of mountains stretches north and south. It forms a natural boundary between Argentina and Chile. The highest mountains are along the northern border of the two countries. Mount Aconcagua (ah kohn KAH gwah) is the highest mountain in the Western Hemisphere. Figure 15-4 on this page compares Aconcagua's height with other peaks in the Americas.

Climate. Because Argentina has high elevations and is close to the oceans, it has many climate types. Dry or moist, mild winter climates spread across the land. Since all of its land area lies south of the Equator, Argentina's seasons are the opposite of those in the Northern Hemisphere.

In the east, where the Pampas is closest to the Atlantic Ocean, the climate is humid subtropical. More than 38 inches (96.5 cm) of

THE URBAN WORLD

BUENOS AIRES: URBAN SPRAWL

Until recently, neighborhoods close to Buenos Aires' center have been the home of the city's wealthiest families. Lately, they have been moving to northern suburbs.

Buenos Aires, seen in the photograph on this page, is an important port located on the west shore of the Río de la Plata. The capital and most-populated city in Argentina, it covers 77 square miles (199.4 sq km). Its metropolitan area, however, is more than 18 times larger than the city. Such a huge build-up of areas all around central cities is called **urban sprawl.** This pattern of urban growth generally happens in areas where building and development are not planned or coordinated.

In many cases urban sprawl has come about because people have placed the highest values on land nearest the central city. This has led those who wanted to build houses or places of business to look away from the heart of the city for cheaper land. The land available is generally farmland or open fields. The cheaper price for land or for rent tempts new industries and businesses to locate in outlying areas. These businesses, in turn, attract people to build homes in suburban areas. Little by little the land all around the city becomes built up.

Urban sprawl is especially seen in areas located on level or nearly level land. Buenos Aires, for example, is surrounded on the north, south, and west by the broad flatlands of the Pampas. The Río de la Plata is to the east. There were no steep highlands or other physical barriers to get in the way of people moving out to the suburbs.

The boundary of metropolitan areas with urban sprawl shows an irregular pattern. In many cities governments tax land based on what it may be used for in the future rather than on what it is used for currently. For example, once a new neighborhood of houses is built, taxes go up on nearby land. This is because people will view that land as future sites for development. So, to save themselves from higher expenses, builders look to other parts of the city for future projects. This causes new residential areas to spring up in a disorganized and unplanned way.

Transportation also plays a part in urban sprawl. Buenos Aires has had good transportation for many years. Around 1900 a streetcar system was set up that allowed people to move to suburban areas and still get back and forth from their homes and places of work. In 1914 the first major subway in South America opened in Buenos Aires. Today there are five major subway lines in the city. An excellent bus system that travels throughout the metropolitan area also has encouraged people to move to outlying areas.

1. What is urban sprawl?
2. What physical characteristics of cities encourage sprawling to outlying areas?
3. What other factors have encouraged urban sprawl in large cities?

Refer students to the special feature on Alexander Von Humboldt on page 16. Note that Von Humboldt planned to walk from California to Patagonia. Using the map of the Atlantic Nations on page 290, discuss the kinds of things he may have seen during his journey through Argentina.

rain fall every year. In the west, where the Pampas is closest to the Andes, a steppe climate is found.

Temperatures in the Pampas are moderate with warm summers and mild winters. In the winter, cold air from the south or southwest sometimes blows across the plains bringing violent thunderstorms and winds that the Argentines call **pamperos.**

In the western part of the Chaco, the climate is steppe. Although yearly rainfall in the area may reach only about 20 inches (50.8 cm), there is frequent flooding. This is because much of the soil is hard clay and does not drain well. There is more rainfall in eastern Chaco and in Mesopotamia.

Because of its landscape and desert climate, Patagonia can best be described as bleak. Winds blow almost all the time, stirring up dust and leaving a haze. Along the coast, sea fogs are common. Air from the cold Falkland Ocean Current mixes with warmer air over the land to form fog.

Summers in Patagonia are cool. Winters in the southern part are cold. There is little rain because southwest winds blow over the Andes, creating an orographic effect. Although the region is generally dry, cold winds from the Antarctic sometimes bring snow to the area. However, the yearly average precipitation is only about 8 inches (20.3 cm).

Refer students to page 94 for an explanation of the orographic effect.

2.2 Economic and Cultural Patterns

Argentina is one of the few countries in Latin America that has an industrialized economy. Both farming and industry are important. In general, the people of Argentina enjoy a fairly high standard of living.

Economic Regions. Unlike so many other countries, Argentina's economic and physical regions are much the same.

The Pampas are the economic heart of Argentina. More than one-third of the country's 31.5 million people are clustered in or around the capital city of Buenos Aires (BWAY nohs EYE rays). This city is on the eastern edge of the Pampas on the bay of the Río de la Plata. Most Argentines live in the Pampas in towns that have 2,000 or more people.

The Pampas are important to Argentina because of their rich soil. Winds of the pampero deposit a fine-grained, wind-blown silt called **loess** (LEHS). This topsoil, along with the mild climate and moderate temperatures, makes the Pampas one of the richest agricultural areas in the world. Farmers grow wheat

People of Buenos Aires are often called *Porteños*— "people of the port." Ask students to explain why.

The Plaza de 25 de Mayo dominates city life in Buenos Aires. The old town hall highlights the public square, which commemorates Argentine independence. How many people live in or around Buenos Aires?

LAND USE AND RESOURCES OF THE ATLANTIC NATIONS ___

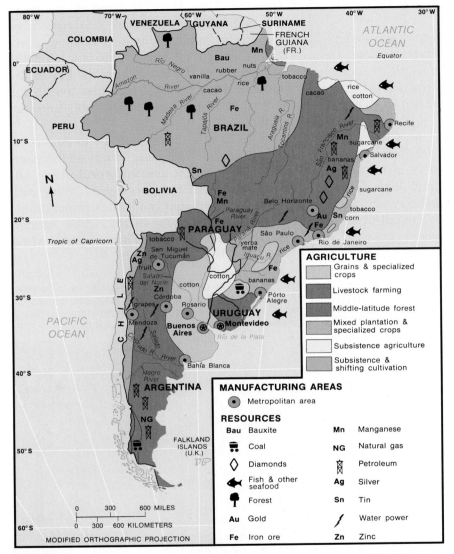

The Atlantic nations have a variety of natural resources. Many different kinds of agricultural products are grown in these nations. Which Atlantic nation has no manufacturing areas?

See the *TRB* for the *Chapter 15 Reading* on the gauchos of Argentina.

FIGURE 15–5

and corn, as well as other grains. Ranchers graze cattle and sheep in the drier western area of the Pampas.

Argentina has been a wealthy country because of its agricultural and livestock industries. Argentina is one of the world's leading grain producers. Argentina also has enough cattle and sheep to supply meat and meat products to countries all over the world.

The Chaco is also an important cattle grazing area. The land generally is either too wet or too hard for farming. Clusters of forest in the Chaco give lumber and also **tannin**—a substance from the quebracho (kay BRAH choh) tree used in tanning leather and in making dyes.

Most of the people of Patagonia herd sheep. There is a small amount of fruit grown

LATIN AMERICA UNIT 5

The ski resorts of the Andes region attract many tourists. Tourists also come to the region for the excellent mountain-lake fishing.

In the 1800s there were several deliberate attempts by Argentines of European descent to reduce the Argentine Indian population.

in the river valleys. The region, however, may hold the key to a better future for Argentina. As Figure 15–5 on page 302 shows, recent discoveries of oil and natural gas in Patagonia have allowed the country to supply its own oil needs.

While few people live in the Andes region, it is important in several ways for the economy of the country. Industries in the Pampas draw much of their electric power from hydroelectric plants in the Andes. Rivers flowing east from the Andes provide water for irrigating some areas. Water that flows from the Andes is used for sugarcane fields near San Miguel de Tucumán (sahn mee GEHL day too koo MAHN) in northwestern Argentina. It also irrigates vineyards and fruit orchards at San Juan and Mendoza (mehn DOH sah). The Andes region is also important as a mining area. Minerals like copper and lead are found there. The central Andes is a popular vacation spot.

Argentina Today. Argentina has one of the highest standards of living in Latin America and one of the best in the world. Most people have attended school. The literacy rate, 94 percent, is one of the highest in Latin America.

Argentina is an urban country. About 84 percent of the people live in cities or towns. About 97 percent of the 31.5 million people are of European ancestry. Buenos Aires is a leading publishing center of Spanish language works.

There is a small number of Indians in the country. They live mostly in the highlands of the northwest and in Patagonia. They often raise goats, sheep, and llamas.

Frequent changes in government have taken place in recent years in Argentina. There has been inflation and a lack of growth in the economy. Changes in world prices for grain, beef, and other cattle products have had an impact on the economy of Argentina.

2.3 Influences of the Past

Argentina was settled by the Spanish. As in most other countries in Latin America, they pushed aside the original Indian inhabitants. As in Brazil the first European settlers did not find an advanced Indian civilization.

Spanish Settlement. The Spanish first entered what is now Argentina in the early 1500s. Spanish colonists crossed the Andes from Chile to outposts of the conquered Inca Empire and set up small Spanish settlements.

The area around the Río de la Plata was part of the Viceroyalty of Peru until 1776. In that year the Spanish government made the new Viceroyalty of La Plata. Buenos Aires was made the capital of this new area. The Viceroyalty took in not only what is now Argentina, but also Uruguay, Paraguay, and southern Bolivia.

Independence. In the early 1800s, Argentina joined many other Spanish colonies in Latin America in working for independence. Under the leadership of General José de San Martín, Argentina declared its independence on July 9, 1816. After this time many people were confused about who was leading the government. **Caudillos** (cow DEE yohz), or military leaders, in the provinces each wanted power in local affairs, and leaders in Buenos Aires worked to spread their own power.

The confusion continued for almost 50 years. Different leaders tried to run the country. However, a central government was finally set up in 1862. This new government had a new constitution and president.

Britain was one of the first countries to recognize Argentina as a separate country. It was with the help of Britain that the economy started to grow in the 1800s. British beef cattle were brought to the Pampas, and railroads were built to carry the cattle to the port of Buenos Aires.

With farming and industry growing, the population also grew rapidly. In 1816 there

COLONIAL SOUTH AMERICA—1790

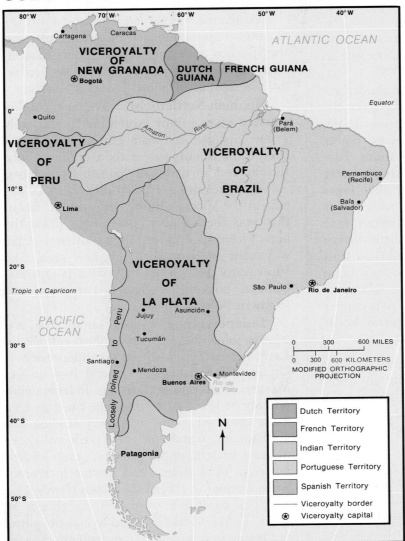

In 1790 Spain and Portugal were the two largest landholders in South America. Which of the present-day Atlantic nations were once part of Spain's colonial possessions?

During the early 1800s, the government of Spain worried about an invasion from France. Meanwhile an Argentine independence movement gained momentum.

FIGURE 15–6

were only about 500,000 Argentines. By 1895 there were four million. European immigration was responsible for most of the population growth.

Government and the Economy. Much of the best land of Argentina was owned by wealthy landowners who also took control of the government. Between 1916 and 1930, this

was a major problem of the Argentine government. A series of laws was finally passed that broke much of this control by the landowners and opened the door to the first real democratic elections.

From 1946 to 1955, Juan Domingo Perón served as Argentina's president. He wanted more industry in Argentina. He also wanted to distribute wealth more evenly. His

LATIN AMERICA UNIT 5

ATLANTIC NATIONS OF SOUTH AMERICA _____

The Atlantic nations dominate South America in terms of area and population. Brazil and Argentina are the two largest nations in area. Sixty-five percent of the continent's total population lives in the four Atlantic nations. Brazil has the largest population of any country of South America. Which cities are the national capitals of the Atlantic nations?

Point out to students that Argentina dislikes the name "Falkland Islands." Argentines refer to the islands as the "Malvinas."

FIGURE 15–7

wife and advisor, Eva, was very popular with workers. With her death, the government moved away from reform. Perón was removed from office by the military. He returned as president in 1973. After his death in 1974, he was succeeded by his vice-president and wife, Isabel Perón. The Western Hemisphere's first woman president, she was removed in 1976 by a group of military leaders.

In 1982 this military group led Argentina into a short war with Great Britain over the Falkland Islands. Argentina was defeated. Because of this conflict, the military junta was replaced and a new democratic government was set up. At present the new government is still trying to help the country recover from the heavy expenses incurred in the Falkland Islands War.

CHAPTER 15   **SOUTH AMERICA: ATLANTIC NATIONS**

See the *TRB* for *Teacher Notes: Section 2 Extending the Lesson* on an economic crisis in Argentina.

See the *TRB* for *Teacher Notes: Section 3 Extending the Lesson* on the Guaraní Indian language.

CONTENT CHECK

1. **Identify:** Argentina, Pampas, Chaco, Mesopotamia, Paraná Plateau, Iguazú Falls, Patagonia, Mount Aconcagua, Buenos Aires, General José de San Martín, Juan Domingo Perón.

2. **Define:** urban sprawl, pamperos, loess, tannin, caudillos.

3. What landscape dominates the south of Argentina?

4. What region is the economic heartland of Argentina?

5. What are important agricultural products of Argentina?

6. What is the capital and largest city of Argentina?

7. How is the Andes region important to Argentina's economy?

8. **Challenge:** In 1982 Argentina fought a war with Great Britain. Some people said that Great Britain was one of the last countries anyone expected Argentina to fight. Why would they have said this?

Refer students to the maps on pages 290, 302, and 304 to review the physical regions, land use, and colonial development of Paraguay and Uruguay.

3. PARAGUAY AND URUGUAY

Both Paraguay and Uruguay are much smaller in size than either Brazil or Argentina in area as well as in population. Both Paraguay and Uruguay, however, share many similarities with their larger neighbors.

See the *TAE* for an *Objective 3* Activity.

3.1 Paraguay

Paraguay (pah rah GWEYE), with 157,046 square miles (406,748.8 sq km), is about the size of the state of California. As can be seen in Figure 15–7 on page 305, the country is **landlocked.** It is bordered on the north and west by Bolivia, on the northeast and east by Brazil, and on the south by Argentina.

The country is divided into two different physical regions by the Paraguay River. The Paraná Plateau covers most of the land east of the river. Low mountains that start in Brazil become highland plateaus with grassland, hills, and tropical rain forests. To the west is the Gran Chaco. Here lowland savannas and thick shrub forest are found.

Climate is tropical savanna in the Chaco area. In the east most of the area has a humid subtropical climate. Temperatures are mild and change little during the year.

Paraguay's land is used mostly for farming. Cotton, soybeans, sugarcane, tobacco, coffee, and yerba maté are grown.

Indian cultural influence is greater in Paraguay than in any other country in Latin America. About 95 percent of the 4.3 million people are of mixed Spanish and Guaraní ancestry. Spanish and Guaraní are the official languages.

Most of the people live within 100 miles (160.9 km) of the capital city, Asunción (ah soon see OHN), once an important Spanish colonial headquarters. By the late 1700s, Asunción became an outpost as Buenos Aires was set up as the capital for the new Viceroyalty of La Plata.

For most of its history, Paraguay has been ruled by dictators. A war with Bolivia in the 1930s drained the country's treasury and slowed economic development.

There are not many energy or mineral resources in Paraguay. Three hydroelectric plants being planned could make Paraguay one of the world's leading exporters of hydroelectric power. But today, many Paraguayans have no jobs. Many have moved to other areas of South America, especially to Brazil. Those who stay behind wait to fill the few unskilled jobs that become available.

Most Uruguayans live in urban areas near the country's southern coast.

Uruguay once had one of the highest per capita incomes in the Western Hemisphere.

3.2 Uruguay

For most of its history, Uruguay (oo roo GWEYE) has been a buffer state between Portuguese Brazil and Spanish Argentina. A buffer state is a small country located between larger, often conflicting, powers. In 1828 it became the independent Oriental Republic of Uruguay, taking the name from its location east of the Uruguay River.

Uruguay, with an area of 68,039 square miles (176,220.9 sq km), is part of the southern coastal plains that stretch from South Brazil to the Río de la Plata. It has rolling plains and low hills and a humid subtropical climate. Where it meets the Atlantic Ocean, there is a small area with a middle-latitude marine climate. The land and climate are good for agriculture and livestock. The economy is based on livestock products and manufactured goods from livestock.

The Uruguayan culture is chiefly Spanish. Most people have European ancestry, especially Spanish and Italian. There are only about 10 percent mestizos and mulattos. The Uruguayan people have a high literacy rate— 94 percent—and a large middle class.

The capital and largest city of Uruguay is Montevideo (mohn teh vee DAY oh), on the Río de la Plata close to the Atlantic Ocean. Almost one-half of Uruguay's 3.1 million people live in Montevideo.

Since the mid-1900s, Uruguayans have seen their economy decline. They also have less political freedom. Too much spending by the government has brought about high prices for goods and services. The government has been taking steps to stop this. In so doing it has taken greater control of the country.

Because of these problems, the country had stopped growing for a time. Debts to foreign countries were high. Many well-educated Uruguayans left and moved to other countries. A more stable government is now running Uruguay.

CONTENT CHECK

1. **Identify:** Paraguay, Guaraní, Asunción, Oriental Republic of Uruguay, Montevideo.
2. **Define:** landlocked.
3. In which country of Latin America is Indian influence strongest?
4. What is the landscape like in most of Uruguay?
5. On what is Uruguay's economy based?
6. **Challenge:** Uruguay has been described as a buffer state between Argentina and Brazil. Why do you think a buffer state might be useful in this part of the world?

See the *TAE* for an *Objective 4* Activity.

CONCLUSION

The four nations that make up the Atlantic region of Latin America are a study in contrasts when it comes to landscape, climate, cultures, and ways of life. But in terms of economics, all four have one thing in common—potential for a bright future. Only Uruguay is without important mineral resources. But it has good land for farming. Until now all of the countries except Paraguay are developed or have been developing rapidly. And, in recent years, Paraguay also has been able to make progress.

At present the greatest need facing the nations is to solve their political problems. Over the years all four countries have moved back and forth between democracy and dictatorship. This has had a great effect on the people and the economies of these nations. In order for these countries to continue to develop and grow, they must find ways to allow all groups of people within their boundaries to have a fair hand in both government and the economy.

SUMMARY

1. The Atlantic nations of South America are Brazil, Argentina, Paraguay, and Uruguay. All four nations face the Atlantic Ocean or are tied to it by deep, navigable rivers.

2. Together the four Atlantic nations make up about two-thirds of South America's land area.

3. Brazil is the largest and most populous country in South America. It takes up about one-half of the continent.

4. Despite its size, Brazil has a few fairly uniform landscapes and climates.

5. Of the country's five major regions, the Southeast region is the heart of Brazil. Brazil's largest cities—São Paulo and Rio de Janeiro—are found there.

6. Brazil has the resources and size to be a major world power.

7. Argentina is the second largest country in South America. Because its land stretches from above the Tropic of Capricorn to near the Antarctic Circle, it has a variety of landscapes as well as climates.

8. The Pampas of Argentina are the economic heart of the country. They are one of the best farming areas in the world. The majority of Argentines live there.

9. Argentina is culturally like Europe. Its economy is developed, and the people have a high standard of living.

10. Paraguay is a landlocked country tied to the Atlantic Ocean and divided into two physical regions by the Paraná River. Its culture is Indian and European.

11. Uruguay is a developed country with an economy based on livestock products and manufactured goods from livestock.

Answers to the following questions can be found on page T170.

REVIEWING VOCABULARY

On a separate sheet of paper, unscramble the following words. For each unscrambled word, write a sentence that shows that you understand its meaning.

equsorva   donecllkda   rescnmepta   agnitaac   yahanrc   sremappo   sesol   tnainn

REMEMBERING THE FACTS

1. What are the four Atlantic countries of Latin America?

2. What are the capital cities of each Atlantic nation?

3. Which is the largest Atlantic nation in land area and population?

4. What is the longest and most noted river in the Atlantic region?

5. What three major kinds of land areas are found in Brazil?

6. What are the five regions of Brazil? Which is the most important economically?

LATIN AMERICA   UNIT 5

7. What is the largest city in Brazil? The major language?
8. What are the four major physical regions of Argentina?
9. In what part of Argentina do most of the nation's people live? Why?
10. How would you describe the standard of living in Argentina?
11. What is the highest mountain peak in the Western Hemisphere? Where is it located?
12. Which one of the four Atlantic nations is landlocked?

UNDERSTANDING THE FACTS

1. Why do some people say Brazil resembles the United States 100 years ago?
2. Why is rain-forest soil not fertile?
3. Why did Brazil decide to build its capital city, Brasília, far inland?
4. What differences are there in the ancestries of people in Brazil and Argentina?
5. Why are the Pampas important to the people of Argentina?
6. What causes frequent fog in coastal areas of Patagonia?
7. In what ways is Brazil like two countries?
8. Why has economic development been slow in both Paraguay and Uruguay?

THINKING CRITICALLY AND CREATIVELY

1. Brazil has many natural resources. Yet, Brazil is not a major industrial power. How do you explain this?
2. The mountains of western Argentina are far away from where most Argentines live. Yet, this part of the country is important. For what reasons do you think it is important?
3. There has been a great interest in using alcohol in fuel for automobiles, buses, and trucks in Brazil, but there has been relatively little in Argentina. Why do you think this is so?
4. **Challenge:** Uruguay is regarded as a buffer state between Brazil and Argentina. If there were no Uruguay, do you think the territory would be part of Brazil or of Argentina? Why?
5. **Challenge:** For many years much of Argentina's beef has been shipped to customers in England. During much of World War I, German submarines made it dangerous for merchant ships carrying beef to go from Argentina to England. What do you think happened to the economy of Argentina during this time?

REINFORCING GRAPHIC SKILLS

Study the map on page 296. Then answer the questions that follow.

1. Besides Brasília, what other cities in Brazil are most accessible by air? By train?
2. In what regions of Brazil are the fewest transportation routes? Why is this so?
3. **Challenge:** What fourth kind of transportation route does Rio de Janeiro have that Brasília does not? What impact might this have on the growth of Brasília?

CHAPTER 16

Many Peruvian Indians are underfed and live on potatoes, barley, and corn. Too expensive for most Indians to buy, wheat, for example, is usually exported.

Market scene in Peru

SOUTH AMERICA:
ANDEAN NATIONS

To help students appreciate the length of the Andes, use a map to show how far north they would extend if they were flipped over and reached 55° north of the Equator. They would reach as far north as southern Alaska.

In this chapter you will learn—

- What physical features and climate patterns are found in the Andean nations.
- How economic development differs throughout the Andean nations.
- How key events in the past of the Andean nations have influenced their cultures.

Very few major highways cross the Andes from east to west. They represent a much more serious barrier to land travel than do the Rockies of North America.

INTRODUCTION

The Andes Mountains form the world's largest mountain range, stretching from the Caribbean Sea in the north to the southernmost tip of South America. The Andes run for more than 5,500 miles (8,851.4 km) and are about 200 miles (321.9 km) wide for most of their length.

The mountains form a natural barrier between the Pacific coast and the rest of South America. Most of the mountain passes are more than 10,000 feet (3,048 m) above sea level. Peaks reach heights of more than 22,000 feet (6,705.6 m).

A narrow and very high range, the Andes have many volcanoes, avalanches, and earthquakes. This is because tectonic plate boundaries are nearby. The mountains play an important part in the lives of the people and countries that make up the Andean region of Latin America. These countries are Chile, Peru, Bolivia, and Ecuador.

Like the mountain chain, the Andean region also is long and narrow. It reaches from the Equator to 55° south latitude. The landscape of the Andean nations is not completely covered with mountains, however. West of the Andes there are deserts and coastal plains. To the east are lowland river basins and plains. The climates vary from tropical moist to dry to highland climate.

Because of the landscape, communication among parts of the region is difficult. Transportation between some areas is nearly impossible. The Andean countries are working hard to improve these situations.

Most of the population of the Andean region live at elevations below 11,500 feet (3,505.2 m) above sea level. So little oxygen in the air above that level limits development. Just as in many other South American countries, the Spanish heritage is strong among the Andean nations.

Chile comes from *Chilli,* an Indian word for "place where the land ends."

1. CHILE

Perhaps the most unique feature of the Republic of Chile is its long, narrow shape. Chile's 292,259 square miles (756,950.2 sq km) run for about 2,650 miles (4,264.8 km) along the Pacific coast. Its average width is only about 100 miles (160.1 km).

311

PHYSICAL REGIONS OF THE ANDEAN NATIONS

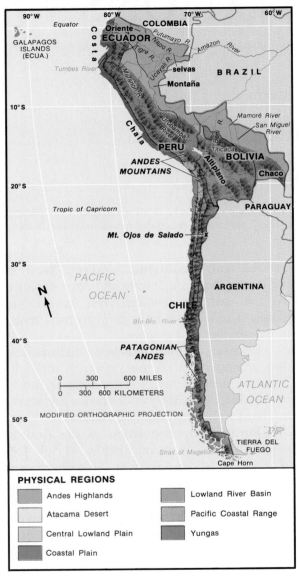

FIGURE 16-1
No large rivers flow into the Pacific Ocean along the western coast of South America. In which physical region is Lake Titicaca located?

See the *TAE* for an *Objective 1* Activity.

Along with its continental land, Chile owns several islands in the Pacific. It shares part of the islands called Tierra del Fuego with Argentina. Cape Horn, the southernmost point of South America, is part of Chile's Horn Island. Chile also owns Easter Island and Juan Fernández Islands in the Pacific Ocean.

Just seven percent of Chile's land is arable, so most of its 12.4 million people live in cities near the center of the country. Few people live in the southern half.

Refer students to pages 96-97 to review the map of Earth's Climate Regions.

1.1 Landscape and Climate

Three major features greatly affect Chile's landscape and climate. Chile spans an area from north of the Tropic of Capricorn to below 55° south latitude. To the west of the country is the Pacific Ocean. For most of its long border in the east, the massive Andes Mountains dominate.

Landscape. Some of the highest peaks in the Western Hemisphere are in the Chilean Andes, which separate Chile on the east from Argentina. One of the largest peaks is Ojos del Salado (OH hohs dehl sah LAH doh) at 22,516 feet (6,862.9 m) above sea level. Many of these mountains are active volcanoes.

The part of the Andes Highlands that extends into southern Chile is called the Patagonian Andes. The rugged mountains there are generally lower than those in the north. The Patagonian Andes reach about 8,000 feet (2,438.4 m) or less. Among the mountains are many beautiful glacial areas with deep lakes, fjords, and rivers. South of the Bío-Bío (BEE oh BEE oh) River, much of the narrow highlands is covered with middle-latitude forests.

Moving west of the Andes and south from Chile's border with Peru is the Atacama (ah tah KAH mah) Desert. It stretches for more than 800 miles (1,287.5 km). Along with high plains that sometimes reach more than 3,000 feet (9,144 m), this area has dry basins and **salt flats**—low-lying areas where water has dried up, leaving salt deposits.

LATIN AMERICA   UNIT 5

Just south of the desert is another dry lowland area. In this arid steppe, enough rain falls so that short grasses grow.

To the west of the desert, running south along the coast of Chile is a highland area called the Pacific Coastal Range. Some of the peaks along this side of the desert reach 6,650 feet (1,998.5 m) above sea level. As Figure 16–1 on page 312 shows, there is no coastal plain between the mountains and the desert, resulting in deep cliffs.

South of the city of Puerto Montt (PWEHR toh MOHNT), the Pacific mountains are partly under water. The peaks make up a large, irregular jumble of islands along the coast. This archipelago continues to the southernmost tip of the continent.

Between the Andes and the coastal mountains is a lowland with rich, moist soil and much vegetation. This central valley has fertile lands used for crops and grazing.

Because of Chile's long shape and high mountains in the east, most of the country's rivers are short and flow from east to west. Many begin in the Andes. They cross the central valley and coastal mountains, then empty into the ocean. In the north most rivers do not even reach the sea before drying up. In the south regular rain and snow feed the river sources in the mountains.

Climate. Because Chile is in the Southern Hemisphere, seasons are opposite those in the Northern Hemisphere. Chile's climates are different from north to south.

In the north the Atacama Desert is one of the driest areas in the world. Wind patterns and the nearness of the Pacific Ocean make a dry climate. From the west, ocean winds blow over the cold Humboldt, or Peru, Current toward land. As this cold air moves inland and begins to warm the desert region, it holds more and more moisture. As a result very little rain falls in that area. Temperatures in the desert are mild.

The area south of the desert has a steppe climate. Between 10 inches (25.4 cm) and 20 inches (50.8 cm) of rain fall there each year. The area is dry most of the summer, which peaks during January in the Southern Hemisphere. Most precipitation falls in winter.

The middle part of Chile has a Mediterranean climate like that of southern California. In the interior between the cities of Copiapó and Puerto Montt, summers are dry, and winters have much rain. On the coast it is mild and humid most of the time. Rain falls each year between 20 inches (50.8 cm) and 40 inches (101.6 cm).

South of the Bío-Bío River the climate is middle-latitude marine. Here the air is generally colder, wetter, and windier than the rest of Chile. Certain places receive as much as 200 inches (508 cm) of rain each year. The islands of the far south are among the stormiest areas in the world.

Despite its long, narrow shape, Chile's area is greater than that of Spain and West Germany combined.

1.2 Economic and Cultural Patterns

Chile has a more developed economy than other Andean countries. It has a good supply of natural resources. It also has a **homogeneous** population—many of the people share similar ways of life.

Economic Regions. Chile can be divided into five regions based on economic activity. They are the Desert North, Central, Frontier, Lakes, and Los Canales regions.

The northernmost economic region of Chile is the Desert North in the Atacama Desert. One of its leading natural resources is nitrates. **Nitrates** are salt compounds that dissolve in water but remain dry on top of desert areas. They are used to make explosives and fertilizers. Because almost no groundwater can be found in the Desert North, nitrates are easily mined there.

FOCUS ON GEOGRAPHY

CAPE HORN

Tierra del Fuego, which means Land of Fire, was named by the explorer Ferdinand Magellan. While searching for a passage to the Pacific in 1520, he saw fires the Indians kept burning along the shore to warm themselves.

Cape Horn, the southernmost tip of South America, is one of the most southerly areas in the world. A **cape** is a piece of land that sticks out from a larger land area into a body of water. Cape Horn is not really part of the continental land of South America. It is part of Chile's Horn Island, just south of Tierra del Fuego Island.

The cape was named in 1616 by a Dutch navigator, Willem Schouten. He named the island for his hometown of Hoorn, a place not far from Amsterdam in the Netherlands.

For centuries Cape Horn has inspired fear and respect among sailors of the world. The waters around the cape are cold and often filled with icebergs. Especially in the days of wooden sailing ships, navigating around Cape Horn was considered a great test of sailing skill.

The names that sailors gave to places near Cape Horn show their feelings about the area. A nineteenth-century map notes "False Cape Horn," "Desolate Cape," "Obstruction Sound," and "Last Hope Inlet."

Some ships avoided Cape Horn on their voyages from the Atlantic to the Pacific oceans. Instead, they passed through the Strait of Magellan between Tierra del Fuego and the mainland of South America. They quickly found, however, that this windy, cold, and narrow way was not easy either.

After the Panama Canal was opened in 1914, there were far fewer ships going around Cape Horn. Most of the ships that must go around the cape today are too large to pass through the canal.

Because of its fearsome history, much has been written about Cape Horn. One of the most famous passages is found in a poem written by Samuel Taylor Coleridge in the early 1800s—"The Rime of the Ancient Mariner." The poet wrote:

And now there came both mist and
  snow,
And it grew wondrous cold:
And ice, mast-high, came floating by,
As green as emerald.
And through the drifts the snowy clifts
Did send a dismal sheen:
Nor shapes of men nor beasts we ken—
The ice was all between.
The ice was here, the ice was there,
The ice was all around:
It cracked and growled, and roared and
  howled,
Like noises in a swound!

1. What makes the Cape Horn area so dangerous for ships?

2. Why would there be cold weather and icebergs near Cape Horn?

3. **Challenge:** Use a map or globe to calculate the approximate distance in miles and kilometers saved by using the Panama Canal rather than going around Cape Horn on a trip from New York to San Francisco.

Demand for nitrates has fallen, however, because synthetic products are being used instead. The people of the Desert North have recently turned to other natural resources like copper, iron ore, gold, and silver. Chuquicamata (choo kee kah MAH tah) has one of the world's largest copper deposits. Copper makes up almost 45 percent of Chile's exports.

The people of the Desert North also depend on the Pacific coast. Anchovies and products made from fish have added to the country's income.

Most Chileans, however, live in the Central region. It extends from Copiapó in the north to Puerto Montt in the south. The country's major cities are found in this region as well as most of Chile's farmland. Climate there is good for growing fruit, wheat, oats, and corn. Much of the farmland is part of large commercial farms, worked by tenants who receive part of the crops as their pay.

Santiago (sahn tee AH goh), the capital of Chile, supports such economic activities as food processing, textiles, clothing, wood and paper products, and chemicals. With a population of 4.3 million, Santiago is Chile's largest city. Valparaíso (vahl pah rah EE soh), a leading port city, is a manufacturing center. Concepción (kohn sehp see OHN) produces most of Chile's iron and steel.

The other economic regions are in southern Chile. An area called the Frontier in the north is called the granary of Chile. This is because much wheat is grown there on large farms. South of the Frontier is the Lakes region, where Chile's largest freshwater lakes are found. Thick forests cover much of the landscape. Its economy is largely based on lumber and dairy farming.

South of the Lakes region is Los Canales (lohs kah NAH lays)—the Canal area. It is named for the many inlets, straits, and other waterways south from Puerto Montt to Tierra del Fuego. One of the few economic activities in this area is sheep-raising for wool. Oil and

The Andes Mountains in the distance provide a natural backdrop in this view of Santiago. Mountains overshadow almost every aspect of life in the region. What are Chile's other important cities?

Santiago's Biblioteca Nacional is South America's largest library with over 1,200,000 volumes.

natural gas are found there, but they may be used up by the end of the century.

Culture. During the 1500s through the 1700s, many Spaniards and Basques—people who lived in northern Spain and southwest France—explored the Americas and settled in Chile. Few Spanish women came to Chile, so many Europeans married Indian women. Today about two-thirds of Chileans are mestizos. Because of this European influence, most people speak Spanish and practice Roman Catholicism.

The Araucanian (ah row KAH nee uhn) Indians make up the largest Indian group in Chile today. They and several other Indian groups were the original settlers of Chile.

Between 1848 and the early 1900s, a large number of Germans moved to the lakes area of southern Chile. These people started the dairy industry there.

Chile has been one of the most stable and prosperous countries in Latin America. A large number of Chileans are literate—94

ANDEAN COUNTRIES BORDER DISPUTES—1828-1928

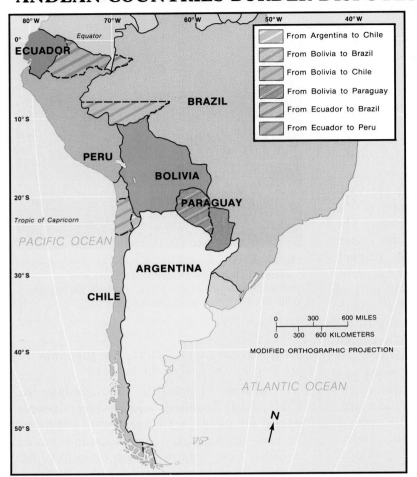

Legend:
- From Argentina to Chile
- From Bolivia to Brazil
- From Bolivia to Chile
- From Bolivia to Paraguay
- From Ecuador to Brazil
- From Ecuador to Peru

0 300 600 MILES
0 300 600 KILOMETERS
MODIFIED ORTHOGRAPHIC PROJECTION

N

FIGURE 16-2

Ecuador is much smaller today than it was in times past. Bolivia once had an outlet to the sea, but today it is landlocked. Bolivia's former seacoast is now part of what country?

Some of the boundaries of the region are still disputed. Peru and Ecuador claim the same frontier area, which covers 42,412 square miles (109,847 sq km). Refer students to the National Claims in Antarctica map on page 636. Ask students which of the Andean countries also have disputed claims in Antarctica.

In 1969 many of the Andean nations decided to seek economic and cultural unity by signing the Andean Pact.

percent of the population. As many as 70 percent are industrial or service workers. Only about 15 percent of Chileans are farmers.

1.3 Influences of the Past

In 1541 the Spanish moved from their base in Peru into Chile. Gold attracted most of the early explorers and settlers, but it was wheat that supported them. Wheat was grown in Chile for export to Peru, the early center of Spain's power in America.

Spanish descendants often came into conflict with the Indians, especially Araucanians. It is a conflict that has yet to end.

For the first 237 years of Spanish control, Chile was ruled from Lima, Peru. In 1778 Spain raised Chile's colonial status and gave Chile its own governor. A declaration of independence was made in 1818. This happened after Bernardo O'Higgins, Chile's champion of independence, helped lead an army against Spanish troops in Chile.

As can be seen in Figure 16-2 on this page, Chile's current political boundaries

316

LATIN AMERICA   UNIT 5

were the result of wars and treaties with neighboring countries. From 1879 to 1883, Chile went to war with Peru and Bolivia. Its victory won the Desert North area. With it Chile took away Bolivia's seacoast and gained control over the valuable nitrate deposits of the Atacama Desert. Chile's land area grew by almost one-third.

In 1881 Chile signed a treaty with Argentina. It gave Chile control over the Strait of Magellan—the waterway separating southernmost South America from Tierra del Fuego.

In the early 1900s, Chile's industry and economy grew. Part of the reason for this was the high demand for nitrates for weapons used during World War I.

In the 1960s the government of Chile began a program of land reform. Much land was given to the poor to farm as tenants. The government also tried to improve health care and housing for workers. The result of all this government spending, however, was inflation and high prices.

In 1973 a military junta (HOON tah) took over the government. A **junta** is a council that controls a government after power has been taken from the former leaders. Since the 1970s there has been great concern over the high prices, lack of growth in the economy, and unemployment. These problems continue to challenge the government of Chile.

CONTENT CHECK

1. **Identify:** Chile, Tierra del Fuego, Cape Horn, Andes Mountains, Ojos del Salado, Patagonian Andes, Bío-Bío River, Atacama Desert, Pacific Coastal Range, Chuquicamata, Santiago, Valparaíso, Concepción, Basques, Araucanian Indians, Bernardo O'Higgins.

2. **Define:** salt flats, homogeneous, nitrates, junta.

3. What landforms are found in Chile?

4. What causes the Atacama Desert to be so dry?

5. What four climate types are found in Chile?

6. What major economic region of Chile brings in the most export income? From what product?

7. **Challenge:** Nitrates have never been discovered in the Los Canales region of southern Chile. Do you think it probable that any will ever be found there? Explain your answer.

See the *TAE* for an *Objective 2* Activity.

2. PERU

Peru has more people—20.7 million—than any other Andean country. It also has the largest land area, with 496,224 square miles (1,285,219.2 sq km). Peru's people are mostly settled along its Pacific coast, although many live in the Andes Highlands. The name of this resource-rich country comes from an Indian word meaning "land of abundance." Peru was the center of the ancient Indian civilization of the Inca.

Peru is about three times the size of California.

2.1 Landscape and Climate

There are three physical regions in Peru. The Andes Highlands dominate the central part. A desert coastal plain covers the part west of the Andes, and a lowland river basin covers the area east of the mountains.

Landscape. The Andes Highlands cover about one-third of Peru's land area. In general the mountains lie in a northwest-to-southeast direction. They stretch from Peru's border in the north with Ecuador to its border in the south with Chile and Bolivia.

Along the border with Bolivia is Lake Titicaca (tee tee KAH kah). It takes up about

The Uros Indians of Peru live on floating islands made of reeds from Lake Titicaca. What is Lake Titicaca's notable characteristic?

Refer students to the Physical Regions map on page 312 to locate the Chala and the Altiplano.

3,200 square miles (8,288 sq km) and is 12,507 feet (3,812.1 m) above sea level. It is the world's highest navigable body of water.

A desert plain called the Chala (CHAH lah) follows most of Peru's 1,410-mile (2,269.2-km) coast. It makes up the northern arm of Chile's Atacama Desert. In the far south, a low cordillera rises along the coast.

About 50 irregularly flowing rivers cut across the Chala to the sea. Along the way the river water is used for irrigating farms and drinking water. As a result many rivers dry up before they reach the ocean.

On the eastern side of the Andes, large rivers such as the Ucayali (oo kah YAH lee) and Marañón (mah rahn YOHN) drain the highlands. At the confluence of these two rivers, the great Amazon River is formed. The thick vegetation of this area is part of the selvas—the rain forest of Brazil.

Climate. Although Peru lies in the tropics, the climate is far from uniform. The climate of the coast is desert—dry and warm.

This arid land gets less rain than the Sahara of North Africa. Cold air from the ocean, however, keeps temperatures in the Chala cool. Temperatures in the city of Lima (LEE mah), for example, vary from an average of 61°F (16.1°C) in winter to an average of 74°F (23.3°C) in summer. Lima receives less than 2 inches (5.1 cm) of rain a year. Every few years, however, it is drenched by heavy rains. These rains come from El Niño, a change in wind patterns and ocean currents.

The climate of the Andes Highlands varies, depending on altitude. In the narrow valleys at the bottom of Andean canyons between 1,000 feet (304.8 m) and 7,500 feet (2,286 m) above sea level, the climate is hot and humid. The climate is generally mild between 7,500 feet (2,286 m) and 11,500 feet (3,505.2 m) above sea level. Above that height temperatures are often cold all year.

Rain is heavy on the eastern slopes of the Andes leading to the Amazon River Basin. Because the climate is tropical rain forest, temperatures are warm or hot with high humidity. Rainfall is as much as 157 inches (398.8 cm) a year.

See the discussion of El Niño on page 88.

2.2 Economic and Cultural Patterns

Peru's physical features play a great part in its different economic activities. Its economic regions are similar to its physical regions. The people come from many different backgrounds and have different ways of life.

Economic Regions. Peru can be divided into three economic regions—Chala, Andean, and Montaña. Although much of the Chala is desert, it is the most important economic region of Peru. Many industrial and trade centers lie along the coast in **oases**—areas of fertile land amid desert. These oases draw their water from short rivers flowing toward the ocean from the Andes. In parts of the Chala that can be irrigated, corn, cotton, and sugarcane are grown.

Lima, the capital and largest city in Peru, is found in the Chala. Lima is known for production of textiles and fishmeal. Other oases include Chimbote (cheem BOH tay), where fishing, iron, and steel are economic goods, and Talara, where oil is refined.

At the place where the cold Humboldt Current mixes with warm waters off the coast of Peru and Ecuador, there is much plankton. **Plankton** is microscopic plant and animal life of the sea and an important food for fish. Because of plankton there are great numbers of fish in these waters. As a result Peru is one of the world's leading fishing countries and a major exporter of fishmeal.

Because there are so many fish, millions of sea birds gather on the coast and on offshore islands. Their droppings, known as **guano,** build up on the land. Because guano has a high amount of nitrogen, it is collected and used as fertilizer. At one time Peru was a leading exporter of guano. Today, however, chemical fertilizers have taken its place.

In the Andean region of Peru, people are generally farmers or miners. Most are Indians who live in villages far from the cities. They are subsistence farmers who grow chiefly potatoes, barley, and corn. They also keep llamas, sheep, cattle, and alpacas. Some farmers work as tenant farmers on large farms called **haciendas** (ah see EHN dahs).

Wheat is grown in the Altiplano (ahl tee PLAH noh)—the high tableland around Lake Titicaca. Although the altitude is high, this large body of water keeps the area's temperature warm enough for crops.

As Figure 16–3 on this page shows, the mines in the highlands of Peru produce copper, lead, silver, and gold. Cerro de Pasco (SEH rroh deh PAHS koh), Peru's most important mining center, at 14,300 feet (4,358.6 m), is one of the highest cities in the world.

LAND USE AND RESOURCES OF THE ANDEAN NATIONS

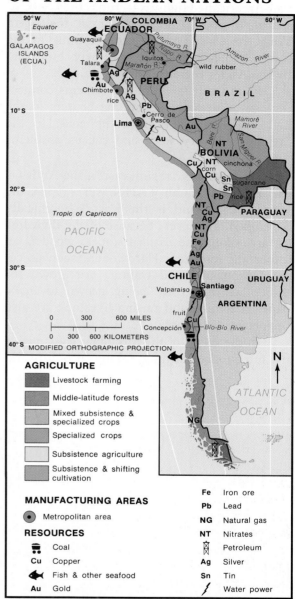

FIGURE 16–3
Little or no farming occurs along much of the coastal areas of Chile and Peru because it is desert country that is too dry to support profitable agriculture. Manufacturing areas are found in each country of this region, except Bolivia. Petroleum has become a valuable resource for the economies of Ecuador and Peru. In which Andean nations are nitrates found?

The mountains cause major transportation problems. A major paved road—the Pan-American Highway—runs only north-south. It goes from Ecuador in the north along the coastal plain through Chile in the south. Some other roads have been built that tie the Andes region to the Chala.

Four small separate rail systems connect the coastal area to the mining centers in the highlands. The rise from the coast to the highlands is very steep and causes problems for railroads.

The economic region east of the Andes is the Montaña (mohn TAHN yah). It has the fewest people and is the least economically developed. However, because of the high forest area along the eastern slopes, wood is an important resource. Hardwoods, such as cedar, mahogany, and walnut, are grown for trade. Softwoods are being grown to make paper. Farming and raising livestock are also important to the area.

In the selvas of the Montaña, Indians live by subsistence farming. Many also fish and gather nuts and fruits. They live in primitive homes made of thatch with dirt floors.

Near the source of the Amazon River is the largest city in the selvas—Iquitos (ee KEE tohs). This port is 2,300 miles (3,701.5 km) upstream from the Amazon's mouth.

With the recent oil boom near Iquitos, transportation between eastern Peru and the ocean has become even more important. The government built a new trans-Andean pipeline that carries oil from the interior lowlands to ports on the Pacific coast. A new railway follows the pipeline. A new highway is little by little opening up farmland along the eastern slopes of the Andes. Also the government has begun a project that brings water from Amazon headwaters into streams flowing toward the Pacific. This water has opened up more irrigated farmland. Many of these economic improvements have been successful, but they have also cost a lot of money. They have strained on the country's finances.

Culture. Peru's population is about 45 percent Indian, 37 percent mestizo, and only

From southern Chile to central Colombia, 3,000 miles (4,828 km), there are no passes below 8,000 feet (2,438.4 m). Railway passengers, especially tourists, struggle to fight sickness caused by altitude changes.

This Amazon riverfront is not a scene commonly associated with Peru. Eastern Peru, however, is at the headwaters of the Amazon River. Why has this region recently become important to the economic development of Peru?

In 1982-1983 El Niño caused severe droughts in some areas and devastating floods in others. Peru's economy was severely affected when schools of fish, one of Peru's major resources, were dramatically reduced.

about 15 percent European. There are also small numbers of people of African and Asian descent.

Most Peruvians speak Spanish, but a large number of Indians speak Quechua (KEHCH wah) or other Indian dialects. Nearly all of the people are Roman Catholics.

Social conditions are much different among the people of Peru than among Chile's population. In Peru there is a large social and economic gap between most Indians and those few of European descent. In part this is because of Spanish colonial rule.

Spain did not allow many to own land. As a result land remained in the hands of a few rich Europeans. Also Spain looked at its colonies as a way to get wealth and raw materials back to Spain. Little was done to start manufacturing and other economic activities that might compete with those in Spain. Spanish government and church officials controlled much of the native Indian population. Although a middle class has been growing, descendants of Europeans still rule and control most of the country's wealth. This social and economic gap has often caused bitterness and division in Peru.

In the 1960s the government began to try to instill a feeling of pride in the nation and its past. The government took over some businesses owned by foreigners, broke up many haciendas, and turned over the land to Indian farmers. But Peru's history and physical features keep the country from uniting. Distrust between highland Indians and coastal and urban Europeans goes on. And the Andes Mountains persist in dividing the people of western Peru from those in the east.

See the *TRB* for *Chapter 16 Reading* on the Chimu people of Peru.

2.3 Influences of the Past

Peru may have been settled by Indian groups as early as 18,000 years ago. By about 1200 AD, one group known as the Inca came to dominate the Andean region around their capital city of Cuzco (KOOS koh). In the 1400s this group claimed an empire more than 2,500 miles (4,023.4 km) long from Colombia to central Chile.

The Inca Empire had a strong central government. It built a major road system throughout the empire. Workers built bridges and dug tunnels. The roads allowed relatively fast communication and transportation. Beautiful cities were built all through the empire, and the Inca won fame for their great engineering feats.

In the 1530s the Inca Empire was interrupted at the height of its development. At

Creole art, combining Spanish baroque with the rich Incan heritage, appeared during the colonial period.

The heritage of the Inca Empire remains strong in Peru. This wooden vase was made by the Incas in the mid-1700s. When did the Incas come to dominate the Andean region?

Spanish cultural influence can be easily seen in the architecture of this Roman Catholic cathedral in Lima. Founded by the Spanish conqueror, Francisco Pizarro, Lima is the second oldest capital city in South America. What effects did the Spanish have in Peru?

Peruvian Indians were the first to grow potatoes.

that time Spanish **conquistadores** (kohn kees tah DOH rehs), or conquerors, arrived in what is now Peru. In a number of battles, the Inca were defeated and the Spanish conquest of Peru began.

The conquistadores of Spain settled mostly in the coastal area. They built the city of Lima in 1535. By 1542 Lima became the center of Spanish government in South America. From Lima Spanish settlers moved into the highlands looking for gold. They set up mining towns on the ruins of the Incan cities.

Before the Spanish arrived in Peru, the Indian population was estimated at 12 million. About 50 years after Spanish control, the numbers had dropped to 2 million. Many Indians died because they had no immunity to diseases brought by the Spanish. Some Indians escaped from slavery to remote areas of the Andes Highlands where most of the Indian people now live.

With the fast decline of the Indian population, the Spanish brought in Africans as slaves to work the large farms on the coast and in the mines of the highlands. Following the end of slavery, Asian workers were brought in as indentured servants. All of these groups intermarried to form the Peruvian coastal population.

Peru was one of the last Spanish colonial areas in South America to seek independence. Although Peru finally achieved independence in 1824, it was not officially recognized by Spain until 1879.

For much of the country's history, however, Peru has had an unstable government. There have been many revolutions and changes in government since the late 1800s. Since 1980, however, rather than rule by the military or a junta, the people voted for a president.

Free primary education is mandatory.

CONTENT CHECK

1. **Identify:** Peru, Lake Titicaca, Chala, Ucayali River, Marañón River, Lima, Humboldt Current, Altiplano, Pan-American Highway, Iquitos, Quechua, Inca, Cuzco.

2. **Define:** oases, plankton, guano, haciendas, conquistadores.

3. What are the three physical regions of Peru?

4. What landscape and climate does the Chala have?

5. What does plankton contribute to Peru's economy?

6. What economic activities are most common in Peru's Andean region?

7. Why has land transportation between eastern and western Peru been difficult in the past?

8. From what ethnic backgrounds do Peru's people come?

9. **Challenge:** Why do you think Peru's economic regions are so closely related to its physical regions?

3. BOLIVIA AND ECUADOR

The Andes Mountains divide the countries they cross as they divide the whole South American continent. Just as Peru's east and west are physically divided and its highland and lowland areas are divided by the Andes, so are Bolivia and Ecuador. In both countries, there are physical divisions based on geography as well as history.

For decades during the colonial period, Potosi, a town southwest of Sucre and site of vast silver deposits, was the largest city in the Americas.

3.1 Bolivia

Landlocked Bolivia lies south and east of Peru. It is north and east of Chile. Other countries that border Bolivia are located in the Atlantic region of Latin America. To Bolivia's north and east is Brazil and to its south is Argentina. Bolivia's neighbor to the southeast is the only other landlocked country of South America, Paraguay.

Bolivia's land area of 424,162 square miles (1,098,578.7 sq km) is about the size of California and Texas combined. It has three different landscapes. These are a high plateau, a small, rugged area of hills and valleys called the Yungas (YOON gahs), and lowland plains.

The high plateau is the continuation of the Altiplano of Peru. It is about 500 miles (804.5 km) long and 80 miles (128.7 km) wide in the southwest part of Bolivia. The average elevation is 12,000 feet (3,657.6 m). Because of the high altitude, the climate is cool. Average temperatures stay around 50°F (10°C).

As shown in Figure 16–4 on this page, both of Bolivia's capitals—La Paz (lah PAHS) and Sucre (SOO kray)—are located on the Altiplano. La Paz, Bolivia's largest city, is the seat of the country's government. Bolivia's national court system is in Sucre.

ANDEAN NATIONS OF SOUTH AMERICA

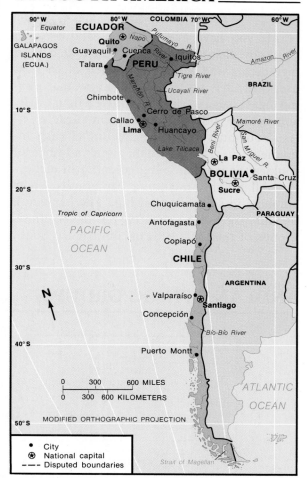

FIGURE 16-4

Large numbers of Indians in most of these nations, as well as isolation posed by the Andes Mountains, make for many regional rather than national ties. Which Andean nation has two national capitals?

See the TAE for an Objective 3 Activity.

Between the Andes and the lowland plains of Bolivia is a small area called the Yungas. Low hills, deep valleys, and gorges are found there. In the north the Yungas region has plateaus as high as 9,000 feet (2,743.2 m). In the south and east, the land spreads out, falls, and becomes part of the Gran Chaco. The climate of the Yungas is

USING GRAPHIC SKILLS

ANALYZING DATA FROM BAR GRAPHS

If you have ever tried to bake cookies, you know that you must first assemble certain ingredients and know how much of each to use. Still, it is not enough to know that mixing eggs, sugar, vanilla, butter, flour, salt, and baking soda will make good sugar cookies. You must know the amount of each ingredient in relation to the total number of cookies the combined ingredients will make.

All graphs, including bar graphs, show amounts in some relationship. The bar graph on this page shows data on the major ethnic groups of the four Andean countries of South America. The whole bar for each country represents its total population. Each bar is then divided to show the amounts, or numbers, in relation to the whole, of each ethnic group in the country. The bar graph shows not only the number of people in each ethnic group but also the percentage of the total population that the number represents.

To analyze data you must break apart the information that is presented in bar graphs into smaller bits of information. When you study them in this way, it will be easier to understand the whole. To analyze the information in the bar graph on this page, you must first examine the data in each bar separately. Then compare the data from each bar with the data from the other bars in the graph.

ANDEAN ETHNIC GROUPS

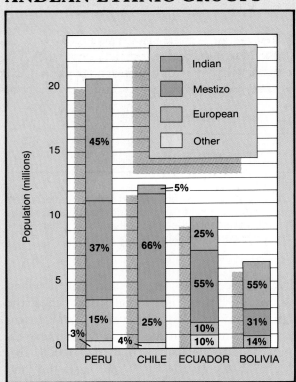

Data from *The 1987 World Almanac and Book of Facts* and *1987 World Population Data Sheet*, Population Reference Bureau, Inc.

Study the bar graph on the left. Then answer the questions that follow.

1. Which country has the largest percentage of European descent in its population?

2. In Peru, 37 percent of the total population are of what ethnic group? How many people does this percentage represent?

3. Which country has the smallest percentage of Indians? The largest percentage of Indians?

4. Which country has the largest number of Indians? How do you explain that it is not the country with the largest percentage of Indians?

5. **Challenge:** Which country has the most diverse ethnic population? The least diverse? In your opinion, how is ethnic diversity a benefit to the people of a country? How might it cause problems for the people?

Altiplano Indians have for centuries cultivated the coca plant. They chew the leaves to alleviate hunger pangs and the rigors of living in a harsh environment.

tropical savanna, with temperatures about 70°F (21.0°C) and heavy rains in the summer.

East of the Yungas and covering nearly 60 percent of Bolivia are lowland plains with many rivers and streams. In the north these plains are part of the Amazon River Basin and have thick tropical rain forests and swamps. Farther south the area opens up to grasslands and flat plains that often flood because of heavy summer rains. Rainfall is heavy, sometimes more than 80 inches (203.2 cm) a year. Temperatures average 77°F (25.0°C). The climate of these lowlands is tropical rain forest in the far north. Moving south, the climate becomes tropical savanna and, in the far south, humid subtropical.

In the highlands of Bolivia, there are many tin mines. Tin is Bolivia's chief export. When world prices of tin dropped in the mid-1980s, the economy of Bolivia suffered. Except for Haiti, Bolivia is the poorest country in Latin America.

Farming makes up the largest part of Bolivia's economy. Corn, potatoes, wheat, and quinoa are grown in the Yungas. **Quinoa** is a grain from which a kind of cereal is made.

In the lowlands there are some large cotton and sugarcane plantations. Cattle-raising is also important in this region. Oil and natural gas deposits have been discovered recently in the lowland plains. Because of the limited access from the highlands, Bolivia's lowlands have been slow to develop. Little by little, however, the plains are becoming less isolated from the rest of the country.

Most of Bolivia's 6.5 million people live in the highlands. As in Peru, more than one-half of Bolivia's people—about 55 percent—are of Indian descent. About 31 percent of Bolivians are mestizos. Most of the rest are of European descent.

The Spanish came to the area in the 1500s in search of silver and precious metals. Upon independence in 1825, when the area was named for its liberator Simón Bolívar, Bolivia stayed an important mining country. Today more than one-half of its national income is from exporting tin. It is estimated, however, that the illegal sale of coca, from which cocaine is made, may earn as much as three times the amount the sale of tin earns. This income does little to help the economy

Bolivia does not have diplomatic relations with Chile. Disagreements continue over Bolivia's lack of access to the sea and Chile's refusal to grant Bolivia a corridor to the Pacific.

Tin accounts for almost 60 percent of Bolivia's income from trade. In this picture, a Bolivian woman washes the raw metal after it is brought out of the mine. What is the economic danger when a country relies so heavily on only one export?

When tin prices drop, as they did in the late 1980s, state-owned mines are forced to close, and thousands of miners are laid off from their $30-a-month jobs.

The 14 Galápagos Islands are home to unique wildlife that has intrigued scientists since Charles Darwin visited them in the 1830s. The islands, located on the Equator, are in the path of the cold Humboldt Current, and temperatures there are more moderate than one might expect.

of Bolivia, however. The money stays in the hands of only a few people.

With the loss of its Pacific coast to Chile in the late 1800s, Bolivia became a landlocked mountain country. Foreign trade has had to be carried out through its neighbors.

Although Bolivia struggles with difficult economic conditions, the country has many natural resources. Careful development of these can do much to ease the poverty faced by many of its people.

Refer students to the map of Physical Regions of the Andean Nations on page 312 and the map of Land Use and Resources on page 319.

3.2 Ecuador

As its name indicates, the mainland of Ecuador (eh kwah DOHR) straddles the Equator. The small country of 109,483 square miles (283,560.7 sq km) is found in the northwestern corner of South America between Peru and Colombia. Also part of Ecuador are the Galápagos (gah LAH pah gohs) Islands. They are some 600 miles (965.6 km) west of the mainland in the Pacific Ocean.

About one-fourth of the country is made up of a western coastal plain and another one-fourth of highlands, which lie between two ranges of the Andes Mountains. The other one-half of Ecuador is an area of tropical rain forests east of the Andes.

The coastal plain, or Costa, reaches from the Colombian to the Peruvian border. Nearly one-half of Ecuador's 10 million people live along this low-lying belt. Also found in this area is Guayaquil (gwah yah KEEL), Ecuador's largest city and most important industrial and trade center. The Costa has two kinds of climate. The coast has a steppe climate, whereas farther inland, a tropical savanna climate is found.

Areas in the coastal plain support a rich agricultural economy. In this region Ecuador's most important cash crop, bananas, and cacao are grown.

The Andes Highlands, or Sierra, is made up of plateaus with high ridges and flat basins. The Sierra is found between two branches of the Andes Mountains. The climate of this area, like many parts of the Andes, depends on the elevation. Most of the plateaus are between 8,000 feet (2,438.4 m) and 10,000 feet (3,048 m) above sea level. The mountains that border these plateaus have several peaks that rise more than 19,000 feet (5,791.2 m) above sea level. One of these, Cotopaxi (koh toh PAHK see), is the highest active volcano in the world. At about 9,300 feet (2,834.6 m) above sea level is Quito (KEE toh), Ecuador's capital city.

Central Bank Museum of Quito is known for its collection of pre-Colombian art.

Street vendors attract visitors to Quito's old section of town. Quito is one of South America's most beautiful cities. What is Ecuador's other important city?

The economy of the Sierra is generally based on farming. In many of the higher basins, grains and potatoes are grown. There are rich mineral deposits in the region, but most have not been touched.

The basins of the highlands have many separate pockets of population. Most are dominated by a single city. Few people travel outside their area because crossing the high ridges of the Sierra is difficult. Most of the people in the highlands are descended from the first Indian people of the area.

The tropical rain forests of eastern Ecuador, called the Oriente (oh ree EHN teh), have few people and have not been used for most of Ecuador's history. The Oriente is made up of thick jungle and has a tropical rain forest climate.

In 1967 oil was discovered in the Oriente. Since that time, Ecuador has become an oil-exporting country. It is a member of OPEC—the Organization of Petroleum Exporting Countries—and oil now accounts for more than one-half of the country's income. As oil has become more important, the country's economy has become more closely tied to it. A series of earthquakes in 1987 caused a 30-mile (48.3-km) break in Ecuador's only oil pipeline. Damages to the country's economy are more than $1 billion.

The government and people of Ecuador also face other problems. Ecuador has a long history of unstable government. Social conflicts happen because many Indians are not treated as equals by many mestizos and people of European descent. Large numbers of Ecuador's population, especially Indians, live in poverty. Some of these conflicts are getting better as government and private groups work together to find solutions. They are trying to encourage a growing pride in Ecuador's diverse cultural heritage. With the added wealth of its rich mineral, energy, and agricultural resources, Ecuador could provide a better life for its people.

CONTENT CHECK

1. **Identify:** Bolivia, Yungas, La Paz, Sucre, Simón Bolívar, Ecuador, Galápagos Islands, Costa, Guayaquil, Sierra, Cotopaxi, Quito, Oriente, OPEC.

2. **Define:** quinoa.

3. What are the two capitals of Bolivia?

4. What is the most important export product of Bolivia?

5. Why have Bolivia's lowlands been slow to develop?

6. In what part of Bolivia do most of the people live?

7. What are the three major physical regions of Ecuador?

8. What is the Sierra's major economic activity?

9. What important mineral resource has contributed to Ecuador's wealth in recent years?

10. **Challenge:** What problems do you think landlocked countries such as Bolivia face?

Ecuador's literate citizens between the ages of 18 and 65 are required to vote.

CONCLUSION

There are some important cultural differences among the Andean Nations of South America. Chile is more European in culture than the other three countries. In fact, Peru, Ecuador, and Bolivia, along with Paraguay, have sometimes been grouped together as the "Indian" countries of South America.

In spite of their differences in culture, the Andean countries as a whole are rich in natural resources. However, the same land containing the resources is also the greatest obstacle to development for the region and its people. Overcoming the problems created by the great Andes Mountains is the region's greatest challenge.

CHAPTER REVIEW

SUMMARY

1. The countries of the Andean region are Chile, Peru, Bolivia, and Ecuador. They all lie along the Pacific Ocean except Bolivia, which is landlocked.
2. The Andes Mountains stretch through the region and make transportation and communication hard. Elevation affects climate, which varies from tropical moist to dry to highland.
3. All of the Andean countries were once colonies of Spain, use Spanish for the official language, and have suffered from instability in government.
4. All of the Andean countries are rich in natural resources. Each relies on one or more of these for most of its income.
5. There are large Indian populations in Peru, Bolivia, and Ecuador. In Bolivia, more than one-half of the people are Indians who do not speak Spanish. Chile is the most European of the Andean countries. Most people are Roman Catholics.

Answers to the following questions can be found on page T177.

REVIEWING VOCABULARY

Number your paper from 1 to 10. Beside each number write the letter of the vocabulary word that best describes the numbered phrase. You will not use all the terms.

a. conquistadores
b. archipelago
c. haciendas
d. homogeneous
e. nitrates
f. quinoa
g. plankton
h. salt flats
i. cape
j. junta
k. guano
l. oases

1. Spanish conquerors in Latin America
2. nitrogen-rich droppings of birds
3. low-lying areas where bodies of water have dried up, leaving salt deposits
4. water-soluble mineral used in making fertilizers and explosives
5. sharing similar characteristics
6. large farms in Peru
7. microscopic sea life that is fish food
8. isolated, fertile areas within a desert that have water
9. cereal grain
10. land that juts out from a larger land area into a body of water

REMEMBERING THE FACTS

1. What is the name of the extremely dry desert in northern Chile?
2. What economic activity is common among Chile's Lakes region?
3. What is the largest Andean nation in size and population?
4. What Indian civilization was centered at Cuzco in today's Peru?
5. Which of the Andean nations is landlocked?
6. What physical features are in Ecuador's Oriente region?

UNDERSTANDING THE FACTS

1. Why do rivers in Chile tend to flow in an east-west direction?
2. What are some factors that have contributed to slow economic development of Chile's Los Canales region?
3. Of what value has the Desert North been to Chile since it gained this territory from its neighbors?
4. What economic improvements has Peru invested its income in recently?
5. How do you explain that the majority of Peru's people live in the area of the coastal plain?
6. Why is the social and economic gap between Peru's Indians and Europeans somewhat related to Peru's past colonial rule by the Spanish?
7. What recent developments have increased the importance of the tropical rain forest in Ecuador to the nation's economy?

THINKING CRITICALLY AND CREATIVELY

1. If freak weather patterns brought heavy rains to northern Chile for several years, what kind of economic consequences might there be for the country?
2. Transportation is much better developed in the Central region of Chile than in Los Canales in the south. What problems might confront a highway builder who was asked to design a freeway through the Los Canales section?
3. Bolivia earns most of its export income from tin. Chile earns most of its export income from copper. Though both are heavily dependent on income from the export of just one product, Bolivia tends to be in more serious economic trouble when the price of tin goes down than Chile when the price of copper goes down. How can this be explained?
4. **Challenge:** All of the Andean nations produce some oil. When world oil prices go down, producing nations suffer. If prices dropped, which of the Andean nations do you think would be hurt the most? Why do you think so?
5. **Challenge:** The area around Guayaquil, Ecuador, produces bananas. But the area around Quito, located close to the Equator, produces none. Why are there no bananas grown there?

REINFORCING GRAPHIC SKILLS

Study the bar graph on page 324. Then answer the questions that follow.

1. In which two countries do mestizos make up more than one-half of the country's total population?
2. **Challenge:** What ethnic groups do you think would be considered in the "Other" category? Make a hypothesis about why Ecuador has a larger percentage of other ethnic groups than the other three Andean countries. Then make a hypothesis about why Bolivia has no significant number of other ethnic groups among its total population.

SUMMARY

1. The four regions in the culture area of Latin America extend from Mexico to the southern tip of South America.
2. Two major mountain ranges dominate Mexico and extend into Central America. Highlands also cover the Caribbean region. The topography of South America is dominated by the Andes Mountains in the west and the Amazon Basin in the northeast.
3. The growing population of Mexico and Central America is concentrated in interior areas. South America's people are concentrated around the coasts.
4. Latin America was the scene of early Indian civilizations. The area is known for its cultural diversity. However, Spanish and Portuguese cultures dominate much of the culture. The Spanish language and the Roman Catholic Church are two of the area's chief unifying elements.
5. The area has many political problems— boundary disputes, internal disorder, and political instability.

Answers to the following questions can be found on page T181.

THINKING ABOUT THE UNIT

1. Some geographers and anthropologists speak of two culture areas in Latin America—Middle America and South America—instead of one. Do you think that the countries of Latin America have enough in common to form a single culture area? Hold an informal debate on this issue.
2. Use the maps on pages 650-651 to answer the following questions: (a) Is Quito, Ecuador, or Boston, Massachusetts, farther east?; (b) Is Buenos Aires, Argentina, or Miami, Florida, farther from the Equator?; (c) Is Lima, Peru, or Washington, D.C., farther west?; (d) Which Central American capital is closest to the Tropic of Cancer?; (e) Which major South American city is closest to the Tropic of Capricorn? (f) Which major South American city is directly south of Miami, Florida?

SUGGESTED UNIT ACTIVITIES

1. Use a world almanac, atlas, or other current reference book to gather average monthly temperature and rainfall data for the following cities: Mexico City, Mexico; Manaus, Brazil; Santiago, Chile; Montevideo, Uruguay; and La Paz, Bolivia. Make climographs and compare the data with the average monthly temperature and rainfall of your hometown.
2. Using information in this book and in other reference books, prepare a map of Latin America's mineral wealth. Color-code the various resources on your map.
3. Pretend that you are a European immigrant who came during the days of colonial settlement to a Latin American country. Write a letter to a friend or relative in Europe describing your new world.

DEVELOPING GEOGRAPHY SKILLS

CLASSIFYING INFORMATION

Geographers must work with a lot of information. They find this task easier when they organize or classify the information. One way to do this is to put the information into a table or a *chart*. A chart presents information in graphic form.

There are several different ways to set up a chart. Information does not always have to be presented in the same way. Look, for example, at the two charts below. The same information appears in both charts. It simply is classified in different forms. But no matter what form a chart takes, four basic steps can be followed in setting it up:

1. Determine what information has to be classified.
2. Decide the major categories to be used in the chart.
3. Write the major categories across the top of a piece of paper.
4. Fill in the information under the proper category.

For additional practice in the skill of classifying information, use the information in Chapter 15, plus information from two other sources to make a chart that shows how physical and cultural features of Brazil and Argentina compare.

Economic and Cultural Characteristics of Guatemala, Nicaragua, and Panama

Chart 1

COUNTRY	POPULATION	ETHNIC GROUPS	ECONOMIC ACTIVITIES	IMPORTANT CROPS
Guatemala	8.4 million	Indian and mestizo	agricultural	coffee, chicle
Nicaragua	3.5 million	mestizo	agricultural, industrial	cotton, fruit, bananas, sugar, coffee, corn, rice
Panama	2.3 million	70% mestizo; 30% blacks, Indians, European descent	agricultural, industrial, service	bananas, rice, sugarcane, coffee

Chart 2

GUATEMALA	NICARAGUA	PANAMA
8.4 million	3.5 million	2.3 million
Indian and mestizo	mestizo	70% mestizo; 30% blacks, Indians, European descent
agricultural	agricultural, industrial	agricultural, industrial, service
coffee, chicle	cotton, bananas, fruit, coffee, sugar, corn, rice	bananas, rice, sugarcane, coffee

EUROPE

UNIT 6

The continent of Europe is located at the western edge of the huge landmass of Eurasia. Europe is smaller in size than any other continent except Australia. However, it has many different landscapes and climates. Europe is made up of two culture areas, Western Europe and Eastern Europe and the Soviet Union.

Europe's countries are grouped into four major regions. Northwest Europe is the most industrialized. Mediterranean Europe is the home of ancient civilizations. Eastern Europe is made up of many countries politically and economically tied to the Soviet Union. The Soviet Union is Earth's largest country, lying partly in Europe and partly in Asia.

For centuries Europe was a world leader. Its countries ruled other lands around the globe and controlled much of the world's trade. European people settled all over the world, carrying with them their ideas and ways of living. Today Europe continues to be important in world affairs.

Schönbuhel castle on the Danube River

Point out to students that the highlighted areas on the world map inset represent the two culture areas studied in Unit 6. One is Western Europe. The other is Eastern Europe and the Soviet Union.

CHAPTER 17

Point out to students that for centuries Northwest Europe was considered the political, economic, and cultural power of the world.

Castle in the Bourgogne region of France

NORTHWEST EUROPE

In this chapter you will learn—

- What landscapes and climates are in Northwest Europe.
- How economic and cultural patterns of Northwest Europe are the same and how they are different.
- How the past has influenced Northwest Europe.

Refer students to the map of Western Europe on page 652. Then point out that since early times, an important shipping industry developed because of Western Europe's many natural harbors.

INTRODUCTION

Northwest Europe includes 17 countries that lie north of the Pyrenees (PIHR uh NEEZ) and Alps mountain ranges and west of the Elbe (EHL buh) River on the European continent. They are the United Kingdom, Ireland, France, Monaco, Andorra, West Germany, Iceland, Norway, Sweden, Denmark, Finland, the Netherlands, Belgium, Luxembourg, Austria, Liechtenstein, and Switzerland. The island of Greenland, located in the North Atlantic Ocean, physically is a part of North America. However, it is viewed as part of Northwest Europe because of its political ties to Denmark.

The landscapes of the region include plains, highlands, and plateaus called uplands. These are shown in Figure 17–1 on page 336. Waterways play important parts in the landscapes of Northwest Europe. The Atlantic and Arctic oceans, the Mediterranean and Baltic seas, and several smaller bodies of water give the region a long coastline. Almost 80 percent of Northwest Europe's people live within 100 miles (160.9 km) of the coast. Many fine harbors and rivers are found in Northwest Europe. During the 1500s and 1600s, some of the countries formed shipping fleets and powerful navies. Today many people of Northwest Europe still make their living with the help of waterways and the ocean.

Water also affects Northwest Europe's climate. Most of the region lies in the middle and high latitudes. However, it enjoys a moist, mild climate because of the effects of the Atlantic Ocean, Gulf Stream, and prevailing westerlies.

This weather pattern covers a small land area. Northwest Europe is only a little larger than the part of the United States east of the Mississippi River. None of its countries can be called large. However, they have played an important role in world history. Modern industry and democratic government began in Northwest Europe. This region also has set global trends in diplomacy, learning, science, and the arts.

Today all of the nations of Northwest Europe are democracies. They have strong industrialized economies that support large urban populations. The people are well-educated, highly skilled, and enjoy a high standard of living. After centuries of war, the countries of Northwest Europe have recently learned to cooperate with one another. They and some of the countries of Mediterranean Europe have formed a trading alliance called the European Economic Community, or Common Market. This has helped the prosperity of the region.

The huge, educated population of the EEC countries contributes to Europe's economic strength.

1. BRITISH ISLES

The British Isles are Europe's largest group of islands. They lie in the Atlantic Ocean northwest of the European continent. The two largest islands of the British Isles are Britain and Ireland. These islands have large

On the map below, point out the relative location of the British Isles to the North Atlantic Current. Because of the warming effects of this current, the British Isles enjoy much milder winter temperatures than parts of eastern North America that lie at about the same latitudes.

PHYSICAL REGIONS OF NORTHWEST EUROPE

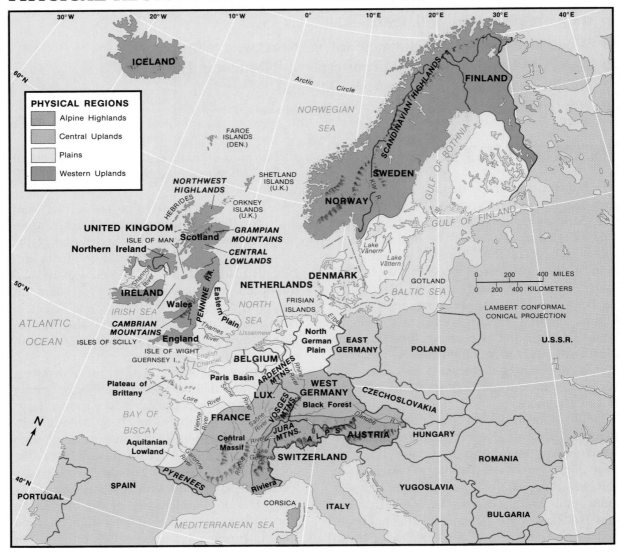

FIGURE 17-1
Land corridors, seas, and rivers interconnect Northwest Europe's landscapes and encourage interaction. Which physical region is the largest in this area?

See the *TRB* for *Chapter 17 Reading* on Scotland.

populations and are very modern. Their location has also influenced the history and development of this region.

The British Isles are made up of two independent countries. They are the Republic of Ireland, called Ireland, and the United Kingdom of Great Britain and Northern Ireland. The United Kingdom is often called Great Britain or Britain. It is made up of England, Wales, Scotland, and Northern Ireland. Northern Ireland and the Republic of Ireland are both located on the island of Ireland. England, Wales, and Scotland are located on the island of Britain.

EUROPE   UNIT 6

The southern part of the Scottish Highlands is important as the heart of Scotland's well-developed wool industry.

Because of its quiet beauty and mild climate, the Southwest Peninsula attracts vacationers all through the year.

1.1 Landscape and Climate

The British Isles have many kinds of landscapes, such as rugged mountains, fertile plains, deep green valleys, and rocky coastlines. They enjoy a mild climate influenced by the sea.

Landscape. The landscape of the British Isles is made up of highlands and lowlands. On the island of Britain, the Northwest Highlands, also called the Scottish Highlands, cover most of northern Scotland. Over much of the highlands is **moor,** a wild, treeless landscape with grasses and heather, a small shrub with tiny purplish pink flowers. Because of the poor soil, the few people living in the area fish or raise sheep.

Inside the Northwest Highlands are narrow, deep valleys called **glens** and long, narrow lakes called **lochs.** The glens and lochs were formed centuries ago by glaciers. Glaciers also cut **firths,** or funnel-shaped bays, along Scotland's coast. Some deeply-cut areas on the coast form sea channels that are between hundreds of small islands and the Scottish mainland.

South of the Northwest Highlands lie the Central Lowlands and Southern Uplands of Scotland. The Central Lowlands are a gently rolling plain divided by the Clyde, Forth, and Tay rivers. These lowlands have Scotland's best farmland and most of its people and industries. The Southern Uplands are groups of low hills that stretch south to the English border. They are used for sheep grazing.

In England, the Pennine (PEHN EYN) Range stretches north to south and forms the "backbone" of the country. West of the Pennines are the small Cheshire Plain and the Lake District. The Lake District is a scenic area of sparkling, blue lakes and low, green mountains.

South and east of the Pennines are the English Lowlands. They include flat land along the coast and broad, rolling plains inland. The English Lowlands are a part of the Great European Plain that stretches from Britain south to France and east through Belgium, the Netherlands, and West Germany to the Soviet Union. The soils in the English Lowlands are the most fertile in Britain. Coal deposits are also found in this area. As a result, the English Lowlands have most of the United Kingdom's farming, industries, and population.

England's most important river, the Thames (TEHMZ), flows 215 miles (346 km) across the English Lowlands and into the North Sea. London, the United Kingdom's capital and largest city, is on the Thames. It acts as a magnet, drawing trade and business from all parts of the world.

Southwest of the English Lowlands is the Southwest Peninsula, an area of high plains, hills, and valleys. Along the coast are high cliffs that tower over tiny fishing villages.

In the northern part of Wales, the Cambrian Mountains dominate the landscape.

See the TAE for an Objective 1 Activity.

A hiker enjoys a walk along a lake in the Cambrian Mountains in Wales. Wales is famous for its rugged mountains and green valleys. What are some other landscape features found in the British Isles?

STRANGE BUT TRUE

BANANAS IN BRITAIN

When people think of a place where bananas are grown, they usually think of the tropics. Bananas need warm weather to grow, such as the type of climate found in Central America or Africa. When they think of bananas in Britain, most people imagine them in the produce section of a store or growing in a greenhouse.

One place in the British Isles where the climate allows bananas to be grown outside is the Isles of Scilly. This group of about 50 small islands and even more *islets*, or very small islands, lies about 28 miles (45 km) off the southwestern coast of Britain and has a mild climate.

Only five of the islands have people living on them. The largest island is St. Mary's, which is only about 2.5 miles (4 km) long and 1.5 miles (2.4 km) wide. The islands have a mild climate, despite their northern location, because of the North Atlantic Current and Gulf Stream.

Tropical plants of all kinds can be grown in the Isles. There are palm trees, eucalyptus trees, cinnamon plants, and others that come from areas near the Equator. Many of these plants were first brought to the Isles of Scilly by sailors in the 1800s. The most famous gardens are found at Tresco Abbey on the island of Tresco.

Conditions in the islands are ideal for growing flowers. They are shipped to the mainland of the United Kingdom during the winter months. People living on the islands earn much of their yearly income from the sale of flowers.

The flower season in the Isles of Scilly begins in November. At that time, narcissus plants bloom. They are easily sold in London, which is damp and cool. Beginning in January, daffodils are harvested. Later, other kinds of flowers are picked and shipped. The season ends after the iris plants bloom in May.

The flowers and the mild climate of the Isles of Scilly attract visitors. People come from other parts of Britain by sea and air. They like to see the flowers and to visit Hugh Town, as pictured above, the largest town in the islands. In Hugh Town there is a museum showing objects made by the early people who settled the islands—one of the first places in the United Kingdom to be settled.

1. Where are the Isles of Scilly located?
2. Why can tropical plants be grown outdoors in the Isles of Scilly?
3. How do people who live on the islands earn their living?
4. Why do many tourists visit the islands?

These mountains are higher and more rugged than the Northwest Highlands of Scotland. In southern Wales, there are high coastal plains and deep river valleys. The land is too steep to farm but has many coal deposits. This region has most of the industry and people of Wales.

The island of Ireland is made up of lowlands, mountains, and coastal plains. Lowlands in the central part of Ireland have forests and farmland. They also have *peat bogs*, or wet ground with decaying plants that can be used for fuel. Along the coasts, the land rises in rocky hills and mountains. In certain coastal areas, however, there are plains, such as those around Dublin, the Irish capital, on the eastern side of the island.

Climate. The British Isles lie between 50° and 60° north latitude and have a middle-latitude marine climate. This means that in spite of being so far north, the islands have a mild climate. Air blowing over the North Atlantic Current from the west warms up and moves in toward the land. In winter this keeps temperatures in the British Isles between 35°F (1.7°C) and 45°F (7.2°C). In summer it keeps temperatures between 51°F (10.6°C) and 73°F (22.8°C).

The sea winds also bring plenty of rain. Precipitation there does not fully evaporate because temperatures are not high enough. As a result, foggy, damp weather is common all through the British Isles.

In general, the southern parts of the United Kingdom are more prosperous than the northern areas.

1.2 Economic and Cultural Patterns

Similar economic and cultural patterns are found all over the British Isles. But there are also differences both within the United Kingdom and between the United Kingdom and the Republic of Ireland.

The United Kingdom is one of the world's major manufacturing and trading

Ireland is called the Emerald Isle because of the rich green color of its countryside and gently rolling hills. What is the capital of Ireland?

countries. Its workers make cars, chemicals, clothing, ships, and machinery for export to other countries. The United Kingdom depends on trade for its survival. Because of the many highlands, good farmland is limited. The country grows only about half of its food needs. Except for coal, low-grade iron ore, oil, and natural gas, the United Kingdom has few natural resources. Thus, many food products and raw materials must be imported.

Large quantities of coal and iron helped make the United Kingdom the world's first industrialized country. However, in recent years, some supplies of coal and other resources have been used up. Also, Britain's industries have been slow to modernize. Thus, the United Kingdom's economy has not grown as fast as those of other industrialized countries. This has made the United Kingdom less of a world economic power.

In spite of economic setbacks, the British have benefited from the discoveries of oil in the North Sea. The United Kingdom now has enough oil to meet all of its needs and to sell

LONDON: CULTURAL CENTER

London, both the capital and largest city of the United Kingdom, serves as the nation's cultural center. It gives the people of the United Kingdom and much of the English-speaking world a place to visit for many intellectual and artistic activities.

What makes a city a cultural center? Size is a factor. Geographers have observed that it takes a varying number of people to support certain functions and services. They call this number the *threshold population*. For example, because many people eat bread every day, even the smallest villages will have successful stores that sell bread. On the other hand, some kinds of surgical operations are very specialized and not many people need them. Surgeons who are skilled in these operations must have their offices in cities where there are many patients for them. Only very large cities have enough people.

Cultural events generally need a very high threshold population. For example, at any one time, only a small part of the total population wants to go to a play. It takes a large population, therefore, to have enough people to keep theaters in business.

Another factor that is important in making a city a cultural center is its location in relation to other cities and towns around it. An important theory in urban geography, called the *central place theory*, says that there are some large cities that are used by more than just the people who live in them. These cities become centers for certain goods and services. People in smaller towns and cities all around these central places are willing to travel many more miles, for example, to buy new cars or to talk with heart specialists.

Large cities are able to offer more kinds of activities than most smaller cities can. London is such a city. Its influence as a cultural center goes well beyond the city boundaries.

London is the center of book publishing in the United Kingdom. From London, books are distributed all through the country and the English-speaking world. London's Fleet Street is the headquarters of most of the morning newspapers in the United Kingdom.

Broadcasting is also centered in London. The government-owned British Broadcasting Corporation (BBC) and the independent commercial networks have their major studios and production offices there.

London is an important center for music, dance, and theater. The city supports five major symphony orchestras. The Royal Ballet and Royal Opera are admired all through the world. In London there are more than 50 theaters where plays are performed.

More than 25 large museums are in London, including the British Museum, the world's largest. Its enormous library receives a copy of every book published in the country. Scholars throughout the world use its reading rooms, one of which is pictured above.

1. What two factors help make a city a cultural center?

2. What cultural activities are centered in London?

Both London and Dublin are viewed as centers of the English-speaking world for theater, music, literature, and other arts.

To encourage the arts, Ireland does not tax the income of professional writers and other such artists.

to other countries. However, the supply may run out by the year 2000. In the meantime, the United Kingdom will need to use its oil profits to modernize its economy.

Unlike the United Kingdom, Ireland is a farming country. Its most important natural resources are its rich soil and pasturelands. Ireland grows enough food to feed its people and to sell overseas.

Since the 1920s Ireland has built up its manufacturing. In recent years the government has encouraged other countries to build factories in the country. Yet now, as in the past, there are few jobs. With one of the youngest populations in Europe, Ireland has seen many of its young people emigrate to other countries for better jobs.

Culturally, the two nations of the British Isles share certain features. Both the United Kingdom and Ireland are cut off from Europe by the sea and have been protected from invasion. This has given them a sense of security that has helped the two nations develop their own ways of life. Both the British and the Irish respect the rights of the individual and value tradition. Another common trait is the English language, which is the major language spoken in the United Kingdom and Ireland. Both countries are especially known for their writers and poets.

Noticeable cultural differences do exist in the British Isles. The United Kingdom has about 56.8 million people, while Ireland has a population of 3.5 million. The United Kingdom is one of the most densely populated countries in the world. Ireland is much less crowded. The United Kingdom is urban, but Ireland still has a large rural population.

There are other differences. Religion plays a more important part in Irish life than it does in British life. Nearly 95 percent of the Irish people are Roman Catholic. Most of them attend church regularly. In the United Kingdom, which is mostly Protestant, fewer people attend church regularly.

Even inside the United Kingdom, cultural differences keep groups of people apart. For example, most of the people think of themselves as British. However, they also view themselves as English, Welsh, Scots, or Irish. England and Scotland have separate Protestant national churches. They and the other two parts of the United Kingdom have their own legal and educational systems.

Explain that some people in Ireland and Scotland speak Gaelic, a language from early British history.

1.3 Influences of the Past

The British and the Irish share common histories. Between 1600 and the early 1900s, the United Kingdom was one of the richest and most powerful countries in the world. During this period, the island of Ireland was ruled by the United Kingdom. Since the early 1900s, the United Kingdom has lost power in world affairs, and the southern part of Ireland has become the Republic of Ireland.

Early History. Early settlers of the British Isles were Celts who came from mainland Europe about 500 BC. The Romans invaded and ruled much of the British Isles from 43 AD until the 400s AD. Ireland was not taken over by the Romans.

After the Romans, German peoples—Angles, Saxons, and Jutes—moved into the island of Britain. The southern part of Britain became known as Angle-land, or England. The early English language can be traced to these German groups. The Celts (SEHLTS), forced out of Britain by the invaders, moved into Ireland. Groups of them also lived in Scotland, which became its own kingdom.

In 1066 French-speaking Normans took over England. Their influence made England's government strong and helped develop a common law for the whole country. In time, Normans and the local population formed a united nation. Their descendants make up most of the population of the United Kingdom today.

Point out to students that, today, the monarch of the United Kingdom *reigns* but does not *rule*. Parliament is the country's real governing authority.

After much conflict, the most populous British colony of all—India—became self-governing in 1947.

COMMONWEALTH OF NATIONS

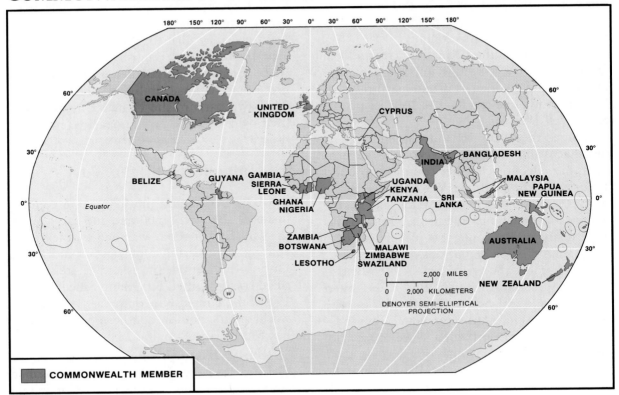

FIGURE 17-2

The British Commonwealth represents a quarter of the world's population and one-third of its nation-states. Members are united by the English language and a common historical past. How many countries belong to the Commonwealth?

See the *TAE* for an *Objective 1* Activity.

The British Empire. During the rule of Queen Elizabeth I in the late 1500s, England became a major trading and sea power. Like other European lands, it began to set up colonies in other parts of the world. The earliest of these colonies was Ireland.

During the 1700s England and Scotland became the United Kingdom. Also, during the next 200 years, the British developed **parliamentary democracy,** a form of government in which the people rule through Parliament, or the legislature. However, in accepting democracy, the British still kept their royal family as a link to their past. Other countries used the British government as a model in developing their own democracies.

Meanwhile, British inventors and scientists sparked the Industrial Revolution. The United Kingdom became the first nation in the world to build an industrial economy. New colonies added in the 1800s gave Britain raw materials and bought goods made in British factories. Because it stretched to all parts of the world, it was said that the sun never set on the British Empire.

The power of the British Empire began to decline in the 1900s. World Wars I and II were very costly for the British. After World War II, many colonies broke away to become independent countries. The British Empire became the Commonwealth of Nations. This group of former British colonies and the

342

EUROPE UNIT 6

United Kingdom work together in trade, education, and other areas. Today, as shown in Figure 17-2 on page 342, there are 48 member countries. Many of them are **dominions,** having their own governments but with the British king or queen as their chief of state. The United Kingdom now includes about two million people who have come from many of the Commonwealth countries.

One of the earliest countries to gain independence from the United Kingdom was Ireland. For years most Irish had opposed British rule. In 1921 the southern part of Ireland became the Irish Free State, a dominion with close ties to the United Kingdom. In 1948 it broke away completely from the United Kingdom and became the Republic of Ireland. Northern Ireland, with its largely Protestant population, has remained part of the United Kingdom. Many Catholics in Northern Ireland, however, oppose British rule. They want Northern Ireland to join the Republic of Ireland.

Share with students information on Great Britain's royalty from the *TRB's* Section 1 Extending the Lesson.

CONTENT CHECK

1. **Identify:** British Isles, Britain, Ireland, Republic of Ireland, United Kingdom, Northwest Highlands, Pennine Range, English Lowlands, Thames River, London, Cambrian Mountains, Dublin, North Atlantic Current, Celts, Normans, Commonwealth of Nations.

2. **Define:** moor, glens, lochs, firths, parliamentary democracy, dominions.

3. What are the two largest islands of the British Isles?

4. What are the independent countries of the British Isles?

5. What are the two general landscapes of the British Isles?

6. What climate type do the British Isles have?

7. Which country of the British Isles is the most industrialized?

8. What cultural traits do the two nations of the British Isles share? How do they differ culturally?

9. **Challenge:** What steps might the United Kingdom take to improve its economy? Can the United Kingdom once again become a world economic power? Why or why not?

See the *TAE* for an *Objective 2* Activity.

2. FRANCE

The French Republic is a six-sided country on the western edge of Europe. It is a little smaller than Texas. However, it is the second largest European country after the Soviet Union and the largest in Northwest Europe. France's land area includes the island of Corsica in the Mediterranean Sea. Two small countries—Monaco and Andorra—are located along France's southern borders. Andorra is in the Pyrenees near Spain. Monaco is along the Mediterranean coast near Italy.

France is bordered by both sea and land areas. As a result, all through its history France has been a sea and a land power.

Because the Pyrenees are more difficult to cross than the Alps, France has historically traded more with Italy than with Spain.

2.1 Landscape and Climate

France has many different kinds of landscape. The south and east are made up of mountains and plateaus. The north and west are flat or made up of low hills. France's climate is influenced by the Atlantic Ocean to the west, the Mediterranean Sea to the south, and the landmass of Europe to the east.

Landscape. Major mountain chains or rivers in France form natural boundaries with nearby countries. In the southwest, the Pyrenees form the border between France and Spain. These peaks are too rugged to farm and have few people. In the southeast, the Alps separate France from Italy and Switzerland. The Alps are the largest mountain system in Europe. Mont Blanc, the highest point in Northwest Europe, is 15,771 feet (4,807 m) above sea level. It is located in France near the Italian and Swiss borders. Rivers in the Alps provide electric power to the area. They also attract many tourists, who ski on the mountain slopes.

Two other mountain chains—the Vosges (VOHZH) and the Jura—lie near France's border with Switzerland and West Germany. They are lower and more rounded than the Alps. In the east the mountains go down to the Rhine River, which separates France and West Germany. The Rhine is the busiest waterway in Europe. On the steep slopes along the Rhine River are vineyards that make eastern France an important wine-making region.

In the south central part of France is an area called Central Massif. This area has mountains and high plateaus, which are really an ancient mountain system that has been worn down over many thousands of years. The soils are poor in the Central Massif, and the region has few people.

South of the Central Massif are the Mediterranean Lowlands. This fertile area is known for its fruit, vegetables, and wines. Marseille (mar SAY), France's largest seaport, is the leading city of the Mediterranean Lowlands. The area also includes the Riviera, a resort area famous for its mild climate, beautiful flowers, and fine beaches.

The Northern French Plain covers the north of France. Another plain, the Aquitanian Lowland, extends along the west coast as far south as the Pyrenees. These are parts of the Great European Plain. Inside the Northern French Plain is Paris, France's capital and largest city. The area around Paris is drained by the Seine (SAYN) River and several other waterways. The plains regions of France are known for industry, trade, and agriculture.

Climate. France generally has two climates—Mediterranean and middle-latitude marine. Because the south of France is warmed and dried by winds from the Mediterranean Sea, it has a Mediterranean climate. So the area has hot, dry summers and mild, rainy winters. The rest of France has a marine climate. France's west coast is affected by the warm winds blowing across the North Atlantic Current. Like the British Isles, this area enjoys a mild climate with plenty of rain. Paris, for example, has from 11 to 17 days of precipitation most months.

The National Profiles chart in the Appendix contains additional statistics on France.

2.2 Economic and Cultural Patterns

France is both an industrialized and an agricultural country. Since World War II, the French government has modernized its economy. One way it did this was to use new ways of manufacturing. Another way was for the government to run some businesses. Because of these and other changes, the French people enjoy a high standard of living.

More than 90 percent of France's land is fertile. French farmers grow many kinds of crops. In the south of the country, as shown in Figure 17–3 on page 346, grapes, olives, and citrus fruits are grown. In the north, the leading agricultural products are dairy products, livestock, wheat, barley, sugar beets, potatoes, and apples. In addition to its fertile soil, France has other natural resources. Coal, iron, and uranium are France's most important mineral resources. Along with hydroelectric power, France is considered a world leader in the use of nuclear plants to generate electricity. It also has many oil refineries, but most of France's oil is still imported from the Middle East.

Although its farming and natural resources are important, France relies mostly on its industry and trade. France's industries produce cars, airplanes, electronic goods, chemicals, clothing, furniture, wine, and perfume. Many French goods are sold to foreign countries. Profits from these sales make it easier for France to pay for its imports.

France's farms and industries are helped by a good transportation system. France's waterways carry about 101.4 million tons (92 million metric tons) of goods a year. The country also has about 22,680 miles (36,500 km) of railroads. A high-speed line called TGV—*très grande vitesse*—French for "very great speed"—runs between Paris and cities in the south of France. Trains on this line are the fastest in the world. They can go over 200 miles (321.9 km) per hour.

More than 73 percent of France's 55.6 million people live in urban areas. The metropolitan area of Paris has a population of about 8.5 million people. In fact, one of every six people in the country lives in or near Paris. As a result, Paris has a very strong influence on the rest of the country. From Paris, the French government sets rules for education, science, and industry.

The French people are known for their love of life—*joie de vivre*. They enjoy good food, wine, and fashions. Paris and other French cities are known for their fine restaurants, shops, and nightclubs. The French also are talented in the arts. Many world-famous artists, writers, and chefs have come from France. Many artistic and building methods have had their beginnings there. The Gothic style of church building, such as Paris' Notre Dame Cathedral, began in France hundreds of years ago. France has many beautiful palaces and **châteaux,** or castles, built in the past for French kings and queens.

The French language is especially prized by the French people. They believe their language is clear and has a beautiful sound. They also try to keep it free of foreign words.

Most French people are Roman Catholics, but few attend church regularly. Even

Railroads are important transportation links in Northwest Europe. Here the French TGV makes its run from Paris to Lyons. How fast can the TGV travel?

so, the Roman Catholic religion still influences daily life. For example, most French holidays are holy days of the Roman Catholic Church. Many farming villages also have festivals to honor saints of the Roman Catholic Church.

Because of long efforts by the French Academy, the French language has changed little over the years.

2.3 Influences of the Past

The first people known to have lived in France were the Gauls. They were related to the Celts of the British Isles. Romans conquered the Gauls after 100 BC. French language, law, and art were greatly influenced by the Romans. The area of France later was taken over by the Franks, a German people. From them, France got its name.

France is viewed as the oldest nation in Europe. It was set up as a unit of government in 843 AD. From that time until the 1700s, French rulers built a strong government.

France was once a **monarchy**—a government with a king or queen as the chief of

LAND USE AND RESOURCES OF NORTHWEST EUROPE _____

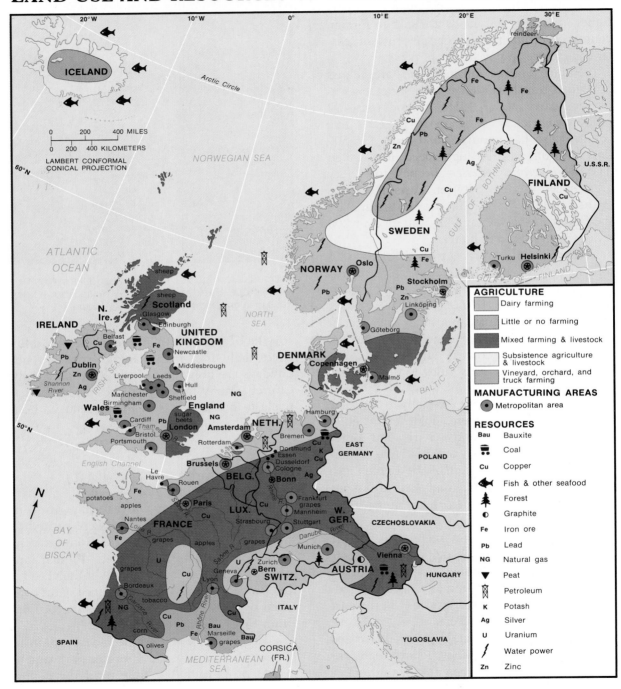

FIGURE 17-3

Northwest Europe includes some of the world's richest farmland and resources which make it one of the world's leading manufacturing centers. According to the map, which countries possess coal resources?

EUROPE   UNIT 6

state. However, a revolution ended the monarchy in 1789. A republic run by representatives of the people was set up.

Not long after, an army leader named Napoleon Bonaparte took over the government. At the height of Napoleon's rule in the early 1800s, France was the greatest military power on the continent of Europe.

During the 1700s and 1800s, France was one of the most influential countries in the world. The educated people of many other countries spoke French along with their own languages. It became the language used at international political meetings. French styles of dress were copied all over Europe and America. French art was admired worldwide.

During the early 1800s, France had several revolutions and many different governments. Finally, in the late 1800s, the people voted for a democratic republic. Also during this time, France took over many countries in Asia and Africa. The French Empire, like the British Empire, began to break up after World Wars I and II. However, France has kept trade and cultural ties with many of its former colonies. It continues to play a leading role in world affairs.

Have students use the political map on page 348 to note the location of each country as it is studied.

CONTENT CHECK

1. **Identify:** French Republic, France, Corsica, Pyrenees, Alps, Mount Blanc, Vosges Mountains, Jura Mountains, Rhine River, Marseille, TGV, Gauls, Franks, Napoleon Bonaparte.

2. **Define:** châteaux, monarchy.

3. What two land areas make up France?

4. What is France's major city? How does it influence the rest of France?

5. **Challenge:** How have France's forms of government changed through the centuries?

3. WEST GERMANY

West Germany is the name used for the Federal Republic of Germany. It has about three-fifths of the land area that Germany held at the end of World War II in 1945. After the war, Germany was divided into two parts. Most of the other two-fifths of the land is now East Germany, or the German Democratic Republic. West Germany is in the center of Northwest Europe. Except for its northern part along the North Sea, West Germany has land all around it.

See the *TAE* for an *Objective 3* Activity.

3.1 Landscape and Climate

Three major European landforms are found in West Germany. They are the Alps, the Central Highlands, and the North European Plain. West Germany's climate is influenced more by the European landmass than by the sea.

Landscape. The southern part of West Germany is largely hills or mountains. The Alps lie along West Germany's southern border. Known as the Bavarian Alps, the mountains have many high peaks. These include Zugspitze, the highest point in Germany, at 9,718 feet (2,962 m) above sea level.

Broadleaf forests cover the lower parts of the mountains. Coniferous trees are found higher up. Near the high peaks is a plant cover known as **alpine meadow.** It is much like the plants found in a tundra. Many of the peaks are capped with snow all year round.

North of the Alps are the Central Uplands. They are a chain of hilly or mountainous plateaus. Several large rivers flow through the Central Uplands. They include the Rhine River and the Danube River. This region also contains many forests. The most famous is the Black Forest, a high, rugged area covered with fir and spruce trees.

NATIONS OF NORTHWEST EUROPE

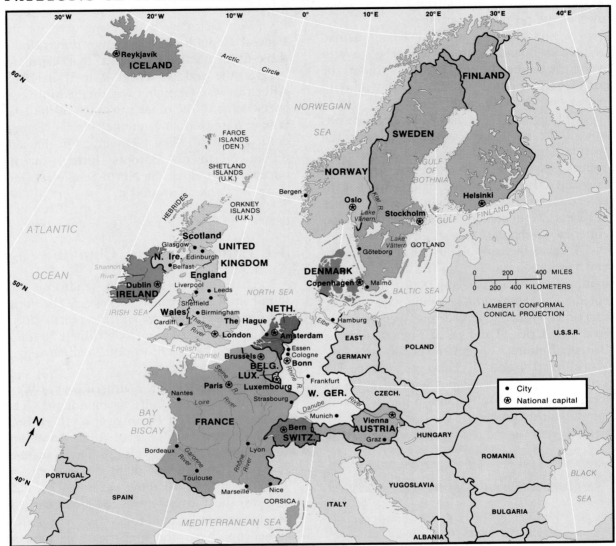

FIGURE 17-4

Continuing cooperation among the nations of Northwest Europe will assure their importance in world affairs. What are five national capitals shown here?

Explain that the lowlands of northern West Germany were created by the action of ancient glaciers.

A section of the Great European Plain extends north from the Central Uplands to the North Sea. It is known as the North German Plain. This plain is the largest and most populated area of West Germany. Elevations in this region are low, most less than 165 feet (50.3 m) above sea level. Several important rivers drain the North German Plain. They are the Ems, Elbe, Rhine, and Weser (VAY zuhr). Along the coast are low, sandy islands and **tidal flats**—areas of muddy land formed by ocean tides. Some coastal areas are **polders,** or low areas of land drained of water and surrounded by dikes.

348

In general, elevation increases from north to south in West Germany. The coldest weather occurs in the mountains in the southern part of the country.

Climate. West Germany's climate varies, depending on whether an area is close to the sea or farther inland. In the marine climate, northwesterly winds from the sea bring warm winters and cool summers. In the humid continental climate area in the south and east, the landmass of Europe cools temperatures. Winters there are colder and summers are warmer than in the north. Precipitation is greater in the northeast than in central areas. However, deep snows cover many mountainous areas in the south all winter.

See the *TAE* for an *Objective 3* Activity.

3.2 Economic and Cultural Patterns

West Germany is the leading industrial country of Northwest Europe and one of the major economic powers of the world. At the end of World War II in 1945, West Germany's economy was in ruins. However, the West Germans have worked hard to rebuild. Today the West German economy ranks fourth, after that of the United States, the Soviet Union, and Japan.

Like the United Kingdom, West Germany has limited land for farming. About one-third of the country's food must be imported. Still, farms on the North German Plain produce potatoes, sugar beets, and livestock. In the Danube River valley, wheat, barley, and oats are grown. Grapes are tended in vineyards along the banks of the Rhine and nearby rivers.

Farming accounts for only a small part of West Germany's income. The most important part of the economy is manufacturing. The main industrial area of West Germany is located near or along the Rhine River in a region known as the Ruhr. The Ruhr includes a number of manufacturing towns such as Dortmund, Düsseldorf, and Essen. It is one of the major industrial centers of the world. The Ruhr produces most of West Germany's

West Germany's industries, such as steel, require tremendous amounts of electrical power, and coal is used to produce much of this electricity.

iron and steel. It also manufactures cars, machinery, clothing, electrical equipment, ships, and tools.

West Germany has a variety of natural resources. Its many forests supply timber for lumber and paper. Coal, however, is the most important mineral resource. West Germany has good supplies of bituminous (buh TOO muh nuhs) coal and lignite. **Bituminous coal** is softer and pollutes the air more than **anthracite** (AN thruh SYT), which is hard-packed, gives off a great deal of energy and pollutes very little. **Lignite** is soft brown coal that gives off less energy than black coal.

After many years of industrial growth, some resources are being used up. West Germany now must import iron ore from Sweden, France, Spain, Algeria, and Canada. It also imports **nonferrous ores**—those other than iron.

Like France, West Germany has a good transportation system of waterways, railroads, and highways. Trade goods arrive at the ports of Bremen on the Weser River and Hamburg on the Elbe River. Of West Germany's rivers, however, the Rhine is the most important. It flows some 820 miles (1,319.7 km) from its source in the Alps to its mouth at the North Sea in the Netherlands. Another important river is the Danube. It connects parts of West Germany with Austria and Eastern Europe. However, large boats cannot use the Danube for much of its length in West Germany.

Canals have been built in most places where there are no navigable rivers. These canals link most major cities and ports in West Germany. About 271.2 million tons (246 metric tons) of goods are carried on West Germany's rivers and canals each year.

In addition to water transportation, West Germany has a good system of roads and railroads. The **autobahns**—super-highways—are among the best roads in the world. Because West Germans enjoy a high standard of living, ownership of cars is widespread.

Most of West Germany's 61 million people live in cities and towns. However, unlike other European countries, West Germany does not have one large city that dominates its national life. Instead, it has several equally important cities located in different parts of the country. West Berlin, surrounded by East Germany, is the largest city. It has about 1.8 million people. In the north is the port of Hamburg, with a population of 1.6 million. Munich is an important cultural center. Located in the south, Munich has about 1.2 million people. Bonn, the West German capital, is a university city on the Rhine River. It has almost 300,000 people.

West Germans are proud of their country's economic success. They are known for being hardworking and highly skilled. However, they also enjoy pleasures, such as festivals, good food, and folk music. West Germans have given much culture to the world. The composer Ludwig van Beethoven (BAY TOH vuhn), the writer Thomas Mann, and the scientist Albert Einstein all were born or lived in what is now West Germany.

3.3 Influences of the Past

The area that is now Germany was settled by people from northern Europe about 3,000 years ago. About 9 AD these groups, later known as Germans, were strong enough to stop the Romans from coming north of the Danube River. Although they learned from the Romans, they kept their own culture.

For centuries after the fall of Rome, Germany was a divided country. It was made up of many states ruled by princes. Because of its disunity, Germany was often the battleground of rival groups. During the 1500s groups of Christians all over Europe left the Roman Catholic Church and formed Protestant churches. This movement, led by Martin Luther and known as the Reformation, began in Germany. Some German states agreed with it and some were against it. Germany soon entered a long time of religious wars between Roman Catholics and Protestants. Peace was finally won, but Germany became a religiously divided country. As a result, most of the people in northern West Germany today

Explain that West Germany's ports on the North Sea give the country excellent access to the Atlantic Ocean.

A dense blanket of conifers covers Germany's Black Forest. The region has become a major tourist attraction, famous for the toys and clocks made by its inhabitants. Where do most West Germans live?

Many areas of the Black Forest are being seriously damaged by pollution such as acid rain.

The modern Germanies resulted from the formal union in the 19th century of many small German states. Of those, Prussia was the most influential.

Reunification continues to be the dream of many Germans. Strong political differences between West and East Germany make this unlikely in the near future.

OCCUPIED GERMANY AND DIVIDED BERLIN

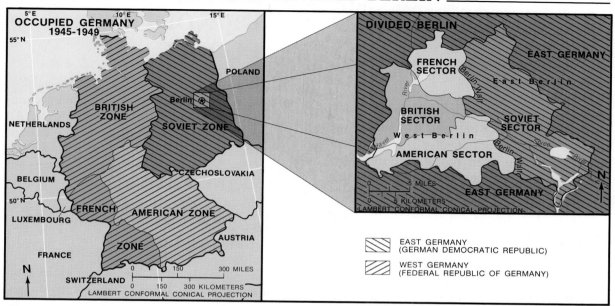

FIGURE 17-5
The Berlin Wall is a very real symbol of two separate Berlins as well as two separate Germanies. Which three countries at one time occupied West Berlin and West Germany?

Many Europeans still distrust a strong, united Germany because of the two world wars.

are Protestants. Most in the south and west are Roman Catholics.

During the 1800s Germany became a united nation after fighting several European wars. From 1871 until 1913, it was the strongest military power in Europe. It also had an overseas empire. From 1914 to 1918, Germany, along with Austria-Hungary and other allies, fought World War I against the United Kingdom, France, Russia, the United States, and several smaller nations.

After its defeat in World War I, Germany went through bad economic times. It had huge debts from the war and had to rebuild its trade. During the 1920s **inflation,** or steeply rising prices, ruined many businesses and many people lost their savings.

In the early 1930s, Adolf Hitler and the Nazi party became powerful and won control of the German government. Hitler promised

to make Germany great again. He blamed the Jews for Germany's problems and wanted to destroy them as a people. Millions of Jews were later sent to prison camps and killed. This period of time is now called the Holocaust. The Nazis also imprisoned and killed hundreds of thousands of others they viewed as enemies.

In 1939 Germany invaded Poland, and World War II began in Europe. The war ended in 1945, with Germany again defeated. As shown in Figure 17–5 on this page, the country was divided among the United States, the United Kingdom, France, and the Soviet Union. Berlin, the old capital of Germany, also was divided. However, cooperation on Germany's future broke down. In 1949 the western Allies—the United States, the United Kingdom, and France—set up the Federal Republic of Germany—West Ger-

CHAPTER 17 **NORTHWEST EUROPE**

If possible, provide photographs of the Berlin Wall, which has become a physical symbol of the division between democratic and communist Europe.

For information on several small but independent European countries, refer to the special feature in Chapter 18, "Europe's Postage-Stamp Countries."

many—with a democratic government. The Soviet Union soon set up the German Democratic Republic—East Germany—with a communist government.

Since that time, tensions between the United States and the Soviet Union have affected West Germany. Because West Germany faces communist nations on its eastern border, any conflict between the Soviets and the Americans would involve the West Germans. Because of their past differences, West and East Germany have failed to reunite. Today, however, with the hope of better relations between the United States and the Soviet Union, cooperation has slowly increased between West and East Germany.

See the *TRB* Chapter 17 Skill Activity.

CONTENT CHECK

1. **Identify:** West Germany, Federal Republic of Germany, Zugspitze, Central Uplands, Danube River, Black Forest, North German Plain, the Ruhr, West Berlin, Hamburg, Munich, Bonn, Reformation, Adolf Hitler.

2. **Define:** alpine meadow, tidal flats, polders, bituminous coal, anthracite, lignite, nonferrous ores, autobahns, inflation.

3. What two countries today occupy the territory of Germany as it existed at the end of World War II in 1945?

4. What landscape is found in the northern part of West Germany? In the central part? In the southern part?

5. In what part of West Germany are winters colder?

6. Where does West Germany rank among the world's economic powers?

7. Why is the Ruhr famous?

8. **Challenge:** How do the rivers of West Germany help connect it to other countries in Europe?

4. OTHER COUNTRIES OF NORTHWEST EUROPE

The other countries of Northwest Europe make up three groups—Benelux countries, Norden, and the Alpine countries. All of these countries have smaller populations than the United Kingdom, France, and West Germany. However, they all are prosperous and enjoy high standards of living.

As early as the 1600s, Dutch engineers helped reclaim lowlands along England's North Sea coast.

4.1 Benelux Countries

Belgium, the Netherlands, and Luxembourg are known as the Benelux countries, from the first letters of their names. They lie between France and West Germany. Luxembourg is surrounded by other countries. Belgium and the Netherlands have coasts on the North Sea. Like the United Kingdom, the Benelux countries have a marine climate with cool summers and mild winters.

Most of the territory of the Benelux countries is low and flat. Some places are even below sea level. Only in Luxembourg and southeast Belgium does the land rise more than 1,000 feet (304.8 m) above sea level.

In the Benelux countries, 25 million people live in an area about the size of West Virginia. These countries are the most densely populated in Northwest Europe. More land is always needed. The Dutch, as the people of the Netherlands are called, have used great skill in reclaiming land from the sea. They have built dikes and then pumped out the water to uncover the land. About one-third of the farmland of the Netherlands is made up of polders, such as those in Figure 17–6 on page 353.

The culture of the Benelux countries is similar to those of nearby countries. In the

Netherlands, the people speak Dutch, a language closely related to German. The people of Luxembourg speak French, German, and Luxembourgian. The largest group in northern Belgium, the Flemings, speaks Flemish, a language that is very close to Dutch. The Walloons, the dominant group in southern Belgium, speak French. Both Flemish and French languages are spoken in Brussels, Belgium's capital.

Like the United Kingdom, the Benelux countries are democratic monarchies. All three countries are highly industrialized and have largely urban populations. Brussels and Antwerp in Belgium, and Amsterdam and Rotterdam in the Netherlands, are important commercial cities. Rotterdam is the busiest port in Europe and one of the busiest in the world.

See the *TAE* for an *Objective 4* Activity.

4.2 Norden

Iceland, Norway, Sweden, Denmark, and Finland make up an area called Norden. Greenland, which is politically linked to Denmark, is also in this region. The countries of Norden lie north of the rest of Northwest Europe. Iceland and Greenland are far west of the European continent, in the Atlantic Ocean. Norden is so far north that in Stockholm, Sweden, the sun rises at 9 o'clock in the morning and sets at 3 o'clock in the afternoon in the middle of winter. Areas farther north receive even less sunlight in winter.

Much of the landscape in Norden has mountains. The area has many kinds of climate, depending on how far north each part is. Denmark and the southernmost parts of Iceland, Sweden, and Norway have a marine climate. Central parts of Norway, Sweden, and Finland have a humid continental with warm summers climate. The northernmost parts are subarctic or tundra. Northern Iceland and Greenland's coast are tundra, and

the rest of Greenland has an ice cap climate. Many parts of Norden are too cold for farming. The best farming areas are in Denmark and southern Sweden.

The countries of Norden have a good supply of natural resources, such as iron ore, coal, copper, and timber. Sweden is the most industrialized of the Norden countries. Its leading industries involve the making of cars and machine parts.

Norway is the only Norden country with its own oil supply. Like the United Kingdom, it has rights to oil found in the North Sea. Norway is also one of the world's leaders in shipbuilding and fishing.

All of the Norden countries are democracies. Sweden, Norway, and Denmark are monarchies, while Finland and Iceland are both republics. The languages and cultures of

LAND FROM THE SEA _____

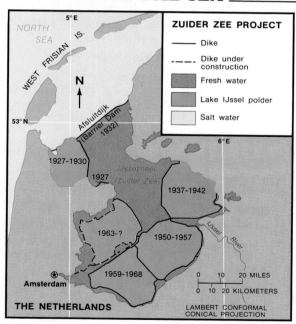

FIGURE 17-6
Over the centuries, polders have allowed the Dutch people to claim 40 percent of their present-day land from the sea. Why is more land needed?

USING GRAPHIC SKILLS

MAKING GENERALIZATIONS

If you say, "My dad is a great cook," you are making a generalization, a general statement, about your father. If you go on to say that your father has a diploma from the Cordon Bleu cooking school in Paris and is a chef for a famous restaurant, you have given evidence to support your generalization.

The table below shows information about five cities of Northwest Europe and three cities of North and South America. Notice that three pieces of information are shown for each city—elevation, latitude, and the average high temperature during January. Only the temperature is a direct element of climate.

To make a generalization about a city's climate, you must first gather information about the physical features and location of the city from your chapter study. Then you put together these pieces of information with the other data in the table below. For example: *Oslo is located in the southeastern corner of Norway along a fjord that leads to the North Sea. It is at the foot of the Western Uplands region, and its elevation is low. Its latitude places it nearly in the high latitudes*. Considering all these pieces of information, along with the average high temperature in January, a generalization about Oslo's winter climate can be made: *Oslo, Norway, has a cold winter climate that may be warmer than areas to its north because of its low elevation and nearness to the sea*.

The table below provides supporting information for you to make generalizations about winter climates. In your generalizations you should be able to state what kind of climate a city has and the reasons why.

Study the table below. Then answer the questions that follow.

1. Paris and Vienna are located at about the same latitude. What factors explain why they have different high temperatures in January?

2. Make a generalization about San Juan's winter climate.

3. Dublin, although located farther north than Geneva, has warmer temperatures in January. Make a generalization about Dublin's winter climate.

STATISTICS ON SELECTED CITIES

SELECTED CITIES	ELEVATION	LATITUDE	AVERAGE HIGH: JANUARY
Dublin, Ireland	155 ft. (47.2 m.)	53°20'N	47°F (8.3°C)
Geneva, Switzerland	1,329 ft. (405.1 m.)	46°14'N	39°F (3.9°C)
Oslo, Norway	308 ft. (93.9 m.)	59°56'N	30°F (-1.1°C)
Paris, France	164 ft. (50.0 m.)	48°51'N	42°F (5.6°C)
Vienna, Austria	664 ft. (202.4 m.)	48°13'N	34°F (1.1°C)
Bogota, Colombia	8,355 ft. (2,546.6 m.)	4°38'N	67°F (19.4°C)
Portland, Maine	103 ft. (31.4 m.)	43°40'N	31°F (-0.6°C)
San Juan, Puerto Rico	82 ft. (25.0 m.)	18°30'N	81°F (27.2°C)

Sweden, Denmark, Norway, and Iceland are descended from the Vikings, a group that traded and roamed the seas hundreds of years ago. Sweden, Norway, and Denmark together are known as Scandinavia. Finland, however, has a culture and language more closely related to the Soviet Union's than to other Norden countries. But because it was ruled by Sweden at one time, both Finnish and Swedish are official languages in Finland.

Beautiful scenery and fine skiing attract winter visitors to the mountains in the Alpine countries.

4.3 Alpine Countries

The Alps form most of the landscape in Switzerland and Austria. Between Switzerland and Austria is the tiny country of Liechtenstein. The Alps give the name of Alpine to these countries, which lie south of West Germany.

Switzerland has a mix of different languages—Swiss-German, French, Italian, and Romansch, a language similar to Latin. The people are generally Protestants or Roman Catholics. Austria is a German-speaking nation and is largely Roman Catholic.

Switzerland and Austria are also different in other ways. Austria has rich resources, such as iron ore, lead, zinc, magnesite, and lignite. Austria is a major source of **graphite**, the carbon used in pencils. Switzerland has no important mineral resources.

Despite having few minerals, Switzerland has a stronger economy than Austria. Its highly skilled workers make light machinery, watches, and electrical products. Swiss cities, such as Geneva and Zurich, are among Europe's important banking centers.

For most of its history, Austria had close ties to Eastern Europe. The Danube River was its major water route to the east. Austria's capital, Vienna, was the heart of a large empire that included Hungary and much of southeastern Europe. Known as the Austro-Hungarian Empire, it ended after World War

I. Today Austria is a small democratic republic located between the democratic countries of Northwest Europe and the communist countries of Eastern Europe.

CONTENT CHECK

1. **Identify:** Benelux, Dutch, Flemings, Walloons, Brussels, Antwerp, Amsterdam, Rotterdam, Norden, Vikings, Scandinavia, Alpine, Geneva, Zurich, Vienna, Austro-Hungarian Empire.

2. **Define:** graphite.

3. What is the landscape of the Benelux countries?

4. What is the busiest port city in Europe? Where is it located?

5. Which country in Norden is the most industrialized? What products does it manufacture?

6. **Challenge:** Why do you think Austria's relations with Eastern Europe have not been as close during this century as they were in earlier times?

See the *TAE* for an *Objective 5* Activity.

CONCLUSION

The countries of Northwest Europe were once the most powerful in the world. Several held large empires that brought them great wealth. These empires are mostly gone today. However, the countries of Northwest Europe have highly skilled populations and prosperous industrial economies. Therefore, they still play an important role in world affairs.

The history of Northwest Europe has included many changes. There have been wars among the different countries. Long years of industrialization have strained their resources. Some of the competition of past years, however, has recently been replaced with cooperation. The cooperation has helped make their economies stronger.

SUMMARY

1. There are 17 countries in Northwest Europe. Of these, the United Kingdom, France, and West Germany lead in population and economy.
2. The climate of Northwest Europe is strongly influenced by the warm North Atlantic Current. This gives much of the area a moist, mild winter climate despite its northerly location.
3. The British Isles are the largest group of islands in Northwest Europe. Britain and Ireland are the two largest islands of the British Isles.
4. The Republic of Ireland and the United Kingdom of Great Britain and Northern Ireland are the two countries that make up the British Isles.
5. The United Kingdom is very urbanized. It was the first country in the world to go through the Industrial Revolution. Ireland is more rural. Farming is more important to its economy than to that of the United Kingdom.
6. France, on the western edge of Europe, has coasts on the Atlantic Ocean and the Mediterranean Sea. Mountains serve as boundaries between France and nearby countries. It is the largest country in Northwest Europe.
7. Both farming and industry are important to the French economy. Paris is the center of France's government, industry, and culture.
8. West Germany is the name given to the Federal Republic of Germany. At the end of World War II, Germany was divided into two parts—West Germany and East Germany.
9. West Germany is the most populous country in Northwest Europe. It has limited farmland but is one of the world's major industrial countries. Manufacturing is very important to its economy.
10. The other countries of Northwest Europe can be grouped as the Benelux countries, Norden, and the Alpine countries.

Answers to the following questions can be found on page T188.

REVIEWING VOCABULARY

On a separate sheet of paper, write the word that is defined to the right of the blanks in each line below. Then circle the letters in the words that show a star (★). Unscramble these letters to find the mystery word. *Write the mystery word and its definition on your paper.*

1. _ ★ _ _ _   long, narrow lakes in Scotland
2. _ _ _ ★ _ _ _   low areas of land that have been reclaimed from the sea
3. _ _ _ ★ _ _ _   soft, brown coal
4. ★ _ _ _ _   an almost treeless landscape covered with grasses and some shrubs
5. _ ★ _ _ _ _   a funnel-shaped bay along Scotland's coast
6. _ _ _ _ _ ★ _ _   mineral that is the source of carbon used in pencils
7. _ ★ ★ _ _ _ _ _   government with a king or queen as chief of state

REMEMBERING THE FACTS

1. How large is Northwest Europe?
2. What countries make up the United Kingdom?
3. What is the capital of France?
4. What are the three groups of Northwest Europe's other countries?

UNDERSTANDING THE FACTS

1. Why is damp, foggy weather common in the British Isles?
2. What generalization can you make about the economies of the Republic of Ireland and the United Kingdom?
3. What cultural differences do the two nations of the British Isles have?
4. How was France ruled before 1789?
5. Why is there more precipitation in the northern half of West Germany than in the southern half?
6. What was the Reformation?
7. Why was Germany divided into two states after 1945? In what ways had Germany been divided in earlier centuries?
8. How is it that Greenland is part of Northwest Europe and is also part of North America?
9. What are some of the differences in the natural resources of Switzerland and Austria and in the religious beliefs of their people?

THINKING CRITICALLY AND CREATIVELY

1. What would you suggest a country do if it has little arable land and few natural resources but wants to build up its economic strength?
2. What makes a country a world power?
3. How do you think the location of Paris has contributed to making the city the largest metropolitan area in France?
4. There has always been more land traffic between France and Italy than there has been between France and Spain. How might you explain this?
5. What is the relationship between French exports and the country's need for oil? Where does France get its oil?
6. How do rivers and canals contribute to West Germany's economy?
7. Which nations of Northwest Europe would be hurt the most by falling oil prices? Why?

REINFORCING GRAPHIC SKILLS

Study the chart on page 354. Then answer the questions that follow.

1. *Cities at nearly the same latitude do not always have similar climates.* What cities support this generalization?
2. Make a generalization about Bogotá's winter climate with supporting information based on the chart.

CHAPTER 18

The name Mediterranean comes from two Latin words—*medius,* meaning middle, and *terra,* meaning land.

Positano, a town in Italy's Campania region

MEDITERRANEAN EUROPE

About 3,000 years ago, the Mediterranean area was covered by thick, well-watered forests. Climate changes and careless use of natural resources over time, however, have caused the Mediterranean area to become the driest part of the European continent.

In this chapter you will learn—

● What landscapes and climates are found in Mediterranean Europe.

● How physical features affect economic conditions in Mediterranean Europe.

● What past civilizations influenced the development of Mediterranean Europe.

Refer students to the map of Physical Regions of Mediterranean Europe on page 360 to note the location of these three peninsulas relative to one another and to Northwest Europe.

INTRODUCTION

Three large land areas just south from northwest Europe into the Mediterranean Sea. They are the Iberian, Italian, and Balkan peninsulas. High mountains separate the peninsulas from the rest of Europe and arms of the Mediterranean Sea connect them.

Several countries are located on the three peninsulas. Four of them form the region of Mediterranean Europe. Spain and Portugal share the Iberian Peninsula. Italy takes up the Italian Peninsula, and Greece is in the southern part of the Balkan Peninsula.

The Mediterranean countries lie between about 35° north and 47° north latitude. About 1,700 miles (2,735.9 km) of land and sea stretch from the west coast of Portugal to the easternmost island of Greece. In land area Spain is the largest country of the region. Italy is the largest country in population.

The countries of Mediterranean Europe are similar in climate and landscape. All have large areas of mountains and highlands. The highest point in Mediterranean Europe is Mont Blanc at 15,521 feet (4,730.8 m) above sea level. It is a part of the Alps in northwest Italy. Most of the countries in Mediterranean Europe have sunny climates with warm summers and moist, mild winters.

European civilization began in the Mediterranean area. It spread from there to the rest of the continent. First, the ancient Greeks set up colonies in the islands of the Mediterranean and in southern Italy. They traded all over the Mediterranean area. Later, the Romans of the Italian Peninsula built a huge empire that covered much of Europe, as well as other lands around the Mediterranean Sea. In the late 1400s, Spain and Portugal in the Iberian Peninsula became great sea powers. They founded colonies in Africa, Asia, and the Americas.

Because of the growing Spanish-speaking minority in the United States, attempts have been made in this book to show the pronunciation of Spanish terms and place-names based on the modern Spanish language.

1. IBERIAN PENINSULA

The Iberian Peninsula is the farthest west of the three peninsulas of Mediterranean Europe. It is shaped almost like a square, with each side some 500 miles (804.7 km) long. On a map, the Iberian Peninsula looks like a little continent set apart from the rest of Europe. On its northeastern side are the rugged Pyrenees. On all its other sides, it touches bodies of water—the Bay of Biscay, the Atlantic Ocean, and the Mediterranean Sea.

PHYSICAL REGIONS OF MEDITERRANEAN EUROPE _____

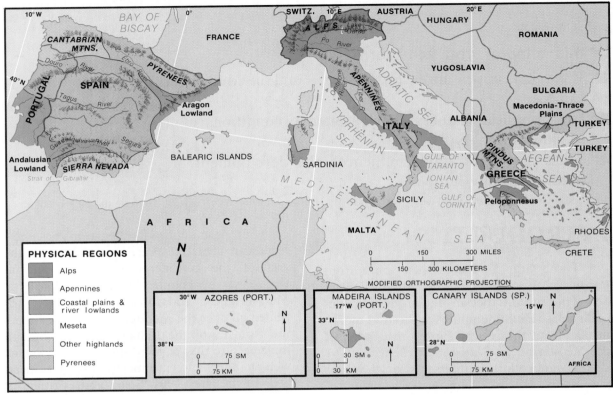

FIGURE 18-1
Mountains and seas are two distinctive features that separate the countries of Mediterranean Europe from the rest of Europe. What three mountain ranges form natural land barriers in this region?

Refer students to the map of Land Use and Resources on page 369.

Spain occupies most of the Iberian Peninsula. It has a land area of 194,896 square miles (504,780.2 sq km) which includes the Balearic (BAL ee AR ihk) Islands in the Mediterranean Sea, the Canary Islands in the Atlantic Ocean, and several small cities along the northern coast of Africa. Spain is the third largest country in Europe, after the Soviet Union and France.

Portugal takes up the rest of the Iberian Peninsula, with a total land area of 35,552 square miles (92,079.6 sq km). This country is located at the western tip of Europe. Portugal includes the Madeiras (muh DIHR uhz) and the Azores (AY zohrz), two groups of islands in the Atlantic Ocean.

1.1 Landscape and Climate

The land of the Iberian Peninsula is mostly high and rugged. Only in southern Portugal and southwestern Spain is the land less than 700 feet (213.4 m) above sea level. Most of the peninsula has a dry, sunny climate. The northern coast, however, receives a lot of rain all through the year.

Landscape. As Figure 18-1 shows on this page, two-thirds of Spain is made up of a large, dry plateau called the Meseta (meh SAY tah). The Meseta is made up of rolling plains, low mountains, and deep valleys. Forests once covered this region. However, over the centuries, the trees were cut down for

EUROPE UNIT 6

farming and building ships. Today the Meseta is a place where such crops as cereal grains, olives, and grapes are grown. Many people earn their living by tending goats and sheep. The largest urban center of the Meseta is Madrid, Spain's capital.

North, east, and south of the Meseta are high mountains. The Pyrenees and Cantabrian (kahn TAH bree͡ahn) Mountains extend across Spain in the north. Some peaks reach more than 10,000 feet (3,048 m) above sea level. In the south the Sierra Nevada includes the highest peak on the Iberian peninsula, Mulhacén (MOO lah SAYN), at 11,410 feet (3,477.8 m).

Narrow lowlands and river basins lie along Spain's long coastline. The largest lowland area is the basin of the Guadalquivir (GWAH dahl kee VEER) River in southwestern Spain. This area is also called the Andalusian Lowland. It consists of plains, hills, and marshes along the coast. In the northeastern part of Spain is the Aragon Lowland. It is made up of broad plains that run along the Ebro River. Even though many Spanish lowlands are dry and hot, farmers have turned them into fertile agricultural areas through irrigation. The lowlands also contain many important Spanish cities, such as Barcelona, Valencia, and Seville.

Portugal has more flat lowlands than Spain. However, mountain ranges cross the central and northern parts of the country. Two major rivers, the Douro (DOHR oo) and the Tagus (TAH goos), flow east to west across Portugal. Lisbon and Porto, Portugal's leading cities, are located in the coastal plains where the rivers meet the Atlantic Ocean.

Climate. Most of the Iberian Peninsula has a Mediterranean climate. Winters there are mild and summers hot and dry. The amount of rainfall is low. The northern coast of Spain and northern Portugal are influenced by warm winds blowing in from the Atlantic Ocean. These winds keep temperatures mild

Southern mountains block moisture to the eastern parts of the Andalusian Lowland. What name is given to Spain's southern mountains?

and bring much rain. The Meseta and other inland areas of Spain have a steppe climate with hot summers and cold winters. In these areas it rains very little.

The ruggedness of the Pyrenees Mountains has always made land travel between Spain and France difficult.

1.2 Economic and Cultural Patterns

Until the mid-1900s, the Iberian Peninsula had an economy based on farming. Then, during the 1950s and 1960s, rapid industrial growth began. Today Spain is a modern, industrialized country with a large urban population. Even though Portugal has also industrialized, it still is largely agricultural. Portugal's **gross domestic product (GDP)**—the value of all goods and services produced by a country for its own use—is one of the lowest in Europe. As a result, many Portuguese are poor.

The Iberian Peninsula is rich in some natural resources. Spain and Portugal both have coal, copper, and iron deposits. How-

USING GRAPHIC SKILLS

ANALYZING LINE AND BAR GRAPHS

When was the last time you went door-to-door in your neighborhood selling candy or popcorn for your school or club? Each school year students raise money for activities and programs, hoping to sell enough to win the grand prize for sales in their school.

PER CAPITA GROSS NATIONAL PRODUCT

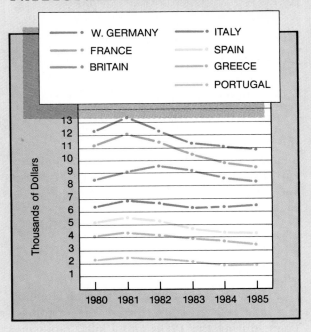

Leaders in your school or club plan their budget for each year based on sources of income and expenses. They examine how much income the fund-raising project brought in during the last several years. Then they judge whether the same project should be tried again during the current year. To help them make this decision, they analyze the *total* amount of money raised and the *average* amount of money raised per student.

The graphs on these two pages chart similar financial information on gross national product. The countries under study are the four Mediterranean countries and three countries in Northwest Europe. The bar graphs chart the total GNP of these seven countries for 1981, 1983, and 1985. The line graphs show the average, or per capita GNP, of the same countries from 1980 to 1985.

To analyze information a person must break apart all the information into smaller pieces. When the information is studied in smaller parts, it is easier to understand the whole. To analyze the information in these graphs, you must first examine the growth or decline of each country's GNP. Then compare this to the GNPs of the other countries to determine which countries are experiencing similar or different levels of economic growth.

Much of Portugal's cork is used to make stoppers for wine bottles. Have interested students research and report on other important uses of cork.

ever petroleum must be imported. Spain has few forests, but Portugal has forests covering one-third of its land area. Portugal's forests supply large amounts of cork, the bark stripped from cork trees. The sea is an important resource for both Spain and Portugal. Many Spaniards and Portuguese from along the coast make their living by fishing.

Poor soil and not enough rain make farming difficult in many areas of the Iberian Peninsula. But Spain is one of Europe's largest growers of farm products. It is the world's largest producer of olive oil and also exports fruit and wine.

Many Spanish farmers depend on irrigation for growing olives, oranges, lemons,

TOTAL GROSS NATIONAL PRODUCT

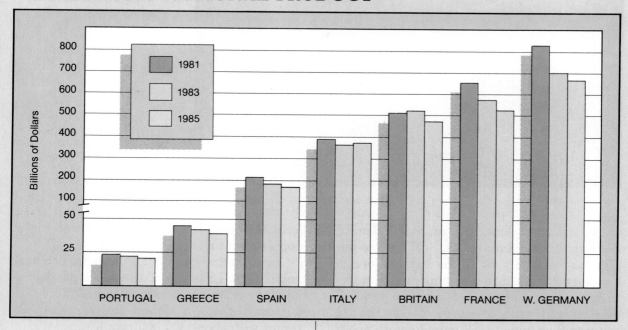

Study the graphs on these two pages. Then answer the questions that follow.

1. Which countries showed an increase in total GNP from one year to the next? Which country showed a steady increase in per capita GNP from 1980 to 1982?

2. Which country had the overall lowest GNP total? Which country had the largest decrease in total GNP from one year to the next?

3. What generalization can you make about the economy of Mediterranean Europe in comparison to the economies of Northwest European countries?

In many Mediterranean areas, crop yields are not as high as in other areas of Europe because use of mechanization and modern technology has only recently begun to grow.

wheat, and wine grapes. They also raise livestock, such as sheep and beef cattle. Farmers in the Andalusian Lowland raise bulls for use in Spain's most famous spectator sport—bull fighting.

The land in Portugal is not as dry as that of Spain. Portuguese farmers, however, grow many of the same products that are raised in Spain. They are especially known for their wine grapes. Wines from Portugal are known and enjoyed all over the world.

Manufacturing plays an increasingly important role in the Spanish and Portuguese economies. Spain produces cars, chemical products, shoes, clothing, and steel. Most Spanish industries are located in cities, such

Under Prince Henry the Navigator, Portuguese explorers such as Vasco da Gama, Bartholomeu Dias, and Pedro Alvares Cabrel helped found an empire that stretched from Africa to Brazil to parts of the East Indies. Touches of Portuguese language and customs remain throughout the world as part of these former colonies.

Portuguese fishermen unload their harvest of clams. The fishing industry is important for coastal Portugal and its outer islands. In which city is Portugal's manufacturing industry centered?

A version of the Castilian Spanish spoken in southern Spain is the Spanish that the conquistadores brought to the Americas in the early days of colonization.

Barcelona, in Catalonia, is Spain's leading industrial city. Although energy costs are high because the energy resources must be imported, these costs are offset by even higher profits in some of Barcelona's industries.

as Madrid, Barcelona, Bilbao, and Valencia. Because of limited resources, Spain has to import raw materials. With the help of foreign investors, the Spanish government and industrialists are trying to modernize Spanish industries and make them more efficient. In this way they hope to sell more Spanish goods to other countries to pay for imports.

Portugal also has been increasing its industrial output. Its leading manufacturing activity is the making of metals and machinery. Most Portuguese industries are centered in Lisbon, Portugal's capital and major seaport.

The Iberian Peninsula has a variety of cultures. Spain has 39 million people, while Portugal has a population of 10.3 million. Most Spaniards live in cities and have adopted modern lifestyles. Two-thirds of the Portuguese still live in rural areas, where old customs are often practiced.

Spain has two large cities. Madrid, the capital and largest city, has a population of 3.2 million. It is one of Europe's leading cultural centers. The art museum, El Prado, is known for its vast collection of paintings by Spanish artists. Barcelona, which is located along the Mediterranean coast, is Spain's

leading seaport and industrial center. It has a population of nearly two million.

Portuguese cities are smaller in size and population. Lisbon is Portugal's capital and largest city, with 820,000 people. North of Lisbon is Porto, a seaport and wine-making center with about 300,000 people.

Portugal's small size gives its people a sense of national unity. All speak Portuguese, a Romance language in the same family as Spanish. Spain, on the other hand, is divided into different cultural regions. The people of these areas often show a greater loyalty to their local region than to the country as a whole.

The cultural regions of Spain are Castile, Catalonia, the Basque Provinces, Galicia, and Andalusia. Castile has served as leader for centuries. The dialect of the Castilian people became the dominant language of Spain and is today spoken by most Spaniards. However, the people of the other regions regard themselves as separate groups within Spain. Catalonia is on the Mediterranean coast and is the most prosperous area of the country. Its people speak Catalan, a Romance language closely related to the French spoken in south-

EUROPE   UNIT 6

Basque aims for independence have sometimes been violent as known Basque militants have backed political assassinations and terrorist bombings.

Cervantes' famous character Don Quixote is known worldwide. Luis Vas de Camoes, Portugal's most famous poet, celebrated da Gama's voyage to India.

ern France. In the Basque Provinces, the Basques have a culture and language unlike any other in Europe. Many Basques want complete independence from Spain. Galicia in the northwest and Andalusia in the south also have cultural differences that set them apart from the rest of Spain.

In Spain and Portugal, city life often contrasts with rural life. Rural standards of living are lower than those in the cities. As a result, many rural people are crowding into urban areas to find jobs in new industries. Unemployment has been high. Many Spanish and Portuguese workers often work in other parts of Europe. These people are **expatriate workers**—citizens of one country who work in another country.

Old customs are fading in some parts of Spain and Portugal. For example, some businesses still close in the afternoon but not for the traditional *siesta*, or afternoon nap. At this time, people eat their largest meal of the day. Then they relax or spend time outdoors. At other times they attend soccer matches or bull fights. They enjoy evening walks before the final meal of the day. In the Iberian Peninsula, the evening meal is usually served after 9 or 10 PM.

More than 90 percent of the Iberian Peninsula's population is Roman Catholic. The Roman Catholic Church once had close ties with the governments of the two countries. Today church and state are separated, and religion has less influence in the cities. Still, the Roman Catholic faith remains strong in rural areas. There church festivals are celebrated year round. Still, in large cities there are parades, bonfires, and feasts on religious holidays.

Spain and Portugal are known for their rich artistic traditions. Spanish writers and painters have portrayed religious subjects or themes from daily life. Two of the most famous of these talented Spaniards are the painter Francisco José de Goya and the writer Miguel de Cervantes. Throughout its history, Portugal has had many writers who have praised their country's explorers, kings, and military heroes.

The Spaniards and Portuguese are also known for their folk music and dancing. The Spaniards perform lively, rhythmic regional dances. In their night spots, the Portuguese sing **fados,** sad songs about daily life. Many songs and dances in the Iberian Peninsula are accompanied by guitar or bagpipe music.

Because family ties are so important in Iberia, the decision to seek work in another country is not easily made.

Stately buildings and tree-lined streets contribute to the beauty of Barcelona. Both an economic and educational center, Barcelona is located in Spain's Catalonia region. What makes Barcelona one of Spain's leading cities?

Tourism employs many workers and adds to national incomes as growing numbers of tourists are attracted to Iberia's beautiful scenery, rustic rural areas, sunny beaches, and historic castles and churches.

Portugal is one of Europe's oldest states. Its approximate modern boundaries were secured by King Afonso III in 1249.

After the expulsion of the Moors, Spain was able to redirect funds to sponsor Columbus' first voyage—the start of Spain's overseas expansion.

1.3 Influences of the Past

The Iberian Peninsula was first settled about 5,000 years ago. Early settlers known as Iberians built towns and cities. They also gave their name to the peninsula.

Over the centuries, other groups followed them. They included Phoenicians (fih NIHSH uhnz) from southwest Asia, Celts from western Europe, Greeks, Carthaginians (KAHR thuh JIHN yuhnz) from north Africa, and Romans. For more than 400 years, the Romans ruled much of Spain. They brought Christianity and influenced the peninsula's languages, laws, and architecture.

After the fall of Rome in the 400s, a German group known as Visigoths set up a Christian kingdom in Spain. Within 200 years, they were conquered by the Moors from north Africa and pushed into the northern part of the country. The Moors were Muslims, followers of Islam. They made important discoveries in mathematics and science and built beautiful palaces, such as Al-

Refer students to the map on page 372 and note the extent of Roman expansion into Spain.

Ancient columns stand amid a Roman theater at Mérida, one of many notable Roman ruins in Spain. What influences did the Romans bring to Spain?

hambra in the city of Granada. The achievements of the Moors were passed on to the less developed civilization of western Europe.

By the 1000s the hold of the Moors over Spain weakened. Meanwhile, the Visigothic territories in the north had become the Spanish kingdoms of Castile, Aragon, and Navarre. Later, Portugal broke away from Castile and became independent.

From the 1000s to the 1400s, the Christian kingdoms of the Iberian Peninsula pushed the Moors southward. In 1469 Prince Ferdinand of Aragon married Princess Isabella of Castile. After becoming king and queen, they drove the Moors from Spain and united the country under their rule. Portugal, however, stayed independent.

During the 1400s and 1500s, Portugal and Spain became major sea powers. They explored and set up colonies in Asia, Africa, and the Americas. The two countries, however, did not use the wealth of their colonies to build strong economies. While western Europe industrialized in the 1800s, Spain and Portugal lost their status as world powers.

During the 1900s Portugal and Spain faced political unrest at home. In 1910 Portugal replaced its monarchy with a democratic republic. However, democracy was weak in Portugal. For most of the 1900s, the country was ruled by dictators. Finally, in the mid-1970s, army officers set up a democratic republic with free elections. Portugal lost its few remaining colonies during this time. Meanwhile, it worked to improve its economy and to develop close ties with western European countries.

Spain set up a democratic republic in 1931 in place of its monarchy. Spanish communists and socialists backed the republic. They favored government control of factories, farms, and other means of production. Under **socialism,** this change comes about by the will of the people through their elected government leaders. Under communism, which

Some people view the Spanish Civil War of 1936 as a dress rehearsal for World War II. German and Italian interests supported Franco; Russians, the monarchy.

Refer students to the map of Physical Regions on page 360 and the map of Earth's Climate Regions on pages 96-97 to review Italy's location and climate.

is an extreme form of socialism, one political party makes these changes on its own without free elections.

The republic in Spain was opposed by the Roman Catholic Church, the wealthy, and the army. In 1936, army units under General Francisco Franco revolted against the republic. A civil war lasted until 1939, when Franco's forces won. Franco ruled Spain until his death in 1975. At that time, the monarchy once again came to power. The new king, however, favored democracy and allowed free elections. Today, Spain is a democratic monarchy similar to that of the United Kingdom.

See the TAE for an Objective 1 Activity.

CONTENT CHECK

1. **Identify:** Iberian Peninsula, Spain, Balearic Islands, Canary Islands, Portugal, Madeiras, Azores, the Meseta, Madrid, Cantabrian Mountains, Mulhacén, Andalusian Lowland, Aragon Lowland, Douro River, Tagus River, Lisbon, Castile, Catalonia, Basque Provinces, Moors, Francisco Franco.

2. **Define:** gross domestic product (GDP), expatriate workers, fados, socialism.

3. What physical features border the Iberian Peninsula?

4. How are the landscapes of Spain and Portugal alike? How do they differ?

5. How do Spain and Portugal compare in land area? Population? Industry?

6. What serious problems do farmers in Spain have?

7. What farm products are produced in Spain and Portugal?

8. How does Portugal's wealth compare with that of other countries in Europe?

9. **Challenge:** Why do you think that people living in Catalonia have sometimes not gotten along well with those living in Castile?

2. ITALY

Italy looks like a boot in the Mediterranean Sea. Three branches of the Mediterranean surround Italy—the Tyrrhenian (tuh REE nee uhn) Sea, the Ionian Sea, and the Adriatic Sea. The Italian Peninsula is about 750 miles (1,207 km) long.

Italy has a land area of 116,305 square miles (301,229.7 sq km). It is about as large as the state of Arizona. In addition to the Italian Peninsula, Italy includes the large islands of Sicily and Sardinia, as well as many smaller islands along the west coast. Two tiny countries—Vatican City and San Marino—lie within Italy's territory.

Point out to students that many of the lakes of northern Italy were created when morainic rock from ancient glaciers blocked river valleys.

2.1 Landscape and Climate

Italy is a rugged land with a long coastline. The climate is generally mild, with some differences from north to south.

Landscape. In the north of Italy, the Alps curve around the border of the country for about 500 miles (804.6 km). They separate Italy from France, Switzerland, and Austria. The highest point in the Italian Alps is Monte Rosa at 15,217 feet (4,638 m) above sea level. In the foothills south of the Alps is an area of lakes. The most important lakes are Maggiore (muh JOHR ee), Lugano, Como, and Garda.

Italy's Apennine (AP uh nyn) Mountains curve out from the Italian Alps into the central and southern parts of the country. This chain is often called the "backbone" of the peninsula. The Apennines are lower than the Alps. They fan out into low hills in the east and west. This pattern of mountains and hills is also found in Sicily and Sardinia.

The southern Apennines sometimes have earthquakes and landslides. Also there are a number of volcanoes in this area. In 63 AD the ancient city of Pompeii near Naples was damaged by an earthquake. When Mount Vesuvius erupted in 79 AD, its lava buried Pompeii. Mount Etna, an active volcano in Sicily, erupted in 1969.

Although mountains and hills cover most of Italy, there are also lowland areas. In the north, the largest lowland is the Po River Valley, a very densely populated part of the country. The Po River, Italy's longest, flows from the French border to the Adriatic Sea.

Climate. Nearly all of Italy has a mild climate with sunny summers and rainy winters. In spring and summer, hot, dry winds blow across the Italian Peninsula from north Africa. In fall and winter, this hot air is replaced by cool, moist air from the Atlantic Ocean. At this time of year, the weather is cold and snowy in the mountains. Along the

See the TAE for an Objective 2 Activity.

A good water supply in the Po River Valley provides Italy with its best farming area. How does the northern area of Italy differ from the southern area?

Mediterranean Sea and in the Po River Valley, winter temperatures are usually mild. The Alps shield most of northern Italy from the cold air of northern and central Europe.

Most of Italy gets enough rain to grow crops. The north has even rainfall all through the year. Farther south, however, it becomes drier. In parts of Sicily and Sardinia, there is very little rain.

Northern Italy enjoys excellent transportation and communication links with the prosperous countries of Northwest Europe. These links encourage industry.

2.2 Economic and Cultural Patterns

Italy is the wealthiest country of Mediterranean Europe. However, economic activities in the north differ greatly from those in the south. Northern Italy is one of the most prosperous areas of Europe. It has modern, efficient industries and farms. Southern Italy is poorer and less developed economically. Little industry is found there, and farming is difficult because of the rocky soil. The average income in the south is about half that of the north. Since World War II, the Italian government has tried to improve the economy in southern Italy.

Italy varies in the quality of natural resources. It has few minerals, except for mercury and sulfur, and few forests. However, as Figure 18-2 shows on page 369, Italy has valuable energy sources in natural gas deposits and hydroelectric power. It also has much fertile soil in the north.

Italy is the third most important agricultural country in Europe, after the Soviet Union and France. Most of Italy's agriculture centers on the Po River Valley. Farmers in the Po River Valley grow wheat, corn, rice, and sugar beets. Those in hilly areas of northern and central Italy grow wine grapes. Italy is one of the world's major wine-producing countries. It also produces cheeses, olives, lemons, melons, and oranges.

The Val Vibrata area near the Adriatic Sea has seen astounding growth in cottage industries—small, privately owned businesses. The Val Vibrata Development Association reports that several hundred such companies produce a variety of designer goods for sale throughout the world.

LAND USE AND RESOURCES
OF MEDITERRANEAN EUROPE

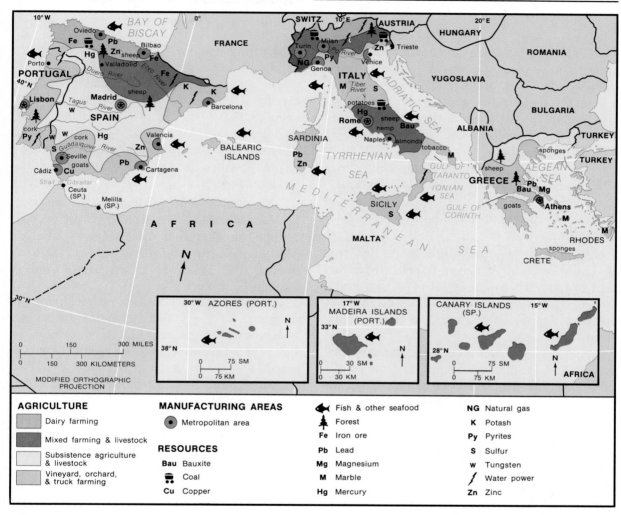

FIGURE 18-2

The mild climate of Mediterranean Europe favors various types of agriculture over extensive areas of the region. Relatively small land areas of Mediterranean Europe are devoted to manufacturing. Which two countries of this region have the most manufacturing areas?

Hydroelectric power is an efficient, relatively inexpensive way to produce electricity, but sending electricity to distant users is costly. Italy's factories near power generation facilities enjoy great cost advantages.

Most manufacturing in Italy takes place in the northern cities of Milan, Genoa, and Turin. These cities are near sources of hydroelectric power in the Alps. They also have a large number of skilled workers. Italian industries make steel, cars, chemicals, machinery, and clothing.

Most of Italy's 57.4 million people live in cities and towns. Rome, located in the center of Italy, is the capital and largest city. Its population is about 2.8 million. Naples is the largest city in the south with about 1.2 million people. Once a great trading city, Naples today is very poor and crowded.

FOCUS ON GEOGRAPHY

EUROPE'S POSTAGE-STAMP COUNTRIES

There are many small countries in different places around the world. Some of the smallest are often called *postage-stamp countries*. This name refers to their tiny size. It also points out that some of them receive part of their income from the sale of postage stamps to collectors.

Europe has five postage-stamp countries. They are Andorra, Liechtenstein, Monaco, San Marino, and Vatican City. Each is small in land area and population, and each is fascinating in its own way.

Andorra. Andorra sits high in the Pyrenees between France and Spain. It has an area of only 185 square miles (479.1 sq km). Its population is about 48,000. Most of the country is made up of rugged mountains and deep valleys.

Andorra's foreign affairs and defense are handled by France and Spain. The president of France and the Bishop of Seo de Urgel in Spain are coprinces of Andorra.

Andorra has had its present borders since the 1200s. Today it is a favorite spot for tourists from the rest of Europe. They come to enjoy the beautiful scenery and historic buildings, including churches dating back to 1100 AD.

Liechtenstein. Liechtenstein is a monarchy with a prince as ruler. For that reason, the official name of this country is the Principality of Liechtenstein.

The country has some 62 square miles (160.6 sq km) of land and a population of 27,000. It lies in the Alps between Switzerland and Austria.

Liechtenstein was set up in 1719 and has been independent since 1815. It has close ties with both Austria and Switzerland. The Swiss handle its foreign affairs and defense.

Despite its tiny size, Liechtenstein is highly industrialized. About 45 factories make light machinery and metal goods for export. The demand for labor has brought about 5,000 expatriate workers to the country. They are from Switzerland, Italy, and Austria. The government's major source of income is from the sale of postage stamps to foreign collectors.

Monaco. The Principality of Monaco lies on the Mediterranean Sea. It is surrounded on the other three sides by France. Monaco has only 0.6 square miles (1.5 sq km) of land area. This is about the size of Central Park in New York City.

There are about 29,000 people living in Monaco. The city is famous for its scenic beauty and for the casino at Monte Carlo. It has been a favorite center for wealthy tourists since 1856, the year the casino was built. The Monaco Grand Prix, a famous car race, takes place there every year.

Monaco is also known for its Oceanographic Museum, a center for the study of sea life. It is run by the scientist Jacques Cousteau and is one of the finest in the world.

San Marino. San Marino is located in north central Italy. It is known as the world's smallest republic. This does not mean that it is the world's smallest country, only that it is the smallest country to have a representative government.

The area of San Marino is about 24 square miles (62.2 sq km). The population numbers about 23,000. The capital also is called San Marino. Most of the country's economic activity takes place there. Serravalle is the only other town.

San Marino has had its own government since the 1100s. Although it is completely

POSTAGE-STAMP COUNTRIES

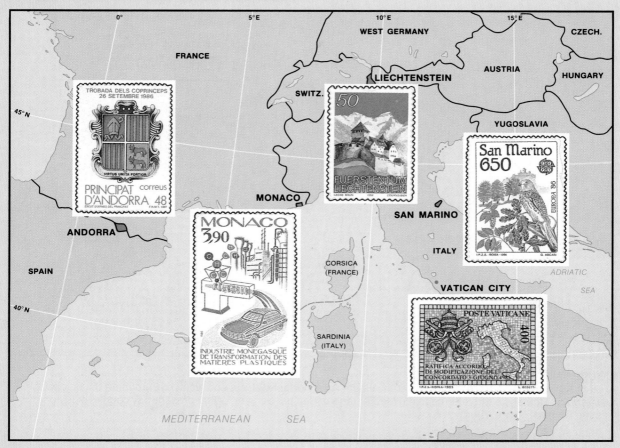

surrounded by Italy, the people are proud of their independence.

Vatican City.   Lying within the city of Rome, Italy, is the tiny country of Vatican City. It has an area of only 0.17 square miles (0.44 sq km). Its population is about 1,000. Nearly all these people are officials of the Roman Catholic Church. The governor is appointed by the Pope.

In general, because of their tiny size, postage-stamp countries do not have a great deal of influence in world affairs. However,

Vatican City is an exception. As the headquarters of the Roman Catholic Church, it provides religious leadership to millions of people around the world.

1. Why are the small countries of Europe called postage-stamp countries?

2. Where is Andorra located?

3. What form of government do Monaco and Liechtenstein have in common?

4. What makes Vatican City influential in world affairs?

GROWTH OF THE ROMAN EMPIRE

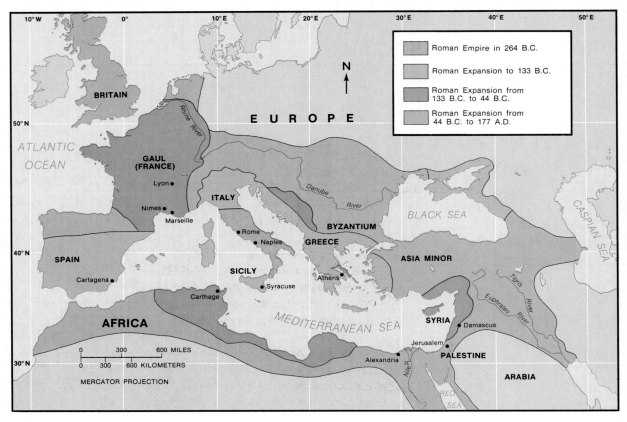

FIGURE 18-3
Ancient Rome once controlled much of southwestern Asia, northern Africa, and western Europe. At the height of their empire, Romans often referred to the Mediterranean Sea as "our sea." What present-day country of Europe was the Roman Empire's northernmost territory?

Have students research Venice's history to explain its past economic prominence and why it has declined.

Most of Italy's large and prosperous cities are in the north. Milan, the second largest city of Italy, dominates the Po River Valley. It has about 1.6 million people. Other important northern cities are Florence, Turin, Genoa, Venice, and Trieste.

Vatican City, the world center of the Roman Catholic Church, lies entirely within Rome. For centuries, the Roman Catholic Church was a major political force in Italy. Today the Church has less influence. However, more than 95 percent of Italians are Roman Catholic.

The fork was invented by early Italians for the purpose of eating pasta.

Like other Mediterranean Europeans, the Italians enjoy the outdoors, celebrate many festivals, and spend time visiting with family and friends. Food is an important part of Italian life. **Pasta,** food made from flour and water, is the basic dish in Italy. It includes spaghetti, lasagna, and ravioli.

For centuries, the Italians have been world leaders in the arts. From 1300 to 1600, a cultural movement known as the Renaissance was centered in Italy. During this time, such outstanding artists as Michelangelo and Leonardo da Vinci worked in Italy. **Opera,**

In the city-states of Italy about 1350, revived interest in Greek and Roman philosophy led to a flowering of the arts and sciences later called the Renaissance. Florence, under Lorenzo de' Medici, was a main Renaissance city. Have interested students research inventions or innovations in science and geography during this time.

an art form blending music, voice, and drama, began in Italy during the 1600s and is still popular today.

Italy's Leonardo da Vinci was also one of history's greatest inventors.

2.3 Influences of the Past

Around 500 BC Rome became Italy's central city. Much of its culture came from earlier peoples, such as the Latins, Etruscans, and Greeks, who settled in Italy. The Romans developed skills in engineering and law.

From the 200s BC to the 400s AD, Rome ruled a large Mediterranean empire that also included part of western Europe. This empire is shown in Figure 18-3 on page 372. The Romans passed on many of their achievements to western civilization. For example, many people in the world today use alphabets based on the Latin alphabet of Rome. The Latin language, as Figure 18-4 on this page shows, also helped form the modern-day languages of French, Spanish, Portuguese, Italian, and Romanian. The Roman Empire adopted Christianity and later helped to spread it all through the western world.

During the 400s AD, the Roman Empire fell apart, and Italy was divided into **city-states.** Each of these territories included an independent city and the countryside around it. During the 1200s Italian city-states, such as Venice, Genoa, and Milan, prospered from trade with Asia. They also traded with Europe north of the Alps.

Wealthy citizens in the Italian city-states became interested in art and literature. In the 1300s artists and writers began studying early Greek and Roman ideas. They soon produced their own great works of art and literature. Much Renaissance art can be seen today in Florence and other Italian cities.

Italy remained divided into city-states until the 1860s. At that time, after many wars and revolutions, the Italians joined together and united their country. In 1870 Rome became the last territory to join the new Italian kingdom. Because of Rome's central location, it was chosen as the capital.

Like the Iberian Peninsula, Italy went through a period of political unrest during the 1900s. The country was under the rule of the dictator Benito Mussolini from 1922 to 1945. Mussolini promised to make Italy a great world power, as it had been in the days of the Roman Empire. During World War II, Italy sided with Germany. After the war, Italy became a democratic republic. Since 1945, Italy's government has changed hands many

WORDS OF LATIN ORIGIN

LATIN	ENGLISH	GERMAN	FRENCH	ITALIAN	PORTUGUESE	ROMANIAN	SPANISH
sol	sun	sonne	soleil	sole	sol	soare	sol
lux	light	licht	lumiere	luce	luz	lumina	luz
nox	night	nacht	nuit	notte	noite	noapte	noche
mater	mother	mutter	mere	madre	mai	mama	madre
pater	father	vater	pere	padre	pai	tata	padre
	Germanic languages		Romance languages				

FIGURE 18-4
The Latin language was the *lingua franca,* or common language, of Europe for hundreds of years. Latin words form the roots of many modern English words as well as words spoken in the languages shown in this chart. For example, what English word derived from Latin is used as an adjective to describe an eclipse of the sun?

times among the different political parties. These changes have made it difficult for the country's leaders to follow a consistent policy.

CONTENT CHECK

1. **Identify:** Italy, Tyrrhenian Sea, Ionian Sea, Adriatic Sea, Italian Peninsula, Sicily, Sardinia, Vatican City, San Marino, Apennine Mountains, Mount Etna, Po River, Rome, Naples, Milan, Renaissance, Latins, Etruscans, Benito Mussolini.

2. **Define:** pasta, opera, city-states.

3. What two large islands are part of Italy's national territory?

4. What kinds of landscape does Italy have?

5. How are northern and southern Italy different?

6. What world religion is centered in Rome?

7. What city-states arose in Italy during the 1200s?

8. How does Italy rank among the nations of Mediterranean Europe in its agricultural development?

9. **Challenge:** Italy has been a divided country throughout much of its history. What geographical factors might have contributed to Italy's national disunity?

3. GREECE

To the east of Italy lies the Hellenic Republic, which is the official name of the country of Greece. Greece lies at the southern tip of the Balkan Peninsula. Its land area of 50,942 square miles (131,939.7 sq km) also includes some 3,000 islands. Most of Greece is very rocky and mountainous.

3.1 Landscape and Climate

The landscape and climate of Greece have much in common with many of the other countries of Mediterranean Europe. Greece is a rugged land. Its winters are mild and wet, yet summers in Greece are hot and dry.

Landscape. The mainland of Greece borders Turkey in the east and Bulgaria, Yugoslavia, and Albania in the north. The Ionian Sea is to the west and the Aegean (ih JEE uhn) Sea to the east. The Pindus Mountains run through the center of mainland Greece. They dominate the landscape of the region. The land west of the Pindus Mountains is limestone. This rock soaks up moisture, making the land very dry and rugged. There are lowlands to the east of the mountains—the Plain of Thessaly and the Macedonia-Thrace Plain. These two plains are Greece's major agricultural areas for growing many kinds of crops. Rising north of the Plain of Thessaly is Mount Olympus, 9,570 feet (2,917 m) high. It is the highest point in Greece. Ancient Greeks believed it was the home of their gods.

At the southern end of the Pindus range is another lowland—the Plain of Attica. Nearly 40 percent of Greece's population lives there. Athens, the Greek capital, is located in the Plain of Attica.

Southwest of the Plain of Attica is the Peloponnesus (pehl uh puh NEE suhs), a large peninsula of rugged mountains and deep valleys. The Peloponnesus is linked to the mainland by the Isthmus of Corinth. This isthmus is cut by the Corinth Canal, making the Peloponnesus almost an island.

Islands are scattered on all sides of the mainland of Greece. They range in size from less than an acre (0.4 ha) to more than 3,000 square miles (7,770 sq km). Crete, south and east of the Peloponnesus, is the largest of the islands. It is about the size of Puerto Rico.

Greece's islands account for about one-fifth of the country's total land area.

Tourism is threatened, from time to time, by concerns about security at Athens International Airport. The government of Greece is working to improve this.

The Ionian Islands are in the Ionian Sea west of the Greek mainland. Another island group is the Aegean Islands. They are 200 miles (321.9 km) from the mainland of Greece but only 5 miles (8 km) from the coast of Turkey.

Climate. Nearly all of Greece has a Mediterranean climate. However, the mountains cause some differences. High areas in Greece are often cooler and wetter than lowlands. The north and west slopes of the mountains receive more rain than the east and south slopes because of the prevailing winds and the orographic effect.

Most of the rain in Greece falls during winter. Athens, for example, gets three-fourths of its rain between October and March. The city gets only 15 inches (38.1 cm) of precipitation a year.

See the *TAE* for an *Objective 3* Activity.

3.2 Economic and Cultural Patterns

Greece has one of the least developed economies in Europe. Most Greeks farm. However, only about 30 percent of the land is good for farming. With only small areas of lowlands, Greece has developed what is called a **hill-land economy.** This means there is farming in the valleys and livestock grazing on the hills. The mild climate of Greece, however, makes it possible to grow most crops year round.

Partly because of the hilly landscape, many farms in Greece are very small. The average farm on the Peloponnesus, for example, is about 8 acres (3.2 ha). In the United States, the average farm is 440 acres (178 ha). Most Greek farmers are poor and cannot afford fertilizers or machinery. They chiefly grow citrus fruits, olives, and wine grapes.

Larger farms, however, are found in the lowland areas. Farmers there grow sugar beets, wheat, fruit, and tobacco. In exporting

A coastal town on Míkonos Island basks in sunlight and the deep blue Aegean Sea. Greece's islands promote tourism. What is Greece's largest island?

See the *TRB* for the *Section 3 Extending the Lesson* on Salonika.

goods, they have easier contact with ports along the seacoast than do farmers living in the mountains and hills.

The sea has long been important to the Greeks. Sardines and sponges are two products from the sea. The waters surrounding Greece, however, are more important for trade than for fishing. Greece is one of the world's leading shipping countries. It lies on the crossroads of trade between western Europe, southwest Asia, and the Soviet Union.

Greece has very few mineral deposits. As a result, manufacturing accounts for only 20 percent of the country's national income. Many manufactured goods are imported. Most factories in Greece are in the Athens area. Leading Greek industrial products are cigarettes, clothing, aluminum, chemicals, and paper.

An industry that has helped the Greek economy is tourism—business of travel and recreation. It has increased rapidly since the

NATIONS OF MEDITERRANEAN EUROPE _____

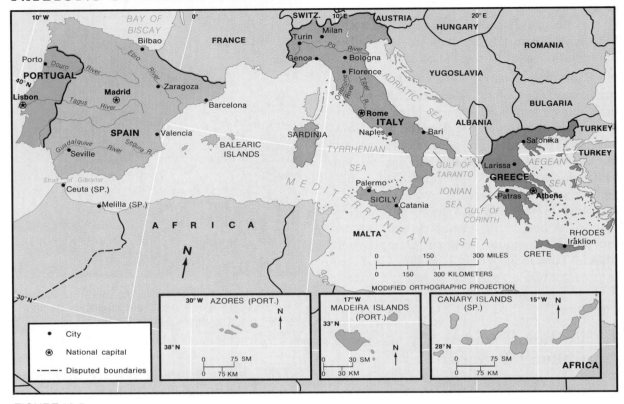

FIGURE 18-5

Although their historical greatness lies in the past, the countries of Mediterranean Europe helped shape the cultures of nations throughout the modern world. European civilization began in Greece and Italy and was carried abroad by Spain and Portugal. Which country in the region does not border on the Mediterranean Sea?

Have interested students research and report on Greek historic sites such as the Acropolis or the Minoan civilization of the Greek island of Crete.

1960s and now brings much income into the country. Outstanding attractions in Greece are historic sites of ancient Greek civilizations and beaches of the sunny Greek islands.

Greece has about 10 million people, the smallest population of the countries of Mediterranean Europe. About 70 percent of Greeks live in urban areas. Most urban dwellers live in Athens, which has more than 3 million people.

The Greeks are known for their love of life. They enjoy celebrations and conversation in their town and village squares. Greeks are known to debate politics in sidewalk cafés and coffee shops. In the past, close ties bound

together parents and children. However, the spread of urban ways since the mid-1900s has weakened the strong role of the family in Greek life, as it has in other urban nations. Today, more grown children are making their own decisions about marriage and careers without asking for their parents' approval.

About 95 percent of Greeks are Eastern Orthodox Christians. Religion is taught in the public schools and influences much of Greek daily life. Easter is the most important Greek holiday. On the eve of Easter, Greeks attend church at midnight and watch fireworks after the service. The next day they feast on lamb and enjoy lively folk dances.

3.3 Influences of the Past

Greece was settled by people from western Asia about 3,000 years ago. Separated by mountains and the sea, the early Greeks set up city-states. Most city-states were small in size and population. Each city-state was protected by a fortified hill called an **acropolis** (uh KRAHP uh luhs).

Athens was the most important of the Greek city-states. The people of Athens became known for their art, architecture, writing, and philosophy. Many of their ideas were later passed to the Romans and from them to the rest of Europe. Two important ideas that the people of early Athens believed in were the value of the individual and the right of citizens to run their own government.

In the 300s BC, the Greeks were conquered by the warrior-ruler Alexander the Great, who set up a large empire that centered on Greece and much of southwest Asia. Later the Greeks were ruled by the Romans. After the fall of Rome in the 400s AD, the Greeks formed the Byzantine Empire in the land that was once the eastern part of the Roman Empire.

During the late 1400s, the Byzantine Empire lost its power, and Greece was conquered by the Ottoman Turks. In the early 1800s, the Greeks revolted against Ottoman Turkish rule and set up an independent kingdom. By the late 1800s, they began developing their economy and modernizing their cities. However, the 1900s was a period of war and political unrest for Greece. In World War II, it suffered under German rule. After World War II, a civil war divided the country between communists and **royalists**, people who favor rule by a king or queen. After these wars Greece began to rebuild its economy. After a short period of military rule from 1967 to 1974, the country became a democratic republic with close ties to Northwest Europe.

CONTENT CHECK

1. **Identify:** Hellenic Republic, Greece, Balkan Peninsula, Pindus Mountains, Plain of Thessaly, Mount Olympus, Athens, Peloponnesus, Isthmus of Corinth, Crete, Ionian Islands, Aegean Islands, Alexander the Great, Byzantine Empire, Ottoman Turks.

2. **Define:** hill-land economy, acropolis, royalists.

3. What are the general features of the landscape and climate of Greece?

4. How does the population of Greece compare in size to the populations of Spain, Portugal, and Italy?

5. How do most Greek farms compare with those in the United States?

6. How does the sea contribute to Greece's economy?

7. In what economic activity is Greece a world leader?

8. **Challenge:** Much of Greece is very dry. How does the presence of limestone contribute to this drought?

See the *TAE* for an *Objective 4* Activity.

CONCLUSION

Mediterranean Europe is the birthplace of western civilization. In ancient times many advanced cultures developed in the region and influenced the rest of Europe. In early modern times, Mediterranean Europeans established overseas empires all over the world.

Today Mediterranean Europe no longer leads its own continent or the rest of the world. Although its economies are modernizing, the people of the region face the problems of high prices, unemployment, and limited resources. However, Mediterranean Europe has not lost its importance to other Europeans because of its past and present contributions to world culture.

CHAPTER REVIEW

SUMMARY

1. Three peninsulas jut out into the Mediterranean Sea. They are the Iberian, Italian, and Balkan peninsulas.
2. Spain and Portugal lie on the Iberian Peninsula. Italy takes up nearly all of the Italian Peninsula, and Greece is at the southern tip of the Balkan Peninsula.
3. Spain is the largest country in Mediterranean Europe in land area.
4. Portugal became independent in the 1100s. Once a great power, it is today one of the poorest countries in Europe.
5. Italy has the largest population and is the leading industrial country in Mediterranean Europe.
6. Greece lies farthest east of Mediterranean Europe. Its land area includes many islands in the Mediterranean Sea.

Answers to the following questions can be found on page T195.

REVIEWING VOCABULARY

For each of the following definitions, write the correct term from this chapter.

1. system of farming in valleys and grazing livestock on hills
2. value of all goods and services produced by a country for its own use
3. those who work in a country other than their own
4. independent territory that included a city and the surrounding countryside
5. fortified hill of a Greek city-state
6. political and economic system in which the government, through the will of the people's elected leaders, owns factories and other means of production
7. art form blending music, voice, and drama

REMEMBERING THE FACTS

1. What are the four major countries of Mediterranean Europe?
2. What is the name of the peninsula where Spain and Portugal are located?
3. What general climate and physical features are shared by the countries of Mediterranean Europe?
4. What is the name of the highland plateau that is the largest physical feature in Spain?
5. What is the leading industrial country of Mediterranean Europe?
6. In what part of Italy is most of the country's population concentrated?
7. Within what Italian city is the world headquarters of the Roman Catholic Church located?
8. What is Greece's official name?
9. What is the capital and largest city of Greece?
10. What is the part of mainland Greece south of the Isthmus of Corinth called?
11. What mountain range runs through the center of mainland Greece?

UNDERSTANDING THE FACTS

1. What are some differences between Spain's Meseta region and its Andalusian Lowland?
2. What brings large amounts of rain to the northwestern Iberian Peninsula?
3. How does climate differ between northern and southern Italy?
4. Today the Po River Valley is a leading agricultural, as well as industrial, area of Italy. Why is this area so productive?
5. Which natural resources are available and scarce in Mediterranean Europe?
6. Why is agriculture a difficult occupation in Mediterranean Europe?
7. How did the growing wealth of the Italian city-states give rise to the period called the Renaissance?
8. What political changes have come to Greece, Italy, and the Iberian Peninsula since World War II?

THINKING CRITICALLY AND CREATIVELY

1. Why do workers leave Mediterranean Europe to find work in other parts of the continent?
2. Two important mountain chains in Mediterranean Europe are the Alps and the Pyrenees. What effect has each mountain chain had on the movement of peoples and goods through Europe?
3. How has Greece's location helped it become a leading shipping nation?
4. Why have the Mediterranean countries of Europe had so much political unrest during the 1900s?
5. **Challenge:** Part of the Alps is in Italy. If the Alps should fall under the control of a country unfriendly to Italy, what impact might there be on the economy of Italy?
6. **Challenge:** An expression "Africa begins at the Pyrenees" was once used to describe the Iberian Peninsula. What do you think it means? Do you think it is accurate today? Why or why not?
7. **Challenge:** Explain why the early city-states in Italy and Greece developed in coastal areas with good ports.

REINFORCING GRAPHIC SKILLS

Study the graphs on pages 362–363. Then answer the questions that follow.

1. Which Mediterranean country experienced the greatest decline in per capita GNP between 1982 and 1983?
2. About how many times greater was Italy's total GNP in 1981 than Portugal's total GNP in 1981? About how many times greater was West Germany's total GNP in 1981 than Italy's total GNP in that same year?
3. **Challenge:** Locate in the National Profiles chart in the Appendix of this book the populations of the countries studied in the graphs. Study the information about each country. Make a hypothesis about what influences on the economy explain why the GNPs of Mediterranean Europe are much lower than those of the leading countries in Northwest Europe.

CHAPTER 19

The Danube River is generally navigable from West Germany to the Black Sea and is used for commerce in Eastern Europe.

Danube River flowing through Budapest, Hungary

EASTERN EUROPE

- What physical features and climate patterns are found in Eastern Europe.
- How economic development differs throughout Eastern Europe.
- How the peoples of Eastern Europe are governed.

A common bond between Eastern European countries is their communist forms of government.

INTRODUCTION

Eastern Europe lies between Northwest Europe and Mediterranean Europe to the west and south and the Soviet Union to the east. About 1,050 miles (1,689.8 km) stretch from Eastern Europe's northernmost point to its southernmost point. From its easternmost point to its westernmost point, the region covers about 700 miles (1,126.5 km). Its total land area is about the same as Peru's.

Eight countries make up this region. They are East Germany, Poland, and Czechoslovakia (CHEHK uh sloh VAHK ee uh) in the north, and Hungary, Romania, Yugoslavia, Bulgaria, and Albania in the south. Eastern Europe may be divided into two parts. The northern part of the region is made up of Poland, Czechoslovakia, and East Germany. The southern part is made up of Hungary, Yugoslavia, Romania, Bulgaria, and Albania. Poland and East Germany have coasts on the Baltic Sea. Czechoslovakia and Hungary are landlocked. Yugoslavia, Romania, Bulgaria, and Albania lie on the Balkan Peninsula, north of Greece.

The landscapes of the region include highlands, valleys, plains, and other lowlands. These are shown in Figure 19-1 on page 382. Because Eastern Europe lies in the middle latitudes, all of the countries have moist climates. The specific kind of climate depends on each area's latitude and its nearness to the ocean.

The countries of Eastern Europe are alike in two other ways. First, although some of the countries have short coastlines along the Baltic, Adriatic, and Black seas, for the most part they are not open to the sea. Leading population centers and industrial areas are not along the coasts. Also, their capital cities are inland.

Second, the countries are greatly influenced by their eastern neighbor, the Soviet Union. Eastern European cultures have become similar to the Soviet Union's, especially during the twentieth century. This is why Eastern Europe and the Soviet Union are viewed by many geographers as a single culture area of the world.

Since the end of World War II in 1945, most of the countries in Eastern Europe have become satellites of the Soviet Union. A **satellite country** is one that depends on another country for authority and direction. East Germany, Poland, Czechoslovakia, Hungary, Romania, and Bulgaria are satellite countries. In their foreign affairs, economies, and governments, they are closely tied to the Soviet Union. Yugoslavia maintains contact with both communist and noncommunist countries. It has kept out of the Soviet Union's control, as has Albania. Albania has very limited contacts with most other countries in the world.

As communist countries, all of the nations of Eastern Europe share certain characteristics. They have **planned economies.**

The mountain ranges in Southeastern Europe have played a vital role in the histories of countries located there. Serving as natural fortresses, the mountains have sheltered those people within them and have discouraged unwelcome visitors.

PHYSICAL REGIONS OF EASTERN EUROPE _____

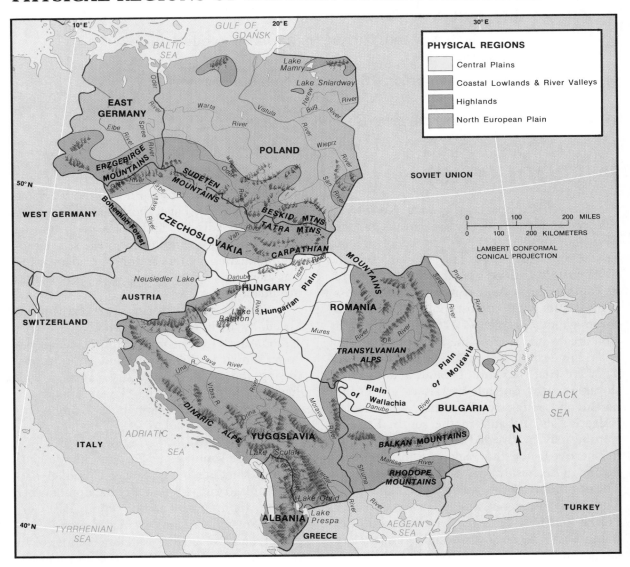

FIGURE 19-1
This physical regions map shows two large areas of plains separated and surrounded by mountainous highlands. Which mountain chains form natural boundaries between some countries of Eastern Europe?

See page 395 for a political map of Eastern Europe.

See the *TAE* for an *Objective 1* Activity.

This means that each country's government sets goals for the economy, determining what and how much should be produced. This planning is done for both farming and industry in the countries of this region.

The countries of Eastern Europe also differ in many ways. Within this region exists a variety of ethnic groups. Each group has its own special traditions, customs, and beliefs, which makes each country unique.

The three countries of Northeastern Europe and three of the countries in Southeastern Europe—Hungary, Romania, and Bulgaria—have united to form COMECON—Council for Mutual Economic Assistance. Through this organization they work to improve their countries' economies.

1. NORTHEASTERN EUROPE

The three countries of the northern part of Eastern Europe—East Germany, Poland, and Czechoslovakia—have just over half the entire region's population. Poland, with 37.8 million people, has more people than any other country in Eastern Europe. With a land area of 120,726 square miles (312,680.1 sq km), Poland also is the largest.

Note that population densities are much higher in flatland areas than in mountainous or hilly areas.

1.1 Landscape and Climate

East Germany and Poland have landscapes of flat land in the north and mountains and hills in the south. Czechoslovakia is mountainous on its borders and has plains and hills in its interior. All three countries have climates with warm summers.

Landscape. The northern sections of East Germany and Poland are part of the North European Plain. The name Poland comes from *polanie* (POH lah nee), which means plains or plains people. Plains and low hills make up about two-thirds of Poland's land area.

Northern Poland has chains of low hills that break up the flat land. The hills rise to 900 feet (274.3 m) in some places. Known as the Baltic Heights, they were made by mounds of rock left behind by glaciers. The soil in the hills is sandy. There are also many lakes and ponds in northern Poland.

Highlands are found in southern East Germany and southern Poland. The Erzgebirge (EHRTS guh BIHR guh), or Ore, Mountains separate East Germany from Czechoslovakia. West to east, the Sudeten (soo DAYT uhn), Beskid, and Carpathian (kahr PAY thee uhn) mountains lie along the border between Poland and Czechoslovakia.

Czechoslovakia is more mountainous than either Poland or East Germany. The Tatra Mountains cover much of Slovakia, the eastern part of the country. They are part of the larger Carpathian mountain chain. The Tatras have Eastern Europe's highest peak, Gerlachovka (gehr luh KAWF kuh), at 8,710 feet (2,654.8 m). Thick, coniferous forests cover the foothills of the Tatras. Tundra grasses and snow cover the high peaks. Czechoslovakia's most important lowland area is in the western part of the country in Bohemia. It is part of the Labe (LAH beh) River Basin.

Climate. All of the countries of Northeastern Europe have moist climates with warm summers. Most of East Germany has a middle-latitude marine climate with mild winters. The western halves of Poland and Czechoslovakia also have a marine climate. Warm winds from the North Atlantic Current influence the weather there. The eastern halves of Poland and Czechoslovakia have a humid continental with warm summers climate. Their location in the central part of Europe accounts for this kind of climate.

Generally, precipitation in Northeastern Europe is adequate. Most places receive more than 20 inches (50.8 cm) a year. Some is in the form of snow. The mountainous areas may get as much as 60 inches (152.4 cm) of precipitation a year.

Refer students to pages 96—97 to review the map of Earth's Climate Regions.

1.2 Economic and Cultural Patterns

The countries of Northeastern Europe are more industrialized and urban than those in Southeastern Europe. They are the economic leaders of the region.

East Germany. The German Democratic Republic is the official name of East Germany. It is the most urban and industrial country in Eastern Europe. Its population is

East Berlin is a major city boasting of many modern buildings and avenues. What is the population of this East German capital city?

In 1961 the Berlin Wall was built to stop East Berliners from fleeing into West Berlin and West Germany.

about 16.7 million. About 77 percent of East Germans live in towns and cities. East Berlin, with a population of 1.2 million, is the largest city and capital.

East Germans enjoy the highest standard of living in Eastern Europe. About one-half of East Germany's national income comes from industry. The country's chief industries are run by the government. They make metal products, cars, cement, chemicals, and some consumer products, such as television sets. The largest industrial centers are East Berlin, Leipzig, and Dresden.

East Germany's agriculture is more productive than that of the other countries of Eastern Europe. As in other communist countries, the government discourages private property. In most cases it has the farmers organized into **collective farms,** or farmland owned jointly by farmers. Workers are paid out of the profits made from selling the farm's products. In other cases the farmers work on **state farms** owned and run by the government. On state farms workers are paid a wage like factory workers.

Much of East Germany's trade is with the Soviet Union, which lacks many of the consumer goods made in East Germany's factories.

East German farmers grow potatoes, sugar beets, barley, wheat, rye, and oats. Pigs and dairy cattle are the major livestock. East Germany has large areas of flat land. However not all these areas have good soil. As a result some food has to be imported to meet the people's needs.

The East Germans are known for their love of music and learning, their respect for authority, and their devotion to work. Through the centuries they have played an important role in Eastern Europe. During the 1000s and 1100s, the people in the eastern part of Germany founded farming settlements and trading cities all over Northeastern Europe. As a result the German language and culture became widely known in the region.

Most East Germans are Protestants. In fact, East Germany is the only Protestant country in Eastern Europe. This is largely because in the 1500s the Lutheran religion began in the eastern part of Germany. Today many East Germans still practice their faith in spite of the communist government's efforts to discourage religion.

Poland. Poland is both an agricultural and an industrial country, but it is not as prosperous as East Germany. Much of northern Poland has poor soil and is underdeveloped. However, farmers are able to grow crops such as potatoes, rye, barley, and oats. Poland's best farmland lies in the central part of the country. In this flat area, farmers raise wheat, sugar beets, and rye. They also tend beef and dairy cattle.

Unlike in other communist countries, most of the farmland in Poland is owned by private individuals rather than by the government. Poland's farmers have been against collective farms or state farms. One result is that Polish farms remain small. Very little modern machinery is used, so output is low.

Poland's major industrial regions are in the central and southern parts of the country.

EUROPE UNIT 6

LAND USE AND RESOURCES OF EASTERN EUROPE

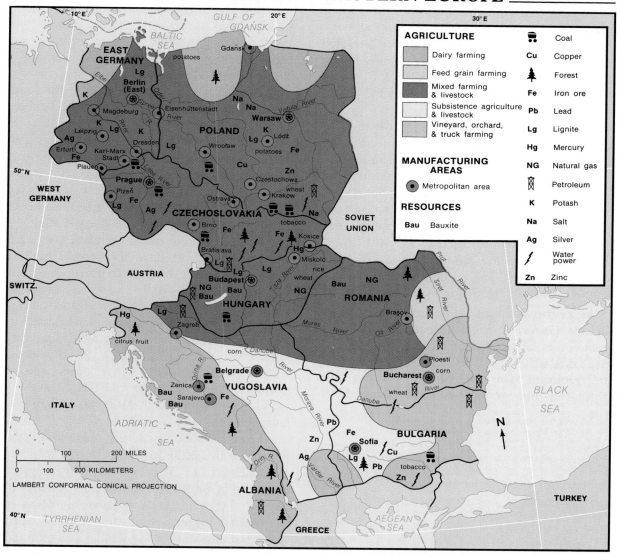

FIGURE 19-2

Agriculture is extensive throughout Eastern Europe with many manufacturing areas scattered throughout the region. A variety of important natural resources is also located here. Which resources are found in Poland?

Poland's fairly level terrain made this area a natural route for armies to cross throughout history.

A baby boom in Poland peaked in 1983 and has strained Poland's resources.

Warsaw, Poland's capital and largest city, has a population of about 1.6 million. Located on the Vistula (VIHSH chuh luh) River, Warsaw is an important center of transportation, with many water and railroad routes serving the city.

Łódź (looj), Poland's second largest city, has about 845,000 people. It lies southwest of Warsaw near the edge of the Silesian-Polish Plateau. Streams flowing down from the plateau are used for hydroelectricity for the city. Łódź is an important textile center.

CHAPTER 19   **EASTERN EUROPE**

385

Nicolaus Copernicus, the father of astronomy, was a Polish scientist educated at the University of Krakow.

Ask students to comment on the strategic importance of Czechoslovakia since it borders both the Soviet Union and West Germany.

Poland's richest industrial region, however, is in the southern highlands of Silesia (sy LEE zhee uh). Deposits of coal, copper, iron, lead, and zinc are mined there. The cities of Krakow, Czestochowa (CHEHN stuh KOH vuh), and Wrocław (VRAWT slahf) make iron, steel, and heavy machinery.

The Poles are part of a large ethnic group known as Slavs. The Slavs are the leading ethnic group in Eastern Europe. In addition to the Poles, the Slavs of Eastern Europe include Czechs, Slovaks, Bulgarians, and a number of groups in Yugoslavia. The Poles use the Latin alphabet and have close cultural ties to western Europe. In spite of communist government disapproval, they are still firmly loyal to the Roman Catholic Church. In 1978 a Polish church leader became Pope John Paul II, head of the Roman Catholic Church.

Czechoslovakia. Czechoslovakia has one of Eastern Europe's most industrialized economies. As Figure 19-2 shows on page 385, it is rich in coal, forests, and other natural resources. The government of Czechoslovakia runs the country's economy. Since 1948

Slavs are closely related to Russians, who are sometimes called their "Slavic brothers."

Most Czechoslovakian farms lie in fertile valleys and are an important economic resource. On what type of farms do most Czech farmers work?

it has encouraged the manufacture of steel, machinery, and transportation equipment. Czechoslovakia also makes glass, textiles, and beer. Most of the country's major industries are found in the two western regions— Bohemia and Moravia.

Agriculture is also important to the economy of Czechoslovakia. Rich farmland covers central Bohemia and Moravia. Slovakia, in the eastern part of the country, is also agricultural. Most farmers in Czechoslovakia work on collective or state farms. They grow many different crops, including barley, corn, rye, sugar beets, and wheat. They also raise hogs, poultry, sheep, and beef and dairy cattle.

Czechoslovakia has a population of 15.6 million. Its people have the second highest standard of living in Eastern Europe. About 74 percent of the people live in urban areas. Prague, Czechoslovakia's capital and largest city, has about 1.2 million people. Located in Bohemia, Prague is an important manufacturing center. It is also known for its old palaces, churches, and bridges. Other large cities in Czechoslovakia are Brno (BUHR noh), a manufacturing center in Moravia, and Bratislava, the capital of Slovakia.

Czechoslovakia is largely made up of two related groups of Slavs—the Czechs, who live in Bohemia and Moravia, and the Slovaks, who live in Slovakia. The Czechs form two-thirds of the country's population. Most of the remaining one-third are Slovaks. The Czechs and Slovaks share similar cultures and speak similar languages. A speaker of one language can easily understand the speaker of the other language.

Most Czechs and Slovaks are Roman Catholics, even though the communist government opposes the practice of religion. Few Czechs attend church. However, the Slovaks, like the Poles, are loyal to the Church.

The people of Czechoslovakia are known for their love of music. The country has produced many noted composers and musicians.

The Czech composers Bedřich Smetana wrote *The Bartered Bride,* and Anton Dvořák wrote the *New World Symphony.*

Refer students to the map on page 388 showing the changing boundaries of Poland.

Although most Czechs and Slovaks live in cities, they still enjoy the culture of their rural past. Folk music is also very popular.

In recent years the Czech government has poured millions of dollars into the sport of tennis and has turned out a large number of world-class players.

1.3 Influences of the Past

Northeastern Europe has had a long history of wars, revolts, and political unrest. The flat land of East Germany and Poland and the rivers and valleys of Czechoslovakia have made it easy for people to move into the region from other areas. As a result Northeastern Europe's political boundaries have changed many times over the years.

Early Period. Northeastern Europe was settled by its present national groups between 500 and 900 AD. The Germans lived in what is now eastern Germany. However, groups of them settled all over Eastern Europe. The Slavs lived in areas to the east and south of the major German settlements. By 1000 AD the Germans and the Slavs had divided to form the Poles, the Czechs, and the Slovaks.

In the 900s AD, Poland became a united kingdom. Between the 1000s and 1300s, groups of German warriors invaded Poland. However, Polish kings and nobles turned them back. Until the late 1700s, Poland was one of the largest independent kingdoms in all of Europe. By the 1790s, however, fighting inside and outside the country had weakened Poland. At that time the country was divided among Russia, Austria, and the east German state of Prussia.

Meanwhile, the Czechs formed an independent kingdom in Bohemia. Their Slav neighbors, the Slovaks, however, were taken over by the Hungarians, who ruled Slovakia for nearly 1,000 years. From about the 900s to the 1500s, Bohemia remained independent. Then in 1526 the Hapsburgs, the royal family of Austria, brought Bohemia and the other

regions that are now Czechoslovakia into the Austrian Empire. The Czech and Slovak territories were part of the empire until after World War I in 1918.

Modern Period. After the end of World War I, Poland and Czechoslovakia became independent nations. Poland gained some land in the west from defeated Germany. Czechoslovakia ruled over areas that had large German populations.

In the 1930s Germany gained control of much of Czechoslovakia. In 1939 the German army invaded Poland, and in the process, World War II began. During the war years, Czechoslovakia remained under German control. At first Poland was divided between Germany and the Soviet Union. Later the Germans took control of the part of Poland occupied by the Soviets.

At the end of World War II, the Soviets drove the Germans from Northeastern Europe. They stayed to set up communist governments in Poland and the eastern part of Germany. In 1948 Soviet pressures brought Czechoslovakia under communist rule.

After gaining the western mountain region of Czechoslovakia, Hitler found it easy to march through the remaining flatlands of the country.

Soviet-backed troops entered Czechoslovakia in 1968 to restore communist authority. When did Czechoslovakia first come under communist rule?

USING GRAPHIC SKILLS

READING POLITICAL MAPS

Maps whose major purpose is to show political boundaries are called political maps. This kind of map shows a nation's land area, capital and other important cities, and borders. It may show how the country is divided into smaller governmental units, such as states, provinces, counties, parishes, and townships. A political map is included in this textbook for each chapter on world regions.

The map at right is a political map of Poland. Its chief purpose is to show land area and changing borders of Poland from 1918 to the present. Because it shows Poland's borders for three different time periods, it can also be viewed as a historical map. Instead of showing three different maps, each with Poland's borders at a certain time, the map combines all this information. This is a convenient way to show more information in less space.

Notice that different colors have been used to show changes in Poland's land area and borders. Different kinds of stripes are used to show land areas that once belonged or now belong to Poland.

Study the map on this page. Then answer the questions that follow.

1. How many areas of land did Poland gain from Germany in 1945? Where are these land areas located?

POLAND—1918 TO PRESENT

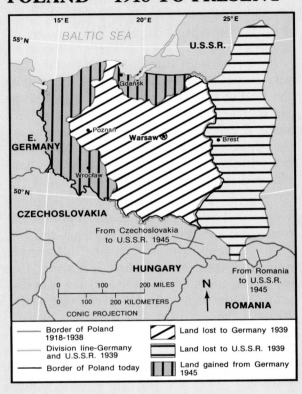

2. What cities were in Poland from 1918 to 1938 and also after 1945?

3. What city was part of Poland from 1918 to 1938 but not after 1945?

4. **Challenge:** What geographical advantages did Poland gain in 1945?

Have students research the changes in Czechoslovakia's borders since 1918.

Today East Germany, Poland, and Czechoslovakia are satellites of the Soviet Union. The Soviet Union sometimes has used force to keep them under control. For example, in 1968, troops of the Warsaw Pact—a military alliance of the Soviet Union and its satellites—moved into Czechoslovakia. They ended *reforms,* or changes to improve conditions, started by the Czechs and Slovaks to ease government controls. The Soviets saw many of these changes as threats to communist rule in Czechoslovakia.

The Poles also have demanded more freedom. In recent years Poland has had seri-

388

Have students prepare a chart comparing members of NATO and members of the Warsaw Pact.

See the *TRB* for *Teacher Notes: Section 1 Extending the Lesson* on the Berlin Wall.

ous economic problems. Farm output has been low, and the quality of industrial goods has been poor. Shortages of food and consumer goods have angered many Poles. In the early 1980s, Polish workers formed Solidarity, a labor union free of government control. They challenged the power of the communist government of Poland and wanted a strong voice in decisions about the economy. With the backing of the Soviets, Poland's communist rulers strengthened their hold over the country and stopped the workers' movement.

Solidarity was led by Lech Wałęsa, who in 1983 received the Nobel Peace Prize for his efforts to avoid violence while trying to gain workers' rights.

CONTENT CHECK

1. **Identify:** East Germany, Poland, Baltic Heights, Erzgebirge Mountains, Czechoslovakia, Tatra Mountains, Gerlachovka Peak, Bohemia, Labe River, German Democratic Republic, East Berlin, Warsaw, Vistula River, Łódź, Krakow, John Paul II, Prague, Slavs, Moravia, Slovaks, Slovakia, Hapsburgs, Warsaw Pact, Solidarity.

2. **Define:** collective farms, state farms.

3. What three countries make up Northeastern Europe?

4. What landscapes are found in Northeastern Europe?

5. Which country in Northeastern Europe has the highest standard of living? Which is the most populous?

6. What urban functions does Warsaw serve?

7. Under what country's control was Czechoslovakia from the 1500s to the 1900s?

8. **Challenge:** Why do you think winters in Northeastern Europe are generally colder than those in Northwest Europe?

2. SOUTHEASTERN EUROPE

The southern countries of Eastern Europe are Hungary, Yugoslavia, Romania, Bulgaria, and Albania. With the exception of Hungary, all are located in the Balkan Peninsula. Yugoslavia is the largest country in the group and the second largest nation in Eastern Europe. The countries of Southeastern Europe are not as industrialized as the countries of Northeastern Europe. Their agriculture is also less varied.

Stress that Southeastern Europe's terrain is more mountainous than that of Northeastern Europe.

2.1 Landscape and Climate

Southeastern Europe is a rugged, mountainous land with only three large lowland areas. The climate of this region is more diverse than that of Northeastern Europe.

Landscape. Mountains form a major part of the landscape of Southeastern Europe. The Carpathian Mountains begin in western Czechoslovakia and curve east and then south into Romania. Other mountain ranges in the area are the Transylvanian Alps in Romania and the Balkan Mountains in Bulgaria.

Southeastern Europe has only a few lowland areas. The largest lowland is the Hungarian Plain. It lies west of the curving Carpathian Mountains and takes up most of Hungary. Two major river basins in the plain are formed by the Tisza River and the Danube River.

The Danube River, which flows between Czechoslovakia and Hungary, is the major river in Southeastern Europe. Then it winds through Hungary into Yugoslavia. The river also forms the border between Romania and Bulgaria. In this area it waters two important plains areas—the Plain of Wallachia and the Plain of Moldavia. Both these plains have large areas of rich, black soil.

Where the Transylvanian Alps and Balkan Mountains meet, the Danube River has cut the deepest gorge in Europe. Known as the Iron Gate of the Danube, the gorge is about 2 miles (3.2 km) long. On both sides of the gorge, steep cliffs rise 2,600 feet (792.5 m) above the river. Past this point the Danube empties into the Black Sea.

Nagyvázsony is a tiny farming village situated on the Hungarian Plain in eastern Hungary. What types of climate favorable to farming are found in Southeastern Europe?

Since 1981 millions of Christian tourists, much to the dismay of communist officials, have visited a shrine located in the remote mountain village of Medjugorje, Yugoslavia.

See the *TAE* for an *Objective 2* Activity.

Climate. Southeastern Europe has many different moist climates. Most of its inland areas have a humid continental climate with cold winters and warm to hot summers. This includes Hungary, Romania, and northern Bulgaria. The inland part of Yugoslavia has a humid subtropical climate with hot, humid summers and mild winters. Areas along the coast of the Adriatic and Aegean seas in Yugoslavia, Albania, and southern Bulgaria have a Mediterranean climate with short, mild winters and long, warm summers. The Adriatic area is noted for violent winds called **bora** that sweep down from the mountains in winter. Through most of the area, rain falls year-round.

Recently the Bulgarian government has set up popular resort areas on the country's Black Sea coast.

2.2 Economic and Cultural Patterns

Southeastern Europe is more rural and less industrialized than Northeastern Europe. In general, standards of living in the south of Eastern Europe are lower than in the north.

An important part of Southeastern Europe is its many cultures. Most of the countries in the area have a number of different ethnic groups making up their populations.

Yugoslavia and Romania are the largest countries of Southeastern Europe in size and population. Yugoslavia has a land area of 98,764 square miles (255,798.6 sq km) and a population of 23.4 million people. Romania, which has a land area of 91,699 square miles (237,500.2 sq km), has about 22.9 million people.

Yugoslavia. The economy of Yugoslavia is based on both industry and agriculture. Yugoslav factories make cars, chemicals, machinery, processed foods, and textiles. The country has many mineral deposits and is the subregion's leading mining country. Yugoslavia's farmers grow corn, sugar beets, wheat, barley, oats, and potatoes. Along the coast, wine grapes, olives, and fruit are grown.

Yugoslavia is a communist country. However, it is not a Soviet satellite. Thus, Yugoslavia's economy is organized differently from that of the Soviet Union and other communist countries. In Yugoslavia managers, workers, and farmers help the government make economic decisions. Also about 85 percent of the country's farmland is privately owned.

EUROPE UNIT 6

Jealousies among Yugoslavia's many cultural groups make governing the country difficult. For example, if the government decides to build a new power plant in a region occupied by one ethnic group, others are likely to protest and to charge the government with "favoritism."

Although Yugoslavia's economy has been growing, there are not enough jobs. More than one million Yugoslav workers have left their country to find jobs in Northwest Europe. The money they send home is much-needed income for Yugoslavia.

Yugoslavia's factories and farms support the most varied population in all of Eastern Europe. Most Yugoslavs belong to one or more of six major Slavic groups: Serbs, Croats, Slovenes, Bosnians, Montenegrons, and Macedonians. There are also many non-Slavic minorities, including Albanians, Germans, and Hungarians.

Each major Slavic group has its own republic within Yugoslavia. The Yugoslav republics are Serbia, Croatia (kroh AY shuh), Slovenia, Bosnia and Herzegovina (HEHRT suh goh VEE nah), Macedonia, and Montenegro. The languages of the people are officially recognized by the Yugoslav government. However, Serbo-Croatian is the country's *lingua franca* (LING gwuh FRANG kuh), or common language of business and communication. It is written in two alphabets—Cyrillic, based on the Greek alphabet, and Latin.

The Cyrillic alphabet was named in honor of Saint Cyril, the Byzantine Empire's leading missionary.

Yugoslavia has many religions as well as cultures and languages. About one-third of the population are Eastern Orthodox Christians. They are mostly Serbs, Macedonians, and Montenegrons. Another 25 percent of Yugoslavs are Roman Catholics. They include most Croats and Slovenes. About 10 percent of the country is Muslim. Most Yugoslav Muslims are Bosnian.

About one-half of the people of Yugoslavia live in urban areas and one-half in rural areas. However, the urban population is going up. Belgrade is the capital and largest city of Yugoslavia. It has about 1.3 million people. The city, located in a major plains area of the Danube River, is an important inland port. Belgrade is also at the center of the most important economic region of Serbia. Zagreb, the next largest Yugoslav city, has more than one million people. It is the capital of the Yugoslav republic of Croatia.

Romania. Romania is still industrializing its economy. Its main industrial activities are machine manufacturing and oil production. Europe's largest oilfields lie near the Romanian city of Ploesti (plaw YEHSHT ee).

Large numbers of Yugoslavian workers have gone to West Germany to find jobs.

The town of Dubrovnik lies on the Adriatic coast of Yugoslavia. Based on the type of location and climate seen here, what other countries in Europe have towns that look like Dubrovnik?

The Dinaric Alps, a continuation of the Italian Alps, run along the Adriatic coast of the Balkan Peninsula. From the coast these mountains rise sharply like a dazzling wall of white limestone.

THINKING LIKE A GEOGRAPHER

BALKANIZATION

The word *balkanization* is a term used by political geographers. It refers to the breakup of an area into a number of small, unstable parts. The term comes from the name of the southern part of Eastern Europe, the Balkan Peninsula. All through its history, the Balkan Peninsula has been an area of conflicts and changing borders.

The Balkan Peninsula has an area of about 295,000 square miles (764,049.4 sq km). It is made up of the countries of Romania, Yugoslavia, Bulgaria, Albania, and Greece. A small part of Turkey is located in the southeastern corner of the peninsula.

The Balkan Peninsula has many different ethnic groups. The people of the Balkans speak many different languages and practice several different religions. Each ethnic group has developed a culture of its own. Many times in history, Balkan ethnic groups have fought with each other or have fought against other groups from outside the region.

The Balkan Peninsula has many mountains with passes that were more easily crossed than those in higher mountains in other parts of Europe. Its position as one of the southern entrances to Europe opened its land to many visitors or intruders from other countries. For example, crusaders during the late 1000s and early 1100s made their way through the southern half of Eastern Europe to Constantinople. Over the centuries parts of Eastern Europe have been within the Roman, Byzantine, Holy Roman, and Ottoman empires. Out of the need to protect itself from outside forces, each ethnic group in Eastern Europe became strong in its nationalism for its own group.

No single group of people has succeeded in ruling over the Balkan Peninsula for very long. Smaller groups have constantly broken

ETHNIC GROUPS OF THE BALKAN PENINSULA

Albanians

Bulgarians (Bulgars)

Croats

Greeks

Hungarians (Magyars)

Macedonians

Montenegrons

Romanians

Serbs

Slovenes

Turks

MODIFIED ORTHOGRAPHIC PROJECTION

away to set up their own countries. The problem of balkanization also applies to other regions. Political geographers have noted other areas of the world with similar problems. World leaders recognize the possible dangers of drawing boundaries that separate people of the same culture or that bring together people of different cultures.

1. Explain the meaning of the term *balkanization.*

2. How has the physical geography of the Balkan Peninsula contributed to the disunity among Balkan ethnic groups?

Romania has attempted to expand trade relations with western European countries and the United States. In recent years the United States has become one of the leading importers of Romanian goods.

On this small farm in the Transylvania region of Romania, workers do harvesting by hand. How successful is farming in Romania?

Although the number-one sport in Eastern European countries is soccer, the governments there stress the training of all athletics. Young athletes may train up to 50 or 60 hours a week.

Nadia Comaneci, a 14-year-old Romanian gymnast, earned 3 gold medals at the 1976 Olympic Games in Montréal.

Pipelines carry oil to other parts of Romania, Bulgaria, and the Soviet Union.

Romania depends heavily on agriculture. Collective and state farms own 90 percent of the land. In the country's fertile soil, wheat, corn, and tobacco are grown. Romania produces enough farm products to meet its own needs and to export. The leading farm exports are wheat and tobacco.

About 50 percent of Romanians live in cities and towns. The largest city in Romania is the capital, Bucharest (byoo kuh REHST). There are about two million people in Bucharest, which is located in the plains area of southeastern Romania. The second largest city— Braşov—is only one-seventh the size of Bucharest. Braşov and Bucharest both began as trading cities and now are centered more on light industries.

Of all the Eastern Europeans, the Romanians have the closest cultural links to Northwest Europe and Mediterranean Europe. They are believed to be descendants of the Romans and an early Balkan people called Dacians. The Romanian language, which developed from Latin, uses the Latin alphabet. It is closer to French and Italian than it is to other Eastern European languages.

In other ways Romanians are like Eastern Europeans. They are ruled by a communist government that places controls on individual freedoms. Like some of their neighbors, the Romanians are largely Eastern Orthodox Christians. Romanian foods, folk arts, and social customs show the influence of the Slavs and other Eastern European peoples.

Most Romanians have kept more of their traditional rural culture than have many of the other peoples of Eastern Europe. In the countryside, they still celebrate weddings, festivals, and national holidays by wearing colorful costumes and dancing to Romanian folk music.

Hungary, Bulgaria, and Albania. The other Southeastern European countries—Hungary, Bulgaria, and Albania—are much smaller than Yugoslavia and Romania. These countries also have fewer people. Hungary, with 10.6 million people, is the most populous of these three smaller countries. Still, it has only half as many people as Romania or Yugoslavia.

In spite of its small size and population, Hungary has the most industrialized economy of Southeastern Europe. Its government allows more small private businesses to operate

Budapest lies on both sides of the Danube River. Eight bridges join the city's two sections, Buda and Pest.

The Hungarian language is related to the Finnish language.

than do most other Eastern European governments. Hungary has the highest standard of living in Southeastern Europe. Budapest, with more than two million people, is Hungary's capital and largest city.

Hungary became an industrial nation only after World War II. Its chief manufactured products are chemicals, machinery, steel, textiles, and transportation equipment. However, Hungary also depends on agriculture. Hungarian farmers grow wheat, corn, sugar beets, barley, sunflowers, peppers, tomatoes, and wine grapes.

The Hungarians are descended from the Magyars, a non-Slavic group that came to Eastern Europe from central Asia centuries ago. The Hungarian language is not related to most European languages. However, the

Hungarians have close cultural and religious ties to Europe. Almost one-half of all Hungarians are Roman Catholics, and another 30 percent are Protestant.

Hungarians are known for their special zest for life. They enjoy fine food and drink. The Hungarians also are known for their lively folk music. Their country has produced world-famous composers whose works were strongly influenced by Hungarian folk music.

The second country of the region, Bulgaria, is not as prosperous as Hungary. However, Bulgaria's communist government has tried to develop the economy. The leading industries of Bulgaria make chemicals, metal products, machinery, and textiles. The country's most productive farms are in the Plain of Wallachia.

The collage portrays the diversity of Eastern Europe's history. Point out the Eastern Orthodox Church, the communist symbol of the hammer and sickle, the Polish labor banner, and some famous Eastern Europeans.

The German composer, Johann Sebastian Bach, Yugoslav president, Josip Tito, and the Polish-born scientist, Marie Curie, represent Eastern European culture. What do you associate with Hungarian culture?

NATIONS OF EASTERN EUROPE

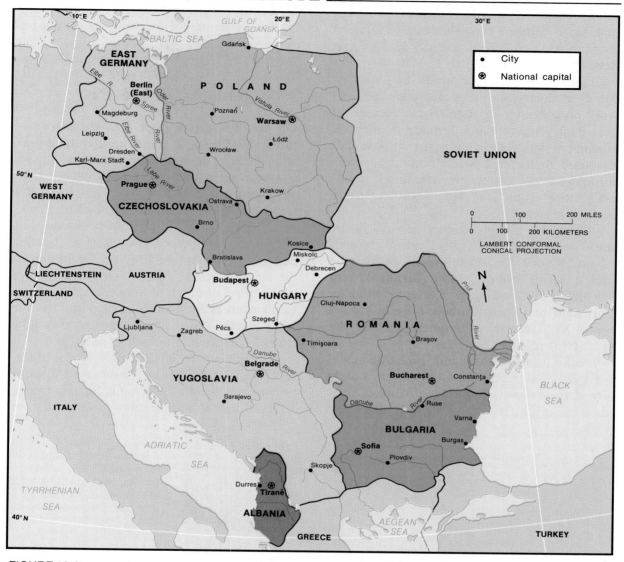

FIGURE 19-3

Although closely identified today as satellite countries of the Soviet Union, the nations of Eastern Europe have histories that date back to before the Middle Ages and cultural traditions that are still kept alive today. Which satellite country of this region is viewed as having the most loyalty to the Soviet Union?

The average Bulgarian earns the equivalent of about $1,800 a year yet pays fairly high consumer prices.

About nine million people live in Bulgaria. The capital, Sofia, has more than one million people and is the country's largest city. The Bulgarians are descended from Slavs and the Bulgars, a group from central Asia. They use the Cyrillic alphabet, practice the Eastern Orthodox religion, and have long admired Russian culture. Today Bulgaria is viewed as the satellite country having the most loyalty to the Soviet Union.

The third country, Albania, is the poorest in all of Europe. It has rich resources but

CHAPTER 19   **EASTERN EUROPE**

lacks the skills and technology to develop them. About 47 percent of Albania is forest, making it Europe's most densely forested country. However, only recently has Albania developed a timber industry.

There are few industries in Albania. Most Albanians are farmers who live and work on collective or state farms. Because of the country's mountains, farming is difficult. However, Albania's communist government has tried to increase agricultural production through the use of modern machinery. Albania's chief crops are corn, potatoes, sugar beets, and wheat.

With 3.1 million people, Albania is the least populous country in Eastern Europe. About 272,000 Albanians live in Tiranë, the capital. Until recently, most Albanians were Muslims. The rest were Eastern Orthodox Christians or Roman Catholics. Today, however, the Albanian government forbids the practice of religion.

Like its neighbor Yugoslavia, Albania is not a Soviet satellite. For a time it was a close ally of the People's Republic of China. Albania's communist rulers now claim that their country is the only truly communist nation in the world. As a result they have largely isolated their country from contact with the rest of the world.

Since 1985 Albanians can tune in to foreign broadcasts, including some western shows.

2.3 Influences of the Past

Southeastern Europe is a patchwork of cultures. The many ethnic groups there have often been conquered and ruled by outside powers. In the 600s the Greeks set up colonies along the Adriatic coast. Later the Romans took over much of the Balkan Peninsula. When Rome declined in the 400s AD, its territories in Southeastern Europe became part of the Byzantine Empire. Beginning in the late 1300s, the Turkish Ottoman Empire won control of much of Southeastern Europe. In many areas Turkish rule lasted into the late 1800s. As the Turks left, the Austrians and the Russians became interested in the area.

In the late 1800s and early 1900s, different groups of people in Southeastern Europe became independent. Romania became free in 1861. Bulgaria and Serbia—now a part of

The United States and the Soviet Union have no diplomatic relations with Albania.

A link to its past, an old Turkish bridge still spans the picturesque little town of Mostar in Yugoslavia. Turks and other outside powers at one time conquered and ruled the people of modern-day Yugoslavia and other countries of the Balkan Peninsula. Which other outside powers have controlled Southeastern Europe during its long history?

In 1204 crusaders from western Europe and Venetians burned and looted Constantinople, the Byzantine capital, leaving it unable to defend itself against the Turks.

Yugoslavia—broke away from Turkish rule in 1878. Albania became independent in 1912. After World War I in 1918, Hungary ended its ties to Austria. The Serbs, the Croats, the Slovenes, and other Balkan Slavic groups united to form Yugoslavia.

During World War II, Germany took over much of Southeastern Europe. Soviet forces helped drive the Germans out by 1945. As in Northeastern Europe, communist governments were set up. All were closely tied to the Soviet Union.

Yugoslavia and Albania were able to avoid tight Soviet control. Under Josip Broz Tito, leader of Yugoslavia from 1945 to 1980, the Yugoslavs followed their own kind of communism.

The Soviets have found it hard to keep control over some of the other countries of Southeastern Europe. In 1956 the Hungarians revolted against their communist government. Soviet forces invaded the country and crushed the uprising. Today Hungary is communist and loyal to the Soviet Union. However, its rulers have eased many strict laws and allowed more personal freedoms to Hungarians. Romania has a strict communist government. But its leaders often disagree with the Soviet Union on foreign policy matters. Of all the countries of Southeastern Europe, only Bulgaria has closely followed the Soviet Union.

Have students compare maps of Eastern Europe before and after World Wars I and II.

CONTENT CHECK

1. **Identify:** Carpathian Mountains, Transylvanian Alps, Balkan Mountains, Hungarian Plain, Danube River, Plain of Wallachia, Yugoslavia, Serbia, Croatia, Slovenia, Bosnia and Herzegovina, Macedonia, Montenegro, Serbo-Croatian, Belgrade, Romania, Ploesti, Bucharest, Hungary, Budapest, Magyars, Bulgaria, Sofia, Albania, Tiranë, Josip Broz Tito.

2. **Define:** bora.
3. What countries make up Southeastern Europe?
4. What major European peninsula includes most of Southeastern Europe?
5. What kinds of landscapes are found in Southeastern Europe? What kinds of climate?
6. Which country of Southeastern Europe has the largest number of different ethnic groups?
7. What natural resource has brought benefits to Romania's economy?
8. **Challenge:** How do the Southeastern European nations handle their communist governments and economies differently?

See the *TRB* for the *Section 2 Extending the Lesson* on Hungary's distinctive communism.

CONCLUSION

Eastern Europe includes the area of the European continent that stretches from the Baltic Sea to the Adriatic Sea. This region has a variety of different landscapes, climates, and peoples. Each group of Eastern Europeans has its own history, language, culture, and religion. Many of these groups spread across national boundaries. This has often increased tensions in the region.

Throughout its history, Eastern Europe has seen many wars, conquests, and revolutions. National boundaries have constantly changed. People have moved from one area to another. Since World War II, Eastern Europe has seen many changes. All of the countries in the area are communist. Most of them are allied to the Soviet Union. Once a primarily agricultural region, Eastern Europe has developed its industries and reorganized its agriculture under communist rule. In spite of improved standards of living, tensions continue to exist. Many Eastern Europeans want more freedoms, but the Soviets are unwilling to relax their hold on the region completely.

SUMMARY

1. Eastern Europe lies between Northwest Europe and Mediterranean Europe to the west and south and the Soviet Union to the east. The region can be divided into Northeastern Europe and Southeastern Europe.

2. Northeastern Europe has large areas of plains, while Southeastern Europe is rugged and mountainous. The climates of Eastern Europe are generally moist.

3. In general, the countries of Northeastern Europe are more urban and industrial than those of Southeastern Europe.

4. There is a great variety of languages and religions in Eastern Europe, especially in the southern part.

5. Eastern Europe has long been an area of political unrest.

6. All of the countries of Eastern Europe have communist governments. All except Yugoslavia and Albania are satellites of the Soviet Union.

7. Poland is the largest and most populous country in Eastern Europe. Yugoslavia is the largest and most populous country in the southern part of the region.

Answers to the following questions can be found on page T202.

REVIEWING VOCABULARY

Listed below are proper nouns from this chapter that name either a city, physical feature, or waterway from Eastern Europe. Divide your paper into three columns. Place Cities, Physical Features, *and* Waterways *at the top as headings for the columns. Then write each noun in the list that follows under its proper classification.*

Adriatic	Carpathian	Krakow	Sofia
Baltic	Danube	Labe	Tatra
Bucharest	Erzgebirge	Łódź	Vistula
Budapest	Gerlachovka	Ploesti	Warsaw

REMEMBERING THE FACTS

1. What are the countries in Northeastern Europe? In Southeastern Europe?

2. Which two countries of Eastern Europe are landlocked?

3. What does satellite country mean? Which countries of Eastern Europe are considered satellites of the Soviet Union?

4. What is a planned economy?

5. What plain makes up much of northern East Germany and Poland?

6. Which is Eastern Europe's largest and most populous country?

7. Which country in Eastern Europe is the most urban and industrial?

8. Which country in Southeastern Europe is the largest in area?

9. What kind of climate do the coastal areas of Yugoslavia and Albania have?

10. In what country is Serbo-Croatian an official language?

UNDERSTANDING THE FACTS

1. How are farms managed in East Germany? In Yugoslavia?
2. Although Poland is an agricultural country, farming is not important in the north, and few people live there. Why?
3. What major religions are practiced in Eastern Europe?
4. How much highland area does Southeastern Europe have when compared to its lowland area?
5. Why is the Danube River important to the countries of Southeastern Europe?
6. Why are there more climate types in Southeastern Europe than in Northeastern Europe?
7. Although Yugoslavia is a communist country, it is not considered a satellite of the Soviet Union. How does life in Yugoslavia differ from life in other Soviet satellite countries?

THINKING CRITICALLY AND CREATIVELY

1. What would be the difficulties of building roads and railroads from east to west in (a) the northern part of Northeastern Europe and (b) Southeastern Europe from Yugoslavia to the Black Sea?
2. More people live in the Labe River Basin of western Czechoslovakia than in the country's more rugged, highland areas. In other parts of the world, the population is denser in relatively flat areas than in mountainous regions. Why do you think this is a pattern geographers find in many parts of the world?
3. In Poland and Yugoslavia, many farmers own their own land. In Soviet satellites, such as East Germany and Bulgaria, large numbers of farmers work on collective farms or state farms. How do you think the efficiency of privately owned farms compares with that of collective or state farms? How do you account for such differences between the two kinds?
4. After World War II, the Soviet Union turned Bulgaria and Romania into satellite countries. Why would the Soviet Union be eager to have friends in their geographic location?
5. **Challenge:** Poland's fishing and shipbuilding industries are important to its economy. Although Yugoslavia has a long seacoast, its shipbuilding is not important, and its fishing industry is much smaller than Poland's. Why do you think there is so much difference?
6. **Challenge:** Albania does not encourage foreigners to visit or trade with it. How does such an attitude affect Albania's people and economy?

REINFORCING GRAPHIC SKILLS

Study the map on page 388. Then answer the questions that follow.

1. According to the map, what country took land from Poland in 1939 but did not return it in 1945?
2. This map shows a time period when Poland was not an independent nation. When did this occur? How can you tell?

CHAPTER 20

Built in the mid-1500s to commemorate Ivan IV's defeat of the Mongols, St. Basil's has 10 domes, each different in color and design.

Church of St. Basil in Moscow.

THE SOVIET UNION

In this chapter you will learn—

- What are the Soviet Union's major physical regions and climates.
- What kind of government the Soviet Union has.
- How the Soviet economy is set up and how it works.
- How the past has shaped present-day Soviet life.

The common use of the term "Russia" for this country is incorrect. The Russian Soviet Federated Socialist Republic is but one of 15 republics that comprise the Soviet Union, and Russians are one of many ethnic groups.

INTRODUCTION

The Union of Soviet Socialist Republics (U.S.S.R.) is the official name of the Soviet Union. It has a land area of 8,649,498 square miles (22,402,182.5 sq km). This makes the Soviet Union the largest country in the world in land area. Soviet territory spreads over two continents—more than one-half of Europe and almost two-fifths of Asia. It covers about one-sixth of all the land on Earth.

Distances between places in the Soviet Union are great. From its westernmost point to its easternmost point, the land stretches nearly 6,000 miles (9,656.1 km) through 11 time zones. The distance from its northernmost point to its southernmost point is about 3,200 miles (5,149.9 km).

Despite its huge size, the Soviet Union has a mostly far northern location. This has shaped its history and development. Because of long, cold winters, the country's coastline has few harbors that are open year-round. Warm-water ports are found on the Black Sea. But foreigners have always guarded where the Black Sea enters the Mediterranean Sea. Thus, the territory of the Soviet Union is nearly shut off from the world's oceans. To overcome this problem, past and present rulers have tried to control nearby lands.

Landforms also have affected the history and development of the Soviet Union. Mountains and deserts are found in the far south. Large, cold flatlands are found in the far north. Since these areas do not easily support human settlement, they have long isolated and protected the country. However, in the center, huge grassy or forested plains have been inviting to settlers—and invaders. Fear of invasion, as well as the need for harbors, has led the people of the Soviet Union to push their borders outward.

As a result of past expansion and invasion of other territories, the Soviet Union today has many different ethnic groups. The largest group—Russians—makes up one-half the country's total population. Russians also hold much of the control over the government and other Soviet affairs.

For the most part, each major ethnic group lives in its own territory. These territories are found in both European and Asian parts of the country. However, about 70 percent of the 284 million people in the Soviet Union live in the European part of the country. This area lies to the west of the Ural (YUR uhl) Mountains and to the north of the Caucasus (KAW kuh suhs) Mountains and the Black Sea. Centered in the European part is Moscow, capital of the Soviet Union and world center of communism.

The Soviet Union is the world leader of countries with communist governments. It is the chief military power among communist countries and the major rival of the United States. Many communist lands, especially those in Eastern Europe, look to Moscow for help and direction.

PHYSICAL REGIONS OF THE SOVIET UNION

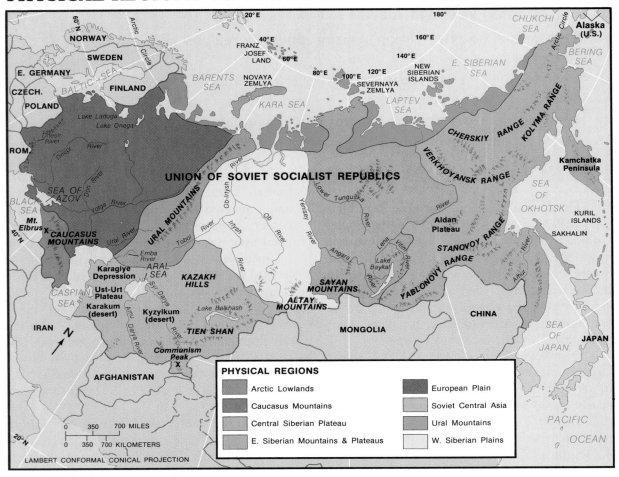

FIGURE 20-1
The Soviet Union's European Plain is a continuation of the same physical region that extends through the northern areas of Eastern and Northwest Europe. What separates the European Plain from the West Siberian Plain?

The land area of the Soviet Union is more than twice the size of Canada, the second-largest country.

1. LANDSCAPE AND CLIMATE

The Soviet Union extends from above 80° north latitude to below 40° north latitude and from 20° east longitude eastward to beyond 180° east longitude. Such a huge land area is bound to have many differences. However, patterns of landscape and climate are simpler in the Soviet Union than in other

parts of Europe and Asia. The Soviet Union has only a few physical regions. Each covers a vast area. Also only two general kinds of climates are found in the Soviet Union.

On the map on page 404, note how much farther north the Soviet Union is than the United States.

1.1 Landscape

A large part of central Soviet Union is covered by plains. Only the Ural Mountains interrupt the generally flat land that stretches

EUROPE   UNIT 6

On the map on page 402, have students identify the Soviet Union's few usable access points to world oceans and seas.

The Ural Mountains also mark the commonly accepted dividing line between Europe and Asia.

from Europe into Asia. In general, the other mountains in the Soviet Union lie along its southern and eastern borders.

Physical Regions. As Figure 20–1 on page 402 shows, the Soviet Union may be divided into eight physical regions: (1) European Plain, (2) Caucasus Mountains, (3) Ural Mountains, (4) Soviet Central Asia, (5) West Siberian Plain, (6) Central Siberian Plateau, (7) East Siberian Mountains and Plateaus, and (8) Arctic Lowlands.

The European Plain stretches 1,500 miles (2,414 km) from the Soviet border with Poland to the Ural Mountains. The land is steppe, flat and gently rolling. The European Plain of the Soviet Union has rich, fertile land, especially in the Don River Basin. It contains most of the Soviet Union's industries and farms. About 75 percent of the Soviet people live in this area.

Flowing through the plains area of the Soviet Union are several major waterways. The most important is the Volga, the longest river in Europe. It flows 2,194 miles (3,530.9 km) from the Moscow area to the Caspian Sea. The Caspian Sea, a salt lake, is the world's largest inland body of water.

Other major rivers in the plains area are the Dnestr (NEES tuhr), Dnepr (NEE puhr), Don, and Ural. All of these rivers flow south and empty into the Caspian Sea or the Black Sea. Both the Ural and Dnepr rivers are more than 1,400 miles (2,253.1 km) long.

South of the European Plain are the Caucasus Mountains. They are located between the Black Sea on the west and the Caspian Sea on the east. These rugged highlands have some mountain peaks more than 10,000 feet (3,048 m) high. Among them is Mount Elbrus, the highest peak in Europe at 18,510 feet (5,641.8 m) above sea level.

A second mountainous area in the European Soviet Union is the Urals. These mountains mark the eastern end of the European Plain. The Urals are made up of mostly low,

rounded peaks, eroded over time by rivers and streams. They run a distance of 1,200 miles (1,931.2 km) from north to south. The mountains rise from only 2,000 feet (609.6 m) to 5,000 feet (1,524 m) above sea level. There are many mountain passes. Thus, the Urals are not a serious barrier to transportation. They are rich in minerals and are the site of many industries.

South of the Ural Mountains and east of the Caspian Sea is Soviet Central Asia. It is mostly an area of flat steppes and sandy deserts. The deserts include the Karakum (KAR uh KUHM) and Kyzylkum (KY zuhl KUHM).

Soviet Central Asia has both the highest and the lowest points in all of the Soviet Union. The highest point is Communism Peak, 24,590 feet (7,495 m) above sea level. It rises on the border where the Soviet Union, China, and Afghanistan meet. The lowest point is the Karagiye Depression along the eastern shore of the Caspian Sea. Here the land is 433 feet (131.9 m) below sea level.

North and east of Soviet Central Asia is a huge area known as Siberia. In Siberia are the

Point out to students that *karakum* means "black sands," and *kyzylkum* means "red sands."

Workers are shown here welding a section of a gas pipeline in the Tyumen region of Siberia. Extremely cold temperatures and rugged terrain create uncomfortable working conditions in Siberia. Where is Siberia located in relation to Soviet Central Asia?

USING GRAPHIC SKILLS

COMPARING LAND AREA MAPS

A familiar event every year is having your class picture taken for the school yearbook. To make sure that everyone will be seen, the photographer asks the shorter students to stand toward the front and the taller students toward the back. When you and your classmates are lined up this way, it is easy to compare how big or small you are in relation to other members of your class.

The same is true for countries. When seen on a map, for example, Colombia is large in comparison to Panama, but small in comparison to Brazil. When you read that Israel is about as large as the state of Massachusetts, it is hard to believe until you look at them on a map. Even so, you must make sure that the map you select shows the land areas at the same scale and that the projection used does not distort one land area much more than the other land area. If you keep these concerns in mind, comparing different countries on a map is the best way to see how large or small they are in relation to one another.

Shown below is a map of the 48 contiguous states of the United States and Alaska, along with a map of the Soviet Union. Both maps are drawn to the same scale and show each country's land area. It is easier to see from the maps that the Soviet Union is about two and one-third times the size of the United States.

Lines of latitude are included to indicate where each country is located in the Northern Hemisphere. Cities are shown in each country to show how far apart different areas of the two countries lie.

UNITED STATES AND THE SOVIET UNION

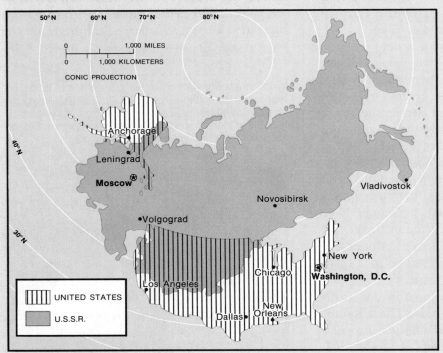

Study the map on this page. Then answer the questions that follow.

1. Which country has land farther north?

2. Which two cities on the map of the Soviet Union are about the same distance apart as Los Angeles and Chicago?

3. Why is it necessary that the scale for both the United States and the Soviet Union maps be the same?

4. **Challenge:** Which is the farther trip cross-country—between Leningrad and Vladivostok or between Los Angeles and New York?

West Siberian Plain, Central Siberian Plateau, and East Siberian Mountains and Plateaus.

The first region east of the Ural Mountains is the West Siberian Plain. It stretches from the Urals east to the Yenisey (YEHN uh SAY) River. This region covers more than 1 million square miles (2.6 million sq km) and is the largest single area of flat land in the world. Elevations in the area seldom rise more than 500 feet (152.4 m) above sea level.

Major rivers in the West Siberian Plain are the Ob and the Irtysh (ihr TIHSH). The Irtysh flows into the Ob, which then empties into the Arctic Ocean. Like all major Siberian rivers, they flow north and are frozen seven to nine months of the year.

To the east of the West Siberian Plain is the Central Siberian Plateau. It lies generally between the Yenisey and Lena rivers. The Lena River and others have cut canyons through the Central Siberian Plateau. The 2,734-mile (4,399.9-km) Lena River is the longest river entirely in the Soviet Union. Also in this region of Siberia is Lake Baykal, the deepest lake in the world. This lake measures 5,315 feet (1,620 m) deep. South of the Baykal, the Central Siberian Plateau ends suddenly as it meets the highlands and rugged mountains along the Soviet border with Mongolia.

The East Siberian Mountains and Plateaus make up the Soviet Union's easternmost physical region. This area has mountains, valleys, and plateaus all the way east to the Pacific Ocean. Many of the mountains are active volcanoes. A large peninsula in this area goes out into the Pacific Ocean. It is called the Kamchatka Peninsula.

The northernmost region of the Soviet Union is the Arctic Lowlands. The Arctic Lowlands stretch from the Barents Sea in the European Soviet Union to the Chukchi Sea in eastern Siberia. The region is very low along the Arctic coast, but it rises little by little to the south.

Vegetation. Vegetation of the Soviet Union changes from north to south. Several kinds of plant life are found in more than one of the country's physical regions.

Tundra vegetation is found in the area north of the Arctic Circle. Permafrost allows only plants with small roots to grow in this area. Plants with deeper roots, such as trees, cannot live here. No trees grow north of 70° north latitude.

From west to east across the Soviet Union is forest area. In fact, the Soviet Union has the largest forest area in the world. It covers about one-half of the country—more than 4.2 million square miles (10.9 sq km).

The forest in the north is taiga, made up of thinly scattered coniferous trees that grow in wet soil. Farther south, forests have conifers and broadleaf trees growing in drier soil. In this area, the forests, over time, are being replaced by steppe grasses. Few trees are found in the steppe even though the soil is fertile. Below the rich layers of topsoil are poisonous salts. These salts do not kill plants with shallow roots, such as most farm crops. However, they destroy plants with deep roots, such as trees.

South of the steppe in Soviet Central Asia is an area of desert vegetation and patches of grasses. Desert covers about 17 percent of the Soviet Union's land area.

Refer students to pages 96-97 to review the map of Earth's Climate Regions.

1.2 Climate

The climate of the Soviet Union is influenced less by landforms and more by its huge size and its location in the high latitudes of the Northern Hemisphere.

The far northern parts of the Soviet Union along the Arctic Ocean have a polar climate. A subarctic climate covers the northern part of the European Soviet Union and nearly all of Siberia. Except for Antarctica, Siberia has the coldest winters in the world.

FOCUS ON GEOGRAPHY

WORLD'S WORST CLIMATE?

Verkhoyansk (vyehr koh YAHNSK) is a small Soviet town in northeastern Siberia. It lies near the Yana River, about 70 miles (112.6 km) north of the Arctic Circle. Its exact location is 67°43′N, 133°33′E. Tourists seldom go out of their way to visit there.

For people who do not like cold weather, Verkhoyansk could be named as the place with the worst climate on Earth. The town has one of the most extreme climates found anywhere in the world.

The term *extreme* refers here to the difference between the coldest and warmest months during a year. At Verkhoyansk, there is a difference of 117.4 degrees Fahrenheit (65.2 degrees Celsius) between the average temperatures of the coldest month, January, and the warmest month, July. During January, the average temperature is −58.2°F (−50.1°C). July's average temperature is 59.2°F (15.1°C). The range of temperature may be greater than these averages show. For example, at times it has been colder than −90°F (−67.7°C) and as hot as 93°F (33.9°C). This is a range of more than 183 degrees Fahrenheit (101.6 degrees Celsius)!

People often think that very cold places must have lots of snow. Verkhoyansk, however, like many places in the interior of continents, gets very little precipitation. Most of it falls during the summer as rain. The average amount of precipitation there is around 5 inches (12.7 cm) a year.

Even though the weather is so cold and dry, some farming can be done because the atmosphere near Verkhoyansk never stays warm enough to evaporate all the moisture. But frosts are possible at any time of year.

The cold winter temperatures require the people of Verkhoyansk and other such places to make certain changes in order to live and work. For example, buildings have triple-paned windows. Engines are left running all the time. If they were allowed to stop, the oil would become so thick that the engines would be very hard to start again. Warm-up sheds help people who have to work outdoors. In very cold weather, people can work outside for only about one-half hour at a time.

VERKHOYANSK, U.S.S.R.

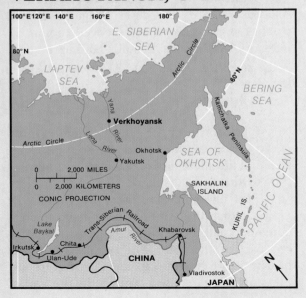

1. Where is Verkhoyansk located?
2. What is the normal range of temperature in Verkhoyansk for summer to winter?
3. Why is moisture always present in the atmosphere above Verkhoyansk even through it has very little precipitation each year?
4. How do the people of Verkhoyansk live in such cold winter temperatures?

CLIMATE: MOSCOW

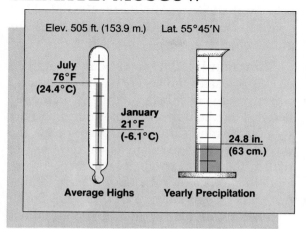

Elev. 505 ft. (153.9 m.)   Lat. 55°45'N

July
76°F
(24.4°C)

January
21°F
(-6.1°C)

24.8 in.
(63 cm.)

Average Highs   Yearly Precipitation

FIGURE 20-2
Moscow has the same average July temperatures as the city of Quebec (46°49'N) in Canada. But Moscow's average January temperatures are slightly warmer than Quebec's. Which city is located farther north?

See the *TAE* for an *Objective 1* Activity.

Oceans are too far away to make temperatures mild. On winter nights temperatures fall far below freezing. At Oimekon near the city of Yakutsk, a nighttime low temperature of $-108°F$ $(-77.8°C)$ was once recorded. The average high temperature in January at Yakutsk is $-45°F$ $(-42.8°C)$.

Winters are also cold in most of the European Soviet Union but not as cold as in Siberia. The southern part of the European Plain has a humid continental with warm summers climate. For example, as Figure 20-2 on this page shows, Moscow has warm summers.

The warmest areas of the Soviet Union are in Soviet Central Asia and around the Black Sea. Soviet Central Asia has a desert climate with warm winters and hot summers. At Tashkent the average high temperature in January is $37°F$ $(2.8°C)$. In July the average high is $92°F$ $(33.3°C)$. The city gets between 8 inches (20.3 cm) to 16 inches (40.6 cm) of precipitation a year. Some areas of Soviet Central Asia get less rain.

Most of the European Soviet Union has between 20 inches (50.8 cm) and 25 inches (63.5 cm) of precipitation a year. The central parts of Siberia get less. For example, Yakutsk receives only 7.4 inches (18.8 cm) a year. The amount of snowfall in Siberia is small. Most of the precipitation there comes as summer rain. Precipitation on the Pacific coast at Vladivostok (VLAD uh vuh STAHK) is 23.6 inches (59.9 cm) a year.

Much of the Soviet Union receives enough rain for farming, but climatic extremes often interfere.

CONTENT CHECK

1. **Identify:** Soviet Union, Russians, Ural Mountains, Caucasus Mountains, Moscow, European Plain, Volga River, Caspian Sea, Dnestr River, Dnepr River, Don River, Ural River, Black Sea, Mount Elbrus, Soviet Central Asia, Communism Peak, Siberia, West Siberian Plain, Yenisey River, Ob River, Irtysh River, Central Siberian Plateau, Lena River, Lake Baykal, East Siberian Mountains and Plateaus, Kamchatka Peninsula, Arctic Lowlands.

2. How does the Soviet Union compare to other nations of the world in size?

3. What are the physical regions of the Soviet Union?

4. What physical region of the Soviet Union has the most people?

5. What landform divides the European and Asian parts of the Soviet Union?

6. What term is used to describe the northern part of the Soviet Union that is located to the east of the Ural Mountains?

7. What general kinds of climates are found in the Soviet Union?

8. **Challenge:** How does landscape and climate limit the usefulness of such Soviet waterways as the Ob and Irtysh rivers?

2. ECONOMIC AND CULTURAL PATTERNS

The Soviet Union is one of the world's leading economic powers. Its huge land area contains many factories, farms, and natural resources. However, the country's cold climate and vast distances often make economic growth difficult.

The Soviet government closely controls the economy and almost every other area of Soviet life. As a result, the Soviet people do not have many personal freedoms.

It is with the General Secretary that the U.S. President meets when there is a "summit conference."

2.1 Government and Economy

The Soviet Union has a communist government. In theory, the Soviet people elect representatives to the government. For example, voters elect members of the Supreme Soviet, the highest lawmaking body in the coun-

Portraits of Soviet leaders, including that of Lenin on the right, are displayed on Moscow's Bolshoi Theater. The theater is famous for its ballet company. Which political party leads the Soviet Union?

try. However, the real power in the country is held by the Communist Party, the only legal political party. It selects all candidates for public office.

Communist Party. About 18 million people, a small number of the Soviet Union's citizens, are members of the Communist Party. They hold a special position in Soviet society. Membership in the party opens the way to a good career and other rewards. In return, the party expects its members to promote its views and to be busy in party activities. The Communist Party of the Soviet Union is set up like a pyramid. Organizations are found at local, regional, and national levels. The lower levels carry out decisions made by a small number of groups at the top. The most important of these is the Politburo, a committee of about 12 members. The leading Politburo official is called the General Secretary, the most powerful position in the Soviet Union.

The Soviet government carries out the decisions made by Communist Party leaders. It cares for Soviet citizens by guaranteeing employment. It also gives free education and health care. It tries to improve the standard of living. At the same time, however, the Soviet government calls upon the people to work hard. It keeps watch over how they act and punishes any serious misbehavior.

Planned Economy. The Soviet Union has the world's largest socialist economy. The government owns land, industries, banks, and communication and transportation systems. Soviet leaders organize and control the economy through a large **bureaucracy** (byoo RAHK ruh see), or network of government officials. To determine what is made and how much is made, the government sets up **five-year plans.** These plans set production goals as well as wages and prices. In the past plans have emphasized heavy industry and military needs. But today increased attention is given

LAND USE AND RESOURCES OF THE SOVIET UNION

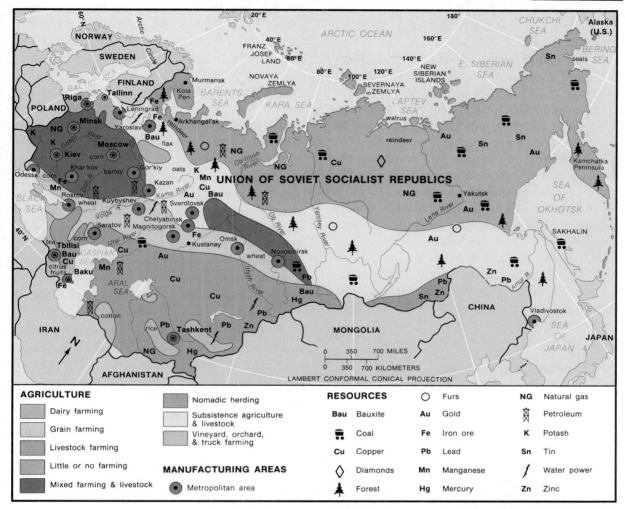

FIGURE 20-3

Vast areas of non-agricultural land extend across the northern part of the Soviet Union. Why is the land shown here not well-suited for agriculture?

Total Soviet production ranks second in the world.

A labor shortage in the 1980s slowed economic growth.

to consumer goods and agriculture. Under the plans the Soviet economy has grown rapidly.

Even with this growth, many Soviets complain about shortages, poor products, and the slow pace of the economy. Because of these problems, their needs are not always met. Many Soviets turn to the **black market,** a network of private trade through which people exchange or pay for goods or services,

instead of through government-run stores. Prices are generally higher on the black market, but service is better. Although the black market is illegal, the Soviet government puts up with it in order to keep its people happy.

Industry is widespread in the Soviet Union, but there are certain areas where it is especially concentrated. Much of the Soviet Union's industrial strength rests on its huge

The Soviet Union has had trouble establishing foreign markets for some of its products because their quality has not been as high as in other industrial nations.

Assurance of housing has been an incentive to attract workers to Siberia from less harsh areas with extreme housing shortages.

number of natural resources. Figure 20–3 on page 409 shows the resources, how the land is used, and the manufacturing areas that are found in the Soviet Union.

The major industrial area in the country is around Moscow, the country's capital and largest city. Factories in the Moscow area make automobiles, buses, and trucks. Chemicals, steel, electrical equipment, and textiles are also made there.

Northwest of Moscow is Leningrad, the Soviet Union's second largest city. It is at the heart of another industrialized area. Located on the Gulf of Finland, Leningrad is mainly noted for shipbuilding. Its metropolitan area also produces light machinery, textiles, and scientific and medical equipment.

The Ukraine, in the south, is the country's third major industrial area. It has large amounts of resources, such as coal, iron, mercury, manganese, uranium, oil, and natural gas. The Ukraine produces metal products

See the *TRB* for *Section 2: Extending the Lesson* on Mikhail Gorbachev's *glasnost* policy.

Every minute and a half, a brand new car rolls off the main assembly line of the Zaporozhsky automobile factory, located in the Ukrainian Soviet Socialist Republic. What industrial cities are located in the Ukraine region?

and heavy machinery. Kiev, Kharkov, and Rostov are the Ukraine's leading industrial cities. On the Black Sea, Odessa is the major port for the southern part of the country.

Northeast of the Ukraine lies the industrial region of the Volga River and the Ural Mountains. The Volga and the Urals are linked because of their large deposits of oil and natural gas. The Volga River and its canals form major inland transportation routes of the Soviet Union.

East of the Volga and the Urals is Siberia, the Soviet Union's most promising economic region. Siberia has the largest supply of mineral resources in the country. However, the region has relatively few people and is largely undeveloped. Because Siberia holds the key to the future economic growth of the country, the Soviet government is pushing to expand its industry rapidly.

Other areas of rapid industrial growth are found in the Caucasus region and Soviet Central Asia. Both areas have rich deposits of oil and natural gas. In the Caucasus area, industrial cities, such as Baku, Tbilisi (tuh BIHL uh see), and Yerevan (YEHR uh VAHN), make appliances, textiles, and chemicals. In Soviet Central Asia, the leading industrial center is Tashkent. It makes textiles, farm machinery, and building equipment.

Agriculture. The Soviet Union has more farmland than any other country in the world. About one-fourth of the country's entire land area is used for farming. Soviet farms lead the world in the production of wheat, barley, and rye. The Ukraine has the Soviet Union's richest farmland and is known as its "breadbasket." Farmers there raise wheat, corn, barley, sugar beets, and livestock. In the northwest of the country, the leading crops are potatoes, rye, and **flax,** a plant whose fiber is used to make linen.

Other important agricultural areas of the Soviet Union are southwest Siberia, Soviet

Point out to students that the climate in some parts of the Caucasus Mountains is similar to the Mediterranean climate areas of California in the U.S.

In analyzing the information below, refer students to the map on page 404 that presents additional comparative information.

Central Asia, and the Caucasus region. Southwestern Siberia is an important grain-producing area. In Soviet Central Asia, farmers use irrigation to grow cotton, fruit, and vegetables. Near the Caucasus Mountains, tea, wine grapes, and citrus fruits are grown.

In spite of its many agricultural products, the Soviet Union has not been able to speed up its farm production. Much of the country's farmland lies in the high latitudes. Growing seasons are short, and yields are low. In other farming areas of the Soviet Union, there are poor harvests because of very little rain. More troubles with Soviet farming have come from government policies that fail to make the best use of land and workers.

Most Soviet farming takes place on huge government farms. About two-thirds of farmland is organized as state farms, or **sovkhozy** (sahf KAW zee). Sovkhozy are run like factories with farm workers paid wages by the government. Soviet state farms are about 42,000 acres (16,996.8 ha) each.

The rest of Soviet farmland is made up of **kolkhozy** (kahl KAW zee), or collective farms. They average about 16,000 acres (6,475 ha) each. Families living and working on the kolkhozy share the profits from the sale of produce. However, the government owns the land and decides what, where, and how much will be produced.

Refer to the map on page 412 and have students note the great disparity in size among the republics.

2.2 Variety of Peoples

The Soviet Union has a population of 284 million. It ranks third among the world's most populous nations—after China and India. Figure 20-4 on this page shows how the Soviet Union's land area and population compare with those of the United States.

The Soviet Union's people come from a variety of backgrounds and speak many different languages. According to the most recent Soviet census, there are more than 90

COMPAR-A-GRAPH: U.S.S.R.-UNITED STATES

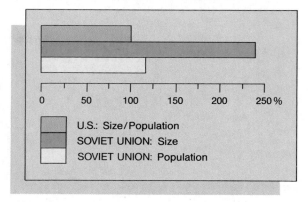

0	50	100	150	200	250 %

U.S.: Size/Population
SOVIET UNION: Size
SOVIET UNION: Population

FIGURE 20-4
The enormous size of the Soviet Union is readily apparent when measured with that of the United States in this compar-a-graph. How many times larger than the United States is the land size of the U.S.S.R.?

ethnic groups in the country. Each of the 15 major ethnic groups has its own republic in the Soviet Union. These republics are not independent. They are more like states in the United States. Figure 20-5 on page 412 shows the locations and capitals of the 15 Soviet republics.

Slavs. The largest family of ethnic groups in the Soviet Union are Slavs. They are divided into three groups—Russians, Ukrainians, and Belorussians. Together, these groups make up 72 percent of the Soviet population. In religion, many of them are Eastern Orthodox Christians.

Russian Slavs number about 140 million. They are the dominant group in the Soviet Union. Most of the high-ranking officials in government and the Communist Party are Russians. Also the Russian language is the lingua franca of the Soviet Union.

Russians live all over the country, but most are found in their own republic—the Russian Soviet Federated Socialist Republic (R.S.F.S.R.). The R.S.F.S.R. is by far the largest of the 15 Soviet republics. It covers

As a result of their prominence in government, some Slavs today live throughout the entire land area of the Soviet Union. In some places the Slavs who hold important positions represent a small minority in the total population of a given area or a separate republic.

UNION OF SOVIET SOCIALIST REPUBLICS _____

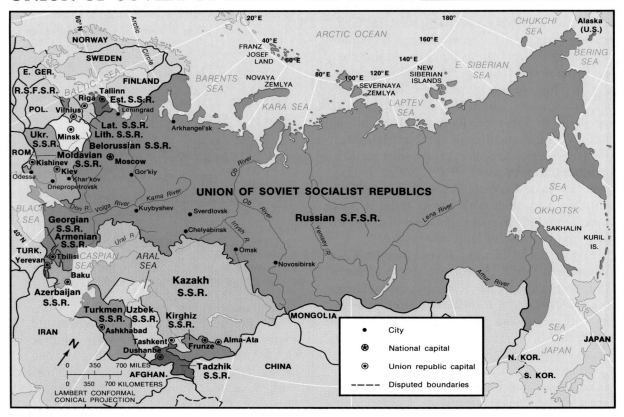

FIGURE 20-5

This map reveals why the country is referred to as a Union of Soviet Socialist Republics. Fifteen republics, each representing a major ethnic group, combine to form the Soviet Union. The Russian Soviet Federated Socialist Republic is the most prominent republic in size and importance. Which three Soviet republics make up the Baltic Republics and how do they differ from their Slavic neighbors in the Soviet Union?

Some Ukrainians have never been happy as citizens of the Soviet Union, a country they view as dominated by Russian Slavs. During World War II, some Ukrainians initially viewed the invading Germans as liberators.

three-quarters of the Soviet Union's land area. Moscow and Leningrad—are located in the R.S.F.S.R.

The second largest group of Slavs is the Ukrainians. They number about 42 million and live in the Ukrainian Soviet Socialist Republic, which lies west and south of the R.S.F.S.R. Today most Ukrainians live in urban areas such as Kiev, Kharkov, and Odessa. Many, however, continue to live in rural areas. In spite of years of Russian influence, Ukrainians remain proud of their own Slavic language and customs.

Belorussians make up the third group of Slavs. They live in the Belorussian Soviet Socialist Republic, which is north of the Ukraine. Once ruled by Poland, the 10 million Belorussians have a strong Polish influence in their culture. Their largest city—Minsk—is one of the fastest growing cities in the Soviet Union.

Baltic Peoples. Three peoples—the Lithuanians, Latvians, and Estonians—live in three small republics along the Baltic coast of the Soviet Union. These are the Lithuanian, Latvian, and Estonian Soviet Socialist

EUROPE UNIT 6

Republics. Once independent, they came under Soviet control in 1940.

The people of the Baltic Republics have little in common with their Slavic neighbors in the Soviet Union. Western European in outlook, they use the Latin alphabet. Most Estonians and Latvians are Protestant, and most Lithuanians are Roman Catholic. The Baltic peoples enjoy a higher standard of living than the Slavs of the Soviet Union.

Peoples of the Caucasus. The Caucasus region of the Soviet Union is the home of more than 40 different ethnic groups. For hundreds of years, the region was made up of many separate states that were conquered repeatedly by powerful neighbors. Today the largest ethnic groups—the Georgians, the Armenians, and the Azerbaijanians (AZ uhr BY JAHN ee uhn)—have their own republics within the Soviet Union.

The Georgians, Armenians, and Azerbaijanians have similar cultures, but there still are many differences among them. The six million Azerbaijanians live in an area near the Caspian Sea. Their territory is called the Azerbaijan Soviet Socialist Republic (S.S.R.). The Azerbaijanians are Muslims and speak their own language. Most live in lowland, rural areas and grow corn, cotton, fruits, vegetables, and tobacco. Their major source of wealth, however, is oil.

The five million Georgians have their own separate language, alphabet, and Christian church. They are known for their business skills, love of festivals, and hospitality to strangers. Because their land—the Georgian Soviet Socialist Republic—is mountainous, most Georgians live in valleys where they grow flowers, tobacco, citrus fruit, and grapes.

The three million Armenians also have their own language, alphabet, and Christian church. They live in the Armenian Soviet Socialist Republic to the west of the Georgian

Joseph Stalin, ruler of the Soviet Union from 1928 to 1953, was a Georgian.

Wine-growing is one of the most ancient and important branches of agriculture in the Georgian Republic. The best Soviet dry wines are made from grapes grown in Kakjetia, which produces one-quarter of the republic's grapes due to its favorable terrain, soil, and climate. Besides grapes, what other agricultural products do Georgians grow?

In contrast to the huge government farms, many farmers have been allowed to hold small garden plots for their own use. Though these plots make up only 2.7 percent of all Soviet farmland, they produce about 30 percent of the country's food.

S.S.R. Although most Soviet Armenians work in industry, many are farmers. Armenians take great pride in their culture.

Central Asians. A variety of peoples live in Soviet Central Asia. Numbering about 35 million, they are Muslims and speak languages related to Turkish. Before modern times, many people in the region raised animals and were wanderers who roamed the steppe in search of pasture. Others settled in cities and created empires.

In the 1920s the Central Asian peoples became part of the Soviet Union and were divided into the Kazakh, Turkmen, Uzbek, Kirghiz, and Tadzhik Soviet Socialist Republics. The Soviet government began building farms, schools, and factories in Soviet Central Asia. Today the region is advancing economically and is known for cotton and grain production. It also produces minerals, such as coal and copper. Their new prosperity has made the Central Asian peoples' position in the Soviet Union strong.

2.3 Daily Life and Culture

The Communist Party of the Soviet Union has set as its goal a society with neither rich nor poor people. It has ended social groups who became rich from inherited wealth. However, there are new groups with special privileges in the Soviet Union. These groups include party and government officials, scientists, engineers, artists, and others who have helped serve the communist system.

City Life. The Soviet government has promoted the growth of cities. Once largely rural, the Soviet Union now is urban. About two-thirds of all Soviet people live in cities and towns. Three Soviet cities—Moscow, Leningrad, and Kiev—have more than two million people each.

Of all Soviet cities, Moscow holds a special place in the hearts of the Soviet people. In the past Russians viewed it as the center of Eastern Orthodox Christianity. Today, they see it as the world center of communism.

The population of Soviet Central Asia has been growing rapidly, but growth in most European areas has slowed. Many Russian Slavs fear, in time, they may be outnumbered by people of vastly different cultures.

Pictured here is the very heart of Moscow and the Soviet Union. The Kremlin Wall encloses government buildings behind it. St. Basil Church, now a museum, stands in the foreground. Red Square and Lenin's Tomb are in the open area to the right. What is the past and present importance of Moscow to the Soviet Union?

The Soviet Union has at least 15 cities that each has more than 1 million inhabitants. Moscow alone has a metropolitan population of more than 8.5 million.

Completed in 1893, Moscow's GUM department store is a massive, glass-roofed, three-storied complex with three huge galleries inside. On the average more than 350,000 shoppers crowd into GUM each day. Although shoppers must usually stand in long lines, they are less often disappointed by empty shelves today than a few years ago.

Over the centuries, Moscow has developed like a huge spiderweb. At its heart is the Kremlin, an old fortress and the seat of the Soviet government.

Industrial growth and a higher standard of living in Soviet cities have drawn a large number of people from rural areas. Today Soviet cities are crowded. Most Soviet families live in tall apartment buildings and have only one or two rooms. Housing shortages often force many newly married couples to move in with their parents. A Soviet family may have to wait for several years before it gets an apartment of its own.

People living in Soviet cities often have problems shopping for food, clothing, and other products. Because of shortages of many consumer goods, most shoppers have to go from store to store looking for what they want. Often, they have to stand in long lines to get scarce or imported goods. Many times after hours of searching, they return home

The elegant interior of Moscow's largest department store attracts both city residents and foreign visitors. What problems do Soviet shoppers face?

SHOPPING IN MOSCOW AND NEW YORK

ITEM	MOSCOW	NEW YORK
Walkman Radio/Cassette	$225.00	$80.00
Jeans	$90.00	$28.00
Sneakers	$45.00	$56.00
Record Album	$ 6.25	$ 7.00
Ballpoint Pen	79¢	$ 2.00
Evening Movie Ticket	68¢	$ 7.00
Gallon of Milk	45¢	$ 2.19
Can of Soft Drink	45¢	65¢
Fast-Food Hamburger	45¢	99¢
Loaf of Bread	29¢	$ 1.09
Fast-Food Milk Shake	15¢	95¢
Bus or Subway Ride	8¢	$ 1.00
Newspaper	5¢	30¢
Dental Checkup	free	$ 60.00

FIGURE 20-6
A comparison of recent prices for identical goods and services show some interesting differences in shopping in these two cities. Why are consumer goods such as radios and jeans more expensive in Moscow?

See the *TAE* for an *Objective 2* Activity.

empty-handed or with goods of poor quality. Figure 20–6 on this page compares the prices people in Moscow pay for goods and services with what people in New York pay.

Privileged members of Soviet society, however, enjoy certain advantages. They can get scarce and valuable goods in special shops open only to them. They can enjoy such luxuries as cars, comfortable apartments, and **dachas,** or summer homes. To make fewer people unhappy about this, the Soviet government has given these privileges to a larger number of people.

Rural Life. About 25 million people— 20 percent of Soviet workers—are farmers. In recent years the living conditions of these people have been better. However, they still

About 93 percent of working-age women in the Soviet Union hold full-time jobs. In addition, one-third of the country's lawyers and 70 percent of the doctors are women, and there are more female scientists and engineers in the Soviet Union than in any other country of the world. However, salaries and promotions usually favor men.

Contrary to the typical image of Siberia is this rural village located in a mild area of Siberia. What are some disadvantages of rural life in the Soviet Union?

See the *TAE* for an *Objective 2* Activity.

do not enjoy the same benefits as city residents. In the villages of the Soviet Union, people live in small log huts called *bas,* or in large community buildings. These buildings sometimes do not have electricity, gas, and running water. Rural areas receive fewer goods and services than cities. Often these items are of poor quality.

Soviet Family.   In the past, family ties were strong in the lands that make up the Soviet Union. Today, however, industrial growth and housing shortages have put pressures on family relationships. Parents, grown children, and even grandparents often have to share an apartment. Such crowded conditions often lead to stress and conflict.

Among the Slavs of the Soviet Union, there is a growing trend toward smaller families. Today the average Russian young couple has only one child. However, in the Caucasus region and in Soviet Central Asia, larger families still are common.

The Soviet Union has long supported the equality of women with men. Over the years

Soviet women have helped in the defense of the country and in its economic growth. Today women make up about one-half of all Soviet workers. Most hold full-time jobs. This is the highest percentage of any industrialized country in the world.

Culture.   The Soviet government promotes the goals of communism by supporting and controlling many cultural activities. Soviets enjoy films, theater, ballet, and public poetry readings. They, however, are especially proud of their land's cultural heritage, much of which comes from Russia of the 1800s and early 1900s.

During this period of time, the Russians enjoyed a golden age of culture. Russian writers, musicians, and artists created many outstanding works that honored their country. For example, the composer Peter Tchaikovsky wrote music that showed a deep love for the Russian land and people. A famous Russian writer, Leo Tolstoy, wrote about events of Russian history in novels, such as *War and Peace.*

In this century the communist government of the Soviet Union has rewarded writers, artists, musicians, and filmmakers who have promoted communism in their work. However, those against government policies have been criticized, put in prison, or forced to leave the country.

As it does in cultural activities, the Soviet government closely controls religion. Officially, the Soviet Union is **atheistic,** not believing there is a God. The government keeps many religious buildings closed. It also closely watches over the few religious groups that are allowed to exist. Religious activities are against the law outside religious buildings, and strong believers are often unable to get good jobs. Even with these restrictions, about 40 percent of the Soviet people can be viewed as religious. They consist chiefly of Christians, Jews, Muslims, and Buddhists.

Soviet citizens pursue a variety of leisure activities, including entertaining at home, reading, watching television, music, and playing chess. Soviets also have a passion for outdoor life and sports. Hiking, cross-country skiing, and ice skating are very popular, as are spectator sports such as soccer and ice hockey.

CONTENT CHECK

1. **Identify:** Supreme Soviet, Communist Party, Politburo, General Secretary, Moscow, Leningrad, Ukraine, Kiev, Kharkov, Rostov, Odessa, Baku, Tbilisi, Yerevan, Tashkent, Slavs, Ukrainians, Belorussians, Minsk, Lithuanians, Lithuanian S.S.R., Latvians, Latvian S.S.R., Estonians, Georgians, Armenian S.S.R., Azerbaijan S.S.R., Kazakh S.S.R., Turkmen S.S.R., Uzbek S.S.R., Kirghiz S.S.R., Tadzhik S.S.R.

2. **Define:** bureaucracy, five-year plans, black market, flax, sovkhozy, kolkhozy, dachas, atheistic.

3. Who holds the real power of government in the Soviet Union?

4. What kind of economy does the Soviet Union have?

5. What are the major industrial areas of the Soviet Union? What goods does each produce?

6. What ethnic groups make up the Soviet Union?

7. What is Soviet family life like?

8. **Challenge:** How are city life and rural life different in the Soviet Union?

See the *TRB* for the *Chapter 8 Reading* on letters from medieval Russia.

3. INFLUENCES OF THE PAST

The land that is now the Soviet Union developed gradually over many centuries. It began when groups of Slavs founded villages along the Dnepr River between 500 and 800 AD. During the 900s a powerful Slavic state grew up along the river with its center at Kiev. After Kiev's fall to invaders in the 1200s, another Slavic state arose farther north in the area of Moscow. It became known as

Russia. From the 1500s to the 1800s, Russians formed a powerful empire that was made up of many non-Slavic peoples. In the early 1900s, the Communists gained power in Russia. They changed the Russian Empire into the Soviet Union.

Remind students of the importance of water routes for transporting both people and goods.

3.1 Early Slavs

About 400 AD groups of Slavs moved from the plains of Poland into what is now the Ukraine. By about 800, Slavic **clans,** or groups of related families, controlled the forested area west of the Volga River.

The Slavs set up trading centers along the rivers that flowed between the Baltic and the Black seas. These centers became links in a trade route that joined the Slavs with the Vikings in the north and the Byzantines in the south.

The trade route of the Slavs stretched more than 1,000 miles (1,609 km). As a result it was hard to protect from outsiders, especially warriors from Central Asia. Knowing they were not strong, a group of Slavs asked Viking warriors to come and rule over them. The warriors, known as *russ* in the Viking language, organized the Slavs into city-states with forts. In time, the Vikings became so important that many of the Slavs came to be known as *Russians*.

During the 900s the Slavic city-states developed the first Russian civilization in the area now called the Ukraine. First, they formed a **confederation,** or loose union, centered in the city-state of Kiev. Then they accepted the eastern form of Christianity from the Byzantines, which became known as the Eastern Orthodox Church.

Along with Christianity, Slavic city-states adopted the Cyrillic alphabet and used it to write the Russian language. They also built churches and palaces that looked like those of the Byzantines. From the 1000s to the early

1200s, Kiev and several other city-states were among the richest and most advanced territories in Europe.

Slavic city-states, however, faced much danger. Their location on the steppe put them in the path of invasions by Mongols from central Asia. In the early 1200s, Mongols destroyed Kiev. During the next 200 years, Russians were cut off from European civilization. The center of Russian culture also shifted northward. By 1400 the northern trading town of Moscow had become the new center of Russian lands.

See the *TAE* for an *Objective 3* Activity.

3.2 Russian Expansion

Muscovy (muh SKOH vee), as early Moscow was called, became powerful as the Mongols left Europe and retreated into Asia.

In the late 1400s, the ruler of Muscovy became known as **tsar,** or emperor, and his territory as Russia.

To stay protected, Russian tsars expanded and created a large empire. In the late 1500s, their first major conquests were the Volga River basin and western Siberia. During the 1600s tsars took over the Ukraine and the rest of Siberia. Finland and parts of Poland and Prussia were added in the 1700s and early 1800s. The Russian Empire also included Alaska until it was sold to the United States in 1867. Figure 20–7 on this page shows the expansion of the Russian Empire during the time of the tsars. It also shows the present boundary of the Soviet Union.

The addition of new lands brought many non-Russians under Russian rule. These included Slavs, Baltic peoples, Georgians, Armenians, Azerbaijanians, Muslim peoples of

TERRITORIAL EXPANSION

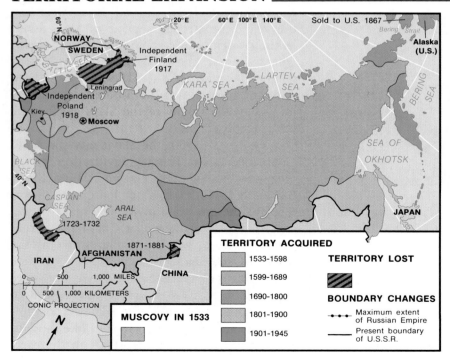

FIGURE 20-7
Whereas part of the territorial expansion in the United States followed an east-to-west direction, Russian territorial expansion was mainly west-to-east. Muscovy's significance to Russia is similar to the significance of the 13 original states to the United States. What present-day area of the United States was at one time Russian territory?

While it is generally known that Alaska once belonged to Russia, it is not well-known that Russia had outposts as far as the modern state of California. Have interested students research and report on these early settlements.

Another important railway, the Baikal-Amur Mainland Railroad (or BAM) was completed in October 1984 at a cost of $14 billion. Two-thirds of the railroad is built over permafrost.

WORLD TRANSPORTATION SYSTEMS

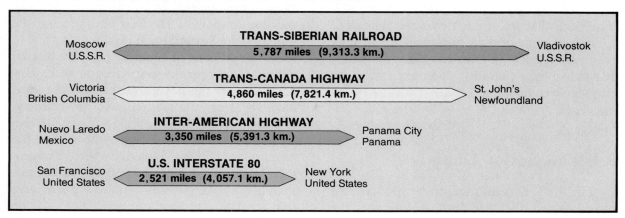

TRANS-SIBERIAN RAILROAD
Moscow U.S.S.R. — 5,787 miles (9,313.3 km.) — Vladivostok U.S.S.R.

TRANS-CANADA HIGHWAY
Victoria British Columbia — 4,860 miles (7,821.4 km.) — St. John's Newfoundland

INTER-AMERICAN HIGHWAY
Nuevo Laredo Mexico — 3,350 miles (5,391.3 km.) — Panama City Panama

U.S. INTERSTATE 80
San Francisco United States — 2,521 miles (4,057.1 km.) — New York United States

FIGURE 20-8
The comparative distances of these four transportation systems give some idea of the Soviet Union's great width. Even though the western end of the Trans-Siberian Railroad stops in Moscow, the territory of the Soviet Union extends an additional 600 miles (965.6 km) to the western Soviet border. How many miles or kilometers longer is the Trans-Siberian Railroad than each of the three highways shown here?

Another famous Russian leader was Catherine the Great, whose leadership made Russia a leading country in European affairs during the late 1700s.

Central Asia, and small groups found all over Siberia. To unify their empire, tsars tried to make non-Russians speak Russian and accept Russian ways. This made non-Russian peoples go against Russian rule.

See the *TRB* for *Section 3: Extending the Lesson* on poet Alexander Pushkin.

3.3 Russia and Europe

In the early 1700s, Tsar Peter I, also known as "Peter the Great," tried to make Russia more like western European countries. Early in his reign, he toured European capitals to see how other Europeans lived and worked. Upon returning to Russia, Peter forced Russian nobles to wear European clothes and to copy European manners. He also reorganized the Russian government and strengthened his military forces.

During Peter's rule Russia expanded its borders to the south and west. The Russians wanted to gain seaports on the Baltic and Black seas. With these new ports, Russia would be able to increase its trade with Northwest Europe and Mediterranean Europe. To bring Russia closer to Europe, Peter moved the national capital from Moscow to a more western location on the Gulf of Finland. The new capital was called St. Petersburg, which is now Leningrad.

Peter's actions, however, did not go very far in changing Russia. Tsars after Peter I and nobles wanted to keep most of the Russian people backward. As a result, they did not easily accept European ways.

Since the 1600s most Russians had been **serfs,** or laborers owned by nobles and bound to the land. Serfs worked in the palaces and on the land of the tsars and nobles. Poor and tired, they had to pay taxes to the government and serve in the army.

Finally, in the late 1800s, Tsar Alexander II freed the serfs. At the same time, Russia began to set up industries like those of other European countries. Railroads also were built. The most famous of these is the Trans-Siberian Railroad. Figure 20–8 on this page compares the mileage of the Trans-Siberian Railroad with that of three other major transportation systems of the world.

Although Russia made progress in the late 1800s, it was still backward politically. The tsars that followed Alexander II refused to give up some of their powers. They did not want democracy in Russia. Many unhappy Russians began to want a complete end to the tsar's government.

Nicholas II, tsar during the early 1900s, believed God had chosen him to rule Russia. On July 16, 1918, he and his family were murdered by Bolsheviks.

3.4 The Soviet Union

In 1905 a revolution in St. Petersburg nearly ended the tsar's rule. However, the army was able to put a stop to it. More than 10 years later, during World War I, the Russians had a hard time fighting the Germans. Many soldiers died, and there was little food for the army and the people. More and more people became angry with the tsar's rule.

In early 1917 revolts broke out in the capital. City workers forced the tsar to **abdicate,** or give up the throne. Government leaders in favor of democracy came to power and promised elections. However, the war continued, and the people became upset.

A second revolution took place in the fall of 1917. At this time the government was taken over by Russian Communists called *Bolsheviks.* They were led by Vladimir Ilyich Ulyanov. Ulyanov was also known as Lenin. Lenin and the Bolsheviks won control of the **soviets,** or groups of workers and soldiers. The soviets had been set up in the first revolution to bring the needs of the workers and soldiers to the government.

From 1918 to 1920, fighting between the Bolsheviks and those who were against them took place all over the country. The Bolsheviks—who began to call themselves Communists—were called Reds, and the anticommunists Whites. The Reds finally won. In 1922 they set up the Union of Soviet Socialist Republics, or the Soviet Union. They named Moscow the capital of the new nation.

Lenin became ill in 1922 and died in 1924. Then Joseph Stalin fought other Bolsheviks for power. He won and became the leader of the Soviet Union. Stalin's aim was to make the Soviet Union a great industrial power. He set up the first five-year plan. Under the plan the government built factories, dams, bridges, and roads all over the country. It also turned small farms into collective farms. This was done against the will of the farmers, who were treated harshly. Government control in all areas of life tightened. People who were against Stalin's plans were sent to prison or labor camps.

Stalin ruled from the years 1927 to 1953. He was Soviet leader when Nazi Germany attacked the Soviet Union during World War II. By 1945 Soviet forces had driven the Germans out of the country. However, more than 20 million Soviets had died as a result of the war. Also huge areas of the country were in ruins.

Despite this, the Soviet Union came out of World War II as a major world power. In military might it was second only to the United States. In the late 1940s, the Soviets set up communist governments in the Eastern European countries that they had freed from the Germans. They also wanted their power to be felt all over the world.

New five-year plans after World War II helped the Soviet Union rebuild its economy. The government gave most of its attention to science and heavy industry. As a result, the Soviets made many advances in areas such as military weapons and space exploration.

Soviet leaders after Stalin kept strict controls over the people. However, they were not as cruel as he was. Soviet society became more relaxed, and people were able to dress and to eat better. They also could enjoy more consumer goods. Abroad, Soviet leaders worked to spread communism. However, they also sought to avoid war with the United States and other non-communist countries.

After World War II, the Soviet Union emerged as the strongest nation in Europe and Asia and a superpower to rival the United States. Since then it has undergone various changes in leadership, and Soviet relations with the western world, particularly the United States, have fluctuated in what has been called the "Cold War."

At Yalta in the Soviet Union, Winston Churchill of Great Britain, Franklin D. Roosevelt of the United States, and Joseph Stalin of the Soviet Union (seated from left to right) met for a conference before the end of World War II. How did World War II affect military and economic development in the Soviet Union?

See the TRB for the Chapter 20 Skill Activity on analyzing historical geography.

CONTENT CHECK

1. **Identify:** Kiev, Mongols, Muscovy, Peter I, St. Petersburg, Alexander II, Bolsheviks, Lenin, Reds, Whites, Joseph Stalin.

2. **Define:** clans, confederation, tsar, serfs, abdicate, soviets.

3. Where did early Russian civilization begin?

4. What did the Byzantines pass on to early Russians?

5. What happened to Russian culture when the Mongols destroyed the city of Kiev in the 1200s?

6. Why did Peter I want to gain seaports on the Baltic and Black seas?

7. What was life like for most Russians under the tsars?

8. What trouble raised support for a revolution among the Russians?

9. **Challenge:** Why do you think after the time of Peter I, tsars and nobles wanted to keep the Russian people backward?

CONCLUSION

In the early 1900s, the Russian Empire was a poor agricultural country. The Soviet Union — the country that followed it — is today one of the world's industrial and military powers. All Soviet citizens have free medical care and education. They also have the right to a job as well as inexpensive, though often crowded, housing.

The Soviet Union has made much progress, in spite of the huge losses it has had in wars and revolutions. The price has been high. To make advances, the Soviet government has put many limits on personal freedoms. Also, although their lives have improved, Soviet citizens still do without many comforts that people in democratic countries enjoy. The planned economy of the Soviet Union does not always work well. Many people in the country have been unhappy about shortages of food and consumer goods. Meeting the needs and wants of its people will be a major issue that the Soviet Union will face in the years ahead.

SUMMARY

1. The Soviet Union is the world's largest country in terms of area and the third largest in terms of population.
2. Most of the Soviet Union has moist, cold winter climates.
3. Vegetation areas in the Soviet Union are different from north to south. A huge forested area covers most of the middle part of the country. This is considered the largest area of forest in the world.
4. The Soviet Union has a planned, socialist economy. It is directed by the Communist Party and government leaders in Moscow.
5. The Soviet Union has a variety of ethnic groups.
6. About two-thirds of Soviets live in cities and towns.
7. The Soviet Union was established in 1922 after a revolution overthrew the last tsar.
8. The Soviet Union is the leading communist country in the world. Even though it has had great losses from wars, it has become a major world power.

Answers to the following questions can be found on page T208.

REVIEWING VOCABULARY

On a separate sheet of paper, number from 1 to 12. Beside each number write the vocabulary word that matches each numbered definition below.

flax	confederation	abdicate	sovkhozy
clans	five-year plans	kolkhozy	atheistic
serfs	bureaucracy	soviets	tsars

1. network of government officials
2. state farms
3. collective farms
4. production goals set by government
5. plant used for making linen
6. farmers owned by nobles
7. group of related families
8. loose union of states
9. rulers
10. not believing in God
11. give up the throne
12. councils of workers and soldiers

REMEMBERING THE FACTS

1. What does U.S.S.R. stand for?
2. How much of Earth's land area is covered by the Soviet Union?
3. What group of countries are led by the Soviet Union?
4. What is the longest river in Europe? Where is it located?
5. What is the highest mountain peak in Europe? Where is it located?
6. How much of the Soviet Union is forests?
7. What general kinds of landforms does the Soviet Union have?
8. What general kind of climate covers most of the Soviet Union?

9. What limits farming in the Soviet Union?
10. What is the leading ethnic group in the Soviet Union?
11. How many republics make up the Soviet Union?
12. What city was established by Peter the Great in his effort to develop his country? What is the city's name today?
13. Which city is the leading center of Soviet culture?

UNDERSTANDING THE FACTS

1. How are the Caucasus Mountains different from the Ural Mountains?
2. Why do few trees grow in the steppe?
3. Why are crops grown in the Caucasus region different from those grown in the Ukraine?
4. How is the Communist Party organized?
5. Why is Siberia called "one vast construction site"?
6. How does the standard of living in the Soviet Union compare with that in the United States?
7. Why do Baltic people have little in common with Slavs?
8. How did the location of Kiev prove to be a problem in the 1100s and 1200s?
9. What was accomplished under Stalin's first five-year plan?

THINKING CRITICALLY AND CREATIVELY

1. How have the Soviet Union's landforms affected its history and development?
2. The Soviet Union occupies more land area than any other country. How is its size an advantage? A disadvantage?
3. Why does a far northern location affect temperatures in the Soviet Union more than in the nations of Northwest Europe?
4. The Soviet Union opposes religion. It has a law that forbids religious education classes for people under 18. Why do you think the Soviets have this law?
5. **Challenge:** After World War II, the Soviet Union set up satellite governments in several Eastern European countries. From what you know about the geography of the Soviet Union, why do you think Soviet military planners wanted these satellites?
6. **Challenge:** The Soviet Union today is made up of the same ethnic groups that made up the Russian Empire. Do you think today's Soviet Union can be called an empire? Why or why not?

REINFORCING GRAPHIC SKILLS

Study the map on page 404. Then answer the questions that follow.

1. According to the map, which direct distance is greater: Leningrad to Vladivostok or Anchorage to New York?
2. **Challenge:** The Novosibirsk area has the same steppe climate as north central United States. Why is this true?

SUMMARY

1. Europe is found at the western edge of the Eurasian landmass. The Ural Mountains in the Soviet Union separate Europe from Asia.
2. Europe consists of four regions—Northwest Europe, Mediterranean Europe, Eastern Europe, and the Soviet Union.
3. Europe has many landscapes and climates. Its large, mostly urban population is crowded into a small land area.
4. In general, Europeans have a high standard of living. The level of economic development in Europe declines from north to south and from west to east.
5. Most European countries have industrial economies. European farms provide large amounts of farm products for many people.
6. Europe is linked by up-to-date ways of communication and transportation. However, it is divided by different languages, cultures, and traditions.
7. In the past many European countries ruled other lands around the globe, carrying with them their ideas and ways of living.
8. Today, the democratic countries of Europe have recently learned to cooperate with each other. They still play an important role in world affairs. The Soviet Union is a world power mostly because of its military strength. However, it also has become an industrial leader.

Answers to the following questions can be found on page T212.

THINKING ABOUT THE UNIT

1. Use maps in the atlas on pages 652-655 to locate the following cities: Oslo, Norway; Moscow, U.S.S.R.; and Berlin, Germany. Which city has the coldest winter temperatures? Why?
2. How has Europe been important in world economic development?
3. What similarities are there between the development of Britain and Russia as colonial powers? What differences?
4. In what ways do you think World War I and World War II affected the physical environment of Europe and the cultural lives of Europeans?

SUGGESTED UNIT ACTIVITIES

1. Prepare a written report on the Tour de France bicycle race or one of the European auto races, such as the Monaco Grand Prix. Include a brief history of the particular race and a map of its route.
2. From writings about the Holocaust, prepare a presentation for class.
3. On a map of Europe, trace the course of the Rhine River or the Danube River. Present an oral report, giving information about some of the major cities located on the river and the river traffic.
4. Plan a pot-luck luncheon. Have class members bring in European foods.

DEVELOPING GEOGRAPHY SKILLS ━━━━━━━

MAKING COMPARISONS

Have you ever walked through a shopping mall parking lot thinking about the reasons why you like a sports car you just saw more or less than the one you saw last night? You decide that in some ways this car was better than the other one. But in other ways, it was not.

What you are doing when you think about two cars in this way is making a comparison. To *compare* means to examine something in order to identify similarities or differences. You can compare, or make comparisons of, things that are very different or things that are very much alike. For any comparison to be complete, at least one similarity and one difference must be noted. Asking yourself questions like the following will help you make an effective comparison.

1. What do I want to compare? (*The car I saw tonight and the one I saw last night.*)
2. What are the areas on which I could base a comparison? (*style, price, trim, standard and extra options, horsepower*)
3. On which area do I want to concentrate? (*options*)
4. What similarities are there in this area? What differences? (Similarity: *Rear window louvers would be extra options on both cars.*) Difference: (*Five-speed transmission would be a standard option on the car you saw tonight but an extra option on the car you saw last night.*)

There are some commonly accepted words and phrases you can use when making comparisons. For example, when indicating similarity, the following may be used:

1. *Both* urbanization and education *have* helped make Northwest Europe prosperous.
2. Most people in France follow the Roman Catholic religion—the *same* religion *as* that followed by most people in the Irish Republic.
3. The belief in respect for human rights is *identical* for the British and the Irish.
4. The histories of England and France *are similar in that* they were both ruled by monarchs.
5. Paris and London *are alike in that* they are major metropolitan areas.
6. The countries of Norden *have* certain natural resources *in common*.

When indicating difference, the following may be used:

1. The United Kingdom has a larg*er* population than Ireland.
2. France is the larg*est* country in Northwest Europe.
3. Agriculture is *more* important in Denmark *than* in Greenland.
4. The northern part of West Germany is *less* mountainous *than* the southern part of West Germany.
5. All Western European nations *are not alike* in their rate of industrialization.
6. The climate of northern France is *not the same as* the climate in southern France.
7. The government of West Germany is *different from* the government of East Germany.

To practice the skill of making comparisons, read Section 2.2 of Chapter 20, and compare ethnic groups of the Soviet Union.

NORTH AFRICA AND SOUTHWEST ASIA

UNIT 7

North Africa and Southwest Asia occupy a large strip of mostly dry land that spans two continents. The area runs east from the Atlantic coast of Africa to the Hindu Kush of Asia. North Africa and Southwest Asia lie between the Black Sea in the north and the southern boundary of Sudan in Africa.

With more than 25 nations, North Africa and Southwest Asia make up a culture area because the two regions have common landforms, climates, and economic features. The area also shares a cultural heritage that is largely based on the Islamic religion and Arab ways of life. From this culture area came two of the world's earliest civilizations.

Throughout history the area has been a crossroads—a land bridge for traders moving back and forth between Europe and Asia.

Recently, North Africa and Southwest Asia have been regions of conflict. Fighting over territory and cultural differences has left many undefined or changing boundaries. Frequent wars and threats of war have created much distrust among the countries of this culture area.

Point out to students that the highlighted area on the world map inset represents the culture area of North Africa and Southwest Asia.

Desert in Algeria

CHAPTER 21

Throughout Africa traditional lifestyles are blended with more modern ways. Point out the power line in the photo below to illustrate this point.

In the Nile Basin at Qena, Egypt

NORTH AFRICA AND THE SAHEL

North Africa and the Sahel culture area is often referred to as part of the "Arab world" because most of the people there are Arabs.

In this chapter you will learn—

- What are the major physical features and climate patterns of North Africa and the Sahel.
- What economic activities are carried on throughout North Africa and the Sahel.
- How land use and population patterns are related to the physical landscape of North Africa and the Sahel.
- How the cultures of North Africa and the Sahel have developed.

Use a large wall map or globe to point out to students that the 48 contiguous states of the United States would easily be enclosed by Africa at its widest part.

INTRODUCTION

The Sahara, a desert in the northern part of Africa, covers an area about the size of the United States. It is about 3.5 million square miles (9.1 million sq km) in area. The Sahara is made up mostly of rock, gravel plateaus, and flatlands. Only 20 percent is sand. The 10 countries of the Sahara make up the region of North Africa and the Sahel (suh HAYL).

The countries of North Africa and the Sahel span the widest part of Africa—about 3,500 miles (5,632.7 km). From the northernmost point in the country of Tunisia to the southernmost tip of Chad is about 2,000 miles (3,218.7 km).

The subregion of North Africa has six countries that can be divided into two groups. One is made up of Egypt and Sudan, which lie in the northeastern part of Africa, bordering the Red Sea. Egypt's northern coast lies along the Mediterranean Sea. These countries are dominated by the Nile River.

West of Egypt is a group of North African countries known as the Arab West. It is made up of Libya, Tunisia, Algeria, and Morocco. All of these countries have coasts on the Mediterranean Sea.

South of the Arab West and west of Sudan is the Sahel. It is made up of the countries of Chad, Niger (NY juhr), Mali (MAH lee), and Mauritania (MAWR ih TAY nee uh). While Mauritania has an Atlantic coastline, Chad, Niger, and Mali are landlocked.

The region of North Africa and the Sahel is mostly desert with irregular rainfall. The people live in the few areas with groundwater.

Most people of North Africa and the Sahel are Arabs and Muslims. Arabic is spoken in most places. Other languages and cultures in the region include those of the Berbers in the Arab West and various groups in the Sahel. Many of the Sahel groups practice either Christianity or **animism**—the belief in spirits existing in nature.

Point out to students that Egypt and Sudan are linked by the Nile River.

1. EGYPT AND SUDAN

The Arab Republic of Egypt is the population center of North Africa. It has twice as many people as any other country in North Africa. In North Africa, as well as in all of Africa, the Democratic Republic of Sudan (soo DAN) is the largest country in land area.

PHYSICAL REGIONS OF NORTH AFRICA AND THE SAHEL

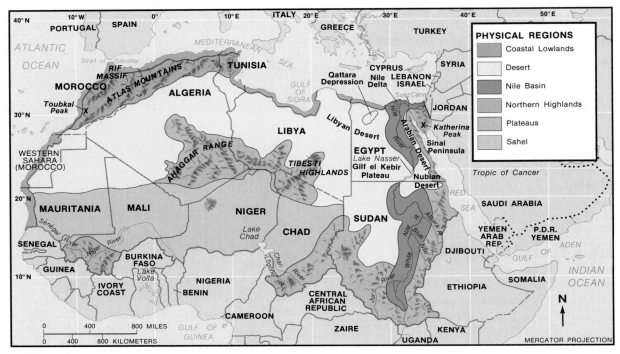

FIGURE 21-1

Desert and Sahel are the predominant physical features of this region. Which country has one-half of its territory in the Sahara and one-half in the Sahel?

Africa is the only continent without a Pacific coastline. Note that even though the continent is located in both the Northern and Southern hemispheres, geographers view it as part of the Northern Hemisphere.

1.1 Landscape and Climate

Egypt and Sudan are typical of the two kinds of land and climate found in North Africa and the Sahel. Figure 21–1 on this page shows that Egypt, like the Arab West, is mostly desert. Sudan, on the other hand, is partly desert with areas of tropical savanna.

Landscape. In addition to the huge part of Egypt that is desert, there are three other physical regions in the country. These are the Nile Basin, Mediterranean coastal lowlands, and Sinai (SY ny) Peninsula.

The Nile River is the longest river in Africa and the world. Figure 21–2 on page 431 compares the length of the Nile with the longest rivers of other continents. The Nile

River gets most of its water from heavy rains that fall at its source in Central Africa. The Nile River flows north to the Mediterranean Sea. More than 950 miles (1,528.9 km) of the river flows through Egypt.

The Nile Basin has two different parts. In the north a delta has formed where the Nile empties into the Mediterranean Sea. Over thousands of years, the flooding of the Nile has left rich silt all along its banks. The silt that was not left along the banks piled up to form the delta. Some parts of the delta have lagoons and swamps. At its base along the Mediterranean Sea, the Nile Delta is 155 miles (249.4 m) wide.

The other part of the Nile Basin is in the southern part of Egypt and is covered with

The Suez Canal is the shortest water route from Europe to southern and eastern Asia. It has been at the center of many international conflicts.

Ask students what effect the desert areas may have had on settlement patterns in North Africa. Where would they expect most people to have settled?

rocky soil. The river flows through narrow valleys and low plateaus of limestone, sandstone, and granite.

The Mediterranean coastal lowlands are a narrow strip of land north of the desert and west of the Nile Delta. This is the only part of Egypt that receives much rain.

Southeast of the Nile Delta is the Sinai Peninsula. It is the only part of Egypt not in Africa. The Sinai is part of southwestern Asia. It is a mountainous desert with a few oases. Jebel Katherina (JEHB uhl kath uh REE nuh), Egypt's highest peak at 8,668 feet (2,642 m), is in the southern Sinai. Between the Sinai Peninsula and the rest of Egypt is the Suez Canal, dug in the mid-1800s to connect the Red and Mediterranean seas.

Egypt's desert is part of the Sahara. However, it is generally studied as two different deserts. This is because one is west of the Nile River and the other is east of the Nile. In some ways these desert areas are different.

West of the Nile is the Libyan (LIHB yuhn) Desert, which covers nearly two-thirds of the land area of Egypt. The surface of this large plateau is gently rolling, averaging about 600 feet (182.9 m) above sea level. In the southwestern part of Egypt, the Gilf el Kebir Plateau (JIHLF ehl kuh BEER) rises to about 3,000 feet (914.4 m) above sea level.

The Libyan Desert also has several depressions. The largest one is the Qattara (kuh TAHR uh) Depression, which is less than 50 miles (80.5 km) south of the Mediterranean Sea. It is a huge saltwater marsh and lake, covering an area of about 7,000 square miles (18,130 sq km). In some places it is 436 feet (132.9 m) below sea level.

Oases are found all through the Libyan Desert. In these places moisture has gathered in cracks in underground rock. At some oases water is found on the surface. At others it can only be reached by drilling wells. Plants like palm trees grow around these areas.

East of the Nile River and west of the Red Sea is the Arabian Desert. From the Nile River Valley, the desert rises to a plateau that has many rocky hills running north and

LONGEST RIVERS OF EACH CONTINENT

FIGURE 21–2

Africa's Nile River easily outdistances the world's other longest rivers. The Nile is one of the few rivers of the world that flow to the north. Into which body of water does the Nile River flow?

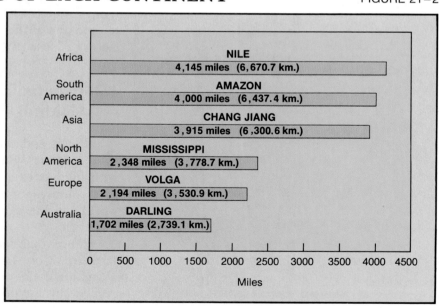

Africa	NILE	4,145 miles (6,670.7 km.)
South America	AMAZON	4,000 miles (6,437.4 km.)
Asia	CHANG JIANG	3,915 miles (6,300.6 km.)
North America	MISSISSIPPI	2,348 miles (3,778.7 km.)
Europe	VOLGA	2,194 miles (3,530.9 km.)
Australia	DARLING	1,702 miles (2,739.1 km.)

Miles (0 500 1000 1500 2000 2500 3000 3500 4000 4500)

CHAPTER 21   **NORTH AFRICA AND THE SAHEL**

Sudan occupies two percent of the total land area of Earth and eight percent of Africa's land.

Refer students to pages 96-97 to review the map of Earth's Climate Regions.

south. Some of these uplands rise as high as 7,000 feet (2,133.6 m) above sea level.

South of Egypt lies the country of Sudan, which covers an area about one-third the size of the contiguous United States. Two physical regions are found in Sudan—plateau and river basin. Much like Egypt, the north is plateau with dry and sandy hills. Highlands in the east begin at the Red Sea and run along the Nile Basin in the center of Sudan. The basin is part tropical savanna, part steppe, and part swamp. In fact, Sudan's swampy area—Sudd—is one of the largest natural marshes in the world.

In Sudan two tributaries of the Nile River join—the White Nile and the Blue Nile. The White Nile, the chief tributary, is joined by the Blue Nile at Khartoum (kahr TOOM), Sudan's capital.

Along the Nile River, from Khartoum to the border with Egypt, there are four great **cataracts,** or waterfalls. At these places the

river is forced into narrow channels and flows over the edges of steep cliffs. Because of these waterfalls and long stretches of rapids, parts of the Nile in this area are not navigable.

Climate. All of Egypt has a desert climate. Throughout most of Egypt, average rainfall is less than 1 inch (2.54 cm) a year. Most of the rain falls along the Mediterranean coast, but even there it measures only 8 inches (20.3 cm) a year.

Egypt's temperatures are hot throughout most of the year. In the city of Alexandria on the Mediterranean coast, the average high temperature in January is 57°F (13.9°C), and in July it is 86°F (30°C). In the south the city of Aswān (a SWAHN) has daytime temperatures as high as 120°F (48.9°C). As in most desert areas, night temperatures are usually cooler, often falling to 45°F (7.2°C).

Sudan's climate is hot throughout most of the country, with almost no rainfall in the desert north to about 57 inches (144.8 cm) in the tropical savanna of the south.

At Khartoum, in the central part of the country where desert changes to tropical savanna, the average high temperature in January is 94°F (34.4°C). There are generally high temperatures of more than 100°F (37.8°C) for ten months of the year.

Explain to students that although Egypt is the most populous country in the Arab world, Nigeria is the most populous country in Africa.

1.2 Economic and Cultural Patterns

Egypt and Sudan are primarily agricultural countries. Both are developing countries with high rates of population growth. Egypt is the most populous country in the Arab world and the second most populous country in Africa.

More than one-third of Egyptians are farmers. Most farming activity takes place along the Nile valley and delta. Almost 99 percent of Egypt's 51.9 million people live

Khartoum, Sudan, is at the site where tributaries of the Nile River join. The confluence of rivers is a natural site for a city's location. Which two river tributaries join to form the Nile River?

within 20 miles (32.2 km) of the Nile River. In other words, the great majority of people live on only 3.5 percent of the country's land. This area is one of the most densely populated in the world.

Most of Sudan's 23.5 million people live along the Nile and its branches in the northern part of the country. Others live in a wider band of land in the middle and southern parts of the country.

Farmers in the Nile Valley are known as **fellahin** (fehl uh HEEN). They rent their land from landlords. Most fellahin are poor and raise only enough crops to feed their families and to pay the rent on their land. Any food left over is sold in villages and towns at a **bazaar,** or marketplace.

Fellahin use many of the same tools and methods used by their ancestors almost 6,000 years ago. Among these tools are hoes, wooden plows, and sickles. Water is brought up from wells with the use of a **shadoof.** This is a long pole, balanced in the middle, with a bucket at one end and a weight on the other.

Some fellahin use what is called **basin irrigation.** They build walls of mud around their fields, which lie close to the river. When the Nile floods, usually in late summer, the walls hold some of the water, which is rich with silt. When the flood waters go down, fellahin drain the fields and plant seeds. Because this method depends on yearly floods, it allows for only one planting a year.

In 1968 the Aswān High Dam was completed on the Nile River in southern Egypt. It was built to provide irrigation for larger areas of land and to produce hydroelectric power.

The Aswān Dam has brought benefits to Egypt. Flooding of the Nile is now predictable and can be planned and prepared for. Fellahin and owners of large plantations that are downstream from the dam now have controlled flooding several times a year. This makes it possible to plant crops up to three times a year instead of only once.

Electrical power from the dam has brought light and industry to what used to be an undeveloped, poor region. In general, this has somewhat improved living conditions and the economic situation of many Egyptians.

However, the damming of the Nile also has brought problems. The dam holds back much of the rich silt that once fertilized the fields each year along the banks of the river. Farmers in Egypt must now use large amounts of artificial fertilizer on their fields.

A second major problem is found in the Nile Delta. Before the dam was built, the force of water from the river held back the salt water of the Mediterranean Sea. With less water flowing from the river, the sea has begun to erode the coast. Some salt water now enters the delta, making some land around it unfit for farming.

The major export crops grown in the Nile Basin are cotton and **gum arabic**—used for making adhesives, perfumes, and some candies. Cotton grown in the Nile area is among the best in the world. It has long fibers that are strong and silky. About 35 percent of Egypt's cotton is traded to other countries. Cotton and cottonseed account for about 50 percent of Sudan's income.

The major food crops in Egypt and Sudan are sorghum, wheat, sesame seeds, peanuts, and castor beans. In desert oases, sheep, goats, and camels are raised by nomads called Bedouins (BEHD wuhnz).

In hopes of growing more food, there has been a shift toward large-scale farming in the Nile Basin. To encourage greater food production, the Egyptian government has restricted cotton planting to one-third of each owner's land. Most landowners must also plant wheat on one-third of their land.

Many fellahin have lost their jobs as fewer people are needed on farms. They have been forced to move to cities in search of jobs. Most have gone to Egypt's capital, Cairo, of 10 million people, or to Sudan's

THE URBAN WORLD

CAIRO: URBAN GROWTH

Among the many rapidly growing cities in developing countries is Cairo, Egypt. With about 10 million people, Cairo today is Africa's largest city. It has grown quickly since the 1970s, when it had 6 million people. Because of this rapid growth, many geographers view Cairo as an example of "overurbanization." This simply means that too much of an area has become urbanized too fast.

People have been migrating to Cairo for many reasons. Hundreds of thousands of refugees from the Sinai Peninsula moved to Cairo after Israel took over the land in the late 1960s. Thousands more have moved from rural areas. Another factor that has increased population is a high birthrate. Recently, Cairo has been growing in population at the rate of 2.6 percent per year.

For Cairo, urbanization—the trend of many more people living in cities than in rural areas—has severely strained city services. People in many areas of Cairo do not receive electricity, water, and sewage disposal. Housing is in short supply. Thousands of people live in cemetery monuments. About 500,000 live on rooftops of buildings. Others live in tents and makeshift wooden sheds. Some areas have as many as 260,000 people living within one square mile (2.6 sq km). Because of little income to improve city services, the quality of life for Cairo's people goes down more and more each year.

Overcrowded conditions are not helped by the physical features of the land around Cairo. Cairo is located on the low-lying floodplain of the Nile River about 12 miles (19.3 km) south of the Nile Delta. On both sides of the Nile Valley, steep hills rise to a high plateau. Not only is the plateau mostly desert and difficult to irrigate but also there are not many areas to which the city may sprawl.

Cairo lies in the heart of some of the best farmland in Egypt. Because the city is expanding, much of this land is being used for settlements. With less and less land to grow crops, it is becoming increasingly more difficult and expensive to feed people.

Today nearly one-third of Egypt's population lives in Cairo. Overurbanization is common in countries like Egypt that have one city that contains a very high percentage of the country's population. Because Egypt is a developing country, it is not able to spend its limited income on the nation's development when a growing population in Cairo is using up many of its resources. For this reason Cairo's problems have become Egypt's problems. In order for the country's economy to grow, it must seek solutions to problems created by the overurbanization of Cairo.

1. What does "overurbanization" mean?
2. What conditions in Cairo suggest overurbanization?
3. How are the problems Cairo is experiencing harming Egypt's economy?

Cairo is the cultural capital of the Middle East and the Arab world. It has many museums and theaters and a large university.

Explain to students that the dry air of Egypt has helped preserve the Pyramids and the Great Sphinx over many centuries.

capital, Khartoum, of 500,000 people. As a result large cities are overcrowded. There are not enough jobs in industry for the fellahin, most of whom have no skills.

Major industries in the area are food processing, textiles, and cement. Not many minerals have been found in Sudan. In Egypt there are some granite, iron ore, phosphate rock, and oil. The country's textile industry is centered in Alexandria and in Cairo. Egypt gains income from the sale of hydroelectric power from the Aswān High Dam. Another source of income is fares charged to ships using the Suez Canal.

See the *TAE* for an *Objective 1* Activity.

1.3 Influences of the Past

One of the ancient world's most advanced cultures developed along the Nile River. Beginning about 5000 BC, early people in the valley began to farm along the Nile. Small communities grew up. By 4000 BC Egypt had two large kingdoms with well-organized governments. About 3000 BC parts of present-day Egypt and Sudan were united as one kingdom of Egypt.

Ancient Egyptians used **hieroglyphics,** or picture symbols, for writing. They made paper from a reedlike plant called **papyrus.** They developed a calendar to keep track of the growing season, and they had great skill in building, as shown by the Great Sphinx and the pyramids. As early as 5,000 years ago, Egypt had cities.

Egypt was a strong united kingdom from about 3100 BC until 525 BC. In that year it was invaded by Persian forces and became a province of Persia. In 332 BC it was conquered by Alexander the Great. He built a large empire in Greece, southwestern Asia, and Egypt. The city of Alexandria is named for him. From that time until the 1900s, Egypt was often ruled by outsiders—Romans, Persians, Arabs, Turks, and the British.

Egypt had been one of the first countries to become Christian. However, under Arab rule, Islam was introduced. Today almost 90 percent of the people are Muslims and about 10 percent are Christians.

In Sudan, between 2000 BC and 350 AD, the kingdom of Kush became strong. Its capital was not far from the present city of Khartoum at Meroë (muh ROH way). The Kush

The Great Sphinx and the pyramids are examples of the ancient Egyptians' skill in building. What other major contributions have the people of ancient Egypt made to civilization?

The major railway system in Egypt runs 2,800 miles (4,506.2 km) from Alexandria to Aswān. Egypt has one-third more gravel or dirt roads than it has paved highways.

were skilled at making iron and traded all over Africa and southwestern Asia. The area of present-day Sudan had been taken by the Arabs by the 1500s. As a result about 70 percent of the Sudanese people are Muslims. About 5 percent of the people are Christians. Most of the rest are animists.

In 1820 Egypt conquered Sudan. However, the British took control of Egypt in 1882 and Sudan in 1898. They had considerable influence in the area during the late 1800s. The source of British power was control of the Suez Canal.

From 1914 to 1922, Egypt was a British **protectorate.** This means that Egypt ran local affairs, while Britain handled the country's defense and foreign affairs. Britain had a strong hold on Egypt until 1953, when a republic was established. Sudan gained its independence from Britain in 1956, after more than 50 years of rule by the British and the Egyptians.

President Gamal Abdel Nasser was the leader of Egypt from 1954 to 1970. Under Nasser Egypt became a leader in the Arab world. Nasser worked to end western influence in his country. His government took control of the Suez Canal.

In 1956 Britain, France, and Israel invaded Egypt to regain control of the canal, which they saw as vital to their trade. Egypt, with help from the United States, stopped the invasion. For his bold stand, President Nasser won great praise from other Arab leaders.

Egypt has had stable government since independence. The country faces problems, such as providing jobs for its many poor farmers and easing Cairo's overcrowded conditions. However, Egypt remains a political, cultural, and educational leader in the Arab world.

The rapid growth of Egypt's population has caused houses to be built on scarce agricultural land. Ask students to explain why this worries some people.

A freighter sails from the Mediterranean Sea to the Red Sea through the Suez Canal. What international problems developed over the Suez Canal in the 1950s?

CONTENT CHECK

1. **Identify:** Egypt, Nile Basin, Nile Delta, Sinai Peninsula, Suez Canal, Libyan Desert, Qattara Depression, Arabian Desert, Sudan, Sudd, White Nile, Blue Nile, Khartoum, Aswān High Dam, Bedouins, Cairo, Kush, Gamal Abdel Nasser.

2. **Define:** cataracts, fellahin, bazaar, shadoof, basin irrigation, gum arabic, hieroglyphics, papyrus, protectorate.

3. What physical features tie Egypt and Sudan together?

4. What climate does Egypt have? Sudan?

5. Where do most of the people of Egypt and Sudan live?

6. What do most Egyptians and Sudanese do for a living?

7. **Challenge:** What benefits has the Aswān High Dam brought the people of Egypt? What problems? Do you think the dam should have been built?

2. ARAB WEST

The central and northwestern part of Africa is taken up by the countries of the Arab West. From east to west, these countries are Libya, Tunisia, Algeria, and Morocco. Algeria is the largest of these countries and the second largest in North Africa with 919,591 square miles (2,381,738.8 sq km) of land. Morocco and Algeria are the most populous of the Arab West countries, each having close to 25 million people.

Refer students to the physical regions map on page 430 for the landscape of the Arab West.

2.1 Landscape and Climate

The countries of the Arab West have similar physical features—narrow Mediterranean coasts and desert farther inland. They also show the same pattern of climate.

Landscape. The Atlas Mountains form the major mountain chain in the Arab West. They stretch from western Morocco to northeastern Tunisia. The highest mountains in the chain are in Morocco. Peaks of the High Atlas and Middle Atlas ranges rise to 13,665 feet (4,165.1 m). The Rif Massif (RIHF muh SEEF) along the northern coast of Morocco rises sharply to heights over 8,000 feet (2,438.4 m). In the higher elevations of the Atlas Mountains are fields that have snow during the last several months of the year. They store water until temperatures rise and the snow melts. Then the water flows in small rivers to the Mediterranean Sea.

In Algeria the mountains are made up of two major chains averaging 7,000 feet (2,133.6 m) above sea level. These are the Tell Atlas along the coast and the Saharan Atlas farther south. Between these mountains is a high, dry plateau about 3,000 feet (914.4 m) above sea level. The mountains join as one range in Tunisia and are lower in elevation.

Another mountain range lies in southern Algeria. The Ahaggar (ah HAHG guhr)

Range rises to as high as 9,852 feet (3,002.9 m) above sea level.

Between the Atlas and the Ahaggar Mountains, especially in Algeria, are parts of the Sahara known as ergs. An **erg** is a huge area of shifting sand dunes, some of which can reach heights of 600 feet (182.9 m). North of the Atlas Mountains along the Mediterranean coast, there is a narrow coastal plain, known as the *Tell.*

Climate. The climate of the Arab West follows a north-to-south pattern. In the north along the Tell, there is a Mediterranean climate. Summers are sunny, dry, and hot, and winters are mild. There is enough precipitation for farming.

Hot, dry climates cover nearly all other areas of the Arab West south of the Tell. Libya alone is 92 percent desert. The amount of rain is limited and comes mostly during the winter months. Rain in the desert is often sudden and heavy. In the rush of water, dry valleys called **wadis** become temporary rivers. Most of the rain quickly evaporates in the desert sun. However, some sinks into the ground to fill oases.

As seen here, the Atlas Mountains in the background rise like an island between Morocco's fertile coast and the Sahara. To what does the *Tell* refer?

USING GRAPHIC SKILLS

COMPARING THEMATIC MAPS

When you and friends discuss why you each like the same movie, you may learn that it was not necessarily for the same reasons. One friend thought the acting was excellent. Another friend loved the special effects. You liked the movie's story. Each of you was impressed by a certain theme, or specific aspect, of the movie.

When studying a region of the world, you will also find there are different themes. When these are compared, it gives you a more complete picture of what the region is really like.

The thematic map on page 439 shows annual rainfall in North Africa and the Sahel. Each of the colors in the legend represents a different range of rainfall. Studying this map will help you make comparisons about the amount of rain different areas receive. But you can learn even more about this part of the world by also studying other thematic maps that show different or related information about the region.

Study the map on page 439. You will also be asked to study carefully other maps in earlier chapters of this book. Then answer the questions that follow.

1. Study the map of Earth's climate regions on pages 96–97. What type of climate is found in the area with the greatest amount of rainfall? The least amount?

2. Study the world population density map on page 117. Make a generalization about the relationship between rainfall and the population distribution of North Africa and the Sahel.

3. **Challenge:** Write a short paragraph in which you describe what you have learned about North Africa and the Sahel by studying and comparing these three thematic maps.

See the *TRB* for the *Chapter 21 Skill Activity* on determining exact location. This activity deals with the location of cities in North Africa.

2.2 Economic and Cultural Patterns

Most of the countries of the Arab West are poor with developing economies. The chief economic activities have long been herding and farming. Population in the Arab West is concentrated along the Tell because of its climate and fertile land.

Although many farmers own small plots, there is also government-run farming. Large-scale farms in Morocco, Algeria, and Tunisia grow Mediterranean crops for exports— dates, grapes, olives, and citrus. Land is also used for growing cereal crops.

Major trade and manufacturing cities are along the coast. With about 2.9 million people, Casablanca (KAS uh BLANG kuh) is the largest city in Morocco. It is also its most important port. Factories there make glass, bricks, and furniture. Tangier (tan JEER), Morocco, is a center for international trade. Algiers (al JEERZ), the capital and largest city in Algeria, has about 1.7 million people. Companies in these cities process food and make clothing, textiles, and leather goods.

There is little manufacturing in Libya's capital and largest city of Tripoli, with a population of 991,000. There are some food-processing and oil-refining plants. Others make textiles, leather goods, and carpets.

AVERAGE ANNUAL RAINFALL IN NORTH AFRICA AND THE SAHEL

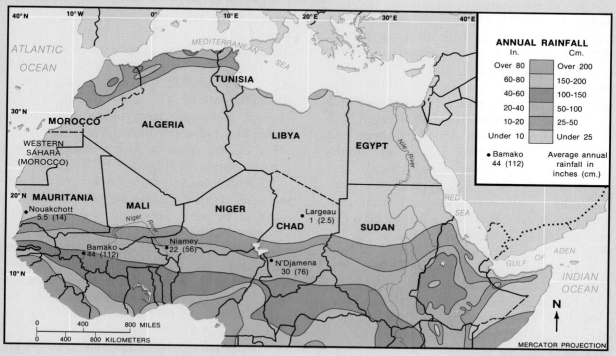

Libya is an example of where the discovery of one natural resource can make a country wealthy. Point out to students that some resources are more in demand and, therefore, are more expensive than others.

Although Libya makes little money from farming or manufacturing, it is the richest country in the Arab West. This is because of the sale of its large amounts of oil and natural gas. Before the discovery of oil in 1959, the country was almost totally undeveloped. Since then the per capita GNP has risen to about $7,500. Libya has enjoyed a dramatic increase in national income from the sale of oil and petroleum products. As in most oil-rich countries, however, much of the actual wealth remains in the hands of a relatively small number of people.

As Figure 21–3 on page 441 shows, energy and mineral resources form the economic base of all Arab West countries except for Tunisia. While Libya is the leading exporter of oil in the Arab West, Algeria leads in the amount of natural gas that it holds. In fact its reserves of gas are the fourth largest in the world. Morocco is the world's largest exporter of phosphate rock.

The large, mostly unsettled areas of the interior of the Arab West are used for grazing animals and mining minerals. Much of the mineral wealth, however, has not been tapped. Morocco, for example, has iron ore, zinc, manganese, coal, lead, and copper. These resources have not yet been developed as phosphates have been.

Much of the money from the sale of resources to other countries is being used to

FOCUS ON HISTORY

ANCIENT LEPTIS MAGNA

In ancient times connections between North Africa's Mediterranean coast and the interior of Africa were difficult. Two physical features that blocked easy travel over land were the Atlas Mountains and the Sahara. But the Mediterranean Sea made possible early contact and trade between North Africa and lands in Europe and Asia. As a result, for many centuries, North Africa has been tied more closely to southern Europe and southwestern Asia than to the rest of Africa.

North Africa's early growth was supported by a group of southwestern Asian people called Phoenicians. They developed a civilization sometime between 1500 BC in the land of today's Lebanon.

The Phoenicians were great traders, who traveled all over the Mediterranean. They established many trading posts that later were viewed as colonies. One of these—Leptis Magna—was in North Africa, east of the city of Tripoli in what is today's Libya. In Leptis Magna the Phoenicians traded with Africans who brought goods by camel caravan from oases scattered all through the Sahara.

Leptis Magna grew to be a large and important city. However, when Carthage became a part of the Roman Empire, Leptis Magna reached its greatest development.

The site of Leptis Magna was a chief reason for its growth. The city lay in the foothills of mountains. The people of Leptis Magna used the slopes for growing olive trees. Leptis Magna became one of the largest olive oil producing areas in Africa. Lands in the city's southeast were used to grow wheat.

Leptis Magna prospered for more than 500 years. Leptis Magna's wheat and olive oil came to be very important to the Roman economy and brought wealth to the city.

With the city's wealth, magnificent buildings—temples, marketplaces, an outdoor theater, and an outdoor sports arena— were built. The arena was called a *circus*. The Leptis Magna circus featured fights between gladiators and African animals.

Many public works projects were begun at Leptis Magna. Dams were built to control flooding of nearby wadis. Roads connected other trading posts and cities along the Mediterranean coast. One road took travelers into the Sahara for a distance of more than 40 miles (64.4 km). Historians believe that this road was built to give Roman troops an advantage if the city were attacked by people from the interior. Over the years such attacks and extravagant public spending led to the decline of Leptis Magna. By the time Muslim Arabs controlled the area in the late 600s AD, Leptis Magna was deserted. Today only ruins of this once thriving city remain.

1. Where was Leptis Magna? Who founded it? Who developed it?
2. How did the site of Leptis Magna contribute to its growth?

LAND USE AND RESOURCES OF
NORTH AFRICA AND THE SAHEL

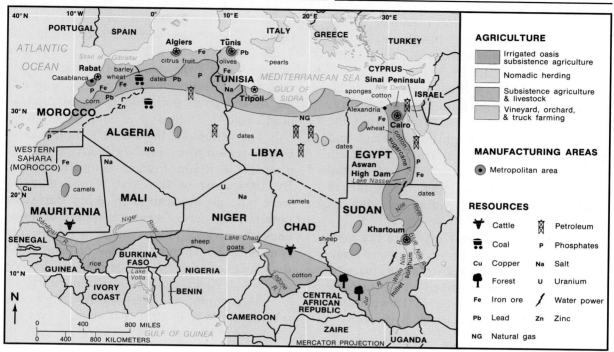

FIGURE 21-3

Nomadic herding is the most common land use in North Africa and the northern Sahel because of the region's huge desert areas. This area is bordered by two sections where subsistence farming and raising livestock are the main agricultural activities. Natural resources grow scarce as one goes farther south into the region. Why are vineyards, orchards, and farms located along the coastal area of North Africa?

expand industry and to raise the living standards of the people. Better health care and education are goals of the countries. Oil money is helping Libya build houses and develop its school and transportation systems. Some money is used to develop artificial oases from underground reservoirs. These will help farm the desert. Algeria has used part of its money from the sale of gas to build one of the best transportation networks in North Africa. It now has more than 2,400 miles (3,862.4 km) of railroads and 50,000 miles (80,467.2 km) of highways. Morocco is improving its ports to support a growing fishing fleet and has plans for large irrigation projects.

2.3 Influences of the Past

Many of the original settlers of the Arab West were Berbers who migrated there from the Nile Basin as long as 3,000 years ago. The area was then invaded by Phoenicians, Romans, Vandals, Byzantines, Arabs, Turks, and finally the French and Italians.

The Phoenicians, based in present-day Lebanon, founded colonies on the northern coast of Africa from about 1000 to 700 BC. Of these, Carthage (KAHR thihj) in modern Tunisia became one of the most powerful. By 265 BC Carthage had its own empire, controlling an area from Libya to southern Spain.

Further Carthaginian expansion brought it into conflict with nearby Italy.

With Rome's defeat of Carthage, Roman rule was imposed on North Africa. When Rome's empire declined, North Africa fell under the control of Germanic Vandals, then Byzantines, and finally Arabs.

Of all the groups that ruled North Africa, the Arabs had the most lasting influence. Between 700 and 1000 AD, Arabs from the Arabian Peninsula brought both Islam and the Arabic language to North Africa. Even when the Turkish Ottoman Empire controlled the region in the 1500s, the culture of North Africa remained Arabic and did not become Turkish.

People of the Arab West share the same written version of the Arabic language. However, common speech varies from place to place. Arabic dialect spoken in Morocco is different from that spoken in Libya. Some groups in the Arab West speak Berber.

After the end of Turkish rule, from the late 1500s to the early 1800s, the Arab West countries became known as the Barbary States. This is from their early Berber heritage. These states were Morocco, Algeria, Tunis, and Tripoli. All were involved in sea piracy. Using swift sailing ships, Barbary pirates raided European and American ships going to and from ports along the Mediterranean coast.

The actions of the Barbary pirates gave France reason to invade North Africa. Beginning in the 1830s, France occupied Algeria. By 1904 most of the Arab West countries were officially recognized by other European powers to be part of France's **sphere of influence** in Africa. This is an area exclusively controlled by an outside power, mainly for the purposes of trade. Trade between France and North Africa remains important today.

Meanwhile, the territory of Libya was invaded by Italy in 1911. Although Libya be-

The inside of this Muslim mosque shows the skill of artisans in the Arab West. The style is common throughout the Arab world. In addition to art, what other elements of Arab culture can be found throughout North Africa?

Arab influence is a strong force in North Africa. Arab influence in architecture can be seen in many houses of worship in the cities.

NORTH AFRICA AND SOUTHWEST ASIA   UNIT 7

In 1777 Morocco became the first country to recognize the United States of America.

Have students locate the countries of the Sahel using the political map on page 444.

came a colony of Italy, Libyan ties to Italy were never strong, the colony having actually more or less ruled itself over the years. During World War II, Libya fell under British control. In 1951 it became independent by declaration of the United Nations.

The other countries of the Arab West also gained independence about this time. Morocco and Tunisia became independent in 1956. Algeria became independent in 1962, after a bloody revolution against the French that lasted for eight years. Many people of French descent left Algeria for France. Today many Algerians go to France in search of jobs.

An area between Morocco and Mauritania, called Western Sahara, is the scene of much fighting today. It was once controlled by Spain as Spanish Sahara. From 1976 to 1979, it was divided between Morocco and Mauritania. Mauritania gave up its claim in 1979. Today Morocco claims two-thirds of the country. Some inhabitants of the area want to be independent and are fighting against Morocco.

See the TAE for an Objective 2 Activity.

CONTENT CHECK

1. **Identify:** Libya, Tunisia, Algeria, Morocco, Atlas Mountains, Tell Atlas, Saharan Atlas, Ahaggar Mountains, Tell, Casablanca, Tangier, Algiers, Tripoli, Berbers, Carthage, Arabs, Barbary States.

2. **Define:** erg, wadis, sphere of influence.

3. What areas of the Arab West have a Mediterranean climate?

4. Why is Libya the richest Arab West country?

5. How are the countries of the Arab West improving their economies?

6. **Challenge:** In what ways do you think the Atlas Mountains have influenced life in the Arab West?

3. THE SAHEL

The *Sahel*—Arabic for "coastline"—refers to the countries west of Sudan and south of the Arab West, extending west to the Atlantic Ocean. As Figure 21–4 on page 444 shows, from east to west they are Chad, Niger, Mali, and Mauritania. These four countries make up a geographic, economic, and cultural **zone of transition**. This means that they are like the places to the north of them in some ways and like the places south of them in other ways.

All of the countries in the Sahel are similar in size, ranging from 398,000 square miles (1,030,819.2 sq km) to 496,000 square miles (1,284,639 sq km) of land. Chad is the largest country, while Mauritania is the smallest and the least populous, with just over 2 million people. Mali has the most people, with about 8.4 million.

Refer students to the map on page 430 while discussing the landscape of the Sahel.

3.1 Landscape and Climate

The Sahel changes from a landscape of desert in the north to tropical savanna and then to forest in the south. The overall climate of the area is hot and dry.

Landscape. The northern Sahel, in general, is made up of shifting sand dunes and gravel plains. The flatness of the land is broken in places by mountains and plateaus. A mountain range called the Tibesti Highlands runs along Chad's northern and eastern borders and rises more than 11,000 feet (3,352.8 m). There are also mountains more than 6,000 feet (1,828.8 m) above sea level in north central Niger.

From central to southern Sahel, the landscape is tropical savanna grassland. Farther to the south, trees become more frequent on the savanna. During periods of rain, which are more frequent in the south than the north, this area can support farming.

NATIONS OF NORTH AFRICA AND THE SAHEL

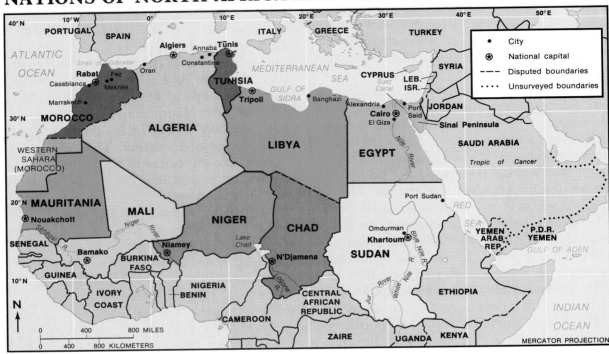

FIGURE 21-4
The nations of North Africa and the Sahel are generally larger in size than most nations in Africa south of the Sahara. What are the three smallest countries of the region?

Since the droughts between 1968 and 1973, the word "Sahel" has become synonymous with "drought."

The only major bodies of water in the Sahel are Lake Chad and the Niger River. Lake Chad, lying on the western border of Chad, is thought to have been a much larger inland lake. The Niger River flows through southern Mali and southwestern Niger.

Climate. The climate all through northern Sahel is hot. Temperatures have been recorded as high as 136°F (57.7°C). In most areas for more than six months of the year, temperatures during the day are greater than 100°F (37.7°C). Nights are often cool.

Limited rainfall usually occurs from July through October. At Largeau (lahr ZHOH), Chad, for example, less than 1 inch (2.5 cm) of rain falls a year. All over the Sahel, rain is very unreliable. During years of drought, the whole area becomes desert.

3.2 Economic and Cultural Patterns

The countries of the Sahel are among the poorest in the world. Their economies are based on agriculture.

The landscape and climate of the Sahel combine to make a difficult environment for its people. Little rain means that they often face times when not enough food can be grown. In 1968 a large drought began that lasted six years. Thousands of people and animals died of hunger and hardship. Today the countries of the region are working together to keep such disasters from happening.

But, with its climate, threat of drought and famine in the Sahel is always present. In some cases, however, the way people use the land has caused part of the problem. During those years when more rain falls, herders graze more animals on the land, and farmers plant more land. During years when rain is scarce, so many animals strip the land of any grasses. There is then less water vapor to help any nearby crops grow. With no plants the soil faces wind erosion. As a result, little by little, the soil becomes barren.

Many people in the Sahel also gather firewood from the land to use for cooking. However, the wood is being used faster than the land can provide.

Overgrazing, growing crops on land that is too dry, and overharvesting of timber have made desert from the semiarid land in the Sahel. Experts believe this desertification will stop only if the people change the ways in which they use the land. Figure 21–5 below shows how far desertification has spread.

Today most farming takes place in the southern Sahel. Livestock is also raised there. Mauritania, Mali, and Chad export mostly livestock, cotton, and fish. Mauritania has begun to use one of the richest fisheries in the world off its coast. Niger exports uranium and cotton.

Most mineral resources in the Sahel are unknown or untapped. When these resources are developed, it may bring much needed income to the countries of the area. Mali is known to have deposits of several minerals,

At the same time lands in North Africa and the Sahel are becoming less productive, their population is increasing at a rapid rate. This suggests that there may be severe food shortages in the future.

DESERTIFICATION IN NORTH AFRICA AND THE SAHEL

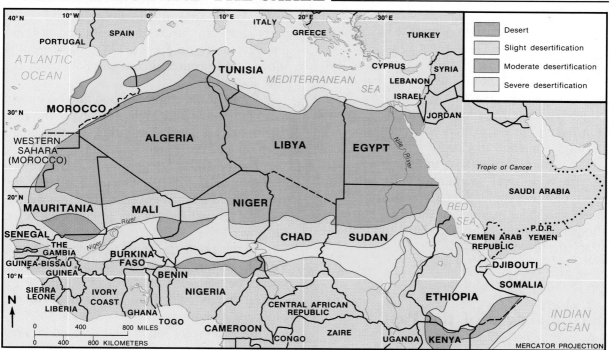

FIGURE 21-5
Studies show that deserts are taking over some areas, most notably in Africa. Estimates reveal that some 250,000 square miles (650,000 sq km) of once-productive grazing land along the southern edge of the Sahara have become desert in the last 50 years. How do people in the Sahel contribute to the problem of desertification?

CHAPTER 21 NORTH AFRICA AND THE SAHEL   445

Remind students of the problems encountered when a country's economy is dependent on one product. Point out that Mauritania is dependent on iron ore.

Note that legends and history passed by word of mouth from one generation to the next provide an important source of information about Africa's past.

The Sahel experiences very dry weather conditions. When much-needed rains arrive, they are sometimes severe. A farmer in Niger is shown here examining his millet plants that were flattened by a rainstorm. Weather conditions, drought, and famine force most people to live in what area of the Sahel?

but a poor transportation system has limited its development. Three-fourths of Mauritania's foreign income is from the sale of iron ore, found in deposits along the border of Western Sahara, an area claimed by Morocco. Niger has large reserves of uranium. Exploration for oil has uncovered only small deposits in Mauritania and in Chad.

All four countries of the Sahel are large in size with small populations. In all cases most of the people live in the south. With water shortages in much of the area, however, the people of the Sahel face hard times in the years ahead.

See the TAE for an *Objective 3* Activity.

3.3 Influences of the Past

The Sahel has been an area of cultural changes for hundreds of years. Berbers and Arabs from the north have traded with many different black African groups in the south.

Within the last century, the people of the Sahel have had to deal with European powers, most notably the French, that ruled their land as colonies.

In the area of present-day Mali, three black African empires were powerful from the 300s AD through the 1500s—Ghana, Mali, and Songhai (SONG hy). The empire of Ghana developed in the 300s. By the middle 1000s, it was overrun by Berber Muslims from the Arab West. As a result the religion of Islam was introduced to the people of the Sahel. Today most people of the Sahel are Muslims.

Another empire known as Mali replaced Ghana as the major power in the area in the 1200s. It ruled over parts of what today make up Gambia, Guinea, Senegal, Mali, and Mauritania. The greatest ruler of Mali was Mansa Musa. During his reign between 1312 and 1337, the city of Timbuktu became the center of Islamic learning in the Sahel. Scholars from Alexandria in Egypt and from other parts of North Africa and Southwest Asia often visited it. As Figure 21–6 on page 447 shows, trade routes linked the Sahel and the Nile Basin.

By 1480 the empire of Songhai had taken over Timbuktu and Mali. However, the new rulers helped keep Timbuktu as the area's learning and trade center.

By the 1600s Songhai was taken over by Morocco to the north. During the next 300 years, the Moroccan government grew weaker and weaker as local leaders fought each other for power.

In the 1800s the Sahel became part of the French Empire. As a result the French language, culture, and goods spread over the region. After World War II, France granted independence to its African colonies.

In 1960 the Sahel was divided among four new nations—Chad, Niger, Mali, and Mauritania. These countries were glad to be independent, but they face many problems because their economies are undeveloped.

Many highly organized states existed in Africa long before the European colonial period. Kingdoms at the southern edge of the Sahara gained power and wealth through control of the Saharan gold and salt trade. Such cities as Kano and Timbuktu became busy commercial centers.

AFRICAN KINGDOMS OF THE MIDDLE AGES

Long before European powers gained economic and political control in Africa, there existed native African kingdoms in the areas shown on this map. These kingdoms had highly developed economies and governments. African culture and civilization were severely disrupted with the beginning of the European slave trade. Which African city was a center of learning and trade in this area?

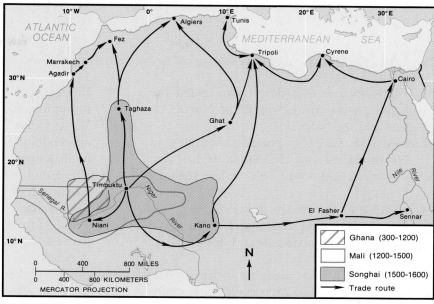

FIGURE 21–6

See the *TRB* for the *Chapter 21 Reading* on the ancient city of Timbuktu.

See the *TAE* for an *Objective 4* Activity.

CONTENT CHECK

1. **Identify:** Sahel, Chad, Niger, Mali, Mauritania, Lake Chad, Niger River, Western Sahara, Ghana, Timbuktu, Songhai.

2. **Define:** zone of transition.

3. What are the landforms that make up the Sahel?

4. Why is farming difficult in the countries of the Sahel?

5. In what ways have the people of the Sahel contributed to the problems of the region's environment?

6. What groups of Africans influenced the history of the Sahel? What European group?

7. **Challenge:** The Sahel is called the zone of transition. In what ways is the Sahel the same as the places north of it? In what ways is it the same as the places south of it?

CONCLUSION

North Africa and the Sahel form a key geographic region of the world. The histories of the peoples of this region go back several thousand years. Not only is North Africa and the Sahel of historical and cultural interest, it is also important for economic and political reasons.

In a sense, the countries of North Africa "guard" the southern shores of the Mediterranean Sea. Egypt controls the Suez Canal, which carries traffic—much of it energy supplies of oil— to and from Europe and Asia.

All of the countries of the area face a harsh physical environment. This limits the economic choices of these countries. Some of the countries of the Arab West have taken advantage of rich deposits of oil and natural gas. They may find the road to development easier than those countries with fewer resources or those unable to feed their people because of drought.

CHAPTER REVIEW

SUMMARY

1. The countries of a desert area called the Sahara make up the region of North Africa and the Sahel.
2. Egypt is the most populous country in North Africa and the Sahel. It has also played an important role in the region's history.
3. Egypt and Sudan are linked by the Nile River. The Nile Basin and Delta have Egypt's best farmland and most of its population.
4. The Arab West is made up of Libya, Tunisia, Algeria, and Morocco. These countries have fertile coastal plains and large interior deserts.
5. Energy and mineral resources are very important to the countries of the Arab West. Libya is one of the world's leading oil-producing countries, and Algeria holds large reserves of natural gas.
6. The Sahel is a zone of transition between North Africa and the countries south of the Sahara.
7. The countries of the Sahel are among the poorest in the world. Their economies depend on agriculture, but unreliable rainfall makes farming difficult.
8. Most people in the countries of North Africa and the Sahel follow Arab ways of life and practice Islam.

Answers to the following questions can be found on page T220.

REVIEWING VOCABULARY

Each of the following groups of terms shares something in common. On a sheet of paper, write a complete sentence that contains the three terms and an indication of what is common for each group.

1. cataracts, basin irrigation, wadis
2. Lake Chad, Niger River, zone of transition
3. Atlas Mountains, Tell, Ahaggar Mountains
4. protectorate, sphere of influence
5. erg, oases, gravel
6. fellahin, bazaar, shadoof

REMEMBERING THE FACTS

1. What kind of land and soil makes up the Sahara?
2. What are the two parts of North Africa, and what countries make up each part?
3. What is the only part of Egypt that is not in Africa?
4. What are the two major tributaries of the Nile River?
5. On what percentage of land area do most Egyptians live?
6. What crop is of major importance to the trade of both Egypt and Sudan?
7. Why have many fellahin in Egypt been moving to cities?
8. What kind of landform dominates the Arab West?
9. What is the major climate type in the Tell?
10. What are the major crops that are grown in the Tell?

11. What energy and mineral resources do the Arab West countries have?
12. What European power once controlled Algeria and the countries of the Sahel?
13. What are the countries that make up the Sahel?
14. Where does most agricultural activity take place in the Sahel?

UNDERSTANDING THE FACTS

1. How can the Libyan and Arabian deserts be both deserts and plateaus at the same time?
2. Why is the southern half of the Nile not navigable?
3. What is meant by the phrase "Egypt is the gift of the Nile"?
4. Why is farmland located where it is in the Arab West?
5. How do the economies of Egypt and the Sudan compare with the economies of countries in the Arab West?
6. What improvements have Arab West countries made with their income from the sale of natural resources?
7. Why can it be said that the Arabs had the greatest influence on North Africa?
8. What factors explain why Tunisia is different from the other countries in the Arab West?
9. Explain why Sudan's landscape is much like that of the Sahel.
10. What conditions make life so difficult in the Sahel?

THINKING CRITICALLY AND CREATIVELY

1. Nearly 99 percent of all Egyptians live on 3.5 percent of the land. Why?
2. Egypt is considered the cultural center of the Arab world. What factors have made Egypt so important in this area?
3. If the Atlas Mountains were not present in the Arab West, how might the region be different?
4. **Challenge:** Based on what you now know about North Africa and the Sahel, what would you predict the region would be like by the year 2020?
5. **Challenge:** Write a step-by-step plan for improving economic activity and life in the Sahel. Indicate the risks and benefits each step may have.

REINFORCING GRAPHIC SKILLS

Study the map on page 439. Then answer the questions that follow.

1. Which city on the map has the heaviest amount of average annual rainfall? The least amount?
2. What is the average annual rainfall over most of Algeria? Mauritania?
3. **Challenge:** Study the map of Earth's climate regions on pages 96 and 97. How closely do the boundaries of climate regions coincide with the boundaries of rainfall regions? Why is this?

Refer to the world map on pages 646-647 in the Atlas to note how close Turkey is to Europe. Its mix of Arabic and European shows the region's variety.

Harran, Turkey, near the border of Syria

SOUTHWEST ASIA

In this chapter you will learn—

- What are the major physical features and climate patterns of Southwest Asia.
- How cultures differ throughout Southwest Asia.
- How three world religions developed in Southwest Asia.
- How history has affected the economic growth and development of Southwest Asia.

On the map on page 452, have students locate and identify the many gulfs and seas that border Southwest Asia.

INTRODUCTION

Southwest Asia is a region of 17 countries, wedged between the Soviet Union to the north and North Africa to the south and west. Eastern Europe touches Southwest Asia in the northwest, and the Asian countries of Pakistan and China border it to the east.

The nations of the region—along with Egypt in North Africa—are most often called the Middle East. This name refers to the area's location and describes the place where three continents—Africa, Europe, and Asia—come together.

Southwest Asia has three parts. One part is made up of countries at the center of the Middle East. They are Syria, Iraq (ih RAHK), Lebanon, Israel, and Jordan. This region is called the Middle East Core.

A second part of the region is made up of countries on the Arabian Peninsula. Among these are Saudi Arabia, Kuwait (koo WAYT), Bahrain, Qatar (KAH tahr) the United Arab Emirates, Oman (oh MAHN), Yemen Arab Republic, and the People's Democratic Republic of Yemen.

The third part of the region is formed by countries of the Northern Middle East. They are Turkey, Cyprus, Iran (ih RAHN), and Afghanistan.

Among all these countries, Turkey and Iran have the largest populations. Saudi Arabia, however, has the greatest land area.

The most common physical and cultural features of this region are dry landscapes and the Islamic religion. But there is much diversity in the land and people of Southwest Asia.

Southwest Asia is an important region of the world. Throughout history it has been a crossroads of trade and armies. It is also a chief source of oil wealth. But to many parts of the world, Southwest Asia is important because it is believed to be the birthplace of western civilization.

Israel is just slightly smaller in area than the country of El Salvador in Central America and about one-half the size of Switzerland in Europe.

1. ISRAEL

The State of Israel is the only Jewish nation in the world. It lies at the eastern end of the Mediterranean Sea. Small in size, Israel has about 8,019 square miles (20,769.2 km) of land. This does not include the eastern part of the city of Jerusalem and other areas disputed with its Arab neighbors. The country is 256 miles (412 km) long from north to south and only 81 miles (130.4 km) from east to west. Although it is small in size, Israel has worked to develop its few resources in order to strengthen its economy.

PHYSICAL REGIONS OF SOUTHWEST ASIA _____

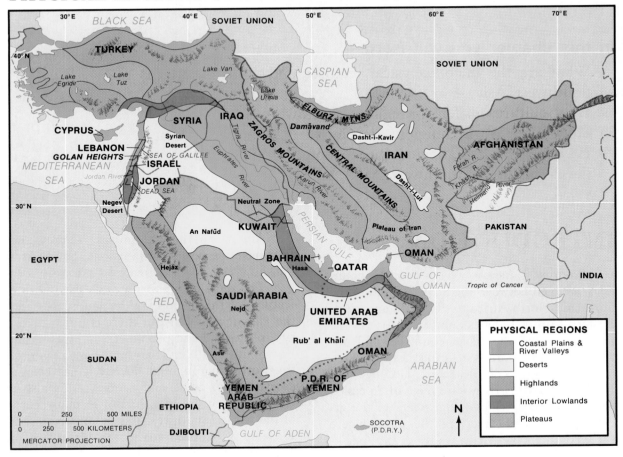

FIGURE 22-1
Plateaus and highlands spread over this region. Deserts are located near the Mediterranean coast, on the Arabian Peninsula, and in Iran and Afghanistan. Which two rivers form the river valley shown in the center of the region?

Have students locate Israel on the map above. Point out that, in spite of its small size, Israel has a variety of physical regions, climates, and resources.

1.1 Landscape and Climate

Israel has several physical regions. Its climate varies among the land regions depending on elevation and distance from the Mediterranean Sea.

Landscape. In the far north of Israel are the mountains of Galilee. As Figure 22–1 on this page shows, east of the mountains is a plateau area called the Golan (GOH LAWN) Heights. South from the mountains are the Judean (joo DEE uhn) Hills.

The Negev (NEH gehv) Desert in southern Israel covers almost one-half of the country. It is made up of dry hills, valleys, and plains. In the past only shrubs grew well in this area. However, because of new irrigation methods, Israelis have been able to farm parts of the Negev to grow crops.

Along the Mediterranean coast of Israel is a narrow, fertile plain called the Plain of Sharon. It is about 115 miles (185.1 km) long and only 20 miles (32.2 km) wide at its widest point in the south.

On a large wall map that includes both Africa and Southwest Asia, have students locate the Great Rift Valley that extends from Syria to southern Africa.

The Mediterranean Sea continues to be an important sea-lane for commercial activity since much of Israel's produce is shipped to markets in northwestern Europe.

A rift valley, which is part of the Great Rift Valley of eastern Africa, runs through the eastern part of Israel. The Jordan River cuts through the floor of the valley. It flows southward from an elevation of about 500 feet (152.4 m) above sea level in the mountains of Lebanon and Syria. Entering the Sea of Galilee, the Jordan River falls 696 feet (212.1 m) below sea level. Farther south, the river flows into the Dead Sea. At 1,300 feet (396.2 m) *below* sea level, the rim of the Dead Sea is the lowest place of any land on Earth.

Climate. In the northern part of Israel, the climate is Mediterranean with hot, dry summers and mild winters. Near Galilee summer temperatures average about 75°F (23.9°C), and winter temperatures average about 45°F (7.2°C). Rain falls in the north about 40 inches (101.6 cm) each year and chiefly in winter. The hilly areas of the north sometimes even receive some winter snowfall.

In the southern part of Israel, the climate is desert. Summer temperatures in the Negev and the rift valley may soar to 120°F (48.9°C) or even higher. Winter temperatures average about 60°F (15.6°C). Less than 1 inch of precipitation (2.5 cm) falls in the south.

1.2 Economic and Cultural Patterns

Israel has limited farmland and natural resources. However, its economy is as well developed as those of Northwest Europe.

Israelis have made good use of the few natural resources they have. Deposits of potash, magnesium, bromide, and salt are found in the Dead Sea area. These minerals support a growing chemical industry. The Negev area is also a source of copper and phosphates, a mineral used in making fertilizer.

In Israel energy resources are scarce. The country has very little water power and no coal. Steel plants in the cities of Tel Aviv-Yafo (TEHL uh VEEV YAH foh) and Haifa (HY fuh) must import raw materials from Europe. Most of Israel's oil comes from Egypt. Some oil has been found in the southern Negev and is moved by pipeline to Haifa for refining. Israel also uses energy from its nuclear power plants, built in the 1950s.

The Israelis have made the best use of what land is available for farming. They have drained swamps and built irrigation systems. They use fertilizers to improve the soil and have introduced modern machinery on most farms. Through these methods, the Israelis harvest up to three crops a year on some irrigated lands. However, the country must still import food to feed its people.

The major area for farming in Israel is the coastal plain. There citrus fruits, especially oranges, are grown. They are Israel's chief farm export. Fruits, vegetables, poultry, and livestock are raised in the valleys of the interior. In the north are many large farms

Irrigation projects similar to this have enabled the Israelis to reclaim parts of the Negev Desert. How large an area of Israel does the Negev Desert cover?

FOCUS ON CULTURE

THREE MAJOR RELIGIONS

During their exile through the 500s BC, many Jews were influenced by Babylonians' belief in many gods. It was not until after the work of the Prophets and Ezra that most historians believe monotheism was achieved.

One of the most interesting aspects of the Middle East is that three of the world's major religions developed there. All of the religions share the same roots. These religions are Judaism, Christianity, and Islam. Through cultural diffusion these religions have spread to become major influences on millions of people all over the world.

Judaism is the oldest of the three religions. It began with the ancient Hebrews and their leader Abraham, who lived in the area of Palestine. Judaism was the first major religion to teach that there is only one God. Most scholars believe that the Hebrews accepted the idea of one God by about 500 BC. About this time the Hebrew prophets taught people

Ezra and the scribes compiled and edited the Torah, the Five Books of Moses.

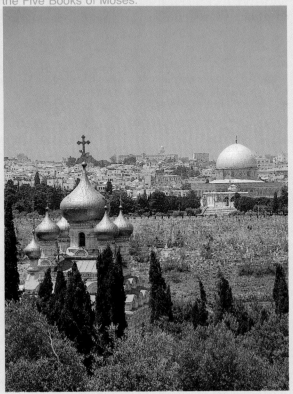

to love God and to treat each other justly. These beliefs became part of the heritage of western civilization. Jews value Jerusalem because it was their original home.

Christianity was the second major religion to develop in the Middle East. It is based on the life and teachings of Jesus, a Jew who grew up in Palestine. He studied the sacred writings of the Jews and learned prayers in the Hebrew language. Jesus traveled throughout Palestine and taught people that if they were truly sorry for their sins and placed their trust in God, they would be forgiven. Jesus was put to death by the Romans in 33 AD in the city of Jerusalem. For this reason the city is considered holy to Christians.

In the early 600s AD, Islam developed as the third major religion of the Middle East. It was founded by Muhammad, an Arab born around 570 in the town of Mecca. Muhammad believed that he had been sent by God to warn the people about their ways of living and to guide them. Muhammad preached that there was only one God and that he was God's messenger. Those who accepted this belief were called Muslims, meaning "those who submit." Islam is the Arabic word meaning "the act of submitting, or giving oneself over to God."

Many of Muhammad's teachings are based on Judaism and Christianity. Muslims accept Abraham, Moses, and Jesus as earlier prophets of God. They regard Jerusalem as a holy city because it is believed that Muhammad was carried to Heaven from there.

1. What are the major religions that developed in the Middle East? Which was the first to develop?

2. In what ways are the three religions related to one another?

Because only about one-fifth of Israel's land can be farmed, development of natural resources and industrial growth are important to Israel's economy.

Around 1900 BC, Abraham, founder of Judaism, led the Hebrews to Canaan. Later, drought forced them to Egypt where they were enslaved for many years.

that grow olives. Farming also takes place in parts of the Negev but only with the help of irrigation. A large network of pipelines and canals pumps water to the Negev from the Sea of Galilee.

Among Israel's rural communities are two special kinds of farms. One kind—a **kibbutz**—is a collective farm. On a kibbutz farmers work the land together and share the income. The other kind is a **moshav,** in which each family owns its own land. These kinds of farms were important in Israel's early growth, and most Israeli farmers still belong to them.

In spite of few natural resources, Israel is the only industrialized country of Southwest Asia. Israel's greatest resource is its highly skilled workers.

Because of their country's industrial growth, Israelis have modern ways of living. Also 90 percent of them live in urban areas. The largest cities are Tel Aviv-Yafo (TEHL uh VEEV YAH foh), with 330,400 people; Haifa, with about 227,900; and Jerusalem (juh ROO suh lehm), with 431,800. Jerusalem has long been a major attraction to people all over the world. It is a holy city for Jews, Christians, and Muslims.

Unlike other lands of Southwest Asia, Israel is a land of immigrants. Nearly one-half of its 4.4 million people come from more than 100 countries on 5 continents. As a result Israel has many different ethnic groups. Yet more than 80 percent of its people are Jewish. The two major groups of Jews in Israel are the *Ashkenazim* (AHSH kuh NAHZ uhm) and the *Sephardim* (suh FAHRD uhm). The Ashkenazim are Jews from eastern Europe and their descendants who were born in Israel. The Sephardim are Jews from North Africa and other parts of the Middle East and Asia.

Israel's people also include Muslim and Christian Arabs. Many of the Arabs live on land captured by Israel from Arab countries. Some Israeli Arabs trace their ancestry to groups that lived in the area centuries ago.

1.3 Influences of the Past

Ancestors of the Israelis have lived in the area that is now Israel for nearly 3,000 years. One of the earliest groups was the Hebrews. About 1000 BC the Hebrews set up a kingdom with its capital at Jerusalem. Their religion, later known as Judaism, emphasized belief in one God and in right conduct. These beliefs became important features of western civilization.

The Hebrews did not remain united very long. By 922 BC the Hebrew kingdom had split into two states—Israel and Judah. Israel was soon destroyed by a group of invaders

Many Arabs living in areas captured by Israel would prefer to have an independent Palestinian nation.

ISRAEL AND ITS NEIGHBORS

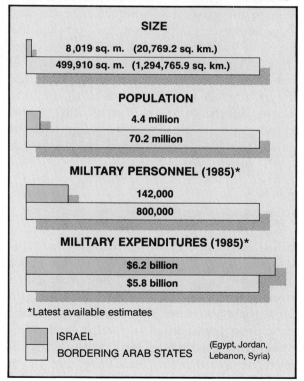

SIZE
8,019 sq. m.   (20,769.2 sq. km.)
499,910 sq. m.   (1,294,765.9 sq. km.)

POPULATION
4.4 million
70.2 million

MILITARY PERSONNEL (1985)*
142,000
800,000

MILITARY EXPENDITURES (1985)*
$6.2 billion
$5.8 billion

*Latest available estimates

ISRAEL
BORDERING ARAB STATES (Egypt, Jordan, Lebanon, Syria)

FIGURE 22-2
Israel spends nearly one-quarter of its annual government budget on military defense. How do the graphs here show Israel as a "David among Goliaths"?

USING GRAPHIC SKILLS

READING TERRITORIAL BOUNDARIES

From time to time you may disagree with your brother or sister or with a classmate. Your sister Nancy borrows a cassette tape of your favorite rock group without your permission, or your friend Ethan may say something that hurts your feelings. The disagreement turns into an argument, which then turns into a fight. Before you know it, both of you have forgotten what started the disagreement, but you are angry about what was said during the argument. With compromise and cooperation, the disagreement is eventually settled, and your relationship returns to normal.

Ever since Israel became an independent nation in 1948, disagreements between Israel and neighboring Arab countries have surfaced over land ownership. These have resulted in a series of wars and occupations between Israelis and Arabs. In 1956 Israel, with the help of the United Kingdom and France, attacked Egypt after an Egyptian takeover of the Suez Canal. In the Six-Day War of 1967, Israel responded to Arab threats by taking over the Sinai Peninsula, the west bank of the Jordan River, and the Golan Heights. After a third war in 1973, Israel drew back from some of the territory it had taken in the Sinai Peninsula. In 1979 Israel and Egypt, supported by the United States, signed a peace treaty. By its terms Israel and Egypt agreed to end their fighting. By 1982 Israel had withdrawn completely from the Sinai Peninsula. After each conflict a settlement has been arrived at and an uneasy peace restored between Israel and neighbors.

As a result of these conflicts, the boundaries of Israel have changed many times. Today the boundary between Israel and Jordan is under dispute. The map on page 457 shows the changes in Israel's territorial boundaries since 1948.

Each color band in the map on page 457 helps you to identify the territory and boundaries of Israel at different times. The dark purple boundary line outlines Israel's territory at the time of its establishment in 1948. The other colors show new territory that Israel has occupied and given back since 1948.

The communities of dispersed Jews became known as the Diaspora, or "Scattering."

called Assyrians. However, the people of Judah, or Jews, kept their freedom for about 150 years longer. Finally, they were taken over by Babylonians, who forced the Jews to leave their homeland. In the following centuries, most Jews settled in foreign lands. Despite living abroad, the Jews continued to regard the area that was once Israel and Judah as their homeland.

Meanwhile, this area was ruled by a series of peoples—Greeks, Romans, Byzantines, crusaders of western Europe, and Muslims of various groups. Following the Roman takeover, Israel and Judah became known as Palestine. During the late 1800s, Palestine was ruled by Muslims called Ottoman Turks. Most of the people living in the area, however, were Arabs, who claimed to be descended from people who had lived in the area for centuries. At this time a small number of Jews moved to Palestine and bought land from the Arabs. Many of these Jewish settlers were *Zionists*, those who wanted to set up a homeland for all Jews.

ISRAEL'S CHANGING BOUNDARIES

Study the map on this page. Then answer the questions that follow.

1. Which was the largest area of land occupied by Israel after 1948?

2. In which country was Israel's most recent occupation of territory?

3. Which territories, which were acquired by Israel in 1967, have not been given back to their former owners?

4. What advantage did Israeli occupation of the Sinai Peninsula provide to Israel?

5. Over what important area did Egypt's reoccupation of territory in 1973 give it control?

6. **Challenge:** What boundary is disputed by Israel and Jordan?

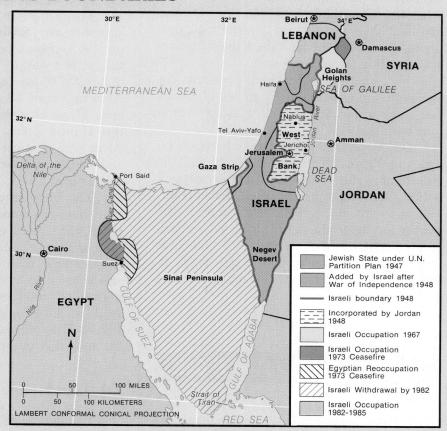

In the 1930s when the Nazis came to power in Germany, large numbers of Jews began emigrating because of Nazi persecution. During the same time, many Arabs began moving into Palestine from Syria and Lebanon.

During World War I, the Ottoman Turks were defeated and lost their empire. Palestine then came under the control of the United Kingdom. To win the support of both Jews and Arabs, the British government promised the Zionists a Jewish homeland in Palestine and Arab leaders that Arab claims to the region would be protected.

During World War II, millions of European Jews were killed by the Nazis of Germany. This added more determination to the Zionist cause. Against the wishes of the Brit-

ish and the Arabs, more and more Jews moved to Palestine. By 1947 almost 650,000 Jews were in the area. The British found it difficult to govern both Jews and Arabs.

In 1947 the United Nations voted to divide Palestine into a Jewish state and an Arab state. In 1948 the Jews of Palestine proclaimed their area to be the State of Israel. However, the Arabs of Palestine—called Palestinians—rejected this action. They claimed that Israel had been illegally set up on their land. A war soon broke out between

Because of danger of attack from hostile Arab nations, Israel developed a large, sophisticated military.

On the map on page 452, have students locate and identify the bodies of water that nearly surround the peninsula occupied by Saudi Arabia.

Israel and neighboring Arab countries that supported the Palestinians. Against overwhelming odds the Israelis won the war. As a result of their victory, the Israelis took over about one-half of the land the United Nations had set aside for an Arab state.

Since then there has been constant tension between Israel and its Arab neighbors. In fact three major Arab-Israeli wars have been fought since 1948.

Despite a 1979 peace treaty between Israel and Egypt, the Arab countries and the Palestinians still refuse to accept Israel as a nation. Wanting to protect itself, Israel is unwilling to give up land taken in the wars. Its people are determined that their nation will succeed. Figure 22-2 on page 455 compares Israel and four neighboring Arab states in terms of size, population, and military forces and costs.

See the *TAE* for an *Objective 1* Activity.

CONTENT CHECK

1. **Identify:** Golan Heights, Negev Desert, Plain of Sharon, Jordan River, Sea of Galilee, Dead Sea, Tel Aviv-Yafo, Haifa, Jerusalem, Ashkenazim, Sephardim, Hebrews, Zionists, Palestinians.

2. **Define:** kibbutz, moshav.

3. What are Israel's six physical regions?

4. What is the climate in the southern part of Israel?

5. What are some of Israel's limited natural resources?

6. What did Israelis do to prepare their land for farming?

7. During what year did the Jews announce the independence of Israel?

8. **Challenge:** Why has Israel had so many problems with its neighbors?

2. SAUDI ARABIA

The Kingdom of Saudi Arabia is the largest country in Southwest Asia. It is found on the Arabian Peninsula, the largest peninsula in the world. With 29,996 square miles (2,149,687.9 sq km) of land, Saudi Arabia takes up nearly 80 percent of the peninsula's area. This makes the country about the size of the United States east of the Mississippi River. Its political boundaries in the south and southeast have not been fully surveyed and defined.

The importance of Saudi Arabia, however, does not come from its size. The country is the center of Islam with two of the religion's holiest cities, Mecca (MEHK uh) and Medina (muh DEE nuh). Saudi Arabia also holds a major share of the world's largest known oil reserves. Today it ranks as the world's third largest petroleum producer. Figure 22-3 on page 459 compares Saudi Arabia and other oil-producing nations.

2.1 Landscape and Climate

The landscape of Saudi Arabia is largely desert. Its climate is hot and dry year-round.

Landscape. Most of Saudi Arabia is a dry plateau. Two parts of the country are desert. The one in the northern part of the country is called An Nafūd (an uh FOOD). The other is in the southern part—Rub' al Khālī (ROOB al KAH lee), known as the "Empty Quarter" because of its small population. With sand dunes that reach heights of 1,000 feet (304.8 m), it covers about 250,000 square miles (647,499.5 sq km).

Between An Nafūd and Rub' al Khālī is a central plateau known as the Nejd (NAJD). Some oases and small farm villages can be found in this mostly dry area of few plants.

In the western part of Saudi Arabia along the Red Sea are highlands. The northern

Founded in 1960 by Saudi Arabia, Iran, Iraq, Kuwait, and Venezuela, OPEC now has 13 members that together claim nearly three-fourths of Earth's recoverable oil reserves. Saudi Arabia is also a member of OAPEC—the Organization of Arab Petroleum Exporting Countries.

WORLD OIL RESERVES

COUNTRY	OIL RESERVES* 1987	OIL PRODUCTION* 1986	YEARS RESERVES WILL LAST**
SAUDI ARABIA	156.6 billion	1,700 million	92
KUWAIT	91.9 billion	454 million	202
U.S.S.R.	59.0 billion	4.500 million	13
MEXICO	54.6 billion	886 million	62
IRAN	48.8 billion	674 million	72
IRAQ	47.1 billion	617 million	76
Total World Reserves = 697.4 billion		* measured in barrels ** based on 1986 production figures	

FIGURE 22-3

Four of the six countries shown above are located in Southwest Asia. Together, these four countries possess slightly more than one-half of the world's oil reserves. How important is oil to Saudi Arabia's economy?

Saudi Arabia's "Empty Quarter" is almost as large as the state of Texas and is uninhabited except for a few nomadic tribes that travel through it.

highlands—Hejaz (heh JAZ)—and the southern highlands—Asir (ah SEER)—are steppes, dotted with some fertile land that is good for farming when irrigated.

In the east between the interior deserts and the Persian Gulf is a lowland area called the Hasa (HAH suh). It has salt flats along the coast and a sand and gravel plain farther inland. Large farming communities have developed around oases.

Climate. The desert climate of Saudi Arabia makes the country hot and dry. Daytime temperatures average more than 90°F (32.2°C) in the summer all through the country. Temperatures in the central desert may be as high as 120°F (48.9°C). Winter temperatures are generally somewhat cooler. Parts of northern and central Saudi Arabia sometimes even see freezing temperatures.

In general, rain is scarce and unpredictable, except for the southwestern part of Asia. There the summer monsoon winds bring an average of 12 inches (30.5 cm) to 30 inches (76.2 cm) of rain per year. The rest of Saudi

Arabia receives 2 inches (5.1 cm) to 4 inches (10.2 cm) per year.

Remind students that, generally, a minimum of 20 inches (50.8 cm) of rainfall is required for farming.

2.2 Economic and Cultural Patterns

The economy of Saudi Arabia is based largely on oil production. Even though only three percent of Saudi workers are involved in the industry, oil accounts for the largest part of the country's income. In fact oil makes up 99 percent of the country's exports.

Oil income finances a number of industrial activities. Saudi Arabia's newest cities have been developed as centers for processing oil—oil refining and the production of chemicals from oil. Oil income has also allowed Saudi Arabia to improve the lives of its people. New schools, hospitals, roads, and airports have been built all through the country.

Agriculture adds only a little to the country's income. Because of a limited amount of water, only about one percent of the land of

Saudi Arabia is arable. To meet the need for fresh water, industrial plants have been built to remove salt from the seawater of the Persian Gulf and the Red Sea. This process is called **desalinization.**

About 30 percent of the people of Saudi Arabia are farmers. Their major crops are dates, melons, vegetables, rice, and wheat. Most of these crops are grown on irrigated land won from the desert. The country still imports much of its food.

Herding is also an activity of the people of Saudi Arabia. About 40 percent of the land is used for grazing. Most herders are nomads, who raise camels or sheep and goats for meat, hides, and dairy products.

In addition to oil, farming, and herding, Saudi Arabia has a specialized tourist industry. The cities of Mecca and Medina are visited by thousands of Muslims each year. It is

See the *TRB* for the *Section 2 Extending the Lesson* on Bedouin.

At the Great Mosque at Mecca, Muslim pilgrims encircle the Kaaba, which contains Islam's sacred black stone. Why do so many Muslims visit Mecca?

a religious duty of each Muslim to make a **hajj**—pilgrimage to Mecca—once in a lifetime. Saudi Arabia does not encourage tourism other than for religious reasons.

In other ways Saudi Arabia discourages immigration and is closed to foreigners. For example, the large number of foreign workers in the country are not allowed to stay permanently. Also Mecca is off limits to people who are not Muslims.

The religion of Islam affects nearly all parts of life in Saudi Arabia from government laws to everyday lives of the people. Most of the 14.8 million Saudis are Arab Muslims. Saudi Arabia has no written constitution because the government is built on Islamic law. Foreign ideas have often met opposition because Islamic traditions are so deeply rooted in the country.

Around 500 AD Mecca began to develop near a large well at a crossroad of caravan routes.

2.3 Influences of the Past

Centuries ago different clans of nomads roamed the Arabian Peninsula. However, no single group ruled the area until the middle 1400s. At that time the Saud clan won control of a large area near present-day Riyadh (ree AHD), Saudi Arabia's capital and largest city. Members of the clan were called Saudis.

In the mid-1700s, the Saudis accepted the strict Muslim beliefs of the Wahhabi religious movement. The Saudis soon became defenders of the Wahhabi form of Islam. As their empire grew to include Mecca and Medina, the Saudis became the official keepers of Islamic holy places. This increased the standing of the Saudis among all Muslims.

During the early 1800s, the Wahhabi movement was crushed by Egyptians invading the Arabian Peninsula. Eventually, the Saud family fled to nearby Kuwait. From there in 1902, the Saudis launched an invasion to recapture the Arabian Peninsula. Little by little over 25 years, they gained one area after another and formed the Kingdom of Saudi Arabia in 1932.

During the early years of the kingdom, Saudi Arabia remained undeveloped and poor. But in 1933 the Saudi ruler, Ibn Saud, allowed the Standard Oil Company of California to search for oil in the country. A major discovery was made in 1938. After World War II, Standard Oil began to develop Saudi Arabia's oil industry. The right to search for oil was later transferred to the Arabian American Oil Company. This group of several major oil companies is known as Aramco. Today Saudi Arabia is the major owner of Aramco, the world's largest oil-producing company. A small number of American companies continue to hold smaller interests in the firm.

The Saudis have used their oil income to invest in such industrialized countries as the United States and the United Kingdom. This has given them great political influence in the Middle East and the rest of the world.

See the *TAE* for an *Objective 2* Activity.

CONTENT CHECK

1. **Identify:** Saudi Arabia, Arabian Peninsula, Mecca, Medina, An Nafūd, Rub' al Khālī, Nejd, Hejaz, Asir, Hasa, Saud, Riyadh, Wahhabi, Aramco.
2. **Define:** desalinization, hajj.
3. How does Saudi Arabia compare in physical size to other countries of Southwest Asia?
4. What landforms are found in Saudi Arabia?
5. What accounts for the largest part of Saudi Arabia's income?
6. What is Saudi Arabia's specialized tourist industry?
7. **Challenge:** Saudia Arabia does not actively encourage visits by tourists who are non-Muslims. How might this attitude be explained?

3. TURKEY

The official name of Turkey is the Republic of Turkey. It has an area of 301,382 square miles (780,578.8 sq km). This makes it a little larger than the state of Texas. Turkey lies in both Europe and Asia. Nearly 97 percent of its territory is in Asia.

The European and Asian parts of Turkey are separated by three important waterways—Bosporus (BAHS puhr uhs), Sea of Marmara (MAHR muhr uh), and Dardanelles (DAHR duh NEHLZ). Together these waterways are known as the Turkish Straits. They form busy sea-lanes that link the Black and Aegean seas. Today the Turkish Straits give Turkey military importance. Ships of the Soviet Union must pass through these narrow waters as they sail to the Mediterranean Sea from their home ports on the Black Sea.

The photograph that opens this chapter on page 450 is of a village in southern Turkey.

3.1 Landscape and Climate

Much of Turkey is made up of highlands and plateaus. With much of the country surrounded by the Mediterranean and Black seas, its climate along the coasts is different from that in the interior.

Landscape. The heart of Asian Turkey is a high plateau surrounded by mountains, known as the Anatolian Plateau. This plateau's western part is rolling and used for wheat farming. Farther east the plateau becomes higher, more rugged, and not good for farming.

The Eastern Mountains take up the easternmost part of Turkey. Here many mountains are from 12,000 feet (3,657.6 m) to 14,000 feet (4,267.2 m) above sea level. Mount Ararat (AR uh RAT), the highest peak in Turkey, is in this area. It reaches 16,945 feet (5,164.8 m) above sea level. The Tigris and Euphrates rivers, two of the most famous rivers in the world, begin in the Eastern Mountain region.

The northern part of Turkey runs along the Black Sea. The Pontic Mountains lie inland from the Black Sea.

The area close to the Aegean Sea wraps around the western end of Asian Turkey and includes all of European Turkey. Between the many high ridges that run to the sea, there are wide, flat valleys of rich farmland.

Southern Turkey is mountainous with high peaks reaching about 12,000 feet (3,657.6 m) above sea level. Along the Mediterranean coast, there are fertile plains.

Climate. Turkey's interior has a middle-latitude steppe climate. Summer temperatures are hot, and winters are cold. In eastern mountain areas, winters are colder with temperatures falling as low as −40°F (−40°C). Much of the precipitation in the interior and the southeastern parts of Turkey comes as heavy winter snowfall.

Some mountain areas in Turkey average as much as 30 inches (38.1 cm) of rain a year.

This castle, towering near Turkey's Aegean coast, dates back to the time of the crusaders. What type of climate is found along Turkey's coastal areas?

Coastal areas of Turkey have a Mediterranean climate. Summer temperatures vary from an average of 70°F (21.1°C) along the Black Sea coast to nearly 90°F (32.2°C) along the Aegean and Mediterranean coasts. In the coldest months, temperatures range between 40°F (4.4°C) and 50°F (10°C).

Refer students to the map of Land Use and Resources on page 463 during their study of this section.

3.2 Economic and Cultural Patterns

Since the 1920s Turkey has had rapid economic growth. Even though more than one-half of the country's workers are farmers, industry has become an increasingly important part of Turkey's economy.

Cereal grains, especially wheat, and livestock account for most of the country's farm income. The best farming regions are in the coastal areas, although much of the wheat is grown in the western part of the Anatolian Plateau. Cotton and tobacco are important export crops. Other leading crops include fruits, sugar beets, and nuts.

Sheep, goats, and cattle are raised in large numbers. Most herding is found in the plateau and mountain areas. Sheep provide wool, hides, and mutton. **Mutton** is the name given to sheep meat. Some of the wool is used to make Turkish carpets. Many of the goats are Angora goats raised for mohair. Turkey is a leading exporter of mohair.

As Figure 22-4 on page 463 shows, Turkey has a number of important mineral deposits. Among these are iron ore, coal, and copper. Turkey is an important world source of boron, a mineral used in refining and producing various kinds of metals. The country is also a major supplier of **chromite**, a mineral used to make chromium. Though close to such important oil-producing countries as Iran, Turkey has very limited supplies of petroleum and must import one-half of its own needs.

LAND USE AND RESOURCES OF SOUTHWEST ASIA

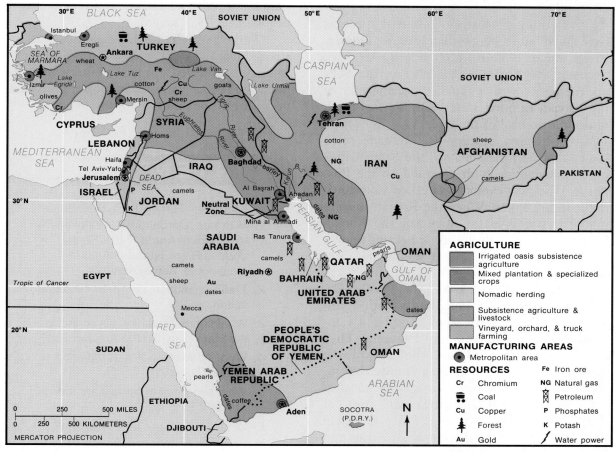

FIGURE 22-4
Land suitable for agriculture is limited in this region. Vineyards, orchards, and truck farms are situated near coastal areas. Which country in Southwest Asia has many areas of land suitable for this type of agriculture?

Although the majority of its people are Muslim, Turkey's constitution guarantees freedom of religion. By law there is no "official" religion in Turkey.

The Turkish government owns or controls most transportation, communication, banking, and large industrial organizations. On the other hand, most small farms and industries are privately owned. Many people work in the manufacturing of yarn, fabrics, and rugs from Turkish cotton.

With more than 51.4 million people, Turkey is the most populous country in Southwest Asia. About 98 percent of its people are Muslim. In addition, there are small groups of Christians and Jews.

Istanbul (ihs tuhn BOOL), which is Turkey's largest city, has about 5.9 million people. It is the only city in the world found on two continents. The European part of Istanbul is separated from the Asian part by the narrow waters of the Bosporus. Four-fifths of the people live in the European side of the city. Istanbul is known for its palaces, museums, and **mosques,** or Muslim places of worship. The second largest city in Turkey is the capital, Ankara (ANG kuh ruh). It has about 3.5 million people.

A hundred years ago, many Armenians lived in Turkey—Christians in a Muslim land, they had their own culture, language, and alphabet. Twice since then, Turkish authorities who feared rebellion ordered Armenians massacred. More than one-half of the Armenian population was destroyed during these bitter times.

3.3 Influences of the Past

All through history different peoples have lived in the area that is now Turkey. From about 1900 to 1200 BC, the Hittites lived on the Anatolian Plateau. In the 500s BC, the entire area of Turkey became part of the Persian Empire. Later still, Turkey came under the control of the Greeks.

By the first century BC, Romans ruled the country. In the 300s AD, the Roman Emperor Constantine built a capital on the Bosporus. The new capital was called Constantinople in his honor. When the Roman Empire in the west fell in the 400s AD, the Roman Empire in the east survived. It became known as the Byzantine Empire. It was largely centered in Turkey.

In the 1200s and 1300s, the Muslim Ottomans began to challenge the Byzantine Empire. In the mid-1400s, they conquered Constantinople and renamed it Istanbul. They also moved westward. By the end of the 1500s, the Ottomans ruled an empire that included Turkey, southeastern Europe, most of the eastern Mediterranean, and most of northern Africa. However, the Ottoman forces were gradually driven out of Africa and Europe. By 1900 the Ottoman Empire was very much in decline.

After World War I, the Ottoman Turks lost much of their remaining territory in the eastern Mediterranean. A treaty in 1923 gave Turkey its present boundaries. At this time the country overthrew its **sultan,** or ruler, and became a republic. Kemal Atatürk, a Turkish military hero, became president.

Atatürk wanted to modernize the country as rapidly as possible. He carried out many reforms. The Turkish language was written with Roman characters instead of Arabic ones. Women were allowed to vote and hold public office. Efforts were made to build roads, dams, and factories. In many ways Turkey became more like a European country

than an Asian country. This difference continues and prevents Turkey from having close ties with its Arab neighbors.

Turkey's link to Europe was further strengthened after World War II. Today the country is involved in many military and economic alliances with the noncommunist nations of Europe and the United States.

See the *TAE* for an *Objective 3* Activity.

CONTENT CHECK

1. **Identify:** Turkey, Bosporus, Sea of Marmara, Dardanelles, Anatolian Plateau, Mount Ararat, Tigris River, Euphrates River, Istanbul, Ankara, Constantinople, Kemal Atatürk.
2. **Define:** mutton, chromite, mosques, sultan.
3. What series of waterways connects the Black Sea and the Aegean Sea?
4. What kinds of landforms make up most of Turkey?
5. What two kinds of climate are found in Turkey?
6. Where is Turkey's best farmland?
7. What religion is followed by most of Turkey's people?
8. **Challenge:** Why might Turkey have difficult relations with some of its Arab neighbors?

Refer students to the political map on page 469 to review the location of Iran.

4. IRAN

The Islamic Republic of Iran is the largest country in the Northern Middle East. It has an area of about 636,293 square miles (1,647,997.5 sq km). With 50.4 million people, Iran is second in population in the region to Turkey. Even though Iran is not an Arab country, Islam is the major religion of the Iranian people.

Have students locate Iran on the maps of Earth's Climate Regions on pages 96-97 and Physical Regions on 452 to review Iran's climate and landscape.

Have students locate the Strait of Hormuz, which connects the Persian Gulf with the Gulf of Oman and was strategic in the Iran-Iraq conflict of the 1980s.

Iran's history goes back more than 5,000 years. For most of this time, it was known as Persia. The country today is important for reasons other than its history. Like Saudi Arabia, it is a major producer of oil. Because Iran borders the Persian Gulf, through which many tankers carry oil to other parts of the world, the government ruling Iran has long had an important role in keeping peace and security in the Persian Gulf area.

Legend says the lost city of Lūt was in the Dasht-i-Kavir, which God cursed by turning the area to salt.

4.1 Landscape and Climate

Iran's landscape is largely made up of a high, partly dry plateau and highlands. Its climate varies from dry in the interior to moist, mild winter along the coasts.

Landscape. More than one-half of the country is the Plateau of Iran. It averages about 3,000 feet (914.4 m) above sea level. High mountains lie around the plateau in the north, west, south, and center.

The Zagros Mountains lie in the southwestern corner of Iran. They are around 9,000 feet (2,743.2 m) in elevation. Along the Caspian Sea in northern Iran are the Elburz Mountains. This chain has Iran's highest peak, Damavand, at a height of 18,386 feet (5,604 m). South of the Elburz Mountains and nearly parallel with the Zagros Mountains are a number of different mountain groups called the Central Mountains. They stretch from the northwest part of Iran to the southeast part, covering almost 25 percent of the country's center.

Central and eastern Iran are desert. Two of the deserts—Dasht-i-Kavir (dasht uh kuh VEER) and the Dasht-i-Lut (dasht uh LOOT)—together form some of the driest, most desolate desert areas on Earth. Parts of the Dasht-i-Kavir have large salt marshes and salt flats.

Iran's major lowland areas are the coastal plains along the Caspian Sea and the Persian

CLIMATE: TEHRAN

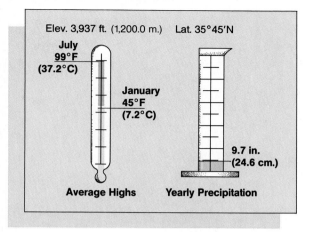

FIGURE 22-5

Even at high elevation, Tehran has very hot summers. What blocks cooler winds from the north and west from reaching the plateau area on which Tehran is located?

See the *TAE* for an *Objective 4* Activity.

Gulf. The Caspian Plain has fertile land and a good water supply, thus, it is an excellent farming area. It also has the greatest population density in Iran.

The Khuzistan (KOOZ uh STAN) Plain along the coast of the Persian Gulf is flat and dry. The Karun (kuh ROON) River, which flows across the plain near the border between Iran and Iraq, drains the Zagros Mountains.

Climate. The high mountains of Iran block winds from the north and west. As a result enough rain and snow fall in the mountains, but little falls in the central plateau area. The desert regions in the country's center receive about 2 inches (5 cm) of rain a year.

As Figure 22-5 on this page shows, Tehran (teh RAHN), situated in the plateau's steppe climate, gets slightly more rain a year than the desert. The only area of Iran that gets an adequate amount of rain is the Caspian coast that has a Mediterranean climate. Almost 40 inches (101.6 cm) of rain falls a year. Summer temperatures there are around 90°F (32.2°C).

The collage below represents various elements of the cultures in Southwest Asia. The crescent and star have long been a symbol of Islam and are part of the national flag of many countries with large numbers of Muslims. The interlacing triangles form the six-pointed Star of David, a symbol both of Judaism and of Israel.

Typifying Southwest Asia's culture are a religious mosque, Muslim women wearing traditional dress, a Middle East oil field, and a desert caravan. A kibbutz exemplifies the ingenuity of the people of Israel in making the desert bloom.

Iran's need for oil profits to pay for the war with Iraq in the late 1980s frequently strained Iran's relations with other oil-producing countries. OPEC nations often had difficulty agreeing on prices and production quotas.

4.2 Economic and Cultural Patterns

Like Saudi Arabia, Iran relies on oil production as a major source of income. The largest deposits of oil in Iran are found south of the Khuzistan Plain. Until the 1980s much of the oil was piped from wells to one of the world's largest refineries at the city of Abadan (AH bah DAHN).

Abadan lies on the Shatt-al-Arab, the river-boundary between Iraq and Iran. Recent fighting between Iraq and Iran has damaged much of the city. This has slowed Iran's oil production. A change in Iran's government in 1979 and the political unrest it has caused have also added to the slowdown.

Iran's income from oil and natural gas has gone up and down in recent years. This has hurt the country's economy. When oil was making money for Iran all the time, much of the money was used to build new industries. Today few new industries are being developed. Many Iranians cannot find jobs, and prices are on the increase. Much of Iran's oil wealth today is being used to pay for a war with Iraq.

Iran has other important mineral resources, such as chrome ore, copper, lead, zinc, iron ore, and manganese. The development of these resources will be postponed until the economy is more stable.

Farming plays a small role in Iran's economy. As in much of Southwest Asia, water is limited. Because of water shortages, less than 15 percent of Iran's land can be used for farming. In these areas Iranian farmers irrigate their fields by using **qanats.** These wells and tunnels bring water to areas where it is needed. Qanats also supply many towns and villages with water.

About one-half of Iran's people live in rural areas and one-half live in urban areas. Because many of Iran's farming villages are poor, Iran's cities have grown recently as a result of many farmers moving from villages. Tehran, Iran's capital, is the largest city, with 5.7 million people. Two other large cities are Esfahān, which has a population of more than 900,000, and Mashhad, with about 1.1 million people.

Iranians speak Persian, also called Farsi. Although Farsi is distantly related to European languages, it has many Arabic words and is written with Arabic characters. Iranians are proud of their old and rich culture, which is famous for its poetry, architecture, gardens, and handwoven carpets.

"Iran" means "Land of the Aryans," and many Iranians believe they are descendants of the Aryans, Indo-Europeans who migrated into the region from southern Russia about 1000 BC.

4.3 Influences of the Past

The area that is now Iran was settled by Persians nearly 3,500 years ago. Their descendants make up the majority of Iran's population today. The Persians once ruled an empire that stretched from Greece in the west to India in the east. The empire reached its height around 500 BC. About 200 years later, it fell to the Greeks under Alexander the Great. Persians later regained part of their former territory and ruled it until the 600s AD.

In the mid-600s, Arab warriors took over Iran. They set up military towns and spread Islam through the region. The Iranians, however, chose to follow their own sect of Islam known as *Shi'a.* A **sect** is a religious group within a larger group. Today most Iranians belong to the *Shi'a* sect, while most of the world's other Muslims are in the *Sunni* sect.

During their stay in Iran, Arabs passed on the Arabic alphabet to Iranians. They also influenced Iranian architecture. Today Iran's cities, towns, and villages have mosques with large domes and tall **minarets,** or prayer towers. From these towers, criers call the people to prayer five times a day.

During the 1800s the United Kingdom and Russia each wanted control of Iran. Russia wanted to use Iran to gain ports on the Persian Gulf. The British feared the growth of the Russian Empire and wanted to strengthen their own hold over nearby India. In 1907 the Russians and the British divided Iran into two spheres of influence, with the Russians taking northern Iran and the British taking southern Iran.

In 1921 an Iranian military officer named Reza Pahlavi became **shah,** or king, of Persia. He took the title of Reza Shah. A strong ruler, Reza Shah brought modern ways to Iran. He also reduced the power of the United Kingdom and Russia in the country.

Reza Shah's son, Mohammed Reza Pahlavi became shah during World War II. In the late 1950s and 1960s, he used oil money to increase Iran's military might. He also divided the land among poor farmers, developed industry, and provided more schools. However, the Shah treated his opponents harshly. Anyone not in favor of his strong rule was put in jail or killed. Also, many Muslims believed that many of the Shah's reforms were against the teachings of Islam.

In 1979 a revolution forced the Shah out of the country. In place of the Shah's government, the Iranians set up a **theocracy,** or a government run by religious leaders. Under the new government, there is very little personal freedom. Iran's religious leaders punish those who oppose their ways of ruling.

Today Iran is an Islamic republic. Before the 1979 revolution, it was the Empire of

Among Iranians' many holidays that celebrate religious and national events, their most joyous is *Now Ruz,* the Iranian New Year celebrated in early spring. Popular Iranian foods, on holidays and ordinary days alike, are bread, lamb, meat and bean soup, and rice mixed with vegetables and meat.

Iran. In many ways Iran is still an empire. There are many different groups of people living in the country. Some of these groups have long demanded separation from the rest of Iran. Among these groups are the Kurds of the northwest and the Turkomans of the northeast.

Even though the name was changed to Iran in 1935, many people still call the country Persia.

CONTENT CHECK

1. **Identify:** Iran, Persia, Plateau of Iran, Zagros Mountains, Central Mountains, Dasht-i-Kavir, Dasht-i-Lut, Caspian Sea, Persian Gulf, Khuzistan Plain, Tehran, Abadan, Shatt-al-Arab, Esfahān, Mashhad, Shi'a, Sunni.

2. **Define:** qanats, sect, minarets, shah, theocracy.

3. What is the importance of the Persian Gulf to the rest of the world?

4. What landforms are in central and eastern Iran?

5. What is the most important source of wealth for Iran's economy?

6. What religion do most Iranians follow?

7. What is Iran's form of government?

8. **Challenge:** How has the war between Iran and Iraq affected Iran's economy?

See the *TRB* for the *Section 5 Extending the Lesson* on war in Afghanistan.

5. OTHER COUNTRIES OF SOUTHWEST ASIA

Israel, Saudi Arabia, Turkey, and Iran are a few of the important countries in Southwest Asia. Yet, a number of other countries are found in the region. They have many

FERTILE CRESCENT

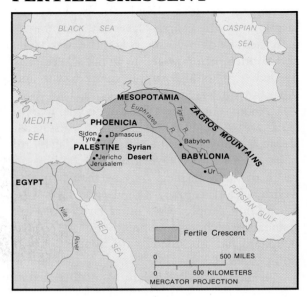

FIGURE 22-6
Beyond its fertile farming areas, this region was also fertile in producing the early civilizations indicated on the map. Here and along the Nile River were the "cradles of civilization." Which waterway system forms a major part of the Fertile Crescent?

See the *TAE* for an *Objective 5* Activity.

things in common with the leading countries. However, in many ways, each has its own physical features, culture, and history.

Point out that the blue dashed line in the map on page 469 represents international boundaries over water and the black dashed line represents disputed boundaries.

5.1 Middle East Core

In addition to Israel, the Middle East Core includes the Hashemite Kingdom of Jordan, the Republic of Lebanon, the Syrian Arab Republic, and the Republic of Iraq. All of these countries share a common Arab culture and language. Also most of their people practice Islam. Each of the lands, however, has a large Christian population.

Jordan, Lebanon, Syria, and Iraq have dry climates and rugged landscapes. The large Syrian Desert takes in parts of Syria,

Jordan, and Iraq. However, arching through the area from the Persian Gulf, north into Turkey, and then south along the Mediterranean coast is an area of fertile land. As Figure 22-6 on page 468 shows, this area is shaped like a half-moon and is known as the Fertile Crescent. Most of the farming in this part of the world takes place in the Fertile Crescent.

The major part of the Fertile Crescent lies in Iraq in the valley of the Tigris and Euphrates rivers, where one of the oldest western civilizations began—Mesopotamia. Farther west is Damascus (duh MAS kuhs), Syria's capital of 1.2 million people. Considered one of the oldest cities in the world, Damascus was founded more than 4,500 years ago. Jordan does not lie in the Fertile Crescent. As a result it does not have much farmland. In fact Jordan is the poorest country in the Middle East Core.

NATIONS OF SOUTHWEST ASIA

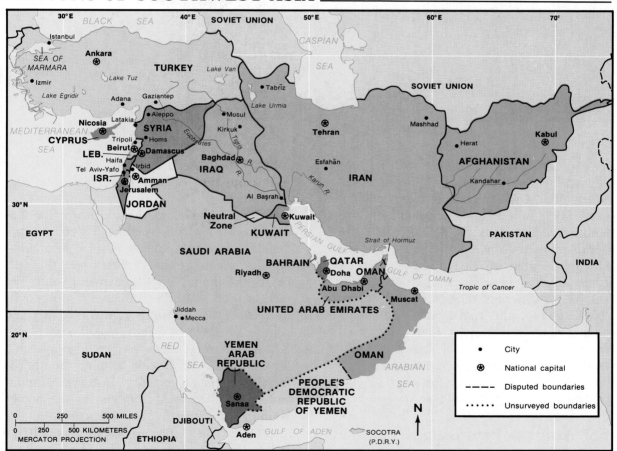

FIGURE 22-7

Many people commonly think of Southwest Asia as a region that is Arabic in speech, Muslim in religion, dry in climate, and rich in oil. Each of these generalizations, to some extent, applies to parts of the region, yet none applies totally throughout. Nonetheless, it is these general factors on which the region's unity is based. Why is the Southwest Asian region considered a crossroads?

CHAPTER 22   **SOUTHWEST ASIA**   469

A particularly dangerous aspect of the conflict in Lebanon has been the taking of hostages. Citizens of countries such as the United States, Soviet Union, United Kingdom, France, and West Germany have been held hostage for months or sometimes even years. Tragically, some of the hostages have been killed by their captors.

Warfare has reduced some sections of Beirut into rubble and bombed-out buildings. In many ways war-torn Beirut reflects the violent and unstable conditions that have existed in Lebanon during recent years. Terrorism and street fighting have made Beirut a dangerous city in which to live. What types of conflicts have torn apart Beirut and Lebanon lately?

Remind students that millions of people throughout history have been forced to leave their homes because of wars and revolutions.

Jordan, Syria, Lebanon, and Iraq were created from the Ottoman Empire after World War I. They became independent between 1932 and 1946. Since that time, these lands have had many political problems. Border disputes and the Arab-Israeli conflict have taken up much of their attention. Recently Lebanon has been torn apart by conflict among its different religious groups. Beirut (bay ROOT), the capital of Lebanon, was once a beautiful seaport that drew visitors from all over the world. Today it is a battlefield in a continuing civil war.

Refer students to the map on page 469 to review the location of the Arabian Peninsula and to identify the countries besides Saudi Arabia that occupy this area.

5.2 Arabian Peninsula

As Figure 22-7 on page 469 shows, Saudi Arabia dominates the Arabian Peninsula. However, several smaller countries are found along the peninsula's southern and eastern coasts. These Arab countries share belief in Islam, but they have different resources and economies.

The countries to the south are the Yemen Arab Republic—or North Yemen—the People's Democratic Republic of Yemen—also known as South Yemen—and the Sultanate of Oman. North Yemen and South Yemen lack oil and other valuable resources. In the past both were important links in trade coming through the Suez Canal. Today North Yemen's moist climate has made it possible for the country to develop farming. South Yemen, however, is very dry. It depends on aid and loans from such countries as the Soviet Union, East Germany, and Cuba.

Oman has some oil, which makes it far richer than the Yemens. However, without new discoveries, the oil will most likely be gone by the early 2000s. Oman's leaders are trying to develop other areas of the economy before the oil runs out.

Unlike the south, the eastern coast of the Arabian Peninsula is the wealthiest area in the world. The countries in this area are Kuwait, Bahrain, Qatar, and the United Arab Emirates. Together they are called the Gulf States because they are found on the Persian Gulf. The United Arab Emirates has a per capita income of more than $23,000 a year, and the per capita income of Qatar is even higher. However, in spite of this great oil wealth, many people in the area make their livings herding livestock or farming the land to feed their families.

On a map have students locate the Khyber Pass in Afghanistan. Ask students what impact Soviet control of Afghanistan and the Khyber Pass might have.

5.3 Northern Middle East

In addition to Turkey and Iran, the countries of the Northern Middle East are the Democratic Republic of Afghanistan and the Republic of Cyprus. Cyprus is an island off the coast of Turkey in the Mediterranean Sea. It has been a source of conflict between Greece and Turkey for hundreds of years. Turkey and Afghanistan are very different from one another in terms of development.

Afghanistan is the least industrialized country in Southwest Asia. It is made up of many different groups of people who make their living mostly as farmers and herders. Their country is a very rugged land of high mountains and deserts.

Recently the Soviet Union has had troops in Afghanistan to give support to a new communist government. The Soviets have fought against the many Afghans opposed to the government. Western countries worry that Soviet control of Afghanistan places the Soviets only 250 miles (402.3 km) from the Persian Gulf and the oilfields around it. The Soviets have had a hard time ruling Afghanistan. Many Soviet soldiers have been killed. Afghanistan continues to be the scene of much conflict and unrest.

CONTENT CHECK

1. **Identify:** Jordan, Lebanon, Syria, Iraq, Syrian Desert, Fertile Crescent, Mesopotamia, Damascus, Beirut, Yemen Arab Republic, People's Democratic Republic of Yemen, Oman, Kuwait, Bahrain, Qatar, United Arab Emirates, Gulf States, Cyprus, Afghanistan.

2. Which of the countries of the Middle East Core lies outside the Fertile Crescent?

3. What city in the Middle East Core has been populated longer than any other city in the world?

4. How does the wealth of the countries on the southern part of the Arabian Peninsula compare with that of the Gulf States?

5. **Challenge:** The Soviet Union has had troops in Afghanistan for some time. What might the Soviet Union's purpose be in aiding the government in this country?

See the TAE for an Objective 6 Activity.

CONCLUSION

For many centuries Southwest Asia has been the scene of change and conflict. In the past, groups of people invaded the area because of its central location. Whoever controlled the area controlled the trade routes leading to three continents.

Today many of Southwest Asia's problems center on groups of people within the area. The Kurds seek independence from Iran, and Iran fights over boundaries with Iraq. Differences between Israel and its Arab neighbors have kept the area in constant unrest. The danger of a major war in this part of the world puts even greater importance on the need for global peace and understanding of all cultures.

SUMMARY

1. Southwest Asia lies at the meeting point of Europe, Africa, and Asia.
2. Southwest Asia can be divided into three parts—Arabian Peninsula, Middle East Core, and Northern Middle East.
3. Israel is the only Jewish nation in the world. It is isolated from its Arab neighbors by political and cultural differences. The conflict between Israel and Arab countries is a major source of tension in this part of the world.
4. Saudi Arabia is the largest country in Southwest Asia. It is important because of its huge deposits of oil.
5. Turkey is the most populous country in Southwest Asia. Its economy has been rapidly industrializing since the 1920s. In outlook it is more European than Asian.
6. Iran is the largest country in the Northern Middle East. Iran was once considered a world leader in oil production, but a war and revolution have interfered with its economy.
7. The Fertile Crescent is a large area of fertile land running through the Middle East Core. Most of the people in this part of the Middle East live on this land.
8. Several small countries share the Arabian Peninsula with Saudi Arabia. The countries in the south are mostly poor, while those in the east are among the richest in the world.
9. Since 1979 Afghanistan has been torn apart by fighting between Soviet military forces and Afghans opposing the country's communist government.

Answers to the following questions can be found on page T229.

REVIEWING VOCABULARY

On a separate sheet of paper, write the word that is defined to the right of the blanks in each line. Then circle the letters in the words that show a star (★) below. Unscramble these letters to spell the mystery word, one of the countries of Southwest Asia.

1. _ ★ _ _ _ _   meat that comes from sheep
2. ★ _ _ _ _ _ _   ruler of the Ottoman Empire
3. _ _ _ ★ _ _ _   collective farm settlement in Israel
4. _ _ _ _ ★ _   cooperative where farms are individually owned
5. ★ _ _ _ _ ★ _ _ _ _ _ _ _ _   process of removing salt from seawater
6. _ ★ _ _   pilgrimage to Mecca
7. _ _ _ ★ _ _   method of irrigation that uses deep wells and tunnels
8. _ _ ★ _   title of Iran's ruler before 1979
9. _ ★ _ _ _ _ _   tall tower on Muslim buildings
10. _ _ _ _ _ ★ _ _ _   government controlled by religious leaders

REMEMBERING THE FACTS

1. What name is frequently given to the countries of the Southwest Asia region and Egypt?
2. What are some reasons why Southwest Asia is an important world region?
3. What are some waterways found in Israel's rift valley?
4. What is the most important source of wealth in Saudi Arabia?
5. What is the name of the peninsula where Saudi Arabia is located?
6. By what name was Iran known for many years?
7. What part of Iran receives the heaviest amount of rainfall?
8. In what part of Iran are most of the country's oil deposits found?
9. What are *Shi'a* and *Sunni*?
10. What is the landscape like in the easternmost part of Turkey?
11. What accounts for the wealth of the Gulf States?

UNDERSTANDING THE FACTS

1. In what ways is Israel isolated from its neighbors?
2. Only three percent of Saudi Arabians are involved in the oil industry. Yet, oil accounts for a high percentage of the country's income. How can this be explained?
3. Saudi Arabia has a relatively small population. Why must it import food?
4. Why is Turkey's location so important to many other countries of the world?
5. How did Iran's government change after the revolution of 1979?

THINKING CRITICALLY AND CREATIVELY

1. If a new energy source developed that ended the need for oil, what do you think the impact would be on Saudi Arabia? Why do you think so?
2. **Challenge:** The Turkish leader Kemal Atatürk moved Turkey's capital from Istanbul to Ankara. Why do you think he did this?
3. **Challenge:** Iran and Iraq have been fighting for many years. What might happen to Israel if these two Muslim countries stopped fighting and became allies?

REINFORCING GRAPHIC SKILLS

Study the map on page 457. Then answer the questions that follow.

1. What advantage does Israeli occupation of the Golan Heights give to Israel?
2. What are the physical features of the land called the West Bank? The Gaza Strip? Why do you think these two areas were continually under dispute?
3. **Challenge:** Why are disputes over territorial boundaries difficult to resolve?

SUMMARY

1. The culture area of North Africa and Southwest Asia extends across major parts of two continents. Its two regions share similar landscapes and climates, economic and cultural patterns, and elements of a common past.
2. The area contains one of the world's largest desert areas. Most of its people live crowded into small areas where the supply of water is adequate.
3. The area's most common economic activity is farming.
4. The world's largest known deposits of oil lie beneath much of the region. Wealth brought by oil revenues has improved living standards only for a minority of the total population.
5. Several of the world's great ancient civilizations and some of its most lasting cultures started in North Africa and Southwest Asia. Three of the world's major religions—Judaism, Islam, and Christianity—began in the area. The area is mostly Arab and Muslim.
6. North Africa and Southwest Asia is an area torn apart by conflict. This is seen in distrust among different cultural groups and in frequent boundary disputes.

Answers to the following questions can be found on page T233.

THINKING ABOUT THE UNIT

1. In what ways does the general climate of North Africa and Southwest Asia influence where people live?
2. Why does this area's relative location make it so important?
3. In what ways did the spread of Islam unify this region?
4. Egypt has many more people than any of the countries of the Sahel. How might this be explained?

SUGGESTED UNIT ACTIVITIES

1. Analyze newspaper articles about the countries of North Africa and Southwest Asia. Classify the articles according to topic and type—factual or editorial. Write a paper in which you describe the kinds of information contained in each type of article. Take special care to note which countries draw the attention of editorial writers. Explain any patterns you find.
2. Hold a class discussion in which you make a list on the chalkboard of items made from petroleum that you use each day. Then in a small group of students, brainstorm responses to this question: How would our lives change if suddenly *no* petroleum products were available? Then consider the impact on people's lives of a tenfold increase in the price of petroleum and petroleum-based products.

DEVELOPING GEOGRAPHY SKILLS

MAKING INFERENCES

If you wanted to solve a crime, you would look for clues. You would be interested in exactly how the crime was committed and in who did it. You would also be interested in what the criminal's reason may have been in committing the crime. Based on these clues, you might make an *inference*, a reasonable deduction based on facts or circumstances.

People make inferences every day, often without even realizing it. For example, suppose your school is getting ready to play its first conference basketball game of the winter season. Your school won the conference last year. Four of the starters from last year's team are back to play this school year. The team your school will be playing finished last in the conference last year and three of its starters graduated. Based on these facts, you infer that your team has an excellent chance of winning its first game.

Or suppose you and some friends want to go shopping at a mall in the next town. When you ask your friend Sarah if she can borrow her mother's car to drive there, she tells you she cannot. You notice that she does not explain why. Then she tells you that even if you find someone else to drive, she cannot go with you. Once again she does not tell you why. It is unusual for Sarah to act this way. You know that Sarah has no other plans for the day, and she is not sick. At first you do not understand why she is not going because you know Sarah loves to watch people at the mall. Based on your conversation with Sarah and what you know about her, you make an inference—Sarah must be grounded.

The following is a paragraph that describes Cairo's *zabbalines*, workers who make their living by collecting and recycling garbage. Most of the zabbalines are Coptic Christians who came to Cairo from rural areas. Read the paragraph and the explanation of facts and inference that follow it:

The lives of the zabbalines are well outside of Cairo's mainstream. As a religious minority, they have little to do with the Muslim majority that dominates the city. The lives of the zabbalines are totally tied to their relationship with garbage. Since they live among piles of Cairo's garbage, they are physically separated from traditional residential areas of the city. Even their religious and social centers, the Coptic churches, are built amid huge hills of garbage. They live, work, and pray in parts of the city that have little contact with others. Part of the isolation zabbalines feel is due to the low regard in which they are held by other people in Cairo. Their ways of living do not earn them high social status.

Explanation of facts: *The zabbalines follow a minority religion in Cairo—Christianity; they live in areas where garbage lies; their social status is very low.*

Inference: *The zabbalines have lonely lives apart from the rest of Cairo's society.*

For practice in making inferences, reread Chapter 22, Section 1.3 on pages 455-458 and the *Using Graphic Skills* feature on pages 456-457. Explain what facts may be the basis of the following inference:

Both Jews and Arabs have legitimate claims to the territory of Palestine.

AFRICA SOUTH
OF THE SAHARA

UNIT 8

Point out to students that the highlighted area on the world map inset represents the culture area of Africa South of the Sahara.

For centuries the Sahara has kept the northern and southern parts of the African continent apart, acting as a barrier to the rapid spread of cultures from north to south and south to north. Largely for this reason, the cultures north and south of the Sahara are different from one another in several ways. This unit focuses on Africa south of the Sahara. It is made up of three regions—East Africa, West and Central Africa, and Southern Africa. Each of these, in turn, is made up of many countries.

Africa South of the Sahara is a very diverse culture area. It is made up of more than 40 independent nations with more than 2,000 different cultural groups, speaking 800 or more languages and dialects. At one time or another, almost all of the countries were under foreign rule. The boundaries of most of the countries were set by Europeans with little or no regard for where members of African ethnic groups lived. As a result, many African nations today are still having trouble uniting the many groups in their countries. The entire culture area is experiencing political, economic, and social change.

Mount Kilimanjaro, Tanzania

Africa's peoples have a rich cultural heritage. In recent years African arts of all types have become sought after by tourists and collectors worldwide.

Maasai girl selling beaded crafts, Kenya

EAST AFRICA

Refer students to the map of colonial Africa on page 501.

East Africa covers a vast land area. This part of the African continent is about one-half as large as the entire continent of Australia. Refer students to the map on page 489 to locate the countries of East Africa.

INTRODUCTION

East Africa is the easternmost region of Africa south of the Sahara. It stretches about 2,000 miles (3,218.7 km) from the northern tip of Ethiopia to the southern border of Tanzania and runs inland about 800 miles (1,287.5 km) from the Indian Ocean. Eight countries make up the region—Ethiopia (EE thee OH pee uh), Djibouti (jih BOO tee), Somalia (soh MAH lee uh), Uganda (yoo GAN duh), Kenya (KEHN yuh), Rwanda (roo WAHN duh), Burundi (buh RUHN dee), and Tanzania (TAN zuh NEE uh). The landscapes, climates, and major economic activities of all eight are very much alike. In some ways so are their histories.

For much of its recent history, East Africa was ruled by non-Africans. Except for the long-standing nation of Ethiopia, other countries have gained their freedom since 1961. All are working to develop their economies and give their people a better standard of living.

South of Kenya's Tana River are beaches known for their beauty, while north of the river are marshy swamps with palm trees.

1. KENYA

The Republic of Kenya covers 224,961 square miles (582,648.5 sq km), an area slightly smaller than Texas. On the east, it borders the Indian Ocean. On the west and northwest, it runs into the interior of Africa. For many Africans Kenya is a symbol of freedom, pride, and self-reliance.

The Great Rift Valley is one of Earth's most unusual landforms. In places it is 2,000 feet (609.6 m) deep.

1.1 Landscape and Climate

The landscape of Kenya has coastal lowlands, interior plains, and highlands. While most of the interior has a very dry climate, the coast is hot and humid.

Landscape. The landscape of Kenya may be divided into four parts—lowlands, plains, highlands, and plateaus. The narrow lowlands are found along the coast of the Indian Ocean. Stretching inland from the coast are plains that run from the northeastern to the southeastern corner of the country. They rise toward the west to about 4,000 feet (1,219.2 m) above sea level.

To the west of the plains are the Kenya Highlands, an area of mountains, valleys, and plateaus with fertile soil, forests, and grasslands. Running through the middle of the highlands is part of the Great Rift Valley, which varies in width from 30 miles (48.2 km) to 80 miles (128.7 km). The Great Rift Valley is the most dominant physical feature of East Africa. It was formed many thousands of years ago when tectonic plates moved away from each other. In the valley are Kenya's best soils along with extinct volcanoes and a

PHYSICAL REGIONS OF EAST AFRICA

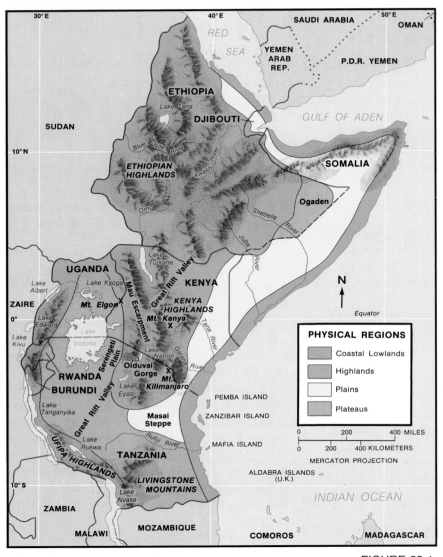

East Africa's climate is affected by its mountains and plateaus. Mountains cause the climate here to be very dry. In some cases the climate is cooler than would be expected for a tropical climate region. What type of climate would you expect to find along East Africa's coastal lowlands?

Lake Nyasa is sometimes called Lake Malawi, particularly by the people of Malawi. However, in the African maps in this unit, the lake has been consistently labeled Lake Nyasa, its conventional name among geographers.

Explain that Lake Victoria is only slightly smaller than Lake Superior, one of the Great Lakes of the U.S. and Canada. At 3,720 feet (1133.9 m) above sea level, Lake Victoria is one of the world's highest lakes.

FIGURE 23-1

Point out that, although Kenya lies on the Equator, the highlands—where most Kenyans live—tend to moderate the temperatures. In colonial days Europeans had little difficulty adapting to Kenya's highland climate.

chain of shallow lakes. On the western edge of the valley is the Mau Escarpment. On the eastern edge is Kenya's highest peak, Mount Kenya, at 17,058 feet (5,199.2 m).

One of the lakes of the valley is Lake Turkana, once called Lake Rudolf. The largest lake in Kenya, it covers 2,463 square miles (6,379.1 sq km). At the western edge of the country, bordered by a broad, fertile plateau, is the largest lake in Africa—Lake Victoria. Called *Victoria Nyanza* in the Bantu language, the lake lies mostly in Uganda and Tanzania.

Climate. Since the Equator passes through the middle of Kenya, almost all of the country has hot or warm temperatures.

480   **AFRICA SOUTH OF THE SAHARA   UNIT 8**

Since Kenya straddles the Equator, there are no important temperature differences between northern and southern areas except those caused by altitudes.

Adorned with flowering trees, shrubs, beautiful houses, and public buildings, Nairobi has become a hub of communications and commercial activity.

The exception is high elevations like Mount Kenya. Its peak is covered with snow and ice all year.

Although the southern coast has a hot and humid climate, plains stretching away from the coastline have a steppe climate. Rainfall in the steppe averages slightly more than 10 inches (25.4 cm). January's highest temperatures average 80°F (26.7°C) at sea level. Those places at higher elevations have average highs of 70°F (21.1°C). Farther north the plains and plateaus receive even less rain and have a desert climate. This large desert in the north is thinly populated.

In the highlands the climate is warm and wet with rainfall that averages between 40 inches (101.6 cm) and 50 inches (127 cm) each year. This area has a tropical savanna climate. Kenya's capital city of Nairobi (ny ROH bee) is in the southern highlands. Figure 23-2 on this page shows that average high temperatures for Nairobi are somewhat higher than those generally found in the Kenya highlands.

Corn, known as maize in Kenya, is one of the basic foods in that country. Often it is pounded into a flour and cooked into a porridge.

1.2 Economic and Cultural Patterns

Only about four percent of Kenya's land is suitable for farming. Even so, agriculture is the most important economic activity. It is carried on in the Kenya Highlands, the western plateau, and along parts of the coast. The leading crop is maize, or corn. Farmers grow it both for their own use and for sale. Other crops they raise for food at home are beans, potatoes, and **cassava,** a plant whose starchy root is used for food.

Subsistence crops, crops raised by farmers for their own use, make up about one-half of Kenya's farm production. The rest is made up of **cash crops,** crops raised for sale. Two major cash crops are coffee and tea, both grown mostly in the Kenya Highlands.

CLIMATE: NAIROBI

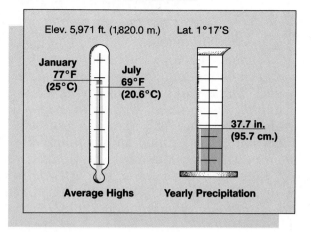

Elev. 5,971 ft. (1,820.0 m.)   Lat. 1°17'S

January 77°F (25°C)

July 69°F (20.6°C)

37.7 in. (95.7 cm.)

Average Highs   Yearly Precipitation

FIGURE 23-2
Nairobi maintains a relatively cool climate throughout the year, despite its location so close to the Equator. What accounts for summer temperatures during January being cool?

Kenya does not have large mineral deposits. Its chief minerals are soda and salt. Some silver and zinc are also mined. Even though it lacks resources, the government encourages the growth of industry for its capitalist economy. Leading industrial products include textiles, light machinery, household goods, and paper goods.

Second only to the sale of coffee as a source of income is tourism. People come from all over the world to visit Kenya's wildlife parks. The government has set aside more than 6 million acres (2.4 million ha) for parks and game reserves to protect wildlife. Since hunting is forbidden, tourists come to look at and photograph the animals.

Kenya is home to about 22.4 million people. Almost 85 percent of these people live in the southern two-fifths of the country. Meanwhile Kenya is growing rapidly. Its almost four percent rate of population growth is one of the highest in the world. If the population keeps growing at this rate, it will double in about 18 years.

NATIONAL PARKS AND RESERVES

Many countries all over the world have set aside public land areas for use as national parks. These parks exist mostly to protect natural landscapes and wildlife. In them animals can roam free, and plants can grow wild. They are not to be used for any human economic activity harmful to nature.

For some countries of East Africa, like Kenya, wildlife is a major resource. Over time some animals have been hunted almost to extinction. Also, in recent years, people have been moving onto land that traditionally has been the home of animals. To protect the wildlife and keep some species from becoming extinct, some governments have established national game parks.

During the 1960s many East African countries expanded their parks to attract more tourists. Thousands of people travel to East African parks each year to see and photograph the region's natural wonders. Of particular interest are such East African animals as elephants, lions, apes, hippopotamuses, and giraffes. Rwanda, on the other hand, allows only about 6,600 tourists a year into its parks. They strictly limit the number who come to see the famed mountain gorillas, an endangered species.

East Africa's largest park is the Tsavo National Park in Kenya. This is only one of many parks there. Uganda has three national parks. Rwanda has one. Tanzania also has several, including the Serengeti National Park. The vast Serengeti, a plain of nearly 5,000 square miles (12,949.9 sq km), is the home of large populations of zebras, wildebeests, and gazelles.

In addition to national parks, East Africa has game reserves, or controlled hunting areas. Plants are protected in the area's forest reserves. The major East African reserves include the Masai Mara Reserve and the Marsabit Reserve in Kenya. The Selous Game Reserve is located in central Tanzania. As the world's largest game reserve, it covers 21,081 square miles (54,599.7 sq km).

The greatest concern of countries that have national parks and reserves is the *preservation,* or keeping from harm, of natural things that are endangered or rare.

1. What is the major purpose of a national park or reserve?

2. What are some of the largest national parks in East Africa?

3. What is the main attraction for people visiting the national parks and reserves of East Africa?

482 Even though Maasai is generally recognized as the correct spelling for both the people and land areas named after them, at times students may find it spelled Masai, as seen above in the Masai Mara Reserve— the official place-name spelling used by the Kenyan government.

Ownership of cattle is important to the Maasai people of East Africa. A person with a large herd of cattle is considered upper class. Initiate a discussion of how different cultures use things to indicate social class.

The spelling Maasai is a more modern spelling than Masai and reflects the proper pronunciation of the people's name.

Kenya's population includes people of African, Asian, Indian, European, and Arab descent. There are more than 40 different black ethnic groups. Together they make up nearly 99 percent of the population. The largest is the Kikuyu (kih KOO yoo). Each ethnic group has its own language. Most are variations of Bantu, an old African language. To aid communication, Kiswahili (kee swah HEE lee) has been made the official language. It is the most widely spoken language in East Africa. English is also spoken.

Nearly 60 percent of Kenyans are Christian. About 6 percent are Muslim. The rest follow traditional African religions.

About 85 percent of Kenyans live in rural areas in small, scattered settlements. Between 5 and 10 percent of the people are nomads who live much the way their ancestors did thousands of years ago. Some, known as **pastoralists,** depend almost totally on their herds of livestock. Much of their diet is milk. One such group is the Maasai (mah SY), whose home is the southern Kenyan plains and the Great Rift Valley. For years the government has tried to make the Maasai into farmers. Many Maasai, however, prefer to keep their traditional way of life. They believe that to be a Maasai one must have cattle.

In recent years Kenya has become more urban. Nairobi is the largest city. It is home to about 1.3 million people. The second largest city is Mombasa, a port on the coast, with a population of about 340,000.

Have interested students report on prominent anthropologists such as Mary and Louis Leakey.

1.3 Influences of the Past

Physical anthropologists, people who study fossil remains to learn about early people, have found remains of very early people in Kenya and other parts of East Africa. Remains found near Lake Turkana show that people lived in the area about two million years ago.

An anthropologist searches a hillside for bone fragments in Kenya's Great Rift Valley, an area that has unearthed some of the earliest-known human remains. How long ago were people first living in East Africa? Kiswahili is the modern version of the Swahili language.

People from other parts of Africa began to move into Kenya about 3,000 years ago. As early as 1000 BC, people were farming and herding in the highlands. By the 300s AD, Africans were trading goods with merchants from Arabia, Persia, and India.

By the 700s AD, Muslim Arab traders set up colonies along the coast of Kenya. In time some of them married Africans. From this came a new people, culture, and language known as Swahili. In the 1400s the Arabs were defeated by Portuguese who were exploring the Kenyan coast. In the late 1600s, Arabs once again gained control of the coast. Both Arabs and Portuguese traded slaves for gold from the interior.

In the late 1800s Kenya came under British control. Within five years the British built a railroad connecting Mombasa with Nairobi and Lake Victoria. British colonists arrived, bringing with them the English language and Christianity. Most settled on large plantations in the Kenyan Highlands. They used African labor to work plantations.

Under British rule, the **indigenous** people—the original African settlers—lost their best farmland and all political power. By the 1940s they organized to oppose British rule. In an effort to get back their original land, Kikuyu and other Africans formed a political party called the Kenya African Union (KAU). A group of Kikuyu also formed a secret movement with the same goal. In the early 1950s, they fought the British and were defeated in 1956. African resistance, however, did not come to an end. Finally, in 1963, Kenya became independent. A Kikuyu leader named Jomo Kenyatta (kehn YAH tuh) was elected the first president of Kenya. After Kenyatta's death in 1978, leaders made his political party the only legal party in Kenya.

See the *TAE* for an *Objective 1* Activity.

CONTENT CHECK

1. **Identify:** Kenya, Kenyan Highlands, Great Rift Valley, Mount Kenya, Lake Turkana, Lake Victoria, Nairobi, Kikuyu, Bantu, Kiswahili, Maasai, Swahili, Jomo Kenyatta.

2. **Define:** cassava, subsistence crops, cash crops, pastoralists, physical anthropologists, indigenous.

3. What four landscapes are found in Kenya?

4. Why does Kenya have hot or warm temperatures?

5. What are the two major economic activities of Kenya?

6. Where do most Kenyans live?

7. What is the largest ethnic group in Kenya?

8. Why did Africans resent British rule?

9. **Challenge:** Of what value do you think a national language could be to Kenya?

2. TANZANIA

The United Republic of Tanzania lies just south of the Equator. It covers 364,900 square miles (945,090.3 sq km). More than 23,000 square miles (59,569.9 sq km) of this area is made up of inland bodies of water. Tanzania was formed in 1964 from two states. One was Tanganyika (TAN guhn YEE kuh), a large territory on the African mainland that included Mafia Island in the Indian Ocean. The other was Zanzibar (ZAN zuh BAHR), a group of offshore islands, the largest of which are Zanzibar and Pemba.

Zanzibar gained independence in December of 1963 and united with Tanganyika in 1964.

2.1 Landscape and Climate

Tanzania is about one and one-half times the area of Kenya and has the same major physical regions. Because it lies so close to the Equator, its climate is hot or warm year-round except in higher elevations.

Landscape. Along the Indian Ocean Tanzania has coastal lowlands that are 500 miles (804.6 km) long. Many are covered by mangrove swamps and coconut palms.

Inland from these lowlands is a large plateau that rises slowly before leveling off at about 4,000 feet (1,219.2 m). Crossing the plateau are several chains of mountains. In the north, south, and southwest of the country are highlands, many with fertile, volcanic soils. In the north also are plains, many covered with steppe grasses and tropical savanna vegetation. In the northeast is the highest point in all Africa—Mount Kilimanjaro (KIHL uh muhn JAHR oh). It rises 19,340 feet (5,894.8 m) above sea level. To its west is the Serengeti (SEHR uhn GEHT ee) Plain. To the south is the Masai Steppe.

Much of far western Tanzania is in the Great Rift Valley. In this area are large lakes. Tanzania's largest lakes are Lake Victoria and Lake Tanganyika.

East Africa has many impressive tourist attractions. Dar es Salaam has museums and art galleries that feature traditional and historic Tanzanian art forms. Part of the Serengeti Plains is in this area, and Zanzibar has several historic remains of former slave market sites.

Lake Natron lies along the border between Kenya and Tanzania. It is one of many large lakes in the region. Where are most of the largest lakes in East Africa located?

Other large lakes include Lakes Nyasa, Rukwa, and Eyasi. Besides beautiful lake shores, Tanzania also has more than 450 miles (724.2 km) of white beaches along the Indian Ocean.

Climate. The islands and much of the coast of Tanzania are hot and humid with a tropical savanna climate. The capital city, Dar es Salaam (DAHR EHS suh LAHM), has an average high temperature of more than 80°F (27°C). Rainfall varies during the year in different regions. The southeastern coast, which has a steppe climate, receives little rain. Much of the plateau area in the middle of the country is hot and dry. The climate is affected by two different monsoon seasons.

Population is sparse in parts of Tanzania that have little potential for agriculture.

2.2 Economic and Cultural Patterns

Although the leading economic activity in Tanzania is agriculture, the greatest part of the country's land is too dry for farming or grazing livestock. Most farming is carried on in the coastal areas, in northern and southern highlands, and in the western lake region. Grains, vegetables, and fruits are grown for use within the country. Crops such as **pyrethrum** (py REE thruhm), a plant used to make insecticides, and sisal, a plant used to make rope, are grown as cash crops. Tanzania also is the world's major source of cloves. The spice **clove** is made from the dried flower buds of clove trees.

As Figure 23-3 on page 486 shows, Tanzania is rich in minerals. It has one of the most important diamond deposits in the world. Yet, even with rich mineral deposits, it has little industry.

The government plays a major role in the socialist economy of Tanzania. It owns many businesses and industries. It promotes cooperative farms in which farmers share in the work and the profits but which government controls. The Swahili word *ujamaa*, which means "family," has become a slogan for the type of cooperation encouraged by the Tanzanian government.

About 23.5 million people live in Tanzania. While some are Asian Indians, Pakistanis, Arabs, and Europeans, the majority are black Africans who belong to more than 130 different ethnic groups. Of all these groups, only the Sukuma numbers more than one million. As in Kenya, the growth rate is high. If it does not go down, Tanzania's population will double in about 20 years.

LAND USE AND RESOURCES OF EAST AFRICA

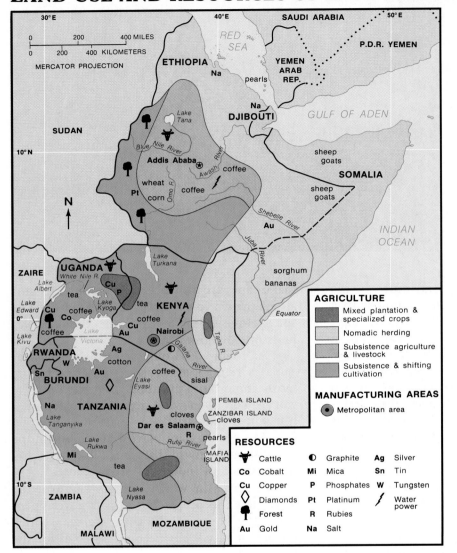

There is much diversity of land use in East Africa, with much land being held in reserve for wild animals. Which country shown on this map has areas in which all four types of agriculture are found?

AGRICULTURE

- Mixed plantation & specialized crops
- Nomadic herding
- Subsistence agriculture & livestock
- Subsistence & shifting cultivation

MANUFACTURING AREAS

- Metropolitan area

RESOURCES

Cattle	Graphite	Ag Silver
Co Cobalt	Mi Mica	Sn Tin
Cu Copper	P Phosphates	W Tungsten
◇ Diamonds	Pt Platinum	Water power
Forest	R Rubies	
Au Gold	Na Salt	

FIGURE 23-3

The tsetse fly places a heavy burden on Tanzania's economy because it keeps people from working places where land is fertile or where other natural resources could be developed.

Although all ethnic groups in Tanzania have their own language, the national language is Kiswahili, a Bantu-based language with strong Arabic influences.

About 35 percent of Tanzanians follow traditional African religions. About 30 percent are Muslims. About the same percent are Christians.

Most Tanzanians live in the highlands, along parts of the coast, or on the shores of Lake Victoria. The threat of disease brought by **tsetse** (TSEHT see) **flies** keeps many peo-

ple from living in the west central area of the country. The bite of these flies can cause sleeping sickness in people and a disease called nagana (nuh GAHN uh) in cattle and horses. To encourage more people to move to the central plateau, the government has built a new city called Dodoma. In the 1990s it will become the capital.

A problem common in most economically underdeveloped countries is the rapid migration of people from rural areas to national capital cities such as Dar es Salaam. Often untrained farm workers are unable to find employment in the city, and urban resources are unable to meet the needs of the huge numbers of newcomers.

More than 82 percent of Tanzanians still live in rural areas. Each year, however, more are moving to towns and cities. The largest city, Dar es Salaam, is a busy port on the Indian Ocean. More than 1,096,000 people live there.

See the *TAE* for an *Objective 2* Activity.

2.3 Influences of the Past

Some of the world's earliest humans lived in Tanzania. At the Olduvai (OHL duh vy) Gorge, British anthropologists Louis and Mary Leakey recently uncovered the bones and stone tools of creatures who may have lived as long as four million years ago. Human beings have lived in the area that is now Tanzania more than one million years.

About 3,000 years ago, different groups of people came to Tanzania from other parts of Africa. Much later, in the 700s AD, Arab traders settled coastal areas of the country. They introduced the religion of Islam and set up a slave trade. They ruled the area until the 1500s. During this time traders from India and Persia also came to the area. In the early 1500s, the Portuguese came, bringing the Roman Catholic religion with them. They won control of the coast along the Indian Ocean and took over the slave trade.

In the late 1800s mainland Tanzania was part of a large area of East Africa taken over by Germany and ruled as German East Africa. German colonial rule stopped with the ending of World War I. The United Kingdom was given control of most of the mainland area under a League of Nations mandate. They renamed the area Tanganyika. They continued to govern the area until 1961, when it became independent. An independence leader named Julius Nyerere (nih RAIR ee) became the first president. In 1964 the country united with the country of Zanzibar, which was formerly ruled by the United Kingdom. Together they formed the United Republic of Tanzania.

CONTENT CHECK

1. **Identify:** Tanzania, Tanganyika, Zanzibar, Mount Kilimanjaro, Serengeti Plain, Masai Steppe, Dar es Salaam, Sukuma, Dodoma, Olduvai Gorge, Louis and Mary Leakey, German East Africa, Julius Nyerere.

2. **Define:** pyrethrum, clove, tsetse flies.

3. From what two states was Tanzania formed?

4. What kinds of landforms does Tanzania have?

5. In what part of Tanzania are large lakes found?

6. What areas of Tanzania are suitable for farming?

7. What part does the Tanzanian government play in the economy?

8. Where do most Tanzanians live?

9. What groups of people from outside Africa have controlled Tanzania?

10. **Challenge:** What similarities and differences do Tanzania and Kenya face in developing their economies?

Have students note the location of the area called the "Horn of Africa" on the map on page 489. Early explorers thought this part of Africa on a map looked like the horn of some animals, such as a rhinoceros.

3. OTHER COUNTRIES OF EAST AFRICA

As Figure 23-4 on page 489 shows, East Africa is made up of eight countries. Besides Kenya and Tanzania, there are six other countries. Three of these countries—Ethiopia, Somalia, and Djibouti— lie in what is called the Horn of Africa. They have in common their coastal locations. The other three countries in East Africa are landlocked. These countries—Uganda, Burundi, and Rwanda— are part of the East African Highlands.

Ethiopia, the oldest independent country in Africa, has a long and rich history. According to legend, Menelik I, the son of King Solomon and the Queen of Sheba, founded the Ethiopian Empire. Missionaries from Egypt and Syria introduced Christianity in the 300s AD.

3.1 The Horn of Africa

The area known as the Horn of Africa, which lies north of Kenya, thrusts out into the Indian Ocean. It is bordered by the Red Sea, the Gulf of Aden, and the Indian Ocean.

Ethiopia. Covering an area of 471,776 square miles (1,221,898.8 sq km), Ethiopia is the largest country not only in the Horn of Africa but in all of East Africa.

In Ethiopia dry lowlands surround a plateau that rises 6,000 feet (1,828.8 m) to 10,000 feet (3,048 m) above sea level. The lowlands, some of which are deserts, are among the hottest places in the world. The chief feature of the plateau is rugged mountains, the highest of which is Ras Dashan (RAHS duh SHAHN). Cutting through the plateau is the Great Rift Valley. Here there are many deep river gorges and waterfalls. Temperatures, rainfall, and soil of the plateau make it good for farming. More people live in the plateau than in the lowlands.

Agriculture is the most important part of Ethiopia's economy. Most farming is done in a traditional way with oxen pulling wooden plows. Most farmers raise crops—mostly grains—for their own families. The most important cash crop is coffee. Cattle, goats, sheep, and chickens are also raised.

Ethiopia has the largest population of the East African countries. Among all of the African countries, only Egypt and Nigeria have more people. Of the 46 million people who live in Ethiopia, only 10 percent live in urban areas. Close to 1.5 million live in Addis Ababa (AD ihs AB uh buh), which is the largest city as well as the capital of Ethiopia.

Over the centuries, many groups have settled in Ethiopia. Settlers came first from the Arabian Peninsula and later from parts of Africa. Because of the many groups of people who settled there, today more than 70 languages are still spoken. Amharic (am HAR ihk) is the official language in Ethiopia.

About one-half of all Ethiopians are Christians. Most belong to the Ethiopian Orthodox Church, which has kept many old traditions. Most Christians live in highland areas. In the northern province of Eritrea (EHR uh TREE uh) and other lowland areas, Muslims make up the largest religious group. There is also a small number of Ethiopian Jews. In southern Ethiopia, most people follow traditional African religions.

Ethiopia is one of the world's oldest nations. Early Egyptian records tell of a civilization in Ethiopia about 3,500 years ago. During Biblical times Ethiopia, known as Abyssinia (AB uh SIHN ee uh), was the center of a kingdom known as Aksum.

In the late 1800s, after a long period of division, Ethiopia became a united kingdom under an emperor. In 1931 a relative of that emperor named Ras Tafari became emperor. He took the title of Emperor Haile Selassie I. He ruled the country until 1935, when it was taken over by Italy, and he was forced to flee. In 1941 he returned and continued his rule until 1974, when his government was overthrown by Ethiopian military leaders.

Ethiopia is larger than the combined areas of France, Spain, and Portugal.

People here are receiving medical care. East African governments promote education to control diseases and training of health-care workers to offset the shortage of doctors and nurses. In which highly populated country is medical care a great necessity?

In the past decade, Ethiopia has experienced widespread famine caused by drought and by disrupted transportation, resulting from fighting between political groups. People from all over the world have made contributions to help starving Ethiopians, but civil strife has prevented much of the food from being distributed.

NATIONS OF EAST AFRICA

Ethiopia is the oldest independent nation in Africa, while Djibouti is one of the youngest independent nations. Most of the nations in the East African region became independent at about the same time during the early 1960s. Which is the largest country in East Africa?

Point out to students that the blue dashed line in the map represents international boundaries over water and the black dashed line represents disputed boundaries.

In a battle at Adowa in 1896, the Ethiopians defeated the Italians—the first time that Africans had successfully defended themselves against European forces. The Battle of Adowa discouraged further invasions of Ethiopia for nearly 40 years. Ethiopia in eastern Africa and Liberia in western Africa were the only two African nations not to experience European colonial rule.

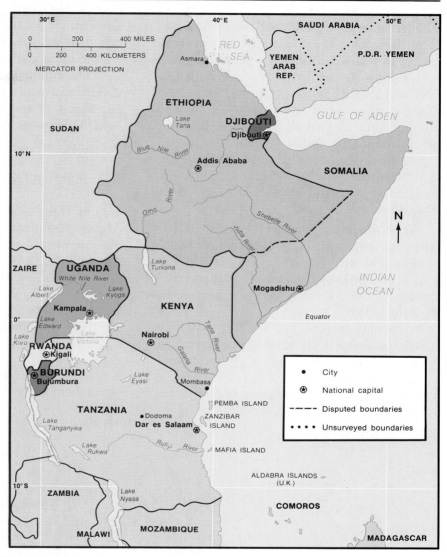

FIGURE 23-4

The military leaders who overthrew the government adopted socialist policies. They started a land reform program to put all land under government control and then divide it among the farmers. The new government became strong supporters of the Soviet Union. As cooperation with the Soviet Union increased, ties with the United States declined.

Somalia. Somalia faces the Gulf of Aden and the Indian Ocean. Before it became independent in 1960, it was the two separate colonies of Italian Somaliland and British Somaliland. Europeans had colonized the two areas during the mid-1800s. Covering an area of 246,201 square miles (637,660.1 sq km), it is about the size of California.

Somalia, which is hot and dry, is mostly agricultural. Many of the 7.7 million people who populate the country are pastoralists who raise livestock. They live together in large groups of relatives. When the grass and water are used up in one spot, they move on to a new one. Other Somalis are farmers who produce bananas, sugar, and grain. Most Somalis are Muslims. All speak Somali, a language first written down in the 1970s.

Only about one-third of the Somalis live in urban areas. The largest city is the capital, Mogadishu (MAHG uh DIHSH oo), with about 450,000 people.

Djibouti. Djibouti lies on the Gulf of Aden between Ethiopia and Somalia. With a land area of 8,494 square miles (21,999.4 sq km), it is a little larger than Massachusetts. A French colony for many years, it became independent in 1977.

Djibouti is very hot and dry with few natural resources. Its economy is based on shipping and transport. Because of its location on the Gulf of Aden, the capital city, Djibouti, is an important port. The railroad line that links it with Addis Ababa makes it an important outlet for Ethiopia's trade.

The country's 300,000 people are largely divided between two black African groups—Afars and Issas—who speak either Afar or Somali. Most are Muslims.

See the *TAE* for an *Objective 3* Activity.

3.2 East African Highlands

All three countries that make up the East African Highlands are small and landlocked. The largest is Uganda, with an area of 91,135 square miles (236,039.5 sq km). Next in size is Burundi, with 10,745 square miles (27,829.5 sq km). The smallest is Rwanda, with its area of 10,170 square miles (26,340.3 sq km). Together the three countries are about as large as New Mexico.

People go about their everyday business in Djibouti's capital city of the same name. Djibouti is the only sizable city in the country, and more than one-half of the population of the entire country lives here. Why is the city of Djibouti an important economic link?

Lake Assal, a body of salt water 80 miles (128.7 km) west of the city of Djibouti, is the lowest point in Africa and the second lowest point on Earth.

This view of Rwanda's rolling landscape could give the impression that people are few and far between in this country. Actually, Rwanda is the most densely populated country on the African continent. Which other country of East Africa has a high population density?

Because of the huge size of Africa, the countries of the East African Highlands may appear smaller than they are. Uganda, for example, actually is nearly as large as the United Kingdom.

The landscapes of Uganda, Burundi, and Rwanda are made up largely of mountains and high, rolling plateaus. Although all three countries are on or near the Equator, high elevations keep their climates mild.

Uganda, Burundi, and Rwanda are poor countries with few minerals and little industry. In each, agriculture is the major economic activity. Farmers raise livestock and grow enough cassava, corn, sweet potatoes, and other crops to feed their families. Coffee is the most important crop grown for export. The countries depend on it because there is little else to provide income.

Uganda, Burundi, and Rwanda are in the interior of the continent. There are few good roads or railroads. Uganda has a railroad line to Mombasa, Kenya, that serves Burundi and Rwanda, but it cannot be easily reached. All this makes it hard for these countries to be accessible to the rest of Africa. This especially makes it hard for them to get their goods to foreign buyers.

All three countries are heavily populated. Uganda is home to 15.9 million people, Burundi to 5 million, and Rwanda to 6.8 million. Rwanda and Burundi are among the most densely populated countries in Africa. Less than 10 percent of these people live in urban areas. In all three countries the capitals are the most important cities—Kampala (kam PAHL uh) in Uganda, Bujumbura (BOO juhm BUR uh) in Burundi, and Kigali (ky GAHL ee) in Rwanda.

There are 20 black ethnic groups in Uganda. In Burundi and Rwanda there are three—the Hutu, the Tutsi, and the Twa. The Hutu are more powerful in Rwanda. Although the Tutsi are in the minority in Burundi, they are more powerful in Burundi.

Until 1962 the countries of the East African Highlands were ruled by European nations. Uganda was governed by the United Kingdom. Burundi and Rwanda were a single territory known as Ruanda-Urundi. It was ruled by Belgium.

USING GRAPHIC SKILLS

READING PICTOGRAPHS

Many parks have signs posted that forbid littering. A common sign shows a slash bar drawn through a picture of a person tossing trash on the ground. No words are used, but the sign clearly reads "No Littering."

In your study of geography, you have learned how to read map symbols. For example, in maps showing a region's land use and resources, you know that symbols such as coal cars, oil derricks, trees, and fish mean that coal, petroleum, timber, and fish are found in certain places of that region.

Symbols are also commonly used in graphs. The illustration on page 493 uses symbols to give information about the countries of East Africa. Because the symbols are like pictures, this kind of graph is sometimes called a picture graph, or *pictograph*. The pictograph gives information about the population and life expectancy of each of the countries in East Africa. In the pictograph the picture of a person stands for one million people. If the picture is of less than a whole person, the symbol represents less than one million people. For example, in the column

showing population for Burundi, five people are pictured. This means that the population of Burundi is five million.

In the pictograph on page 493 a picture of a birthday cake stands for 10 years, and 1 birthday candle means 1 year. The column showing life expectancy in Burundi shows 4 birthday cakes and 8 birthday candles. This means that life expectancy in the country of Burundi is 48 years.

Study the pictograph on page 493. Then answer the questions that follow.

1. What country is the most populated? How many people live there?

2. In which country is life expectancy longest? Shortest?

3. What is the approximate population of Somalia? Of Uganda?

4. How many East African countries have a life expectancy rate equal to or above the African average? The world average?

5. **Challenge:** Make a hypothesis about how Ethiopia's population may affect its life expectancy rate.

See the *TAE* for an *Objective 4* Activity.

CONTENT CHECK

1. **Identify:** Horn of Africa, Ethiopia, Ras Dashan, Addis Ababa, Abyssinia, Haile Selassie I, Somalia, Djibouti, Afars, Issas, East African Highlands, Uganda, Burundi, Rwanda, Hutu, Tutsi, Twa.

2. What is the major economic activity of the Horn of Africa?

3. In what ways are the countries of the Horn of Africa alike?

4. What religions are found in the countries of the Horn of Africa?

5. Which East African country is one of the world's oldest nations?

6. What do the countries of the East African Highlands have in common?

7. Why are the countries of the East African Highlands so isolated from the rest of Africa?

8. **Challenge:** What do you think can be done to help the countries of the Horn of Africa and the East African Highlands develop?

AFRICA SOUTH OF THE SAHARA UNIT 8

EAST AFRICAN POPULATIONS AND LIFE EXPECTANCIES

COUNTRY	POPULATION	LIFE EXPECTANCY
Burundi	🯄🯄🯄🯄🯄	🁢🁢🁢🁢 ｜｜｜｜｜｜｜｜
Djibouti	(less than 1)	🁢🁢🁢🁢 ｜｜｜｜｜｜｜
Ethiopia	🯄🯄🯄🯄🯄 🯄🯄🯄🯄🯄 🯄🯄🯄🯄🯄 🯄🯄🯄🯄🯄 🯄🯄🯄 / 🯄🯄🯄🯄🯄 🯄🯄🯄🯄🯄 🯄🯄🯄🯄🯄 🯄🯄🯄🯄🯄 🯄🯄🯄	🁢🁢🁢🁢 ｜
Kenya	🯄🯄🯄🯄🯄 🯄🯄🯄🯄🯄 🯄🯄🯄🯄🯄 🯄🯄🯄🯄🯄 🯄🯄🯄	🁢🁢🁢🁢🁢 ｜｜｜｜
Rwanda	🯄🯄🯄🯄🯄 🯄🯄	🁢🁢🁢🁢 ｜｜｜｜｜｜｜｜
Somalia	🯄🯄🯄🯄🯄 🯄🯄🯄	🁢🁢🁢🁢 ｜
Tanzania	🯄🯄🯄🯄🯄 🯄🯄🯄🯄🯄 🯄🯄🯄🯄🯄 🯄🯄🯄🯄🯄 🯄🯄🯄🯄	🁢🁢🁢🁢🁢 ｜｜
Uganda	🯄🯄🯄🯄🯄 🯄🯄🯄🯄🯄 🯄🯄🯄🯄🯄 🯄	🁢🁢🁢🁢🁢

🯄 = 1 million people 🁢 = 10 years ｜ = 1 year

African average = 51 years
World average = 63 years

Data from Population Reference Bureau, Inc., 1987.

See the *TRB* for the *Chapter 23 Reading* on the Great Rift Valley of Africa.

CONCLUSION

Some of the countries of East Africa have made much economic progress since they became independent in the 1960s. Some have not. All have experienced change, and all still have problems they are trying to solve. Some have the highest rates of population growth in the world and economies that cannot keep pace with the growth of population.

East Africa is still largely agricultural. Most people farm, generally to feed their own families. They depend on traditional farming methods and spend long hours tending crops and animals, carrying water, and collecting wood for fuel. They also face the dangers of drought or heavy rainfall. Both ruin the soil and cause famine.

For most of these countries, new political problems came with independence. Differences in language, religion, and ethnic loyalty often work against unity. Yet, even with these difficulties, these countries are working to develop their natural resources, build industries, and improve agriculture. Some are now joining together to bring about change.

CHAPTER REVIEW

SUMMARY

1. The region of East Africa lies along the coast of the Indian Ocean, from Ethiopia in the north to Tanzania in the south. The countries of East Africa are Kenya, Tanzania, Ethiopia, Djibouti, Somalia, Uganda, Burundi, and Rwanda.

2. The Great Rift Valley and the East African Plateau are important physical features of the area. East Africa has dry and tropical moist climates.

3. Most East Africans are members of one of the many different black ethnic groups. Both Islam and Christianity are major religions. Kiswahili is a widely used language, but many other languages are spoken by smaller numbers of people.

4. Kenya has a capitalist economy. Farming is the major activity, but tourism is an important source of income for the entire country.

5. Tanzania has a socialist economy. Even though it is rich with minerals, the sale of crops is its major source of income.

6. All but Ethiopia have been independent nations only since the 1960s.

7. The countries of the Horn of Africa are Ethiopia, Somalia, and Djibouti. Ethiopia is the most populous and largest country in East Africa.

8. Most Somalians are farmers. Some are pastoralists, while others grow cash crops. Due to its location on the Gulf of Aden, Djibouti's economy centers on shipping.

9. The countries of the East African Highlands are Uganda, Burundi, and Rwanda. They have few minerals and little industry. They are among the most densely populated countries in Africa.

10. The countries of East Africa have many problems to solve. Some must adapt to physical environments that make it hard to earn a living. Others must strive to unify their many ethnic groups under one national government. All are struggling to develop their economies.

Answers to the following questions can be found on page T241.

REVIEWING VOCABULARY

On a separate sheet of paper, number from 1 to 10. Beside each number write the vocabulary word that matches each numbered definition below.

clove	sisal	tsetse flies	physical
cassava	pyrethrum	subsistence crops	anthropologists
cash crops	indigenous	pastoralists	

1. plant whose starchy root is used for food
2. used in making rope
3. spice
4. scientists who study remains of early people
5. native or original
6. nomadic herders
7. plants raised for farmers' own use
8. used in making insecticides
9. cause of disease in people and cattle
10. plants raised for sale

REMEMBERING THE FACTS

1. What are Kenya's two major cash crops?
2. At what rate per year is Kenya's population growing?
3. What is the most widely spoken language in East Africa?
4. What was the purpose of the Kenya African Union?
5. What is the highest peak of Africa? In what East African country is it?
6. Who introduced Islam to the people of Tanzania? Who introduced Roman Catholicism to them?
7. What three East African countries are landlocked?

UNDERSTANDING THE FACTS

1. Why is the Great Rift Valley an area of many volcanoes, lakes, and highlands?
2. In general, what accounts for temperature differences among places in Kenya?
3. How are the economies of Kenya and Tanzania the same? Different?
4. What discourages Tanzanians from living in the central part of their country? What are the government's plans to change this pattern?
5. Why is the location of the countries in the Horn of Africa important?

THINKING CRITICALLY AND CREATIVELY

1. Almost 85 percent of all Kenyans live in the southern part of the country. How do you explain this population pattern? Why is it not likely to change?
2. In Kenya a community campaign to plant trees in areas threatened by desertification was recently organized. The Green Belt Movement has planted more than two million trees in Kenya. Why do you think such programs are more successful than government-sponsored programs?
3. **Challenge:** Tanzania plans to develop its economy with better use of the natural resources of its central plateau. What steps would you take in order to carry out this development?
4. **Challenge:** Kenya and Tanzania consider their wild animals a natural resource, which people from all over the world enjoy. As the economies of these countries develop, what problems might occur to endanger the animals?

REINFORCING GRAPHIC SKILLS

Study the pictograph on page 493. Then answer the questions that follow.

1. How does Kenya rank among other East African countries in population? In life expectancy?
2. **Challenge:** Make a hypothesis about why Africa's average life expectancy is so much lower than the world average.

CHAPTER 24

Markets provide more than a place to purchase or sell goods. They also offer people opportunities to share news and to socialize.

Market in Abidjan, Ivory Coast

WEST AND CENTRAL AFRICA

In 1986 Ivory Coast officials asked other nations of the world to refer to their French-speaking nation as Côte d'Ivoire, the French form of Ivory Coast.

In this chapter you will learn—

- What are the major physical features and climates of West and Central Africa.
- What economic problems and opportunities face the countries of West and Central Africa.
- What ethnic groups make up the population of West and Central Africa.
- How Europeans have affected the development of West and Central Africa.

Students often underestimate Africa's size. Have them locate the United States on a globe and use a tape measure or string to measure the distance from Seattle to Boston. Now have them measure the distance from Dakar, Senegal, to southeastern Zaire, a distance more than 1,000 miles (1,609.3 km) greater than the first.

INTRODUCTION

The region of West and Central Africa lies south of the Sahel countries and west of East Africa. It stretches from Senegal on the Atlantic coast to Zaire in the heart of the continent.

The western part of the region, called West Africa, has a land area of 899,920 square miles (2,330,791 sq km). It lies between Lake Chad and the Atlantic Ocean, along the southern part of what might be called the "bulge of Africa"—the part of the African continent that sticks out into the Atlantic Ocean. Thirteen countries make up West Africa—Nigeria (ny JIHR ee ah), Benin (beh NEEN), Togo, Ghana (GAH nuh), Burkina Faso (bur KEE nuh FAH soh), Côte d'Ivoire (koht deev wahr), Liberia (ly BEER ee uh), Sierra Leone (see AIR uh lee OHN), Guinea (GIHN ee), Guinea-Bissau (GIHN ee bih SOW), Senegal (SEHN uh GAWL), The Gambia (GAM bee uh), and Cape Verde (VUHRD).

The eastern part of the region, known as Central Africa, has a land area of 1,576,259 square miles (4,082,507.6 sq km). It is made up of seven countries—Zaire (zah IHR), Congo, Central African Republic, Gabon (ga BOHN), Cameroon, Equatorial Guinea, and São Tomé and Príncipe (SOWN taw MEH) (PREEN see puh).

The climates and landscapes of West and Central Africa are very much alike. The long Atlantic coast of the region is low and marshy with few good harbors. Inland the land gradually rises to form high plateaus.

Many contrasts are found among the countries in this region. The largest population and the richest mineral resources are found in the largest countries, Nigeria and Zaire. Many other countries depend on subsistence farming and the sale of a few exports.

Many people of the region are descended from Bantu-speaking peoples who came to the area almost 1,000 years ago. Still others are descended from Europeans who came to the region in later times.

Central Africa's seven countries occupy an area equal to about 45% of the area of the United States.

1. WEST AFRICA

Some of the earliest and greatest kingdoms and empires of ancient times arose in West Africa. Today the 13 countries that

497

Have students compare the Physical Regions map below with the Land Use and Resources map on page 507 and the political map on page 505.

PHYSICAL REGIONS OF WEST AND CENTRAL AFRICA _____

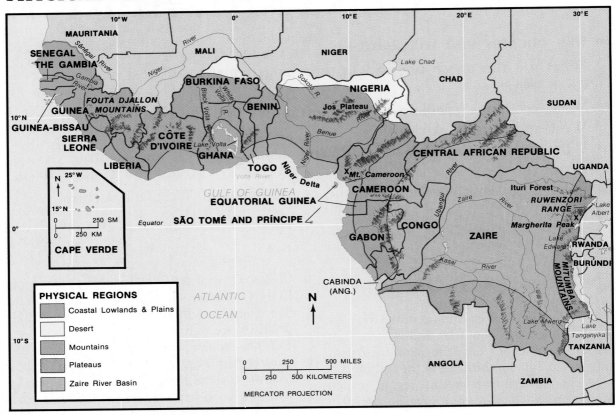

FIGURE 24-1
A band of lowlands borders the region's Atlantic coast. Plateaus, interrupted by mountains in Cameroon and the Zaire River Basin, parallel the coastal regions. In which countries are desert regions located?

Refer students to pages 96-97 to review the map of Earth's Climate Regions.

make up West Africa are home to many different ethnic groups, each with its own traditions. Both they and their nations have been influenced by their colonial pasts.

Nigeria is larger than every country in Europe except the Soviet Union.

1.1 Nigeria

The Federal Republic of Nigeria covers 356,668 square miles (923,769.4 sq km). It is the largest country of West Africa and the seventh largest on the African continent. It has a rich variety of landscapes, climates, peoples, and the human and natural resources needed to make it prosperous.

Landscape and Climate. Nigeria has many kinds of landscapes. Along the Gulf of Guinea is mostly coastal lowland, much of which is mangrove swamps. Near the sea the Niger River forms a large delta. Away from the coast the land rises to a gently sloping plain covered by tropical rain forests and palm bushes. North of this is a high plateau. As Figure 24-1 on this page shows, the plateau covers about one-half of the country. In the middle is the highest elevation, the Jos Plateau, with highlands more than 5,000 feet (1,524 m). The many small rivers and streams that drain the Jos Plateau flow south into the Niger and Benue (BAYN way) rivers.

AFRICA SOUTH OF THE SAHARA UNIT 8

The Niger is the third largest river in Africa. It begins in far western Africa, flows north into Niger, runs south through Nigeria, and empties into the Gulf of Guinea. The Benue runs from the east across Nigeria. Near the center of the country it flows into the Niger River. A smaller river—the Sokoto—drains areas to the north. North and east of the Sokoto the landscape is desert.

Like most of West Africa, Nigeria's climate is tropical moist with two seasons, dry and wet. In the north the dry season lasts from October through April. In the south it lasts from November through March. The dryness is the result of the **harmattan** (HAHR muh TAN), a dusty wind from the Sahara. Annual rainfall varies from 25 inches (63.5 cm) in the north to about 150 inches (381 cm) in coastal areas. Temperatures are warm or hot year-round.

Economic and Cultural Patterns.
Agriculture is one of the most important parts of Nigeria's economy. About 70 percent of the workers are farmers who own land. Most farms average about 2.5 acres (1 ha). Farmers grow food crops for their own use. Many also produce cash crops such as peanuts, cotton, rubber, palm products, and **cacao,** which is used to make chocolate. Nigeria used to be a world leader in these crops. It grew enough to take care of its peoples' needs as well as sell to others. In the 1980s, however, Nigeria began to import food. This led the government to take steps to improve agriculture and grow more food.

Improving agriculture means teaching new ways, which takes time. In Nigeria, as in many parts of Africa, farmers have practiced shifting cultivation for many years. They cut down branches and other plant growth, let them dry, and burn them. They then plant the cleared land, made fertile by the ashes. After a few seasons, the land will lose its fertility. It will not be good for farming again for at least 10 years. During this time farmers will find new areas to clear and then farm. With a rapidly growing population and little good land, slash-and-burn farming is no longer efficient.

Nigeria also has several important mineral resources, including tin, iron ore, coal, and **columbite,** a mineral used in producing stainless steel. The most important is petroleum. Nigeria is one of the world's top 10 petroleum producers. Oil exports make up over 90 percent of the country's income.

Nigeria is home to 108.6 million people—more than any other country in Africa. As Figure 24-2 on this page shows, they are crowded into an area one-tenth the size of the United States. The people are divided into 250 ethnic groups. The largest are the Hausa-Fulani (HOW suh FOO LAHN ee), the Yoruba (YAWR uh buh), and the Ibo (EE boh). About one-half of all Nigerians are Muslims. Close to 30 percent are Christians. Nearly 20 percent practice local religions. Many Nigerians combine traditional African beliefs with Christianity and Islam. About 75 percent of Nigerians live in towns and villages in walled-in groups of dried mud, wood, or grass houses. The villages are centers of traditional African culture.

In recent years many Nigerians have moved to cities. This movement, plus growth

Cacao beans, from which chocolate is made, are white. The dark color comes only after processing.

COMPAR-A-GRAPH: NIGERIA-UNITED STATES

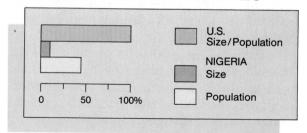

FIGURE 24-2
Nigeria's large population lives in a small area. How does its population compare to that of the U.S.?

The mosque at Kano, Nigeria, attracts many people to worship every Friday afternoon. Friday is a special day of prayer in the Islamic religion, similar to the Sabbath in other religions. How was Islam introduced to this part of West Africa?

See the TAE for an Objective 1 Activity.

in population, has led to a growth of cities. Today Lagos, Ibadan (ih BAHD uhn), and Kano (KAHN oh) all have populations of more than one million people. Lagos, on the southwestern coast, is the largest city in Nigeria, with more than four million people. It is the national capital and a center of light industry. Ibadan, inland in the southeast, and Kano, in the far north, each have about one million people. Many of Nigeria's cities are overcrowded and unable to provide enough housing or services for all people.

Influences of the Past. One of the earliest peoples to live in West Africa was the Nok of central Nigeria. Their civilization reached its height of development between 500 BC and 200 AD.

Later, about 1000 AD, a people called the Hausa set up states in the north that traded with countries in North Africa and the Middle East. The Hausa states remained powerful until the 1800s, when they were taken over by a Muslim people called the Fulani. The Fulani set up a powerful Islamic empire that took in most of northern Nigeria.

About 1400 AD, another people, known as Yoruba, founded a kingdom in southwestern Nigeria. At about the same time, the Ibo culture developed in the southeast. When Europeans came to Nigeria during the 1600s and 1700s, the Yoruba and the Ibo traded precious metals and slaves with them. European traders shipped the slaves from the port of Lagos to the Americas. In time European missionaries arrived, bringing Christianity and European culture.

By the mid-1800s the British had become the leading European group in Nigeria. In 1861 they captured Lagos and made it a colony. By 1914 they ruled the whole country. The Nigerians did not want British rule and, finally, in 1960 gained independence.

After independence, problems arose among some of the country's regions and ethnic groups. In 1967 Ibo military leaders declared their region in the east a country separate from the rest of Nigeria. They called their country the Republic of Biafra (bee AF ruh). This led to civil war. The war ended in 1970 when the national government defeated Biafra. After the war Nigerians adopted a new plan of government in the hope of making national unity more important than ethnic differences.

Missionaries worked their way into the interior by following waterways. In Nigeria the Niger River was a major transportation artery.

1.2 Other Countries of West Africa

The other 12 countries of West Africa lie west of Nigeria and south of the Sahel. The climates and economic activities of these countries are much the same. Like Nigeria, all are home to many different ethnic groups.

Landscape and Climate. Fanning out east and west across Africa south of the Sahel is an irregular plateau known outside of Nigeria as the Guinea Plateau. Much of this plateau is rugged, hilly, and covered with grasses and some trees. The highest part is formed by

European explorers followed coastal rivers inland. In time, these routes to the interior became political boundaries. Usually, tribal groups extended for considerable distances parallel to the coast. Boundaries created by Europeans often divided members of a single tribe into two, three, or even more countries.

COLONIALISM IN AFRICA

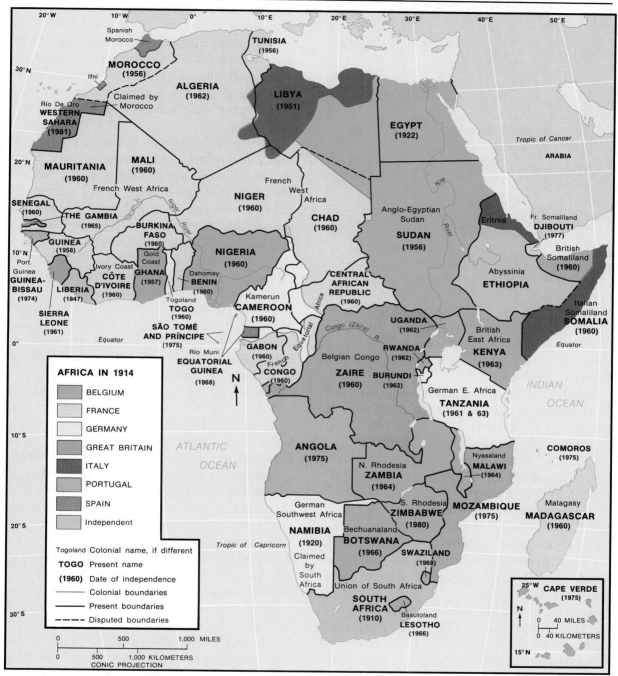

FIGURE 24-3

Africa "belonged" to Europe for much of this century. Upon gaining independence, leaders of the new African nations worked together to help build a sense of African unity, to work on similar problems, and to encourage economic co-operation. Which nation of present-day Africa was the most recent to gain independence?

CHAPTER 24   **WEST AND CENTRAL AFRICA**

Music is a major art form that has had practical uses. Drums and other musical instruments were once used to send messages. Protest songs inspired Africans as they struggled for independence from colonial rule. West Africans also have a rich tradition of oral literature, stories told from generation to generation.

This plantation worker in Guinea loosens bark from cinchona trees that will be made into quinine for medicine. What other West African cash crops are grown?

See the *TRB* for the *Section 1 Extending the Lesson* on juju music.

the Fouta Djallon (FOO tuh juh LOHN). These mountains are the source of the area's most important rivers—the Niger, Senegal, Gambia, and Volta.

South of the plateau and along the Gulf of Guinea is a coastal strip with few natural harbors. This lowland is 50 miles (80.5 km) to almost 400 miles (643.7 km) wide.

Much of the plateau has a tropical savanna climate with a short dry season. Although at Ouagadougou (WAHG uh DOO goo) in Burkina Faso almost no rain falls between late October and February, the total rainfall for the year is 35.2 inches (89.4 cm). Along the coast from Guinea to the Ivory Coast, the yearly rainfall varies between 60 inches (152.4 cm) and 170 inches (431.8 cm), and it is warm and humid all year.

Economic and Cultural Patterns. The major economic activity of most of the West African countries is farming. More than one-half of the workers of each country are farmers. Goods that cannot be made or grown are obtained by trading at **periodic markets,** markets held in rural areas every third or fourth day. Here farmers barter, or exchange without using money, extra produce.

Major cash crops, such as peanuts and cotton, generally are grown on large farms and plantations. Rubber plantations are especially important in Liberia. Because all the countries grow much the same crops, each trades more with other countries than with each other.

Some West African countries also export minerals. Guinea, for example, exports bauxite, of which it has one-third of the world's reserves. Iron ore makes up 60 percent of Liberia's exports. Sierra Leone exports diamonds and some bauxite, Ghana diamonds and some gold, and Togo phosphates.

Influences of the Past. By the late 1200s and early 1300s, many small kingdoms had arisen in West Africa. In time, inland areas were included in the empires of Ghana, Malinke (muh LIHNG kee), and Songhai (sawng hy). As late as the 1800s, the states of Benin and Ashanti controlled much of the land along the coast.

In the 1200s, attracted by mineral wealth and the large population, Arab traders came to West Africa. They brought with them Islam and the culture of the Middle East. They were followed in the 1400s by the Europeans —Portuguese, British, French. They brought with them Christianity, their languages, and their form of government. Over several hundred years, they colonized parts of the area.

Figure 24-3 on page 501 shows Africa as it was ruled by colonial powers in 1914. It also presents the independent African countries of today. In West Africa the Portuguese ruled Cape Verde and part of Guinea, known as Portuguese Guinea. In the mid-1970s Cape Verde and Guinea-Bissau, now called Portuguese Guinea, became independent. The Portuguese influence remains strong even today. Most people of Cape Verde and Guinea-Bissau speak *Crioulo,* a language made up of Portuguese and African words.

AFRICA SOUTH OF THE SAHARA UNIT 8

France ruled a large area known as French West Africa. After the defeat of Germany in World War I, the French also gained control of the German colony of Togo. Between 1958 and 1960, all of France's colonies in the region became independent. They include the present-day countries of Senegal, Guinea, Côte d'Ivoire, Benin, and Burkina Faso. French language and culture, however, remain widespread in these countries.

Until 1957 the United Kingdom controlled the colonies of Gambia, the Gold Coast, Sierra Leone, and Nigeria. That year the Gold Coast became independent. It became known as Ghana, after the ancient African empire of that name. By 1965 independence also came to the other British colonies in the region. As with the Portuguese and French, much of the British culture, including language, remains.

The only West African country that was never a colony is Liberia. In 1816 members of the American Colonization Society in the United States bought land in Africa. It paid for some 15,000 freed American slaves to move to and settle the land. Today descendants of those slaves make up only about 5 percent of Liberia's population.

Liberia's capital, Monrovia, is named for the fifth president of the United States, James Monroe.

CONTENT CHECK

1. **Identify:** Gulf of Guinea, Niger River, Hausa-Fulani, Yoruba, Ibo, Lagos, Ibadan, Biafra, Fouta Djallon Mountains, Senegal River, Gambia River, Volta River, Songhai, American Colonization Society.

2. **Define:** harmattan, cacao, columbite, periodic markets.

3. What are the 13 countries of West Africa?

4. What are the major landscapes and climate of Nigeria?

5. Where is Nigeria's largest city? What is its population?

6. What is the major economic activity in West Africa?

7. Which West African country was never a European colony?

8. **Challenge:** What changes might be made to encourage greater unity among the people of West Africa?

See the TAE for an Objective 2 Activity.

2. CENTRAL AFRICA

Central Africa is made up of seven countries. Of these, one country—Zaire—takes up 57 percent of the land area. Of the 48.5 million people who live in Central Africa, 66 percent live in Zaire. Although all Central African countries, shown in Figure 24-4 on page 505, are independent today, only Zaire has made major economic progress since gaining independence.

See the TRB for the Section 2 Extending the Lesson on the Zaire River.

Stretching into the distance is part of Zaire's tropical savanna. How much of Central Africa's land area does Zaire cover?

STRANGE BUT TRUE

THAT IS NO JUNGLE

The large, broadleaf, evergreen forests of Brazil, West Africa, Central Africa, and Southeast Asia are mistakenly called *jungles*. Geographers correctly call these areas *tropical rain forests*. If a jungle is not the same as a tropical rain forest, what exactly is a jungle?

A **jungle,** like the one pictured above, is a dense growth of plants found in tropical rain forests. In most tropical rain forests, the tops of closely spaced trees form a kind of umbrella that blocks sunlight from reaching the forest floor. Plants must have sunlight to grow. Therefore, a tropical rain forest that has closely spaced tall trees will not have a lot of dense underbrush.

Jungles develop in the tropical rain forest areas where sunlight enters the forest, generally in clearings, on slopes, or along banks of rivers and streams. Suppose, for example, that areas of a tropical rain forest have been cleared. In time, as sunlight reaches the ground, plants will begin to grow. These plants grow, die, and are replaced by new plants in the space left by the cleared trees.

Jungles that develop in clearings are often so dense that a person must cut away the growth to be able to walk through them. Jungles in clearings last only as long as trees re-main small. Once trees are large enough to provide shade, underbrush begins to die from lack of sunlight, and the area again becomes part of the tropical rain forest.

Permanent jungles often appear on steep slopes in tropical rain forests. In these places the treetop-umbrella effect is less complete than it is on level ground. Trees on slopes generally allow sunlight to reach the floor of the forest.

In jungles located along the sloping banks of rivers and streams, dense, tangled plant growth extends from sunlit areas over shallow water onto drier land areas. This type of jungle is called a *wet jungle* because it is difficult to tell where the land begins and where the water ends. Wet jungles are common because few large shade trees can take root in shallow water.

The presence of wet jungles in tropical rain forests is responsible for the fact that many people think of all tropical rain forests as jungles. Early European explorers in Brazil, Africa, and Asia were the first to make the mistake. These visitors to new lands usually moved inland from the coast by way of the rivers and streams. They seldom left their boats. Since they saw mostly jungle-fringed banks, they concluded that dense jungles covered all tropical rain forests. The mistake has been continued over the years by stories, books, and movies about these areas. Many people still use the term *jungle* incorrectly.

1. Where are Earth's major tropical rain forests?
2. Why are most tropical rain forest areas not actually jungles?
3. Why do people often confuse tropical rain forests and jungles?
4. What areas within rain forests are most likely to be covered by jungles?

504

NATIONS OF WEST AND CENTRAL AFRICA

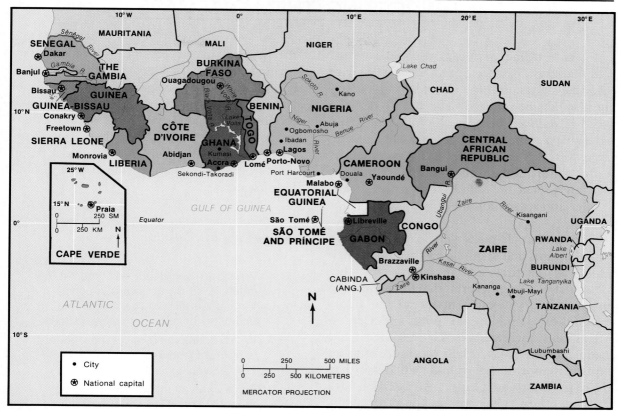

FIGURE 24-4
Zaire is the region's largest country in size; Nigeria, in population. Liberia, founded by black Americans, is the region's oldest independent nation. Generally, where are most national capitals located?

Changed in 1971, Zaire's name is derived from a Kikongo word, *nzadi,* meaning "river."

2.1 Zaire

Zaire is the third largest country of the African continent. It covers an area of 905,564 square miles (2,345,408.9 sq km). In population it ranks fifth among African countries. Because of its mineral wealth, it could become a major economic power in the next century.

Landscape and Climate. The major feature of Zaire's landscape is the Zaire River Basin. Although most of it lies in Zaire, some also runs into the Central African Republic and the Republic of Congo. One of the world's largest tropical rain forests covers much of the rolling plains of the basin. The Ituri Forest in the northeast is part of this area.

To the south the basin is surrounded by the Angolan and Shaba plateaus. To the east are the Mitumba Mountains. The Zaire River and its tributaries drain these areas and flow into the Atlantic Ocean to the west. Except for the Zaire River, the country is almost landlocked. Its only outlet to the sea is a narrow strip of land north of the mouth of the river.

Running 2,718 miles (4,374.2 km), the Zaire is Africa's second longest river. Only the Amazon River of South America carries a greater volume of water. Many rapids and waterfalls are found along the course of the

USING GRAPHIC SKILLS

INTERPRETING THEMATIC MAPS

While riding in a car, you pass a road sign that says "Reduce Speed Ahead." As you read this sign, you think about why the speed ahead might be reduced. You decide that the speed is reduced because the highway ahead has a sharp curve in it or because the highway passes through an area that has a great deal of traffic going through all the time. You have just interpreted the sign. To interpret means to offer an explanation for words, symbols, or statistics.

In earlier chapters you learned how to read the signs and symbols on thematic maps. This was the first step in interpreting thematic maps. To interpret the thematic map on page 507, you must first read the colors that indicate land use in West and Central Africa and the symbols for resources and manufacturing areas. Then you must offer an explanation for the colors and symbols as they apply to West and Central Africa. You also must take into consideration the other items on the map. For example, answering questions like the following will help you interpret the map relative to the location of manufacturing areas: What is the symbol for manufacturing areas? What color represents bodies of water? Where are the manufacturing areas located? Where are the bodies of water located? Based on your answers to these questions, what is the relationship in West and Central Africa between manufacturing areas and bodies of water?

Study the map on page 507. Then answer the questions that follow.

1. Where are petroleum resources located in West and Central Africa? What generalization can you make about the location of these resources?

2. Which country shows the most variety in terms of land use and resources? How do you know this?

3. This region might not commonly be thought to have industrial importance. Does the information on this map support or argue against this view?

Zaire. Because of the rapids, ocean ships can travel only about 100 miles (160.9 km) up the river from the Atlantic Ocean.

The Mitumba Mountains, which run north and south, include Zaire's highest peak, Margherita, at 16,762 feet (5,109.1 m). East of the mountains, along Zaire's border with the countries of East Africa, is a part of the Great Rift Valley.

Zaire has a tropical rain forest climate through the northern half of the country in which the Equator lies. The southern half has a tropical savanna climate. Rain falls regularly year round in the Zaire River Basin. The av- erage amount of rain for the whole country is about 42 inches (106.7 cm) a year. North of the Equator the rainy season lasts from April through November. In the south rain falls regularly between October and May.

Economic and Cultural Patterns. Zaire's economy is based largely on agriculture, with about 85 percent of the people farmers. Most farmers work small plots of land on which they grow food for their families. Some also sell food products in the local marketplace.

About 80 percent of the agricultural products that Zaire exports are from large

AFRICA SOUTH OF THE SAHARA   UNIT 8

LAND USE AND RESOURCES OF WEST AND CENTRAL AFRICA

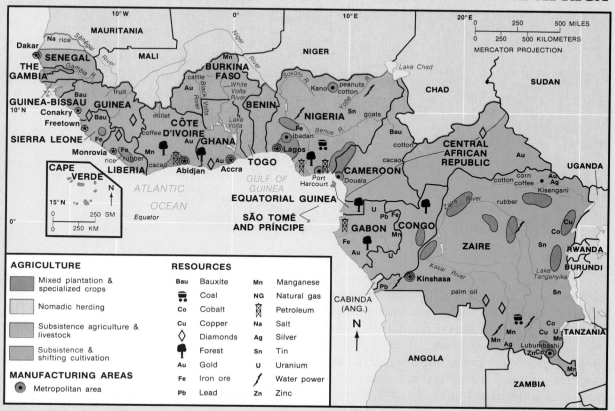

AGRICULTURE

- Mixed plantation & specialized crops
- Nomadic herding
- Subsistence agriculture & livestock
- Subsistence & shifting cultivation

MANUFACTURING AREAS

- ⊙ Metropolitan area

RESOURCES

Bau	Bauxite	Mn	Manganese
	Coal	NG	Natural gas
Co	Cobalt		Petroleum
Cu	Copper	Na	Salt
	Diamonds	Ag	Silver
	Forest	Sn	Tin
Au	Gold	U	Uranium
Fe	Iron ore		Water power
Pb	Lead	Zn	Zinc

Ask students why port cities, such as Abidjan and Port Harcourt, enjoy some economic advantages.

plantations. The major cash crops are coffee, rubber, and palm oil. Small farms grow cotton and peanuts to sell to other countries.

Although about 25 percent of Zaire's land could be used for farming, only about 3 percent is being used at present. In Zaire, as in most of tropical Africa, farming and herding are difficult because of such threats as tsetse flies and locusts.

Zaire is rich in mineral resources. These minerals greatly boost the country's income. Among other minerals, Zaire mines large amounts of manganese, tin, and gold. The most important mineral is copper. Zaire ranks sixth in its production. It brings in nearly 50 percent of the country's export income.

Zaire also is one of the world's largest sources of industrial diamonds, the diamonds used in drills. It also is the world's major source of **cobalt,** a magnetic element used in making metals.

Zaire has some important energy resources. There is oil in the narrow strip of land near the Atlantic Ocean and offshore. There are deposits of natural gas in Lake Kivu in the east. In addition, the country's large river system could provide about 13 percent of the world's hydroelectricity.

Kinshasa, Zaire, has many features associated with larger cities anywhere in the world. This city lies along the Zaire River, visible in the background. Kinshasa, the center of Zaire's government, is also an educational and cultural center. What benefits and problems result from Zairians moving to cities?

Lead a discussion on problems of building a modern economy in a nation where many people have very little technical literature available to them.

Since the 1960s industry has become more important in Zaire. The leading manufactured goods are light machinery, food products, beverages, tires, and textiles.

Zaire has a population of 31.8 million people divided into many different ethnic and language groups. There are more than 700 languages and dialects in all. Four of these— Lingala (lihng GAHL uh), Kingwana, Kikongo, and Tshiluba (chih LOO buh)— are spoken in large areas of the country. Along with French they have become Zaire's official languages.

About 70 percent of the people of Zaire are Christians. Nearly three-fourths of these are Roman Catholics. Some practice Christianity along with traditional religions.

Most Zairians live in rural areas in small villages of about ten to a few hundred people. Houses are made from mud bricks or dried mud and sticks. Many have thatched roofs.

Since the 1960s many Zairians, mostly young people, have moved to the cities in search of jobs in business, industry, and government. This has led to unemployment and overcrowding. Large numbers of factory and office workers live in crowded parts of the cities in cheap houses or apartments made from cinder blocks or baked mud bricks. The more well-to-do live in attractive bungalows or high-rise apartment buildings.

In Zaire the government has decreed that voting is mandatory for anyone over the age of 18.

AFRICAN URBAN CENTERS

CITY	POPULATION
Kinshasa, Zaire	5,000,000
Lagos, Nigeria	4,189,000
Abidjan, Ivory Coast	1,800,000
Accra, Ghana	1,500,000
Ibadan, Nigeria	1,500,000
Addis Ababa, Ethiopia	1,465,000
Nairobi, Kenya	1,300,000
Dar es Salaam, Tanzania	1,096,000
Dakar, Senegal	975,000
Conakry, Guinea	656,000

Data from Population Reference Bureau, Inc., 1987.

FIGURE 24-5
This chart offsets any myths describing Africa as a land of jungles and small villages. Which African country has two very large cities?

Kinshasa is Zaire's capital and largest city. As Figure 24-5 on page 508 shows, it is also one of the largest urban centers in Africa. About five million people live in its metropolitan area. The city itself has a population of more than three million.

Influences of the Past. Among the first to live in the area of Zaire was a people called Pygmies. Less than 5 feet (1.5 m) in height, Pygmies were nomadic hunters and gatherers. Today only a few thousand live in Zaire, mostly in the Ituri Forest.

Next to move into the area, about 2,000 years ago, were people from East Africa and the Nile River Valley. By the 1400s AD, more than 200 ethnic groups lived in the area. Several of these groups set up powerful kingdoms. The largest were the Kongo, Kuba, Luba, and Lunda.

The first Europeans to arrive were the Portuguese, who came in the late 1400s. They made a trade agreement with the Kongo. The major item traded was slaves. From about 1500 to 1800, the Portuguese slave trade drained the population of large areas of Central Africa.

In 1878 King Leopold of Belgium took over much of present-day Zaire. Known as the Congo Free State, the area was more the king's own private plantation than a Belgian colony. Leopold's harsh treatment of Africans drew protests from around the world. In 1908

The collage highlights the rich cultural heritage of West and Central Africa. Note the fourteenth century king of Mali, the intricately carved wooden mask, and the contrasting urban and rural settings.

Pictured here are past and present aspects of West Africa's culture. Kwame Nkrumah was an African nationalist and became the first president of independent Ghana. Modern-day flags of Ghana (right) and Mali (left) call to mind the earlier native African kingdoms of the same name. What do the shackles on the lower right symbolize?

CHAPTER 24   WEST AND CENTRAL AFRICA

WORLD ECONOMIC DEVELOPMENT

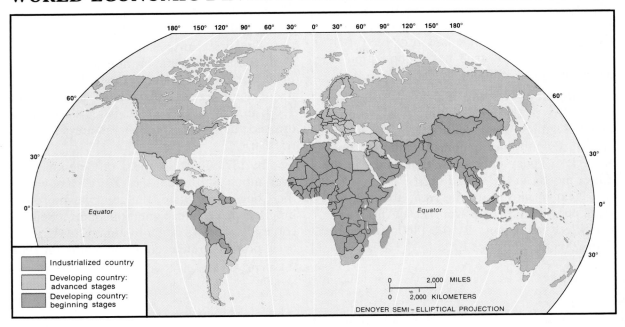

FIGURE 24-6
This map shows levels of economic development of the countries of Africa, as well as the countries of the world. In general, industrialized countries have manufacturing-based economies and higher gross national products. Developing countries have more or less agricultural-based economies and lower GNPs. What other regions of the world match Africa in their economic development?

Refer students to the maps on pages 498 and 507. Lead a discussion on the impact that physical regions and land use and resources may have on a country's development.

the Belgian government seized control from Leopold, and the area became known as the Belgian Congo.

In 1960 the Belgian Congo became an independent nation known as Congo. It was one of the first African nations to become independent. But regional conflicts and civil war kept the country divided. Then, in the 1970s, the country began to work to erase signs of European culture and to show pride in African traditions. The name of the country was changed to Zaire. The Congo River became the Zaire River. The capital city, Leopoldville, became Kinshasa.

Today the government of Zaire wants to unify the country's ethnic groups. It hopes to create a common African culture that will bind all Zairians.

2.2 Other Countries of Central Africa

Bordering Zaire on the north and northeast are the six other countries of Central Africa. Compared to Zaire each of these is small in land area and population. The population of all six together account for only 34 percent of the total population of Central Africa.

Landscape and Climate. Central Africa has a low, marshy plain that slowly rises to a huge, well-watered plateau in the landlocked Central African Republic. Farther west, mountains rise above the landscape of northern Cameroon.

All of the countries of Central Africa have hot and humid tropical moist climates,

AFRICA SOUTH OF THE SAHARA   UNIT 8

and tropical rain forests cover much of the area. Gabon, for example, is 75 percent forest, and about one-half of Congo is made up of thickly matted tropical plants.

Economic and Cultural Patterns.

Figure 24-6 on page 510 shows the levels of economic development for countries all over the world. For many different reasons, most African countries are only beginning to develop their economies. The climate and rain forests of Central Africa limit the area's economic development and the space where people can live. Most people make their living by farming. Among the major cash crops in Equatorial Guinea, Gabon, Cameroon, and São Tomé and Príncipe are coffee, cacao beans, coconuts, and bananas. In Congo they are peanuts and palm kernels. In Central African Republic they are cotton and coffee.

Only recently discovered by satellite observation, mineral and energy wealth has not yet been developed. Oil and natural gas are found in waters off the coasts of Cameroon, Equatorial Guinea, Gabon, and Congo. Diamonds and uranium make up most of Central African Republic's export income. Uranium, gold, manganese, and petroleum are exported by Gabon.

Like other parts of Africa, these Central African countries are home to many different ethnic groups. Most people speak at least two of the hundreds of languages found throughout the area. Most also have been influenced by many African and European cultures.

Influences of the Past.

The first settlers in this area were Bantu-speaking peoples who moved in 1,000 years ago. In the 1400s Portuguese explorers arrived, and Spanish, Dutch, and British traders soon followed. By the 1800s France and Germany had colonies in the area. Until 1960, when they became independent, Gabon, Congo, Central African Republic, and the Sahel country of Chad made up French Equatorial Africa.

Cameroon was a German colony in the late 1800s. After World War I, the colony was divided between France and the United Kingdom. In 1960 the two parts joined together as the independent Republic of Cameroon.

CONTENT CHECK

1. **Identify:** Zaire River, Kinshasa, Pygmies, King Leopold.
2. **Define:** jungle, cobalt.
3. What countries are in Central Africa?
4. Why is farming difficult in Zaire and in much of Central Africa?
5. What problems did Zaire have after independence?
6. What is the general climate of Central Africa?
7. What valuable resources are found in Central Africa?
8. **Challenge:** What effects might the slave trade have had on the development of West and Central Africa?

In August 1986 more than 1,700 people in Cameroon died from poisonous gases released during a gas burst from under a volcanic lake.

CONCLUSION

The region of West and Central Africa is large in size and rich in human and natural resources. Although it has political problems, it has the possibility of very great economic growth in the years to come. At present people of the region are working to raise their standard of living. Income from the sale of minerals may help them reach their goal.

In order for economic growth to take place, stable governments are needed. The long-standing rivalries that exist among many ethnic groups of the region are a threat to stability. Many Africans hope that their common heritage will help them bring unity and prosperity to the region.

SUMMARY

1. The region of West and Central Africa extends from the Atlantic coast of Senegal east to Nigeria and south through Zaire. West Africa includes those countries from Nigeria west to Senegal along the southern part of the bulge of Africa. Central Africa is made up of those countries that run from Zaire to Nigeria. All the countries of the region have similar climates and landscapes.

2. Many different ethnic groups live in West Africa and Central Africa. Many of them are distantly related to Bantu-speaking peoples that came to the region about 1,000 years ago.

3. All of the countries of West Africa and Central Africa, except Liberia, were once European colonies.

4. Nigeria is the largest nation of West Africa both in size and in population. It also has more people than any other nation in Africa.

5. Although agriculture remains important, Nigeria's economy is based on the sale of oil. Like many West African countries, Nigeria has a good supply of minerals.

6. While most Nigerians still live in the countryside, Nigerian cities have been growing rapidly in recent years.

7. Zaire is the largest nation of Central Africa in size and population.

8. Zaire is among the world's leading producers of copper and diamonds. It also is the world's major source of cobalt and has some important energy resources. In years to come, it may become a major economic power.

9. The smaller countries of Central Africa have had slower economic growth than other parts of Africa. As in other parts, most of the people have been influenced by both African and European cultures.

10. The economies of West Africa and Central Africa are largely agricultural. Many valuable minerals have been discovered in the region. However, ways to uncover both the mineral and energy wealth have not yet been fully developed.

Answers to the following questions can be found on page T248.

REVIEWING VOCABULARY

Number your paper from one to six. Beside each number write the vocabulary word from the list below that best describes each phrase. Then use each word in a complete sentence that shows you understand its meaning. You will not use all of the terms listed.

1. magnetic element used in making metals
2. area of thickly growing tropical plants
3. dry, dusty wind from the Sahara
4. used in making chocolate
5. farmers' exchange held in rural areas every few days
6. mineral used in making steel

cacao
columbite
harmattan
Crioulo
jungle
cobalt
periodic market

REMEMBERING THE FACTS

1. In general, what is the climate of Nigeria and the rest of West Africa?
2. What are the three largest ethnic groups of Nigeria?
3. What major agricultural products are exported by the countries of West Africa?
4. What European countries once had colonies in West Africa?
5. What type of vegetation covers much of Central Africa?
6. How do most of the people of Central Africa make a living?

UNDERSTANDING THE FACTS

1. Why is Nigeria considered the leader among countries of West Africa?
2. Why is shifting cultivation a wasteful way to farm?
3. Why do some West African countries trade more with the United States and Japan than with each other?
4. Why can the economic future of Zaire be considered bright?
5. What limits economic development in Central Africa?
6. From what early culture do most of the people in West Africa and Central Africa come?

THINKING CRITICALLY AND CREATIVELY

1. Oil accounts for almost 95 percent of Nigeria's exports. Should Nigeria rely so heavily on oil? Why or why not?
2. Nigeria is planning to move its capital inland to get people to settle the area. Is this a workable plan? Why or why not?
3. Nigeria's unity is still threatened by ethnic loyalties. How can Nigeria strengthen national feeling among its people?
4. Why do you think the majority of Christian Zairians are Roman Catholics?
5. **Challenge:** Much of Central Africa is not economically developed. One of the key factors preventing development in some areas is the presence of many tropical diseases. Suggest a plan by which disease can be reduced and the area made healthful for humans.
6. **Challenge:** If Zaire is able to use the hydroelectric power of the Zaire River fully, what effect would it have on the country?

REINFORCING GRAPHIC SKILLS

Study the map on page 507. Then answer the questions that follow.

1. Why would international businesses dealing in precious metals have interest in setting up business in this part of Africa?
2. Where are water power resources located? On what does the location of these resources depend?

CHAPTER 25

Southern Africa, like the rest of the continent, has many different ethnic groups, languages, cultures, and religions.

Mapoch women of Ndebele village in Pretoria, South Africa

SOUTHERN AFRICA

The countries of Southern Africa have long and rich historical traditions. Today each is working to achieve a better standard of living for its peoples without forsaking its past.

In this chapter you will learn—

● What landscapes and climates are found in Southern Africa.

● How the economies and cultures of Southern African countries have developed.

● How the past has influenced the growth of Southern African nations.

Most of the lands in Southern Africa were first used by Europeans as ports for ships bound for southern and eastern Asia. As the region's own natural resources were discovered, Europeans set up colonies there.

INTRODUCTION

The region of Southern Africa lies south of Zaire and Tanzania. It runs about 1,928 miles (3,102.8 km) from northern Angola to the southern tip of South Africa. Fourteen countries, all in the Southern Hemisphere, make up the region— Angola (ang GOH luh), Zambia (ZAM bee uh), Malawi (muh LAH wee), Mozambique (MOH zuhm BEEK), Namibia (nuh MIHB ee uh), Botswana (baht SWAHN uh), Zimbabwe (zihm BAHB wee), Swaziland, Lesotho (luh SOH toh), South Africa, Comoros (KAHM uh ROHZ), Madagascar (MAD uh GAS kuhr), Mauritius (maw RIHSH ee uhs), and Seychelles (say SHEHLZ). The largest country is Angola, having an area of 481,351 square miles (1,246,698.1 sq km). The second largest is South Africa, with 471,444 square miles (1,221,039 sq km). Four countries— Madagascar, Comoros, Seychelles, and Mauritius— are islands in the Indian Ocean.

The region is surrounded by lowlands along the coasts, with inland highlands that lead to wide, high plateaus. Two deserts can be found in Southern Africa. Running parallel to the eastern lowlands is the Namib Desert. Near the center of the region is a second desert— the Kalahari.

At one time all the countries of Southern Africa depended totally on agriculture for their economies. The discovery of rich minerals such as gold, diamonds, and copper changed that for many of the countries. Today South Africa has the most highly developed economy in the area and strongly influences its neighbors.

Diamonds and gold have provided South Africa with the money it needs for diversifying its economy. These minerals are to South Africa what oil is to OPEC nations.

1. SOUTH AFRICA

The Republic of South Africa lies at the southernmost tip of Africa. Nearly twice the size of Texas, it is home to 34.3 million people. It has more people than any of the other countries in Southern Africa.

Because of its mineral wealth, South Africa has a strong economic base. Most of the country's wealth—and its government—is at present controlled by people of European descent—whites, who make up only a small part of the population. This is due in great part to the official policy of **apartheid**— "separate development" of the races. Recently, this policy has made South Africa the center of international attention.

See the TAE for an Objective 1 Activity.

1.1 Landscape and Climate

South Africa's landscape varies from desert to mountain. It is dominated by a high, central plateau that sweeps in a diagonal from the border with Zimbabwe in the northeast to lowlands along the southwest coast. The climate, affected by the country's closeness to

515

PHYSICAL REGIONS OF SOUTHERN AFRICA _____

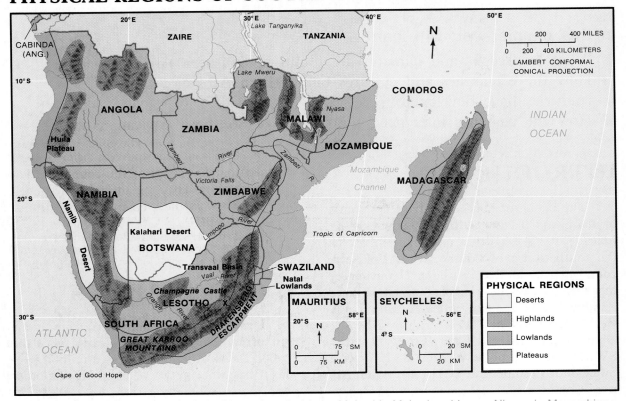

FIGURE 25-1   Lake Nyasa is called Lake Malawi in Malawi and Lagos Niassa in Mozambique.
Plateaus and highlands form the predominant physical features of Southern Africa. Lowlands form a narrow coastal band that encircles the region. Which country has the largest area of desert region?

See page 521 for a political map of Southern Africa.

Another name for the Drakensberg Mountains is Quathlamba.

two oceans, also varies, with both dry and moist, mild climate types.

Landscape. South Africa's land regions form a U-shape, with the Atlantic Ocean meeting the west, south, and southeastern coasts of the "U." The northeast coast is met by the waters of the Indian Ocean.

Narrow lowlands make up the country's U-shape as they wrap around 2,700 miles (4,345.2 km) of seacoast. In width they range from less than 30 miles (48.3 km) along the west coast to about 80 miles (128.7 km) in the fertile Natal Lowlands in the east.

Rising inland from the lowlands in the southeast, standing sharply above the Natal Lowlands, is the Drakensberg (DRAHK uhnz buhrg) Escarpment. It is the face of the Drakensberg Mountains. From this, many small, short rivers run down to the sea. Farther south are the Great Karroo Mountains. They are partly arid lands. In the drier northern section are large salt pans. In the south, where the land meets the coastal lowlands, enough rain falls for vegetation to grow.

Beyond the mountains is the high, central plateau. In the northeast it is as high as 8,000 feet (2,438.4 m) above sea level. In parts of the west, it drops to around 2,000 feet (609.6 m). High, flat grasslands called **highveld** cover the plateau. These elevated,

AFRICA SOUTH OF THE SAHARA   UNIT 8

sometimes rolling steppes have very few trees. The northeast part of the plateau, called the Transvaal Basin, holds much of the country's mineral deposits. The western section is chiefly grazing land.

As shown in Figure 25–1 on page 516, part of the Kalahari (KAHL uh HAHR ee) Desert lies in South Africa's northwest. Most of the desert, however, is in the country of Botswana to the north.

Climate. In South Africa, climate changes from one area to another. The southern tip of the country, around the Cape of Good Hope, has a Mediterranean climate, with long summers and short winters when most of the rain falls. In the Natal Lowlands, along the southeast coast, the climate is humid subtropical. Farther inland much of the eastern highlands has a middle-latitude marine climate. Fog and clouds form when warm currents off the Indian Ocean meet the cooler highland temperatures.

Except for the southeast and the area around Cape Town, South Africa gets little precipitation. As a result, in the eastern part

Refer students to pages 96-97 to review the map of Earth's Climate Regions.

of the central plateau, the climate is steppe. Temperatures are moderate but can be cool at night. In July it is winter, and temperatures may fall below 40°F (4.4°C). Rainfall ranges from 24 inches (61.0 cm) in parts of the east to 8 inches (20.3 cm) farther west.

In the western regions, the climate is desert. As little as 5 inches (12.7 cm) of rain falls each year. These dry conditions are caused by the cold Benguela (behn GWEHL uh) Current in the Atlantic Ocean. Winds blowing over the current pick up little moisture. As they move eastward over land, they warm up, gather, and hold moisture.

The Namib Desert of western South Africa is known as a "cold" desert.

1.2 Economic and Cultural Patterns

Until the late 1800s, the major economic activity of South Africa was agriculture. At that time diamonds and gold were discovered in the Transvaal. Today the greatest part of the country's income is from the sale of these and other minerals. South Africa has the

South Africa has about half of Africa's cars and telephones but only about six percent of its people.

The highveld west of the Drakensberg Mountains is scarred by erosion. Periods of severe drought alternate with heavy rains that cut gullies in the land. To what does highveld refer?

The highest point of the Drakensberg Mountains is Thabana Ntlenyana, which is 11,425 feet (3,482.3 m) above sea level.

CAPE TOWN: SITE AND SITUATION

Geographers often refer to site and situation when they explain why a city grew where it did. An African city with an interesting site and situation is Cape Town. The oldest city of South Africa, Cape Town is squeezed into a semicircular area formed on one side by Devil's Peak, Table Mountain, and the Lion's Head, and by Table Bay on the other. Table Mountain rises to a height of 3,549 feet (1,081.8 m) right behind the city.

Much of Cape Town's development can be related to its situation. The city is located near the southern tip of Africa at the northern part of Cape Peninsula. The peninsula ends in the Cape of Good Hope, where the Atlantic and Indian oceans meet. As a result Cape Town has been part of an important east-west trade route for hundreds of years.

In the 1600s merchants used the east-west trade route to bring spices from the east to Western Europe. In 1647 a Dutch ship wrecked near the present site of Cape Town. Survivors who struggled ashore were impressed by what they found. Their reports led the Dutch East India Company to build a small food and fuel station on the Cape where the Dutch ships sailing to the Dutch East Indies could stop.

For many years all the residents of Cape Town worked for the Dutch East India Company. As late as 1700, only about 200 people lived there. In 1795 the British took possession of Cape Town. Over the next 30 years or so, population grew as British settlers began arriving in greater numbers.

The discovery of diamonds and gold in the late 1800s brought thousands of people through Cape Town. Shortly after, the need for supplies during the Boer Wars led new industries to start. In the early 1900s, Cape Town became the legislative capital of the Union of South Africa.

Today Cape Town and the surrounding communities of the Cape Peninsula have a population of close to 1.8 million. Cape Town maintains its importance as a city located on one of the world's busiest trade routes.

1. What is Cape Town's site?
2. What can be said about the influence of Cape Town's situation on its growth?

Students sometimes mistakenly believe that the Cape of Good Hope, located near Cape Town, is the southernmost point in Africa. Cape Agulhas is actually that point. Help students find Cape Agulhas on a map.

world's largest deposits of diamonds and produces between 45 and 60 percent of all the gold produced in the world each year. About two-thirds of the country's miners work in gold mines.

South Africa also has a variety of industries, including food processing, iron and steel, textiles and clothing, light machinery, paper, and oil refining. The industries are centered in the cities. The most modern city is Johannesburg (joh HAN uhs BUHRG), with a population of more than 1.7 million. Other important cities are Pretoria (prih TOHR ee uh), with 850,000 people, and Durban, with more than 1 million. Cape Town, South Africa's oldest city, has over 850,000 people.

Only about 11 percent of the country is farmed. Still, enough is grown for home and export, and there is variety. Citrus fruits, wine grapes, and wheat are grown in the Mediterranean climate of the southern half of South Africa. On the higher plateau of Transvaal, corn, grains, tobacco, peanuts, and dairy products are produced. Farmers on the highveld also raise livestock and export wool and meat. There is a good fishing industry along South Africa's coast.

By law, the people of South Africa are divided into four racial categories—Whites, Coloreds, Asians, and black Africans. Whites make up 18 percent of the population. Most of them are descended from Dutch, German, French, or British settlers or are recent immigrants. Coloreds, who are mixed African and European, make up another 11 percent of the population. Asians, who are mostly descendants of Indians brought to South Africa as indentured servants in the 1800s, account for only 3 percent. Black Africans, most of them of Bantu-speaking descent, make up about 68 percent of the population.

The ways of life of all the people of South Africa are strongly influenced by apartheid. Whites rule the country and hold the most highly paid and skilled jobs. Coloreds

South Africa's apartheid policy translates into the harsh reality of a black township. These crowded, barren areas cannot support large populations. What is one of the largest black townships in South Africa?

See the *TRB* for *Teacher Notes: Section 1 Extending the Lesson* on Winnie Mandela.

and Asians are allowed to live in segregated parts of "white" South Africa. They also are allowed to take part in government. In general, however, whites have a much higher standard of living than nonwhites.

Under the policy of apartheid, about 13 percent of South Africa's land has been divided into 10 homelands, or **bantustans.** These are areas of land set aside in various parts of the country for blacks only. Under apartheid black South Africans must live in these homelands or in special areas outside cities known as **townships.** One of the largest townships is Soweto (soh WEHT oh), located outside of Johannesburg. Nearly two million people live there. Since the government views blacks as citizens of the homeland in which they live, blacks can have no part in the national government.

Life in the homelands is hard. Many live in rural areas where much of the land is so dry it cannot be farmed. Most economic

FOCUS ON ECONOMY

FABULOUS DIAMONDS

For many people diamonds are the most precious of all gemstones. Because few areas in the world produce diamonds, they are very rare. Their beauty and their rareness give diamonds great value.

Formed by the great heat and pressure under the surface of Earth, diamonds are among the hardest substances found in nature. This hardness makes them useful in industry for cutting and grinding other hard substances. Almost 80 percent of all diamonds mined are used in industry.

The world's largest supplier of diamonds is the Republic of South Africa. Much of its national income can be accounted for by the export of raw and finished diamonds. Diamonds were first discovered there in the late 1860s, supposedly by a farmer's child. By the 1870s, after several more discoveries were made, fortune hunters from all over the world rushed to South Africa to begin mining.

The first large-scale diamond-mining operation opened near the town of Vooruitzicht. Originally called New Rush, it later became known as Kimberley. By 1887 the DeBeers Company controlled the Kimberley operation. To this day the DeBeers Company mines most of the world's diamonds.

Diamonds are also mined at Bulfontein and near Pretoria. The largest uncut diamond ever found was mined at the Premier Mine near Pretoria. About the size of a person's fist, it weighed 3,106 carats (621,200 milligrams)—about 1.4 pounds. When it was cut, it made 9 major jewels and more than 100 smaller ones. The largest jewel became known as the "Star of Africa."

Diamonds are dug from deep mines. The rock in which they are found is called *kimberlite*, from the name of South Africa's first mine. Many tons of kimberlite must be mined to find each diamond. An expert estimates that one part diamond is found for every 40 million parts of kimberlite rock.

As pictured on this page, in South Africa most miners are black. The work is hard, and the pay is low. They are not paid on the same scale as whites, and it is almost impossible for them to rise to positions of responsibility. Recently the miners have begun to protest and to push for change. For many people who oppose South Africa's policies, diamonds have become symbols of apartheid.

1. Where in South Africa are diamonds mined?
2. In what kind of rocks are diamonds found?
3. Why do some people see diamonds as symbols of apartheid?

activity takes place in white areas. This forces many blacks to spend many hours traveling to cities to work. Many blacks are away from their families for months in order to work in mines or in cities.

According to the South African government, four of the homelands are independent of South Africa. No other country, however, recognizes these homelands as independent nations. The South African government also has been giving help to industries that build factories near the homelands. The government hopes that with more jobs available, more blacks will stay in the homelands.

1.3 Influences of the Past

Groups of people have lived in South Africa since about 6000 BC. One early group was the San (SAHN), later called Bushmen by Europeans. They were hunters. Another was the Khoikhoi (KOY KOY), known as Hottentots by Europeans. They were nomads who kept large flocks of sheep and herds of cattle.

Sometime before 100 AD, Bantu-speaking people moved from other parts of Africa to northern and eastern South Africa. About 70 percent of the population of South Africa is descended from these people. The largest

Refer students to the map of Physical Regions of Southern Africa on page 516 and the map of Land Use and Resources of Southern Africa on page 525.

NATIONS OF SOUTHERN AFRICA

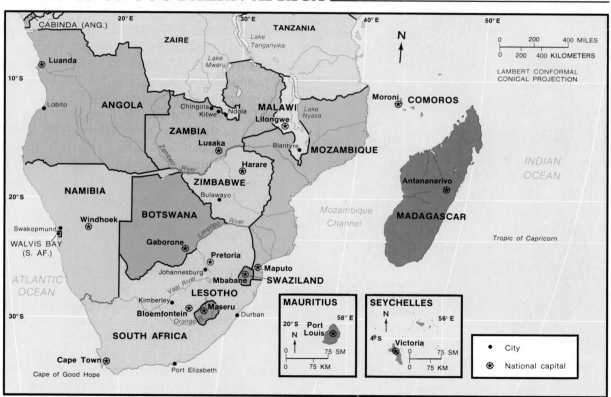

FIGURE 25-2
The Republic of South Africa is clearly the leading nation in this region. South Africa's technology and wealth have the potential for helping to raise living standards throughout the neighboring nations of the Southern African region. Which Southern African nations directly border the Republic of South Africa?

USING GRAPHIC SKILLS

ANALYZING CIRCLE GRAPHS

For many people, a shopping mall is a fun place to visit. Because it is so large, hours can be spent browsing in shops and looking at the items they sell. But only by going into one store at a time can you get a detailed idea of what each store has. Whenever you take something large and look at it more closely, you are, in a sense, analyzing. In much the same way, geographers often must look more closely in detail at a large piece of information and analyze it. Here several circle graphs are used to show different kinds of information. In these graphs amounts are represented by a certain portion of a circle. For example, in the large circle graph labeled "Total Population," three percent of the circle, or about 11 degrees, represents the Asian population which makes up three percent of South Africa's total population.

The two smaller circle graphs show information another way. First, the graphs give a more detailed breakdown of the groups making up the black and white populations of South Africa. The size of each graph is drawn in proportion to the part of the total population its population represents. The circle labeled "Black Population," for example, is about two-thirds the size of the circle labeled "Total Population." The circle labeled "White Population" is even smaller.

Study the circle graphs on this page. Then answer the questions that follow.

1. What percentage of the total population do nonwhites make up?

2. How much larger is the black population than the white population?

3. Why are the percentage figures of the various black national groups higher on the "Black Population" graph than on the "Total Population" graph?

4. **Challenge:** In other parts of the world, members of different ethnic groups have intermarried, sometimes making a new, larger part of a country's total population. Why do you think the Coloreds of South Africa have remained a minority?

SOUTH AFRICAN ETHNIC GROUPS

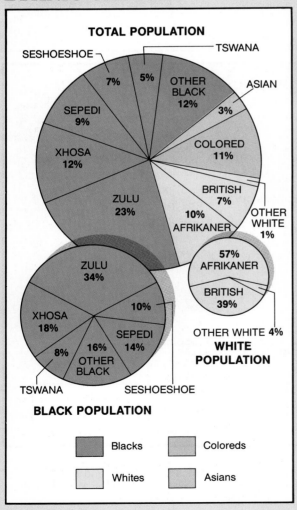

TOTAL POPULATION

SESHOESHOE — 7%
TSWANA 5%
OTHER BLACK 12%
ASIAN 3%
SEPEDI 9%
COLORED 11%
XHOSA 12%
ZULU 23%
BRITISH 7%
10% AFRIKANER
OTHER WHITE 1%

ZULU 34%
10%
XHOSA 18%
SEPEDI 14%
8% 16% OTHER BLACK
TSWANA
SESHOESHOE
BLACK POPULATION

57% AFRIKANER
BRITISH 39%
OTHER WHITE 4%
WHITE POPULATION

Blacks   Coloreds
Whites   Asians

522

groups among these Bantu-speaking people are the Zulu and the Xhosa (KOH suh). Each numbers more than five million.

In 1652 the Dutch set up a supply base at the Cape of Good Hope. It soon grew into a settlement called Cape Colony. There the Dutch, who called themselves *Afrikaners* (AF rih KAHN uhrs), or *Boers* (BOHRZ), set up farms and businesses. Before long the Africans were forced to work for them.

In the late 1700s, the Dutch lost Cape Colony to the British. Rather than be under British rule, many Boers left Cape Colony and headed toward the interior on a journey that became known as the Great Trek. After defeating several African groups, including the Zulu and Xhosa, the Boers set up two independent republics, the Transvaal and the Orange Free State.

In the late 1800s, the discovery of diamonds at Kimberley and gold in the Witwatersrand (WIHT WAWT uhrz RAND), an area around Johannesburg, brought further changes. Many people, mostly British, rushed to the area. Soon friction arose between the Boers and the British, each of whom controlled two territories in South Africa. In 1899 war broke out between the two groups. After three years of fighting, the British won the Boer War. By terms of the peace treaty, the Boers accepted British rule and the British promised to honor certain Boer practices.

In 1910 they joined together their colonies and the Boer republics and formed the Union of South Africa. At that time they set up the three capitals shown in Figure 25–2 on page 521. Each capital served a different purpose. Pretoria, in the Transvaal, became the administrative capital. Bloemfontein (BLOOM fuhn TAYN), in the Orange Free State, became the seat of the court system. Cape Town, in the Cape Province, became the legislative capital.

After World War I, English and Afrikaans (AF rih KAHNS), spoken by the Boers, became the official languages of South Africa. In 1948 apartheid became official government policy. In 1961 South Africa became the Republic of South Africa.

Over the years there has been growing resistance and resentment to the policy of apartheid both from within and outside of South Africa. Recently, several countries have refused to trade with South Africa, and some foreign companies have closed their businesses and moved out of the country. South Africa has begun to change parts of its apartheid policy.

English and Afrikaans are really the languages of South Africa's small European minority. There are many other black African languages spoken.

CONTENT CHECK

1. **Identify:** South Africa, Natal Lowlands, Drakensberg Escarpment, Great Karroo Mountains, Transvaal Basin, Kalahari Desert, Benguela Current, Johannesburg, Pretoria, Durban, Cape Town, Coloreds, Soweto, San, Bushmen, Khoikhoi, Hottentots, Zulu, Xhosa, Cape Colony, Afrikaners, Boers, Great Trek, Boer War, Bloemfontein, Afrikaans.

2. **Define:** apartheid, highveld, bantustans, townships.

3. What landforms make up South Africa?

4. What minerals are important to South Africa's economy?

5. What four groups of people live in South Africa?

6. What white European groups settled in South Africa?

7. Under the policy of apartheid, where can black South Africans live?

8. What cities serve as South Africa's capitals?

9. **Challenge:** How does the Benguela Current make the western parts of South Africa dry?

Victoria Falls is known locally as "the smoke that thunders." During the rainy season, the Zambezi River is high, and the waterfall creates much mist.

2. ZIMBABWE

The Republic of Zimbabwe covers 150,803 square miles (390,579.5 sq km). Wedged between Mozambique, Botswana, Zambia, and South Africa, Zimbabwe is land-locked. Once called Rhodesia, it was the last European colony in Southern Africa to gain its independence.

Have students identify other landlocked countries in Africa. What problems do these countries face?

2.1 Landscape and Climate

Zimbabwe is a tropical country about the size of the state of Montana. Most of the country is a plateau with large areas of fertile

See the *TAE* for an *Objective 2* Activity.

As this picture shows, the Zambezi River plunges into a deep, lengthy gorge at Victoria Falls. The Zambezi separates what two countries in Southern Africa?

land. Climate varies with both tropical moist and dry climates.

Landscape. The high, rolling plateau that covers most of Zimbabwe has elevations between 3,000 feet (914.4 m) and 4,000 feet (1,219.2 m). Crossing the plateau from the southwest to the northeast is a highveld that rises 6,000 feet (1,828.8 m) above sea level. It was called the Great Dyke by early British settlers. Highlands near Zimbabwe's border with Mozambique reach heights of more than 8,000 feet (2,438.4 m). These eastern high-lands and the central plateau hold much of the country's fertile crop and grazing lands.

North and south of the plateau are low-lands. The Zambezi River forms the northern border with Zambia. On the Zambezi is Victoria Falls, which many view as one of Africa's greatest natural wonders. At the Falls, the water of the Zambezi drops 350 feet (106.7 m), making the falls more than twice as high as Niagara Falls. Another river, the Limpopo (lihm POH poh), forms the border between Zimbabwe and South Africa. Here clusters of woodlands stand tall over shrubs and grasses.

Climate. Temperatures in Zimbabwe are a little cooler than those that might be expected in the tropics. This is often because of high elevation.

Most of the highveld has a tropical savanna climate. At the cities of Bulawayo (BUL uh WAY oh) and Harare (huh RAH ray), average high temperatures are about 80°F (26.7°C) in January and 70°F (21.1°C) in July. Low temperatures in July, which is winter, sometimes drop below 40°F (4.4°C). In the winter there is a rainy season. The heaviest rainfall is in the eastern highlands. The highveld receives between 23 inches (58.4 cm) and 33 inches (83.8 cm) of rain a year.

In the dry areas to the north and south is a steppe climate. Here rainfall is less than 20 inches (50.8 cm) each year.

Have students compare the map of Land Use and Resources of Southern Africa below with the map of Land Use and Resources of North Africa and the Sahel on page 441.

LAND USE AND RESOURCES OF SOUTHERN AFRICA

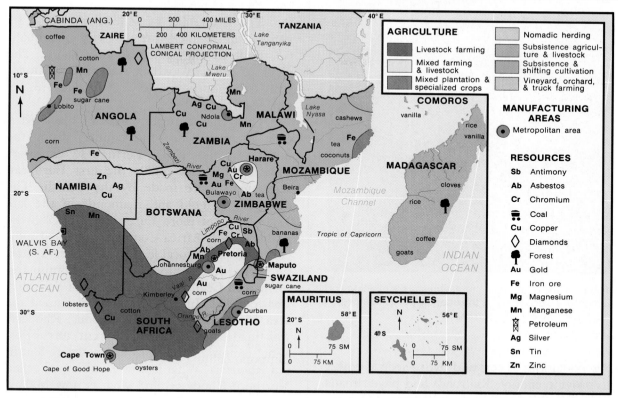

FIGURE 25-3
Valuable resources in Southern Africa were an early attraction to European colonizers. Within this region are some of Africa's greatest reservoirs of natural resources. Precious resources, such as gold and diamonds, are found principally in which Southern African country?

Most people in Zimbabwe live at higher elevations where climates are relatively pleasant.

2.2 Economic and Cultural Patterns

Zimbabwe has large areas of fertile land and low population density. Despite several years of drought that held down farm production, the country has been able to make progress in several areas.

Economic Patterns. Over 40 percent of Zimbabwe's land can be used for farming and about 60 percent for grazing livestock. Corn is the leading food crop and tobacco and coffee the chief exports. Other grains are also grown, and cattle are raised on large farms.

World prices of tobacco and coffee vary over time. When prices are low, Zimbabwe's economy suffers.

Until the time of independence, Europeans controlled about 40 percent of the best farmland, most of which was on the Great Dyke between the cities of Bulawayo and Harare. Many of the farms were large and grew crops for export. Blacks farmed mostly in the central plateau and in river basins. Today, although most of the large commercial farms are still in the hands of whites, many black communal farms are successful.

As shown in Figure 25–3 on this page, Zimbabwe also has a wealth of mineral resources. In fact, its mineral resources bring in its chief income. Coal, chrome, gold, copper, asbestos, and iron ore are mined, and there is

CHAPTER 25   **SOUTHERN AFRICA**

525

The ruins of the ancient city of Zimbabwe cover about 100 acres (40.5 ha). The city was built in the 1300s when the gold and ivory trade with Arab merchants was at its peak. Great Zimbabwe was built of slabs of granite fitted without mortar.

Tobacco and other agricultural crops are a mainstay of Zimbabwe's economy. Is the economy of Zimbabwe dependent solely on agriculture?

See the *TRB* for *Teacher Notes: Section 2 Extending the Lesson* on rivalries in Zimbabwe.

a good supply of coal and hydroelectric power to provide energy. Railroads and paved roads link the cities and industrial areas. Harare, the capital and largest city, is a major manufacturing center.

Culture. Zimbabwe has 9.4 million people. Most are black Africans, with whites making up about 1 percent of the population. More than 75 percent of the blacks and about 25 percent of the whites live in rural areas. Until 1980 whites ruled the country.

There are two major black ethnic groups—Shona (SHOH nuh) and Ndebele (EHN duh BEE lee). The Shona make up about 80 percent of the black population. The Shona and the Ndebele have been political rivals for a long time.

Most of the people of Zimbabwe follow traditional African religions. A small percentage, mostly whites, practice Christianity. Although a number of languages are spoken, the official language is English.

2.3 Influences of the Past

The Republic of Zimbabwe took its name from the ancient trading city of Zimbabwe, built by the Shona about 700 AD. The ruins of this city, which was built of stone, still stand approximately 200 miles (321.9 km) south of Harare.

Over the centuries waves of black Africans migrated into the country from the north. In the 1500s Portuguese explorers came, and in the 1800s the first European settlements were made by the British. The discovery of gold and diamonds in the late 1800s brought more Europeans. In 1888 the British South Africa Company obtained mineral rights from local leaders. Two years later, under the leadership of a British administrator named Cecil Rhodes, the city of Salisbury was founded. In 1895 the British named the area Rhodesia, in honor of Rhodes. Rhodesia was made up of three different territories. What is now Zimbabwe was known as Southern Rhodesia. What is now Zambia was called Northern Rhodesia, and what is now Malawi was Nyasaland. The whole area came under British influence. In 1923 Southern Rhodesia was declared a Crown Colony. In 1953 it joined with Northern Rhodesia and Nyasaland to become the Federation of Rhodesia and Nyasaland.

Although the blacks of the area resisted rule by whites, the whites kept control. They refused to share political power with blacks. When the British tried to make them change their attitude, they declared Rhodesia independent. The United Nations declared this illegal and asked its members not to recognize the government of Rhodesia. Both Britain and the United Nations set up **economic sanctions.** This means they limited trade with the country.

In 1972 civil war broke out, and blacks fought to overthrow the white governments. Finally, in 1979, elections were held, and a government controlled by blacks came to power. In 1980 Britain declared Rhodesia independent, and the name of the country was changed to Zimbabwe.

Zimbabwe is making efforts in education. The government has set up a school for young Zimbabweans disabled during the nation's freedom struggle.

CONTENT CHECK

1. **Identify:** Great Dyke, Zambezi River, Victoria Falls, Limpopo River, Bulawayo, Harare, Shona, Ndebele, British South Africa Company, Cecil Rhodes, Salisbury, Southern Rhodesia, Northern Rhodesia, Nyasaland.

2. **Define:** economic sanctions.

3. What countries border Zimbabwe?

4. What type of landscape covers most of Zimbabwe?

5. Why are temperatures a little cooler in Zimbabwe than in most other tropical countries?

6. What brings in the chief income of Zimbabwe?

7. **Challenge:** What do you think Zimbabwe might be like today if gold and diamonds had not been discovered there in the 1800s?

See the *TAE* for an *Objective 3* Activity.

3. OTHER COUNTRIES OF SOUTHERN AFRICA

The other countries of Southern Africa can be grouped together on the basis of history or economic dependence. Two of the countries, Angola and Mozambique, were colonies of Portugal. Two others, Zambia and Malawi, were British territories. Madagascar, Comoros, Mauritius, and the Seychelles, on the other hand, are all island countries located in the Indian Ocean. The countries of Botswana, Lesotho, Swaziland, and Namibia are all linked economically to South Africa.

Although both Angola and Mozambique have highlands and lowlands, Mozambique has more lowlands.

3.1 Angola and Mozambique

Both Angola and Mozambique lie along the coast of Southern Africa. Angola is on the Atlantic coast, and Mozambique is on the Indian Ocean coast. The best natural harbors in Africa south of the Equator are in these two countries—Lobito (loh BEET oh) in Angola and Maputo (mah POO toh) and Beira (BAY ruh) in Mozambique. Through these cities minerals and farm products are shipped from such landlocked areas as southern Zaire, Zimbabwe, Zambia, and Malawi.

Angola is more than one-fifth larger than Mozambique. Both countries have lowlands along the coasts with dense tropical forests. In Mozambique, however, these coastal areas make up 44 percent of the landscape. The capital cities of both countries are found along the coast. In Angola the capital is Luanda. In Mozambique it is Maputo.

A chain of uplands meets the eastern coastal areas of Angola. In Mozambique uplands form the western border with Malawi. Both Angola and Mozambique also have a central plateau with deep rivers that serve as important watersheds.

Both Angola and Mozambique have two climate types. One is dry. The other is tropical moist. In the southwest part of Mozambique and along the western edge of Angola, the climate is desert or steppe. In most of the rest of both countries, there are tropical savanna climates. Elevations in the uplands affect temperature.

Both Angola and Mozambique have minerals and enough fertile land for their populations. Although Angola has rich oil resources, most have not been developed.

Eight million people make their home in Angola. Of these, most are of Bantu descent. Angola was first explored in the late 1400s by the Portuguese. It became a Portuguese colony and remained one until 1975, when it became independent. The Portuguese influence was strong, and Portuguese still is the official language.

Mozambique, although smaller in size than Angola, has a population of 14.7 million. Like Angola, Mozambique was a Portuguese colony until 1975, and Portuguese remains its official language.

An archaeological site in Broken Hill, Zambia, has yielded the skull of an early *homo sapiens*, perhaps 200,000 years old.

3.2 Zambia and Malawi

Both Zambia and Malawi were for many years British colonies. During the 1950s and early 1960s, Zambia was known as Northern Rhodesia and Malawi as Nyasaland. Along with present-day Zimbabwe, they formed the Federation of Rhodesia and Nyasaland.

Zambia has a land area of 290,583 square miles (752,609.4 sq km). Malawi is much smaller than Zambia, with a land area of 45,745 square miles (118,479.5 sq km). Both countries have highlands, high, fertile plateaus, river basins, and a climate that is primarily tropical savanna.

Malawi depends heavily on its agriculture both to feed its people and for export. Its major crops are tea, tobacco, and sugarcane. Zambia, on the other hand, has to import much of its food. Its chief resource is copper. It has one-fourth of the world's known reserves of this mineral.

Because it is landlocked, Zambia must ship its goods through other countries for export. A major transportation link is the Tan-Zam Railway, built with help from the People's Republic of China. It connects Zambia with the Indian Ocean through Dar es Salaam in Tanzania.

Madagascar was a favorite lair for pirates preying on ships in the Indian Ocean. Among these pirates was the famous Captain Kidd.

3.3 Island Countries

Madagascar, Comoros, Mauritius, and the Seychelles all are located in the Indian Ocean near the African continent. Each, however, is different from the other in certain ways. All have been influenced by Africans and South Asians, as well as by Europeans. Their populations are a mix of Bantu, Arab, Indian, Indonesian, European, and Chinese.

Madagascar. Of the four island nations, Madagascar is the largest. The fourth largest island in the world, it covers 226,656 square miles (587,038.6 sq km). In the lowlands that circle the island, the climate is steppe. In the highlands and plateaus that make up the rest of the island, it is tropical savanna. A colony of France until it became independent in 1960, the island was first settled about 100 BC by Indonesians. Around 900 AD people from East Africa and the Arabian Peninsula arrived. In the 1500s people from Portugal, Britain, and France began arriving. They were followed later by immigrants from China and India. The major economic activity of the island is agriculture, with 90 percent of the work force farmers.

Comoros. Comoros is a group of four mountainous islands that lie at the northern end of the Mozambique Channel between Africa and Madagascar. All four islands are volcanic in origin and have a tropical climate. Once a French territory, Comoros became independent in 1975. French, Swahili, and Arabic are spoken by the country's 400,000 people, most of whom are of African, Arab, or Indian descent. Most of them make a living by farming. Vanilla, copra, cocoa, sisal, cloves, and oils used for making perfumes are the major crops.

Mauritius. Mauritius, which lies about 500 miles (804.7 km) east of Madagascar, has a series of plateaus interrupted by small streams and waterfalls. Almost 67 percent of

Because the borders of Southern Africa were chosen by Europeans without regard to the unity of the different people living in each area, each country today is home to a variety of ethnic groups, languages, and customs.

Shown here are rice paddies on the edge of Antananarivo, a city built along the slopes of a ridge. This city serves as a trade center and as the capital of the island nation of Madagascar. What rank does Madagascar hold among the large islands of the world?

The people and language of Madagascar are known as Malagasy.

In the nations of Africa, the arts are interwoven with many aspects of daily life. Music, drama, dance, poetry, and other art forms are very much a part of the African heritage.

It is common for island countries to have mixed populations, as they were stepping stones throughout time.

See the *TAE* for an *Objective 4* Activity.

its 1.1 million people are Indian. There also are smaller numbers of Chinese, French, and British. Most of the people follow the Hindu religion. Smaller numbers are Muslims or Christians. While the official language is English, French, Creole, and several Indian languages also are spoken. The island was named after a prince in Holland in the late 1500s when it was discovered by the Dutch. The Dutch controlled the island until the early 1700s, when it was taken over by the French. In the 1800s it became a British possession. Finally, in 1968, it became independent.

The Seychelles. The Seychelles lie about 1,000 miles (1,609.3 km) off the east coast of Kenya. About 90 islands, about half of which are mountainous, form the country. The rocky landscape makes farming difficult. Tourism is a major source of income, along with the sale of coconuts and vanilla. Of the 100,000 people who populate the country, about 65 percent live on the largest island of

Mahé (mah HAY). Most of the people of the Seychelles are Roman Catholics and are of mixed European and African descent. Discovered in the early 1500s by Vasco de Gama, the islands were later claimed by the French and then the British. They were ruled by the British until 1976, when the Seychelles became independent.

By 1914 all of Africa, except Liberia and Ethiopa, had been partitioned among European countries.

3.4 South Africa Dependencies

Botswana, Lesotho, and Swaziland, as well as the territory of Namibia, all have strong economic ties with South Africa. While all are against South Africa's racial policies, they try to keep good relations with the country for economic reasons.

Botswana. A landlocked country, about the size of Texas, Botswana is bordered by Namibia on the west and north, Zambia on the north, Zimbabwe on the northeast, and

South Africa on the south. Once ruled by the British, Botswana became independent in 1966. More than 80 percent of its 1.2 million people make their living from farming. About 40,000 people work in the mines and fields of South Africa for part of the year because there are not enough jobs in Botswana to support them. The climate of Botswana is dry, and the Kalahari Desert covers a large part of the country. Mineral wealth has been discovered in the northern part of the country, and mining is becoming an important part of the economy.

Lesotho. Lesotho is about the size of Maryland. Completely surrounded and dominated by the country of South Africa, much of Lesotho is rugged and mountainous. Parts of it have yet to be touched or changed by modern civilization. Most of Lesotho's population of 1.6 million live in farming lands near the South African border. The largest majority of the population are of black African descent. Most follow traditional African reli-

gious beliefs. Once a British colony, Lesotho became independent in 1966.

At least 200,000 of Lesotho's work force spend part of the year in South Africa, working in mines, on farms, or in industry. The wages they earn are vital to Lesotho's economy. Because most of the young men work in South Africa for months at a time, the whole burden of subsistence farming falls to women. Taking care of the herds of sheep and cattle is the responsibility of young boys. To find grazing lands, many boys may have to be away from home for months.

Swaziland. Swaziland is one of the smallest countries in mainland Africa, with only 6,703 square miles (17,360.8 sq km) of land area. Except for a short eastern border with Mozambique, it is surrounded by South Africa. Although the country is mountainous, it has fertile lowlands that contain good farm and ranch lands, forests, and mineral resources. Among its major crops are sugarcane, tobacco, and peanuts. Cattle are raised

Most of the inhabitants of the Kalahari are mainly San and Khoikhoi.

A man looks after his herd of goats on a rugged hillside in Lesotho. For those people in Lesotho who do not work in South Africa, livestock raising and subsistence farming are their main occupations. Why is so much of this type of work in Lesotho done by women and young boys?

Refer students to the map of colonial Africa on page 501.

Although English is the official language, most people in Swaziland speak Siswati, a Zulu dialect.

AFRICA SOUTH OF THE SAHARA UNIT 8

for export. Most of the 700,000 people who live in the country are found near the South African border. About 16 percent of all workers are employed in the Transvaal and Orange Free State provinces of South Africa, and close to 95 percent of the country's imports and exports pass through South Africa.

Namibia. Namibia is bordered by Angola on the north, Botswana on the east, Zambia on the northeast, and South Africa on the south. It has a land area of 318,259 square miles (824,290.2 sq km). Moving west to east, the landscape is made up of coastal lowlands, desert, uplands, and plateaus. For the most part, the climate is hot and dry.

Its population of 1.3 million people is made up of a variety of African ethnic groups and whites of South African, German, and British descent. About one-half of the people are Christian, while the rest follow traditional African beliefs. Most of the population are pastoralists. Goats and sheep are raised chiefly in the south and cattle herded chiefly in the north. Among the country's chief minerals are diamonds and copper.

South Africa considers Namibia part of its territory, calls it "Southwest Africa," and controls the government. The United Nations, however, does not recognize South Africa's authority over Namibia. Groups of blacks within the country, supported by Angola and other countries, have been fighting against South African control.

Point out Walvis Bay on the political map on page 521. South Africa refuses to relinquish this bay, one of Africa's best natural harbors.

CONTENT CHECK

1. **Identify:** Angola, Mozambique, Lobito, Maputo, Beira, Luanda, Zambia, Malawi, Northern Rhodesia, Nyasaland, TanZam Railway, Madagascar, Comoros, Mauritius, Seychelles, Mahé, Botswana, Lesotho, Swaziland, Namibia, Southwest Africa.

2. What do Angola and Mozambique have in common?

3. What are the major economic activities of Zambia and Malawi?

4. In what ways are Madagascar, Comoros, Mauritius, and the Seychelles different from one another?

5. What four countries are dependent economically on South Africa?

6. **Challenge:** Suppose South Africa were to cut its ties with Botswana, Lesotho, Swaziland, and Namibia. What effect do you think this would have on the people of these four countries?

See the *TRB* for *Teacher Notes: Section 3 Extending the Lesson* on Madagascar's ecological crisis.

CONCLUSION

Like many of the nations in other regions of Africa, most of the countries of Southern Africa are developing nations that have been independent for only a short time. Also like many of the others, they hold promise despite their problems. As a region, Southern Africa is one of the richest on the continent in mineral resources and fertile land. That wealth, however, is not spread evenly across the countries or among the peoples who live in this region.

South Africa dominates the region economically. Several of the countries of the region are not yet strong enough to break their dependence on South Africa even though they do not agree with that country's political policies. The conflict between South Africa's black majority and white minority has drawn a great deal of attention not only from African countries but also from the rest of the world as well. Black rights and black rule have long been an issue in this region. How South Africa resolves its problems cannot help but have an effect on the other countries of this region.

SUMMARY

1. South of Zaire and Tanzania is the region of Southern Africa. It is made up of countries on the African continent as well as island countries in the Indian Ocean.
2. The most populous and economically strong country in the region is the Republic of South Africa. Its industries draw workers from many other countries.
3. South Africa's government is run by a white minority. Blacks have no voice in the national government.
4. The wealth of South Africa is based mostly on rich mineral deposits. Its climate also allows the production of a number of different crops.
5. Zimbabwe was once a British colony called Rhodesia. For many years its government was controlled by the minority

white population. In 1979 the first black majority government was elected.
6. Zimbabwe has large areas of fertile farmland. Like South Africa, Zimbabwe is also rich in mineral resources.
7. Mozambique and Angola have good natural harbors that serve as outlets for landlocked parts of Southern Africa.
8. Malawi and Zambia were once British colonies. Zambia has rich copper deposits. Having little development, Malawi is made up of mostly subsistence farmers.
9. Madagascar is the largest island country of Southern Africa and the fourth largest island in the world.
10. Swaziland, Lesotho, Botswana, and Namibia are economically tied to South Africa's economy.

Answers to the following questions can be found on page T256.

REVIEWING VOCABULARY

On a separate sheet of paper, write a definition for each of the following terms. Then write a sentence that uses the term and gives some further information about Southern Africa.

apartheid   economic sanctions   bantustans   highveld   townships

REMEMBERING THE FACTS

1. What countries of Southern Africa are on the continent of Africa itself?
2. What other territory that is claimed by South Africa is also on the continent in Southern Africa?
3. What country in Southern Africa is largest in area?
4. What is the general pattern of the land in Southern Africa?
5. What desert occupies northwest South Africa and much of Botswana?
6. Name several minerals that provide a lot of income to South Africa.
7. What is Zimbabwe's leading food crop?
8. Compare the size of South Africa's nonwhite population to its white population.
9. Is farming more important in Zambia or Malawi?

10. Madagascar ranks fourth in size among the world's islands. Which islands are larger?

11. What three of South Africa's neighbors are very economically dependent on South Africa?

UNDERSTANDING THE FACTS

1. Why are there relatively few major port cities in South Africa?
2. What physical feature makes land transportation difficult between the Natal Lowlands and the highveld?
3. Why is there more agricultural activity on South Africa's east coast than on the country's west coast?
4. Why have some people described South Africa as two countries?

5. What are some advantages Zimbabwe enjoys as an agricultural country?
6. Why is Zambia dependent on the world price of copper?
7. Why is South Africa sometimes considered to be an outcast among the countries of the world?
8. What are some of the problems faced by countries of Southern Africa as they try to develop their agriculture?

THINKING CRITICALLY AND CREATIVELY

1. More people live in the eastern part of Southern Africa than in the western part. What accounts for this distribution?
2. When white people in Rhodesia declared the former colony of Great Britain independent, the United Nations and Great Britain declared economic sanctions. Why was this done?
3. At one time South Africa, Zimbabwe, Zambia, Botswana, Swaziland, Lesotho, and Malawi were controlled by Britain. What are some effects of British rule that remain in these areas?
4. **Challenge:** Whites are outnumbered by nonwhites in South Africa five to one. How do whites maintain effective control when they are so heavily outnumbered?
5. **Challenge:** How have racial and ethnic differences hindered political unity in the Southern African countries?

REINFORCING GRAPHIC SKILLS

Study the graphs on page 522. Then answer the questions that follow.

1. Look at the proportion of whites to the total population. Which one black national group has the same proportion to the black population?
2. In 1838 the Zulu fought against the Boers when these Europeans came to settle. In 1879 the Zulu War was fought between the British and the Zulu. Even though the Zulu greatly outnumbered the British and won the Battle of Isandhlwana, the British defeated the Zulu several months later. Within today's population, how do the Zulu compare with the Afrikaner population? With the British population?

UNIT REVIEW

SUMMARY

1. Africa is the second largest continent in the world. Africa south of the Sahara is a culture area in the part of the continent that lies south of the Sahara.
2. The major physical features of the area's three regions are the Great Rift Valley and tropical savannas in East Africa, plateaus and tropical rain forests in West and Central Africa, and plateaus and desert in Southern Africa.
3. Even though most of the people in Africa south of the Sahara depend on farming for their living, poor soils and unreliable rainfall make farming difficult.
4. Because the best farmland in the area is used to grow export crops and not food,

much of Africa south of the Sahara suffers serious food shortages.
5. Most of the large cities in Africa south of the Sahara were founded by non-African colonists. A large part of the area's population lives in small, scattered villages.
6. Africa south of the Sahara is made up mostly of developing countries. South Africa is the only industrialized country in the culture area.
7. After centuries of European rule, most countries in Africa south of the Sahara have become independent nations since the mid-1900s. Economic development and unifying diverse ethnic groups are common problems.

Answers to the following questions can be found on page T260.

THINKING ABOUT THE UNIT

1. Compare landscape and climate features of East Africa, West and Central Africa, and Southern Africa.
2. How have natural resources aided in the economic development of certain countries in Africa south of the Sahara?
3. What common problems face the people of Africa south of the Sahara? What are some causes of these problems?
4. How did European colonization affect the cultural and economic development of the countries of this culture area?

SUGGESTED UNIT ACTIVITIES

1. Study the map on page 501 to prepare a list of current names of countries in Africa south of the Sahara. Then compare today's names of the countries in the area with those of earlier times. Prepare a short report on the origins of many of the new African names. Explain why so many names have been changed.
2. Tanzania and Nigeria have made plans to move their capitals to the interiors of their countries. Study their reasons for making such a move. Then write a proposal suggesting that the capital of the United States be moved to a more central location. State your reasons for supporting such a move.

DEVELOPING GEOGRAPHY SKILLS

SUPPORTING GENERALIZATIONS

If you tell a friend, "My dad knows lots about football," you are making a generalization. If you go on to say that your father played varsity football when he was in college and then went on to coach at both the high school and college levels, you have provided evidence to support your generalization.

People make generalizations all the time. Some are sweeping generalizations, statements so broad and applied to so many cases or people that most people hearing or reading them recognize that they are not logical and probably are false. Generalizations like this often are applied to a culture. For example:

All Germans like to work hard daily.
All Americans are inventive.

Surely, there are some Germans who prefer to spend the day hiking through a forest rather than working in an office or factory. And, just as surely, there are some Americans who are not creative thinkers.

It is important, therefore, when making generalizations to be able to back them up with supporting evidence. As indicated in the following examples, to truly support a generalization, a statement must (1) relate directly to the generalization, (2) be logical, and (3) have a basis in fact.

Generalization:

The majority of Kenya's people live in areas where productive agriculture is possible.

Statements:
1. Kenya's interior has a very dry climate.
2. To the north a large section of the Kenyan plains receives less than 10 inches (25.4 cm) of rain a year.
3. Only about four percent of Kenya's land is suitable for farming.
4. Agriculture is the most important economic activity in Kenya.
5. Nearly 85 percent of Kenya's people live in the southern two-fifths of the country.

(Statements 1, 2, and 5 are supportive. Although statements 3 and 4 both give information about Kenya, neither relates directly to why most Kenyans live in areas that support agriculture.)

Generalization:

Zaire is a developing country with great economic potential for the future.

Statements:
1. Because of its mineral wealth, Zaire could become a major economic power in the next century.
2. It is estimated that 25 percent of Zaire's land could be used for farming; today only about 3 percent is being used.
3. Copper brings in nearly 50 percent of Zaire's income from exports.
4. Zaire's rivers could provide about 13 percent of the world's hydroelectric power.
5. Since the 1960s industry has become more important in Zaire.

(Statements 1, 2, and 4 are supportive. Although statements 3 and 5 both give information about Zaire's present economy, neither relates directly to Zaire's potential.)

For practice in supporting a generalization, reread Chapter 25, Section 1 on pages 515-523. Then write three supporting statements for this generalization:

The ways of life of all South Africans are strongly influenced by the policy of apartheid.

535

ASIA

The nations of Asia have richly diverse histories and cultures. While some Asian countries are industrialized and modern, most are struggling to overcome large populations, religious differences, and poor economies.

UNIT 9

Asia covers more land than any other continent. It is made up of five major culture areas. Northern Asia, as part of the Soviet Union, is discussed with the countries of Europe in Unit 6. Southwest Asia, which is largely Muslim, is covered in Unit 7. The three other culture areas of South Asia, East Asia, and Southeast Asia are the focus of this unit.

South Asia stretches southward from the southern slopes of the Himalayas, Earth's highest mountain range, to the island of Sri Lanka. India is the leading country of South Asia in size, population, and economic development.

Midway along the western rim of the Pacific Ocean is East Asia. It is the home of one-fifth of all the world's people. About 80 percent of East Asians live in China, the largest country in size in the culture area. Over the centuries, Chinese culture has influenced all the countries of East Asia. Today, however, the economic leader of East Asia is Japan.

Southeast Asia is bounded by India to the northwest and China to the northeast. It is made up of a peninsular mainland and hundreds of islands. Indonesia and Thailand are the leading nations of this culture area.

Likiang River near Kweilin, China

CHAPTER 26

The Taj Mahal is but one example of the Muslim influence in South Asia. It was built in the mid-1600s by Shah Jahan as a mausoleum for his wife.

Indian girls in front of the Taj Mahal

SOUTH ASIA

Great numbers of young people study at India's universities. India has more skilled scientists and skilled workers than any other country except the United States and the Soviet Union.

In this chapter you will learn—

● What are the major physical regions and climates of South Asia.

● How physical environment has shaped the economies and cultures of South Asia.

● How religious and ethnic groups have influenced political events in South Asia.

Because India is so large, students sometimes mistakenly assume the other countries in South Asia are quite small. Pakistan is nearly one and one-half times the size of France. Nepal and Bangladesh are each larger than Greece. Even Bhutan is larger than either Switzerland or Denmark.

INTRODUCTION

The culture area of South Asia is made up of six countries—India, Pakistan (PAK ih STAN), Sri Lanka (sree LAHNG kuh), Bangladesh (BAHNG gluh DEHSH), Nepal (nuh PAWL), and Bhutan (boo TAHN). Together these countries cover 1,733,182 square miles (4,488,937.9 sq km), about 10 percent of the land area of the continent of Asia.

As the map on page 540 shows, tall mountains in the north cut South Asia off from the rest of the Asian continent. Because of this separation, South Asia is sometimes called a **subcontinent**—a landmass that is like a continent, only smaller. Because India dominates the subcontinent, it is often called the *Indian subcontinent*.

South Asia has many different kinds of landscape and climate—from deserts to tropical rain forests to fertile plains to snow-capped mountains. The people are as varied as the land—in language, religion, heritage, and way of life.

South Asia is the home of some of the world's oldest civilizations. Over thousands of years, its territories have been invaded and ruled by many different groups of people. Today those territories are independent republics or kingdoms, each with its own government, economy, and resources.

1. INDIA

India covers 1,269,340 square miles (3,287,588.0 sq km) and is home to 800.3 million people. It is the largest country in South Asia in land area and the second largest country in the world in population. In Figure 26-1 on page 541, India's size and population are compared with those of the United States.

Skilled climbers from all over the world come to this area to climb the peaks of K-2 and Everest.

1.1 Landscape and Climate

India is a land of varied landscapes and climates. In both landscape and climate, as well as in people, it is a study in contrasts and extremes. The environment in general has had a great influence on the country.

Landscape. Two huge walls of mountains—the Karakoram (KAR uh KOHR uhm) and the Himalayas (HIHM uh LAY uhz)—rise in northern India. They stretch some 1,500 miles (2,414.0 km) along its northern border from the Indian state of Jammu and Kashmir east to Bhutan. The Karakoram Range dominates Jammu and Kashmir. In this range is K-2, the second highest peak in the world and the highest point in India. The Himalayas, which average more than 5 miles (8.0 km) in height, are the tallest mountains in the

539

USING GRAPHIC SKILLS

MAKING HYPOTHESES

In studying about geographic inquiry in Chapter 1, you learned that one of the last steps geographers take in their work is making generalizations and hypotheses. Hypotheses are generalizations that are made before any research is done to explain how or why things happen as they do. They are educated guesses that offer a possible answer or answers to a problem or provide an explanation for an observation.

Making hypotheses can help you in your study of geography. It focuses your attention on a problem or observation and challenges you to act as a detective in thinking out possible explanations. After hypothesizing, you would research and observe further to see if your hypotheses are correct.

A problem or observation is often presented as a statement. In making an hypothesis, you should first carefully read and understand the statement. (*India has found it hard to feed all of its people.*)

Then think of possible reasons that might explain the statement. Read in your textbook and other reference books such as encyclopedias for causes, influences, or factors that you *think* explain the statement. (*Most of India's physical features do not permit much farming; India does not receive enough rainfall on a regular basis to support farming; India's population is too large for the farmers to feed; Indian farmers do not use modern farming methods or equipment that would increase the amount of crops they raise, and so on.*)

Use the physical regions map on this page as well as other sources of information in your textbook or other reference books to make hypotheses that explain each of the statements below.

1. Pakistan now exports more food than it imports.
2. Bangladesh is one of the world's poorest countries.
3. China has never undertaken an invasion of India.

PHYSICAL REGIONS OF SOUTH ASIA

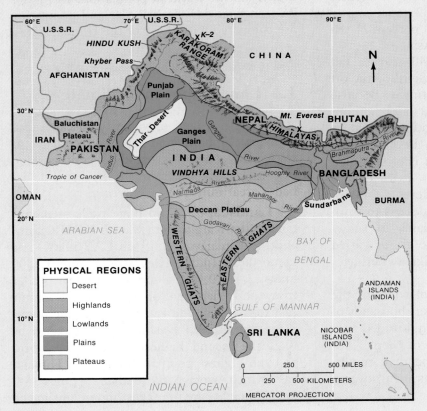

world. Actually three parallel chains separated by deep valleys and canyons, they cover the countries of Nepal and Bhutan. On the border between Nepal and China is Mount Everest, the world's highest peak at 29,028 feet (8,847.7 m).

A series of hills and low mountains runs along the eastern border with Burma. South of the mountains and hills major plains areas spread out like a fan. At the western edge of the plain is the Thar (TAHR) Desert, which runs into Pakistan. About 500 miles (804.6 km) long and 275 miles (442.5 km) wide, the Thar has salt flats, sand dunes, and salt lakes.

Stretching east of the Thar to the Bay of Bengal (behn GAWL) is the vast Ganges (GAN JEEZ) Plain. It has some of the most fertile soil in India. Crossing the plain is the Ganges River. From its sources in the Himalayas, the Ganges flows 1,550 miles (2,494.4 km) to the Bay of Bengal. Here is where it forms a huge delta that makes up much of the country of Bangladesh. Also crossing the plain is the Brahmaputra River. It begins on the Plateau of Tibet and flows nearly 1,700 miles (2,735.8 km) to join the Ganges in Bangladesh.

South of the Ganges Plain is a range of low mountains known as the Vindhya (VIHN dyuh) Hills that separate the plain from the Deccan (DEHK uhn) Plateau. The plateau makes up the southern two-thirds of India. Shaped like a triangle pointed south, it has forests, farmland, and many minerals.

Bordering the western part of the Deccan Plateau just inland from the Arabian Sea are the Western Ghats (GAWTS), mountains ranging from 3,000 feet (914 m) to 8,000 feet (2,438 m) above sea level. The Eastern Ghats, which lie along the coast of the Bay of Bengal, are lower. The Ghats are separated from the sea by a strip of lowland.

Climate. Because mountains along India's northern border block cold air from entering the subcontinent, most places in India

COMPAR-A-GRAPH: INDIA–UNITED STATES

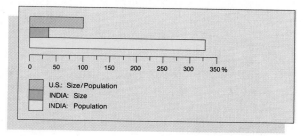

FIGURE 26-1
India has more than three times as many people as the United States in an area less than half the size. How would you describe India's population density?

See the TAE for an Objective 1 Activity.

are warm or hot most of the year. Only areas at high altitudes in the northernmost parts of India have temperatures below freezing. These low temperatures occur only during the coolest season of the year.

As Figure 26-2 on page 542 shows, an important influence on India's climate is monsoon winds. The term monsoon comes from the Arabic word *mawsim*, which means season. Most of India has three seasons—cool, hot, and rainy. During the cool season, which lasts from November through February, and the hot season, which lasts from March to the end of April, monsoon winds bring dry air from the northern mountains. During the rainy season, which runs from May through October, monsoon winds shift direction and bring much moist air from over the Indian Ocean.

Monsoon rains fall most heavily in the Western Ghats, the Ganges Plain, and eastern India. From June through September, these areas receive 50 inches (127 cm) or more. The rest of the year is dry. A city in eastern India—Cherrapunji (CHEHR uh PUN jee) is one of the wettest spots in the world. It gets about 425 inches (1,079 cm)—35.4 feet (10.7 m)—of rain a year.

CHAPTER 26 **SOUTH ASIA**

Despite its having a rather diverse economy, India is not a prosperous country. The birthrate is extremely high by European and Anglo-American standards. India has found it difficult to expand its economy fast enough to provide well for its fast-growing population.

MONSOON WINDS OF INDIA

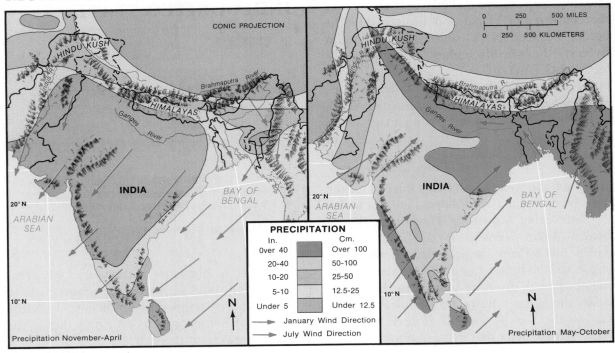

FIGURE 26-2
India's southwest coast has a tropical monsoon climate in which winds during particular times of the year bring great amounts of rain. Why does this area receive such a large amount of rainfall from May through October?

More than 15 percent of the world's people live in India, which ranks second only to China.

1.2 Economic and Cultural Patterns

In India agriculture and industry are important to the economy. Both are being developed over five-year periods under a series of plans set up by the government. The goal is to develop the nation and improve the standard of living of the Indian people.

Agriculture and Industry. Although about one-half of India's land can be farmed, most farmers have small farms and grow only enough for their own needs. According to tradition, a farm should be divided equally among a father's sons when he dies. Because farm families often are large and farms relatively small, shares of land often are too small to provide enough food for a family.

In December 1984 a toxic chemical leak from a Union Carbide plant in Bhopal killed more than 2,500.

Over the years, India has found it hard to feed all its people. In recent years, however, because of improved farm methods, their food needs are coming closer to being met. Since the 1960s and 1970s, farmers have increased food production through more irrigation and better use of seeds and fertilizers.

India now grows more peanuts, peppers, and tea than any other country, and is second only to China in rice production. It is also a world leader in growing bananas, sugarcane, tobacco, cotton, wheat, and **jute,** a plant fiber used for burlap bags and twine.

India has a good supply of natural resources needed for industries to grow. Hydroelectric plants produce about 40 percent of the country's electricity, and nuclear power stations provide energy for factories. India

ASIA UNIT 9

also has rich mineral deposits, many of which are just beginning to be uncovered.

Textiles are a major industry. Of all the industries in India, it has the largest number of workers. Iron and steel is another leading industry, with four mills owned by the government. A fifth mill, the Tata iron and steel plant, is one of the world's largest privately owned industrial centers. India also has oil and sugar refineries and factories that make locomotives, automobiles, paper, cement, and chemical fertilizer. In addition are the many products made by **cottage industries,** industries based in rural homes where family members use their own tools. These include hand-woven cotton and silk cloth, rugs, leather goods, and metal goods.

The Indian People.   Nearly 75 percent of India's people live in rural villages, most in crowded straw and mud huts. Both men and women work in the fields. Women also carry the burden of other work, such as getting water from village wells and gathering firewood for cooking and heating. For most, village life is hard, and often there is no way to make a living. For this and other reasons, thousands of people move from their villages to the cities. Today about one-fourth of Indians live in urban areas. Calcutta, with more than nine million people, is the largest city. Next is Bombay, with about eight million.

Fourteen major languages and more than 1,000 minor languages or dialects are spoken in India. Hindi is used by only one-half of the people. In trade and government, English is the common language.

Religion plays an important role in Indian life. As Figure 26–3 on this page shows, several religions are practiced by Indians. The most important religion of India is Hinduism, which is practiced by more than 80 percent of the people. Hindus believe that all living things have souls that belong to one eternal spirit. They also believe in **reincarnation,** the

RELIGIONS OF SOUTH ASIA

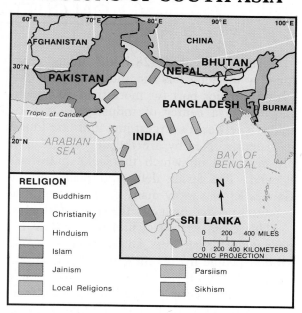

FIGURE 26-3
South Asia is predominantly Hindu. In which country is South Asia's second largest religion practiced?

There are about 3,000 different subcastes. Access to certain jobs is influenced by a person's caste.

idea that all living things are reborn after death in another form. Hindus follow daily rituals of washing and prayer. Many bathe in the Ganges, which they view as holy. Important to Hinduism is the **caste system,** the division of society into four categories. Each category, or caste, has its own rules for diet, marriage, and other social practices. People cannot move from one caste into another. The caste system has been a strong part of Indian culture for centuries.

Today the government opposes many caste rules, and the caste system is weakening.

1.3 Influences of the Past

People first settled the area that is now India about 400,000 years ago. By 2500 BC, well-planned cities had been set up in the northwest along the banks of the Indus River. Then about 1500 BC, invaders known as Aryans (AR ee uhnz) entered the country from

THE URBAN WORLD

CALCUTTA: POVERTY

About 80 miles (128.7 km) inland from the Bay of Bengal is the Indian city of Calcutta. A major port for more than 300 years, Calcutta is a center of industry as well as trade. The world's largest jute mills are found in Calcutta. Nearby are the deposits of iron ore and coal on which the city's industries depend. The fertile delta and plains of the Ganges River supply many of the agricultural products needed by a city the size of Calcutta.

In recent years Calcutta has become India's major urban area. Today more than nine million people live in the city. This is an average of 98,000 people per square mile (37,838 per sq km). While some neighborhoods have large houses and plenty of space, other parts of the city are dirty and crowded. In many areas, clean water and waste disposal systems are lacking. Three million people live in poorly built huts in Calcutta's slums. An-

other 300,000 have no home at all. At night they crawl into doorways or sleep on sidewalks. Many people sift through garbage for scraps of food.

Calcutta has not always had some of the problems it has had recently. From 1772 to 1912, it was the capital of British India—"the jewel of the British Empire." But when British India was divided in 1947, millions of Hindus fled into India from East Pakistan. Most were farmers with few other skills. They went to Calcutta in search of work and shelter. In many cases they found neither. But they had nowhere else to go. In 1971, when Bangladesh separated from Pakistan, millions of frightened people again sought safety in Calcutta. And once again there was no work and no place to live for many.

Calcutta's officials were not prepared to take care of so many people. They could not provide enough water, sewers, housing, electricity, and transportation for all the people living in the city. As a result, in the 1970s and early 1980s, Calcutta became known worldwide for its poor living conditions.

Although poverty remains a major problem in Calcutta today, the city's outlook is more hopeful. The rate of population growth has slowed. More sections of the city have sewers and clean water. Roads and streets have been improved. Although building is slow, more and more people are off the streets and in rooms, apartments, or houses. All of these changes make Calcutta's future look brighter.

1. What events led to the decline of living standards in Calcutta?
2. How do poor people live in Calcutta?
3. How has Calcutta changed in recent years?

About 2500 BC a people called Harappans settled in the Indus River Valley. They were the earliest known people to grow cotton, and the ruins of their largest cities, Harappa and Mohenjo-Daro, are the oldest examples yet found of planned communities where buildings were laid out on a planned street grid.

INDUS VALLEY CIVILIZATION—3000 BC

The Indus River Valley gave rise to one of the world's earliest civilizations. Its chief urban centers were Mohenjo-Daro and Harappa. The Aryans, who invaded this region, brought with them the Sanskrit language, horses, and iron and copper tools. What were some other Aryan contributions to Indian culture?

Archaeologists have found some Indus Valley artifacts among ruins of Mesopotamia in Iraq.

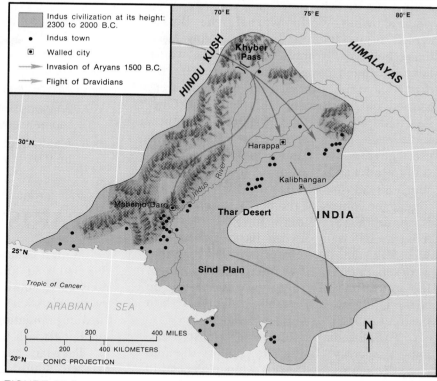

FIGURE 26-4

central Asia. Figure 26-4 on this page shows the invasion of the Aryans through the passes of the Hindu Kush Mountains.

When the Aryans arrived in India, people known as Dravidians (druh VIHD ee uhnz) were living in cities on the northern plains. The Aryans gradually pushed the Dravidians into southern India. Those who remained in the north became slaves.

The Aryans had a strong influence on early Indian culture. In time they separated into classes and developed the caste system. Hinduism also began with the Aryans. An old religion, its beliefs and practices grew and changed over the years. Another major world religion, Buddhism, began in India about 500 BC and soon spread to other parts of Asia.

Over the centuries, many other invaders came to the subcontinent. They set up power-

ful empires and founded centers of education and the arts. Beginning in the 700s AD, Muslim invaders brought Islam to India. In the 1500s they founded the Mogul (MOH guhl) Empire, which lasted 200 years.

During the 1400s and 1500s, European traders reached India. By the 1700s the British had gained control of large areas of the country. They built roads, railroads, seaports, and irrigation systems. Their changes, however, largely benefited them rather than Indians. Indians worked the plantations, mines, and factories, but the British made the profits.

In the early 1900s, many Indians began to support freedom from British rule. An Indian leader by the name of Mohandas Gandhi (moh HAHN das GAHN dee) took charge of the movement for independence. He urged

Indians to use peaceful methods of resistance against the British.

Following World War II, the British agreed to give India its freedom. Many Muslims, however, feared that Hindus would have too much power in an independent India. As a result two separate countries were formed out of British India in 1947. One, Pakistan, was set up for Muslims. The other, India, was set up for Hindus. This led to a great migration as Hindus moved from Pakistan to India and Muslims from India to Pakistan. Since then India and Pakistan have fought for control of the northern territory of Kashmir (KASH MIHR). In 1971 India entered a civil war between East Pakistan and West Pakistan, two territories of Pakistan that were separated by 1,000 miles (1,609.3 km) of Indian territory. The result was the setting up of the independent Republic of Bangladesh in East Pakistan.

Today India is the world's most populous democracy. It was also one of the first large democracies to have a woman as head of government. Recently certain regional religious and ethnic groups in India have wanted more freedom. The actions of those favoring fast change through fighting have led to much killing. Meanwhile the Indian government has been working to meet the demands of its peoples and to keep national unity.

Have students research the life of Mohandas Gandhi.

CONTENT CHECK

1. **Identify:** India, Karakoram Range, K-2, Himalayas, Mount Everest, Thar Desert, Ganges Plain, Ganges River, Brahmaputra River, Vindhya Hills, Deccan Plateau, Western Ghats, Eastern Ghats, Cherrapunji, Calcutta, Hindi, Hinduism, Aryans, Dravidians, Mogul Empire, Mohandas Gandhi.

2. **Define:** jute, cottage industries, reincarnation, caste system.

3. What kinds of landforms are found in India?

4. How do monsoon winds affect India's climate?

5. What industry employs the most workers?

6. What is the major religion of India?

7. Why was British India divided into two separate countries?

8. **Challenge:** How is India different from most developing countries?

See the *TRB* for *Teacher Notes: Section 1 Extending the Lesson* on India's railway system.

2. PAKISTAN

With a land area of 310,402 square miles (803,940.6 sq km), the Islamic Republic of Pakistan is South Asia's second largest country in size. With 104.6 million people, it is third in population in South Asia. Only India and Bangladesh have larger populations.

Pakistan has depended on both South Asia and Southwest Asia for its development. History and geography link it to South Asia. Religion ties it to Southwest Asia.

Khyber Pass is 28 miles (45 km) long and was used by armies such as Alexander the Great's in their invasions of India.

2.1 Landscape and Climate

Pakistan is a land of tall, snow-covered mountains, high plateaus, sandy deserts, and fertile plains. Its climate is dry, with hot summers and cool winters.

Landscape. The landscape of northern Pakistan is dominated by the towering Hindu Kush Mountains, which are part of the same chain as the Karakoram Range of northern India. Several passes cut through the mountains. The most famous is the Khyber (KY buhr) Pass, which the Aryans used around 1500 BC to enter the Indian subcontinent. The pass makes it possible to travel between the city of Pashawar (puh SHAH wuhr) in north-

This view shows the landscape of Pakistan's Upper Swat Valley with the Hindu Kush Mountains rising dramatically in the background. The rugged mountainous terrain illustrates a sense of isolation and the difficulty in farming some of the land in Pakistan. What famous mountain pass cuts through the Hindu Kush Mountains?

A railroad built in the Khyber Pass in 1920-1925 passes through 34 tunnels and over 92 bridges.

Baluchistan is not only a plateau, but the name of one of the four provinces in Pakistan. Pastoral nomads such as the Baluchi and Pathans make up most of the population there. They speak languages related to Persian.

west Pakistan and Kabul (KAHB uhl), the capital of Afghanistan.

Farther south the Indus (IHN duhs) River flows through central Pakistan. The valleys formed by the Indus and its tributaries have the most fertile soil in the country.

To the east and west of the Indus River are dry low areas. To the west the Baluchistan (buh LOO chuh STAN) Plateau covers much of the country. Running through the plateau are several mountain chains. From the foothills of the mountains in the north, lowlands reach south about 1,000 miles (1,609.3 km) to the Arabian Sea. The Thar Desert covers part of this lowland in the east.

Climate. Pakistan has largely a dry climate with rainfall in most parts less than 10 inches (25.4 cm) a year. An exception is the northern foothills, which get more than 30 inches (76.2 cm) a year, most of it between July and September.

Except at high elevations, temperatures are generally warm or hot. As in India, the high mountains to the north keep the cold air of central Asia from entering the country. At the coastal city of Karachi (kuh RAHCH ee),

average high temperatures are 77°F (25°C) in July. At the inland city of Islāmābād (ihs LAHM uh BAHD) in the northeast, high temperatures average 62°F (16.7°C) in January and 98°F (36.7°C) in July.

Refer students to pages 96-97 to review the map of Earth's Climate Regions.

2.2 Economic and Cultural Patterns

About 55 percent of all Pakistanis make a living from the land. Most raise crops on small farms. Although they use few modern machines, they have irrigated more than 25,000,000 acres (10,117,140 ha), 47 percent of Pakistan's farmland.

To increase food production, the Pakistani government has given more land to poor farmers. This action, along with more fertilizers, has led to more and better crops. Pakistan now exports more food than it imports.

Wheat is the chief food crop and is used to make flat loaves of bread called **chapatty.** Pakistani farmers also grow rice, sugarcane, barley, tobacco, and fruit for their own use. They also raise cotton, which is the country's

CHAPTER 26   **SOUTH ASIA**

547

Karachi's airport, one of the busiest in Asia, is a major link in international trade routes.

In Pakistan Muslim holidays are considered national holidays.

LAND USE AND RESOURCES OF SOUTH ASIA

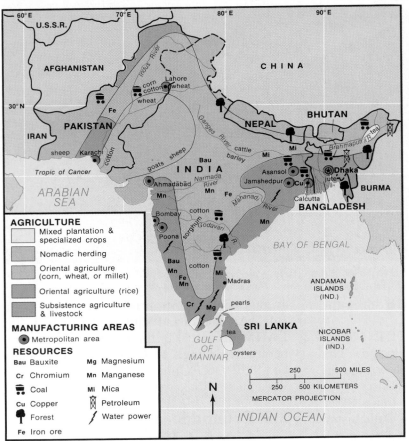

South Asia's large populations require as much land as possible be used for agriculture. India is the region's major industrial nation. Its iron ore reserves support the country's important steel industry. For what types of agriculture is Pakistan's land used?

FIGURE 26-5

Fairly extensive natural gas deposits and newly discovered oil reserves have improved Pakistan's energy outlook.

most important cash crop. Besides crops, many Pakistanis tend sheep and goats. Cattle are raised as work animals and for milk, meat, and leather.

Figure 26-5 above shows that industry takes second place to farming. Many products are made by cottage industries. Until recently industry did not grow a great deal because of a shortage of natural resources. To overcome this and help industry grow, the government has built dams on the country's rivers to supply industry with hydroelectricity. Government leaders also are backing the production of such goods as steel, cars, chemicals, and fertilizers. In this way they hope to cut back the need for foreign aid.

Most heavy industry is found in the cities of Karachi and Lahore (luh HOHR). However, factory jobs are still scarce. Since the 1970s about two million Pakistanis have left the country to work in the oil fields of the Persian Gulf. The money they send home is important to Pakistan's economy.

Although nearly 97 percent of Pakistanis are Muslims, the country is made up of many different ethnic and language groups. Urdu (UR doo), the official language, is spoken by only nine percent of the people. Almost 64 percent speak Punjabi (PUHN JAHB ee). Because of language differences, English is widely used in government, universities, and the military.

About 75 percent of the people live in rural villages in small homes of clay or sun-dried mud. Most villagers follow traditional customs. For example, women do not have as much freedom as men do. The women must wear veils when they are in public places. They take care of their families but do little outside their homes except work in the fields.

Recently, many Pakistanis have left villages for urban areas. In cities poor people live in older, crowded areas and often keep their traditional ways. People of the upper and middle classes, on the other hand, have accepted many western ideas and practices.

Pakistan's largest city is the seaport of Karachi with about five million people. The capital, Islāmābād, lies in the northern part of the country near the Himalayas. A well-planned city that has a population of 205,000 people, it was built during the early 1960s to draw people from the crowded coast to the less populated interior.

Point out to students the great distance that separates the cities of Karachi and Islāmābād.

2.3 Influences of the Past

Pakistan and India share much of the same history. The ruins of the ancient civilization of the Indus River Valley are in Pakistan, and many Pakistanis are descended from the early Aryans. After the Aryans, several other invasions added to the variety of Pakistan's people and the growth of its culture. Of all the invaders, the Arabs had one of the greatest effects on Pakistan's development. In 711 AD they crossed the Arabian Sea and brought Islam to South Asia. Three hundred years later, Turkish Muslims invaded and strengthened Islam's hold on the people. Islam especially made itself felt in Pakistani art, architecture, and literature.

During the 1800s and early 1900s, the British ruled Pakistan as part of their Indian empire. The Muslims of British India, however, refused to accept western ways. They

also feared Hindu rule of the country. To protect their culture, Muslim leaders formed their own political organization and called for a separate Muslim country. This led to dividing British India into India and Pakistan. Pakistan was divided into two sections—East Pakistan in the northeast and West Pakistan in the northwest. The two sections were more than 1,000 miles (1,609.3 km) apart.

In spite of religious ties, the people of East Pakistan and West Pakistan were divided by ethnic and language differences. These differences led to a civil war in 1971 in which East Pakistan became the independent country of Bangladesh.

Since the late 1970s, Pakistan has had many political problems. In the years ahead, however, its biggest challenge is to overcome the many divisions among its people.

See the *TRB* for *Teacher Notes: Section 2 Extending the Lesson* on Pakistan's handmade carpets.

CONTENT CHECK

1. **Identify:** Pakistan, Hindu Kush Mountains, Khyber Pass, Indus River, Baluchistan Plateau, Karachi, Islāmābād, Lahore, Urdu, Punjabi.

2. **Define:** chapatty.

3. How does Pakistan compare in size to the other nations of South Asia?

4. Where is the most fertile soil found in Pakistan?

5. How do most Pakistani's make their living?

6. What has helped Pakistani farmers grow more and better crops?

7. In what ways did the Arabs influence Pakistan's development?

8. Why was Pakistan founded as a nation?

9. **Challenge:** What are some problems that Pakistan might face if it tried to set up many heavy industries?

During the ages of exploration and discovery, Sri Lanka achieved fame for its spices.

Education through the university level is free in Sri Lanka. The literacy rate there is 80 percent.

NATIONS OF SOUTH ASIA

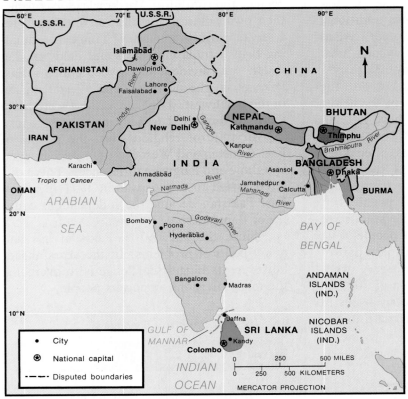

FIGURE 26-6

India is the dominant nation of South Asia economically and politically. However, differences within India's culture—religions, ethnic groups, languages—have stopped India from being a unified nation. Pakistan and Sri Lanka have also experienced problems of unifying their different ethnic groups. What two ethnic groups live in Sri Lanka?

Point out to students that the blue dashed line in the map represents international boundaries over water and the black dashed line represents disputed boundaries.

The narrow strait separating India and Sri Lanka—Palk Strait—is so shallow that many large ships cannot pass through it.

3. OTHER COUNTRIES OF SOUTH ASIA

As Figure 26-6 above shows, the four other countries of South Asia—Bhutan, Nepal, Sri Lanka, and Bangladesh—all lie on the edges of either India or Pakistan. All four are small in size. All have economies that are just beginning to develop.

See the *TAE* for an *Objective 3* Activity.

3.1 Sri Lanka

The island country of Sri Lanka lies in the Indian Ocean about 20 miles (32.1 km) southeast of India. Its 25,332 square miles (65,609.8 sq km) are made up of a low plain

along the coast and forested highlands in the interior. Sea breezes help keep the climate mild and humid.

Sri Lanka's economy is largely based on agriculture. Cash crops, such as tea, rubber, and coconut, are grown on large plantations. Sri Lanka is also one of the world's leading exporters of tea. Recently, the country has tried to expand its economy by building more industries. Textiles, fertilizers, cement, leather, and wood and paper products produced in Sri Lankan cities have become important exports to be sold all over the world.

For nearly 150 years, Sri Lanka was a British colony known as Ceylon. In 1948 it became an independent country. With nearly 600,000 people, the seaport of Colombo is the capital and largest city.

About 75 percent of Sri Lanka's 16.3 million people are Sinhalese (SIHN guh LEES). More than 2,000 years ago, their ancestors left northern India and brought Buddhism to the island. Today 66 percent of Sri Lankans are Buddhists. Another 18 percent of the people are Tamils (TAM uhlz). Some are descended from Dravidians of southern India who came to Sri Lanka hundreds of years ago. Others are descended from Indian workers brought there by the British during the 1800s. Today the Tamils, most of whom are Hindu, live in the northern and eastern parts of the island. Many of them do not like Sinhalese control of the government and want to set up a separate Tamil state.

Bangladesh is one of the rainiest spots on Earth, averaging as much as 85 inches (215.9 cm) annually.

3.2 Bangladesh

The Republic of Bangladesh is found near the border of India and Burma at the delta of the Ganges River on the Bay of Bengal. With an area of 55,598 square miles (143,998.7 sq km), the country is about the size of Wisconsin. Largely made up of flat, low plains, it has a tropical moist climate. Much of the country is flooded during the wet monsoons. It is also hit by cyclones that develop over the Indian Ocean.

Bangladesh was called East Bengal until 1955, when it became East Pakistan.

Bangladesh's rich, wet soil produces such crops as rice, jute, sugarcane, and tobacco. From its forests comes **teak,** a wood used for shipbuilding and fine furniture. Despite this, Bangladesh is one of the poorest countries in the world. About 85 percent of its 107,100,000 people live in rural areas. Most are poor farmers who work small plots of land without modern tools or methods.

Bangladesh's urban population is smaller than that of most other nations of South Asia. Its capital and most important seaport, Dhaka (DAK uh), has more than two million people. Its cities, however, are slowly becoming centers of industry whose factories produce farm-related products. The major industry is the making of rope and thread from jute.

A cyclone and tidal wave in 1970 devastated Bangladesh and caused about 300,000 deaths.

Carrying baskets filled with clumps of sod, these boys and men are working to build an earthen dam in Bangladesh. The dam will control flooding and help with irrigation. What conditions in Bangladesh make flooding a constant threat?

Point out the course of the Brahmaputra River to students.

FOCUS ON ECONOMY

A STORY OF TEA

Tea is a flowering, evergreen plant that grows fastest in areas of high temperatures and high humidity. The drink made from the plant's leaves has a better flavor, however, when the plant grows slowly. The best-tasting teas are grown in tropical and subtropical areas at altitudes over 5,000 feet (1,524 m) where it is cooler. The photo above shows tea pickers in Sri Lanka, which has a good climate for growing tea.

India and Sri Lanka produce more than one-half of the world's tea. The export of tea brings much income to these countries. Tea has been grown in South Asia for about 125 years. In many other parts of the world, it has been raised for hundreds of years.

Tea was discovered nearly 2,000 years ago by people who lived in the mountains of southeast Asia. They boiled the leaves of native tea plants to make a drink. Sometimes they even ate the leaves, mixing them with salt, garlic, oil, pork, or fish, and then rolling them into balls.

In time the plant became known in China. Farmers there began to raise it as early as 350 AD. In addition to using tea as a drink, these early Chinese sometimes made a thick paste from the boiled leaves, spread it on the skin, and used it as a medicine. It was supposed to cure rheumatism or sore, stiff joints.

By the 400s tea was traded all through China, and its use spread quickly to nearby Japan. In the 1500s, it was brought to Europe. In the 1600s England and other parts of Europe began importing tea. At this time, however, it was a luxury used only by the very wealthy.

England's demand for tea grew a great deal in the early 1700s after Queen Anne announced that she drank tea instead of ale with breakfast. The upper classes soon followed her example. In time so did the middle and working classes.

At the time, the British East India Company was the only company allowed to import tea from China. Because more people were drinking tea, the company made money. To make sure it continued to make money, it kept tea from being grown in India and other places until the 1800s.

The first shipments of tea from India reached London shortly before 1840. In the 1860s there was a great increase in the growing of tea in India and Ceylon. The crop was so successful that South Asia became the leading tea producer. It remains so today.

1. Where was tea first grown?
2. Why was tea important to the British East India Company?
3. How does South Asia rank as a tea-producing region today?

In the 1950s pesticides were applied to the malaria-infested lowlands of Nepal. Health improved, and the land was made suitable for settlement. The lowland forests are now being cut down at alarming rates because more land for farming and firewood is needed. Soil erosion and landslides now threaten the lowlands.

Bangladesh is the world's eighth largest nation in population. Most of the people are Bengalis who speak a language by the same name and who share many cultural features with the people of eastern India. With about 85 percent of the people Muslim, Islam has affected much of the country's art, architecture, music, and literature.

The number of people living in Bangladesh is growing rapidly. By the year 2000, the population is expected to reach close to 145 million. This population growth is already causing problems. Bangladesh's farmers, with their limited resources, cannot feed all the country's people. In addition to food shortages, the people of Bangladesh also suffer from overcrowding. With 1,926 people per square mile (743 per sq km), Bangladesh is one of the most densely populated countries in the world.

By way of contrast, the United States has about 67 people per square mile (26 per sq km).

3.3 Bhutan and Nepal

Bhutan and Nepal are both kingdoms in the Himalayas. Bhutan, which lies between Tibet and India, takes up 18,147 square miles (47,000.7 sq km). Most of its 1.5 million people live in river valleys and are farmers. Their principal religion is Buddhism and their major language Dzongkha (JAWNG kah). Most of Bhutan's wealth lies in its forests, coal, some minerals, wildlife, and rivers. Its principal city is the capital, Thimphu (THIHM boo).

Like Bhutan, Nepal is primarily an agricultural country. It also is one of the least urbanized countries in the world. Only seven percent of its 17,800,000 people live in towns or cities. The principal city is the capital, Kathmandu (KAT MAN DOO). The Himalayas cover 90 percent of the country's 54,363 square miles (140,800.1 sq km). Nearly all Nepal's people live on the 10 percent that is arable. Most people are Hindu and speak a language called Nepali (nuh PAWL ee).

CONTENT CHECK

1. **Identify:** Sri Lanka, Ceylon, Colombo, Sinhalese, Tamils, Bangladesh, Dhaka, Bengalis, Bhutan, Dzongkha, Thimphu, Nepal, Kathmandu, Nepali.

2. **Define:** teak.

3. What two groups make up most of the population of Sri Lanka?

4. What problems are being caused by population growth in Bangladesh?

5. From where does most of Bhutan's wealth come?

6. Where do all but seven percent of the people of Nepal live?

7. **Challenge:** What are some problems that might stand in the way of an effort to raise standards of living in Bangladesh quickly?

Bhutan's mountainous environment limits the potential for agricultural development.

CONCLUSION

People have lived in South Asia for thousands of years. The people who live there today, however, are faced with many challenges. Farming is, for the most part, the single most important economic activity. Yet millions of South Asians barely make a living as farmers and others do not get enough to eat. Population is large and continues to grow at a rapid rate.

Since World War II, the countries of South Asia have thrown off foreign rule. They have also come a long way in developing their economies. In recent years attention has been focused on developing the area's resources. Thus, the number of industries has increased. However, growing populations and conflict among ethnic groups make progress difficult. These issues will continue to challenge South Asia in the years to come.

SUMMARY

1. South Asia includes the countries of India, Pakistan, Nepal, Bhutan, Sri Lanka, and Bangladesh. These countries are located on an extension of the Asian continent called the Indian subcontinent.
2. India is the dominant country of the South Asia region. Its population is second largest in the world.
3. The traditional caste system of India is tied to Hinduism. The caste system has a weakening hold on Indian life today.
4. India's economy is based on agriculture and industry.
5. Pakistan became an independent country in 1947. It is mostly Muslim. At one time Pakistan included two parts, East Pakistan and West Pakistan. In 1971 East Pakistan broke away and became the independent country of Bangladesh.
6. Pakistan is primarily agricultural. The most productive farming areas are along the Indus River and its tributaries.
7. Sri Lanka is an island country off the coast of southern India. Sri Lanka's economy is based on agriculture.
8. Bangladesh lies to the east of India. Much of its territory is occupied by the Ganges delta. It is a poor, very crowded country.
9. Bhutan and Nepal are kingdoms in the Himalayas. They are small in size. Both are agricultural countries.

Answers to the following questions can be found on page T266.

REVIEWING VOCABULARY

On a separate sheet of paper, number from 1 to 6. Write the word that best matches each definition below. Then write a complete sentence for each word that shows you understand its meaning.

cottage industry   subcontinent   reincarnation   caste system   teak   chapatty

1. wood used for shipbuilding and fine furniture, found in Bangladesh
2. categories into which Hindus are divided
3. belief that living things are reborn in some other form after death
4. wheat bread
5. manufacturing activity performed in the home by families and centered in rural areas
6. landmass smaller than a continent

REMEMBERING THE FACTS

1. What are the countries of the South Asia culture area?
2. What are the largest cities of India and Pakistan?
3. Where do most of India's people live?
4. What are the major lowland and plateau areas of India?
5. What is the major religion of India?
6. What pattern of rainfall is common in India?

7. Is India more of an agricultural or an industrial country?
8. What mountains of Pakistan are part of the same chain as the Karakoram Range of northern India?
9. What countries in South Asia make products from jute?
10. What is the highest mountain in the world, and in which of South Asia's countries is it found?
11. In what country of South Asia are the majority of people Sinhalese?
12. In what country of South Asia is the delta of the Ganges River?

UNDERSTANDING THE FACTS

1. What accounts for India having a dry season and a wet season?
2. How does the distribution of India's population affect the growth of industry in the country?
3. How do the climates of India and Pakistan differ?
4. What groups brought Islam to the area that is now Pakistan?
5. Do the main agricultural products of Sri Lanka meet the nation's food needs? Why or why not?
6. How is the economy of Bangladesh like those of other South Asian countries?

THINKING CRITICALLY AND CREATIVELY

1. How might the climates of India and Pakistan be different if no high mountains were found along their northern borders?
2. For 200 years the United Kingdom ruled much of the Indian subcontinent. How did the British affect development?
3. Why was British India divided into India and Pakistan in 1947? What problems developed as a result of the division?
4. **Challenge:** Suppose you were asked to invest money in a plan to establish large rice plantations in India in an area midway between Delhi and the Pakistan border. Would this be a wise investment? Why or why not?
5. **Challenge:** Many Tamils in Sri Lanka would like to set up their own state. If an independent Tamil country were carved out of Sri Lanka, what problems might it face?
6. **Challenge:** What economic problems might arise for Sri Lanka and other countries that produce only a small number of agricultural products?

REINFORCING GRAPHIC SKILLS

Study the map on page 540. Then make hypotheses to explain each of the statements below.

1. Other than farming, Bhutan's economic activities include wood and leather working and papermaking.
2. The Pakistani government has given more land to poor farmers, and this has led to more and better crops.

CHAPTER 27

Since the Pacific War, Japanese cities have grown tremendously because of the large numbers of people who have migrated from rural to urban areas.

Crowded street in Tokyo, Japan

EAST ASIA

In this chapter, you will learn—

● What are the major physical features and climates of East Asia.

● How people in East Asia make their livings.

● How historical events have affected the countries of East Asia.

● Why there are two Chinas and two Koreas.

Ask students to locate the countries of East Asia on a map. Point out to students the vast size difference of these countries. Compare for example, the size of the People's Republic of China to that of Macao.

INTRODUCTION

Bordering the Pacific Ocean south of the Soviet Union is the culture area of East Asia. The home of one-fifth of all the world's people, it is made up of Japan, the People's Republic of China, the Republic of China (Taiwan), North Korea, South Korea, Mongolia, Hong Kong, and Macao (muh KOW).

East Asia is huge in area. It stretches about 3,600 miles (5,793.6 km) from the western provinces of China to the eastern coast of Japan. Along the coasts and on the plains, large numbers of people are crowded into some of the densest population centers in the world. In other parts of the area, however, are large stretches of land with few or no people.

A variety of governments are found in East Asia. The People's Republic of China, North Korea, and Mongolia are communist countries. To different degrees Japan, South Korea, and the Republic of China are democracies.

In East Asia the old and the new exist side by side. East Asia has one of the world's oldest nations—China. Its culture, begun more than 4,000 years ago, has spread over the centuries to nearby countries. Yet, in many ways, China is a new nation. It has had a communist government only since 1949, and it is just beginning to create an industrial economy. East Asia also has one of the world's most modern industrial nations—Japan. Although it ranks with the United States and other leading economic powers, its people have not forgotten their past and keep many of their traditions.

Point out to students that Japan lies generally within latitudes also occupied by the contiguous United States.

1. JAPAN

Forming a curve off the coast of East Asia is the island country of Japan. It is an archipelago of four main islands—Hokkaidō (hah KY doh), Honshū, Shikoku (shih KOH koo), and Kyūshū (kee OO shoo)—and more than 3,900 small islands. With its 143,749 square miles (372,309.6 sq km), it is a little smaller than California.

Explain to students that there are no large and important navigable rivers in Japan.

1.1 Landscape and Climate

The landscape of the islands of Japan is made up mostly of highlands surrounded by sea. The sea plays an important part in the country's climate.

Landscape. As Figure 27-1 on page 558 shows, nearly 70 percent of Japan is covered by rugged mountains and steep hills. The mountains are divided by rocky gorges and narrow valleys, and forests grow on their lower slopes. Flowing through them are swift, shallow rivers and thundering waterfalls.

557

Refer students to the map of Population Distribution of East Asia on page 567, the political map of East Asia on page 571, and the map of Land Use and Resources of East Asia on page 574.

PHYSICAL REGIONS OF EAST ASIA

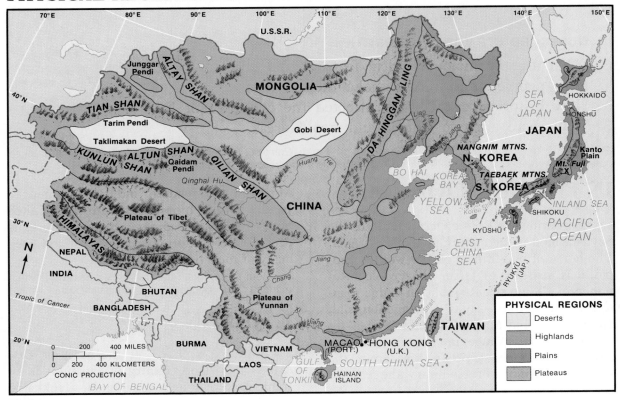

FIGURE 27-1
Most of the landforms in China are composed of mountains and plateaus. Highlands are also found in Japan, North Korea, South Korea, Taiwan, and even Hong Kong. Two huge river systems, the Huang He and the Chang Jiang, drain much of China. Plains are located in northeast China and along the Chinese coast, the western coasts of North and South Korea, and Japan's coastal areas. What desert region lies within parts of two countries?

To review the concept of plate tectonics, refer students to the diagram on page 53.

Taken together, all the Japanese islands have a land area slightly smaller than Montana.

The islands themselves are part of a large mountain range rising from the floor of the Pacific Ocean. Japan lies on the Pacific's "Ring of Fire," where Earth's crust is not stable and moves constantly. Because three tectonic plates meet near Japan, volcanic eruptions are very common.

Of the more than 150 volcanoes in the country, one of the best known is Mount Fuji. As the highest peak in Japan, it rises 12,388 feet (3,775.8 m) above sea level. The Japanese have long viewed this inactive volcano as a sacred symbol of their country.

No part of Japan is more than 70 miles (112.6 km) from the sea. Coastlines are rough, craggy, and highly irregular. Many bays offer good harbors and ports. One of the most important seacoast areas is along the Inland Sea, which lies between Honshū, Shikoku, and Kyūshū.

Narrowly squeezed between the coasts and the foot of the mountains are plains, the largest of which is the Kanto Plain. Although plains make up only about one-eighth of Japan's land area, most of Japan's people, farms, and industries are found there.

Climate. Japan stretches north and south more than 2,360 miles (3,798.0 km), from 24° to 45° north latitude. This distance creates differences in climate from one part of the country to another. Hokkaidō, for example, has a humid continental climate with warm summers, while northern Honshū has hot summers. Southern Honshū, Shikoku, and Kyūshū, on the other hand, have a humid subtropical climate.

Another influence on climate is two Pacific Ocean currents—the Oyashio Current and the Japan Current. The cool Oyashio Current flows southward near northern Japan and cools this area. The warm Japan Current flows northward, warming southern Japan.

Most of Japan receives a good deal of rain. Because of the orographic effect from the mountains, more rain falls on the western side of the islands than on the eastern side. Parts of northwestern Honshū, for example, receive 150 inches (381 cm) of rainfall a year, while some parts of eastern Hokkaidō get less than 40 inches (101.6 cm). As Figure 27-2 on this page shows, the city of Tokyo in east central Honshū has an average yearly precipitation of 61.6 inches (156.5 cm).

Refer students to page 94 for an explanation of the orographic effect.

1.2 Economic and Cultural Patterns

Despite its limited natural resources and small amounts of flat, fertile land, Japan has become one of the world's major industrial countries. Today it ranks third after the United States and the Soviet Union in the production of goods and services. Much of this success stems from the efforts made recently by the Japanese people. Today, as a result of their prosperity, they have the highest standard of living in East Asia and one of the highest in the world.

Economic Patterns. Because it has so few natural resources, Japan must import the

CLIMATE: TOKYO

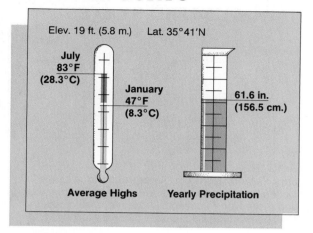

FIGURE 27-2
Tokyo's climate is comfortable throughout the year. Temperatures are moderated by a fairly steady amount of precipitation during the year. Why does Japan receive a good deal of rain?

Refer students to pages 96-97 to review the map of Earth's Climate Regions.

raw materials it uses to make many kinds of finished goods. Income from the sale of exports makes it possible for Japan to buy these raw materials. About 19 percent of Japan's income comes from exports. The Japanese are world leaders in making steel, cars, ships, computers, cameras, televisions, and textiles—all of which they sell to other countries.

A major strength of Japanese industry is its highly skilled work force. Almost everyone can read and write, and high value is placed on education, hard work, group loyalty, and new technology. Japanese industry is known for its efficiency, high growth rates, and low unemployment. Many other industrial nations now look on Japan as a model for improving their own economies.

Agriculture, in spite of certain limits, also has prospered. Because of the mountainous landscape and the growth of cities, only 13 percent of the land is suitable for farming. Most Japanese farms are small, privately owned, and run by families or small

COMPAR-A-GRAPH: JAPAN-UNITED STATES

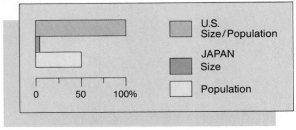

U.S. Size/Population

JAPAN Size

Population

FIGURE 27-3

Japan's land area is only 4 percent as large as the United States yet supports a population that makes Japan the world's seventh largest populated country. How does Japan's population compare to the U.S.?

Explain that fish, traditionally, has been an important part of the Japanese diet.

nesses. Those who farm are able to raise about 70 percent of the country's food. They do this by using high quality fertilizers and modern farm machinery and practicing **intensive cultivation.** This means they make complete use of nearly every piece of farmable land. Hillsides are farmed by **terracing,** or cutting flat areas into the slopes. Even patches of land between buildings and highways are planted. The most important crop is rice.

The Japanese also have the world's largest fishing industry. Tuna and salmon are the biggest catches, but other fish are also caught.

Cultural Patterns. Japan has a population of 122.2 million people, five times that of California. Figure 27-3 on this page compares how Japan's land area and population compare with those of the United States.

Japan is a very crowded country. Because it is so mountainous, about 90 percent of the people live on coastal plains in several large cities. About 75 percent of the Japanese people live in these urban areas. Today a megalopolis called Tokaido (toh KY doh) stretches from the Japanese capital of Tokyo to Ōsaka, a major commercial center. Within this megalopolis the cities of Tokyo and Yokohama form one of the world's largest population centers, with about the same number of people as Canada.

Point out to students that most of Japan's population lives in its best farm areas.

Japan's coastal plains are one of the most densely populated areas in the world.

Robots are shown here welding car bodies at the Nissan Motors assembly line in Yokohama, Japan. Modern industrial technology and an industrious work force place Japan among the leaders of the world's industrial nations. How efficient is Japan in its agriculture?

Ask students to suggest why Japan reacts very strongly to actions taken by other countries that might reduce its ability to export its products.

A high-speed electric train passes Mount Fuji on the main island of Honshū. High-speed train service, linking Tokyo and Ōsaka, began during the 1960s, and today runs the entire length of Honshū. How would you describe Japan's transportation systems?

Singapore, Bangladesh, Maldives, Taiwan, and South Korea are more densely populated than Japan.

Urban growth has led to overcrowding and water and air pollution. At the same time, it has also led to the development of advanced transportation systems. High-speed "bullet trains" carry thousands of people between Tokaido's cities, and a network of roads and railroads connects the major islands.

Japan has a low rate of population growth. Because about 99 percent of the population is Japanese, there is a strong feeling of national unity. Although they live in a very modern society, the Japanese remain loyal to their traditions, many of which are based on the religions of Shintoism and Buddhism. Shintoism, an old religion begun in Japan centuries ago, has helped people have a respect for nature, love of simple things, and concern for cleanliness and good manners. Buddhism, which came to Japan from China, teaches respect for nature and inner peace. Many Japanese practice both religions.

Gautama Buddha founded his religion in India in the 500s BC. By 1200 AD, it spread to Japan. Followers of Buddhism in Japan regard Buddha as a god and have built many statues of him. What is Japan's other main religion and how has it influenced the Japanese?

The first capital of Japan was established at the city of Nara in 710 AD.

1.3 Influences of the Past

As long as 6,500 years ago, hunters and gatherers lived in Japan. About 200 BC, groups of people from the Asian mainland came, farmed, and set up villages. About the end of the 400s AD, Chinese ideas and practices began to have an influence. Among these were Buddhism, art, writing, and a Chinese form of government.

During the mid-1500s, traders and Christian missionaries arrived from Europe. Japan's **shoguns,** or military rulers, feared that European influence would be too strong, so they cut off contacts between Japan and other countries. Foreign countries, however, wanted to trade with Japan. In 1853 Commodore Matthew Perry of the United States brought four warships into Tokyo's bay. The threat of war forced Japan to open ports to foreign trade.

COMPARING ECONOMIES: JAPAN AND UNITED STATES

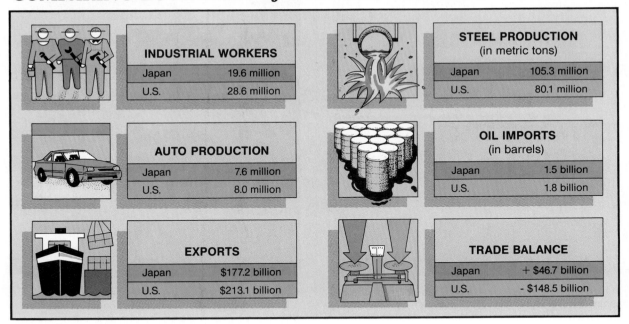

FIGURE 27-4
Recent figures indicate how well Japan holds its own in economic competition. Japan's favorable trade balance, in comparison with the United States' deficit trade balance, shows the value of its exports are higher than the value of its imports. In which economic category does Japan outproduce the U.S.?

In 1933 Japan invaded Manchuria, which was part of China, and created the state of Manchukuo. From Manchukuo Japanese forces launched an attack against the rest of China in 1937.

From 1867 to 1912—known in Japan as the Meiji (MAY jee), or "Enlightened" Period—many changes took place in the country. Education, industry, and banking were modernized, and the government was modeled on those of western Europe. Military power grew, and wars against China and Russia were fought and won.

During the 1930s military leaders gained control of the government. To get more land and resources, they attacked China and won Chinese territory. The leaders later signed a pact with Germany and Italy, the countries that began World War II in Europe in 1939. In 1940 Japan moved into southeastern Asia and the Pacific and in 1941 attacked United States military bases in Hawaii. By 1942 Japan had greatly expanded its empire. Although the Japanese had many victories in

World War II at first, the Allies were able to stop Japanese offense in 1942. Major Allied naval victories and other Allied actions began to push the Japanese back. With the dropping of atomic bombs on two of Japan's major cities in 1945, Japan agreed to surrender.

After the war Japan's cities lay in ruins, and its economy was near collapse. Under American direction the government and economy were rebuilt. Since 1945 Japan has been an ally of the United States and has had a democratic government. Since that time it also has made use of new machinery and industrial methods to become an economic power. Today Japan has a favorable **balance of trade,** which means that the value of its exports is higher than the value of its imports. Figure 27-4 on this page compares Japan's economy with that of the United States.

Using the map of Physical Regions of East Asia on page 558, discuss the landscape of China.

CONTENT CHECK

1. **Identify:** Japan, Hokkaidō, Honshū, Shikoku, Kyūshū, Mount Fuji, Inland Sea, Kanto Plain, Oyashio Current, Japan Current, Tokaido, Tokyo, Yokohama, Shintoism, Buddhism, Matthew Perry, Meiji Period.

2. **Define:** intensive cultivation, terracing, shoguns, balance of trade.

3. Of what is most of Japan's landscape made?

4. How does the sea affect the climate of Japan?

5. What is a major strength of Japanese industry?

6. Why are Japanese farmers able to raise so much of their country's food?

7. Where do most of Japan's people live?

8. What effect did World War II have on Japan?

9. **Challenge:** Japan must import a great deal of coal. What might happen to Japan's steel industry if supplies of coal were cut off?

China probably always has been the most populous nation on Earth.

2. CHINA

Much of the mainland of East Asia is taken up by the People's Republic of China. With its 3,705,390 square miles (9,596,952.6 sq km) in area, China is the second largest nation in Asia and the third largest in the world.

Because of size and other factors, China has played an important part in the history and culture of Asia. Today about 80 percent of the people of East Asia live in China. In years to come, China is expected to play a more important part not only in Asian affairs but in world affairs as well.

2.1 Landscape and Climate

China has many kinds of landscapes, from tall, snow-capped mountains to sandy deserts to fertile plains. The country also has many climates, ranging from desert to humid subtropical.

Landscape. The landscape of China is different from west to east. In the western two-thirds of the country are rugged mountains, high plateaus, low basins, and barren deserts. In the eastern third are fertile river valleys, flat plains, and low hills. The country is often divided into five physical regions—southwestern, northwestern, northeastern, east central, and southeastern.

The Great Wall has often been used as a symbol of China's isolation.

This section of China's Great Wall, which extends for 1,500 miles (2,414 km), stands near Beijing. What problems in its construction may China's landscapes have caused?

Southwestern China is dominated by the high, rugged Plateau of Tibet, which reaches about 13,000 feet (3,962.4 m) in height. Although mostly empty and treeless, it does have several salty lakes and high, grassy valleys. Forming the southern edge of the Plateau, separating China from South Asia, are the Himalayas. North of the plateau are several chains of mountains that run from west to east.

Northwestern China has deserts and mountains. Stretching 900 miles (1,448.4 km) across the area is the Taklimakan Desert. To the east are more deserts, including part of the Gobi, which also covers much of southern Mongolia.

Northeastern China has mountains and uplands that run generally north to south. Between the ranges is a large lowland that includes the Manchurian Plain and the North China Plain.

East central and southeastern China are the most fertile parts of the country. Crossing these sections are three rivers, all of which begin in the highlands of southwestern China. They are the Huang He (HWAHNG HUH), known as the Yellow River; the Chang Jiang (CHAHNG JYAHNG), known as the Yangtze (YANG SEE); and the Xi Jiang (SY JYAHNG), known as the West River.

The Huang He, the northernmost river, flows 2,900 miles (4,667 km), the last several hundred miles of which pass through the North China Plain. The river's name comes from the large amounts of yellow soil it carries. Its deposits of rich silt make fertile farmland. The Huang He is also known for its destructive floods. Because of these it has been called "China's Sorrow."

The middle river, the Chang Jiang, flows 3,915 miles (6,300.6 km) across south central China. On it ships can travel 1,300 miles (2,092.1 km) into the interior. At the point where it empties into the South China Sea, it has formed a delta.

The southernmost river is the Xi Jiang. Along its course are steep, jagged, limestone hills called **karst**. In this area are many underground streams and caves.

Climate. Because of the many landforms and its huge size, China has several different climates. Northwestern China is largely desert with cold winters and hot, dry summers. The land between the desert and the northeastern coast is steppe with cold winters and hot summers. It receives more rain than the desert—more than 4 inches (10.2 cm) but less than 20 inches (50.8 cm) every year. The northeastern coast has a humid continental with hot summers climate. Temperatures average above 75°F (23.9°C) in July and between 30°F (-1.1°C) and 15°F (-9.4°C) in January. Rain falls about 40 inches (101.6 cm) every year.

Southwestern China, with its high elevations, is dry and cool or cold all year. Southeastern China has a humid subtropical climate. Rain falls between 40 inches (101.6 cm) and 80 inches (203.2 cm) each year. Summers are hot and humid, and winters are mild.

Most of China is affected by monsoons. Winter monsoons blow from central Asia, bringing cold, dry air, while summer monsoons from the sea carry warm, moist air. As a result most areas have 80 percent of their rainfall in the summer. Southeastern China receives more rain than the rest of China—as much as 80 inches (203.2 cm) a year. Deserts in northwestern and southwestern China, on the other hand, get less than 4 inches (10 cm) yearly.

Ask students to discuss some of the climate types that occur both in China and in the United States.

2.2 Economic and Cultural Patterns

China is considered a developing country based largely on agriculture. As in most communist countries, the government controls the economy. It is trying to build industries

Workers farm a rice field in southern China's Szech-wan Province. Today China is self-sufficient in food production. What is China's other major food crop? See the *TAE* for an *Objective 2* Activity.

and raise the standard of living. Chinese leaders hope that trade with western nations will help China meet these goals.

Economic Patterns. Figure 27-5 below shows that China has more than four times as many people as the United States. However, China has only one-half as much arable land. About three-fourths of China's workers are farmers, many of whom work the land with simple tools. They terrace hillsides, irrigate, and fertilize their fields. Though for much of China's history, they could not grow enough grain to feed all Chinese, recent changes have made this possible.

After the Communists came to power in 1949, they placed all farmland under control of government-run collectives. At first food production and living standards improved. But as the years went by, fewer gains were made. In the 1980s the government gave farmers more freedom in growing and selling crops and let some start small businesses. In most rural areas, where about 70 percent of the Chinese people live, these programs have boosted production and living standards.

In many parts of China, farmers grow two crops a year. In the south the major crop is rice, which is the basis of the people's diet. In the north the major crop is wheat, which is used to make noodles and bread. Since the 1960s China has become a leading world producer of rice, tea, tobacco, pork, cotton, oilseeds, corn, soybeans, oats, sugar, and vegetables. It has also developed an important fishing industry.

China is rich in natural resources. It mines coal, iron ore, tungsten, gold, and tin, which it is now using in the development of industries. As Figure 27-8 on page 574

To assist in the production of food and to help develop an appreciation for the contributions of farmers, the Chinese government sends some urban workers and students to work on farms during certain times of the year.

COMPAR-A-GRAPH: CHINA—UNITED STATES

China, with slightly over one billion people, has 262 million more people than India, the world's second most populated country. It has 818 million more people than the United States. Is China larger or smaller in size than the United States?

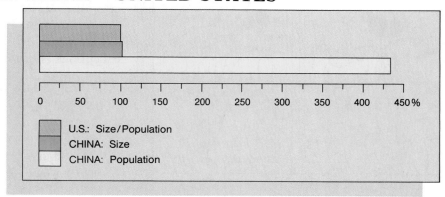

U.S.: Size/Population
CHINA: Size
CHINA: Population

FIGURE 27-5

THINKING LIKE A GEOGRAPHER

PINYIN

In China many dialects are spoken. Chinese dialects in northern China pronounce, words and place-names a little differently than how they would be pronounced in southern China. In 1958, to help people all over the country understand each other, the government of the People's Republic of China adopted a system for pronouncing Chinese. The system is based on the northern, or Mandarin, dialect. This is the Chinese spoken in the region of the capital and the north in general.

In 1979 the government also began to use a new system for writing Chinese words in English or any other language that uses the Roman alphabet. This system, Pinyin, provides a standard spelling and pronunciation of Chinese names for people and places. These names used to be written in other languages according to the Wade-Giles system. That system received its name because it was developed in 1859 by a British diplomat named Sir Thomas Wade and improved years later by a linguist named Herbert A. Giles.

Only a few Chinese names, such as *Shanghai*, are the same in both Wade-Giles and Pinyin. Most names are different. For example, the Wade-Giles' English spelling *Canton* is *Guangzhou* in Pinyin. *Tibet* in Wade-Giles is *Xizang* in Pinyin.

Mao Tse-tung, the man who led the country's communist revolution, and *Peking*, the capital of the People's Republic of China, are English Wade-Giles spellings. In Pinyin the spellings are *Mao Zedong* and *Beijing*. The Pinyin spellings are closer to the sounds used by the Chinese people.

The Pinyin system uses many *q*'s, *x*'s, and *z*'s. But the sounds these letters represent are not the same sounds people who speak English are used to. For example, in Pinyin the letter *x* is pronounced as "sh" as in *sheer* rather than "eks." The letter *q* is pronounced as "ch" as in *cheese*.

The change from Wade-Giles to Pinyin has caused some confusion. In some cases Pinyin has not been totally accepted. Most non-Chinese prefer to use the word *China* for the country. In Pinyin it is *Zhongguo*. Non-Chinese geographers also continue to use the term *Plateau of Tibet* for the prominent physical region of southwest China.

Switching to Pinyin has been expensive for librarians, book publishers, and mapmakers. Most are gradually introducing readers to the new system. For the most part, the Pinyin system is used in this textbook. One of the exceptions is the use of the word *China*.

1. Why did the Chinese government introduce Pinyin?
2. What system was used before Pinyin?
3. What is the Pinyin name for China? Peking? Canton?
4. Why has the change from Wade-Giles to Pinyin spellings caused confusions?

In China young people are regarded as "the wealth of the country." Thus, China has been working hard to improve its educational system. Today about 75 percent of the people are literate.

shows, most of China's industries are found around cities in the eastern half of the country. For example, more than one-third of the country's iron and steel is produced in Beijing (BAY JIHNG), Tianjin (TYEHN JIHN), and other northeastern cities. Another important industrial area is the Chang Jiang Basin. Around the cities of Shanghai, Hangzhou (HAHNG JOH), and Nanjing (NAHN JIHNG) are many factories that make textiles, chemicals, trucks and cars, and electrical goods.

Several things have limited the building and growth of industry. One is a lack of transportation. Another is the large number of old factories that need to be modernized. Still another is that electrical power is not yet fully developed in China.

Cultural Patterns. China has a population of 1,062,000,000 people—more people than any other country in the world. About one out of every five people in the world lives in China, most in very crowded conditions. As Figure 27-6 on this page shows, most of China's people live in the eastern third of the country. It is in this eastern third that the farming areas and major cities are found.

China has some of the world's largest cities. Shanghai, the capital city of Beijing, Tianjin, Shenyang (SHUHN YAHNG), Guangzhou (GWAHNG JOH), Wuhan (WOO HAHN), and Harbin all have more than two million people.

More than 90 percent of China's people belong to the Han ethnic group. While many Chinese follow traditional religious beliefs, the government discourages religious worship. The major language of the country is Chinese. Although spoken Chinese has many dialects, all are written in the same way—with characters that stand for words or syllables. For centuries writing has been a popular art form that has made itself felt in drama, literature, and painting.

Much of China's traditional culture is based on the teachings of an early Chinese thinker known as Confucius. He taught that people should know their place in society and act for its well-being rather than for their own selfish interests. In time his ideas became part

Explain to students that arable land supports larger population densities than land where farming is difficult. Thus, major cities are often found in areas where land is suitable for farming.

POPULATION DISTRIBUTION OF EAST ASIA

East Asia has some of the most densely populated areas on Earth. The distribution of population in East Asia follows a very uneven pattern. What generalizations can you make about population distribution in East Asia, based on information shown on this map?

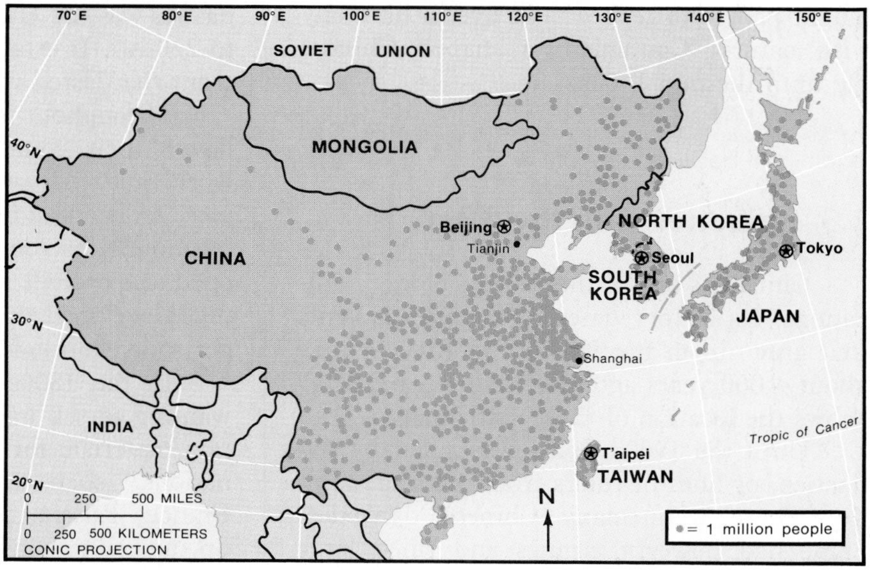

Have students compare this map with the map of Land Use and Resources of East Asia on page 574.

FIGURE 27-6

USING GRAPHIC SKILLS

DRAWING CONCLUSIONS

As you walk down your school hallway, you see the principal, your social studies teacher, and your friend Eric standing together. As you pass by them, you hear the teacher speaking angrily to Eric and see him roll his eyes to you. You infer from Eric's gesture that he is not taking the teacher very seriously. Knowing that yesterday the teacher warned him about getting in assignments, you infer that Eric did not complete the one for last night. You know that your inference is probably correct because Eric often forgets to do his assignments and in the past has been grounded for this reason. Based on what you know, you *conclude*, or make a final judgment, that Eric will soon be punished by either the principal, his teacher, or his parents.

A conclusion is reached after you have made a series of inferences, or deductions based on facts or circumstances. Inferences act as clues that help you find a possible judgment for what you see, read, or experience.

Study the map on page 569. Then answer the questions that follow.

1. The map shows where four of the earliest civilizations in human history were located. From observing location and physical features, what inferences can you make about why the civilizations began where they did?

2. What conclusions can you draw about why the earliest civilizations formed around river valleys?

of a religion known as Confucianism. Along with Buddhism and Daoism, a religion that taught people to respect and live in harmony with nature, Confucianism shaped Chinese life until the mid-1900s.

2.3 Influences of the Past

China has one of the world's oldest civilizations. Its history dates to early settlements that grew up in the Huang He River Valley about 4,000 years ago. The map on page 569 shows the location of those settlements.

Until the 1900s China was ruled by **dynasties,** or lines of rulers from the same family. There were many Chinese dynasties. Some had powerful armies and ruled large

areas. Others were militarily weak and easily overthrown. One of the most important dynasties was the Han, which ruled from 202 BC to 220 AD. It established a system of government that lasted well into modern times.

Throughout their history the Chinese believed their country was the center of the world and they were superior to other peoples. Isolated and protected from other areas by mountains, deserts, and seas, they developed their civilization. Among other things they developed the compass, gunpowder, paper, porcelain, and silk cloth.

In the 1800s European traders arrived, wanting to sell in China's markets and to get raw materials for their industries. European nations, such as the United Kingdom, France, Russia, and Germany, soon carved up the country into special areas for trade.

The Chinese in the past referred to their country as the "Middle Kingdom." They believed their country was at the geographic center of the world and that it was the most refined civilization on Earth.

EARLY RIVER-VALLEY CIVILIZATIONS

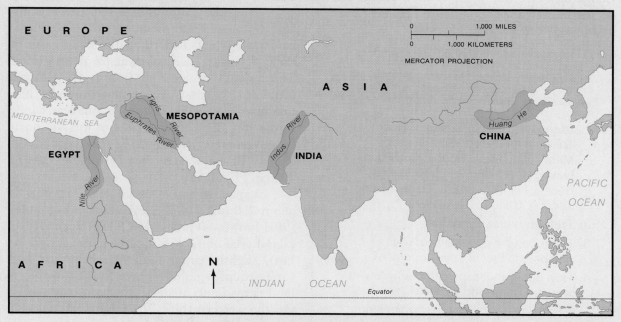

Note that the communist revolution in the Soviet Union began among workers in large cities. China's communist revolution was different in that it started in rural areas and only later spread to the cities.

In 1895 China was defeated in a war with Japan. This led to demands from the Chinese people for their government to modernize the country. Although a few changes were made, it was not enough, and in 1911, a revolution ended dynastic rule. Soon China was divided by civil war.

The country did not really become united until after World War II. Chinese Communists, who had been trying to gain power for many years, became stronger. In 1949, led by Mao Zedong (MOW dzuh DOONG), they formed the People's Republic of China and set out to transform the country. The communist government took land from wealthy landowners and gave it to poor farmers. The farmers, however, had to join farm cooperatives. The government also took over important industries and built new ones. In-

dustrial production went up, but farming did not improve as quickly.

Meanwhile, China began a long fight with the Soviet Union about their borders and about the role of communism in the world. By the early 1960s, their feud had divided the world communist movement. Members of the Chinese Communist party who believed that China was moving away from the goals of communism began what was called the Cultural Revolution. There were riots all over the country, and factories, farms, and universities closed. Many people were jailed or killed.

In 1976 the Cultural Revolution came to an end. That same year Mao Zedong died. Since his death, there have been many changes. Some government controls over the economy have been reduced. More consumer goods have been made available. Farmers have a greater say in what to plant and to sell. Companies can keep more of their profits and decide how to use them. Close ties have been developed with western nations.

China now trades with more than 150 countries.

CONTENT CHECK

1. **Identify:** China, Plateau of Tibet, Taklimakan Desert, Gobi Desert, Manchurian Plain, North China Plain, Huang He, Chang Jiang, Xi Jiang, Beijing, Han, Confucius, Daoism, Mao Zedong, Cultural Revolution.

2. **Define:** karst, dynasties.

3. How does the population of China compare to that of other countries?

4. How does landscape differ between western China and eastern China?

5. What climate covers the southeastern part of China?

6. How do most people in China make a living?

7. Where is the density of population highest in China?

8. What changes have taken place in China since 1976?

9. **Challenge:** China is not yet an industrialized nation. Why is it likely that efforts to develop a more industrial economy will take many years?

Chinese culture strongly influenced the development of other countries and territories of East Asia.

3. OTHER COUNTRIES AND TERRITORIES OF EAST ASIA

Also part of East Asia are the offshore island of Taiwan; the two countries of the Korean Peninsula—South Korea and North Korea; Mongolia; and the two territories of Hong Kong and Macao.

Before 1949 Taiwan was known as Formosa. It became known as Taiwan when the Republic of China was established there.

3.1 Taiwan

When the Communists took over mainland China in 1949, members of the Nationalist Party, which had ruled the country until then, fled with their followers to the island of Taiwan, 100 miles (160.9 km) off China's southeastern coast. Since that time the Nationalists have ruled it and 78 smaller islands in the area. The official name of the Nationalist government in Taiwan is the Republic of China. Its capital is the Taiwanese city of T'aipei (TY PAY).

Shaped like a tobacco leaf, Taiwan is about 250 miles (402.3 km) long and 60 miles (96.5 km) to 90 miles (144.8 km) wide. It has a land area of 12,456 square miles (32,261 sq km), slightly larger than Massachusetts and Connecticut together. Three-fourths of the island is made up of steep, forested mountains. On the western third, the land is suitable for farming. The climate is humid subtropical, with hot summers and mild winters. There is plenty of rain year-round.

Taiwan is the home of about 19.6 million people, most of whom live on the western third of the island. About 16 million are Taiwanese Chinese, whose ancestors came to the island from the Chinese mainland around 1600. Another 2.5 million are Nationalist immigrants who fled the mainland in 1949 or their descendants. While the Taiwanese Chinese control business, the Nationalists run the government. The Nationalist government considers itself the legal government of all of China. At the same time, however, the communist government of the People's Republic of China claims the island of Taiwan as one of its provinces.

Taiwan has a booming economy. Taiwanese farmers own their own land, and the government provides them with help in growing their crops. Over the past 30 years, farmers have raised their yields so much that Taiwan now can produce 85 percent of its food.

NATIONS OF EAST ASIA _____

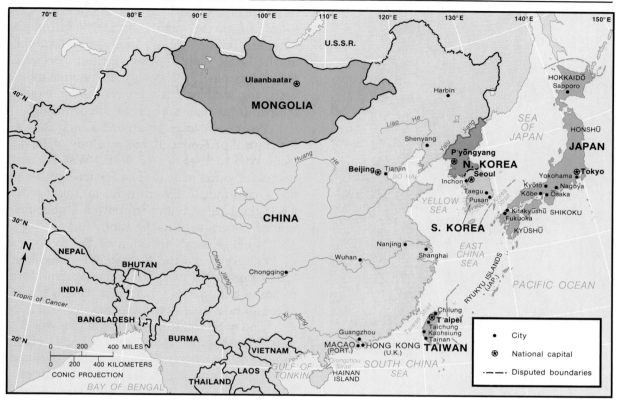

FIGURE 27-7

The existence of "two Koreas" and "two Chinas"—the People's Republic of China and Taiwan—point out a possible instability in the region of East Asia. Japan is a leading economic nation and very influential in world economic affairs. Because of its size, population, and government, China is an important world power. With what other world power does China share much of its borders?

Have students compare Taiwan's economy with the economy of the People's Republic of China.

Point out to students that South Korea occupies an area slightly larger than Indiana.

Many foreign nations trade with Taiwan. The growth of both manufacturing and trade are aided by government and by business people. By the early 1970s, Taiwan was producing more than the People's Republic of China. It now exports a variety of goods, including textiles, electronic equipment, appliances, and machines.

As a result of this economic growth, Taiwan has one of Asia's highest standards of living. Many Taiwanese believe that their strong economy will help the Republic of China continue to survive.

3.2 South Korea and North Korea

The two Koreas came into being because of power struggles between communist parties and other political parties. The Republic of Korea, or South Korea, takes up the southern part of the Korean Peninsula. It has an area of 38,023 square miles (98,479.5 sq km) and a population of 42.1 million. The Democratic People's Republic of Korea, or North Korea, takes in the northern part of the peninsula. It has an area of 46,541 square miles

These uniformed women are assembling printed circuit boards at an electronics factory in South Korea. Is there much industry in South Korea?

See the TAE for an Objective 3 activity.

(120,541.1 sq km) and about 21.4 million people. As Figure 27-7 on page 571 shows, the dividing line between the two countries is close to 38° north latitude. Together the Koreas are about the size of Utah.

The Korean Peninsula separates the Yellow Sea on the west from the Sea of Japan on the east. Most of the peninsula is very mountainous. Narrow lowlands and river valleys are found on the eastern, southern, and western coasts. Most Koreans live in the coastal lowlands, which are among the world's most densely populated areas. Seoul (SOHL), the capital of South Korea, and P'yŏngyang (pee AWNG YAHNG), the capital of North Korea, are both located in the lowlands area.

Most of North Korea has a humid continental with hot summers climate. Most of South Korea has a humid subtropical climate.

Climate on the Korean Peninsula is affected by monsoon winds. In the summer, monsoons from the south bring hot, humid weather. In the winter, monsoons from the north bring cold, dry weather. Because mountains block the flow of the winter monsoon, the western coast enjoys milder winter temperatures than the rest of the peninsula.

For many years Japan and China fought for control of Korea. It was a colony of Japan from 1905 to 1945. After World War II, Korea was divided in two. The Soviet Union set up a communist government in the north, while the United States supported a noncommunist government in the south.

North Korea's invasion of South Korea in 1950 grew into the Korean War. Fighting lasted until 1953, with great damage and loss of life in both Koreas. However, North Korea failed to take over South Korea.

Today South Korea is one of the world's most prosperous countries. Among other things, its privately owned farms produce rice, barley, and millet. Its factories, also privately owned, produce such industrial goods as textiles, chemicals, steel, transportation equipment, and electronics. Many Korean cars are exported to the United States.

North Korea is rich in minerals, especially iron and coal, and has a largely industrial economy. Its government-run factories produce chemicals, iron and steel, machinery, and textiles. Its farmers, organized into collectives, raise rice, barley, corn, and millet. Most of North Korea's trade is with other communist countries.

Until 1945 the people of South Korea and North Korea shared a common history. They still share a common language and culture. As one country they would benefit each other. North Korea has better mineral and energy resources. South Korea has better farmland and more people. However, deep political differences continue to keep the two countries apart.

This fenced area and the Freedom Bridge across the river are located along the demarcation line which marks the political border between North and South Korea. A demilitarized zone extends for just over one mile (2,000 m) on either side of the demarcation line. In what ways are North and South Korea alike and different?

Explain that North and South Korea do not recognize each other's right to exist. Citizens of the two countries cannot directly exchange mail.

3.3 Mongolia

The Mongolian People's Republic is bordered on the west, south, and east by China and on the north by the Soviet Union. With an area of 604,247 square miles (1,564,998.5 sq km), it is more than twice as large as Texas. For its size its population of two million is small, with only three persons per square mile (one person per sq km).

Mongolia is a rugged land of mountains, hills, high plateaus, and deserts. The climate is dry—middle-latitude steppe—with summers that are very hot and winters that are very cold. There is little snow or rain.

Largely because of the landscape and climate, farming is limited, with wheat and oats the chief crops. There is a lot of wildlife, some of which is hunted for its fur. Mongolia also has valuable timberlands and a variety of mineral resources.

Until the 1900s most Mongolians lived as nomads and raised animals. Today about one-half of the population live in rural villages where they tend animals on government-run livestock farms. Although most of the livestock are sheep and goats, there are some cattle and horses. The rest of the population lives in cities, such as the capital, Ulaanbaatar (YOO LAHN BAH TAWR).

Mongolia's communist government is closely tied to the Soviet Union. Since coming to power in the early 1920s, the government has built schools, hospitals, and roads. It has also opposed many traditional practices that it considers backward. One of these is religion. Some Mongolians, however, still practice Buddhism.

Point out to students that Hong Kong and Macao are located quite close together. They are connected by hydrofoils and other forms of water transport.

3.4 Hong Kong and Macao

Both the territories of Hong Kong and Macao are located on the mainland of China. Both are very small. Hong Kong has a land

LAND USE AND RESOURCES OF EAST ASIA _____

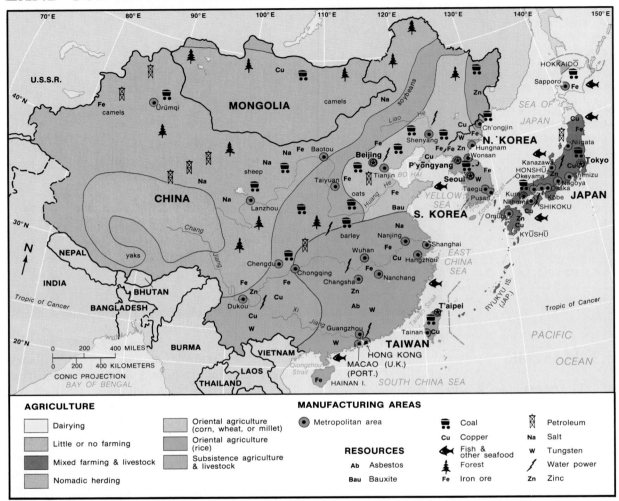

FIGURE 27-8
Favorable landscape and climate conditions create areas of agriculture in eastern China, North and South Korea, Japan, and Taiwan. Resources and manufacturing areas are more numerous in these regions as well. In which East Asian country are manufacturing areas most heavily concentrated?

Hong Kong includes more than 200 islands.

See the *TAE* for an *Objective 4* Activity.

area of 402 square miles (1,041.2 sq km). Macao has a land area of 8 square miles (20.7 sq km). The 5,600,000 people of Hong Kong are mostly Chinese. So are the 400,000 people of Macao. In both territories, Chinese is a major language.

Hong Kong, governed by the United Kingdom, has many natural harbors. The

great majority of its people live along the coast near the port capital of Victoria. Its urban areas are among the most densely populated in the world, with many people living in hillside huts or on junks in the harbor. Today Hong Kong is a leading light-manufacturing center. Its leading industry is textiles and clothing. Other industries include plastics,

Thousands of refugees from Indochina fled to Hong Kong during the Indochina War of the 1970s, seeking a way to safer parts of the world.

Because they are located so close together, many tourists visit both Macao and Hong Kong.

electrical and electronic goods, toys, ship-building, and food processing. Since only about eight percent of its land is arable, its farmers cannot grow enough food to meet the needs of its people. As a result much of its food is imported.

About 40 miles (64.3 km) west of Hong Kong is Macao. Ruled by Portugal, it is the oldest European settlement in this part of the world. The explorer Vasco da Gama visited it in 1497, and the Portuguese established a trading post there in 1557. Like Hong Kong, Macao is a popular port and draws many tourists. Also like Hong Kong, it is a leading trade and fishing center. Both Macao and Hong Kong will come under control of the People's Republic of China in the 1990s.

The official language of Macao is Portuguese, although Chinese is spoken extensively.

CONTENT CHECK

1. **Identify:** Taiwan, Nationalist Party, Republic of China, T'aipei, Republic of Korea, Democratic People's Republic of Korea, Seoul, P'yŏngyang, Mongolia, Ulaanbaatar, Hong Kong, Victoria, Macao.

2. Who makes up the population of Taiwan?

3. Why does Taiwan have such a high standard of living?

4. What kind of landscape does the Korean Peninsula have?

5. In what ways are North Korea and South Korea the same? Different?

6. What is the main economic activity in Mongolia?

7. What do Hong Kong and Macao have in common?

8. **Challenge:** What effect do you think the fact that there are two Chinas and two Koreas has had on the development of East Asia?

CONCLUSION

East Asia is a culture area of many contrasts. Some contrasts are in landscape. For example, East Asia includes steep mountains, thick forests, and harsh deserts not suitable for human life. At the same time, it also includes a small number of coastal lowlands, interior plateaus, and fertile plains densely crowded with people.

Other contrasts are related to population. Recently, East Asia has faced many population pressures. Large numbers of people in crowded areas have increased the need for goods and services. Japan, South Korea, and Taiwan have built strong economies and, for the most part, are successfully dealing with these pressures. China also has the resources for building a modern, prosperous economy. To help reach this goal, it has been trying to slow its population growth.

Still other contrasts are political. Hong Kong and Macao are currently foreign-ruled territories. This will change in the late 1990s when both territories will come under control of China. China and Korea are divided into communist and noncommunist states. Japan, Taiwan, and South Korea are all noncommunist. Japan, however, is the only one of the three that is fully democratic. Among the communist lands, China does not trust the Soviet Union and disapproves of Mongolia's close ties to that country. Mongolia, in turn, sees China as a threat to its independence.

Despite the many contrasts, East Asia is the home of some of the world's oldest civilizations. In the past the peoples of these civilizations faced many challenges and underwent many changes. They survived without losing the sense of who they were. Today the peoples of East Asia are experiencing further great changes. At the same time, their countries are helping to shape the modern world. Like their ancestors, they hope to survive with a sense of their identity.

SUMMARY

1. East Asia is made up of countries and territories on the continent of Asia as well as islands off its eastern coast.
2. Japan consists of four major islands and many small ones. Most of its land is hilly or mountainous. The region's leading industrial country, Japan's economy is based on foreign trade.
3. The People's Republic of China is the most populous country in the world.

Most live in the eastern part of the country in villages and are farmers.

4. Much of western China is mountainous, with large arid or semi-arid areas.
5. East Asia has both communist and noncommunist countries.
6. Some economies of East Asia have made great progress recently. In addition to Japan, both South Korea and Taiwan have built prosperous industrial economies.

Answers to the following questions can be found on page T276.

REVIEWING VOCABULARY

On a separate sheet of paper, number from 1 to 9. Look at the two lists of place-names below. A surprising number of places in East Asia are known by more than one name. Write the place-name from the top list that matches each numbered place-name in the bottom list.

Peking	South Korea	Yangtze River	Guangzhou	Xizang
North Korea	West River	Yellow River	Taiwan	

1. Republic of Korea
2. Democratic People's Republic of Korea
3. Xi Jiang
4. Republic of China
5. Tibet
6. Canton
7. Huang He
8. Chang Jiang
9. Beijing

REMEMBERING THE FACTS

1. On what lowland do most of Japan's people live?
2. What name is given to the heavily settled area lying between Tokyo and Osaka?
3. What major religions are practiced in Japan?
4. How does the People's Republic of China compare in area to other countries in the world?
5. What landforms are found in southwestern China?
6. What two regions of China have the most fertile lands?
7. What river has sometimes been called "China's Sorrow"? Why has it been given this name?
8. During what season does China receive most of its rain?
9. Upon whose teachings is much of China's traditional culture based?
10. About how old is China's civilization?
11. Who governs the island of Taiwan?

12. To what country is Mongolia's government closely tied?

13. Under whose control will Hong Kong and Macao come in the 1990s?

UNDERSTANDING THE FACTS

1. Why are volcanoes and earthquakes common in Japan?
2. In Japan more moisture falls on the western side of the islands than on the eastern side. Why?
3. How do ocean currents affect Japan's climate?
4. What major strength of Japan has made it a major industrial country?
5. Why is so little of Japan's land arable?
6. What agricultural advantages come from the flooding of the Huang He?
7. What are some differences in the climates of southeastern and northwestern China?
8. How evenly is population distributed in China?
9. How are the terrains of Japan and South Korea similar? How have people adapted their farming to the terrains?
10. How do most Mongolians make a living?

THINKING CRITICALLY AND CREATIVELY

1. Japan has a highly developed transportation system. How do you think this contributes to its economy?
2. In 1853 Commodore Matthew Perry persuaded leaders of Japan to open the country to trade with the United States and Europe. In what ways did this decision contribute to the development of Japan as an industrialized nation?
3. Japan's economic successes have been praised worldwide in recent years. What do you know about *how* the Japanese succeed that you would like American business people to know?
4. The Plateau of Tibet occupies about one-fourth of China's land area. However, few people live here. How do you account for this?
5. The Great Wall of China was built to keep out invaders. Why might invaders have been interested in controlling China?
6. **Challenge:** Why do you think the Communists were able to unite the Chinese people after years of war and disunity?
7. **Challenge:** How do you think Taiwan has been able to surpass the People's Republic of China economically?

REINFORCING GRAPHIC SKILLS

Study the map on page 569. Then answer the questions that follow.

1. How do you suppose that scientists know that very early civilizations developed in areas such as the Huang He Valley?
2. Based on conditions in Asian river valleys today, what conclusions can you draw about their present environment?

CHAPTER 28

Old harbor in Singapore

SOUTHEAST ASIA

In this chapter you will learn—

- What are the major physical features and climates of Southeast Asia.
- What economic products come from Southeast Asia.
- How the peoples of Southeast Asia live and work.
- How the cultures of Southeast Asia have developed over the centuries.

On a large wall map, have students note the location of Southeast Asia and the names and locations of the main gulfs and seas throughout this area.

INTRODUCTION

South of China and east of India is the culture area of Southeast Asia. It is made up of peninsulas on the continent of Asia as well as islands between Asia and Australia. It stretches from Burma in the west to the large island of New Guinea in the southeast.

Geographers often divide Southeast Asia into two regions. One region is called Continental Southeast Asia. It is made up of countries that lie on the Asian mainland. They are Burma, Thailand (TY LAND), Laos, Kampuchea (KAM puh CHEE uh), and Vietnam (vee EHT NAHM).

The other region is known as Insular Southeast Asia. *Insular* means island. This region is made up of countries that are islands as well as countries that lie partly on the Asian mainland and partly on islands. These countries are Malaysia (muh LAY zhuh), Indonesia (IHN duh NEE zhuh), Singapore (SIHNG uh POHR), the Philippines, and Brunei (BROO ny).

The countries of Southeast Asia are rich in landscape and natural resources. They also have large, productive populations. Like other parts of the continent, Southeast Asia is made up of many different ethnic groups. Differences among them have often led to conflict. Because of this, Southeast Asian governments have had difficulty winning the loyalty of all their peoples.

Because of its location near the seas, Southeast Asia has been a meeting place of peoples and cultures for thousands of years. People from India, China, Europe, and the United States have left traces of their cultures throughout the area. Many Southeast Asian countries were at one time colonies of foreign countries. Today they are all independent nations, trying to develop their economies and raise living standards for their peoples.

Point out to students that some of the most densely populated areas in Southeast Asia are river valleys.

1. CONTINENTAL SOUTHEAST ASIA

Geographers often refer to Continental Southeast Asia as Indochina. It includes mainland areas and part of the long, thin arm of the Malay Peninsula. The Bay of Bengal separates Indochina from India to the west. To the east is the South China Sea.

The five countries of Indochina—Burma, Thailand, Laos, Kampuchea, and Vietnam—have a total land area of about 750,000 square miles (1,942,499 sq km). Together they have about 165 million people.

PHYSICAL REGIONS OF SOUTHEAST ASIA

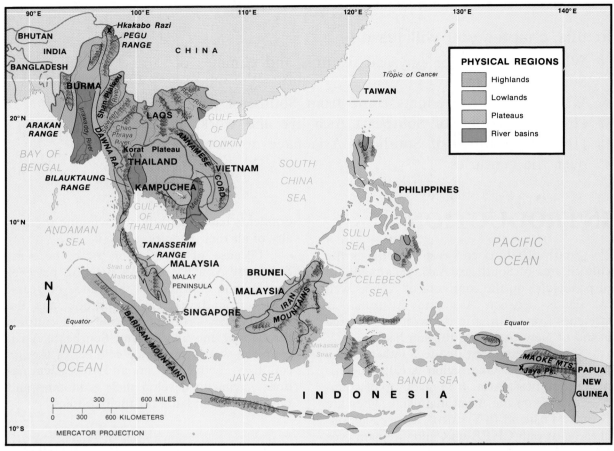

FIGURE 28-1
Continental Southeast Asia is covered by many mountains and plateaus. This region is drained by large rivers such as the Irrawaddy and the Mekong. Highlands extend into Insular Southeast Asia as well. Which region has more lowlands, Continental or Insular Southeast Asia?

Most of mountainous Southeast Asia is part of a giant chain of mountains reaching from the Atlas of northern Africa, through the Alps and Himalayas, to the Malay Peninsula and beyond, as a series of islands off the mainland.

1.1 Landscape and Climate

In landscape and climate, the countries of Indochina are alike in many ways. However, each has special features that set it apart from the others. For example, Indochina lies in or near the tropics. All of the countries have tropical moist or moist, mild winter climates. Yet the landscape patterns of the region divide the peoples of Indochina into distinct population clusters.

Landscape. As Figure 28-1 on this page shows, a number of mountain ranges and plateaus run north to south through Indochina. The highest mountains, the Arakan and Pegu ranges, are along Burma's border with India. There some peaks rise to more than 12,000 feet (3,657.8 m) above sea level. Another mountainous area is the Annamese Cordillera, which covers about 75 percent of Vietnam. In its northern part, some peaks are higher than 10,000 feet (3,048 m).

The major rivers of Indochina flow north to south between the mountain ranges. Their basins generally have the most fertile land in Indochina. The Irrawaddy River rises near Burma's border with China. It flows through central Burma and forms a large delta where it enters the Bay of Bengal. Thailand's Chao Phraya (chow PRY uh) is formed by several tributaries in the northern part of the country. It crosses western Thailand before entering the Gulf of Thailand.

The Mekong (MAY KAWNG) River flows farther east in Vietnam. About 2,600 miles (4,184.3 km) in length, it is the longest river in Southeast Asia. The Mekong begins in China's Plateau of Tibet and flows along the border between Laos and Thailand. Finally, it curves through Kampuchea and into southern Vietnam.

Besides mountains and river basins, Continental Southeast Asia has thick, tropical rain forests. These forests are found in the Malay Peninsula and nearby areas along the Bay of Bengal. Forests of teak and other hardwoods cross much of Burma and Thailand.

Climate. Most of Indochina has tropical moist climates, with warm temperatures year-round and much precipitation. Northern areas, however, have a humid subtropical climate, with hot summers and mild winters.

In Indochina the southwest coast along the Bay of Bengal has a tropical monsoon climate. Central and eastern Indochina has a tropical savanna climate. The amount of rain all places in Indochina receive is about the same, but some areas have dry seasons. The yearly rainfall is more than 60 inches (152.4 cm). Average high temperatures through the year are about 86°F (30°C). Some highland areas are cooler. For example, mountains in northern Burma and Laos sometimes have frosts. Because of the hot temperatures over most of the region, water evaporates very quickly. Heavy rains also leach the soil.

A hillside is terraced to add more rice fields in this area of Java. How is farming made possible in the mountainous areas of Indochina?

A chart on page 589 compares rural and urban population of selected Asian countries.

1.2 Economic and Cultural Patterns

The economies of Indochina are based largely on farming. Because of mountainous areas and poor soils, many parts of the region are hard to farm. Even so, farmers make the best use of available land. About 80 percent of Indochina's population is rural.

Economic Patterns. In mountainous areas, the farmers of Indochina practice shifting cultivation. First they clear trees and brush from an area; then they burn the ground cover. Corn, potatoes, and beans are planted in the cold ashes, which fertilize the soil. After a few harvests, the soil is worn out. Then the farmers move to a new area and repeat these steps. The old plots may be farmed again after a few years.

Shifting cultivation has helped crops to grow in the poor soils of Indochina. However, the growing population of the region needs more food. Many areas of tropical rain forest have been cleared for farming.

In the lowland areas of Indochina, farmers grow rice on wet plots of land called **paddies**. Rice is the major crop in most of Indochina. The Mekong Delta is one of the world's best rice-growing areas.

As Figure 28-2 on page 583 shows, there are many different natural resources available in Indochina. Burma's forests have about 80 percent of the world's teak. Both Burma and Thailand export hardwoods and rubber. **Silvaculture** is the name given to commercial tree-growing.

Mineral deposits are scattered all through the region. Vietnam has coal, while Burma has rubies and sapphires. Tin is mined in Thailand and Laos. Except for Thailand, most of the countries of Indochina have not yet developed mining.

Cultural Patterns. Most of the people in Indochina are descended from the earliest settlers of the region. Almost 70 percent of

Burma's people are Burmans. Of Thailand's population, 75 percent are Thai. The Khmer (kuh MEHR) make up 90 percent of Kampuchea's people. Laos is nearly 50 percent Laotian (lay OH shuhn). Vietnamese make up about 90 percent of Vietnam's population.

In addition, three important outside groups have affected Indochina. They are Asian Indians, Chinese, and Europeans. The Indians brought Hinduism and Buddhism to the region. Today nearly 90 percent of the people in Burma and Thailand are Buddhists. Many Buddhists also live in Vietnam and Laos. Kampuchea was a Buddhist country, until the communists came to power in the 1970s. In Kampuchea stands the beautiful Angkor Wat, a temple built by the Khmer in the 1100s. The temple is known for its many Buddhist and Hindu carvings.

Today the Chinese form a very large and important group in the larger cities of Indochina. The economies of Burma, Thailand, and Laos are strengthened by many Chinese-owned businesses.

The major religions of Southeast Asia are Islam, Christianity, Buddhism, and animism. Concentrations of these religions vary from place to place throughout Southeast Asia. Indonesia is the world's largest Muslim nation, and the Philippines is the only predominantly Christian country in Asia.

The 800-year-old temple at Angkor Wat, Kampuchea, stands as a monument to the Khmer Empire and Indian architecture. Khmer culture was largely influenced by Indian culture. In what other ways has Southeast Asia been affected by outside cultural groups?

Typical of areas with great cultural diversity, Southeast Asia's major religions show the impact of many different cultural currents from neighboring and distant regions.

LAND USE AND RESOURCES OF SOUTHEAST ASIA _____

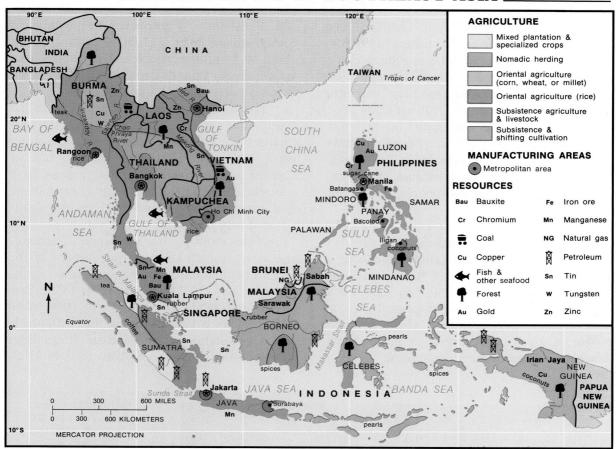

FIGURE 28-2
The region's climate makes possible various types of agriculture over the entire area. What type of farming is most common in Java? In Borneo?

The British, French, and Dutch were the main groups of Europeans who were active in colonizing areas in Southeast Asia. For many years Indochina was known as French Indochina.

Many Europeans and Americans came to Indochina during the 1800s and 1900s. As a result of their cultural influence, Vietnam and other areas of the region have many Christians. About 10 percent of Vietnamese are Roman Catholics. Also many educated people in Indochina speak French or English.

Each of the nations of Indochina has its own unique culture. In the past cultural differences often led to conflict in the region. Today fighting continues, but much of it now centers on the struggle between communist and noncommunist ways of life. Rival communist groups have also fought each other for control in the region.

Burma is the largest nation of Indochina in size. With an area of 261,216 square miles (676,548.9 sq km), it is a little smaller than Texas. About 39 million people live in Burma. Most of them are farmers, who tend fields in the lowlands and delta of the Irrawaddy River. These areas are the most densely populated parts of the country. Rangoon, Burma's capital, is in the delta area. It

CHAPTER 28   **SOUTHEAST ASIA**

has about 2.5 million people and is known for its Buddhist architecture.

Burma's eastern neighbor, Thailand, has a land area of 198,456 square miles (514,000.6 sq km). With more than 53.6 million people, Thailand is the most industrialized country in Indochina. Its factories produce cement, sugar, and paper products. However, the people of Thailand have kept many of their old traditions, most of which are based on Buddhism. Bangkok, Thailand's capital, is known for its beautiful Buddhist temples and royal palaces. About 5.5 million people live in the city of Bangkok.

Northeast of Thailand, Laos is the only landlocked country in Southeast Asia. It also has Indochina's least developed economy. Smaller than Oregon, Laos has an area of 91,429 square miles (236,800.9 sq km) and a population of 3.8 million. Its largest city, Vientiane (vyehn TYAHN), has about 200,000 people. Laos has a communist government that controls the country's economy.

Bordering Laos to the south is Kampuchea, another communist country. About the size of Missouri, Kampuchea has an area of 69,900 square miles (181,040.9 sq km). It has about 6.5 million people. The capital and largest city is Phnom Penh (NAWM PEHN). It has a population of about 700,000.

For many years Kampuchea, also called Cambodia, was a farming country. It produced rice, beans, and corn. Fish and rubber were exported. However, many years of fighting among rival communist groups have brought suffering to the Kampuchean people and damaged their economy. Now the country is slowly beginning to recover.

With about 62 million people, Vietnam, the easternmost nation of Indochina, has the largest population of any nation in the region. Vietnam has 127,243 square miles (329,559.1 sq km) of land. Ho Chi Minh (HOH chee MIHN) City is the largest city in Vietnam. It has a population of more than 3.5 million people. Once known as Saigon, Ho Chi Minh

A monk in saffron robes walks through the temple grounds of a Buddhist pagoda in Rangoon, Burma. Which other city of Indochina is famous for its beautiful Buddhist temples?

With the world's largest population, China has been the original homeland of many people who migrated to other world areas. These immigrants often develop sizeable Chinese communities in their new homelands, adding touches of Chinese culture wherever they settle.

Images of Southeast Asia include a rubber tree, Thai dancers, Buddha, and Hindu temples. King Philip II and a trading ship show early European influences. Which European countries became involved in Indochina?

City is found in the area of the Mekong Delta. Hanoi, the Vietnamese capital, is to the north. It has about 2.5 million people.

Once divided into communist and noncommunist sections, Vietnam today is united under a communist government. The government controls the largely agricultural economy. About two-thirds of Vietnamese are farmers. They grow crops such as rice, coffee, coconuts, corn, cotton, and rubber.

See the TRB for Section 1: Extending the Lesson.

1.3 Influences of the Past

More than 1,000 years ago, Indochina was settled by various peoples from other parts of South Asia and East Asia. Settlers from China came to northern Vietnam. In later centuries their descendants moved into Vietnam's coastal plain and the Mekong Delta. By the 800s AD, people from parts of Tibet, China, and India had settled in Burma. In the 1100s the powerful Khmer Empire ruled much of Indochina. It was centered in present-day Kampuchea and Laos. In the 1700s the Thai people formed the kingdom of Siam in the Chao Phraya valley. Today Siam is known as Thailand.

In the 1500s the Portuguese became the first Europeans to reach Indochina. They set up trading posts but no permanent settlements. In the 1800s the British added Burma to their colony of India. During this same period, the French took over the part of Indochina that is now Vietnam, Laos, and Kampuchea. Siam was the only country in the

CHAPTER 28   **SOUTHEAST ASIA**

A house and farmland in An Loc, Vietnam, show the devastation caused during the Indochina War. What was the final outcome of this war?

The Indochina War was more commonly known in the United States as the Vietnam War.

region that kept its freedom and never became a European colony.

During World War II, Japanese forces took control of the European colonies of Indochina. After the war the colonies became independent nations. However, communist and noncommunist groups began fighting for control of the region.

During the 1960s, war spread all through Indochina as the superpowers entered the conflict. The United States sent forces to help noncommunist governments. The Soviet Union sent military aid to communist forces. Many communists carried out **guerrilla warfare.** This kind of warfare was generally not part of an organized national army. Soldiers made attacks and then withdrew into the forests or mountains.

By the 1970s the Indochina War had no clear winner. Peace talks were held, and the United States agreed to withdraw its forces from the region. However, the noncommunist governments were too weak to rule. During the mid-1970s, Vietnam, Laos, and Kampuchea all became communist countries.

CONTENT CHECK

1. **Identify:** Indochina, Malay Peninsula, Bay of Bengal, Arakan Range, Pegu Range, Irrawaddy River, Chao Phraya, Mekong River, Khmer, Burma, Rangoon, Thailand, Bangkok, Laos, Vientiane, Kampuchea, Phnom Penh, Cambodia, Vietnam, Ho Chi Minh City, Khmer Empire, Siam.

2. **Define:** paddies, silvaculture, guerrilla warfare.

3. What kinds of landforms are found in Indochina?

4. How do the people of Indochina make their livings?

5. What is the major religion of the people of Indochina?

6. Which country in Indochina has the largest population?

7. What countries in Indochina are communist?

8. **Challenge:** From what you know about the landscape of Indochina, would you expect the population to be spread evenly over the region or to be clustered in certain areas? Explain.

Refer to the map on page 587 to identify locations of the countries of Insular Southeast Asia. Emphasize the importance of water transportation there.

2. INSULAR SOUTHEAST ASIA

Insular Southeast Asia lies between Indochina and Australia. The region is made up of the southern tip of the Malay Peninsula and more than 20,000 islands of various sizes. Five countries—Indonesia, Malaysia, Singapore, the Philippines, and Brunei—are found in the region. Their total area—980,954 square miles (2,540,668.9 sq km)—is larger than that of Europe. The population of Insular Southeast Asia is about 255.3 million.

Since the early 1900s, Southeast Asia has gone from a region dominated by western European and American colonialism to an arena of competition between two superpowers—the U.S. and the U.S.S.R. The area is now fragmented into neutralist, pro-Western, pro-Soviet, and pro-Chinese states. The varying allegiances, however, are seldom firm.

NATIONS OF SOUTHEAST ASIA

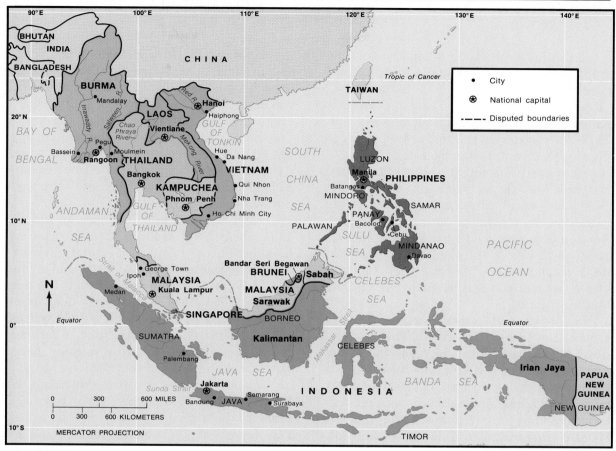

FIGURE 28-3

Thailand is the only nation of Southeast Asia that remained free of colonial control. Indonesia was the first nation in the region to gain independence. Oil-rich Brunei became independent in the mid-1980s. In 1987 the people of the Philippines adopted a new constitution and elected a new legislature. Vietnam, Laos, and Kampuchea became communist nations after a long and divisive war. Which large islands are part of Indonesia?

The Pacific "Ring of Fire" is illustrated on the map of Zones of Earthquakes and Volcanoes on page 75.

2.1 Landscape and Climate

The landscape of Insular Southeast Asia is made up of mountains, lowlands, and tropical rain forests. Lying on the Equator, the region has a tropical rain forest climate.

Landscape. There are two large mountain ranges that form the island chains of Insular Southeast Asia. Some of the peaks on the islands are more than 12,000 feet (3,657.6 m) above sea level. The highest peak, Djaja (JAH yuh), is about 16,000 feet (4,876.8 m) above sea level. It is in Irian Jaya, Indonesia's half of the island of New Guinea.

Most of the mountains of Insular Southeast Asia are volcanic. Several tectonic plates meet in this area. When these plates move, earthquakes, volcanic activity, and mountain building take place. Much of the region is **part of the Pacific "Ring of Fire,"** known for its earthquakes and volcanic eruptions. This volcanic ash makes the soil fertile.

STRANGE BUT TRUE

MIGHTY BLAST AT KRAKATAU

In August of 1883, a mighty volcanic eruption made news around the world. Newspapers ran headlines like "An Island Dies," "Krakatau Is No More," and "Thousands Killed by Giant Wave." Krakatau (KRAH kuh TOW), a volcano in the Sunda Strait between Java and Sumatra, had exploded.

It was truly a mighty blast. The sound was heard as far as Australia, 2,200 miles (3,541 km) away. Since no one lived on the island, no one was killed during the eruption. But 36,000 people died when the eruption set off a giant wave 120 feet (36.6 m) high that hit coastal villages of Java and Sumatra. Other tsunami traveled as far as Hawaii and South America.

For two and one-half days, the area around the island was dark. The ash and dust, which had blown 50 miles (80.5 km) high, blotted out the sun. The dust was carried around the world by winds and for many months made the sunsets more colorful. Ash and pieces of lava fell across an area of 300,000 square miles (776,999.4 sq km). Ships could not move through it.

Krakatau had disappeared. When scientists studied the material that had fallen on the nearby islands, they found that most of it was new magma, not pieces of the volcano's four cones. They discovered that the top of the volcano had sunk below the sea, collapsing because so much magma from its center was gone. For five years the islands nearby had no plants or animals, because they were buried beneath ash.

After the big blasts of August 26 and 27, 1883, there were small eruptions for several months. Then Krakatau was quiet. New activity began near the end of 1927, and a cone grew enough to form a small island. The new cone is called Anak Krakatau, which means Child of Krakatau. Although there have not been any more big blasts from Krakatau, there are rumblings from time to time. There were small eruptions in the 1960s.

There are many other volcanoes in Southeast Asia. This is because it is located near the boundary between tectonic plates. On the island of Sumatra alone there are about 90 volcanoes. Twelve of these are thought to be active.

Scientists who specialize in studying volcanoes are called **volcanologists** (VAHL kuh NAHL uh juhsts). From study stations they set up at volcanic sites, volcanologists are learning how to predict when some volcanoes will erupt. If eruptions can be predicted, lives can be saved. Volcanologists are also learning ways to make use of volcanic power. Heat energy from underground steam is used in countries with many volcanoes.

1. What happened to the top of Krakatau in 1883?

2. What do scientists learn by studying volcanoes?

The major lowlands in the region are the southern tip of the Malay Peninsula and parts of the islands of Indonesia. As Figure 28-3 on page 587 shows, nearly all the ports of Insular Southeast Asia are found in the coastal lowlands along the Java Sea and the Strait of Malacca (muh LAK uh).

Climate. Because the region has a tropical rain forest climate, most of Insular Southeast Asia is hot and wet. For example, Singapore has an average humidity of more than 80 percent. Its average high temperature is 89°F (31.7°C). Yearly rainfall in Singapore amounts to 95 inches (241.3 cm).

Typhoons are also found in the region. The Philippines is hit by several typhoons each year. These storms bring heavy rain and strong winds and often cause a great deal of damage to this region.

The word *typhoon* is believed to have come from the Chinese phrase *taai fung,* which means "great wind."

2.2 Economic and Cultural Patterns

The economies of Insular Southeast Asia are largely agricultural. Although the region has many mountains, lowlands have rich, fertile land. Most people are farmers and live in rural areas. However, recently, city populations have grown rapidly. Figure 28-4 on this page shows the distribution of population in rural and urban areas in Indonesia, the Philippines, Singapore, and other Asian countries.

Economic Patterns. The most important farming countries of Insular Southeast Asia are Indonesia, Malaysia, and the Philippines. Farmers in these lands grow rice and other food crops on small farms. Indonesia is the world's leading rice producer. The Philippines grows most of its own food. It also exports sugar, tobacco, coconuts, and bananas. Malaysia has a strong agriculture based on oil, palm oil, and other food crops.

RURAL AND URBAN ASIAN POPULATIONS

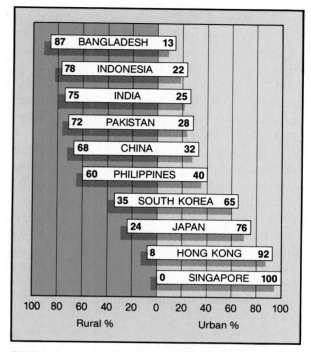

1987 *World Population Data Sheet,* Population Reference Bureau

FIGURE 28-4
Rural populations are higher in those Asian countries that are developing, whereas urban populations are higher in those countries that are industrialized. Which countries here are located in Southeast Asia?

Use of synthetic rubber today has somewhat reduced the demand for natural rubber.

The three countries are especially important for silvaculture. Nearly two-thirds of Indonesia is covered with forests. Ebony, teak, and bamboo are among the valuable forest products that are harvested and exported. The Philippines and Malaysia also grow and harvest trees. Malaysia is well known for rubber production. Rubber trees there are grown on large plantations.

Insular Southeast Asia is rich in mineral resources. Tin, found chiefly in Malaysia, has brought prosperity to Malaysia's economy. Deposits of oil and natural gas are found all over the region. Brunei is a leading producer of oil and natural gas, which it exports to

USING GRAPHIC SKILLS

REVIEWING EXACT AND RELATIVE LOCATIONS

When you call your parents for a ride home from the concert, you tell your parents that you are at the intersection of Main Street and Third Street, which is just east of the auditorium. They will have no problem finding you since you have given them your exact and relative locations.

In Chapter 1 you learned that the intersection of latitude and longitude lines tells you the exact location of a certain place. By using the grid system, you can find each place on Earth by first locating the line of latitude nearest to the city. Then, you must follow this line until it intersects with the nearest line of longitude. Such a location, which is described by using latitude and longitude coordinates, is called the exact location of a place.

You also learned that relative location is the location of a place relative to, or compared with, another place. To describe the relative location of a city, geographers find the hemisphere, continent, and country where the city can be found. Direction is very important in finding relative location. North, south, east, and west—cardinal directions—and northeast, southeast, northwest, and southwest—intermediate directions—can be used to describe relative location.

The map on this page shows the Philippines and surrounding land and water areas. The grid system shows lines of latitude and longitude at intervals of one degree. For example, the exact location of Manila is approximately 14°N, 121°E. The relative location of Manila is in the Northern and Eastern hemispheres on the island of Luzon, southeast of the city of Tarlac and northwest of the city of Iloilo.

Review the information in the graphic skill exercise in Chapter 1 on page 12. Then study the map on this page. Finally answer the questions that follow.

1. What is the exact location of Laoag?
2. What is the exact location of Cebu?
3. Which city shown on the map is closest to the Equator?
4. What is the relative location of the island of Palawan?
5. What is the relative location of the island of Samar?
6. The map shows three seas surrounding the Philippines. Describe the relative location of each sea in relation to the Philippines.
7. What is the relative location of the island of Mindanao in relation to the island of Luzon?

THE PHILIPPINES

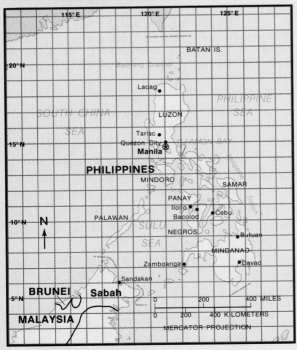

Japan, the United States, and Singapore. Wealth from these resources has given the people of Brunei a high standard of living.

Recently the nations of Insular Southeast Asia have begun to set up industries. Of all the countries in the region, Malaysia, Brunei, and Singapore have been the most successful in manufacturing. In the Philippines and Indonesia, poor roads in mountain and forest areas have held back industrial development. As a result these nations have to import many manufactured goods. To improve their industrial economies, the governments of Indonesia and the Philippines are working to improve transportation and communications. They are also investing some of their income in training more teachers and workers, many of whom study in foreign countries.

Cultural Patterns. Most of the people of Insular Southeast Asia are Malays. Most Malays are followers of the religion of Islam. Islam is the leading religion in Brunei, Singapore, Malaysia, and Indonesia. In fact Indonesia has more Muslims than any other country in the world. The Muslims of Insular Southeast Asia mix their beliefs and practices with those of Hinduism and other traditional religions found in the region.

In addition to Malays, other groups have settled in Insular Southeast Asia over the years. They have added to the ethnic and cultural variety of the region. For example, many Chinese live in Malaysia, Singapore, and Brunei. They are found in urban areas, where they are known for their business skills. Also after years of European rule in the region, many urban areas reflect a blend of Asian and western ways.

Because of similar mixtures of peoples, most nations in Insular Southeast Asia have cultures that are alike in many ways. For example, Malay, Chinese, and Indian languages are widely spoken the region. Also they have similar traditional arts such as rhythmic folk

dances, shadow puppet dramas, and colorful fabric-making. However, there are also differences. This is especially seen in forms of government. Malaysia and Brunei are each ruled by a king. Singapore, the Philippines, and Indonesia are republics.

Indonesia is the largest nation of Insular Southeast Asia in size. It has an area of 735,355 square miles (1,904,567.9 sq km), about as large as Texas and California combined. Figure 28-5 below shows how the land area and population of Indonesia compare with those of the United States.

Indonesia consists of about 13,600 islands that lie along the Equator. It has four large islands and one-half of the island of New Guinea. The four main islands are Java, Borneo, Celebes (SEHL uh BEEZ), and Sumatra (su MAH truh).

Indonesia is the largest nation of the region in population. It has about 175 million people. About three-fifths of Indonesians live in small farm villages on the island of Java. Most of Indonesia's cities are found on Java. The capital and largest city of the country is Jakarta (juh KAHR tuh). It has a population of 6.5 million.

North of Indonesia is Malaysia, one of the most prosperous countries of Southeast

Java has more than 100 million people living in an area about the size of the state of New York.

COMPAR-A-GRAPH: INDONESIA-UNITED STATES

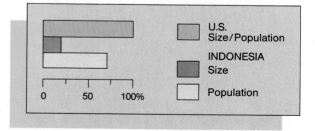

FIGURE 28-5
Indonesia's population is the fifth largest of any country in the world. How do Indonesia's size and population compare with those of the United States?

Singapore is a city-state, with a population density of more than 10,000 people per square mile (4,000 per sq km). Refer to page 154 for a feature on Singapore.

Although Filipino and English are the official languages in the Philippines, about 87 native languages and dialects are commonly spoken.

Asia. It has an area of 127,317 square miles (329,750.8 sq km) and 16 million people. Malaysia is made up of two regions—Malaya, on the southern tip of the Malay Peninsula, and Sarawak (suh RAH wahk) and Sabah (SAHB uh), on the northern edge of the island of Borneo.

About two-thirds of Malaysians live in small rural villages of wooden houses. Most of them are Malays. However, a large number of Chinese live in Malaysia's cities, such as Kuala Lumpur (KWAHL uh LUM PUR), the capital. The Chinese have more wealth than the Malays. But the Malays control the government. These differences often lead to tension between the two ethnic groups.

Close to Malaysia is Singapore, the smallest nation in the region. It is about 224 square miles (580.2 sq km) in area. Singapore has close to 2.6 million people. More than 90 percent of its population live in its capital city,

Singapore. Most of them are Chinese. However, there are also Malays, Asian Indians, and Europeans among Singapore's people.

In spite of its small size and limited resources, Singapore is the only industrialized nation in Southeast Asia. Its prosperity is based on banking, insurance, manufacturing, and trade. On an island at the tip of the Malay Peninsula, Singapore has one of the world's busiest ports. The city of Singapore is an **entrepôt** (AHN truh POH)—a center for storing and reshipping goods of other countries. It is also a **free port.** That means other countries are not taxed for using its warehouses and harbors.

Another small nation in Insular Southeast Asia is Brunei. With an area of 2,228 square miles (5,770.5 sq km), Brunei lies on the northern coast of Borneo. Because of its oil, most of Brunei's 200,000 people enjoy a high standard of living. About 65 percent of them live in rural areas. The capital and largest city of Brunei is Bandar Seri Begawan.

Northeast of Brunei is the Philippines, made up of about 7,000 islands in the South China Sea. It has an area of 115,830 square miles (299,999.5 sq km), a little bigger than Arizona. The largest islands of the Philippines are Luzon (loo ZAHN), and Mindanao (MIHN duh NAH oh).

About 61.5 million people live in the Philippines. About 60 percent of the population are farmers and live in rural areas. The country, however, has many towns and cities. The capital and largest city is Manila (mah NIHL ah). It has a population of close to 7 million in its metropolitan area.

The Philippines has the strongest western influence of any nation in the region. Spain ruled the islands for more than 300 years and named them for King Philip II, one of its great rulers. Spanish priests brought the Roman Catholic religion to the islands. Today the Philippines is the only country in Asia with a largely Christian population.

Shop signs, traffic, and pedestrians add to the color and congestion of Petaling Street in Kuala Lumpur, Malaysia. A closer look at the signs reveals that this is a Chinese section of the city. What differences create tensions between the Chinese and the Malays?

2.3 Influences of the Past

The Malays began to arrive in Insular Southeast Asia about 4,000 years ago. About 2,000 years later, people from India came to the region. Movements of Chinese people into the area continued through the centuries. In more recent times, around 1900, a large number of Asian Indians came to Malaysia to work on rubber plantations.

In the 1500s the Portuguese, looking for spices and new sea routes, came to the region. They set up trading colonies in the area that is now Indonesia. A century later the Dutch took control of much of Indonesia. These islands were called the Dutch East Indies for many years. During World War II, Japan occupied the Dutch East Indies. In 1949, the islands became independent as the Republic of Indonesia.

From 1595 to 1898, Spain ruled the Philippines. Then the United States won control of the islands until Japan's invasion during World War II. The war nearly destroyed Manila and severely hurt the country's economic progress for years. Since 1956 the Philippines has been independent. In 1986, after years of one-person rule, a revolution brought a democratic government to power. However, the new government has had difficulty controlling power struggles among rival political groups.

Both Singapore and Malaysia were colonies of the United Kingdom from the early 1800s to the mid-1900s. Japan also invaded these territories during World War II. After the war, both countries gained full independence from the British, Malaysia in 1957 and Singapore in 1965.

Brunei is the last nation of this region to become independent. It is a very old kingdom, with a royal family that has ruled for 29 generations. However, it became a British protectorate in 1888. This means that the United Kingdom had some control over Brunei, even though Brunei was not a colony.

Like many other nations of Southeast Asia, Brunei was under Japanese rule during World War II. It gained full freedom from the United Kingdom in 1984.

See the *TAE* for an *Objective 3* Activity.

CONTENT CHECK

1. **Identify:** Insular Southeast Asia, Irian Jaya, Java Sea, Strait of Malacca, Malays, Indonesia, Jakarta, Malaysia, Kuala Lumpur, Singapore, Brunei, Bandar Seri Begawan, Philippines, Manila, Dutch East Indies.

2. **Define:** volcanologists, entrepôt, free port.

3. Why are volcanoes common in Insular Southeast Asia?

4. What climate is found in Insular Southeast Asia?

5. What are the major ethnic groups of Insular Southeast Asia?

6. What is the basis of Singapore's industrialized economy?

7. **Challenge:** Why do you think there is such a mixture of peoples and religions in Insular Southeast Asia?

See the *TRB* for the *Chapter 28 Reading.*

CONCLUSION

In many cases the countries of Southeast Asia are physically broken into several pieces—islands or parts of peninsulas. Its physical fragmentation and cultural diversity make it unique among culture areas of the world. These characteristics have also made problems for the regions of the area. Economies have been slow to industrialize, and rivalries among different groups continue, making it difficult to build stable governments. Rapid population growth and food shortages are newer problems many Southeast Asian countries face.

SUMMARY

1. Southeast Asia has two regions. One is made up of peninsulas on the mainland of Asia. The other is largely made up of islands south of the Asian mainland.

2. Southeast Asia is very mountainous. This reduces the amount of good farmland in each country. Volcanic ash has added fertility to the soil.

3. Most of the people in Southeast Asia make their living by farming. Rice is the area's most important crop. The Mekong Delta is one of the world's best rice-growing areas.

4. Rapid population growth affects most of the countries. This growth holds back economic development and puts great demands on food supplies.

5. Insular Southeast Asia is rich in mineral and energy resources, especially oil. Most of the mineral resources in Continental Southeast Asia have only begun to be developed in recent years.

6. Several cultures have affected Southeast Asia. Today there are differences in religion, language, and politics.

7. The Indochina War was damaging to the area, and many of the countries there are still rebuilding.

8. There are both communist and noncommunist governments in Southeast Asia.

Answers to the following questions can be found on page T284.

REVIEWING VOCABULARY

Draw an illustration that shows the meaning of each term below. Then write the term and its definition at the bottom of each illustration.

entrepôt   silvaculture   paddies   guerrilla warfare

REMEMBERING THE FACTS

1. What are the two regions that make up Southeast Asia? What are the countries found in each region?

2. What is the longest river found in Southeast Asia?

3. Which country in Southeast Asia has the least developed economy in the entire region?

4. Which is the most populous country of Southeast Asia?

5. What religion do most of the people of Indonesia practice?

6. What two climate types are found in Continental Southeast Asia?

7. What is the most important food crop in Southeast Asia?

UNDERSTANDING THE FACTS

1. Rice is a very important crop in Southeast Asia. What does this tell us about rainfall and available water here?
2. What outside cultures have influenced the cultures of Southeast Asia? In what ways have they influenced this region?
3. Why are there so many volcanoes in Southeast Asia?
4. There is relatively heavy rain over most of Continental Southeast Asia, yet farming conditions are not very good in many areas. Why is this so?
5. Compare the economic development of Burma and Thailand with Kampuchea and Laos.
6. Why is Singapore so prosperous?
7. Two countries of Insular Southeast Asia that have small area and population are Brunei and Singapore. In what ways are they different?

THINKING CRITICALLY AND CREATIVELY

1. There are people who follow the Hindu religion in many parts of Insular Southeast Asia. Where did these people come from? How did they probably get to these islands?
2. What are some similarities of the locations of Southeast Asian cities? How might these be explained?
3. Would you expect to find a greater diversity of people in Continental Southeast Asia or Insular Southeast Asia? Explain your answer.
4. The Philippines was heavily influenced by the United States and Europe. In what ways are these influences still reflected in the Philippines?
5. **Challenge:** Almost 90 percent of Vietnam's population is Vietnamese. Other countries have more mixed populations. What are some advantages for a country that has a large majority of its people belonging to one ethnic group? What are some disadvantages?
6. **Challenge:** What problems might there be if one country gained total control of the Strait of Malacca and then refused to allow ships from other countries access in using it?

REINFORCING GRAPHIC SKILLS

Study the map on page 590. Then answer the questions that follow.

1. What is the exact location for the city Zamboanga?
2. Which city of the Philippines shown on the map is located closest to Malaysia? What is its relative location to Malaysia?
3. Between which degrees of latitude and longitude is the small country of Brunei located?
4. What is the exact location for the city Sandakan?

UNIT REVIEW

SUMMARY

1. Asia is made up of three different culture areas: East Asia, South Asia, and Southeast Asia.
2. Asia has many areas of high population density. However, the spread of population over the large land area is uneven.
3. Much of Asia's land is mountainous and not suited to agriculture. As a result, farmers make the best use of the fertile land that is available. Some of the highest yields in the world come from Asian farms.
4. India is the major country of South Asia. Much of South Asia's nations have rapidly growing populations, which create many problems for their economies.
5. At one time all the countries of South Asia were British colonies. Then the United Kingdom divided the area along religious lines. The two major religions of South Asia are Hinduism and Islam.
6. The countries of East Asia trace their cultures to China. Their art, religion, and written languages are similar.
7. The countries of East Asia also have many differences. Japan has a fully developed industrial economy. China's economy is the least developed. It depends on agriculture.
8. Southeast Asia occupies the area of mainland Asia once called Indochina and those island countries off the coast. Most are developing countries. Singapore has the most developed economy in Southeast Asia.
9. The culture of Southeast Asia has been influenced by both South Asia and East Asia.

Answers to the following questions can be found on page T287.

THINKING ABOUT THE UNIT

1. How are the landscape and climate of South and East Asia different from Southeast Asia's landscape and climate?
2. How have outside influences affected different cultural groups in South, East, and Southeast Asia?

SUGGESTED UNIT ACTIVITIES

1. Make a bulletin board display showing the written languages of Asia. Use language dictionaries from the library to find the same words or phrases written in the different languages. Remember to label each language.
2. Create a recipe card file for the kinds of food common in the various regions of Asia. Determine why certain foods are or are not popular in certain regions.
3. Prepare a report on the basic beliefs of such Asian religions as Hinduism and Buddhism. Include maps showing the distribution of each religion in South, East, and Southeast Asia. Identify each religion on your map with a separate color.
4. During one day in class, divide class members into castes and role-play in character.

DEVELOPING GEOGRAPHY SKILLS

TESTING HYPOTHESES

Suppose that 1,500 years from now, someone came across a Kennedy half-dollar dated 1983. Looking at it carefully, this person might make some guesses about the culture that produced it. For example, the fact that two languages—English and Latin—are on the coin might suggest a bilingual culture. The statement, "In God We Trust," might mean that the culture followed a religion that believed in one God. The eagle might indicate that birds were greatly valued. The perfectly circular shape of the coin could suggest a fairly high level of technical development.

As you know, guesses such as those listed above are hypotheses—generalizations made before any research has been done. Review the steps given on page 540 for making hypotheses:

1. Consider the statement, object, or theory: *India has found it hard to feed all its people.*
2. Make your hypotheses to explain the statement:
   a. *Most of India's physical features do not permit much farming.*
   b. *India does not receive enough rainfall to support farming.*
   c. *India's population is too large for its farmers to feed.*
   d. *India's farmers do not use modern farming methods or equipment that would increase the amount of crops they raise.*

Now it is time to determine which of the hypotheses listed is actually true. To do this, add these three steps to the process.

3. Think of what questions you need to an-swer to prove or disprove the hypotheses given:
   a. *What are India's physical features?*
   b. *How much rainfall does India receive?*
   c. *How much land in India is arable?*
   d. *What is India's population?*
   e. *What is India's population density?*
   f. *What is India's population distribution?*
   g. *What farming methods and equipment are used in India?*
4. Find the answers to the questions listed under step 3. You can use your textbook, especially Chapter 26, for answers. If the information in your book is not enough, the library has many reference books that can be of help. Your teacher also may be able to help you locate other sources of information.
5. Based on your answers, decide whether each hypothesis is correct. Revise incorrect hypotheses to make them consistent with the answers you have found.

For practice in testing a hypothesis, read the following statement: *Pakistan has a sizable textile industry.*

Now use the five steps given to test the following hypotheses:

1. *In Pakistan growing conditions—soils, rainfall, and temperature—are well suited for growing cotton.*
2. *Large numbers of people in Pakistan work in the textile industry.*
3. *Pakistan earns much money from its textile exports.*
4. *There is a strong demand for cotton cloth.*

597

OCEANIA AND ANTARCTICA

UNIT 10

Point out to students that the highlighted area on the world map inset shows Antarctica and the two culture areas of Oceania.

Oceania and Antarctica contain two culture areas and an uninhabited continent. One of the culture areas is the island continent of Australia. The other is most of the islands of the Pacific Ocean. These areas of the world share the common characteristic of being physically isolated from the rest of the world's culture areas.

Most of the people of Australia and New Zealand are related by culture and tradition to the people of Great Britain. Most speak English and practice Christianity. Both nations have well-developed economies, giving most of their people high standards of living.

The Pacific Islands are studied together more from their general location in the Pacific Ocean than from any common culture traits. The people of these islands show great cultural diversity.

Antarctica, "Earth's last great frontier," is far from most of the world's populated areas. Even though much of its frozen wilderness is unexplored, scientists are researching how its environment and resources may benefit Earth's people in the near future.

Outriggers on an island beach, French Polynesia

CHAPTER 29

Sheep-raising is vital to both Australia's and New Zealand's economies.

Sheep grazing by the Shotover River near Queenstown, New Zealand

AUSTRALIA AND NEW ZEALAND

In this chapter you will learn—

- What are the major physical regions and climates of Australia and New Zealand.
- What economic and cultural patterns have developed in Australia and New Zealand.
- How Australia and New Zealand have been influenced by their European heritage.

INTRODUCTION

The culture area of Australia and New Zealand lies southeast of Asia between the Indian and Pacific oceans. Cut off from Earth's other landmasses for millions of years, the area is viewed as faraway and isolated.

Although many of the area's features are similar, their landscapes and climates often differ. Australia is a huge, mostly flat country with several climates. New Zealand is a small mountainous country with a uniform climate.

People first settled the area during the last Ice Age, about the same time people first came to North America. Few people lived in Australia and New Zealand for thousands of years. Europeans did not make permanent settlements in the area until the late 1700s. From that time on, however, the two countries shared a common European culture.

The culture area still has a population no larger than that of New York. Australia and New Zealand's 19.5 million people live in an area the size of the United States.

Australia and New Zealand are modern, industrialized countries with large urban centers. Even though their economies include industry and manufacturing, farming and mining account for much of their trade with other countries.

1. AUSTRALIA

Many people refer to Australia as the "land down under" because it is entirely within the Southern Hemisphere. It is the only continent that contains just one country. As a continent it is the smallest in the world. As a country it has the world's sixth largest land area.

The Australian people have the same cultural background as Anglo-Americans. Like the United States and Canada, Australia was an English-speaking colony of Great Britain.

1.1 Landscape and Climate

Australia covers an area of 2,967,896 square miles (7,686,844.7 sq km). As Figure 29-2 on page 603 shows, the country has more than 80 percent of the land area of the United States. The land is mostly flat and dry. It has the lowest average elevation and relief of all Earth's continents, which is highlighted in Figure 29-3 on page 604.

Most of Australia has a dry climate. However, areas along the coasts have moister climates.

Landscape. Approximately 1,250 miles (2,011.7 km) from Australia's northeast coast

PHYSICAL REGIONS OF AUSTRALIA AND NEW ZEALAND

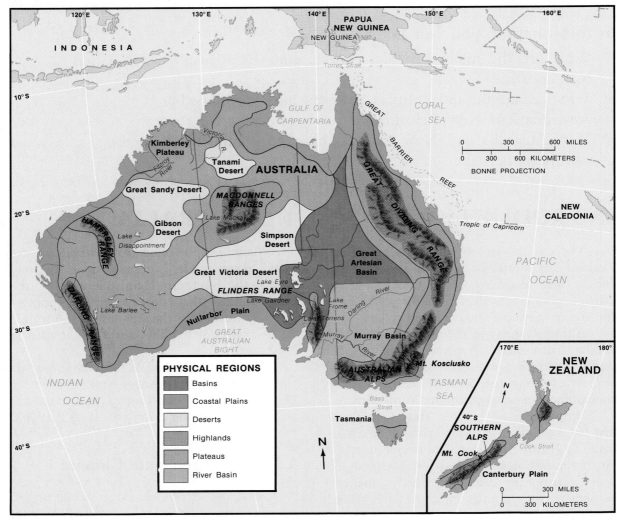

FIGURE 29-1
Deserts and highlands are striking features of the physical regions of Australia and New Zealand. Coastal plains rim most of Australia and areas of New Zealand. Which two rivers form the large river basin in southeastern Australia?

Australia's highest peak, Mount Kosciusko, is only 7,310 feet (2,228 m) above sea level.

Refer to the political map on page 610.

lies the Great Barrier Reef, the largest chain of coral in the world. Off the southern coast of Australia is the Great Australian Bight, a bay of the Indian Ocean.

Coastal plains circle Australia. They also cover the northern part of Tasmania, an is-

land off the continent's southeast coast. Many thousands of years ago, Tasmania was connected to Australia. Since that time sea level has risen to make Bass Strait, the waterway that separates Australia from Tasmania. Politically, Tasmania is a part of Australia today.

OCEANIA UNIT 10

Wrapping around the southeast is an area of highlands. The Great Dividing Range of low mountains and rugged hills form the continental divide. Part of this range, the Australian Alps sweep across the southeast corner of the country. Along the southern shore of Australia is a long, wide plain called Nullarbor.

Australia has four other highland areas. As shown in Figure 29-1 on page 602, the Macdonnell Ranges of high plateaus are found in the arid center of the country. The Flinders Range shoots up from the southern coast. The Hamersley and Darling ranges separate parts of the western plateau from the coastal lowlands. None of these ranges reach elevations of more than 5,000 feet (1,524 m).

Australia has no large river network. Most of its rivers are like the wadis of North Africa. They flow only after heavy rain, then shrink in dry seasons, and become creeks or completely dry. Lakes in the interior often become salt flats.

The chief river system is the Murray-Darling, which drains the Great Dividing Range. The Murray-Darling flows about 3,000 miles (4,828 km) across southeast Australia. Its basin, which includes other small

See the *TAE* for an *Objective 1* Activity.

Sunlight warms the domed Olga mountains, located just south of the Macdonnell Ranges in Australia. In which part of Australia are these mountains found?

COMPAR-A-GRAPH: AUSTRALIA-UNITED STATES

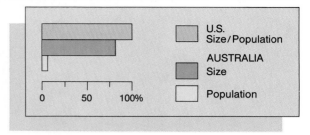

U.S. Size/Population

AUSTRALIA Size

Population

0   50   100%

FIGURE 29-2
Australia's population density is very low. How does its population percentage compare with the U.S.?

rivers, makes up the largest farming area. Because only six percent of Australia's land is arable, some must still be irrigated.

Much of Australia uses artesian wells for its water. The Great Artesian Basin, north of the Murray Basin, is perhaps the best known. **Artesian** (ahr TEE zhuhn) **wells** are made by drilling into the earth until water flows to the surface under its own pressure.

Two-thirds of Australia and the southern part of Tasmania have dry plateaus or desert. In the plateaus are dry grazing lands with shrubs. Three major desert areas that get little or no rain are found all around the central Macdonnell Ranges. Droughts here often are long and severe. Dryness and erosion over much of Australia mean only six percent of the country is forested.

Climate. Nearly all of Australia has a dry climate. In fact, Australia is viewed as the driest continent. Australia's center is desert. Less than 10 inches (25.4 cm) of rain falls here each year. Around the desert is a steppe climate area, which gets enough rain to grow short grasses and shrubs.

Closer to the Equator along the northern coast is an area of tropical savanna. It has hot, wet summers and warm, dry winters. Darwin, a city on the northern coast, averages 61 inches (154.9 cm) of rain each year.

ELEVATION OF AUSTRALIA AND NEW ZEALAND

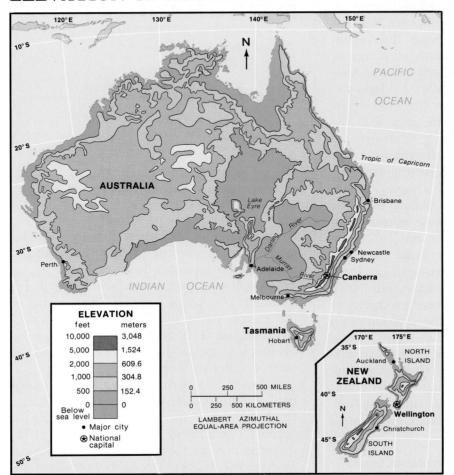

This map uses different color bands to compare the different ranges of elevation in Australia and New Zealand. Low elevations are common in both countries. Very few areas, especially in Australia, have elevations that are above 2,000 feet (609.6 m). In moving from the capital of Australia to Sydney, do you go to a higher or lower elevation?

New Guinea is separated from Australia by a relatively narrow body of water called the Torres Strait. Have students locate it on a map.

FIGURE 29-3

Australian football is played on an oval field about 200 yards (182.9 m) long and 150 yards (137.1 m) wide across the middle. Each team has 19 players who may punch, kick, or dribble the ball past the goal.

Except for a small area around Cooktown that has a tropical monsoon climate, most of Australia's eastern and southern coasts have moist, mild winter climates. Along the eastern rim of the continent, the climate is humid subtropical. Farther south, including Tasmania, a middle-latitude marine climate makes summers hot with high humidity. Winters there are warm and mild. Moving across the southern coast from west to east, Australia has a Mediterranean climate. Most of the rain falls in this area during the winter.

At one time Australia had a "white Australia" policy designed to keep Asian immigrants out of the country.

1.2 Economic and Cultural Patterns

The Australian economy has both industry and farming. Europeans, especially the British, gave Australia its culture. A full 99 percent of Australia's 16.2 million people speak English, practice Christianity, and have European ancestors.

Economic Patterns. Industry gives Australia close to 36 percent of its GNP. Almost 25 percent of the country's people work

OCEANIA AND ANTARCTICA UNIT 10

in industry. However, farming and mining make up most of Australia's economy.

Generally too dry for crops, Australia's land is good for grazing. As shown in Figure 29-4 on page 607, about 58 percent of the country is pasture, and less than 6 percent is planted. Grazing lands support large herds of cattle and sheep. Most of the livestock is raised on what the Australians call stations or ranches. The largest of these are found in the **outback,** Australia's isolated rural center.

Australia's major farming product is wool. The country supplies nearly one-third of the world's wool. Each year it also produces more than 496,000 tons (450,000 tonnes) of mutton.

The most important crop in Australia, however, is wheat. It is grown chiefly in the Murray Basin. Australia ranks seventh in world wheat production.

In 1851 Australia's farm economy was changed by the discovery of gold. Because of gold many people came to Australia. Gold also was the reason the country's mining industry got underway. Australia also has other minerals. Today it is one of the world's leading suppliers of lead, zinc, bauxite, and iron ore. It produces 90 percent of the world's rutile and zircon. It also has large diamond and opal deposits.

As to energy resources, Australia now exports more coal than any other country in the world. It also exports great quantities of uranium, shale, and natural gas. Many of its mineral and energy resources lie untapped.

Cultural Patterns. The first inhabitants of Australia were Aborigines (AB uh RIHJ uh neez). Today they number about 150,000—less than 1 percent of the country's 16.2 million people. Almost 40,000 Aborigines live on reservations. Nearly 160,000 Australians are of both Aborigine and European descent.

During the country's early history, Australia's population remained small. There were only about 400,000 people by 1850. The population increased dramatically, however, after gold was discovered. Between 1850 and 1860 almost one million people came to Australia. Most were European. Of the Europeans, the majority were English, Irish, or Scottish. Today only about one percent of Australia's population is non-European. Recently, Asians have been migrating to the area.

A farmer trucks hay out to feed his sheep during a drought in New South Wales. Sheep are raised for their wool and meat. How much of the world's wool is supplied by Australia?

THE URBAN WORLD

CANBERRA: URBAN PLANNING

Canberra, Australia's capital, is one of the world's planned cities. Other capitals of the world have also been planned, such as Washington, D.C., the capital of the United States, and Brasília, the capital of Brazil.

A country may have one of several reasons why it wants to plan the building of a city. In many cases such planned cities are capitals. A country may want to build a capital somewhere near the center of its land area. This makes it easier for the government to communicate with the rest of the country. At the time Washington, D.C. was built, the city was located close to the center of the 13 original states.

A country may also choose to build a capital in a certain area so that people will move into and develop that area. Canberra, like Brasília, was planned for this reason.

Most Australian cities grew up along its coastline. The government, however, wanted to develop the outback. In order to get this process started, the Australian Constitution called for a national capital in this region. The city had to be located at least 100 miles (160 km) from Sydney, the country's largest city. The site finally selected in 1913 was a treeless plain about 190 miles (30 km) southwest of Sydney near the Australian Alps.

A worldwide competition was held to design the new capital. The winner was an American architect from Chicago—Walter Burley Griffin. His design showed the waterways, placement of government buildings, businesses, and residential and recreation areas. He also mapped out streets and transportation and communication systems.

The city is built around a human-made lake, Lake Burley Griffin. The lake was formed by damming the Molonglo River. Thousands of acres of parks surround the lake. Two tree-lined streets lead to bridges that cross the lake. The government had to bring in thousands of trees, shrubs, and other plants.

The city was planned so that there would be lots of open space. As a result Canberra has more total space than many other cities with similar populations. The city was planned to have a population of about 500,000, but today metropolitan Canberra has only about 281,000 people.

Canberra is one of the world's most successful planned cities. It draws thousands of visitors each year from all over the world.

1. What are two reasons why a government may want to build a capital city in a certain location?
2. Where in Australia is Canberra?

LAND USE AND RESOURCES OF AUSTRALIA AND NEW ZEALAND

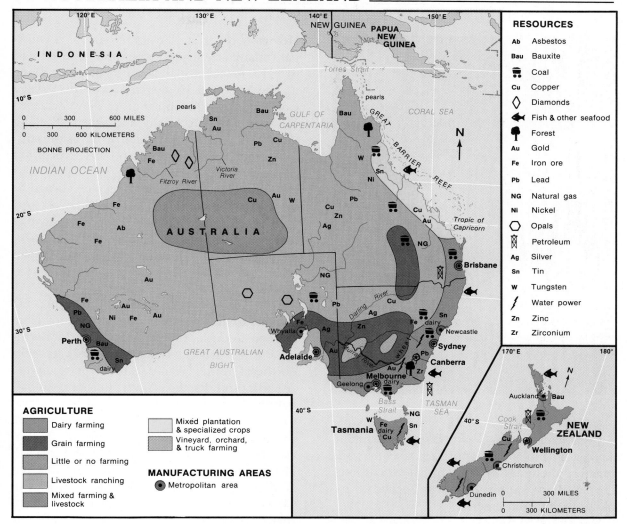

FIGURE 29-4

Because of its dry climate, Australia has extensive areas that cannot be used for growing crops, but which are suitable for livestock ranching. What types of agriculture are found in New Zealand?

Brisbane has more than 1 million people and Canberra has about 281,000.

Perth is a fast-growing, modern city. Some say it has more millionaires than most cities in the world.

Two out of every three Australians live on the narrow plain along the east and southeast coasts in one of the country's major cities. These are Sydney, Melbourne (MEHL buhrn), Brisbane (BRIHZ buhn), and Canberra (KAN buh ruh), the capital. Sydney is Australia's largest city. It and Melbourne together have more than one-third of the country's population.

Two heavily populated areas along the western and southern coasts are Perth on the west coast and Adelaide (AD uhl AYD) on the southern coast. Each has almost one million people.

FOCUS ON HISTORY

AMAZING CAPTAIN COOK

Captain James Cook was a sea captain, navigator, explorer, mapmaker, scientist, and practical dietitian. Because of his expeditions, the Southern Hemisphere was opened to exploration and settlement.

Through Captain Cook's voyages, people learned more about the Pacific, South Atlantic, South Indian, and Arctic oceans than they had ever dreamed. Cook became famous after a successful expedition to the South Pacific. In 1769 the Royal Society of Great Britain sent Cook and several scientists to Tahiti. It wanted them to watch what happens in the Southern Hemisphere when the planet Venus moves between Earth and the sun.

After it left Tahiti, the Cook expedition began to explore other parts of the Southern Hemisphere. It started searching for a continent many scientists of the time believed had to exist to balance the continents that made up the Northern Hemisphere. On this voyage Cook found and mapped all of New Zealand. He then found Australia and sailed all along its eastern coast. Cook sailed as far as present-day Indonesia before he and his expedition returned to Great Britain.

In 1772 Cook made a second voyage to search for the continent known today as Antarctica. He sailed farther south than anyone had ever sailed before. He circled Earth at 70° south latitude. On this trip Cook mapped many islands in the South Pacific and South Atlantic.

In 1776 Cook sailed for a third time. He wanted to find a short northern route from Europe to Asia. It would be either a northwest route around Canada and Alaska or a northeast route around Siberia between the Atlantic and Pacific. Many unsuccessful attempts from Europe had been made before. Cook was not successful, either. However, on this voyage he stopped along the northwestern coast of North America, then sailed north of the Bering Strait before turning south and landing on Hawaii. The voyage ended with Cook's death in the Hawaiian Islands in February 1779.

1. For what reasons did Captain Cook make his first voyage to the South Pacific in 1769?

2. What were the major accomplishments of Captain Cook's second voyage to the Southern Hemisphere?

3. Why do you think the discovery of a northwest or northeast passage from Europe to Asia was important to European explorers of the 1700s?

1.3 Influences of the Past

Some scientists believe Australia's first Aborigines came about 40,000 years ago from southeastern Asia. Originally hunters and gatherers who led a nomadic life, they knew little about planting and had no domestic animals except for a wild dog known as a dingo. Portuguese sailors may have been the first Europeans to meet the Aborigines in Australia. Written stories about the continent appeared in Portugal in 1542. During the 1600s Spanish and Dutch navigators explored coastal Australia. In 1642 the Dutch explorer Abel Tasman reached the island later named in his honor.

By 1770 British explorer James Cook landed along the east coast of Australia. At that time Europeans called the area *terra Australis incognita*, or "the unknown southern land." The British started settling it sometime after they lost their American colonies in 1776. The first permanent European settlement in Australia was Sydney.

In the early 1800s, Australia came under British control. Australia was first used as a **penal colony**, or a settlement for criminals. Many of Australia's early British settlers had been jailed for not paying their bills. They were freed on the condition that they move to Australia.

During Australia's colonial period, the country's six states—Victoria, New South Wales, Queensland, Tasmania, Western Australia, and South Australia—were ruled as separate British colonies. In 1901 an Australian constitution unified the colonies, making the Commonwealth of Australia. It included the states plus the Northern Territory and the Australian Capital Territory. Australia's government is a democracy.

Australia grew in population and in economic and political strength during its first 40 years as a country. Since then it has been a leader in regional and international affairs.

CONTENT CHECK

1. **Identify:** Australia, Great Barrier Reef, Tasmania, Great Dividing Range, Nullarbor, Macdonnell Ranges, Murray-Darling, Great Artesian Basin, Murray Basin, Aborigines, Sydney, Melbourne, Brisbane, Canberra, Perth, Adelaide, James Cook.

2. **Define:** artesian wells, outback, penal colony.

3. What landforms are in Australia?

4. What general climate does most of Australia have?

5. What are Australia's most important agricultural products?

6. Where do most Australians live?

7. **Challenge:** Australia's population density is 5 persons per square mile (2 per sq km). With all of its land area, one might think it could be promoted as a new home for many people in overcrowded parts of the world. What makes this a good idea? A bad idea?

See the *TRB* for *Teacher Notes: Section 1 Extending the Lesson* on saving the Franklin River.

2. NEW ZEALAND

New Zealand lies about 1,200 miles (1,931.2 km) southeast of Australia. It has an economy and culture like its neighbor but a much smaller land area. As Figure 29-5 on page 610 shows, New Zealand is made up of two main islands. Called the North and South islands, they are part of two separate colliding tectonic plates.

New Zealand is a much more mountainous country than Australia. Nowhere are mountains out of view.

2.1 Landscape and Climate

New Zealand's 103,737 square miles (268,678.6 sq km) are almost the size of Colorado. Except in high elevations, its climate is warm and mild.

NATIONS OF AUSTRALIA AND NEW ZEALAND

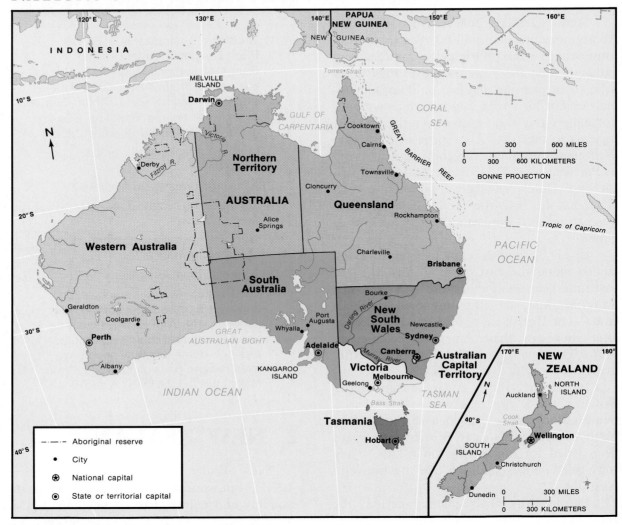

FIGURE 29-5

Distance, isolation, a distinct cultural identity, and relatively sparse population have been important features of this region. Traditionally, Australia and New Zealand's ties have been close to Great Britain. What names of provinces or cities seem to suggest the region's British heritage?

Some animals native to New Zealand are the kiwi, albatross, and tuatara. No land snakes live there.

While most of New Zealand's rivers are difficult to navigate, they are sources of hydroelectric power.

Landscape. New Zealand is a long, narrow country with a varied landscape. It stretches almost 1,000 miles (1,609.3 km) from north to south. It is no wider than 210 miles (338 km). In fact no place in New Zealand is more than 80 miles (128.7 m) from the sea. The larger North and South islands make up 98 percent of the country's area. They are separated by Cook Strait.

North Island covers 44,190 square miles (114,452 sq km). A narrow, low-lying peninsula juts away from the island toward the northwest. Coastal plains run from this northernmost tip of North Island along the western

610   **OCEANIA**   **UNIT 10**

Mount Cook, the highest peak in New Zealand at 12,349 feet (3,764 m), is found in the Southern Alps.

New Zealand's volcanoes are part of the Pacific "Ring of Fire." Earthquakes are common, and, in fact, they helped shape New Zealand's landmass.

coast to Cook Strait. Thick woodlands and croplands are found in this lowland area.

The plains rise to a range of volcanic highlands in the center of the island. Forests turn into shrubs and volcanic rock. The highest points on the island are found in this region. East of these highlands is a high plateau that meets the Pacific Ocean. Rich, green rolling hills and grazing lands can be found along this eastern coast.

South Island covers about 58,190 square miles (150,712 sq km). A range of high mountains called the Southern Alps in the center of the island extends nearly its full length. The western slopes of these highlands are very steep—more than 10,000 feet (3,038 m) above sea level.

The beautiful high country of South Island gives New Zealand a rugged look. There are many glaciers, lakes, and forests on South Island. Fjords cut into much of the southwest coast.

Coastal plains fall on both sides of the highlands and at the southernmost tip of New Zealand. Along the east central coastal area of South Island is the Canterbury Plain. This lowland is New Zealand's largest area of flat land and its chief farming area.

Climate. All of New Zealand has a middle-latitude marine climate. Rainfall over much of both North and South islands' west coasts averages more than 100 inches (254 cm) a year. The cooler temperatures in the south slow down evaporation. The result is fog and many cloudy days.

New Zealand lies in the path of the westerly winds. Because of this the eastern side of South Island is in the rain shadow of the Southern Alps. Some eastern areas get as little as 25 inches (63.5 cm) of rain each year. That is the yearly average for the amount of rain the city of Christchurch on the Canterbury Plain receives.

Christchurch's average high temperatures range from 50°F (10°C) in July to 70°F (21.1°C) in January. As shown in Figure 29-6 on page 612, Auckland (AW kluhnd) on North Island is only slightly warmer.

Have students compare the fjords on New Zealand's coast with those of Norway's west coast.

The Canterbury Plain is New Zealand's chief farming region. It lies between the Southern Alps and the east coast of South Island. What other landscape features are found on South Island?

The Maori people call Mount Cook *Aorangi,* which means "cloud piercer."

Beef and dairy products are also sent to New Zealand's trading partners—Japan, Australia, United States, and Great Britain. In return the country imports machinery, some minerals, chemicals, fuels, and many manufactured goods.

CLIMATE: AUCKLAND

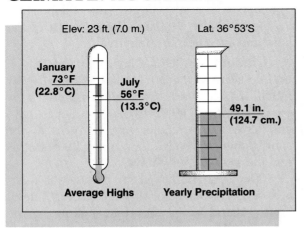

FIGURE 29-6
Auckland's climate remains mild throughout the year. How does Auckland's elevation affect its climate?

Refer students to pages 96-97 to review the map of Earth's Climate Regions.

2.2 Economic and Cultural Patterns

New Zealand is a modern country with both a Polynesian and European heritage. Its economy, once based completely on agriculture, is now becoming more varied.

Economic Patterns. Nearly 50 percent of New Zealand's land is pasture. Much of its economy is based on raising and selling livestock. The country is one of the largest producers of wool in the world.

Only about three percent of New Zealand's land supports crops. Much of this land is found on South Island on Canterbury Plain. About one-half of the country's farmland is in grain crops, such as wheat, corn, and barley. Fruits are also grown, and today New Zealand produces 68 percent of the world's supply of kiwi fruit.

The rest of the land is used for fodder crops, grains and grasses grown for livestock feed. New Zealand needs fodder to feed its large number of animals—more than 70 million sheep and about 8 million cattle. The animals of New Zealand outnumber the people by almost 26 to 1.

New Zealand also has a variety of mineral resources—asbestos, gold, copper, lead, and zinc. Its chief energy base is hydroelectric power, created from rapidly flowing streams and rivers draining the central highlands of North and South islands.

The economy of New Zealand is changing. Low prices for sheep and farm products, the loss of some overseas trade, high prices, and less spending by government have forced the country to produce other goods. The government of New Zealand is trying to encourage more manufacturing and industry so that New Zealand does not have to depend so much on trade with other countries.

Cultural Patterns. European expansion into the South Pacific gave New Zealand its mostly European culture. Today 87 percent of New Zealanders are descended from

See the *TAE* for an *Objective 2* Activity.

These fishing boats lie docked in Auckland's harbor. Fishing plays an important role in the country's economy. How is the economy of New Zealand changing?

OCEANIA UNIT 10

Faces in this group of New Zealand girls and boys reflect the country's various ethnic groups. Who were the first settlers of New Zealand and when did they establish their first permanent settlements?

Auckland is New Zealand's major center of manufacturing and trade.

2.3 Influences of the Past

The early history of New Zealand has some mystery. No one really knows when or from where the Maori came. Some historians think the first Maori came from the Cook and Society islands, far away in the South Pacific. They may have arrived about 750 AD.

These first people did not build permanent settlements. They used the islands of New Zealand and surrounding waters for hunting and fishing. It is believed that the first permanent Maori settlers arrived about 1300. These settlers farmed as well as hunted and fished. Most of their settlements were on North Island. Still today most of New Zealand's 280,000 Maori live there.

The first Europeans to see New Zealand were Dutch sailors. They sighted the islands in 1642, but they were stopped from landing by Maori warriors. Nevertheless, Dutch explorers named the island *Nieuw Zeeland* for a province in the Netherlands.

The first Europeans to land on the island were part of James Cook's British expedition. In the 1770s the British set up whaling colonies along the coasts of North Island. New Zealand also attracted many traders interested in the island's timber as well as missionaries seeking converts. In the early 1800s, many British began communities on South Island, where there were few Maori settlements.

The British in New Zealand negotiated for land rights with the Maori. When the Treaty of Waitangi was signed in 1840 by Britain and a group of Maori chiefs, it gave the Maori land rights in exchange for accepting British rule over the islands. This treaty officially made New Zealand a British colony. It is one of the rare examples in history where expansion by a world power was negotiated with the original settlers.

The British, in their settlement of New Zealand, did not attempt to isolate the Maori. In fact since 1907, when New Zealand gained

Europeans, many from Scotland. Almost 81 percent are Christian. English is the language of most New Zealanders.

Among New Zealand's non-European minorities are Maori (MOW uhr ee), the area's first settlers, and other people from the South Pacific—Samoans, Cook Islanders, and Tongans. There are also Indians, Chinese, and Southeast Asians in New Zealand.

New Zealand's North Island has about 72 percent of the country's 3.3 million people. Most live and work in cities such as Auckland or Wellington. Auckland is the most populous city with almost 900,000 people. Wellington, New Zealand's capital, has about 360,000 people. Rural South Island has 28 percent of the country's people. Christchurch is its largest city.

New Zealanders enjoy a high standard of living. The country has many national health and social programs and free public education. As a result 98 percent of the people can read and write.

USING GRAPHIC SKILLS

READING TIME-ZONE MAPS

When you studied the Soviet Union, you learned that the country is so large that it includes 11 time zones. When people are going to bed at 11:00 PM in Moscow, people are already at work and school at 9:00 AM the next morning in easternmost Siberia.

In Chapter 2 you learned about world time-zone maps. Since Earth completes a rotation once every 24 hours, scientists created 24 standard time zones, each 15 degrees of longitude apart. The point of reference for Earth's time zones is the Prime Meridian in Greenwich, England. The International Date Line, where one calendar day ends and the next day begins, is along most of the 180° line of longitude.

The map below shows time zones for Australia, New Zealand, and areas of Oceania. Study the map. Then review the information on pages 26-27. Finally answer the questions that follow.

1. If it is 11 AM in Auckland, what time is it in Sydney?

2. When it is 10:00 PM Monday in Canberra, Australia, what time and day is it in Western Samoa?

3. You must place an important phone call at the beginning of the business day—8:00 AM—in Perth, Australia. You are calling from Wellington, New Zealand. At what time should you make your call?

STANDARD TIME ZONES

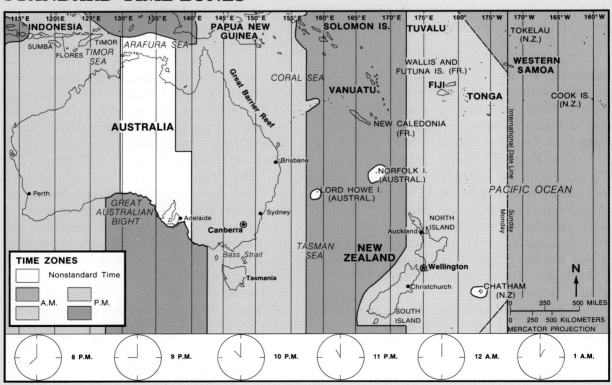

Maori visual arts and music can be seen and heard in New Zealand. The woman in this photograph is playing a musical instrument on a porch that showcases Maori sculpture. Do the Maori take an active part in the life of New Zealand?

Some 800,000 tourists visit New Zealand annually.

New Zealand, like Australia, still recognizes British monarchs as sovereign.

its independence in the British Commonwealth, many Maori have become active leaders in the government and businesses of New Zealand.

Modern New Zealand has a stable government and economy. Although it is one of the world's most remote countries, New Zealand became involved in major world events. After World War II, New Zealand helped in founding the United Nations. Today it is active in world trade and politics. New Zealand has proved that just because it is faraway, it is not isolated.

In 1893 New Zealand became the first country to grant women over 21 the right to vote. An old-age pension plan was begun in 1898.

CONTENT CHECK

1. **Identify:** New Zealand, North Island, South Island, Cook Strait, Southern Alps, Canterbury Plain, Christchurch, Auckland, Maori, Wellington, Treaty of Waitangi.

2. What are the major features of the New Zealand landscape?

3. What climate is found in New Zealand?

4. On what is much of New Zealand's economy based?

5. What ethnic groups live in New Zealand?

6. **Challenge:** How is North Island different from South Island?

See the *TRB* for *Teacher Notes: Section 2 Extending the Lesson* on kiwi fruit.

CONCLUSION

Australia and New Zealand are similar in their economic, political, and cultural development. It is their similarities that make them a unique culture area. These same elements also make it possible for them to continue to grow together in the future. The chief obstacle between them is the sea. However, this is slowly being overcome with modern transportation and communication.

SUMMARY

1. The culture area of Australia and New Zealand lies totally in the Southern Hemisphere. Both Australia and New Zealand are modern, industrialized countries, even though their industries are still developing.
2. Australia is the only country in the world that is an entire continent. The terrain of Australia is chiefly flat. Most of Australia is dry.
3. New Zealand is an island country, located southeast of Australia. Mountains and hills cover much of the country. New Zealand has two main areas—North Island and South Island.

4. The most important economic activity in Australia and New Zealand is sheep and cattle raising. Australia grows wheat, and it supplies the world with many minerals. New Zealand uses much of its farmland to grow grains and feed for its livestock.
5. Australia's original settlers were Aborigines from southeastern Asia. New Zealand's original settlers were Maori from Polynesia. European settlers brought their culture to Australia and New Zealand in the 1700s.
6. Australia became an independent nation in 1901. New Zealand became an independent nation in 1907.

Answers to the following questions can be found on page T294.

REVIEWING VOCABULARY

On a separate sheet of paper, write the word that is defined to the right of the blanks in each line. Then circle the letters in the words that show a star (★) below. Unscramble these letters to spell the mystery word.

1. _ ★ _ _ ★ _ _   isolated rural land
2. _ _ _ ★ _ _ _ ★ _ _ _   settlement to which prisoners are sent as punishment
3. ★ _ ★ _ ★ ★ _ _ _ _ _ _ _   water coming from underground after earth is drilled
4. _ _ _ _ _ ★   livestock feed

REMEMBERING THE FACTS

1. Compared to other continents, how large is Australia?
2. In what part of Australia is the continental divide?

3. Where is the driest climate found on the continent of Australia?
4. What population distribution is found in Australia?

5. From where did people first come to settle Australia?
6. Where in New Zealand is the country's largest lowland?
7. What are some of the mineral resources of Australia and New Zealand?
8. When were Australia and New Zealand established as independent nations?
9. What are the largest cities in Australia? In New Zealand?
10. Who were the first Europeans to see New Zealand?

UNDERSTANDING THE FACTS

1. Why do Australia and New Zealand lead the world in wool production?
2. In what ways are Australia and New Zealand landscapes alike? In what ways are they different?
3. How did the discovery of gold change the economy of Australia?
4. What are the common cultural characteristics of Australia and New Zealand?
5. Why do New Zealand's east coasts receive less precipitation than its west coasts?
6. What was the main result of the Treaty of Waitangi?

THINKING CRITICALLY AND CREATIVELY

1. How do you think the fact that Australia has a small population limits the economic growth of the country?
2. Why do you suppose Australia and New Zealand both have high standards of living despite their remoteness from the rest of the world?
3. **Challenge:** Large numbers of Aborigines died after Europeans settled Australia. Some were killed. Others died of diseases brought from Europe. Today many Aborigines face prejudice and are poor. They live on reservations set up by the Australian government. What groups in other parts of the world does this remind you of? The word *aborigines* means the first people to live in a country. Why do you think there are many "aborigines" in the world in situations similar to Australia's Aborigines?

REINFORCING GRAPHIC SKILLS

Study the map on page 614. Then answer the questions that follow.

1. Which other country is in the same time zone as eastern Australia?
2. What parts of New Zealand are in a different time zone from North and South islands?
3. How many time zones does the continent of Australia span from east to west?
4. If it is Wednesday at 3:00 PM in the Cook Islands, what day and time would it be in Tasmania?

CHAPTER 30

Young woman in ceremonial headdress, Papua New Guinea

PACIFIC ISLANDS

Most of these islands remained undisturbed by outsiders for thousands of years. During the struggle for colonies in the 1700s and 1800s, European and Asian countries and the United States scrambled for control of these islands to add to their "empires."

In this chapter you will learn—

⬤ What regions make up the Pacific Islands culture area.

⬤ What landforms and climates are common throughout the Pacific Islands.

⬤ What economic activities take place in the Pacific Islands.

⬤ How the traditional cultures of the Pacific Island peoples have been influenced by outside cultures.

Point out that Micronesia lies generally north of Melanesia. Polynesia lies generally east of both Micronesia and Melanesia.

Melanesia, Micronesia, and Polynesia are each further divided into individual islands and smaller island groups called archipelagoes.

INTRODUCTION

The culture area of the Pacific Islands covers the largest area of Oceania. As Figure 30-1 on page 621 shows, as many as 30,000 islands spread over thousands of miles of the Pacific Ocean. Most are little more than specks of land breaking the ocean's surface.

The area can be divided into three regions—Melanesia (MEHL uh NEE zhuh), Micronesia (MY kruh NEE zhuh), and Polynesia (PAHL uh NEE zhuh). These names come from special characteristics of the people or the land. The word *melos* means "black." Melanesia is populated by people who have dark skin and dark hair. Melanesia includes Papua New Guinea (PAP yuh wuh NOO GIHN ee), Vanuatu (VAN uh wah TOO), New Caledonia (NOO KAL uh DOH nyuh), Fiji (FEE JEE), and the Solomon Islands.

The word *micro* means "small." The name Micronesia comes from the general size of the islands in that area rather than any cultural features. Micronesia includes the Federated States of Micronesia, Marshall Islands, United States Trust Territory of Palau (puh LOW) Islands, Guam (GWAHM), Wake Island, Northern Mariana (MAR ee AN uh) Islands, and Nauru (nah OO ROO).

The word *poly* means "many," and Polynesia is an area of many islands. Polynesia includes Tonga (TAHNG guh), Tuvalu (too VAHL OO), Western Samoa (suh MOH uh), Midway Island, American Samoa, Wallis and Futuna (fuh TOO nuh), Tokelau (TOH kuh LOW) Islands, Niue (nee OO way) Island, Easter Island, Cook Islands, Pitcairn (PIHT KARN) Island, Kiribati (KIHR uh BAS), and French Polynesia. The people living in this area have lighter skin and wavier hair than do other people of the Pacific Islands. The Hawaiian Islands and New Zealand are both part of Polynesia. However, they are studied with other regions because of their political or cultural ties.

The Pacific Islands have landscapes that vary from jungle to mountain. Because they lie in the tropics, they have mostly hot, humid climates with much rain. Most of the people who live there grow their own food.

This area of beautiful beaches and warm waters attracts many tourists. However, economic troubles are problems on many of the islands.

Some of the countries in the Pacific Islands culture area have become independent republics. Others are still governed as colonies or commonwealths.

1. MELANESIA

Melanesia, located north and east of Australia, lies between the Equator and the Tropic of Capricorn. The eastern half of New Guinea, called Papua New Guinea, is part of Melanesia. The western half is a part of the Southeast Asian culture area. The mainland of Papua New Guinea and several small islands make up the largest country in the Pacific Islands. It is spread over 870,000 square miles (2,253,298.3 sq km) of land and ocean. However, the land alone covers only 178,259 square miles (461,690.5 sq km).

So-called "dry areas" receive very adequate supplies of rainfall—there are no deserts on the islands.

1.1 Landscape and Climate

Melanesia has more land area than both Micronesia and Polynesia. Most of the lands are **high islands,** or islands of volcanic origin that have mountains and plateaus.

Mainland Papua New Guinea is divided into two parts by high mountains. Running east to west, the ranges have many peaks that are more than 12,500 feet (3,657.6 m) high. Rivers flow north and south of these highlands. Most have large, swampy deltas, which make travel difficult.

Much of Papua New Guinea has heavy forests. Swamps and jungles border the north and south edges of the mainland. Reefs stretch along the coast and around most of the small islands.

Most of the other large islands that make up the rest of Melanesia are high islands. Many of the smaller ones are flat coral atolls.

The islands of Melanesia have either tropical savanna or tropical rain forest climates. Some islands do have a dry season. Temperatures in Melanesia, however, are hot all year. Average high temperatures are between 85°F (29.4°C) and 90°F (32.2°C). Some highland areas are cooler at night.

Cannibalism was once practiced in parts of the Pacific Islands. Some believed it was a religious practice, whereby a dead person's good qualities would be passed on to anyone who ate part of his or her flesh.

This view shows an area of highlands in Papua New Guinea. Wooded hillsides are common on Melanesia's high islands. What landscape features are found in New Guinea?

Some tribes in Melanesia, called Negritos, are pygmies, or short people. They look somewhat like the Pygmies of Africa.

In Fiji the official language is English. Fiji also has an 80 percent literacy rate. However, the number of people that can read or write in the rest of Melanesia is much lower. The literacy rate runs as low as 15 percent in Vanuatu. Many island children do not continue their education beyond elementary school.

RELATIVE SIZE OF THE PACIFIC ISLANDS _____

A map of the contiguous United States gives some perspective in measuring the area of the Pacific Islands. The vast expanses of ocean that separate the thousands of islands in this culture area make it easy to understand why it is sometimes referred to as *Oceania.* Within how many degrees of longitude do the Pacific Islands extend?

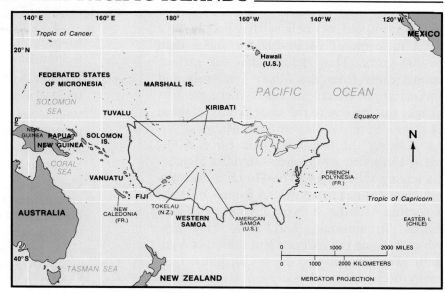

Refer students to the political map of the Pacific Islands on page 624.

FIGURE 30-1

Recently Fiji has undergone political, social, and economic changes. Ethnic Fijians, who make up 47 percent of the 700,000 population, are struggling to preserve the traditional authority of Fijian chiefs against Indians, who are mostly descendants of plantation laborers and who make up 49 percent of the population.

Some areas receive as much as 137 inches (348 cm) of rain each year. Drier areas receive at least 40 inches (101.6 cm). In general, high islands receive more rain than atolls.

See the *TAE* for an *Objective 1* Activity.

1.2 Economic and Cultural Patterns

Most of the five million people who live in Melanesia are subsistence farmers, or they fish for a living. The people of Melanesia live chiefly on fish, sweet potatoes, yams, and cassava. They export some cash crops like cacao, rubber, and coffee. The large islands have some minerals. On the island of Bougainville (BOOG uhn VIHL) in Papua New Guinea, there are copper mines.

Mining and light industry make up about 39 percent of Papua New Guinea's GNP. Light industry is found in or around Melanesia's major cities. The most common indus-

trial activities in the islands are lumbering and food processing.

There is no common cultural pattern among all the people of Melanesia. Isolated groups of people speak different languages, totaling more than 700. Many in Melanesia speak in a **pidgin** language. This is a mix of local language with European words. It was created when the Europeans came to the area. Today it is the spoken language of business and government in most of Melanesia.

Less than 13 percent of the people of Melanesia live in cities. The largest cities are the capitals of Port Moresby in Papua New Guinea, Nouméa (noo MAY uh) in New Caledonia, and Suva (SOO vuh) in Fiji. Port Moresby has a population of about 144,000 people. Both Nouméa and Suva have fewer than 75,000 people.

Most of the people of this area live in small villages. They range in size from 50 to 200 inhabitants. Villages of 1,000 or more are found along major rivers or the coasts.

1.3 Influences of the Past

Anthropologists believe that people have lived in parts of Melanesia for more than 50,000 years. They believe that the earliest people came from the Malay Peninsula and Indonesia. In Melanesia today there are languages that belong to the same family as those of the Philippines, Taiwan, and Malaysia.

During the late 1800s and early 1900s, many European governments divided Melanesia among themselves. The Dutch took western New Guinea. The British gained Fiji, the Solomons, southeast New Guinea, the Bismarck Archipelago, and New Hebrides, which became the independent nation of Vanuatu. The French took New Caledonia. Germany occupied northeast New Guinea for a time. After World War I, Australia ruled all of eastern New Guinea.

Europeans brought plantation agriculture, metal tools, and many new crops to the area. They also introduced Christianity and European forms of government. However, European diseases had the greatest effect on the islands. With no immunity to these diseases, thousands of Melanesians died during the first years after Europeans arrived.

Few Europeans now live in Melanesia. Most of the people have Melanesian backgrounds. There are small groups of French, Vietnamese, Chinese, and other Pacific Islands people. Fijians are a slight minority on Fiji—44 percent. About 50 percent of the population are people of French and Melanesian ancestry.

Many of the countries of Melanesia are now independent. Fiji gained its independence in 1970, Papua New Guinea in 1975, the Solomons in 1978, and Vanuatu in 1980. New Caledonia is still a French territory. It will probably become independent in the 1990s. There is still some unrest in Melanesia. Many countries of the world are trying to maintain their influence in the area.

CONTENT CHECK

1. **Identify:** Melanesia, Papua New Guinea, Bougainville, Port Moresby.
2. **Define:** high islands, pidgin.
3. What islands make up Melanesia?
4. What are the most important cash crops in Melanesia?
5. From what part of the world did the earliest Melanesians come?
6. **Challenge:** Why do you think pidgin is Melanesia's language of choice for business and government?

See the *TRB* for *Teacher Notes: Section 1 Extending the Lesson* on jimi theater of Papea New Guinea.

2. MICRONESIA

Micronesia lies in the western Pacific. It is east of the Philippines and north of Melanesia. Micronesia's total area, including water, is about the same as that of the 48 contiguous United States. But Micronesia's land area is only about the size of Rhode Island. It has about 1,214 square miles (3,144.3 sq km). Guam, with 210 square miles (543.9 sq km), is Micronesia's largest island.

Guam is only about one-fifth the size of Luxembourg, a small country in northwestern Europe.

2.1 Landscape and Climate

Micronesia's many islands are different in size and landscape. Some are no larger than one square mile (2.6 sq km). Most can best be described as **low islands.** That is, they are made of coral and barely rise above sea level. Low islands generally are small, have poor soil, very little plant life, and little fresh water. Low islands are often **atolls** (A TAWLZ) coral reefs that surround a body of water.

The Marshall Islands and Nauru are low islands or atolls covered with broadleaf evergreens and sand. The Carolines, part of the

622   **OCEANIA AND ANTARCTICA**   UNIT 10

Federated States of Micronesia, have both low and high islands. Pohnpei (POHN PAY), the Federated States' capital, has peaks reaching 2,000 feet (609.6 m), rolling hills, swamps, and thick broadleaf evergreen forests. Other islands in the same chain are tiny flat **islets,** or little islands.

The Mariana Islands' high volcanic cones make them unique among Micronesia's islands. The landscape has high cliffs and rocky shorelines, as well as low hills with fertile areas and streams. Although there are highlands on Guam, for example, there is no point higher than 1,500 feet (457.2 m).

Micronesia has a tropical rain forest climate. Temperatures average between 80°F (26.7°C) and 89°F (31.7°C) most of the year. The amount of annual rainfall changes in different areas. It is 85 inches (215.9 cm) in the Marianas and 182 inches (462.3 cm) in Pohnpei and Truk in the eastern Carolines. The wettest months in Micronesia are May through November.

Most of Micronesia lies along the Pacific Ocean typhoon belt. These storms have winds that range from light to more than 190 miles (305.8 km) per hour. People in the islands call the light winds "coconut typhoons." They usually are only strong enough to knock coconuts from trees. More powerful storms cause great damage. In Melanesia more typhoons come from July through October than in other parts of the year. In 1968 a typhoon that hit Saipan (sy PAN) in the Marianas destroyed more than 90 percent of the houses.

Have students research the cause of typhoons, explaining factors that go together to produce typhoons with very strong winds.

2.2 Economic and Cultural Patterns

Most of the 120,000 people of Micronesia live by farming or fishing. Micronesia's low islands cannot support large-scale farming. Small plots of land provide only enough crops for families. On the large high islands, people

Many islanders are skilled artists and craftsworkers. Colorful baskets, mats, masks, and cooking utensils are made, and some are sold to tourists and export companies.

A Fijian plantation owner and his wife are spreading broken coconuts out to dry in the sun. Coconuts are valuable for their oil, which is extracted from the fruit's dried meat. In which Pacific Islands region is the island of Fiji located?

Ask students if they think it likely that the islands of Micronesia will ever support a large population.

USING GRAPHIC SKILLS

REVIEWING SCALE

Pens, pencils, a calculator, and a ruler are common tools which you need for your schoolwork. A ruler is an important tool that you often use in school for making various types of measurements.

In Chapter 2 you learned that *scale* is an important tool used for measurement in making and reading maps. Scale is the relationship between a unit of measure on a map and a unit of measure on Earth. A map shows scale with a line divided into several parts equal to a certain number of miles or kilometers. This line is called a bar scale. Its length is used to measure distances on a map.

The map below shows the land and water areas of the Pacific Islands. It also shows the bar scale that is used for measuring distances on this map. Study the map and review the information on scale on pages 30–31. Then answer the questions that follow.

1. What is the approximate distance in miles from Guam to Pitcairn Island?

2. What is the approximate distance in kilometers of Polynesia at its widest extent from west to east?

3. Which is closer to Easter Island: Fiji or Hawaii?

REGIONS OF THE PACIFIC ISLANDS

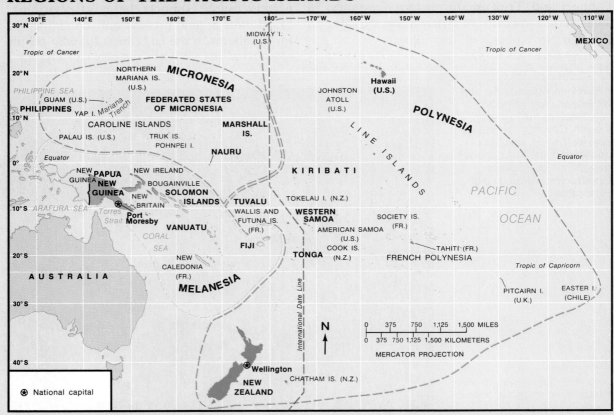

raise cattle, sheep, and goats, which were brought to Micronesia by Europeans.

The chief cash crop of Micronesia is **copra,** dried coconut meat. It is used in margarine, cooking oil, and soap. The only major industry in Micronesia is phosphate mining. Most of this mining is done on the island of Nauru. Much of Nauru's soil has been ruined because of many years of mining.

Recently, Micronesia has begun to use its location and climate to develop tourism. The islands get visitors from the Philippines, Japan, Australia, New Zealand, and the United States.

Micronesia's location is also important for the defense strategy of the United States. Many people work on United States military bases. Anderson Air Force Base, for example, is the largest employer in Guam.

Because Micronesia is made up of scattered islands, at least nine major languages and many regional dialects are spoken. English, French, Spanish, Japanese, and German are also spoken in different parts of the islands. However, these differences have not stopped the people of Micronesia from keep-

See the *TAE* for an *Objective 2* Activity.

ing many traditions that are thousands of years old. These traditions bind the people of the scattered islands together.

Before Christianity was introduced, the islanders followed many religions, each based on polytheism and a complicated mythology about Earth's creation.

2.3 Influences of the Past

Anthropologists believe Micronesia was settled by people from the Malay Peninsula as early as 1500 BC. The first Europeans, the Portuguese, did not arrive in Micronesia until after 1500 AD. Since then, however, Micronesia has known many different European and Asian rulers. Each has left its mark on the culture, economy, and land.

Spaniards came in the 1700s. Because of their influence, about one-half of Micronesia's population is Roman Catholic. In the Northern Mariana Islands, family names and customs also show Hispanic influence. When Spain lost control of Micronesia in the late 1800s, Germans moved into the area. They were attracted by the copra trade. Germans are remembered in Micronesia for setting up this industry.

Some islanders still believe in magic and witchcraft.

Heavy equipment is used for loading phosphate from Nauru onto ships bound for markets in other countries. What damaging effect has phosphate mining had in Nauru?

Some western sports, such as volleyball and rugby, have intruded upon more traditional forms of recreation such as dancing.

The German occupation lasted only until World War I. At that time the Japanese captured much of the region. The remains of Japanese roads, docks, seaplane ramps, and buildings can still be seen in Micronesia. Japanese control ended with Japan's defeat in World War II. During the war the United States and Japan fought many important battles on the islands.

Much of Micronesia became the United States Trust Territory of the Pacific Islands in 1947. Today only the Palau Islands are still governed as a trust. The Northern Marianas are a commonwealth of the United States. The people who live there have many rights of United States citizenship. However, they cannot vote or send representatives to the United States Congress.

Many of the other islands have become independent republics. Several, including Yap, Truk, and Pohnpei, formed the Federated States of Micronesia. The Republic of Nauru began in 1968. The Marshall Islands became a self-governing, "free associated state" of the United States in 1986.

See the TRB for Teacher Notes: Section 2 Extending the Lesson on public health problems.

CONTENT CHECK

1. **Identify:** Micronesia, Guam, Marshall Islands, Nauru, Carolines, Mariana Islands, Palau Islands.
2. **Define:** low islands, atolls, islets, copra.
3. What is Micronesia's largest island?
4. What general landscape do most of the Micronesian islands have?
5. What climate does Micronesia have?
6. What countries have controlled Micronesia in the past?
7. **Challenge:** Why is Micronesia's location important to the defense strategy of the United States?

Tahiti's location gives it a delightful climate and lush vegetation. How does landscape and climate vary throughout Polynesia?

See the TAE for an Objective 3 Activity.

3. POLYNESIA

Polynesia lies east of Melanesia and Micronesia in the central Pacific. It forms a large triangle from Midway Island to New Zealand to Easter Island. Midway, the northernmost point of Polynesia, is almost 4,000 miles (6,437.4 km) from New Zealand, the southernmost point. It is 6,000 miles (9,656.1 km) from Easter Island, the easternmost point.

An important World War II battle was fought at Midway. Some students may be interested in researching this battle or the United States' "leapfrog strategy."

3.1 Landscape and Climate

The landscape of Polynesia ranges from coral reefs to volcanic mountains. On the high islands of Hawaii, Samoa, and French Polynesia, some peaks rise almost 13,800 feet (4,206.2 m) above sea level. They have great amounts of rain and thick, green vegetation. On the other hand, the smallest of the low

Although it is made up of more than 150 coral and volcanic islands, the kingdom of Tonga is one of the world's smallest countries in total area.

Ask these questions: How are the Pacific Islands different from the Caribbean Islands? How are they similar?

islands in the Cook chain are quite dry with clumps of palms spread far apart.

Fertile soil found on the lowlands of the volcanic high islands is deep enough for large-scale farming. The low islands, on the other hand, only have scattered areas of fertile land. Most of this fertile land is used for subsistence farming.

Polynesia lies on both sides of the Equator. It is roughly between the Tropic of Cancer and the Tropic of Capricorn. As a result its climate is tropical rain forest. Much of Polynesia lies in a belt of heavy rainfall. Rain averages from 80 inches (203.2 cm) to 160 inches (406.4 cm) each year. Temperatures, as in many of the Pacific Islands, are generally between 80°F (26.7°C) and 90°F (32.2°C).

3.2 Economic and Cultural Patterns

High islands in Polynesia produce cash crops. Low islands are used chiefly for subsistence farming or fishing. Nearly all the islands depend on tourism. The exceptions are Tonga and French Polynesia. Tonga has a developing oil industry. French Polynesia has a nuclear test base.

The major cash crops in Polynesia are sugarcane, cocoa, coffee, citrus fruits, pineapples, and bananas. French Polynesia also exports mother-of-pearl and coconuts. Taro, bananas, and yams are grown for local markets. **Taro** (TAHR oh) is a plant whose underground stems are used as food. However,

Even today, for long voyages, catamarans and canoes equipped with outboard motors are used.

This illustration shows a catamaran, a double-rigged canoe set with sails, which provided ocean-going transportation to cover the vast distances between Polynesian islands. Catamarans were extremely stable and could travel at fast speeds in the heavy waves of the Pacific Ocean. How great are the distances in Polynesia?

STRANGE BUT TRUE

STATUES OF EASTER ISLAND

Archaeologists are not sure what purpose the statues served in the culture of their sculptors, but the statues show that these early Easter Islanders were master builders.

Easter Island lies at the easternmost edge of Polynesia. The tiny island of 63 square miles (163.2 sq km) stands isolated in the Pacific Islands, 1,200 miles (1,931.2 km) from its nearest Polynesian neighbor. Almost 2,300 miles (3,701.5 km) of ocean separate it from Chile, the country that has administered the island since 1888.

To its original settlers, the island was known as *te pito o te henua,* or "the navel of the world." To the 2,000 Polynesians and Chileans who live there today, it is called Rapanui (RAHP uh NOO ee). The name Easter Island came from the Dutch explorers who named the island for the Sunday on which they arrived there in 1722.

Easter Island is famous for its gigantic stone statues called *moai* (MOH eye). More than 600 of them dot the island. They were carved from the slopes of one of the island's three volcanoes. Archaeologists found several hundred unfinished moai and thousands of crude stone picks near the Rano Raraku volcano on the eastern part of the island. It looked as if the sculptors' work had been suddenly interrupted. Whatever interrupted them put an end to their work forever.

Most of the statues are around 10 feet (3 m) to 20 feet (6.1 m) tall. One of the largest ones still standing is 40 feet (12.2 m) tall. The average statue weighs almost 25 tons (22.7 metric tons), while some weigh close to 90 tons (81.7 metric tons).

It is believed the statues were all carved at Rano Raraku and then moved to some 300 stepped stone platforms. Called *ahu,* the platforms were believed to be altars. From 1 to 12 statues stood on a single *ahu.*

Experiments made by the present-day Easter Islanders show that it took 180 people to pull a medium-sized statue over the ground. Twelve islanders were able to lift a 25-ton (22.7-metric-ton) statue about 10 feet (3 m) off the ground and tilt it on end on top of an *ahu.* This work took about 18 days to do. No tools other than two wooden logs were used by the workers.

Why the statues faced inland, why the statues' sculptors left in a hurry, and why nearly 1,000 statues were carved are a few of the many mysteries of Easter Island's past. Chances are that they will remain unsolved but will intrigue archaeologists and tourists alike for many years to come.

1. In what part of Polynesia is Easter Island? How far is it from its ruling country?

2. How large are the unusual statues found on Easter Island?

3. What reasons do you think early Easter Islanders had for carving moai and placing hundreds of them all over the island?

Many tourists now stop at Tahiti while traveling from the United States to Australia or New Zealand.

Most of the islands of Polynesia were settled much later than those of Melanesia and Micronesia. Ask students why this is so.

Polynesia depends on imports for most food and all manufactured goods.

Tourism has been a mixed blessing for the Polynesians. They need the money that comes from tourism, but it also has destroyed many traditions. Tahiti, in the Society Islands of French Polynesia, is an example of an island changed by tourism. Hotels, large buildings, and modern conveniences have been placed on much of the land. Such development has brought many more people to the area. Tahiti now has one of the few large airports in Polynesia. It is clear that Tahiti will soon become as developed as Hawaii.

What has happened to Hawaii and what is happening to Tahiti are being watched by many Polynesians on other islands. They do not want their islands to change this way.

Most Polynesians, however, have been able to keep some traditions. Although they are far apart, their way of life on the different islands is similar. This is seen in their types of houses, language, and forms of art. Polynesian culture has picked up some European heritage. Europeans introduced Christianity, different languages, and ways of doing things. Clothing, for example, became European in parts of Polynesia during the 1800s.

Have students compare and contrast the people of Melanesia with those of Polynesia.

3.3 Influences of the Past

The ancestors of the Polynesians came to the area at least 2,000 years ago. They used small ocean-going boats and their skills in navigation to get there. Migration took place in stages, from Southeast Asia to Micronesia to Polynesia. The earliest people moved into the area to find new sources of food.

The island civilizations developed at different rates over the years. Some of the eastern islands show the Polynesians' building skills. Stone houses on the Society Islands and huge head figures on Easter Island show the engineering abilities of early islanders.

Europeans ruled many of the islands through the early 1900s. All but Pitcairn, Tonga, Tuvalu, and Western Samoa are now ruled by New Zealand. In 1962 Western Samoa became the first fully independent Polynesian state. Independence came to Tonga in 1970, to Tuvalu in 1978, and to Kiribati in 1979. Today France controls much of southeast Polynesia—French Polynesia—and Wallis and Futuna in the west. Hawaii is the fiftieth state of the United States. American Samoa is a territory of the United States.

After two centuries of European and American contact, there is a new Asian cultural influence affecting the islands. Many people from Japan, China, and the Philippines now live in Polynesia.

CONTENT CHECK

1. **Identify:** Polynesia, Tonga, French Polynesia, Tahiti, Tuvalu, Western Samoa, Kiribati.
2. **Define:** taro.
3. What is Polynesia's climate?
4. What are Polynesia's chief cash crops?
5. **Challenge:** Why is tourism a mixed blessing for Polynesia?

See the TRB for Teacher Notes: Section 3 Extending the Lesson on Thor Heyerdahl's travels.

CONCLUSION

Different groups of people in the Pacific Islands are separated from one another by great stretches of ocean. However, the population is growing in the Pacific Islands, and arable land is limited. The area does not have enough natural resources to have many economic products. The people will continue to import much of their food and keep tourism a large part of their future development.

SUMMARY

1. The Pacific Islands culture area is divided into Melanesia, Micronesia, and Polynesia. It is the largest fragmented area in the world.
2. In the Pacific there are generally two types of islands. High islands are large and have adequate fresh water, fertile soil, and thick rain forests. High islands are volcanic in origin. Low islands are small and have poor soil, limited vegetation, and little fresh water. Low islands are made of coral.
3. Papua New Guinea is the largest country in the region. The island of New Guinea is the second largest island in the world.
4. The Pacific Islands experience a tropical moist climate over most of their area. This is because the Equator cuts through the middle of the area.
5. Most of the people in the area live in small villages and subsist on farming and fishing.
6. Much of the industry in the region is limited to phosphate mining, lumbering, and food processing.
7. Many of the islands depend on tourism for their national income. Tourism is important to future economic development in the Pacific Islands.
8. Some Pacific Islands have become independent nations. Others, however, are still under the control of other countries. Some of these islands are working out ways to become self-governing.

Answers to the following questions can be found on page T300.

REVIEWING VOCABULARY

Imagine these words and place-names from Chapter 30 are correct answers to 12 items in a crossword puzzle. Write the 12 clues for the answers. Then make the puzzle with some answers written down and some across.

copra	Melanesia	high islands	typhoons
islets	Micronesia	low islands	taro
atoll	Polynesia	pidgin	tourism

REMEMBERING THE FACTS

1. What are the three major regions of the Pacific Islands?
2. Of the three major regions of the Pacific Islands, which one has the greatest total land area? The greatest total area?
3. What is the largest country in the Pacific Islands? In what region is it located?
4. Where do anthropologists think that the original people came from whose descendants today live in Melanesia?

5. What climate does Micronesia have?
6. How do most people in Micronesia make their living?
7. What major power occupied much of Micronesia during World War II?

8. In what ways are crops different on Polynesia's high islands and low islands?
9. In which of the three major regions of the Pacific Islands is tourism most important to its economy?

UNDERSTANDING THE FACTS

1. In what parts of Melanesia is the region's light industry located?
2. Why has pidgin become an important language in Melanesia?
3. In what ways are Melanesia and Micronesia different?

4. What Hispanic influences are still felt in parts of Micronesia today?
5. Why are many Polynesians watching what happens to Hawaii and Tahiti?
6. In what ways are the landscapes of high islands and low islands different?

THINKING CRITICALLY AND CREATIVELY

1. Many European powers at one time established colonies in the Pacific Islands. What were some of their reasons for being interested in this part of the world?
2. Papua New Guinea is not very far south of the Equator. Yet, in the central part of the island, it can be very cold at night. What causes this?
3. **Challenge:** In recent years the tourist industry has grown larger in Tahiti. What factors do you think are responsible in order for a tourist industry to grow in very remote parts of the world?
4. **Challenge:** In 1986 the people of the Palau Islands voted on a plan to become a

self-governing, "free associated state" of the United States. This status gives their own government control over local and foreign affairs, but the United States would defend their land from outside attack. Instead of the necessary 75 percent approval, only 66 percent of the Palau voters approved the plan. This means that of the four trust territories administered by the United States since 1947, only the Palau Islands remain a trust territory. What factors may have led to only 66 percent voter approval? What benefits do you think there would be in becoming a free associated state? Disadvantages?

REINFORCING GRAPHIC SKILLS

Study the map on page 624. Then answer the questions that follow.

1. Which is closer to Port Moresby, New Guinea—Nauru or New Caledonia?

2. About how far in miles is Guam from Fiji?

CHAPTER 31

Large colonies of penguins live in Antarctica. In addition, scientists have found bacteria, pollen grains, and fungi frozen in Antarctica's ice.

632

Antarctic researcher with emperor penguins, South Georgia Island

ANTARCTICA

In this chapter you will learn—

- What physical features, climate, and natural resources are found in Antarctica.
- How Antarctica was explored.
- What role Antarctica plays in scientific research.
- What issues face the world regarding Antarctica's future.

Point out to students that other maps show north arrows, while maps of Antarctica in this chapter do not. Ask them: Why not?

Refer to the feature on *Pangaea* on page 48. Many scientists believe that when Pangaea broke up, Antarctica drifted to its present location. The ice cap formed, and glaciers swept away most life from the continent.

INTRODUCTION

At the southern end of Earth is the large landmass of Antarctica (ant AHRK tih kuh). With a land area of 5.4 million square miles (14 million sq km), Antarctica is the world's fifth largest continent. Figure 31-1 on page 635 shows how its size compares with that of the United States. Antarctica is shaped like a circle, with the Antarctic Peninsula sticking out like a tail. The distance from the tip of the peninsula to the opposite coastline of the continent is about 3,250 miles (5,230.4 km).

Located around the South Pole, Antarctica is one of the coldest places on Earth. Most of its land lies buried under thousands of feet of snow and ice. Strong winds blow across its empty surface, and stormy seas break against its icy, rocky coasts.

Antarctica is far from the world's populated areas. Distant location and harsh environment have made it uninviting to most forms of life. The continent is often called Earth's "last great frontier." Large areas of wilderness remain unexplored. Since the early 1900s, however, explorers and scientists have opened up much of Antarctica. They have set up research stations to carry out scientific studies. In their work they have learned much about Antarctica's physical environment. In years to come, the continent's resources may greatly help the world's growing population.

1. LANDSCAPE AND CLIMATE

About 98 percent of Antarctica is covered by a huge ice cap nearly 1 mile (1.6 km) thick. Under this ice are mountains, valleys, and lowlands. The climate of Antarctica is cold year-round. Because of its harsh landscape and climate, Antarctica has been called the "cold, white desert."

The land area of Antarctica is larger than either Europe or Australia.

1.1 Landscape

The Antarctic ice cap is a slightly rounded dome that spreads over the whole continent. It has about 90 percent of Earth's permanent ice and 2 percent of its fresh water. The heavy weight of ice forces it to move outwards from the center. Huge glaciers are formed and move slowly down to the sea. Along the coasts large pieces of ice break off to form icebergs. The breaking of these huge ice chunks is called **calving.**

About one-tenth of the ice cap spreads beyond the land and into the oceans surrounding the continent. These icy stretches are known as **ice shelves.** They form huge cliffs that rise out of the sea.

Oceans. The ice cap greatly affects the oceans all around Antarctica. The continent

In November 1987 a section of ice larger than the state of Rhode Island broke off from an Antarctic glacier into the ocean. Scientists estimate that enough water is contained in the massive iceberg to meet the needs of Los Angeles, California, for the next 675 years.

touches the Pacific, Atlantic, and Indian oceans. Waters of these oceans cool and become less salty as they get closer to Antarctica. Plant and animal life also changes. Because of these differences, the waters around Antarctica are viewed by some scientists as a separate body of water known as the Antarctic Ocean. In winter the Antarctic Ocean freezes to form a solid ice pack that floats on the surface. This ice pack is all around Antarctica, extending for several hundred miles out to sea.

Land. Along Antarctica's coasts and in the interior are high rocky mountains, many of which rise above the icy surface. Running through the center of the continent is the Transantarctic Range. Many peaks in this range reach as high as 16,000 feet (4,476.8 m). The Transantarctic Range splits Antarctica into two areas. The eastern area, facing Australia, Africa, and the Indian Ocean, is mostly an empty icy plateau. The western

Antarctica's average land elevation is about 5,900 feet (1798.3 m)—higher than any other continent's.

An ice cliff near the Antarctic coast shows patches of dark color where the ice has been tightly pressed together. How is the Antarctic ice cap formed?

area, facing the Pacific Ocean and South America, is a group of low-lying islands under thousands of feet of ice.

See the *TRB* for *Section 1 Extending the Lesson* on Antarctica's warm-water lakes.

1.2 Climate

Antarctica has an ice cap climate, the coldest in the world. Along the continent's coasts, winter temperatures in July drop below −40°F (−40°C). Summer temperatures in December may rise to 32°F (0°C), or even slightly higher. In the interior of the continent, winter temperatures fall to an average of −100°F (−73.3°C). Summer temperatures rise to about 0°F (−17.8°C).

Summers in Antarctica are short, lasting from November through January. During these months the sun is bright and never sets. Winter lasts from about May through October. During the winter season, the sun never rises, and darkness covers Antarctica. High winds of 60 miles (96.6 km) per hour sweep across the continent's icy wastelands.

Although covered with ice, Antarctica gets little snow. Its dry air makes for less than 3 inches (7.6 cm) of precipitation a year. The little snow that does fall never melts but pushes down upon the old snow to build up further the thick ice cap.

See the *TAE* for an *Objective 1* Activity.

CONTENT CHECK

1. **Identify:** Antarctic Peninsula, Antarctic Ocean, Transantarctic Range.
2. **Define:** calving, ice shelves.
3. Why is Antarctica called "the cold, white desert"?
4. How does the ice cap affect the oceans surrounding Antarctica?
5. **Challenge:** How might landscape and climate affect exploration and settlement of Antarctica?

Experts believe that the Antarctic Peninsula, which stretches northward to within about 600 miles (965.6 km) of South America, is an ice-covered continuation of the Andes Mountains. If this is so, then this part of Antarctica probably contains many of the same resources, such as copper and lead, that are being mined in the Andes.

RELATIVE SIZE OF ANTARCTICA

Land-area maps of Antarctica and the continental United States are shown together here in order to compare their sizes with each other. Antarctica is about one-half times larger than the United States. How would you show Antarctica's size with that of the United States on a compara-graph?

See the *TRB* for *Section 2 Extending the Lesson* on the blue whale.

During the Antarctic winter, from approximately June to September, the ice pack grows larger. During the summer, from about November to January, high winds and warmer temperatures reduce the size of the ice pack.

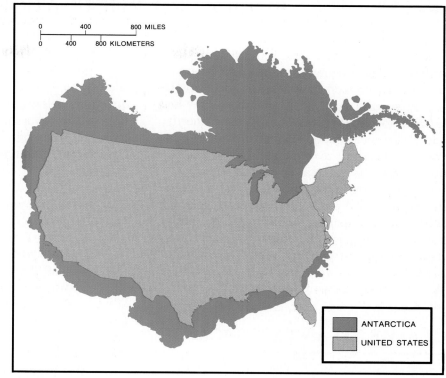

FIGURE 31-1

In the 1980s 18 nations interested in scientific research and exploration in Antarctica were negotiating rules for the management of economic activities in Antarctica by member nations of the Antarctic Treaty.

2. NATURAL RESOURCES

Compared with other continents, Antarctica has few known natural resources. However, experts have recently claimed that valuable minerals may be locked beneath the ice cap waiting to be discovered.

Minerals. The world's largest coal deposits are thought to lie in the Transantarctic Range. Geologists have recently discovered small deposits of low-grade iron, copper, manganese, and uranium on Antarctica. Higher grades are believed to be located under the ice cap. Oil and natural gas may be in Antarctica but so far have not been found.

Until better technology is developed, the harsh climate and thick ice will discourage efforts to mine or drill for these minerals.

Plant and Animal Life. The Antarctic environment also limits plant and animal life. Although few are found in the interior, many life forms thrive along the coasts. The few plants found in Antarctica are mostly mosses and lichens that grow on rocky surfaces. In the seas around Antarctica are millions of whales, seals, and fish. On land tiny insects and microscopic creatures are found in mosses and lichens. The best known land animals are penguins. Penguins cannot fly or use their wings to swim in the sea for fish. Many kinds of flying birds are also found in Antarctica.

USING GRAPHIC SKILLS

EVALUATING INFORMATION

When Amy says that a fundraising idea will not bring in enough money, members of the student council have learned to listen. In her three years as a council member, Amy has learned to assess ideas, judge their merits, and make decisions on them. In other words, she has learned to evaluate information—determining its value after careful study.

Evaluating information is a skill that cannot be mastered until you have learned other skills first. Comparing, analyzing, hypothesizing, concluding, and generalizing are often necessary before you are ready to evaluate. When evaluating, you "put together" all these skills to come up with your own opinion and ideas.

The map below shows the claims various countries have placed on Antarctica. It also shows some of their research stations. The questions below ask you to evaluate information you have learned from reading the chapter and studying the map concerning the claims on Antarctica and the Antarctica Treaty.

Study the map below. Then answer the questions that follow.

1. Do you agree that countries can stake claim to unexplored frontier areas?

2. Do you believe a treaty is the best way to protect Antarctica's environment?

CLAIMS TO ANTARCTICA

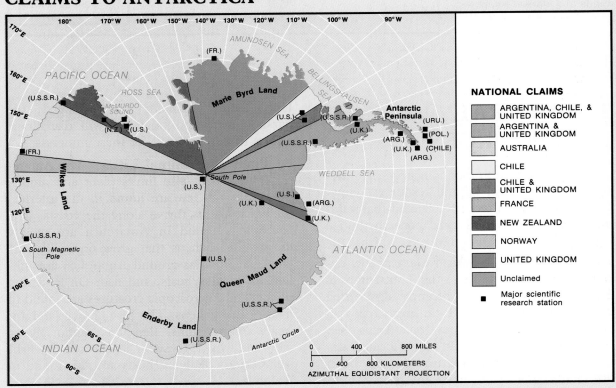

The waters around Antarctica support an amazing food chain that connects the animal life of the continent. A tiny shrimp-like shellfish known as **krill** feeds on microscopic sea life. Krill, in turn, become food for whales, seals, and penguins.

See the *TAE* for an *Objective 2* Activity.

CONTENT CHECK

1. **Define:** krill.
2. What kinds of minerals, plants, and animals are found in Antarctica?
3. **Challenge:** How would the mining and drilling of minerals affect Antarctica's plant and animal life?

Robert F. Scott and another British explorer, Ernest H. Shackleton, led parties to Antarctica before the 1911 race between Scott and Amundsen.

3. EXPLORERS AND SCIENTISTS

Antarctica is the last continent to be explored. It was first seen by British explorer Captain James Cook in 1772. About 50 years later, American and British seal hunters became the first people to set foot on Antarctica. It was not until the early 1900s, however, that teams of explorers from many different countries arrived on the continent.

In 1911 a race began between Norwegian explorer Roald Amundsen (AHM uhn suhn) and British explorer Robert F. Scott to reach the South Pole. In October Amundsen and his team left the Pacific coast of Antarctica on skis and sleds for the trip into the interior. One week later Scott and his team set out. Amundsen became the first person to reach the South Pole, where he left a flag, tent, and note for Scott. About a month later, Scott's team finally reached the Pole.

Discovery of the South Pole opened the rest of Antarctica to other explorers for exploration. In 1928 Naval Commander Richard E. Byrd set up Little America, the first permanent base in Antarctica. He and three companions later became the first persons to fly over the South Pole.

By the 1950s exploration of Antarctica had become an international effort. During the International Geophysical Year from 1957 to 1958, 12 nations worked together to learn more about Antarctica's environment. More than 10,000 scientists set up about 40 research stations, where they studied weather, Earth's magnetism, cosmic rays, and oceans. After the year ended, scientists from many lands continued to come to Antarctica to do research.

As Antarctica was explored and researched, seven countries laid claim to parts of the continent. The map on page 636 shows the claims held by Argentina, Chile, the United Kingdom, France, New Zealand, Australia, and Norway. Soon fears arose that disputes over claims would get in the way of scientific research. To keep Antarctica peaceful, 12 nations active on the continent signed the Antarctic Treaty in 1959. Later six other nations decided to sign the treaty. Under the agreement, treaty nations promised not to push any territorial claims or to use Antarctica for military purposes. They also stated that Antarctica was open to scientists from all nations.

Territorial claims to Antarctica's land are not widely recognized or seen as legal.

CONTENT CHECK

1. **Identify:** Roald Amundsen, Robert F. Scott, Richard E. Byrd, International Geophysical Year, Antarctic Treaty.
2. What are the terms of the Antarctic Treaty?
3. **Challenge:** What do you think would have happened to Antarctica if the Antarctic Treaty had not been signed?

STRANGE BUT TRUE

ANTARCTICA AND OUTER SPACE

Can research in Antarctica help scientists understand the solar system, particularly conditions on planets other than Earth? Some scientists think the answer to this question is "yes." For years people have wanted to know if life exists or has existed on the planet Mars. Recent space missions to Mars show that the planet at present cannot support life. However, the question remains: Did life exist on Mars some time in the past? Teams of scientists currently working in Antarctica are trying to find an answer to this question.

Mars today does not have water. Nor does that planet have an atmosphere. Both water and air, however, are necessary for sustaining life. Scientists believe that at one time Mars was covered by huge bodies of water. These bodies of water may have been favorable to such life forms as simple **microorganisms,** or animals so small that they can be seen by a person only through a microscope.

Scientists working in Antarctica have been doing research in freshwater areas of the continent. These bodies of water are covered by 10 feet (3 m) to 15 feet (4.6 m) of ice. Below the ice is very cold water. Microorganisms living at the water bottom may be much like those microorganisms that are believed to have developed long ago on Mars.

Scientists have found some places in Antarctica where microorganisms have come to the surface and died. They are looking at these dead microorganisms to see if any special chemical signatures were left behind in the microorganisms. **Chemical signatures** are traces of chemicals in an object that can be used to name that specific object from which they may have come.

If scientists find these chemical signatures, they may be able, through study and testing, to determine whether there was life on Mars. In time space missions to Mars will gather dust particles from the surface of that planet. Then the particles will be analyzed by scientists for chemical signatures. If such traces are found, this will give scientists important clues that life might have existed on Mars some time in the past.

1. For what question are teams of scientists working on to find an answer in Antarctica?

2. Where in Antarctica are scientists doing research in an effort to answer the question?

3. What kind of life forms are scientists studying in Antarctica?

4. What clues are being studied?

5. Why are scientists doing research in Antarctica to find out about life in outer space?

4. ANTARCTICA TODAY AND TOMORROW

Today Antarctica is protected by the Antarctic Treaty. The only people on the continent are about 2,000 scientists from 18 nations. They carry out research in 57 stations all over Antarctica. These stations are made up of runways and underground living areas, laboratories, and workshops connected by tunnels. Nuclear energy is often the source of electricity and heat. Airplanes and radio provide contact with the rest of the world.

In the future, Antarctica may have permanent settlers who are not scientists. However, cold and ice will keep most people away. Because of the harsh climate, road and rail systems cannot be built. Most traveling is done by tracked vehicles. Yet the continent's scenic beauty is beginning to draw a small number of visitors. In 1986 about 1,000 tourists on cruise ships visited the Antarctic coast.

In the future, as the world's natural resources decrease, nations will want to develop Antarctica's resources. They also will want to support projects in Antarctica to help their peoples. For example, the world's dry areas may someday be able to get needed water from Antarctica's huge icebergs. The shrimp-like krill, rich in protein, may become an important food for the world's growing population. Antarctica will also be used as a scientific laboratory to predict changes in Earth's climate. For example, in 1987 an "ozone hole" was discovered in the atmosphere above Antarctica. Scientists are studying the hole to find out what caused it and what effect it might have on Earth's climate and its people.

Many experts are against some of these efforts to develop Antarctica further. They fear opening the continent to economic development and scientific testing will harm a frag-

This bank, whose sign is in Spanish, English, Russian, and Chinese, shows promise for permanent settlements in Antarctica. How many nations have scientists there?

See the *TRB* for *Section 4 Extending the Lesson* on harvesting ice for fresh water supplies.

ile environment. Digging and mining of minerals, they warn, will lead to oil spills and other forms of pollution. These hazards will threaten Antarctica's plant and animal life. Many experts also fear that the harvesting of krill will upset the food chain on which animals of the continent depend.

Another concern is that nations, in their hunt for resources, may press claims to Antarctica. In 1991 the Antarctic Treaty comes up for review. At that time treaty nations will decide what to do. Many experts believe the treaty will be kept and updated.

See the *TRB* for the *Chapter 31 Reading*.

CONTENT CHECK

1. **Define:** microorganisms, chemical signatures
2. How will Antarctica become important in the years ahead?
3. **Challenge:** If you were a leader of an Antarctic Treaty nation, what changes would you make in the treaty when it comes up for review in 1991? Explain.

CONCLUSION

Antarctica is viewed as Earth's "last great frontier." Found at the southern end of Earth, it is a cold, distant continent of ice and snow. Though limited in known resources, Antarctica may have many valuable minerals.

Since the early 1900s, Antarctica has been gradually opened up by explorers and scientists. A number of nations have taken an interest in the continent. The Antarctic Treaty keeps it free of national disputes and open to scientific research. However, global need for resources will eventually lead to economic development. In the next decades, the world's nations will have to work together to develop resources without harming Antarctica's fragile environment.

CHAPTER REVIEW

CHAPTER 31　　　　　　　　　　　ANTARCTICA

SUMMARY

1. Antarctica is the world's fifth largest continent. Except for scientists, it has no permanent human population.
2. Antarctica is located at the southern end of Earth and surrounds the South Pole. It has an icy, rocky landscape and an ice cap climate.
3. Very little plant life is found in Antarctica. Most animals live in the sea or along the coast.
4. Antarctica has few known natural resources. In recent years experts have claimed that valuable minerals may lie under its ice cap.
5. Exploration of Antarctica began in the early 1900s. Since then scientists from 18 nations have set up research stations throughout the continent.
6. The 1959 Antarctic Treaty keeps Antarctica open for peaceful, scientific research. When the treaty comes up for review in 1991, treaty nations will have to decide the ownership of Antarctica and how to control the use of its natural resources.

Answers to the following questions can be found on page T308.

REVIEWING VOCABULARY

On a separate sheet of paper, number from 1 to 5. Beside each number write the vocabulary word that matches each numbered definition below.

calving　　　　ice shelves　　　　krill　　　　microorganisms　　　　chemical signatures

1. shrimp-like creatures
2. traces found in the remains of animals
3. icy stretches of ice cap that spread into the ocean
4. breaking of glacial ice that forms icebergs
5. small animals seen only through a microscope

REMEMBERING THE FACTS

1. What living and natural resources are found in Antarctica?
2. Which American explorer helped open up Antarctica to exploration?
3. What did the International Geophysical Year accomplish?
4. What agreement will come up for review in 1991?

UNDERSTANDING THE FACTS

1. How are Antarctica's coastal temperatures different from those of its interior?
2. Why do trees and shrubs not grow in Antarctica?
3. Why is the food chain important to the animal life of Antarctica?
4. How did the International Geophysical Year change the landscape of Antarctica?
5. Why have Antarctica's mineral resources not been discovered or uncovered?
6. What fears do scientists have about the economic development of Antarctica?

THINKING CRITICALLY AND CREATIVELY

1. Scientists have found fossils of thick, green plant life in the interior of Antarctica. What might this scientific discovery reveal about Antarctica's past landscape and climate?
2. Recently Argentina has tried to strengthen its Antarctic claims by encouraging settlement. At the Argentine base of Esperanza, family groups have arrived, and a bank, post office, and school have been set up. In June 1978, the first baby was born on Antarctica—an Argentine girl. She was immediately declared a citizen of Argentina. Does Argentina's settlement policy go against the principles of the Antarctic Treaty? Why or why not?
3. **Challenge:** Many developing nations who have not signed the Antarctic Treaty believe that the 18 treaty nations have a control over Antarctica that they do not have. They are asking for the United Nations to govern Antarctica as an international territory. Do you agree or disagree with this position? Explain.
4. **Challenge:** Japan, the Soviet Union, and others are harvesting krill along the Antarctic coast. Do you think they should be permitted to continue? Why?

REINFORCING GRAPHIC SKILLS

Study the map on page 636. Then answer the questions that follow.

1. Do you think the way Antarctica has been divided among those nations with claims is reasonable?
2. What is your opinion about the kinds of research scientists should be permitted to conduct in Antarctica?

SUMMARY

1. Oceania consists of two culture areas. One is Australia and New Zealand. The other is the Pacific Islands. Antarctica is the only uninhabited continent.

2. Oceania's total area is the largest of all world areas. However, the land that it occupies is among the smallest.

3. Most of the land area of Oceania lies in Australia, New Zealand, and Papua New Guinea. Australia is the only continent in Oceania.

4. The cultures of Australia and New Zealand are related to Europe, especially Great Britain. Both countries share the English language, same kind of government and religions, and high levels of economic development.

5. The Pacific Islands are grouped together as a culture area chiefly because they are all located in the Pacific Ocean. They are divided into three regions: Melanesia, Micronesia, and Polynesia.

6. The cultures of the Pacific Islands often vary from island to island. The origin of most of the people in the region can be traced to Southeast Asia.

7. Most of the people of the Pacific Islands face a major problem of making a living from the limited resources on the islands and from the surrounding water.

8. Antarctica is the last continent to be explored. Its known natural resources are few. Scientists conduct research to learn more about its environment.

Answers to the following questions can be found on page T311.

THINKING ABOUT THE UNIT

1. Compare the landscape and climate of New Zealand to Papua New Guinea.

2. What has been the major hindrance to successful economic development in the Pacific Islands?

3. Why can it be said that Australia and New Zealand are remote but not isolated from the rest of the world?

4. Why is Antarctica not considered a culture area?

SUGGESTED UNIT ACTIVITIES

1. Study the photographs that appear in this unit. Take note of your impressions of the terrain, people, history, cultural features, and economic activities of these parts of the world. Based on this information, make 8-10 general statements about geographic characteristics of Oceania and Antarctica.

2. Suppose you were to interview a visitor from one of the Pacific Islands. Prepare a list of questions you might ask. Include questions about landscape, climate, culture, economy, and history.

3. Plan a trip through Oceania. List the places you would stop, explaining your reason for each visit.

DEVELOPING GEOGRAPHY SKILLS

IDENTIFYING TRENDS AND MAKING FORECASTS

As a student, you probably have come across many *trends*, general changes or shifts in patterns. Some trends are *fads*, ideas that take hold for a while and then lose popularity. Others take hold and become an accepted part of life. Home computers, for example, started out as the hobby of some people interested in electronics. Today computers are a permanent part of American culture.

Trends that remain and become accepted often are used in making *forecasts*, or suggestions about future developments. The fact that computers are now in so many homes, for example, has led some people to forecast home use of more electronic items.

Some forecasts are no more than good guesses. Others are backed up by solid evidence. But even those that seem to have strong support can be wrong at times. An example is weather forecasts. New developments that no one expected can always come up and affect a forecast.

The steps used in the example that follow will help you identify trends and make forecasts based on those trends.

1. Read the following passage carefully:

   In developing countries new industries have not been as profitable as had been expected. There are several reasons for this. For one, developing countries often do not have large numbers of skilled workers. For another, many raw materials often have to be imported. In addition, so many people have moved from the countryside to the cities to work in industry that food often has to be imported at high cost from other countries.

2. Identify the trends, and describe them in your own words:
   (The trends are:
   a. *too few skilled workers;*
   b. *not enough raw materials;*
   c. *agricultural workers leaving their farms to work in cities;*
   d. *less food being produced.*)

3. Ask yourself what might happen in the future if the trends continue:
   (*Developing countries might decide not to continue to industrialize or continue to industrialize, making themselves less well off than before.*)

4. Ask yourself what developments could change the trends you have identified:
   (*Training programs could be set into motion that would provide more skilled workers. More resources or ways to develop existing resources could be discovered. New equipment or methods of farming could make more people want to stay in the countryside rather than go to the cities and could also increase food production.*)

5. Based on the answers to the questions you asked yourself in steps 3 and 4, make your forecast:
   (Forecast: *If current trends continue and developing countries try to industrialize further, they may find themselves poorer than they were before they began to industrialize.*)

For practice in identifying trends and making forecasts, read Section 4 of Chapter 31 on page 639. Then, using the five steps, identify trends and make a forecast about the future of Antarctica.

APPENDIX

ATLAS

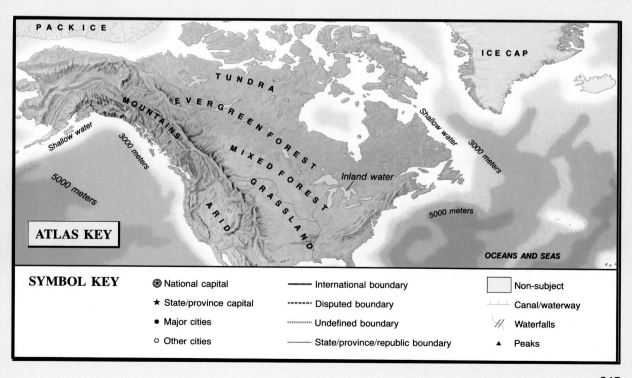

ATLAS KEY

SYMBOL KEY

⊕	National capital	——— International boundary		☐ Non-subject	
★	State/province capital	------ Disputed boundary		⊥⊥⊥ Canal/waterway	
●	Major cities	·········· Undefined boundary		⫽ Waterfalls	
○	Other cities	——— State/province/republic boundary		▲ Peaks	

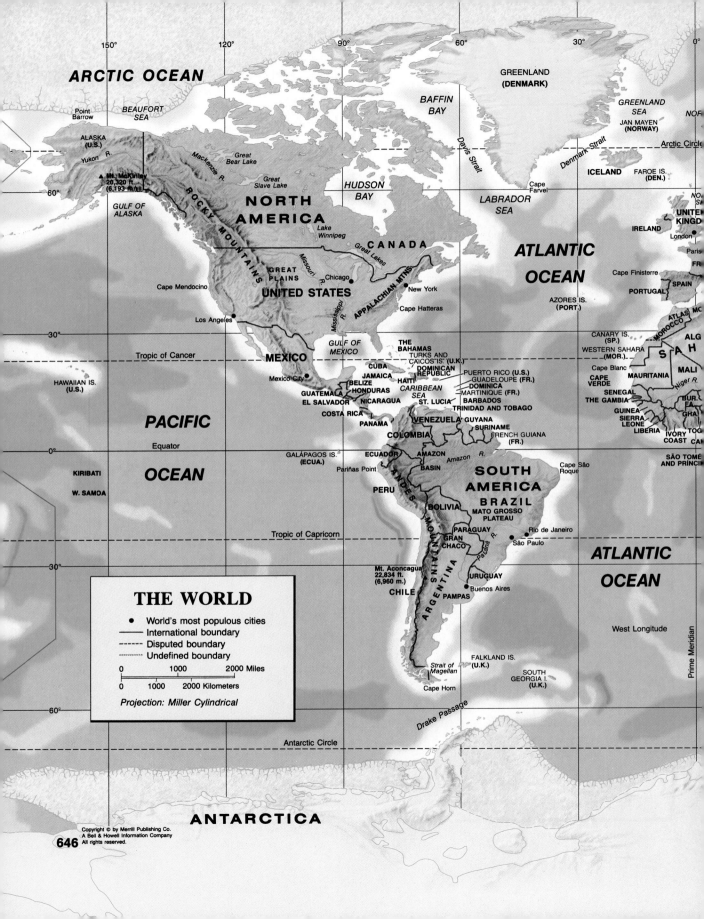

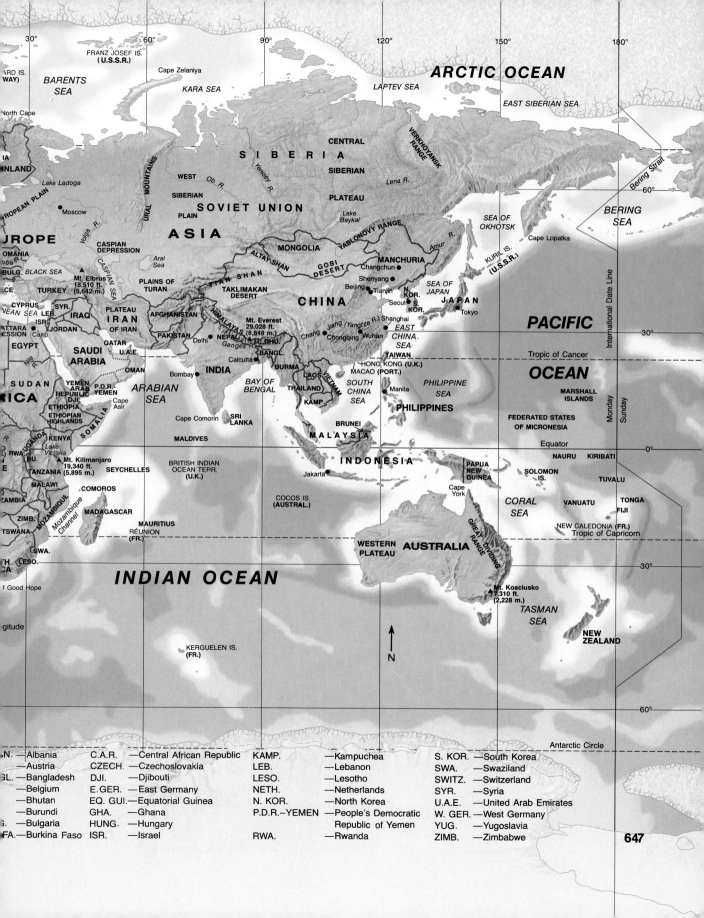

ARCTIC OCEAN

BARENTS SEA
KARA SEA
LAPTEV SEA
EAST SIBERIAN SEA

FRANZ JOSEF IS. (U.S.S.R.)
Cape Zelaniya
North Cape
Bering Strait
60°

SIBERIA
CENTRAL SIBERIAN PLATEAU
VERKHOYANSK RANGE

WEST SIBERIAN PLAIN
Ob R.
Yenisey R.
Lena R.
Amur R.

URAL MOUNTAINS
Lake Ladoga
Moscow
Volga R.

SOVIET UNION
ASIA
PLAIN
Lake Baykal
BERING SEA

CASPIAN DEPRESSION
Aral Sea
MONGOLIA
YABLONOVY RANGE
SEA OF OKHOTSK
Cape Lopatka

EUROPE
ROMANIA
BULG.
BLACK SEA
CYPRUS
TURKEY
MEDITERRANEAN SEA
LEB.
ISR.

Mt. Elbrus 18,510 ft. (5,642 m.)
CASPIAN SEA
PLAINS OF TURAN
ALTAY-SHAN
TIAN SHAN
TAKLIMAKAN DESERT
GOBI DESERT
MANCHURIA
Changchun
Shenyang
Beijing
Tianjin
N. KOR.
Seoul
S. KOR.
KURIL IS. (U.S.S.R.)

SYR.
IRAQ
IRAN
PLATEAU OF IRAN
AFGHANISTAN
HIMALAYAS
CHINA
JAPAN
Tokyo

JORDAN
EGYPT
Cairo
SAUDI ARABIA
QATAR
U.A.E.
OMAN
PAKISTAN
Delhi
NEPAL
BHU.
Ganges R.
Mt. Everest 29,028 ft. (8,848 m.)
Chang Jiang (Yangtze R.)
Chongqing
Wuhan
Shanghai
EAST CHINA SEA
TAIWAN
PACIFIC

ATTARA DEPRESSION
Nile R.
SUDAN
AFRICA
YEMEN ARAB REPUBLIC
DJI.
P.D.R.-YEMEN
Cape Asir
Bombay
INDIA
BANGL.
BURMA
LAOS
VIETNAM
HONG KONG (U.K.)
MACAO (PORT.)
Tropic of Cancer
OCEAN

ARABIAN SEA
BAY OF BENGAL
THAILAND
KAMP.
SOUTH CHINA SEA
Manila
PHILIPPINE SEA
MARSHALL ISLANDS

ETHIOPIA
ETHIOPIAN HIGHLANDS
SOMALIA
Cape Comorin
SRI LANKA
BRUNEI
PHILIPPINES
FEDERATED STATES OF MICRONESIA

UGANDA
KENYA
MALDIVES
MALAYSIA
Equator
NAURU
KIRIBATI
Monday
Sunday

Lake Victoria
Mt. Kilimanjaro 19,340 ft. (5,895 m.)
BU.
RWA.
TANZANIA
SEYCHELLES
BRITISH INDIAN OCEAN TERR. (U.K.)
Jakarta
INDONESIA
PAPUA NEW GUINEA
SOLOMON IS.
TUVALU

MALAWI
COMOROS
MOZAMBIQUE
MADAGASCAR
ZAMBIA
Mozambique Channel
COCOS IS. (AUSTRAL.)
Cape York
CORAL SEA
VANUATU
TONGA
FIJI

ZIMB.
MAURITIUS
RÉUNION (FR.)
NEW CALEDONIA (FR.)
Tropic of Capricorn

BOTSWANA
SWA.
LESO.
AFRICA
f Good Hope
INDIAN OCEAN
KERGUELEN IS. (FR.)
WESTERN PLATEAU
AUSTRALIA
GREAT DIVIDING RANGE
Mt. Kosciusko 7,310 ft. (2,228 m.)
TASMAN SEA
NEW ZEALAND

N

Antarctic Circle

International Date Line

60°
30°
0°
30°
60°

30°
60°
90°
120°
150°
180°

AN.—Albania	C.A.R.—Central African Republic	KAMP.—Kampuchea	S. KOR.—South Korea
—Austria	CZECH.—Czechoslovakia	LEB.—Lebanon	SWA.—Swaziland
GL.—Bangladesh	DJI.—Djibouti	LESO.—Lesotho	SWITZ.—Switzerland
—Belgium	E. GER.—East Germany	NETH.—Netherlands	SYR.—Syria
—Bhutan	EQ. GUI.—Equatorial Guinea	N. KOR.—North Korea	U.A.E.—United Arab Emirates
—Burundi	GHA.—Ghana	P.D.R.–YEMEN—People's Democratic Republic of Yemen	W. GER.—West Germany
—Bulgaria	HUNG.—Hungary		YUG.—Yugoslavia
FA.—Burkina Faso	ISR.—Israel	RWA.—Rwanda	ZIMB.—Zimbabwe

647

649

NORTH AMERICA

- ⊛ National capital
- ● Major city
- ○ Other city
- —— International boundary

| 0 | 250 | 500 | 750 Miles |
| 0 | 250 | 500 | 750 Kilometers |

Projection: Azimuthal Equal Area

650

SOUTH AMERICA

⊛ National capital
• Major city
○ Other city
— International boundary

| 0 | 250 | 500 Miles |
| 0 | 250 | 500 Kilometers |

Projection: Azimuthal Equal Area

651

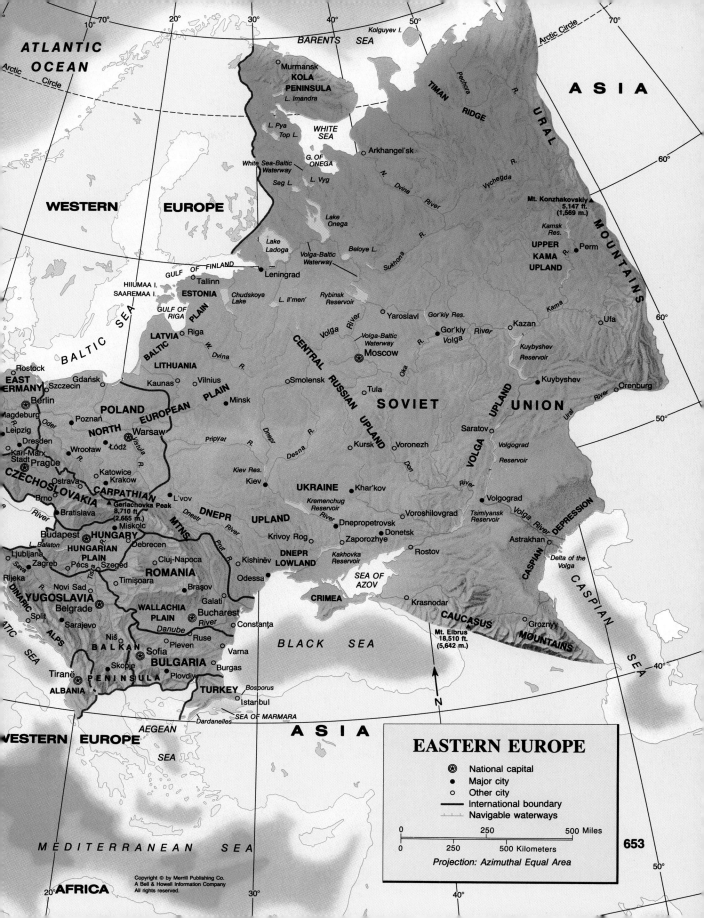

EASTERN EUROPE

⊕ National capital
● Major city
○ Other city
━━━ International boundary
⟂⟂⟂ Navigable waterways

0   250   500 Miles

0   250   500 Kilometers

Projection: Azimuthal Equal Area

653

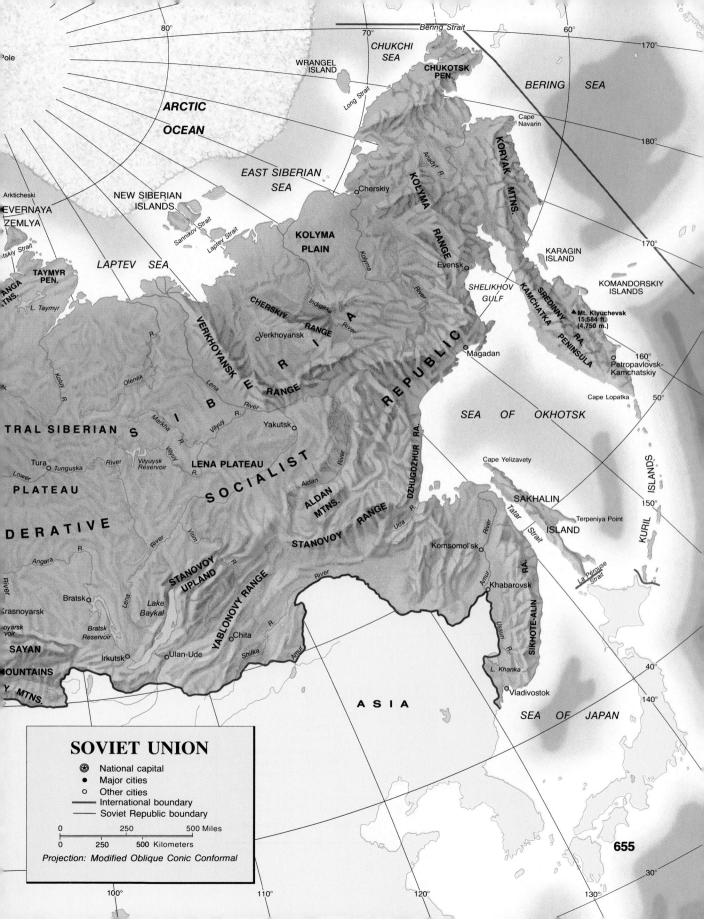

80° 70° Bering Strait 60° 170°

Pole

ARCTIC

OCEAN

CHUKCHI
SEA

BERING SEA

WRANGEL
ISLAND

Long Strait

CHUKOTSK
PEN.

Cape
Navarin

180°

Arkticheski

EAST SIBERIAN
SEA

NEW SIBERIAN
ISLANDS

Cherskiy

EVERNAYA
ZEMLYA

Sannikov Strait

KOLYMA
PLAIN

KOLYMA

RANGE

KORYAK

MTNS.

170°

tskiy Strait

Laptev Strait

Anadyr R.

KARAGIN
ISLAND

KOMANDORSKIY
ISLANDS

ANGA
NS.

**TAYMYR
PEN.**

LAPTEV SEA

L. Taymyr

CHERSKIY

RANGE

Indigirka

Kolyma

Evensk

SHELIKHOV
GULF

SREDINNY

KAMCHATKA

▲ Mt. Klyuchevsk
15,584 ft.
(4,750 m.)

Verkhoyansk

River

VERKHOYANSK

RANGE

S

I

B

E

R

I

A

River

Magadan

RA.

PENINSULA

160°

Petropavlovsk-
Kamchatskiy

TRAL SIBERIAN

S

Olenek

Lena

Markha

River

Vilyuy

Yakutsk

REPUBLIC

SEA OF OKHOTSK

Cape Lopatka

50°

Tura

Tunguska

River

Vilyuysk
Reservoir

LENA PLATEAU

R.

SOCIALIST

Aldan

River

DZHUGDZHUR RA.

Cape Yelizavety

SAKHALIN

Terpeniya Point

KURIL ISLANDS

150°

PLATEAU

Lower

Angara

R.

DERATIVE

Vilim

River

**ALDAN
MTNS.**

**STANOVOY
RANGE**

Uda R.

Tatar

River

ISLAND

R.

R.

**STANOVOY
UPLAND**

Lena

R.

Komsomol'sk

Strait

La Pérouse
Strait

140°

Krasnoyarsk

Bratsk

R.

Bratsk
Reservoir

Lake
Baykal

YABLONOVY RANGE

River

Amur

Khabarovsk

RA.

oyarsk
voir

SAYAN

Irkutsk

Ulan-Ude

Chita

Shilka

R.

Amur

Ussuri

R.

SIKHOTE-ALIN

MOUNTAINS

Y
MTNS.

A S I A

L. Khanka

Vladivostok

40°

SEA OF JAPAN

100° 110° 120° 130° 30°

SOVIET UNION

⊛ National capital
● Major cities
○ Other cities
━━ International boundary
── Soviet Republic boundary

0   250   500 Miles

0   250   500 Kilometers

Projection: Modified Oblique Conic Conformal

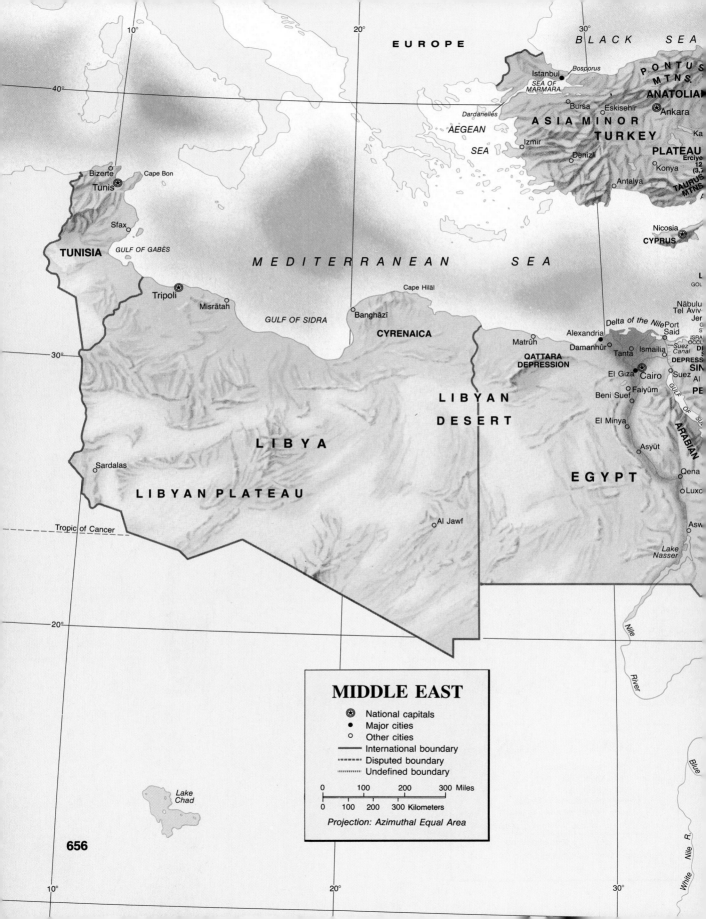

MIDDLE EAST

⊛ National capitals
● Major cities
○ Other cities
―――― International boundary
▪▪▪▪▪▪ Disputed boundary
⋯⋯⋯⋯ Undefined boundary

0   100   200   300 Miles
0 100 200 300 Kilometers
Projection: Azimuthal Equal Area

656

SOUTH ASIA

- ⊛ National capital
- • Major cities
- ○ Other cities
- —— International boundary
- ----- Disputed boundary

0   250   500 Miles

0   250   500 Kilometers

Projection: Mercator

SOVIET UNION

Mazar-i-Sharif

HINDU KUSH   KARAKORAM RANGE

Godwin Austen Pk. (K-2)
28,251 ft.
(8,611 m.)

Herāt

○Kabul

AFGHANISTAN

Peshawar
Srinagar
Rawalpindi Islāmābād

Kandahar

Jhelum R.
Sialkot
Sargodha Gujranwala
Faisalabad Amritsar
R. Lahore

**CHINA
(TIBET)**

Quetta

Multan   Ravi
River
Sutlej

PAKISTAN

BALUCHISTAN

Sukkur

**CENTRAL
MAKRAN
RANGE**

SULAIMAN RANGE

Indus
River

**THAR

DESERT**

Delhi
New Delhi

Jaipur

Yamuna
Agra   River

Mt. Dhaulagiri
26,971 ft.
(8,221 m.)

NEPAL

Mt. Everest
29,028 ft.
(8,848 m.)

Mt. Kangchenjunga
28,208 ft.
(8,598 m.)

Thimphu

BHUTAN

Kathmandu

GANGES
Lucknow
Kanpur   Ganges
River
Vārānasi

Ghaghara River
River

Patna

Brahmaputra Gauhati

**PATKAI
RANGE**

River

Imphal

**SONMIANI
BAY**

Hyderabad
Karachi

**RANN OF
KUTCH**

Gandhi
Reservoir

INDIA

PLAIN

Govind Ballaldh
Pant Res.

BANGLADESH

Sylhet

Dhaka

Tropic of Cancer

GULF OF KUTCH

**KATHIAWAR
PENINSULA**

Ahmadābād

○Vadodara

VINDHYA RANGE

Indore Narmada

SATPURA RANGE

Surat Tapti   River

River

Howrah
Calcutta

Khulna
Barisal

Karnaphuli
Reservoir

Chittagong

BURMA

Mahanadi

**GULF
OF
CAMBAY**

Nāgpur

Delta of The Ganges
(Sundarbans)

Palmyras
Point

Bombay
Poona

DECCAN

Godavari
River

Sholapur

PLATEAU

Hyderābād

**ARABIAN

SEA**

Bhima
River

Krishna River

Vijayawada

Vishakhapatnam

**BAY OF

BENGAL**

HINDUSTAN

**WESTERN

GHATS**

Bangalore

Madras

**EASTERN
GHATS**

Coromandel Coast

NORTH ANDAMAN

MIDDLE ANDAMAN

**ANDAMAN IS.
(INDIA)**

SOUTH ANDAMAN

**LACCADIVE IS.
(INDIA)**

Coimbatore

Calicut

Madurai
Cochin Malabar

Coast

Point Calimere
Point Pedro
Jaffna

**ANDAMAN

SEA**

**LACCADIVE

SEA**

Palk
Strait

**GULF
OF
MANNAR**

Trincomalee

**SRI
LANKA**

**NICOBAR IS.
(INDIA)**

**GREAT
NICOBAR I.**

Cape
Comorin

Colombo

Dehiwala—Mt. Lavinia
Moratuwa

Cape Dondra

⊛Male

MALDIVES

Equator

INDIAN OCEAN

659

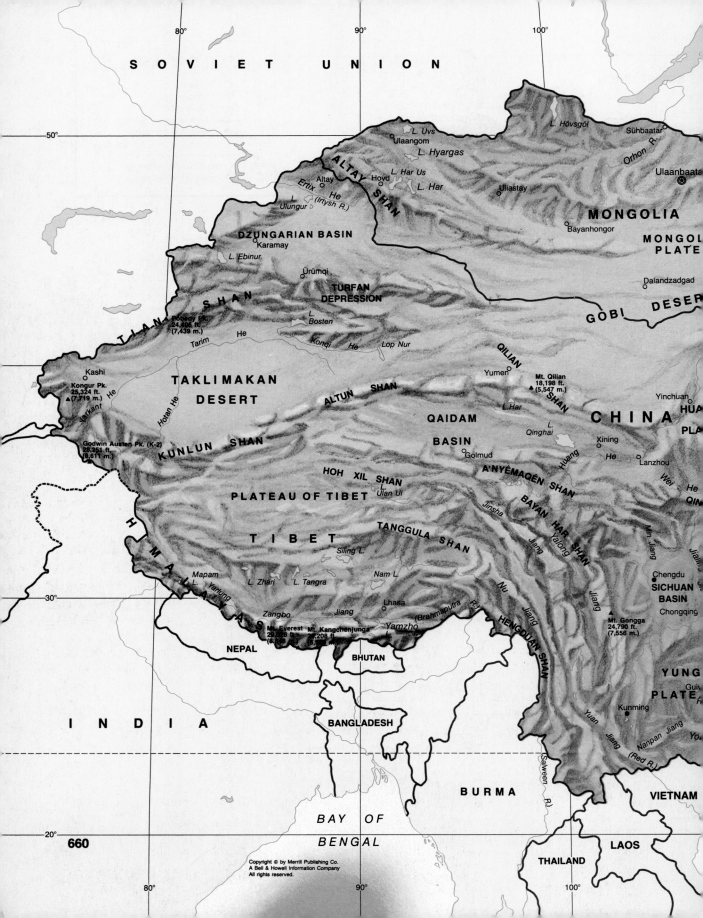

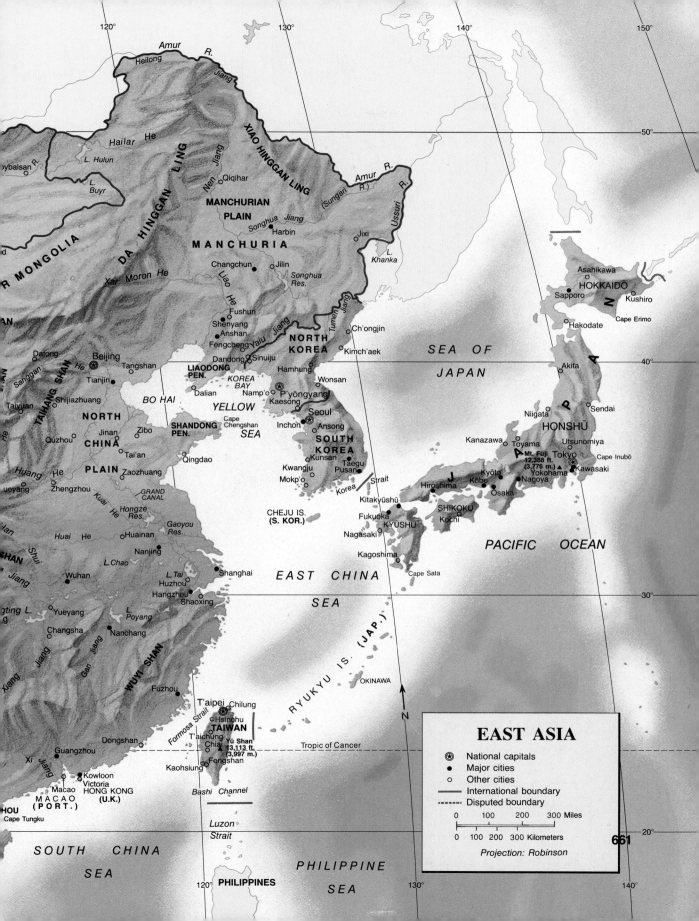

120°   130°   140°   150°

Amur   Heilong   R.
Jiang

Hailar   He
L. Hulun

ybalsan
R.

OR   MONGOLIA

L.
Buyr

Amur   R.
Nen   Jiang   Qiqihar

XIAO HINGGAN LING

(Sungari R.)

Ussuri   R.

50°

MANCHURIAN
PLAIN

DA HINGGAN LING

MANCHURIA

Songhua   Jiang
Harbin

Jixi

L.
Khanka

Changchun   Jilin

Songhua
Res.

Asahikawa
HOKKAIDŌ

Sapporo   Kushiro

Cape Erimo

Hakodate

SEA   OF

Datong   Xar Moron He   Liao He   Fushun

Beijing
Tianjin
Tangshan

Shenyang
Anshan
Fengcheng   Yalu   Jiang

Tumen   Jiang

Ch'ongjin

Kimch'aek

JAPAN

40°

Akita

TAIHANG SHAN
He
Sanggan

Taiyuan
Shijiazhuang

NORTH
CHINA
PLAIN

Jinan

Tai'an

Zibo

LIAODONG
PEN.

Dandong   Sinuiju

NORTH
KOREA

Hamhung   Wonsan

Sendai

HONSHŪ

Niigata
Kanazawa
Toyama
Utsunomiya

BO   HAI
Dalian

KOREA
BAY

YELLOW

Namp'o   P'yŏngyang

Kaesong

Seoul

Kyōto
Ōsaka

Mt. Fuji
12,388 ft.
(3,776 m.)   Tokyo

Yokohama
Nagoya   Kawasaki

Cape Inubō

Quzhou
Zhengzhou

SHANDONG
PEN.

Cape
Chengshan

SEA

Inchon   Ansong

Kanazawa

JAP

Datong

Huang   He

Zaozhuang   Qingdao

SOUTH
KOREA

Kunsan
Kwangju   Taegu
Mokp'o   Pusan

Hiroshima
Kōbe

SHIKOKU   Kōchi

Nagoya

Huai   He

Huainan

Nanjing

GRAND
CANAL

Gaoyou
Res.

Hongze
Res.

Korea   Strait

Kitakyūshū

Fukuoka
KYŪSHŪ

PACIFIC   OCEAN

Wuhan   L.Chao

L.Tai
Huzhou

Shanghai

CHEJU IS.
(S. KOR.)

Nagasaki

Kagoshima

30°

Yueyang

Hangzhou
Shaoxing

EAST   CHINA

Cape Sata

Changsha   Nanchang

SEA

WUYI SHAN

Fuzhou

RYUKYU IS. (JAP.)

OKINAWA

N

Dongshan

Xi   Jiang
Guangzhou

T'aipei   Chilung
Hsinchu
TAIWAN
T'aichung
Chiai
Yü Shan
13,113 ft.
(3,997 m.)
Fengshan

Formosa Strait

Tropic of Cancer

20°

Kowloon
Victoria
HONG KONG
(U.K.)

Macao
MACAO
(PORT.)

Kaohsiung

Bashi   Channel

HOU
Cape Tungku

SOUTH
CHINA
SEA

Luzon
Strait

120°   PHILIPPINES

PHILIPPINE

SEA

130°   140°

661

EAST ASIA

⊛   National capitals

●   Major cities

○   Other cities

———   International boundary

- - - -   Disputed boundary

0   100   200   300 Miles

0   100   200   300 Kilometers

Projection: Robinson

SOUTHEAST ASIA

- ⊛ National capitals
- ● Major cities
- ○ Other cities
- —— International boundary

| 0 | 200 | 400 Miles |
| 0 | 200 | 400 Kilometers |

Projection: Mercator

662

NEPAL
BHUTAN
BANGLADESH
CHINA
INDIA
Tropic of Cancer
Chindwin R.
Mandalay
Myingyan
BURMA
Irrawaddy
River
Salween
R.
Black R.
Red R.
Hanoi
Haiphong
GULF OF TONKIN
20°
Chiang Mai
Vientiane
LAOS
D'ANNAMITE MTNS.
Henzada
Pegu
Nan
Moulmein
KHORAT
PLATEAU
Savannakhet
Hue
Da Nang
Bassein
Rangoon
C. Negrais
GULF OF MARTABAN
Chao Phraya R.
Ping R.
THAILAND
Nakhon
Ratchasima
Ubon
Ratchathani
Mekong
River
VIETNAM
Preparis
Channel
Tavoy
Thonburi
Krung Thep
(Bangkok)
KAMPUCHEA
Tonle Sap
Qui-Nhon
Coco Channel
Phnom
Penh
Nha-Tran
ANDAMAN
SEA
GULF OF
THAILAND
Ho Chi Minh City
10°
ISTHMUS
OF
KRA
Can-Tho
Pt. Bai Bung
Hat Yai
SOUTH CHINA
SEA
Great
Channel
George Town
MALAY
Ipoh
PENINSULA
MALAYSIA
BUNGURAN
ISLAND
(INDONESIA)
SRI LANKA
Medan
Kuala
Lumpur
ANAMBAS
IS.
C. Datu
INDIAN
OCEAN
L. Toba
Strait
of
Malacca
Johor Baharu
SINGAPORE
Singapore
SUMATRA
Pekanbaru
Pontianak
Kapu
0°
Equator
Padang
Jambi
Karimata Strait
BARISAN
Palembang
MTNS.
JAVA S
Jakarta
Sunda Strait
Bandung
JAVA
Surakarta
10°

TAIWAN

Tropic of Cancer

Luzon
Strait

20°

Cape Engaño

LUZON

PHILIPPINE
SEA

PACIFIC

OCEAN

Tarlac

Caloocan · Quezon City
Manila · Pasig

MINDORO

PHILIPPINES

Iloilo · Bacolod
Cebu

PALAWAN

10°

SULU SEA

Butuan

Balabac Strait

Zamboanga

MINDANAO
Davao

Kinabalu

Bandar Seri
Begawan

Point Tinaca

CELEBES
SEA

HIGHLANDS

BORNEO

Manado

HALMAHERA

N

Samarinda

GULF OF
TOMINI

MOLUCCA
SEA

Equator

0°

Balikpapan

Strait

GULF OF
TOLO

CERAM SEA

Jayapura

Makassar

CELEBES

CERAM

Banjarmasin

BURU

Ambon

MAOKE MTNS.

Jaya Pk.
16,499 ft.
(5,029 m.)

Cape
Selatan

GULF
OF
BONE

NEW GUINEA

Ujung Pandang

BANDA   SEA

PAPUA
NEW GUINEA

INDONESIA

ARU

FLORES   SEA

663

a

SUMBAWA

FLORES

TANIMBAR

BALI

TIMOR

SAVU SEA

ARAFURA   SEA

10°

SUMBA

120°

TIMOR SEA

130°

140°

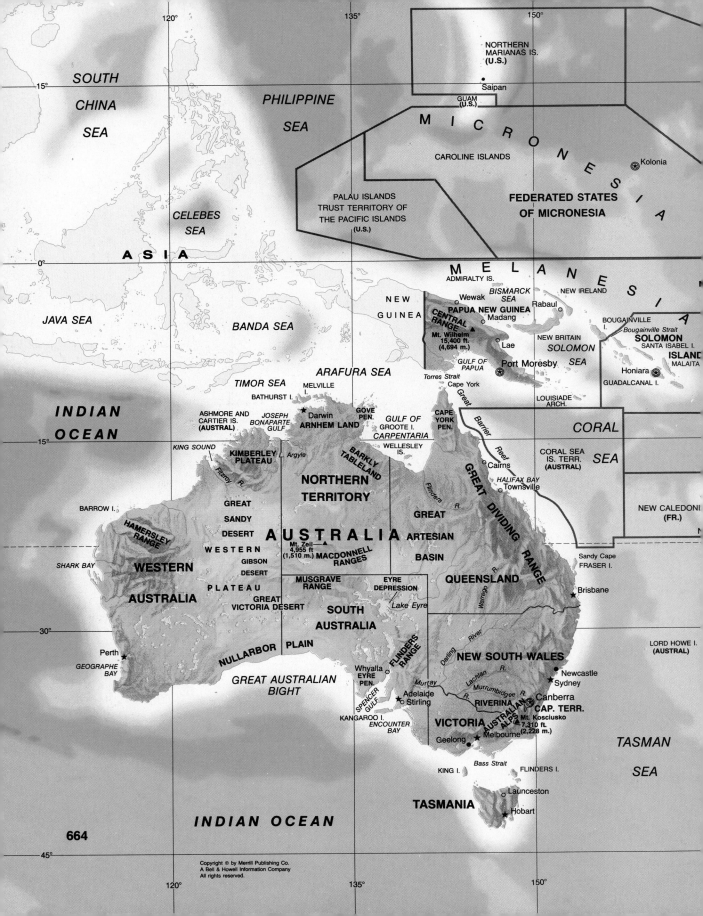

SOUTH
CHINA
SEA

PHILIPPINE
SEA

NORTHERN
MARIANAS IS.
(U.S.)

• Saipan

GUAM
(U.S.)

M I C R O N E S I A

CAROLINE ISLANDS

◉ Kolonia

PALAU ISLANDS
TRUST TERRITORY OF
THE PACIFIC ISLANDS
(U.S.)

FEDERATED STATES
OF MICRONESIA

CELEBES
SEA

A S I A

M E L A N E S I A

ADMIRALTY IS.

NEW IRELAND

JAVA SEA

BANDA SEA

NEW
GUINEA

• Wewak

BISMARCK
SEA

Rabaul

BOUGAINVILLE
I.

PAPUA NEW GUINEA
CENTRAL
RANGE
Mt. Wilhelm
15,400 ft.
(4,694 m.)

• Madang

NEW BRITAIN

Bougainville Strait

SOLOMON
SANTA ISABEL I.

SOLOMON
ISLAND

INDIAN
OCEAN

• Lae

SOLOMON
SEA

MALAITA

Honiara ◉

GUADALCANAL I.

TIMOR SEA

ARAFURA SEA

GULF OF
PAPUA

Port Moresby ◎

Torres Strait

Cape York

Great

CORAL

SEA

MELVILLE
I.

BATHURST I.

ASHMORE AND
CARTIER IS.
(AUSTRAL)

JOSEPH
BONAPARTE
GULF

★ Darwin

GOVE
PEN.

GULF OF
CARPENTARIA

GROOTE I.

CAPE
YORK
PEN.

Barrier

CORAL SEA
IS. TERR.
(AUSTRAL)

KING SOUND

KIMBERLEY
PLATEAU

L. Argyle

ARNHEM LAND

BARKLY
TABLELAND

WELLESLEY
IS.

Reef

HALIFAX BAY
Townsville

Cairns

NEW CALEDONI
(FR.)

BARROW I.

HAMERSLEY
RANGE

Fitzroy R.

GREAT
SANDY
DESERT

NORTHERN
TERRITORY

Flinders R.

GREAT
DIVIDING
RANGE

Sandy Cape
FRASER I.

WESTERN

GIBSON

Mt. Zeil
4,955 ft
(1,510 m.)

MACDONNELL
RANGES

AUSTRALIA

GREAT

ARTESIAN

Burdekin R.

SHARK BAY

DESERT

WESTERN

PLATEAU

MUSGRAVE
RANGE

EYRE
DEPRESSION

BASIN

QUEENSLAND

Warrego R.

Brisbane ★

GREAT
VICTORIA DESERT

SOUTH

Lake Eyre

LORD HOWE I.
(AUSTRAL)

AUSTRALIA

Perth ★

GEOGRAPHE
BAY

NULLARBOR

PLAIN

FLINDERS
RANGE

Darling

River

NEW SOUTH WALES

R.

Newcastle •

Sydney ★

GREAT AUSTRALIAN

BIGHT

Whyalla •
EYRE
PEN.

SPENCER
GULF

Adelaide •
Stirling •

Murray R.

Lachlan

Murrumbidgee

Canberra •

R.

RIVERINA

AUSTRALIAN
CAP. TERR.

KANGAROO I.

ENCOUNTER
BAY

VICTORIA

AUSTRALIAN
ALPS

Mt. Kosciusko
7,310 ft
(2,228 m.)

TASMAN

Geelong •

★ Melbourne

SEA

KING I.

Bass Strait

FLINDERS I.

INDIAN OCEAN

Launceston ◉

664

TASMANIA

Hobart ★

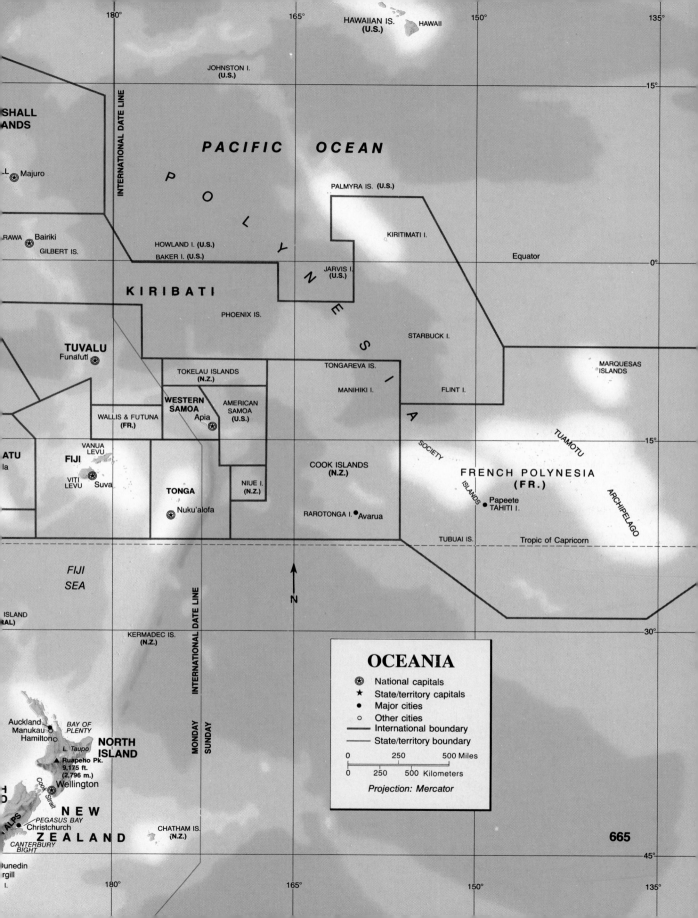

PACIFIC OCEAN

HAWAIIAN IS.
(U.S.)
HAWAII

JOHNSTON I.
(U.S.)

PALMYRA IS. (U.S.)

KIRITIMATI I.

Equator

JARVIS I.
(U.S.)

HOWLAND I. (U.S.)
BAKER I. (U.S.)

KIRIBATI

PHOENIX IS.

STARBUCK I.

MARQUESAS
ISLANDS

TUVALU
Funafuti

TOKELAU ISLANDS
(N.Z.)

TONGAREVA IS.

MANIHIKI I.

FLINT I.

WESTERN
SAMOA
Apia

AMERICAN
SAMOA
(U.S.)

WALLIS & FUTUNA
(FR.)

SOCIETY

TUAMOTU

VANUA
LEVU

FIJI

VITI
LEVU   Suva

COOK ISLANDS
(N.Z.)

FRENCH POLYNESIA
(FR.)

ISLANDS

ARCHIPELAGO

TONGA

NIUE I.
(N.Z.)

Papeete
TAHITI I.

Nuku'alofa

RAROTONGA I. Avarua

TUBUAI IS.

Tropic of Capricorn

FIJI
SEA

KERMADEC IS.
(N.Z.)

N

OCEANIA

⊛ National capitals
★ State/territory capitals
● Major cities
○ Other cities
— International boundary
— State/territory boundary

0   250   500 Miles

0   250   500 Kilometers

Projection: Mercator

MONDAY
SUNDAY

Auckland
Manukau
Hamilton

BAY OF
PLENTY

NORTH
ISLAND

L. Taupo
▲ Ruapeho Pk.
9,175 ft.
(2,796 m.)

Wellington

NEW

PEGASUS BAY
Christchurch

ZEALAND

CHATHAM IS.
(N.Z.)

CANTERBURY
BIGHT

SHALL
ANDS

Majuro

RAWA Bairiki

GILBERT IS.

ATU

INTERNATIONAL DATE LINE

INTERNATIONAL DATE LINE

POLYNESIA

665

POLAR REGIONS

○ Cities and towns
— International boundary

	250	500	750 Miles
0	250	500	750 Kilometers

Projection: Polar Azimuthal Equidistant

THE ARCTIC

North Pole

CHINA

SOVIET UNION

ASIA

Amur River

Lower Tunguska R.

Yenisey R.

Noril'sk

CENTRAL SIBERIAN PLATEAU

STANOVOY RANGE

Aldan R.

Lena River

VERKHOYANSK RANGE

Verkhoyansk

Mt. Mus-Khaya 9,708 ft. (2,959 m.)

Indigirka R.

NEW SIBERIAN ISLANDS

Tiksi

LAPTEV SEA

Lake Taymyr

TAYMYR PEN.

SEVERNAYA ZEMLYA

NOVAYA ZEMLYA

KARA SEA

Cape Zelaniya

FRANZ JOSEF IS. (SOV. UN.)

BARENTS SEA

North Cape

KOLA PEN.

Murmansk

FINLAND

Kiruna

SWEDEN

NORWAY

EUROPE

NORTH SEA

UN KIN

IRE

ARCTIC OCEAN

SVALBARD (NOR.)

JAN MAYEN (NOR.)

Prime Meridian

Arctic Circle

FAROE IS. (DEN.)

SHETLAND IS. (U.K.)

NORWEGIAN SEA

GREENLAND SEA

Cape Brewster

Denmark Strait

ICELAND

ATLANT OCEA

SEA OF OKHOTSK

KOLYMA RANGE

Kolyma R.

KOLYMA PLAIN

Cherskiy

EAST SIBERIAN SEA

80°

LINCOLN SEA

GREENLAND (DEN.)

Thule

Cape Fa

KAMCHATKA PEN.

Mt. Klyuchevsk 15,584 ft. (4,750 m.)

70°

WRANGEL I.

60°

CHUKCHI SEA

ELLESMERE ISLAND

BAFFIN BAY

Davis Strait

LABRADO SEA

Cape Navarin

CHUKOTSK PEN.

Point Barrow

QUEEN ELIZABETH IS.

DEVON I.

SOMERSET

PRINCE OF WALES

Nettilling Lake

BAFFIN ISLAND

ALEUTIAN IS.

50°

180°

BERING SEA

Bering Strait

SEWARD PEN.

Barrow

BROOKS RANGE

Prudhoe Bay

BEAUFORT SEA

BANKS

VICTORIA ISLAND

KING WILLIAM I.

Hudson Strait

UNGAVA PENINSULA

ST. LAWRENCE I.

NUNIVAK I.

Yukon

ALASKA (U.S.)

Kuskokwim R.

Mt. McKinley 20,320 ft. (6,193 m.)

MACKENZIE MTS.

Mackenzie

Inuvik

Echo Bay

Great Bear Lake

CANADA

NORTH AMERICA

HUDSON BAY

BELCHER IS.

120°

90°

ANTARCTICA

666

SOUTH AMERICA

TIERRA DEL FUEGO

Cape Horn

PACIFIC OCEAN

Drake Passage

FALKLAND (U.K

AMUNDSEN SEA

Cape Flying Fish

THURSTON I.

BELLINGSHAUSEN SEA

ADELAIDE I.

ALEXANDER I.

ANTARCTIC PEN.

SOUTH SHETLAND IS.

JOINVILLE I.

SCOT SEA

SIPLE I.

EXECUTIVE COMMITTEE RANGE

BYRD LAND

THWAITES ICEBERG TONGUE

ELLSWORTH LAND

SOUTH ORKNEY IS.

CAMPBELL I. (N.Z.)

AUCKLAND IS. (N.Z.)

ROSS SEA

SCOTT ISLAND

Cape Colbeck

EDWARD VII PEN.

ROCKEFELLER PLATEAU

MARIE BYRD LAND

ELLSWORTH MTNS.

Vinson Massif 16,863 ft. (5,140 m.)

MACQUARIE I. (AUSTRAL.)

BELLANY IS.

ROOSEVELT I.

ROSS ICE SHELF

REEDY GLACIER

RONNE ICE SHELF

BERKNER

WEDDELL SEA

GEO

Cape Adaré

COULMAN I.

PRINCE ALBERT MTNS.

ROSS I.

McMurdo Sound

MOUNTAINS

PENSACOLA MTNS.

VAHSEL BAY

VICTORIA LAND

TRANSANTARCTIC

QUEEN MAUD MTNS.

NILSEN PLATEAU

Mt. Kirkpatrick 14,855 ft. (4,528 m.)

South Pole

RECOVERY GLACIER

RANGE

SHACKLETON

RIISER-LARSEN ICE SHELF

WILKES LAND

80°

Cape Norvegia

FIMBUL ICE SHELF

ATLANT OCEAN

DIBBLE ICEBERG TONGUE

QUEEN MAUD LAND

MÜHLIG-HOFMANN MTNS.

TOTTEN GLACIER

Cape Poinsett

Cape Flying

Prime Meridian

Antarctic Circle

AMERICAN HIGHLAND

LAMBERT GLACIER

PRINCE CHARLES MTNS.

SHIRASE GLACIER

60°

120°

SHACKLETON ICE SHELF

AMERY ICE SHELF

ENDERBY LAND

LÜTSOW-HOLM BAY

SO SANDW

50°

90°

INDIAN OCEAN

DAVIS SEA

WEST ICE SHELF

PRYDZ BAY

30°

NATIONAL PROFILES

FLAG	COUNTRY Capital (Largest City)	AREA sq m (sq km) PERCENT ARABLE PERCENT URBAN	POPULATION DENSITY sq m (sq km) BIRTH/DEATH RATE ANNUAL GROWTH %	MAJOR LANGUAGES LITERACY RATE LIFE EXPECTANCY	PER CAPITA GNP MAJOR EXPORTS
ANGLO-AMERICA					
	CANADA Ottawa (Toronto)	3,851,792 (9,976,133.5) 5 76	25,900,000 7 (3) 15/7 0.8	English, French 99% 76 years	$13,670 wood, petroleum, paper, transport equipment, wheat
	UNITED STATES Washington, D.C. (New York City)	3,615,104 (9,363,112.1) 20 74	243,800,000 67 (26) 16/9 0.7	English 99% 75 years	$16,400 machinery, chemicals, transport equipment, agricultural products
LATIN AMERICA					
	ANTIGUA AND BARBUDA St. John's	170 (440.3) 18 34	100,000 588 (227) 15/5 1.0	English 90% 72 years	$2,030 clothing, rum, lobsters
	ARGENTINA Buenos Aires	1,068,297 (2,766,887.0) 13 84	31,500,000 29 (11) 24/8 1.6	Spanish 94% 70 years	$2,130 wheat, corn, wool, oilseed, hides
	BAHAMAS Nassau	5,382 (13,939.4) 1 75	200,000 37 (14) 23/6 1.8	English 89% 70 years	$7,150 pharmaceuticals, cement, rum, crawfish
	BARBADOS Bridgetown	166 (429.9) 77 32	300,000 1,807 (698) 17/8 0.9	English 99% 73 years	$4,680 sugar, sugarcane by-products, clothing, electrical parts
	BELIZE Belmopan (Belize City)	8,865 (22,960.3) 2 52	200,000 23 (9) 33/6 2.7	English 90% 70 years	$1,130 sugar, seafood, wood, garments, citrus fruits
	BOLIVIA Sucre[1] (La Paz)[2]	424,162 (1,098,578.7) 3 48	6,500,000 15 (6) 40/14 2.6	Spanish, Quechua, Aymara 63% 53 years	$470 tin, natural gas, metals, coffee, sugar, cotton

[1]Judicial capital
[2]Legislative and administrative capital

Data from *Background Notes,* United States Department of State, Bureau of Public Affairs; *1987 World Population Data Sheet,* Population Reference Bureau; *The World Factbook 1987,* Central Intelligence Agency, Public Affairs Office; and *The World Bank Atlas, 1987,* The World Bank.

FLAG	COUNTRY Capital (Largest City)	AREA sq m (sq km) PERCENT ARABLE PERCENT URBAN	POPULATION DENSITY sq m (sq km) BIRTH/DEATH RATE ANNUAL GROWTH %	MAJOR LANGUAGES LITERACY RATE LIFE EXPECTANCY	PER CAPITA GNP MAJOR EXPORTS
	BRAZIL Brasília (São Paulo)	3,286,475 (8,511,963.6) 9 71	141,500,000 43 (17) 29/8 2.1	Portuguese 76% 65 years	$1,640 coffee, soybeans, transport equipment, iron ore, machinery
	CHILE Santiago	292,259 (756,950.2) 7 83	12,400,000 42 (16) 22/6 1.6	Spanish 94% 68 years	$1,440 copper, iron ore, paper and steel products, fishmeal
	COLOMBIA Bogotá	439,734 (1,138,910.2) 5 65	29,900,000 68 (26) 28/7 2.1	Spanish 88% 65 years	$1,320 coffee, coal, fuel oil, cotton, sugar, tobacco, textiles
	COSTA RICA San José	19,575 (50,699.2) 13 48	2,800,000 143 (55) 31/4 2.7	Spanish 93% 74 years	$1,290 coffee, bananas, beef, sugar, cocoa
	CUBA Havana	42,803 (110,859.7) 29 71	10,300,000 241 (93) 18/6 1.2	Spanish 96% 73 years	(not available) sugar, nickel, shellfish, coffee, tobacco, citrus
	DOMINICA Roseau	290 (751.1) 23 N.A.	100,000 345 (133) 22/5 1.7	English, French patois 80% 75 years	$1,160 bananas, coconuts, lime juice and oil, cocoa
	DOMINICAN REPUBLIC Santo Domingo	18,815 (48,730.8) 30 52	6,500,000 345 (133) 33/8 2.5	Spanish 68% 63 years	$810 sugar, nickel, gold, coffee, tobacco, cocoa, silver
	ECUADOR Quito (Guayaquil)	109,483 (283,560.7) 9 51	10,000,000 91 (35) 35/8 2.8	Spanish, Quechuan 85% 65 years	$1,160 petroleum, shrimp, coffee, bananas, cocoa, fish products
	EL SALVADOR San Salvador	8,124 (21,041.1) 34 43	5,300,000 652 (252) 36/10 2.6	Spanish 65% 66 years	$710 coffee, cotton, sugar, shrimp
	GRENADA St. George's	131 (339.3) 41 N.A.	100,000 763 (295) 26/7 1.9	English 85% 72 years	$970 cocoa beans, mace, nutmeg, bananas
	GUATEMALA Guatemala City	42,042 (108,888.7) 17 39	8,400,000 200 (77) 41/9 3.2	Spanish 50% 60 years	$1,240 coffee, cotton, sugar, bananas, meat
	GUYANA Georgetown	83,000 (214,969.8) 2 32	800,000 10 (4) 26/6 2.0	English 85% 68 years	$570 bauxite, sugar, rice, shrimp, molasses, timber, rum
	HAITI Port-au-Prince	10,714 (27,749.2) 33 26	6,200,000 579 (223) 36/13 2.3	French, Creole 23% 53 years	$350 mangos, coffee, sugar, sisal, light industrial products

FLAG	COUNTRY Capital (Largest City)	AREA sq m (sq km) PERCENT ARABLE PERCENT URBAN	POPULATION DENSITY sq m (sq km) BIRTH/DEATH RATE ANNUAL GROWTH %	MAJOR LANGUAGES LITERACY RATE LIFE EXPECTANCY	PER CAPITA GNP MAJOR EXPORTS
	HONDURAS Tegucigalpa	43,278 (112,089.9) 16 40	4,700,000 109 (42) 39/8 3.1	Spanish 56% 63 years	$730 bananas, coffee, lumber, meat, sugar, minerals, seafood
	JAMAICA Kingston	4,243 (10,989.4) 24 54	2,500,000 589 (227) 26/5 2.0	English, Creole 76% 73 years	$940 sugar, bananas, rum, cocoa, citrus fruits, alumina, bauxite
	MEXICO Mexico City	761,602 (1,972,547.6) 13 70	81,900,000 107 (41) 31/7 2.5	Spanish 88% 67 years	$2,080 cotton, coffee, shrimp, petroleum, minerals, machinery
	NICARAGUA Managua	50,193 (129,999.8) 10 53	3,500,000 70 (27) 43/9 3.4	Spanish 66% 61 years	$850 coffee, cotton, sugar, seafood, bananas
	PANAMA Panamá City	29,761 (77,080.9) 7 51	2,300,000 77 (30) 27/5 2.2	Spanish 90% 72 years	$2,020 petroleum products, bananas, shrimp, sugar
	PARAGUAY Asunción	157,046 (406,748.8) 5 43	4,300,000 27 (11) 36/7 2.9	Spanish, Guarani 81% 65 years	$940 cotton, oilseeds, meat products, coffee, tobacco, timber
	PERU Lima	496,224 (1,285,219.2) 3 69	20,700,000 42 (16) 35/10 2.5	Spanish, Quechua 80% 60 years	$960 fishmeal, cotton, sugar, coffee, metals, petroleum
	ST. CHRISTOPHER AND NEVIS Basseterre	139 (360.0) 39 45	50,000 360 (139) 26/11 1.6	English 80% 67 years	$1,520 sugar
	ST. LUCIA Castries	239 (619.0) 27 40	100,000 418 (162) 30/6 2.5	English, French patois 78% 71 years	$1,210 bananas, cocoa
	ST. VINCENT AND THE GRENADINES Kingstown	150 (388.5) 50 N.A.	100,000 667 (257) 26/7 2.0	English 82% 69 years	$840 bananas, arrowroot, copra
	SURINAME Paramaribo	63,039 (163,270.8) 0 66	400,000 6 (2) 27/7 2.1	Dutch, Creole, English 65% 69 years	$2,570 bauxite, aluminum, rice, wood and wood products
	TRINIDAD AND TOBAGO Port-of-Spain	1,981 (5,130.8) 31 34	1,300,000 656 (253) 27/7 2.0	English, Hindi 89% 70 years	$6,010 sugar, cocoa, coffee, citrus, petroleum, ammonia, chemicals
	URUGUAY Montevideo	68,039 (176,220.9) 8 85	3,100,000 46 (18) 18/10 0.8	Spanish 94% 71 years	$1,660 meat, textiles, wool, hides, fish, rice, leather products

FLAG	COUNTRY Capital (Largest City)	AREA sq m (sq km) PERCENT ARABLE PERCENT URBAN	POPULATION DENSITY sq m (sq km) BIRTH/DEATH RATE ANNUAL GROWTH %	MAJOR LANGUAGES LITERACY RATE LIFE EXPECTANCY	PER CAPITA GNP MAJOR EXPORTS
	VENEZUELA Caracas	352,143 (912,049.7) 4 76	18,300,000 52 (20) 32/6 2.7	Spanish 86% 69 years	$3,110 petroleum
EUROPE					
	ALBANIA Tiranë	11,100 (28,749.0) 25 34	3,100,000 279 (108) 26/6 2.0	Albanian, Greek 75% 71 years	N.A. asphalt, bitumen, petroleum products, metals, vegetables
	ANDORRA Andorra la Vella	185 (479.1) 2 N.A.	48,000 259 (100) 15/4 1.1	Catalan, Spanish, French 100% N.A.	N.A. tobacco
	AUSTRIA Vienna	32,375 (83,851.2) 18 55	7,600,000 235 (91) 12/12 0.0	German 98% 74 years	$9,150 iron and steel products, textiles, machinery, lumber
	BELGIUM Brussels	11,749 (30,429.9) 25 95	9,900,000 843 (325) 12/11 0.0	Flemish, French 98% 73 years	$8,450 cars, iron and steel products, petroleum products, chemicals
	BULGARIA Sofia	42,822 (110,908.9) 37 66	9,000,000 210 (81) 13/12 0.1	Bulgarian 95% 72 years	N.A. machinery, fuels, minerals, metals, agricultural products
	CZECHOSLO- VAKIA Prague	49,371 (127,870.8) 40 74	15,600,000 316 (122) 15/12 0.3	Czech, Slovak 99% 71 years	N.A. machinery, fuels, manufactured goods, minerals, metals
	DENMARK Copenhagen	16,629 (43,069.1) 61 84	5,100,000 307 (118) 11/11 -0.1	Danish 99% 75 years	$11,240 meat, machinery, dairy products, textiles, clothing
	FINLAND Helsinki	130,127 (337,028.7) 7 60	4,900,000 38 (14) 13/10 0.3	Finnish, Swedish 99% 75 years	$10,870 timber, paper and pulp, machinery, ships, clothing
	FRANCE Paris	211,208 (547,028.3) 34 73	55,600,000 263 (102) 14/10 0.4	French 99% 75 years	$9,550 machinery, textiles, transport equipment, chemicals
	GERMANY, EAST East Berlin	41,826 (108,329.3) 46 77	16,700,000 399 (154) 14/14 0.0	German 99% 73 years	N.A. machinery, chemical products, textiles, clothing
	GERMANY, WEST Bonn (West Berlin)	95,977 (248,580.2) 30 85	61,000,000 636 (245) 10/12 -0.2	German 99% 74 years	$10,940 machines, machine tools, chemicals, motor vehicles
	GREECE Athens	50,942 (131,939.7) 30 70	10,000,000 196 (76) 12/9 0.2	Greek 95% 75 years	$3,550 tobacco, minerals, fruits, textiles

FLAG	COUNTRY Capital (Largest City)	AREA sq m (sq km) PERCENT ARABLE PERCENT URBAN	POPULATION DENSITY sq m (sq km) BIRTH/DEATH RATE ANNUAL GROWTH %	MAJOR LANGUAGES LITERACY RATE LIFE EXPECTANCY	PER CAPITA GNP MAJOR EXPORTS
	HUNGARY Budapest	35,919 (93,030.1) 57 56	10,600,000 295 (114) 12/14 -0.2	Hungarian 99% 70 years	$1,940 fuels, machinery, consumer goods, agricultural products
	ICELAND Reykjavík	39,768 (102,999.0) 0 89	200,000 5 (2) 16/7 0.9	Icelandic 100% 77 years	$10,720 animal and fish products, aluminum, diatomite
	IRELAND Dublin	27,135 (70,279.6) 14 56	3,500,000 129 (50) 18/9 0.8	English, Irish Gaelic 99% 73 years	$4,840 foodstuffs, animals, machinery, chemicals, clothing
	ITALY Rome	116,305 (301,229.7) 41 72	57,400,000 493 (191) 10/10 0.1	Italian 93% 75 years	$6,520 textiles, chemicals, footwear
	LIECHTEN-STEIN Vaduz	62 (160.6) 25 81	27,000 435 (168) 15/7 0.9	German 100% 66 years	N.A. postage stamps, metal manufactures, machines, chemical products
	LUXEMBOURG Luxembourg	992 (2,569.3) 44 78	400,000 403 (156) 11/11 0.0	Luxembourgian, French, German 100% 73 years	$13,380 iron and steel products
	MALTA Valletta (Sliema)	124 (321.2) 41 85	400,000 3,226 (1,245) 16/8 0.8	Maltese, English 83% 73 years	$3,300 clothing, textiles, ships, printed matter
	MONACO Monaco-Ville	0.6 (1.5) 0 100	29,000 48,333 (19,333) 20/17 0.3	French, Italian 99% N.A.	N.A. postage stamps
	NETHERLANDS Amsterdam	14,405 (37,308.9) 23 89	14,600,000 1,013 (391) 12/9 0.4	Dutch 99% 76 years	$9,180 foodstuffs, machinery, chemicals, petroleum products
	NORWAY Oslo	125,181 (324,218.5) 3 70	4,200,000 34 (13) 12/11 0.2	Norwegian 100% 76 years	$13,890 oil, natural gas, metals, chemicals, machinery, fish
	POLAND Warsaw	120,726 (312,680.1) 47 60	37,800,000 313 (121) 18/10 0.8	Polish 98% 71 years	$2,120 machinery, fuels, minerals, metals, chemicals
	PORTUGAL Lisbon	35,552 (92,079.6) 38 30	10,300,000 290 (112) 12/10 0.3	Portuguese 83% 73 years	$1,970 cotton textiles, cork, canned fish, wine, timber, resin
	ROMANIA Bucharest	91,699 (237,500.2) 45 53	22,900,000 250 (96) 16/11 0.5	Romanian 98% 71 years	N.A. machinery, fuels, minerals, metals, consumer goods

671

FLAG	COUNTRY Capital (Largest City)	AREA sq m (sq km) PERCENT ARABLE PERCENT URBAN	POPULATION DENSITY sq m (sq km) BIRTH/DEATH RATE ANNUAL GROWTH %	MAJOR LANGUAGES LITERACY RATE LIFE EXPECTANCY	PER CAPITA GNP MAJOR EXPORTS
	SAN MARINO San Marino	24 (62.2) 17 74	23,000 958 (370) 9/8 0.1	Italian 97% N.A.	N.A. postage stamps, stone, lime, wood, wheat, wine, hides
	SOVIET UNION Moscow	8,649,498 (22,402,182.5) 10 65	284,000,000 33 (13) 19/11 0.9	Russian, Ukrainian 99% 69 years	N.A.[3] petroleum, natural gas, metals, wood, manufactures
	SPAIN Madrid	194,896 (504,780.2) 41 91	39,000,000 200 (77) 13/8 0.5	Spanish 97% 76 years	$4,360 iron & steel products, cars, citrus, fruits, wine, textiles
	SWEDEN Stockholm	173,730 (449,960.4) 7 83	8,400,000 48 (19) 12/11 0.1	Swedish 99% 77 years	$11,890 machinery, motor vehicles, paper products, wood
	SWITZERLAND Bern (Zürich)	15,942 (41,289.7) 10 57	6,600,000 414 (160) 12/9 0.2	German, French, Italian 99% 76 years	$16,380 machinery, chemicals, precision instruments
	UNITED KINGDOM London	94,525 (244,819.6) 29 90	56,800,000 601 (232) 13/12 0.2	English, Welsh, Scottish Gaelic 99% 74 years	$8,390 manufactured goods, machinery, fuels, chemicals
	VATICAN CITY Vatican City	0.17 (0.44) 0 100	1,000 5,882 (2,273) N.A. N.A.	Italian, Latin 100% N.A.	N.A. postage stamps, publications
	YUGOSLAVIA Belgrade	98,764 (255,798.6) 30 46	23,400,000 237 (91) 16/9 0.7	Serbo-Croatian, Slovenian, Macedonian 91% 71 years	$2,070 raw materials, consumer goods

NORTH AFRICA/SOUTHWEST ASIA

FLAG	COUNTRY Capital (Largest City)	AREA sq m (sq km) PERCENT ARABLE PERCENT URBAN	POPULATION DENSITY sq m (sq km) BIRTH/DEATH RATE ANNUAL GROWTH %	MAJOR LANGUAGES LITERACY RATE LIFE EXPECTANCY	PER CAPITA GNP MAJOR EXPORTS
	AFGHANISTAN Kabul	250,000 (647,499.5) 12 16	14,200,000 57 (22) 48/22 2.6	Pashto, Dari 12% 39 years	N.A. fruits and nuts, natural gas, carpets
	ALGERIA Algiers	919,591 (2,381,738.8) 3 43	23,500,000 26 (10) 42/10 3.2	Arabic 52% 60 years	$2,530 petroleum, natural gas
	BAHRAIN Manama	239 (619.0) 3 81	400,000 1,674 (646) 32/5 2.8	Arabic 40% 67 years	$9,560 petroleum, fish, aluminum
	CHAD N'Djamena	495,753 (1,283,999.2) 2 27	4,600,000 9 (4) 43/23 2.0	Arabic, French 17% 43 years	N.A. cotton, meat, fish, animal products
	CYPRUS Nicosia	3,571 (9,248.9) 47 53	700,000 196 (76) 20/9 1.1	Greek, Turkish, English 99% 74 years	$3,790 citrus, raisins, potatoes, wine, cement, clothing

[3]Estimated 1984 per capita GNP: $7,400.

FLAG	COUNTRY Capital (Largest City)	AREA sq m (sq km) PERCENT ARABLE PERCENT URBAN	POPULATION DEN-SITY sq m (sq km) BIRTH/DEATH RATE ANNUAL GROWTH %	MAJOR LANGUAGES LITERACY RATE LIFE EXPECTANCY	PER CAPITA GNP MAJOR EXPORTS
	EGYPT Cairo	386,660 (1,001,448.6) 2 46	51,900,000 134 (52) 37/11 2.6	Arabic 40% 59 years	$680 crude petroleum, raw cotton, fabric, cotton yarn
	IRAN Tehran	636,293 (1,647,997.5) 9 51	50,400,000 79 (31) 45/13 3.2	Farsi 48% 57 years	N.A. petroleum, carpets, fruits, nuts, cement
	IRAQ Baghdad	167,923 (434,920.2) 13 68	17,000,000 101 (39) 46/13 3.3	Arabic 50% 62 years	N.A. petroleum, dates
	ISRAEL Jerusalem	8,019 (20,769.2) 21 90	4,400,000 549 (212) 23/7 1.7	Hebrew, Arabic, English 85% 75 years	$4,920 polished diamonds, citrus, fruits, textiles, clothing
	JORDAN Amman	37,737 (97,738.8) 4 60	3,700,000 98 (38) 45/8 3.7	Arabic 71% 67 years	$1,560 fruits, vegetables, phosphates, fertilizers
	KUWAIT Kuwait	6,880 (17,819.2) 0 80	1,900,000 276 (107) 34/3 3.2	Arabic 71% 72 years	$14,270 crude petroleum
	LEBANON Beirut	4,015 (10,398.8) 29 80	3,300,000 822 (317) 30/8 2.2	Arabic 75% 65 years	N.A. fruits, vegetables, textiles
	LIBYA Tripoli	679,359 (1,759,538.4) 1 76	3,800,000 6 (2) 39/9 3.0	Arabic 55% 61 years	$7,500 petroleum
	MALI Bamako	478,764 (1,239,997.8) 2 18	8,400,000 17 (7) 51/22 2.9	French, Bambara 10% 43 years	$140 livestock, peanuts, dried fish, cotton, skins
	MAURITANIA Nouakchott	397,954 (1,030,700.0) 0 35	2,000,000 5 (2) 50/20 3.0	Arabic, French 17% 45 years	$410 iron ore, processed fish, gum arabic, gypsum, cattle
	MOROCCO Rabat (Casablanca)	172,413 (446,549.3) 19 43	24,400,000 141 (55) 36/10 2.5	Arabic 28% 60 years	$610 phosphates, foodstuffs, manufacturing
	NIGER Niamey	489,189 (1,266,998.5) 3 16	7,000,000 14 (5) 51/22 2.9	French, Hausa 10% 44 years	$200 uranium, livestock, cowpeas, onions, hides, skins
	OMAN Muscat	82,031 (212,460.1) 0 9	1,300,000 16 (6) 47/14 3.3	Arabic 20% 52 years	$7,080 petroleum, pro-cessed copper, agricultural goods

FLAG	COUNTRY Capital (Largest City)	AREA sq m (sq km) PERCENT ARABLE PERCENT URBAN	POPULATION DENSITY sq m (sq km) BIRTH/DEATH RATE ANNUAL GROWTH %	MAJOR LANGUAGES LITERACY RATE LIFE EXPECTANCY	PER CAPITA GNP MAJOR EXPORTS
	QATAR Doha	4,247 (10,999.7) 0 86	300,000 71 (27) 34/4 3.0	Arabic 40% 69 years	$15,980 petroleum
	SAUDI ARABIA Riyadh	829,996 (2,149,687.9) 1 72	14,800,000 18 (7) 39/7 3.1	Arabic 52% 63 years	$8,860 petroleum and petroleum products
	SUDAN Khartoum	967,494 (2,505,807.5) 5 20	23,500,000 24 (9) 45/16 2.8	Arabic 20% 49 years	$330 cotton, gum arabic, livestock, peanuts, sesame
	SYRIA Damascus	71,498 (185,179.7) 31 49	11,300,000 158 (61) 47/9 3.8	Arabic 47% 63 years	$1,630 petroleum, textiles, tobacco, fruits, vegetables, cotton
	TUNISIA Tunis	63,170 (163,610.2) 29 53	7,600,000 120 (46) 32/7 2.5	Arabic 62% 62 years	$1,220 hydrocarbons, agricultural goods, phosphates, chemicals
	TURKEY Ankara (istanbul)	301,382 (780,578.8) 35 46	51,400,000 170 (66) 30/9 2.1	Turkish 70% 62 years	$1,130 cotton, tobacco, fruits, nuts, metals, livestock products
	UNITED ARAB EMIRATES Abu Dhabi	32,278 (83,600.0) 0 81	1,400,000 43 (17) 30/4 2.6	Arabic 68% 68 years	$19,120 crude petroleum, natural gas, dried fish, dates
	YEMEN, NORTH Sanaa	75,290 (195,000.9) 7 15	6,500,000 86 (33) 53/19 3.4	Arabic 15% 47 years	$520 qat, cotton, coffee, hides, vegetables
	YEMEN, SOUTH Aden	128,560 (332,970.1) 1 40	2,400,000 19 (7) 47/17 3.0	Arabic 25% 48 years	$540 petroleum products, fish, cotton, hides, skins, coffee

AFRICA SOUTH OF THE SAHARA

FLAG	COUNTRY Capital (Largest City)	AREA sq m (sq km) PERCENT ARABLE PERCENT URBAN	POPULATION DENSITY sq m (sq km) BIRTH/DEATH RATE ANNUAL GROWTH %	MAJOR LANGUAGES LITERACY RATE LIFE EXPECTANCY	PER CAPITA GNP MAJOR EXPORTS
	ANGOLA Luanda	481,351 (1,246,698.1) 3 25	8,000,000 17 (6) 47/22 2.5	Portuguese, Bantu 20% 43 years	N.A. oil, coffee, sisal, diamonds, fish, timber, cotton
	BENIN Porto-Novo (Cotonou)	43,483 (112,620.9) 16 39	4,300,000 99 (38) 51/20 3.0	French, Fon 11% 45 years	$270 palm products, cotton, agricultural products
	BOTSWANA Gaborone	231,803 (600,369.3) 2 22	1,200,000 5 (2) 48/14 3.4	English, Setswana 30% 58 years	$840 diamonds, cattle, animal products, copper, nickel

FLAG	COUNTRY Capital (Largest City)	AREA sq m (sq km) PERCENT ARABLE PERCENT URBAN	POPULATION DENSITY sq m (sq km) BIRTH/DEATH RATE ANNUAL GROWTH %	MAJOR LANGUAGES LITERACY RATE LIFE EXPECTANCY	PER CAPITA GNP MAJOR EXPORTS
	BURKINA FASO Ouagadougou	105,869 (274,200.5) 10 8	7,300,000 69 (27) 48/20 2.8	French, More 7% 46 years	$140 livestock, peanuts, shea nut products, cotton, sesame
	BURUNDI Bujumbura	10,745 (27,829.5) 47 5	5,000,000 465 (180) 47/18 2.9	Kirundi, French 25% 48 years	$240 coffee, tea, cotton, hides, skins
	CAMEROON Yaoundé (Douala)	183,568 (475,440.8) 15 42	10,300,000 56 (22) 43/16 2.7	English, French 65% 51 years	$810 crude oil, cocoa, coffee, timber, aluminum, cotton
	CAPE VERDE Praia	1,556 (4,030.0) 10 27	300,000 193 (74) 35/8 2.6	Portuguese, Crioulo 37% 60 years	$430 fish, bananas, salt, flour
	CENTRAL AFRICAN REPUBLIC Bangui	240,533 (622,980.0) 3 42	2,700,000 11 (4) 44/19 2.5	French, Sangho 20% 43 years	$270 diamonds, cotton, coffee, timber, tobacco
	COMOROS Moroni	694 (1,797.5) 43 23	400,000 576 (222) 47/14 3.3	Swahili, Malagasy, French 15% 52 years	$280 perfume oils, vanilla, copra, cloves
	CONGO Brazzaville	132,046 (341,998.9) 2 48	2,100,000 16 (6) 47/13 3.4	French, Lingala, Kikongo 80% 55 years	$1,020 oil, lumber, cocoa, tobacco, veneer, plywood, coffee
	DJIBOUTI Djibouti	8,494 (21,999.4) 0 74	300,000 35 (14) 43/18 2.5	French, Afar, Somali 20% 47 years	N.A. hides, skins, coffee
	EQUATORIAL GUINEA Malabo	10,830 (28,049.7) 8 60	300,000 28 (11) 38/20 1.8	Spanish, Fang 55% 45 years	N.A. cocoa, coffee, wood
	ETHIOPIA Addis Ababa	471,776 (1,221,898.8) 11 10	46,000,000 97 (38) 46/23 2.3	Amharic 35% 41 years	$110 coffee
	GABON Libreville	103,347 (267,668.5) 2 41	1,200,000 12 (4) 34/18 1.6	French, Fang 65% 49 years	$3,340 crude petroleum, wood and wood products, minerals
	GAMBIA Banjul	4,363 (11,300.2) 15 21	800,000 183 (71) 49/28 2.1	English, Mandinka 12% 36 years	$230 peanuts and peanut products, fish, palm kernels
	GHANA Accra	92,100 (238,538.8) 12 31	13,900,000 151 (58) 42/14 2.8	English, Akan 30% 54 years	$390 cocoa, wood, gold, diamonds, manganese, bauxite, aluminum

FLAG	COUNTRY Capital (Largest City)	AREA sq m (sq km) PERCENT ARABLE PERCENT URBAN	POPULATION DENSITY sq m (sq km) BIRTH/DEATH RATE ANNUAL GROWTH %	MAJOR LANGUAGES LITERACY RATE LIFE EXPECTANCY	PER CAPITA GNP MAJOR EXPORTS
	GUINEA Conakry	94,927 (245,860.7) 6 22	6,400,000 67 (26) 47/23 2.4	French, Fulani 34% 41 years	$320 bauxite, alumina, diamonds, coffee, pineapples
	GUINEA-BISSAU Bissau	13,946 (36,120.1) 8 27	900,000 64 (25) 41/21 2.0	Portuguese, Crioulo 9% 44 years	$170 peanuts, palm kernels, shrimp, fish, lumber
	CÔTE D'IVOIRE Yamoussoukro (Abidjan)	124,502 (322,459.9) 12 43	10,800,000 87 (33) 46/15 3.0	French, Dioula 24% 52 years	$620 cocoa, coffee, wood, cotton, bananas, pineapples, palm oil
	KENYA Nairobi	224,961 (582,648.5) 4 16	22,400,000 100 (38) 52/13 3.9	Kiswahili, English 47% 54 years	$290 petroleum products, coffee, tea, sisal, livestock products
	LESOTHO Maseru	11,718 (30,349.6) 10 17	1,600,000 136 (53) 41/15 2.6	English, Sesotho 60% 50 years	$480 wool, mohair, wheat, cattle, peas, beans, corn
	LIBERIA Monrovia	43,000 (111,369.9) 3 40	2,400,000 56 (21) 48/16 3.2	English 24% 50 years	$470 iron ore, rubber, diamonds, lumber, coffee, cocoa
	MADAGASCAR Antananarivo	226,656 (587,038.6) 5 22	10,600,000 47 (18) 44/16 2.8	Malagasy, French 53% 50 years	$250 agricultural & livestock products, coffee, vanilla, sugar
	MALAWI Lilongwe (Blantyre)	45,745 (118,479.5) 20 12	7,400,000 162 (62) 53/21 3.2	Chichewa, English 25% 46 years	$170 tobacco, tea, sugar, peanuts, cotton, corn
	MAURITIUS Port Louis	718 (1,859.6) 58 42	1,100,000 1,532 (591) 19/7 1.2	English, Creole, French 79% 68 years	$1,070 sugar, knitwear, molasses, tea, textiles
	MOZAMBIQUE Maputo	309,494 (801,588.8) 4 13	14,700,000 47 (18) 45/19 2.6	Portuguese, Bantu 14% 46 years	N.A. cashews, shrimp, sugar, tea, cotton
	NAMIBIA Windhoek	318,259 (824,290.2) 1 51	1,300,000 4 (2) 44/11 3.3	Afrikaans, German, English 22% 49 years	N.A. diamonds, copper, lead, uranium, beef, cattle, fish
	NIGERIA Lagos	356,668 (923,769.4) 34 28	108,600,000 304 (118) 46/18 2.8	English, Hausa, Ibo, Yoruba 28% 49 years	$760 oil, cocoa, palm products, rubber, timber, tin
	RWANDA Kigali	10,170 (26,340.3) 38 6	6,800,000 669 (258) 53/16 3.7	French, Kinyarwanda 37% 48 years	$290 coffee, tea, cassiterite, wolframite, pyrethrum

FLAG	COUNTRY Capital (Largest City)	AREA sq m (sq km) PERCENT ARABLE PERCENT URBAN	POPULATION DENSITY sq m (sq km) BIRTH/DEATH RATE ANNUAL GROWTH %	MAJOR LANGUAGES LITERACY RATE LIFE EXPECTANCY	PER CAPITA GNP MAJOR EXPORTS
	SÃO TOMÉ AND PRÍNCIPE São Tomé	371 (960.9) 38 35	100,000 269 (104) 36/9 2.7	Portuguese, Fang 50% 65 years	$310 cocoa, copra, coffee, palm oil
	SENEGAL Dakar	75,749 (196,189.8) 27 36	7,100,000 94 (36) 46/18 2.8	French, Wolof, Pulaar 10% 45 years	$370 peanuts and peanut products, fish, phosphate rock
	SEYCHELLES Victoria	108 (279.7) 25 37	100,000 926 (357) 27/7 1.9	Creole, English, French 60% 70 years	N.A. fish, copra, cinnamon bark
	SIERRA LEONE Freetown	27,699 (71,740.4) 25 28	3,900,000 141 (54) 47/29 1.8	English, Krio, Mende, Temne 15% 35 years	$370 diamonds, iron ore, palm kernels, cocoa, coffee
	SOMALIA Mogadishu	246,201 (637,660.1) 2 34	7,700,000 31 (12) 48/23 2.5	Somali 60% 41 years	$270 livestock, hides, skins, bananas
	SOUTH AFRICA Pretoria, Bloemfontein, Cape Town[4] (Johannesburg)	471,444 (1,221,039.0) 11 56	34,300,000 73 (28) 33/10 2.3	English, Afrikaans, Bantu 59% 56 years	$2,010 gold, coal, diamonds, corn, uranium
	SWAZILAND Mbabane	6,703 (17,360.8) 8 26	700,000 104 (40) 47/16 3.1	English, siSwati 65% 50 years	$650 sugar, asbestos, wood products, citrus, canned fruit
	TANZANIA Dar es Salaam	364,900 (945,090.3) 5 18	23,500,000 64 (25) 50/15 3.5	Swahili, English 79% 52 years	$270 coffee, cotton, sisal, cashew nuts, meat, cloves, tea
	TOGO Lomé	21,927 (56,790.9) 25 22	3,200,000 146 (56) 47/15 3.1	French, Ewe 18% 53 years	$250 phosphates, cocoa, coffee, palm kernels
	UGANDA Kampala	91,135 (236,039.5) 28 10	15,900,000 174 (67) 50/16 3.4	English, Luganda, Swahili 52% 50 years	N.A. coffee, cotton, tea
	ZAIRE Kinshasa	905,564 (2,345,408.9) 3 34	31,800,000 35 (14) 45/15 3.1	French, Lingala, Swahili 46% 51 years	$170 copper, cobalt, diamonds, coffee, petroleum
	ZAMBIA Lusaka	290,583 (752,609.4) 7 43	7,100,000 24 (9) 50/15 3.5	English 54% 52 years	$400 copper, zinc, cobalt, lead, tobacco
	ZIMBABWE Harare	150,803 (390,579.5) 7 24	9,400,000 62 (24) 47/12 3.5	English, Shona 50% 57 years	$650 tobacco, asbestos, cotton, copper, tin, chrome, gold, nickel

[4]Administrative, judicial, and legislative capitals, respectively.

FLAG	COUNTRY Capital (Largest City)	AREA sq m (sq km) PERCENT ARABLE PERCENT URBAN	POPULATION DENSITY sq m (sq km) BIRTH/DEATH RATE ANNUAL GROWTH %	MAJOR LANGUAGES LITERACY RATE LIFE EXPECTANCY	PER CAPITA GNP MAJOR EXPORTS
	ASIA				
	BANGLADESH Dhaka	55,598 (143,998.7) 63 13	107,100,000 1,926 (743) 44/17 2.7	Bengali 23% 50 years	$150 raw & manufactured jute, leather, tea
	BHUTAN Thimphu	18,147 (47,000.7) 2 5	1,500,000 83 (32) 38/18 2.0	Dzongkha 5% 46 years	$160 agricultural and forestry products, coal
	BRUNEI Bandar Seri Begawan	2,228 (5,770.5) 1 64	200,000 90 (35) 30/4 2.6	Malay, English, Chinese 45% 62 years	$17,580 crude oil, liquefied natural gas, petroleum products
	BURMA Rangoon	261,216 (676,548.9) 15 24	38,800,000 148 (57) 34/13 2.1	Burmese 78% 53 years	$190 teak, hardwoods, rice, beans, metals, ores, rubber
	CHINA Beijing (Shanghai)	3,705,390 (9,596,952.6) 11 32	1,062,000,000 287 (111) 21/8 1.3	Chinese 76% 66 years	$310 manufactured goods, agricultural products, oil
	INDIA New Delhi (Calcutta)	1,269,340 (3,287,588.0) 51 25	800,300,000 630 (243) 33/12 2.1	Hindi, English 36% 55 years	$250 engineering goods, textiles, clothing, tea
	INDONESIA Jakarta	735,355 (1,904,567.9) 11 22	174,900,000 238 (92) 31/10 2.1	Indonesian, Javanese 62% 58 years	$530 petroleum, natural gas, timber, rubber, coffee, tin, tea
	JAPAN Tokyo	143,749 (372,309.6) 13 76	122,200,000 850 (328) 12/6 0.6	Japanese 99% 77 years	$11,330 machinery, motor vehicles, consumer electronics
	KAMPUCHEA Phnom Penh	69,900 (181,040.9) 17 11	6,500,000 93 (36) 39/18 2.1	Khmer 48% 43 years	N.A. natural rubber, rice, pepper, wood
	KOREA, NORTH P'yŏngyang	46,541 (120,541.1) 19 64	21,400,000 460 (177) 30/5 2.5	Korean 95% 65 years	N.A. minerals, metallurgical products, manufactures
	KOREA, SOUTH Seoul	38,023 (98,479.5) 22 65	42,100,000 1,107 (427) 20/6 1.4	Korean 91% 67 years	$2,180 textiles, clothing, electrical machinery, shoes, steel, cars
	LAOS Vientiane	91,429 (236,800.9) 4 16	3,800,000 42 (16) 41/16 2.5	Lao 85% 50 years	N.A. electric power, forest products, tin, coffee

FLAG	COUNTRY Capital (Largest City)	AREA sq m (sq km) PERCENT ARABLE PERCENT URBAN	POPULATION DEN-SITY sq m (sq km) BIRTH/DEATH RATE ANNUAL GROWTH %	MAJOR LANGUAGES LITERACY RATE LIFE EXPECTANCY	PER CAPITA GNP MAJOR EXPORTS
	MALAYSIA Kuala Lumpur	127,317 (329,750.8) 13 32	16,100,000 126 (49) 31/7 2.4	Malay 65% 67 years	$2,050 natural rubber, tin, palm oil, timber, petroleum
	MALDIVES Male	116 (300.4) 10 26	200,000 1,724 (666) 48/10 3.8	Divehi 36% 51 years	$290 fish products, garments
	MONGOLIA Ulaanbaatar	604,247 (1,564,998.5) 1 51	2,000,000 3 (1) 37/11 2.6	Mongol 80% 62 years	N.A. livestock, wool, animal products, hides, metals
	NEPAL Kathmandu	54,363 (140,800.1) 16 7	17,800,000 327 (126) 42/17 2.5	Nepali 20% 52 years	$160 rice, food products, jute, timber, manufactured goods
	PAKISTAN Islamabad (Karachi)	310,402 (803,940.6) 25 28	104,600,000 337 (130) 44/15 2.9	Urdu, Punjabi, English 24% 50 years	$380 rice, cotton, textiles
	PHILIPPINES Manila	115,830 (299,999.5) 38 40	61,500,000 531 (205) 35/7 2.8	Filipino, English 88% 65 years	$600 coconut products, sugar, lumber, copper, garments
	SINGAPORE Singapore	224 (580.2) 10 100	2,600,000 11,607 (4,481) 17/5 1.1	English, Chinese, Malay, Tamil 84% 71 years	$7,420 manufactured goods, petroleum, rubber, electronics
	SRI LANKA Colombo	25,332 (65,609.8) 34 22	16,300,000 643 (248) 25/7 1.8	Sinhalese, Tamil 87% 70 years	$370 tea, textiles, petroleum products, coconut, rubber
	TAIWAN T'aipei	12,456 (32,261.0) 24 67	19,600,000 1,573 (607) 17/5 1.2	Chinese 94% 73 years	N.A. textiles, metals, electrical machinery, foodstuffs
	THAILAND Bangkok	198,456 (514,000.6) 38 17	53,600,000 270 (104) 29/8 2.1	Thai 82% 63 years	$830 textiles, garments, rice, tapioca, tin, rubber, sugar, fruit
	VIETNAM Hanoi (Ho Chi Minh City)	127,243 (329,559.1) 20 19	62,200,000 489 (189) 34/8 2.6	Vietnamese 78% 63 years	N.A. agricultural & handicraft products, coal
OCEANIA					
	AUSTRALIA Canberra (Sydney)	2,967,896 (7,686,844.7) 6 86	16,200,000 5 (2) 16/8 0.8	English 99% 76 years	$10,840 wheat, barley, beef, lamb, dairy products, wool
	FIJI Suva	7,054 (18,269.8) 13 37	700,000 99 (38) 28/5 2.3	English, Fijian, Hindustani 80% 67 years	$1,700 sugar, copra

FLAG	COUNTRY Capital (Largest City)	AREA sq m (sq km) PERCENT ARABLE PERCENT URBAN	POPULATION DENSITY sq m (sq km) BIRTH/DEATH RATE ANNUAL GROWTH %	MAJOR LANGUAGES LITERACY RATE LIFE EXPECTANCY	PER CAPITA GNP MAJOR EXPORTS
	KIRIBATI Tarawa	264 (683.8) 0 32	66,000 250 (96) 31/11 2.0	English, Gilbertese 90% N.A.	N.A. copra, fish
	NAURU Yaren[5]	8 (20.7) 0 N.A.	9,000 1,125 (435) 23/5 1.8	Nauruan, English 99% N.A.	N.A. phosphates
	NEW ZEALAND Wellington (Auckland)	103,737 (268,678.6) 2 84	3,300,000 32 (12) 16/8 0.8	English, Maori 98% 74 years	$7,310 beef, wool, dairy products
	PAPUA NEW GUINEA Port Moresby	178,259 (461,690.5) 1 13	3,600,000 20 (8) 36/12 2.4	Pidgin, Motu 32% 54 years	$710 gold, copper, logs, coffee, palm oil, cocoa, copra, tea
	SOLOMON ISLANDS Honiara	10,985 (28,451.1) 2 9	300,000 27 (10) 42/6 3.6	English, Pidgin 60% 68 years	$510 copra, timber, fish, palm oil, seashells, shell products
	TONGA Nuku'alofa	288 (745.9) 25 28	99,000 343 (133) 28/5 2.3	Tongan, English 93% 63 years	$730 coconut oil, vanilla, copra, bananas, taro, fruits
	TUVALU Funafuti	10 (25.9) 0 29	8,000 800 (309) 28/11 1.7	Tuvaluan, English 45% 61 years	N.A. copra
	VANUATU Port-Vila	5,699 (14,760.4) 6 18	200,000 35 (13) 39/5 3.3	English, French, Pidgin 15% 68 years	N.A. frozen fish, meat, copra
	WESTERN SAMOA Apia	1,104 (2,859.4) 43 21	200,000 181 (70) 31/7 2.4	Samoan, English 90% 65 years	$660 copra, cocoa, timber, bananas, mineral fuel

[5]Location of government offices; Nauru has no capital city.

MEASUREMENT

The metric conversions of measurements seen in this book were calculated based on factors provided by the Central Intelligence Agency of the United States in *The World Factbook 1987.*

To Convert from English System	To Metric*	Multiply by:
Acres	Hectares (ha)	0.4046856
Degrees, Fahrenheit	Degrees, Celsius (C)	subtract 32 and multiply by 0.555555
Feet	Meters (m)	0.3048
Gallons, US liquid	Liters (l)	3.785412
Inches	Centimeters (cm)	2.54
Miles	Kilometers (km)	1.609344
Miles, square	Kilometers, square (sq km)	2.589998
Pounds	Kilograms (kg)	0.45359237
Tons	Tons, metric	0.907185

*All metric measurements have been rounded to the nearest one-tenth for greater accuracy.

GLOSSARY

A

abdicate give up control of a government or abandon power (p. 420)

abolition act of doing away with (p. 276)

abyssal plain (AH bihs uhl) actual floor of the ocean (p. 73)

acculturation (uh KUHL chuh RAY shuhn) changing a culture by borrowing traits from another; blending or merging of one culture with another (p. 128)

acropolis fortress built at highest point of an ancient Greek city-state for defense of the city (p. 377)

aerial photography method used to study Earth's surface by taking pictures of Earth from the air (p. 32)

alluvial fan (uh LOO vee uhl) cone-shaped landform made by deposits of rock and soil carried to a foot of a slope by moving water (p. 51)

alpine meadow plant cover growing above timberline in elevated mountain slopes (p. 347)

anarchy absence of orderly government; state of lawlessness or political disorder (p. 297)

animism belief that objects and nature have spirits (p. 429)

annexation joining or adding to something earlier, larger, or more important (p. 208)

Antarctic Circle imaginary line circling Earth at 66½° south of the Equator (p. 91)

anthracite hard, black coal of high quality; produces high heat with almost no pollution (p. 349)

anthropologist person who studies science of humans and their cultures (p. 129)

apartheid (uh PAHR TAYT) racial separation; specifically, separate development of the races and political and economic discrimination against non-European groups in South Africa (p. 515)

aquifer body of rocks and soil that holds water between layers of rock (p. 68)

arable fit for plowing and farming (p. 102)

archipelago (AHR kuh PEHL uh goh) group of islands scattered within a large area of the ocean (p. 270)

Arctic Circle imaginary line circling Earth at 66½° north of the Equator (p. 91)

artesian well well drilled deep until water is reached and is forced up from internal pressure (p. 603)

artisan (AHRT uh zuhn) skilled worker or craftsman, such as a potter, tailor, or carpenter; one skilled in a trade (p. 150)

asbestos substance used in making products fireproof and resistant to chemicals (p. 227)

atheist one who believes there is no God (p. 416)

atmosphere air surrounding Earth (p. 8)

atoll (A TAWL) island made up of a coral reef surrounding a body of water called a lagoon (p. 622)

authoritarian having a concentration of power in a leader or group of leaders who rules and makes laws for the people (p. 131)

autobahn (AWT oh BAHN) German expressway; superhighway (p. 349)

azimuthal projection method of mapmaking that is based on projecting a globe's features onto a flat surface from a given point on globe; line drawn from central point to any other point represents shortest distance; type of flat-plane projection (p. 35)

B

balance of trade difference in value between a country's exports and imports (p. 562)

bantustan one of ten areas in South Africa designated by the government as homelands for blacks; each has limited degree of self-government (p. 519)

barge large, flat-bottomed boat used for carrying goods on inland waterways, usually towed (p. 189)

barrier island low, long strip of sand that parallels and protects the shoreline (p. 81)

basin irrigation system of irrigating fields close to rivers in which farmers build mud walls to absorb silt-rich river water when the river floods (p. 433)

bauxite ore used to make aluminum (p. 265)

bayou (BY oo) small, marshy creek or river that is a tributary to another body of water (p. 166)

bazaar place for the sale of goods (p. 433)

bedrock solid rock in the upper layers of Earth's crust beneath soil layers (p. 56)

bilingual able to use two languages (p. 219)

biome (BY OHM) community of plants and animals that live in a particular climate (p. 57)

biosphere layer of Earth in which life exists (p. 7)

birthrate number of live births each year per thousand population (p. 111)

bituminous coal (buh TOO muh nuhs) soft, black coal of lesser quality than anthracite; contains more impurities to pollute the air when heated (p. 349)

black market unlawful trade in goods or services at generally higher than open market prices (p. 409)

bora violent, cold, northerly wind from the mountains during winter in Southeastern Europe (p. 390)

broadleaf forest forest biome in middle-latitude areas with trees having broad leaves such as oak and maple (p. 58)

buffer area between two larger settlements that blocks expansion or reduces conflict between them (p. 205)

bureaucracy (byoo RAHK ruh see) group of government officials, each having special duties and separate authority (p. 408)

C

caatinga (kah TIN gah) semiarid shrub forest of northeastern Brazil (p. 292)

cacao (kuh KOW) tree whose seeds are used to make cocoa, chocolate and cocoa butter (p. 499)

calve (kav) to break or separate an ice mass so that a part becomes detached (p. 633)

campos grassy plain usually surrounded by dense forest (p. 291)

canyon deep, narrow valley with steep sides (p. 53)

cape land jutting out into a body of water (p. 314)

capital city where the main offices of a government are located (p. 24)

cardinal direction one of the chief geographic directions of north, south, east, or west (p. 9)

cartographer (kahr TAHG ruh fuhr) mapmaker (p. 32)

cash crop plant or plant product grown and harvested primarily for market (p. 481)

cassava (kuh SAHV uh) plant grown for its edible roots, which yield a nutritious starch (p. 481)

caste system Hindu division of society into four hereditary social classes, each of which has its own rules for occupation, marriage, and social practices (p. 543)

cataract large waterfall; steep rapids in a river (p. 432)

caudillo (cow DEE yoh) Spanish or Latin American military leader (p. 303)

cay (KEE) small, low island or reef of sand or coral (p. 270)

cede withdraw or give up (p. 207)

census count of population (p. 123)

central business district (CBD) original core or downtown area of city (p. 155)

chapatty flat wheat bread made in Pakistan (p. 547)

château (shah TOH) feudal castle or fortress built in France for king and queen; large country house or mansion (p. 345)

chemical signature trace of known chemical or chemicals found in an unidentified object; sometimes used to identify the object from which it came (p. 638)

chicle (CHEE klay) main ingredient in chewing gum (p. 261)

chromite mineral from which chromium is made; chromic iron oxide (p. 462)

city-state self-governing state consisting of a single city and its surrounding countryside (p. 373)

civilization nation or group of people whose culture includes writing and keeping written records (p. 127)

clan group of families claiming a common ancestor (p. 417)

climate pattern of weather a certain place has over a period of years (p. 85)

clove dried flower bud of a tropical tree; used as a spice (p. 485)

cobalt silver-white magnetic element used in making metals (p. 507)

cocaine illegal narcotic derived from dried leaves of the coca plant whose use can result in psychological dependence (p. 283)

collective farm farmland, especially in a communist country, theoretically owned jointly by farmers, operated under governmental supervision; workers paid from collective profits (p. 384)

colony group of people settling in new country but keeping ties with parent country; land controlled by an outside country (p. 203)

columbite (kuh LUHM BYT) black mineral used in making stainless steel (p. 499)

common market group of countries who agree to remove trade barriers such as tariffs or taxes among members (p. 259)

communism system of government in which an authoritarian party controls the political, economic, cultural, and social life of the people; economic system in which society as a whole owns all means of production, distribution, and exchange of goods (p. 132)

compass magnetic device for finding north (p. 29)

compass rose symbol on a map that shows cardinal and, sometimes intermediate, directions (p. 28)

confederation non-binding political alliance (p. 417)

confluence place where two or more rivers flow together (p. 152)

conformal map one on which parallels and meridians are drawn so an area is shown as closely as possible to its true shape (p. 33)

conic projection method of mapmaking that is based on projecting a globe's features onto the surface of a cone touching along one or two parallels (p. 34)

coniferous forest (koh NIHF uh ruhs) forest biome with evergreen trees having needle-like leaves and bearing cones (p. 58)

conquistador (kohn kees tah DOHR) a leader in the Spanish conquest of Mexico and Peru in the 16th century (p. 322)

conservation careful use and protection of Earth's resources to hinder waste or loss (p. 63)

consistent-scale map one on which parallels and meridians are drawn so the same scale applies in all parts of the map (p. 33)

contiguous (kuhn TIHG yuh wuhs) touching or adjoining throughout in an unbroken sequence (p. 165)

continent one of seven major land areas on Earth (p. 10)

continental glacier wide thick sheets of ice that cover Earth's poles (p. 78)

continental shelf shallow, underwater land surface of varying widths forming a border to a continent and ending in a steep slope to the deep ocean floor (p. 73)

continental slope steep slope from the continental shelf to the ocean floor (p. 73)

contour line one used in maps to connect all points of a land surface at the same elevation (p. 25)

copra (KOH pruh) dried coconut meat, from which coconut oil is extracted (p. 625)

coral reef small, low-lying island or barrier built up over time from skeletons of certain sea animals (p. 173)

cordillera (KAWRD uhl EHR uh) system of mountain ranges consisting of nearly parallel chains (p. 222)

cottage industry industry based in rural home where family members do work with own equipment (p. 543)

crop rotation practice of cultivating different crops in succession on same piece of land to keep up productive capacity of soil (p. 190)

crust outermost layer of Earth's surface under ocean floor and continents; made of rock (p. 46)

cultural diffusion (dihf YOO zhuhn) flowing or carrying of ideas, objects, or behaviors from one culture to another culture where they become part of its way of life (p. 128)

cultural hearth areas from which new objects, ideas, and behaviors spread outward to other cultures (p. 133)

cultural landscape environment as it has been affected by a particular society, including such things as buildings, highways, and pollution (p. 127)

culture total way of life developed by a group of people to satisfy its needs; learned and handed down from generation to generation (p. 127)

culture area large, geographic region in which one or more common culture traits are strong (p. 129)

culture trait characteristic of a culture such as an object, idea, or behavior (p. 129)

cyclone fierce storm or wind system that rotates as it travels (p. 87)

cylindrical projection method of mapmaking that is based on projecting a globe's features onto the surface of a cylinder; parallels and meridians are straight lines at right angles to one another (p. 34)

D

dacha (DAHCH uh) Russian country cottage or summer home (p. 415)

death rate number of deaths each year per thousand population (p. 111)

deforestation clearing of forests (p. 102)

delta landform shaped like a triangle made by deposits of rock and soil carried to a river's mouth by moving water; named after Greek letter, Δ (p. 50)

democracy government in which the people hold political power and rule themselves through the election of representatives and leaders (p. 131)

demographer scientist who studies human population growth (p. 111)

deposition act of laying down in new area rock and soil carried by agents of erosion (p. 50)

desalinization process of removing salt (p. 460)

desert dryland biome with scarce plant life and very low rainfall (p. 59)

desertification process by which fertile farmland becomes desert (p. 102)

developing country one whose economy is based largely on farming and is not yet industrialized (p. 113)

dialect certain version of a language that is spoken in a particular region and has special features of vocabulary, grammar, and pronunciation (p. 132)

distortion to change from its original shape or form (p. 33)

doldrums section of the ocean near the Equator having little or no winds (p. 89)

dome mountain that formed by one tectonic plate sliding under another, causing magma from outer core to push up rock of Earth's crust, forming domes (p. 47)

dominion self-governing nation of the British Commonwealth other than the United Kingdom that acknowledges the British monarch as its chief of state (p. 343)

drought dry period in which little, if any, precipitation falls and often causing extensive damage to crops (p. 95)

dry farming method that enables farmers to grow crops in dry areas without irrigating (p. 190)

dynasty a line of rulers from the same family; a powerful family that holds its influence for a long time (p. 568)

E

earthquake vibrations caused by tectonic movements creating great amounts of heat and energy in Earth's mantle (p. 74)

ecologist (ih KAHL uh juhst) scientist who studies living things and their environments (p. 57)

economic sanction limitation of trade with a country violating international law to force that country to stop violations (p. 526)

economy organized way a country uses its resources to meet needs and wants of its people (p. 112)

elevation distance of land above or below sea level (p. 24)

El Niño (ehl NEEN yoh) change in wind patterns and ocean currents near the Equator (p. 88)

entrepôt (AHN truh POH) place, usually port city, where goods from other countries are stored and re-shipped (p. 592)

environment surroundings including physical, social, and cultural conditions (p. 11)

equal-area map one on which parallels and meridians are drawn so the areas shown have same proportions as they do on Earth (p. 33)

Equator imaginary line that circles Earth halfway between North and South Poles; 0° line of latitude (p. 8)

erg huge area of shifting sand dunes (p. 437)

erosion (ih ROH zhuhn) wearing away of Earth's surface by movement of water, wind, ice, and force of gravity (p. 49)

escarpment (ihs KAHRP muhnt) steep slope or long cliff separating two gently sloping surfaces, often one higher and one lower (p. 291)

estuary (EHS chuh WEHR ee) deep, broad water passage where river meets ocean; water is part salt water and part fresh water (p. 77)

ethnic group people who share a common racial, national, tribal, religious, or cultural background (p. 132)

ethnocentric having the belief that one's own culture, race, or group is superior to others (p. 128)

evaporation process by which water changes from liquid to gas (p. 67)

exact location position of place on Earth where nearest line of latitude crosses nearest line of longitude (p. 9)

expatriate worker person who is a citizen of one country but works in another (p. 365)

F

fado (FAHTH OO) sad Portuguese folk song (p. 365)

fall equinox (EE kwuh NAHKS) time when days and nights are of equal length in both hemispheres; beginning of fall in the Northern Hemisphere and spring in the Southern Hemisphere; September 23 (p. 91)

fall line point on plateau between mountains and sea where land drops sharply, creating falls in rivers crossing plateau (p. 167)

farm belt area of a country where most productive farms are located (p. 190)

fault-block mountain that formed when two tectonic plates slide past each other and make breaks, or faults, in Earth's crust (p. 47)

favela (fah VAY lah) slum (p. 293)

federation system of government in which powers are shared between a central national government and regional governments, each of which controls its own internal affairs (p. 234)

fellahin (fehl uh HEEN) peasants or farm laborers in an Arab country (p. 433)

fieldwork study conducted by directly observing subject (p. 15)

firth funnel-shaped bay; arm of the sea at lower end of a river (p. 337)

five-year plan economic goals set forth by communist government for production, wages, and prices (p. 408)

fjord (fee AWRD) narrow, winding inlet of the sea between cliffs or steep slopes (p. 222)

flat-plane projection method of mapmaking based on projecting globe's features onto flat surface from point at center or on surface of globe (p. 35)

flax plant whose fibers are used for making linen thread and cloth (p. 410)

floodplain flat, low-lying area of fertile soil made by soil deposits left in river basin after flood (p. 52)

fodder feed for livestock (p. 190)

folded mountain that formed when tectonic forces press against Earth's crust, making waves of mountains (p. 46)

fossil fuel fuel such as coal, oil, or natural gas formed from plant or animal remains (p. 227)

free enterprise freedom of private businesses and individuals to operate for profit with little interference from government (p. 131)

free port port city where goods are received and shipped without taxes or customs duty (p. 592)

G

generalization statement that describes a basic relationship or condition that exists between two or more things (p. 15)

general reference map one that gives basic information about an area or place such as location, size, physical features, political boundaries, and distance from other places (p. 24)

geographic grid crisscross system of parallels and meridians used on globe or map (p. 28)

geography study of Earth and people who live on it (p. 6)

geologist (jee AHL uh juhst) scientist who studies the history of Earth and its life (p. 45)

ghetto part of a city inhabited largely by minorities because of social, legal, or economic pressure (p. 155)

ghost town previously flourishing settlement totally deserted (p. 211)

glacier river of slowly moving ice (p. 50)

glen deep, narrow, secluded valley (p. 337)

global interdependence situation in which people in one part of the world rely on people in other parts of the world for necessities, such as natural resources and agricultural or manufactured products (p. 18)

gnomonic projection (noh MAHN ihk) flat-plane projection on which a straight line drawn between two places indicates a great-circle route (p. 35)

graphite soft, black carbon used in pencil lead; conducts electricity and is used in electrical wiring (p. 355)

great circle imaginary line that circles globe and divides it into two equal parts (p. 35)

greenhouse effect process by which water vapor and carbon dioxide in the atmosphere absorb and reflect infrared rays, thus warming Earth's surface (p. 86)

gross domestic product total value of all goods and services produced per year by residents of a country for their own use; GDP (p. 361)

gross national product total value of all goods and services produced by residents of a country in one year; GNP (p. 112)

groundwater water that moves through soil and fills spaces between layers of rock (p. 68)

guano excrement of sea birds; used as fertilizer (p. 319)

guerrilla warfare irregular warfare against an enemy; usually carried out by independent soldiers who harass the enemy by surprise attacks (p. 586)

gum arabic gum from acacia trees, used in making candy, medicine, perfume, and adhesives (p. 433)

H

hacienda (ah see EHN dah) large, farming establishment in the country (p. 319)

hajj Muslim pilgrimage to Mecca (p. 460)

harmattan (HAHR muh TAN) hot, dry, dusty wind blowing from the Sahara (p. 499)

hemisphere one half of a divided Earth (p. 9)

hieroglyphic (HY uh ruh GLIHF ihk) picture-writing of the ancient Egyptians (p. 435)

high island large island of highlands made from volcanic tectonic movement (p. 620)

high latitudes regions from 60° north latitude to the North Pole and from 60° south latitude to the South Pole (p. 90)

high-technology industry one that uses or produces advanced or sophisticated devices, especially in the area of electronics and computers (p. 185)

highveld grass-covered, high-elevation plateau (p. 516)

hill landform that rises above surrounding land, with altitudes ranging from 500 feet (152.5 m) above sea level to less than 2,000 feet (609.6 m) above sea level and local relief less than 1,000 feet (304.8 m) (p. 53)

hill-land economy efficient use of resources by farming in valleys and livestock grazing on hills (p. 375)

hinterland (HIHN tehr land) area from which a city gets its farm products and raw materials and to which it exports goods; area far from urban areas (p. 152)

hollow narrow valley or basin in a hilly or mountainous area (p. 193)

homesteader settler granted a tract of land to farm and improve for a period of time (p. 211)

homogeneous of the same or similar nature, character, or kind (p. 313)

human geography study of people on Earth and their activities within their environment (p. 11)

humidity water vapor in the air (p. 87)

humus (HYOO mus) dark brown or black material in upper layers of soil, made up of dead or decaying plants and animals; topsoil (p. 55)

hurricane fierce, tropical storm with winds of 74 miles (119.1 km) per hour or greater (p. 87)

hydroelectric power electricity produced by water turning turbines (p. 225)

hydrosphere (HY druh SFIHR) waters of Earth's biosphere including bodies of water, groundwater, snow and ice, and water in atmosphere (p. 8)

hypothesis (hy PAHTH uh suhs) proposed generalization that is tested to see if it is true (p. 17)

I

ice shelf sheet of floating ice, protruding from land-supported ice cap into the ocean (p. 633)

incorporate to unite in one body with legal boundaries, powers, rights, and liabilities; to organize as a legal corporation (p. 145)

indentured servant person who agrees to work for employer for specified time in return for travel and living expenses (p. 204)

indigenous (ihn DIHJ uh nuhs) native; originating in a particular country (p. 484)

industrialized country one whose economy is based on manufacturing and is highly developed (p. 112)

inflation increase in amount of money and credit in relation to available goods, resulting in steeply rising prices (p. 351)

infrared radiation heat waves of lengths longer than those wavelengths of visible light (p. 86)

inner city usually older section of city that surrounds the central business district (p. 155)

inner core center of Earth made of very hot solid iron and nickel (p. 46)

intensive cultivation farming system characterized by complete use of every piece of arable land (p. 560)

interior drainage area in which streams or rivers flow into lakes or basins within region rather than to rivers or ocean outside region (p. 172)

intermediate directions geographic directions of northeast, southeast, northwest, or southwest (p. 9)

International Date Line imaginary line that follows along most of 180° line of longitude, marking where new calendar day begins (p. 9)

irrigation process of transporting water to dry land areas by canals or pipes (p. 68)

islet (EYE luht) small island (p. 623)

isthmus (IHS muhs) narrow piece of land connecting two larger land areas (p. 247)

685

J

jet stream long, narrow belt of high-speed winds traveling from west to east (p. 90)

jungle dense growth of tropical vegetation (p. 502)

junta (HOON tuh) group of leaders controlling a government after revolutionary seizure of power (p. 317)

jute glossy plant fiber used to make burlap bags and twine (p. 542)

K

karst irregular limestone area with steep, jagged hills, caverns, and streams (p. 564)

kibbutz collective farm or settlement in Israel (p. 455)

kolkhoz (kahl KAWZ) collective farm of the Soviet Union; owned and managed by the government but workers who live and work there share profits (p. 411)

krill tiny, shrimp-like shellfish that exists in huge quantities in Antarctic waters (p. 637)

L

ladino (luh DEE noh) Spanish-speaking Latin American who has taken on aspects of European culture (p. 261)

lagoon shallow sound, pond, or channel of water near or connected to a larger body of water (p. 166)

lake small body of fresh water surrounded by land (p. 76)

land breeze cool air blowing out to sea at night (p. 92)

landform individual physical feature in Earth's landscape (p. 45)

landlocked enclosed or nearly enclosed by land (p. 306)

landscape total scenery of region including its land, soil, plants, and animals (p. 45)

language family group of languages that come from a common language (p. 132)

large-scale map one that shows many details about small area (p. 29)

latitude imaginary lines on Earth for measuring distance north and south of Equator; measured in degrees, minutes, and seconds (p. 8)

lava molten rock, or magma, from outer core that reaches Earth's surface, especially during volcanic eruption (p. 47)

leeward side that faces away from wind (p. 94)

legend part of map that explains the colors, patterns, and symbols used on it (p. 28)

levee (LEHV ee) ridge built to prevent flooding; landing place along a river—pier (p. 81)

life expectancy probable average life span of people born in a given area (p. 112)

lignite soft, brown coal of lesser quality than bituminous coal but higher than peat; gives off less energy than black coal (p. 349)

literacy rate percentage of people in a given place who can read and write their own language (p. 137)

lithosphere (LIHTH uh SFIHR) land area of Earth's biosphere including outer crust (p. 8)

loch (LAHK) long, narrow lake in Scotland; arm of sea when nearly landlocked (p. 337)

loess (LEHS) fine-grained, yellowish-brown silt deposited by wind (p. 301)

longitude imaginary lines on Earth for measuring distance east and west of Prime Meridian; measured in degrees, minutes, and seconds (p. 8)

low island generally small island made of coral; barely rises above sea level; poor soil, little fresh water, and little plant life (p. 622)

low latitudes areas close to Equator ranging from 30° north latitude to 30° south latitude (p. 87)

M

magma hot molten rock from Earth's outer core (p. 46)

magnetic north pole northern point of Earth's magnetic field (p. 29)

malnutrition inadequate nourishment (p. 119)

manifest destiny belief that began in 1830s that United States would expand its territory from Atlantic to Pacific Oceans (p. 211)

mantle thick layer of hot solid rock between Earth's core and crust that extends for 1,800 miles (2,897 km) below Earth's surface (p. 46)

marine relating to the sea (p. 98)

marsh area of soft, wet land, often filled with grasses or cattails (p. 81)

mass movement natural motion of rock and soil down slopes due to gravity (p. 50)

megalopolis (MEHG uh LAH puh luhs) huge continuous urban area including number of cities (p. 188)

menhaden (mehn HAY duhn) fish caught along Atlantic coast of United States; used as bait or to produce fertilizer and fish oil (p. 192)

meridian (muh RIHD ee uhn) line of longitude (p. 8)

mestizo (meh STEE zoh) person of mixed European and Native American ancestry (p. 253)

metropolitan area (MEH truh PAHL uh tuhn) central city and closely related communities around it (p. 145)

Metropolitan Statistical Area (MSA) term used by The Bureau of the Census for a metropolitan area in the United States (p. 145)

microorganism (MY kroh AWR guh NIHZ uhm) organism or animal so small it can be seen only through a microscope (p. 638)

middle-latitude grassland grassland biome in areas with hot-summer and cold-winter climates; prairie or steppe (p. 59)

middle latitudes those areas of Earth between about 30° and 60° north latitude or between 30° and 60° south latitude (p. 34)

midocean ridge continuous mountainous ridge on floor of major ocean basins (p. 73)

migration movement of people from one country, place, or locality to another (p. 123)

minaret tower attached to mosque and surrounded by one or more balconies from which criers call Muslims to prayer five times a day (p. 467)

mission religious settlement (p. 206)

molybdenum (muh LIHB duh nuhm) mineral used especially to strengthen and harden steel (p. 196)

monarchy (MAHN uhr kee) government having king or queen as chief of state; nation having undivided rule by one person (p. 345)

monsoon (mahn SOON) periodic change in wind pattern in Pacific and southeastern Asia characterized by heavy rainfall (p. 95)

moor landscape characterized by open, treeless, infertile land, dominated by grasses and shrubs (p. 337)

moshav cooperative settlement of small, individually owned farms in Israel (p. 455)

mosque (MAHSK) building used by Muslims for public worship (p. 463)

mountain landform that rises sharply above surrounding land, with altitude of at least 2,000 feet (609.6 m) high and local relief of more than 1,000 feet (304.8 m) (p. 46)

mouth place where stream empties into larger body of water (p. 77)

mulatto person of mixed African and European ancestry (p. 277)

muskeg land that is swampy and infested with insects in summer and frozen hard in winter; bog, especially in northern North America (p. 173)

mutton meat of mature sheep; used for food (p. 462)

N

nation community of people possessing a territory and government of its own (p. 130)

nationalism belief that people who consider themselves a nation should have their own land and government; loyalty to nation (p. 132)

nitrate salt compound that dissolves in water but remains dry on top of a desert area; used to make explosives and fertilizers (p. 313)

nonferrous ore mineral that does not contain iron (p. 349)

O

oasis fertile land amid desert (p. 318)

opera drama having most of its script set to music; made up of vocal pieces, orchestra accompaniment, and usually elaborate costumes (p. 372)

orient to align or position map in same direction as land it represents (p. 29)

orographic effect (OHR uh GRAF ihk) precipitation caused by air moving up and over mountains (p. 93)

outback isolated rural country, especially of Australia's interior (p. 605)

outer core molten iron and nickel center of Earth that lies between solid inner core and mantle (p. 46)

P

paddy wet land in which rice is grown; rice field (p. 582)

pampero violent thunderstorm and fierce wind from the west or southwest that sweeps over Pampas of Argentina (p. 301)

papyrus (puh PY ruhs) reed-like plant used in making paper (p. 435)

parallel line of latitude (p. 8)

parent material original rock material from which soil is made; weathered rocks or bedrock (p. 55)

parliamentary democracy form of government in which power is vested in the people and exercised by them indirectly through Parliament, or the legislature (p. 342)

pasta paste made from flour and water and processed, as spaghetti, or shaped into dough, as ravioli (p. 372)

pastoralist (PAS tuh ruh luhst) one who is devoted to raising livestock (p. 483)

peat bog area of wet ground composed of various decaying plants (p. 222)

penal colony (PEEN uhl) settlement for criminals; place of confinement and punishment (p. 609)

peninsula piece of land jutting out into a body of water; having water on three sides (p. 247)

periodic market one held every few days by traveling merchants in rural area; goods are bartered (p. 502)

permafrost permanently frozen layer of soil beneath ground in cold regions (p. 60)

photogrammetry use of aerial photography for studying and measuring Earth (p. 32)

physical anthropologist one who studies the early development of humans through observation and measurement (p. 483)

physical geography study of Earth itself including things not made by people, such as plants and animals (p. 11)

pidgin language made up of local words and words borrowed and adapted from other languages (p. 621)

pioneer one of the first to settle in a territory (p. 206)

plain landform with mostly level land and elevation of no more than 1,000 feet (304.8 m) above sea level with local relief of less than 300 feet (91.4 m) (p. 51)

plankton microscopic plant and animal organism of the sea that floats in water near the surface and serves as food for fish (p. 319)

planned economy economic system organized so a central authority sets goals that determine what and how much the country will produce and distribute (p. 381)

plantation system farming estates specializing in single crops and worked by resident or slave labor (p. 204)

plant community group of plants that needs a similar environment to grow (p. 57)

plateau broad, level landform that has high relief and higher elevation than surrounding land with steep cliffs on at least one side and usually close to or surrounded by mountains; elevations range from 300 feet (91.4 m) to more than 3,000 feet (914.4 m) above sea level (p. 52)

plate tectonics theory that explains movements of continents and changes in Earth's crust caused by forces within Earth's structure (p. 46)

pluralistic having different cultural groups keep many of their traditional customs within the boundaries of a common civilization (p. 183)

pocket settlement settling at individual locations instead of within a large area (p. 211)

polar easterlies prevailing winds blowing from the east near the North or South Pole (p. 90)

polder low area of land drained of water and surrounded by dikes (p. 348)

population density average number of persons living in a given area (p. 116)

population distribution pattern established by numbers of people settling in various places throughout the world (p. 116)

population explosion sudden, tremendous growth in numbers of people (p. 112)

population pyramid graph used to show ages and percentages of men and women in a country (p. 115)

potash potassium or potassium compound used to make fertilizer (p. 228)

precipitation any of forms in which water falls on Earth's surface, such as rain, sleet, snow, or hail (p. 67)

prejudice irrational attitude of hostility or dislike directed against groups or individuals (p. 214)

presidio military post or fort in area originally controlled by Spain (p. 206)

prevailing westerlies winds blowing from the west in the middle latitudes (p. 90)

primary landform that made originally by movement of tectonic plates on Earth's crust; e.g. mountains (p. 46)

Prime Meridian imaginary line crossing through Greenwich, England, that serves as point of reference for lines of longitude; 0° line of longitude (p. 8)

projection process of transferring Earth's features from globe onto flat surface of map (p. 34)

protectorate country under the partial control and protection of politically stronger country (p. 436)

pyrethrum (py REE thruhm) type of chrysanthemum from which insecticide is made (p. 485)

Q

qanat (kah NAHT) underground tunnel to bring water from hills to plains (p. 467)

quinoa grain from which cereal is made (p. 325)

R

refugee person who flees to a foreign country to escape oppression, persecution, or danger (p. 215)

region geographical area that has similar characteristics (p. 14)

regional method geographic study of many features of single world region (p. 14)

reincarnation rebirth after death into new bodies or forms of life (p. 543)

relative humidity comparison between amount of moisture in air at certain temperature and amount air could hold at that temperature (p. 87)

relative location position of place on Earth as compared with another place or places (p. 9)

relief difference found between lowest and highest elevation in area (p. 25)

remote sensing kind of photography by highly sensitive cameras in satellites that transmit images to receiving stations on Earth (p. 32)

representative fraction (RF) fraction or ratio that shows the relationship between inches (or centimeters) on map's scale and actual number of inches (or centimeters) on Earth (p. 28)

reservation public land area set aside for use of Native Americans by government (p. 215)

rift crack or separation in Earth's crust (p. 73)

royalist supporter of rule by king or queen (p. 377)

S

salt flat low-lying areas where body of water has dried up, leaving salt deposits (p. 312)

satellite country country that depends on another more powerful country for political and economic leadership (p. 381)

scale relationship between unit of measure on map or model and unit of measure on Earth; line on map that shows this relationship (p. 28)

sea large body of salt water that is surrounded by land except for a narrow opening to ocean (p. 70)

sea breeze cool air blowing inland from sea during day (p. 92)

seafloor spreading ocean floor spreading apart when oceanic plates move away from each other (p. 73)

sea level position on land equal to surface of nearby ocean or sea; used as point of reference for measuring elevation and ocean depth (p. 24)

seamount volcano that forms on sides of midocean ridges and along abyssal plain (p. 74)

season one of four different times of year when a certain amount of sun's energy reaches Earth; spring, summer, fall, winter (p. 90)

secondary landform that made from wearing down of primary landforms (p. 51)

sect religious group believing in particular doctrine or leader; group within a larger group (p. 467)

selva dense, tropical rain forest (p. 291)

semiarid receiving little rainfall: about 10 to 20 inches per year (p. 102)

separatist person who supports independence for part of a nation or political unit (p. 236)

serf member of the lowest feudal class; laborer bound to the land and subject to a noble (p. 419)

service industry business that sells service rather than tangible product (p. 186)

shadoof long pole with bucket on one end, weight on other, and balanced in the middle; used for raising water (p. 433)

shah sovereign or king of Iran (p. 467)

shifting cultivation farming method in which farmers burn forests to clear land, plant, and harvest for 1-2 years, then move on to another piece of land, giving first plot chance for nutrients to return to soil; also known as slash-and-burn (p. 262)

shogun one of line of military governors ruling Japan until revolution of 1867-68 (p. 561)

shrub forest forest biome in dry middle-latitude areas with mostly shrub and other low-lying plants (p. 58)

silicon chip component important in manufacture of electronic equipment (p. 198)

silvaculture growing trees for business (p. 582)

sisal (SY suhl) plant whose strong, durable, white fiber is used to make rope (p. 293)

site exact area of ground on which city is built; location, scene, or point of something (p. 152)

situation city's relationship with its surrounding area; way in which something is placed in relation to its surroundings (p. 152)

slum usually urban area characterized by poverty, crowding, and run-down housing (p. 156)

small-scale map one that shows few details about large area (p. 29)

smog fog combined with smoke and chemical fumes (p. 103)

socialism economic system in which government partly owns and controls production and distribution of goods (p. 366)

soil horizon one of four layers of soil that have particular characteristics; Horizon O, A, B, or C (p. 55)

soil profile vertical cross section of soil that shows each of its horizons (p. 55)

sorghum grain used mainly as food for livestock (p. 193)

source point where river begins (p. 76)

soviet council of workers and soldiers set up to bring needs to communist government; governing councils in Soviet Union (p. 420)

sovkhoz (sahf KAWZ) huge state farm of Soviet Union (p. 411)

spatial interaction (SPAY shuhl) relationship between people and places on Earth and between one place or group of places and another place or group of places (p. 6)

sphere of influence area over which a powerful nation has political control (p. 442)

spring equinox time when days and nights are of equal length in both hemispheres; beginning of spring in Northern Hemisphere and fall in Southern Hemisphere; March 21 (p. 91)

squatter settlement unauthorized settlement on land settlers do not own (p. 157)

standard of living minimum comforts, necessities, and luxuries thought necessary to maintain certain quality of life (p. 112)

standard parallel line of latitude used in conic projection along which there is least distortion (p. 34)

state farm one associated with communist economies that is owned and managed by government (p. 384)

stream body of water that drains water from land area; e.g. river (p. 76)

subarctic area near Arctic Circle; located between 50° and 70° north latitude (p. 99)

subcontinent landmass of great size, but smaller than continent (p. 539)

subsidiary company controlled by another (p. 231)

subsistence crop plant or plant product grown and harvested primarily for farm family's own use (p. 481)

subsistence farmer one whose farm provides all or almost all of goods needed by farm family without surplus left to sell (p. 123)

subtropical near or bordering the tropics (p. 96)

suburb smaller community, often with its own government, close to city; residential area on the outskirts of city (p. 145)

summer solstice (SAHL stuhs) day with longest period of daylight in Northern Hemisphere and shortest period in Southern Hemisphere; June 22 (p. 91)

surveying method of determining land area by measuring points and boundaries on Earth's surface (p. 32)

T

tannin substance from quebracho tree which has tanning effect and is used in tanning leather and making dyes (p. 302)

taro (TAHR oh) tropical plant grown in Pacific Islands; underground stems are edible (p. 627)

teak hard, yellowish-brown wood used for shipbuilding and making fine furniture (p. 551)

technology use of scientific knowledge and skills, including all tools, machines, and processes, to provide objects necessary for human sustenance and comfort (p. 63)

tectonic activity movement of Earth's crust—tectonic plates—due to pressure from inside Earth's structure (p. 46)

terrace to cut flat area out of hillside for purpose of farming (p. 560)

thematic map one that gives specific information on single topic (p. 25)

theocracy government by officials who are thought to be divinely guided (p. 467)

thermal pollution discharge of dangerously hot liquid such as wastewater from factory into natural waters (p. 79)

threshold population minimum number of people needed to financially support certain functions, businesses, and services (p. 340)

tidal flats level areas of muddy land formed by ocean tides along coast (p. 348)

tide regular rising and falling of ocean surface and of water bodies connected to ocean that occur twice a day and are caused by gravitational attraction of sun and moon (p. 71)

tierra caliente (tee AY rrah kah lee AYN teh) lands at sea level to 1,500 feet (457.2 m) above sea level; Spanish for "hot country" (p. 248)

tierra fría (FREE ah) lands rising over 6,001 feet (1,829.1 m) above sea level; Spanish for "cold country" (p. 248)

tierra templada (tehm PLAH dah) lands between 1,501 feet (457.5 m) and 6,000 feet (1,828.8 m) above sea level; Spanish for "temperate country" (p. 248)

timberline upper limit of where trees can grow on mountains or in high-latitude areas (p. 230)

topical method geographic study in which one subject is observed and analyzed in one, several, or many world regions (p. 14)

topography (tuh PAHG ruh fee) shape or contour of land's surface including relief and other physical and cultural features of the land (p. 25)

tourism industry of traveling for recreation (p. 198)

township local unit of government in United States; in South Africa, special area outside city set aside for blacks (p. 519)

trade winds prevailing winds in low latitudes, blowing almost continually toward Equator (p. 89)

transpiration process by which plants give off water vapor (p. 68)

trench deep ditch on ocean floor formed by tectonic movement (p. 74)

tributary stream that flows into larger stream (p. 76)

tropical rain forest forest biome in areas near Equator where rainfall is high; broadleaf trees and many varieties of other plant life stay evergreen year-round (p. 57)

tropical savanna grassland biome in which grasses grow in clumps, and trees and shrubs are scattered; found in climates where there are rainy and dry seasons (p. 59)

Tropic of Cancer line of latitude 23½° north of Equator and farthest north that overhead sun reaches (p. 91)

Tropic of Capricorn line of latitude 23½° south of Equator and farthest south that overhead sun reaches (p. 91)

tropics region of Earth near Equator lying between Tropic of Cancer and Tropic of Capricorn (p. 94)

truck farm farm whose purpose is to produce vegetables for market (p. 229)

true-compass direction map one on which parallels and meridians are drawn as straight lines that follow cardinal directions as correctly as possible (p. 33)

tsar emperor; specifically, title given to rulers of Russia from late 1400s until early 1917 revolts (p. 418)

tsetse fly (TSEHT see) African insect of which one species is a carrier of sleeping sickness and another is a carrier of nagana (p. 486)

tsunami (su NAHM ee) seismic sea waves often carrying huge amounts of water to shoreline; caused by earthquakes (p. 74)

tundra dryland biome of high-latitude areas in which little plant life grows due to year-round cold temperatures; found in Arctic region and on mountains (p. 60)

typhoon fierce storm or hurricane which forms in Pacific Ocean or China Sea (p. 87)

U

upwelling movement of water from ocean bottom to top and then outward (p. 75)

urban characteristic of city; describes places in which most people make their living in ways other than farming (p. 145)

urban heat island condition of cities in which environment creates warmer temperatures than neighboring rural areas (p. 155)

urbanization (UHR buh nuh ZAY shuhn) trend toward greater percentage of population living in cities; state of becoming more like city (p. 150)

urban sprawl irregular growth pattern of urban areas, caused by lack of planning and coordination of development (p. 300)

V

valley low, level land between two areas of higher elevation such as mountains or hills (p. 50)

valley glacier long, narrow body of ice that flows downhill from mountains into valleys (p. 78)

vaquero (vah KAYR oh) cowhand of Brazil (p. 293)

volcano mountain formed when one tectonic plate slides under another, creating enough pressure to push magma through weak part of mantle; lava and ash pile up in layers on Earth's surface, forming volcano (p. 47)

volcanologist (VAHL kuh NAHL uh juhst) scientist who studies volcanoes (p. 588)

voodoo religion derived from ancient African practice of ancestor worship characterized by spells, trances, and use of charms (p. 280)

W

wadi bed or valley of stream that is usually dry except during rainy season (p. 437)

water cycle process by which Earth's surface water constantly changes its state and location (p. 67)

water table top layer of rock and soil that holds water between layers of rock (p. 68)

water vapor water in gaseous state (p. 67)

weather condition of atmosphere at given time and location (p. 85)

weathering breaking down of rock and soil by pushing or rubbing against other rocks, by interference from plants and animals, and by chemical action (p. 49)

windward side which faces wind (p. 94)

winter solstice (SAHL stuhs) day with shortest period of daylight in Northern Hemisphere and longest period in Southern Hemisphere; December 22 (p. 91)

XYZ

yerba mate (YEHR bah MAH tay) tea-like beverage popular in many parts of South America (p. 295)

zero population growth (ZPG) condition of country's birthrate equalling death rate (p. 113)

zone of transition area that is similar in some ways to areas on each side (p. 443)

INDEX

Erzgebirge (EHRTS guh BIHR guh) Mountains, 383
Esfahān, 467
Eskimos, 230
Essen, 349
Estonians, 412-413
estuaries, 77, 81
Ethiopia (EE thee OH pee uh), 488-489
Ethiopian Orthodox Church, 488
ethnic groups, 132; in Bolivia, 324; in Brazil, 295; in Canada, 219, 229, 230, 231, 233; in Caribbean, 269; in Central Africa, 511; in Central America, 261, 264, 265; in Chile, 315; in China, 567; in East African Highlands, 491; in East Europe, 391, 392, 394, 395; in Ethiopia, 488; in India, 543; in Israel, 455; in Kenya, 483; in New Zealand, 613; in Nigeria, 499; in Peru, 320-321; in South Africa, 519, 521, 523; in Southeast Asia, 591; in the Soviet Union, 411-414; in Tanzania, 486; in United States, 213-215; in Uruguay, 307; in West Indies, 269, 272-273, 275; in Zimbabwe, 526
Etna, Mount, 368
Euphrates River, 133, 461-462, 469
Eurasia, 10
Europe, 10, 333-425; climate in, 97-98; culture in, 132; population distribution, 116. *See also countries in;* Northeastern Europe; Southeastern Europe; Western Europe
European plain, 403
Europeans, immigration to United States, 213-214
Everest, Mount, 541

F

Falkland Islands, 305
Falkland Ocean Current, 301
farming. *See* agriculture
Farsi, 467
faults, 47
Federal Republic of Germany, 347; 351. *See also* West Germany
Federated States of Micronesia, 619, 623
fellahin, 433
Ferdinand of Aragon, 366
Fertile Crescent, 468, 469
Fiji (FEE JEE), 619, 621, 622
Finland, 353, 355; climate in, 99
Finland, Gulf of, 410
fire, discovery and use of, 127
fishing: in Belize, 261; in Canada, 224, 229; in Chile, 315, 319; in Greece, 375; in Iberian Peninsula, 362; in Japan, 560; in Mexico, 249; in Peru, 319; in South Africa, 519; in United States, 185, 192, 197
Flinders Range, 603

Florence, 372, 373
Florida, 174, 176, 192, 193, 205, 214, 216
Florida Cession, 207
fodder, 190, 612
food supply, and population growth, 119, 120, 121-122
forest biomes, 57-59
Forth River, 337
Fouta Djallon (FOO tuh juh LOHN) Mountains, 502
France, 343; in Algeria, 442; climate of, 344; economy of, 344-345; exploration and colonization by, 203-204, 275, 442, 503, 528, 585-586; history of, 345, 347; landforms of, 343-344; population distribution, 116, 345
Franco, Francisco, 367
Franks, 345
Fraser River, 222, 229
free enterprise, 131, 183
French and Indian War, 233
French Guiana (gee AH nuh), 269, 284, 285, 291
French Polynesia, 619, 626, 627, 629
French West Africa, 503
Fuji, Mount, 558
Fulani, 500
Fundy, Bay of, 71
Futuna. *See also* Wallis and

G

Gabon (ga BOHN), 497, 511
Gadsden, James, 209
Gadsden Purchase, 209
Galápagos (gah LAH pah gohs) Islands, 326
Galicia, 364, 365
Galilee, Sea of, 453
Gambia (GAM bee uh), 497, 503
Gambia River, 502
Gandhi, Mohandas (GAHN dee, moh HAHN das), 545-546
Ganges (GAN JEEZ) Plain, 541
Ganges River, 116, 541, 543, 544, 551
Garda Lake, 367
Gary, Indiana, 190
Gauls, 345
Gautama, Siddhartha, 137
generalization, making, 354; as step in geography inquiry, 15, 17
Geneva, 355
Genoa, 369, 372, 373
geographers, activities of, 6-7
geographic centers, 210
geography, 5-20; and aerial analysis, 146; asking effective questions, 41; definition of, 6-10; describing locations, 12; human, 11; importance of places, 7-10; kinds of, 11-12; making hypotheses in, 540; making observations in, 154; physical, 11;

study of, 3, 5, 14-15, 17; value of, 17-19
geologists, 45
Georgetown, 284
Georgia, 167, 192, 204
Georgians, 413, 418
Gerlachovka (gehr luh KAWF kuh), 383
German Democratic Republic, 352, 383. *See also* East Germany
Ghana (GAH nuh), 497, 503; deforestation in, 102
Ghana Empire, 446, 502
Gila River, 209
Giles, Herbert A., 566
Gilf el Kebir Plateau (JIHLF ehl kuh BEER), 431
glaciers, 50, 78
global interdependence, 1, 18-19
Gloucester, 185
Gobi, 564
Golan (GOH LAWN) Heights, 452
gold, in Australia, 605; in California, 211; in Central Africa, 507; in China, 565; in South Africa, 523; in South America, 293, 315
Gold Coast, 503
Goodyear, Charles, 294
government, in Anglo-America, 131; in Australia/New Zealand, 140; in East Asia, 137; in Eastern Europe, 132; in Latin America, 131; in South Asia, 136; in urban areas, 148; in Western Europe, 132
Goya, Francisco José de, 365
Granada, 366
Gran Chaco, 306, 323
Grand Banks, 224
Grand Canyon, 172
graphic skills. *See listing on p. ix*
graphs, bar, 324, 362; circle, 72; comparing data from maps and, 138; line, 362
grassland biomes, 59
gravity, 5; effect of, on oceans, 71; and glacier movement, 78
Great Artesian Basin, 603
Great Australian Bight, 602
Great Barrier Reef, 602
Great Britain, 336. *See also* British Isles; United Kingdom
Great Dividing Range, 603
Greater Antilles, 269, 270
Great Escarpment, 291
Great European Plain, 337, 344
Great Dyke, 524
Great Lakes, 76, 189, 227, 232; climate in, 177
Great Plains, 51, 177, 190
Great Rift Valley, 453, 488, 506
Great Salt Lake, 76
Great Trek, 523
Greece, 374; climate, 375; culture of, 376-377; economy of, 375-376; history of, 377; landforms, 374-375
Greenland, 353; climate in, 99

Kenya, 481; in Pacific Islands, 625, 629; in Saudi Arabia, 460; in Seychelles, 529; in United States, 198; in West Indies, 272, 277

trade, in Central America, 259; in Greece, 375; and growth of cities, 149-150; in Mexico, 250; in urban areas, 148-149. *See also* economy

trade winds, 88, 89-90

Trans-American Highway, 293

Transantarctic Range, 634

transportation, in Central America, 259-260; in France, 345; in the United States, 212; in urban areas, 148

transportation maps, reading, 296

Trans-Siberian Railroad, 419

Transvaal, 517, 519

Transylvanian Alps, 389

Trieste, 372

Trinidad, 269, 271

Tripoli, 438, 442

tropical moist climates, 94-95, 174, 499, 510, 527, 581

tropical monsoon climate, 95, 271, 604

tropical rain forest climate, 57-58, 95, 174, 258, 281, 292, 318, 325, 504, 506, 589, 620, 623, 627

tropical savanna climate, 59, 95, 174, 258, 271, 281, 306, 325, 432, 485, 502, 506, 524, 581, 603, 620

Tropic of Cancer, 91, 94, 96, 174

Tropic of Capricorn, 91, 94, 96

tropics, 91

Truk, 623, 626

Tshiluba (chih LOO buh), 508

tsunami (su NAHM ee), 74

Tula, 253

Tulsa, Oklahoma, 193

tundra climate, 60, 99, 179, 223

Tunis, 442

Tunisia, 429, 437; climate, 437; landforms of, 437

Tupí, 297

Turin, 148, 369, 372

Turkey, 374, 451, 461; climate of, 462; culture of, 463; economy of, 462-463; history of, 464; landforms of, 461-462; population of, 451, 463

Turkish Straits, 461

Turkmen Soviet Socialist Republic, 414

Turkomans, in Iran, 468

Tuvalu (too VAHL oo), 619, 629

typhoons, 87, 589

Tyrrhenian (tuh REE nee uhn) **Sea,** 367

U

Ucayali (oo kah YAH lee) **River,** 318

Uganda, 479, 490-491

Ukraine, 410, 412

Ukrainian Soviet Socialist Republic, 412

Ulaanbaatar (YOO LAHN BAH TAWR), 573

Ulyanov, Vladimir Ilyich, 420

Union of Soviet Socialist Republics (U.S.S.R.). *See* Soviet Union

United Arab Emirates, 451, 471

United Empire Loyalists, 234

United Kingdom, 233, 335-343. *See also* British Isles

United Provinces of Central America, 260

United States, 165-179, 183-200, 203-216; agriculture in, 184-185, 190-191, 192-193, 195-198; 204; Appalachian Highlands, 166-168, 169; area, 165; Central Uplands and Lowlands, 165, 173; climate patterns, 174-179; Coastal Plains, 165-166; colonial settlement of, 203-206; economy in, 183, 185, 190, 192-193; ethnic groups in, 213-215; fishing in, 185, 192, 197; immigration, 212; industry in, 183, 185-186, 190, 191, 192-193, 196, 197, 198, 212; Interior Highlands, 165, 169-170; Interior Plains, 165, 169; Intermontane Plateaus and Basins, 165, 172; landforms in, 165-169, 171-173; Middle Atlantic region, 185-190, natural resources in, 185, 189, 190, 192-193, 196, 197, 198; New England region, 184-185; North Plains region, 190-192; North Slope, 173; Pacific Mountain and Valley System, 172-173; Pacific Northwest region, 197-198; Pacific Southwest region, 198; pluralistic culture in, 183; population in, 113, 183, 193, 195, 197-198, 210; Rocky Mountain region, 196-197; Rocky Mountains, 172; settlement patterns, 211-212; South region, 192-193; South Plains region, 193-196; Superior Upland, 171; territorial expansion, 206-209; tourism in, 187, 193, 197, 198; transportation in, 212; urban areas in, 145, 183, 185, 186-187, 188, 189, 190, 191, 193, 195-198, 212; Volcanic Islands, 173;

United States Geological Survey, 146

United States Mint, 197

United States Trust Territory of the Pacific Islands, 619, 626

Upper Canada, 234

Ural (YUR uhl) **Mountains,** 10, 401, 402, 403, 405, 410

Ural River, 403

Uranus, 5

urban areas, 145-157; in Argentina, 300, 303; in Australia, 607; in Bangladesh, 551; in Brazil, 293, 294, 297; in Canada, 224, 225, 227, 228, 229-230; of Chile, 315; in China, 567; classification of, 145; in Eastern Europe, 391, 393; economic functions in, 148-149; in Egypt, 433, 434, 435; in France, 345; in Greece, 376; in Iberian Peninsula, 364, 365; in India, 541, 544; in Iran, 467; in Israel, 453, 455; in Italy, 369, 372; in Japan, 560-561; in Kenya, 483; kinds of, 145; in Mexico, 250-251, 256; in Pakistan, 549; in Peru, 319; in Saudi Arabia, 459, 460; in South America, 300; in Soviet Union, 410, 414-415; in Tanzania, 486-487; in Turkey, 463; in United States, 145, 183, 185, 186-187, 189, 190, 191, 193, 195-198, 212; urban growth in, 156; in Uruguay, 307; in West Germany, 350. *See also* cities; *cities by name*

urban development, impact of, 152-153; world patterns of, 156-157

urban environment, 151; climate, 153, 155; landscape, 152-153; lifestyle, 155-156

urban geography, 12, 145, 188, 300, 340, 434, 518, 544, 606; and the central place theory, 340

urbanization, 103, 150

urban planning, 606

urban sprawl, 300

Urdu (UR doo), 548

Uruguay, 289, 307; culture of, 307; economy of, 307; landforms of, 307

Uruguay River, 289, 299, 307

Utah, 196, 211

Uzbek Soviet Socialist Republic, 414

V

vaccination, 112

Valdez, Alaska, 197

Valencia, 361, 364

valley, 50. *See also by specific name*

Valparaíso (vahl pah rah EE soh), 314

Vancouver, British Columbia, 229-230

Vanuatu (VAN uh wah TOO), 619, 622

vaqueros (vah KAIR ohs), 293

Vatican City, 149, 367, 371, 372

Venezuela, 269; climate of, 283; economy of, 283-284; history of, 284; landforms of, 283

Venezuela, Gulf of, 281

Venice, 372, 373

Venus, 5

Veracruz, Mexico, 250

Verkhoyansk, 406

Vermont, 184, 204

Vesuvius, Mount, 368

Victoria, Australia, 609

Victoria, British Columbia, 229, 230

PHOTO CREDITS

2-3, Jack D. Swenson/Tom Stack & Associates; **4,** NASA; **7,** Steve Lissau; **8,** Michelle Wigginton; **11**(l) United Nations, (r) Steve Elmore; **14,** Steve Lissau; **16,** Courtesy of Staatliche Museen zu Berlin; **18,** Charles E. Zirkle; **19**(t) James Westwater, (b) The Port Authority of New York and New Jersey; **22,** Ralph Perry/National Geographic Society; **25,** U.S. Geological Survey; **29,** Tim Courlas; **32,** NASA; **33,** Cobalt Productions; **42-43,** David Hiser/Photographers Aspen; **44,** Collier/Condit; **50**(t) William E. Ferguson, (b) Roger K. Burnard; **51**(t) NASA, (b) Betty Crowell; **56,** Tim Courlas; **58**(t) Frank S. Balthis, (b) USDA; **59**(t) Larry Hamill, (b) Lynn Stone; **60**(tl) National Park Service, (tr) Craig Kramer, (b) file photo; **62,** Art Resource; **66,** Steve Lissau; **71,** Earth Images; **73,** Courtesy of Aluminum Corp. of America; **76,** Larry Hamill; **78,** Steve McCutcheon; **79,** file photo; **80,** United Nations/Wolff; **84, 87**(l), Tracy I. Borland; **87**(r), file photo; **88,** J. Meyers/FPG; **95,** Tom McHugh/Photo Researchers; **98**(l) Paolo Koch/Photo Researchers, (r) file photo; **99**(l) Tracy I. Borland, (r) David Hiser/Photographers Aspen; **102,** Steve McCurry/Magnum; **107,** Paolo Koch/Photo Researchers; **108-109,** George Gerster/Photo Researchers; **110,** Brian Seed/CLICK Chicago; **112,** Cameramann International; **119,** Carl Purcell; **120,** The Granger Collection; **121,** UN Photo 150101/Carol Redenius; **122,** Courtesy of The Population Institute; **126,** Wolfgang Kaehler; **128,** UN Photo 154311/Oddbjørn Morsen; **131,** Sheryl S. McNee/Tom Stack & Associates; **134,** Legacy Stock Photo/Mikel B. Davis: **135,** George Gerster/Photo Researchers; **136,** Cameramann International; **140,** Middenway & Jones/FPG; **144,** Wolfgang Kaehler; **147,** U.S. Geological Survey; **149**(l) Jim Pickerell/FPG, (r) Ted Spiegel/Black Star; **162-163,** Adele Hodge/FPG; **164,** file photo; **166,** Lucian Niemeyer; **167,** Doug Martin; **168,** Weldon King/FPG; **169,** A.C. Haralson/Arkansas Dept. of Parks & Tourism; **172,** Michael Collier; **173,** Stephen J. Krasemann/DRK Photo; **174,** Susan Rhoades; **177,** Steve Lissau; **179,** James Westwater; **182,** David R. Frazier; **185,** William H. Howell/Lightwave; **188,** U.S. Dept. of Commerce; **192,** Frank Cezus; **194,** Matt Bradley/Tom Stack & Associates; **196,** Grant Heilman Photography; **202,** R. Rowan/Photo Researchers; **204, 211,** The Granger Collection; **214,** H.M. DeCruyenaere; **218,** Eastcott-Momatiuk/The Image Works; **221,** National Film Board of Canada/Pierre Gaudard; **223,** Neil Rabinowitz/Aperture; **224,** Nova Scotia Dept. of Tourism; **229,** George Hunter/Shostal Associates; **230,** David Hiser/Photographers Aspen; **232,** NASA; **237,** Lee Snider/Photo Images; **242-243,** Joe Viesti; **244,** Robert Frerck/Woodfin Camp & Associates; **248,** Lee Foster/Alpha; **251,** Tony Jarzombek/Picture Group; **253,** Alpha; **257,** Rich Brommer; **258,** UN Photo 154880/Jean Claude Constant; **259,** United Nations; **264,** Peter Beck/Alpha; **268,** Robert Frerck/Woodfin Camp & Associates; **271,** Richard Rowan; **272,** Slim Aarons/Photo Researchers; **274,** Larry Hamill; **275,** Library of Congress; **280,** Alon Reininger/Contact; **285,** Frans Lanting; **288,** Will & Deni McIntyre/Photo Researchers; **291,** Steve Vidler/Leo de Wys; **294,** Balzat/Alpha; **295,** Messerschmidt/FPG; **298,** Robert Fried/D. Donne Bryant; **300,** Plessner/The Stock Shop; **301,** Shostal Associates; **310,** Virginia Ferrero/D. Donne Bryant; **314,** The Granger Collection; **315,** Tui de Roy Moore; **318, 320,** Andrew Rakoczy; **321,** file photo; **322,** F. Broadbeck/Tom Stack & Associates; **325,** Christiana Dittman from Rainbow; **326,** D. Donne Bryant; **332-333,** Adam Woolfitt/Woodfin Camp & Associates; **334,** Lee Snider/Photo Images; **337,** Jerry Derbyshire/Berg & Associates; **338,** Robert Harding Picture Library; **339,** Joe Burke from Rainbow; **340,** Greg Sailor; **345,** French National Railroad; **350,** Photri; **358,** Joe Viesti; **361,** Charlotte Kahler; **364,** Betty Crowell; **365,** Joe Viesti; **366,** Charlotte Kahler; **368,** Dan McCoy from Rainbow; **375,** Masa Uemura/Aperture; **380,** Jessie Blackburn/FPG; **384,** Robert Harding Picture Library; **386,** Betty Crowell; **387,** Magnum; **390,** Paul Quirico/Tom Stack & Associates; **391, 393,** Susan McCartney/Photo Researchers; **396, 400,** Travel Pix/FPG; **403,** Tass from Sovfoto; **408,** George Holton/Photo Researchers; **410, 413, 414,** Tass from Sovfoto; **415,** Travel Pix/FPG; **416,** Wolfgang Kaehler; **421,** FDR Library; **426-427,** Thomas Hopker/Woodfin Camp & Associates; **428,** Joe Viesti; **432,** Martin Rogers/FPG; **434,** Louis Goldman/Photo Researchers; **435,** Jamie Kalikow; **436;** Robert Azzi/Woodfin Camp & Associates; **437,** Nicholas Devore/Photographers Aspen; **440,** Rene Burri/Magnum; **442,** Nicholas Devore/Photographers Aspen; **446,** Steve McCurry/Magnum; **450,** R & S Michaud/Woodfin Camp & Associates; **453,** Jim Howard/FPG; **454,** World Image/FPG; **460,** Robert Azzi/Woodfin Camp & Associates; **462,** George Holton/Photo Researchers; **470,** Gamma-Liaison; **476-477,** Peter Davey/Bruce Coleman, Inc.; **478,** George Holton/Photo Researchers; **482,** Ann Purcell; **483,** Tim White; **485,** M. Philip Kahl, Jr./Bruce Coleman, Inc.; **488,** Bernard P. Wolff/Photo Researchers; **490,** Leo de Wys; **491,** Shostal Associates; **496, 500,** Marc & Evelyne Bernheim/Woodfin Camp & Associates; **502,** Shostal Associates; **503,** Frans Lanting; **504,** Roger K. Burnard; **508,** Robert Maust; **514,** Robert Harding Picture Library; **517,** Thomas Friedmann/Photo Researchers; **518,** Joe Viesti; **519,** Nicholas Devore/Photographers Aspen; **520,** Richard Harrington/FPG; **524,** George Holton/Photo Researchers; **526,** H.V. Meiss/Photo Researchers; **529,** Frans Lanting; **530,** Nicholas Devore/Photographers Aspen; **536-537,** Betty Crowell; **538,** Wolfgang Kaehler; **544,** Jehangir Gazdar/Woodfin Camp & Associates; **547,** John Elk III; **551,** Carl Purcell; **552,** Travelpix/FPG; **556,** Timothy Eagan/Woodfin Camp & Associates; **560,** Cameramann International; **561**(l) Photri, (r) Dave Bartruff/Alpha; **563, 565,** Wolfgang Kaehler; **566,** Jeff Kobelt; **572,** Cameramann International; **573,** Gary Bloomfield/Gamma-Liaison; **578,** John Elk III; **581,** Wolfgang Kaehler; **582,** Photri; **584,** Wolfgang Kaehler; **586,** Bruno Barbey/Magnum; **588,** file photo; **592,** Robert Harding Picture Library; **598-599,** Wolfgang Kaehler; **600,** Shostal Associates; **603,** A. Foley/FPG; **605,** David Austen/FPG; **606,** Travelpix/FPG; **608,** The Granger Collection; **611,** Photri; **612,** B.D. Drader/FPG; **613,** Eugene Gilliom; **615,** B. Hunter/Photo Researchers; **618,** Viesti Associates; **620,** Cameramann International; **623,** Dave G. Houser; **625,** William E. Ferguson; **626,** David R. Frazier; **628,** James C. Simmons/Tom Stack & Associates; **632,** George Holton/Photo Researchers; **634,** William D. Popejoy; **638,** NASA; **639,** Wolfgang Kaehler.